THE *Making* OF
English HISTORY

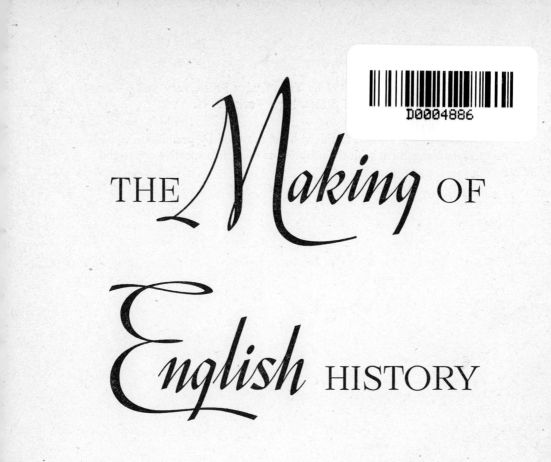

ROBERT LIVINGSTON SCHUYLER

Gouverneur Morris Professor Emeritus of History,
Columbia University

HERMAN AUSUBEL

Assistant Professor of History,
Columbia University

THE DRYDEN PRESS • NEW YORK

FORMAT

The text has been set in Times Roman, the part titles in Le Mercure, and the title page was hand lettered. Designed by Stanley Burnshaw and manufactured by The Norwood Press, Norwood, Massachusetts.

First Printing: March, 1952

TO
S. K. S. *and* A. A.

PREFACE

THE COLLEGE TEACHER of English history is fortunate in having at his disposal many valuable teaching aids. There are several excellent textbooks from which he can choose, and there are many useful collections of primary sources to which he can send his students. If, however, he wishes to supplement text-book and source-book assignments with required readings in the work of experts who have devoted long years of research and thought to the mastery of specific subjects, he soon finds himself in difficulty. Few American college libraries can afford to buy enough copies of monographs for classroom use, and even fewer can subscribe to the learned journals in which so much of the finest historical scholarship of our age is contained and often, sadly, interred. In short, the teacher discovers that finding adequate supplementary readings for his students is a major problem.

The present volume aims to help in solving this problem. It consists of seventy essays, most of which appeared originally in American and British scholarly journals that are for the most part unavailable in the average American college library. The authors of these essays are among the leading authorities in their field. Some of them, indeed, are among the greatest of twentieth-century historians. The essays often embody fresh and stimulating approaches to the subject treated, and they have been selected with a constant view to their usefulness for classroom discussion. The subjects dealt with in the essays are not confined to political and constitutional history; social, economic, religious, literary, and intellectual history have also received attention. Since, however, the usual undergraduate course in English history emphasizes domestic development, we have, although reluctantly, limited the number of selections devoted specifically to imperial history. Since the tendency has also been to give especial attention to the seventeenth and nineteenth centuries, we have intentionally made the sections dealing with these centuries relatively long. And, since the period following World War I has been admitted to the classroom, we have devoted an appreciable amount of space to recent history. If we have done this without any serious sense of guilt, the reason is that some very able historians have written and are writing on contemporary developments.

For the convenience and guidance of the student, each essay is preceded by an introduction and, in almost all cases, accompanied by a glossary. The introduction is designed to place the selection in its setting and to indicate why the student has been asked to read it. The glossary identifies those names and defines those terms which seem to deserve or require special definition or identification. Except in a few cases—and these are clearly indicated—the essays have been reproduced in their entirety. In order to make room for the inclusion of as many essays as possible, however, the footnotes which originally appeared with some of the essays have been omitted. Such omissions have also been clearly indicated.

We conclude with the hope that the students who use this volume will become interested enough in its subject matter to continue—even after they have left college—to read in the literature of English history.

R. L. S.
H. A.

Columbia University
January, 1952

A NOTE ON SOURCES

The essays in THE MAKING OF ENGLISH HISTORY have been selected from both books and periodicals. The periodicals are listed below.

Agricultural History

American Historical Review

American Political Science Review

Cambridge Historical Journal

Canadian Historical Review

Canadian Journal of Economics and Political Science

Catholic Historical Review

Church History

English Association: Essays and Studies

English Historical Review

English Review

Fortnightly

Historical Association: Pamphlet Series

History

Huntington Library Quarterly

Isis

Journal of Economic History

Journal of Modern History

Journal of the History of Ideas

Listener

Modern Philology

Nation

Nature

Pacific Historical Review

Pennsylvania Magazine of History and Biography

Philosophical Review

Political Quarterly

Quarterly Review

Review of Politics

Royal Historical Society: Transactions

Royal Society: Proceedings

Social Education

South Atlantic Quarterly

Southwestern Social Science Quarterly

Speculum

Studies: An Irish Quarterly Review

University of Birmingham Historical Journal

University of Toronto Quarterly

CONTENTS

INTRODUCTION

PART ONE
PRE-NORMAN TIMES

PART TWO
THE HIGH MIDDLE AGES

PART THREE

THE LATER MIDDLE AGES

PART FOUR

TUDOR TIMES

PART FIVE
STUART TIMES

PART SEVEN

THE NINETEENTH CENTURY

PART EIGHT
THE TWENTIETH CENTURY

Introduction

MANY EDUCATIONAL, INTELLECTUAL, AND SOCIAL uses and values have been ascribed to historical study, and historians continue to be very far from agreement as to the aims which it ought to pursue. According to one eminent authority, analysis has shown that the teaching of history in American schools early in the present century has had more than two hundred aims "ranging from mere entertainment of various kinds to direct guidance in dealing with current problems." There seems to be little doubt, however, regarding the nature of the growing interest in history in American colleges today. It appears to be generally believed that the principal, if not the only, value of the study of the past is to explain the present. Acceptance of this view of history has, naturally but unfortunately, led historians to read far too much of the present into the past and thus seriously to distort the past. The dangers of this "retrogressive modernism" were effectively pointed out by Professor Charles H. McIlwain, of Harvard University, in the address which he delivered as president of the American Historical Association—an address which is of especial interest to students of English history. Author of *The High Court of Parliament and Its Supremacy* (1910) and *The Growth of Political Thought in the West from the Greeks to the End of the Middle Ages* (1932), Professor McIlwain has had to guard constantly against the "untimely intrusion of modern ideas" in his own writings; and he has often insisted that if the historian is to do justice to the study of history he must try to view the past in the light of the past, not of the present.

THE HISTORIAN'S PART IN A CHANGING WORLD
CHARLES H. McILWAIN

Probably never since this Association was founded have men and women of our profession been asking themselves as earnestly and as anxiously as they are asking now, the old question, so often asked before, whether we, as historians, have anything practical to offer to our own country and to the world in times of crisis like the present, and if we have, how we can make our particular contribution most effectively.

Each one's answer to these pressing questions must be his own personal answer, based on his own individual experience, if it is to be anything vital to him or any practical help to others. But if this is true, each one must also see that his answer can never be more than a tentative one. He must realize how very narrow the range of his vision must be; how infinitely small a part of the whole varied experience of our race, which is history, can be mastered in one short span of life or even in many. All history should be a lesson in humility to us historians, but there is no more striking lesson than the present world crisis, in many of its most important aspects wholly unpredicted, if not unpredictable, even at the opening of this twentieth century.

To one in a boat at sea the horizon seems to recede into infinity on every side, but if he is a seaman, he knows he is only looking over the brim into nothingness.

In a troubled time like our own, in thinking of our inherited institutions and ideas, one sometimes feels as old Thomas Fuller did in 1655 on the completion of his *Church History of Britain,* when, as he says in his preface, "An ingenious Gentleman some

Reprinted by special permission from *The American Historical Review*, XLII (1937), 207-224.

moneths since in Jest-earnest advised me to make hast with my History, for fear (saith he) lest the Church of England be ended before the History thereof."

In this period of perplexity, we naturally wonder what service history can render in solving the problems of our country and of the world. We are asking ourselves how we, as historians, can do our part and what that part may be. No words seem more aptly to express this mood or to make clear our own present doubts and fears and hopes than the moving preface of an English pamphleteer of 1643 who signed himself "An Earnest desirer of his Countrie's Peace":

When a Patient lies sicke under the destroying paroxismes of a Fever, every stander-by will be telling his Medicine, though he be no Physitian: O then let no Sonne of this State account it presumption in me, for putting in my judgement, and speaking that which I conceive might, if not remove, yet mitigate this fatall distemperature of our common Mother: at another time perhaps it might be censurable, but in this exigence laudable.

For whether we like to admit it or not, we know we are to a large degree the creatures of habit, and the makers of history are no exception; they always have been and always will be guided in their actions rightly or wrongly by what they conceive to be the results of past experience, by the "lessons of history"; at least they will attempt to justify these actions or to secure popular assent to them by an appeal to the past. "It is these lessons of history that we want," I once heard it said by an eminent professor of pedagogy, and we do want them; but I was glad it was pedagogy and not history he professed, for he added that it was only the lessons, not the history, that we needed. In the schools, two or three weeks, he thought, would be enough for the history itself. This certainly is "to make haste with our history," and perhaps it is this very widespread unthinking haste of today that best indicates the most helpful contribution we can make as students of history. Some "lessons of history" we know will always be drawn, some "lessons of history" will always be acted on. Our part is to see that these really are the lessons *of history*.

It is not as easy a part as it might seem at first sight. Especially in times like this we are in a hurry lest the institutions we study "be ended before the History thereof." We are anxious—too anxious—to find a short cut.

In this connection we are often told that each generation will rewrite its history of the past. Even if it does not wholly reconstruct this past, it will make its own choice of the parts to be noted, and these parts will be precisely those which are uppermost at the time when the history is written. One scarcely needs to be told that this is so, but some have told us more. They have not only admitted the fact that this is done. They have said it ought to be done. At times they have implied, if they have not actually said, that what is out-of-date now ought to be eliminated from history. Others have put it a little differently, perhaps a little less crudely. It is humanly impossible, they say, even to approximate in our words the complex of innumerable facts and forces that made the life of any part of the past. The historian at most can make only a selection, and a woefully inadequate one at the best. This is too true, though one might question whether it is any more true of some parts of the past than of the actual present.

But again these defeatists, for they are defeatists, would tell us more. Because it can never be done perfectly, it should not be attempted at all. At times they seem even to make a merit of our obvious, but unfortunate, defects. Why not admit that all our histories are after all little better than fiction, little more than impressionistic pictures? And isn't it better so? The writing of history, they tell us, is only an "act of faith." One convincing proof of the inadequacy of this phrase of an eminent predecessor on this rostrum is the tale of his own distinguished contributions to history [Charles A. Beard].

Styles change in history as they do in women's garments, but sometimes the latter revert too. When some of us were youngsters we were taught to look up to the aims and aspirations of Leopold von Ranke as a guide. Now this is all changed. We find ourselves as professed historians engulfed in the general wave of pessimism, economic, political, and intellectual, which has been sweeping over the world since the Great War. Because we now know we can never achieve the full objectivity which Ranke preached, we are told that we should never make an effort to do so. Let us rest content with the subjective. It is all we can ever reach, all that can have any truth or value for us. Objective truth is a chimera. History is only an "act of faith." This intellectual weariness is no new thing in the world. Plato spent his life in combating it among the Sophists. Today the world is again in a sophistic mood—I am using the word, of course, without any modern sinister meaning. There is a general distrust of reason. Behaviorists would have us believe that blind animal instinct alone determines human destiny, and fervid nationalists are setting up the menace of a particular tribal culture against the historical verdicts of universal human reason. Such subjectivism usually ends in a complete skepticism. As Gorgias said in the Socratic dialogue, even if there were an objective truth, we could never recognize it. History is a vain quest. Let us frankly admit that we are only drawing imaginary portraits and vistas that never were on sea or land. No doubt it is a good thing thus to know our own limitations. In the past, without question, we have known too many things that were not so, and we shall never know more than a little of what is so. Some distrust of ourselves is not a bad thing. As one result, we shall probably be spared some further excursions into prophecy under the name of the "philosophy of history."

But with all due deference to the considerations just recited, the historian is after all faced with the brutal fact that some things

---

HENRY DE BRACTON: Thirteenth-century clergyman, judge, and author of the most celebrated and important legal treatise produced in medieval England, *De legibus et consuetudinibus Angliae*. Based mainly upon the records of cases decided in the king's courts, it embodied the first attempt to prepare a complete study of English laws and customs.

SIR JOHN FORTESCUE: Fifteenth-century English judge and constitutional lawyer who wrote important treatises on English law and government which emphasized the superiority of limited monarchy to absolute monarchy. He served as chief justice of the king's bench under Henry VI. S. B. Chrimes, in his *English Constitutional Ideas in the Fifteenth Century* (1936), discusses Fortescue's thought and places it in its historical context.

EDWARD AUGUSTUS FREEMAN: English historian (d. 1892) whose writings, mainly in English medieval political and constitutional history, had great influence in their day. Living at a time of advance in political democracy, Freeman was inclined to attribute ideas and interests of his own age to past ages. Although many of his conclusions have been discredited, he still deserves to be read. He had much to do with the popularization of the idea of the continuity of history.

THOMAS FULLER: Seventeenth-century English clergyman, moderate Royalist, and prolific writer on religious and historical subjects. He is best known for his extensive compilation of English biographies, *The History of the Worthies of England* (1662), and for his multivolume *Church History of Britain* [to 1648].

THOMAS FREDERICK TOUT: Twentieth-century English historian and leading authority on medieval English administrative history, a subject to which he devoted a massive work in six volumes. He was always conscious of the historical dangers involved in studying the past "with minds too much set on present presuppositions."

did actually happen in the past, and that some record of these happenings sometimes survives. And if these things happened, they had definite historical causes and results of which we often have some account remaining, even if incomplete.

How, in common sense, dare anyone say that we can know absolutely nothing positive about these past transactions, even if we cannot know all, even if we can know but little? And why should we be content merely to tint our picture with the colors that suit the changing taste of our own time? I am impressed by the sober words of the late Professor Tout in the opening part of his great work on English medieval administrative institutions. They seem to reflect more of the general aims and purposes of Ranke than of some later ones. "We investigate the past," he says, "not to deduce practical political lessons, but to find out what really happened."

We may not agree unreservedly with the first half of this sentence, but what serious historian can question the second? And if we investigate the past "to find out what really happened," knowing all the time that we can never truly find out anything whatsoever, why should we waste our time? Why not turn at once to historical romance? Too much of our written history even now is actually historical romance, and there may be a danger that much more will be. Biography seems to be turning that way, and already there are more than hints in certain parts of the world that all past history must be rewritten for a present purpose. In these days of propaganda, propagandist history is not likely to be neglected. Just let me give you a short extract from one interesting older example of it.

The author, John Aylmer, later bishop of London, is particularly bitter against the French—the date of the book, 1559, is significant—and asks, "Are they Giaunts, are they conquerours, or monarks of the world? No good Englishe men they be effeminate Frenchmen: Stoute in bragge, but nothing in dede. . . . They be your slaves and tributaries." They are in fear of the English, he says, "and it is no marvaile, for we have thorow Gods help ever had the better of them. . . . When durst these meacockes mete us in the field? or if they did; went they not weepynge away? . . . . We have a fewe hunting termes and pedlars French in the lousye lawe, brought in by the Normanes, yet remayning: But the language and customes bee Englyshe and Saxonyshe." "We live in paradise. England is the paradise and not Italy, as commonly they call it." And here in the margin the author has added, "God is English"!

You laugh, but how much more fantastic is this than some things written or taught or promoted in our own time? If such is the rewriting of one's history for his own generation—or his own nation—then some of us may prefer, with Professor Tout, to stick to the more humdrum task of trying "to find out what really happened," even if we know in advance that we can never find it all out. And few serious students of the history of English institutions, I think, would venture to deny that this more patient method in Professor Tout's own hands has actually resulted in a truly measurable increase in our positive knowledge of "what really happened."

There is, of course, a sense in which each generation not only does, but undoubtedly should, rewrite past history for itself. For example, no one could deny that our modern concern in the material things of life—whether that itself be good or bad—has led to an appreciation of their importance in the past, fuller and probably more just than the views of some of the older historians. But when this leads, as it sometimes does, to a treatment of some past periods on the assumption that these same material or economic factors must have been just as prominent then as they are now in the political or intellectual development of the time—when this is done, we get in the name of history a distortion in place of an interpretation.

When kept within proper limits, this general kind of revision has, it is true, resulted in a very great enrichment of our history; but it is a mistake to think of it as the only kind; indeed, it is the principal contention of this paper that the most valuable of the newer interpretations of that history are now to be found in a quarter not only different from this, but almost directly opposite to it. The most serious defects in our existing histories of past institutions—the kind of histories with which I am most familiar—lie, not in any undue suppression of modern modes of thought and action, but rather in their untimely intrusion. Thus the chief advances made in the recent study of these institutional developments have come from a recognition of such defects. And I venture to predict with some confidence that any further improvement we may ever be able to make over our predecessors in this study in the years to come, any firm building we may succeed in erecting on the foundations they have laid, is likely to be in large part the result of a still clearer recognition of these defects and of a still further application to history of the canon which Sir Edward Coke once laid down for law: *contemporanea expositio fortissima est.*

Infractions of this rule naturally come oftener in some kinds of history than in others and are far more frequent for certain periods. For contemporary or recent history the danger is slight, for there familiarity with present-day conditions forms the necessary basis of all accurate historical judgments; and even in ancient history the faults are likely to be of a very different kind. You will notice that most of the illustrations of our retrogressive modernism come from the institutional development of the Middle Ages and after. This is the period from which we can trace our own familiar institutions in a continuous development. It is the stage of growth immediately behind us, in which were laid the foundations on which our social and political fabric still stands. Thus it is just because these institutions are so peculiarly our own and yet during their earlier growth so fundamentally different in character from what they have now become, that the temptation is so great to slur over the historical stages in their evolution. Probably for no other period is it so necessary or so difficult to observe in our thinking and writing the caution of Maitland when he says, "We shall have to think away distinctions which seem to us as clear as the sunshine; we must think ourselves back into a twilight. This we must do, not in a haphazard fashion, but of set purpose, knowing what we are doing."

Actual changes like this in our attitude toward particular historical problems have, however, not as a rule come about wholesale, or from any "set purpose." They have usually come piecemeal because someone has been steeping himself in the thought and motives of some past epoch by extensive and careful reading of the records or writings of the time, and one day wakes up to find—usually to his utter amazement—that this thought or these motives and institutions are not at all the ones he has been reading about all these years in the standard modern books. Then he gets to work. If I may be pardoned a personal allusion, I can never forget the shock—it was really consternation rather than mere surprise—when I suddenly realized that men like Lambarde or Fitzherbert in Elizabeth's time, when they spoke of a parliament, were thinking of something in many ways very different from what I had learned. It is a little shocking to find the actual makers or the contemporary recorders of the past saying or doing or thinking something entirely different from the thing we have always had in mind, or, what is worse, have even been teaching to others as history.

But such shocks do not commonly arise out of the consciousness that our received notions of earlier historical developments fail to square with modern conditions. On the contrary, nine times out of ten it is just because these notions are too modern that the historian finally discovers that they do not fit the actual facts, that they furnish no explanation at all, or an obviously inadequate or even a distorted explanation, of past movements and actions.

To see if this is true or not, it might be profitable to look at a few specific instances of revisions made in recent years in the field of our own earlier institutions which historical scholars have accepted generally as improvements. It is most interesting to compare, for example, the older traditional conception of these institutions in England just after the Conquest with the one now prevailing. The former is concisely stated in Freeman's *Growth of the English Constitution,* first published in 1872, and still survives in some of our textbooks; the latter is brilliantly set forth in Professor Stenton's *First Century of English Feudalism,* which appeared in 1932. To Freeman, apparently nearly as much as to Bishop Aylmer in the sixteenth century, all "the language and customes be Englyshe and Saxonyshe." The words of our greatest modern master in this field are strikingly different. They were written by F. W. Maitland in 1895, or just before. He admits, as everyone must, that the Conqueror could not and did not "sweep away English law and put Norman law in its stead," nor ever intended to do so; but he sees, nevertheless, "one indelible mark" which the Conquest "has stamped forever on the whole body of our law." He continues:

It would be hardly too much to say, that at the present day almost all our words that have a definite legal import are in a certain sense French words. . . . Earl was not displaced by count, sheriff was not displaced by viscount; our King, our Queen, our lords, our knights of the shire are English; our aldermen are English if our mayors are French; but our parliament and its statutes, our privy council and its ordinances, our peers, our barons, the commons of the realm, the sovereign, the state, the nation, the people are French; our citizens are French and our burgesses more French than English. . . . In the province of justice and police with its fines, its gaols and its prisons, its constables, its arrests, we must, now that outlawry is a thing of the past, go as far as the gallows if we would find an English institution.

The date of the final conquest of French over English in the courts Maitland significantly puts rather in 1166 than 1066, at the time of Henry II's Assize of Clarendon instead of the Battle of Hastings, and he goes on to warn us that this fundamental change in language must be the index of much more. These may be only terms of law, but they touch life in all its phases. For "Language," he says, "is no mere instrument which we can control at will; it controls us. It is not a small thing that a lawbook produced in the England of the thirteenth century will look very like some statement of a French *coutume* and utterly unlike the *Sachsenspiegel*." When we pass from these more general matters to specific events of this period, the difference appears even more marked between the old interpretation and the new. Let us take the famous Salisbury oath of 1086, which brings up "perhaps the obscurest question in Anglo-Norman history," as Professor Stenton says. Speaking of it in his *Norman Conquest,* Freeman attacks certain "ingenious writers," because—to quote his own words—"they have picked out, as the act by which a Feudal System was introduced in England, the very act by which William's far-seeing wisdom took care that no Feudal System ever should grow up in England." These "ingenious writers" are chiefly lawyers, and in speaking of them Freeman says he is tempted to refer to St. Luke, XI, 52, which, by the way, reads as follows: "Woe unto you Lawyers: for ye have taken away the key of knowledge: ye entered not in yourselves, and them that were entering in, ye hindered." Following the Peterborough Chronicle, Freeman seems also to accept its statement that some 60,000 freemen took that oath in that unique "Gemót of Salisbury," which destroyed feudalism forever in England.

To Professor Stenton, on the other hand, the same transaction appears simply as an application on a large scale of the normal and widely extended feudal institution of liege homage, and he says "its authority was in accordance with the strictest feudal principles." Furthermore, in his view it was not all the freemen who took the oath at Salisbury, nor even the mere knights, but only "the leading mesne tenants, men with military resources of their own, and the personal influence which birth and experience gave. . . . And the social custom of the time regarded such men as barons 'whosesoever men they were.' " Such a feudal and aristocratic interpretation is a far cry from Freeman's glowing Germanic democracy.

Another important institution of the same period furnishing a similar illustration of the change in historical treatment is the county court and the membership of that court under the Norman kings. Even Bishop Stubbs seemed to regard attendance at the court as a privilege or honor so much cherished in twelfth century England that King Henry I found it necessary in a writ which still survives to restore the frequency and regularity of its meetings after a period of interruption. A more recent view is somewhat different. Attendance at these courts was no honor that members prized or communities sought for. Instead, this attendance was a nuisance to those members and a burden of service upon those communities which should not be exacted any oftener than precedent warranted. The well-known writ of Henry I for holding the county and hundred courts, it is thought, is not then, as Stubbs and his predecessors assumed, an order for the holding of these courts oftener than before; it is a command that they should meet less often. The amount of suit at court shall not be increased for the local communities; as the contemporary author of the so-called Laws of Henry I puts it, they are not "to be worried further by any wearisome burdens" (*nec ullis ultra fatigationibus agitari*). The grievance redressed here is not too little representation, but too much. Like changes have taken place in our modern accounts of the nature of the central assembly, the Great Council or *Magnum Concilium*. It is now usually thought of as essentially a meeting of tenants-in-chief in response to a royal summons to acquit their lands of a strictly feudal obligation, the obligation of counsel. This has diverged pretty far from Freeman's conception of a great national assembly at whose meetings "the whole people had an acknowledged right to attend." What was formerly considered a national privilege turns out to be only a feudal burden.

Such revisions of Anglo-Norman history all tend in one direction, and they may be considered sound or unsound, but no one can deny that they are momentous. They amount to a fundamental change in our notion of the whole of the social and political institutions in operation in that important period. They modify our ideas respecting almost every side of men's life at the time.

None of them, however, seems to have been prompted by any feeling that earlier historians had neglected the forces of the present in their treatment of the past. The changes noted above in our ideas about Norman England have come almost invariably from an enlarged estimate of the importance of feudal relations in the life of that period; and yet, if there is one thing conspicuous by its absence in the life and thought of our own time, it is feudalism. What really produced this great change, then, was no reading in of modern modes of thought or action, but a reading out. It has resulted from no attempt, conscious or unconscious, to rewrite this part of the past in our own terms, but rather from a realization, born of careful research into the records of the time, that those records actually tell a story different from the one we have hitherto accepted as history.

Turning from the twelfth to the thirteenth century, we find similar changes of emphasis or of interpretation. One of these, at least, seems to have won the assent of historical scholars generally.

In 1853 Sir Edward Creasy described the Great Charter of King John as "a solemn instrument deliberately agreed on by the King, the prelates, the great barons, the gentry, the burghers, the yeomanry, and all the freemen of the realm." Of the famous words of its thirty-ninth chapter, "except by the lawful judgment of his peers, or by the law of the land," he said, "I believe that the trial by peers here spoken of means trial by jury. The words will bear this meaning; it is certainly impossible to give them any other satisfactory meaning." The clause guarantees "full protection for property and person to every human being who breathes English air." This is a fair statement of the opinion of historians pretty generally in 1853, and no doubt it is law, for this identification of the feudal trial by peers and our trial by jury is made in many of our own state constitutions. But good law may be pretty bad history. Needless to say, no reputable historian accepts this view today, though it lives on in Fourth of July orations and no doubt will for years to come. Less generally accepted perhaps, but no less significant, is an apparent change in the attitude of historians toward the annulment of Magna Carta by Pope Innocent III. It has been usual to see in it something of a papal attack on the independence of an English church. Even as late as 1914 Mr. McKechnie could say that "the conception of an English Church that was something more than a mere branch of the church universal began to take clearer shape," when English churchmen found that John was receiving sympathy and support from Rome. If there is any contemporary evidence that can be fairly interpreted in this sense, I do not know what it is. The reasons for the revocation given in the bull itself seem ample; they are chiefly the compulsion under which John's promises had been extorted and the surrender of royal authority which these promises involved. The first of these grounds is too obvious to need comment, the second is far more interesting constitutionally; but on either ground it is hard to avoid the conclusion that the pope could scarcely have given any other decision than he did; while the belief that Langton and John's other clerical opponents saw in it any attack on their national church looks like just another of these anachronisms we have been tracing, which it is the business of the historian to disprove.

Historians have thought and apparently still often think they find a sort of national declaration of independence of the canon law of the Universal Church in the famous declaration by the barons at Merton in 1236, *Nolumus leges Angliae mutari*—"We are unwilling that the laws of England be changed." This nationalistic explanation seems still to be the one generally accepted, and a good deal of eloquence has been expended on these patriotic barons. But a revisionist with contemporary evidence in mind must have his doubts. No man in England in 1236, noble or non-noble, layman or ecclesiastic, would have dreamt of challenging the church's exclusive right to define legitimacy—the particular question then at issue—or to determine it in a particular case in its own courts. The barons do not say they repudiate canon law; they do not even say they repudiate the church's definition of legitimacy; they claim for themselves no jurisdiction over legitimacy generally; they only say that in determining a right of succession to English land, which is a proprietary right, the king's courts will follow the ancient English land law relative to succession in cases of illegitimacy in preference to any other rule. It might be added that although the Statute of Merton, of which this is one of the sections, is always printed among the Statutes of the Realm, it antedates any surviving statute roll, and how it originally got the name and authority of a statute must be considered now a question of much greater doubt, since the recent notable investigations of Messrs. Richardson and Sayles into the history of the early statutes.

Other instances of the same thing will no doubt occur to you. This same antedated nationalism that formed our traditional estimate of the Statute of Merton and inspired McKechnie's criticisms of Innocent III's revocation of Magna Carta has also suggested similar modern objections to the arbitration of St. Louis in 1264, in which he declared that the Provisions of Oxford of 1258 were void, even though enacted with Henry III's formal assent, because they were an infringement of the king's royal authority. It has not always been sufficiently noticed that this constitutional objection of St. Louis is the same that Innocent III had made against parts of Magna Carta, nor has enough weight been given to this and to other contemporary evidence for the existence at this time in England of a constitutional principle which seems to forbid even the king himself, much more any of the king's subjects, to "blemish" the rights of the crown, and renders null and void even a royal act which attempts it. If such a principle was in existence then, St. Louis' decision, like Innocent III's, was probably the only one that could be justified then or now, in view of all the circumstances of the case.

Similarly, of course, these considerations must affect our estimate of Simon de Montfort and his work. We may admire as much as before the nobility of his character and aims and recognize the great significance of his acts and proposals, but we are less likely now to call this nobility patriotism or to defend those acts as constitutional. In the same way, and for much the same reasons, important recent historical research into the origins of English representation has made it impossible any longer to refer to him, as the German historian Pauli did, as "The Founder of the House of Commons."

What the retrospective nationalism of the older histories has done in this way for the work of Simon de Montfort, retrospective constitutionalism has done for the administration of King Edward I. He was the hero of Stubbs's great constitutional epic. Now he is regarded rather as a champion of prerogative than of constitutionalism; but to think of him thus, as a man of his own time rather than of a later time, is in no way really to detract from the nobility of his character or the true greatness of his designs. If one thing in his reign more than another might serve to illustrate our changing historical views, it is what I could now probably speak of without risk as "the Myth of the Model Parliament."

So we might go on to the revaluations of the great ordinances of 1311 and the Statute of York which repealed them and enacted what Stubbs, in his constitutional enthusiasm, regarded as the provision establishing the share of the commons in legislation. We might pass to the great ecclesiastical statutes of the middle of Edward III's reign, the statutes of Provisors and Praemunire, and Maitland's classic exposure of their nationalistic interpreters and the naïve *non sequitur* that they had proved the existence of an opposition to papal authority among the English clergy because they had been able to show an opposition to the clergy among the English laity.

When we reached the Tudors in a survey of this kind it might seem at last that we had come to a period in which historical revision was to take a more modern form, something possibly almost like a rewriting in terms of our own day. For so far as there has been any recent revision in the historian's conception of this epoch it has seemed to incline to a softening of the old accepted phrase "Tudor absolutism" as a characterization of the time. At last we might seem to need a little more modern constitutionalism instead of reactionary antiquarianism if we were to reach a just estimate of the period. Like most such sweeping phrases, "Tudor absolutism" does cover a multitude of sins, not only past but present. In the reign of Henry VIII, at least, there is plenty of oppression, much injustice, at times intolerable cruelty. There can be no doubt of that, but can we properly call it a despotism? Strictly, it was not. The king had great power, and at times he greatly abused what he had, but he certainly did not legally have *all* power: there were limits to what he could legitimately do. His mere will was not law. It is impossible to characterize the Tudor reigns as an absolutism or a despotism in any proper sense of those terms.

Bishop Aylmer has been quoted for his fantastic chauvinism, but when he could forget that, he was a remarkably keen observer, and he might be quoted again in this connection:

But to what purpose is all this? To

declare that it is not in England so dangerous a matter to have a woman ruler, as men take it to be—If on the other part, the regement were such as all hanged upon the King's or quene's will, and not upon the lawes written; if she might decre and make lawes alone, without her senate; if she judged offences according to her wisdom, and not by limitation of statutes and laws; if she might dispose alone of war and peace; if, to be short, she were a mer monarch, and not a mixed ruler, you might peradventure make me fear the matter the more, and the less defend the cause.

That is a very remarkable statement of constitutionalism to be written in 1559, and there is plenty of other contemporary evidence in support of it which I cannot stop to cite. Clearly we must temper our phrase, "Tudor absolutism." But is this because it is too modern to fit the facts, or because it is not modern enough? The answer to that question depends on another—whether despotism or absolutism is itself a medieval or a modern form or ideal of government. Without doubt it is modern, not medieval. In fact, in sixteenth century England medieval constitutionalism was fighting for its life against the new, the more modern despotic tendencies, but it survived there. In sixteenth century France the same battle was going on, but the outcome was different; there modern absolutism replaced an older constitutionalism, to last till the Revolution of 1789; the "tempered monarchy" of earlier times gave way before the personal rule of the Bourbon kings. What we still chiefly need, then, even for Tudor England, if we are to comprehend it better, is a more thorough understanding not so much of its modern innovations as of its great medieval heritage.

Need I cite more examples of such anachronisms as these? Because they were political liberals, St. Thomas Aquinas must now be made over into a modern Whig and Cardinal Bellarmine into a democrat; because they believed in a restricted royal prerogative, men like Sir John Eliot and Sir Matthew Hale have to be turned into preposterous parliamentary Austinians. This is about the last and the worst case of this kind of procedure. Lessons may be got in this fashion, no doubt, but they will not be the lessons of history. The quickest and the surest way of finding the present in the past, but hardly the soundest, is to put it there first.

The illustrations above have practically all been taken from the earlier history of our own constitutionalism in the mother country, but further illustrations, equally pertinent, will no doubt occur to you from historical fields other than the constitutional and from other lands than England.

But here someone may object. He may say, as Glaucon said to Socrates in Plato's *Republic,* that this rehearsal thus far has been all negative. If it is true that some measure of objective history can really be reached, as has been maintained, then one ought to be able to point to something positive in that history, something not completely vitiated by the fallacies we have been tracing.

It is with a good deal of hesitation that I would venture to put forward one or two general political principles that do seem to accord with the words and actions of men throughout the earlier part of our constitutional history and yet have persisted to our own time or almost to it—principles, therefore, that may possibly survive the tests by which we have ventured to discard some others. Probably the best way to suggest these principles here is in the form of a commentary on one of the texts that expresses them best. It is the well-known line of Bracton in which he says, *Rex non debet esse sub homine, sed sub Deo et lege*—"The king ought not to be under a man but under God and the law." It would be hard to fix on any sentence outside Scripture more quoted in our later constitutional struggles than this, but the way it has usually been quoted is rather amazing. How many times we have all seen the last part of this maxim repeated, "under God and the law"! But how often do we ever see a quotation of the first part—"non sub homine," not under a man? Yet Bracton himself put both these parts together, and he put "non sub homine" first. Some English royalists of the seventeenth century quoted the first part of Bracton's sentence and stopped there; many more on the parliamentary side repeated the last part and began with it. Practically none, to my knowledge, made use of both parts of Bracton's statement, and this is probably not surprising. It is always a favorite trick of propagandists to quote half a sentence and carefully omit the rest. But how shall we explain the fact that sober historians in later times have in this case done the same thing and kept on doing it? Why have we all gone on for ages repeating the words, "under God and the law," and as regularly omitting, "not under a man"? If we could answer those two questions satisfactorily, we might find that we had incidentally answered some others of very general historical significance and possibly even of some practical importance to the world today.

The king, Bracton says, should have no man over him, but he should have over him the law. In ignoring the former part of this statement we are no doubt assuming that it does not fit our modern conditions, that it is untrue for us. That assumption might be questioned; but historians seem to have assumed even more than this, and the present argument is addressed to historians. In virtually suppressing this first part of Bracton's explicit statement, "not under a man," we appear also to condemn him, tacitly at least, of a misunderstanding of the political conditions in his own day. We reason, I take it, somewhat as follows: Bracton has said that the king should be under the law. This can mean one thing only; namely, that others either stand over the king to impose a penalty on him if he breaks or exceeds this law, or have at least an authority, independent of him, to oppose his acts. It can mean nothing less than this; therefore, our author's assertion which contradicts it, that none should be over the

king and none equal with him, must be just a slip. It cannot be coupled with the words "sub lege"; it is obviously untrue, and therefore Bracton must have been in error in making it. I have called this an assumption. It looks more like presumption. We in the twentieth century are venturing to tell the ablest English constitutionalist of the thirteenth that he is all wrong about his own country and his own times, that we know more about it than he did. Suppose, then, we should adopt the more modest alternative, at least as a temporary hypothesis, should assume that the discrepancies in Bracton may after all be more apparent than real, and should set to work seriously to examine the institutions and ideas of Bracton's time for contemporary indications as to the accuracy of his statements or the possibility of reconciling seeming contradictions in them.

There is no need to bring evidence to show the general acceptance of the second part of Bracton's maxim, "sub Deo et lege," either in his own time or by modern historians. It is generally admitted, though hardly sufficiently to account for all the facts of the sixteenth century. The part requiring proof is the first part, "non sub homine." Yet, what Socrates says of justice in Plato's *Republic* may be equally applicable here—"what we were looking for has all this while been rolling before our feet and we never saw it." For what but a constitutional doctrine like Bracton's could have led Innocent III to quash a king's charter because it contained a loss or surrender of royal right (*regalis juris dispendium*); what but this could have been in the mind of St. Louis in 1264 when he declared that King Henry III "should have full power in his realm and government free of control" (*plenam potestatem et liberum regimen habeat in regno suo*); or on what other principle can we account for parliament's repeal in 1322 of an ordinance already assented to by the king, ostensibly of his own "free will"?

There are many other evidences of the existence and the continuance of this constitutional principle of Bracton's, and one of the most interesting comes late in the fifteenth century, in the very heyday of the so-called "Lancastrian constitution" and from the greatest of Lancastrian "constitutionalists," Sir John Fortescue. In the famous and oft-quoted phrase by which he characterizes the existing English monarchy, "regimen politicum et regale," Fortescue couples together "politicum" and "regale," just as Bracton did the two like parts of his maxim; and if Bracton's two statements contradict each other, so do Fortescue's. We must, in fact, condemn practically all medieval authorities as muddle-headed if there is not justification for every part of Bracton's dictum.

The explanation of all this confusion is simple enough. We historians have been confusing two things that contemporaries were always careful to distinguish, *restriction* and *control*. They held that the king's authority was legally restricted, or bounded, or "limited" in its extent—"sub Deo et lege," a "regimen politicum," as Fortescue put it; but it does not follow that they did not, or that they should not believe that his rule was at the same time "free"—"non sub homine," in Fortescue's terms a "regimen regale," a "regimen liberum" in St. Louis'.

One part of Bracton's sentence has to do with the extent, the other with the manner of royal government. The confusion of these two is no mistake of contemporaries; it seems to be our own, and probably no similar lack of discrimination has ever caused more serious misrepresentations of history than this unfortunate failure to distinguish medieval *limitation* from modern *control*.

To the end almost of the sixteenth century English constitutional history is not fully clear without some reference to this old distinction. In 1587, in Cavendish's case, Elizabeth bowed when the judges ignored her express command to transfer an office from one man to another—the command was *ultra vires;* but in 1575 the intrepid Peter Wentworth had been sent to

the Tower for even discussing the exercise of the queen's authority as "supreme governor"—that was an attempt at *control.*

Even the process by which this older notion of limitation gradually grew into something more, in the development of a real control by a representative parliament becoming more and more conscious of its power—even this, in its full historical significance, is likely to escape us if we have no appreciation of the older ideas and institutions out of which the new ones grew. *The Winning of the Initiative by the House of Commons,* as Professor Notestein has so aptly termed this great change, can never have much real meaning for us if we allow ourselves to forget that this initiative did, after all, have to be *won.*

In Bracton's line, *Rex non debet esse sub homine, sed sub Deo et lege,* we have, apparently, at least one positive principle of lasting importance, a faithful summation of medieval politics; and in the later modification of it we might find a considerable part of the modern. Consideration of it seems to point to the fact that we must distinguish pretty carefully in our history between autocracy and despotism; it seems to indicate that the medieval king was an autocrat, was absolute in the sense of having no superior, but was anything but despotic, in that his *jura regalia* left off where the rights of his subjects began. He was in fact limited but not controlled.

When we look for survivals of such principles in later times, after the initiative had been won, we must substitute the modern "government" for the medieval king, but a modern historian might find some illustration of this same old principle in the solidarity of the English cabinet; and even the American historian may wonder whether our bills of rights which embody this principle may not be a surer safeguard of liberty than an overextension of checks and balances which violate it in making government innocuous only by making it ineffective, and by splitting it up do little else than render it irresponsible.

As historians, our real task is with history, not with its application; but when troubles come upon us, the question will always emerge—it will not down—whether it belongs to the historian, even if not strictly *as* a historian, to find in all these facts and developments, assuming them to be accurate, any lessons of value that may be practically useful. I sincerely believe that it does; but like that other "Earnest desirer of his Countrie's Peace" already referred to, if I tried to urge any such lessons for our present troubles, I should be "telling my medicine" only as a bystander, and not as a physician. If there are any practical inferences to be drawn from this jumbled survey, therefore, I leave them for you to draw.

Pre-Norman Times

PART ONE

IN A FAMOUS PASSAGE IN *The Decline and Fall of the Roman Empire,* Edward
Gibbon described the manner in which the province of Britain was added to
the Roman Empire during the first century of the Christian era: "After a
war of about forty years, undertaken by the most stupid, maintained by the
most dissolute, and terminated by the most timid of all the emperors [Claudius,
Nero, and Domitian], the far greater part of the island submitted to the Roman
yoke." Roman interest in Britain Gibbon attributed to "the proximity of its
situation to the coast of Gaul"; and the success of the conquest was made
possible, he wrote, because "the various tribes of Britons possessed valor
without conduct, and the love of freedom without the spirit of union." For
about three centuries and a half, Britain, including the territory of modern
England, Wales, and the lowlands of Scotland, formed a part of the Roman
Empire; and its historical development was naturally influenced by the course
of events in other parts of the Empire. Literary sources of information about
Roman Britain, being scanty and fragmentary, throw only a dim and flicker-
ing light upon its history as a whole. These sources have been greatly supplemented, however, during the last two or three generations by discoveries in
archaeology and such auxiliary sciences as epigraphy and numismatics, and
it is largely upon these discoveries that the historian of Roman Britain now
relies. In the essay that follows, J. N. L. Myres, an eminent specialist in early
English history and now Librarian of the great Bodleian Library at the University of Oxford, sketches some of the main currents in the political, military,
institutional, social, and economic history of Britain during the centuries when
it was a part of the Roman Empire.

ROMAN BRITAIN
J. N. L. MYRES

INTRODUCTION

The Roman conquest and occupation of
Britain has long been taken as the conventional starting point of English History, and
there is a conventional justification for so
doing. For in the writings of the Roman
historians, notably those of Caesar, Tacitus,
and Dion Cassius, occur the first literary
records of historical events and historical
personalities connected with this country.
But it is perhaps worth asking whether the
accidental preservation of these extremely
fragmentary and inadequate records is
really a good enough reason for the main-

tenance of this convention: for, in the first
place, the development of archæology and
its auxiliary sciences in the last half-century
has reduced the contribution made by those
records to a very minor one in our present
knowledge of the Roman occupation; and,
in the second place, we are able by the
help of those same sciences to give a much
surer account of pre-Roman Britain for
centuries, even millennia, before the Christian era than was possible only a very few
years ago. At the present time the old distinction between a strictly historic period
for which the evidence is literary in character, and a vague pre-history dependent on

Reprinted by special permission from the series of pamphlets brought out by the Historical
Association in Great Britain. This essay appeared originally as Historical Association Pamphlet
No. 113 (1939).

the guesswork of archæologists has become quite meaningless. In Britain as elsewhere history and pre-history in this sense meet and mingle over more than a thousand years.

If Roman Britain is to remain the conventional beginning of English History other reasons must be sought. In some ways it might be thought desirable to abandon the old convention altogether. It can always be argued with force that the history of England should begin with the history of the English, and for many purposes that is no doubt an unassailable position. After all, the break between the ancient and the modern world is a far sharper one in this country than it is in most parts of Europe, and no one would venture to place it before rather than after the Roman period. What sense can there be in beginning the story with the last phase of the old world, an old world which in any case left only the slightest cultural influence in Britain on the new, rather than with the first phase of that new world itself? If ever historians are justified in cutting history into sections, they are surely right to make one such cut in British history in the fifth century A.D.

But the cut is one in cultural history only. Roman Britain is the final phase of the old world because it is the climax of a series of movements from the continent to this country, a series of which each successive member, at any rate from the later Stone Age onwards, had brought some addition great or small to the material equipment and culture of the land. The early history of Britain is essentially the history of her invaders;[1] her culture was slowly and patchily built up out of the successive contributions which those invaders brought. The Roman Conquest differed from earlier conquests mainly in the far more emphatic emphasis that it laid on this cultural development and in the greater degree of uniformity which it achieved. For whereas the earlier movements mostly imposed themselves by weight of numbers and more heavily on one part of the land than another, the Romans overcame the Britons by superior military organization and the attractions of a higher standard of life: they made no radical change in the basis of the population in any part. But the Roman Conquest was none the less the cultural climax of British pre-history.

But politically it was not a climax at all. Britain continued to be conquered by successive invaders from the Continent after the Roman occupation as before. The Anglo-Saxons, the Danes, and the Normans carry on the series initiated in the mists of a remote antiquity, and thus prolong the essential political features of the prehistoric period to the end of the eleventh century A.D. If Britain has not been conquered since then it is mainly because the growth of strongly organized forces on the Continent has replaced the political fluidity of prehistoric times, induced a general stability of population, and provided the machinery for a more or less peaceful traffic in ideas. But it is well sometimes to remember that any relapse of Europe into barbarism, indeed any substantial alteration in its political organization or in its cultural basis would be likely on all prehistoric analogy to usher in a fresh spate of invasions of these islands.

If on the long view the history of Britain has thus been the history of her invaders, it is desirable to examine the different forms which these invasions may take. It can be argued that a study of Roman Britain is of value as the best example of the imposition of an elaborate, highly organized culture on Britain by military conquest, unaccompanied by any great influx of a fresh population: while the Anglo-Saxon settlement which followed it can be regarded as a typical case of quite another sort of conquest, the immigration *en masse* of a new people, culturally and politically backward, but swamping by force of numbers and vitality a civilization technically much higher but deflated by social corruption and economic collapse. The contrast between the two may help to remind us of the in-

[1] See, for this whole question, Sir Cyril Fox, *Personality of Britain, its influence on inhabitant and invader*, 3rd ed., 1938.

finite variety of influences which have gone to the making of Britain as we know it, and to save us from the historical inadequacy of such a view as is implied in Shakespeare's picture of this country as,

> This fortress built by Nature for
> herself
> Against infection and the hand of
> war.

It is only against the brief background of eight short centuries that we can attach any significance to such words.

* * * * *

In the pages which follow, a sketch is first given of the Political History of Roman Britain, and this is followed by some account of its Institutional, Economic and Social History: finally the problems raised by its collapse are briefly mentioned. In the available space it is impossible to do more than draw attention to the more salient features in each aspect of the subject, and a short bibliography of the more useful books for further reading will be found at the end.[2] No one who writes on this subject at the present time can do so without the feeling that most of what he writes has already been expressed much more felicitously by Prof. R. G. Collingwood, and the first task that must be undertaken by

anyone who seeks a balanced introduction to Roman Britain is the study of his works. No originality of standpoint is claimed for the views expressed in this pamphlet: its purpose is merely to focus attention on the essentials of the subject, and its debt to the work of the many scholars who have made those essentials clearer will be obvious to every reader.

A. POLITICAL HISTORY

The political connection between Britain and Rome begins half-heartedly with the raids of Julius Caesar in 55 and 54 B.C., and becomes closely knit with the Claudian conquest of A.D. 43. The reasons which prompted the controllers of Roman policy to envisage and finally, after much hesitation, to undertake the military subjugation of the country altered in emphasis in the course of those ninety years. To Julius Caesar the problem of Britain was essentially a military one: its subjection was almost, if not quite, a necessary corollary of the conquest of Gaul, for without the control of southern Britain, the Roman hold on Gaul was believed to be precarious and insecure. There were two main reasons for this, one geographical and one political. Geographically southern Britain is really part of Gaul, the north-western side of the great drowned valley of the English Channel, across which successive invaders of Britain had passed without difficulty for thousands of years: politically too at this time it was almost a part of Gaul, for the

[2] There is no room in this pamphlet for separate accounts of Romano-British art and Romano-British religion. Both topics have been admirably discussed by Prof. Collingwood in *Roman Britain and the English Settlements,* chaps. XV and XVI.

R. G. COLLINGWOOD: Philosopher and historian who devoted much study and thought to the history of Roman Britain. He collaborated with J. N. L. Myres in writing *Roman Britain and the English Settlements* (1936), the first volume of the "Oxford History of England" series.

ST. GERMANUS: Gallic bishop who went to Britain in A.D. 428. An account of his life, written by Constantius, a former pupil of his, gives us some bits of information about events in Britain in the second quarter of the fifth century.

GILDAS: British Christian priest who lived in the first half of the sixth century, probably somewhere in the western part of Britain. His book, *On the Destruction and Conquest of Britain,* written in Latin, was the work of a moralist rather than a historian and must be used with great caution as a historical source.

last of those invaders, the Belgae, were still pouring across to Britain at the time of Caesar's campaigns in Gaul. It was the Belgic peoples in Gaul who were the spearpoint of resistance to Caesar, and as long as Britain remained untouched their irreconcilable elements had an ideal refuge from Roman invasion, an ideal base from which disaffection could be stirred up in the newly conquered lands.

Caesar raided Britain in 55 B.C.: in 54 he attempted its conquest, and he failed. Political confusion in Rome and the difficulties attendant on the conversion of the Republic into the Empire deferred fresh attempts and in the course of the next ninety years the position changed. The militancy of Gaulish nationalism died quickly under the beneficent rule of Rome: irreconcilables such as Commius the Atrebate may have found refuge in Britain, and may have contributed with their followers in greater or less degree to the spread of Belgic influence in the south and west, but they constituted no serious danger to the stability of Roman Gaul. In time southern Britain became politically unified under the rule of progressive Belgic princes, amongst whom the descendants of Caesar's enemy Cassivellaunus were the most successful: it provided a market for the products of Gaulish industries now flourishing under the *Pax Romana,* and it was in its turn the source of important raw materials, especially corn, cattle, minerals and slaves, the last being the product of continuing Belgic expansion into the hinterland. Although Cunobelin, the most important prince of Cassivellaunus's dynasty, may have held himself politically aloof from Roman alliance, he undoubtedly fostered the spread of Roman standards of living in south-eastern Britain and probably encouraged the investment of Romano-Gaulish capital in British trade.

His death (about A.D. 42) provoked a crisis. The commercial interests seeing danger in the break-up of the Belgic power among his sons and the emergence of a frankly anti-Roman party, pressed for military intervention. At Rome too there were political reasons which induced Claudius to take the initiative in Britain. The long ignoring of British affairs under Augustus and Tiberius had been given up by the unbalanced and unsuccessful Caligula, but his much advertised preparations for the conquest of Britain had been abandoned at the last moment for obscure reasons which in any case were damaging to the prestige of Roman arms. The circumstances of Claudius's own accession made the early winning of martial successes a matter of the first importance for this most unmilitary of Emperors: the resources and the troops for the enterprise were ready. Everything thus combined to bring about the resumption of the British project: threatened commercial interests, the hope of greater gain from the exploitation of raw materials whose value was magnified by speculative rumour, and the desire to restore the prestige of Roman arms by establishing the Emperor's authority on a firm basis of positive achievement.

With the details of the expedition's history there is no space to deal. It was well led by an able officer, Aulus Plautius, and had little difficulty in attaining its primary objectives. The Emperor was able to appear in Britain at the moment appropriate to the decisive advance, to lay down the main lines of the embryonic provincial organization, and to return to Rome with the necessary materials for the traditional triumph. From this point the political history of Roman Britain, which is essentially the same as its military history, may be conveniently divided into the following periods, on each of which a few words must be said:

I. 43-84. The attempt to conquer the whole of Britain.

II. (*a*) 84-211. The establishment of the northern frontier.

(*b*) 211-286. The maintenance of the northern frontier.

III. 287-410. The breakdown of the *Pax Romana.*

I. 43-84. Whatever the original intentions of the government may have been— it has been argued that in the first place only the tribes of the Belgic south were the direct object of the Roman attack—the struggle quickly turned into an attempt to conquer the whole of Britain. The last Belgic resistance was broken with the capture of Caractacus, son of Cunobelin, in 51: but more than all the Belgic territory had already been occupied four years before, when a diagonal frontier across the midlands from Devonshire to Lincoln had been laid out along the line now known as the Fosse Way by the second governor, Ostorius Scapula. This, however, even with its centre advanced to Wroxeter on the Severn, corresponded to no natural division of the country, and already by 60-61 the fifth governor, Suetonius Paulinus, was attempting by campaigns in North Wales and Anglesey to establish Roman arms on the Irish Sea and to divide the two main centres of anti-Roman feeling, the Silures of South Wales and the Brigantes of Northern England. But the revolt of Boudicca and the Iceni of East Anglia in 61 not only showed that this attempt was premature but very nearly brought the whole enterprise to an inglorious close, for before they were suppressed the rebel forces had pulverized one of the four Roman legions and by destroying the new centres of provincial administration and commerce at Colchester, Verulamium (St. Albans) and London, had effectively paralysed the government and cut the communications of the remaining legions with the Continent.

It took ten years of careful and conciliatory work, after the revolt was over, to pacify the tribes behind the midland frontier once more, and to re-establish the security necessary before the advance could be resumed. This was finally undertaken early in the reign of Vespasian, himself a veteran of the Claudian conquest, by three successive governors of enterprise and ability, Petilius Cerealis, 71-4, Julius Frontinus, 74-8, and Julius Agricola, 78-84. Cerealis, who had commanded the Lincoln legion at the time of Boudicca's revolt, concentrated his attention on the Brigantes of the north, who had recently adopted a more hostile attitude

to Rome. He was probably the first to conduct effective campaigns beyond the Humber, and to seize the great strategic position which became the legionary fortress of York. Frontinus, who followed him, advanced the left wing of the Roman frontier correspondingly into South Wales and pacified the difficult country of the Silures from his new legionary base at Caerleon-upon-Usk. It was thus possible for Agricola to resume the assault upon the north without fear of troubles in his rear, and to make the conquest of the whole island look for the first time what we know from Tacitus that he himself believed it to be, a practicable proposition.

Tacitus's biography of Agricola has perhaps caused historians to attribute to its hero more than his rightful share of the credit for the great extension of Roman rule in Britain at this period. At least it can be said that he was not the originator of the forward movement and that his work was possible only because secure foundations had been laid by his two predecessors. He was moreover allowed nearly twice as long a term of office as was normal at this time for governors of Britain. But it none the less remains true that Agricola was the only governor who did come within striking distance of a complete conquest of Britain, and if we examine the details of his military dispositions we can see that he had grasped in a remarkable degree the essentials of the problem. He saw the importance both of the Tyne-Solway line, later guarded by Hadrian's Wall, and of the Forth-Clyde isthmus, the site of the Antonine frontier, and he defended both with his own forts. And if, as Professor Collingwood has shown, Agricola had little genuine cause for the resentment which Tacitus attributes to him, at his recall by Domitian in A.D. 84, it cannot be denied that his recall does mark a turning-point in the history of the province. His successors were not encouraged to exploit the possibilities which it was believed at the time that his decisive victory at Mons Graupius had opened up: at the critical moment Rome reduced the army of

Britain and refused to pursue the conquest of the north.

II. (a) 84-211. The results were not at first as disastrous as Tacitus's phrase *perdomita Britannia et statim omissa* once led historians to believe. There has of late been some controversy over the extent of Agricola's Scottish conquests and their duration after his recall, but, whatever the detailed story may have been, it seems clear that many of the garrisons which he left north of Brigantia maintained themselves with more or less success at any rate until the end of the first century and in some important instances rather longer. But they could do little more than fight a losing battle against tribesmen increasingly conscious of the ineffectiveness of Roman policy and increasingly prepared to demoralize the isolated garrisons into abandonment of important positions by surprise attacks in overwhelming force. The reign of Trajan (98-117) was marked in Britain by none of the enterprising activity which characterized it in the East. What policy there was may perhaps be described as a 'petrification of the status quo': many forts in Wales and some in northern England hitherto built of earth and timber were now substantially reconstructed in stone: but here and there new forts were built and old ones abandoned, and it seems probable that some attempt was made to check the demoralizing process of enforced withdrawal from Agricola's Scottish fortresses by treating his transverse road from the Tyne to the Solway as a *limes* and fortifying it with a few new posts and the refurbishing of some old ones.

Such half-hearted measures, however, were quite inadequate. We have no knowledge of details, but it is clear that a major military disaster overtook the Roman forces in the north at the end of Trajan's reign or the beginning of that of his successor, Hadrian (117-38). Not only is there literary evidence that the Britons were in successful revolt at this time, but we know that the York legion and a number of auxiliary units disappeared altogether in these years,

and that Hadrian felt it necessary to come to Britain in person and to reinforce the depleted armies with a fresh legion for York, and other less permanent drafts. He also took the opportunity to plan and to initiate the great system of frontier works which bears his name between the Tyne and the Solway, and lies for the most part just north of the Trajanic *limes*. This new complex, with its elaboration of ditch, wall, forts, mile-castles, turrets, and vallum behind, was in construction between 122 and 126 in the governorship of A. Platorius Nepos. Hadrian built a massive frontier on a scale intended to be decisively permanent; but however much we may admire the magnificence of the achievement, his Wall is in reality but the solidest expression of a military panic in European history, and it marks a still more emphatic determination than had been registered hitherto to abandon Agricola's dream of a thoroughly conquered and pacified Britain.

Efficient as Hadrian's frontier system no doubt was in its direct purpose, it did not solve the problem of the unconquered north, and the existence of this problem, which necessitated the continuous maintenance of great armies on the northern frontier, remained henceforward the dominant political fact in Romano-British history. Less than twenty years after its completion, indeed, the construction of the turf wall of Antoninus Pius between the Forth and the Clyde, whatever may have been the purpose which it was built to serve, illustrates official dissatisfaction with the position left by Hadrian. Whether it was intended as a permanent advance to a line which on a superficial view appeared shorter and more defensible, or as a first stage in a belated resumption of Agricola's policy of breaking up the northern tribes into manageable and isolated blocks, or, as Professor Collingwood has recently suggested, as a temporary cover to a systematic deportation of the bellicose Lowlanders to Germany, it emphasized in any case the fundamental weakness of the Hadrianic solution.

And in itself it only made the military

situation more alarming. For the existence of the new line did not mean the abandonment of the old, the army of Britain was not augmented to provide for its garrisons, and the latter could thus only be obtained by a drastic withdrawal of troops from Wales, and a dangerous weakening of the forces in occupation of southern Brigantia. This region, though now far behind the official frontier, remained practically unaffected by the emollient penetration of Roman civilian culture, which further south had long since turned the compatriots of Caractacus and Boudicca into peaceful and prosperous provincials.

From the military point of view, in fact, much the same mistake had been made as in the days of Boudicca's revolt, and the results were somewhat similar. In 154, and perhaps more than once in the early years of Marcus Aurelius (161-80), there is both literary and archæological evidence for troubles in Britain which, at any rate on the first occasion, are definitely associated with a revolt of the Brigantes in the rear of the frontier region. After their suppression we hear in the reign of Commodus of the opposite danger—a regular invasion of Caledonians from beyond the Walls, an invasion which at least the northern barrier with its depleted garrisons and inadequate lateral command of the Firths of Forth and Clyde was powerless to withstand. When the situation was retrieved it would appear that the Roman command at last realized that in the existing conditions the double frontier constituted a weaker obstacle than Hadrian's Wall alone would have done, and the Antonine *limes,* after a stormy career of little more than forty years, marked achæologically by at least two major disasters, was deliberately dismantled by its own garrisons, who were thus released for strengthening the more tenable line to the south.

The political disturbances which followed the murder of Commodus in 193 unfortunately deprived this solution of durability. In the confused years that followed, the legions of Britain abandoned the task of frontier defence and were taken over to Gaul in 196 to support the claims of their governor, Clodius Albinus, to the imperial throne, thus providing the first example of a fatal practice whose repetition two centuries later was eventually to deprive Britain of its military protection against barbarian attack. The results on this occasion were disastrous both for Clodius Albinus and for Britain. The former was defeated by Septimius Severus at Lyons in 197 and lost his life: while in Britain the northern tribes took advantage of the deserted frontiers to carry out a deliberate and systematic destruction of Roman military works in the north, the effects of which are archæologically recognizable not only all along Hadrian's Wall but even as far south as the legionary fortresses of York and Chester. The governor sent over by Severus to repair the damage found that he had first to bribe the barbarian horde to return home.

An immense work of reconstruction was then undertaken. The Hadrianic system, wall, forts, and roads, and also the legionary bases at Chester and York, were refortified with a solidity and thoroughness worthy of the earlier period. No pains were spared to complete the work with dispatch. Even cemeteries were sometimes looted for building material as at Chester, and the military drafts were augmented by civilian labour gangs recruited from the southern British *civitates,* which have left building inscriptions here and there on the Wall itself. By 208 it appears that troops could be spared for a series of punitive expeditions, conducted by the Emperor in person against the tribal centres in the heart of Scotland; these expeditions were designed not so much to effect permanent conquests beyond the fortified zone as to show the barbarians that the restored frontier was to be respected. When Septimius Severus died at York in 211 the problem of the unconquered north, though still unsolved, had no longer the perpetual urgency which had marked it for the previous hundred and thirty years.

(*b*) 211-286. With the final establishment of the Severan frontier a period of unwonted calm falls over British politics. The Caledonian campaigns ended at Severus's death and many bodies of troops, which since the Antonine advance had been employed in the north, were returned to their old quarters in Wales, which in several cases, as at the legionary base at Caerleon itself, they seem to have found grass-grown and ruinous, and in need of complete reconstruction. But after this epilogue to the outburst of Severan building was over, the archæologist and the historian alike have little to record of any substantial moment, until the last quarter of the third century.

This is a fact of some interest. It means not only that Severus's work was so well done that it lasted for three generations, but that Britain as a whole must have escaped much of the political insecurity which characterized Roman history, especially frontier history, during the third century. For a secure frontier and political quiescence were rare enough in any part of the Empire in that troubled time, when Emperor succeeded Emperor in bewildering rapidity, and the incompetent instability of the armies replaced the comparative solidity of middle-class government as the dominant factor in politics. There is of course no reason whatever to believe that Britain was immune from the economic and social upheavals of the age—there is plenty of evidence that she was not—but it would appear that for the best part of a century the hardly-won frontier was held in comparative tranquility and that Britain enjoyed a period of unusual freedom from the worst political troubles of the time.

III. 287-410. Before the third century was over, however, the characteristics of the final phase of Romano-British history were beginning to appear. The military problem of provincial defence was no longer confined to the maintenance of the northern frontier, for the east and south coasts were coming to demand protection from the increasing menace of Frankish and Saxon pirates, and on the west the

tribes of Ireland were on the move, not only raiding the shores of Wales and Dumnonia but pouring across from Ulster into Scotland and so upsetting in its turn the long stable equilibrium of the north.

Britain experienced only one example of that tendency to political separatism, which nearly broke up the Roman Empire in the third century into a congeries of dynastic monarchies. This came, it appears, directly from the attempt of the central government, now in the capable hands of Diocletian and Maximian, to provide against this new danger of barbarian raids upon the coast. In 286 an officer named Carausius, who had been entrusted with the command of a strengthened naval force in the Channel and the task of suppressing piracy, established himself in Britain as an independent Emperor and successfully defied the forces sent against him. His position was so unassailable that he was for a while acknowledged as a colleague by the reluctant Emperors, and it was not until after his murder by one of his own officers, Allectus, in 293, that the western Caesar, Constantius Chlorus, found himself strong enough to reassert the central authority, a task which he successfully carried through in 296-7.

The brief interlude of Carausius and Allectus is important in Romano-British history as providing the background to a complete reorganization whose military aspect was even more drastic than that which had marked the reign of Septimius Severus. There was certainly every need in Britain for a *Redditor Lucis Aeternae,* the proud phrase with which Constantius described himself on the medal commemorating his victory over Allectus. On the northern frontier for example the latter had apparently removed the garrisons to oppose Constantius and the hostile tribes had poured in as at the end of the second century, once again razing the deserted fortifications as far south as York. Constantius had thus to begin by repeating the wholesale reconstruction effected by Severus a hundred years before, and he had further to meet the new danger of coastal piracy in a way which would not involve the danger of a second Carausius.

An elaborate system of coastal fortification, of which perhaps the outline had already been laid down by Carausius himself, was his solution of this problem. On the east and south coasts nearly every prominent harbour between the Wash and the Isle of Wight was provided with a fortress which served apparently both as a base for the naval patrol and as the headquarters of a military unit, part of the force at the disposal of a new officer, the Count of the Saxon Shore, who was in charge of the whole. The forts conformed in construction to the new tactics of the barbarized Roman army: they were strongly walled and equipped with bastions to resist a siege, but contained a minimum of permanent buildings within, and looked from without more like the lofty defensible castles of the Middle Ages than the low-built earlier Roman forts, which still retained in the second century features of the marching camps from which they had evolved. The same system was extended in a more half-hearted fashion to Wales, where forts of Saxon Shore type were built at any rate at Cardiff, Caernarvon, and Holyhead, and it would appear that either now or perhaps earlier the native Welsh were permitted or encouraged to refortify for their own defence many of the old hill-forts from which they had been ejected in the first century by the troops of Frontinus or Agricola.

Of the many institutional features of Constantius's reorganization something must be said later. Here it need only be mentioned that the military commands were now divorced from the civil authority, with which under the early Empire they had always been combined, and the legionary legates, hitherto directly responsible to the provincial governors, now gave way, as the chief officers of the army, to regional commanders of whom the Duke of the Britains had responsibility for the northern frontier, and the Count of the Saxon Shore, as already mentioned, took charge of coastal defence.

For more than half a century the system inaugurated by the reforms of Constantius secured the internal peace of Britain, and the landowning classes, if we may judge from the widespread evidence for the extension of unfortified country house life at this time, could live their rather futile lives of sterile virtuosity, untroubled by the alarms of Saxon piracy or the inconvenience of military revolt. Their prosperity, it may be, was only secured by periodic frontier concessions to barbarian settlement, of the type whose negotiation, it seems, brought Constans to Britain in 342, but it was not until after 360 that the military weakness to which such concessions contributed culminated in disaster. In 367 after several years of minor disturbances a concerted assault by Picts and Scots on the north and west and by Franks and Saxons on the south and east coasts overwhelmed the barbarized and partly treacherous forces of the Duke of the Britains and the Count of the Saxon Shore, and with the death of both officers in action there was nothing to prevent the invaders from once again destroying the defences of the north or from looting undefended villas at pleasure up and down the countryside. When Count Theodosius was sent over to restore the situation in 368 he was faced with bands of marauders plundering in Kent.

The Theodosian restoration of Britain was marked by the usual reconstruction of the Wall, though it would seem that attention was now concentrated on the main forts (the mile-castles and turrets being no longer occupied), and by the usual punitive expeditions beyond it. But it had two new features of its own. One was the additional protection afforded to the north-east by the building of coastal signal stations on the Yorkshire cliffs, a system the traces of whose probable employment elsewhere have perhaps been destroyed by subsequent erosion; and the other was the successful incorporation of some undefined frontier district, hitherto occupied by more or less hostile barbarian *foederati,** as the new

* [Allies.]

province of Valentia: this is more likely to have been in Wales than in the north.

The final collapse of effective Roman rule in Britain began within fifteen years of this apparently successful restoration of her power. It was not due to the overthrow of Roman arms by overwhelming barbarian force: still less was it due, as is often carelessly assumed on the basis of an isolated incident reported by a court poet, to the withdrawal of the garrisons of Britain by the central government for the defence of Italy or Rome. It was directly caused, as had been most of the military disasters in Britain since the second century, by the irresponsibility of the Roman forces themselves, and by the increasing tendency of their officers to pay more attention to the possibilities of their own advancement than to the safety of the provincials in their charge. This was perhaps not altogether surprising, for by now the armies were themselves largely barbarian by birth and sentiment and had little reason to feel more sympathy with the effete and oppressive landowning aristocracy which constituted the most Romanized elements of the provincial population, than with their own kinsmen, whom it was their business to keep beyond the frontiers.

The revolt of Maximus, who transferred the bulk of the British garrisons to Gaul in 383, was the beginning of the end, not so much because his exploit differed in kind from others of its type, as because after his failure in 388, and the death of his conqueror Theodosius in 395, the latter's general Stilicho did not find it possible in his patchwork restoration to reoccupy the Wall. This abandonment of the northern frontier, which was apparently followed before 400 by the destruction of the signal stations on the Yorkshire coast, made any future attempt to maintain the internal security of Britain strategically impossible. This being so, it was only a question of time before the final disappearance of effective Roman authority, and it has generally been assumed that this closely followed the next large-scale exodus of troops under the usurper Constantine, who crossed over to Gaul in 407 to repeat the attempt and to meet the fate of Maximus. When the Britons, exasperated at his failure to protect them, returned to the allegiance of the central government, the Emperor Honorius could only reply to their appeals for help by placing the responsibility for the defence of Britain on the civil organization of the *civitates,* thus implying that the last shreds of military organization had gone.

Whether these events represent the effective end of the Roman occupation of Britain, or whether, as some scholars now believe, there was a brief reoccupation of the south-eastern districts under a new official, the Comes Britanniae, for a few years in the second and third decades of the fifth century, the pattern of Romano-British history remains substantially the same. For such a reoccupation cannot have lasted more than fifteen years at the outside, can only have affected a very limited area, and made so little impression on contemporary or later historians that, while none mention it directly, several explicitly or implicitly deny its occurrence. It was in any case a matter of small consequence either in Roman or in British history.

B. INSTITUTIONAL, ECONOMIC, AND SOCIAL HISTORY

This brief outline of the political history of the province has dealt almost wholly with the creation, maintenance and collapse of the frontier system. The political history of Roman Britain is, in fact, essentially its military history and that history until the last phase is concentrated mainly in the frontier districts. But behind these frontier districts, and protected by them, lay the greater part of the province in area and population, and by far the most important part in wealth and culture. If we seek information about the provincial life behind the frontiers we shall find ourselves discussing not so much political history, as the institutional and economic problems of a complex social organization.

The main reason for this contrast lies in the physical geography of Britain. In the south, east, and over much of the midlands, the countryside was fertile and easy to traverse, capable of supporting a large agricultural population and open, as the Belgic invasions and the Roman conquest itself show, to every sort of continental influence. All this area was conquered in the first stage of the Roman occupation and rapidly pacified: but in the more mountainous, wetter, and more scantily populated country to the north and west of the island, the invaders were up against a different problem, one which in the long run defied even the power of Rome. The legions, it is true, struck deep into the Highland Zone: they conquered and pacified Wales and, less successfully, Brigantia, but they could not civilize either as they civilized the south; and even if Agricola had been successful in conquering the whole island, the contrast between the two halves of Roman Britain would still have remained. But with the Roman frontier established, as it came to be, across the foothills of the Highland Zone, the inevitable contrast was greatly exaggerated. In the north relations between the two peoples remained fundamentally hostile, and interest is concentrated on the political fluctuations of the balance between them. But in the south there was no such basic hostility between Roman and Briton, and the institutional, economic, and social consequences of their co-operation form its main claim on our attention.

1. *The Institutions of Roman Britain*

The main institutional framework of Roman Britain can be very briefly described. Down to the time of Severus it formed a single Imperial province under a legate of the Emperor as governor. Civil and military affairs were alike under his charge, his chief military subordinates being the legates commanding the three legions at Caerleon, Chester, and York, and his chief civilian assistant being the *legatus iuridicus,* of whose work we know little but who presumably controlled the administration of justice. The

only part of the governmental machine outside the authority of the governor was the financial department, which was in the hands of procurators directly dependent on the Emperor. Under Severus, and probably with the object of reducing the political power wielded by a single governor with so large an army as that of Britain under his command, the government divided Britain into two provinces, the Upper and the Lower, and the whole machine was presumably doubled. From literary and epigraphic evidence we know that Lincoln and York were in Lower Britain, Chester and Caerleon in Upper Britain, and it has thus been conjectured that the division ran roughly between the Wash and the Mersey, leaving in all probability London as the headquarters of the Upper Province, as York was more certainly the capital of the Lower. As has already been mentioned, the provincial system of Britain was reorganized again a hundred years later, as part of the general administrative rearrangement of the Empire carried out under Diocletian and Constantine. Britain now became one of the new divisions known as Dioceses under a Vicarius responsible to the Pretorian Prefect of the Gauls. It was subdivided into four provinces, Prima, Secunda, Flavia Caesariensis, and Maxima Caesariensis, to which a fifth, Valentia, was added, as already noticed, by Count Theodosius after 368. We do not know even roughly where these provinces lay, the only safe clue at present being an inscription which records the activities of a governor of Britannia Prima at Cirencester in Gloucestershire.

The reforms of Diocletian and Constantine also involved the separation of civil and military authority. The provincial governors now lost their authority over the troops, and the latter were reorganized into at least two new commands, those of the Duke of the Britains, and the Count of the Saxon Shore, whose functions have been described above. It should also be noticed that the increasing multiplicity of civil posts and military commands which was brought about by these successive alterations was symptomatic of a far-reaching social change which affected the whole character of Imperial government. In earlier times Roman officials had been comparatively few in number, exercising wide and often ill-defined powers with a maximum of individual responsibility and a minimum cost to the tax-paying provincials, who enjoy a wide measure of self-government; but, after the time of Diocletian, the number of functionaries enormously increased, their individual responsibility and with it their common standard of morality declined, while the chief employment of many was to duplicate one another's activities, and to collect the revenue necessary to their own maintenance. Such a system progressively aggravated its own defects and its increasing top-heaviness and corruption led straight to the disastrous incompetence of later Imperial administration.

So much for the provincial machinery of Britain considered as a unit of the Roman Empire. But there were also the local divisions and loyalties which affected the life of the individual provincial far more than the remote activities of legates and procurators. Foremost among these were the old Celtic and Belgic tribes, which the Romans, with their genius for adapting the institutions of subject peoples to their own purposes, had skilfully converted into self-governing units of local administration. To this end something over a dozen of the larger tribes had been recognized as *civitates:* their royal families, where they were monarchical, were abolished (sometimes with a transition stage in which a Romanophil king might be recognized for his lifetime as a tribal *legatus*), their councils of nobles were turned into local *ordines* or senates, with their own elective annual magistrates, and, to complete the illusion of self-government, they were encouraged and probably assisted to lay out well-planned and finely built tribal capitals of Roman design in which the public buildings would be dedicated to the Emperor by the local senate in carefully worded Latin inscriptions. Here sites for houses and shops would be available on easy terms for all tribesmen anxious to follow the new fashion for urban life. For although in one or two cases in the Belgic districts such towns seem to have grown more or less directly out of a pre-Roman settlement, the sites of most of them were new, as was indeed the whole conception of urban culture which their existence implied. However much we may speak of Belgic cities or trace the origins of town life in Britain back to the Neolithic Age, it remains true that urban life, as a life different in kind from village life and provided with standards and amenities which the other lacked, was a new and foreign conception introduced into Britain by Rome. As such it was, as we shall see later, perhaps the most important piece of machinery through which Roman culture came to Britain, and it will thus be of vital significance to assess the spontaneity of its reception and the extent of its influence.

Here, however, it must be noticed that the tribal capitals, if in some ways the most interesting, were not the only form which urban life took in Britain. There were towns more Roman in structure and therefore more artificial and alien to the British scene: there were others whose growth was perhaps more spontaneous but which never achieved the essentials of self-government. Five important towns at least fall into the former class: there were the four military colonies, Colchester, Gloucester, Lincoln and York, and the *municipium* of Verulamium near the present St. Albans. The colonies were primarily, like all Roman colonies, self-governing settlements of time-expired legionaries, although Colchester was also, at any rate at first, the centre of organized Emperor-worship and in some sense the capital of the province. All four were surrounded by cultivable lands adequate for the support of their inhabitants, who possessed full self-governing rights, and thus fell outside the general structure of the tribal system. In the same way Verulamium, as a *municipium,* would possess the usual *ordo* and magistrates, and a *territorium* which may well have included the bulk of the former lands of the Catuvellauni whose centre its pre-Roman equivalent had been. We know less of the status of certain other important places. London, for example, the largest town and doubtless mainly of spontaneous commercial growth, was in a class by itself, containing, as it must have done, the head-quarters of many administrative departments (such as the financial *procuratores*) in addition to a cosmopolitan host of traders; it must have been self-governing, but nothing is known of its position in the provincial structure. The same is true of Bath, whose existence depended on its hot springs: it probably won the usual free constitution justified by the possession of an artificial prosperity like that of many modern water-ing-places. The other class includes the smaller towns of Roman Britain, which were very numerous and doubtless varied a great deal in character: a good many were walled, which may indicate a certain official im-portance, perhaps as the centres of *pagi,* the subdivisions of the tribes, or the headquar-ters of imperial estates; but most were no doubt of natural growth springing up in response to the demands of trade, or occu-pying positions of local consequence on the network of Roman roads.

These roads bound the whole province together much as the railway system bound together Victorian England. Planned in the first instance to serve the needs of the army and constructed by military engineers as the legions advanced, their primary purpose was to secure rapid transport from the Channel ports and London to the frontier districts of Wales and the north. Once arrived in the military districts, they spread out into an elaborate network linking every fort to its neighbours and to the nearest point on the main arteries from the south. But after the pacification of the civil areas was completed they came to serve more and more the needs of the towns in the regions through which they passed. Branch roads and cross roads of little military significance were built to link the towns together and to ensure rapid communication from every place of any con-sequence to all its neighbours.

This obvious relationship of the roads to the towns emphasizes, like its counterpart

the railway system in the nineteenth cen-tury, the contrast between town and country. The chief element of Romanized country life was the *villa,* and the main roads paid no more attention to the convenience of the villas than did the railways to the country houses of a later age. The villas were served, as were the peasant villages, by local tracks and private lanes, many no doubt of pre-historic origin. These, although they may still in some cases exist, are impossible to recognize now as Roman because they lack the characteristic directness and heavy con-struction of the main roads.

The institutions of the countryside, al-though more must be said of their economic significance later, deserve notice at this point to complete the picture. Much work, how-ever, needs to be done before the usual divi-sion of their material remains into the Villas and Villages of our Romano-British maps can tell us much about the organization of country life. It has already been noticed that we know hardly anything about the adminis-trative geography of the province, the boundaries of the tribal areas or of the territories attributed to the self-governing towns. Nor do we know how much of Britain had been absorbed into the imperial estates, *saltus,* which were characteristic of many provinces and lay for most purposes outside the normal sphere of local govern-ment. It has been suggested that the distrib-ution of the villas and villages over the countryside may perhaps provide a clue to some of these uncertainties, for a glance at the maps will show that in some areas villas are very common and villages very rare and vice versa. It can be argued that in the vil-lage areas we may have the signs of imperial estates cultivated by tenant small-holders, and certain regions of this type such as the Fenlands, where considerable initial out-lay on drainage and regional planning alone made cultivation possible, are perhaps best explained on this hypothesis. On the other hand, the aristocratic structure of British tribal society might be expected to reveal itself architecturally in a countryside dotted with the villas of the upper classes, whose lands were cultivated by dependents, whether slaves or freemen, who were at first often housed on the premises of the villa itself.

All this, however, although offering a profitable field for local study, is at present very speculative, and progress will be slow until more detailed classification of villas and of villages has been carried out. For both terms in fact cover such a variety of architectural remains that it would be most unwise to draw confident conclusions from our present maps. Thus the term *villa* is normally used to cover every type of building from a large country mansion with central heating, elaborate mosaic floors, extensive bathing arrangements, and substantial outbuildings, through every grade of farmhouse, down to the shoddily built bungalows of small-holders or squatters. A countryside such as that of Gloucestershire, where the most luxurious type of villa is fairly common, is likely to have possessed a different social structure from one which is dotted over with villas of the small unheated farmhouse type. Of one fact alone we can be reasonably certain. The villas, large and small, were in the majority of cases the residences of native Romano-Britons of whatever social rank, and the extent to which they display Roman standards of comfort and decoration is indicative both of the degree of native prosperity under Roman rule and of the attractiveness of Roman fashions. If the towns were the chief channels of Romanization for all classes of the population, the villas illustrate in detail the receptiveness of the upper ranks of society to the lessons which Rome taught.

The villages illustrate the same point for the peasant classes. Here there is an even more bewildering variety than among the villas; for under this heading must always have been gathered the great bulk of the population of Roman Britain, even if the material traces of their settlements are far less substantial and far less informative than those of villas, towns and forts. Included among them were not only the descendants of primitive native agriculturalists and many

dependent cultivators of the villas and the imperial estates, but also such varied groups as the populous mining communities of the Mendips, or Derbyshire, the half-nomadic charcoal burners of the Weald, the followers of a rural industry like the New Forest potters, and the innkeepers and postboys of a minor halting-place on a main road. Their response to Roman culture varied with their economic position and their accessibility to towns and villas. Rural communities especially in the hills saw in Roman civilization little but the opportunity for obtaining a cheap supply of serviceable household goods to replace the products of primitive domestic industries: others, more ambitious and better off, might attempt to decorate their huts in the classical manner, and to scribble scraps of Latin on their pots and walls. But, apart from such superficialities, the habits and the sentiment of the lower rural classes remained far less touched by Roman institutions than was the case in the upper ranks of native society. To appreciate the significance of this cleavage we must look a little more closely at the economic background to the history of Roman Britain.

2. The Economic Background

The economic basis of pre-Roman Britain was quite simply one of subsistence agriculture. In the highlands of the north and west, and to a less extent on the chalk downs and limestone plateaux of the south, a semi-pastoral existence may have been still followed by many, but the bulk of the population depended for its food supply upon the cultivation of the land, and, its agricultural equipment being for the most part extremely primitive, this cultivation was limited to the lighter and more easily drained soils whether these were found high up on open downland or down on the gravel spreads and terraces which lined the valleys of many rivers in the south and midlands. Thus the pattern of human settlement was strictly conditioned by the distribution of such soils, and the wide regions of heavy land bearing forest or ill-drained marsh and swamp were left practically uninhabited. Only in the south and east, the parts which had been substantially affected by Belgic settlement, had any changes of moment been made in this essentially primitive pattern: there, it is now believed, the newcomers who, partly Teutonic in origin, were more accustomed on the Continent to exploiting forest conditions, had begun to open up some of the heavier lands, with their more efficient tools and implements, and had also developed, alongside the older village agriculture, the system of cultivation based on isolated farmsteads whose broad cornlands so impressed Julius Caesar in Kent.

The Roman conquest made no direct changes in this situation. It was not inspired by any enthusiasm for agricultural pioneering or by the land-hunger which marked, for example, the European settlement of North America. And from first to last the great bulk of the inhabitants of Roman Britain must have been engaged in subsistence agriculture with substantially the same primitive equipment which their ancestors had long possessed. This has been clearly shown by air-photography and field-work in many areas of predominantly light soils, where the Romano-British village populations continued to conform throughout the occupation to the essential pattern of prehistoric times.

But indirectly and unintentionally the balance was altered by the Roman conquest in a good many ways. Many causes led to an increased demand for the fruits of the earth, and made it worth while to grow more from the land than was wanted for the bare subsistence of its growers. The Roman towns began to spring up and their non-producing inhabitants had to be fed; and their fires and furnaces supplied with fuel, the demand for which made it worth while to clear good soils of woodland; tax-gatherers came round and officials requisitioning supplies for the army; the new roads made transport easy where before it had been impossible for bulky goods; the imposition of internal peace increased security and minimized the risk of disturbance to growing crops; and, finally, currency was more abundant and it was easier to convert the profits of agriculture into the material comforts supplied by the new industries.

Such causes lay behind the development of the villa system in Roman Britain. It represented no direct importation from Italy or Gaul, but was the natural response of the more progressive British agriculturalists to the new demand for their produce. For Roman villas are but Belgic farmsteads writ large, and the spread of the system means simply adaptation all over the country, by those who could afford the initial outlay, of the progressive methods of cultivation already spreading in the south-east: the centering of broad lands on a house built solidly, *more Romano,* as houses were being built in the new towns, and provided, as taste and resources dictated, with the new decorations and amenities which the towns displayed.

Thus the capital expenditure incurred in the construction of towns and roads stimulated something of an economic revolution in the countryside of Roman Britain, a revolution which, it must be remembered, had its social basis. In pre-Roman times tribal society was no doubt already aristocratic, and the nobility was able to maintain its social prestige mainly by martial prowess, renown won by heroic exploits in intertribal warfare. But if the *Pax Romana* had destroyed the tribal warfare and with it much of the *raison d'être* of the old aristocracy, the latter now won a more durable economic basis for its threatened superiority. For not only were its members recognized by Rome as a governing class by their membership of the tribal senates, but they also were alone in a position to exploit the new demand for corn and cattle, and to adopt the profitable technique of villa agriculture. Hence the momentous economic distinction sprang up between the villa-owning classes, who were able to take full advantage of the new fashion for Roman culture and material comforts and prospered accordingly, and on the other side the bulk of the agricultural peasantry, who remained culturally barbaric and economically backward, and thus became relatively more impoverished than before. This unfortunate distinction developed in time into a social cleavage of the utmost gravity, which eventually threatened the whole stability of Romano-British civilization.

But for perhaps a hundred or a hundred and fifty years all was well. If one may judge from the tremendous output of public and private building which distinguishes the history of almost all Roman towns in the second and third quarters of the second century, there must have been a genuine burst of urban prosperity produced by a wide initial demand for the products of their industries, a demand no doubt fostered by the local nobility, who were equally interested as urban magistrates and as rural landlords in the welfare of town and country alike. It is true that we know little about specifically urban industries. This is in part because so few towns have been adequately excavated, in part because the comparative density of towns in lowland Britain probably confined the products of each to a restricted area, and prevented the development of really large-scale activity. But although the primary function of the towns was to be the centres of culture and administration rather than centres of trade and industry, the facts suggest that for a century or more the initial momentum of their creation lasted, and for a while at least they must have paid their way.

Unfortunately this prosperity was not permanent: it was apparently killed partly by a general change in Imperial economic policy which affected all provinces of the Empire alike, and partly by local factors which operated more strongly in Britain than elsewhere. We may take the latter first. It will be obvious from what has been said that the urban structure of the province was extremely artificial. While its basis still remained a thinly spread rural population engaged mainly in subsistence agriculture, some twenty or thirty towns had sprung up with great rapidity at the bidding of a government primarily concerned with problems of administration and obsessed with the equation between culture and town life.

They had not grown naturally as modern towns grow, in response to the demands of industry and commerce. Hence, while their creation played its part, as has been suggested, in producing an initial phase of general prosperity in which they shared, they had in the long run to be fed at the expense of the countryside which could not afford to buy their products in return. The land had neither the wealth nor the population to maintain indefinitely this unnatural burden of a parasitic urban culture.

Just at the time when such factors were probably beginning to make themselves felt a change was coming over Imperial economic policy. The Empire, which had, in a sense, grown out of a federation of Mediterranean city states, had hitherto stimulated and encouraged in its conquered provinces the urban culture which was its own life-blood. But by the beginning of the third century political power had passed from the city bourgeoisie of Italy and Gaul into the hands of the army and its leaders, men trained in the savage realities of frontier defence, who cared little for the amenities of urban civilization. Cities to them were nothing but the sources of wealth from which armies could be maintained, and, whereas in earlier times the towns had grown rich on the conquests of the army, it was now the army which lived on the resources of the towns. Heavy taxation and the imposition of forced services penalized bourgeois industry and, to make matters worse for the trading classes, the currency was ruined by successive inflations which brought commerce and manufacture to a standstill.

The effect of all this is clearly seen in the spectacular dilapidation which seems to have overtaken many towns in the second half of the third century. At Wroxeter, where the forum was burnt before A.D. 300, not only was it never rebuilt but its debris, including ruined columns, and even human bodies, was left where it fell and was worked pell-mell into the improvised road surface formed by the continuing traffic of the surviving inhabitants. At Verulam, the town was ruinous, and its walls and gates in a state of collapse. A great part of the urban population must have melted back into the countryside.

But the countryside itself was strangely unaffected by the tragic breakdown of this artificial urban prosperity, a fact which suggests that the ruin of the towns was brought about more by the disastrous policy of unsympathetic Emperors than by the natural decay which would have resulted from purely economic weakness. For the increase in villa building in the third and fourth centuries suggests that there was still money about but that the moneyed classes, who, as we have seen, had from the first been both urban and rural in their interests, were now deliberately concentrating their resources on their country properties. There are, in fact, all the symptoms of a flight of capital from town to country which can best be explained by the desire of all who could do so to escape from the burdens and services which were now exacted with increasing rigour from the holders of what had once been civic posts of honour and authority. Although stringent legislation was passed to prevent the richer citizens from thus escaping the new and disastrous consequences of their wealth, it is clear that the more influential contrived in many cases to make good their escape, thus leaving the major burdens to be borne by the smaller bourgeois, who had no such means of retreat. Thus, while the towns decayed, the villas prospered and there are many instances in the third and fourth centuries of the building of new ones and of extensions and reconstructions of the old, normally increasing their accommodation and amenities.

The breakdown of the towns was not accompanied by a complete collapse of industry, but rather by its reorganization to suit the new conditions. It is a remarkable fact that the period of their decay is coincident in the pottery industry, about which we know most, with the growth of specialized rural manufactures whose standardized products found a surprisingly wide market. The best-known instances are the New Forest wares of Hampshire, apparently the products of a genuine peasant industry, and

the Castor potteries near Peterborough, which, to judge from the very extensive distribution of their output and the number of prosperous villas which surround them, were more heavily capitalized. In the fourth century a similar phenomenon appears in Yorkshire with the Crambeck, Throlam, and Knapton industries, which supplied not only a civilian demand, but the needs of most of the northern garrisons. This curious and rather unexpected development was caused in part, no doubt, by the cessation in the third century of supplies of the better fabrics from the so-called Samian potteries of Gaul, whose wares had hitherto been imported in enormous quantities: in part it was due to the natural increase of specialized industry in a highly capitalized society: but in part too it exemplifies once more the flight of enterprise from town to country, for these late potteries are rarely found in any close relationship with one of the older towns. How the industry was financed in an age when wild fluctuations in price levels were brought about by repeated inflations of an already chaotic currency is far from clear: it may be that the general return to rural conditions assisted the growth of an industry based mainly on barter and other non-monetary expedients. Certain it is that the prosperity of the villas at this time can only be explained on the assumption that their economy rested increasingly on the payments in kind and labour services of the down-trodden peasantry, which gave at any rate greater security to the landlords than an exclusive reliance on the contemporary currency could have done.

At the beginning of the fourth century and no doubt as part of the Constantian overhaul of the whole provincial machinery, a deliberate attempt was made to reverse the trend of the previous hundred years and to pump fresh blood into the arteries of the towns. Verulamium was extensively rebuilt on a scale which certainly implies governmental assistance, and at any rate the defences of many other cities were repaired and brought up to date with the addition of the now fashionable bastions. At the same time the general reformation of the currency must have improved the outlook for urban trade and commerce, although the increasing numbers of the bureaucracy meant heavier taxation and sapped what little remained of local independence.

But, in Britain at any rate, things had gone too far to be easily remedied by assistance from a temporarily benevolent government, and, while the evidence of prosperity in the villas reaches its peak in the first half of the fourth century, a great city like Verulamium had already reverted by 350 to the helpless disrepair and deplorable squalor of a century before. All but a group of streets round about the civic centre of the town seems to have been deserted by its inhabitants, and even in this withered nucleus the municipal theatre was being used as a rubbish tip.

We have thus to think of civilian society in Roman Britain at this time as consisting broadly of three elements whose interests were coming to be ominously divergent: the townsfolk, decadent and impoverished, who were still regarded by government as the natural centres of provincial organization and bore the main burden of its taxation: the rural aristocracy of the villas, who alone maintained the earlier standards of Roman culture and taste, but whose wealth largely depended on the exploitation of the third element, an increasingly barbarous peasantry whose traditional craftsmanship and native culture had long been weakened by dependence on the cheaper products of Roman industry and who now thought of the Empire simply in terms of its tax-collectors and oppressive landlords.

C. THE END OF ROMAN BRITAIN

It only needed the collapse of the *Pax Romana* to break the feeble ties which bound this society together, and after 360, as we have seen, the countryside was more and more at the mercy of marauding Picts, Scots, and Saxons. Their raids made little difference at first to the towns except perhaps to swell their population with refugees

escaping from the insecurity outside their walls; but they fell with shattering effect on the villas, for these not only contained the bulk of the material wealth of the province but were isolated and for the most part entirely unfortified. Thus such early raiding is likely to have endangered the economic and cultural position of the province out of all proportion to the extent of the material damage which it caused: not only did it mean that the most Romanized classes suffered soonest and most severely, but the disorganization of the villas upset the food supply on which the towns still depended, and broke the discipline which bound the reluctant peasantry to their lords. In Gaul a century later it was this menace of an uprooted peasantry turned brigands which seems to have been the major terror to the countryside, and no doubt the same was true of Britain in the last quarter of the fourth century. And, whether we atttribute the general scantiness of coin finds in the villas after 375 to their destruction and desertion, or whether, as has been recently suggested, we treat it merely as proving their general reversion to a regime of subsistence agriculture for which currency was not required, it is clear that by 400 the villa-owners had ceased to be the dominant social class in Britain, and their disappearance marks a major stage in the collapse of the Roman economy. It must have been a memory of this collapse of villa agriculture which led Gildas[4] in his confused summary of the events between 383 and 446 to note that a moment came when 'the whole province was deprived of the support of its food supply, except only for the resources of hunting.' Roman Britain was rapidly sinking back to what anthropologists call a food-gathering economy.

It is rarely wise to use an argument from silence in a Dark Age context, and an *argumentum ex silentio Gildae* is especially dangerous, but it may none the less be signifi-

[4] It is generally agreed that the *De excidio et conquestu Britanniae* is a genuine work of the British priest Gildas, whose *floruit* was in the first half of the sixth century A.D.

cant that he scarcely shows any other conscious memory of the days when villa-owners were the outstanding social aristocracy of Roman Britain: his apparent ignorance is at least consistent with the view that in his time the villas had perished so long and so utterly that the part they had once played in the life of the province had been wholly forgotten.

But the same is not true of the Roman towns. Gildas knew enough about them to deplore their destruction in one of his purplest passages, and to give the heading *De urbium subversione* to his general account of what he believed was the most chaotic phase of Anglo-Saxon settlement, a phase which he places late in the fifth century, not long before his own birth. His evidence for their survival to that age is borne out not only by inherent probability, but by other scraps of literary evidence. Verulamium at least was alive enough to discuss Pelagianism with St. Germanus in 428, and to offer him the hospitality of a thatched hut; and an entry in the *Anglo-Saxon Chronicle* has been held to show that London could still provide shelter for British refugees from Kent as late as 457. But whether we take Gildas's account of their entire desertion in his own day at its face value, and believe with Haverfield that even London 'lay waste a hundred years' or whether we are convinced that some at least retained a continuous if diminished population to the days when commerce could revive under the encouragement of settled Saxon dynasties, the entire disappearance of the urban bishoprics, which must have provided in Britain as in Gaul the framework of the Christian organization in Roman times, is clear enough proof that sooner or later they lost the last remnants of that civic consciousness which distinguished the *civitates,* even in the days of Honorius, from the uprooted peasants of the countryside. The institutions of Roman Britain in town and country alike were entirely unsuited to the economic conditions of the age of Anglo-Saxon settlement and, while the British people may have contributed substantially to the blood of our later mongrel population, their long-forgotten villas and depopulated towns had no direct part to play in the slow and painful evolution of the manors and boroughs of medieval England.

ROMAN BRITAIN PRODUCED NO SCHOLAR comparable in stature to Anglo-Saxon England's Bede. A Benedictine monk whose life (A.D. 673-735) was spent largely in the Northumbrian monastery of Jarrow, Bede was exceptional because of the range of his interests and knowledge and the extent of his literary output. His complete works, published in the original Latin with an English translation, run to twelve volumes, and include Biblical commentaries, scientific treatises, grammatical and critical handbooks, saints' lives, and verse. Many of his books circulated widely in medieval times, but his *Ecclesiastical History of the English Nation* (*Historia ecclesiastica gentis Anglorum*) was even then his most celebrated production, and it is primarily as a historian that the modern world has known him. This work, which traced the change from barbarism to civilization in English history, was one of the books which Alfred the Great caused to be translated into Anglo-Saxon, and the compilers of the *Anglo-Saxon Chronicle,* which was begun during Alfred's reign, made use of it. As the title of the work indicates, Bede was primarily interested in the history of the Christian church in England, but he included in his account a good deal of what we would call secular history. In his day civilization centered in the church, and ecclesiastical history, broadly viewed, was cultural history. As a storyteller and as a literary artist, Bede has had few peers. Yet it is important to remember that his objective was not to entertain but to set forth historical truth, as he saw it. The brief appreciation of Bede that follows was delivered by Monsignor Philip J. Furlong as a paper at the annual meeting of the American Catholic Historical Association in December, 1935.

ON THE TWELVE HUNDREDTH ANNIVERSARY OF THE DEATH OF BEDE

PHILIP J. FURLONG

To be remembered by posterity after twelve hundred years is in itself exceptional; it is more than exceptional when one reflects that during the twelve hundred years which have elapsed since the death of the Venerable Bede dynasties have risen and vanished, Christendom has been divided and subdivided, new continents have been discovered and settled. And the wonder is not lessened by recalling the fact that the figure we are concerned with was not a great pontiff, nor a crusader, nor an emperor; he was of all things a historian. To understand why after twelve hundred years the slight figure of Bede should be remembered at all it may be practical to borrow the suggestion in the inscription carved for an Englishman of a later time: "Si monumentum requiris, circumspice" and transpose it into the injunction, "tolle, lege," for Bede has a monument and that monument, the written word, is indeed an impressive one. Bede's monument is composed of a series of works which includes theological and scriptural studies, literary pieces, that is to say the technical side of letters as well as some verses, treatises on natural science, and of particular importance, history. The variety of fields of human knowledge covered by Bede is little less than astonishing. The physical labor alone incident to the production of his intellectual output judged

by any standards is considerable, but when it is reckoned, as it should be, both with reference to the troubled times in which he lived and to his own position in life, the results of Bede's industry cannot fail to amaze us. So it appeared to Symeon of Durham, who wrote of Bede as one living "in a remote corner of the world, who never crossed the seas in order to learn knowledge, who did not visit the schools of the philosophers, [yet] should be famous for such great learning and should be known everywhere in the world for the composition of so many books." But mere quantity production cannot explain Bede's importance. There are certain characteristics about his writing that set him far above his fellows. Bede's sympathy, his variety of intellectual interests no less than his technical equipment as historian, are in fact the characteristics which place his work far above that of his contemporaries. An understanding of his life which was marked by singular sincerity of purpose and a high respect for truth is the key to Bede the historian. His life, which covered in all some sixty-two years, after his seventh year was passed behind the protecting walls of the monastery. The years spent quietly at Jarrow vitalized his career. As a monk meditating upon the realities of life and upon the verities of eternity Bede must have acquired that feeling for truth

Reprinted by special permission from *The Catholic Historical Review*, XXII (1936), 297-303. The footnotes which originally appeared with this essay have been omitted.

and that sense of proportion which characterized his work. In this cultural oasis set in the midst of a world torn by strife and given to destruction, the scholar was protected against those disturbing influences which beset the path of historians of our own times. The monastery, too, apparently was a treasury of source material and in this treasure house Bede was able to sort his materials, using that which was worthy and discarding the spurious. The picture of these influences has been admirably set forth by Francis S. Betten, S.J.

A full appreciation of Bede the historian requires an excursion along the avenue of his non-historical works and while it is not here practical to make more than a passing reference to their subject-matter even this little will disclose the fact that all human knowledge was within the sphere of Bede's interest. Bede was no Doctor Dryasdust, he was not a specialist of the present-day variety hobbled to a single point, wandering hopelessly through a maze of detail with neither perspective nor direction. Bede was what the model historian must be, an explorer. His inquisitiveness, for example, led him to make special studies of the reasons and the ways of reckoning time. Bede's studies of chronology are of special importance and even though the results have been the subject of controversy, as witness among others that carried on in the *Athenaeum* (1930) between Sir James H. Ramsay and Mr. A. Anscombe, the conclusions prove only this: that Bede was a careful historian and in the matter of chronology he is far more careful than his contemporaries.

Professor Charles W. Jones has called attention to the fact that in the subject of chronology Bede seems to have assembled a library of exceptional completeness for that time. At any rate Bede's knowledge stood him in good stead when he came to write history, for history must have strict regard to chronology. Indeed, the fifth book of his *Ecclesiastical History* contains a chronological recapitulation of English history from the Roman invasion under Julius Caesar to the death of Archbishop Bertwald in 731. Mathematics challenged Bede. This no doubt made him careful in computing figures or accepting the totals of others. In some of the Old English versions of Bede's *Ecclesiastical History,* as George Hempl notes, there has been a misreading of numerals. These errors, however, are not to be attributed to Bede who is most careful about figures. Thus, for example, in the third book of the history he is careful to note that in 655 A.D. five thousand families lived in southern Mercia on the careful enumeration of the bishops who took part in the ecumenical councils of the Church from Nicea to the second at Constantinople (Book IV, cxviii).

The historical works of Bede are unquestionably his most important productions and of these the *Ecclesiastical History of the English People* by far out-distances his other works, for although the *Martyrology* has a place in the catalogue of Bede's writings, in its present form it undoubtedly is not entirely his work. Bede's *Chronicle of the Six Ages of the World* is limited in its appeal. His two biographies of St. Cuthbert, one in

WILBUR CORTEZ ABBOTT: American historian who is best known for his monumental work in four volumes, *The Writings and Speeches of Oliver Cromwell* (1937-1947). As a student at Cornell in the 1890's, he wrote a thesis on the sources of Bede's *Ecclesiastical History,* and his volume of essays entitled *Conflicts with Oblivion* contains an interesting study of Bede.

ST. CUTHBERT: Seventh-century Northumbrian monk and bishop who is believed to have performed many miracles and is held in the highest veneration in the church. Several biographies of St. Cuthbert were written during the Middle Ages, of which two by Bede, one in hexameters, the other in prose, are considered the best. A modern biography by Charles Eyre was published in 1849.

verse, relatively speaking, are likewise unimportant. But the *Ecclesiastical History* is a different matter. This is a genuine masterpiece and upon it Bede's fame chiefly rests. The history was written in his fifty-eighth or fifty-ninth year, at the suggestion of Albin, a disciple of Archbishop Theodore and Abbott Adrian. Perhaps not more than a year was consumed in the writing of the history, which in itself is an achievement. The history in Everyman's Library comprises nearly 300 pages of closely printed matter, a most representative production. But while in the actual writing of this work great speed was brought to bear, in the larger sense a lifetime went into its making. Perhaps here is the explanation of the attractiveness of this book. In any case Bede's *History* is the one history written during the medieval period that towers above its fellows. The importance of his text was so clearly perceived that it was copied probably hundreds of times so that even today at least one hundred thirty manuscripts are extant which are, or were, to be found from Leningrad to Mexico City. And after the invention of printing this book was among the first to come from the presses. But this does not explain its greatness. There are, however, characteristics in this book more or less discernible which do indicate the reasons for the appeal of Bede's masterpiece. There is a poetry in the history; there is also a certain epic quality that raises it from a standard chronicle to a piece of literature. There is, besides, the honesty and sincerity of the author that speak forth from every page and finally there is the technical equipment of the writer himself who evidently regarded the office of historian with reverence. The effectiveness of a historian depends to some extent upon his style, for no matter how painstaking his research, he must be able to clothe the fruits of his labor in beautiful language. Bede was a poet. We have his verse, but we have his poetry in his prose also. And here is one explanation of the beauty of Bede's writing, because a writer of history, for being a poet, is not less a historian; rather his writing will be rich

and complete. So in the *Ecclesiastical History* Bede speaks of a "hill adorned, clothed with flowers" (Book I, cvii). "Craggy and uncouth mountains" are noticed (Book IV, cxxvii), "The boisterous wind," "raging pain," make definite what he wants us to see.

Professor Abbott has called attention to the epic quality of Bede's writing. Bede, unconsciously perhaps, is recounting the progress of a tremendous struggle, the battle between paganism and Christianity. Christianity had by no means triumphed even in Bede's day, for it was not until several centuries later that the northern peoples who constituted the chief threat to England came under the yoke of Christ. England itself, during the seventh century, was undergoing the process of conversion and Bede was born during the seventh. He therefore knew much of the power of the forces which Christianity must overcome. And the conqueror? Who He was and how He was regarded had already been proclaimed in *The Dream of the Rood* but not more eloquently than in Bede's own words at his death preserved for us in Cuthbert's letter to Cutwin: "The time for me to be set free is at hand, for indeed my soul much desires to behold my King Christ in His beauty." Here is the secret: Bede's King, the White Christ, is He who is fighting the powers of darkness. He is the hero of the *Ecclesiastical History*.

Factual history is taken for granted in the historian. Bede's honesty amounts to genius. Perhaps this quality explains why his history begins as it does by omitting a grandiose survey of world history and beginning directly in Chapter I with a statement concerning the geography of Britain and the character of its early inhabitants, and, in Chapter II, giving the story of Caesar's invasion. Had Bede followed the practise of contemporary writers, and later writers also, he should have written a history largely apocryphal in parts and one that long since had been forgotten. When dealing with the miraculous, Bede is carefully objective. In describing the virtues of saintly characters there is a complete absence of pietism. Indeed there is a rugged honesty which is especially appealing. See, for example, Pope Gregory's exhortation to Augustine that he glory not in his miracles: "It remains, therefore, most dear brother, that amidst those things which you outwardly perform through the working of our Lord, you always inwardly strictly judge yourself. . . . And if any time you have offended our Creator . . . call it to mind that the remembrance of your guilt may crush the vanity which rises in your heart."

But the professional historian will perhaps be chiefly interested in Bede's method of writing. Concerning his method of writing history he has this to say, that his sources were "the writings of the ancients, or the tradition of our ancestors or of my own knowledge." What were the writings of the "ancients"? They were, among others, Eddius' *Life of Wilfrid,* or the anonymous *Life of Pope Gregory,* or *The Life of Cuthbert.* Bede was acquainted also with Pliny, Orosius, Eutropius, Vegetius, Isidore of Seville, Tertullian, and, no doubt, others, for what has been called the monastic travelling library was evidently an efficient institution and was in successful operation in Bede's day. This explains why it was not necessary for him to leave his monastery for source material; the sources came to him. His friends journeyed as far as Rome to procure material. Unfortunately, it is not always possible to particularize concerning the sources used by Bede. Plummer remarked some years ago that a really critical edition of Bede, which should show exactly how much he borrowed and how much is original, is a great desideratum. After forty years this situation has not been remedied. Such a task would be a monumental one because Bede rarely indicates specifically which sources he has used; the authority may be mentioned but not the particular work. This neglect must not always be charged against Bede. Probably in copying the manuscripts later scribes failed to note all the indications. Bede enjoyed the friendship of many of the best informed men of his day, those who had personal knowledge of the events he describes or who had been in contact with a previous generation that had known of these events first hand. Their contributions are for the most part duly noted. The professional historian, therefore, cannot fail to be satisfied with Bede's method of writing history and his careful use of source material.

So we turn from an attempted analysis of the method employed by Bede and the all too sketchy consideration of the sources used by him to the man himself to justify— if justification were needed—the salutation on the twelve hundredth anniversary of his death: Bede, model for historians. We like to think that this may be found in the concluding words of the *Ecclesiastical History of the English People,* where Bede writes: "And now, I beseech thee, good Jesus, that to whom thou hast graciously granted sweetly to partake of the words of thy wisdom and knowledge, thou wilt also vouchsafe that he may some time or other come to thee, the fountain of all wisdom, and always appear before thy face, who livest and reignest world without end. Amen!"

LIKE MANY OTHER PROBLEMS in Anglo-Saxon history, the problem of the origin of English urban communities has given rise to no little controversy. The word *burh,* of which *borough* and *burgh* are later forms, was the old English name for a fortress, or fortified place, and many of the boroughs recorded in Domesday Book may well have had a military origin. F. W. Maitland in his *Domesday Book and Beyond* (1897) expounded a "garrison theory" of borough origins. The nucleus of the borough community, he argued, was to be found, at least in the case of many boroughs, in groups of fighting men maintained in them as armed garrisons by the great landed proprietors of the shire. Professor Carl Stephenson, in an article published in the *English Historical Review* in 1930 and later in a book (*Borough and Town: A Study of Urban Origins in England,* 1933), rejected this "garrison theory" but emphasized what he believed to be the military character of Anglo-Saxon boroughs. In his opinion the normal borough remained essentially a fortress and administrative center throughout the Anglo-Saxon period, devoid of any really urban character, which it did not acquire until after the Norman Conquest. The views of Stephenson, Maitland, and others regarding the origins of English boroughs were critically examined by James Tait in his authoritative study *The Medieval English Borough: Studies on Its Origins and Constitutional History* (1936). In the selection that follows, Professor F. M. Stenton, of the University of Reading, discusses Anglo-Saxon boroughs in the light of the best and most recent historical scholarship. He concludes that the normal county town at the end of the Anglo-Saxon period was "an agricultural unit, a trading centre, and a place of defense." The selection is taken from Professor Stenton's *Anglo-Saxon England,* one of the best volumes in the important "Oxford History of England" series.

TOWNS AND TRADE [IN ENGLAND BEFORE THE NORMAN CONQUEST]

F. M. STENTON

No problems in the whole of Anglo-Saxon history are more difficult than those which relate to the origins of the English town. The evidence is fragmentary, and often ambiguous. The only documents which give direct information about the beginnings of English urban life come from the southeast, the district from which communication with the continent was easiest. It is unwise to assume that places less favourably situated had come to the point of urban development reached before 850 by London, Canterbury, or Rochester. Now and then a historian or clerk uses phrases which show that a particular place was something more than an upland village. When Bede refers to the *praefectus Lindocolinae civitatis* he makes it clear that Lincoln, if not a city in the medieval sense of the word, was at least a centre of population of more account than the ordinary *hām* or *tūn* of the country-side. But the word *civitas,* which was generally reserved for places known to have been sites of Roman occupation, does not in this period imply any close concentration of inhabitants. Worcester is called a *civitas* in 803, but some ninety years later, when the place was fortified as part of a scheme of national defence, it is clear that no more than a faint anticipation of urban life had as yet arisen there. There can be no doubt that York, to which Frisian traders are known to have resorted in the eighth century, was already an important centre for the distribution of goods, and that the Danes who plundered Southampton in 842 knew of the place as a trading port where stores of movable wealth were likely to be

Reprinted by special permission from *Anglo-Saxon England* (Copyright, Oxford University Press, 1943; second edition, 1947), 518-536. The present selection is reprinted from the second edition. The footnotes which originally appeared with it have been omitted.

laid up. It is reasonable to assume that there were merchants sitting before the gate of Offa's 'palace' at Tamworth. But it is only in Kent that anything is known about the way in which the earliest English traders lived together.

The Kentish evidence is derived from a series of early charters which show that Canterbury and Rochester were divided, more or less completely, into a number of enclosed holdings resembling, though often larger than, the messuages of a medieval borough. The individual holding was known from the fence which surrounded it either as a *haga*—that is, a hedged plot—or as a *tūn*—a usage which shows this familiar word in its primitive sense of 'enclosure.' To some, and probably to most, of these tenements there were attached shares in the common fields and meadows of the borough, and rights in its common woods and marshes. A charter of Offa, which includes one of these tenements among the appendages of a large estate in rural Kent, gives a curious anticipation of the later practice by which urban properties were commonly annexed to country manors. In some parts of Canterbury dwellings were packed closely together. A private charter of 868 shows that by the customary law of the place two feet must be left empty between houses to serve as 'eavesdrip.' By the early ninth century the population had grown too large to be contained by its walls. Coins were struck in both Canterbury and Rochester for the Mercian overlords of Kent, and the hint of commercial activity which they give is borne out by references to the market-place of Canterbury, and by a ninth-century reference to the place as a *port*—that is, a trading centre. But by virtue of its walls Canterbury was not only a *port*, or market-town, but a *burh*, or defensible position, and in the ninth century its inhabitants are described indifferently as *port-ware* or *burgware*. There is no clear reference to their communal action in any document of this period, but it can certainly be assumed that they held regular meetings for the management of their common agricultural interests. The most remarkable feature of their recorded life is the existence among them of a gild, whose members were known as *cnihtas*. The position of the Old English

---

ANGLO-SAXON KINGS

Northumbria
Ethelfrith, 593-617
Edwin, 617-633
Oswald, 635-642
Oswy, 642-670
Ecgfrith, 670-685

Mercia
Penda, 626-655
Ethelbald, 716-757
Offa II, 757-796
Cenulf, 796-821

Kent
Ethelbert, 560-616

Wessex
Ine, 688-726
Egbert, 802-839
Ethelwulf, 839-858

Ethelbald, 858-860
Ethelbert, 860-866
Ethelred, 866-871

ENGLISH KINGS

Alfred, 871-899
Edward, 899-924
Ethelstan, 924-939
Edmund, 939-946
Edred, 946-955
Edwig, 955-959
Edgar, 959-975
Edward, 975-978
Ethelred, 978-1016
Edmund, 1016
Canute, 1017-1035
Harold, 1035-1040
Harthacanute, 1040-1042
Edward, 1042-1066
Harold, 1066

cniht is a difficult question, and it must be left uncertain whether the ninth-century *cnihtas* of Canterbury were young members of landed families maintaining themselves by trade, or resident servants of lords with property in, or adjacent to, the *civitas*. Whatever they may have been, they have a distinguished place in social history as the founders of the earliest gild on record in England.

These details are valuable for two reasons. They show that London was not the only town in ninth-century England. They also show that many of the features which distinguished the typical English borough of the eleventh century had been developed in at least one urban centre before the age of organized town-planning which opened with the Danish wars. Like ninth-century Canterbury the normal county town of the Confessor's reign was a market and minting-place; it was enclosed with walls or an earthen rampart; it was divided into fenced tenements, which Domesday Book frequently describes as *hagae;* and it possessed open fields and meadows, shared out among its leading inhabitants. It had developed a series of local usages, which, like the Canterbury regulations about eavesdrip, could fairly have been described as matters of 'customary law.' It was welded into the economy of the surrounding country by the attachment of town houses to rural manors. It was at once an agricultural unit, a trading centre, and a place of defence. The Canterbury evidence is important because it proves that in this, its characteristic form, the Anglo-Saxon borough was not a new conception of the age of Alfred.

Even without the stimulus of the Danish wars economic forces would in time have increased the number of English towns. The laws of Alfred give the impression of a considerable volume of internal trade in the hands of men of substance who travelled from one district to another with bands of servants. But the activities of the itinerant trader were hampered by the necessity of standing as surety for the men who accompanied him, by the scarcity of places where articles could be stored in bulk, and by the difficulty of obtaining assurance against the risk of buying stolen property. The foundation of new boroughs offered to traders bases for their operations more secure than could be found in the open country, and the means of establishing the validity of their transactions by the testimony of responsible persons of their own sort. Statesmen, on their part, were anxious that trade should be restricted to a limited number of recognized centres. A law of Edward the Elder prohibits trade outside a *port,* and orders that all transactions shall be attested by the portreeve or by other trustworthy men. His successors were unable to maintain this prohibition, but its significance is clear. By the end of Edward's reign it is probable that every place of trade which was more than a local market was surrounded by at least rudimentary fortifications. Like pre-Alfredian Canterbury, the normal *port* of Edward's time was also a *burh,* and the urgency with which Edward commands traders to resort to it is explained by its military importance. A derelict *port* was a weak point in the national defences.

The combination of military and commercial factors in the history of the Old English borough is well brought out in the one surviving document which illustrates the internal condition of a new Alfredian *burh*. Towards the close of Alfred's reign Æthelred and Æthelflæd of Mercia were asked by Bishop Werferth of Worcester to fortify that place for the defence of the people and the security of his cathedral. When the fortifications had been made Æthelred and Æthelflæd, in return for spiritual services, granted to the bishop half the rights which belonged to their lordship 'in market-place or in street,' reserving to the king the toll of goods brought to Worcester in wagons or on horses, and to the bishop all the rights which had belonged to his predecessors within the property belonging to his church. The rights which they shared with the bishop included a tax levied for the repair of the borough-wall, a payment vaguely described as *landfeoh,* presumably the rent yielded by tenements within, or close to, the fortifications, fines for fighting, theft, and dishonest trading, and whatever came in to the representatives of the state in respect of offences which could be emended by money payments. The document gives the impression that not only the fortifications but also the market at Worcester was new, and that the rents, dues, and judicial profits which Æthelred and Æthelflæd derived from the borough were regarded as a compensation for the expenses which they had borne in making it defensible.

At Worcester much of the borough belonged to the bishop, and the extent of his property must have narrowly limited the area from which Æthelred and Æthelflæd derived their revenue. In most boroughs the land enclosed by the fortifications had belonged wholly, or in by far the greater part, to the king. Oxford and Wallingford, for example, were each founded on a compact block of royal land regarded as equivalent to eight yardlands, which at Oxford was still known as the king's eight yardlands in the twelfth century. On the foundation of such a borough it seems that the defensible area was divided into plots— represented by the *hagae* and *mansurae* of Domesday Book—which were taken from the king at a money rent by persons wishing to engage in trade. The men who thus became the king's tenants were all personally free. Most of them must have ranked as ceorls, but there was no convention which hindered a thegn from living in a borough as a merchant, and in days when the male inhabitants of a borough might at any time be required to defend its walls, it was desirable that there should be a few men of rank resident within them. It is also possible that the thegnly element, of which there are clear signs in eleventh-century London and faint traces in some other boroughs, may have been recruited from within, for a well-known English tract states that in the past a merchant who had carried out three voyages at his own charge was regarded as of thegnly status. Whatever their social position may have been, the individuals holding

burghal plots from the king were bound by conditions of tenure which, in substance, were the same everywhere. The rents which they paid seem to have been uniform for the same kind of tenement within each borough, and had become stabilized by custom before the Norman Conquest. As a rule the holder of a tenement was free to mortgage or to sell it, often, it would seem, without obtaining the king's licence, but it was regarded as a heritable property, and there is some evidence that the holder's liberty of alienation might be restricted in the interest of his kin. In addition to his rent, the holder of a plot might be liable to a number of personal services, such as the duty of helping to form an escort for the king; his commercial transactions were subject to toll, and he contributed to such payments for special purposes as might be laid upon his borough. It is clear, in fact, that all the essential features which distinguished the burgess tenure of the middle ages had been developed in the Old English borough, and although no more precise term than *burgware,* 'inhabitants of a borough' or *portmenn,* 'townsmen' had been found for men holding burghal plots on these terms, Domesday Book was recognizing a genuine tenurial distinction when it described them as *burgenses.*

The decisive impulse towards the creation of boroughs had been given by the king, and in the eleventh century a majority of the burgesses in any normal borough were his men. Nevertheless long before the Conquest churches and noblemen had been acquiring borough plots, and placing their own men in them. The extent to which the king retained an interest in the 'customs'— rents, dues, and services—which these plots had formerly rendered, varied with the circumstances of each case. The king sometimes allowed a lord of the very highest rank to receive all the customs arising out of his land within a borough. More often the king reserved a portion of them to himself, and in many, if not in most, cases he retained all the customs, leaving to the lord no more than the profits for which he had bargained when he planted out his tenants on their holdings. It might well happen that an eleventh-century burgess paid both a customary rent to the king and a stipulated rent to his lord. Conversely, although the profits of justice done upon or between burgesses were normally the king's, and were in fact included among his 'customs,' a lord of sufficient rank often enjoyed the right of sake and soke over his burgess tenants. For all these complications it remains the fact that the essence of burgess tenure lay in the subjection of the individual burgess to the 'customs' of his borough— customs which were always felt to be of royal institution, however completely their origin might have been disguised by royal alienations and private encroachments.

It is clear from Domesday Book that in 1086 a piece of borough property—a messuage, a house, or a group of houses—was often annexed to a manor in the open country. At Leicester, for example, 134 houses were thus attached, singly or in groups, to 27 different manors. So far as can be seen the borough property was treated as a profit-yielding appendage of the manor. It provided the lord with a lodging when he came to the borough on business and with a place of refuge in time of trouble. The elaborate economy of a large Old English manor implied the possibility of access to something more than a mere rural market; and an appurtenant house in a neighbouring borough formed a convenient centre at which goods needed on the estate could be brought together and stored. Most of the evidence which illustrates this practice relates to the time after the Conquest, but it can be traced far back into the Anglo-Saxon period, and Anglo-Saxon kings had encouraged it. In a charter of 958 the boundaries of an estate at Staunton on Arrow which King Edgar had given to one of his thegns are followed by a statement that the king has also given him a *haga* in Hereford. The association of the manor and its burghal appendage is brought out still more clearly by a charter of Æthelred II relating to Moredon near Swindon which refers expressly to a *haga* in Cricklade added by the king to the estate. Other pre-Conquest charters show tenements in Wilton, Winchester, Southampton, Chichester, Worcester, Oxford, and Warwick attached in the same way to rural properties. There can be no serious doubt that such annexations were common already at the turn of the tenth and eleventh centuries.

It is clear, in fact, that for at least two generations before the Conquest the population of a normal borough must have included the tenants of other lords than the king, and it is probable that in many boroughs this intermingling of tenures goes back to the time of their foundation. Little is known of the institutions through which these artificial communities were governed. But it could not have been easy for groups of men of diverse antecedents to adapt themselves to the conditions of life within borough walls, and at an early date in the history of at least the larger boroughs there must have arisen the need for a court with the authority of the state behind it for the settlement of disputes between individuals and the establishment of a local customary law. Unfortunately, the pre-Conquest documents which refer to borough courts are few, and their language is ambiguous. The ambiguity is chiefly caused by the fact that many boroughs were the meeting-places of shire courts or of courts with jurisdiction over smaller districts such as hundreds or groups of hundreds. It is sometimes hard to decide whether a passage which on the surface refers to a borough court may not actually be referring to one of these courts of wider jurisdiction which had a borough for a meeting-place. From all this confusion there emerges something more than a probability that King Edgar was referring to a borough court, in the strict sense, when he ordered that the shire court should meet twice, and the *buruhgemot* three times, a year. It is certain that in the early eleventh century a distinction was felt to exist between *landriht,* that is 'ordinary law,' and *burhriht,* which can only mean the more specialized law of the borough. The fact that this distinction was regarded as a matter of course implies that borough law and borough courts in which it was administered had arisen at least as early as the date of Edgar's ordinance about the meetings of the *buruhgemot*. In 1018 the bishop of Crediton announced to the *burhwitan* of Exeter, Totnes, Lydford, and Barnstaple that he had mortgaged one of his estates to a local thegn, an announcement which suggests that at each of these places the *burhwitan* formed an official body, capable of preserving the memory of a transaction formally brought to its notice. It is not unreasonable to see in these 'borough councillors' the upper bench of a borough court. It is possible that such a bench may have existed in the pre-Conquest court of Chester, where, according to Domesday Book there were twelve *judices,* taken from among the men of the king, the bishop, and the earl, who were all bound to attend every session of the court under the penalty of a ten-shilling fine. But the Chester *judices* clearly resemble the bodies of twelve lawmen whose existence is recorded at Lincoln and Stamford and implied at Cambridge and York. These lawmen undoubtedly came into being through Scandinavian influence. Their name connects them at once with the lawmen of the great Scandinavian codes —men with specialized legal knowledge, on whom there lay the responsibility of directing a court in its application of rules to cases. Danish influence was stronger at Chester than in any other borough except London outside the Danelaw, and there can be little doubt that one of its manifestations was the development of a body of doomsmen or lawmen, who, whatever the name by which they were known, took the leading part in the framing of judgements in the local court.

The difficulty of forming a clear impression of the Old English borough court is increased by the fact that the Old English boroughs themselves did not conform to any single type. It would be easy to make a long list of pre-Conquest boroughs, each

of which was obviously important in the national economy as the commercial centre of a wide region. A few of them, such as York and Chester, are known to have been in touch with the outside world through trade; others, such as Lincoln, Thetford, Norwich, Ipswich and Colchester, contained populations which could not have been supported by a traffic confined to England; many were administrative as well as commercial centres, and already before the Conquest had risen to the status of county towns. Within most of them there must have been abundant scope for a court of internal jurisdiction co-ordinate with the rural hundred-moot, and it is probable that in 1066 all of them possessed such courts. But in southern, and particularly in south-western England, there were many small boroughs within which the need for a separate court was less apparent. Many of them, such as Bedwyn and Warminster, had arisen on royal manors, where a king, wishing to improve his property, could offer the protection of the special peace around his house to such traders as might be willing to take plots from him. The king's direct influence was naturally paramount in boroughs of this type. Even in boroughs such as Langport or Axbridge, which had once been fortresses in a scheme of national defence, his tenants generally by far outnumbered those of all other lords. In a normal south-western borough there cannot have been the same clash of interests as in the boroughs of the east and midlands. The population of an average borough was much smaller and the volume of trade was less. Life in Bedwyn or Langport was far simpler than in York or Norwich. Under the conditions which prevailed in the south-west a borough could exist for many years without a court of its own. On the eve of the Conquest, so far as can be seen, there were many boroughs in this part of England which had not yet developed courts separate from those of the hundreds in which they were situated. Some of them gave name to hundreds, and in these cases it is reasonable to assume that the court of the hundred met in the borough and that the king's reeve in the borough accounted for the profits of the hundred court. In other cases nothing is known about the relationship of the borough to the hundred in which it lay. All that can safely be said is that although in time all the most prosperous south-western boroughs acquired courts separate from those of the surrounding hundreds, the separation was purely a matter of expediency. An independent court was not inherent in the Anglo-Saxon conception of a borough.

But, for all the vagueness of its constitution, the Old English borough had an official character. Every borough which had arisen in southern or western England since the beginning of the Danish wars had been created by an act of state, and the government continued to be interested in its fortunes. The closeness of its connexion with the king is evident from whatever angle it is regarded. It is more remarkable that at the end of the Old English period the earl, as the king's vice-regent, was accustomed to receive one-third of the public revenue which came in, year by year, from at least a majority of the boroughs within his province. The history of 'the earl's third penny,' as Domesday Book calls it, is very obscure. The 'customs of the burgesses,' from which it was derived, were highly miscellaneous, and little is known about the methods by which the earl's part in them was separated from that of the king. Nothing is known at first hand about the origin of the earl's third penny, and in this connexion it can only be observed that the ealdormen of the Alfredian time had played an important part in the work of borough fortification, that their successors had the responsibility of seeing that the fortifications were kept defensible, and that a share in the borough revenues would be an appropriate return for these labours. But it is certain that in 1066 the earl's right to his third penny was derived from public law rather than royal favour. In all places where it was recognized it seems to have passed automatically to each new earl on his appointment, and its operation can be traced in boroughs of the most diverse size and character. It was admitted at Axbridge and Bruton as well as at Ipswich and Warwick. There were important boroughs within which no sign of it has yet been found, and in some of them it is probable that the king had actually kept the whole of the borough revenues in his own hand. But the boroughs within which the earl is known to have taken his third penny are so numerous that the custom may fairly be regarded as a normal feature of Old English borough finance, and as an indication that the idea of the borough as an integral element in the constitution of the state had survived the military urgencies which had brought the Alfredian boroughs into being.

The function of the Old English borough as a minting-place points still more clearly in the same direction. After the fall of the Norwegian kingdom of York the king of Wessex was the only person in England who could authorize the issue of a currency. His servants used his power efficiently, and handed on the tradition of a well-managed coinage to the Norman administrators who replaced them. By establishing a rule that all dies must be cut in London, and that every moneyer must come to London for his dies when the design of the coinage was changed, they brought its type and fabric under a very effective supervision. But the need of local markets for a regular supply of coins was fully, perhaps over-generously, recognized, and in the history of the late Old English coinage an absolute control of design by the government coincided with a decentralization of issue to an extent that has never since been tolerated in England. The first official statement of the attitude of the government towards the currency occurs in the laws of Athelstan.

We declare . . . that there shall be one coinage throughout the king's dominions and that there shall be no minting except in a *port*. And if a minter be convicted of striking bad money, the hand with which he was guilty shall be cut off and set up on the mint-smithy. . . . In Canterbury there shall be seven minters; four of them the king's, two, the archbishop's, one, the abbot's. In Rochester, three; two of them the king's, and one, the bishop's. In London there shall be eight, in Winchester, six, in Lewes, two, in Hastings, one, in Chichester, another, in Southampton, two, in Wareham, two, in Dorchester, one, in Exeter, two, in Shaftesbury, two, in each other *burh,* one.

The passage is made important for the history of the Old English borough by its last words. Declining to attempt a complete list of minting-places, the king shows that he considers, or at least is prepared to allow, that there should be a minter in every *burh.*

The evidence of the coins themselves suggests that at one time or another in the next century a mint was actually set up in every place with a claim to be regarded as a borough. The evidence is fragmentary at first, for it was not until the reign of Edward the Martyr that it became the rule for every coin to bear both the name of the moneyer responsible for its quality and the name of the place where it was struck. It is clear that even in Athelstan's time mints were working in boroughs which are unlikely to have been centres of any considerable trade. One of his coins was struck at a place named *Weardbyrig,* which cannot now be identified, and is only known otherwise as one of the *burhs* which Æthelflæd had built for the defence of Mercia. In the reigns of Æthelred II and Cnut, when the evidence has become copious, there is no doubt that moneyers were established, not only in the large commercial centres of the east, the county towns of the midlands, and most of the *burhs* mentioned in the Burghal Hidage, but also in places where the trading community must have been a mere appendage to a royal manor. There cannot have been any large concentration of burgesses and there can hardly have been more than the most rudimentary of fortifications at Aylesbury or Crewkerne or Bruton. Cadbury in Somerset, where coins were struck for both Æthelred and Cnut, and Horndon

in Essex, where they were struck for Edward the Confessor, were not even royal manors in 1066, and Domesday Book gives no hint of anything unusual in their past. Each of them had probably been a short-lived *burh,* like the *novum oppidum* called *Beorchore,* which Æthelred II visited in 1007, but of which there is no other record. Even so, neither Cadbury nor Horndon can have been an important place, and their coins increase the probability that in the first half of the eleventh century every *burh,* whatever its size, had been a centre for the issue of currency.

The fact that every coin of this period bore the name of both moneyer and minting-place provides the materials for a rough estimate of the relative importance of the different boroughs of the Confessor's reign. It is reasonable to assume, for example, that a borough in which at least six moneyers were working simultaneously had a stronger economic like than a borough in which there were no more than three. It would obviously be unwise to use the number of moneyers in a borough as a positive index to its size or urban population, but it must to some extent reflect the significance of the borough as a centre of exchange. London, as would be expected, comes at the head of the list, with more than twenty moneyers working at the same time in the years after 1042. York follows with more than ten; Lincoln and Winchester had at least nine; Chester, at least eight; Canterbury and Oxford, at least seven; Thetford, Gloucester, and Worcester, at least six. It is possible that this method of comparison, which rests on the evidence of coins accidentally discovered, does less than justice to Ipswich and Norwich, where a large concentration of pre-Conquest burgesses, revealed by Domesday Book, seems to have been served by no more than four or five moneyers. It is certainly unjust to Hereford, where Domesday Book shows that no less than seven moneyers were at work in 1066, although only five can be identified on local coins. On the other hand, each of the boroughs with six or more moneyers had unusual advantages of situation, each of them served a tract of country which was either unusually large or unusually prosperous, and their names probably approximate to a list of the market centres which were of most consequence in King Edward's time.

It is impossible to form a close estimate of the population of these and other pre-Conquest boroughs. Domesday Book gives many figures which apparently record the number of burgesses living within a particular borough in 1066. But the compilers of Domesday Book were chiefly interested in the king's demesne burgesses, who rendered, or ought to render, full 'customs,' and they took less account of the burgesses who were the tenants of noblemen or churches. In regard to many boroughs their figures relate, not to burgesses, but to messuages or houses, and the interpretation of these figures is made difficult by the possibility that a single tenement may have been divided between two or more burgess households. An estimate of the population of a pre-Conquest borough which is founded on Domesday statistics will nearly always tend to be too low. Even so, the figures recorded for a number of boroughs in eastern England amount to totals which sharply differentiate these places from their rural environment. A recent discussion of these figures, which assumes that each recorded tenement was occupied by a single household and that each household comprised no more than five people, has shown that pre-Conquest York must have contained more than 8,000 persons, and Norwich at least 6,600; that the population of Lincoln must have approached the same figure; that Thetford must have included nearly 4,750 inhabitants, and Ipswich more than 3,000. Apart from London and Winchester, which are not described in Domesday Book, the only other borough which seems to have belonged to this class is Oxford, where the Domesday enumeration of houses suggests a pre-Conquest population of more than 3,500. Indefinite as they are, these figures answer one of the fundamental questions raised by the history of the Old English

borough. They show that where local conditions were favourable, the accumulation of dwellings within an Anglo-Saxon *burh* might well reach a density which entitles it to be called a town.

Among the English boroughs of the eleventh century a distinctive place belongs to London. In the number of its inhabitants, the range and volume of its trade, and the elaboration of the system by which it was governed, it stands apart from all other English towns. The accidents of war, through which it became for a time the centre of the English resistance to Danish invasion, gave its citizens a lively sense of their importance to the state, and formed the basis of the singular claim, put forward by their successors, that the men of London had the right of choosing a king for England. In the eleventh century the conception of a capital city had not yet taken a definite shape anywhere in the west. The centre of government in England was the king's mobile court. The king was free to hold a national assembly at any point in his realm, and to lay up his treasures in any place which he considered safe, as Eadred had laid them up with Dunstan at Glastonbury. But half a century before the Norman Conquest London was beyond comparison the largest town in England. It was the principal resort of foreign traders in time of peace, and the base which sustained the defence of the land in war-time. It had the resources, and it was rapidly developing the dignity and the political self-consciousness appropriate to a national capital.

It was inevitable that in a city of this size and importance society should be more complex, and the organization of government more elaborate than in even the largest of provincial boroughs. It is significant that at London men of thegnly rank, who are elsewhere indistinguishable from the mass of the burgesses, appear as a separate class, and probably formed a recognized urban patriciate. Moreover, so far as is known, there is no parallel in any other town to the series of courts through which justice was administered in pre-Conquest London. The folkmoot, which was first in authority, shows all the features to be expected in an ancient popular assembly. It met in the open air immediately to the north-east of St. Paul's cathedral, on the highest ground in the city. It held three sessions a year which every citizen was expected to attend without individual summons; it was, at least formally, responsible for the good order of the city, and it was the only court in London in which a man could be proclaimed an outlaw. The husting, which is first mentioned in England a little before the end of the tenth century, was less august, but of much more importance in the life of the ordinary citizen. In the Norman age, and no doubt earlier, it met once a week for the transaction of civil business. It was well established before the conquest of England by Cnut, but its name, which means 'house assembly,' is of Danish origin, and it probably came into being as a court for the settlement of pleas in which Danish and English merchants were involved with one another. By the Norman period, when the direct evidence for its judicial activity begins, it was entertaining all manner of civil suits, and the commercial side of its business gave it outstanding importance as the body which regulated intercourse between English and foreign traders in the greatest of English ports. A link between the husting and what may be called the police courts of the city was provided by the aldermen, who sat apart in the husting as a bench of persons learned in the law. It was the essential function of the alderman to take charge of one of the wards into which the city was divided, and in this capacity he held a court—the wardmoot of Anglo-Norman records—for the settlement of small disputes and the punishment of minor offences. Many boroughs, such as York and Cambridge, had been divided into wards by the date of the Norman Conquest, but, so far as is known, the wardmoot is peculiar to London. There is little doubt that long before the Conquest, through the acquisition of London properties by persons of high rank, the process had begun which was ultimately to create innumerable enclaves of private jurisdiction in every part of the city. It is in London that the urban immunity, or 'soke,' comes to its highest point of development in England. But in 1066, apart from a number of ancient estates in the hands of important churches, the private soke is unlikely to have been much more than an occasional exception to a judicial system which rested on public authority.

London is not described in Domesday Book, and many details of its early constitution are impenetrably obscure. The nature and organization of its government in the years before 1066 would be virtually unknown were it not for the fragments of ancient custom, preserved by the conservatism of its citizens, which are recorded in medieval custumals. But the commercial relations of the city with foreign countries are indicated in a document of approximately the year 1000, which is fundamental in the history of English trade. The document states that the men of Rouen came to London with wine and the larger sorts of fish. It also states that the port was visited by traders from Normandy at large, Flanders, Ponthieu, and France, but its language suggests that they were required to expose their goods and pay toll on the wharf or on shipboard. Traders from Lower Lorraine, and in particular from Huy, Liége, and Nivelles, were apparently allowed to enter the city before paying toll, and the 'men of the Emperor,' a phrase which covers all other Germanic merchants, are declared to be worthy of such good customs as the men of London themselves enjoyed. The document does not refer to traders from the Scandinavian lands, but a twelfth-century city custumal, which incorporates ancient matter, states that both Danes and Norwegians were at liberty to dwell in the city for an entire year. The probability that this passage relates to the time before the Conquest is strengthened by a statement that while the Danes were free to travel over the country to markets and fairs, the Norwegians were restricted to trade in London.

The differentiation between Danes and Norwegians agrees very well with the character of Anglo-Scandinavian relations in the reigns of Cnut and Edward the Confessor, but is unlikely to have arisen at any later time. It would seem clear, in fact, that in the first half of the eleventh century London was a place of frequent resort for traders from every country between Norway and northern France.

Important as it is, the London evidence should not be regarded as more than a general indication of the main lines of English foreign trade. It was written down in order to define the position of foreign traders visiting London, and it naturally takes no account of the travels of English traders into foreign parts. The concessions which Cnut secured for English and Danish merchants from the Emperor and the king of Burgundy prove that his subjects of either race were accustomed to visit Rome for business as well as devotion. An incidental remark by Ælfric to the effect that in his time English traders were in the habit of taking their goods to Rome shows that Englishmen were using the Italian trade-routes a generation before Cnut became king. But the document which gives the clearest impression of active trade between England and the Continent is the treaty concluded between King Æthelred and Olaf Tryggvason in 991. Two of its provisions are especially significant. One of them lays down that every merchant ship of any country brought safely into an English estuary should be immune from attack, and that even if it had become a wreck, and therefore a lawful object of plunder, its crew with the cargo which they had saved should have peace if they had been able to make their way into a *burh*. The second provides that if the viking fleet should come upon a subject of King Æthelred in any land outside the treaty—a phrase which covers Germany, the Low Countries, and France—he should have peace for himself, his cargo, and his ship, if his ship were afloat, or if he had beached the ship and laid up the cargo in a hut or a tent, but should keep nothing except his life if he had

entrusted his goods to a man of the country. In the obscurity that overhangs the whole subject of international trade in the Dark Ages it is useful to have this definite evidence that late in the tenth century the English seas were being traversed by the merchant ships of many countries, and that a viking fleet raiding a continental harbour would not improbably find an English trader there.

It is probable that a considerable volume of trade passed in this period between England and the Scandinavian countries themselves. A well-known passage in the earliest life of St. Oswald states that in the writer's time, that is, shortly after the year 1000, York was filled with the treasures of merchants, chiefly of Danish race, who had come to the city from every quarter. The picture may be overdrawn, but it is good evidence that Danish traders in the tenth century, like Frisian traders in the eighth, had formed a colony in the city. It would be easier to form a definite opinion about the amount of this trade, and about the commercial relations which existed between England and Scandinavia in general, if it were possible to estimate the exact significance of the vast quantities of late Old English money which have been discovered in the northern countries. Much of this money must have been brought to the north by warriors who had taken Danegeld in England; some of it may well have come from gifts made by Cnut to northern chiefs; and some, from the wages of his housecarles and seamen. But there is a residue which cannot be explained on these lines. Most of the coins belong to the reigns of Æthelred or Cnut, but the series continues through the reign of Edward the Confessor into the Norman period, and it is clear that many of the coins cannot have reached the northern countries until Danegelds had ceased to be levied and the Scandinavian troops in English service had been disbanded. It is also significant that a large number of the coins, including many of Æthelred and Cnut, have been discovered in association with continental coins of the same period, under conditions which show that they had been accumulated gradually, and, to all appearance, in the course of trade. But the clearest piece of evidence for regular commercial intercourse between England and Scandinavia is the remarkable fact that by the beginning of the eleventh century the English currency had come to be accepted everywhere as a model by the Scandinavian peoples themselves. In each of the three northern countries—in Denmark under Swein Forkbeard, in Norway under Earl Eric of Hlathir, in Sweden under Olaf Skattkonung—the first step towards the introduction of a regular currency was the imitation of pennies of Æthelred II. The possibility that the northern peoples were simply copying coins brought to their land as spoils of war is disproved by the English names borne by a number of the first moneyers who are known to have worked in Scandinavia. Of the six men who struck pennies for Olaf Skattkonung of Sweden, at least four must have been of English origin. The employment of English moneyers by northern kings amounts to proof of an intercourse between England and Scandinavia which was based on trade conducted through the medium of a currency.

It is clear that for at least seventy years before the Norman Conquest England had been in continuous relationship through trade with the continental world. Little can be said about the relative importance of the different channels through which the relationship was maintained. Two of the great-est trade-routes of the Dark Ages converged upon England, and there are no means of determining whether the traffic from Italy through the Rhineland to the Low Country ports, or that from Russia along the Baltic to its outlets on the North Sea was of the greater advantage to English traders. As to an earlier time, there is little evidence for the nature or direction of English foreign trade in the century which followed the collapse of the Carolingian empire, when the energy of Mediterranean commerce sank to its lowest point. But even in this impoverished age it is unlikely that England was ever thrown entirely back on to her own internal resources. It was in the ninth and tenth centuries that the Baltic trade-route, on which Haithaby near Slesvig was the chief distributing centre, became of the greatest consequence. It is more than probable that Englishmen engaged themselves in the commerce which passed along this line, and that the foundations of later English trade with the Scandinavian countries were already laid in this period. That England had shared in the commerce of the Carolingian and pre-Carolingian age is beyond question. In the centuries of Old English history the stream of traffic which reached England was often thin, and it rarely came to a volume at which it could support large masses of population disassociated from the soil. But it would be going against both evidence and probability to suggest that its continuity was at any time completely broken.

THE

High Middle Ages

PART TWO

CASTLES WERE AN ESSENTIAL AND TYPICAL ELEMENT in the feudal way of life, and there were many of them in England when feudalism was at its height—that is to say, during the two or three generations following the Norman Conquest. These castles had to be garrisoned, of course, and it may well have been that the feudal service known as "castle-guard" was originally more burdensome than knight's service in the field, for unlike the feudal army, which was called into existence only occasionally and for special purposes, the garrisons of castles had to be maintained continuously. Rather early, it would seem, the obligations of personal service for castle-guard were commuted into money payments. Baronial castles, as well as royal castles, were regarded by the Norman kings as necessary for the defense of the country, but during the so-called "anarchy" of Stephen's reign (1135-1154) some of the baronial castles became centers of revolt, and under Henry II (1154-1189) many of them were destroyed or seized by the King, who caused new royal castles to be built. By the end of the twelfth century the baronial castle, except along the Welsh and Scottish borders, had lost its importance for national defense. The remains of Anglo-Norman castles exist all over England, and archaeological discoveries have supplemented the scanty firsthand information regarding them to be gleaned from documentary sources. Even so, we know less about the medieval castle as an institution than about many other feudal institutions. Professor Sidney Painter, of Johns Hopkins University, one of the ablest of American medievalists and author of *William Marshal* (1933), *French Chivalry* (1940), *Studies in the History of the English Feudal Barony* (1943), and *The Reign of King John* (1949), believed when he wrote the article that follows that the time had not yet come to write a full and adequate account of the castle in medieval England. That time has still not come, but meanwhile Professor Painter's discussion of certain aspects of the subject serves a useful purpose.

ENGLISH CASTLES IN THE EARLY MIDDLE AGES
THEIR NUMBER, LOCATION, AND LEGAL POSITION
SIDNEY PAINTER

Despite the fact that in England as on the continent the castle was a fundamental feature of feudal society, it has been sadly neglected by historians. The students of military architecture have done their work thoroughly and well, but that is merely one aspect of a highly complicated subject. The questions which more closely touch the realm of the historian have received comparatively little attention. Here and there the deft hand of Mr Round has thrown light into obscure corners. While Mrs Armitage's interests were primarily archaeological and architectural, her very valuable book [*The Early Norman Castles of the British Isles*] contains much general information. Her article on "Ancient Earthworks" in the *Victoria History of Yorkshire* is particularly suggestive. Finally, Professor Stenton has laid a firm foundation for future students in

Reprinted by special permission from *Speculum*, X (1935), 321-332. The footnotes which originally appeared with this essay have been omitted.

his excellent chapter [in *The First Century of English Feudalism, 1066-1166*] on "Castles and Castle-guard." A complete and satisfactory discussion of the part played by the castle in mediaeval England cannot yet be written. It must await the publication of more early charters, a thorough and accurate survey of archaeological material, and a more adequate knowledge of English feudal geography. This article is intended to be simply a set of supplementary notes to the work of the three scholars mentioned above. I hope that it may serve to clarify some obscure points and advance our knowledge of the subject as a whole.

The obvious first question to ask of a writer on English castles is in regard to their total number, and it is the one which can be answered least satisfactorily. The very importance of castles in the early Middle Ages may well have been responsible for our lack of adequate information about them. The results of royal inquests enable us to estimate with reasonable accuracy the number of knights' fees in England, but no inquest of castles has been preserved and it is improbable that one was ever made. A castle could not be concealed nor forgotten. Its existence was a vital element in the safety and good order of its neighborhood. Hence the king and his officers probably knew perfectly well what castles were in existence and had no need to inquire. Consequently our knowledge of these fortresses must be built up from a multitude of incidental references. Before the beginning of the great series of records of the royal government such as the pipe, patent, and close rolls, the material is most unsatisfactory. Even in the early thirteenth century it furnishes no adequate basis for statistical studies. The most that one can do is to obtain a minimum figure. Between the Norman Conquest and the year 1225 I have found references to 245 English castles. In the last twenty-five years of this period about two hundred were mentioned.

It is easy to demonstrate the utter inadequacy of these figures. The moated mounds which are now generally conceded to have been the sites of early mediaeval wooden castles outnumbered the strongholds for which one can find written evidence by at least two to one. Professor Stenton has maintained with justice that these motte castles were the result of the fundamental military and political necessities of the years after the Conquest rather than the product of the disorders of Stephen's reign. I am inclined to believe that the number of castles reached its peak about the year 1100, when there may have been five or six hundred scattered through the shires of England. While the anarchy which resulted from the contest between Stephen and Matilda undoubtedly caused the erection of many hastily constructed and essentially temporary fortresses, it is probable that as many more permanent ones were destroyed. Certainly Henry II was an energetic foe of baronial castles. He is known to have razed twenty-one, and he probably destroyed many more. But I suggest that a far larger number were simply abandoned by their lords. The maintenance of a castle was expensive and could only be justified by a great necessity. The stern peace enforced by the Angevin kings made baronial castles less vital to their masters' safety. Finally one is led to wonder whether economic changes may not have had an important effect. Before the development of markets when a baron had to feed his family and retainers directly from the produce of his estates, he needed a residence on each manor or at least in each geographical group of manors. As soon as he could sell the produce of his more distant estates and use the money to maintain himself in his principal stronghold, he could let his outlying castles fall into decay. Whatever the exact causes may have been, I feel reasonably certain that by the year 1200 the number of castles in England had fallen to between two hundred and two hundred and fifty. This cannot be proved, for no material exists which will permit an argument from silence, but the nature and extent of the records for the early thirteenth century seem to me to justify a belief that the number of castles which they fail to mention was not very large. Thus if these rather wild surmises have any validity, the twelfth century saw the total of English castles reduced by half.

After the question as to how many castles existed in England comes naturally the query as to where they were located. Mr Alfred Harvey seems to have believed that the Conqueror and his successors had a geographical plan of fortification on a national scale. This is highly improbable for the simple reason that no monarchs of their time could have had the requisite knowledge of English geography. In the thirteenth century Matthew Paris made a map of England which experts consider one of the best of all mediaeval maps. His geographical ability was esteemed so highly by Henry III that the king had him make a map for the wall of his chamber. But Matthew's map of England would have been most unsatisfactory as the basis for a scheme of national defense. On the frontier of Scotland he omitted entirely the counties of Lancashire, Cumberland, and Westmoreland. In the equally important south-eastern section his knowledge was little less vague. Sussex was placed safely inland, with Essex bordering it on the north. Surrey seems entirely lost. Now it is perfectly possible that the officials of Henry's administration could have corrected individual errors made by Matthew, but it is extremely unlikely that they had a more accurate knowledge of England as a whole. One can imagine the complete geographical ignorance with which the Conqueror faced his newly acquired realm.

As a matter of fact, even if William had been supplied with the best of modern maps, he probably would have made little use of them in placing his castles. From the point of view of national defense against a foreign invader the exact location of a fortress made very little difference. To say that a castle blocked a road, a river valley, or a route to the continent is to be inexact. A force larger than the garrison could pass with perfect ease and safety. As an early mediaeval army lived off the country, the fact that a garrison lay between it and its base was not serious. Dover has always been spoken of as a vital strategic fortress—the key to England. But an army large enough to handle a sortie by the garrison could have landed in the harbor and marched inland. Louis of France conducted a very creditable invasion of England without ever taking Dover castle. One might argue that his frequent sieges of that stronghold showed its importance in his mind, but that is to miss the point. As had an earlier invader of England, the Conqueror himself, Louis undoubtedly viewed Dover as an invaluable refuge in case he was defeated. There he could in safety await passage home. Again Windsor has been said to have blocked the Thames valley, but even were an army bound by some strange rule to follow the course of the river it could still pass without difficulty. In short, to consider the location of a castle on such and such a road or over such and such a harbor as a matter of vital importance is to misconstrue the strategic use of these fortresses in mediaeval war.

A castle of the eleventh, twelfth, or early thirteenth centuries consisted of an inner stronghold—a motte or a stone keep—and one or two less formidable outer works. The former could be adequately defended by a small force. The latter could in case of need

LEGES HENRICI: A law book written probably between A.D. 1100 and 1118. It has been called "the earliest legal textbook of medieval Europe." The object of its author, who is unknown, was to give an account of Anglo-Saxon law as amended by William I and Henry I.

ROBERT OF BELLESME: The most powerful of the great Norman feudal lords in England at the beginning of the twelfth century. He was overwhelmingly defeated in 1102 by Henry I, to whom he had been disloyal, and his vast possessions in England were confiscated.

give shelter to a fairly large body of men. The strategic value of castles lay in their number and the elasticity of their garrison requirements. The king of Scotland might cross the border with a large army. The barons of Northumberland would retire into their castles with their men, cattle, and if possible crops. The invader had the choice between the endless process of reducing the fortresses one by one or ignoring them and pressing on into Yorkshire. If he chose the latter course, he could be sure that when the levy of England finally moved against him, he would have in his rear the combined garrisons of the castles of Northumberland. One of the best examples of the military value of castles was the campaign which ended in the battle of Lincoln in 1217. The royalist leaders, Ranulf of Chester and William de Ferrars, laid siege to the rebel stronghold of Mountsorrel, but its lord and the count of Perche marched to its relief with a superior force. As soon as he learned of the enemy's approach, Earl Ranulf placed his army in safety in Nottingham castle. Thus he was enabled to remain near the scene of action ready to join the regent for the decisive stroke at Lincoln. The regent's own army was largely composed of the royal garrisons scattered over the counties through which the count of Perche had passed on his march from London. In short, a network of fortresses was necessary for the defense of the realm, and it should be particularly closely woven in exposed regions, but the exact position of the individual castles was of little significance.

Whatever the reasons may have been, the locations of the castles of England were governed by local or at most regional considerations. A flourishing town was a natural place for a castle. Not only could the fortress hold the inhabitants in check, but also the mere fact that a town had grown up there usually guaranteed the place to be a convenient center for administrative and military control of the country around. This was particularly true of the midland boroughs. Only three of the eleventh-century royal castles listed by Mrs Armitage were outside of towns—Rockingham, Windsor, and Wisbeach. Wisbeach and probably Rockingham served to control Hereward's fenland followers. Thus the considerations which governed the location of the Conqueror's own castles were mainly political and administrative.

Far more numerous than the royal strongholds were those of the king's vassals. Their importance from the point of view of national defense lay in their number rather than in their location. Some watched over towns. Most of those located in the open country fulfilled the double purpose of providing a safe residence for the lord and protecting a fertile manor. A large percentage of the castles of England lay in the rich river valleys. The type of isolated impregnable stronghold intended primarily as a place of refuge which was so common in many parts of Europe was extremely rare in England. Scarborough and Mulgrave in Yorkshire, the Peak in Derbyshire, Richard's Castle in Herefordshire, and Corfe in Dorsetshire were examples of this class of fortress. As a rule a baron's castle guarded his most valuable estates.

Obviously in some regions a feudal lord's local interests might coincide with those of the country as a whole. It is possible that William fitz Osbern and Roger de Montgomery had regional geographical plans for the defense of their palatinates of Herefordshire and Shropshire. A study of the castle sites of these two shires shows that screens of minor strongholds covered Hereford, Ludlow, and Shrewsbury from the west. A Welsh army seeking to attack one of these great fortresses would have to thread its way through a maze of auxiliary castles, and if it undertook siege operations, it would be continually harassed in the rear by their garrisons. This arrangement does not, of course, prove the existence of a comprehensive plan. Each vassal of the palatine earls needed a castle to protect his own lands, and pure chance may have led to the formation of these screens of fortresses. The safety of the interior counties of England required that Herefordshire and Shropshire be thickly studded with castles. The local interests of the marcher barons led to that end.

The Conqueror and his vassals were faced with common dangers—invasions by Welsh, Scots, or the still more terrible Scandinavian peoples, and risings of the Anglo-Saxons. The safety of William's realm depended on the local security of his barons. But by the time of Henry I conditions had changed. There seemed no danger of a rising. The menace from the Vikings was so slight that Henry felt it safe to reduce the permanent garrisons of such great fortresses as Norwich and Lincoln. The Welsh had been pressed back by vigorous marcher lords, and the Scots were little more than a local problem in the far north. The danger from foreign invasions was overshadowed in the king's mind by that of baronial revolts. Robert of Bellesme was a far more serious menace than the king of Denmark. The needs of civil war rather than those of defense against a common enemy governed the policies of crown and baronage.

Castles were of extreme importance in times of internal confusion. They served as a protection for a baron's own lands and as convenient bases for plundering his neighbors. If he could fill a district with his own fortresses and exclude those of the king and other barons, his control of the region was secure. His own men had plenty of bases for offensive operations, and it was practically impossible for a hostile force to move safely in the midst of his castles. The series of charters issued by King Stephen and the Empress Matilda to Geoffrey de Mandeville and his friends show us a strategic group of fortresses in the process of construction. Geoffrey extorted permission to build new castles. He was to be hereditary custodian of the Tower of London, and his ally Aubrey de Vere was to be given Colchester. The bishop of London's fortress of Bishop's Stortford was to be razed or given to Geoffrey. He would thus secure effective military control of western Essex. The same process was going on in other parts of England. The famous treaty between the earls of Chester and Leicester is an excellent illustration.

Robert of Leicester received as a fief the earl of Chester's stronghold of Mountsorrel which threatened his control of Leicestershire, and both magnates agreed to limit their castle building. A study of the castle sites of this region shows that the earl of Leicester and his neighbor the earl of Warwick each had a nice nest of castles surrounding his chief seat. De Lacy of Pontefract in Yorkshire and Hugh Bigod in Suffolk had equally effective groups of fortresses. The Count of Aumale was hard at work on one in the West Riding of Yorkshire. He obtained Scarborough from Stephen and greatly strengthened its fortifications. While undoubtedly the affection for compact strategic groups of castles had existed before Stephen's reign, the civil war made possible the achievement of such baronial ambitions.

Henry II was naturally the bitter foe of these combinations of fortresses. He seized Scarborough from Aumale and Walton from the earl of Norfolk and turned them into royal fortresses which could hold those lords in check. His purpose in building Oreford was probably to control the Bigods. At least one of the Mandeville castles was razed by him. After the revolt of 1173-75 Henry broke the power of the earl of Leicester. All his castles except Mountsorrel were razed, and that was seized into the king's hands. It is probable that Henry also weakened if he did not actually destroy the groups of castles centering in Pontefract and Warwick. In the latter part of the twelfth and the early thirteenth centuries a number of barons possessed more than one castle, but outside of the Welsh and Scottish marches no one had a compact strategic group.

It seems worth while as a summary of this discussion to review briefly the general principles which seem to have governed the location of the castles of England in the eleventh and twelfth centuries. The Conqueror and his sons could not have had sufficient geographical knowledge to formulate a national scheme of castle building, and there was no need for such a plan. The safety of the realm required that it be studded with castles which lay more thickly in the more exposed regions. The interests and needs of the barons guaranteed that this end would be attained. With the possible exception of the seats of the rapes of Sussex, I can see no reason for believing that King William dictated the location of any baronial stronghold. It is, of course, possible that the crown encouraged castle building in regions which were vital to the national defense and discouraged it in others, but I can find no evidence to indicate such a policy. In fact Bedfordshire, which can hardly be called an exposed shire, had for its size a vast number of castles. In short, it seems clear that feudal considerations governed the location of the majority of castles. When men's minds turned to civil war instead of Saxon risings and foreign invasions, these feudal necessities demanded strategic groups of fortresses. At the same time the king's interests demanded the destruction of these groups, a general reduction in the number of baronial castles, and new royal fortresses to control the great magnates. This accounted for the vigorous razing and confiscation of baronial holds and building of royal castles which marked the policy of Henry II. When Henry died, no baron outside of the marches had effective military control of a district.

Next in importance to the questions of the numbers and locations of castles comes that of their legal position. One is moved to inquire about the laws and customs which governed the ownership, actual command, and construction of these fortresses. A baron could have effective control of a castle by owning or being in command of one already in existence or by building a new one. Hence once the strongholds became primarily factors in civil warfare rather than in the national defense, these questions assume great importance for the historian. The chief check on the authority of the English crown was the military power of the baronage, and the principal element of that power was the mass of fortresses controlled by the barons.

When used in discussing the Middle Ages, the word ownership requires careful definition. In theory, the king as feudal suzerain of England owned the entire realm, and everyone else held his property directly or indirectly from him by some form of tenure. By this definition the king was the owner of all the castles in England. But feudal custom limited a suzerain's control over property which he had granted to a vassal as a fief. Thus for practical purposes a lord may be said to have owned what he held in demesne. The castles situated on the king's demesne were royal, and those on the demesne of his barons baronial. This distinction was clearly recognized in the twelfth and thirteenth centuries, if not before. There was a definite difference between the position of the man who held a castle of the king in fee and one who was simply the hereditary constable of a royal fortress. In the former case the castle was granted to the baron as part of his fief. In the latter only the *custodia,* that is, the office of constable, was given. A baron who held a castle in demesne was deprived of it only when he was disloyal or at least strongly suspected of treason, but the tenure of a hereditary constable was much less secure. Henry II displaced most of them with officers appointed during his pleasure. The best illustration of the contemporary attitude on the ownership of castles is found in letters patent of 1217 addressed by the earl of Pembroke as regent to Philip de Ulecotes. Philip was ordered to surrender the strongholds of the see of Durham to the newly elected bishop. He was not to seek to avoid obeying this command on the ground that the king's castles could not legally be surrendered on the authority of letters patent because 'these castles are not our demesne, but demesne of the lord bishop, nor have we any right in them except through custody [of a vacant see].'

Obviously neither king nor great baron could devote his personal attention to the safe custody of his castles. That was the function of the constables. In common with other feudal offices the position tended to become hereditary and as time went on honorary rather than active. Professor Stenton has pointed out that in the eleventh and early twelfth centuries the constables of such great honors as Chester and Richmond were both the chiefs of their lords' military households and the custodians of the castles of Chester and Richmond. The former at least seems to have had subordinate constables who commanded the lesser castles of the honor of Chester. In the early thirteenth century the constable of Richmond was still the guardian of that stronghold, but the constableship of Chester was vested in the lord of the great honor of Pontefract. Roger de Lacy and his son could have been only the most nominal custodians of Chester castle. Little is known about the honorial constables, but it is probable that every barony had such an officer and, if necessary, his deputies in subordinate castles. For instance, the Amundevilles were constables of the bishop of Lincoln and, one would suppose, keepers of Newark castle. Fourteenth-century evidence indicates the existence of a separate hereditary constable for Banbury. The whole subject is highly complicated because of the diverse meanings of the word constable. A constable might be the chief military officer of an honor, the custodian of a castle, or simply the commander of a constabulary, the unit of the feudal army.

Far more information is available about the hereditary constables of the king's castles. In all probability the Conqueror ordinarily entrusted his fortresses to baronial commanders who held office as a hereditary right. Sometimes it was combined with the hereditary shrievalty, sometimes the two offices were separate. Twelve royal castles are positively known to have had hereditary constables at various times during the eleventh and twelfth centuries. Four of these offices were still recognized early in the thirteenth century. In the cases of four more castles claims to the constableship were advanced during John's reign, but their validity was doubtful, and they received at most only very temporary recognition. Then there were two fortresses which are generally considered as baronial, Ludlow and Tamworth, which I suspect were in reality royal castles. This belief is based simply on the casualness with which the De Lacys and

the Marmions were dispossessed from these strongholds from time to time. In the thirteenth century the royal castles which still had hereditary constables tended to lose their original status and become regular baronial strongholds. Once it became rare, the right of custody could be easily changed into full ownership. It is also interesting to notice that just as the constable of the honor of Richmond was custodian of Richmond castle, so two of the constableships of England were originally connected with royal strongholds. Henry of Essex was constable of the king's household and of Dover castle. The more famous line of constables of England, the Bohuns, owed the origin of their office to their ancestors' possession of the hereditary custody of Gloucester.

The function of actually commanding the garrison of a castle was probably rarely performed by the hereditary constable in person. Most of them were men of importance with castles of their own. In the early thirteenth century the De Hayes at Lincoln and the Beauchamps at Bedford seem to have used the royal castles in their custody as permanent residences and as chief seats of their fiefs, but this was comparatively rare. In general the actual command of a castle must have been vested in a constable appointed during the pleasure of the hereditary constable or the lord. As a matter of fact great barons had a strong disinclination to take personal command of a castle in time of war. Unless the fortress was of enormous importance, the person of a baron was too valuable to risk during a siege. He preferred the open country and a fast horse. The ransom of a man of rank was a more serious burden to a fief than the loss of a castle.

The responsibility of the actual constable toward the man in whose name he acted was clearly defined by contemporary custom. He was expected to hold the castle well and loyally as long as there was any chance of eventual success. The Middle Ages were not given to 'forlorn hopes.' When a constable realized that his position was hopeless, it was his duty to notify his master and request relief within a certain time. If the required aid was not forthcoming, he could surrender with perfect propriety. As a rule the besieging army was willing to grant a truce during the time involved in this process in the hope of being able to secure the stronghold without loss of life. There is some evidence of the existence of a custom which later became a definite part of the laws of war by which a garrison which insisted on holding out after all hope was gone might be put to death, but it was rarely enforced. The mediaeval warrior was too realistic to have any desire to start a series of reprisals that might some day involve himself or his own men. One might add that in the case of men of rank their ransoms were considered far more desirable than their corpses.

Considering the vital importance of castles to the safety and good order of the realm, one would expect to find that the regulations governing their possession and construction had a prominent place in the compilations of contemporary customary law. As a matter of fact, however, the subject was almost entirely neglected in legal documents. One is led to suspect that these regulations were so well known that no one felt any need of stating them. The historian is forced to content himself with two brief passages, one of which applied to Normandy rather than to England.

In the year 1091 William II of England and his brother Robert, duke of Normandy, held an inquisition to determine what Norman custom had been on certain points in the time of their father. The fourth paragraph of the document which embodied the results of this inquest dealt with castles. It stated that no one could build a castle in the duchy, and that an existing stronghold had to be surrendered into the duke's hands if he wished to have it. Mrs Armitage was probably correct in interpreting the first part to mean that the duke's permission was required for castle building. The sense of the second part is determined by the meaning one gives to the word *voluit*. If one uses *wish* in its modern sense, the passage states that the duke could seize his barons' castles

at his mere whim without any specific reason. It is highly improbable that in practice the duke possessed any such power, and it is perfectly certain that the king of England did not. The answer lies in the fact that the Middle Ages could not conceive of a sovereign whose wish was uncontrolled by reason. In short this passage should be interpreted to mean that the duke could seize a baronial stronghold when he believed that the safety of the state demanded it. In practice it meant that he could demand the surrender of the castles held by men whose loyalty he suspected. The next paragraph of this document which deals with the duke's right to demand hostages from his barons must be read in the same light. If a ruler used either of these powers very frequently on the basis of suspicions that were obviously unfounded, he faced baronial discontent. The troubles of King John form an excellent illustration of the possible results of arbitrary action.

It is unlikely that the Conqueror claimed less authority over the castles of England than over those in Normandy. At the same time circumstances could not but affect the application of the customary regulations. The safety of the conquerors and their newly acquired realm demanded a multitude of castles, and it is hard to believe that the king gave specific permission for the construction of each stronghold. In the thirteenth century one finds grants of land in Ireland accompanied by express permission to build castles wherever the grantee felt they were needed. William must have had a similar understanding with his barons. By the time of Henry I the danger of a Saxon uprising had passed, and the country was supplied with a large number of fortresses. The king could then begin to enforce his right to control new construction.

The only actual evidence that Henry I insisted that his barons seek his permission before building castles consists of a brief passage in the *Leges Henrici*. In the following reign, however, the charters which were granted to Geoffrey de Mandeville by King Stephen and the Empress Matilda prove conclusively that a specific license from the crown was required for castle building. Unfortunately I can find no similar document from the reigns of Henry II or his son Richard although some castles are known to have been built during that period. There is a license issued by John as count of Mortain to Richard de Vernon giving him permission to fortify his house at Haddon, but the building which it envisaged could hardly be called a castle. In the year 1200 King John gave William Brewer leave to build three castles. Some three or four other licenses issued by John have survived, and by the middle of the reign of Henry III they become numerous.

If it were to be even reasonably effective, royal regulation of castle building could not be confined to controlling the erection of new strongholds on sites never before used. A motte castle was practically indestructible. The wooden palisade and tower could be burned by the king or a hostile neighbor or deserted by their lord and allowed to fall into decay, but the mound and moats must have usually remained intact. As more and more of these fortresses were abandoned or destroyed, England became dotted with unused castle sites. But in time of civil war these moated mounds could be easily and quickly refortified with towers and palisades. In short, beyond the castles actually in use the barons of England had a large reserve of fortresses for service in case of need. In all probability this refortification of old mottes required royal license. Stenton has pointed out that at least one of the castles figuring in the great revolt against Henry II was of this variety, and he was undoubtedly correct in his belief that many of the adulterine or illegal strongholds mentioned in the chronicles of the twelfth century were ancient moated mounds hastily put in a state of defense. In the early thirteenth century this process was certainly considered illegal. In 1218 the regent ordered the sheriff of Staffordshire to prevent anyone from fortifying a castle at Dudley. Undoubtedly this referred to a projected refortification of the imposing mound on which had stood the castle of Gervase Paganel which had been destroyed by Henry II. Again Nicholas de Anstey was directed to level the castle of Anstey to the condition it had been in before the war began. Considering the feudal insignificance of the Anstey family, one is forced to conclude that before the war their castle could have been little more than the deserted motte once raised by the counts of Boulogne. Not until the wooden castle had become completely obsolete did the good order of England cease to be menaced by the moated mounds of the Norman period.

One more important point remains to be discussed—what sort of building did the king consider to be a castle and hence subject to regulation. In the days of wooden fortresses this problem of definition was not difficult. The *Leges Henrici* clearly considered any fortification consisting of a mound surrounded by a moat to be a castle. But the development of the use of stone made the question far more complicated. John as count of Mortain gave license to Richard de Vernon to fortify a house with a wall twelve feet high but without crenellations. This would seem to indicate that he considered that the building of a stone wall required a license. In 1220 the government sent a commission to examine a house being built by Reginald Marc in Sherwood Forest. The commissioners were to see whether it was sufficiently fortified to constitute a menace to the peace of the region. During the reign of Henry III the government seems to have established a definite criterion for judging whether or not the license of the crown was required. A house could be surrounded by a stone wall, but if the wall was to be crenellated, the king's leave had to be obtained. Again during the reigns of John and his son the designation *castle* tended to become restricted to the more important fortresses. Under John several minor strongholds were called indifferently house or castle. Hence the term crenellation replaced castle as the key to the royal regulation of fortification.

THE STUDENT OF HISTORY must be constantly on guard against unqualified generalization and oversimplification in his study of the past. It is, for example, extremely unsound and unsafe, historically speaking, to make sweeping assertions about medieval institutions. The thousand years which we speak of as the Middle Ages were not all of a piece, even in the same region, and conditions throughout the wide expanse of Europe were not all of a kind, even in the same period. Unless account is taken of geographical and chronological differences, labor will have been saved at the expense of historical truth, and anachronism and historical distortion will be the result. As Professor Herbert Heaton, a wise economic historian, has observed, any attempt to describe country life in Europe during the Middle Ages is made difficult by "the refusal of its inhabitants to fit into a simple standard pattern or to stand still. . . . No description fits all the people all the time or even some of the time; it can at best depict some of them some of the time. This is especially true of any account of the 'typical manor,' that community in which unfree villagers (villeins) cultivated the lord's domain as the price of their serfdom and of their use of a holding." A good example of scholarly caution in dealing with a medieval institution is found in the following essay on English manorial forms by the late Professor Nellie Neilson, of Mount Holyoke College, who was the foremost American student of medieval English agricultural and manorial history. It was written as a plea for the study of local customs and variations and as a protest against yielding to the temptation to impose a uniform type of manorial organization on all of England. Professor Neilson's subject is among the most difficult in the whole range of English history, and her treatment of it can, by the very nature of things, hardly make for easy reading.

ENGLISH MANORIAL FORMS
NELLIE NEILSON

A study of the material available for English manorial history—of court rolls, charters, surveys, and bailiffs' accounts of the thirteenth century, printed, in manuscript, and of photographs of ancient fields taken from the air—will show on even cursory examination striking differences in the form and structure of village units in Medieval England. This paper is a plea for the vigorous study of local customs and arrangements, after the fashion set by Professor Stenton and others, and a protest against yielding to a somewhat insidious temptation to cover England too generally with the Seebohm types of manorial organization, types which were common in parts of the midlands and the south, but not necessarily elsewhere.

Until such studies of local customs have been carried further than their present limits, generalizations regarding the causes of differences in agrarian forms are apt to be dangerous. It is clear, however, that three fields of investigation, which have already proven fruitful, are capable of yielding more abundant information. The study of the

Reprinted by special permission from *The American Historical Review*, XXXIV (1929), 725-739. The footnotes and some of the more technical material which originally appeared in this essay have been omitted.

village or manor may be pursued profitably, first, in relation to the natural characteristics of the countryside in which it is found; secondly, in relation to the racial elements once strong in the neighborhood; and, thirdly, in relation to the character of the lordship established over it.

Of the influence of the natural characteristics of the countryside, the villages described in *Boldon Book,* at the close of the twelfth century, are good examples. Mr. Lapsley, their able commentator finds five types to which such villages belonged: the pastoral village, with tenants performing week work and paying cornage, the agricultural village, where the community as a whole performed services but paid no cornage, the forest village where special forest service was performed at the *magna caza* or great hunting lodge of the bishop, and the nascent borough. The fifth class is of less interest in this connection. Other examples are the villages of the fen country, with their many plots of arable fields divided by dikes constructed to keep out the salt and sweet water, whose maintenance was a heavy customary burden; and the woodland villages of Essex with their many estover customs. The age of the village must in large measure depend upon the character of the countryside, as is obvious—"anciently arable" being found more often in country susceptible of easy cultivation—but it is important to remember that waste regions often had some peculiar "use" or "custom" of their own, existing from time beyond the memory of man, which necessarily conditioned the development of settlements within their limits, and thus lent to them a flavor of great antiquity. Good examples of "use" or "custom" of this kind, which will be spoken of again, may be found in the weald and marsh land of Kent, in the forest of Coupland, and in the Fenland.

The importance of racial influence in determining village forms and methods of agriculture in particular regions is difficult to estimate, and the discussion of it apt to become somewhat theoretical; yet, however difficult it may be to follow Meitzen and assign particular forms of settlement to particular races, some importance must surely

GEORGE GORDON COULTON: Author (d. 1947) of many works in medieval religious and social history, including a multivolume study entitled *Five Centuries of Religion.* A vigorous controversialist, he tended to be distinctly hostile in his comments on the Roman Catholic church.

HIDE: A unit of land, varying in size, often about 120 acres in area.

VIRGATE: A unit of land, usually one fourth of a hide.

CARUCATE: A unit of land equivalent to a hide.

BOVATE: A unit of land equivalent to one eighth of a carucate.

SULUNG: A unit of land in Kent equivalent to the hide and carucate elsewhere.

JUGUM (*plural,* JUGA): A unit of land equivalent to one fourth of a sulung.

CHARLES PETIT-DUTAILLIS: French medievalist (d. 1947) who devoted much attention to English history. His edition of the first two volumes of the French translation of Stubbs' *Constitutional History of England* (1907-1913) contains valuable supplementary studies which did much to bring Stubbs up to date by presenting results of later historical scholarship. These studies were later published in English translation as *Studies and Notes Supplementary to Stubbs' Constitutional History.*

SIR PAUL VINOGRADOFF: Historian and jurist, professor of history at the University of Moscow and afterward at Oxford (d. 1925). His many important contributions to English medieval history include *Villeinage in England* (1892), *The Growth of the Manor* (1905), and *English Society in the Eleventh Century* (1908). His *Outlines of Historical Jurisprudence* (1920-1922), although not completed, is a monumental work, the result of years of research.

be allowed to such influences, at least as a contributory cause of difference. Of value here are photographs taken from the air which disclose ancient field forms, square fields and strips, which are no longer decipherable from the ground level. The possibility, on the other hand, of a natural development from one agricultural form to another, inherent in processes of husbandry, and underlying and independent of all superficial racial conquest or change, has been suggested by a high authority, and may well have been operative. Such natural development would not, however, necessarily exclude completely the coincident action of other forces.

An important variation from the usual manorial form, although perhaps it may be considered social rather than agrarian in its main features, is the custom that distinguished Kent from other counties. The question arises as to whether the Kentish peculiarities were due to original differences in settlement, geographical or racial, as described above, or, as seems to me more likely in view of the wide distribution of particular features of that custom outside of Kent in regions that can be reduced to no common geographic or racial unity, to the fact that Kent, lying in the pathway to the Continent, advanced quickly, and attained an early self-consciousness and entity that enabled her to withstand the equalizing and standardizing influence of the Norman conquerors, and to preserve to a late date characteristics once prevalent elsewhere. Is there perhaps some basis of truth in the legend of Swanscombe Wood [see p. 76] and the recognition of Kentish custom forced by the men of Kent from an astute conqueror? It will be recalled that Cornwall, Yorkshire, and Gloucestershire also had once their customs, but being less favorably placed apparently succumbed to Norman influences and lost their peculiarities quickly.

The third possible cause of variation in village organization, the character of the lordship, is a matter of some interest, in need of more definite information than we at present have. Was there an appreciable difference in the position of peasants on lands belonging to the church and on lay land, and, if so, on which side did advantage to the peasant lie? On one hand is to be considered the constant pressure of a lordship that never dies and is always on the spot, a point emphasized by Maitland; on the other, is to be considered the ameliorating influence of the humanitarian ideas of the church, a point raised by Mr. Coulton, who yet questions the existence of any very marked benefit derived therefrom, and even asks if the greater freedom of the Danelaw can be explained in part by the destruction of churches there, accomplished by the Danish invaders. The study of numerous surveys of lay lordships, especially of those contained in the inquests *post mortem,* should go far towards answering this question, and towards restoring a balance at present inclining too far in the direction of the use of ecclesiastical material.

Whatever their origin, the variations in village forms and manorial organization, which are the main theme of this paper, may be conveniently considered from the following points of view: first, the general organization of the manor and its relation to the village; secondly, the classes of society within the manor; thirdly, the tenemental units, that is to say, the normal holdings of different classes within the manor; fourthly, assarts and approvements; fifthly, rents and services; sixthly, the demesne; seventhly, judicial arrangements.

Such a division may be convenient for purposes of discussion, but it is clear that these elements of agrarian life were interdependent, and that the consideration of any one of them can not be bounded by hard and fast lines. It is also evident that the adequate discussion of any one of them would require a volume. The remarks that follow are desultory reflections on special points that are in need of elucidation, or that are suggestive of matters of particular interest.

Of attempts to define the manor the safest is Professor Stenton's, "it is impossible" to define the manor, or Round's, "it is not a technical term." It is rather a general term for a substantial estate of one lord. The manor was "primarily a rural mansion with appurtenant rights over its lord's tenants." If it had any essential feature besides lordship, it was perhaps the *aula* or hall for the holding of the *halmote*. The *villa,* the geographical village, and the *villata,* the people living therein, usually imply some inhabited nucleus, although the *villa* may appear as the equivalent of the tithing [territorial unit for police purposes], or of the *borgha,* which in less settled regions of Kent replaced the tithing. That the *villa* was a definite geographical entity with boundaries is made clear in perambulations for the partition of intervillar waste, and in pleas in court. . . .

Specific information from different parts of England of the relationship of vills and manors, whether they were coterminous, or one inclusive of several of the other, and the relation of both to parish boundaries, would have value. In general the manors that go back in origin to royal vills granted to the church or retained by the king, and that sometimes themselves served as the centres of administrative districts, . . . were most often of one lordship and coterminous with the vill. Also it is clear that such coincident vills and manors were more common in the well-manorialized midland and southern region than in the Danelaw, East Anglia, or the north and far west, where on account of conquest and scattered settlements homogeneity was difficult to attain. The effect of the Norman tendency towards standardization was probably to create or restore coincidence wherever possible.

Recent important studies have done much to make clear the character of the agrarian units in the Danelaw and East Anglia. In East Anglia the village was large and nucleated, to use Maitland's happy term, but its strip-holding and rotation of crops were worked by units of tenements, not by the three-field system. . . . In the Danelaw occurred the discrete manors. . . . There are many other regions of hamlets which would repay more study than has been given them. Sometimes unusual little jurisdictional groups appear, like the salt boilers on the sea in the village of Fleet. . . . Moreover, the coalescing of small manors to form larger units goes on, as well as the "fission" of vills and the formation of new manors. . . .

Can we then trace the relative age of vill and manor, or, rather, can we sometimes find traces of a time before lordship had developed, when the village group was the vital unit? It is held that the manor was somewhat late and artificial in East Anglia, the Danelaw, and the north. It is the *villata* there that attests charters, makes by-laws, serves as a unit for the geld, goes to the tourn [special meeting of the hundred court, presided over by the sheriff], enters into agreements with the lord. In his recent volume on Ramsey court rolls Professor Ault shows a village assembly in Walsoken, Norfolk, which is not manorial. But most interesting of all perhaps is the fact that it is the *villata* that is endowed with ancient rights of common in the intervillar waste, and makes regulations for the use of that waste.

Concerning the second suggested topic, the classes of society in the thirteenth-century manor, much investigation has been carried on, and we know a great deal about the economic and legal characteristics of different groups. The difficult sokemen have been in part explained, as tenants representing an earlier organization than the manorial, slowly being assimilated within the manor to the position of ordinary villeins. The jurisdictional aspects of their position have not yet perhaps been made perfectly clear, and the characteristics of those living on ancient demesne certainly need further elucidation. Of the unusual classification of peasantry in Kent, and the Year Book dictum regarding villeinage there, the writer has suggested an explanation elsewhere. A question which is of a good deal of interest and deserving of study is the origin of the class of molmen. They occur fairly generally; for example, on the manors of Glastonbury, Ely, Durham, Burton; in East Anglia, in Lincolnshire, and as *smalmolmen* in Middlesex. The rent *mala,* from which they take their name, is common also in Kent. A number of passages seem to explain that they are a class of unfree tenants who have at an early time commuted the bulk of their rents and services for a mony rent. *Mala* is rent "paid by our ancestors for all unjust dues and exactions," as the *Black Book* of St. Austin puts it, the result of a definite agreement with their lord. A very interesting indenture, mentioned by Mr. Douglas, records a definite contract between certain molmen and their lord regarding works. . . .

Other matters regarding the tenants on the manor would certainly become clearer if studies of local material were made. We should know more of the position of cottars . . . ; of those tenants who worked for other tenants, even perhaps for villeins; of the men "whose number increased and decreased," who came at certain seasons of the year; . . . of all of these and many others.

Of tenemental arrangements three main systems may be traced; that of hides and virgates, that of carucates and bovates, that of sulungs and *juga*. . . . Recent research seems to have established a good deal that is interesting with regard to tenements. Of the three chief systems, that of the hide and virgate is considered the oldest, and can perhaps be traced below the other later impositions. It held, speaking generally, in the great block of Saxon counties, or, more specially, as Mr. Turner suggests, in the region of the three-field system of agriculture.

The system of bovates and carucates is found in the Danelaw, but also in Cumberland and the lowlands of Scotland where the Danes did not go. The sulungs and *juga* were confined to Kent. Modern opinion seems to hold that the bovate and the virgate, the smaller divisions, were older than the hide and carucate, and that the larger allotment of hide and carucate made to the family, with definite obligations of tribute and service affixed, was not a measure of economic necessity. The relation of these units to the system of assessment is a difficult problem in which there is still room for much study. . . .

Of all aspects of manorial life common assart [land improved by the grubbing up of trees and bushes] and the use of the waste seem to the writer best to repay study devoted to them. The two main uses of the waste were for pasture and colonization. The study of pasture rights will some time lead to the great work on early commons which is needed. There is much to be learned with regard to common within the manor, but more with regard to common in the intervillar waste, or, as it is later called, common *pur cause de vicinage*. The grouping of neighboring vills according to the kind of pasture rights enjoyed—those, namely, with very ancient rights for all tenants of ancient arable land to turn out all the cattle levant and couchant within their villages during all the year, and those others which paid under differing conditions sums of money for specific numbers of cattle during restricted seasons—seems to have been the custom in all parts of England. The attempt of the royal administration when such districts were afforested to cut down ancient rights of common pasture and the corresponding common use of woodland was, I believe, a chief cause of the hatred of royal forests, and of the constant agitation against afforestation. It would too be of interest to know whether the systems of denns in Kent and the weald of southern England had parallels elsewhere. The denn was an outlying part of the village, situated in the woodland, and used for swine pasture. It might lie at a distance of half a county from its parent vill, and it had its own different and peculiar rents and services. The question of the right of the tenants of the denn to cut the timber trees without the assent of the lord, or *vice versa*, the lord's right to cut at his own will, became a subject of litigation in the king's courts, and furnishes admirable evidence of the possibility of independent action on the part of groups of tenants.

The use of the waste for assart and colonization has received even less attention than its use for common pasture and will prove a most interesting field of work. Where a large territory lay open to settlement there was room for a definite policy. In the archbishops' innings in Walland marsh in Kent, south of Rhee Wall, for example, protection against the sea had to be secured by regulations regarding walls and sewers, and such regulations became the basis of later royal ordinances: the tenure of gavelkind was extended to land so inned, the plots show a certain uniformity in size, and the tenant who took one had to put in gage and pledge for its proper maintenance all his tenements and chattels elsewhere, and, unless he had a house in the village to which it was appurtenant, had also to build on his inning. He took a corporal oath that he would fulfil the conditions of his enfeoffment.

Rents and services still offer an admirable field for research, notwithstanding the fact that much study has already been given them. Labor services of the tenants for the lord are usually divided into week work and boon work, but this division is not necessarily exhaustive. All labor that was not boon work was not necessarily week work; much was performed by the task, *ad tascham,* a certain number of days of work, "daywerks," being required in a particular season, or a total of "works" required in a whole year, or a total assignment made of land to be ploughed or reaped. Sometimes these works are designated as "great or small works." In Kent, and other regions where partibility of inheritance or some other cause had split up the land into small tenements, week work would have been difficult to manage, and a more flexible arrangement was clearly almost a necessity. But even where the two- and three-field system prevailed and land was held in hides and virgates, week work was by no means universal. Thus a study of Oxfordshire as it appears in the Hundred Rolls in the survey of the seventh year of Edward I, shows that week work was of far from uniform occurrence or importance, and also that it was the first service commuted, a fact natural enough in view of its cumbersome nature. Seasonal works, on the other hand, are

frequent, and are rendered to the lord until a comparatively late date.

The relation of week work, then, to *gafol* or original tribute on one hand, and to commutation on the other, becomes important. Was it a necessary stage through which all manorialized villein land passed, or was it in some cases non-existent, and in its place may we find a heavy *mol, mala, redditus,* dating from an early time and commuting early obligations other than the *gafol* or food rent, which had not yet crystallized into week work? We should then find villeins divided according to their labor services into three classes: first, a class, very numerous on church lands, who performed both week work and boon works, and paid customary rents which were in some cases commutations of occasional services; secondly, a class less common, perhaps, but still very numerous and unmistakably of villein status, who paid a *mala* or *redditus,* a fixed and heavy rent, for their tenement, as well as boon works and perhaps occasional daywerks, but no week work; and thirdly, a class of those who had once performed week work which had later been commuted, either permanently or in given years at the lord's will, and who still performed boon works. These classes can be conveniently studied in the surveys of 1279 in the *Hundred Rolls,* and much light is thrown on the second class by the information available regarding molmen. The possibility of early and fairly general commutation of week work as found in the third class should be noticed. That labor services in general were a better indication of villein status than anything else is probably true, but, in view of the foregoing variations, Mr. Douglas would seem to me to over-emphasize the value of week work as a test. Vinogradoff's position is probably safer when he says that "agricultural service may be regarded as a symptom of villeinage"; that, for the courts, agricultural service was "a presumption of villein tenure till proof to the contrary was forth coming," but that a "hesitating jurisprudence" was fastening on, and sometimes producing simultaneously, "many discordant tests of status." . . . The origin of week work and of other villein services on the lord's demesne is still obscure. Was it imported by the church from the Continent, as sometimes stated, or may it have been the result of the substitution of *gafol* works for some of the *gafol* rent in kind? Thus it might even have become attached to definite bits of land, which would come to be considered the lord's special strips. . . .

According to much of the evidence, the rent in kind or *gafol* was probably of great age, antedating manorial arrangements. The very long survival of original food rents on the manors of Bury St. Edmunds has recently been shown by Mr. Douglas. . . . In connection with another group of rents attention should be called to Miss Cam's recent article on the importance of great private lords as vicegerents of government in the maintenance of the principles of the collections of public fines and dues. On certain particular rents further light is needed; for example, on the very curious payment of *fulstingpound,* which seems to suggest the early appearance of a somewhat advanced principle of insurance. A pound is paid every year by the *villata,* or an annual twelve-penny rent by the individual, in order that a villein, if amerced for any offense not involving the shedding of blood, may pay no more than twelve pence. The custom occurs in rural districts and can not well therefore be referred solely, as Miss Bateson refers it, to the law of Breteuil. The custumals of towns must often exhibit traces of customs of the adjacent countryside, and I think have not been examined from this very interesting point of view. Another interesting rent is that called *foxalpeni* in Kent, which carries an extremely heavy penalty for arrears.

A study of local material is necessary to show to what extent the demesne in any manor lay in compact blocks or in strips in the open fields. There were still villages, some belonging to Ely, some in the Danelaw and elsewhere, where there was no demesne: on the other hand sometimes important tenants of the lord of the manor had demesnes of their own within the village. Other groups of villages had a common demesne. The renting of plots of demesne was probably more common at an early date than is generally supposed; the *Domesday of St. Paul's,* for example, gives a good deal of evidence regarding tenements in new and old assart. On what terms were such demesne tenements held—always for a money rent only, or were some of the ancient services and dues of the manor ever imposed? Again, at what time and in what manner did the lord's claim to the waste of the manor, as contrasted with his land held anciently in demesne, develop? Did the Statute of Merton confirm or modify the common law practices with regard to the use of the waste? Was not *inland*—that is to say land *sine geldo regis* and hence the antithesis of *warland* which was subject to royal dues—often kept apart and distinct from the newer "de dominio" holdings, which were subject to public burdens? Again, what was the position of castles with regard to their own demesne and that of their members?

Of the jurisdictional side of manorial life one aspect of great importance has received as yet comparatively little attention, namely, the procedure in manorial courts, and its likeness to procedure in the common law courts. The researches of Professor Ault, Miss Levett, and others will throw light on manorial practice and on the development of the common law. Was the common law procedure taken over bodily? Did manorial lords imitate royal procedure with regard to a jury of presentment? To what extent did local custom, for example the furnishing of "witnesmen," thrust itself through the more conventional procedure, and become part of the "custom of the manor," a subject which has been strangely neglected, considering its interest and importance. Did great private lords hold inquests *post mortem?*

Another question connected with jurisdiction already has been suggested in speaking of the antiquity of village life under the crust of manorialism. What was the nature of the first meetings of the villagers? Were they for purely economic matters, or did some jurisdiction also spring from the soil? If the East Anglian village had sufficient self-consciousness to attest charters, it must, Mr. Douglas believes, have been able to have a court for economic arrangements.

In conclusion, a specific example may be given, taken from material still unprinted, of one of the many variations from the closely organized manorial groups of parts of England. Cumberland in the thirteenth century was divided into lordships derived from the great lordships of Norman times, four of which had castles as centres of their administration. One of these lordships, the honour of Cockermouth, with the castle of Cockermouth as its centre, passed in the forty-fourth year of Henry III, on the death of William de Fortibus, Earl of Albemarle, to his widow Isabella, Lady of the Isle, as her dower. Isabella was a woman of strong character, who took the king's side in the Barons' War, was pursued by Simon de Montfort, according to her own story, and quarrelled with her mother, Amicia, Countess of Devon, in "a manner displeasing to God and odious to all." Of the administration of her fief in Cumberland we have unusually full records. The honour consisted of the castle and town of Cockermouth, several neighboring manors, and scattered tenements in the great waste and mountainous districts of Cumberland, in Derwentfelles, Allerdale, Coupland, and Inglewood Forest. The duties of the chief officer, the constable, to whom all lesser officers accounted, are clearly described, the provenance and collection of the revenue, its delivery to the countess at places very far distant from its source, her need for it on account of her fondness for litigation, and the necessity for large payments to secure justice. There is included in the documents a customal of Cockermouth, not noticed in Miss Bateson's or Ballard's list. For the present purpose, however, the chief interest of the documents is the clearness with which they describe agrarian conditions within the various holdings of the fee. The tenements were in bovates, rated often at seven acres, the tenants were *firmarii* and villeins. Both classes paid light labor services, and the villeins paid also hens and eggs. There was no week work, but a considerable number of boons. A point of much interest is the large amount of hired labor, and the frequent appearance of selfods, extra laborers. Much of the demesne was already stocked by the lord, an ox to a bovate, and rented in farms to the bond tenants. Outside these home manors, the Cockermouth honour included wide stretches of territory suitable for hunting and grazing, and for little else, with few and scattered tenants—two in Falls, eleven in Buttermere, as many as eighteen in Goderescale, three in Skalegayl, and small numbers elsewhere. . . .

Equally far from the conventional manorial type is the village or manor of Kent, with its gavelkind tenure, its unique tenements, its absence of week work, its denns or swine pastures in the weald, and its subordination to the custom of Kent, some phases of which were very old, others of which had accumulated in later times. . . .

The further one goes beneath the surface of manorial life, the deeper one finds the layer of ancient customs, the more striking the variation from the normal manor imposed by the manorial lordship. As the law of the Norman military fief becomes the common law of England, obliterating in most places the ancient rules of inheritance, of wardship, of dower, so the manorial lordship of the Normans seeks to bring into uniformity ancient systems of landholding and cultivation of the fields. The "custom of the manor," of which such variations are the vital part, has a strong hold on life, and may maintain itself against complete annihilation and become a clue in the hands of students of history to the conditions of a village life long past. "Recent law may go one way while ancient custom goes another." "It is curious," to adapt the words of M. Petit-Dutaillis, "how little contradiction embarrassed the men of the middle ages"; and of great weight is Vinogradoff's *dictum:* "English courts . . . had to reckon with deeply rooted customs of feudal and pre-feudal origin, and this fundamental fact ought to be made the starting-point of inquiries as to the origins of English . . . Law,"

ONE OF THE SUPREMELY GREAT DEVELOPMENTS in the history of civilization has been the formation and spread of the English common law. It had its origins in the decisions of the king's courts in cases that came before them, and the period of its most rapid growth was the hundred years from the middle of the twelfth to the middle of the thirteenth century. It may seem paradoxical, but it is true, that the basis of the common law was laid down by French-speaking judges, as was natural at a time when French was the language of the governing classes of England. The common law was the subject of Bracton's great treatise, *De legibus et consuetudinibus Angliae* (probably written during the 1250's), by far the most important law book produced in medieval England. At first the common law, *lex communis,* was so called because it was common to all England, applied throughout the land by the king's justices when they went on circuit, as distinguished from local and special customs peculiar to particular localities. It was not until later that the term "common law" was used to designate the law found in judicial decisions as distinguished from the law found in statutes—that is, enacted law. The common law grew up in medieval England with little aid from the universities, where the canon law of the church and the civil law of Rome were taught. It was studied in institutions known as "Inns of Court," which came into existence in the late thirteenth and the fourteenth centuries. It developed in contact with various bodies of pre-existing customary law, by which it was profoundly affected. In the essay that follows, the late Professor Nellie Neilson deals with a number of these bodies of customary law which exercised so great an influence on the common law. This essay was Professor Neilson's presidential address before the American Historical Association, and in it she deserted her favorite field—medieval agricultural history—for another in which she had a compelling interest.

THE EARLY PATTERN OF THE COMMON LAW

NELLIE NEILSON

It has been pointed out to me by a kind and helpful critic that of late years scholars sitting in this "sliddery" seat, as King James would have called it, have more often presented for your consideration certain generalizations drawn from their own experiences in the study of history than specific subjects of discussion drawn from their own field. My life has been spent in the Middle Ages, however; my field of work lies there, and I can not forego the opportunity to talk about them, especially since they seem to me to offer material pertinent to our own time.

Medieval English law seems very far from the world of today, and in the opinion of many may well be left unstudied until the war is over and we can once again enjoy the pleasant pursuit of the nonessential. Perhaps the differing of opinion among medievalists is only self-delusion, but I hope not. Surely it is essential that the history of the great contestants should be known, not only for its own sake but also for the growth

Reprinted by special permission from *The American Historical Review,* XLIX (1944), 199-212. The footnotes which originally appeared with this essay have been omitted.

of political and social ideas whose birth lies hidden in the remote past but whose influence has had an important share in forming present opinion and action resulting therefrom. The roots of the present lie deep in the past, a truism that we cannot today despise if we seek a solution of our own difficult problems.

Especially, I believe, we should study those characteristics of English history which make her different from other countries, her constant stress on the particular forms of self-government and civil liberties which she has developed and which, we must gratefully acknowledge, she has in part passed on to us. Much of her history is our history. Our own law is in part derived from her law and legal procedure. We think in large measure the same legal thoughts, in spite of many political and social differences. The same lawbooks and legal dictionaries are used by both of us, and we cannot appropriate so much of her essential framework without some recognition and knowledge of the model from which we have acquired it. The pattern of her common law she began to build very long ago, and throughout her history she has continued to elaborate it quietly without violent breaks or changes. It is a living organism and one the knowledge of which is especially essential to us Americans in war and in peace.

The medieval pattern of her law was well formulated by England in the two hundred years that followed the Norman Conquest, the period when there was most danger, perhaps, of the imposition of alien rules and regulations. The legal interest of this faraway and somewhat obscure period centers in the growth of the king's justice and its contact with already existing laws and customs. I have chosen this period for several reasons. It has to my mind intrinsic interest, and we are a little inclined to neglect it, or, rather, in the dearth of material it has to offer, we are often inclined to endow it with

CORNAGE: A manorial obligation based upon the number of horned cattle in the peasant's possession.

HUNDRED ROLLS: Medieval records concerned with local government in England. Early in the reign of Edward I royal commissioners were sent throughout England with lists of detailed questions to be put to juries in every hundred regarding the exercise of judicial authority by lords and other matters. The information thus obtained was recorded in rolls brought back to Westminster by the commissioners early in 1275; these came to be known as the Hundred Rolls. Although many of these rolls have perished, enough of them survive to make possible a description of English local government at the time. They have been brilliantly exploited by the English medievalist Professor Helen M. Cam, now of Harvard University, in her *Studies in the Hundred Rolls: Some Aspects of Thirteenth-Century Administration* and *The Hundred and the Hundred Rolls: An Outline of Local Government in Medieval England* (1930).

PIPE ROLLS: Annual records of exchequer accounts. The earliest extant roll comes to us from the reign of Henry I (1130), but this is an isolated one. From 1156 to 1833, however, the series is practically unbroken. The pipe rolls contain much information of the greatest value for the social, economic, fiscal, and legal historian. The Pipe Roll Society has done excellent work in publishing some of the rolls, mainly of the twelfth century, but the great majority of the 676 rolls preserved in the Public Record Office remain unpublished.

YEAR BOOKS: Series of reports begun in the reign of Edward I and continued until 1535; so called because one book was compiled for each regnal year. The Year Books contain reports of cases adjudicated in the king's courts and are of the utmost importance as sources for the history of the medieval common law. The reader will find W. C. Bolland's *The Year-Books* (1921) an illuminating exposition of the subject.

some of the conditions that belong clearly to later times. But most of all I have chosen it because it illustrates the English method of gentle change. It is the period when the first lines of the magnificent common law were graven deep into their legal foundation, never to be erased by later edifices.

The meeting during this period of the common law with church law, the *ius commune* of the universal church, is a great subject by itself and one that I am not competent to deal with. I must leave that to church historians. It has also, however, contacts with another and more manageable condition existing in England, namely, English customary law in its various forms, some pre-Conquest English custom, some post-Conquest adaptations of that custom. Maitland speaks of 1066 as the midnight of legal history and emphasizes how little written law the Normans had of their own and how English law is far more than a meeting of two thin streams, English and Norman, and is really formed out of all the complex events and currents of the history of the time. It is by no means simply made out of a law imposed by a conqueror upon a conquered people. Perhaps some of William's patience with lack of uniformity in his conquered country was due to his tolerance of tradition and to the old idea, now passing, that the law of the conqueror was too good for the conquered. The Conqueror promised, it will be remembered, to maintain the law of Edward the Confessor.

What were then some of the variations in law and custom that were present in England after the Conquest and how among them did the so-called common law become of transcendent importance for later history? First and most important is its evident basis in the law of the royal court, of the king's court, and in the method of that court in dealing with conditions as it found them. It grew slowly with the increasing understanding of the "tremendous empire of the kingly majesty." It was the general law as accepted by the courts, not yet clearly enacted in statute, in contact with local customs, with the ideas and conditions that lay along its always extending boundaries. With such conditions it dealt variously, rarely by denying their force, more often by adapting them to common-law notions, or by adopting them entirely and enshrining them in common-law rules. In later times these variations became unimportant, but in speaking of the early formative days it is necessary to see that the law was exposed to different variations and that it molded these slowly and reasonably into the growing pattern of king's law and court procedure. It is a mistake to think of early English law as too immature to be reasonable. Even early pleading shows a desire to understand differences and to make a peaceful adjustment with existing conditions.

Recognition of special custom occurs again and again in early English legal material. Very commonly in early Year Books and other material one meets the words *consuetudo loci*—the best-known phrase— . . . [many other customs], custom and law of London, of Wales, of Scotland, of Normandy, of the manors of the king, custom and liberty of the vill, *usage defait commune ley que usage usee parmi le pays,* and other like phrases.

The *consuetudo loci* refers in general to the local custom of particular places. Such custom has always had for me a peculiar fascination, I suppose because it takes one so far back into the past, unknown but imaginable. From certain regions such custom excludes all or part of the operations of the king's law, the law of the king's courts. What will the natural desire for legal uniformity do with these? Perhaps the most important of such customs and in some ways the clearest, because it lasted down into times of definition and was too strong to be obliterated, is the well-known custom of Kent. The story goes, but there is no proof of its truth so far as I know, that William, marching through Kent after Hastings, was met by the moving wood of Swanscombe, composed of men in armor, carrying trees, and that William thereupon agreed to let them have their customs intact. In later times the custom included at least fourteen points, of which some were evidently ac-cretions. The most famous of them were partibility of tenement amongst heirs, which was of course not peculiar to Kent but was found elsewhere in that great socage tenure which was accepted as part of the common law and which is crying for its historian. Secondly, the payment of gafol, from which the gavol-kind tenure of Kent takes its name, a name not used elsewhere in England in early documents, but, I am informed, occa-sionally found in South Scotland. Thirdly, a lesser age for attaining majority than that of the common law and also a different ruling on dower, on the awarding of the custody of a minor to the *procheym ami,* usually the the mother instead of the lord; again a re-lief paid on entrance into property of double the rent, a special jury system, and in cases of felony, poetically, "the father to the boghe, the son to the ploghe." In addition several economic rules regarding rights of way and the cutting of trees in Kent, the county of dennes, appear. Such rules were regarded as *selon l'usage de Kent,* and the various manuscripts in which they were re-corded await an editor. I suppose that the explanation of their long endurance against the pressure of common law is the fact that Kent was in part the much-traveled road to the Continent, where formulation of rules would occur early, and in other part was covered by the weald, which was backward and inaccessible.

Other counties too had once their own customs, but we know little of these because they were assimilated into the common law at an early date. The *Prerogativa Regis* [Prerogative of the King] in the statute book speaks of the custom of the county of Gloucester. The custom of the counties of York and Norfolk is very occasionally men-tioned without much definition, and also the custom of a Sussex rape, of the honor of Brittany, and of "the north where cornage prevailed." Cradle right, the succession of the youngest son to the holding, while a varia-tion of the common rule of the succession of the eldest, was sufficiently prevalent to have a place of its own. It seems sometimes to have been in force in certain distinct localities, especially in mid-southern Eng-land.

Of a nature similar to county peculiarities were the long-prevailing rules regarding tenements called ancient demesne of the king. In these instances royal influence pre-served them as separate entities in some legal matters. Much has been written about them. Land in ancient demesne was land which at the time of the Conquest was royal land and had descended as such from Edward the Confessor and was so entered in Domes-day Book. The more exact definition seems to have been land that was King Edward's on "the day he was alive and dead," which allows for some changes between 1066 and 1086. For all intents and purposes, however, the picturesque summoning of Domesday Book into court to give evidence that King Edward had held the land in question was sufficient to establish its identity. I am at present engaged in preparing for the Dug-dale Society the great book of ancient de-mesne customs, the Stoneleigh Leger Book. It shows the special writs for lands which had to be brought in the Stoneleigh court and were excluded from the king's courts. . . . The king insisted in the maintenance of the peculiar writs of ancient demesne, even where the land had been given away by him, feeling that if it should escheat at any time in the future he himself would have more control over it in the manorial court than in the Common Bench. . . . There is much that is of interest in ancient demesne procedure and some points that are not yet clear, but it is clearly accepted as outside common-law jurisdiction.

Other variations in custom are found in boroughs where the borough court admin-istered its own law in all its own ancient peculiarities. The twelfth century burgess in Cardiff went free of summons, for ex-ample, if he could prove that he had one foot in the stirrup and was about to leave the town. Another defendant elsewhere could gain a delay in procedure if he spoke out and said, "Have law." Such picturesque sur-vivals can be seen best in Mary Bateson's

Borough Customs, but even her two large tomes are by no means exhaustive. Manuscript material discloses many more local customs, which, it is true, add little to her main classifications. Miss Bateson lays great stress on the transference to English boroughs of the customs of boroughs in France, but I think that sometimes the transference is rather due to the appearance in the English borough of customs already imbedded in the surrounding countryside. Similar variations in customs are found in manors and vills. Manorial court records are full of regulations which are often applicable to unfree and free alike and are important because they sometimes preserve old uses and have a definite influence on the development of ideas of freedom and self-government. The old men, *seniores,* of the village are often called into court or are consulted in order that they may give descriptions of old procedure. I have been specially interested in the part played by the old men in drawing lines of division through ancient waste, used from antiquity for common pasture by the men of adjacent sokes, villages, or groups but now to be partitioned among them and their practice of intercommoning thus stopped. Interesting instances of this procedure appear to antedate the strict control by feudal lords. Also it is of interest to see how the village itself regulates the intercommoning of tenants, in other vills outside its group, and the admissions of the cattle of other villages for a sum of money for specified times of pasture. Villages in the great stretches of fen in Holland in Lincolnshire furnish much interesting information on arrangements that are derived from old local conditions of pasture and the use of the waste, which indicate free discussion and common action on the part of villagers.

Another variation from ordinary common-law procedure of a somewhat different kind occurred in the great franchises of Norman England. The legal side of these units is interesting. They were built up before and after the Conquest, in the main for purposes of defense along an unruly border in the north and west. Each was composed of fiefs under an overlord whose position in his domain was in some cases almost that of a king. The "sword of Chester" was in some ways almost equivalent to the "crown of St. Edward" over the lord. The king was still ruler, demanding loyalty and exercising a certain amount of control, in different degree in different franchises, especially over defaulters and traitors.

The most marked characteristic of these great franchises was the usual exemption from the authority of the common-law courts and variations in procedure. From some points of view the palatinates of Chester, Durham, and Lancaster may be considered as the most instructive in their varied history. In ordinary matters the lord took the place of the king, always theoretically by the king's consent. If royal justices appeared within their boundaries it was with the lord's consent, unless there had been a default in feudal justice. The king's writ did not run, although procedure on the lord's writ might be like that of the ordinary courts. Most of the exempt jurisdictions had their general centers in the gateways into Wales, at Shrewsbury, Hereford, and Gloucester, and their lands were in part at least conquered lands. Shrewsbury ceased to be a palatinate in the time of Henry I; Chester went back to the crown in 1237 and was given to Prince Edward in 1254. He finally conquered it, together with Flintshire, Denbighshire, Cardigan, and Carmarthen, and in 1284 the ordinance annexing Wales, which resulted in a compromise between Welsh and English law, was issued. The later survey of the honor of Denbigh, edited by Sir Paul Vinogradoff's seminar, shows some of these points of contact of English and Welsh law and custom, part of the inhabitants living under Welsh custom, part under English. The king's writ did not run in some parts of the liberty, and the king's problem of how to attain a peaceful government was a difficult one. There was no writ of error, no writ of *certiorari,* and the peace that was broken was the lord's, not the king's. Recourse might be had to parliament, however, and the king was regarded as the ultimate *dominus.* The building up of the great Lancaster fief and the accumulation of lands finally in the hands of the Black Prince, from the earldom of Chester and the earldom of Cornwall and other great lordships, is also very instructive. The threads of local liberties and customs were without question gathered up in Westminster and London.

Durham, a very great liberty on the northern border of England, brings in an additional factor, the ecclesiastical courts and church law, for its lord was a bishop. Durham was a border district and often the subject of dispute between English Northumberland and the Scottish kings. It was almost more Scottish than English. In Dr. Lapsley's famous and admirable book on this franchise we can watch the working of palatinate law and the contact of the franchise with common law and church law. Only crime or an attack upon the king was subject to immediate royal jurisdiction. The maxim developed, "quicquid rex habet extra, episcopus habet intra."* The bishop speaks of *pax nostra.*† Even here, however, fell the shadow of the crown; not all was left to custom and local law. The king could be reached by petition and the powers of the bishop varied at different times, being at their height from 1292 through the fourteenth century. There are traces of northern custom still remaining in this northern franchise; for example, rewards are paid for the heads of decapitated robbers. Among these great jurisdictions should be mentioned the Channel Islands, where the custom and law of Normandy prevailed, and the Isle of Man, once belonging to Norway.

Within England were many smaller franchises which varied in the amount of exemption they had from common-law procedure. Most extensive of the liberties in privilege, but very small in the extent of

* ["Whatever the king has outside, the bishop has inside."]
† [Our peace.]

territory, were the *banlieux* [suburbs] of monasteries and ecclesiastical foundations. Within a limited territory the king's writ did not run, but the abbot or ecclesiastical officer was the lord. Within the Four Crosses of St. Edmund, for example, such jurisdiction was exercised, and common-law officers were excluded. Very rewarding in this connection would be a study of some of those bundles of writs preserved in the Record Office, not yet calendared and still largely unused. They furnish a good field of investigation for some student of early English history. There often is a bundle of five or six hundred for each of the four law terms of the Common Bench in a given year. Even the later ones, those of early Edward III, the only ones which I have used, are full of detailed matters of importance. Those in any bundle dealing with liberties show the sheriff delivering the writ to the bailiff and the bailiff returning it, or not, with notes on its adventures within the liberty. If the bailiff has not delivered it, the writ *ne omittas propter libertatem* is issued to the sheriff, which enables him to enter the liberty and perform his duties. In cases where the king's writ did not run the substantive common law is found within the liberty, and the difference was one of procedure, but even here old custom would also be recognized:

And as in good St Edwards days
So must it go, St Use allows,
When Norman lords ride English ways.

While not very much may be known of the early law of exempt jurisdictions, some light is thrown on them in the great volumes wherein are printed the Hundred Rolls and subsequent proceedings. The English Justinian before and after his accession in 1272 tried to cut down on private jurisdiction wherever it lay by questioning the ancient warrant for it, and, even when accepting the efficacy of its charter or claim of prescription, by preventing its extension—and incidentally by taking large fines for settlement of the cases. There is a good deal of information on this in early Year Books dealing with franchises and their legal status.

An interesting example arose in the liberty of Durham; the question is asked: May the king's sheriff enter the liberty on the king's command? The answer is that the bishop has such franchise that he has royal power, and no minister of the king may enter except on default of franchisal justice. It is objected that the king's prerogative is above any franchise, and if a sheriff distrains in a liberty he does it in contempt of the king, who has by his prerogative created the liberty.

Other exemptions from the application of the common-law courts and their rules were functional in character. Districts lay outside the *corpus comitatus,* for example, because they were furnishing mines and their products. Mines for precious metals, gold and silver, belonged to the king, and his claim was accepted generally. Non-precious metals were mined in the usual way, although Richard I tried to claim special control over them. They went with the land, and the owners had their rights, as they had over the rest of their soil. But there was a third class of miners more interesting from the point of view of exemption from common-law rules. In some places where there were tin and lead mines, for example, in Cornwall and Devon, there had grown up groups of miners from very early times who formed semi-independent communities with their own customs and their own courts. Besides courts they had executive convocations and perhaps legislative meetings as well, and no tinner might be subpoenaed by any other court for any matter determinable in his own court. Their workings were divided into five districts in each county, each with its own court and steward, and there were larger courts under wardens. The Pipe Rolls refer to their privileges in 1243 and 1297, and there are earlier references. Richard I's charter of 1198 gives some picture of the organization as it was at that time, but the tin mines were much older even than this and were probably pre-Conquest in origin, forming little states of great solidarity.

Similar communities of miners may be found in the Mendips and in the Forest of Dean in Gloucestershire and elsewhere,

for example, in Cumberland and Derbyshire. I suppose that the crown insisted on maintaining its courts in order to keep the metal flowing. Common-law procedure took too long. Here, too, definition of the miners' privileges and place of work restricted their extension. They were clearly not always welcome neighbors to the owners of the soil. A late protest states, for example, that more than sixty tinners entered on the Black Prince's demesne and soil, "which was bearing corn, barley, oats, beans, and peas as fine as any in Cornwall, and have conducted water in, by reason of which they deluge the land, and nothing remains but stones and gravel."

Still other regions in England that were in early times under special jurisdiction of their own in regard to certain matters of daily living were those which had to be defended against natural dangers arising from the sea and the flooding by rivers. Very clear provisions were made for the regions of salt marshes and the fenlands. Great fens stretched sometimes far inland in low-lying countryside, and the "sweet waters" of the downrushing rivers meeting low plains and the high tides of the sea were piled back and the land along their course was thus flooded. From the earliest time local safeguards had to be set up to protect the inhabitants. One remembers the old stories of the stilt-walking and skating Gyrvians, the fenmen of the Wash, and their rude ways. Here there grew up the custom of the maintenance of walls and dykes and ditches, the extension of the duty of maintenance over all living in the region, and the heavy punishments of those who failed in their duty. In like manner great salt marshes along the seacoast where the sea overflowed and had to be kept walled out were from Saxon days treated specially and severely. The negligence of one might endanger all. Romney Marsh is a very good example; its great churches are an evidence of the close habitation of the region in early times, and we know of the great "innings" from the sea made by early archbishops. In time ordinances and rules were made and officers appointed for the maintenance of old safe-guards, including within them all of the ancient customary arrangements that were possible. Thus the old sea wall of Dym-church, made famous in our time by Kip-ling, was retained, and also some of the old regulations made necessary by the white steeple of Lydd church, which drew into the sandy shore ships laden with raisins and spices.

A very delightful variation in common-law procedure is found in the beautiful re-gions called forests. You may remember Chaucer's lines:

Thorgh me men gon into that blysful place
Of hertis hele and deadly woundis cure,
Thorgh me men gon unto the welle of grace
There grene and lusty May shall ever endure.
This is the weye to all good aventure.

The dark obscurity of the Conquest period makes it difficult to see the exact develop-ment of the forest administration. We know of William's assignment of New Forest and certain other regions mentioned in Domes-day Book to be forests and so to be dis-tinguished from the usual *silva* or *boscus,* the ordinary woodland. We know of pre-Conquest charters which speak of hunting parties in certain regions, but it is probable that the pre-Conquest wood was not forest in the technical sense in which the word is later used, and it is clear that English forest organization owes much to the already existing forests of Normandy. One finds many familiar arrangements in the Forest of Eu in Normandy, for example.

To understand the technical use of the word forest in England we must give up its usual connotation as *statio ferarum,* home of wild beasts, wild wood, or waste. After the Conquest the word refers to a region prob-ably largely wood and waste, it is true, but also a region under forest law and not necessarily excluding all habitation. Such districts were usually the king's but not al-ways. There are a few private forests also, like Whitby's in the East Riding, or Coup-land in Cumberland, and down through early English history there are forests which

disappear later in the rapes of Sussex and in Lancaster regions in the north and else-where. Within the forests both the red and fallow deer and the boar are preserved for royal hunting and for any disposition the king may wish to make of them. He may grant them to his sister, or to a bishop, or to lords passing through the forest, or to Westminster Abbey, with a hunting *menee* sounded as they are put on St. Peter's altar. To the poor are sometimes given those that are putrid and not fit for ordinary use!

In these lands there was built up a very clear and exacting system of punishment and fine. Sad was the lot of the jolly hunts-man who let himself be caught doing any injury to vert, that is, bush high enough to cast a shadow, or venison. Forest fines were very profitable to the king, if looked at from that point of view! There were many royal officers, forest justices in eyre, foresters for special forests, some of whom held their office in fee and had many perquisites. There were courts held for forest trespasses and offenses, and records of their procedure give a clear view of many forest arrange-ments.

There are, however, some points where questions arise. It is clear enough that the common law operated in forest regions for offenses not concerned with the forest code. Such cases may be studied in common-law records of villages, for example, that lay within the forest boundaries and where other kinds of offenses might also well occur. In the wilder regions the offenses would usually be only forest cases tried by forest law. There still remain from early days, however, some puzzling questions, resulting largely from the confusion regarding the status of given regions. Districts were put in or out of forest law, and uncertainty of boundaries prevailed. Such questions, however, would be satisfac-torily answered as time went on and the clear definition appeared. It is obvious that the king would enjoy a wide district to hunt in and perhaps still more obvious that he would enjoy the fines his officers could col-lect. But it is also clear that feudal lords objected to the curtailment of their liberty implied in afforestation, and still more clear that commoners in land once free would object to interference with their cattle going to and from pasture and with the cutting of wood for fuel. Did common-law officers and forest officers always reach a happy adjustment in these matters? The number of forests even in the restricted days after the great disafforestations of Edward III was listed at approximately seventy, and the extent of their liberty must once have been greater.

The forests had other uses. They were used as breeding places of the king's studs, his great horses, his mares, his cows. They seem sometimes to have been part of defense units, as in the rapes of Sussex, and also they became sometimes, by the king's command, refuges for those in danger from invasion by the Scots.

Merchant law and maritime law also present many interesting features that differ from the common-law procedure. They are concerned very often with those who were not Englishmen, or those Englishmen who lived away from the neighborhood where the particular cases were coming to trial or peaceful settlement. The word foreigner was used for both these classes. Foreign merchants in our sense of the word came into England in groups for trade purposes and as a rule used the code of laws which English ports preferred, the so-called code of Oléron, originating in Barcelona but widely used elsewhere, just as merchants of the Mediterranean used often the Consolato del Mare. These codes, established in coast towns of the countries using them, were of much importance in the growth of merchant law. We find the code of Oléron clearly in use in the days of Edward II. There is not very much evidence of earlier procedure.

There was in very early days a somewhat mysterious custuma maritima on the sea coasts for trade or protection. The courts of admiralty do not develop clearly until the days of Richard II. The main problem of these early coastal courts was to secure speedy justice. Foreign merchants were "come today and gone tomorrow" and pro-

cedure in ordinary courts of common law was extremely slow. So special arrangements were made. In Grimsby, for example, cases relating to foreign fish had to be settled within three tides, those related to foreign corn within three days. The judges in these courts were the merchants, and the procedure, except in land cases, was summary. It was pointed out long ago by Professor Gross that these courts helped to extend a reasonable method of proof against the slower methods of compurgation and ordeal, assize, and outlawry used in the common-law courts. Thus at Yarmouth, courts sitting at tide time had to render their decision by the next tide.

There is a certain picturesque side to the contact of the king's courts with old customs and regulations such as I have enumerated. Except where customary procedure is definitely *encountre la ley,** as the court puts it, there is a desire to maintain the old tried familiar ways and to adapt them to new ends. Reasonable conditions will be maintained, and dull uniformity is not in itself considered meritorious. The king's prerogative, which might well become a danger to just, established, and reasonable procedure, is in practice required to conform with reason. Four times the early courts as described in the Year Books decide in a case before them that the king has not proved his right to have certain advowsons to churches. Once his order to execute a delinquent is not obeyed. The answer given to him may be couched in courteous terms: "The king would not have asked for this if he had known the circumstances which would make assent to it unjust"; "the king has forgotten that he had already appointed to this post." It is assumed that the king will govern with justice and support the courts in the maintenance of old tradition where it is just. The royal prerogative, while a very important factor in the administration of law, is in practice restrained within reasonable limits. The king too must adapt himself to the customs of the kingdom, sometimes upholding them as in ancient

* [Against the law.]

desmesne, in the thought that to himself may sometime escheat the land in question.

One would not today perhaps like Serjeant Maynard of old choose a year book to divert one in one's travels, but one can still read legal records with profit to see how the free governments of the English-speaking peoples have come into being. Professor McIlwain has spoken recently of the "bar-rier" of the common law against tyranny and injustice. I should like to add, in concluding my remarks, those well-known words of Sir Francis Bacon: "The king is bound by the law he makes. He cannot exceed the limits of that law. If he does wrong he is nothing but tyrant." . . . Nurtured in the common law, we Americans too have pledged against what seems to us to be tyranny "our lives, our fortunes, and our sacred honor."

———————

MONASTERIES EXISTED IN PRE-CHRISTIAN TIMES, but it was with the advent of Christianity, with its stress on the ascetic ideal, that they achieved their greatest historical importance. Probably the crucial factor in the early development of Christian monasticism was the adoption of Christianity as the official religion of the Roman Empire. Indeed, the establishment of monasteries was to a considerable extent a protest against the state-sponsored church—a church which became increasingly worldly in the period after it gained official recognition. In short, the monasteries were designed to make possible, in the words of one authority on the history of the monastic ideal, "a return to ancient simplicity and purity and an emulation of the poverty of Christ." For close to a thousand years monasteries figured prominently in the life of England. Their history may be said to have begun in the time of St. Augustine (d. 604), first Archbishop of Canterbury; it ended, to all intents and purposes, in the age of Henry VIII and Thomas Cromwell, with the famous acts of Parliament of 1536 and 1539, by which the monasteries were dissolved. Although monasteries flourished in England for a long time, the role they played in the country's intellectual and cultural life was far from being the same century after century. This is made admirably clear in the following essay by Professor David Knowles, of the University of Cambridge. An eminent Benedictine scholar who has written extensively and thoughtfully on English medieval religious life, Professor Knowles shows that the history of monastic cultural influence in England may profitably be divided and subdivided into chronological periods and that that influence varied markedly from one period to another. Thus he sees the monasteries of the century preceding the Norman Conquest as the intellectual heart of England, whereas by the late fifteenth and early sixteenth centuries they had ceased to play an important part in English cultural life.

THE CULTURAL INFLUENCE OF ENGLISH MEDIEVAL MONASTICISM

DAVID KNOWLES

Students of history are well aware of the ambiguity of the term medieval. Although it may be true that for some thousand years, between *c.* 500 and *c.* 1500 A.D., the social, economic, political and religious life of Western Europe had characteristics easily distinguishable on a broad view from the ancient Greco-Roman civilization that preceded, and from what we call the modern world of nation-states that followed, yet within that millennium the developments are so great, and the changes and declines so numerous, that the careful historian distrusts anything approaching to a general judgment which might confuse century with century, and region with region. Yet in spite of this, many, whose knowledge of the social or artistic life of past ages is very wide, forget such distinctions, and speak readily of the medieval papacy, the medieval village, the medieval craftsman or medieval philosophy, as if each of these expressions denoted a single clear-cut system or institution.

Nowhere, perhaps, is this confusion more common than when the monastic life is being considered. It is true that from *c.* 600 to 1540, with a few early intervals of extinction, monasteries and monks filled a conspicuous place in English life and on the English scene, whereas before Augustine they were unknown and since Thomas Cromwell they have been, for all practical purposes, non-existent. There is, therefore, a great temptation to assess all values in the gross, and to pass a single comprehensive judgment. Thus the extreme Protestant of past centuries, whose views on the monastic ideal coloured all his vision, made little distinction between the Dark Ages, the age of Bernard, and the decline of the Middle Ages. Romantic historians, on the other hand, not a few archaeologists, and multitudes of the general public, seduced by the extraordinary beauty of the monastic ruins, and the

vision of a life utterly remote from modern experience, tend to confuse all epochs in a picture reproducing the first fervours of Jarrow, Bec and Rievaulx. And on the point of monastic cultural influence, while to many Englishmen of the past the whole sum of the monastic contribution seemed worthless, if not positively evil, the more recent tendency—never wholly absent from learned circles since the days of Spelman and Cotton—has been to regard monasticism throughout the centuries as a beneficent source of light. In point of fact, during the eight hundred odd years of its active existence, English monasticism passed more than once through every phase from nonentity to supreme importance.

The so-called medieval period is divided very sharply by the first renaissance of the eleventh century. Until *c.* 1050 the history of civilization in Western Europe is that of a series of efforts at various times and places to arrive at order and light by imitating the past. It was a period from which efficient organization, scientific thought, and intellectual self-confidence were absent. From *c.* 1000 onwards, first in north Italy and later in France, a vital change occurred, manifested by the reform movement in the Church, by the evolution of scientific feudalism and the machinery of government in the State, and by the appearance of a new architecture and sculpture, and a new philosophy. Self-confidence and a critical sense reappeared, and with them the possibility of real originality and steady progress in things of the mind.

These two great divisions are seen reflected or refracted in the history of monasticism. The first corresponds very roughly to what have been called the Benedictine centuries; the latter to what may be called, less aptly perhaps, the centuries of the schools and universities. The divisions of

Reprinted by special permission from *The Cambridge Historical Journal,* VII (1943), 146-159.

monastic history, however, do not perfectly coincide with those of European culture. At the crisis of change there is as it were a time-lag of almost a century. Since the monks, at least north of the Alps, were at first almost the only possessors of the two great requisites for intellectual work, sheltered leisure and books, they were the first to benefit by and to exploit the revival with which they had no direct causal connexion. In consequence, between 1050 and 1150, the monasteries of Europe had, in matters purely intellectual, an influence greater than before. This they soon lost, and a convenient date for the change may be found in 1153, when the death of St Bernard was immediately preceded by that of his disciple, Eugenius III, and followed in the same autumn by that of the most eminent English Cistercian, archbishop Henry Murdac of York.

We may therefore begin by dividing the history of monastic influence into two periods: from the coming of Augustine till *c.* 1150, and from 1150 till the Dissolution; and speaking very generally, we may say that in the earlier of these periods the intellectual and cultural life of England was often at its purest and most intense within the monasteries, and that they were the principal depositories and diffusers of all culture, whereas in the latter period the intellectual initiative had passed to secular schools and universities and, later, to the world of individual scholars and their writings.

These two broad divisions may themselves be split into several sections. Speaking again very generally, it may be said that from 600 to 1066 the achievement of the monks was to preserve the legacy of the past—the attenuated Greco-Roman learning as well as that of the early Church—and to imbue with

it a small but influential group within and without the monastery, while in England, also, as nowhere else in Western Europe, there was a native, non-Latin, literary and artistic life which was stimulated rather than transformed by foreign contact. From 1066, for a century or more, the monasteries, while losing their missionary character, were the great centres of the new literary culture, and counted among their inmates in England a very large proportion of the ablest ecclesiastics and writers; this phase, which began abruptly with the Norman Conquest, waned gradually and in varying degrees between 1150 and 1200 or even later in isolated houses. A characteristic of the whole period from the beginning till 1150 is that during this time a very high proportion of the best minds of the country was nurtured from childhood in the monasteries, or attracted later to the cloister.

The second division, from *c.* 1150 to the Dissolution, is less susceptible of analysis. In general, however, three phases are discernible. The first, from *c.* 1150 to *c.* 1275, is a pale reflection of what had gone before. The culture of the monasteries is of the same kind as hitherto, but less intense and far less influential. From *c.* 1275 to *c.* 1420 another phase can be recognized. The phenomenal development of university education and of the student orders of friars had left the monasteries in a backwater from which they endeavoured to emerge into the stream by opening houses at the universities. For a century and a half, therefore, the ablest and most influential monks passed many years of their lives at Oxford or (later) Cambridge as students, lecturers or priors of the monastic colleges. Finally, from *c.* 1420 onwards, when the age of the schools

BLACK MONKS AND WHITE MONKS: The monks of the Benedictine Order and the Cistercians (a religious order dating from the end of the eleventh century), respectively.
FRIARS: The mendicant friars, of whom the Dominicans and the Franciscans were the most important. They are not accurately described as monks, and in certain respects— such as the fact that they mixed with their fellow men in the world—their work was inconsistent with the monastic ideal. In the present article friars are sharply distinguished from monks.

and of theological controversy had ceased, though the monks continued to frequent the universities, this had little significance in the life of the times. The few notable figures are rather those of the pioneers of the English renaissance.

Having thus passed in rapid review the medieval centuries, it is possible to return for a closer scrutiny.

Monasticism entered England from Italy with Augustine and his companions, but apart from the breath of Roman life that accompanied the introduction of Christianity there is no evidence that the monastic and semimonastic communities that came into being in Kent or near London had any intellectual life. The first real flowering of monastic learning and art was towards the end of the seventh century. With the story of this we are not concerned, save to recall that its development was almost simultaneous in Northumbria and in Wessex. In the north the Celtic monachism of Iona and Lindisfarne was fused with the Mediterranean tradition by Benet Biscop, the founder of Jarrow and Wearmouth. Biscop was a most assiduous agent of civilization; in addition to the Rule of St Benedict and the customs of European monasteries, he brought to Jarrow continental methods of building and glazing, books of all kinds and the Roman antiphoner and chant, together with a living norm of ceremony and music in the person of John, arch-cantor of St Peter's. The Lindisfarne monks, for their part, already possessed one art in great perfection, that of manuscript illumination, and the whole region was instinct with the life of which such precious fragments remain in the poetry of *The Rood* and the crosses of Bewcastle and Ruthwell. When the two traditions fused, the Roman was the stronger, perhaps because the Northumbrian mind was more susceptible to European than to Celtic influence; the soil of the north, however, was peculiarly receptive, and for half a century the group of monasteries between Wear and Tweed formed a centre of art and learning surpassing in purity all else in Western Europe, and gave birth to the Lindisfarne Gospels, the *Codex Amiatinus* and the *Historia Ecclesiastica* of Bede.

A sober scholar of our day has written of 'the miracle of Bede,' and another of 'the portent of learning and sanctity' in the North. The appearance, indeed, of such a lucid intelligence at such an epoch and at the very periphery of the civilized world, is a marvel for which no adequate cause can be assigned. The breadth of Bede's learning, though great and most remarkable at such a time and place, is not without parallel; what is unparalleled is the combination of rare industry with a love of absolute historical truth, and the command of a method and style that allow facts and judgments to pour through unstained, like light through clear glass. Bede has indeed the mental limitations of his age; he does not judge men or policies with the depth and subtlety of a Thucydides or a Tacitus, nor does he see in the past a ceaseless, varied stream of caused and causing movement; his primary interest is in persons and in the affairs of the Church, and he does not exclude direct supernatural intervention in human affairs. But he has none of the faults of his age; he is without prejudice, without spite, without superstition, without a love of the marvellous and the monstrous; he lives, in short, in a rational world, even if it be the world of a pure-minded, unsophisticated child. Standing as he does at the fountain-head of English scholarship—the true father of English history—he has a threefold significance for all who follow him: he is the sole literary authority for all English ecclesiastical history down to his day; he sets a standard of sobriety, completeness and truth which subsequent generations recognized, even if they did not equal it; and in his personality, never obtruded but always visible, he fixed for the Middle Ages and beyond the type of monk-historian, laborious, sane, constructive, benevolent.

The immediate influence of Bede was not great. Northumbrian monasticism scarcely survived its golden age, though it doubtless helped to mould the school of York and Alcuin. Indirectly, however, his influence was immense. His works were multiplied and broadcast in England and the West; his narrative was appropriated and abbreviated by others, and he served as an ideal which generations of subsequent historians consciously strove to attain.

At the very moment of the foundation of Jarrow, a revival of learning was taking place in the monasteries of the south. Theodore of Tarsus, a Basilian monk, sent to be archbishop of Canterbury, and his companion Hadrian, abbot of a Neapolitan monastery, accompanied the impact of a new wave of Mediterranean culture. But whereas in the north the art and learning are a virile, native growth, in the south there is an exotic touch. The mists suddenly vanished from the Wessex landscape; the sun shines, and the plain, unpruned native trees are seen to bear the strangest, brightest fruit:

miranturque novas frondes et non sua poma.

Such is Aldhelm, the first to compose original works in West England, a writer in verse and the strange prose studded with transliterated Byzantine words which has not yet received the careful study it deserves; such are the numerous small monasteries and nunneries from Exeter to Nursling where a literary culture flourished which allowed monks and nuns to correspond in excellent Latin and occasional hexameters with Boniface and his colleagues in Germany or at Rome. Here, as in Northumbria, though for different reasons, the time of flowering was brief. The grafted trees run wild; the light flares out. Aldhelm takes his place in the *Patrologia,* indistinguishable in type from writers of other countries; no literary or artistic work survives from southern England comparable to the writings of Bede, nor, so far as we know, to the Lindisfarne Gospels. The learning of the south had, however, a permanent monument in the monasteries and the Christian civilization of western and southern Germany, the apostolic work of a monk from Devon.

In the course of the eighth and early ninth centuries monasticism and its culture virtually disappeared from both the north and south of England—from the north owing to the Scandinavian invasions; from the south through lack of any fresh impulse from abroad and any true centre or system of education at home. The small and scattered monastic houses of England had neither the libraries nor the reserves of life that made Fulda, St Gall, Corbie, Cluny and others all but immortal. Perhaps, also, the purely imitative Latin learning was always doomed to a short life.

The next revival, that of Alfred, was wholly unmonastic. Alfred planned to revive the religious life, but he lived only to make a modest beginning which soon languished. The real awakening came fifty years after his death, first, from 943 onwards, under Dunstan at Glastonbury, and later, in the reign of King Edgar, from Abingdon and Ramsey also, under Ethelwold and Oswald. The splendour of this revival has been fully recognized only in recent years, by historians such as the late Dean Armitage Robinson and S. J. Crawford, and students of literature and art such as Professor R. W. Chambers and Mr A. W. Clapham. It differed from the earlier southern revival in several important respects: it was, for the first time, definitely educational in its aim and national in scope; it carried on and amplified the tradition of Alfred by translating patristic works into English and by continuing the Old English *Chronicle;* and it embraced all forms of literature and music and the minor fine arts such as illumination, carving and metal-work. It was, therefore, half a rebirth and half a new creation; the models were the old ones, and there was no original thought, simply an attempt to understand and hand down that of Augustine or Gregory or Isidore, but the vehicle, the language, was, at least in the hands of Aelfric and Wulfstan and the writers of the Old English *Chronicle,* both original and beautiful. And in the arts of illumination, of goldsmith's work, and of the Gregorian chant and its developments, masterpieces of supreme beauty were produced.

It would indeed be difficult to exaggerate the merits of this cultural achievement. What has been called the Winchester style of manuscript painting, of which masterpieces survive in the New Minster charter of Edgar (966), the Benedictional of St Ethelwold (*c*. 980), and the somewhat later Missal and Benedictional of Robert of Jumièges, is now recognized as an idiom common to all the larger houses of the monastic revival, and the Old English style of outline drawing was equally widely practised. In Gregorian plainchant the purest traditions were preserved and additions were from time to time made in a manner not unworthy of the original corpus, while in polyphony the large abbeys and cathedral monasteries, with a command of trained boys' voices, made advances which, when the many surviving manuscripts of music have been studied, will probably appear of the greatest significance in the evolution of European music.

At the same time, the copying of manuscripts in a clear and beautiful script was everywhere part of the normal work of the cloister, and though it is true that, owing to the absence of primitive archetypes of classical and patristic texts, the manuscripts of English origin are not often of the first class, yet they served to keep alive in the country a knowledge of the Latin writers, while in the case of Old English poetry and the so-called *Saxon Chronicle* almost all the surviving manuscripts are of monastic provenance.

This great movement of culture was wholly monastic in origin, and was guided throughout by monks; it was also consciously expansive, and it seems certain that it was freely diffused not only by treatises, homilies and translations but also by way of classroom education to all who came, though from the circumstances of the time these were necessarily few and for the most part aspirants to the monastic life. The century preceding the Norman Conquest was in fact one—and the only one—in which the monasteries were the cultural and educational heart of England; previously, they had been isolated and enclosed reservoirs; subsequently, they were to be merely one among several agencies, but in the days of

Ethelwold and Aelfric they dominated the higher life of the country.

The literary impulse had died down before the Conquest; as with the preceding waves of life, there was no organization and no self-possessed criticism to carry over the first growth, though something of it sprang up again at Worcester and Evesham shortly before 1066. It has recently been the fashion to deplore the Conquest. It is indeed arguable that had there been no invasion the arts—or at least the minor arts—would have continued to surpass in richness and delicacy all that the Continent could create, and that the native literature would have developed into full independence, but there can be no real question as to the balance of loss and gain in the field of intellectual effort. It was through the Norman Conquest that England shared in the two greatest benefits of the new renaissance: critical self-confidence, and a rational system of education.

For almost half a century after 1070 the black monk monasteries of Europe enjoyed all the advantages of the new world and the old. They were still far richer in the implements of learning and opportunities for study than were the small episcopal or urban schools, and the system of lectures and disputations, which was possible only in a freer, larger atmosphere than that of a monastery, had not yet absorbed all talent at the expense of a purely literary training. Consequently, they still drew to themselves many of the most brilliant minds of the age—a Lanfranc, an Anselm, an Abelard and an Ailred—and were able for a few decades to offer more attractions to the disciple than did the cathedral schools which often depended on a single master. In other words, educational and cultural resources were still dispersed at numerous centres of equal strength, and many of these were monasteries.

In England, as is well known, a monastic revival of great fervour and wide extension followed the Norman Conquest, and abbots were drafted across the Channel by the Conqueror from the houses of highest reputation—Bec, Caen, St Evroul, Mont St

Michel, Jumièges. The two most celebrated teachers of the age, Lanfranc and Anselm, had direct influence both in Normandy and England on men who were later to rule English sees and abbeys. Nothing indeed is more impressive than the high level of intellectual and artistic life that rose so soon at so many English houses. Not only the great monasteries at or near the centres of national life—Canterbury, Westminster, Winchester, St Albans—but houses in the Cotswolds and the Fens—a Malmesbury, a Thorney, a Ramsey—became self-sufficient islands of life, literary, artistic and musical. Gilbert Crispin of Westminster, Faricius of Abingdon, Symeon of Winchester among the Normans, and Eadmer of Canterbury, Symeon of Durham and William of Malmesbury from among the native monks are some of the most familiar names, and it is perhaps significant that while the three foreigners are noted for theology, medicine and satirical poetry, the three great English writers are one and all historians. The culture transmitted was, in fact, almost wholly literary, and something in the national character turned the most receptive of its adepts in England to the writing of history. The two great disciplines that were to inform the young universities—law and philosophy—took no foothold in this country for almost a century after 1066, even though Vacarius settled at York.

The Anglo-Norman literary achievement was undoubtedly wider, deeper and more mature than that of the Edgarine revival. Though it produced no writer or thinker of absolute greatness comparable to Anselm or Abelard or Bernard of Clairvaux, one at least of the historians, William of Malmesbury, is in scope and power of criticism and judgment the greatest English medieval historian after Bede, and the monastic school of historians and chroniclers, and still more the monastic scribes and illuminators, reached a level of excellence unsurpassed in any other country of Europe, and founded traditions of method and technique which were copied by subsequent generations and have benefited all centuries since that time.

The great Bibles and Psalters, in which the Norman boldness of design and brilliance of colour was blended with the native delicacy and fancy, were the product of houses as widely separated as Winchester, Bury and Durham, and until the close of the century the art, admittedly at the height of excellence, was almost exclusively the product of monastic *scriptoria*. At the same time the script in use for all purposes in the cloister was brought to the highest level of beauty, clarity and accuracy that has ever been attained by a hand in use for all purposes, and this was a circumstance not without its effect upon the transmission of the legacy of the past. Yet in one important respect the Anglo-Norman monastic culture was less genial than the Old English: it was enjoyed exclusively by the monks. After the Conquest, the number of lay children educated in the cloister was negligible, while in the course of the twelfth century the whole domestic economy of the monasteries was changed by the gradual abolition of child oblation, a practice as old as Western monasticism itself. After *c.* 1150 the monasteries were recruited in growing numbers from those who had learnt their letters outside the cloister or who had passed through a course and even taken a degree at some celebrated foreign school or university. Thus the specifically monastic culture was contaminated and weakened.

The rise of the universities, indeed, with their schools of law, medicine and speculative theology, was fatal to the old monastic education, which was purely literary and static. The new learning depended on a constant flow and interchange of students, teachers and ideas, and while hitherto a gifted mind could find and absorb all the available knowledge in a steady, unbroken intake from boyhood to age between the walls of a well-stocked library, aided by the advice of elders, henceforward the process was broken and divided—vertically by the separation of the grammar school from the lecture room, horizontally by the specialization of old and new branches of learning. For a brief space some of the best minds of the new dis-

cipline found their way to the cloister—
Marlborough of Evesham and the group of
physicians at St Albans—but gradually the
stream dried up. The great historians of the
period 1150-1215 are clerks or regular
canons—Ralph of Diceto, 'Benedict of Peterborough,' Gerald of Wales, William of New-
burgh—while the most notable monastic
writings are domestic and personal chronicles, such as those of Jocelin of Brakelond
and Gervase of Canterbury, or biographies
such as the life of the last great monk-
bishop, St Hugh, by the latest monastic
biographer, Adam of Eynsham. In other
words, from 1150 onwards, in ever-growing
measure, the monastic culture became a
purely private possession limited to a very
few fields of achievement, the writing of
chronicles and the illuminating of manuscripts. Even in these departments a decline
in the quality and quantity of the work becomes evident before 1200, and save for a
single house no literary and very little artistic work of the first quality was produced
by the black monks after the reign of John.
The thirteenth and early fourteenth centuries were, in England as elsewhere, the
age of the friars and the schools.

Hitherto only the black monks have been
considered. The various orders of canons,
though monastic in character, do not strictly
fall into the scope of this paper. Their contribution was, in fact, indistinguishable in
type from that of the monks. As for the
Cistercians, they were in origin and by primitive legislation debarred from learning, literature and art. The exuberant genius of
Bernard, however, broke through the dykes,
and in subsequent generations the white
monks became more and more assimilated
to the black. In England few Cistercians
appear as scholars or writers, with the notable exceptions of Gilbert of Swineshead,
who completed the Sermons on the Canticle
left unfinished by Bernard, and Ailred of
Rievaulx, the Bernard of the north, who
composed a series of treatises, half spiritual,
half philosophical in character, and several
short historical works. The latter, purely
English in inspiration, take their place alongside of the larger works of the monks of
Durham and the canons of Hexham; the
former derive a peculiar interest and charm
from the personality of their author and the
picture they give of eager debates in the
cloister of Rievaulx, but in the history of
thought they are survivals, the last of their
kind, the last of a long line stretching back
seven hundred years. The future lay, not
with meditative disquisition in the style of
Augustine, but with the less literary, more
formal, practical, comprehensive work of
Ailred's contemporaries Gratian and Peter
Lombard.

Whatever may have been the influence of
the monasteries on the country at large, there
can be no question of the thoroughness of
the education in letters within their walls.
The ablest minds were rendered humane,
expansive, European. This was given, while
the fresh impulse from France lasted, to
nunneries also, and, as in the days of Boniface, nuns of Wessex were able to add their
copy of hexameters or elegiacs to the bede
rolls that were passed round from house to
house.

As has been suggested above, the characteristic monastic culture gradually lost its
strength between 1150 and 1250. There
was, however, one exception to the general
decline, and that so illustrious that it has
often been considered as typical rather than
as unique. The great abbey of St Albans
harboured during the first half of the thirteenth century a school of painters and illuminators of which the Colchesters are the
most celebrated names, and a series of historians culminating in the celebrated Matthew Paris, who is commonly regarded as
the greatest monastic historian of the Middle
Ages. St Albans stands alone. From the first
coming of Lanfranc's nephew, Paul of Caen,
until the days of Whethamstede that great
abbey remained something of an Athens
among the monasteries of England, a home
of books and art. Nevertheless, its current
reputation in manuals of history and archaeology is probably an exaggerated one.
The illumination of the school of St Albans
cannot compare in subtlety of colour and

delicacy of design with the Old English, or even with the Anglo-Norman, masterpieces, and those familiar with the works of all the monastic writers will probably consider William of Malmesbury, and perhaps Eadmer also, superior to Paris in the nobler qualities of a historian, those of careful criticism and sober judgment. The vivacity, the broad and coloured canvas, and the national and personal prejudices of the later writer have no doubt combined to make his admirers too indulgent to one who, with all his shortcomings, is necessarily a principal source of information for the period.

Within twenty years of the death of Paris the focus of the artistic and intellectual activity of the country had finally shifted from the cloister. Illumination and craft work had passed into the hands of secular clerks and laymen, and even the straightforward copying of books, which could be accomplished as a routine task by those without any artistic talent, had ceased to be a normal employment of monks and had become a commercial operation for professional writers.

Henceforward, therefore, such influence as the monks might exert as a body was limited; the great English names of the thirteenth and early fourteenth centuries are those of friars—Adam Marsh, Alexander of Hailes, Roger Bacon, Robert Kilwardby, Haymo of Faversham, Duns Scotus, John Baconthorpe, and William of Ockham. This essay, in consequence, loses its theme at the death of Matthew Paris. Since, however, later monastic literary activity has been either exaggerated or neglected, it may be permissible to carry the story forward to the end.

The thirteenth century, which opened with the call to simplicity of the unlettered Francis and his early followers, saw the gradual drift of all the religious orders into the whirlpool of the schools. The Preachers led the way, followed by the Minors and the Augustinian Hermits, the Carmelites and all the lesser orders of friars. Hitherto, as has been noted, some of the ablest graduates had passed into the monastic life; now this source of recruitment dried up; boys of promise with a desire for a religious and intellectual life now joined the friars. Moreover, the monks, scattered and static, were debarred from any share in the life of the schools, while their own traditional literary culture had gone wholly out of fashion. It was natural, therefore, that they should endeavour to find a place for themselves at the universities, and from c. 1270 onwards a series of efforts was made by some of the most eminent abbots, both black and white, to open common houses of studies at Oxford and compel each monastery to pay its quota and send up a percentage of its subjects. The system was ultimately taken into the discipline of the Church by Benedict XII in his Constitution of 1337. Strangely enough, the Cistercians were first in the field with Rewley Abbey, and between c. 1280 and 1437 five monastic priories or colleges came into being, four at Oxford and one at Cambridge, and in consequence almost all the leading monks appear as bachelors or doctors of divinity, and often spent years in teaching at the university or governing the monastic college. Research has shown that from the early years of their connexion they took part in public disputations and filled university offices. A wholly new type appeared—the university monk—of which Adam Easton and Ughtred of Boldon are conspicuous examples. No monk, however, rose to an eminence as leader of thought comparable to the great friars; the mental climate of the monastic life has never proved genial to speculative or scholastic theology, and it would be hard to point to a single speculative theologian of the first rank from among the white or black monks since the days of Anselm. Nevertheless, monks took considerable part in the domestic controversies of the late fourteenth century, in particular those between the mendicant and possessioner religious, and that occurring in the latter phases of Wyclif's career. On the other hand, no monk, so far as is at present known, contributed to the remarkable body of spiritual writings of the century known as the school of the English mystics; such spiritual writings as have survived are either meditative treatises of the traditional type, or discussions of questions of monastic discipline. Nor can the career in another field of the poet John Lydgate of Bury be taken as representative of his order. Throughout the fourteenth and early fifteenth centuries certain monasteries stand out from the rest in academic distinction. Durham is *facile princeps;* as it was not a member of the southern province, to which belonged the common house at Oxford, the priory sent monks to Oxford independently, and ultimately possessed a college of its own. Of the rest, Norwich, Worcester and St Albans were most distinguished in the academic life; Canterbury, though it too had a college of its own, as claiming exemption from the provincial chapter, never rivalled Durham.

If scholastic theology as such was alien to the spirit of monasticism, the rebirth of humanistic, literary culture in the fifteenth century might seem to have been more attractive to the black monks. There were, in fact, not a few adepts in the monasteries of Italy, which possessed libraries whither the eminent humanists resorted to explore the classical manuscripts. England, however, especially the England of the fifteenth century, was far from Italy, and the individual abbeys were not rich enough in classical manuscripts, least of all Greek classical manuscripts, to give an imaginative impulse to a young scholar. There was, indeed, in fifteenth-century England nothing of the artistic ferment and keen intellectual life of the cities of central and northern Italy.

Nevertheless, two distinguished monks have been sometimes noted as harbingers of English humanism. The first of these, Whethamstede, abbot of St Albans from 1420 to 1465, has until recent years been allowed to retain the reputation he held among contemporaries. In reality, he is a figure of no great importance in the history of learning. Though he travelled extensively in renaissance Italy, and took an interest in some of the literary branches of Italian humanism, he was completely blind to much of what

passed before his eyes and remained, in style and in thought, a typical child of the dying Middle Age. The second, William Tilley of Selling, monk and later prior of Christ Church, Canterbury, is of another calibre. He was not the first monk at Canterbury College to admire the new learning, which the benefactions of Humphrey, Duke of Gloucester, George Neville and others had introduced at Oxford, but he was the first English monk to imbibe the spirit and practise the arts of humanism. He wrote and spoke in pure and fluent Latin; what was more, he taught Greek and collected Greek texts in his monastery at Canterbury, and, with that strange fortune which so often blesses genius in teaching, counted among his few pupils Thomas Linacre. He is in every way a figure of the first importance in the early days of English humanism.

Selling had no worthy successor, but a few of the superiors of the last generation were friends of learning, among them Thomas Milling prior of Westminster, later bishop of Hereford, Richard Bere of Glastonbury and above all Abbot Kidderminster of Winchcombe. These, however, were in a sense accidental examples. There was no strong intellectual discipline among the monks at any single house, still less throughout the whole body. Such intellectual life as existed in conservative or neo-Catholic circles flowed into other channels. There was a small group of Cambridge traditionalists—an interesting pendant to the brilliant reformers—who owed the cast of their minds to Fisher and the Lady Margaret and who formed the intellectual core of the opposition which Henry encountered at the London Charterhouse and Syon. At the Charterhouse the Prior, John Houghton, was a Cambridge man, and among the Carthusians executed was the scholar William Exmew of Christ's and Augustine Webster, to whom Cranmer gave the epithet 'learned.' At Syon, besides the confessor-general, Fewterer of Pembroke Hall and Richard Whytford of Queen's, there was Richard Reynolds, who suffered with the Carthusians; his college was Christ's and he was an excellent scholar in Hebrew as well as Greek and Latin; Reginald Pole, who knew him well, described him as the most learned religious of his day. In all these, however, their scholarship was personal and in no sense due to their profession. On a broad view, the specifically monastic influence in the world of learning was negligible, and interesting as it may be to speculate on the part that a reformed monasticism might have played in an un-Reformed England, materials for such speculations are wholly lacking, and the very different circumstances of Spain and France forbid the drawing of any analogy from abroad.

Nothing has yet been said in this paper of monastic influence on architecture. The subject is a large one, and many points still require critical elucidation; moreover, the monks had influence not so much as individuals as in their capacity of corporate bodies making certain architectural demands. A few words, however, may be permitted.

Before 1066, apart from Biscop's importations at Wearmouth and Jarrow, there is little to record. Old English architecture, with all the merits that have been so warmly set out by Mr Clapham, remained comparatively small in scale, and there is nothing to suggest that a monastic church differed in dimensions or decorations from other important churches. Nor is there any record that Dunstan and Ethelwold, who composed music, worked in metal, and constructed organs, also added practical architecture to their accomplishments. On the other hand, the influence of the monks on the new Romanesque of Normandy and England was immense. However elementary the technique and rude the decoration of the early Norman churches may have been, a norm was set up of plan and dimensions for large churches which subsequent centuries modified but did not wholly alter, and which has influenced all large Norman and Gothic churches from that day to this. It is not always recognized that several features of this design—and those the most remarkable—are due to its origin among the great

monasteries of Normandy. Of these, the elongated choir, often still too short to hold all the stalls, and the still longer nave, designed solely for ceremonial processions, were due entirely to monastic tastes and demands, as were also the early transeptal and apsidal chapels, while length of nave and choir carried with it, as a necessary artistic consequence, a great increase in roof-height. All these features were reproduced in every great Anglo-Norman church, whether monastic or not, and were duly carried over into the Gothic style.

Individual monk-architects or master masons and sculptors after the Norman Conquest were as rare and accidental as have been Deans of cathedrals and Fellows of colleges with architectural or sculptural talents in the modern world, though notable examples have been found of all these classes. Gundulf of Rochester is perhaps the most eminent practical architect of the Anglo-Norman period. For long, however, the abbot or prior or major officials of the monastery (and in particular the sacrist) were directly in charge of the works affecting the fabric and decoration of the monastic church, and did in fact exercise an influence on plan, design and execution far greater than that of the normal patron in the ancient or modern ages of professional architecture. How far such eminent men as Alan of Walsingham at Ely and Abbot Wigmore at Gloucester were technically and artistically responsible for the masterpieces achieved under their supervision will perhaps always remain a matter of debate, though it is remarkable that both were skilled craftsmen. It is at least noteworthy that two of the major innovations in English architecture between the Conquest and the Dissolution—the completed stone vaulting introducing the pointed arch, and the so-called Perpendicular style, with its vast spaces of glass and its unbroken vaulting shafts—make their first full-scale appearance in monastic churches, at Durham and Gloucester, while the evolution from Romanesque to Gothic was accelerated and conditioned by the set type of Cistercian church imported in its main lines from Burgundy.

On the whole, however, the chief and permanent influence of the monks on the fine arts of sculpture and architecture, and the lesser arts of decoration, metal-work and embroidery, was that of munificent patrons who often called the tune, rather than that of architects and artists who executed the work. Had all the objects of art, along with the service books and libraries of the monasteries, been preserved to the modern world, the extent of our debt to these patrons would have been more widely appreciated.

Looking back, therefore, after this short review we may make a general judgment in some such form as this. From the days of Augustine to the Norman Conquest the monks, when their institute flourished, were always a principal, and sometimes the sole, cultural force in the land. They preserved and multiplied manuscripts, they kept alive the study of letters, they carried the art of illumination to its highest pitch of excellence and they contributed not a little to the other arts. Benet Biscop in the north, Theodore and Hadrian in the south, together with their pupils and assistants in the west, gave notable and enduring impulses to culture, without which Anglo-Saxon civilization would have been infinitely the poorer, and that of South Germany would not have existed at all. And in Bede, an untravelled, untitled monk, there was given to the north the greatest literary figure of the early Middle Age. Later, under Dunstan and his associates, the monks once more gave to the nation all that was available of the culture of the past, and developed to a fine point all the arts of their own age; they also laid firm courses in the foundations of English literature; and for more than half a century they were the heart of civilized England.

With the Norman Conquest the influence of the monks changed. Though their purely literary work grew in bulk, in power and in originality, they were cultivating a field soon to lose its fertility, while their secular contemporaries were clearing the virgin forest to plant new crops. The monks ceased to be either directly or indirectly educators; they gave, however, to posterity masterpieces of the illuminator's art and a magnificent harvest of historical work. When full account is taken of all the records and charters, which are only now yielding their secrets to patient research, it must still be allowed that we owe to the monks and their imitators the mass of detailed and accurate information that has made of the Norman and Angevin periods such a vivid, living epoch to all succeeding generations of Englishmen.

Thenceforward, the monastic order ceased to exert any specific influence outside their own body, though monks for long took their part in public and university life and theological controversy. Before the end, much even of this had ceased, and with the opening of the sixteenth century the black and white monks were, as an intellectual and cultural force, all but negligible in the life of England.

WHAT MAY BE CALLED THE MYTH OF ROGER BACON has been exposed by critical historical scholarship gradually during the last hundred years. It is no longer believed, in informed historical circles, that Bacon was as modern in spirit as used to be supposed, that in the history of natural science his was a thirteenth-century voice crying in the wilderness. No aspect of the legend which had grown up around his name was clung to more tenaciously than that which represented him as a unique medieval advocate of the experimental method in science. It turns out, however, that experimentation by alchemists and others was by no means unusual in Bacon's day; nearly fifty years ago a French writer on the history of medieval philosophies went so far as to pronounce the thirteenth century an important epoch in the history of the experimental sciences. In the article reproduced below, Professor Lynn Thorndike, of Columbia University, one of the greatest twentieth-century authorities on the history of medieval science, expresses the opinion that Bacon's discussion of "experimental science" came to little more than "a recognition of experience as a criterion of truth and a promulgation of the phrase 'experimental sciences.'" Professor Thorndike calls attention to Bacon's credulity, which is in sharp contrast with the skeptical attitude of mind of modern experimental scientists, and reaches the conclusion that Bacon, in his treatment of experimental science, was not a prophet centuries ahead of his day but rather a product of his own age, "an excellent representation of both the good and bad points of an important movement of the time in the direction of experimental method."

ROGER BACON AND EXPERIMENTAL METHOD IN THE MIDDLE AGES

LYNN THORNDIKE

The year 1914 marks approximately the seventh centennial of the birth of Roger Bacon, and offers opportunity for a reconsideration of his place in thirteenth century thought and of his relation to modern science. In the early 1700's, before Jebb had edited the *Opus Maius* in 1733, Roger Bacon was unappreciated and unknown. Today many will incline to celebrate his anniversary as that of the first rebel against mediæval scholasticism and the first prophet of modern science. They may feel that such recognition is the more due to his memory because they believe him to have been a prophet without honor and persecuted in his own age, or because they believe that in later times Francis Bacon received the praise that was Roger's due. They will set Roger's four causes of human error against Francis's idols; they will point to Roger's urging the study of Greek, Arabic, and Hebrew as well as Latin, and

to his sharp criticism of the translations of Aristotle in vogue in his day, to his investigations in optics, to his insistence upon the importance of the mathematical method, whose value Francis scarcely realized; but above all they will remember Roger's criticism of scholastic methods, of reliance on authority, and his advocacy of experimental method. It is of this last point, long regarded as the brightest gem in Roger's crown, that the present article will treat, inquiring what Bacon's discussion of "experimental science" really amounts to, whether his conception was a novel one or the common property of his age, and finally what the actual status of experimentation was at that time.

But before attacking this particular problem it will be well to give some idea of recent study of Bacon and the progress of opinion concerning him, especially since doing this will pave the way for our argu-

Reprinted by special permission from *The Philosophical Review*, XXIII (1914), 271-298. The numerous footnotes which originally appeared with this essay have been omitted. The author has made a few minor changes in the present version of his essay.

ment. Much attention has been given to Bacon since the editing in 1859 by Brewer of a number of his writings hitherto unpublished, and the almost simultaneous appearance in 1861 of Émile Charles's *Roger Bacon; sa vie, ses ouvrages, ses doctrines.* Unfortunately Charles wrote without knowledge of Brewer's labors, and it must be added that several writers on Bacon since have failed to keep abreast of the latest research in their field. These works by Brewer and Charles educed a number of minor essays and studies in the following decades. Then a new impetus to the study of Bacon was given in 1897 when the *Opus Maius,* previously accessible only in Jebb's rare and incomplete edition, was re-edited by Bridges. In the same year Father Gasquet published a new fragment which he regarded as an introduction to the *Opus Maius.* In 1902 Nolan and Hirsch edited Bacon's Greek Grammar. Then in 1909 Professor Duhem gave to the world a newly discovered fragment of the *Opus Tertium;* in 1911 the British Society of Franciscan Studies printed the *Compendium Studii Theologiæ,* and, in 1912, more of the *Opus Tertium.* Meanwhile Robert Steele, who in 1905 had edited a fragment of Bacon's Metaphysics, began in 1912 to produce the *Communia Naturalium.*

As Bacon's works have thus become more generally known and as standards of historical criticism have grown more strict, his life, doctrines, and point of view or personal equation have been more carefully examined and analyzed, and much legend and exaggeration have been exposed, although still repeated in some quarters. Indeed, the very writer who rejects some one legend may hold fast to the old view of Bacon in all other respects. There is, therefore, the more reason for a brief collective review of this criticism which hitherto has been somewhat piecemeal and fragmentary.

For one thing, it is admitted by many that Bacon did not anticipate modern inventions by actual discoveries. As far back as 1864 *The Westminster Review* said: "It can easily be shown that of the things which

Bacon is asserted to have invented, several were perfectly well known before his time, and the rest are nowhere described in his works." He mentions spectacles and explosives but does not claim them as his own discoveries; he dreamed of future marvels of science but he worked none of them out in detail. Perhaps he thought that he could, but then, he thought that he could make gold artificially.

Secondly, Bacon cannot be proved a martyr to science, nor have we any evidence that his contemporaries hated him and that the church persecuted him for his scientific studies. On the contrary, his best works were produced at the command of the pope, and one of their chief aims is to induce the church to enlist science in its service and to profit by scientific discoveries. Abbé Feret has shown how through the nineteenth century successive historians, including even Charles, kept adding to the story of Bacon's persecution by the Franciscans, without giving any references to the sources for details which they elaborated from their imaginations. The legend that he was imprisoned from 1257 to 1267 rests simply on unwarranted inference from his own statements to the pope,—statements which really only show that in recent years he has not won the fame which he thinks his due, that he is jealous of his more successful contemporaries, and that he is desperately anxious to secure the pope as his patron. However, an Assisi manuscript of the early fourteenth century states that in 1277, a decade after his writings to the pope, a council of his Order condemned "the doctrine of Rogerius Bacho, an English master of sacred theology, since it contained some suspected novelties, on account of which the said Roger was condemned to prison." But what the novelties were we are not informed; they were probably theological rather than scientific. Some writers have assumed that they were astrological, but there was nothing "novel" about Bacon's astrology. Theories that Bacon was accused of magic are also unwarrantable inferences from his own statements. He complains that the

Canon Law confuses mathematics and magic, and that philosophers are sometimes falsely accused of magic; it is thereupon assumed that what he says may happen to others did happen to himself.

In the third place, Bacon's outspoken criticism of the learning of his age is no longer unquestioningly accepted. A review in the *English Historical Review* for October 1912, "hopes that it is not an article of faith with the Society of Franciscan Studies to accept all of Roger Bacon's statements. As regards the state of knowledge among his contemporaries, his assertions are often of no greater value than the similar assertions of his distinguished namesake in a later age." It is seen that his tendency to indulge in personalities and to belittle his distinguished contemporaries must be discounted. When he sneers at meritorious scholars like Albertus Magnus and William of Meerbeke, one wonders how far to accept his hostile estimate of the schools at Paris, his boasts of his own superior knowledge and better methods of teaching, his professed exploitation of neglected fields in linguistics, mathematics, optics, alchemy, and experimental science. His censure of the translations of Aristotle in use at Paris loses much of its force, when we learn that he himself bases some of his views upon mistranslated passages from Aristotle,—passages which Albert and Aquinas translate as well or better than he. Also we must remember that Bacon is addressing the pope and trying to interest him not only in the reform and advancement of learning but in Roger Bacon. So if, as Macaulay said, Francis Bacon seeking the truth was a very different person from Francis Bacon seeking the seals, we must remember that Roger combines both attempts at once.

Fourthly, the faults of Bacon's own learning, his superstition and credulity, his belief in alchemy and astrology, have been noticed, so that a recent reviewer speaks of "the usual Baconian atmosphere, in which science and superstition are happily or unhappily compounded." These weaknesses are usually charged in large measure and correctly to the age in which Bacon lived; but, while some treat them as only throwing his merits into higher relief, these failings at least support Hastings Rashdall's assertion that "Bacon was more the child of his age than he imagined himself to be," and perhaps may be taken as an indication that his virtues, too, were those of his age.

Father Mandonnet, the erudite author of *Siger de Brabant et l'averroïsme latin au XIIIe siècle,* thinks that Bacon's importance has in many ways been over-estimated. While Charles held that, if Bacon's scientific importance had been exaggerated, his value as a schoolman had been lost sight of, Mandonnet affirms that, as a philosopher and theologian, Bacon was behind rather than in the forefront of his age. Bacon has been reproached for making philosophy and science ancillary to theology, but he could scarcely do otherwise when addressing the pope and trying to induce the church to support science.

This changing tide of opinion concerning Bacon's life and works both suggests that there may be room for further revision of our estimate of him, and provides a more correct setting for his discussion of experimental science. But to evaluate this properly we must rid ourselves of one more false assumption, namely, that mediæval learning was exclusively scholastic and theological, and that Bacon in his advocacy of natural science was "a voice crying in the wilder-

---

ALBERTUS MAGNUS: Thirteenth-century theologian and scholastic philosopher. Often considered the outstanding natural scientist of the Latin Middle Ages, he drew heavily on Aristotle but at the same time emphasized the need to use experimental methods.

PLINY THE ELDER: Roman writer of the first century A.D. His *Natural History* is for all practical purposes a history of civilization. It is filled with useful information concerning ancient manners, customs, inventions, and scientific beliefs.

ness." This notion still survives in writers whose estimate of Bacon is otherwise sane and critical. Thus the articles in *The Westminster Review,* quoted above against the attribution of modern inventions to Bacon, and which further state that the merit of the *Opus Maius* "lies rather in the spirit in which it was written than in the facts it records or in any merit which it may have as a scientific whole," go on to say that "Bacon preached a philosophy of which not half-a-dozen men in Europe saw the value, and of which the majority of really good men feared the results," and that "when Roger Bacon was laid in his grave the real philosophy was buried with him." Such is still the impression given by otherwise excellent recent estimates of Bacon, such as those in the *Catholic Encyclopedia* and in Henry Osborn Taylor's *The Mediæval Mind.*

But such an assumption is ungrounded. Most educated persons are, it is to be hoped, by this time aware that the middle ages were not "dark ages," that the classical revival of the 15th and 16th centuries was no new birth of civilization, and that our modern states, literatures, laws, cities, and universities had begun by the twelfth century. It should equally be realized that the rise of modern science can no more be associated with the so-called Renaissance than with the so-called Middle Ages. The scientific interests and the characteristics of works on nature in those two periods were very similar. Of course there was progress, but there was no break, they merge into each other. Galileo's telescope was the natural outgrowth of earlier investigations concerning lenses which had resulted in the use of spectacles as early as the thirteenth century. Printers of the 15th and 16th centuries found plenty of readers for the many mediæval works on nature which they published and which often ran through several editions. The narrow humanist had no more interest in natural science than the narrow schoolman. In the middle ages logic and discussion were not the only forms of intellectual exercise,

though they largely displaced the rhetoric and oratory of Roman days. The collection of facts was another engrossing pursuit, as the voluminous mediæval encyclopedias testify; there was keen curiosity about the things of this world. Open a book for general reading in a vernacular language, the long French poem, *The Romance of the Rose,* and you will find there more allusions to natural science and to human history than to logic and theology. Perhaps in the early middle ages literature was almost exclusively ecclesiastical and based upon patristic authorities. But through the twelfth century the tide of secular and scientific learning was rising, until in the first part of the next century ecclesiastical opposition was powerless to prevent the study of the newly discovered books of Aristotle in natural philosophy. Aristotle, moreover, was far from being the sum and substance of mediæval science which drew from many other sources, such as Ptolemy, Pliny, Galen, and the Arabs, and which made original contributions and practical discoveries of its own. It was an age when even a superstitious book on magic and necromancy such as *Picatrix* declared that science was God's greatest gift to man, since "It always is making acquisitions and never diminishes; it ever elevates and never degenerates; it is always clear and never conceals itself." And even Bacon asserts that many scientific facts and truths were now known of which Plato and Aristotle, Hippocrates and Galen, had been ignorant.

It would be exceeding the limits of this article to discuss further this mediæval interest in natural science, and there are already a number of books or papers dealing with that field, although undoubtedly a great deal remains to be done. Even the subject of experimentation in the middle ages has been approached, but never sufficiently discussed. Pouchet in his *Histoire des sciences naturelles au moyen âge, ou Albert le Grand et son époque considérés comme point de départ de l'école expérimentale* was one of the first to point out Albertus Magnus's insistence on the necessity of experience as a criterion of truth in natural science, but his discussion goes little farther than that. Abbé Narbey's "Le moine Roger Bacon et le mouvement scientifique au XIIIe siècle" is another promising title which leads to disappointment. Mr. Taylor gives a discriminating analysis and estimate of Bacon's discussion of experimental science, considered *per se,* but regards it as a unique contribution, calling it "this most original and 'advanced' product of Bacon's genius."

It has, however, been observed that there was much practical experimenting in Bacon's time among artisans and alchemists. Picavet writes on this point, "It is well known that the technical arts attained great perfection. What is less realized is that the thirteenth century marks an important epoch in the history of the experimental sciences, that Roger Bacon is not an isolated apparition or exception. There was a whole school of alchemists who performed the experiments mentioned by ancient writers and devised new ones." But this article will not compare what Bacon said with what others did but only with what others said; it will confine its attention to allusions to experimental method in the writings of Bacon and his contemporaries. Many of the latter are today comparatively inaccessible and unknown, since they exist only in rare old printed editions; and the admirers of Bacon who reproach previous centuries with their neglect of Roger's works are unconscious that they are similarly neglecting a considerable group of mediæval men of science.

We have first to examine Bacon's discussion of "experimental science" (*scientia experimentalis*), to which one section of his *Opus Maius* is devoted and to which he adverts more briefly in other works. He regards it as the best criterion of truth in natural science. "All sciences except this either merely employ arguments to prove their conclusions, like the purely speculative sciences, or have universal and imperfect experiences;" while "It alone, in truth, has the means of finding out to perfection what

can be done by nature, what by the industry of art, what by fraud"; for it alone can distinguish what is true from what is false in "incantations, conjurations, invocations, deprecations, and sacrifices."

But how is one to set about experimenting? On this point Bacon is disappointing. His explanation of the rainbow, which is his longest illustration of the value of experimental science, is based merely on ordinary intelligent observation and reasoning, although he adds at the close that tests with instruments are needed and that consequently he will not assert that he has reached the full truth of the matter. Elsewhere he speaks of astronomical experiments "by instruments made for this purpose," but seems to regard the unaided eyesight as sufficient for the investigation of terrestrial phenomena. Bacon has sent "over sea and to various other lands and to annual fairs, in order that I might see the things of nature with my own eyes." "And those things which are not present in our locality we may know through other sages who have experienced them, just as Aristotle by authority of Alexander sent two thousand men to different regions to experience all things on the face of the earth, as Pliny testifies in his Natural History." The one contemporary who most nearly fulfills Bacon's ideal of what an experimental scientist should be, does not spend his time merely in reading, attending lectures, and engaging in disputations, but "is ashamed to have some layman or old-wife or knight or rustic know facts of which he is ignorant"; hence he goes out into the world and observes the doings of common workingmen and even takes hints from the operations of witches, enchanters, and magicians. Bacon even believes that valuable medicines can be discovered by observing what remedies various animals employ. It would seem that experimental method is in a low stage of its development, if it takes lessons from common human experience and from the actions of brutes. Bacon sufficiently indicates, however, that it does not consist merely of observation and casual experience, but includes purposive experimentation, and he often speaks of "experimenters." Undoubtedly he himself experimented. But the fact remains that he gives no directions concerning either the proper environment for experimenting or the proper conduct of experiments. Of laboratory equipment, of scientific instruments, of exact measurements, he has no more notion apparently than his contemporaries.

Bacon says far more of the marvelous results which he expects experimental science to achieve than he does of method. Some of his dreams have been made true by modern mechanical inventions, but in the main marvelousness rather than practicability characterizes the aims which he proposes for *scientia experimentalis*. Indeed, of the three ways in which he represents it as superior to all other sciences, while one is that it employs sure proofs rather than mere arguments, two are that by it life may be greatly lengthened, and that from it a better knowledge of the future may be gained than even from astrology. Thus experimental method is especially connected with alchemy and astrology. Bacon declares that "it has been proved by certain experiments" that life can be greatly prolonged "by secret experiences," and he believes that Artephius was enabled by such methods to live for a thousand and twenty-five years.

Some of his "experiments" are as fantastic as the aims are marvelous. "A good experimenter says in the book *De regimine senum*" that the following elixir will greatly prolong life: "that which is temperate in the fourth degree, and what swims in the sea, and what grows in the air, and what is cast up by the sea, and plant of India, and what is found in the entrails of an animal of long life, and those two serpents which are the food of the inhabitants of Tyre and Aethiopia." We also are told that "at Paris recently there was a sage who asked for snakes and was given one and cut it into small sections except that the skin of its belly on which it crawled remained intact; and that snake crawled as best it could to a certain herb

by touching which it was instantly made whole. And the experimenter collected a herb of wonderful virtue."

Credulity, in contrast to the skeptical attitude of modern science, is a characteristic of Bacon's experimental method. He declares it true that experiment disproves many false notions, but he also asserts that credulity is necessary in experimentation. "First one should be credulous until experience follows second and reason comes third. . . . At first one should believe those who have made experiments or who have faithful testimony from others who have done so, nor should one reject the truth because he is ignorant of it and because he has no argument for it." Taken as a plea for an open-minded attitude toward scientific investigation on the part of the ordinary man and of the ecclesiastical authorities, this utterance may be commended; but as a prescription for the scientific investigator it is dangerous. Many of Bacon's "experiments" are copied from books, and the reproach made against the Greek Empirics that they followed tradition, applies also to him. Describing a certain marvel of nature, he exclaims, "After I beheld this, there was nothing difficult for my mind to believe, provided it had a reliable author." In the midst of his discussion of experimental science we encounter the following instance of his gullibility.

"It is certain that Æthiopian sages have come into Italy, Spain, France, England, and those Christian lands where there are good flying dragons; and, by an occult art that they possess, excite the dragons from their caves. And they have saddles and bridles ready, and they ride the dragons, and drive them at top speed through the air, in order to soften the rigidity and toughness of their flesh, just as boars, bears, and bulls are hunted with dogs and beaten with many blows before they are killed for eating. And when they have tamed the dragons in this way, they have an art of preparing their flesh . . . , which they employ against the accidents of age and prolong life and inspire the intellect beyond all estimation. For no education which man can give will bestow such wisdom as does the eating of their flesh, as we have learned without deceit or doubt from men of proved trustworthiness."

Bacon's discussion of experimental science, therefore, on its positive side amounts to little more than a recognition of experience as a criterion of truth and a promulgation of the phrase "experimental science." Let us now look at other writers. Bacon himself, by his copying "experiments" from other books and by his locating an "experimenter" even at degenerate scholastic Paris, has suggested that we may find the subject treated elsewhere. We shall not find, it is true, any such express and lengthy discussion of the matter as his, but we may get the same substance in briefer form from the fairly numerous incidental references to experience and experiment.

As for experience as a criterion of truth, as early as the twelfth century we find writers on nature either asserting this or implying it. Early in that century Adelard of Bath in his *Natural Questions* attacked exclusive trust in authorities, and, while relying especially upon reason, also adduced experience. Alexander Neckam (1157-1217), who in 1213 was elected Abbot of Cirenchester, in his *De naturis rerum* calls upon "diligent investigators of nature" to testify to the virtues of words, herbs, and stones, which have been demonstrated "by most certain experience." Michael Scot, writing early in the thirteenth century, often uses the word *experimentum* in his elaborate introduction to astrology. So does Vincent of Beauvais later in the century in his huge work on nature, the *Speculum naturale*. The *Thesaurus pauperum* of Peter of Spain, who seems to have become Pope John XXI (died 1277), is further described in its title as, "Or concerning the ills of the human body by experiments ingenious, simple, and particular; an empirical book, from all sorts of authors and my own experience." The scholastic form of the celebrated *Conciliator* of Peter of Abano, composed about 1300 and one of the most elaborate of mediæval

medical treatises, scarcely makes one anticipate mention of experience or experiment. Yet Peter couples reason and experience as of equal authority, disagrees with those who deny that medicine is a science because it employs experience as well as reason, and in other passages alludes to his personal astronomical observations and his own successful experimenting with an incantation and an astronomical image.

A favorite theory in the twelfth and thirteenth centuries is that the things of nature possess "occult virtues" which cannot be reasoned out but must be learned experimentally. The hypothesis was still in force that all natural objects were composed of only four elements, earth, air, fire, and water, and characterized by four qualities, hot, cold, dry, and moist. It was impossible even by the most ingenious reasoning to explain on this basis certain properties of objects, such as the action of the magnet. So men decided that things possessed occult virtues in addition to the qualities which they derived from their component elements. Many believed that these occult properties were due to the influences of the stars; but in any case all agreed that they could only be discovered by experience. General principles and logic give no clue to them. Peter of Abano writes, "We perceive that precious stones and medicines have marvellous and occult virtues which cannot come from the qualities and natures of the elements. . . . Effects of this sort cannot be investigated by reasoning based on the qualities of the elements, but rather by experience." In the same strain write Arnald of Villanova, a medical author who died in 1312, Thomas Aquinas, Albertus Magnus, and others.

Indeed, writers on Albertus Magnus have not failed to notice that his scientific writings are neither mere commentaries upon Aristotle, nor compilations from a variety of sources; but that he both recognizes experience as a criterion of truth, and frequently states the results of his personal observations. This becomes especially evident in the last few books of his treatise on animals where he often states, "I have tested this," or "I and my associates have experienced," or "I have proved that this is not true," or "I have not experienced this." In treating of whales he limits himself entirely to the results of his own experience, saying, "We pass over the writings of antiquity on this topic because they do not agree with experience." Albert also often expresses doubt as to certain statements concerning animals on the ground that they have not been tested by experience, even if he has had no opportunity to disprove them; and he draws a sharp distinction between authors who state what they themselves have seen or tested, and those who appear simply to repeat rumor or folk-lore. He is particularly chary of accepting the assertions of Solinus and Jorach, assuring us, anent their assertion that certain birds can fly unharmed through flames, "Those philosophers tell many lies and I think that this is one of their lies."

On the other hand, Albert accepts as the statements of men of experience the stories which hunters, fowlers, and fishermen have told him. Toward such contemporary personal testimony he is, like Bacon, unduly credulous. He says that "a trustworthy person" told him that he saw in an eagle's nest 300 ducks, over 100 geese, about 40 hares, and many large fish, all of which were required to satisfy the hunger of the young eagles. However, Albert is somewhat less credulous than Bacon on the subject of dragons. That the Æthiopians eat the flesh of dragons to cool themselves, that dragons are afraid of thunder and therefore enchanters imitate the noise of thunder with drums in order to capture dragons and ride on them through space, that a dragon by a coil of its tail can crush an elephant: all these reports Albert treats as rumors rather than tested facts. He also suggests that meteors or flaming vapors have been mistaken for dragons flying through the air and breathing forth fire. He has, however, "heard from trustworthy persons" that a serpent with the virgin countenance of a beardless man "was slain in an island of

Germany and there displayed in our times to all who wished to see it until the flesh putrefied." Albert also still states that adamant can be broken only by goat's blood, an error which Bacon rejects. On the other hand, one notion which Bacon himself attacks but which he represents as generally accepted, namely, that the beaver when hunted castrates itself to save its life, Albert also rejects, saying that experience near his home has often proved the contrary. Again, Bacon tells how he himself has profited by an "experiment" which the magicians pretend to perform by virtue of an incantation. The experiment consists in holding the split halves of a hazel rod apart at the two ends, whereupon the middle portions bend toward each other. Bacon says, "I omitted the incantation and discovered a marvel of nature." But Albert and also John of St. Amand, a medical writer about 1261, both narrate this same marvel of nature and assure us that it works without the incantation.

It is true that Albert's allusions to experience occur mainly when he is discussing the specific properties of particular things. In his treatise on animals we find such allusions in the books where he is listing and describing particular animals, rather than where he discusses the general natures and common characteristics of animals. This is true again in his treatise *On Vegetables and Plants* where allusions to experience occur especially in the sixth book, in which particular plants are listed and described and, as Albert says, "We satisfy the curiosity of our students rather than philosophy, for philosophy cannot deal with particulars." However, in his *Physics* Albert states that "every hypothesis which is confirmed by the senses is better than that which contradicts sense; and a conclusion contrary to sense is incredible: indeed, a principle which does not agree with *experimental knowledge* acquired by the senses is no principle but quite the opposite."

Other authors than Bacon not only rely on experience, they also mention "experimenters" and cite experimental books or "books of experiments." In short, others than he have conceived the possibility of purposive experimentation, although we find their ideas as to experimental method in the same crude state as his. Bernard Silvestris, a teacher at Tours in the first half of the twelfth century, entitled an astronomical treatise which he composed *Experimentarius.* Early in the thirteenth century Thomas of Cantimpré, in the preface to his *De naturis rerum,* cites "a certain book without name of author which I have heard was compiled in modern times, whose statements you will know wherever you meet them from this indication, that you will find the name *Experimentator* (experimenter) prefixed." The *Speculum astronomiæ,* a treatise probably written by Albertus Magnus, mentions a *Book of Experiments* by the Arab Albumasar; Arnald of Villanova attributes a book of experiments to another Arab, Rasis. Bernard Gordon cites the opinions of "experimenters" in his *Lilium medicinæ* which he began to write in 1303.

As Bacon's experimental scientist was "ashamed to have some layman or old-wife or knight or rustic know facts of which he is ignorant," so Arnald of Villanova admits that the practical man of experience may know more of nature than the bookish scholar. "For since the properties of things cannot be discovered by reason but only by experiment or revelation, and experience and revelation are common to the ordinary man and to the scholar, it is possible that knowledge of properties may be attained by the common people sooner than by others." Arnald not only speaks of "experimenters" but of a "philosopher and experimenter"; and in another treatise states that a certain hypothesis "can be satisfactorily proved by the long experience of any intelligent operator." He also speaks of "rational experiment" which "always presupposes a determined object."

John of St. Amand asserts that *experimentum* alone is "timorous and fallacious," but that "fortified by reason" it gives "experimental knowledge." His idea seems to be, not only that experience must be combined with theory, but also that there should be methodical experimentation. He gives seven rules to be observed in discovering experimentally the properties of medicinal simples: that the simple tested should be pure and free from every extraneous quality, that it should be tested in a simple and not a complex disease, that several tests be made, that the dose administered should be proportioned to the patient's constitution, and so on.

On the whole one rather gets the impression that the experimental method which Bacon pleads for, as if it were a novelty, is calmly assumed by other writers as a well-established method. It is even doubtful if Roger can be credited with having coined a new phrase in "experimental science," since not only do others employ the adjective "experimental" and the noun "experimenter," but both Albertus Magnus and John of St. Amand use the expression "experimental knowledge."

It is significant that others not only duplicate Bacon's positive contributions, but that their experimental method is characterized by precisely the same failings as his. They display the same credulity and love of the marvelous, and are especially prone to mention experiment when they wish to prove something unreasonable, and to support incredible assertions by assurances that they have been tested by experience. They show the same inclination to fantastic "experiments." What Arnald's "experimenters" have proved is that a frog's legs bound to the patient's feet for three days, with the right leg on the right foot and the left leg on the left foot, cure gout. What his "philosopher and experimenter" has demonstrated is that application of the magnet has the same effect. To Socrates Arnald attributes this "marvellous and choice experiment." "In young swallows are found two stones, one red and one white. Application of the white stone will raise up a falling lunatic; and the red stone will benefit him, if tied in a bit of skin about his neck." Albert matches Bacon's snake experiment by one with a toad and emerald, which he tells to illustrate "the many effects of stones and plants that are known by experience and by which wonders are worked."

"An emerald was recently seen among us, small in size but marvelous in beauty. When its virtue was to be tested, someone stepped forth and said that, if a circle was made about a toad with the emerald and then the stone was set before the toad's eyes, one of two things would happen. Either the stone, if of weak virtue, would be broken by the gaze of the toad; or the toad would burst, if the stone was possessed of full natural vigor. Without delay things were arranged as he bade; and after a short lapse of time, during which the toad kept its eye unswervingly upon the gem, the latter began to crack like a nut and a portion of it flew from the ring. Then the toad, which had stood immovable hitherto, withdrew as if it had been freed from the influence of the gem."

The following experiment with a religious tinge was a favorite with medical writers. I quote John of Gaddesden's version.

"Since many boys and others who cannot take medicine are troubled with epilepsy, let the experiment be performed which Constantinus gives in the chapter on epilepsy in the fifth book of his *Practica,* and Walter in his *Practica,* and Bernard, and Gilbert, and everyone. And I have found it true, whether the patient be a demoniac, or epileptic, or lunatic. If he has a father and mother, let them take him to church after fasting with him for three days, and let him make confession, provided he has reached years of discretion. Then let them go on Friday in the fast of four seasons and hear mass, and let them repeat this on Saturday. On Sunday let a good religious priest read in church over the patient's head the Gospel which he reads in September after the harvest feast of the holy cross in the days of the four seasons. Moreover, let him devoutly write the same, and let the patient wear it about his neck and he will be cured. The Gospel meant is the passage, 'This kind of demon is not cast out except by fasting and prayer.'" Many more such "experiments" might be given.

In reality, therefore, Bacon's discussion of experimental science, instead of being a wonderful original contribution to knowledge, is an excellent representation of both the good and bad points of an important movement of the time in the direction of experimental method. Crude as this tendency may be, it at least demonstrates that the interests of the period were not exclusively scholastic.

Two further questions concerning experimental method in the middle ages suggest themselves. Was there any positive advance in this respect over the science of the classical period? How are we to explain the association of so much superstition with experimental method?

To the former question I incline to answer, Yes. Pliny the Elder, whose *Natural History* (written in the first century of our era) was a compilation of all previous science, should know of experimentation if it has ever amounted to much hitherto. He frequently uses the word *experimentum* but seldom in such a way that it is best translated "experiment." He never uses the words "experimental" and "experimenter," which are post-classical. Several of our mediæval writers cite Galen as an authority for the recognition of experience as a criterion of truth. It is true that Galen, writing a century later than Pliny and showing an advance in anatomical and medical knowledge over his predecessors, approaches more closely the conception of experimental method. He himself engaged in original research in anatomy, dissecting and vivisecting, and proving by actual experiment that the arteries contain blood, not air. It is true, as John of St. Amand and Peter of Abano state, that Galen makes both reason and experience criteria of truth in medicine; but as he insists that they ought not to be employed simultaneously, he misses the essence of experimental method. He further objects that experience is unscientific, irrational, and that it "requires good fortune to find what is sought." Once he identifies it with mere observation. The Empirics were the chief advocates of experience in the ancient medical world, and Galen broaches the topic mainly in connection with allusions to their sect. He usually depicts them as over-emphasizing experience and neglecting reason, as regarding phenomena only and ignoring causes, as learning what drugs to use from dreams and chance, and as trusting unquestioningly in authorities and tradition for information concerning the experience of past ages. The Empirics themselves insisted that experience was a scientific method. They distinguished three kinds, of which Galen unfortunately gives no further description, namely, accidental, off-hand, and imitative. They held that observation of a single instance was not enough, but that repeated observation with things remaining in the same condition was necessary. Thus they seem both to have had some of the faults of our mediæval scientists and to have had at least some notion of controlling the results of experience. Indeed, Galen himself believes that the properties of medicinal simples can and should be learned from experience, and gives some rules for testing their effects from which John of St. Amand seems to have developed his longer directions. Admitting, however, the debt of the middle ages to Galen, it seems true that they rely more frequently on experience than the ancients did; that they apply it more generally through the field of science, rather than merely to medicinal simples as Galen did, or to medical practise as the Emperics did; that they have developed the theory of occult virtues which can be discovered only by experience; that they have "experiments" and "experimenters" and entire books called experimental. Others besides Bacon seem conscious that science is finding a new method in their day, and Peter of Spain, in stating his sources of information, speaks of "ancient philosophers" but of "modern experimenters."

As for the other matter, the credulity, the superstition, the element of marvelousness, which seem to vitiate the experimental tendencies of Bacon and his contemporaries, —these are to be explained as the result of a real connection between experiment and magic. There is abundant evidence for this. Bacon, it is true, asserts that experimental science exposes and shuns all the follies of the magicians, but he admits that many persons confuse it with magic because of the marvels which it works, and he himself especially associates it with the occult sciences of alchemy and astrology. It makes gold such as neither the art of alchemy nor nature can produce; it can predict the future better than astrology. It teaches one to choose the proper constellations for his undertakings, and to use the right words at the proper time; it can construct "philosophical images and incantations and characters" which are vastly superior to those of magic; it can alter the world about us, and incline and excite the human will, though without coercion. Moreover, Bacon's ideal experimental scientist does not scorn to take hints from wizards, while Roger himself derives his hazel rod experiment from the magicians. The snake experiment of his sage at Paris sounds more like the trick of a Hindu conjurer than the procedure of a modern laboratory.

One gets the same impression from Bacon's contemporaries. The conception of occult virtue, which leads them so often to rely on experience, is a more or less magical notion, akin to the *mana* of primitive magic. Believers in astrology, divination, and fascination also appeal to experience. Vincent of Beauvais says that divination from portents is proved by many experiences, and that the influences of the planets upon our world were discovered by philosophers by "sure experiments" as well as by "convincing arguments." Albertus Magnus assures the reader that divination from dreams is "no idle report but the testimony of experience." In another treatise which has sometimes been attributed to Albert we read, "When the soul of any person is raised to great excess of some passion, it is found by manifest experiment that it binds and alters objects as it wishes." The experiments of Bacon's contemporaries, too, are often more like feats of magic than like scientific tests. Gaddesden's experiment employed an incantation and amulet; Peter of Abano experimented with an incantation and an astronomical image; and a necromantic book attributed to him bears the subtitle, "A book of marvelous experiments." Michael Scot describes "a chiromantic experiment," and mentions "love experiments" and the experiments of necromancers and magicians. Arnald recounts an "experiment" performed by an old-wife of Salerno to help women in childbirth. It consisted in taking three grains of pepper; saying a Lord's Prayer over each with substitution of the sentence, "Deliver this woman from the pangs of childbirth," for the words, "Deliver us from evil"; giving the grains one by one to the woman to be swallowed in wine or water without touching the teeth; and finally uttering an incantation* with three Paternosters in her right ear.

Arnald condemns this procedure as diabolical and contrary to the Faith, but he calls it an experiment nevertheless and earlier in the same treatise describes approvingly a very similar experiment by which a priest cured him of warts. Albert concludes his tale of the toad and the emerald by stating that there are many other effects of stones and herbs, which we learn by experiment, and which magicians study, and work won-

* [Bizomie lamion lamium azerai vachina
    deus deus sabaoth
  Benedictus qui venit in nomine domini
    osanna in excelsis.]

ders by means of them. In the *Speculum astronomiæ* he calls "experimental books" those which deal with different varieties of divination, namely, aeromancy, pyromancy, hydromancy, geomancy, and chiromancy; and he declares that such books ought not to be called science, which recalls Bacon's remark that to some men experimental science seems false and unworthy of a Christian. In a treatise entitled *Apollonii Flores Aurei,* which treats of the Notory Art of miraculous acquisition of knowledge by incantations and invocation of spirits, experiments and experimental science are again mentioned in the same breath with the above named varieties of divination. Books "which are nigromantic or contain the experiments of lot-casters" were condemned at Paris in 1277 together with the opinions of Siger de Brabant.

This is not the place to discuss magic, but from further investigation which I have made of its history and its relations to science I have little doubt that the connection between it and experimentation which our authors suggest is real. But this is not so much to the discredit of science as it is to the credit of magic. After all it is not surprising that magic, which was curious and tried to do things and to attain practical results, and which as long ago at least as Pliny the Elder's day had investigated nature, should experiment. It is indeed possible that magicians were the first to experiment, and that science, originally speculative, took over experimental method, as well as the conception of occult virtue, from magic.

THE
Later Middle Ages

PART THREE

DURING THE LAST HALF CENTURY or so there has been a striking change in the dominant point of view from which historians have regarded the medieval English Parliament. Bishop Stubbs, influenced no doubt much more than he realized by the great part played by Parliament in the constitutional conflicts of the seventeenth century and by the subsequent growth of parliamentary government, looked upon Parliament in the Middle Ages as the central institution of English government and represented it as such in his famous and extremely influential *Constitutional History of England,* written some three quarters of a century ago. Since his day a great deal that he did not know, and could not have known, has been learned about medieval Parliaments as well as about other institutions of medieval English government, and in the light of this more recent knowledge, Parliament in the thirteenth and fourteenth centuries is seen from a different standpoint. In the following lucid and informative summary of modern scholarly work on the history of Parliament to the end of the fourteenth century, Geoffrey Templeman, author of the valuable short study, *The Sheriffs of Warwickshire in the Thirteenth Century* (1948), shows how older views have been profoundly modified and changed. Especially useful is his summary of the recent contributions to medieval Parliamentary history made by the English scholars H. G. Richardson and G. O. Sayles in their notable collaborative articles, which, unfortunately, have never been brought together in a single work. Mr. Templeman shows also that scholarly opinion is by no means in complete agreement on all important questions in early English Parliamentary history. His survey affords a good example of the growth of historical-mindedness in the study of old institutions, for, as he remarks, "greater emphasis is now laid upon the necessity for interpreting the early history of Parliament in medieval terms and in the light of medieval conditions."

THE HISTORY OF PARLIAMENT TO 1400 IN THE LIGHT OF MODERN RESEARCH

GEOFFREY TEMPLEMAN

Twenty years ago two scholars, who themselves have made notable contributions to the subject, felt bound to remark that the story of the origin and early growth of the English Parliament had hardly begun to be written.[1] This may seem strange doctrine when it is remembered that a host of scholars, including the great Stubbs himself, had already laboured mightily in this field. Yet it is none the less true that during the last thirty years our knowledge of the early history of Parliament has undergone a

transformation so radical as to constitute what is virtually a new beginning in the

[1] H. G. Richardson and G. O. Sayles, 'The Early Records of the English Parliaments, III' in the *Bulletin of the Institute of Historical Research,* VI p. 145. This is henceforward referred to as *B.I.H.R.* Professor Plucknett strikes a note of deeper pessimism when he remarks that 'no English institution has been studied with such ardor and so little result as Parliament.' *The English Government at Work 1327-1336,* (ed. J. F. Willard and W. A. Morris), I p. 82.

study of the subject. Much of this re-shaping is still in its early stages, for as Mr. G. L. Haskins rightly says 'we cannot be in a hurry to get at the problems involved in the early history of Parliament, at best we must often be content to adjust our perspectives simply by checking new information and new points of view against the more general background of our frames of reference.'[2]

Such a situation makes the kind of short article here attempted at once more difficult and more necessary. More difficult because it must summarise interim conclusions and tentative opinions, while following an uncertain road amid many controversies. More necessary because the beginner, to whom this paper is addressed, must somehow find his way to that multitude of articles and studies in learned journals and monographs, which form the bulk of the modern literature of the subject. He may also think it useful to have some brief indication of the shape of the subject as it now appears. Indeed any justification these pages can claim lies wholly in the extent to which they minister to such real if elementary needs.[3]

At the outset one notable fact deserves mention. When Stubbs addressed himself to the task of expounding the constitutional history of medieval England after 1215, he unhesitatingly gave pride of place in his survey to Parliament, since he made its history the principal theme of the two volumes in which he considered the period 1215-1485. In so doing Stubbs did not arbitrarily narrow the scope of his work, rather he displayed the whole subject in what he held to be its true proportions. As he saw it the development of Parliament was at once the measure and the means of the constitutional progress for which he looked, and to it all

else was therefore subordinate and supplementary. For Parliament, so Stubbs believed, was the means by which each class in the community, as soon as it was fitted for the trust, could be admitted to a share of power and control, and through which national action could be determined by the balance of the forces thus combined.[4] This, in his opinion, was the peculiar excellence of English government, and its principal achievement since the time of Edward I. Thus in his work the Council, the Courts, the departments of state and even the monarchy itself achieved significance not by reason of their intrinsic importance, but chiefly because their history is so closely interlocked with that of Parliament.

Modern opinion, however, inclines to regard the whole matter from a different standpoint. Scholars are now much less disposed than formerly to find the true significance of medieval parliamentary history in the way it foreshadows, prepares or illuminates the development of parliamentary government in more recent times. They are less anxious than Stubbs was to show how much those who opposed the Stuarts owed to 'the heroes of the thirteenth century,' not to mention Parliament's lesser medieval pioneers.[5] Much greater emphasis is now laid upon the necessity for interpreting the early history of Parliament in medieval terms and in the light of medieval conditions. This is no passing intellectual fad; it is a permanent change wrought by great improvements in our knowledge of the working and structure of English government in the thirteenth and fourteenth centuries. These improvements are themselves the first fruits of that systematic study of the judicial and administrative agencies of the king's government, which Maitland and Tout did so much to

[2] *English Historical Review*, LIII p. 2. Henceforth referred to as *E.H.R.*
[3] There are, of course, admirable modern sketches of the early history of Parliament in J. E. A. Jolliffe, *The Constitutional History of Medieval England,* pp. 304-408, and in G. O. Sayles, *The Medieval Foundations of England,* pp. 448-65. Yet neither of these fulfils quite the same purpose as is here intended.

[4] *Constitutional History of England,* (4th edition), II p. 166-7. Henceforth referred to as *C.H.*
[5] Cf: *C.H.,* II pp. 319-20, 652: 'The most superficial reading of history is sufficient to show that the series of events which form the crises of the Great Rebellion and the Revolution might link themselves on to the theory of Richard II as readily as to that of James I.'

inspire.[6] Much of this work still remains to be done, and some would say that it is hardly started. There is still much to be learned even about the Chancery and the Exchequer, and few would claim, despite the labours of Maitland, Holdsworth and Sayles, that complete understanding of the medieval history of the superior courts has yet been achieved.[7]

Nevertheless sufficient is known to enforce a considerable revision of the traditional idea of English government as it existed from the death of John to the deposition of Richard II. Parliament can no longer occupy the foreground of the picture. Instead the scene is dominated by the King and his Council jointly controlling an already elaborate judicial and administrative organisation, which was steadily developing its own complicated procedure. The tentacles of royal power can be seen stretching octopus-like into every part of the kingdom, lacing themselves ever more firmly round the remnants of feudal authority, and even prying curiously into the affairs of the church. A multitude of functionaries, royal judges, commissioners and clerks, sheriffs, coroners, justices of the peace and escheators, with bailiffs of divers kinds in towns and liberties all busied themselves at the king's command to do his will.

Nor is it any longer possible to think of the making of this massive system simply as the work of the 'great organisers of the Norman and early Plantagenet lines.'[8] Administrative development in the king's government went on apace in the fourteenth century carried forward inexorably by its own momentum; for as Viollet says 'insensiblement la fonction créa l'organe.'[9] Indeed, as Tout hints, the later medieval kings found themselves in some degree prisoners of the great organisation originally devised to enforce their sovereign will. On many sides the king's personal power was hemmed in and constricted in its operation by unyielding formality and routine.[10] The early Parliament now appears as an appendage of this system, as a parasite which, in the course of time, overwhelmed its host. Thus like Ptolemy's cosmology, Stubbs's view of Parliament's medieval primacy in the realm of government has suffered a Copernican revolution.

[6] There is an excellent survey of all but the most modern work in these fields in G. Lapsley, 'Some Recent Advances in English Constitutional History, (before 1485)' in *Cambridge Historical Journal*, V pp. 119-61.

[7] Sir Frederick Pollock and F. W. Maitland, *The History of English Law before the Time of Edward I*, 2 vols.: W. S. Holdsworth, *A History of English Law*, 3rd edition, 9 vols.: G. O. Sayles, *Select Cases in the Court of King's Bench under Edward I*, (Selden Society, LV, LVII and LVIII). A model of the kind of study in this field to which students may hopefully look forward is provided by Margaret Hastings, *The Court of Common Pleas* (Cornell Univ. Press, 1947).

[8] *C.H.*, II p. 537.

[9] P. Viollet, *Histoire des Institutions Politiques de la France*, III p. 296, quoted by G. Lapsley in *C.H.J.*, V p. 122. ['Unconsciously the function created the organ.']

[10] T. F. Tout, *Chapters in the Administrative History of Mediæval England*, V pp. 228-9; (henceforth referred to as *Chapters*). Also *Collected Papers*, III pp. 191-248, where in two reprinted lectures Tout sets out his more important general conclusions on the matter and considers their implications.

ANGEVIN KINGS	LANCASTRIAN KINGS
Henry II, 1154-1189	Henry IV, 1399-1413
Richard I, 1189-1199	Henry V, 1413-1422
John, 1199-1216	Henry VI, 1422-1461
Henry III, 1216-1272	
Edward I, 1272-1307	YORKIST KINGS
Edward II, 1307-1327	Edward IV, 1461-1483
Edward III, 1327-1377	Edward V, 1483
Richard II, 1377-1399	Richard III, 1483-1485

In this new setting the traditional account of Parliament's medieval history, which received its last and most perfect formulation from Stubbs, could not have survived unchanged for long. As it happened there was no chance of this, because a vigorous reformation had started within the subject itself before the full impact of wider changes outside was felt. Yet it would be wrong to give the impression that these two processes were in reality separate, although for purposes of study it is convenient to consider them apart. Indeed much of the difficulty of writing on this subject arises from their complicated interaction. This has happened because the early Parliament had its roots deeply embedded in the administrative, judicial and consultative activities of the government. Therefore those whose principal concern has been to explore the history of these matters have found themselves confronted at every turn by the problems of Parliament.

Baldwin discovered this when he wrote on the Council,[11] and in his great work Tout has much of importance to say about Parliament, although his real subject was the history of the Wardrobe. Nor have such influences been wholly one-sided, for, from Maitland's time onwards, efforts to probe into the complexities of Parliament's early development have undoubtedly stimulated enquiry into the history of the Council, the Courts and the other great medieval departments of state.

Such general considerations help to illuminate the way in which the modern idea of Parliament's early history has been built up, and that process can now be sketched in brief outline. Since Stubbs's view of the matter has exercised a profound if not always beneficent influence on much of the later work, it is perhaps well to begin by summarising what he taught. His 'system' for the early history of Parliament, although wonderfully learned and imposing, was, at bottom, simple. He held that in the

eighty years from 1215 to 1295 the nation grew and became sufficiently compacted to feel its own strength, the spirit of liberty made notable advances, and Parliament as an institution was brought into being and given recognisable shape.[12] Yet Stubbs was too great a scholar not to realise and allow for the fact that this development was very complicated and in part fortuitous, or at least unpremeditated by those, who, in their political struggles, helped it forward.[13] The idea of representative government, we are told, ripened under Simon de Montfort's hand, and he had the merit of being one of the first to see the uses and glories to which it would ultimately grow. Nevertheless this account is balanced by the significant statement that 'the means he took for admitting the nation to self-government wear very much the form of an occasional or party expedient, which a longer tenure of undivided power might have led him either to develop or to discard.'[14] Even Edward I, who 'saw what the nation was capable of and adapted his constitutional reforms to that capacity,' was 'forced to carry out his own principles of design even when they told against his momentary policy and threatened to thwart his own object in the maintenance of his design.'[15] Nor did Stubbs neglect to emphasise analogous developments in other parts of the Christian West during this period, or to insist that what happened in England 'approved itself to the genius and grew out of the habits of the people.'[16]

The result of this, 'the consummation of a growing policy,' was the Parliament of 1295. Then, so Stubbs believed, Edward I, now fully determined to summon the nation

[11] J. F. Baldwin, The King's Council in England during the Middle Ages, (Oxford, 1913), especially pp. 307-44.

[12] C.H., II p. 5.
[13] Ibid., pp. 537-9. Stubbs draws a sharp distinction between what he calls the political and the mechanical sides of this development, treating each separately in a long chapter. Ibid., p. 2: chapters XIV and XV.
[14] Ibid., pp. 103-4.
[15] Ibid., pp. 304-5.
[16] Ibid., p. 304. Chapter XV opens with a summary account of comparative developments elsewhere in Europe. Ibid., pp. 166-9.

to a share in the business of government, prescribed the permanent form of its participation through the medium of an assembly of estates. In particular, after twenty years of experiment, there were added to a baronage, now limited and defined on a distinct system of summons, representatives of clergy and people chosen in accordance with a carefully evolved scheme.[17]

To Stubbs the fourteenth century was the first stage, for the process was a long one, in the unfolding of the powers and possibilities of this new system; the running-in period, as it were, of a new mechanism. He thought, and most historians have continued to agree with him, that the political achievement of this century in English history fell far below that of its predecessor. He saw very little of the spirit of the deliverer in Thomas of Lancaster or in Thomas of Woodstock. He was under no illusion that the men of the fourteenth century carried forward the great struggle to limit royal authority with the same resolute purpose, which, he believed, had earlier animated Simon de Montfort and his like. Rather he argued that Parliament in the fourteenth century was strengthened in its organisation, its function and its privilege because the factions saw in it a convenient forum for their quarrels, and used it vigorously in that fashion. In his phrase, 'factious aims and factious divisions' were the energising power of parliamentary growth in the fourteenth century. Nevertheless, looking back on the tale he had unfolded, Stubbs felt able to claim a real growth of parliamentary authority during the century, and especially an extension of the influence of the Commons, of whom he already thought as the constituted defenders of the nation's liberties. At the

same time he was careful to emphasise that such improvement must be estimated, particularly in the case of the Commons, 'not by the rights they had actually secured, but by those which they were strong enough to claim and wise enough to appreciate.'[18] Thus Stubbs, always cautious, sought to safeguard his system, and this done he added, in the twentieth chapter of the Constitutional History, a long survey of medieval parliamentary procedure.

The great work was finished in 1878, and for a time it dominated the subject. J. R. Tanner described the situation as it then was in words which bear repetition:—

The subject was deposited in three sacred volumes, which were approached by the devout disciple in much the same spirit as that in which the youthful Brahmin draws near to the Vedas. To read the first volume of Stubbs was necessary to salvation; to read the second was greatly to be desired; the third was reserved for the ambitious student who sought to accumulate merit by unnatural austerities . . . The lecturer lectured on Stubbs; the commentator elucidated him; the crammer boiled him down. Within those covers was to be found the final word on every controversy, and in this faith the student moved serene.[19]

By 1900 things had begun to change, at any rate so far as the medieval history of Parliament was concerned. Ludwig Riess, by stressing the petitory function of representatives coming from the shires and the towns to thirteenth century English Parliaments, was the first to cast doubt upon

[17] Ibid., II 236, 306. An assembly of estates is precisely defined as 'an organised collection, made by representation or otherwise, of the several orders, states or conditions of men, who are recognised as possessing political power. A national council of clergy and barons is not an assembly of estates, because it does not include the body of the people, the "plebs," the simple freemen or commons, who on all constitutional theories have a right to be consulted as to their own taxation, if on nothing else.' Ibid., p. 171.

[18] Stubbs's view of the character of fourteenth century history is set out Ibid., II pp. 539, 653-6. For the progress of Parliament in this age see Ibid., p. 652. A little while ago, in an interesting address delivered before the Canadian Historical Association, Professor Wilkinson pleaded for a drastic revision of the accepted view of fourteenth century history, which owes so much to Stubbs. Report of Annual Meeting of the Canadian Historical Association 1946, pp. 18-29.

[19] The Teaching of History, (ed. W. A. J. Archbold, Cambridge, 1901), p. 54.

Stubbs's account of the origin of the institution.[20] Then J. H. Round and L. O. Pike demonstrated that the received view of the origin of the peerage and the early history of the Lords in Parliament, which owed much to Blackstone and was preached by Stubbs, needed considerable revision.[21] Most important of all, the year 1893 saw the publication of F. W. Maitland's edition of the Parliament Roll of 1305. In the long run the views expressed in the Introduction to this work probably did more to outmode Stubbs's theory of medieval parliamentary history than any other single contribution to the subject. It should be emphasised, however, that Maitland himself had little thought of setting in motion any radical change.[22] In ways like this, among scholars, the authority of Stubbs's work on the history of Parliament was soon undermined, although in the ranks of the less knowledgeable it persisted longer. Yet if his authority has gone his influence still remains. His system has been discredited, but his judgements on matters of detail are still respected by those who, without calling themselves his disciples, find good reason to admire his massive learning and acute understanding. In particular Stubbs had an intimate knowledge of medieval personalities and politics

which, in these more specialised days, it is harder for the historian to come by. Nevertheless the decline and fall of Stubbs cannot be allowed to obscure the positive significance of the new developments which were its principal cause. Maitland pointed the way to a fresh line of advance destined to be painstakingly explored by those coming after him, and the modern idea of the subject rests largely on the new knowledge thus obtained. It is therefore desirable to examine this aspect of the matter in some detail.

Maitland began by describing the proceedings of the Lent Parliament of 1305 as they are revealed in the Roll. He laid special stress on the fact that the full or general Parliament was still regarded as in session on 6 April, although a proclamation of 21 March had dismissed all but the members of the Council, and those others who still had business to transact. Then, after discussing the Council and its work, Maitland formulated some conclusions about the nature of Parliament at the beginning of the fourteenth century. These are best expressed in his own words:[23]

[20] His views were set out in his doctoral dissertation, published under the title *Geschichte des Wahlrechts zum englischen Parlament im Mittelalter,* (Leipzig, 1885), supplemented by an article entitled 'Der Ursprung des englischen Unterhauses,' (*Historische Zeitschrift,* LX pp. 1-33). The parts of the monograph which are of permanent interest have been translated and edited by Miss K. L. Wood-Legh under the title *The History of the English Electoral Law in the Middle Ages,* (Cambridge, 1940). For a more detailed account of Riess's theories see below.

[21] L. O. Pike, *Constitutional History of the House of Lords,* (London, 1894). J. H. Round's article, 'The Origin of the House of Lords,' was first published in magazine form 1884-5, when it seems to have attracted little attention. It was reprinted in *Peerage and Pedigree,* (London, 1910), I pp. 324-62. Despite its polemical character it is well worth reading, since it adumbrates, in general terms, many of the ideas concerning the King's Council and the Medieval Parliament, which have since become accepted.

[22] The full title of the work is *Records of the Parliament holden at Westminster on the twenty-eighth day of February in the thirty-third year of the reign of Edward the First.* (Rolls Series). It is more usually known by its shorter alternative title *Memoranda de Parliamento.* The introductory essay, except for the part dealing with technicalities concerning the date and authority of the MS. itself, has been edited by Mr. G. Lapsley and is reprinted in Maitland, *Selected Essays,* (ed. H. D. Hazeltine, G. Lapsley and P. H. Winfield, Cambridge, 1936), pp. 13-72. Maitland is at pains to remind his readers that, should they accept his conclusions, they will not, to use his own words, 'be departing very far from the path marked out by books that are already classical.' Ibid., pp. 70-1.

[23] Maitland, *Selected Essays,* pp. 14-15, 70-1. —Maitland's interpretation of the proclamation of 21 March 1305, particularly of the crucial clause specifying those who were to remain behind, has been challenged by Professor B. Wilkinson, *Studies in the Constitutional History of the 13th and 14th centuries,* (Manchester, 1937). In a review of this book, *E.H.R.,* LIII p. 703, Mr. Lapsley advances strong reasons for rejecting Dr. Wilkinson's opinion.

That about the parliaments of Edward I's time there is still much to be discovered . . . that a session of the king's council is the core and essence of every *parliamentum,* that the documents usually called 'parliamentary petitions' are petitions to the king and his council, that the auditors of petitions are committees of the council, that the rolls of parliament are the records of the business done by the council—sometimes with, but much more often without, the concurrence of the estates of the realm—that the highest tribunal in England is not a general assembly of barons and prelates, but the king's council.

Plainly the major innovation here is the predominant place assigned to the Council in Parliament. Linked with this, although by no means so fully developed, is the notion that parliamentary proceedings were then mainly judicial in character.

These ideas, particularly the second, were taken up and worked out on a much larger scale by that great American scholar, C. H. McIlwain. His book, *The High Court of Parliament and Its Supremacy,*[24] was an historical examination of the boundaries between legislation and adjudication in England. It also had an intimate bearing upon the working of modern American government. As McIlwain pointed out, the practice whereby the Supreme Court of the United States scrutinises the acts of the Legislature is the outcome of that long metamorphosis in the course of which the English Parliament shed much of its original character as a supreme court of law, while it slowly acquired legislative and deliberative functions.[25] Thus the problem of the medieval Parliament is of first importance in McIlwain's work. Accepting Maitland's view that the early Parliament was an occasional, en-

larged session of the Council, he then proceeded to argue that 'the Rolls of Parliament show that a large part of the work of the "Parliament" was what we should call "judicial," consisting of those cases that had proved too hard or too novel for the judges in the separate courts.'[26] In support of this contention he showed that, to the medieval way of thinking, law was not something to be made, but a body of custom to be declared, affirmed, defined and applied, since it was thought to be based on principles beyond the power of men to change.[27] In short, medieval legislation, if it can be so called, was the outcome of judicial activity. As will later appear, McIlwain probably overstressed the curial factor in Parliament's early development.[28] Nevertheless, at the time, his book served both to establish the new doctrine more firmly and to ensure its further development.

At this point Professor A. F. Pollard intervened with his *Evolution of Parliament.*[29] This book was a highly successful attempt, in so far as it dealt with the Middle Ages, to popularise the views of Maitland and McIlwain. It must be mentioned here because it is still widely used by students and its place in the literature of the subject should be clearly understood. With iconoclastic fervour Pollard uprooted the older notions, and in their place set the new ideas, pressed into a more rigid and coherent pattern than the evidence seemed to warrant. Since he wrote, so much new work has been done on the subject that his book, even with the corrections and explanations he later made, can now be reckoned as no more than a brilliant summary of the position as it was thirty years ago.[30]

In February 1928 there appeared the first

[24] New Haven, 1910.
[25] McIlwain explains that the development of the practice of the judicial review of statutes in England was frustrated by the growth of the absolute legislative sovereignty of Parliament from the seventeenth century onwards. *The High Court of Parliament,* pp. 385-7.

[26] Ibid., pp. 19, 25.
[27] This idea is carefully worked out in the chapter entitled 'The Fundamental Law.' Ibid., pp. 42-100.
[28] See below.
[29] London, 1920.
[30] A second edition was published in 1926. This contains two long appendices (pp. 387-446) in which Professor Pollard made certain corrections and answered some of his critics.

of those notable studies in the early history of Parliament, which have resulted from the collaboration of Mr. H. G. Richardson and Professor G. O. Sayles. It is true that their work represents only a part of the important contribution to the subject made by a number of scholars in the last two decades. Yet, without in any way belittling what others have done, it is fair to say that Mr. Richardson and Dr. Sayles have first claim on our attention because their investigations have probed so deeply and persistently into the very heart of the matter. Moreover their work has produced, at least in outline, a new scheme for the history of Parliament up to the death of Edward III, which by attraction and repulsion has exerted a profound influence on the opinions now held by most scholars.

Although they themselves early asserted that they were not 'greatly concerned with the notions of modern writers, who seem to us to be often quite uncertain of their own criteria,' Mr. Richardson and Dr. Sayles did in fact build on the foundations laid by Maitland and McIlwain.[31] Mr. Richardson has described the discovery of the part played by the Council in Parliament as something of cardinal importance.[32] In this connection also judgements like 'the history of Parliament is the history of a court placed over other courts, devised to dispense a higher justice' and 'the essence of [Parliament] is the dispensation of justice,' speak for themselves.[33]

The general method used with conspicuous success by Mr. Richardson and Dr. Sayles in approaching the subject is also worth noticing. They are clear that the first questions to be asked and answered are 'what did Parliament do?' and 'how did it work?'[34] Only then will it be possible to enquire, with a reasonable prospect of success, how Parliament was composed and what powers, duties and privileges can be attributed to the different groups ordinarily present there. This method recommends itself as the most profitable and efficient way of tackling the difficult and often fragmentary material from which the early history of Parliament must be constructed. It has a larger significance too, which should not be overlooked. All the work done by Mr. Richardson and Dr. Sayles seems to point clearly to the fact that, at every stage in its early growth, Parliament's function determined its composition and organisation. As that was varied and enlarged, so they were almost automatically altered. In fact this is the general idea which they have fitted into the gap left by the destruction of the older notion of Parliament as a deliberately created institution speaking the nation's will.

Mr. Richardson laid the foundation of the joint work in a paper called 'The Origins of Parliament.'[35] His argument was briefly as follows: The English Parliament took definite shape in 1258, the year of the Provisions of Oxford. After that date 'we have to do with an institution of a distinctive kind, which will evolve and suffer setbacks and some interruptions, but which will have a legible and continuous history.'[36] Before 1258 the problem is to discover why and how 'the occasional plenary meetings of the king's court in the early thirteenth century became transformed into . . . organised parliaments,' dominated, it may be added, by the king, and developed chiefly to forward the untrammelled operation of his sovereign will.[37] Here it is suggested that a large part of the explanation lies in the urgent need, which then existed, to find some means of remedying evils, particularly those arising from local misgovernment, with which the ordinary courts were powerless to grapple effectively. Inevitably such

[31] *B.I.H.R.*, V p. 129.
[32] *B.I.H.R.*, XIV p. 82. This opinion is reported in the account of a discussion entitled 'Have recent studies altered the accepted outlines of the early history of Parliament?' held during the Anglo-American Conference of Historians, 1936.
[33] Ibid., VI pp. 145, 78.
[34] Ibid., pp. 145-6.

[35] *Transactions of the Royal Historical Society, 4th series,* XI pp. 137-83. (Henceforth cited as *T.R.H.S.*).
[36] Ibid., 4th series, XXVIII p. 23.
[37] Ibid., 4th series, XI p. 170.

difficulties often raised broad questions of policy and discussion of these matters found a natural and unquestioned place in the early Parliaments. Again it cannot be doubted that in some degree at least baronial ambitions to curb royal power also played a part in this whole development.

This general theory, supported by English evidence, is buttressed by testimony from the history of the Parlement in France. There, a similar change took place in the thirteenth century and it is 'not at all unlikely . . . that in its origin the English parliament owes something to ideas borrowed from France, although it is of course true that like problems in countries sharing a common civilisation may suggest like remedies.'[38] The essential fact that stands out from all this is that by 1272 the Council in Parliament, meeting in fairly regular sessions, was habitually occupied with remedying grievances by judgement and discussion.

Thus, when they turned to the history of Parliament from 1272 to 1376, Mr. Richardson and Dr. Sayles considered that they already had to deal with an established institution. They did not think of it as inchoate, only slowly acquiring the rudiments of its organisation and function during the reign of Edward I. On the contrary, they held that the Edwardian Parliament began and continued as 'something fixed, determined, absolute, which all men may know and respect.'[39] This conviction is founded, as might be expected, upon the view the authors hold of Parliament's function under Edward I. While admitting that many different things might be done in Parliament at this period, aids demanded, homage rendered, laws promulgated and high politics discussed, they insist that such matters were not the real and expected business of Parliament. All these things, until well into the reign of Edward III, could be and were done

in non-parliamentary assemblies. Conversely they are not to be found among the 'agenda' and 'acta' of many Parliaments. The proper and distinctive business of Parliament at this time, we are told, is 'pro justitia omnibus exhibenda,' to dispense the highest kind of justice.[40]

This approach, vigorously pursued in a series of technical studies, has yielded some startling results.[41] It has produced a list of the Parliaments of the first three Edwards, without the complications and inconsistencies which had marred previous versions. When the test of a true Parliament was seen to be whether or not its proceedings included the normal judicial business proper to such an occasion, then Parliaments stood out clearly from the multitude of other assemblies, 'colloquia,' Great Councils and the like, convoked by the Crown at this time. It was also possible to abandon the widely held but difficult alternative theory that there must have been several different kinds of Parliament. Also the Parliament Rolls, so vital to an understanding of the subject, appeared in a new light. Their haphazard arrangement and fragmentary character were revealed, not as something to be explained away, but rather as something to be expected from a body with the bulk of its business originating in written petitions. Parliament's early records, like the rolls of any court of law, were 'a putting together of odds and ends.'[42] More recently Mr. Richardson and Dr. Sayles have traced the ancestry of the parliamentary petition back to that protoplasmic judicial form, the

[38] *T.R.H.S.*, 4th series, XI p. 157. See the article in which Dr. Sayles collaborated entitled 'The Provisions of Oxford' in *Bulletin of the John Rylands Library*, XVII pp. 291-321.
[39] *B.I.H.R.*, V p. 133.

[40] Mr. Richardson and Dr. Sayles hint that the origin of parliamentary privilege is to be sought in the peculiar sanctity thought to attach to a court of law. *B.I.H.R.*, V pp. 130-1.
[41] The work with which this paragraph is concerned appeared under the general title of *The Early Records of the English Parliaments*. (1) 'The English Parliaments of Edward I.' *B.I.H.R.*, V pp. 129-54. (2) 'The English Parliaments of Edward II.' Ibid., VI pp. 71-88. (3) 'The Exchequer Parliament Rolls and other Documents.' Ibid., pp. 129-55. To these should be added 'The Parliaments of Edward III,' Ibid., VIII pp. 65-82; IX pp. 1-18.
[42] *B.I.H.R.*, VI p. 131.

plaint, or 'querela.' They have further shown its close relationship in the later part of the thirteenth century to the bill in eyre, and to those other petitions regularly addressed to the Chancellor, the Treasurer and the Council outside Parliament.[43] This point, incidentally, further confirms their attribution of a precise judicial function to Edward I's Parliament. Moreover their collection of hitherto unprinted fragments of the early Parliament Rolls has revealed something of the crucial fourteenth century development of the written petition of public interest brought before the Council in Parliament. This instrument contained within itself the germ of the bill and the statute.[44]

Most important of all, this new method of approach suggested the need to study the doings of the judges, ministers and clerks, the permanent staff of the early Parliament, whose activities now appeared of particular consequence. This investigation, conducted in a series of articles under the title 'The King's Ministers in Parliament, 1272-1377,' pulled together the strands of the earlier work, demonstrated its surprising inner coherence and provided the opportunity for a synoptic view of Parliament's history in this period.[45]

In Edward I's time Parliament was dominated by the ministerial group of clerks and judges in the king's service. They alone had the necessary skill to staff its tribunals and to arrange and transact the great bulk of its normal business. As for the baronage and the commons they appear intermittently, mainly in connection with matters less essential to the conduct of Parliament, and there is no reason why it should not have functioned without them. The beginnings of significant change belong to Edward II's reign. Then there occurred what the authors

term a feudal reaction, engineered by the Ordainers. The baronage, which tried and failed to seize control of the Council, managed to thrust itself into partnership with the ministerial group in the control of the various parliamentary tribunals. Under Edward III the consequences of this change were partly worked out. The main purpose of Parliament became political instead of judicial. The judges and the clerks were roughly elbowed out of their superior place, only remaining as assistants, while the principal ministerial offices came to be occupied by those who ranked as members of the baronage or the commons. At the same time the number of private petitions began to decrease, partly because of the growing equitable jurisdiction of the Chancellor, and partly because politics, in the broad sense, were intruded ever more boldly into the forefront of Parliament's business.[46] In short, Parliament in Edward III's time worked 'under the shadow of the rising power of the peerage and commons' with all that implied.[47] Nevertheless we are warned against supposing that this alteration was either rapid or easily perceptible. Its subtle alchemy is hard to detect at this distance in time, and, for practical purposes, the old and the new co-existed side by side. Finally, if strict regard is paid to their premises, Mr. Richardson and Dr. Sayles must be held to view the whole change as a process of transformation and not as a process of evolution.

The opinions just summarised have worked like leaven in the study of the early history of Parliament during the last fifteen years. Few scholars have accepted this new teaching in its entirety. Many are occasional conformists, and some have been provoked to expound contrary doctrines of their own. This being so it is convenient to consider the other important modern work on the subject in relation to what Mr. Richardson and Dr. Sayles have done.

The most extreme reaction to their views is found in the work of Miss M. V. Clarke and Professor Wilkinson. Miss Clarke's prin-

[43] *Select Cases of Procedure without Writ under Henry III.* (Selden Society, LX), pp. xxi-lxviii.

[44] *Rotuli Parliamentorum Anglie Hactenus Inediti.* (Camden Society, 3rd series, LI). See also their article, 'The Early Statutes' in *Law Quarterly Review,* L pp. 201, 540.

[45] *E.H.R.,* XLVI pp. 529-50; XLVII pp. 194-203, 377-97.

[46] *B.I.H.R.,* IX pp. 2-7.
[47] *E.H.R.,* XLVII p. 396.

cipal contribution is in her book *Medieval Representation and Consent,* which was only published after her tragically early death.[48] To begin with she recorded her conviction that the modern study of the early records of Parliament, particularly in the work of Mr. Richardson and Dr. Sayles, had shown that 'we must look elsewhere for knowledge of the beginnings of national assemblies organised on the principle of representation and consent.'[49] These records, she believed, could throw little light upon 'what was in the minds of kings and their subjects as to the nature and function of Parliaments of estates.'[50] Knowledge of this vital matter must be sought in other ways, and particularly in that enigmatic fourteenth century document the 'Modus Tenendi Parliamentum,' which purports to describe the composition and procedure of Parliament, and to expound the principles governing its action and authority. On the whole scholars have always distrusted the evidence of the 'Modus.' Mr. Lapsley calls it that 'ignis fatuus' of parliamentary history. Stubbs thought it worthless, and Pollard considered it to be no more scientific (whatever that may mean) than Tacitus' *Germania.*[51] Miss Clarke thought otherwise and set out to justify her opinion.

As was already well known the 'Modus' enunciated a doctrine of parliamentary authority even more exalted than that which Stubbs had preached. All the orders of the realm were to participate in the business of government, harmoniously co-operating in a common task for which all shared responsibility.[52] Miss Clarke held that such

was in fact the case after 1322. She thought that the 'Modus' was composed in that year, which was also the year of the Statute of York, by an ecclesiastic well acquainted with the processes of government. Its testimony, she believed, could be accepted as a reliable and informed account of what Parliament was and how it worked. The arguments by which Miss Clarke endeavoured to establish these propositions are complicated and many-sided. Important among them is the reliance she placed on the Statute of York, for she held that it closely reflected the doctrine of the 'Modus.' 'The sum of these opinions (i.e. those of the 'Modus') was expressed succinctly in the Statute of York.'[53] In fact this statute and the 'Modus' between them epitomise the results of the political struggles of 1311-1322, which, we are told, were crucial for the medieval development of Parliament. Edward II's conflict with the Ordainers endowed the Parliament of estates with a new significance.[54] The Commons began to exercise the political functions which had hitherto been monopolised by the king and the magnates, and those who framed the Statute of York clearly intended to assert this principle of common responsibility. Miss Clarke of course allows that a much longer period was required for the full working out of all the implications of this change. She also contends that what was achieved in 1322 represents the consistent outcome of earlier parliamentary development. Edward I's Parliament was a Parliament of estates, and as such 'the public assembly of a coherent society.'[55] To it came the Commons with power to act by virtue of mandates from their constituencies. In truth, as Miss Clarke sees it, the Edwardian Parliament was founded upon representation and consent.

In two very significant chapters she traces the history of the doctrine of consent and of the principle of representation in thirteenth century England.[56] Consent was a

[48] London, 1936.
[49] *Medieval Representation and Consent,* p. 3.
[50] Ibid., p. 2.
[51] *E.H.R.,* LVI p. 24; *C.H.,* III p. 445; A. F. Pollard, *The Evolution of Parliament,* (2nd edition), p. 433.
[52] 'In great matters, both legal and political, the final decision must rest with Parliament. Parliament must be summoned in due form by the king himself, it must include the commonalty of the realm as well as the magnates; the king must enact, but the common assent of the estates is essential to the validity of enactments.' *Medieval Representation and Consent,* p. 172.

[53] Ibid.
[54] Ibid.
[55] Ibid., p. 315.
[56] Ibid., pp. 247-316.

typical practice at all levels of feudal society, but it lacked representation. Representation was a well established feature of
royal government, particularly in the administration of justice, but it did not involve
consent. In the thirteenth century the English Church brought the two together in its
financial dealings with the crown. The clergy
insisted that, so far as they were concerned,
taxation should be related to representation
and consent. It was from this example,
so Miss Clarke holds, that the laity learned
the lesson 'quod omnes tangit ab omnibus
approbetur' ['what concerns all should be
approved by all'].[57]

As a whole these conclusions have not
commended themselves to those best able
to judge of their worth. For one thing it is
improbable that Miss Clarke's interpretation of the Statute of York, which closely
resembles that propounded by Stubbs, will
bear the weight of argument which rests
upon it. The significance of this Statute is
still a matter of acute controversy, but
those principally concerned, while they differ widely among themselves, are agreed
that Miss Clarke's view is untenable.[58] Then

there is the vexed question of the sense to
be attached to the term 'estates,' which
seems to have been used with a variety of
meanings, and some think that Miss Clarke
did not fully recognise the difficulties thus
presented.[59] Again her other arguments for
the date and reliability of the 'Modus' have
not been everywhere accepted.[60] On the
other hand what she has to say of the
ecclesiastical origin of the ideas of representation and consent may well be of great
future significance; for, as will later appear,
it seems to harmonise with the trend of
other recent work on the history of the
Commons under Edward I. No less important is Miss Clarke's insistence on the
need to discover what Parliament, in the
early stages of its growth, meant to contemporaries, and what they conceived its
purpose to be; for the nature of the record
material encourages the hazardous practice

---

[57] Miss Clarke was not, in the strict sense, a
pioneer in this field. Apart from earlier work
three modern scholars have paid particular attention to the problems of clerical taxation and
the use of representative devices in ecclesiastical government. Sir Ernest Barker, *The Domini-
can Order and Convocation* (Oxford, 1913);
Professor W. E. Lunt, *The Valuation of Norwich* (Oxford, 1926); Sir Maurice Powicke,
Stephen Langton (Oxford, 1928) chapter VI.
The novelty of Miss Clarke's approach lies in
the fact that she is concerned to explore the
interaction of lay and ecclesiastical activity in
these matters. Another interesting modern contribution to this topic, apparently unknown to
Miss Clarke, is to be found in the studies by
O. Hintze in *Historische Zeitschrift*, CXLI pp.
229-48; CXLIII pp. 1-47.

[58] The last clause of the Statute has been
the particular focus of discord. The interpretation put upon it by Hallam and Stubbs, although the latter was somewhat hesitant, made
it appear as a direct assertion of parliamentary
authority, as assuring to Parliament, at a very
early stage in its development, full legislative
competence, indeed as endowing it with a legislative monopoly. In 1913 Mr. G. Lapsley chal-

lenged this view, and from a more rigid exegesis of the Statute proposed a fresh interpretation. Put briefly, this restricted the legislation
contemplated in the disputed clause to matters
involving the royal prerogative. This provoked
a most learned controversy which is still unresolved. Few have supported Stubbs. Mr. Lapsley made some converts, but he also raised up
powerful opponents to argue that the purpose
of the disputed clause was to do exactly the
opposite of what he had supposed. Others, including Mr. Richardson and Dr. Sayles, have
been even more radical in refusing to attribute
any constitutional importance whatsoever to the
Statute of 1322. Lately Mr. Lapsley returned
to the charge, now contending that by the
Statute the Crown intended to sublimate the
violence of political controversy through the
agency of Parliament. This contribution, together with a summary of the previous stages
of the controversy, can be found in *E.H.R.*,
LVI pp. 22-51; 411-46, especially pp. 22-9. See
also G. L. Haskins, *The Statute of York and the
Interest of the Commons*, (Oxford, 1935).

[59] *American Historical Review*, XLII p. 733.
This is a review of *Medieval Representation
and Consent* by Mr. G. L. Haskins. Also
E.H.R., LVI pp. 37 ff. There is a useful treatment of this problem on a broad scale by Professor C. H. McIlwain in *Cambridge Medieval
History*, VII chapter XXIII.

[60] Miss Clarke's attribution of an early date
to the 'Modus' is supported by the independent
work of Professor W. A. Morris in *E.H.R.*,
XLIX pp. 407-22.

of deducing what was intended from what was done.

Professor Wilkinson's concern is not simply with Parliament.[61] His purpose is to exhibit the working connections of some of the chief organs of the central government in the thirteenth and fourteenth centuries. In so doing he goes further than many of the moderns, because his work is a kind of sketch plan of a new system for the medieval constitutional history of England.

His argument is based on the contention that medieval royal government here was shaped by a distinct political tradition, which has to be taken into account before the system it produced can be understood. This tradition embodied the notion of co-operation in government between king and people. But it was a form of co-operation based upon well recognised functional differences. The king, in Bracton's phrase, 'ordinariam habet jurisdictionem et dignitatem et potestatem super omnes qui in regno suo sunt, habet enim omnia jura in manu suo.'[62] Not only did he reign; he also ruled, and everyone recognised that it was his right, even his obligation, to do so. The king's personal power was exercised with the advice of the Council, whose members were his 'domestici.' The poltical duty of the community, the 'universitas regni,' on the other hand, was different although complementary. It must consent to changes in the law and to major decisions affecting the welfare of the kingdom. Its obligation covered those matters which are comprehended in the phrase 'magna negotia regis et regni.'* If the king erred, then its duty was extended to include the business of setting him right. In practice the magnates usually shouldered this whole burden on behalf of the rest. This, in itself, is not surprising, since they had long enjoyed a place of influence in the Curia Regis. At times, particularly in the reign of Henry III and again in that of Edward II,

the magnates over-reached themselves, for they sought to clamber up into the seat of power and sit there as of right. That they failed is, we are told, a testimony to the strength of the medieval political tradition, in the light of which such efforts were an intolerable usurpation of kingly authority.

Parliament fits into this scheme of things as 'the greatest of all expressions of the medieval tradition of government by consent and the co-operative state.'[63] It was the great assembly of the nation, political in its beginnings, where the king and those considered to represent the 'universitas regni' treated of the great affairs of the realm. According to Professor Wilkinson, medieval English government tottered to its fall in the fifteenth century, when the tradition upon which it was founded fell into disrepute. One sign of this was the slow strangulation of the king's personal authority, partly by magnate control of the Council, and partly by the growth of bureaucratic routine in the great departments of state. Another appeared when the 'universitas regni,' acting through Parliament, began to pervert its right and duty of consent into a power of control, especially in financial matters.

We are thus presented with Parliament and the Council as separate institutions, which, because they served different needs, had distinguishable functions in the state. The Council as a body had its place in Parliament, but Parliament was not, as Maitland and his successors have contended, an occasional, enlarged session of the Council. Instead Parliament, from its first beginnings, stands forth in its own right as the appointed means for achieving co-operation between king and people in discussing the great affairs of state. Evidence from the parliamentary writs is marshalled to show that, already in Edward I's time, invariable Chancery usage bestowed the title of Parliament only on an assembly in which the king and the 'universitas regni' met together to treat concerning the 'magna ne-

[61] B. Wilkinson, *Studies in the Constitutional History of the Thirteenth and Fourteenth Centuries,* (Manchester, 1937), especially pp. 1-54; 108-79; 247-72.

[62] Quoted ibid., p. 250.

* ['Great affairs of the king and the realm.']

[63] Ibid., p. 262.

gotia regis et regni.'[64] The Commons only come regularly into the picture towards the end of Edward II's reign, helped into what proved to be their secure and essential place by the Statute of York. Parliament's judicial function, based on remedy in response to petition, thus falls into a subordinate position. Dr. Wilkinson allows that judicial matters had some place in the business of thirteenth century Parliaments. He thinks that work of this kind increased in amount and became of greater significance after the Ordinances of 1311, which, he believes, stressed Parliament's judicial power. What he strenuously denies is that, at any time in the thirteenth or fourteenth centuries, Parliament's primary political function was overlaid, or in any way obscured by its judicial activity.

It is perhaps well to recognise that, so far as can be seen at present, no synthesis or even accommodation of Dr. Wilkinson's opinions with those of Mr. Richardson and Dr. Sayles is possible. If Parliament was in form an extension of the Council, and in essence a court, then it could not have been a distinct assembly of king, lords and commons occupied principally with high politics. To follow Dr. Wilkinson all the way thus involves not merely denying Mr. Richardson and Dr. Sayles, but also rejecting the fundamental doctrine of Maitland and McIlwain as well. Faced with this choice the need to probe the strength of Dr. Wilkinson's argument is plain.

Its most debatable feature is its treatment of the relations of the Council and Parliament before the middle of the fourteenth century. Here the test case is in the handling of the evidence provided in the proclamation of March 1305, which Maitland used to prove that the Council was the core of Parliament. Dr. Wilkinson holds that Maitland was wrong, but to support this contention he has to strain the text by putting on its words a meaning which, it is permissible to think, they will not bear.[65] To reinforce his view that Parliament was

distinct and self-sufficing at this time, Dr. Wilkinson further seeks to show that the Council did not then possess the power usually attributed to it.[66] Most scholars would say that certainly under Edward I and his son, and perhaps in Henry III's time too, the Council was the mainstay of the king's power and the agent of the prerogative. Ubiquitous and omnicompetent as it was, its members included magnates and 'ministeriales' as the king willed. Not so Dr. Wilkinson, for he argues that the business of the Council was to advise, not to act. Thus when, for example, he is faced with the Council actually exercising wide powers during Edward I's later years, he is compelled to say that this is altogether exceptional. The king was busied with foreign wars, and the Council, temporarily deprived of its ordinary work, acted in the king's place, wielding his authority. Yet, on the evidence, it is at least possible to argue that, in these and other exceptional circumstances, the Council was itself simply using the ordinary power normally exercised by the king with its executive help. Points like these seem to show that Dr. Wilkinson has not been completely successful, either in achieving a functional separation of Council and Parliament, or in establishing that the Council was predominantly advisory in character. Hence there is legitimate cause for refusing to accept his theory in its entirety.

Yet this should not blind us to the real strength of his argument for supposing that politics bulked large in the work of the early Parliament. Emphasis on this side of the matter will serve to introduce that part of the work of two other scholars, which bears closely upon the central problem of Parliament's early function and structure. They are Sir Maurice Powicke and Professor Plucknett. On this matter both rank as

[64] Ibid., pp. 25-36.
[65] Ibid., pp. 7-12. See above note 23.

[66] Ibid., pp. 108-79. New work on the Council in this period includes Sir Maurice Powicke, *King Henry III and the Lord Edward*, (Oxford, 1947), I pp. 290-342: and J. F. Baldwin, 'The King's Council,' in *The English Government at Work 1327-1336*, (ed. J. F. Willard and W. A. Morris, Cambridge, Mass., 1940), I pp. 129-61.

disciples of Maitland, because they recognise that Parliament grew up round the Council. But if they reject Dr. Wilkinson's theory on this essential point, they do not thereby commit themselves to the doctrines of Mr. Richardson and Dr. Sayles. On the contrary it is possible to see in their work the outlines of an approach to the early history of Parliament, substantially different from that favoured either by Miss Clarke and Dr. Wilkinson, or by Mr. Richardson and Dr. Sayles. The drawback here is that neither of them has had occasion to develop his views on the problem as a whole. Sir Maurice has dealt only with the very early stages of Parliament's growth as part of his massive study of the reign of Henry III. Professor Plucknett had to work within even narrower limits, for he was given the task of describing Parliament as it was in the first decade of Edward III's reign.[67]

In one important respect they both dissent sharply from the standpoint of Mr. Richardson and Dr. Sayles. Neither is prepared to regard Parliament at Edward I's accession as something already fixed and definite, as an established institution destined to retain its original form until well into the fourteenth century, when the long process of adding to its duties and enlarging its authority in the state began. They both prefer to think that the thirteenth century Parliament was still only in its formative stage, neither independent nor distinct in form and function. Professor Plucknett believes that its powers and composition only became reasonably settled and plain in the early part of the Hundred Years War.[68] Writing of Henry III's time Sir Maurice Powicke says this:—

The mystery which attends on the beginnings of parliament is not peculiar to these particular happenings. It is the mystery which attends on all beginnings, when men are doing things because they are convenient and do not attach conscious significance to them, still less consider what the distant outcome of their acts may be. The word was in the air, the materials were to hand . . . Nor should we injure the fragile uncertainties of these beginnings by too eager definition.[69]

According to his analysis the second half of Henry III's reign sees the central government making frequent and more systematic use of two devices. The first was the practice of reserving important judicial business for the early part of the law terms, when the judges, the barons of the Exchequer and the regular members of the Council could act in concert. The name Parliament was sometimes given to these proceedings, and it was coming to be thought that at least some of this business was best done when the magnates were present. The second, a device of much greater antiquity, was the practice of summoning the magnates to treat with the king on the affairs of the realm. To such meetings the name Parliament could also be applied, although often they did not coincide with the 'parliamentary' sessions for judicial business. This does not mean, however, 'that there were two kinds of parliament, but that there was a distinction between the conditions which made the king and his servants on the one hand, and the magnates on the other, aware of the value of parliament. In Edward I's time the co-incidence in time and place between parliament regarded from these two points of view is complete.'[70] It is chiefly for this reason that the reign is important in Parliament's early history.

Thus Sir Maurice Powicke does not feel that, despite official emphasis, the transaction of judicial business ought to be accepted as the exclusive mark of a true Parliament in this period. Unlike Mr. Richardson and Dr. Sayles he is therefore unwilling to use the judicial criterion as the means of making a sharp distinction, in

[67] Powicke, op. cit., I pp. 338-41 et passim; T. F. T. Plucknett, 'Parliament,' in *The English Government at Work 1327-1336*, I pp. 82-128. See also Ibid., pp. 12-29.
[68] Ibid., p. 108.

[69] Powicke, op. cit., I p. 340.
[70] Ibid., I p. 341.

the unbroken series of parliamentary assemblies, between those which were true
Parliaments, and those which were not. He
prefers to rest on the conviction that under
Edward I Parliament was still very mal-
leable. Justice, politics and finance were
jumbled together among its business, because the king and his principal subjects
found this convenient. For the same reason
its members, royal clerks and judges, prelates and lay magnates, joined only very
occasionally by knights and burgesses, were
not present in accordance with any clear or
predetermined scheme. The fact was that,
as yet, nobody had found reason to ponder
where such practices might eventually lead.

Writing of Parliament as it was in the
early years of Edward III's reign Professor
Plucknett still regards it as in process of
formation. He believes, however, that this
process was then near its end. While it is
true that 'in 1327 the clear cut technical
distinction which separated parliaments
from other assemblies was still unformed,'
there are many indications that it would not
remain so much longer.[71]

For one thing, at this time, about half
these parliamentary assemblies included the
commons, whereas between 1258 and 1300
they only attended one in every nine of the
gatherings usually reckoned as Parliaments.
Furthermore, the proctors of the lower
clergy were beginning to sever their connection with the parliamentary body, leaving
the knights and burgesses there to fend for
themselves. Again individual lords, both
spiritual and temporal, were summoned with
far more regularity and consistency than
was the case under Edward I.[72] Not only is

the composition of Parliament taking recognisable shape, but its characteristic functions are beginning to emerge more clearly.
Professor Plucknett leaves no room for
doubt here for he writes 'the legislative
side of parliament's work has by now become its most characteristic and important
activity, second only to its general political
and administrative supervision of the country': while parliamentary statutes 'had an
assured position at the very centre of legal
and constitutional life.'[73] At the same time
the judicial activity, which had occupied so
prominent a place in the parliamentary
assemblies of the previous century, was
slowly receding into the background. In
Edward III's early years Parliament 'was
nominally, rather than actually, the crown
of the judicial edifice.' This happened, we
are told, because in matters of justice the
Council remained strong enough to dominate the situation. Its judicial power was
exercised with vigour both in and out of
Parliament, so that there was small chance
of a specific kind of supreme judicial authority being reserved for Parliament alone.

No account of the matter would be complete if it failed to mention the work of
those who have concerned themselves with
particular aspects of the problem of Parliament's origin and early history. This includes the notable investigations which have
been made into the history of the Commons
in Parliament. Nowadays it is generally
recognised that the early history of Parlia-

---

[71] *The English Government at Work 1327-
1336,* I p. 85. In this connection Professor
Plucknett criticises the attempt made by Mr.
Richardson and Dr. Sayles to show that by this
time the term 'parliamentum' had acquired a
technical meaning in official usage.
[72] Since Professor Plucknett wrote Mr. Richardson has committed himself to a very definite
statement about the improvement of the constitutional power of the lords in the reign of
Edward II, which deserves mention here.
'A great and fundamental change in the constitutional position of the baronage had taken

place . . . (they) had not only made good in
practice their claim to control an evil king;
they had climbed into power and sat perpetually and without question beside the king . . .
From unmistakeable historical evidence we can
point to a narrow period within which this
political evolution was consummated; it must
be placed in the reign of Edward II. It is then
that the conception of peerage takes shape and
men begin to talk of peers of the land. Under
Edward I men had hardly thought of peers in
this sense, but before the reign of Edward II
had run its course the notion of peerage had
become thoroughly established in England.'
T.R.H.S., 4th series, XXVIII pp. 25-6.
[73] *The English Government at Work 1327-
1336,* I p. 117.

ment ought not to be confused with the early history of representation, and on every hand scholars acknowledge that the Commons, as an organised and self-conscious group, were of small importance before the end of the fourteenth century. Nevertheless it is still most necessary to discover how they came to be associated with Parliament at all, and how, having become established there, they contrived to make their place secure and to enlarge their authority.

The discussion of the first of these two problems has been carried a good deal further since Riess's time.[74] He argued that representatives from the shires and the towns were summoned to Parliament so that each might place before the king in Council the concerns of those by whom he had been sent, and, in returning, might carry home to them the king's commands. The French scholar, Dr. Pasquet, who was concerned with the Commons up to the death of Edward I, thought Riess failed to stress sufficiently their duty of granting money in Parliament, which Hallam had long before called 'unmistakably the principal cause of their being summoned during the first generation.'[75] All the same Pasquet endorsed Riess's principal contention when he said, 'it was above all as being themselves petitioners that the knights and burgesses came to Parliament and appeared before the Council.'[76] It would be foolish to deny that petitions bulked large in the business of Edward I's Parliaments, for, as Maitland pointed out, the powers of the other courts were narrowly limited, and Parliament was the place where the aggrieved might seek relief.[77] But as Dr. Wilkinson says 'it was the business of the subject to approach the monarch for this purpose (i.e. to petition) not the monarch to summon the subject.'[78] Recently Mr.

G. L. Haskins has shewn that during Edward I's time 'in their capacities as representatives and as individuals the knights and burgesses presented very few petitions at Parliament.'[79] In face of this it is difficult to suppose that the task of petitioning brought the Commons into Parliament. Further examination of their financial duties, however, has made it appear very likely that Edward I summoned them primarily for this purpose. They were to come armed with 'plena potestas,' 'full power,' from those who sent them, so that these latter might be legally bound to render such sums as were agreed in Parliament.[80]

It now looks as if this cause, which first operated to secure the Commons an occasional summons to Parliament, later did much to ensure their regular attendance, and to stimulate the fourteenth century beginnings of their organisation as a 'house.' Mr. Edwards has lately demonstrated that by 1338, when the Commons were just starting to come regularly to Parliament, the 'plena potestas' was evidently so far established as a legal attribute of the representatives, and some of its implications were so far realised, that it could provide counsel with a basis for legal argument in the king's own court.'[81] During the rest of Edward

[74] Above note 20.

[75] D. Pasquet, *Essay on the Origins of the House of Commons* (trans. by R. G. D. Laffan with notes by G. T. Lapsley, Cambridge, 1925), pp. 183 ff. H. Hallam, *Constitutional History of England* (edn. 1873), p. 24.

[76] Pasquet, op. cit., p. 201.

[77] Maitland, *Selected Essays*, p. 50.

[78] Wilkinson, op. cit., p. 21.

[79] G. L. Haskins, 'The Petitions of Representatives in the Parliaments of Edward I' in *E.H.R.*, LIII pp. 1-20.

[80] Two important studies bearing on this point are J. G. Edwards, 'The *"Plena Potestas"* of English Parliamentary Representatives,' in *Oxford Essays in Medieval History presented to H. E. Salter,* (Oxford, 1934); and C. Stephenson, 'Taxation and Representation in the Middle Ages,' in *Haskins Anniversary Essays,* (Boston, Mass., 1929). See also Miss Helen Cam's paper 'From Witness of the Shire to Full Parliament,' in *T.R.H.S.*, 4th series, XXVI pp. 13-35. Another important aspect of the matter has been explored by J. F. Willard, *Parliamentary Taxes on Personal Property, 1290-1334,* (Cambridge, Mass., 1934), and in his study 'Taxation Boroughs and Parliamentary Boroughs,' in *Historical Essays in Honour of James Tait,* (Manchester, 1933).

[81] J. G. Edwards, 'Taxation and Consent in the Court of Common Pleas, 1338,' in *E.H.R.*, LVII pp. 473-82.

III's reign the Commons were vigorously self-assertive in money matters, although in nothing else. Yet, as Mr. Richardson says, this should not lead us to suppose that they were already reaching out to grasp the power which would one day be theirs through the control of taxation. At this time their criticism of the king's financial demands and their grudging assent to what he asked, derived from the fact that they were moved 'by considerations of the kind that actuate modern rate-payers' associations.'[82] In other respects from about 1340 onwards the Commons reveal the defects rather than the promise of their situation in Parliament. Except in money matters the knights and burgesses were noticeably slow in achieving any real community of interest or purpose.[83]

Miss Rayner has lately argued that even in the matter of petitioning, so long thought to have been the foundation of their corporate power, the fourteenth century Commons made little headway.[84]

Far from exercising any sole right to petition king and council, they [the Commons] fall humbly into line with other petitioners who put forward petitions "en noun des communes," and so far as we can tell, the petitions actually framed by knights and burgesses were accorded no special pre-eminence, for they are mingled indiscriminately with the other "communes petitions."[85]

The circumstances of Richard II's reign appear to have involved the Commons, whether they liked it or not, more closely in political strife than had previously been the case. There is some dispute whether they showed any independence at all in this new situation. Mr. Richardson finds them wholly pliable and subservient to the king and the magnate opposition in turn. They were expected, he believes, to accept and acquiesce, and he thinks they did so without stint.[86] This, if Miss Cam's interpretation is followed, was also the view of a contemporary satirist, who in the poem 'Richard the Redeless,' sketched the Commons in one of Richard II's later Parliaments in most unflattering terms.[87] Mr. MacFarlane, however, dissents from this opinion.[88] He thinks that then, despite manipulated elections and the like, 'politics were a joint stock enterprise. Power was not concentrated in the hands of a few. It was distributed among king, magnates and commons in various and varying degrees, according to each man's wealth, affiliations and political capacity.'[89]

Finally, careful research by a number of scholars has revealed no general evidence of that widespread reluctance on the part of the Commons to serve in Parliament at this time, which was formerly held to have existed. For the knights, particularly, at-

[82] H. G. Richardson, 'The Commons and Medieval Politics,' in *T.R.H.S.*, 4th series, XXVIII p. 28.

[83] Miss M. McKisack has made an admirable study of the burgesses in her book *The Parliamentary Representation of the English Boroughs during the Middle Ages*, (Oxford, 1932). There are also articles bearing on this point by G. Lapsley, 'Knights of the Shire in the Parliaments of Edward II,' in *E.H.R.*, XXXIV pp. 25, 152; and by Miss K. L. Wood-Legh, 'Sheriffs, lawyers, belted knights in the Parliaments of Edward III,' in ibid., XLVI pp. 372-88. There is much valuable bibliographical information in the *Interim Report of the Committee on House of Commons Personnel and Politics 1264-1832*, (Command 4130, 1932).

[84] Doris Rayner, 'The Forms and Machinery of the "Commune Petition" in the Fourteenth Century,' in *E.H.R.*, LVI pp. 198-233; 549-70. On this matter there is also the work of Mr. H. L. Gray, *The Influence of the Commons on Early Legislation*, (Cambridge, Mass., 1932). The book contains much of great value, but it has been criticised on the ground that it fails to distinguish clearly between petitions originating with the Commons, and those which were common in the sense that they were of general interest and concern.

[85] *E.H.R.*, LVI p. 569.

[86] *T.R.H.S.*, 4th series, XXVIII p. 29.

[87] Helen Cam, *Liberties and Communities in Medieval England*, (Cambridge, 1945), pp. 223-35.

[88] K. B. MacFarlane, 'Parliament and "Bastard Feudalism,"' in *T.R.H.S.*, 4th series, XXVI pp. 53-73.

[89] Ibid., p. 73.

tendance seems to have formed part of the public service in the royal interest, in which they had long been schooled in their shires.[90]

A paper such as this calls for no elaborate conclusion. To provide one would distort its simple purpose of smoothing the way for those who wish to acquaint themselves with the modern literature of a fascinating but very intricate subject. Inevitably, since the great dispute about Parliament continues with unabated vigour, much space has had to be devoted to the reporting of controversy, and to the statement of conflicting opinions upon many vital points. Yet these matters, prominent although they are, should not be allowed to obscure the fact that very real progress has been made towards a more perfect understanding of the subject. It is no small achievement to have wrung so much new knowledge from such unpromising material, and what has already been done augurs well for what may yet be accomplished.

[90] J. G. Edwards, 'The personnel of the commons in parliaments under Edward I and Edward II,' in *Essays in Medieval History presented to T. F. Tout,* (Manchester, 1925); Miss K. L. Wood-Legh, 'The knights' attendance in the parliaments of Edward III,' in *E.H.R.,* XLVII pp. 398-413; N. B. Lewis, 'Reelection to parliament in the reign of Richard II,' in ibid., XLVIII pp. 364-94. For a contrary opinion lately expressed by Mr. H. G. Richardson see *T.R.H.S.,* 4th series, XXVIII pp. 38-9.

"NO FEATURE OF EARLY ENGLISH SOCIETY has attracted greater attention than the gilds," writes a well-known English economic historian in a recent book, and he adds that "none perhaps has been more consistently idealized." The gilds were products of an age of lively and intense localism, of a stage in social and economic history in which towns were the mainsprings of trade and industry and the state had not yet come to be thought of as an economic unit. Perhaps the most conspicuous economic function of the town, as differentiated from the surrounding countryside, was to provide a market, where commodities could be bought and sold. In general, however, the distinctions between urban and rural conditions were by no means as sharp in the Middle Ages as they came to be in later times. Even the larger medieval towns were rural to a great extent in their ways of life. There has been much conjecture and difference of opinion among historians regarding the origins of gilds; and gild history, like manorial history, is marked by variety rather than uniformity of interpretation. It was characteristic of gild regulations that they were social and ethical in motivation as well as economic, a point clearly illustrated in the rules governing apprenticeship in the craft gild. The object of the craft gild was to promote civic virtue as well as to train competent craftsmen. In the following essay, which is mainly concerned with the later Middle Ages, Professor Sylvia L. Thrupp, now of the University of Chicago, raises some basic questions concerning gild history and suggests some important problems that await solution. Professor Thrupp is the author of the admirable monograph *The Merchant Class of Medieval London, 1300-1500* (1948).

MEDIEVAL GILDS RECONSIDERED

SYLVIA L. THRUPP

I

Present-day economic historians display an uneasy feeling that medieval gilds have enjoyed much more attention than they deserve. Professor Heckscher compares them unfavorably with later gilds, Professor Gras grudges them credit for anything save the keeping of records to mislead historians, and the authors of a recent textbook almost apologize for pausing to describe them. In general, this reaction from former attitudes reflects a shift of interest from the interpretation of economic policy to other problems that now appear more fundamental. We have a quantity of information about gild policies, but it leaves us uncertain whether or not the gilds were of any real importance in the history of economic development.

There is relatively little work in English on the question, English gilds having long been treated mainly in relation to institutional or political history. Brentano's brilliant essay aroused interest, but chiefly in its political aspects. His central thesis, that gilds had everywhere been an instrument of class struggle, was never thoroughly explored, and controversy on the point died down without leading to any deeper investigation of the differences between English and Continental conditions. Gross applied Continental theory to the study of English gilds more cautiously. His familiar doctrine of the early formation of a heterogeneous merchant gild with a monopoly of trade in the borough, of the gradual evolution of specialized crafts within this body, and of the later evolution of mercantile interests within the crafts traces a most attractive abstract pattern. Gross himself realized that it did not apply to all towns in its entirety, since many lacked any record of a gild merchant. But, notwithstanding the exceptions to the first part of the theory, there has been a temptation to follow its second part quite blindly, without reference to the possible effects of differences in regional setting.

Thus it has been assumed that the separate crafts, conventionally but unhistorically described by the hybrid term "craft gilds," were evolved at the simplest stage of development compatible with a market, and that the later appearance of mercantile interests altered and finally broke up the gild system. "The essence of the craft gild," according to Mr. Lipson, lay in the combination of trading and handicraft functions in the hands of the master craftsman, who bought his raw material direct from the producer and sold his finished goods direct to the consumer. But this arrangement would obviously not have been convenient except when the raw materials in question were produced in the immediate vicinity of the town. In most places, then, it would have been characteristic only of the brewers, butchers, bakers, pastry cooks, and tallow chandlers, and of trades selling articles made of wood, leather, or wool, when these commodities were not in the hands of merchants. The situation was slightly different in the tailoring shops, where customers ordinarily brought their own cloth; other customers probably often saved other craftsmen, too, the trouble of procuring materials. This plan allowed the craftsman to operate with less capital. What is more important, it also allowed the general merchant to build up a business in raw materials. But it did not directly impair the independence of the master craftsman. In very small towns off the main highways of commerce it is well known that this elementary organization of industry persisted for centuries. Any one wanting goods not produced locally would have to seek them,

Reprinted by special permission from *The Journal of Economic History,* II (1942), 164-173. The footnotes which originally appeared with this essay have been omitted.

either in the stock of merchants traveling or living in the neighborhood, or else at a fair.

But in the larger centers of consumption there were not sufficient supplies obtainable locally for the craftsman to be able to buy at firsthand from the producer. Moreover, in the larger towns craftsmen who worked on materials that were imported from a distance, as was usually the case with wax and metals, certainly did not rely upon their customers for supplies. They bought from native or foreign merchants or their agents or through other middlemen. Maltmongers, cornmongers, and mealmen came to the assistance of the brewers and bakers. These two trades were under too close surveillance in the Middle Ages for any of their members to profit by buying supplies for their fellows. But in other crafts, especially if they produced wares that could be sold at country fairs, there was a tendency for some of the masters to specialize in dealing. Finally, there was a third set of conditions, under which craftsmen had no direct contact with either producer or consumer, but bought and sold through the agents of a local capitalist entrepreneur.

Far too little is known of the origins of gilds for any one to assert that they arose only under conditions that assured the handicraftsman's complete economic independence. It is certain, however, that at the earliest periods of which there is any definite record of their existence they were adapted to the varying circumstances of different types of trade and of cities differing widely in the size and nature of their population. For merchants to intervene in the organization of industry in the smaller and more remote places may have been an abnormal or late development, but in the larger medieval towns it was neither. In the great industrial cities of the Continent it must have coincided with the rise of their export trade. No English city could rank with the more famous manufacturing centers of Italy or the Low Countries, so that one would not expect the role of English merchants in regard to industry to have attained the same early importance. Yet the London weavers of the late thirteenth century were working on orders from local cloth merchants; this is known only because of friction between the two groups at that time, and it is stated that there had been a previous quarrel "in time whereof memory does not run." A list of London gilds amerced by the king in 1180 included several that, being assessed at a high rate and headed by prominent citizens, were presumably composed of wealthy merchants. Among them, paying the highest sum of all, were the goldsmiths. More likely than not they were already, as we know their successors to have been in the fourteenth century, wealthy merchant manufacturers controlling the conditions under which poorer workmen carried on their art.

Mercantile influence on English town industries may have been on the increase in the later Middle Ages, and it no doubt contributed to the splitting of companies into sections distinguished by the wearing of a livery. But to assume that every aspect

CHARLES GROSS: Professor of history at Harvard (d. 1909) who made important contributions to the study of English medieval history; among them are *The Gild Merchant* (1890), *A Bibliography of British Municipal History* (1897), and *Sources and Literature of English History from the Earliest Times to about 1485* (1900).

ELI F. HECKSCHER: Present-day Swedish historian whose two-volume *Mercantilism* (1935) is by far the most important scholarly contribution ever made to the study of that subject. Already it has become a classic in the literature of economic history.

EPHRAIM LIPSON: Present-day English scholar whose *Economic History of England* has become a standard work. A brief statement of the conclusions that have grown out of a lifetime of study devoted to economic history appears in his recently published *Growth of English Society*.

of its activity in that period was then necessarily new is unjustified and will remain so until there has been fuller research into conditions of the twelfth and thirteenth centuries. To imply that it was undermining the gild system of industry is absurd, for there was no such thing. The only sense in which one can speak of the gilds as forming a system is in regard to urban economic administration.

II

The gilds everywhere represented congeries of special interests, loosely bound together, under the aegis of municipal authorities, by a common care for the quality of goods sold. To assess their influence upon economic development requires a more detailed knowledge of industry, trade and finance, and also of urban politics, than is yet generally available either for England or continental Europe. A good deal of interest has been shown in the problems of their potential influence in critical phases of transition, but the results are on the whole inconclusive.

The change with which they are perhaps chiefly associated is the increasing tendency, at the end of the Middle Ages, for industry to be located in the country. It is apparent that many gilds became obstinately conservative and exclusive, and hence may have helped to deflect new enterprise from their town. Yet they are not necessarily to blame for every case of urban decline before village competition, for in any large-scale diversion of industry to the country other factors would surely have been at work.

Another problem is that of their influence upon technological progress. Here the negative character of the findings may be illustrated from the story of the introduction of the fulling mill, run by water power, in the neighborhood of London. There is no evidence of the reactions of the townsmen during the first phase of this innovation, but it may be surmised that the cloth merchants were quick to make use of it and and impatient with opposition from the city fullers,

Sir John Pulteney, a rich draper, ten years an alderman and four times mayor of London, is known to have acquired one of the mills, at Stepney, early in the fourteenth century. In 1298 the civic authorities reluctantly allowed the fullers the right of making search at the city gates with the object of preventing either fullers, weavers, or dyers from sending cloth to the mills; they were not to interfere, however, if the sender swore that the cloth was his own. Efforts to enforce the ban were renewed in 1311 and 1342, but the cloth-making crafts were plainly so permeated by mercantile interest that they were soon able to adapt themselves to the use of the mills. In 1376 both the fullers and the drapers are found disapproving of the practice of fulling caps at the mills, on the grounds that the fulling mills damaged their cloth. Further action and controversy in London over mechanical fulling related solely to this question of caps, the hurers, "men of low degree and simple," having intermittent success in opposing the desire of the hatters and haberdashers, a mercantile craft, to patronize the mills.

To discuss whether or not gilds hindered the rise of entrepreneurial activity is clearly useless. They embodied all of the diverse interests concerned in the movement. The greater merchants, having ordinarily a dominant influence in town government, tended sometimes to abuse their power, but the situation varied from place to place and at different periods. In the lesser trades, those in which there was very little capital invested, the mutual jealousies of the masters tended to hinder the rational combination of related industrial processes under one management. Yet it is doubtful whether in the smaller towns, where there were too few men in the minor crafts to keep up efficient gild organizations, there would have been many hindrances of the kind.

III

The hardest work that lies ahead of gild historians is in studying the question of monopoly. The most involved of all their problems, it is at the same time the only one to which reasonably exact answers, as expressed in price trends, might ultimately be expected. Meanwhile a certain sifting of theories advanced and facts available is in order.

The idea that gilds passed through two phases, an early phase in which they were anxious to throw their ranks wide open, and a later one in which they became exclusive and monopolistic, though probably in a great many cases true, needs to be qualified. On the one hand, in trades that were obnoxious, such as butchering and tanning, or in which equipment was limited, as in baking, there was often a natural tendency, from a very early date, to keep membership down. In all victualing trades monopolistic tendencies were chronic. That was one of the reasons why they were kept under closer supervision than other crafts. Wyclif denounced merchant victualers as "false conspiratours . . . cursed of God and man," because they manipulated prices by secret agreements. There is no reason at all to imagine either that the practice was new in his time, or that it was ever seriously checked, for price control was attempted only through the retailer. Fifteenth-century records show that breach of price agreements among merchants, though naturally not one of the offenses punishable by a term in the city prison was subject to heavy fines and disciplinary boycott. In industry, again, when the raw materials used were found locally in great abundance, or when there was an expanding market for the goods produced, or when the capital of merchants was attracted for these or other reasons, it is highly improbable that craftsmen could ever have succeeded in attaining a monopoly within an exclusive gild.

On the other hand, although the fact that many gilds tended to become more exclusive as time passed cannot be contested, open claims to monopoly need not be taken at their face value. In industry it was always difficult to enforce them. When the tailors of Namur in the later Middle Ages forbade

mothers to teach their girls to sew, they no doubt encountered trouble. Again, statements implying that there was an increasing tendency for gilds to become hereditary or caste-like in character in the later Middle Ages may be taken with a grain of salt unless they are supported by actual genealogical research. Chances of family survival were less favorable in the fourteenth and fifteenth centuries than in the thirteenth century.

The most important aspect of the whole problem is to judge how far craftsmen deliberately restricted output; it is probable that the practice was in inverse ratio to the influence of merchants over their trade. Gild control over the recruiting of masters and the training of labor, however, was general. Conceded in the interests of maintaining high technical standards of work, it obviously lent itself to abuse. But ordinances controlling the number of apprentices and journeymen that a master might employ were not necessarily effective. In the fourteenth century there appears to have been a general shortage of labor, and in later fifteenth-century London, where population may have been on the increase again, the rules were in some cases invoked only when there was already considerable unemployment in the trade. There were many ways of evading the rules. Men could join a gild temporarily, simply for the purpose of registering apprentices whose terms of service would presently be sold. It is very unlikely that a gild could restrain members from expanding their workshops when they had the capital to do so. A merchant who had dual membership in the companies of mercers and pewterers in mid-fifteenth century London employed eleven apprentices and seven hired workers in his pewter business; the average per member in the company at that time was two apprentices and about three-quarters of a servant, and later regulations permitted a maximum of three apprentices.

Another difficult question that bears upon the problem of gild control over prices is that of the ownership of transport facilities.

Members of merchant companies coöperated both in hiring convoys for their overseas trade and in arranging for the services of porters to convey their goods from waterfront to warehouse. But the organization of inland and coastal transport is a very obscure subject.

IV

Gilds were of obvious service to their members in a number of other ways that have been so often described one hardly dares mention them again in a journal devoted to research. They restrained competitive bidding that threatened to raise rents; they maintained extensive loan funds; they dispensed relief in sickness and poverty. The right of taking a part of fellow gildsmen's purchases at the original price, on which Gross laid so much stress, may refer less to the conscious fostering of coöperative policies in trade than to the common and convenient practice of buying in small groups in order to obtain better terms of credit. Coöperative purchase of industrial supplies was resorted to only in emergencies. Despite these qualifications, the usefulness of the gild should not be underestimated. Indeed historians and economists unfamiliar with the contours of the medieval scene may not always fully appreciate it. Especially in the later Middle Ages, medieval townsmen had incessantly to contend with the disasters of war, epidemics, and local crop failures; they suffered at the best of times from shortage of capital; moreover, outside the Mediterranean area, the custom of insurance had not established itself. In these circumstances the gilds may have been of invaluable help in maintaining the continuity of economic activity on as even a keel as possible.

To any one sharing Marshall's broadminded interest in whatever aspects of history throw light upon human nature, the gilds are of still further importance. It has often been remarked that many trade gilds were based upon a fraternity life similar to that of the parish gilds. In common with the latter they gave expression not only to

religious faith and conviviality but also to certain social needs and ideals and forms of class consciousness. Industrial gilds, for example, were at pains to cultivate a spirit of thrift and temperance and to discourage idleness. Brethren of their fraternities were eligible for relief only if their need were the result of circumstances beyond their control. No skinner in Norwich could expect alms in any misfortune resulting from "his foly," nor could any carpenter there risk indulging in "ryoutous lyvyng." Parish gilds, which in London drew the majority of their members from people of middling social rank, showed the same strictness. One withheld alms from any who had suffered "through plunder by harlots or any other bad way of life"; and the ordinances of another paint a most beguiling picture of the temptations that beset the weak-willed townsman:

> If ony man . . . use hym to ly long in bed; and at rising of his bed ne will not work ne wyn his sustenaunce and keep his house, and go to the tavern, to the wyne, to the ale, to wrastling, to schetyng, and this manner falleth poor, and left his cattel in his defaut for succour; and trust to be holpen by the fraternity: that man shal never have good, ne help of companie, neither in his lyfe, ne at his dethe; but he shal be put off for evermore of the companie.

In these and in the ordinances seeking to restrain apprentices from gambling and journeymen from coming to work still stupid from their "drinkings" of the night before, one sees the petty bourgeois master, the only medieval figure who cherished any love of the economic virtues for their own sake, fighting an uncertain battle for some measure of efficiency in industry.

The spirit of the great merchant companies was differently keyed. It set a high value on the qualities of dignity, decency, and courtesy and also held the economic virtue of prudence in esteem. But with the passage of time, as the history of innumerable towns will tell, the prudence of the merchants gave way before habits of ostentation and luxury.

Pride in their gild led them on. The cost of membership of gilds mounted with the cost of building and maintaining fine halls, wearing liveries of startling color, and holding splendid banquets. All the gilds alike, by giving office to their wealthier members, encouraged the custom of showing respect to the rich. Snobbery flourished among them. Spurred on to imitate their social superiors, the greater merchants, the members of the lesser gilds strained their resources to outshine each other in magnificence, and gradually relaxed their hold on the humble economic virtues on which they might have built a greater industrial prosperity. Snobbery and extravagance made for exclusiveness and deadened enterprise. By this road, the gilds leading the way, medieval urban culture strayed into an economic and social cul-de-sac.

DURING THE MIDDLE AGES THE CLERGY in England, as in Christendom generally, was the learned class par excellence, and members of this class, known in England as "clerks" (a word derived from the Latin *clericus,* meaning usually a person in orders), were employed extensively in carrying on the political and administrative functions of secular government. The medieval chancellors of England were almost all clergymen. At the same time it was customary to reward government officials by appointment to ecclesiastical office. Before the close of the Middle Ages, however, what we may call the English civil service came to include laymen, men who had not had the same opportunities for higher education as were open to the clergy. Yet these lay officials could not have been uneducated men, although little is known about the kind of training they received. A considerable number of medieval English officials, clerical and lay, made contributions of greater or less importance to English learning and literature, as writers, as patrons of scholarship, as collectors of libraries, and in other ways. In the following survey the foremost authority on medieval English administrative history, the late Professor Thomas Frederick Tout, of the University of Manchester, offers it as his opinion that an appreciable part of fourteenth-century English literature was the work of men who were, or had been, employed in the service of the state. By English literature he means works of all kinds written by Englishmen in any language, "it being understood that most books made in England were then written in Latin, some in French, and some in English." The most famous of medieval English poets, Geoffrey Chaucer, was a product of the civil service.

LITERATURE AND LEARNING IN THE ENGLISH CIVIL SERVICE IN THE FOURTEENTH CENTURY

THOMAS FREDERICK TOUT

The Mediaeval Academy of America aims at bringing into a common organisation all scholars devoting themselves to the study of some aspect of the Middle Ages. It is, therefore, a society of specialists, for to the outsider mediaeval study is in itself a specialised field. Yet all of us who seek to make a permanent contribution to knowl-

Reprinted by special permission from *Speculum,* IV (1929), 365-389.

edge cannot hope to attain our purpose, if we take the whole of mediaeval life as our province. The outlook is too vast, the ground to be covered indeed enormous. We are, therefore, compelled to further special-isation within our special subject. And the more deeply we delve into our own particu-lar patch of knowledge, the more com-pletely we become engulfed in it and, there-fore, indifferent to the labors of workers in adjacent fields. In the long run each spe-cialist tends to erect round himself a thick hedge of incuriousness that blocks his fel-low workers out of vision. It is useless to complain of such a process. It is the condi-tion precedent to the advance of science. Yet it is an evil thing for all that, for knowl-edge is not really split up into water-tight compartments. We can properly appreciate our own particular work only if we bring it into relation with the work of those who are dealing with closely allied studies. To establish easily such relations, the workers on adjoining fields must meet together, com-pare notes, put into plain language the general results of their investigations, and set up, so to say, a clearing-house, where ideas can be exchanged and different points of view presented. Thus only can we attain such a general synthesis as will make our knowledge complete.

I may perhaps be permitted to make my own case a personal illustration of this two-fold process. I have been engaged for more years than I care to remember in investigat-ing the administrative machinery of the mediaeval English state. To understand that machine properly one has to learn some-thing about the men engaged in working that machine. Gradually one comes to the conclusion that, before the beginning of the fourteenth century, perhaps even earlier, the government of England was largely in the hands of a body something like the per-manent civil service of the modern state. This civil service was in its origin a branch of the household service of the king. As government became more complex, there arose, in fact if not in name, a differentia-tion between the servant of the crown, who worked in the ever-itinerating household of his master, and the servant of the state, who became gradually established in some per-manent government office, located for the most part in London or Westminster. This civil service was, like the civil service of the modern British state, permanent in character and 'non-political' in the sense that it went on with its work with little regard to changes of monarch or changes of ministers. Its members were professional men who made their career and earned their living in the service of the state and went on with their work until death, promotion, pension, or dismissal brought their official careers to an end. They were thus essentially like our modern civil servants, but yet in some ways they were extraordinarily dif-ferent. One great point of contrast is that to most of them the service of the state was not their exclusive profession. They were to a large extent clerks, that is actual or potential ecclesiastics, capable of ordin-ation to minor or holy orders, and often were ordained priests or deacons. They were, therefore, competent to receive ecclesi-astical preferment as the reward for their political services. As a result, a large num-ber of smaller benefices and prebends in the church fell to them. Moreover, as the modern distinction between the permanent servants of the state and 'political' ministers of the state had not yet arisen, the pro-moted civil servant might well become a minister of state, a chancellor, or a treas-urer, as well as a bishop or an archbishop. To follow their careers to the end, the ad-ministrative historian must go to the ec-clesiastical historian. If this is easy in the case of the shining lights who became min-isters or bishops, it is difficult when we come to the lesser personages who had their re-ward in livings, prebends, deaneries, or other less conspicuous posts. And even when we have painfully compiled a list of their preferments, and perhaps added to this some account of their property and estates, such as official records often supply, we are still quite unable to picture to ourselves what manner of men they were, what were their ideals, their ambitions, their characters, their personalities, their education, their habits, and their amusements. This difficulty is enhanced in the course of the fourteenth, and still more during the fifteenth, century, when the lay civil servant came increasingly to the fore, gradually making his way into posts hitherto regarded as the exclusive preserve of the clerk, so that the word clerk began to connote not ecclesiastic so much as writer. For the career of the lay officer, we can get no help from the abundant records of the church, though, if his promotion be political, we may perchance know the names of his offices and the dates of his appointments from the records of the state. Failing this, we are hardly able to catalogue the dry bones of his career, as we can with the clerical official.

I must, however, pull myself up. To make alive the career of the mediaeval official would require a book and not a lecture, and, moreover, would need gifts of imagination and presentation that seldom fall to the lot of the poor scholar. To-day I want to take only one single aspect of this large subject by suggesting one way in which the administrative historian needs the coöperation of the academic historian and of the literary historian, almost as much as he needs the help of the historian of the church. The former may in some cases tell him how the mediaeval civil servant was educated and what his relations were to educational foundations. The latter will occasionally help him to realise what manner of man he was by the books which he wrote. Both will illustrate my theme of the relations of the mediaeval civil service to literature. To save overcrowding the canvas, I shall draw most of my illustrations from the fourteenth century, not only because it is the period that I have most in my mind, but because it gives us the best evidence of the activities with which I am concerned.

My chief thesis to-day is that an appreciable proportion of fourteenth-century English literature came from the civil servants of the state. By English literature I mean books written by Englishmen, in whatever tongue they were written, it being understood that most books made in England were then written in Latin, some in French, and some in English. To write good books in any tongue involves a good education, and I may perhaps begin with a few words about the education of the civil servants of the Middle Ages. That he was a fairly well educated man is clear from his works. He had, for example, to have a reading and writing knowledge of three languages. Assuming English to be his mother tongue (an assumption not always warranted in the fourteenth century), his official vernacular was certainly French until the very end of the period, and his official communications, so far as they were formal, were generally made in Latin, though

COTTON MANUSCRIPTS: Manuscripts from the collection of Sir Robert Cotton, antiquary, member of Parliament, and friend of Parliamentary leaders in the early-Stuart period. He was a life-long collector of manuscripts and records and founder of the great Cottonian Library, which later became one of the basic collections in the Library of the British Museum.

JOHN LELAND: Eminent sixteenth-century antiquary. A supporter of the Reformation, he was commissioned by Henry VIII to search the libraries of the monasteries and colleges of England for important literary and historical materials. His extensive manuscript collections were scattered. The seventeenth-century antiquary Thomas Hearne brought out a considerable body of Leland's papers in a six-volume collection, known as Leland's *Collectanea*.

again, as the century grew older, the official language became to an increasing extent French. To this we must add a wide acquaintance with official forms and precedents, the traditions of his office, the corresponding formalities and traditions of foreign courts and offices, skill in the art of *dictamen* or literary composition and form, and a good knowledge of law, municipal, civil, and ecclesiastical. How was all this knowledge obtained? Mainly, I feel convinced, by apprenticeship under a master, the method in which all knowledge was acquired in the Middle Ages. The junior official copied forms under direction, until he was skillful enough to write them on his own responsibility. Ultimately he became, in his turn, the master, that is, the instructor and director, of his juniors. The clerk may also have gone to a university, but a university training and degree were, I am convinced, the exception rather than the rule. That can be proved by the rarity with which the individual official is designated by the coveted title of 'master,' which, like its equivalents 'doctor' or 'professor,' then denoted the attainment of a full university degree in any recognised faculty.

The Chancery, whose sphere took in all administration and the higher secretarial work, was the most learned of the government offices, and we know that occasionally a graduate of distinction was brought in from the outside and given from the beginning a conspicuous post. But it is an illusion to think that 'masters of chancery'—a rare term before the end of the fourteenth century—were so called because they were commonly masters of arts or doctors of laws. They were so called because they had the privilege of acting as masters of the junior clerks who served under them and whom they introduced into official life. Moreover, the members of a north European university were, in the Middle Ages, clerks by the fact of their studentship, and there was, therefore, no place in the university for the lay element, which was now becoming increasingly prominent in the civil serv-

ice. Of course, a university-trained clerk could easily renounce his clergy for a lay career, culminating perhaps in knighthood. Doubtless there were other places than the university where a lay aspirant to the civil service might receive an education. Perhaps already, as certainly in the fifteenth century, he might frequent the London law schools which, I imagine, owed their very existence to the fact that the university had no place for the lay student or for the student of common law. I feel fairly convinced that the normal school of the civil servant was a sort of apprenticeship, either in the royal household or in some government office under a senior officer. We have instances of civil servants using the standard manuals of *dictamen,* or the art of literary composition, and themselves compiling treatises on the common forms of documents for the use of themselves or their office. I shall return to this question later when dealing with the concrete problem of the education of that eminent lay civil servant, Geoffrey Chaucer.

However this may be, it is clear from his works that the mediaeval civil servant had somehow the opportunity of a good education. Like most mediaeval education, its tendency was technical rather than humanistic. Its object was not to widen the mind, but to give a man the tools of his trade. Subject to these limitations, the mediaeval civil servant had the training which enabled him, on occasion, to befriend literature and science and, in some cases, to make personal contributions to them. This was in the very dawn of our civil service and remains true of the present day, despite the increasing call of the exacting modern state on the services of its members.

Professor Haskins has suggested, even as regards the twelfth century, that literature, though never a department of government, has its importance to those who, like myself, are concerned with administrative history. 'It is,' he says, 'at least a phase of the larger life of the mediaeval court and thus not without its contacts with actual administration.' To see what these contacts were in the twelfth century, when administrative history as a serious study begins, I need only refer to Stubbs' two lecturers on 'Learning and Literature at the Court of Henry II' and to the admirable supplement in Dr Haskins' paper on 'Henry II as a Patron of Literature,' which he contributed not long ago to a volume in which I take a particular interest.[1] It is enough to note that among the men who practised the literary craft at that great king's court, were Richard FitzNeal, the exchequer magnate, who wrote the *Dialogus de Scaccario* and I know not what beside; the mighty justiciar, Ranulf Glanville with his famous law book; and that humbler 'clerk of chancery' (if we may anticipate a later phrase) who wrote one of the lives of the great chancellor who became St Thomas of Canterbury. If the literary stream flowed less copiously from the court during the thirteenth century, it revived after the death of Edward I. It is with this revival that we have chiefly to do.

The civil servants of the fourteenth century with direct literary interests may be divided into three classes. Firstly, there were, conspicuously and clearly, men of the academic type who had, before their entrance into state service, studied and taught at a university. There were, secondly, the men who, without being themselves profound scholars, posed as patrons of learning, friends of learned men, collectors of libraries, benefactors of universities, or pious founders of academic colleges. Thirdly, there were (most important of all) the men who themselves made solid contributions to literature. Each class shades into the other, and the line between them is hard to draw, just as it was difficult in those days to make our modern distinction between civil servant and political minister, since, as in modern imperial Germany, the minister was often the promoted civil servant, and the modern differentiation of professions had hardly begun. There is, moreover, the trouble that always besets the mediaevalist when he finds that

very different things are being done at the same time by a person with a given name. He is always in doubt whether these things are all the work of the same man or whether they suggest two different persons with precisely the same name, and how, assuming the second possibility to be true, he can divide the acts done between these hypothetically separate individuals. Perhaps we shall clear up the ground best if we begin with these doubtful identifications. This we can do the more rapidly since, with one possible exception, they concern personalities of no great importance.

This possible exception is that of John Wycliffe. We all know that 'John Wycliffe' appears in the later part of Edward III's reign, doing so many different things that many have been led to insist on there being two John Wycliffes and some have gone so far as to believe that only the hypothesis of three John Wycliffes will explain all the facts. This is a problem on which I have no views, but it is one irrelevant to our present purpose, for the great John Wycliffe, who is undoubtedly the only Wycliffe who was at any time in the service of the state, cannot be regarded as, in modern speech, a member of the permanent civil service, though he was so frequently employed by the crown on special missions that he called himself 'specialis regis clericus.' We may, however, dismiss him and go on to the less distinguished persons more regularly in the royal service, whose identity is doubtful. They are all too obscure to make it worth while to tarry long over them, but they are numerous enough to make their cases worth consideration.

First among them comes Roger Waltham, king's clerk, who was keeper of Edward II's wardrobe in 1322 and 1323. As the head of the wardrobe was nearly always a promoted wardrobe clerk, he was likely to have been a permanent officer of the household. About the same time, there flourished a scholastic philosopher named Roger Waltham, who wrote a *Compendium Moralis Philosophiae*, which survives in several manuscripts, though it has, I believe, never

---

[1] *Essays in Medieval History presented to Thomas Frederick Tout* (Manchester University Press, 1925).

been printed. It has had some reputation at different times and has been used by Sir John Fortescue in the fifteenth century and by Dr Charles Plummer and Mr C. L. Kingsford in our own days. It is not a treatise on moral philosophy, but a series of disquisitions on the duties of princes, enforced by historical examples. Mr Kingsford, who was an excellent scholar, wrote Roger's life in the *Dictionary of National Biography* and accepted the identification of the author with the keeper of the king's wardrobe. Dr Plummer, another excellent scholar, is more doubtful. The probability is that we have no means for coming to a positive decision, but I regret that in my brief reference to Waltham in my *Administrative History,* I did not mention the possibility of his having been an author.

It is a far cry from Roger Waltham at one end of the century to Roger Walden at the other. Roger Walden's career, both in the public service and in the church, is perfectly well known. Under Richard II he was in turn treasurer of Calais, king's secretary, and treasurer for the exchequer. His devotion to Richard II and prerogative elevated him, in 1397, to the archbishopric of Canterbury, and he was so well liked and so pliant that, though forced out of the primacy on the restoration of the deposed Archbishop Arundel by Henry IV, he was soon made bishop of London and died in peace and prosperity. The good will of Arundel to his supplanter discounts the statement of Lancastrian partisan chroniclers that he was illiterate and insufficient. But I am pretty sure that we cannot sustain as proof of his literacy the attribution to him of an unpublished chronicle, still lurking in two manuscripts in the British Museum. 'This chronicle is,' says my old colleague, Professor Tait, 'a manuscript collection of chronological tables of patriarchs, popes, kings and emperors, misleadingly entitled *Historia Mundi.*' A note at the beginning of the copy in a Cotton manuscript ascribes this jejune performance to Roger Walden. The late Mr. Wylie was prepared to accept this and suggested that the period between Walden's removal from Canterbury and his establishment at London, gave him the time to compose what he wrongly called a *General History*. Unluckily, the attribution has no weight, for it is written in a sixteenth-century hand, while the Cotton manuscript itself goes back to the early thirteenth century, a fact fatal to the assignation of its authorship by a man who lived into the fifteenth century! Moreover, the other manuscript of the same document has a similar note ascribing its authorship to our friend Roger Waltham, who lived almost two generations earlier! Nothing can be made of 'evidence' such as this.

It is the same with another wardrobe clerk, William Pakington, who spent a long life in the public service, being for many years general receiver to Edward, the Black Prince, and, after his death, to his widow, Joan of Kent. Their son, Richard II, took Pakington into his own service, and he acted from 1377 to 1396 as keeper of the king's wardrobe. Of him Leland in the sixteenth century said that he wrote a French chronicle, ranging from the ninth year of King John to his own time, and dedicated it to the Black Prince. In his *Collectanea* Leland translated some passages of what he said was a French epitome of this book. There the matter rested until in 1904 Dr Brie, the German editor of the English *Brut Chronicle,* claimed that he had discovered this epitome,[1] and explained, rather pompously, his 'Recovery of an Anglo-Norman Chronicle' in a short pamphlet, in which he maintained that this was an abstract of the Chronicle which Leland had assigned to Pakington. Dr Brie held forth prospects of a fuller statement of his position in an elaborate introduction which he contemplated to his edition of the English *Brut*. This introduction, so far as I know, has never been published. But on the evidence before us, it may be said categorically that both Leland and Dr Brie are wrong. I have examined the Cotton manuscript in question and find nothing in it that associates Pakington with the work. I find that even Leland's descrip-

[1] In *MS. Cotton Tib. A. VI,* 455-470.

tion is very inexact. It begins, not in the ninth year of the reign of King John, but with Harthacnut in the middle of the eleventh century. It becomes very fragmentary after 1333, and its last entry is in 1346, when the Black Prince was a boy, and long before a man who lived till 1390 was likely to have entered into his service. Indeed I cannot prove that Pakington served the Black Prince before 1364. We may, therefore, dismiss the literary claims of Pakington as decisively as we have dismissed those of Roger Walden.

From civil servants whose literary credentials are unfounded we pass to those whose pretensions are doubtful though plausible. At the head of these I would place Richard of Bury, bishop of Durham, the reputed author of one of the most human and attractive of mediaeval literary efforts, the *Philobiblon*. Bury's claims to be a civil servant cannot be gainsaid. He is a typical professional servant of the crown who, in the course of a long career, worked his way up from humble beginnings to the highest posts in church and state. He was from his earliest years in the service of Edward of Windsor, when the future Edward III, a mere boy in years, was still only earl of Chester. Beginning as clerk of the justice of Chester, he rose to be chamberlain of Chester, the chief clerical officer of the palatinate, who not only managed its finances as a chamberlain naturally would, but was keeper of the Chester seal, and therefore the head of its chancery, or department of general administration. He was taken from Cheshire to southwestern France when his master became duke of Guienne and, as constable of Bordeaux, did the same sort of mixed financial and administrative work which he had performed when chamberlain of Chester. This duty kept him away from England during the troubles which led to Edward II's deposition. But he came back with his master in 1326, and his public advance was thereafter ensured. As wardrobe clerk, ultimately cofferer and treasurer of the wardrobe, and as keeper of the privy seal, he went through every stage of household service and finally

attained the great political posts of treasurer and chancellor, while in the church he rose to the great palatine bishopric of Durham. Bury held every office imaginable in turn, except perhaps that of tutor to Edward III, which was assigned to him by the tradition of the next generation, though in reality this tutorship was held by an obscure successor of his as chamberlain of Chester, named John Paynel, parson of Rostherne.

Bury has his real place in literary history as an indefatigable bookhunter, the collector of a library which was bequeathed to an Oxford college belonging to the monks of his cathedral at Durham. His most famous literary act was that he was the cause of the composition of the most attractive of mediaeval treatises on the love of books. But I do not believe that Richard himself wrote the *Philobiblon,* though personal vanity made him willing to accept the credit of it. He was a professional administrator and not more highly educated than the mass of household clerks. Adam Murimuth, the chronicler, speaks with contempt of his illiteracy and his foolish wish to be thought a 'great clerk.' This is, however, a rather prejudiced judgment, for, if Richard were not learned, he certainly wished to learn and was keenly interested in books and in all things academic. His assiduity in book-collecting, perhaps even book-stealing,—for then, as now, it was hard to separate the two hobbies,—is well attested by some famous passages in the *Philobiblon,* which, if not his, doubtless contains his sentiments. Moreover, it is brought home by the concrete fact of his library and the assignment of it by him to public use. His interest in matters academic is indicated by the frequency with which he went to Cambridge to examine the scholars of the King's Hall, a society set up by Edward II, where boy choristers of the King's Chapel, after their voices had broken, might be trained up to serve in the clerical offices of state. It is even more strikingly demonstrated by the fact that, when of mature years and after a long official career, he obtained an indult for three years non-residence on his benefices to allow him to pursue his studies at a university. Luckily or otherwise, Richard's elevation to the see of Durham cut short his academic ambitions. One new indication of his anxiety to pose as a scholar may, I venture to suggest, have made its mark in the English public records. I notice that in records he is often officially described as 'dominus' and sometimes as 'magister.' Now *magister*—master—was a title which involved a full degree in some university faculty, while *dominus*—foolishly Englished by moderns as 'sir,' which normally meant a knight—was the common title given to such clerks as had not the definite status of a master. Once, at least, I observed that 'magister Ricardus de Bury' had been struck out and 'dominus' substituted, as if some pedantic purist had erased the misleading title and reduced Richard to his proper level. On the other hand, his kinsman, Simon de Bury, is always called 'magister.' But he clearly had a right to that designation.

Richard of Bury's patronage of learning in no wise stands alone. Predecessors in such work may be well represented by Walter Merton, the household clerk of Henry III, whom the jealous king continued to regard as a member of his household even when he became chancellor of England, the more so since in the late thirteenth century the distinction, emphasised by Bury, between the offices of the court and the great offices of state had not yet been drawn. As the founder of the first college on a large scale at Oxford, Merton has a place of his own in academic, if not in literary, history. Similarly the natural successor of Bury in the patronage of academic learning was William of Wykeham. A link between Merton and Bury was Walter Stapeldon, the famous reforming treasurer of Edward II and founder of Exeter College, Oxford, though Stapeldon, a professional civil lawyer, was perhaps never what we should call a civil servant. A more natural successor to Bury was William of Wykeham, both in his career as a servant of the state and in the noble benefactions which set up a new and magnificent type of the endowment of study and learning in the twin foundations of the School of St Mary's at Winchester and its correlative, the new College of St Mary's, at Oxford.

Like Bury, Wykeham was in the strictest sense a civil servant by profession, working his way up from humble beginnings to confidential posts in the royal household and then rising to the keepership of the privy seal and finally to the great offices of state and the bishopric of Winchester. Like Bury, Wykeham was primarily an administrator, and his unblushing pluralism supplied him with the resources of which he made good use in his two foundations as well as in his virtual rebuilding of his cathedral. He was anticipated in the latter task by his predecessor, Bishop Edington, also a politician and prelate who had worked his way through the household and wardrobe to the treasury and chancery. Unlike Bury, Wykeham made no claim to literature, and it was reserved to the moderns to proclaim him a great architect without any reason at all, except his skill in directing the craftsmen who designed the king's works and his bounty in erecting buildings at Winchester and Oxford. A chronicler well puts his position in the phrase that he compensated for his lack of letters by his wonderful liberality.

Even more interesting than great prelates such as Bury and Wykeham were civil service patrons of learning of humbler status, who were able and willing to devote their modest means to founding colleges and schools with a liberality that stood in closer relation to their total means than the moneys lavished on their foundations by men like Stapeldon or Wykeham. Such was Adam de Brome, clerk of the king's chancery, who, towards the close of his long career as a civil servant, founded the College of St Mary at Oxford, which was later called Oriel College, whose sixth centenary was celebrated only a year or two ago. Another man of the same type was Harvey of Staunton, chancellor of the exchequer and, therefore, in those days a civil servant, who founded Michaelhouse at Cambridge about the same time. These are only instances, not an exhaustive list, but I will call attention to one foundation which, though never carried out, deserves due recognition. This is the proposed foundation of John Winwick, the son of a country gentleman from Huyton, near Liverpool, who was for many years a clerk of the privy seal and rose to be its keeper during the critical years between Poitiers and Brétigni. He was one of the strongest and most influential ministers of his time and was amply rewarded by prebends and livings, though cut off by death from higher promotion. By his will he set apart estates for establishing at Oxford a college of scholars to study civil and common law, 'desiring to enrich the English church with men of letters.' The foundation never materialised, apparently through the greediness of his heirs.

There are other ways of being a benefactor to learning besides the foundation of colleges, and I think fourteenth-century Oxford would have put high on its list of benefactors Robert Stratford, an Oxford doctor and a prominent chancery clerk, who rose, under his brother John's protection, to be chancellor of England and a bishop. He is interesting as holding the office of chancellor of Oxford, when a nonresident and a prelate, being the first of the magnate university chancellors who were soon to supersede the resident working chancellors of earlier days. Robert Stratford used his great position in church and state to crush remorselessly the 'adulterine,' or unrecognised, University of Stamford, which a group of seceders from the older university were striving to set up. Perhaps a broader vision would have encouraged, rather than repressed, the multiplication of university centres: but the work of the pious founders tended in the same direction as that of Robert Stratford, since the immense increase of endowments of corporations within the corporate university undoubtedly increased the stability of each existing *studium* and made successful rivalry to it more difficult.

Already by the fourteenth century the Oxford element in the public service was strong enough to make itself felt. Cambridge doctors were also beginning to come to the front. It was a sign of the increasing tendency of universities to nationalise themselves that the Continental, generally the Paris, doctor becomes almost a negligible quantity. The two tendencies converge in St Thomas of Cantiloupe, whom Simon de Montfort took in 1265 from the chancellorship of Oxford to be chancellor of England. After Montfort's fall, Thomas retired to Paris, where he taught theology, and came back to England to be again chancellor of Oxford and finally bishop of Hereford. There is little evidence of St Thomas' contribution to scholastic or theological literature.

Equally lacking in output were most of the other eminent doctors who, in later times, became administrators or ministers of state. John Stratford, later archbishop of Canterbury, was an Oxford doctor of laws, and long employed in the king's service before his threefold tenure of the chancellorship enabled him to pack the office with his kinsmen. But he never wrote much himself, save that in his controversy with Edward III in 1340-1341 he formulated the Lancastrian theory of baronial control of the crown, and thus made some contribution to political ideas. A more distinguished academic personage was Thomas Bradwardine, the *doctor profundus,* the writer of the greatest Augustinian theological work of his century, and also a king's clerk, accompanying Edward on his campaigns and promoted, just before his death, to the archbishopric of Canterbury. If, as is likely, Bradwardine's introduction to the king's service came from worldlings, like Bury and John Stratford, links between the practical academic leader and the deep scholar are brought home to us.

Of other persons of high academic standing, though not of learned output, who were distinguished in the king's service, I may mention instances. Among them were John Thoresby, doctor of laws, chancery clerk, chancellor, and archbishop of York; Walter Skirlaw, doctor of laws, clerk of chancery, and bishop of Durham; and John Ronhale, doctor of laws, worthy of special notice because he went from the mastership of the King's Hall at Cambridge to serve the king as notary of chancery, thus fulfilling for once the special function of that foundation. Ronhale is the most conspicuous instance of a Cambridge master in Edward III's service. It is indeed sometimes said that Robert Thorp, a common lawyer by profession, was in earlier life master of Pembroke Hall, Cambridge, and based his attitude as chancellor on his loyalty to the house of Pembroke, which had founded the college of which he was once head. However, the identity of names is not enough, especially in the case of so common a name as his. Robert Thorp, the chancellor, had long been a practising lawyer. It is conceivable that he might, like other successful common lawyers, have renounced his clergy for the bar and knighthood. Yet by the end of Edward III's reign, when the common law had become substantially a lay profession, some more positive proof is needed before we can accept so improbable an identification.

I must not dwell longer on the academic personage in politics. Still less must I stress the relation to our subject of the many men of letters who were attached for a time to the courts of Edward III, his queen, his sons, and his grandson, though in the aggregate they suggest a literary atmosphere, more literary in the narrow sense than that of the shrewd worldlings and saintly recluses who fluctuated between the service of the university and the service of the crown. Yet in days when service in the household was hardly yet differentiated from the service of the state, a plausible claim might be made for their inclusion. Such were John Froissart of Valenciennes, poet, clerk, chronicler, and traveller, attached for some years to the service of his countrywoman, Queen Philippa, and upholding a very English point of view until better pay or prospects lured him away to serve French masters and change his attitude to politics.

In the same category as Froissart we may place the anonymous Chandos Herald, a Hainaulter like Froissart, if we may argue from his language, who chronicled in rhyme the doings of Chandos' master, the Black Prince. The presence of skilled pens about the court made easy the establishment of what we may almost call an effective publicity department, by which knowledge of the king's great doings against the French were duly reported home in despatches that had the same function of interesting and educating public opinion as was thought necessary during our most recent war. The same spirit inspired the incorporation of these despatches in the drum and trumpet history of Robert Avesbury, himself an official of the ecclesiastical courts, and in the lurid patriotism of Geoffrey Baker's *Chronicle,* and of Laurence Minot's war songs. In home affairs we have already had an instance of such appeal to public opinion in the controversy between Edward III and John Stratford, in which the frenzied denunciations of the courtiers who drew up the *libellus famosus* were countered by the dignified utterances of Stratford from his retreat at Canterbury.

These appeals to public opinion came to a head in the opposition to Richard's attempt at autocracy when Thomas Favent, the chaplain of a lord of the opposition, wrote in Latin a strongly partisan account of the acts of the Wonderful Parliament of 1387, so anti-royalist in temper that it was disinterred and translated into English as a weapon to fight the cause of the Long Parliament against Charles I. It was equally conspicuous on the king's side in the falsification of the parliament roll of 1397, worked by chancery clerks in Richard II's interests. Finally, we see its effects in the considerable literature, mainly of French provenance, which sought to stir up European opinion against the Lancastrian usurper by depicting the sufferings and murder of the deposed Richard II. Even such acts as the reconciliation of Richard

II with the Londoners in 1392 have their literary commemoration in the person of Richard Maidstone. Long before this the strenuous Sir Peter de la Mare's speakership of the Commons inspired popular songs in honour of the popular hero. The remarkable account of the Good Parliament preserved in the annals of a Yorkshire abbey, and recently published in the *Anonimalle Chronicle* by Mr Galbraith, shows that there was a public for the faithful reporting of memorable parliamentary debates. The spread of interest in current affairs from the magnate to the simple squire and citizen had, as one of its results, the increasing attention paid in court circles to publicity. This had some effect in the increasing value of the government agent who could write.

We have still to consider the direct contribution of the fourteenth-century official to literature, and especially to current vernacular literature. Preëminent among these, we have now to deal with two personages who were undoubtedly men of letters, and equally undoubtedly civil servants. These were Geoffrey Chaucer and Thomas Hoccleve, respectively representing the lay and clerical branches of that service.

No mere historian can add anything material to the biography of either Chaucer or Hoccleve. All he can hope to do is to harp on the claims of the civil service on its own and perhaps put into focus their professional career, which the literary historian, too often unmindful of fourteenth-century social and political conditions, may sometimes fail to coördinate with their literary activities. Yet their professional record cannot be overstressed; for Chaucer, a *bona fide* layman at every stage of his career, could not have written his poems but for the court favour which gave him and his something approaching a sufficiency to live upon, and even Hoccleve, the clerk, when he cut off all chance of a career by becoming *clericus uxoratus,** had nothing to keep him alive save his modest salary and other occasional state bounties. And to obtain the payment of all of these he had

* [Married clerk.]

frequent occasion to call upon the aid of his muse. Mediaeval conditions made literature an impossible profession. There could hardly be publication in our sense. There were certainly no direct profits of authorship and no legal copyright, as long as there was no printing or other means of rapidly multiplying copies to meet a commercial demand. Preferment in the church for the clerk, offices in the state for clerk and layman alike, the bounty of kings and magnates in all cases—such were the only means by which the man of letters could earn his living and that by occupations quite foreign to his literary profession. Hence the importance of political service for the literary aspirant of the later Middle Ages. For it was rarely indeed that literature was cultivated by a man of private means, like John Gower, who seems to have lived on his patrimony and to have written for writing's sake.

Geoffrey Chaucer's literary primacy needs neither statement nor demonstration. My humbler duty to-day is to emphasise his position as a permanent civil servant, a position the more emphatic since it was, after a fashion, hereditary. His father, John Chaucer, a prosperous London wine merchant, was attached to Edward III's household service as deputy butler. So intimate were the ties involved in that office that John Chaucer attended the king in his long sojourns in the Netherlands between 1338 and 1340, his foreign service probably lasting until nearly the period of his famous son's birth. It was easy for a youth, born in the atmosphere of the royal household, to be attached from early years to the service of the court. I am convinced that the excellent education which Geoffrey undoubtedly received was the education which the household of a king, or one of the greater magnates, could give to its junior members. How this education was conducted we know very little, but it clearly combined that familiar knowledge of the Latin tongue, which in the Middle Ages was the essence of literacy, with that broader accomplishment in modern literature whose chief vehicle was still French, the *lingua franca,* so to say, of cultivated lay society in Western Europe. I emphasise the point since this part of the 'Chaucer legend' has not yet been so decisively dissipated as the rest of it has been by the admirable scholars who are collecting, with extraordinary patience, every scrap of evidence from record sources.

This process of investigation is still going on, and a notable example of the sort of picture it enables us to build up can be found in Mr J. M. Manly's *Some New Light on Chaucer.* He throws over most of the derelict planks of the Chaucer legend. He rightly dismisses the conjecture, with which one is still sometimes confronted, that Chaucer might have been educated at Oxford or Cambridge. There is not a scrap of evidence in support of these imaginings, and all our knowledge of fourteenth-century conditions is against them. The university legend fades away when we remember that, north of the Alps, the mediaeval universities were universities of clerks, and there is the extreme unlikelihood that such a *bona fide* layman as Chaucer was at any time in his career a tonsured clerk. Moreover, we cannot find any time during which a youth, who had been for some years a page in a subordinate royal household, and who took arms in the campaign of 1359, before he was twenty, could have attended the courses of any university. Unluckily, Mr Manly is still inclined to the alternative theory that Chaucer was educated at the Temple. His only positive reason for thinking this is a reference in an Elizabethan writer, which, if only a scrap of contemporary corroboration could be found, would make the theory probable. But no such contemporary evidence exists. Mr Manly makes much of the inadequacy of a training about the court, and considers it far more likely that an exceptional education, such as that of Chaucer, would have been obtained in one of the common law schools of London, the 'Inns of Court,' for such he assumes the Temple had already become. This assumption may well be right, but we have no

certain knowledge to support it. Mr Manly goes further and says that a legal training is a natural explanation of Chaucer's career. Both these arguments, I think, are pressed too far. Households, royal and baronial, were the usual training ground for officials, and I see no unlikelihood whatever in their having been responsible for the education of a man like Chaucer. I am certain too that there is nothing in his career which suggests that he was a trained lawyer, and we know that most of his contemporaries, who held similar posts, were not trained lawyers either. The whole theory remains conjectural, therefore, and I think that our absolute lack of knowledge of the early history of the London law schools makes it improbable that it will ever be proved. We must guard against that subtle, but widespread, sin of the historian, namely, the reading back into an earlier age, for which he has no evidence, the testimony of the documents of a later date. It is highly dangerous to assume that Fortescue's famous account of the education of the London law schools, nearly a hundred years later, applied to the reign of Edward III. For Fortescue's own days it suggests just the sort of education Chaucer might well have received, including the study of history on Sundays and saints' days, when no more serious lectures were available! But even if such schools were in operation in the middle of the fourteenth century, we have no evidence of Chaucer being in any sense a lawyer. On the contrary, his whole early history centres round the households of the king and his sons, and those only.[1]

[1] My reason for having, rather unfairly, traversed Mr Manly's argument, since it appears in a book of public lectures which he modestly says is not for specialists, is that it is a theory about which he seems fairly confident. He expounds it so clearly that I do not think I can have mistaken his arguments, in spite of the popular form in which they are cast. This question of Chaucer's education is one where the literary and administrative historians meet on common ground, and it is one on which, therefore, stress must inevitably be laid in this address. I read with delight Mr Manly's invigorating book, which I regard as an excellent illustration

As a boy, Chaucer was a page in the household of the king's son, Lionel of Antwerp. He was still in Lionel's retinue when he made his first campaign in France in 1359, and was already important enough for the king to contribute towards his ransom when he was taken prisoner in a skirmish near Rethel. Geoffrey was subsequently transferred to the king's household, and to that confidential branch of it called the king's chamber. In 1367, and probably earlier, he was yeoman, or *valettus,* of the king's chamber, and afterwards held the higher rank of esquire of the chamber. Chamber office, originally the personal service of the king's bedroom, still normally involved close attendance at court and intimate relations with the king. It was, however, usual to employ chamber officers on delicate missions at home and abroad. Such incidents of the duty of an esquire of the chamber gave Chaucer his diplomatic experiences in France and Italy, and perhaps, therefore, his personal acquaintance with Italian poets. His marriage with a lady of the court not only strengthened his position, but involved him ultimately in a left-hand connexion with John of Gaunt. Modest pensions and grants from both king and duke of Lancaster rewarded the divided service to two masters which was so usual with the officials of that age.

In 1374 Chaucer was relieved from his constant attendance at court by his appointments as controller of the great and petty customs in the port of London. Henceforth he was settled in a home of his own over Aldgate. He became increasingly prosperous as a landed proprietor and justice of the peace in Kent, and, though never knighted, he was elected *loco militis* to represent Kent in the memorable parliament of 1386 at which the baronial opposition began their attack upon prerogative government by the

impeachment of the chancellor, the earl of Suffolk. I have no doubt that Chaucer's presence in parliament was part of a policy which Edward III and Richard II handed on to later generations. I mean the policy of securing the complacency of the Commons by the infusion of a liberal sprinkling of courtiers and placemen among their ranks. In 1386, however, such precautions were to no purpose. The lords and commons drove Suffolk from office, and it is most unlikely that Chaucer, though he sat, or at least drew pay, for sixty-one days' attendance at that parliament, ever raised a voice on behalf of the unpopular minister. In his *Hous of Fame* (ll. 652-660) he has for once deviated from the impersonal note which characterises nearly all his writings, by describing how, indifferent to distractions, social or political, he divided his life between his work in his office and his literary pursuits at home:

> For whan thy labour doon al is,
> And hast y-maad thy rekeninges,
> In stede of reste and newe thinges,
> Thou gost hoom to thy house anoon;
> And also domb as any stoon,
> Thou sittest at another boke
> Till fully daswed is thy loke,
> And livest thus as an hermyte,
> Although thyn abstinence is lyte.

Chaucer's prudence did not, however, keep him long in his posts. Before the end of 1386, a fresh storm burst, provoked by the reluctance of the king to carry out the wishes of the parliament which had driven the earl of Suffolk from the chancery. The reforming commissioners appointed by that parliament answered the king's action by greater activity in purging the administration of undesirable elements. It was doubtless the result of their energy that in December Chaucer lost his two posts in the customs and was reduced to such financial straits that he had to give up his house in Aldgate and barter his pension for an advance of cash. Yet his prudential abstention from politics may have lightened his fall, for he never seems to have lost his posi-

---

of the way our knowledge of Chaucer has been amplified and humanised by the researches of a host of workers into the records of the state. Among these Professor Manly and his colleague, Professor Rickert, occupy places of distinction.

tion, somewhat nominal, I imagine, latterly, in the royal household, and his little pensions from the exchequer and the duchy of Lancaster enabled him to live somehow.

Very different was the fate of a brother man of letters, Thomas Usk, in status a clerk, but engaged mainly in the public service, being in turn secretary to John Northampton, the turbulent mayor of London (whom he betrayed), king's sergeant-at-arms, and under-sheriff of Middlesex. He was, therefore, if not quite a civil servant, engaged in official work. He was a literary man, too, being, as Dr Henry Bradley has proved, the author of that *Testament of Love,* which in precritical days was ascribed to Chaucer. Usk, whose repeated treachery to his masters had lost him all his friends, was one of the culprits whom the Merciless Parliament of 1388 condemned to a cruel end. The chronicler expatiates on the piety shown by this victim of the angry estates. As he was dragged to his doom, he recited the penitential psalms, the *Te Deum,* and other incentives to devotion at the hour of death, among them, curiously enough, being the Athanasian Creed. He was strung up on the gallows and cut down immediately, when still conscious. His subsequent beheading was so mishandled by a clumsy executioner that it was only after thirty strokes of the sword that his sufferings were brought to an end. The fate of this poet turned politician may well have convinced his friend Chaucer of the wisdom of holding aloof from politics and ostentatiously proclaiming his indifference to all but the daily official task and the literary pursuits of his leisure hours. There is no civil servant, clerical or lay, depicted in the great gallery of portraits drawn in the General Prologue to the *Canterbury Tales.*

We must now turn to a later stage of Chaucer's official career. His worst trials were soon over, but for some time it was thought prudent to keep him out of the way. On July 5, 1387, he had letters of protection to go for a year to Calais in the retinue of the captain of the town.[1] However, he was back in England before the end of the year, and, in 1389, the successful assertion by the king of his right to choose his own ministers was soon followed by Chaucer's restoration to place. He was not put back in his old offices, but his appointment in 1389 as clerk of the king's works made him the successor of William of Wykeham in the post which led his predecessor to greatness both in church and state. Chaucer soon took advantage of the not unusual permission to appoint a deputy, but in 1391 he lost his controllership and was again in financial difficulties. Henceforth, he ceased to be a civil servant, for subsequent office, such as the deputy keepership of a forest in Somerset, he owed technically, not to the crown, but to the young earl of March. His other means of support were pensions, which were small under Richard II and became adequate only when the accession of Henry of Lancaster was at once followed by marks of royal favour that enabled the poet to end his life in comfort in a home, under the shadow of the palace, and within the precincts of the great abbey wherein he was buried. Whether Chaucer's troubles in his public career were accentuated, as some of his biographers suggest, by his unbusinesslike ways which made further promotion difficult, it is hard to say. But chequered as was his official record, it had this importance, that it gave him the leisure to write what the world will not willingly let die. But we know his public career only in outline and from official documents. The rule of reticence as to his personal affairs and his political attitude, already laid down by him in 1384, was never broken. Yet his position at court had this advantage for his stock, that it gave to Thomas Chaucer, whom I cannot but regard as his son, a rich wife and a great estate in Oxfordshire, an almost permanent position as 'knight' of

[1] This is a new fact due to a discovery of Professor E. Rickert, first revealed in her paper in the *Times Literary Supplement* (September 27, 1928). Though I was of course unaware of it when this address was delivered, it rounds off the statement as to Chaucer's disgrace so well that I have ventured to incorporate it in my narrative.

that shire in parliament, and ultimately the speakership of the Commons at the period of their greatest activity under the early Lancastrians. The marriage of Thomas' daughter Alice to William de la Pole, earl and afterwards duke of Suffolk, raised the granddaughter of the poor poet to the highest circle of the nobility, and Alice's son's marriage to Edward IV's sister might have made her grandson heir to the throne but for the Tudor revolution. Altogether, this is not a bad record for an official whose father was a tradesman in the City of London. And yet people still talk of the Middle Ages as the time of the domination of an hereditary caste. Even the lay official could find opportunities for his kin, hardly surpassed by the direct avenue to power and position afforded by the church.

In the literary circle of which Chaucer was the chief star, many lesser lights revolved. Some at least among them had administrative affinities of a kind. Among them some have been inclined to place Ralph Strode, common sergeant of the City of London, though he, even more than Thomas Usk, was an officer of the city rather than of the state. But this depends on identifying the scholastic Oxford writer, Wycliffe's opponent, Chaucer's 'philosophic Strode,' with this successful lawyer, and fathering him in addition with the authorship of anonymous poems of rare poetic quality. Sir Israel Gollancz has not hesitated to maintain for some thirty years that there was only one Ralph Strode who did all these things. My sympathies go with him, but my intelligence does not allow me to have implicit faith in the identification. All one can say is that if the one Ralph Strode did all these things he was a very remarkable man. But I find it hard to believe that a clerk of established position would leave the university, start a new career as a common lawyer, abandon his clergy for a wife and a family, and find time to write poetry in his leisure. Something more positive than conjuncture is necessary to carry conviction. More relevant to us is that literary dining-club called the 'Court of

Good Company,' which included Thomas Hoccleve among its members and was entertained at dinner on May Day, 1410, by Henry Somner, chancellor of the exchequer, still a civil servant at that period, and not the political minister that he has become in these later days. Chaucer was already dead, but we may feel sure that he would not in his lifetime have been lacking at such a feast. Let us now turn to his disciple Hoccleve, for in him alone we can study in detail the literary career of a civil servant of more ordinary calibre.

Chaucer's stages as a civil servant bear but little relation to his literary career. But with Hoccleve we are at last able to go beyond the bare catalogue of appointment to offices and payment of salaries and pensions, which constitute all our knowledge of Chaucer as a public servant. The reason is that in strong contrast to his master's reticence, Hoccleve was the most garrulous, self-centred, and autobiographical of poets, ever ready, when his arid muse refused him impersonal inspiration, to write about himself, his office, his work, his pleasures, and, above all, his misfortunes. Though these excursions into autobiography give us rather a low opinion of Hoccleve, we owe him a debt of gratitude for enabling us to visualize the mentality and career of an ordinary civil service clerk of the later Middle Ages. He was, for something like forty years, one of the four clerks of the privy seal, who, under the keeper of the seal, were the chiefs of the secondary secretariat, called the office of the privy seal. He was important enough to have at least one subordinate clerk working under him, and zealous enough to wear out his energy and health on the dreary monotony of endless official correspondence. His lot was the harder since matrimony cut him off from the society of his brother clerks and debarred him from all ecclesiastical preferment. Accordingly, he had to continue at his dull task until old age and ill health compelled him to retire on a small pension, very irregularly paid. He was always lamenting in his verse the hardships and monotony of the life of a professional scribe. Yet he was clearly a keen official, for we can study in the British Museum a large manuscript, written with his own hand, wherein he sets down in businesslike fashion common forms and examples of every kind of writ and bill that emanated from the privy seal office. Thus the administrative historian obtains from this literary source the precious information which enables him to go beyond the common forms of the record and realise the sort of life led by the ordinary official of the later Middle Ages. It is a good illustration of the interdependence of one branch of mediaeval study and another, and a striking vindication of the function of the Mediaeval Academy of America, in bringing together all sorts of mediaevalists into a single society.

THE INSTITUTIONS, CUSTOMS, AND IDEAS of a past age can be apprehended only in the light of the cultural milieu of that age. The division of history into branches or departments is necessary if historical knowledge is to advance. But the various departments into which the whole field of history, considered as knowledge of the past, has been divided for convenience and scientific utility—political, social, economic, religious, artistic, and scientific history, for example—are not self-sufficient or self-explanatory. Thoughtful historians have realized that this departmentalization of knowledge does not correspond to anything in history considered as the flow of events in the past, to anything, that is to say, inherent in the historic process itself—that this departmentalization tends, on the contrary, to obscure relationships that have always existed in that process as an undivided whole. The superficial reader of the literature of an earlier period, applying the assumptions and the criteria of his own day to a past age, is unconsciously tempted to suppose that he has a more accurate understanding of what he reads than is actually the case. Much in medieval writing, for example, that would have been clear to medieval readers will be obscure or meaningless to him unless and until he becomes a medievalist. In the essay that follows, addressed to modern readers of medieval literature, Henry Stanley Bennett, an English scholar who has devoted much study and thought to medieval English literary, social, and economic history and who has written *The Pastons and Their England* (1922), *Life on the English Manor* (1937), and *Chaucer and the Fifteenth Century* (1948), emphasizes the need for knowledge of the cultural context of medieval literature. "As we make ourselves familiar with things such as the medieval conception of the ordering of society, the Feudal System, Chivalry, and Courtly Love, or as we study the medieval Church, its organization and work, we shall be equipping ourselves to follow the literature of medieval times."

MEDIEVAL LITERATURE AND THE MODERN READER

H. S. BENNETT

The Master of Trinity, in the Introduction to his *English Social History,* has written eloquently about the study of the past—a past as real as the present, in which 'We can see our forerunners, remote and recent, in their habits as they lived, each intent on the business of a long-vanished day, riding out to do homage or to poll a vote; to seize a neighbour's manor-house and carry off his ward, or to leave cards on ladies in crinolines.' He goes on to say that 'The age of Chaucer speaks to us with many voices not unintelligible to the modern ear. Indeed we may be tempted to think that we "understanden" more than in fact we do. For these ancestors of ours, in one half of their thoughts and acts, were still guided by a complex of intellectual, ethical and social assumptions of which only medieval scholars can to-day comprehend the true purport.'

Dr. Trevelyan's words demand the earnest attention of students of literature, for in common with students of history they are constantly tempted to be satisfied with half the thoughts of our ancestors, since even half provides them with so much of interest and value. Our literature before the fourteenth century is a closed book to all but students, because of the linguistic difficulties of Anglo-Saxon and Middle English. In the fourteenth century Chaucer's immense superiority to his fellows and immediate predecessors concentrates most readers' attention upon his work, and they find to their surprised delight that with a little practice they can read and enjoy him without undue effort. But are they not tempted to think that they understand more than in fact they do, and is there not a further step to be taken if they wish to penetrate into the full content of the poet's meaning? Let us see.

The person of the toun hir fader
  was . . .
She was yfostred in a nonnerye.

How many have read these lines of Chaucer without gaining from them more than their surface meaning, and without realizing how important they are if we are to understand Chaucer's full ironic intention in telling *The Reve's Tale?* 'Her father was the parson of the little township, and she had been brought up in a nunnery.' What is remarkable in those two statements, it may be asked, but to make such an inquiry is to show oneself uninstructed in fourteenth-century life and thought, and imperfectly equipped to read Chaucer. No contemporary could have been in doubt of Chaucer's underlying purpose in using these words, for they touch on two of the most important religious problems of medieval England. Let us take the parson first. Although the secular cleric was not vowed to celibacy as were the monks, at the same time Canon Law enjoined it, and for centuries the Bishops had warred against the marriage of the clergy. Dr. H. C. Lea, the learned authority on this subject, writes: 'The rule was now [*temp.* Henry III] firmly established and generally acknowledged: concubinage, though still prevalent—nay, in fact almost universal—was not defended as a right, but was practised with what concealment was possible, and was the object of unremitting assault from councils and prelates. To enter into the details of innumerable canons and constitutions directed against the ineradicable vice during the succeeding half century would be unprofitable. Their endless iteration is only interesting as proving their inefficacy. A popular satirist of the reign of Edward II declares that bribery of the ecclesiastical officials

Reprinted by special permission from *Essays and Studies by Members of the English Association,* XXXI (1945), 7-18.

ensured the domestic comfort of the clergy and their female companions:

> And thise ersedekenes that ben set
>   to visit holi churche
> Everich fondeth hir he may
>   shrewidelichest worcke;
> He wole take mede of that on and
>   that other,
> And late the parsoun have a wyf
>   and the prest another, at wille.'

Facts such as these were well known: those who stood around in the court or elsewhere when Chaucer's poem was read must often have remembered their own local parson and his little house in the village which sheltered his *focarius* and her children.

The latter were almost as great a problem as was the 'wife.' What to do with the boys was a matter which bristled with difficulties. What to do with the unwanted girls was somewhat easier. So long as a dowry could be found for them they could be conveniently forgotten in a nunnery; and there, as Dr. Eileen Power has pointed out, a large number of girls found their first and last permanent home. Others only stayed there for a time, receiving such education and training as the nuns could give them, and when they were of suitable age were withdrawn and married. This was what happened to Malyne in *The Reve's Tale*. She was married to Symkyn, the Miller, who received as a dowry 'ful many a panne of bras' to outweigh any defects of birth. She, like many whose origins are suspect, comported herself with overwhelming dignity, for, as Chaucer says,

> she was somdel smoterlich
>   [besmirched
> She was as digne as water in a
>   ditch;
> And ful of hoker and of bisemare.
>   [scorn, disdain.

Thus she was well suited to her husband— 'As eny pecok he was proud and gay,' while 'she was proud and pert as is a pye.'

Here again was a personage well known to many of Chaucer's audience, and thus it was not merely the fortunes of Symkyn and his wife that they followed, but those of a whole group whose place in the social scheme was so equivocal. Chaucer follows up his preliminary 'placing' by telling one of his most outrageous (and most skilful) 'churl's tales,' the point of which will be partly lost if we do not keep in mind while we read it the facts outlined above. It cannot be too often repeated that Chaucer was a highly sophisticated author, writing for a highly sophisticated audience, a large part of whose pleasure arose from their instantaneous taking of all the points that Chaucer had to offer. The wife's pride, the husband's pride in her, their common pride in their daughter and their hopes of what her grandfather would do for her (for he was 'in purpos to maken hire his heir' and 'to bistowe hire hye In-to som worthy blood of auncetrye'), must all be referred back to the parson and his family life, and kept constantly in our mind, while we read of what befell the Miller's household at the hands of the clerks of Cambridge.

Similarly, a considerable knowledge of medieval life and literature is required if we are to get the full flavour from Chaucer's great series of portraits in the *Prologue*. It is true that recourse may be had to the notes of Skeat or Robinson, but these at best are only a 'first-aid' expedient: the reader's momentary curiosity is satisfied and he reads on, but still lacks any coherent understanding of the particular point which Chaucer is making. To illustrate this we may turn to the portrait of the Prioress. Many critics have discussed the subtle irony which underlies Chaucer's work here, and delineates, in Professor Lowes's admirable phrase, 'the delightfully imperfect submergence of the woman in the nun.' The adjectives 'simple and coy' have a long ancestry in the pages of medieval romance, as has the name 'Madame Eglentyne,' while the account of the Prioress's table manners acquires an added flavour when we realize, as did Chaucer's audience, from whence it derives. No medieval poem was so well known as the *Roman de la Rose,* and little doubt of Chaucer's ironic intention could be felt by his listeners as they heard the Prioress's manners described in terms so reminiscent of those used in the *Roman de la Rose*. There, the way in which the fashionable woman should behave in order to attract masculine attention is thus described: 'She takes good care not to wet her fingers in the sauces up to the joints, nor to have her lips anointed with soups, garlic, or fat meat, nor to heap up too many or too large morsels and put them into her mouth. She touches with the tips of her fingers the morsel which she has to moisten with the sauce, be it green, or brown, or yellow, and warily lifts her mouthful, so that no drop of the soup, or sauce, or pepper falls on her breast. And she must drink so daintily that not a drop is spilled on herself. . . . She ought to wipe her mouth so well that she leaves no grease clinging there—at least upon the upper lip, for when grease stays there little drops of it are seen when wine is drunk.' Not only in this close parallel between the behaviour of fine lady and nun, but in his description of the Prioress's brooch, her unveiled forehead, her pleated wimple, her pet dogs, and her presence on a pilgrimage Chaucer gave plenty of clues concerning his underlying intention—all immediately available to the instructed, but only available to us if we will take the trouble to put ourselves as nearly as possible in the position of a contemporary.

Those of Chaucer's contemporaries who had the entrée at the Court of Richard II, might well have overheard the Bishop of Winchester discussing the state of affairs in the monasteries of his diocese, and we can read what they were like if we turn to his visitation of the Priory of Selborne in 1387. There, Wykeham deplores the custom of some of the inmates who absent themselves from their cloister, or ride to their farms and manors under the pretence of inspecting them, and thus absent themselves as long as they please. The Bishop finds that many of them are hunters and sportsmen, keeping hounds and attending hunting matches, while others care inordinately for the fine quality of their hose and shoes, and wear garments edged with costly fur. It was with knowledge such as this that some of Chaucer's audience first heard of a Monk

> fair for the maistrie,
> An outridere, that loved ven-
> erie . . .
> Therfore he was a prikasour
> aright:
> Greyhoundes he hadde as swifte
> as fowel in flight;
> Of prikying and of huntyng for
> the hare
> Was al his lust, for no cost wolde
> he spare.
> I seigh his sleves pufiled at the
> hond

ANDREAS CAPELLANUS: Chaplain to the Countess Marie of Champagne, daughter of the famous Eleanor of Aquitaine. About 1185 Andreas, at the Countess' court at Troyes and no doubt at her direction, composed a Latin treatise on the art of courtly love which enjoyed considerable popularity in the Middle Ages and was translated into several of the vernacular languages. The theme of courtly love had been developed by the troubadours of southern France. An English translation of Andreas' treatise by John Jay Parry has been published in the Columbia University Records of Civilization, under the title *The Art of Courtly Love* (1941).

WILLIAM CAXTON: English printer who introduced the art into England in the late 1470's. Caxton was also a writer, editor, and translator. Indeed, his translations were influential in the development of English prose style.

JOHN GOWER: Fourteenth-century English poet who wrote in French and Latin as well as in English. Although he was by no means Chaucer's equal as a poet, the two men, who were contemporaries, have often been called the fathers of English poetry.

With grys, and that the fyneste of
    a lond.

Those with a little more knowledge than
their fellows would note Chaucer's allusion
to *grys*. Benedict XII had specially forbidden the use of this *gris,* the costly fur of the
grey squirrel, to all cloistered clergy. If a
monk needed warmth let him wear lamb-
skin, a less attractive but far more effective
stuff. That decree, dated 1337, was already
ignored in Chaucer's time: apparently it demanded too much from monastic nature to
go without this fur which was favoured by
those of high rank. The simple monosyllable
gris, therefore, is used by Chaucer with intent, and helps to enforce the elaborate
portrait he has been drawing.

It is not only a knowledge of the details
of everyday life that is necessary: we want
also some understanding of the ideas and
conventions which animated the society of
Chaucer's day, for Chaucer often raises
matters in the course of his narrative about
which there was considerable controversy,
and which lose much of their interest if we
are not fully aware of this. The Prologue
of the Wife of Bath's tale may serve as an
admirable example of Chaucer's skill in
making use of contemporary ideas to further his own designs. It is, of course, possible to become so absorbed in the self-
portrait that the Wife of Bath develops with
such verve that we overlook the outrageous
implications of what she has to say. Professor Kittredge, however, was right when he
insisted that her whole introduction was in
effect a challenge to the party on two cardinal doctrines of medieval thought. In the
first place she skilfully attacked the ideal of
the celibate life, and in the second the
notion of male supremacy. The first of these
was not attacked by frontal assault. The
Wife of Bath knew, as did all her hearers,
that the celibate state was unquestionably
the holiest of estates. All the authorities
throughout the ages had proclaimed this,
and the married state was but a concession
for the necessary procreation of children.
She admits this, but adds slyly:

Virginitee is greet perfeccioun,
And continence eek with devo-
    cioun.
But Christ, that of perfeccioun is
    welle,
Bad nat every wight he sholde go
    selle
All that he hadde, and give it to
    the poore,
And in swich wyse folwe hym and
    his foore.
He spak to hem that wolde lyve
    parfitly;
And lordynges, by your leve, that
    am nat I.

This done, she commences to state the
case for the non-celibate life—an audacious
proceeding when we remember that a large
number of her fellow pilgrims were pledged
to celibacy. There is no need to follow her
here in detail; the case for the *femme
moyenne sensuelle* was never stated with
more fervour, but it is only if we recognize
the wide divergence of what she advocates
from the orthodox view that we shall be
able to do justice to her audacity.

Her second point was equally full of
contentious matter. Much of what she said
no doubt won a willing assent from the
married members of the pilgrimage, and
from contemporary listeners when the tale
was read. Their turn, however, was not
long in coming, for she opens up a terrific
attack on the domination of wives by their
husbands—a doctrine almost as sacrosanct
in medieval thought as that of celibacy.
Woman's rights never had a more absolute
or a more doughty advocate.

I shal seye sooth, the housbondes
    that I hadde,
As three of hem were gode and
    two were badde.

In other words, three allowed her *dominium*
over them, while the other two fought for
the mastery. The rebellious two could have
quoted authorities from the earliest times
in their defence. Medieval society was
based on the power of the husband over

his wife and family. It was accepted that a man might beat his wife 'only in reason,' and a theological treatise of the early fourteenth century tells us that 'a man may chastise his wife and beat her by way of correction, for she forms part of his household; so that he, the master, may chastise that which is his, as is written in the Gloss [to Canon Law].' 'What is sauce for the goose is sauce for the gander' was the Wife of Bath's view, and her Prologue is an extended account of her successful attempts to put this into operation. Much of the daring, challenging nature of her argument depends for its effectiveness on our comprehension of these aspects of medieval thought.

When we turn to consider conventions—whether literary or social—our need of the contemporary approach increases. Medieval society was regulated by conventions very different from our own, and many an illuminated manuscript shows us three medallions, each containing a picture of a knight, or of a priest, or of a labourer. The fighters, the prayers, and the workers—medieval society was organized on this basis, and, as a thirteenth-century poet says, 'the labour of the knight is to do justice, of the priest to pray to God, and of the labourer to find their bread. In the field, the town, and the church these help each other in a well-ordered scheme.' This state of affairs, of course, was capable of infinite subdivision, but for the literary student it is perhaps sufficient to bear the main divisions in mind, and even more to remember that, until Chaucer's day and even later, literature was a thing for the first two of these great classes, and was little concerned with the third. The court and the Church had long been the two centres which attracted all literary aspirants, and the common people had to be content with what little came their way as the itinerant minstrel chanted the debased and adulterate versions of romance and lyric which had originally won rewards and acclamation from lords and ladies or ecclesiastical audiences.

The content of much medieval literature betrays these facts in the way in which it seeks to please those for whom it is written by delineating with great fidelity their life in war and peace. The romances are perhaps the most perfect mirror of the aristocratic, chivalric ideal, and if we are to read them with sympathy we must remember that they are designed to give 'solace and sentence' to an audience whose lives were similar to those of the characters portrayed, and who deliberately turned to the romance for inspiration and example. Here, if anywhere, was a literature which taught men 'how to live.' That being so, authors were content to work within well-defined limits. No breath of the outside world penetrates into the walled-off gardens and castellated bowers in which lords and ladies play out the elaborate game of courtly love, and even when the warriors don their armour and ride out on sterner quests, it is a curiously limited world in which they move. Towns and citizens seem unknown to them; the peasants only exist to point the way to a lonely ford, or wisely hide when they see the glitter of armour. Even Lancelot shares the common contempt for the 'churl,' and gives one a buffet which kills him—all because he will not give Lancelot a lift in his wood-cart to the neighbouring castle. Malory sees nothing wrong in this, although he tells us that Lancelot and his son are 'the greatest gentlemen in the world,' and Malory only repeats at the close of the Middle Ages what had been the view of countless romance-writers for centuries.

With this circumscribed view of the world goes an equally limited account of human activities therein. It goes without saying that life is freed from all the day-to-day problems of house-keeping and finance which beset less favoured mortals. In this, perhaps, medieval literature is not more false in its failure to reflect the national life than are, say, the novels of Meredith, or Proust, or the memoirs of any great Victorian landowner. The romance-writers were concerned with the two great topics of love and war—for in these the medieval aristocrat found his duty and his happiness. Their pages, therefore, are full of the detail of battle and tournament, of the chase and all manly sports which prepare a man for battle; of the softer pleasures of the ladies' bower or the feasting in hall. As the story was told, knight and squire, and all who aspired to gentle deeds, had placed before them an ever-changing vista of adventure, love-making, sport, etiquette, ceremonial, and all that made for the chivalric life. Once we recognize this, much that otherwise seems trivial, otiose, and even ridiculous will take on a new light. This we may see if we look at the poem of Chaucer's contemporary, the anonymous author of *Sir Gawayne and the Grene Knight*.

Dr. Wells writes: 'The piece is admirably constructed. Though it tends to over-elaborate description, it proceeds with little digression and with much variety. The poet's skill is shown in his presenting three hunting episodes and three tests of chastity with a variety that few writers in a much later period could approach. He was a lover of details; but he handled the details with a constructive power and a picturesqueness that create vivid impressions or realistic scenes. His observation of dress, of colour, of position, of relative location, of deportment, enabled him at the opening of the piece to make of a conventional situation an intense, rich, dramatic scene with a splendid background. His observation of details of architecture is shown in his description of the castle; of sports, in the remarkable hunting scenes, in the account of the brittling of the deer and the unlacing of the boar; and of armour, in the account of the arming of Sir Gawayne, and in that of the equipment of the Green Knight.'

The 'over-elaborate description' of which Dr. Wells writes was no blemish in the eyes of medieval people. *Sir Gawayne and the Grene Knight* enabled the squire to learn how to receive a guest and how to arm him when he departed; how to behave with ladies, and how to unlace the boar, or to talk in the hall. Every detail was of interest, and every turn in the story was followed by an audience quick to realize the *expertise*

with which the technical and chivalric elements of the poem were handled. We must not hope to understand the poem fully if we are not willing to put ourselves as nearly as possible in the same frame of mind as Chaucers' contemporaries. Only by so doing shall we do justice to this 'jewel of medieval romance.' In short, Caxton's words to the readers of the *Morte D'Arthur* should be our guide when reading much medieval literature. He tells us that he has printed it 'to the entente that noble men may see and lerne the noble actes of chiualrye, the Jentyl and vertuous dedes that somme knyghtes vsed in tho dayes, by whyche they came to honour, and how they that were vycious were punysshed and ofte put to shame and rebuke . . . wherin they shalle fynde many joyous and playsaunt hystoryes and noble renomed actes of humanyte, gentylnesse and chyvalryes.'

As for literary conventions, they exercised a profound influence upon the way in which writers developed their ideas. Mr. C. S. Lewis has illustrated this brilliantly in his survey of the 'Allegory of Love,' and has shown how persistent one way of writing could be. The idea of *amour courtois* had little in it that was fully acceptable to English ways, however much, or little, we may believe it represented certain French or Provençal manners of earlier centuries. Yet literary men continued until Chaucer's day and after to write poems in which the action was controlled by the sanctions of courtly love, and the actors animated by the code first put into definite form by Andreas Capellanus. Chaucer's friend Gower relies on his reader's understanding of such things when he describes the lover in these terms:

> I mot hire nedes serve,
> For as men sein, nede hath no
>   lawe.
> Thus mot I nedly to hir drawe,
> I serve, I bowe, I loke, I loute,
> Min yhe folweth hire aboute,
> What so sche wole so wol I,
> Whan sche wol sitte, I knele by,

And when sche stant, than wol I
    stonde:
Bot whan sche takth hir werk on
    honde
Of wevinge or enbrouderie,
Than can I noght bot muse and
    prie
Upon hir fingres longe and smale,
And now I thenke, and now I tale,
And now I singe, and now I sike,
And thus mi contienance I pike,

and so on for many lines in which he tells how 'he may read to her if he will, but it must be some sound romance, and not his own rondels, balades, and virelays in praise of her. Custom allows him to kiss her when he takes his leave, but if he comes back on any pretext and takes his leave again, there is not a second kiss permitted. She lets him lead her up to the offering in church, and ride by her side when she drives out, but she will take no presents from him. . . . Sometimes she will not stay with him, and then he plays with the dog or with the birds in the cage, and converses with the page of her chamber—anything as an excuse to stay.'

This was the understood mode of behaviour. Pandarus tells us that this service of a lady can be even more exacting:

What! many a man hath love ful
    deere y bought
Twenty wynter that his lady wiste,
That nevere yet his lady mouth he
    kiste.

The lover's conduct, however, must not deviate from the strict code:

What? sholde he therfore fallen in
    dispayr,
Or be recreant for his owne tene,
Or sleyn hymself, al be his lady
    fair?
Nay, nay, but evere in oon be
    fressh and grene
To serve and love his deere hertes
    queene,
And thynk it is a guerdon, hire to
    serve,

A thousand fold moore than he
    kan deserve.

All this, despite the fact that 'love comes to every gentle heart' in most cases in a flash as it did to Arcite or to Troilus. Once they have been stricken the rest is according to rule. Thus Troilus returns from the sight of Criseyde at the feast of the Palladion and exhibits all the classic signs of 'the lover's malady of Hereos,' like Arcite, lacking sleep, without appetite, losing flesh, weeping and wailing, and overwhelmed by song or sound of any musical instrument. Strange as such behaviour may seem to us unless we understand the conventions which inform it, the whole action of poems which are based on *amour courtois* will seem even stranger still. In *Troilus and Criseyde* Chaucer deliberately makes use of the conventions of courtly love, boldly reversing Boccaccio's version to do so. He brings the lovers together, with the aid of the conventional confidant, and allows them to enjoy their love in secret and with no thought of marriage, although there was little to prevent this happening. But the course of the action in the last two books is only explicable if we realize what was demanded of the lovers by the conventions of *amour courtois*. It was to satisfy these that Troilus was dumb at the council which arranged for Criseyde to be exchanged for Antenor, 'lest men sholde his affeccion espie.' Secrecy was all-important; the lady's 'honour' must remain unsullied, and so Troilus sits mumchance, and only when he leaves the council does he give way to his feelings. He weeps copiously, appeals wildly to Fortune and to Love, threatens to put out his eyes, and indulges in every extravagance of behaviour, yet dares not openly avow their love even to save her from going,

For certeyn is, syn that I am hire
    knyght,
I moste hire honour levere han
    than me
In any cas, as lovere ought of
    right.

Similarly, in *The Knight's Tale,* the action, viewed from a modern point of view, is either ridiculous or revolting. Emelye is little more than a very superior prize to be handed over to the knight who can strike the hardest. Chivalric tradition saw nothing wrong in this. The *mariage de convenance* was the lot of the vast majority of medieval people above the lowest ranks of society, and came about by hard bargaining between the contracting families for the most part. This, however, was scarcely a poetical view of things, and the troubadours and later poets found it more agreeable to put the matter in another, and less prosaic, light. In reading much medieval literature, therefore, we must be willing to see the action from the point of view which was demanded by the literary conventions of the time.

This requires a good deal of study on our part, and is made the more difficult since literary convention and everyday fact were often at variance. As we have said, medieval marriages were not often love-marriages. The pages of *The Paston Letters,* for example, will serve as a useful corrective for any who hold too romantic a view. There they will find the detailed accounts of the marriage affairs of that family; of how Elizabeth was beaten into submission till she accepted Stephen Srope, a battered old widower of nearly thrice her age; of how John Paston scoured London and elsewhere, both in person and by proxy, in search of a wealthy bride, and was reduced by his ill success to ask his brother to secure for him anyone, even a 'thrifty old draff-wife,' such was his extremity. Even William Paston, while still at Eton, keeps his eyes open, and writes home about a possible match in terms which leave no doubt that the girl's

'money and plate' outweigh even his fears that in later years the lady 'may be disposed to be thick'!

Chaucer was well aware of this dichotomy between theory and practice, and his poetry reflects both aspects. He follows the chivalric convention in the works we have mentioned, or in *The Book of the Duchess,* or *The Squire's Tale,* but allows himself to paint a more realistic scene in the various 'churl's tales,' in which such characters as January in *The Merchant's Tale,* or the Wife of Bath play conspicuous parts. Here we are in a world far removed from that of chivalry—a world in which romance and romance tradition is ignored or ridiculed. The revolting matter-of-factness of January and the frank sensuality of the Wife of Bath are part of Chaucer's vision of the every-day world which was henceforth to become more and more important an element in life and literature.

To enter upon this world would be to enlarge the scope of this essay to impossible dimensions. Until the time of Chaucer literature remained the preserve of the aristocracy and of the Church, and here I have attempted to show only how the ideas and conventions governing a small part of the literary field are of importance. As we make ourselves familiar with things such as the medieval conception of the ordering of society, the Feudal System, Chivalry, and Courtly Love, or as we study the medieval Church, its organization and work, we shall be equipping ourselves to follow the literature of medieval times. Unless we are prepared to make such an effort we shall get only the barest surface meaning of our authors, and in particular the subtle, ironic intentions which lurk below the surface of some work will often escape us.

A COMMON MODERN OPINION ABOUT medieval society has been that it was ultraconservative and rigid in structure. It was, to be sure, divided into recognized classes, and the general acceptance of these class divisions has been regarded as a strong conservative force, making for social immobility. Historical generalizations, however, are notoriously dangerous unless supported by detailed investigations, and thoughtful students of medieval social history have cast doubt on this view. In the following essay, Professor Sylvia L. Thrupp addresses herself to the question of "how far, in fifteenth-century England, conscious acceptance of class divisions was a conservative force." The social scene which she sketches included lords and gentry, merchants, retail traders, artisans, urban proletarian workers, yeomen, and agricultural laborers; but these social classes were not sharply set apart from one another. On the contrary, there was much class interrelationship combined with class consciousness. The lively social mobility of which Professor Thrupp speaks does not support a theory of unqualified conservatism. Her essay is pervaded by scholarly caution. A study of medieval conservatism must, she urges, take into account "the coincidence and interlocking of forces of change with forces opposed to change."

THE PROBLEM OF CONSERVATISM IN FIFTEENTH-CENTURY ENGLAND
SYLVIA L. THRUPP

Most modern misconceptions of mediaeval society are due to a distorted notion of the rigidity of its structure. In the circumstances of the last century, it was perhaps inevitable that such an idea should have arisen. The capitalist economy, in its phases of rapid expansion, was creating new occupations and ways of life, radically altering the position of the older social classes and bringing new ones into existence. Society in the middle ages, largely agrarian and slow-moving, indubitably offered an extreme contrast to these fluid conditions. By an easy and natural process, aided by prejudices of eighteenth-century and Renaissance lineage, the contrast was exaggerated. The middle ages therefore came to stand, in the mind of the average educated reader, as the very type and symbol of immobility.

But the days of dynamic expansion are now long past, and the various political and social movements of today all tend alike towards congealing the social system in some mould or other that will ensure security and respect for all citizens. If these desires for a more static system persist, the

mediaeval world will take on a much less alien aspect. More sympathetic readers will more readily appreciate that it, too, underwent periods of expansion and of contraction, and, as it comes to be seen in its true colors, the popular legend of its immobility will die.

At the same time, specialists should find themselves in a better position to analyze the nature of the conservative influences in mediaeval society. It is undeniable that very strong forces were periodically at work, opposing change. For example, one cannot but be struck by the apparent willingness of mediaeval people to accept as divinely ordained whatever social order the economic and military situation might impose. A brief paper can do no more than point out one of the problems that would be raised by a study of this attitude of mind. The problem may be illustrated by considering the question, how far, in fifteenth-century England, conscious acceptance of class divisions was a conservative force. Fifteenth-century England provides a setting in which one would expect to find class

Reprinted by special permission from *Speculum*, XVIII (1943), 363-368. The footnotes which originally appeared with this essay have been omitted.

divisions mature and class consciousness assuming stereotyped forms, for, until the economic and political revival under the Tudors at the end of the century, the age was for the most part one of decline, with population either static or receding.

A few of the difficulties that beset this type of enquiry must be mentioned at the outset. In the first place, it is imperative to be specific in the use of terms; yet there is an immediate danger of becoming doctrinaire, and of begging one's major questions. Thus, in referring to a society as stratified one is presupposing that its members were conscious of being grouped in social classes distinguished by typical sources of income and cultural standards, and that these classes were in the common judgment ranked in a certain order. But these suppositions must be put to the test of facts, and the relevant facts are elusive. They are contained mainly in literature and in the more intimate documents of private life, such as letters, wills, marriage settlements, which reveal the extent of circles of friendship on terms of equality, and give expression to attitudes of superiority and inferiority. To speak of social classes unless there is proof of this kind that their division issued in attitudes affecting people's conduct of their lives is merely to invent political or economic abstractions. A further difficulty lies in the fact that in respect of these matters England was not a homogeneous unit. The only true picture of the situation would be a composite one, based on comparison of many local studies. And adequate local studies have not yet been carried out.

Yet although shadows of obscurity hang over many sides of fifteenth-century social life, the broad outlines of a class system bulk fairly clear, and may be hastily called to mind. Whatever local variations may have affected the rating of groups in the middle and lower ranks of society, the uppermost class, that of the lords, was held in uniform esteem throughout the nation. Its supremacy was the product of a number of factors. As a seventeenth-century writer

remarked, 'Honor sprang originally from the Field, for it being the effect of Power.' The fifteenth-century English had not forgotten that their background was in part that of a society organized for military service, in which prestige was measured by capacity for such service. The people's attitude of deference toward the nobility was rooted in the tradition that made them leaders in the organization of war and defence. That they were still able to fill this rôle was obviously due to their wealth. As a class the nobles had no distinctive source of income, living on the rents and produce of their estates, augmented in some cases by pensions granted by the Crown, but they were individually wealthier than any of their inferiors. They were thus able to employ wealth in a unique manner, maintaining their famous liveried staffs of servants and soldiers, which were at once symbols and instruments of power.

The foundation of 'the estate of a lord' was the power that made his patronage a boon eagerly solicited by lesser men. In theory the dignity pertained only to barons or those of still higher rank, but in practice, as Stubbs pointed out, the wealthier and more influential of the knights were also regarded by their neighbors as lords. Formerly there may have been a great deal of ambiguity in the delimitation of the class, but in the fifteenth century it was coming to be much more clearly marked. The larger groupings of estates were concentrated in very few hands.

The gentry, numbering several thousand families, shared with the lords the distinction of being regarded as noble, or gentle. They were a composite class, formed of a series of groups whose members derived their income and their prestige from different sources. Some were rich and leisured landowners. Some were satellites of the lords, serving them for wages in the administration of their estates, as armed retainers, or as menial servants in their households. A smaller group, but one growing in importance, served in the royal households or in various branches of the civil service. Still another group was made up of the leading members of the legal profession. These groups roughly paralleled each other in rank. From the point of view of precedence their members were divided into knights, esquires and ordinary gentlemen, but these titles did not in any sense denote separate classes. That of knight carried heavy and expensive military responsibilities that most people were anxious to avoid. That of esquire marked a degree of promotion in military or household service, but outside these it was often self-assumed, and often the same man might be described either as esquire or gentleman.

Three criteria determined whether a man was gentle. It was essential either to have security of fortune, which meant to have wealth in the form of lands, or else to be able to claim descent from a landed family. In both cases it was desirable to live up to certain cultural standards. Those who combined all three qualifications stood highest in the public esteem. They had inherited estates, and were able to live at leisure in the style that was considered fitting for men of rank, with servants about them. Their property gave them power, their birth gave them influence through connection with other families of note, and their way of living, which imitated, on a humbler scale, the ceremony and luxury of lordly households, seemed a visible demonstration of power and influence.

Birth was honored, independently of wealth, not only because it might spell influence, but because of the very strong belief in the inheritance of superior gifts, and because it was realized that pride in family traditions, especially traditions of military service, gave a man spirit and ambition. Yet younger sons had a struggle to maintain their position as gentlemen. Often they received little or no inheritance, having to be satisfied, as an Elizabethan cadet lamented, with 'that which the cat left on the malt heap.' Poverty would in time obliterate gentility. The easiest way for the younger son to maintain his status was probably by entering the service of a lord. But there is no evidence of prejudice against any occupation save that of retail trade. It was requisite only that one continue to live 'like a gentleman.'

Wealth, too, was honored, independently of birth, on condition that the man of property lived 'like a gentleman.' To live 'like a gentleman' meant to incline towards certain cultural ideals rather than to live in luxury or to spend any fixed amount of money. The ideals were aristocratic in quality, colored by love of country life, by the rudiments of a classical education, and by an interest in romances. But there were no specific customs peculiar to the gentry, nor did they have any elaborate code of manners.

The more successful members of the merchant class, particularly those in London, were to all intents and purposes regarded as the equals of gentlemen. This merchant class was composed of men with capital who handled foreign trade and wholesale distribution. Forming the governing class of the towns, they exercised great political power locally; as an important source of loans to the Crown they were frequently in touch with the central government; as authorities on foreign trade they were sometimes sent abroad on embassies. Intensely proud of their unique position, they kept themselves, at least in the larger towns, very much aloof from the retail traders, artisans and workers. But in London and in several other parts of the country, the century saw a growing rap-

---

EILEEN POWER: Eminent British medievalist (d. 1940) who made important contributions to English economic and social history and served as co-editor with Professor J. H. Clapham of Volume I of *The Cambridge Economic History of Europe from the Decline of the Roman Empire* (1944). Her collection of essays, *Medieval People* (1924), is a volume of social history at its best.

prochement between them and the gentry. There are many instances of men who called themselves indiscriminately 'merchant' or 'gentleman,' or 'merchant and gentleman.'

The structure of the rural classes is not at all clear. It probably differed greatly in different regions. One can draw a line of economic distinction between free-holders and tenant farmers, but there is no evidence of any social distinction between them. Both came under the heading of yeoman, an ambiguous term which also described menial and military servants below the rank of gentleman and man-at-arms. Some of the yeomen were quite as well off as the poorer country gentry, and there could have been only very small differences between them in their way of life. The yeoman's wife, if Bishop Latimer's recollections of his home were correct, milked the cows; the gentlewoman may have rebelled at this. But there are instances of men who were described in legal documents as 'gentleman and yeoman.'

As on their upper level the yeomanry merged into the lesser landed gentry, so on the other hand they merged into the copyholders, who in turn merged into the landless agricultural laborers, and together with the proletarian workers of the towns made up the bulk of the nation. Contemporary writers dismissed them as 'the common people,' and condescendingly described them as 'simple.' They lived in huts or tenements and had few personal possessions. Although something might be gleaned from manorial records, we know very little of their social relations among themselves, and we can only surmise what their attitudes were to the higher classes.

When so little is known of the masses of the people is one justified in affirming that the whole of English society at this time was rigidly stratified and pervaded by deference to social superiors? It must be admitted that there is much to support an impression of rigidity of structure—the power of the lords, the value set by the gentry on birth, the exclusiveness of the

merchants, the poverty of the workers, and the general religious orthodoxy of the age. Again, it seems as though the power that normally flowed from possession of property must have been abnormally magnified by the regard that men of the fifteenth century had for property. Whoever has money, Peter Idley advised his son, is 'as a Godde under God.' If gentlemen held views of this kind, there is at least a presumption that their attitudes were reflected among the lower classes.

Among the gentry class-consciousness was indeed highly conservative in tone. Its more extreme forms were evoked by resentment of the economic and social trends of the time. Throughout the century agricultural depression kept landlords under a cloud of anxiety. Their troubles were increased, from Edward IV's reign onwards, by the rising cost of keeping up with luxurious fashions in dress. The situation was the more irritating in that gentlemen could see the standard of living of the peasantry slowly improving. Furthermore, *nouveaux riches,* climbing out of the ranks of the merchant class and the lesser officials and the yeomanry, were buying land and laying claim to the title of gentleman. These circumstances naturally swelled the pride which the older families took in their pedigrees and their ancestral coats of arms, and also made them receptive to the new currents of aristocratic culture coming from France and from Italy. The doctrines of courtesy were welcomed the more because they might widen the gulf between the older gentry and their inferiors. Pedantic and snobbish doctrines of gentility were formulated and were bequeathed, a legacy of ultra-conservatism, to the sixteenth and seventeenth centuries.

The merchant class, too, was conservative in thought, and, like the gentry, was made so by difficulties. Shrinking foreign markets made it all the more desirable to check competition in the home market, and a means to this end was found in strict company organization. Merchants guarded the entrance to their gilds by the requirement of long terms of apprenticeship or high premiums, and they also jealously tightened their grip on local political powers.

Class consciousness was certainly, at these levels, bound up with strong forces of conservatism. But while it lent weight to desires for a static world, it had also an opposite character and opposite effects. Satisfaction with the social system and an attitude of deference towards superiors did not, for the individual, necessarily mean contentment with the state to which he was born. An exaggerated respect for power and wealth made them objects so much the more to be coveted; in other words, a great deal of energy was generated in the shape of social ambition. This is evident on every hand—in the marriage settlements of the gentry, in the provision that merchants made for education of their sons, in the family histories of gentlemen and of merchants, which frequently run back to humble and obscure origins.

That there was so much freedom to rise in the social scale was partly due to a difference in fertility between the upper classes and the lower rural classes. The former consistently failed to maintain their numbers, so that there was continuous opportunity for new men to establish themselves beside the proud old families of rank. There is reason to believe that the average baronial family died out, in the male line, in its third generation. This was not because the barons did not wish to perpetuate their families. On the contrary, they might have up to twenty-two children. But only the strong survived childhood, and not all marriages were fertile. Thus, even without the casualties suffered in the civil wars and on Tudor scaffolds, the old aristocracy would gradually have made way for new men. The wealthy landed gentry, leading less strenuous lives, may have made a slightly better showing. Their families ran up to twenty-five. But, just as was the case among the lords, the rate of child mortality was pathetically high, and not all marriages were

fertile. As to the gentlemen in menial or military service, they could not marry young nor lead a normal family life. In the merchant class gild regulations and a preference for rich wives combined to lower the birth rate by delaying the age of marriage. Families of over twenty nevertheless occurred, but a very high proportion of men died either childless or leaving daughters only. All these matters demand statistical treatment, and are to some extent, by methods of sampling, capable of being measured.

The late Professor Eileen Power used to say when people spoke of the immobility of the mediaeval scene, that it always looked to her as lively as an ant-heap. Fifteenth-century England was one of the less rapidly changing corners of that scene, yet it displayed a lively degree of social mobility, of movement not only from one community to another, but from one social class to another. This movement was as characteristic a feature of the class system as were the various exhibitions of class pride and class prejudice that have been emphasized.

One of the basic problems, then, of which the student of mediaeval conservatism must take account, is the coincidence and interlocking of forces of change with forces opposed to change. Since the subject is a broad one, it can be approached from many angles. Attitudes of prejudice and conservatism in regard to the social system being as a rule closely related to similar attitudes in regard to religion and government, a study of religious and political thought is indispensable. From the point of view of the social historian, however, there is a direct line of attack through the laborious analysis of class structure as it varied in one region and locality after another. Tension set up by chance variations from the normal manner and rate of social mobility may have had much to do with stiffening or relaxing attitudes of conservatism in regard to every type of change.

Tudor Times

PART FOUR

THE MILITARY VICTORY OF HENRY TUDOR, the nearest male representative of the House of Lancaster, over the last of the Yorkist kings, Richard III, brought to a close a generation of civil war and placed on the throne of England the dynasty that was to occupy it for more than a hundred years. It was thus that posterity came to look back upon the outcome of the battle that was fought on Bosworth Field in August, 1485, but many contemporaries must have regarded the Tudor triumph as merely another turn of the wheel in the inter-dynastic conflicts of the Wars of the Roses. Although Henry VII and his followers may have seen in their victory the judgment of God, their opponents could not be expected to acquiesce at once in this interpretation. There were Yorkist conspiracies during Henry's reign, but his marriage to Elizabeth of York, daughter of Edward IV, was intended to strengthen his position, and his son, Henry VIII, thus represented in his person the Red Rose of Lancaster and the White Rose of York. The Wars of the Roses were at last clearly a thing of the past. The solid achievements of Henry VII, in strengthening the royal power, curbing the aristocracy, and encouraging trade and industry, made possible the revolutionary accomplishments of his more glamorous son, whose character and policies have often been subjects of lively historical controversy, owing principally to his relation to the Reformation. Indeed, it is difficult to recognize the same man in extreme Protestant and in extreme Roman Catholic portrayals of Henry VIII. In the following appraisal, the late Professor A. F. Pollard, of the University of London, a distinguished specialist in Tudor history and author of the best existing biography of Henry VIII, sets forth his view of Henry's place in history.

HENRY VIII

A. F. POLLARD

A philosopher has said that "to popularise philosophy is at once to debase it." That, no doubt, is true of every kind of truth, but history runs a greater risk than most. Philosophy, like physical science, is the perquisite of experts; but history is the happy hunting-ground of the novelist, the playwright, the film-producer, and the correspondent who writes to the Press about things he admits he did not even learn at school. The "taste for Tudors" is less a taste for history or even for biography than for the common things which make the great akin to little men. The age of heroes and of hero-worship concentrated on the distinguishing features which raised men up above their fellows: democracy dotes on the defects which bring them down to a common level understanded of the people. If we cannot share the greatness of men, our self-esteem seeks fellow-feeling in their foibles. Some of the Tudors are immune from this ignominious popularity: even Shakespeare wrote no play about Henry VII, who would paralyse any film; for he merely conducted the most successful foreign policy in English history and established a throne on foundations invisible to opera glasses. Edward VI died at fifteen, disqualified by disease and early death from admission to the school for scandal, while

Reprinted by special permission from Katharine Garvin, ed., *The Great Tudors* (London: Ivor Nicholson and Watson Ltd., 1935), 23-33.

Mary was too conscientious or too plain. Elizabeth was anything but either, and Lytton Strachey's book *Elizabeth and Essex* were better named *Elizabeth and her Sex*. Martin Hume was more polite in his *Courtships of Queen Elizabeth* than in his *Wives of Henry VIII,* and it is Henry's wives who qualify him for posthumous popularity. The grave and right reverend Bishop Stubbs did, indeed, confess (while he was only a professor) that the portraits of those wives "were, if not a justification, at least a colourable occasion for understanding the readiness with which he put them away." But the more wives he put away, the more they cling to his memory.

Marriage was doubtless—though murder was not—one of the matters the Apostle had in mind when he counselled moderation in all things. The morality of the problem is obscure. Six mistresses would have been no news at a royal court; they would have eluded the film altogether, like the forty-five debited to Henry of Navarre or the unspecified number George II had in mind when he protested in tears to his dying Queen that he could not bear the thought of marrying again. Mere mistresses might, perhaps, have cast over Henry VIII the meretricious halo which now adorns the brow of that prince of profligates, Charles II. Even four wives might not have mattered: Henry's last queen, Catherine Parr, had four husbands without leaving a stain on her character; his brother-in-law the Duke of Suffolk had four wives and his sister Margaret Tudor, Queen of Scotland, three husbands. Six seems to have been the limit which divided the silly sheep from the giddy goats. The gravamen of the charge against Henry is not that he seduced the ladies of his court, but that he married them. The Papal Curia itself was lenient to mistresses; it was, indeed, as Mr. Hilaire Belloc has noted, "a common practice" for his "greater ecclesiastics" of that time to take a mistress, and Anne Boleyn only encountered Papal censures when Clement VII discovered that Henry really meant to marry her.

Henry could have had, if he wanted them, as many mistresses as Francis I without raising a ripple on the surface of English history. He had at least one, Bessie Blount, the mother of the Duke of Richmond, and almost certainly another, Mary, the elder sister of Anne Boleyn—both before he was thirty years of age. If there were others they have entirely escaped the records, his correspondence, and the chronicles of the time; not one has ever been named, and a hundred thousand contemporary documents can be searched in vain for any reference to a child of Henry's other than the Duke of Richmond, Edward VI, Mary, and Elizabeth. There was no secrecy about any of these, and total silence with regard to others is fairly conclusive proof that they never existed.

The King, indeed, was not in search or in need of a mistress, or even of a wife, so much as of a son to succeed him, carry on the Tudor succession, and avert a recrudescence of the Wars of the Roses. That was his engrossing problem throughout almost the whole of his reign; and it was only solved in the end by an Act of Parliament, to the terms of which—in spite of religious passions and rival claims—England stood staunch so long as a Tudor remained to fulfil them. Catherine of Aragon, whom he had not chosen himself, failed him: one miscarriage or still-born child succeeded another, and in 1514, after five years of parental misfortune Henry—or Wolsey—petitioned Leo X to annul the marriage with his brother's wife which another pope had sanctioned, doubting the validity of his own dispensation. Then in 1516 came Mary, who was welcomed, not for her own sake, but as an earnest of the son to follow. No woman had yet reigned in England, and Henry VII had secured the throne, not only by ending a civil war, but by excluding from the throne his mother, from whom he derived whatever hereditary right he possessed. The expected heir never followed Mary, and by 1527 it was certain that Henry VIII would have no legitimate son so long as Catherine remained his wife. He ceased to cohabit, though not to live, with her from that date, and fell a victim to the one grand passion of his life. It might provide a better hope for the succession than the *mariage de convenance* with Catherine. He was the second English king to marry for love and nothing else, and its ripe and refreshing fruit was Queen Elizabeth. But for five years he waited; the child must be legitimate, and a divorce from Catherine was confidently expected from Clement VII in 1529. It was refused: if, wrote the Pope's secretary, it is granted, "The Church cannot escape utter ruin, as it is entirely in the power of the Emperor's servants." Charles V's armies had almost turned Italy into a province of Spain; Catherine was his aunt, and Mary his cousin whose succession to the English throne he was bent on securing.

The Papacy was immovable: so was Henry on the question of the succession to his throne. So, too, was the Queen: her honour was involved, the legitimacy of her child, that child's prospects of a crown, and the Spanish alliance of which they were the emblems and the agents. The women of England supported her on the grounds of morality and sentiment; their husbands opposed on those of national policy. It was not yet a question of religion or the faith: the Lutherans and Tyndale, the Protestant martyr, denounced the divorce; and, could Clement VII have been constrained or persuaded to grant it, there might have been no immediate breach with Rome and no Act of Supremacy. France, for the sake of the English alliance and her ambitions in Italy, supported Henry, and the diplomatic struggle raged for three years. But, mean-

while, the Reformation Parliament assembled in November 1529 and gave voice to the anti-clerical tide which Wolsey had dammed for fifteen years. It overflowed, swept away some of the more notorious privileges and abuses, and enabled Henry to extort from the Church itself a reluctant admission of his supremacy. Warham died, protesting in vain, and Cranmer became Archbishop of Canterbury, while Cromwell succeeded to Sir Thomas More's and Stephen Gardiner's place in Henry's counsels. The Act of Annates robbed the Papacy of its revenues from English benefices, and the Acts of Appeals made England independent of its jurisdiction. Henry married Anne Boleyn about the end of January 1533, in the confidence born of her pregnancy, and on September 7, she gave birth to the future queen, Elizabeth. Finally, in 1534, the Royal Supremacy was enshrined in a Parliamentary statute, where it has remained ever since, save for Mary's Catholic reign and the Puritan regime a century later.

Never was revolution more skilfully draped as reform; it was made respectable, like treason, by success. Its path had, indeed, been prepared by centuries of struggle between Church and State, in which the Church had grown weaker and the monarchy stronger through the decline of ecclesiastical unity and the rise of secular nationalism; and the Church in England had already proved too weak to resist the royal demand that it should become the Church of England. Nevertheless, Henry VIII was the parent of what Lord Acton justly termed "a new polity." Hitherto there had been no "State" in England, but various

---

HILAIRE BELLOC: Versatile and prolific British author who has written essays, novels, poetry, literary criticism, social criticism, biography, and history. A leading figure in twentieth-century Roman Catholic intellectual circles, he stands out for his critical power and his admirable style.

LYTTON STRACHEY: Literary critic and biographer (d. 1932). A leading champion of the "new biography," he delighted in blasting the myths that surrounded the great men and women of the past. He achieved fame with the publication in 1918 of *Eminent Victorians,* and he continued his attempt to humanize and debunk great figures in his *Queen Victoria* (1921) and *Elizabeth and Essex* (1928).

Estates, of which the ecclesiastical were subject to papal, and the secular to royal, sovereignty. The Act of Supremacy brought all under one Sovereign and created out of them a single, novel State which also claimed to be an Empire, independent alike of Holy Roman Emperor and Holy Roman Pope; and, what was more, the emancipator became dictator and the father of all the Fascists in the world. The Middle Ages passed away in child-birth, and its child was what Michelet calls "le nouveau Messie, le Roi."

Happily, the Middle Ages had also left in England another child, born before the decadence and still surviving, though threatened in England and doomed elsewhere; and, with equal good fortune, Parliament found in Henry a foster-father who did not, like other Fascists, strangle the offspring left by the Middle Ages on the doorstep of modern despots. He nursed it, because he discerned its promise as a sure shield and weapon for his own defence and that of the realm. "He has always fortified himself by the consent of Parliament," wrote the Emperor's ambassador with an envious wish that Charles V could do the same. Of all the legends about Henry VIII, the most extravagant is that he sought to weaken Parliament. In truth he gave it and its acts a prestige and authority they had never possessed before; he enhanced its power and extended its sphere of authority; and critics in 1540 were jeering at "this new-found article of our creed, that Parliament cannot err." All his great acts were Acts of Parliament, and they fill in the statute-book more space than all the earlier Acts of Parliament put together.

This invitation to Parliament to share his work and strengthen his hands constitutes Henry's chief claim to statesmanship. It may be that he had no choice, and that Parliament was the only means at hand adequate to his purpose. But that implies that Parliament was the dominant factor in the situation, and that is a view which is not easily reconcilable with the decline of parliamentary institutions elsewhere or with the disdain in which they were held by

Wolsey and even by Henry VII. It is truer to say that Henry VIII felt the national impulse, discerned possibilities which were not yet explicit, and saw in Parliament the means of effecting his own particular objects. Only a national legislature could effect the breach with Rome, eradicate foreign jurisdiction, and make England the exclusive and common property of Englishmen. Wolsey's gaze was riveted on Rome; Henry's after 1529 on what he called his little island. That did not mean that he could not see beyond it. England herself was not an island; Wales and even Calais were brought within its Parliamentary system, and during his later years most of his attention was devoted to Ireland and Scotland: England for the English was to be expanded into Britain for the British.

But England was the core of the situation when theological dissension was rending Europe and precipitating it into a century of Wars of Religion. So long as she was united, said Henry, anticipating Shakespeare's words in *King John,* she could not be conquered; the problem was to keep it united and English Catholics and Protestants at peace with one another. His last speech to Parliament, a lay sermon on charity, summed up Henry's position. He denounced Catholics for calling Protestants heretics and anabaptists, and Protestants for calling Catholics papists, hypocrites, and pharisees, and asked "how can poor souls live in concord when you preachers sow amongst them in your sermons debate and discord?" Not that the laity were much better, and he was "sorry to hear how unreverently that most precious jewel, the word of God, is disputed, rhymed, and jangled in every alehouse and tavern." The balance he strove to maintain and the *via media* he sought to follow could only be achieved by supporting now the one and now the other disputant. In his breach with Pope and Emperor he had to rely on the Reformers, and Thomas Cromwell used the European situation to press him nearer to German Lutheranism than he liked. Catherine's death and the restoration of Mary to her place in the succession to the throne removed the grievance of Charles V, while Cromwell's unfortunate speculation on Anne of Cleves destroyed the German attraction. Cromwell fell, and Henry seemed bent for the rest of his life on showing that Catholicism was safer in essence but more capable of practical reform under his royal supremacy than under papal jurisdiction. It was a position which history showed that none but he could maintain.

But it had a profound effect on English politics. A critic has recently declared that in England "we have our rationalists and our free-thinkers, but only out of Continental soil can there spring the anti-clerical." It may seem odd to attribute this distinction to Henry VIII; but he had relieved the Church of the obloquy under which it suffered by reason of its privileges, wealth, control over laymen's lives and beliefs, and immunity from secular punishment for its crimes. It had enjoyed exclusive jurisdiction over heresy; when a layman was accused of heresy there was no benefit of · clergy, no sanctuary, no *habeas corpus,* and no trial by jury; and men were charged with heresy for merely refusing to pay "mortuaries"—a sort of ecclesiastical death-duty—on the death of infants who had no property. Such were some of the irritants, rather than any legitimate question of faith, which fomented the anti-clerical spirit. More tolerable evils were the unlimited number of benefices the favoured clergy might hold, their consequent absence from their livings, their lack of learning, their immersion in secular pursuits, and the extorionate charges for proving wills over which the ecclesiastical courts had exclusive jurisdiction. The worst of these evils were curbed by Henry's legislation, so far as they angered the English people; but Catholic countries in Europe had for the most part to wait till grievances festered into the fever of revolution; even after 1789 Spaniards attributed their sufferings at Napoleon's hands to the neglect of their duty to God in not burning heretics. Anti-clericalism thus became associated with Revolution rather than Reformation. Henry

VIII did not succeed in eliminating religion from English party-politics by subjecting the clergy to English common law, but by so doing he helped to relieve them of the bitterness which the survival of clerical privilege fomented on continental soil.

That was no disservice to the Church in England, however obnoxious it might seem to the Church abroad. But Henry was a nationalist and therefore a schismatic; Popes and Councils having failed in their efforts at reform, he determined to attempt it himself in his own dominions, hoping that others would follow suit. So far as England is concerned, his anti-ecclesiastical character has been exaggerated. He secured the concurrence of Convocation in all his measures; and instead of exasperating the mediæval conflict between Church and State, he brought it to an end. Whatever might happen elsewhere, he was determined that England should be united, self-sufficient, and independent. Within its borders there was to be no jurisdiction to rival that of the Crown in Parliament. But he did not contemplate the purely secular modern State: he was himself Head of the Church and a theologian of no mean learning; he took his unction at coronation seriously, and composed anthems still occasionally sung in our cathedrals. To the end of his reign bishops sat in his Privy Council and he had ecclesiastics as his Secretaries of State and chief diplomatists; even Convocation was still regarded as a "house" of Parliament. The royal head and the Parliamentary body were still supported by two legs, and stood on one foundation: Convocation as well as Parliament declared that England was an empire of itself; and the modern "taste for Tudors" is a comparatively innocuous expression of the spirit of nationalism that has gone to the heads of younger nations less experienced in the manners and methods of self-government which depend upon self-control.

This national reconciliation under the Crown in Parliament substituted a single for a dual control of the life and liberty, the faith, the law, and property of English people. It imposed upon them self-reliance; henceforth they could look to no appeals at Rome, to no papal censures or excommunications to remove a tyrant or chastise an heretical king. They must seek their remedies at home and realise that they were responsible for their own government. Some sought a remedy in rebellion, and the Pilgrimage of Grace was the first forcible protest against the new Tudor polity; it was followed by others which have been alleged as proofs of its unpopularity. The fact that they always failed points to a different moral. The rebellions were all against Parliament as well as against the Crown; and, while Parliament might rebel with success against the Crown, no rebellion against Parliament in England has ever succeeded. If the English had been taught to look to themselves for their own remedies, they had also learnt that remedies were not to be found by means of force imposed upon their own representatives. While other European countries were dispensing with representative systems and falling into the arms of despots or the abyss of civil war, Henry VIII wound round his royal carcase and the Tudor State a garment more effective than coats of armour. Had his constitution of Church and State been overthrown, Parliament would have died before becoming the mother of Parliaments scattered all over the world, upon whose vitality depends to-day the freedom of mankind. The New World would have been a mere replica of the Old, and government of the people, for the people, by the people, might have perished from the earth.

Man is often said to be greater than his work. It is hard to believe that of Henry VIII; his failings as well as his capabilities exceeded the measure of common humanity. His egotism was immense, and his people conspired to make it worse. The only apparent bulwark against a recrudescence of the Wars of the Roses, embittered perhaps by religious strife, his person was sacrosanct and his security the foundation of public peace. "These bishops," wrote his French ambassador in 1540, "make of him not

only a king to be obeyed, but an idol to be worshipped"; and the worship of man as a god is apt to make him a devil. Henry had some redeeming graces: he was apparently sincere in the Catholic faith he professed, and was at least scrupulous in his religious observance. He showed no personal animus against the victims of his statecraft, but he was a pitiless *étatiste;* the more eminent and the more conscientious the objector, the more needful to make him an example: the King was no respecter of persons. Men might argue a bill as much as they liked, but a law they must not impugn or resist. Bishop Gardiner relates the story of a dispute between him and Cromwell in Henry's presence whether the King's will should be the law, in which Cromwell maintained that it should, while the bishop held it better that the King should make the law his will. Henry chose the latter part, and no one was put to death in his reign except by due process of law or Act of Parliament; he was not in person the supreme court of his country for a single hour.

That does not, of course, exhaust the argument. Few kings of England have been in a better position to make their will the law. But that was not due to force of arms: his standing army consisted of a hundred yeomen of the guard, and for his defence against rebellion he depended on the good will of his people. When he grumbled about them, it was not on the ground of their disloyalty, but on that of their dissensions among themselves. Provided that national unity was preserved, he was not scrupulous over the means of preserving it, nor perhaps very particular about the shade of orthodoxy which England presented abroad; German or Scandinavian Protestants were as welcome allies, in case of need, as Catholic France or Spain. Against foreign foes he relied partly on fortifications which monastic masonry helped him to provide, but more on the English Navy, which was to him, from the earliest years of his reign, a plaything, a weapon, and almost a passion. He was an expert in shipbuilding and in artillery, and the Navy he founded enabled him to steer his national course without serious molestation from Catholic Europe. It was for the sake of that Navy that Philip II married Mary Tudor and proposed to Elizabeth; and it was by its means that Scotland was rescued from the clutches of France, and England was saved from the Spanish Armada.

Early in Henry's reign Erasmus described him as "a universal genius." The courtly remark indicates no more than the wide range of his interests and intelligence; but his learning was remarkable in a king, and although he confessed that writing was to him "somewhat tedious and painful," there survive pages and pages of diplomatic instructions, drafts of statutes, and plans of fortification written in his own hand. His immense vitality expressed itself on fields as divergent as sport and statesmanship, and the sport impressed itself most on the popular mind. But the only sphere in which he was really great was in statecraft. Fortunately, perhaps, he was no soldier, and so was not tempted to follow Henry V in his criminal folly of trying to annex France. But his understanding of English mentality and European politics was profound, and his bluff and hearty appearance concealed an intellect as subtle as Machiavelli's and as lithe as a panther's body. His phrases give an occasional glimpse into the workings of his mind: "three may keep counsel if two be away"; "if I thought that my cap knew my counsel, I would cast it into the fire"; "the opinion of the world is often stronger than truth." But, while he kept his own counsel, he exacted all that others could give. His theological conclusions were only reached after conference with both Catholics and Protestants: when a book of note appeared, he would tell one of them to read it, then give it to the other with similar injunction, and finally make them debate the crucial points in his presence. He was always

the King in Council and not the monarch alone, and he organised his Privy Council, with its regular sittings and formal minutes, out of the more fluid and less business-like Council of the Middle Ages. So, too, in spite of the disappearance of abbots from the House of Lords, attendance at its meetings grew steadily fuller, until in 1540 the clerk of the Parliaments began to note the absences instead of the daily presence of peers, as being the less laborious method.

Facts speak louder than words, and the fact that, so long as Henry and his three children were available, England would tolerate no one else on the throne is eloquent testimony to the impress he made on the minds of his people; so, too, was Elizabeth's public avowal at her accession that she intended to follow in his footsteps. Phrases like Cromwell's and Warwick's, which passed from mouth to mouth, to the effect that he was "the light of all the kings and princes in Christendom" and "the father of wisdom of all the world" may properly be discounted, though they were amplified by an Italian after Henry's death. But critical ambassadors at his court were hardly less emphatic: "he has no respect or fear," writes Charles V's, "for anyone in the world"; and, while Francis I's remarks that "this King, as all the world knows, is far from reckless," he adds, "when he decides on anything he goes the whole length." But the most remarkable testimony comes from Cardinal Pole, who had more reason than any other living man to loathe Henry VIII on personal, political, and religious grounds; for the King had proscribed the Cardinal, executed his mother and his brother, and extirpated the papal jurisdiction to which the Cardinal was heart and soul devoted. Yet, says Pole, writing from Rome to Protector Somerset two years after Henry's death, "he was the greatest King who ever ruled that realm."

QUESTIONS OF THEOLOGICAL DOGMA AND RELIGIOUS BELIEF had little to do with the ecclesiastical revolution which abolished all papal authority over the Church of England and made the king its supreme head. The Henrician Reformation, as it has been called, was anticlerical and nationalistic, but it was not Protestant, and during the reign of Henry VIII Protestants were burned at the stake as heretics while Roman Catholic opponents of the anticlerical and antipapal measures of the government were beheaded as traitors. The government, however, in making the Bible available to laymen in English translation, unintentionally promoted diversity in religious opinion which it tried in vain to check. During the next reign, that of the boy king, Edward VI, Henry's attempt to steer the English church along a middle course between Rome and Protestantism was abandoned, and a prayer book, the use of which in all religious services was made compulsory by act of Parliament, shows unmistakable Protestant influence. But this trend toward Protestantism was reversed under the next sovereign, Queen Mary, the daughter of Catherine of Aragon. By act of Parliament all legislation against the Papacy passed since the beginning of the Reformation Parliament (1529) was repealed, and the old heresy laws, which had been repealed under Edward VI, were restored. There ensued the Marian persecution, in the course of which some three hundred persons were burned at the stake as heretics and other Protestants went into exile on the Continent. In the bibliographical essay that follows, Professor W. M. Southgate, of Denison University, deals skillfully with the question of how far these Marian exiles were influenced by the ideas of Calvin.

THE MARIAN EXILES AND THE INFLUENCE OF JOHN CALVIN

W. M. SOUTHGATE

The English exiles of the reign of Mary have commonly been characterised as a group united upon the basic problems of doctrine and church government. Anglican historians have joined Roman Catholic historians in labelling the exiles without distinction as extreme protestants deeply imbued with the tenets of Geneva and determined to work towards the realisation of the Genevan ideal in England. The position taken by some of the more recent Anglican writers concerned with the general interpretation of the early years of the Elizabethan settlement, in particular Dixon,[1] Frere,[2] and Wakeman[3] is worth consideration. The first of these is, and most probably will remain,

the definitive work on the English Church through the early part of Elizabeth's reign. Frere's volume is the ablest treatment of the reign, and Wakeman's perhaps the best short history of the Church of England.

Frere asserts that the exiles consisted mainly of those who "set least store on the bonds that tied them to historic catholicity.

[1] Richard Watson Dixon, History of the Church of England (Oxford, 1895-1902).

[2] W. H. Frere, The English Church in the Reigns of Elizabeth and James I (London, 1924).

[3] H. O. Wakeman, An Introduction to the History of the Church of England (London, 1927).

Reprinted by special permission from History, XXVII (1942), 148-152. The footnotes have been renumbered.

... In more or less degree they came under the spell of Calvin's genius, and were influenced by the imposing comprehensiveness of the new scheme of doctrine and discipline which he substituted for the system of the catholic and apostolic church." In Geneva they had sat at the feet of Calvin, and in Frankfort they had disturbed the peace with their disputes.[4] Wakeman agrees with this point of view in general, and adds that, tainted as they were with Swiss opinions contracted during their travels, it would be dangerous to appoint them to administer an ecclesiastical system of which they did not approve.[5] Even Dixon joins the chorus with the statement: "They were of one colour. This colour had grown deeper with banishment."[6]

An examination of the acts and writings of the exiles during their stay on the continent and afterwards when they returned to England reveals that they were in no sense unified,[7] that while the influence of Calvin was probably the strongest single influence upon their thought, it was only one of a number of influences, and one from which many of the exiles were in large part free.

The troubles at Frankfort in certain respects redound to the credit of the exiles.

In the years 1554 and 1555 Cox, Grindal, Jewel, and others maintained the prayer-book against a Genevan substitute. They fought unscrupulously and with instruments not worthy of men of God. But, in fairness to Cox and his party, it should be noted that all subsequent accounts of the struggle have been based upon the accounts of Whittingham[8] and Knox,[9] the leaders of the Genevan opposition. While there is no evidence of the inaccuracy of these contemporary authorities, their interest in the case tends to disqualify them as judges of the motives of the conservatives. Cox and his party, as Mr. Knappen has pointed out, were intent upon the maintenance of the Anglicanism they had brought over with them.[10] It is a purpose not likely to have justified them in the eyes of Whittingham and Knox. Their actions, however, provide indisputable evidence of the existence of a powerful group among the exiles openly opposed to Calvin and his influence. The effort of this Anglican group to defend its actions to Calvin by a letter written after the departure of Whittingham is no proof "that they continued to regard themselves as Calvinists, and that they considered that the English Church had been founded and formed on

[4] Frere, *English Church*, p. 8.
[5] Wakeman, *Church of England*, p. 306.
[6] Dixon, *History*, v, 34.
[7] One need look no farther than Dixon's own detailed treatment of the controversies abroad for evidence of the lack of unity.

[8] (William Whittingham) *A Brieff discours off the troubles begonne at Frankford in Germany, etc.* (1575, Zurich ?).
[9] John Knox, *Works*, by David Laing (Edinburgh, 1846-54), IV, 1-50.
[10] M. M. Knappen, *Tudor Puritanism* (Chicago, 1939), p. 127.

ERASTIANISM: Doctrine associated with the name of the sixteenth-century theologian Thomas Erastus. In its popular form it came to mean the supremacy of the state in the regulation of ecclesiastical affairs.

INSTITUTES OF THE CHRISTIAN RELIGION: Work by John Calvin. First published in 1536, it was expanded and modified by Calvin on numerous occasions before his death in 1564. It stands out as the most important theological exposition of sixteenth-century Protestantism.

LAMBETH ARTICLES: Doctrinal statements issued by Archbishop Whitgift in 1595 in an attempt to win Puritan support for the Elizabethan religious settlement. Since they failed to win the approval of Elizabeth or of Parliament, they were ineffective.

MATTHEW PARKER: Marian exile who became Archbishop of Canterbury under Elizabeth. He championed a middle-of-the-road position between Roman Catholicism and staunch Protestantism.

the Continental model."[11] It was by no means clear in 1555, or even later, that an Anglican must have no intercourse with Calvin; that a request for advice upon one point involved acceptance of his authority upon all points, or even upon the particular point in question.

The later struggle at Frankfort was over a somewhat different issue, the authority of the minister. Horne, now minister of the English there, made a vigorous though undignified fight for his authority and for uniformity. The basic issue in this quarrel was the threat of what is later known as Congregationalism. Horne, like Cox before him, was in fact defending a fundamental tenet of Anglicanism.

Further evidence of the conservatism of the group at Frankfort and its independence of Geneva is shown by a step taken just prior to the return of the exiles to England upon the accession of the new sovereign. The former Frankfort malcontents, Knox, Whittingham, and others, now at Geneva, addressed letters to the English in other centres, setting forth a standard of doctrine and church government to be followed upon their return to England. To accept the proposals meant in effect the denial of the English prayer-book[12] and an assumption of authority by the congregation without precedent in English church history. Lever and his congregation at Aarau expressed their willingness to discuss the matter.[13] But Pilkington and Nowell, who were then in charge of the church at Frankfort, declared unequivocally that such matters must be settled in due order in England. There is no record of an answer from the English congregation at Strassburg and no evidence that a letter was even sent to the congregation at Zürich.

Only a small number of the English leaders during the Marian exile and later in England can be said to have accepted Calvin's ideas completely. Mr. Knappen estimates that "something like a quarter of the total number of English religious exiles . . . came under Genevan influence."[14] However, even this small percentage should be qualified, for in his list of Englishmen who were at one time or another in Geneva and hence presumably "under Genevan influence," he names among others, Lever and Pilkington. Lever was there from April 1554 to January 1555.[15] It was after the latter date that he headed the early opposition to Knox in Frankfort. His short visit to Geneva later in 1555 is insufficient evidence, as Mr. Knappen would have it, "of the success of the Geneva undertaking."[16] Pilkington was only in Geneva from April to June 1556.[17] His action afterwards as head of the Frankfort congregation in refusing to accept the proposals of the Geneva group for a united front suggests that the influence of Geneva had not been overpowering.

The Strassburg group under Horne and Grindal and the group around Peter Martyr and Jewel at Zürich were even less inclined than Pilkington and Nowell to take their orders from Geneva. The English at Strassburg throughout the period of exile constituted a virtual centre of opposition to the Calvinists. It was to the Strassburg group that the conservative party at Frankfort looked for advice, and it was under the leadership of men sent from Strassburg that the party of Knox was finally defeated.

The authorities on the continent to whom many of the English turned rather than to Calvin were Peter Martyr and Heinrich Bullinger. The closeness of the relationship is shown by the voluminous correspondence of the exiles with Zürich upon their return to England. Martyr was perhaps closest to

[11] A. B. Hinds, *The Making of the England of Elizabeth* (New York, 1895), p. 32.

[12] Dixon, *History,* v, 36-7.

[13] *Troubles,* lxxxvi, ff. Knappen, *Tudor Puritanism,* p. 165, declares that Lever and his congregation "wholeheartedly accepted the Genevan proposals." His reference for this statement, however, is the *Troubles,* which gives no such impression.

[14] Knappen, *Tudor Puritanism,* p. 142.

[15] C. H. Garrett, *The Marian Exiles* (Cambridge, 1938), p. 220.

[16] Knappen, *Tudor Puritanism,* p. 143.

[17] Garrett, *Marian Exiles,* p. 250.

the English of all the continental leaders. He had known many of them in England, and his association with the English Church of Edward VI had been intimate. Martyr, it is true, held Calvin in great respect; he found himself, as did many later leaders of the English Church, in thorough agreement with the author of the *Institutes* concerning the doctrine of predestination. But his agreement did not by any means extend to all matters. Martyr seems to have been quite willing to remain a safe distance from the tyrant of Geneva. Mr. C. H. Smyth has pointed out that while Martyr found it altogether impossible to leave Strassburg when Calvin invited him to Geneva, only a year later he found it a simple matter to leave Strassburg in order to join Bullinger at Zürich.[18]

Because Bullinger and his colleagues at Zürich had signed the *Consensus Tigurensis* with Calvin, it does not follow that the Zürich group was subject to Calvin's domination.[19] It would be equally logical to conclude that the church at Geneva was subservient to Zürich. In the middle decades of the century, and indeed later, Calvin and Bullinger were regarded by many protestants as leaders of comparable authority, quite independent of one another. "Bullinger did not always see eye to eye with" Calvin, "nor did the Züricher's contrary judgments always fall on deaf ears"[20] outside his own city. Agreed as were Zürich and Geneva upon certain fundamentals of doctrine, the Zürich reformers showed themselves during the period of exile, and later during the reign of Elizabeth, far more tolerant of the Anglican point of view than did Calvin and his great followers, Knox and Beza.

The atmosphere of the group gathered around Martyr first at Strassburg and then at Zürich was humanistic. The learning at Geneva was profound, but it was a severe and rigid learning, unsympathetic to the interest which Martyr and Jewel displayed in the study of humane letters, an interest so vividly portrayed by Laurence Humfrey in his *Vita Juelli.*

In general, the differences among the exiles have been stressed only to their discredit. The exiles were factious and quarrelsome—at times guilty of mean and questionable actions. Yet their differences were the result of fundamental disagreements upon which little compromise was possible. The conservatives among the exiles fought to retain the Book of Common Prayer and its teachings. They defended the Anglicanism of Cranmer against radical attack just as the Archbishop had defended it against the assaults of the Marian counter-reformation. That they did not pay the price of martyrdom, that their means were less noble than those of Cranmer and Ridley, should not detract from their essential purpose. Bishop Creighton has written that at the accession of Elizabeth there were to be found no men of middle ground, so that some had to be brought up by experience, by a period of training, "into harmony with the Anglican system."[21] Doubtless the administrative duties with which the exiles were entrusted upon their return to England made them more conservative as the years went by. But they were not fundamentally changed by the weight of authority. Their responsibilities tended rather to strengthen the moderate conservatism which was already theirs.

However, the error should not be made of placing even the more conservative of them under one label. The early Elizabethan churchmen range all the way from the extremely conservative Matthew Parker to Grindal and Parkhurst among the bishops themselves, and on to Sampson and Humfrey, not to mention Whittingham, Coverdale, and others even farther to the left. In this gradation from left to right, Jewel, Cox, Horne, Nowell, Pilkington, and even Sandys, will be found bridging the gap

[18] C. H. Smyth, *Cranmer and the Reformation under Edward VI* (Cambridge, 1926), pp. 123-24.

[19] Smyth, *Cranmer,* p. 21, note 1.

[20] Knappen, *Tudor Puritanism,* p. 137.

[21] Mandell Creighton, article on John Jewel in the *Dictionary of National Biography.*

between Parker and his unfortunate successor in the see of Canterbury.[22]

The Anglican historians have tended to be severely critical of the early Elizabethans, perhaps for the reason that, with the exception of Dixon, they have generally stressed the puritan controversies during the latter part of the reign, and therefore naturally stress the puritan aspect in the earlier years. They have underscored that which was to become puritanism, forgetting that the first problem faced by these men and the Church under Elizabeth was to combat Rome and to satisfy moderate opinion in England.

In doctrinal matters the Anglican Church, from the time of Archbishop Parker to the end of the century, was Calvinistic. The Lambeth Articles cannot otherwise be interpreted. Doctrine, however, is only a part of the structure of the Church, and may take a particular form independent of the remainder of the structure. Because Anglican doctrine was in essential agreement with Calvinistic doctrine, it does not follow that the authority for doctrine need be Calvin or the authority cited by Calvin. In the case of the English Church the doctrinal authority sketched by Bishop Jewel in the early part of Elizabeth's reign, and later developed and elaborated by Richard Hooker, could never have received the approval of Calvin, and was never accepted by those who continued to look to Geneva for leadership.

In less theoretical matters the English Church of the Elizabethan settlement was even farther removed from the Genevan ideal. The governmental organisation of the Church is the clearest case in point. Its episcopal structure, its Erastianism, is in direct contrast to the theocratic congregationalism of Calvin. In regard to the liturgy, the differences between Anglican and Calvinist which had caused the quarrels at Frankfort were short-lived. The Edwardian prayer-book, modified in the direction of earlier English forms rather than towards the Genevan model, was generally accepted. There was no effective opposition on this score. The Church as a whole accepted a uniform service which was Anglican. There was less agreement upon the problem of ecclesiastical vestments. Here, however, the opposition to the Anglican teaching looked for leadership to continental protestants in general, and not merely to Calvin. Furthermore, having accepted the Anglican settlement in regard to church government, the early churchmen came, if reluctantly, to accept the moderate Anglican habits. On this point, and on this alone, did continental protestantism force a disagreement between the early leaders of the Church and the Government. And it was settled, with the advice of the more moderate continental protestants,[23] by the acceptance of uniformity in clerical dress.

The Elizabethan churchmen, the exiles of Mary's reign, carried on the tradition of Cranmer rather than that of Calvin. Varied in ability, in learning, in character, they were Anglicans. Theirs should be the credit for preserving Anglicanism during the exile and reestablishing it upon firm ground in the difficult early years of the new reign. It is important that while the greatest of English reformers perished at the stake, there remained, as Dixon has pointed out, a group of great learning, more radical perhaps than Cranmer, but able nevertheless to cooperate with Parker in administering a newly organised church and defending it with traditional weapons against Rome and before the people.

[22] Frere (English Church, p. 71) recognises the degrees of radicalism among the bishops, allowing that Jewel represents a protestantism too learned to be "merely protestant." Similarly, J. Trésal in Les Origines du schisme anglican (Paris, 1908), p. 383, places Grindal far to the left and Jewel in the centre.

[23] The correspondence between the English and their continental advisers is published in the Parker Society edition of The Zürich Letters (Cambridge, 1842), vol. i, letters lviii, lx, lxi, lxix, lxxvii, xcviii, and appendix, letters ii-vi.

IN MOST RESPECTS QUEEN ELIZABETH PRESENTED a sharp contrast to the half-sister whom she succeeded on the throne. She was pre-eminently of the earth, earthy, and seemingly devoid of any strong religious convictions. She looked upon religion from a political point of view. Outward religious diversity, in her scheme of things, was a source of political weakness and therefore not to be permitted, but she declined to pry into men's souls. The old heresy laws, revived under Mary, were finally repealed at the beginning of Elizabeth's reign, and there were no more burnings at the stake. Roman Catholics were put to death during her reign, to be sure, but it was on the ground that they had committed treason or other high crimes, not because they believed in transubstantiation or some other Catholic doctrine. By the Act of Uniformity passed in the first Parliament of her reign, Roman Catholic services in England were legally banned, but Elizabeth's policy in the enforcement of anti-Catholic legislation was for some years after her accession to the throne decidedly lenient. What changed her policy was a papal bull issued in 1570 in which the Pope, not content with excommunicating her and her adherents as heretics, declared her to be deposed, absolved her subjects from the allegiance they had sworn to her, and positively commanded them not to obey her laws. Obedience to the Pope and obedience to the Queen thus became irreconcilable. Not all English Roman Catholics followed the lead given by Rome, but in the eyes of nonpapalists in England all Englishmen who recognized the authority of the Pope were potential traitors. In Elizabeth's relations with foreign governments—and with rebels against foreign governments—English interests were always paramount. Mary had been the child of an international marriage of convenience, as much Spanish in descent as she was English, and she became the subservient ally, as well as the adoring wife, of her Spanish cousin Philip II. Elizabeth's Englishry, on the other hand, was unimpeachable. In the essay that follows, Professor Conyers Read, of the University of Pennsylvania, the outstanding contemporary American student of Tudor history, sees in the sympathetic understanding that existed between Elizabeth and the rank and file of her subjects the chief source of her strength. Whatever her courtiers and ministers thought of her, to the average Englishman she was "Good Queen Bess."

GOOD QUEEN BESS

CONYERS READ

Queen Elizabeth of England had established her claim to greatness many years before her death. Two of the greatest of her contemporaries, Pope Sixtus V. and King Henry of Navarre, who were agreed upon little else, were agreed upon that. In the generation which succeeded her there was no difference of opinion about the matter. Camden, Speed, and Stow all wrote of her in terms of extravagant admiration, so did

Reprinted by special permission from *The American Historical Review*, XXXI (1926), 647-661. The footnotes which originally appeared with this essay have been omitted.

Sir Francis Bacon. James I. himself, who had many excellent personal reasons for not cherishing her memory, declared her to have been one "who in wisdom and felicity of government surpassed all the Princes since the days of Augustus."

During the whole of the seventeenth century the day of her accession was celebrated as a public holiday. It is a curious thing that in the time of the civil wars her memory seems to have been cherished with equal fervor by both parties. The Cavaliers looked back upon her as the champion of the Anglican Church and the royal prerogative, the Puritans as the defender of the true religion against Roman Catholicism. In fact, the Cavaliers had much more justification for their attitude than the Puritans had, but such was Elizabeth's position in the hearts of the English that those who were fighting hardest against her political and religious system contrived to frame an image of her to their liking. Cromwell himself pronounced her Queen Elizabeth of famous memory and added "we need not be ashamed to call her so." In the unfamiliar guise of Protestant champion she managed to survive almost unscathed the period in English political thought best calculated to produce her sternest critics.

It is rather delightful to observe that the rationalistic temper of the eighteenth century found her as much to its taste as did the religious temper of the seventeenth, and for precisely the opposite reason. Hume the philosopher and historian commended her for her very lack of that religious partizanship which the Puritans had singled out for praise.

The nineteenth century was on the whole not less kind to her. It is hardly to be expected that she would appeal strongly to the conventional respectability of Agnes Strickland, or to the zealous Romanism of Lingard, but Macaulay and Green both acknowledged her essential greatness, Carlyle is quite carried away with admiration of her, and the two most conspicuous of her modern biographers, Creighton and Beesly, endorse, with some decent reserva-

tions, the judgment of her contemporaries. [J. E. Neale is the author of the best biography of Elizabeth now available.] Yet the nineteenth century produced perhaps the most severe of all her critics in James Anthony Froude. Froude has probably done more than any one else to set the prevalent impression of her, and justly so, for no historian of sixteenth-century England has worked harder to wring the truth from the sources. It were going too far afield to summarize with any fullness his estimate of Elizabeth. He exonerates her of the charges against her private character, but his estimate of her as a queen is a low one. To Froude the central fact of her reign was the struggle against the Counter-Reformation, and since Elizabeth herself resolutely refused to define her problem in those terms, Froude will frankly have none of her. He concedes that she found England poor and weak and left her rich and powerful, but because her ways were not his ways, he ascribes her achievements more to good luck than good management. When things went right, they went right in spite of her, when they went wrong, they went wrong because of her. This is good partizan logic, but it does not explain much. The one thing certain is that the policy of Elizabeth— and no one can seriously question that it was she herself who defined the policy of her government—was eminently successful. Whether the policy proposed by James Anthony Froude would have been more successful none but the high gods know.

The woman Elizabeth is a sufficiently familiar figure. Most of the portraits of her which survive are of middle or late life, when she wore a red wig and her face had grown long and hatchety, but it is clear enough that even in her youth she was not beautiful. There is intelligence and force and a good deal of pride in her countenance, but no indications of the gentler attributes of womanhood, nor of what we call nowadays feminine charm. She is said to have been sickly. Not long ago we were treated to an elaborate analysis of her health which left her scarcely a leg to stand on. Nevertheless her physique proved to be equal to the strain of over forty years of the most exacting and nerve-racking kind of labor. She lived to bury every one of the group of courtiers and statesmen who surrounded her at her accession. Up to her time hers was, with one exception, the longest reign in English history, and only two English sovereigns since have reigned longer than she.

She had a sharp tongue, a vile temper, almost no feminine delicacy, and little or no feminine modesty. Of personal loyalty and affection she seems to have commanded little or none. Her popularity, which was great, lay entirely outside the circle of those who knew her intimately. In this respect she stood in marked contrast to her rival, Mary Stuart. A great deal has been written about her morals. Whether or not she lived and died a virgin will probably never be determined with certainty—nor is it a matter of any political consequence. No one ever commanded her heart, nor did her passions, if she had any, ever betray her judgment in a major issue. The probabilities are that she lacked any strong sex impulse, though Pollard's argument that she was sterile lacks conviction. Her coquetry was of so blatant a sort that one is almost tempted to assume a conscious effort on her part to emphasize what she conceived to be the attributes proper to her sex. It reminds one rather of the antics of college boys

playing girls' parts in undergraduate dramatics.

Though the circumstances attending her birth ought to have marked her as a child of the Reformation, she was both by temper and by training the child of the Renaissance. No one of her time was more unsympathetic with medieval standards, whether of morals, of religion, or of politics; none a more vigorous exponent of *Realpolitik,* none a more adroit opportunist. If this attitude of mind had not been natural to her she could hardly have escaped the pitfalls which beset her early life. Her mother was executed while she was still a baby; before she was three she was branded a bastard and she lived under that stigma during much of her early childhood. While she was still a mere girl she became involved, probably through no fault of her own, in an unsavory scandal with her stepfather, and had she not been wary, might well have drawn by his ambitious schemes into a position analogous to that of the unfortunate Lady Jane Grey. During her sister's reign she was cast by discontented Protestants for the part which discontented Catholics cast for her rival, Mary Stuart, later; but she was clever enough to conceal any connection with their treasonable purposes, if indeed there was any. Her whole youth was spent leaping from tussock to tussock through a bog of intrigue and conspiracy, with no other guide than her mother-wit and perhaps no other purpose

GLORIANA: One of the names used by Edmund Spenser in his *Faerie Queene* to refer to Elizabeth.

JOHN LINGARD: Eminent Roman Catholic priest and historian (d. 1850). His multivolume *History of England,* published between 1819 and 1830 and revised often in subsequent years, is a classic in the literature of English history. It presents its subject from the standpoint of a moderate Roman Catholic who wished to overcome Protestant suspicions. The *History* was the most important historical study written by a Roman Catholic since the age of the Reformation.

SIR FRANCIS WALSINGHAM: Elizabethan political leader (d. 1590) who served as secretary of state for almost twenty years. He supported a militant anti-Spanish policy, and he viewed Mary, Queen of Scots, as a menace to England. Indeed, he was largely responsible for the decision to execute her in 1587. He is the subject of a monumental three-volume biography by Conyers Read.

than self-preservation. It is not surprising if in this mad dance with death she was forced to scrap any convictions she may have had, and if she lost any nice sense of honor or feminine delicacy. Nor is it surprising, when she reached something like solid ground at last, if she had developed extraordinary agility, both of mind and of conscience, extraordinary quickness in sizing up a situation, extraordinary readiness to go backwards or forwards or sidewise, wherever a new foothold seemed to offer, extraordinary indifference to anything like a logical and orderly progress, along with extraordinary self-confidence in her ability to get on somewhere somehow.

In nothing was Elizabeth more true to character than in her attitude towards the religious questions which in her time divided Europe into two hostile camps. If she was committed by the facts of her birth to the side against Rome she was well disciplined by the circumstances of her upbringing to accept the religious formulae imposed by the law of the land. A Henrican Catholic under her father, she became first a moderate and then a rather radical Protestant under her brother and then, with as good a grace as might be, a Roman Catholic at the direction of her older sister. There is no sound evidence that she ever displayed enthusiasm for any one of these creeds or ever revealed a strong distaste for any of them. She appears even then to have accepted the proposition that the establishment of religion was a matter which belonged properly to the prerogative of the crown. Her youthful experience must have fortified her in the belief that such a proposition was acceptable to the average Englishman. Before she was five and twenty she had seen him swallow at least three radical changes in his religion without any great fuss about the matter. She must have remarked too the relative indifference of England's neighbors to her religious vagaries. Her father and her brother both had carried through their religious programmes without any protracted disturbance of their international relations. No wonder then if Eliza-

beth, when she ascended the throne, approached the problem of religion with the conviction that her subjects would accept what she imposed and that her neighbors would never regard religion as such as a *casus belli*. It is doubtful if she attached much importance to questions of theology. Her final endorsement of a position opposed to Roman Catholicism is probably to be explained rather by her opposition to papal authority than to Roman Catholic theology. Like her father she not only resented outside interference in the affairs of the Church in England, but she believed the direction of the religious life of her people to be essential to the integrity of her crown. Her disposition to subordinate religion to political control was quite consonant with the spirit of the times. It had its counterpart in the so-called Gallican movement in France, in the Augsburg settlement in Germany, and even in the attitude of so loyal a Catholic as Philip II. towards papal authority in Spain. Whether we should regard it in Elizabeth's case as a manifestation of Tudor despotism or of Tudor nationalism it is difficult to say. In any case it commanded popular support because it harmonized with the strong national spirit of Elizabethan England.

Elizabeth might perhaps have stopped where her father did and have limited her ecclesiastical changes to a breach with Rome, preserving all the essentials of the old church except its ultramontane government. But as Maitland has remarked, there was nothing to be gained by mere schism, no popular support to be expected from such a course. It must either be Catholicism and the pope, or something like the creed for which Cranmer and Ridley had died. If Elizabeth was to abandon Rome she must recruit her strength from the other camp. She could never forget that it was after all the Protestants who had borne her to the throne; hence her concessions to the new theology in the 39 Articles, put as ambiguously as might be. But she was not prepared to go far in that direction and she was not concerned at all about harmonizing her ecclesiastical arrangements with Protestant movements on the Continent. Her church was to be English; if it was not to be Roman it was certainly not to be Swiss or German. And it was to be under royal headship, whether that headship was to be expressly stated or decently veiled under an *et cetera* clause in her titles, and it was to be unchallenged. Of any open diversity of creeds in her realm she would no more hear than she would hear of a diversity of governments. Religious dissent was no more to be tolerated than political rebellion. The two were indeed classified together in her mind as they were in the minds of most of her contemporaries. As to the democratic ideas of church government emerging from Geneva, they were particularly obnoxious to her. She remarked on one occasion to the French ambassador that the Puritans did not wish to recognize either God or the king, an observation which forecasts the better known comment of her successor. It will not be forgotten that John Knox had barely preceded her accession with his *First Blast of the Trumpet against the Monstrous Regiment of Women,* which he protested was not directed against her but which stood long in her mind as a fair indication of the attitude of militant Puritanism towards her and her office.

On the other hand, Elizabeth, as she herself protested, had no desire to open windows into men's souls. Outward conformity to the legally established religion she demanded, but given that men might think as they pleased. She was not interested in saving souls from hell fire, she was interested in an orderly state; and religious dissension, as she had good reason to know, meant civil disorder of the worst kind. There was a considerable amount of religious persecution in her reign, but it was directed not so much against religious beliefs as against the political implications of those beliefs. The Roman Catholics were treated with singular mildness until their religious propaganda became badly entangled with treasonable purposes against the crown. The Puritans she tolerated so

long as they confined their attention to conforming and criticizing. It was when they showed themselves to be openly rebellious against her ecclesiastical arrangements that they felt her heavy hand. She was in fact *a politique,* whose attitude towards religious questions was shaped entirely by political considerations. Once again she belongs to the Renaissance, not to the Reformation, with William of Orange and Catherine de Médicis and Henry of Navarre, not with Admiral Coligny and Philip of Spain. It was her very indifference to religious considerations *per se* which kept her more zealous Protestant councillors constantly on tenterhooks. They were never by any means sure that she would not turn back to the old faith for a consideration. Walsingham, her principal secretary, wrote to one of his Puritan brethren as late as 1578: "If you knew with what difficulty we retain that we have and that the seeking of more might hazard (according to man's understanding) that which we already have, you would then . . . deal warily in this time when policy carrieth more sway than zeal."

It was the irony of fate that a woman of Elizabeth's temper should have been called to rule over England at a time when the national destiny was or seemed to be so intricately involved in issues purely religious. Many of her wisest councillors insisted that her welfare was bound hand and foot to the fortunes of European Protestantism, struggling for its very life against the forces of the Counter-Reformation. They stormed and fumed because of her refusal to support whole-heartedly the cause of the Dutch rebels and of the French Huguenots. They figured her forth as the anointed champion of the Protestant faith. But Elizabeth steadily refused to accept the rôle they assigned to her. As she was never prepared to wage war for religious reasons herself, so she never could be brought to think that her neighbors were. Notwithstanding all the talk of Catholic leagues for the extermination of heretics, she believed that in the long run dynastic and national considerations would dominate the policy of the Catholic princes as they did her own. She was always prepared to exploit the resources of Protestantism for the benefit of England, but she was never prepared to allow the resources of England to be exploited for the benefit of Protestantism. She supported the Dutch rebels because they were a thorn in the side of Philip of Spain, whom she thought to be over-strong for her safety, but it is to be observed that when the French threatened to annex the Low Countries she was quite willing to join forces even with the Duke of Alva to prevent them. She supported the Huguenots because they served to weaken France and the strength in France of the party opposed to herself, but she was talking marriage with the offspring of Catherine de Médicis within six months after St. Bartholomew's. Her main objectives were to keep herself on the throne, England at peace, and her subjects contented and happy. If she could do that by feeding religious fires in her neighbors' houses, feed them she would, but as for crusaders' swords or martyrs' crowns, she was no more disposed to draw the one than she was to assume the other.

Her technique was essentially that of the Italian school of statecraft—cautious, crafty, and altogther untrammelled by moral considerations or by *a priori* convictions about anything human or divine. It was the product of the days of her weakness but she never abandoned it in the days of her strength. War she sought by all means to avoid, partly from sound reasons of state but partly also because war was uncongenial to her temper. In the indirect crooked ways of sixteenth-century diplomacy she found her true *métier*. She was always averse from bold and resolute courses and particularly from courses which admitted of no alternative. It suited her best to have a foot in every camp, and a finger in every pie, to keep open every door to advance, and to close no door to retreat.

Neither her enemies nor her intimate councillors ever knew what she would do next. She did not mean that they should know. Very likely she did not know herself.

It was of the essence of her plan of action that she had no plan of action. She was ten years and more making up her mind to send troops to assist the Dutch rebels; within a fortnight of their despatch she was contemplating their recall. She delayed Norfolk's execution for months, not because she was not convinced of his treason, but because she did not wish to cut herself entirely off from the parties in England which he represented. It took her a still longer time to consent to the trial of Mary Queen of Scots and almost to the last she dallied with the idea of coming to terms with her adversary. It was altogether characteristic that even after Mary had been judged and condemned Elizabeth should have sought to evade responsibility for her death, first by getting her secretly murdered, and, when she found her servants too "dainty" for that grim business, by laying the blame for Mary's execution upon her secretary. Her father had a short way with traitors, but there was something too dreadfully definitive about the headsman's axe to suit his temporizing daughter.

Not the least remarkable thing about Elizabeth was her ability to utilize the resources peculiar to her sex. First to last she played a woman's game. A great deal of righteous mid-Victorian indignation has been directed against her devious ways in courtship. No doubt, judged by mid-Victorian standards, she deserved it. But she was in no position to cultivate the smug respectability of Queen Victoria, and very likely had little taste for it. Courtship was to her a diplomatic asset of first-rate importance, and its value to her from this point of view was increased precisely in proportion to the disposition of her contemporaries to regard it simply as a more or less modest device for getting a husband.

It will hardly be necessary to point out the advantages conceded by the conventions of love-making to the lady in the case. They have not greatly changed in the last three centuries. When the lady happened to be a queen to boot, and, as Walsingham put it, "the best marriage in her parish," these advantages were naturally stretched to the limit. Elizabeth recognized in this a rare diplomatic opportunity. She could play fast and loose with royal suitors, blow hot or cold as the exigencies of the international situation demanded, and excuse herself in the end for the most outrageous and transparent breaches of faith on the ground that her heart was not convinced. It is quite possible that her appreciation of the diplomatic advantages accruing from her unmarried state had a good deal to do with keeping her unmarried. Marriage again was a dreadfully definitive business.

Taking her merely as a woman there was much in Elizabeth's position calculated to arouse our sympathies. She was without a husband, without children. Her nearest living relatives were first cousins. She never had close friends. She was ringed around with intriguing courtiers and hostile neighbors. It is not hard to picture her as a lonely, forlorn woman in an unfriendly world. And yet she never does arouse our sympathies, precisely for the reason that she never seems to stand in need of them. Notwithstanding all her apparent irresolution and vacillation she conveys the impression of being always mistress of the situation. Behind the irascible shrew one is conscious of a personality cold and hard and flexible as steel. Her councillors often disagreed with her, but the boldest of them rarely dared to act without her authorization. Following good Tudor precedent she surrounded herself with statesmen and courtiers who owed everything to her favor and who would lose everything at her displeasure. Nor did she ever delude herself with the idea that they were held by other considerations. Burghley perhaps enjoyed a larger measure of her confidence than any other man, but this was chiefly due to the fact that Burghley was as ardent a nationalist and almost as agile an opportunist as she was herself. And even Burghley never dominated her, not even to the extent of forcing Leicester from his privileged position beside her.

In fact she seems to have maintained Leicester as a counterpoise to Burghley and Burghley as a counterpoise to Leicester. Sir Robert Naunton, who knew her personally, says "that she ruled much by factions and parties, which herself both made, upheld, and weakened as her own great judgment advised." And a careful study of her reign goes far to substantiate his view of the matter. Of her favorites the three principal ones, Leicester, Hatton, and Essex, were all admitted to a larger share in her government than their abilities perhaps warranted, but there were bounds beyond which they might not step, as Essex learned to his sorrow. The statement often made that she distinguished sharply between her courtiers and her councillors is not justified, but it is certain that the men upon whose advice she chiefly depended were not selected for their engaging personal qualities. If one were to name the outstanding men in her council he would probably single out Lord Burghley, the Earl of Leicester, Sir Francis Walsingham, and Sir Robert Cecil. All of these except Leicester were men who would have ranked high among the statesmen of any country at any time. Elizabeth indeed had as keen an eye for a wise head as she had had for a well-proportioned figure. She adored flattery of the most fulsome sort, but could listen to very plain talk from those whose judgment she had tested. It is to be remarked that her outstanding councillors lived out their lives in her service. Bacon, not Sir Francis but his father, Burghley, Leicester, Walsingham, and Sir Thomas Smith, all died in harness. Robert Cecil outlived her. Once she singled out a man she hung to him through thick and thin, even though in her tempestuous intervals she might hurl plates at him. There are no Wolseys or Cromwells in the records of her reign. For one thing she allowed none to climb so high, for another she was too thrifty of her resources to destroy a man of ability even when his ideas ran directly counter to her own. But always she was the dominating figure and always her grasp was very firm upon the reins of power. None but a master hand could have driven Burghley and Leicester for over twenty years, and Cecil and Essex for nearly ten, in double harness, without overturning the coach of state.

At close range Elizabeth was clearly not a likeable sort of person, though she was a very keen and intelligent one. She commanded the loyalty of a sovereign from her court, but never the affection of a friend from a friend. It was what she stood for and particularly what she stood against that held their support, not the woman herself. In the orthodox sense of the term, it is hard to identify her even with what we think of as Elizabethan England. Of all that great company who made of her reign the golden age of English literature, only two, Sir Philip Sidney and Sir Walter Raleigh, enjoyed any large measure of her favors, and neither of these owed their fortunes to their literary talents. Sidney had his uncle, the Earl of Leicester, to thank, Raleigh his *beaux yeux*. The greatest literary figure of her time was hardly known and apparently never patronized by her. Nor was she in any essential sympathy with the purposes of the great Elizabethan seafarers, Drake and Hawkins and Gilbert and the rest, though she was ready enough to make her profit from their enterprises. In all of these respects she does not conform to the prevalent conception of her age. She was not a good Elizabethan.

But then it is open to question whether the average Englishman of her times was a good Elizabethan. The articulate elements of any age have a way of stamping their impress upon the age, but it is dangerous, though common, to assume that their thoughts and their aspirations to any considerable extent reflect the thought and aspirations of the inarticulate masses. The England of Elizabeth was the England of Shakespeare and of Marlowe, of Sidney and of Raleigh, of Drake and of Hawkins, of Gresham and of Burghley, of Thomas Cartwright, of Edmund Campion, and of Richard Hooker; but it was also the England of common folk who were not dramatists, not gallants, not bold navigators, not rich merchants or rich landlords, and not religious zealots of any faith. No doubt the great mass of Elizabeth's subjects fell within this undistinguished category. The average Englishman of her age, as indeed of all ages before and since, was probably a commonplace fellow with commonplace aspirations. Generally speaking he was left out of account in the calculations of his rulers. It was the peculiar distinction of Elizabeth that she never lost sight of him, that she was indeed much more careful of him than was any one of the wise and gallant company that surrounded her. She knew what he wanted and she knew that it was not a damp grave in Flanders, or a damper one off the Spanish Main, or the fires of Smithfield, or heavy taxes, or the enclosure of his commons, or a mercantile system of trade designed to exploit the poor for the benefit of the rich, or any of the other things which those with whom she was in habitual contact would have had her impose upon him.

Indeed she was determined to deliver him from them if she could. How hard she strove to avoid war has been remarked upon already. Had it been possible she would have ignored religious controversies altogether. As it was she undertook to provide a church catholic enough to suit what she held to be the requirements of all reasonable men. Sorely as she needed money she kept her taxes low, preferring to borrow from the rich by such politely illegal devices as privy seals, to increasing the fiscal burden upon the nation at large. She turned a deaf ear to the sound economics of spirited cultivators and approached the agrarian problem with the strange idea that it was more important to preserve the peasantry than to increase the yield of the soil. She was a poor mercantilist if only because she saw that there was no necessary relation between the increase of national wealth and the distribution of it. The cloth trade interested her not so much because it swelled the purses of merchant adventurers, as because it provided bread and butter for the English weavers. It is shocking to observe how little respect she had for the common law. Her prerogative courts punished powerful offenders without regard to its tedious procedure. Perhaps she discerned what the next century was to make apparent, that the common law was rapidly becoming the chosen weapon of a new and dangerous oligarchy of country squires and town merchants, who already dominated the local administration and who were presently to dominate through the high court of Parliament not only the crown but every lesser creature in England.

Elizabeth would have been the last to confess to any high flown purposes of social justice and she would have been the last to endorse such modern gospels as liberty, fraternity, and equality. It not only flattered her vanity to play at Gloriana among her courtiers, but it also expressed her own conception of her position in the state. But she never allowed the glittering pageantry of her court circle to isolate her from the nation at large, she never forgot that she was queen of all the English. The pomp and splendor which surrounded her person was never a cage for her as it was later for Louis XIV. It was nothing more than a frame from which she looked out, a benevolent mistress, upon her people. And it was so that the average Englishman in turn regarded her. He did not know what Elizabeth was to her court circle, to her ladies in waiting, to her harassed councillors, to Bernardino de Mendoza, or to Castelnau de la Mauvissière—to him she was Good Queen Bess.

In that fact, in the affectionate familiarity of that name, lies more of the truth about her than any amount of court scandal and court gossip. She is not seen in her true proportions through the state papers and the confidential despatches. One must look at her afar off as she appeared to the rank and file of her subjects. For once the archives are less trustworthy than the gossip of the market-place. The English people by and large felt that Elizabeth was their queen, they knew her and loved her and

believed that she knew and loved them. It was this fundamental sympathy and understanding between her and them which constituted the chief source of her strength. So far was she from being lonely that she was conscious of a whole nation behind her and around her. That was why she dared to play fast and loose with her Council and even on occasion to defy Puritan parliaments. No monarch of her time and very few since have been so sensitive to what we call nowadays public opinion. And none probably has attached more importance to it, or courted it more assiduously. She was perhaps the first of English monarchs to realize the importance of the press as an instrument in shaping popular sentiment. During the last twenty-five years of her life she scarcely took a single important step in policy without justifying her action by an official publication in which documents were often set forth at length in a manner suggestive of the modern blue-books. The Throgmorton Plot, the Parry Plot, the despatch of troops to the Low Countries, the execution of Mary Queen of Scots, the defeat of the Spanish Armada, the seizure of the Hansa grain ships in 1589, the Cadiz expedition of the same year—to mention no others—were all explained to the nation by government pamphlets, many of which were even put forth in French, Italian, and Latin versions, for distribution on the Continent. Contemporary chronicles were made to serve something like the same purpose. Those parts of Holinshed which covered Elizabeth's reign were carefully edited by royal censors; and Stow's innumerable editions of his *Annals,* of which at least a dozen appeared before Elizabeth's death, in every form from pocket books to folios, were no doubt officially inspired. Elizabeth lacked the daily newspaper press, but she did her best with what she had.

There is every indication that she shaped her public behavior with the same ends in view. Her condescending familiarity in her casual contacts with simple folk, her majestic mien on state occasions, her multitudinous portraits, her elaborate wardrobes, her constant progresses, were so much stage property in her dramatic appeal to popular attention and popular admiration. From the days when she passed through London streets in sober mourning, a mere prisoner in her jealous sister's charge, to the closing scene of her reign, when she fought hard to be allowed to die on her feet, Elizabeth never forgot that the eyes of her people were upon her. It was for them that she staged her visit to the good ship *Pelican,* and knighted Sir Francis Drake for one of the most daring pieces of piracy ever perpetrated. It was for them that she put on helmet and corselet and rode through the ranks of her soldiers at Tilbury Camp. The speech ascribed to her at Tilbury may be apocryphal, but no one can doubt that on that dramatic occasion, when the Spanish Armada was in the channel and when she faced the armies of England gathered in her defense, she rose to the full measure of her greatness.

Her contacts with her parliaments were not invariably smooth and easy. More than once, as on the question of her marriage, they crowded her for decisions upon matters which she thought it wise to leave undecided. More than once she came perilously near losing her temper with them.

Was I not born in this realm [she demanded of them], were my parents born in any foreign country? Is there any cause that should alienate myself from being careful over this country? Is not my kingdom here? Whom have I oppressed? Whom have I enriched to others' losses? What turmoils have I made to this commonwealth that I should be suspected to have no regard of the same? How have I governed since my reign? I will be tried by envy itself. . . . Though I be a woman I have as good a courage answerable to my place as ever my father had. I am your anointed Queen. I will never be by violence constrained to do anything. I thank God I am endued with such qualities that if I were turned out of the realm in my petticoat I were able to live in any place in Christendom.

But she never carried an issue with them to a point beyond which she would run the risk of estranging their loyalty.

She was not much given to philosophizing about the position of the crown in the state. Generally speaking she left such high matters to the wise fool who succeeded her. It is clear enough that she believed in the divine right of kings; she believed also in the divine responsibility of kings. But she never lost sight of the fact that from whatever sources her power sprang, and however absolute it might be argued to be, it rested ultimately upon the consent of her people.

In my governing this land [she said on one notable occasion] I have ever set the last judgment day before mine eyes, and so to rule as I shall be judged and answer before a higher Judge, to whose judgment seat I do appeal—that never thought was cherished in my heart that tended not to my People's good. . . . For myself I was never so much enticed with the glorious name of a King or royal authority of a Queen, as delighted that God hath made me this instrument to maintain His truth and glory and to defend this Kingdom from peril, dishonour, tyranny, and oppression.

In this statement she came as near as perhaps she ever came to a definition of her political creed. Two centuries later such an utterance would have classified her among the benevolent despots. But she differed from them in this, that she did not seek to impose enlightened theories of good government without reference to time and place and circumstance. She knew her land, she sensed intuitively the needs and desires of her people and she shaped her policy in accordance with them. Her government was brilliantly successful, not because it was wise and far-sighted, for very often it was not, but because it was nicely attuned to the popular will.

In what was almost her last public utterance to her people, Elizabeth summarized her greatest achievement in one glowing sentence. "Though God," she told the Commons, "hath raised me high, yet this I account the glory of my crown, that I have reigned with your loves."

No one doubted it. Her long reign declared it. The constitutional restraints devised to prevent the abuse of royal power might be held in reserve for less happy times. England had Good Queen Bess.

In ENGLISH POLITICAL AND CONSTITUTIONAL HISTORY it has been customary to regard the medieval period as ending, and the modern as beginning, with the accession to the throne of the first Tudor sovereign, in 1485. Henry Hallam thought of his *Constitutional History of England* (first published in 1827) as dealing with modern history, as distinguished from medieval history, and he began it with the reign of Henry VII. More than a generation later, during the decade of the 1870's, Bishop Stubbs wrote a monumental work on medieval English constitutional history and ended it where Hallam had begun. "With the battle of Bosworth," he said, "the medieval history of England is understood to end." But, as thoughtful students of history know, the flow of past events cannot be divided into periods by sharp chronological boundary lines without doing violence to historical continuities. To quote the words of a great historian of English law, "Such is the unity of all history that anyone who endeavours to tell a piece of it must feel that his first sentence tears a seamless web." English society, culture, institutions, and laws were not suddenly remodeled on Bosworth Field, and much that was medieval lasted into, and through, the Tudor period. On the basis of a study of works on the English constitutional system by Sir John Fortescue, the fifteenth-century Lancastrian jurist, and Sir Thomas Smith, a diplomat and secretary of state under Queen Elizabeth, Professor George L. Mosse, of the University of Iowa, concludes in the following essay that during the hundred years of English constitutional history that lay between the writings of these two men (approximately 1470-1570) continuity was more striking than change. Professor Mosse is the author of the well-organized and well-written study *The Struggle for Sovereignty in England from the Reign of Queen Elizabeth to the Petition of Right* (1950).

CHANGE AND CONTINUITY IN THE
TUDOR CONSTITUTION
GEORGE L. MOSSE

Tudor England, while effecting a great revolution in the social system, characteristically preserved the form and even the spirit of much that was old. In the realm of constitutional thought the element of continuity is especially striking. The state of

Reprinted by special permission from *Speculum,* XXII (1947), 18-28. The footnotes which originally appeared with this essay have been omitted.

English constitutional theory of the sixteenth century is probably best indicated by the works of Sir Thomas Smith, one of Queen Elizabeth's secretaries of state. But roughly a hundred years before Smith gave us his analysis of the English Constitution, before the dawn of the Tudor era, the great Lancastrian lawyer and chief justice, Sir John Fortescue, had in his turn analyzed the Constitution. A comparison of these two analyses, each of them typical and authoritative of its century, will both show the continuity of the Tudor and Lancastrian Constitutions and bring out such changes as a century of Tudor rule had wrought.

Between the Constitutions which Fortescue and Smith described there was but little essential change. Polity, writes Fortescue, in the Greek tongue is identical with plurality, which means a government administered by many. 'Manage therefore,' he exhorts the King, 'the Commonwealth by the rule of many.' A commonwealth, echoes Smith, is 'a society or common doing of a multitude of free men collected and united together by common accord and convention amongst themselves as well in peace as in war.' Truly republican statements these, and both Fortescue and Smith have been hailed as precursors of modern democracy. Yet to Fortescue no body politic can exist without a king, and Smith conceived of princes as holding of God Himself.

The apparent incompatibility between a polity governed by many and the necessity for a king is solved by the two men in an identical manner: the king is conceived of as limited, though not controlled. Their apparent democracy consists in the safeguarding of certain rights to the people against the encroachment of the executive. The king, in short, has his sphere of operations and the subjects theirs. This becomes even clearer if we look at Fortescue's theory of the origins of the state. The state began with an original compact practically identical with Smith's free men united together by common accord. The people are thus demonstrably more than mere chattels, for they united in order that they might more

securely enjoy their pristine and inalienable rights. How wrong, therefore, for the king to despoil his subjects of their property, once the compact was formed! But (here Fortescue was voicing a commonplace of medieval political thought) no body politic can exist without a head. Therefore, the people delegate some powers to the king, above all the power of protection, for they originally united in order to enjoy their rights and their property more securely. The king 'has no just claim to any power but this.' Thus Fortescue, quoting St Thomas Aquinas, states, 'The Kingdom is not made for the King, but the King for the Kingdom.'

The common law and the ancient customs of the realms provide the demarcation line between the rights of the 'many' and those of the king. This formed England's bulwark against royal absolutism. Both Smith and Fortescue looked across the channel, where Frenchmen lived with no such bulwark operating to protect them, and both attributed the misery which they saw there to the unfettered power of the monarch. To Smith and Fortescue, such a monarch was a tyrant. Smith's definition of a tyrant as one who 'breaketh laws allready made at his pleasure, maketh others without advice or consent of the people,' is practically identical with Fortescue's, though the latter adds a concrete example, 'if like the French King he rules his people by such laws as he makes himself.'

It is not surprising that these definitions were legal ones, for it was the common law which guaranteed the rights of the subject. Of this both men, as lawyers, were fully aware; Fortescue had been Chief Justice under Henry VI, and Smith had been Master of Requests in the reign of Edward VI. Nevertheless, Smith's awareness of the importance of the common law as the ligament of the constitution seems to have developed in spite of his training, for Smith was trained as a Civilian. As Master of Requests he used the *Ius Civile*. One might, therefore, expect him to voice the sentiments of Padua rather than those of the Inns of Court.

When his conversion to the principles of the common law actually took place is difficult to determine. But even in his inaugural lecture as Professor of Civil Law at Cambridge, there are some discordant notes. The technicalities of the civil law are derided, while the eloquence and vigor not infrequently exhibited in common law courts are praised. It must not be forgotten that Fortescue in turn finds words of recognition for the civil law. Smith seems, however, to have thought of the common law itself in civilian terms: 'That our Law which is called of us the Common Law, as ye would say *Jus Civile.*'

The common law was the municipal law of England, as the civil law was the municipal law of France. Whatever Smith might have thought of the civil law, the fact that he was describing the English Constitution necessarily meant a description of the common law as its ligament. Perhaps it is a tribute to the reality of the fundamentals of that Constitution, even in Elizabeth's time, that a Civilian trained at Padua, attempting an analysis, became convinced of the function of the common law in the Constitution and of its excellence.

The king, then, must not tamper with the subjects' laws and customs: here was the fundamental concept of limited monarchy. These laws and customs could only be changed with the consent of the people. On the other hand, in his sphere of government the king was absolute, but always with regard to the rights of the subjects. This is well illustrated by the king's pardoning and dispensing powers. The king can, writes Fortescue, mitigate and remit all punishment provided he can do so without danger

to his subjects and without infringing the customs and statutes of the realm. The king's pardoning power is thus strictly limited. So is his dispensing power. Says the Chief Justice, if someone ought to repair a bridge, and the king dispense him of that duty, this is of no avail except so far as the fine which the king would have taken himself is concerned. He cannot dispense with the fine which the delinquent owes to the community. The king may dispense with his own rights but not with those of his subjects. Over a hundred years later, Smith echoed these sentiments. In popular actions, where part of the fine goes to the declarator and part to the prince, the prince may only dispense with his part. In criminal actions the king may only give a pardon if the plaintiff is unwilling to take up renewed accusation against the convicted criminal.

Was there, then, any sphere of government in which the king might be said to be supreme? Here Smith concedes to him absolute control over the choice of all chief officers and magistrates, as well as over foreign policy. In principle Fortescue is in agreement with Smith. Yet, living in times when the peace of England was disturbed by royal minorities or by incapable rulers, he even limits the king in his administrative functions, for he would join to the king a council partly removed from his immediate control, in order to avoid the flattery of self-seeking courtiers. Smith, too, saw that danger, but his solution lay not in a better council but in a husband for the Virgin Queen who would have her true interests at heart. Fortescue is, however, vague on the important point of the selection of the council. Once the councillors

JEAN BODIN: French lawyer, government official, and scholar (d. 1596) who wrote on politics, economics, and history. His conception of sovereignty, set forth in his *Republic,* shaped political thought for many generations. His analysis of the price revolution of the sixteenth century is a classic formulation of the quantity theory of money. His *Method for the Easy Comprehension of History* is a major work in the development of the philosophy of history.

MUNICIPAL LAW: Expression used to signify the internal law of a state, kingdom, or nation, as contrasted with international law.

were appointed, the king could only change them upon the advice of the majority of his council.

The president of the council, however, was to be chosen by the king and was to hold office at his pleasure. This council was to concern itself with all matters pertaining to the policy of the realm. Thus, presumably, even foreign policy would come within its jurisdiction. We have here a decided limitation of the king's power, even in the sphere of government. The jurisdiction over the royal domain, moreover, Fortescue would put in the hands of Parliament. The inability of the king to alienate the domain he sees in the nature of an endowment, thus enhancing the king's prerogative, by enabling him to live of his own. In an age of continual strife for the crown, Fortescue would limit the king even in his sphere of government, in order to increase the prestige of the office of kingship. Sir Thomas Smith, living in quieter times, had no need for such safeguards.

Yet, inasmuch as the king has the obligation to protect as well as to govern the realm, both Smith and Fortescue concede him emergency powers in time of war. Here his word is law, and he may conscript the nation's manpower and its wealth. This emergency power, for Fortescue, holds good as well in times of rebellion. Small wonder, since Fortescue lived at a time when internal strife was the order of the day. Here Smith argues along slightly different lines, for Tudor government was less rent by rebellion and, moreover, treason laws had been tightened markedly by Elizabeth's reign. Smith would disallow such wide prerogatives in times of rebellion, since wise men feared the consequence and example of such a power when the punishment might be accomplished by order of law.

The king is thus limited, to be sure, but is he also to be controlled? Of what use is it to limit royal power without the proper sanctions to enforce such limitations? The whole history of modern constitutionalism is bound up with the acquisition of appropriate sanctions against arbitrary power. If a king did become a tyrant, could the limitations be enforced? Again we arrive at a difference of approach between the Lancastrian and the Elizabethan. Fortescue lived shortly after the great religious schism, and the Papal reaction following the Council of Constance had left its mark on the Chief Justice. The punishment of tyrants is ultimately in heaven, yet the Lord's vicar on earth might have the authority to perform that office. Only the Pope, on earth, could punish tyrants. Thus the reinvigorated theory of Papal omnicompetence finds an echo in the works of the English Chief Justice.

One could hardly expect Sir Thomas Smith, Elizabeth's Secretary of State, to voice such sentiments. Instead Sir Thomas cautiously evades the issue. 'The learned' will judge when the time comes, according to the tyrant's purpose and the state of the times. It is, however, certain, continues Smith, that to meddle with laws and government is a hazardous thing.

In spite of this difference of approach to the question of controlling tyrants, both agree that the king is limited by the laws and customs of the realm but not controlled by his own people, in the last resort. Is it then a static commonwealth which both men envisage? The king is controlled by customs and laws. What if these customs and laws, what if the common law, needed to be adjusted to new conditions? The answer is simple: these laws and customs are the safeguard of the people; therefore only the people themselves can change them; or rather, the people must consent to have them reformed, changed, or abrogated. This is the underlying principle of both Smith's and Fortescue's conception of the organization and function of the High Court of Parliament.

If there are inconvenient laws, says Fortescue, they may be reformed, abolished and amended in every Parliament. This statement seems clear enough. But did Fortescue believe in the actual 'making' of new laws? Here we come to the one really fundamental and important difference between the Lancastrian and the Elizabethan, for Smith was sure that Parliament 'changeth old laws and maketh new.' It is highly doubtful that Fortescue as yet thought of enacted statutes as entirely new law. Fortescue believed, in common with his contemporaries, in the existence of certain permanent and unchangeable laws. The highest body of law was the divine law, which in turn confirmed the decrees of the law of nature. A rule of law is to Fortescue simply the elucidation of this higher body of law. It is by appealing to the law of nature itself that he tries to settle the conflict between the Houses of Lancaster and York. The authority of Parliamentary statutes is therefore not so important as those principles of the natural law from which those statutes were in the first instance derived. Law, even if enacted in Parliament, is therefore never entirely new; in a sense it is only declaratory of the law of nature.

Statutes are enacted with the 'concurrent consent' of the whole kingdom, by the representatives in Parliament. Once enacted, bills may only be repealed or amended in the same manner in which they were first enacted into law. We have here the constitutional principle that one act of Parliament can only be repealed by another. Once the bill is the law of the land it ought to be respected by all; Fortescue's respect for the authority of Parliament is well illustrated by one of his decisions as Chief Justice. A bill had passed Parliament in an irregular manner. The king had, however, certified by writ that the bill had been properly confirmed by act of Parliament. 'This is an act of Parliament,' judged Fortescue, 'and we wish to be well advised before we annul any act made in Parliament.' Judges, Fortescue held, must never render any judgment against the law of the land, even if the king should command them to do so.

That the king was limited by acts of Parliament was natural, for such an act, which had to be made with the concurrent consent of the people, was a change in the ligament of the Constitution which guaranteed their rights. But the king was a vital part of this process, and the words which Fortescue used are significantly 'concurrent consent,' not 'absolute power.' The head cannot make any changes without the consent of the body politic, and the body cannot change the ligament of the Constitution without the head. England was a *dominium politicum et regale—politicum* inasmuch as the concurrent consent of the people was necessary for the enactment of law, *regale* inasmuch as the king with this consent might change the laws of the land, while on the other hand, without his permission, nothing could be enacted by Parliament. Laws and customs constituted the dividing line between the king's power and the people's, and both had an interest in them.

Between the end of the fifteenth century and the time of Elizabeth a decided advance in the growth of Parliament had taken place. Parliament had attained maturity. Elizabeth still spoke of her 'Parliaments,' but Parliament was well under way to become a permanent institution. It had established a religion while sitting, intermittently to be sure, for seven years. Rules of debate and procedure had evolved. Queen Mary herself had frequently to go out of her way to placate the House of Commons, which in 1555 rejected a measure against the exiled Protestants. Of some of the Marian Parliaments Sir Thomas Smith had been a member. One would doubt the value of the *De Republica* if these developments had not left their mark.

Yet here too, in spite of momentous divergence, there is agreement on important fundamental points between the Lancastrian and the Elizabethan. That which is done by Parliament, says Smith, is 'called firm and stable and sanctum, and is taken for law.' The representatives of the kingdom are present at Parliament to 'advertise, consult and show' what is good and necessary for the commonwealth. Is not this similar to Fortescue's concurrent consent? Moreover, here too the king is a vital part of Parliament. Those bills of which he disapproves are 'utterly dashed and of no effect'; 'to be short, the Prince is the head, and the authority of all things that be done in England.' England here too is a *dominium politicum et regale,* where the people could not make laws without the king, and the king without the people. Both Fortescue and Smith thought of Parliament in terms of the 'High Court.' For example, while to Smith bills were merely a matter of giving judgment in Parliament, Fortescue discusses the reforming and abolishing of laws in connection with the delays which might at any time arise in pleading. Yet it should be emphasized that according to Smith, Parliament could actually make new and change old laws, for there is in Smith's factual account no trace of eternal unchangeable law. Has Smith's Parliament, then, all-embracing powers? He does give us a list of what Parliament can do, a list solidly grounded in Tudor precedent. Among other things, Parliament can establish forms of religion and regulate the succession. But what about the most important power, Parliament's right over private property? After all, the commonwealth had originally come about through the desire of the multitude to enjoy their rights and possessions more securely. May the community deprive itself of its possessions?

Smith's answer is clear. Everyone being represented in Parliament, that body has the power to dispose of the rights and possessions of private men. Here, then, is a momentous step towards the doctrine of Parliamentary sovereignty. That this assertion seems to be connected with the waning influence of the idea of natural law seems highly probable, if we contrast it with Fortescue's ideas on this problem. For Fortescue, property originated in the law of nature, long before nations were established. Was not the secure enjoyment of property, for him too, the essence of the founding of the commonwealth? Property is thus based on both the natural law and the original purpose of the state. But all acts of Parliament are derived from the law of nature. Could they therefore change something which was an integral part of that

very law? Moreover, Fortescue's projected administrative reforms were all designed to make any levying of subsidies and taxes unnecessary, for the king should live of his own.

Smith, no longer bound by the fetters of natural law, could concede powers over property to Parliament, for the 'multitude' itself was represented by that body. It is in this step towards Parliamentary sovereignty that the chief divergence between the two men consists, and perhaps also one of the chief contributions to the Constitution of the century of Tudor rule.

Professor Hatschek has placed Smith as the transmitter of Jean Bodin's ideas of sovereignty into England. It is true that Smith concedes Parliament to be the 'absolute power' in England, though absolute in a legal sense, meaning without appeal. Absolute enough, however, to tamper with private property, to make and change laws. Yet, the right of the sovereign to dispose of private property was explicitly denied by Bodin. Bodin, like Fortescue, was imbued with the idea of natural law. To him, natural and divine law was something very real, a decided limitation on the sovereign.

The divine and natural law protected private property from the reach of the sovereign. Republics were established principally to render to each man his due, in order that the property of each subject might be safeguarded. Fortescue, too, held that the state was founded for the protection of the people's rights and property, as we have seen; moreover, besides the fact that property originated in the natural law before the founding of states, it was also one of the principal qualities of the natural law to render to everyone his due. Both Fortescue and Bodin, nearly a century after him, excepted certain rights from the law-making power in the state, and this on grounds of natural law and the original purpose of the state, which in its form was in accord with the law of nature. Smith the Elizabethan had already advanced one step beyond these medieval concepts; no longer is it true so far as he is concerned that to the 'King belongs authority over all—to private persons prop- erty.' The king and the representatives of the realm in Parliament assembled might dispose of property. Here Smith, as in all his listings of Parliamentary power, apart from his ignoring of the natural law, is grounded on solid Tudor precedent. Had not Parliament under Henry VIII tampered with the private property of the monasteries, taken their lands and goods without their consent? A similar interference with prop- erty might be seen in the Statute of Uses, passed also by Parliament in the reign of Henry VIII. As late as 1550, the judges were still hard put to justify this transfer of land by Parliament, to him who had the use of it, from him who might have the right of ownership. Thus Sir Thomas Smith with his acceptance of the constitutional reality reflected a fundamental change in the constitution, the 'beginnings of a new theory of Parliamentary Sovereignty,' no longer restrained by the property-protecting bonds of eternal laws.

From this, then, Fortescue has more in common with Bodin than has Smith. Both were largely in the medieval tradition of superior law. With Smith and Fortescue it cannot, of course, be said that Parliament as such was sovereign, for the king has his sphere of operation: the government of the realm and emergency power in time of war. Here he was sovereign. Even in making laws he was linked to Parliament. 'The King of England is the most absolute King in his Parliament, but, of himself, his Power is limited by the Law.' When Smith and Fortescue wrote of Parliament, it was of the 'king in Parliament' they were think- ing. And the king in Parliament had abso- lute lawmaking powers for Fortescue, but the natural law did protect property, its basic ingredient, even from Parliament. For Smith, too, the king in Parliament was 'abso- lute,' but here there was no natural law, and property was at Parliament's mercy. Sir Thomas Smith seems to be a step ahead of Jean Bodin, his feet firmly placed on the road to Parliamentary omnicompetence, though he could not foresee that this would

be reached by restricting the king in Par- liament, the king 'the head of all that is done in England.'

To this symptomatic divergence between Smith and Fortescue, which illustrates at least one important change that had taken place, over the century of Tudor rule, an- other interesting divergence of views might be added. This change belongs more to the revolution in the social system than to the realm of constitutional theory, however. Fortescue speaks of the *dominium politicum et regale*. The word *dominium* stands for the pre-ordained rightness of the relations of superior to inferior. The concept was in harmony with the rigid hierarchical social structure of the Middle Ages, by and large the Church provided the only system where- by a man might work his way up in the social structure. But Smith holds that yeo- men, by sending their sons to the University, and by leaving them sufficient land, might raise them to the status of gentlemen. Edu- cation and landed wealth seem to him to cut through the rigidity of the *dominium* as Fortescue conceived it. Here, too, is the result of changing conditions.

Yet, even when the chief divergences have been pointed out, the continuity is more striking than the change. England, at least to Sir Thomas Smith, was still a *dominium politicum et regale,* a 'mutuall society.' The king, whether Edward VI or Elizabeth, was beneath God and the law, for the law guaranteed the rights of the subject and the rights of the king. Only united in Parliament could the head and the body effect any change. The king, with modifications in Fortescue's case, was abso- lute in his sphere of government and pro- tection. In short, the king was limited. But he was not controlled by positive sanctions. It took a century of bloody civil wars to attain that end.

It is difficult to ascertain whether Sir Thomas Smith was familiar with Fortescue's works. In Strype's list of his library, no work of Fortescue appears. However, he did possess a copy of the 'Years and Termes of Henry VI' and there he might have read some of Fortescue's decisions. In type of mind each of these men was the product of his age. The Lancastrian's works abound in Scriptural quotations; the classics take a very subordinate place. Smith, the Elizabethan, knew his classics well, as he might, having been trained in Padua. Besides the classics and such ecclesiastical literature as the works of St Augustine, his library contains works by Boccaccio, Machiavelli, and 'that great, learned and wise man, Erasmus.' Moreover, the whole *Republica* shows the cold, analytical spirit of a man no longer in the fetters of Scriptural quotations or of supernatural laws. His description of England tries to show how it actually stood in the year 1565, not how it should be or how it should have been.

That two such dissimilar men, the Lancastrian Common Lawyer and the Elizabethan Civilian, could have reached such similar conclusions with regard to the English Constitution, should tell us much as to its true nature in Tudor times, and should further illustrate the inadequacy of the term 'Tudor absolutism.' Where they did differ in their chief points, the social system and, more important, the idea of natural law may give us an inkling of the basic changes of Tudor times, changes which lead us to that pamphleteer, who, writing at the beginning of the Civil War, stated bluntly: 'The Question never was whether we should be governed by arbitrary power, but in whose hands it should be.'

UNDER HENRY VII THE ENGLISH GOVERNMENT made greater use than it had done in earlier times of economic regulations as a means of promoting the unity, prosperity, and power of the state, and this policy was continued under his successors. Such governmental regulation of economic life later came to be called "mercantilism." That this term has lacked definiteness is not surprising, for the subject to which it refers has been approached from many points of view, and its objects have been variously conceived. The most comprehensive treatment of mercantilism to be found in any single work is contained in Eli F. Heckscher's historical treatise *Mercantilism,* in which the subject is viewed as a unifying system, as a system of power, as a system of protection, as a monetary system, and as a conception of society. Regulation of economic life was not in itself new, but in the Middle Ages the regulating powers had been, in the main, local—manorial courts, merchant and craft gilds, and urban authorities. In the age of mercantilism (roughly the sixteenth, seventeenth, and eighteenth centuries) the central governments of western Europe tended to concern themselves with the whole range of economic life—commercial, agricultural, and industrial—and thereby greatly expanded the sphere of state activity. Their objective was to encourage economic pursuits that would be beneficial to the state and to discourage those regarded as injurious to it, but the state was personified and idealized and thought of as something quite different from the mere aggregate of its inhabitants. In days before the mass of the people were thought of as forming part of the body politic, mercantilist thinkers and writers were usually businessmen or politicians, and the state, as they conceived of it, could be rich and strong although the great majority of its inhabitants were poverty-stricken. It would hardly be going too far to say that the state could not, in the eyes of these mercantilists, prosper otherwise. Few mercantilists were interested in human welfare as such. There were, nevertheless, evidences of concern for social justice in Tudor England. Some of these are discussed in the following essay by Professor Conyers Read.

TUDOR ECONOMIC POLICY
CONYERS READ

Probably the most important two political developments in 16th-century England were (1) the increased centralization of power in the Crown, and (2) the increased importance of the role of Parliament in the government. The power of the Crown was of course exercised through the Privy Council or by various agencies of that body such as the Court of Star Chamber, the Council of the North, and the Court of High Commission. The actual distribution of power between the monarch himself and his deputies depended a great deal upon the character of the monarch. In the case of Henry VII, Henry VIII, and Elizabeth the dominance of the monarch, although occasionally called into question, was never successfully challenged. The reigns of Edward VI and Mary constitute exceptions to the general rule. Had they been longer they might have done serious harm to the Tudor pattern of government. As it was, they served rather to emphasize its validity. Actually most rebellions against the Crown in the 16th century represented attempts by the old feudal order to re-establish itself. They all failed and most of their leaders either died in the attempt or withered away into obscurity. Almost none of the great feudal houses survived the 16th century—survived I mean in the sense of constituting important power factors in the state. Those who rose to power under the Tudors were new men, successive waves of new men, each one in turn competing with its predecessor for influence and prestige. None of them suc-

ceeded in establishing itself in positions independent of royal favor. Probably the most impressive illustration of the stability of the Tudor pattern was the failure of Warwick, who, like his 15th-century namesake, fancied himself a kingmaker, and who had for a time all the resources of the state at his command, to divert the course of succession. Feudalism in the old sense never recovered from the mortal blow of the Wars of the Roses.

But something analogous to feudalism which was indeed rooted in feudal attitudes did develop in the 16th century, crossed swords with monarchy in the 17th century, and emerged triumphant in the squirearchy of the 18th century. The rise of the gentry was a phenomenon rather peculiarly British. It was due primarily perhaps to the utilization of the gentry by the Crown for the business of administering government at the local level. But it was immensely enforced by the dominant position of the gentry in the House of Commons.

The term gentry is a vague term. Sir Thomas Smith in the 1560's defined a gentleman as "one who can live idly and without manual labor and will bear the port, charge and countenance of a gentleman." He goes on to say that though by definition gentlemen are "those whom their blood and race doth make noble and known," it is easy enough for those who have the other qualifications to procure a respectable pedigree. Actually the gentry included all the well-to-do of the countryside. The class was,

Published for the first time by special permission of the author. This essay, with some minor changes, was read at the meeting of the American Historical Association in December, 1950.

as Professor Tawney says, kept few and tough by the ruthlessness of the English family system. If it did not drown all the kittens but one, it threw all but one into the water. By the laws of primogeniture the landed estates of the gentry passed to their oldest living male descendant, and the younger fry had to seek sustenance elsewhere, in the army or the church, or as a last resort in industry and trade. And this of course gave the gentry families valuable connections with the church and with the townsfolk. Their number was steadily recruited in the 16th century, as always, by prosperous townsmen like the Walsinghams, who, having made their fortune in shoemaking and wine-selling, bought themselves a country place and an appropriate pedigree. The flexibility of the class and its wide attachments constituted one of its chief sources of strength. The offices, local and national, which the gentry held never became hereditary in the precise sense, but they became hereditary in the family sense. If you were one of the country families, you normally expected to be a Justice of the Peace and a member of the House of Commons. Your prestige as a family tended to be measured in those terms.

In proportion as power in the state became more centralized and more extensive, the problem of applying power became more complicated. The central government had to provide for the performance of those functions of government which had previously been the responsibility of the feudal lords. In France it did so by establishing a paid bureaucracy, in England by utilizing the country gentry. The scope of their public duties was progressively enlarged in matters legal, economic, social, and even religious. They were already by wealth and by birth the recognized leaders of the countryside. Generally speaking, they were not paid for their services, but the accumulation of duties meant an accumulation of powers. Social prestige, economic prestige, and political power went in fact hand-in-hand—the realities of power with the symbols of power. It is this blending of eco-

nomic and social power with political power which accounts in large measure for the stability of the English government in the centuries to follow. The gentry were not absentee landlords, they were not idle rich, they were hard-working officials, strengthened by royal authority but exercising that authority in areas to which they belonged by birth and tradition and in which they could command local loyalties rooted deep in old feudal attitudes.

Professor Pickthorn in discussing the justices of the peace under Henry VII in his work on *Early Tudor Government* has written: "What the class from which the justices of the peace were drawn wanted done, Henry VII could get done very easily; what they did not mind being done, easily enough; what would happen if the crown should want done something which that class determined should not be done was a question still to be settled, even still to be raised." Ultimately it was raised with the result that the whole Tudor structure of government crashed to the ground.

The turning point in English parliamentary history was the definite recognition by Henry VIII of the national assembly as an integral part of the Tudor pattern of government. This matter has been elaborated by the late Professor Pollard, and we need not pause upon it. Increasingly the significance of Parliament was focused upon the House of Commons, which was based of course upon two types of constituency, the county and the borough. Numerically, borough members constituted over two thirds of the House, which would seem to suggest that the urban interests there dominated the situation. Actually, as Professor Neale has recently pointed out in his brilliant account of the Elizabethan House of Commons, the boroughs were largely represented by country gentlemen. The country gentry in fact dominated the House of Commons. There is little or no evidence in its debates of any really significant conflict between urban and rural interests. No doubt conflict existed, but it does not appear to have assumed significant dimensions.

Otherwise it would be hard to explain why so many of the boroughs were willing to be represented by the gentry.

It should always be borne in mind that Parliament was not a routine part of the political machine. It met only when the King called it and with relatively few exceptions confined its attention to matters which the King laid before it. This was at least the case during most of the 16th century, though early in the next century the initiative, as Professor Notestein has pointed out in his essay, *The Winning of the Initiative by the House of Commons,* passed rather rapidly from Crown to commons. Indeed the passing of initiative constitutes the first great manifestation of the developing rift between Crown and gentry—the prologue to the Great Rebellion.

Virtually all of the economic and social legislation in the 16th century originated with the Crown. There is very little evidence of any considerable opposition to it. Some of it ran counter to the interests of the gentry and when it did the Crown encountered a great deal of passive resistance to its implementation. It is not enough to examine the legislation in order to get an accurate picture of the actual state of things. The whole course of the enclosure movement is a case in point. Legislation was steadily designed to check it, and yet it proceeded with increasing momentum. This does not necessarily mean that the gentry did not approve of the legislation in principle. They were after all creatures of their time and the same considerations which led the government to initiate legislation had a good deal to do with their support of it. Above all things they wanted security from internal revolt and external attack, and they were prepared to make large concessions to a king who could provide it. Nevertheless, when these concessions ran counter to immediate pecuniary interests, the gentry's attitude toward government policy took on something of the character of New Year's resolutions. Gentlemen in the House of Commons did not feel too much reluctance about approving laws when they realized

that the actual application of the laws fell to them. As Pickthorn has observed, "Well meaning rules might be laid down by the Crown in Parliament, though it was a landowner's Parliament, but there was no one to enforce the rules except the justices of the peace. It was a little as if there were no one but cotton lords to enforce factory legislation."

Traditional attitudes of the gentry were profoundly disturbed by two considerations which together produced something like an agrarian revolution. The first of these in point of time and probably also in point of importance was the general rise of prices, induced primarily as we now know by the inflow of the precious metals from America. This meant a marked increase in the cost of living, which was at the same time being enhanced by the new expensive tastes created and fostered by the Italian Renaissance. As always the burden fell heaviest upon the rentier class, particularly upon the landlord class, whose income was largely derived from customary rents. The gentry were the first sufferers and they were driven to find expedients for increasing their revenues. The obvious first step was to increase their rents, a difficult and a very unpopular course. Another obvious step was to abandon landlording and to become entrepreneurs. Having become entrepreneurs the next obvious step was to operate their holdings not from the point of view of the common interest but from the point of view of private profit. All of these steps ran counter to the traditional patterns of the countryside. The wholesale conversion of arable land into pasture land created great social distress among the lower classes, widespread unemployment, civil disorder, and a strong sense of social injustice. Next to religion the enclosure movement was the chief popular factor in virtually all of the rebellions which plagued, if they did not actually threaten, the Tudor regime. Indeed the old religion and the old agrarian economy were the last bulwarks of the old England against the new monarchy and the new capitalism.

The trends provoked by the price revolution were accentuated by the feverish activities of the 16th-century real estate market. A great deal of land changed hands from old owners to new owners. Easily the most considerable, but by no means the only factor in this land market, were the confiscated monastic lands. To a large extent and particularly in the home counties, the new landlords were prosperous townsmen—recruits to the gentry class who brought into the countryside the instincts and the impulses of trade and were free from the customary inhibitions of the old gentry. They were, in fact, carpetbaggers, interested socially of course in emulating the gentry, but still regarding their lands, as they regarded their other investments, rather as sources of profit than as opportunities for service. To a considerable extent, though in widely differing degrees, this new element served as the leaven to leaven the whole loaf.

These, then, were the chief elements which went into the making of public policy —the Crown and the gentry.

It is customary to describe the policy of the Crown as mercantilism. The term is of 18th-century origin, a later generalization imposed upon an earlier state of things as it appeared in perspective to social philosophers like the French physiocrats and Adam Smith. It has since been used in a variety of ways. According to Eli Heckscher, probably the most distinguished authority on the subject, mercantilism meant in its earliest phase the establishment of national economic unity as opposed to the decentralized and disordered state of things under feudalism. England had substantially achieved this unity by the end of the 13th century. In its later phase mercantilism came to mean the control of the national economic life in the interests of national security and prosperity. Its emphasis was upon the security and prosperity of the state rather than upon the welfare of the individual. According to that interpretation, the economic regime in Germany under Hitler and in Italy under Mussolini has been described as neo-mercantilism.

As far as one can speak of any basic principle underlying Tudor economic policy in the 16th century, he can speak of mercantilism in this sense. Even so, one still has to wrestle with the problem of the implementation of that policy. Were the safety and welfare of England to be better achieved by autarchy or by internationalism, by protection or by free trade, by promoting the interests of agriculture or the interests of industry, by navigation acts or by unrestricted transport facilities, by a high price level or a low price level, by wealth in terms of bullion or wealth in terms of general prosperity? At one time or another, even in the 16th century, the English government played with all these alternatives. During the first part of the century it came near to laissez-faire in its trade relations, during the latter part it leaned more and more toward protection. Its main preoccupation internally was to maintain the traditional agricultural economy, partly in the interests of public order, partly in the interests of the food supply, largely in the interests of preserving the social pattern upon which the whole Tudor structure was built.

Insofar as the welfare of the countryside was concerned, this policy enjoyed the enthusiastic support of the social reformers, men like More, and Starkey, and Hales, and Lever and Latimer. By and large the social reformers were advocates of the preservation of the old order in society if not in religion. Apart from that interesting literary exercise, More's *Utopia,* none of the reformers contemplated any disturbance in the old property laws. One and all, they disclaimed any connection with the Anabaptists, the 16th-century equivalent of communists. One and all, they endorsed the hierarchical pattern of society, assigning to each individual the station in which God had placed him, recognizing both his responsibilities and his rights within that frame of reference. It was the medieval pattern, finding its expression as well perhaps in the speech on the subject which Shakespeare put into Ulysses' mouth in *Troilus and Cressida,* as anywhere else. There is nothing of democracy about it, either political or economic democracy. The dependence of the reformers was upon the strength of the King and the moral sense of the "possessioners." The emphasis was upon trust in the King and obedience to him. The right of rebellion to achieve social justice, if it was contemplated, was not expressed in matters secular.

Obviously the Tudor policy in this particular ran directly counter to economic trends. From one point of view the history of the century is that of one long struggle, by the government to maintain old patterns and by the gentry profoundly to modify if not to destroy them.

The same thing is true in the field of industry and trade, though these fields were currently regarded as of secondary importance. England in the 16th century was still emphatically green England, and the towns were still accidents upon a country landscape. From the point of view of the people involved, and of the interests involved, there could be no two minds about that. The policy of the government was definitely one of protecting and fostering the agricultural interest. The yeoman was still the English fighting man par excellence. So far as industry was concerned the Tudors accepted the pattern of gild control within the towns. The old view that the Tudors definitely attacked the gilds has long been exploded. Certainly they never allowed the gilds to dominate the industrial life to anything like the extent which they dominated French industrial life. The Statute of Apprentices, the most comprehensive of all Tudor economic laws, never mentioned the term gild. It did endorse the gild pattern and it did undertake to protect the gild against its industrial competitors in the countryside. Actually the forces which were to destroy the gild were already at work. The most important of all the English industries, cloth-making, had already moved, or it was rapidly moving, out of the towns into the country. The Statute of Apprentices undertook to check that movement. It failed, but the attempt discloses the attitude. One of the

most surprising aspects of Tudor policy is its reluctance to recognize the rising economic importance of the cloth trade. Even William Cecil, sometimes represented as one of the champions of the new order, argued strongly against it. He wanted to reduce the number of those engaged in it and even went so far as to suggest that those who lost their jobs in consequence might be sent overseas to the new plantations in Ireland. Probably the major consideration was the disturbance of the status quo, the increased sense of insecurity as England became increasingly dependent upon a market which she could not control and which oscillated violently.

English foreign trade during the first half of the 16th century was concentrated to an increasing degree upon a single product handled through a single port and directed along a single trade route. Interruptions of that trade by disorders on the Continent in the second half of the 16th century, and particularly by the Dutch wars, forced a reorientation not only of trade but also of government finances, which for short-term loans had been largely dependent upon the Antwerp money market. The consequences of that interruption were an expansion of trade in other directions and to a lesser degree a diversification of commodities of trade. To a considerable extent the closing of the Antwerp money market made the government increasingly dependent upon English financial resources and delivered it more or less into the hands of the City of London. So it was that the Tudors were forced to make friends with the mammon of unrighteousness. The monopolistic charters of new trading countries were one illustration of that fact. A more significant one was the amelioration of the official attitude of the government toward commercial credit. The Act of 1571 fixing maximum rates of interest constituted, according to Professor Tawney in his Introduction to Thomas Wilson's *Discourse on Usury,* the turning point. It did not authorize money lending, but it was so interpreted and so applied. "The paradox of Tudor administration and perhaps the ultimate cause of the collapse of the whole system," Mr. Lawrence Stone has observed, "is to be found in the extent to which its program of a paternalistic state was sacrificed to the implementation of the more pressing needs of planned autarchy and opportunistic war finance."

One might have expected that the country gentry would have found its interest on the side of the Crown in its struggle against domination by the English financial interests. But actually the country gentry were rather deeply involved on the other side. The cloth trade alone, though it found its vent through London, was so widely distributed through the countryside that it constituted a major country interest, and the inter-locking family connections gave country families a direct stake in commercial prosperity. This stake was considerably enlarged when joint-stock projects gradually opened the door through which country money could flow into commercial adventures. Furthermore one must distinguish between the government and the men and woman who composed it. Cecil, Walsingham, Leicester, Sidney, and many others, including Queen Elizabeth herself, often had a private stake in the very enterprises at which, ideologically, they looked askance.

What strikes one about the whole situation is the relatively little attention paid to the welfare of the man in the street. The price of food, the scale of wages, the problem of the poor, were very much the concern of the government. They always had been. In general the regulation of food prices was dictated by the consumer's interest, though with ample recognition of the fact that the food producers were the most important factors in economic life. The resistance of the government to the enclosure movement was prompted to a very considerable degree by preoccupation with the national food supply. The assessment of wages by government officials has a long history, dating back at least as far as the Statute of Laborers, which immediately followed the Black Death. It is not easy to determine whether wage fixing was in the interest of the employer or the employee, though in the case of agricultural wages certainly the rate fixed in 1563, as in 1349, appears to have been regarded as a maximum rather than a minimum. It was only in the case of weavers' wages that the reverse was true. Agricultural wage earners had so many alternatives to working for wages that there was probably a real labor shortage. Actually the wages paid were in most instances higher than the official rate. It is interesting to observe that the one specific social reason advanced for the national wage regulation provided for in the Act of Apprentices was the rise of prices. The recognition of the relation between wages and the cost of living is refreshing, though it is well to remember that the wage assessment was left in the hands of the justices of the peace, that is to say in the hands of the employers who were at the same time the magistrates, the police, the landlords, and the army recruiting officials.

The problem of the poor was from the point of view of the government mainly the problem of the unemployed. It was a matter rather of avoiding civil disturbance than of dispensing charity. It contemplated relief to the impotent poor but was mainly concerned with sturdy fellows out of employment. The essence of it was the responsibility of the parish for its own poor and the prevention of vagrancy at large. It was aimed at the civil disorder apparent or implicit in wandering bands of sturdy beggars. Incidentally it did much to hinder the flow of labor into areas where there was a labor shortage out of areas where there was a labor surplus. Probably in metropolitan areas like London, local authorities, aiming to build up a surplus labor supply, often connived at the breach of the act in this particular. It is interesting as the definite assumption by the state of the responsibility for poor relief, though by impersonalizing charity and by separating it from the church it had rather disastrous consequences. The cause of the poor became too much a matter of poor rates and not enough a matter of Christian charity. The methods of relief envisaged were on the whole sound. They normally took the form of out-relief. Not for another century do we hear much of the horrors of the almshouse. There was nothing like unemployment insurance or old age pensions or even that guaranteed minimum associated two centuries later with the so-called Speenhamland Act. There was no very intelligent appraisal of the reasons for unemployment, though pressure was sometimes brought upon the clothiers to provide work for the weavers even when there was no market for cloth.

Taking the whole picture, the outstanding feature of government policy at the outset of the century was the application of medieval remedies to social ills. Tudor policy was fundamentally conservative, fundamentally opposed to those new forces in economic life which were to transform England. It was, however, capricious and irregular, directed by the exigencies of the moment rather than by any consistent adherence to a principle. It did nothing more, as Professor Tawney has observed, than impose an occasional brake on economic forces.

The implementation of that policy, so far as the welfare of the average Englishman was concerned, fell into the hands of the justices of the peace. During the Tudor period they were selected with some care and subject to constant oversight by the Crown. But they were all recruited from the same class, and in the long view their concept of the welfare state was a class concept. The Crown alone stood between them and those below them in economic and social status. That fact gives particular poignancy to the seventeenth-century civil struggle, the outcome of which, though often represented as a triumph of the people over the despot, was, if viewed socially and economically, the triumph of the landlord over the tenant, the employer over the employee, the rich over the poor, the exploiter over the exploited. The glories of the Glorious Revolution of 1688 become somewhat tarnished as we reflect that during the century and a half which followed, English policy was controlled by a class whose social ideology was defined in terms of the great chain of being and was resolutely opposed to equalitarian principles. The welfare of the people at large during that period was a matter of benevolence, not of right. One might perhaps go even further and say that the subsequent development in England of a more democratic attitude both in politics and in economics stemmed rather from the humanitarian impulses of the "Haves" than from the clamors and pressures of the "Have Nots."

COMPARED WITH THE PEOPLES OF Italy, Portugal, and Spain, Englishmen were slow to awaken to the importance of finding new trade routes and opening up commercial relations with distant regions. Early English oceanic discoveries were largely the work of foreigners resident in England, among whom John Cabot and his son Sebastian are the best known. Shortly before the reign of Elizabeth, however, English merchants were beginning to trade with some new areas. The earliest recorded English commercial voyage to Morocco was in 1551, and trade with the Guinea coast of Africa began at about the same time. In 1552-1553 a group of English merchants, capitalists, and courtiers received a royal charter from Edward VI, and this organization, later known as the Russia Company, long continued to carry on England's trade with the dominions of the Tsar by way of the White Sea. It was probably the earliest of England's joint-stock companies, as distinguished from the "regulated" companies, an earlier type of commercial association, similar in many respects to the medieval merchant gilds, which continued to control most branches of England's trade with distant regions throughout the Tudor period. An outstanding feature of English economic history during the reign of Elizabeth was the organization of a number of new companies to carry on sea-borne trade with remote areas. These included the Eastland Company, for trade with the countries of the Baltic; the Levant Company, for trade with the dominions of the Sultan of Turkey; and (most famous of all) the East India Company, for trade with territories beyond the Cape of Good Hope. The initiative in opening up this new trade was taken by interested groups of merchants, who sought governmental recognition and support for their commercial ventures and obtained it by a charter from the government, which utilized the companies as agents in carrying out its commercial policies. Monopolistic privileges were normally conferred upon the companies, which, on the other hand, incurred special obligations to the government. In the following essay, Professor Jelle C. Riemersma, now of the University of Toronto, makes some comparisons between the relations of government to oversea trade in England and in Holland from the middle of the sixteenth to the middle of the seventeenth century. He emphasizes that commercial enterprise in Holland, being in a position to exert much greater political influence than in England, was more self-reliant and less dependent on governmental support. Whereas "the whole institutional structure of the Dutch Republic . . . tended to increase commercial enterprise," the central power in England "was as yet not under control of the merchants."

GOVERNMENT INFLUENCE ON COMPANY ORGANIZATION IN HOLLAND AND ENGLAND (1550–1650)

JELLE C. RIEMERSMA

I

The development of rationality in economic life, according to Werner Sombart and Max Weber, is one of the most important aspects of modern economic history. Gradually, religious and ethical considerations lose their influence in commercial behavior; finally, in the nineteenth century, economic judgment proceeds on the basis of its own logic. Business is liberated from noneconomic sanctions.

The authors mentioned have compared modern economic life with that of the

Middle Ages and the mercantilist epoch. In the latter period the influence is noticeable of one particular set of noneconomic sanctions, namely, those which followed from raison d'état. In the eyes of the statesman, business enterprise should be judged according to the contribution which it made to the power of the realm. The opinions of leading merchants were not unaffected by this maxim, and Thomas Mun gave it this somewhat pompous formulation:

Behold, then, the true form and worth of forraign trade, which is, the great reve-

Reprinted by special permission from *The Journal of Economic History, Supplement,* X (1950), 31-39. The footnotes which originally appeared with this essay have been omitted.

nue of the king, the honor of the kingdom, the noble profession of the merchant, the school of our arts, the supply of our wants, the employment of our poor, the improvement of our lands, the nurcery of our mariners, the walls of our kingdom, the means of our treasure, the sinnews of our wars, the terror of our enemies.

Obviously, the motivation for foreign trade was heavily colored by the regard for "the sinnews of our wars." If the purpose of mercantile activity should be to increase the state's potential, political authority could be expected to play some role in commercial development.

My discussion will be concerned with the respective roles of political power and entrepreneurship in the economic expansion of Holland and England, especially in the period from 1550 to 1650. It is to be remembered that the two concepts used, power and entrepreneurship, are both rather vague. A survey of contemporary literature would show a lack of unanimity about their definition. I will abstain from increasing the confusion by adding a new pair of definitions to the existing number. I will simply associate "power" with the central government and "entrepreneurship" with the merchants engaged in foreign trade. Of course, this is only a rough approximation of real circumstances because in most societies there is a diffuse distribution of political power. The distribution of entrepreneurship can be equally all-pervading. Nevertheless, my simplified procedure is somewhat justified by the peculiarities of the historical period with which we are to deal. In the century which followed the oceanic discoveries, the exploitation of new trade routes constituted, indeed, the most crucial aspect of entrepreneurship. New communications rather than industrial innovations were in the forefront of development. Consequently, economic leadership rested with the merchants, especially those engaged in foreign trade.

During the Middle Ages, commercial activity had found its main center in the Mediterranean; the shift toward the Atlantic is one of the major occurrences in modern history. Among the Atlantic nations, Spain and Portugal were the first to exploit the possibilities of transoceanic enterprise. The relations between business and the state are so intimate in these cases that we may speak almost of state enterprises. In the "Casa de Contratación de la Especeria" of 1522, which was intended to be the Spanish association to monopolize the spice trade, the Crown contributed about half the invested capital. The Portuguese spice trade was under even more complete control of the monarchy.

About a century after the explorations of Columbus and Da Gama, economic leadership had been transferred from the Iberian peninsula to Holland and England. Dutch and English merchants had entered the Arctic regions as well as the Mediterranean and were reaching out to obtain their footholds in the Indies. The long time interval that elapsed between the discoveries and their commercial utilization by the countries of northwestern Europe suggests the

WERNER SOMBART: Twentieth-century German economic historian. His account of the development of European capitalism from its origins to the twentieth century was originally published in German in 1902 and frequently revised and enlarged. An important scholarly contribution, it served to arouse much disagreement and to encourage further study. Sombart wrote the article on capitalism for the *Encyclopaedia of the Social Sciences*.

MAX WEBER: Twentieth-century German sociologist and economic historian who has been much criticized as an oversimplifier but has rarely been equaled in his ability to challenge, provoke, and stimulate. He is best known in the United States for his *Protestant Ethic and the Spirit of Capitalism* and his *General Economic History*.

magnitude of the obstacles that had to be overcome. Larger capitals had to be invested because heavier ships were required and because of the slower returns. The need for diplomatic representation and for military protection led to large expenses. Moreover, bullion was an important article in oriental trade: this was a retarding factor in those countries which shared only indirectly in the flow of American treasure.

After 1550 a number of mercantile enterprises for distant regions were started; one of the earliest was the English Russia Company of 1553. The organization of this company and of the others that were to follow differed from the established precedents of earlier periods, probably under the influence of the exigencies of a new situation. In England the subsequent decades were characterized by the occurrence of a "wave of corporateness." For almost all the new branches of trade, merchant associations were formed with a state charter granted either by the king or by Parliament or by both. In this way, the arising associations obtained the exclusive rights of trade with a given region; we might call this a geographical monopoly.

Among English merchant associations, a distinction can be drawn between joint-stock companies and regulated companies. Adam Smith touched on an essential aspect of the latter when he remarked that "regulated companies resemble, in every respect, the corporations of trades, so common in the cities and towns of all the different countries of Europe." The guild-like characteristics of such companies are indeed obvious. Personal qualifications determined the admission of new members into the "brotherhood"; only "mere merchants" were generally allowed to enter. The regulations of the company applied to the personal as well as to the commercial conduct of the members. The entrance fee, often rather high, was the same for every new member, and everybody had one vote in the general assembly that determined the policy of the association. The assembly also elected the officials who were entrusted with everyday management: the governor and assistants, as they were often called.

From the economic point of view, the joint-stock and regulated companies present important differences. Organizationally, however, the two types were almost alike. English joint-stock associations showed guild-like characteristics almost as much as did the regulated companies. Consequently, Schmoller was led into the confusion of calling the East India Company a regulated one. Yet the early minutes are unequivocal regarding the existence of a joint stock:

> no ship shall be received to be brought in by any adventurer in this company to be employed in the same as his stock or portion of adventure at any rate whatsoever . . . no commodity shall be accepted in the said voyage to be brought in as any man's portion of adventure, but all goods, wares and other things shall be bought by such as shall be thereunto appointed as committees and directors . . . .

At another session of the East India Company the question of a charter was discussed. Queen Elizabeth was asked

> to grant to the adventurers a privilege in succession and to incorporate them into a company, for that the trade of the Indies being so far remote from hence cannot be traded but in a joint and united stock.

Probably the earliest chartered company to have a joint stock was the Russia Company under which, in 1553, six thousand pounds were brought together in equal shares of twenty-five pounds. The personal aspect of the fellowship appears from the clause of the charter stipulating that any new member should "in all things behave himself as others of the society are bound to do." In order to qualify for admission he should "for the course of ten years continually (have) traded the course of merchandise."

In distant trade, with Russia and the Indies, joint-stock companies were important, but the larger part of English trade was in the hands of regulated companies.

Thus the Merchant Adventurers were incorporated in 1564; the Eastland Company was established in 1579; the Levant Company in 1581. Besides these well-known companies there were a number of others. The persistence of the tendency toward a regulated trade was strong; thus the Lord Mayor and Common Council of London proposed in 1662 a similar organization for commerce with Spain, Portugal, France, and Italy. This proposal was rejected by Parliament.

In Holland also, during the century which began in 1550, some merchant associations for distant trade were chartered. It might be expected that similar difficulties in this kind of trade would lead to the formation of organizations similar to those of England, but this did not happen. The differences in the organization of foreign trade in the two countries were fundamental.

In the first place, merchant associations with a government charter occupied a relatively minor position in Dutch trade as a whole. While English traders became to a large extent incorporated into large associations with exclusive rights, the bulk of Dutch trade remained in the hands of an immense plurality of small firms and partnerships, operating without any explicit sanctions from the state.

Since medieval times this type of organization had prevailed in Holland, and the system did not change basically during the sixteenth and seventeenth centuries. The number of large-scale associations which arose in these centuries remained relatively small. While the English merchants who wanted to establish a new branch of trade seemed to consider a state charter indispensable at the very beginning of the enterprise, their Dutch competitors usually obtained such a monopoly, if at all, as an afterthought. The Dutch East India Company (1602) was chartered long after a number of smaller companies, the so-called "voor-compagnieën" had made a successful start with the oriental trade. Private enterprise was also responsible for the beginnings of whaling near Spitzbergen. The Noordsche

Compagnie was formed in 1614 by the union of several pre-existing companies.

Aside from the trade to the West Indies, which was partly a military undertaking, the initiation of new branches of overseas commerce occurred with a minimum of direct participation by the Dutch Republic. The States-General granted commercial monopolies to combinations of firms, but the unification of such firms often led to insurmountable difficulties. Thus the trade to Russia and to West Africa remained without any over-all association and, consequently, without a chartered monopoly. The strength and the competitive spirit among the existing firms prevented their unification; some attempts were made but they were shipwrecked.

For the same reason, the Levant trade remained free. In 1629 a proposal was made to establish a company which would have a monopoly of commerce with North Africa and the Levant and a monopoly of marine insurance besides. The scheme for this "Compagnie van Assurantie" was vigorously opposed by the merchants of Holland and especially those of Amsterdam. As a result it was rejected. The arguments of the opponents showed a strong spirit of individualism; they stated that

> commerce exists by virtue of industry, diligence and activity. By means of the "Compagnie van Assurantie" the slack and clumsy would have the same advantage as the bold and active merhcants.

Successful unification of the existing firms occurred in the case of the East India trade. Between 1595 and 1602 a number of merchant firms had arisen which engaged in ruthless competition with each other. The danger from the English and Portuguese and the desire to obtain the European spice monopoly resulted in 1602 in the establishment of the Dutch East India Company. Similarly, the Noordsche Compagnie of 1614 united some firms which had been engaged in the whaling trade for two years, and again it was need of protection from English attacks that led to unification.

Not only the origin of monopolistic associations in Holland but also their internal organization was quite different from that of the English companies. The Dutch companies were associations of capital rather than of persons; consequently, the guild-like features of the English companies were absent. For instance, the overwhelming majority of the stockholders in the Dutch East India Company had no influence whatsoever in the policy decisions of the company.

I have already mentioned the general assembly of the English-regulated company, which met to make important decisions and which chose, moreover, the directors and assistants entrusted with the daily management. The absence of a similar body politic in the Dutch companies was conditioned by the much larger number of shareholders and the wide variation in the amount of the shares. For instance, in Amsterdam the shares varied from Fl.50 to Fl.36,000. A distinction existed between major shareholders who were eligible for leading positions and the large majority of *participanten,* who contributed capital and joined in the dividends but had no chance of exercising influence in the company. In the English East India Company this distinction was absent; the amount of the shares, as appears from the earliest list of subscribers, varies only between £100 and £3,000. The large majority of the shareholders contributed £200 or £300.

The English merchant associations with all their exclusiveness toward outsiders were internally rather democratic, with equality between their members. The Dutch companies have been described as oligarchic in character; at the same time, such companies were far less exclusive. No personal qualifications were needed to enter the company, only the willingness to contribute capital in any amount. Even foreigners seem to have participated in the Dutch companies.

II

The contrast between Dutch and English companies can be explained by the different relations between commercial enterprise and the central government. I have already observed that the government of the Dutch Republic afforded relatively little direct stimulation to new branches of commercial enterprise. The development of commerce was independent of state action in its behalf. Paradoxically, the state, which was the model and ideal of all mercantilist policy, did not itself apply the mercantilist principles. In Holland mercantile enterprise was left largely to its own resources; the spheres of government and of commerce were clearly kept apart.

English merchants engaging in new branches of trade were rewarded with state-sanctioned monopolies. On the other hand, they also had many obligations to the Crown, for instance, in furnishing credit. The English system of commerce, with its entanglements of government and enterprise, should be called less rational (in Weber's sense) than the Dutch system of the same period. Given this state of affairs, the corporate spirit of English merchant associations is not surprising. From a number of instances it appears that the peculiar organization of English companies was effective in checking the influence of the monarch and his favorites.

Thus in 1624 the directors of the East India Company refused to admit James I as a member of the company. They explained the refusal by arguing that no monarch could enter into a fellowship with his subjects. Evidently the personal qualifications for membership, as well as the fraternal aspects of the association, could be used as weapons when the company was in danger of outside interference.

At the very beginning of the East India Company the independence of the participants was asserted in the following way. The lord treasurer proposed that Sir Edward Michelborne be appointed the commander of the first voyage. The directors of the company refused, asking the treasurer

to give them leave to sort their business with men of their own quality and not to expect that they (the Directors) make any further motion of this to the generalty lest the suspicion of the employment of gentlemen being taken hold upon will drive a great number of adventurers to withdraw their contributions.

Evidently, the general assembly was rather sensitive on this point. The desire to be "with men of their own quality" may also account for the fact that among the one hundred earliest subscribers to the company only four nobles are to be found.

It is true that in some English companies nobles or even royal persons played a considerable role, but in these companies the guild-like characteristics were usually absent. For instance, the Guinea Company of 1564 had many noble members; its organization paralleled the oligarchic pattern of the Dutch companies, comprising major partners and subpartners. Generally speaking, the influence of nobles in English economic development was strong in colonial and industrial enterprises rather than in commercial ventures.

In general, the features which distinguished the English system of commercial organization from the Dutch system had the effect of shielding mercantile undertakings from noncommercial influences. The interference from the side of the Crown, especially, was considered undesirable.

In Holland such a segregation of an autonomous commercial sphere had been achieved in another way. On a national scale, commerce had been liberated from the disturbing influences of a central monarchy by the successful revolt against Spain. The Dutch Provinces, after 1581, formed a federal republic with only a very weak central power. The medieval tradition of a large urban and provincial autonomy was preserved and, as a result, mercantile groups could exert a large political influence. Consequently, mercantile enterprises had no pressing need to defend their independence with respect to political authority; this authority rested with the merchants themselves, and the chance that it would harm commercial activity was therefore negligible. Actually, the whole institutional structure of the Dutch Republic, its laws and taxes, all tended to increase commercial enterprise.

Comparatively speaking, the English merchant was in a less advantageous position; English institutions were not devised according to his particular needs only. The central power was as yet not under control of the merchants. In this context, the corporate structure of mercantile enterprise could give some security and independence from the exigencies of political power.

WHEN THE STUDENT OF ENGLISH LITERATURE and intellectual history uses the label "Renaissance," he usually has in mind, from the standpoint of chronology, the period from the late fifteenth century to the middle of the seventeenth. When he uses the term to differentiate sixteenth- and early-seventeenth-century English thought from medieval thought, he usually has in mind two distinguishing characteristics: that Renaissance thought was vastly more secular than medieval thought, and that Renaissance thought was vastly more individualistic than medieval thought. It is dangerous, however, to introduce any sharp and neat division between medieval and Renaissance thought. For one thing, medievalists have been demonstrating in recent years that the thought of the Middle Ages was far more secular and individualistic than it has often been painted. Secondly, it becomes increasingly clear that the thought of the Renaissance was often far less secular and far less individualistic than it has often been pictured. In short, there is no doubt that medieval intellectual interests continued to flourish on a significant scale into the age of the so-called Renaissance. In the essay that follows, Dr. Louis B. Wright, now director of the Folger Shakespeare Library and author of the admirable study *Middle-Class Culture in Elizabethan England* (1935), emphasizes the importance of religion as a force in the literature of the English Renaissance and points out how misleading it is from the historical point of view to focus attention exclusively on the secular thought of the period.

THE SIGNIFICANCE OF RELIGIOUS WRITINGS IN THE ENGLISH RENAISSANCE

LOUIS B. WRIGHT

To say that the history of religion is one of the most important, as well as one of the most complex, subjects facing the student of the English Renaissance is a platitude so obvious that it ought not to need repeating. Yet of all the fields of investigation in the history of English thought during this period, it would be hard to find another that has been treated in such piecemeal fashion, or approached with so many pre-conceived and *ex parte* notions. And within the broad outlines of religious history, no special subject has been so persistently ignored as the significance of the vast body of religious writings that poured from the English press from the time of Caxton to the beginning of the Puritan Revolution, the period that we may somewhat loosely describe as the English Renaissance. Only within the last decade have literary historians shown an inclination to take cognizance of a body of literature amounting to more than forty per cent of the total output of the printing press. Thanks now to a few inquiring pioneers, a trail, here and there, has been blazed through the wilderness, and scholars are beginning to see that, if the dark hinterland is not precisely flowing with the milk and honey of literary genius, at least it has abundant stores of good grain to nourish

historians who deal in ideas or social trends, or even strictly literary developments.

The neglect of religious writings is understandable, for literary historians usually emphasize types of writing pleasing to the age in which they live. Their criticisms and observations are more often a reflection of themselves and their contemporaries than an interpretation of the literature they write about in terms of the age that produced it. For example, today, quite reasonably, we are more interested in Shakespeare's dramatic development than in the career and influence of his contemporary, the Reverend William Perkins; but for every Elizabethan who saw or read one of Shakespeare's plays, a hundred bought and read Perkins' sermons. Yet even if a host of historians arose to "discover," with whatever enthusiasm, such forgotten preachers, the twentieth century would not fall to sermon-reading for its pleasure—which is as it should be. Nevertheless, if we hope to have an adequate understanding of the Elizabethan period, we must know something more of its literary tastes than can be obtained from books that merely entertain us. As Professor Chambers comments in his brilliant essay on the continuity of English prose, "in the

[1] R. W. Chambers, "The Continuity of Eng-

Reprinted by special permission from *The Journal of the History of Ideas,* I (1940), 59-68.

history of literature, we have to consider not merely what writers charm us, but what writers influenced their age, and how."[1] And, illustrating the distortion of truth that comes from failure to recognize this simple fact, Mr. Chambers points out that historians have banished into oblivion the greatest prose writers of the fourteenth century because these forgotten men wrote of religious matters—a theme distinctly boring to the children of enlightenment in the twentieth century. In this connection we might also recall Gibbon's contempt for Caxton because he brought out so many pious works and saints' legends, thereby catering to "the vicious taste of his readers."[2]

Although we have yet no work on English religious literature so comprehensive as M. Henri Brémond's *Histoire littéraire du sentiment religieux en France depuis la fin des guerres de religion jusqu'à nos jours,*[3]

there are signs that scholars are awaking to the tremendous importance of this subject. In 1933 Dr. G. R. Owst of Cambridge published *Literature and Pulpit in Medieval England,* a book for which a much-abused phrase of blurb writers is literally true; it is indeed an "epoch-making book," for it has shown the necessity of re-writing medieval literary history as we conventionally know it. It is significant that Dr. Owst in his introduction felt a compulsion to write a defense of his theme. A few of his remarks should be quoted here, for what he says of medieval literature is equally true of the Renaissance:

> The historical student, who wanders from outside into the preserve of the literary critics, can hardly fail to be struck from time to time by the highly artificial treatment of the story of English medieval literary development by those whose chief concern appears to be "to sift out"—by modern standards—"the good from the bad." In the first place, the very contents of the typical text-book upon the subject seems often to bear little resemblance to the medieval library, as a student of the actual manuscript would learn to know it. Where, we may well

---

[1] lish Prose from Alfred to More and His School," *Early English Text Society,* No. 186 (London, 1932), p. cxlix. See also pp. cxxv, clxvii.

[2] Nellie Slayton Aurner, *Caxton, Mirror of Fifteenth-Century Letters* (Boston and New York, 1926), p. 126.

[3] Translated by K. L. Montgomery as *A Literary History of Religious Thought in France* (London, 1928-   ). The first four volumes have appeared. In Vol. I, *Devout Humanism,* p. xv, M. Brémond remarks of a proper historical attitude toward literature: "Would the historian of French literature be justified in neglecting Jean Louis Guez de Balzac, the greatest literary force of his time, although he be no longer read in ours? In the same way,

---

> though it is open to us to prefer a page of the *Elévations sur les mystères* to a hundred pages of Père Binet, still we must not ignore the fact that this Jesuit exercised on the religious consciousness of his century an influence far wider and more active than that of Bossuet himself."

HUGH LATIMER: Protestant preacher and social reformer who was condemned as a heretic and burned during Mary's reign. His extant writings reveal his skill in using simple language and choosing vivid illustrations.

WILLIAM PERKINS: Elizabethan theological writer. Known in his youth for his profanity and lack of moderation, he underwent a sudden conversion when he heard a woman using "drunken Perkins" as an example for her child not to follow. He achieved tremendous fame as a preacher, a theologian, and a teacher at the University of Cambridge. Although he was not a peer of Calvin or Hooker, he continued to be widely read generations after his death. His sympathies were clearly with those who wished to purify the Elizabethan church of medieval Catholic survivals.

ask, in our modern literary historian's digest are the hundreds of religious works in prose and verse fairly presented and discussed, outnumbering, as they do, every other species of contemporary writing? Even if for the earlier centuries they receive due recognition, there is little to suggest in his pages that the output multiplies an hundredfold as later generations succeed, much less that their contents have any significance for his theme. From this discrepancy, however, a worse follows. Having decided, according to modern standards of taste and value, what is strictly worthy of a place in his survey, and having dismissed the rest from his mind, our literary historian proceeds to regard this highly arbitrary selection of letters as though it were a self-contained, organic whole, comprising within itself the whole story of literary development. So, he will trace this image and that, this conceit and that, as he fondly imagines, from recognized author to author, lightheartedly leaping the centuries and the bounds between land and land, scattering freely, as he goes, his tribute or his censure, here crowning a supposed original genius, there chastising a decadent, ignoring, all the while, the vast literature of those whom current ages were wont to regard as *the* "literati," writers and orators of unchallengeable authority.[4]

In the light of Dr. Owst's revelations, we are prepared for a better understanding and appreciation of Chaucer and the author of *The Vision of Piers Plowman;* but what is perhaps more important, we come nearer seeing the intellectual and social world of Chaucer and his contemporaries as it was, not as critics have been pleased to imagine it. Literary history of this type is justified by its value to literary appreciation; and

even more valuable is its very real contribution to all phases of historical understanding. Owst has shown how such unpromising material as the sermons of the Middle Ages, preserved in countless manuscripts, provide an insight into the lives and feelings of common men, for the preachers of these forgotten homilies were themselves of the people and, by and large, they reflected the interests of the laity. He has also shown how these sermons are a corrective to the abstractions of institutional history, and how they enable us to see, not merely the skeleton of society, but something more of the whole living body. To ecclesiastical history —often written as if the church were an abstract institution of theological dogma devoid of human interest—the religious writings give a fuller significance, as one sees church history through the eyes of the congregations and the ordinary preachers instead of the bloodless theologians. The clues suggested by Owst could be profitably applied to a new appraisal of the writings of the English Renaissance.

That the development of English prose of the sixteenth century owed much to the religious writers of the two preceding centuries has been ably demonstrated by Professor Chambers. Had he chosen to do so, he might also have shown that habits of thought and points of view had also been vastly influenced by the same means, that Englishmen had developed an inordinate taste for pious literature, and that, though the Reformation and Renaissance altered the quality and the theological implications of religious writings, the public's keen zest for such matter was undiminished. Englishmen of the Middle Ages as well as their descendants in the sixteenth and seventeenth centuries were regarded by continental Europeans as extraordinary for their piety and their appetite for religious works.[5] The

---

[4] Pp. viii-ix. See further pp. 210-11, 230. An earlier work by the same author, *Preaching in Medieval England* (Cambridge, 1926), also throws a great deal of light on the significance of the religious literature in the Middle Ages.

[5] See H. Maynard Smith, *Pre-Reformation England* (London, 1938), pp. 91-103, 126; and Louis B. Wright, *Middle-Class Culture in Elizabethan England* (Chapel Hill, 1935), pp. 228-96.

early popular printers, for instance, produced large quantities of pious books: devotional treatises, sermons, and saints' legends all for the delectation of the laity. In contrast with the zeal shown by Aldus of Venus to produce cheap texts of the classics, England's first printer, Caxton, energetically set to work to turn out inexpensive works of spiritual edification.[6] The example he set was followed for two hundred years by scores of succeeding printers. And we can be quite sure that these printers were inspired by a hope of profit this side of heaven.

An analysis by subjects of the output of the English printing presses from the time of Caxton to the year 1641, made by Miss Edith L. Klotz of the Huntington Library, has shown that 43.7 per cent of the total number of books printed were in some way religious in theme.[7] In some years religious books accounted for more than half of the works published, and rarely in any year during that whole period did they fall below one third of the total output. Bibles and service books account for many of these volumes; there were, of course, many controversial and theological works; but the great bulk of this reading matter was what we might describe as "non-professional"— that is, designed for the general reader bent upon self-improvement. Sermons, devotional manuals, pious allegories, guides to the good life, and a vast quantity of miscellaneous works of edification made up this

tremendous flood of religious reading matter that influenced every walk of English life. Throughout the social, political, and intellectual upheavals that took place during this century and three-quarters, the volume of religious reading matter remained fairly constant. Whether England was Catholic or Protestant, her citizens read with avidity the works of piety which the printers supplied. Changes in spiritual outlook, in theology, in social attitudes, and in politics are reflected in these works, but the major preoccupation of English readers was with certain timeless values. However far, in practice, Englishmen might stray from the path of religious rectitude, they subscribed to the theory of pious conduct. A courtier living a loose life of debauchery salved his conscience by writing paraphrases of the penitential Psalms or by reading sermons and books of devotion; and, at the other social pole, the profane tinker, or the ribald waterman at London, might have by him such a work as Arthur Dent's *The Plain Man's Pathway to Heaven* (1601).

Englishmen did not buy religious books merely as a perfunctory act of piety, nor did they acquire fine volumes of sermons just to lie on the parlor table as a symbol of the household's godliness; in this age, all classes actually read pious books. It should be remembered, too, that the degree of literacy was far greater than has been generally supposed,[8] and even women in humble stations knew how to con their books of prayers and manuals of religious conduct. Indeed, the belief that every citizen should be able to read the Bible and the Prayer Book was the impelling motive behind much popular education after the Reformation. Driven by the intensity of religious fervor that characterized the English sixteenth and early seventeenth centuries, thousands of men and women greedily consumed all manner of books that ministered to their souls' welfare, and thus unconsciously developed a rudimentary literary taste. And we should not forget that some

[6] Aurner, *op. cit.,* pp. 79-129.

[7] A chronological catalogue of extant English books from the introduction of printing to the year 1641 has been made at the Huntington Library by copying on cards all the items in *A Short-Title Catalogue . . . 1475-1640* (London, 1926) and rearranging them by years. By classifying the cards for every tenth year, an estimate was made of the relative proportion of subjects during the whole period. A further analysis of shorter spaces of time showed that the results would not be materially different if *all* the titles for the period were classified. See Edith L. Klotz, "A Subject Analysis of English Imprints for Every Tenth Year from 1480 to 1640," *The Huntington Library Quarterly,* I (1937-38), 417-19.

[8] See Wright, *op. cit.,* pp. 43-80.

of the best minds of this age were writing religious books, often with the object of reaching the average sort of men. Whatever we may think today of the literary value of the religious reading matter that poured so profusely from the presses, it cannot be denied that this literature exerted a vast influence on the public by providing instruments for the cultivation of their intellects.

Next to the Bible—fundamental to all religious reading—the most popular works of piety were devotional books. Preachers never tired of compiling them and printers never failed to scent a profit in a new one. From Caxton's *Art and Craft to Know Well to Die* (1490) until long after Michael Sparke's *The Crums of Comfort* (tenth edition, 1629) there was a constant stream of these manuals, which undoubtedly reached a large audience. Indeed, Sparke, in 1652 declared in the preface to a new edition of *The Crums of Comfort* that forty impressions of the first part, amounting to 60,000 copies, had been previously sold. Most of them were literally read out of existence, so that the earliest extant copy recorded in the *Short-Title Catalogue* is the seventh edition of 1628. Other manuals were equally popular. Some of these, like Dent's *The Plain Man's Pathway,* have considerable literary charm; their directness of style and simplicity of diction must have taught salutary lessons to an age whose conscious literature was often a jungle of verbiage. Dent's manual was one of the books owned and read by John Bunyan, and its influence is reflected in his later works. Nearly all of the devotional handbooks contain illuminating sidelights on the ideals and the practices of the day. Yet until Miss Helen White published, in 1931, her *English Devotional Literature [Prose], 1600-1640,* there was no satisfactory book on the subject for any part of the field. Further investigations into the impact of these manuals upon the intellectual development of their readers would produce significant results. They not only influenced Englishmen at home, but after the period of colonization, they were brought to the New World to supply the sole reading of some settlers.

Almost as popular as devotional manuals were sermons, published as single treatises or in collected editions. Inheriting a taste for homilies from the Middle Ages, Englishmen did not lose their appetite for such reading matter until well into the eighteenth century. Rich and poor, high and low, found in sermons food for their minds and spirits. Sermons as delivered in the pulpits were an important means of disseminating propaganda and were shrewdly utilized by the Tudors.[9] Professor Godfrey Davies has recently shown the importance of political sermons in the reigns of James I and Charles I.[10] During the whole period we are considering, the spoken sermon reached thousands of listeners and helped to shape, not only their spiritual, but their social, political, and intellectual attitudes. The official homilies, published in the reign of Edward VI and continued by Elizabeth and her successors, were heard and read by thousands, who could not help being impressed with the ideas therein, as well as by their straightforward, simple diction. From the time of Hugh Latimer onward, the tradition of direct, salty, idiomatic utterance from the pulpit held the multitude. Even after the rise of the so-called "witty" style of preaching in the early seventeenth century—with its consciously involved literary technique—the preachers of the plain style, both Anglican and Puritan, continued to attract immense crowds. By the late years of the sixteenth century, the popularity of sermons was so great that certain preachers received homage not unlike that now accorded motion picture actors. Men, women, and children attended sermons and carefully took down the discourses in shorthand. Women, in fact, became so vain of their skill in this exercise that a few conservatives felt that their pride needed rebuking.[11] During the

[9] *Ibid.,* pp. 269-75.
[10] Godfrey Davies, "English Political Sermons, 1603-1640," *The Huntington Library Quarterly,* III (1939-40), 1-22.
[11] Observe the complaint of Sir Ralph Verney in the mid-seventeenth century that women, having learned shorthand to take down sermons, had developed a pride that "hath made multi-

reign of James I, the king and his courtiers attended sermons with the air of connoisseurs and criticized the learning and the technique of the preachers. Throughout the reigns of the Tudors and the early Stuarts, the pulpit was a vital institution that affected every citizen.

If spoken sermons reached thousands, printed ones gained a much wider audience. Relatively few could actually hear the Reverend William Perkins preach at Cambridge, but half of England perused his sermons, and colonists in New England and Virginia alike continued to read him for a hundred years.[12] Other preachers, Anglican and Puritan, enjoyed audiences almost as extensive. One fact that cannot be emphasized too often is that the most popular sermons were the least controversial; hence many Puritan preachers—and Perkins is a good example—who stuck to exhortations to godliness and discourses on practical ethics were read by all sects. The reading public was less interested in theology than in ethics.

For the historian, these sermons are extremely valuable. In them may be traced fluctuations of attitudes; and social philosophies current in their day find a reflection in them. Though only a neophyte in investigation would take the utterances of preachers at their face value, their discourses, used with proper discrimination, are mines of material that cannot be duplicated elsewhere. Even where sermons are tissues of misrepresentation, where they contain imaginative creations of prejudice instead of facts, they are significant as evidence of what the populace was asked to believe, of the most potent influence shaping public opinion. Moreover, as in the case of the devotional manuals, many of the sermons are not devoid of literary merit. But despite the obvious historical value of this vast body of literature—perhaps because of its vast-

ness—scholars have avoided it as if it carried the infection of some malady. It is true that a few hardy souls like Professor Charles McIlwain have often demonstrated its value in the study of institutional history, and Professor W. K. Jordan has found therein materials for his study of religious toleration,[13] and church historians have utilized particular segments, but these men have engaged in placer mining, taking out nuggets here and there. Until the present decade, there has been little effort to follow any vein systematically. Lately, however, a few scholars have attacked the problem. One worthwhile exploration into sermon literature is Mr. W. Fraser Mitchell's *English Pulpit Oratory from Andrewes to Tillotson: A Study of Its Literary Aspects* (London, 1932); and another, more recent study, Professor William Haller's *The Rise of Puritanism* (New York, 1938), gives a somewhat broader interpretation of the value of sermons preached and published by the leading Puritans of the first half of the seventeenth century. These two books indicate both the literary and historical worth of the sermon literature.

Students of the English Renaissance are gradually coming to realize the significance of a body of literature that touched every man and woman of the age. They are beginning to see that any interpretation of the period that hopes to approach truth must describe the impact of this literature upon the various strata of the public. They are observing that, even upon literary style, religious works had a tremendous effect. For instance, as Professor Chambers has shown,[14] the Authorized Version of the Bible, published in 1611, was not an isolated miracle of style; lessons learned from religious writings preceding that translation gave it clarity and purity of diction. Religion as a motive and religious literature as a stimulus to some of the belles-lettres of the day should be more carefully studied. We need a

tudes of women most unfortunate." Margaret M. Verney, *Memoirs of the Verney Family during the Commonwealth, 1650 to 1660* (London, 1894), III, 72.

[12] Louis B. Wright, "William Perkins: Elizabethan Apostle of 'Practical Divinity,'" forthcoming in *The Huntington Library Quarterly*.

[13] W. K. Jordan, *The Development of Religious Toleration in England* (3 vols., London, 1932-38).

[14] R. W. Chambers, *op. cit.,* p. cxxxv.

clearer perception of the qualities of an age that made religion an intimate part of its life, and that read religious writings as eagerly as we read the newspapers. Religion was a dominant theme in poets like Spenser, and unless we appreciate the Elizabethan's attitude toward religion, much in the *Faerie* *Queene* is meaningless. The history of thought in the English Renaissance cannot be understood without first comprehending the importance of religion in the lives of the people. The approach to that necessary comprehension is through the extant religious literature.

HISTORIANS HAVE OFTEN BEEN CONDESCENDING in their attitude toward the study and writing of the history of education. This is not to say that they have failed to recognize the importance of the subject. The explanation is, rather, that they have viewed it as a field to be explored at teachers' colleges. The upshot has been that the history of education has often been investigated and written about by professors of education who, despite their undoubted enthusiasm for their subject, have lacked the general historical background that could give greater validity and meaning to their investigations. In other words, many of the writers on the history of education have had only a superficial grasp of political, social, economic, and intellectual development. Yet a fundamental knowledge of these aspects of history is indispensable to an understanding of the history of education; otherwise the subject is certain to suffer from the absence of meaningful context. In the essay that follows, Professor J. H. Hexter, of Queens College of the City of New York, invades a realm that has traditionally been reserved for professors at teachers' colleges, and he shows how fruitful the study of the history of education can be when it is related to the general history of an age. Author of an excellent monograph on *The Reign of King Pym* (1941) and of a number of articles on early-modern England, Professor Hexter is a challenging and stimulating scholar, who delights in the explosion of historical myths and revels in the suggestion of new approaches and novel theses.

THE EDUCATION OF THE ARISTOCRACY IN THE RENAISSANCE

J. H. HEXTER

In an inquiry concerning education the historian may take one of several starting places, launch his investigation with one of several major questions. He may ask what people thought education should be at a particular time. Or he may ask what education at that time was like in fact; and as every teacher knows to his sorrow, there is usually a world of difference between the answers to those two questions. He may also ask who got the education that was offered, and this third question is

Reprinted by special permission from *The Journal of Modern History*, XXII (1950), 1-20. Copyright, University of Chicago Press. The extensive documentation which originally appeared with this essay has been omitted. So, too, has a large section of the text that deals with the Continent.

surely no less significant than the other two. If one believes that knowledge in some measure is power, particularly if, like the author, one is an educational anarchist and believes that in society at large a man who has received almost any kind of rigorous intellectual discipline stands in a position of competitive advantage, other things being equal, over a man who has received none, then the question of who got an education becomes acute for the writing of social history. Now about what certain men during the period of the Renaissance thought education should be like we know a great deal, and about what education in fact was like we know somewhat less, but still a considerable amount. About who got the education—about the social appropriation and distribution of this very valuable scarce goods—we know almost nothing.

That this was the case was sharply brought home to the writer in the course of a study he was making of the aristocracy of the new monarchies in the age of the Renaissance. Not being able to find any study of the matter in print, he decided to try himself to reach at least a tentative answer to his question, and the rather fragmentary sketch that follows is the result of his inquiry. A casual investigation of the situation in Spain did not produce any result worth recording, so any generalizations that appear hereafter apply only to England, France, and the Netherlands. What, then, was the education of the aristocrats during the Renaissance, how many of them received it, when historically did they begin to receive it, and what did they want with it?

The most superficial examination of the most conspicuous data tells us with certainty at least this: that in the sixteenth century there was a great deal of complaint about the education of the aristocracy and that with a few exceptions the Jeremiahs of the time were all saying pretty much the same thing. The well-born were ignorant, they were indifferent to learning, and they preferred to stay that way. John Skelton compressed the essence of a century of criticism into a capsule of doggerel:

> Noblemen born
> to learn they have scorn,
> but hunt and blow a horn,
> leap over lakes and dikes,
> set nothing by politics.

It was in almost identical terms but more emphatically that an unnamed gentleman stated his attitude on learning to the humanist diplomat Richard Pace. "It becomes the sons of gentlemen," he said, "to blow the horn nicely, to hunt skillfully, and elegantly to carry and train a hawk." He added that "the study of letters was for rustics," that it was stupid, and that all learned men were beggars. "Rather my son should hang," than be learned, he concluded. Another Englishman later in the century added dress, dining, drinking, and gadding about

---

ROGER ASCHAM: English scholar (d. 1568) who served as tutor to the young Princess Elizabeth, Latin secretary to Queen Mary (even though he was Protestant), and private tutor to Queen Elizabeth. His *Toxophilus* (1545), a treatise on archery, stressed the need for physical training in education. His posthumously published *Scholemaster* cautioned against what he regarded as the menace of idle attendance at court and of travel in Italy.

SIR THOMAS ELYOT: Popularizer of the classics in England and author of the *Boke Named the Gouernour* (1531), an important treatise on education as well as an important work in the history of English prose. As a result of his having written this volume, he was named ambassador to Charles V.

JOHN SKELTON: English poet (d. 1529) who served as tutor to the future Henry VIII. He was especially gifted as a satirist, and in various poems he poked fun at the court of Henry VII, the clergy, and Cardinal Wolsey.

to hunting and hawking in the list of current noble attainments. Noble folk charge
anyone who talks wisely with preaching, he
said, and contemptuously call all men more
learned than themselves penmen. Across
the Channel the story is the same. La Noue
spoke of the present sunken generation of
noblemen, great hunters and brawlers, who
take little care to educate their young to
choses honnestes. They let themselves be
ruled by custom and think it enough if
their children can read and write. Nöel du
Fail's country gentleman in the *Contes
d'Eutrapel* read a translation of the Bible,
a dismal series of medieval romances and
saints' lives, and nothing else. Another
Frenchman deplored "the nobles' Gothic
fashion of hating learning and learned men
as if books and arms were things incompatible." And yet another in an untranslat-
able pun says that the only use most nobles
had for a *plume* was to put it in their hats.

So ran the refrain—a chorus of condemnation against the unlearnedness and hostility to learning of the noble and the gentle.
What is the meaning of this denunciation?
It fits well into a time-honored pattern of
historical explanation. It may be but one
more note in that running-down-the-scale
of feudalism which, played contrapuntally
with the ascent of the middle class, is taken
to be the all-sufficient explanation of practically everything that happened in Europe
for seven hundred years. Before adopting
this explanation out of hand we had better
examine somewhat more closely the circumstances surrounding the complaints. We
have the criticism of the aristocracy, and
we have the situation criticized—the ignorance of the wellborn. Was the complaint
new or long standing? The situation—
was it old or new? And, finally, was the
situation real or unreal; to what extent was
the sixteenth-century aristocrat actually an
ignorant man?

For purposes of comparison we may
begin our investigation with Geoffrey
Chaucer's pilgrims on the Canterbury road
at about the end of the fourteenth century. In that motley band there were only
three men who were certainly aristocrats or
near-aristocrats—the knight; his son, the
squire; and the franklin. The knight and
the squire received identical training; and
to it we must give our earnest attention.
The franklin tells us why: he has a son, he
says, and he

> . . . levere than twenty pound worth lond,
> Though it right now were fallen in myn
>   hond,
> He were a man of swich discrecion

as the squire. Then, instead of dicing and
spending wildly, he would commune with
gentlemen and rightly learn what belongs
to gentility. The Yorkshire landlord feels
that the training of the squire is just what
that of a gentleman should be. His own
education is somewhat deficient; the squire's
is at once the average and the ideal, the
pedagogic goal toward which gentlemen and
would-be gentlemen direct their children.
It is *the* education of the aristocrat.

The squire's formal education had two
branches. He learned music—to sing it,
to play it, to compose both tune and lyric.
He learned to dance, to draw and write; he
learned to speak and move gracefully. This
was courteous aesthetic training, the learning of love, dedicated to the lady fair. He
exercised his body. He rode, shot, handled
lance and sword; he ran, vaulted, and
leaped. He carved before his father at table.
This was practical knightly training, preparation for warfare and for the honorable
service a gentleman owed his lord. The
squire's education began when he became
a page in about his seventh year, it continued for fourteen years, and its goal was
knighthood. In the course of these fourteen years the noble youth was supposed
to acquire not only a set of accomplishments but a code of morals as well. He
was to come out of the educational mill
lowly and serviceable, gentle and worthy,
loving chivalry, truth, and honor, freedom
and courtesy.

In Chaucer's time this pattern of gentle
education was about two hundred and fifty
years old, and almost a century later it was

still the only kind of aristocratic education the court of France knew. In this long time much had changed but not the training of a gentleman. Henry II's good servant, William the Marshall, would have found nothing in the education of Chaucer's squire in fourteenth-century England or of La Tremouille in the fifteenth-century court of Louis XI that he would not have prescribed for his own sons. But it was not the kind of education that the lament-makers of the sixteenth century were prescribing for gentlemen in their time. Indeed, some of the squire's very attainments were a target for their criticisms. In his old age the squire himself, like his sixteenth-century successors, probably retired to his estate, sloughed off his no longer useful graces, and spent his time in hunting, hawking, and the reading of old romances that so disgusted our band of Renaissance critics. Many of these critics were coolly indifferent even to those aspects of knightly training which they did not overtly sneer at. In their eyes the squire's education suffered from a fatal flaw. Partly practical, partly moral, partly aesthetic, it was quite unlearned. Bookish learning could rarely be expected among men in whom the ability to read and write was a good but supererogatory work.

Such learning, the squire's sixteenth-century congener said to his critics, was clerkly, for the men of the church and the men of the schools, not for men of the world. So would the squire have said, and so said his ancestor in William the Marshall's time. But —and here lies the core of the difference— they did not say it in answer to criticism, because in those days there was no criticism to answer. Before the Renaissance few people demanded or expected that a gentleman should be a clerk, and if aristocrats drew a sharp line between clerkly education and their own, they had the support of the clergy in so doing. Yet in the sixteenth century we have a spate of words dedicated to the proposition that all gentlemen worthy of the name must be clerks, deep in learning and the intellectual virtues; and the

words come, mind you, not merely or mainly from clerks but from the gentlemen themselves—from men like Sir Thomas Elyot and Sir Humphrey Gilbert, Jean de Saulx Tavannes and François de la Noue. Ignorance and indifference to letters in the aristocracy was not new in the sixteenth century; what was new and radical was the suggestion that things should be otherwise.

What educational reality underlay the mass of exhortation and criticism directed at the aristocracy in the sixteenth century? Were the English gentlemen, say, of that age as innocent of and indifferent to school learning as Chaucer's squire was, and as the squire's contemporaries felt that he had a perfect right to be? Some of their doings suggest that the answer is, "No."

Beginning some time in the reign of Henry VIII, the scions of the titled nobility of England swarm into those citadels of clerkly training, the English universities. Greys, Brandons, Mannerses, Cecils, and Devereux all appear on the college registers. Between 1525 and the end of the century six peers of the Howard family alone matriculate at Oxford or Cambridge. In his years at Cambridge as tutor and master of Trinity, Archbishop Whitgift supervised the education of Herberts, Norths, Cliffords, Cavendishes, and Zouches. Among the great crown servants who surround Elizabeth— the Cecils, the Bacons, Walsingham, Smith, Coke, Hatton, Sydney—there is scarcely one without a university education. Never before had the lay councilors and titled nobility of an English ruler been so learned. But these are the men at the top, the very apex of the pyramid of gentility. What happens if we descend a little? Around 1550 the fiery preacher Hugh Latimer, who had once complained that the nobility was so ill-trained that churchmen had to be employed in the royal service, thunders angrily and not altogether consistently, "There be none now but great men's sons in the colleges, and their fathers look not to have them preachers." In the third quarter of the century William Harrison accuses the sons of the rich of filling up not only Ox-

ford and Cambridge but the great grammar schools, too, and pushing the poor
out of the scholarships. Such charges suggest that we should take a look at what was
happening during the Renaissance in those
institutions originally founded for the instruction of poor clerks.

No formal record of all Etonians was
kept until late in the seventeenth century.
The biographical register of Eton College
is a modern compilation put together from
such bits of information as happen to have
survived at Eton or are deducible from
other school lists. Because of the bond
between Eton and King's College, Cambridge, a disproportionate number of King's
Scholars, usually headed for the church,
appear in the register, while the commen-
sals, sons of great and powerful gentlemen,
are underrepresented, and the oppidans,
who lived in town, are scarcely to be found.
Keeping all this in mind, we may profitably
open the register not quite at random. We
come to a page full of Clarks, and especially
of William Clarks, no less than seven
Williams between 1444, when the college
opened, and 1567. Almost to the end the
list runs as it should in a school the prime
intent of which is to raise up clerics. The
first six William Clarks are all King's
Scholars both at Eton and later at its sis-
ter-school, King's College. Several become
fellows of King's, one makes his career in
the university, the others become vicars,
rectors, or chaplains. But the last William
Clark, William of 1567, turns from the well-
worn path of ecclesiastical preferment; he
goes from Eton to the Middle Temple and
knighthood. Is this a symptom of change?
What does a further glance through the C's
in the register tell us?

There are about a hundred C's from 1444
to 1600 concerning whose later careers the
register carries information. Almost three-
fourths of these men end up in suitably
clerical positions—as university fellows
and schoolmasters or in benefices. If the
period is divided through the middle around
1520, just about half our clerical Etonians
fall on each side of the line. The case of

those who do not follow clerical careers
is a different story. Of twenty-eight such
entries twenty-six fall into the second half
of our period. The secular careers followed
by the twenty-six are in the main those in
which gentlemen predominated. A dozen go
on to the Inns of Court, five are members
of parliament, two are soldiers, three become knights, and one a peer. The social
complexion of Eton has begun to change.

The presence of five members of the
house of commons in our group suggests
another approach to the register. How
many future members of the commons went
to Eton between its founding and the death
of Elizabeth, and how are they distributed
chronologically? A search of the register un-
earths about fifty of them. Only one Etonian
of the half-century and more between the
founding and 1500 appears on the register
as a member of the house; fewer than ten
enter in the first full century of the school's
history. But among the Etonians of the
forty-odd years of Elizabeth's reign one
finds no less than forty future parliament
men. Now this appearance of parliament
men among the Etonians coincides neatly
with a significant sociopolitical change—the
rush of the gentry to get themselves elected
to the house of commons for borough
seats. Who are these forty Etonians who
later turn up in parliament? Eighteen are
sons of knights or of peers, six sons of
knights' or peers' daughters. Twenty become
knights themselves, six become peers, and
a considerable number marry daughters of
knights or peers. In the case of only six of
the forty is no connection with folk bearing
titles of honor indicated in the slight biographical sketches of the register, and, when
we note a Temple, a Hampden, and a son
of the Archbishop of York among the six,
we need not take the exceptions overseri-
ously. When we further note that several
of our future parliament men were King's
Scholars, Harrison's complaint about the
sons of the great bumping the poor off the
foundations takes on an appearance of
accuracy. The impression that men of gentle
birth in England were beginning to take

bookish learning with unprecedented seriousness in the sixteenth century is strongly reinforced when we observe that every single one of the forty Etonian members of parliament went from Eton to the universities and that more than two thirds of them proceeded thence to the Inns of Court.

Two rather scandalous episodes in the history of other English schools indicate that the development at Eton was not unique. Late in the fourteenth century William of Wykeham founded Eton's elder sister, Winchester, to restock with learned men a clerical body depleted by the Black Death. As an afterthought he provided that his own kin should be admitted as scholars on the foundation. During a century and a half Winchester fulfilled Wykeham's intention by becoming a forcing house for the higher clergy. The founder's kin availed themselves of their privilege but little at first, and then, for a hundred years, almost not at all. Then in 1569 the son and heir of Lord Saye and Sele requested and received admission. The grounds were kinship to the founder. Unwittingly Winchester had opened the floodgates. Wykeham's aunt, it seems, had thirteen extremely philo-progenitive daughters, whose sequelae two centuries later knew a good thing when they saw it. For several years scions of gentle houses—Sacheverells, Barkers, Blounts—poured into Winchester, all claiming descent from Wykeham's family. Only the judgment of a commission headed by the lord chancellor recommending that but ten of the founder's kin at one time be allowed on the foundation prevented Wykeham's gentle-born descendants from taking over the school altogether.

Twenty years before the Winchester affair there was a dispute in the commission to refound the Canterbury Cathedral school. Some of the commissioners argued that only the sons of gentlemen should be admitted. When Archbishop Cranmer pointed out that the children of the poor were often more gifted than gentlemen born, he was flatly told that plowmen's sons should plow, artificers' sons follow the paternal trade, while "gentlemen's children are meet to have the knowledge of government and rule in the commonwealth."

In the Canterbury and Winchester episodes the sixteenth-century English gentlemen do not appear in an altogether flattering light. They are edging the clergy out of one school and trying to bar all but themselves from another. But the stories certainly do not point to an aversion to learning on the part of the well-born. Rather they seem to show the aristocracy in a stampede toward bookish education in which the poor and weak are likely to be crushed by the great and strong.

We have already noted that the Etonians of Elizabeth's day who later sat in parliament all went on from school to the universities. This appears to be a further symptom of the English aristocracy's new attitude toward education. True, entries with respect to "literate laymen" begin to appear in the registers of the church as early as the end of the fourteenth century, and the parvenu Pastons for a couple of generations sent most of their young men to the universities in the reigns of Henry VI and Edward IV. Still it is the writer's impression that, except for such as were planning careers in or through the church, English gentlemen did not ordinarily go to Oxford or Cambridge in the later middle ages. In this connection the case of the Stonors is significant. An Oxfordshire county family since the late thirteenth century, they lived within convenient distance of the university. They served on commissions to settle university disputes; they befriended impoverished gentlewomen on the request of the chancellor of the university; generation after generation of Stonors as sheriffs of the county collected for the king what was due him from the colleges. They were even benefactors of the university. Yet in two volumes of correspondence there is no evidence that they ever sent their children to school at Oxford.

By the third quarter of the sixteenth century the squirearchy has elbowed its way into Oxford in force. For every five men matriculating there as *filii plebei,* three describe themselves as gentlemen's sons. At the beginning of the seventeenth century the proportion is six gentlemen to five plebeians. Such a record is reasonably imposing, yet it is by no means the whole record. English university registers of the sixteenth century are not altogether reliable and are less likely to mark the presence of the well-born than of the baseborn. Moreover, no English school record will tell us of the education in letters of men like Sir Thomas Elyot, who acquired his learning from private tutors, or like Lord Mountjoy, who got his while traveling abroad.

We have caught our gentlemen acquiring clerkly learning in the schools. Let us see what they are doing after school days are over. The lord lieutenants of the shires and their deputy lieutenants were responsible for taking the musters and exercising the county militia—the feeble and somewhat perfunctory English surrogate for the standing armies of the continental powers. They were also in part in charge of that *bonne police* of their neighborhood with which contemporary French writers were so much concerned. The line between their part and that of the justices of the peace in the maintenance of order in the country was not sharply defined, but it did not greatly matter since they themselves were all on the commission of the peace. Deputy lieutenants were also likely to crop up in the house of commons as representatives of neighboring boroughs or of their county and to do a turn or two as sheriff. Of the men who served in the lieutenancy commission between 1607 and 1619 in Northamptonshire most had come of age in the reign of Elizabeth. There were nineteen of them in all, including the lord lieutenant himself. What kind of education had they received, or, to put it more pertinently, to what extent had their Elizabethan fathers been satisfied to allow them to grow up as great hunters and hawkers untouched by formal education? Two of the nineteen left no discoverable trace on the educational record of the age, and concerning two

others the evidence is ambiguous. Of the remaining fifteen at least eleven matriculated at Oxford or Cambridge, and of the eleven, seven were admitted to the Inns of Court. Four others, who do not appear on the university registers, also went to the great English schools of law, and one of the four traveled on the continent under the supervision of a tutor, making occasional though educationally unprofitable stops in university centers. In other words of our group of nineteen men almost four-fifths was exposed to some kind of higher learning, almost three-fifths attended the former centers of clerical training, the universities, and well over a third topped their university experience with a dab, and sometimes much more than a dab, of education in the laws of England. And these figures, note, are an absolute minimum, representing only those men who left indubitable traces on the various school registers. Given the fairly casual way in which the registers were sometimes kept and our uncertainty about two names actually on them, we must recognize that there well may have been more schooling scattered among our deputy lieutenants than the numbers we have given indicate. Yet the very minimum involves a goodly number of gentlemen of a single county in a kind of education that Chaucer's squire knew not. Moreover, among these were very few younger sons, put to school because—perennial Saturday's children of the English system of primogeniture—they would have to work or beg for a living. In their school days most of our deputy lieutenants had been heirs apparent to substantial fortunes, under no immediate economic pressure to seek place by the route of learning. And there is no reason to believe that the situation with respect to the schooling of the deputy lieutenants in the other counties was markedly different from what it was in Northamptonshire. Even in remote and backward Cornwall, at least four of the eight gentlemen in the commission during Sir Walter Raleigh's lieutenancy were university educated. Nor does it seem likely that there would be an abrupt change if we descended slightly in the social scale and gave our attention to the education of the justices of the peace. Whatever the validity of the indictment at the beginning of the sixteenth century, it was certainly not true at its end that English gentlemen as a group were indifferent to formal schooling. By that time men who received what once was called clerkly training no longer remained concentrated in the schools, nor did they make a bee-line for the church or the offices of the central administration of the realm. Bookish learning had gone with them out into the shires and was widely scattered among the men who ruled the countryside.

∗   ∗   ∗   ∗   ∗

We have heard much of the aspiration of the Renaissance Italian to be an *uomo universale,* to devote himself to the development within himself of a rounded personality, a complete individuality. In the north, among the aristocracy, there is little of this. When a gentleman considers the education of gentlemen, it is with one end in view. . . . Sir Thomas Elyot sets the pattern in England. He heads one of his chapters of the *Boke named the gouernour,* "The education or form of bringing up of the child of a gentleman, which is to have authority in a public weal." Thomas Starkey and Roger Ascham echo the same idea. Sir Humphrey Gilbert has a scheme whereby gentlemen's sons will be crammed like Strasbourg geese with knowledge and skills, the better to serve "in Parliament, in council, in commission and other offices of the Commonwealth." And just in case his nephew may be under the illusion that his impending tour of the continent is solely for his own edification or amusement Francis Walsingham reminds him no less than six times in a scant two-page letter of his obligation to make the trip fruitful for the public service and the commonwealth. In France, La Noue emphasized the importance of providing adequate training for an aristocracy destined to serve as "great generals, commanders, governors and high officials, ambassadors and captains," and Montaigne's

indictment of the French grammar-school pattern of education in his treatise for Diane de Foix on the rearing of her son is grounded on the thesis that the schools are useless for nobles whose life will be spent in high office—military, diplomatic, and civil.

If during the period there is any development of ideas on the proper training for aristocrats—and our habit of thinking in terms of evolutionary growth often leads us to read development into texts where it is not—it is a development in precision and clarity. The end—education for service in the princely commonwealth—remains unchanged; the means and methods needed become better understood. The first impulse, as we find it expressed in Jean de Lannoy and Commines, is to say, "Get ye to school!" and to refrain from overmuch curiosity about the suitability to the end they had in view of the education the schools were offering. When the tide of humanism begins to move north, any questioning of the educational program of the apostles of antiquity and light is drowned in a deluge of expletives and ink, accompanied by shrill cries of "Barbarian!" "Ignoramus!" "Hunter and hawker!" Only later in the sixteenth century did men who doubted whether either scholastic logic or classical philology were the best possible foundations for the new role of the nobility formulate their ideas precisely enough to deserve a full hearing. Then, however, in all three lands, men of gentle birth—Humphrey Gilbert in England, Montaigne and La Noue in France, Philippe de Marnix in the Netherlands—proposed schemes of education specifically framed to meet the needs of an aristocrat whose career was to be public service.

The assertion in the sixteenth century that the aristocrat has a special claim on office is, of course, nothing new. On the contrary, what is new is an overt recognition on the part of some nobles that the claim is not indefeasible and absolute. The day is past when there was almost a one-to-one coincidence between the number of a lord's "tall men" or the extent of his acres and the role he could arrogate to himself in that management of common concerns which is government. Instead of simply assuming that political authority belongs of right to them, the aristocrats profess that, other things being equal, preference in office should be theirs; and the very claim to preference is made on the grounds of its utility to the commonweal. It is no longer always presupposed as it formerly had been, that a prince who chose parvenus to serve him did so out of mere whim or to spite those born to rule. Not only bitter preachers like Latimer but the more perceptive members of the upper class recognized that a prince who would be well served had no alternative but to take help where he could find it. The recognition by a gentleman of the paramount claim of prince and commonwealth to good service is almost always coupled with an exhortation or a plan addressed to the members of the aristocracy to educate themselves to the point where they can render such service. Jean de Lannoy, after paying respects to the ability of the legists and *ystoryens*, urges his son to be as learned as they. Ascham inserts his criticism of the incompetence of aristocrats to fill the great offices of the land into an elaborate pedagogic manual designed to overcome that incompetence. And William Cecil plans obliquely to undermine the place of the baseborn in the service of the realm by forcing education on the nobility by act of parliament.

One of the most impressive and universal traits in the complex of writings about the education of the aristocracy for service to the commonweal is the subordination of questions of right and privilege to questions of responsibility. Something is made of the rights of the aristocrats to office, more of their responsibility through education to prepare themselves for office, and most of their responsibility to turn the education they get to the service of the public weal. In Starkey's dialogue Lupset brusquely overrides Pole's suggestion that the contemplative life may be a legiti-

mate end of a nobleman's education. A man of Pole's position, he answers, is duty bound "to handle matters of the commonweal here in his own nation." Men such as he are born "to common such gifts as to them be given . . . and not to live to their own pleasure and profit." Osorius in his book of *Civil nobility* speaks slightingly of those who take their learning with them into seclusion and do not "employ the benefits of their arts and sciences to the avail and commodity of the commonwealth." Even Montaigne, himself so little given to conventional judgments, feels bound to make a rather elaborate apologia for his conduct and career in view of "the complaints daily buzzed in mine ears . . . that touching public office I am over singular and disdainful."

From the assertion of the duty of gentlemen to acquire an education and turn it to the service of the princely commonwealth, it was not far to the assertion that the head of the commonwealth was obligated to provide the necessary education for his noble servants. Erasmus gave early expression to such an idea, but without limiting it to the nobles. In this tract, *De pueris instituendis,* he declares that the provision of an adequate supply of teachers "is a public obligation in no way inferior to the ordering of an army." The idea that there exists a public duty to provide learned training specifically for the aristocracy comes later in the century. In preparation for Elizabeth's first parliament Cecil drew up the scheme before mentioned, which, besides binding the nobility by law to bring up their children in learning at some university from the age of twelve to eighteen, would have set aside one-third of all university scholarships for gentlemen. Toward the end of the century La Noue in France and Sir Humphrey Gilbert in England came up with far more elaborate and carefully wrought plans. Gilbert suggested one academy in England, La Noue several in France, in which the curriculum, fully set out in their respective schemes, was entirely focused on training noble youth for public service. The full cost of maintaining these schools was to be a public charge on the royal revenues. As we run across one after another of these plans in which the education of the aristocracy was to be subsidized out of the common purse as a matter of public responsibility, the startling demand of the gentlemen of the Canterbury school commission, that all but men of good birth be excluded from the benefits of the foundation, comes into a more intelligible perspective. In a rough and highhanded way they were reflecting the demand of the aristocrats for a sufficient share of the available education to prepare them for public careers in a commonwealth that required to be served not only faithfully but intelligently.

At the outset of this article we entered into a small empirical study of the extent to which the nobility went in for education during the Renaissance. As we proceeded with our search, we came perhaps to recognize that this question had implications with respect to the entire social history of the age, that it cast a shadow of doubt on some of our most cherished prepossessions about the direction and character of social change during the Renaissance. There are two clichés concerning this era so much a part of our historical tradition that to cast doubt on them smacks of heresy. One of those clichés concerns the rising middle class climbing to power over the prostrate bodies of the degenerate nobles. The other tells us how royal absolutism transformed some feudal lords into feeble court butterflies and left the rest to grumble and rot in the country, secluded from any role in government. These two clichés are by no means irreconcilable with one another; on the contrary, they are usually served up well-blended in the same dish.

Yet how prostrate is a social group that, facing the challenge of new times, rises to meet it by engaging in an altogether new kind of activity—that of acquiring a kind of learning hitherto almost monopolized by clerics? The nobles who went chasing education with the ardor we have noted, can they be the same men as the nobles who, we are told, sat about in a somnolent stupor while brisk businessmen were snatching the seat of power out from under them? On the contrary is not their quest for learning a mark of the flexibility of Renaissance aristocrats, who, having lost the influence over the course of affairs that their bands of stout fellows had afforded them, were seeking, in a measure successfully, to exercise power in a changed world through new channels?

A description of the relationship between the aristocracy and the new monarchs that seeks to do justice to the actual complexity of the situation is a delicate and difficult business, but even this little study should have sufficed to show how inadequate to cope with it are banalities about Renaissance despots and a monstrous nobility, half court insect, half bucolic vegetable. Doubtless the nobility had its full share of such insectivora and flora, as what grouping of the sons of men does not; but the kind of education that Renaissance aristocrats were seeking and to some extent getting did not have as its object the multiplication of rural fainéants or courtly sycophants. There is a difference between serving honorably in a princely commonwealth and decorating a court—all the difference, let us say, between Louis XII and Louis XIV or Philip the Good of Burgundy and Philip III of Spain.

The sixteenth-century aristocrat, when he assumes governmental tasks, is not rendering the service that a man owed his personal lord in the days of high feudalism. Nor is he performing that unlimited earthly worship that subjects were presumed to owe to God's vice-regents by some writers of the seventeenth century. He is serving a commonwealth prince, who in the words of one of the ablest of those princes stands highest "in his estate royal" when he is "conjoined and knit together" with his people "in one body politic."

The conception of service to the commonwealth cannot be written off as mere verbiage in all the outpourings on the education of the aristocracy that we have examined. If that conception gave a certain moral legitimacy to obedient service rendered by the aristocracy to the prince, it also established psychological limitations on that service and set some bounds on the duty of obedience. Montaigne makes quite explicit a fundamental disinction implied in the thought of his time. The tutor of the nobleman "shall frame his charge's will to a most loyal servitor of his prince, very well affected and courageous, but he will dampen in him any desire to attach himself to the court except out of a sense of public obligation." The educated nobleman will thus retain that liberty impossible in "a man waged and bought, . . . a courtier who can have neither the right nor the will to speak or think otherwise than favorably of a master who has chosen to foster and raise him up from among so many other subjects. Such favor and usage dazzle a man's eyes and corrupt his freedom." It is not without significance that Francis Walsingham, the great councilor of Queen Elizabeth, in his letter of advice on education through travel speaks of public service,

speaks of serving the country, speaks no less than three times of duty to the commonwealth, but does not even once mention the obligation to serve the prince. Education to serve the commonwealth is not training in servility to its ruler; quite the contrary.

It is the express distinction of Montaigne and the patent habit of thought of Walsingham that become action on the part of many of the aristocrats in the revolt of the Netherlands, in the civil wars in France, and in the Puritan revolution in England. They owe obedience to the prince as head of the commonwealth, but when the prince divorces himself from the commonwealth the whole question of obedience must be examined anew. Here we enter paths that in an article of this scope we cannot follow. What we have already said may suffice to indicate that a revaluation of our whole conception of social ideas, social structure, and social function in Europe in the age of the Renaissance is long overdue and to suggest that we may start our revision by thinking in terms not of the decline of the aristocracy but of its reconstruction.

THE REPUTATION AND FAME ACQUIRED BY GREAT FIGURES in the realm of scientific thought and discovery in seventeenth-century England have tended to obscure, if they have not consigned to oblivion, the sixteenth-century precursors of those great men. Everyone has heard of Francis Bacon, William Harvey, and Isaac Newton, but how many, even among those who have some knowledge of the history of Tudor England, have ever heard of the Elizabethan John Dee, who was an ardent exponent of the scientific spirit? Conditions in England in the sixteenth century were, indeed, distinctly favorable to the growth of that spirit. For one thing, there was a well-established tradition, reaching back to the thirteenth century at least, that authority in scientific matters, especially the authority of Aristotle, was to be distrusted unless it was supported by observation and experiment. Moreover, the rise of the commercial classes and the notable developments in industry in the later Tudor period made for the growth of the scientific spirit, as did geographical discovery, closely related as it was to the growth of commerce. It is to be remarked that this spirit flourished outside of the universities and that much of Tudor scientific literature was written in English instead of in Latin (which was still the language of conventional learning), one reason being that it was intended to be read by people outside the learned classes. During the reign of Elizabeth, noteworthy efforts were made to diffuse scientific knowledge, and Gresham College, founded toward the close of the reign, may be regarded as a fore-runner of the seventeenth-century Royal Society. In the essay that follows, Professor Raymond Phineas Stearns, of the University of Illinois, discusses the development of scientific ideas in Tudor England. Although medievalists will take exception to some of the author's comments on the scientific thought of the Middle Ages, his treatment of sixteenth-century scientific thought is a useful contribution to a neglected field.

THE SCIENTIFIC SPIRIT IN ENGLAND IN EARLY MODERN TIMES (c. 1600)
RAYMOND PHINEAS STEARNS

The concept of "science" has undergone obvious changes since the Renaissance, and it is little more than a generation since the term replaced the expression "natural philosophy" in our vocabulary. Accordingly, those attitudes of mind which have fostered scientific accomplishment and which we may term the "scientific spirit" have likewise changed. In Tudor times, the scientific spirit embraced, I believe, three factors. First, it required a critical use of authorities which must be carefully compared with one another and checked against natural pheno-mena known by means of observation and experiment. This implied a reliance upon experimentation and a willingness to accept the results thereof, even if acceptance re-quired the rejection of formerly received "authorities," however sacrosanct. Secondly, the scientific spirit included a faith in the faculty of human reason to classify data and to draw conclusions from facts in order to formulate "laws" to which natural phen-omena appeared to conform. Thirdly, the scientific spirit assumed that human knowl-edge might be extended indefinitely. This notion suggested the perfectibility of man and led, in time, to the idea of progress. It seems to have been identical to the Renais-sance concept expressed by Alberti, "Men can do all things if they will." And, though in some particulars the scientific spirit may have derived from Plato's Academy and the methods which Plato set forth, it appears to have been largely a product of the Renais-sance era, during which men cast off their authoritarian attitude of mind. In lieu of unquestioning acceptance of Aristotelian, Ptolemaic, Augustinian, or scholastic dicta, and firm in the faith that nature's secrets are discoverable by and comprehensible to hu-man kind, men set out boldly to test long accepted beliefs in natural philosophy and to establish new ones with the double-edged tool of experimentation and rationalization.

For Europe at large, the emergence of this scientific spirit is usually assigned to the year 1543, when the first important fruits of the new methods were set forth in Coper-nicus's *De revolutionibus orbium coelestium* and Vesalius's *De humani corporis fabrica*. But in England, the introduction of the scientific spirit is frequently assigned to the era of Francis Bacon and his great contem-poraries, William Gilbert and William Har-vey. These three men, working more or less independently, are represented as having simultaneously stumbled upon the methods

Reprinted by special permission from *Isis*, XXXIV, Part IV (1943), 293-300. The footnotes which originally appeared with this essay have been omitted.

of experimental science without any previous *English* preparations or foundations upon which to build. Gilbert's famous book, *De magnete,* first appeared in 1600; Harvey, though he had recognized the function of the heart as early as 1616 and had lectured on it publicly before 1620, did not publish his revolutionary book on the subject until 1628; and Lord Verulam's [Francis Bacon's] scientific works were scattered through the first quarter of the seventeenth century, or appeared shortly after his death in 1626. If we accept the notion, then, that Bacon, Gilbert, and Harvey introduced the scientific spirit into England, we find that it appeared full-grown in the first quarter of the seventeenth century, a full sixty years after its appearance elsewhere in Europe and just in time to inspire those men who, in 1645, founded the "Invisible College" which later developed into the Royal Society of London and presaged the age of Newton.

Fortunately, not all the historians of English science have subscribed to this explanation of the genesis of the English scientific spirit, for its inaccuracy is amply demonstrated by a number of recent studies, particularly works by Eva G. R. Taylor, Francis R. Johnson, Sanford V. Larkey, R. T. Gunther, G. B. Parke, and Louis B. Wright. Collectively, these works point out that to place the origins of the English scientific spirit in the seventeenth century is to ignore a long list of significant sixteenth-century forerunners and an English scientific tradition running back to Robert Grosseteste, Roger Bacon, and their fellow English Franciscans of the thirteenth century. Indeed, it seems safe to say that just as English Protestantism derived from John Wyclif and was nourished upon a long, indigenous tradition of Lollardy before the peculiar internal conditions and the continental examples of the sixteenth century led to a breach with the Church of Rome, so the English scientific spirit derived from Roger Bacon and fed upon a native Baconian tradition until English circumstances and continental examples of the sixteenth century led to its emergence in dynamic and sur-

prisingly mature scientific achievement. It is my purpose in the remainder of this paper to outline briefly the circumstances in sixteenth-century England which fostered the emergence of the scientific spirit and to point out, in passing, a few specific examples of Tudor scientific accomplishment. This is not to maintain that the scientific accomplishments of England surpassed, or even equalled, those of Italy and some other continental countries at the time; nor is it to suggest that the English scientific spirit developed without reference to continental examples and inspiration. Rather, it is to point out certain facts inherent in the English scene which, though often neglected, cannot be ignored in the history of early modern science in England. Within the space allotted me, I can do little more than sketch the broad outlines of this scene, postponing a more detailed development to another occasion.

The conditions of English Tudor life which matured the scientific spirit can be classified, I believe, under three main heads: the nature of the philosophical outlook, the influence of the rising middle class, and the effects of geographical discovery and commercial expansion.

With reference to the English philosophical outlook, a number of factors demand emphasis. First, the influence of Roger Bacon must not be overlooked. Anyone familiar with his *Opus Majus* is aware how clearly he unfolded the methods of modern science and how nearly he cast off the authoritarian shackles which encompassed the minds of contemporary schoolmen:

. . . There are two modes of acquiring knowledge [wrote Bacon], namely, by reasoning and experience. Reason draws a conclusion and makes us grant the conclusion, but does not make the conclusion certain . . . unless the mind discovers it by the path of experience. . . . He therefore who wishes to rejoice without doubt in regard to the truth underlying phenomena must know how to devote himself to experiment. . . .

Bacon was the first modern European who attempted to set forth a system of natural knowledge based on observation and experiment. And, though it seems doubtful whether his works were widely read in the original by his successors, nevertheless it is evident that the gist of his philosophy became a tradition which was never lost upon succeeding generations of English scholars. At Oxford, especially, it kept alive a neo-Platonist attitude favorable towards mathematics and experimental science during an era in which the pseudo-Aristotelianism of the Schoolmen dominated the Continent in a manner destructive to the scientific spirit. Perhaps it was the Baconian tradition which led English humanists such as Thomas Linacre, Cuthbert Tunstall, John Colet, and Sir Thomas More, to display, as has often been observed, an unusual interest in natural science—an interest marked by a distinctive neo-Platonist attitude of mind in violent contrast to pseudo-Aristotelian authoritarianism. With such a background, it is not surprising that later Tudor scientific investigators, who drew upon these sources, subscribed largely to the Baconian spirit of scientific inquiry and frequently referred to *"Bakon of Oxforde"* as their model.

Roger Bacon had emphasized reason and experience as the best means to obtain natural knowledge. Many Tudor scientists, in addition to these tools, also asserted unmistakably a faith in the perfectibility of man—the third factor set forth above as part of the modern scientific spirit. A few examples follow. Let us begin with one of the earliest sixteenth-century English statements, that of Robert Recorde (c. 1510-1558), the Welsh physician at the courts of Edward VI and Mary. Recorde was not only one of the first English writers to accept Copernican astronomy but also was author of the earliest important English arithmetic, *The Grounde of Artes,* first published in 1543. In his dedication to Edward VI, Recorde began with these words:

> The Excellency of mans nature being such, as it is by Gods divine favour (most mighty Prince) not only created in highnesse of degree far above all other corporall things, but by perfection, reason, and search of wit, much approaching toward the image of God . . . [Recorde continued for two pages to extol the virtues of human reason and expressed the hope that] My meer English Country-men . . . will so learne to love reason, that they will also gladly and greedily embrace all good Sciences.

Similar statements with reference to the perfectibility of man and the role of reason occurred in Thomas Wilson's *Rule of Reason,* first published in 1551 and many times after in Elizabeth's reign. And, when Barnaby Googe published (1560 and later) his English translation of the *Zodiacus vitae,* originally published in Venice in 1531 by Marcellus Palingenius Stellatus, it was widely employed as a textbook in Elizabethan grammar schools and read in part as follows:

> Whatsoeuer *Aristotle* saith, or any of
> them all,
> I passe not for: since from the truth they
> many times doe fall.
> Oft prudent, graue, and famous men, in
> errors chance to slide,
> And many wittes with them deceiue when
> they themselves goe wide:

BALDASSARE CASTIGLIONE: Italian humanist (d. 1529). His *Book of the Courtier* (1528), which was widely read in upper-class Elizabethan circles and influenced the writings of Sidney and Spenser, discussed the characteristics of the ideal courtier.

ROBERT GROSSETESTE: Thirteenth-century clergyman who wrote an important study in which he classified the knowledge of his age. He was also the author of works on theology and agriculture. His contributions were highly regarded by Roger Bacon and John Wycliffe, among many others.

Examples only serue, so much must errors
followed bee,
Let no man iudge me arrogant, for reason ruleth mee,
She faithful guide of wisemen is: let him
that seekes to finde
The Truth, loue hir, and followe hir with
all his Might, and minde.

It is no very difficult task to multiply the
English scientific works which, between
1550 and 1600, challenged the infallibility
of Aristotle and other widely received
authorities and extolled the research values
of experimentation, reason, and belief in
the power of the human mind to comprehend nature's secrets. But one Elizabethan
cannot be omitted—Dr. John Dee (1527-
1608), mathematician, geographer, inventor, astrologer, and collector of probably the
finest scientific library in England in his
day. Among other writings, Dr. Dee prepared a lengthy introduction for Henry Bil-
lingsley's excellent English translation, published in 1570, of Euclid's geometry. In his
introduction, after a gracious bow "To the
Vnfained Lovers of truthe, and constant
Students of Noble Sciences" and praise of
"Divine Plato, the great Master of many
worthy Philosophers," Dr. Dee went on to
develop a subject to which he gave the name
of "Archemastrie." "Archemastrie," Dr.
Dee explained, is a science, not an art, "And
by cause it procedeth by *Experiences,* and
searcheth forth the causes of Conclusions,
by *Experiences:* and also putteth the Conclusions themselves in *Experience,* it is
named of some, *Scientia Experimentalis.*"
Here, under date of February 9, 1570, is as
clear and concise a statement of the scientific spirit as can be found anywhere in the
works of Francis Bacon. Between Robert
Recorde's words, published in 1543, and
John Dee's statement, dated 1570, more
than a score of English scientific writers,
many of them known to one another and
often working coöperatively, are known to
have subscribed to, and to a considerable
extent put into practice, those methods
known to modern times as scientific.

One more circumstance which conditioned the philosophical outlook of late
Tudor England was the almost total absence of religious opposition to the scientific spirit. This is a phase of the late Tudor
mind about which, in the present state of
our knowledge, it is dangerous to generalize. The problem is made doubly difficult
by the Puritan cross-currents of opinion
running through the late Tudor church.
Marshall Knappen has ably pointed out that
"there were many Puritan spirits but there
was no Puritan spirit," and just as the Puritan mind was in a state of flux, so Anglican
opinion can hardly be classified as a rounded
statement of philosophical belief. Their differences, however, were fundamentally concerned with theological and ecclesiastical
matters, and nearly all parties appear to have
drawn a clear distinction between spiritual
knowledge, wherein faith plus grace might
work wonders and carnal reason possessed
doubtful potency, and secular knowledge,
wherein reason and experiment might go far
to glorify God by elucidating His laws as
discovered in nature. Puritan and Anglican
alike appear to have attributed great powers
to human reason in the realm of temporal
affairs and, if experimentation glorified God
by demonstrating His mysterious ways,
neither party objected. Recent studies of
the Puritan mind have clearly demonstrated
that, among Puritans of early Stuart times at
least, there was a surprisingly ready acceptance of experimental science; and it is undeniably true that a major portion of seventeenth-century English scientists were of
Puritan origin. Random samplings of late
Tudor Puritan writings, especially in the
works of William Perkins, would seem to
make Professor Knappen's conclusion unduly cautious when he states that Puritanism
merely "made the negative contribution of
furnishing a less effective barrier" to the
scientific spirit than did Catholicism. On the
Anglican side, the "judicious Hooker" is
more positive. Not only does he praise the
faculty of human reason and proclaim it
capable of such perfection that men "come
at length to be even as the angels themselves,

are," but also he states that the works of nature may "be framed according to that which the Law of Reason teacheth" and "those Laws are investigable by Reason, without the help of Revelation supernatural and divine." A few pages farther on Hooker adds these significant words:

. . . inasmuch as to live virtuously it is impossible except we live; therefore the first impediment, which naturally we endeavour to remove, is penury and want of things without which we cannot live. Unto life many implements are necessary; more, if we seek (as all men naturally do) such a life as hath in it joy, comfort, delight, and pleasure. To this end we see how quickly sundry arts mechanical were found out, in the very prime of the world.

Obviously, the theological mind, whether Puritan or Anglican, was not disposed to discountenance the scientific spirit, and experimental philosophy found a place in the Tudor mind without protest from English churchmen.

Emergence of the middle class to a position of power and affluence in Tudor England was an important circumstance which fostered growth of the scientific spirit. Here was a group of men, literate to a high degree, yet not bound by the traditions of a proud nobility or by the Peripatetic learning which still prevailed in English universities. When no other motive existed, their ambition in the world of trade and commerce led them to entertain an active interest in the utilitarian values of the new science, especially in the fields of mechanics and navigation. The record shows many bourgeois Englishmen who became scientists or patrons of science, and English scientific achievement in the sixteenth, as well as in the seventeenth and eighteenth centuries, was a remarkable instance of the coöperation of merchants and mariners with physicists and physicians for the enlargement of natural knowledge. The close relationship between the growth of the scientific spirit and the English middle class is especially evident in the fact that most of the Tudor scientific literature was written in English specifically for the benefit of a class of people untrained in the classical tongues. A check of titles listed in Pollard and Redgrave's *Short-Title Catalogue of Books Printed in England, Scotland & Ireland, 1475-1640* reveals that nearly twelve per cent of all the books were scientific treatises and that, of these, about ninety per cent were published in English. Several motives, of course, impelled English authors to use the vernacular, such as patriotic devotion and a pride, like Dante's, in the native tongue. But many, like John Dolman, writing in 1561, conscious of "a meane sorte of men" between "the raskal multitude, and the learned sages," wrote in English with the object of reaching the middle class. Dr. Thomas Phaer, in his *Regiment of Life* (1553), a popular book on child health, advocated the vernacular in order "to distribute in English to those who are unlearned, part of the treasure that is in other languages, to provoke them that are of better learning, to utter their knowledge in such like attempts." Indeed, after Robert Recorde's *Grounde of Artes,* published in English in 1543, more and more English scientific works appeared in the vernacular, the authors evidently in tacit agreement with Sir Thomas Hoby, who wrote in his translation of Castiglione's *Book of the Courtier,* in 1561, that ". . . where the Sciences are most turned into the vulgar tongue, there are best learned men." The net results were the enlistment of a wide popular support for the new science and the creation of a large scientific literature in English.

Other efforts to popularize scientific learning and make it more available to the rising middle class—and, incidentally, with the effect of patronizing men skilled in the new learning—were various public lectures endowed in Elizabethan days. The most ambitious of these was the establishment of Gresham College in London by the will of the Queen's great financial aide, Sir Thomas Gresham. Sir Thomas's will, made in 1575, provided that upon the death of his widow, his mansion house in Bishopsgate should be used for a college and rents arising from the Royal Exchange should serve as an endowment, the whole to be administered jointly by the Corporation of London and the Mercers' Company. Successively each week-day, seven professors were to lecture publicly in English on divinity, astronomy, music, geometry, law, medicine, and rhetoric. Lady Gresham did not die until late in 1596, but by Trinity term, 1597, the trustees had a faculty chosen and lectures began. Great care was exercised to insure the utilitarian value of the lectures. For example, the professor of astronomy was to read, "first, the principles of the sphere, and the theoriques of the planets, and the use of the astrolabe and the staf, and other common instruments for the capacity of mariners; which being read and opened, he shall apply them to use, by reading geography and the art of navigation, in some one term of every year." Gresham College professors were among the best scientists in England. Its first geometry professor, for example, Henry Briggs, was one of the first mathematicians to make logarithms useful by improving upon Napier's system and by publishing logarithmic tables (in 1617 and 1624); and Briggs later (1619-30) became the first Savilian professor of mathematics and astronomy at Oxford. Gresham College, besides providing the average man with utilitarian learning in the spirit of experimental science, soon became the rendezvous of leading English scientists and, until the foundation of the Royal Society (of which it was, to a degree, the nucleus), the clearing-house for the latest scientific discoveries. When one considers the purposes for which it was established, and the nature and quality of its staff, it seems clear that it was the culmination of a series of events in Tudor England and a revelation of the maturity of the English scientific spirit.

As my time runs short, I can only suggest the effects of the third set of conditions in Tudor England which stimulated growth of the scientific spirit—geographical discovery and industrial and commercial expansion. Nor is a detailed elucidation necessary in view, on the one hand, of Miss Taylor's recent works on Tudor geography and, on the other, of many studies of English commercial and industrial developments. Among the latter, however, I wish to underscore some of the recent findings of Professor J. U. Nef, especially those in which he points out that the century after 1540 is one of such tremendous industrial growth and technological achievement that he is inclined to label it the first Industrial Revolution in England. It would be trite to point out either the intimate connections between expanding industrial and commercial activity and the rise of the middle class—that group which contributed so much to Tudor scientific growth—or the fact that a "spirit of oversea discovery and maritime expansion had permeated the [English] national life." It is not so commonplace, however, to point out the effects of these developments on English science. For new technological problems in industry, commercial expansion, and the lure of overseas discovery went far to whet appetites for more accurate natural knowledge, and caused the English increasingly to question classical scientific authorities. Problems arising from new industries encouraged experimentation among physicists, chemists, and mechanics in the search for new technological processes and inventions. New flora and fauna from overseas led to new classifications of plants and animals—to herbal gardens, pharmaceutical experiments, museums, and zoos. The search for the Northwest Passage, and other attempts at geographical discovery, gave great impetus to all the sciences connected with navigation and map-making. But, most important of all, just as trade expansion required financial coöperation and stimulated the growth of commercial companies, so the search for new routes and new lands required a pooling of practical and theoretical knowledge and stimulated coöperation among mariners, merchants, adventurous noblemen, royal councillors, and sometimes the Queen herself. The picture, so frequently given in his *Diary,* of Dr. John Dee in earnest consultation with instrument makers, mariners, merchants, Privy Councillors, and other noble gentlemen of the Gilbert-Raleigh type, is no isolated event in late Tudor England. Its effect, besides bringing into active coöperation the upper and middle classes with the scientific investigator, was an incalculable impetus to experimental science.

Necessarily, I have treated the scientific spirit in limited fashion. I have said nothing about the fact that it arose largely outside English universities—and, in fact, its interrelation with the universities is a subject deserving much further study. I have not pointed out the rather obvious unevenness of the growth of the scientific spirit, how it appears much more mature in mathematics and the physical sciences than in botany and the natural sciences. And I have said little about the tendency, clearly evident in Tudor days, of English scientists to carry on a constant intercourse and exchange of information with one another and with Continental scholars as well. For these and other omissions, I plead lack of space as a means of cloaking more serious shortcomings. But I believe enough has been said to demonstrate that the last seventy years of sixteenth-century England were a formative period in the growth of the scientific spirit; and that before 1600—I should say by 1570—the scientific spirit was not only widely embraced by English investigators but also had become a point of view popular with middle-class amateurs. Francis Bacon, William Gilbert, and William Harvey, perhaps because they eyed only the Peripatetic learning which dominated the English universities, evinced an extraordinary disregard of their English scientific predecessors. Bacon gave a classic English statement of the scientific method and prophesied great things for its future; Gilbert and Harvey produced the earliest important fruits of the new science in England. But, collectively, these three men did not introduce the scientific spirit into England. Their works are illustrative of the maturity of the English scientific spirit, not of its inception in the English nation.

Stuart Times

PART FIVE

SHORTLY BEFORE THE OUTBREAK OF WORLD WAR I Sir Charles Firth delivered an important presidential address before the Royal Historical Society.
In it the then leading authority on early-Stuart history surveyed his favorite
field of investigation and pointed to some of the gaps which in his opinion
still needed to be filled. What impressed him as being particularly worthy of
study was a series of topics in the political, constitutional, military, naval,
and diplomatic history of the age of James I and Charles I. In his address Sir
Charles had remarkably little to say about research in the economic history
of early-Stuart times. Yet here was a field seriously in need of further study
some forty years ago and still sadly neglected today. True, Soviet historians
have been doing a great deal in the field, but much of their work has been
vitiated by its propagandistic character. True, too, several outstanding British
and American scholars have attempted to remedy the neglect of the economic
history of the early-Stuart age. In an important article that was published in
1941 in *The Economic History Review,* Professor R. H. Tawney, of the
University of London, wrote brilliantly, if not altogether convincingly, on
the rise of the gentry; and Professor John U. Nef, of the University of Chicago,
has made valuable contributions to the industrial history of the period. Even
so, there remains a glaring need for scores of scholarly studies of the various
aspects of early-Stuart economic history. One such aspect—business fluctuations—is considered briefly in the essay that follows. Its author is the late
Professor Edwin F. Gay, of Harvard University, who had the distinction of
being "America's first native-born thoroughly trained economic historian"
and of serving as first president of the Economic History Association.

ECONOMIC DEPRESSIONS, 1603-60

EDWIN F. GAY

There are three types of economic fluctuations, which are well recognized, and a
fourth which is conjectural. The first are
seasonal, occurring within the year, and the
latest research on seasonals indicates that
they seem to have cumulative influence upon
the next larger group—that is, the business
cycle. Since the middle of the nineteenth
century, and especially during the past quarter century, the business cycle has received
most attention by students. It may be defined, roughly and rather artificially, as any
major swing of prices and economic activity
coming within the limits of a decade. But
business cycles vary greatly in time and
magnitude. Everybody since our recent experience is fairly well acquainted with the
depression period of a business cycle. Running from the height of business activity
and prosperity, with ample investment in
new enterprise, large returns, full employment, there comes, usually suddenly, a
break. That break is generally followed by
a longish depression. The curve both upward and downward is a saw-tooth line. It
may be halted for a while and then rise or
drop again. Not all business activities go
up or down at the same time. But the top

Reprinted by special permission from *The Huntington Library Quarterly,* V (1942), 193-198.
This essay was one of a number of papers read at a Renaissance conference at the Huntington
Library.

and bottom points can be determined within fairly close limits.

There is another economic fluctuation, about which not so much research has been done—the so-called secular trend. Not only price movements but volume of production and numerous other economic changes alter in long swings, usually of two or three decades in length. There is also some basis for the conjecture that there may be still longer secular swings, which may run through some centuries of gradual but fundamental changes in institutions and the ideas underlying the institutions. The business cycle and the secular trends are differentiated in other ways than by length. Despite the efforts of a number of investigators to emphasize the money factor in the business cycle, it seems clear that the volume of money supply plays a larger part in the movement of the secular swing. This swing coincides very closely with facts in regard to the increase and decrease in the total money supply. There is a down swing following the close of the Napoleonic period. There is a rise from the close of the forties, coinciding with the increase in the production of gold in California and Australia, lasting in England till 1866 and in the United States till 1873. From these dates the long downward movement of prices continues until the middle of the nineties. Thenceforward, the movement is upward to the time of the Great War. One of the chief factors in these swings seems clearly the rate of increase or decrease of the total available monetary supply.

The longest swing of which we have historical record was the great movement in prices of the sixteenth century, closely related to the inflow of precious metals from Spanish America. This swing lasted from the second or third decade of the century, with saw-tooth movements upward, until the close of the century, in Spain (and probably in Italy), and to the middle of the seventeenth century, in Germany and England. It is marked by a rapid and considerable rise of the general scale of prices, till it levels off by the middle of the seven-

teenth century, when it has reached its high point and goes down, gradually.

The cyclical movements within this long swing (measured by prices, and not by production, for we have no series of statistical facts for other business activity) look, at first sight, like the modern business cycle. But the leading scholar in this field, Wesley Mitchell, rejects them as true business cycles and calls them "random perturbations"; the course is broken, here and there, by plagues, famines, or war, and other outside disturbances, which so predominate up to 1763 that it is impossible to deal with them as with modern cyclical fluctuations. So far as I know, the only person who has tried to make a careful listing of these fluctuations is the authority upon whom Mitchell depends, W. R. Scott, whose study of joint-stock companies in England, Scotland, and Ireland, to 1720, is regarded as an authoritative work. For the presentation of the main facts concerning the joint-stock companies, that is true. But his interpretative statements must be carefully scrutinized. He presents what he calls the years of crisis from 1558 to 1720. As I study his analysis I am reminded of the cartographers of the sixteenth century who tried to map the world as they knew it. The general picture of the continents is roughly made, but many of the details are lacking or untrue. Scott's interpretations, and sometimes his facts, are erroneous. Periods of high agricultural prices he calls "famines." A plague in which 1,000 died is equated with the plagues in which 30,000 or 60,000 died. Contradictions between the list at the close of Volume I and the preceding text are not infrequent. For instance, in the list, Scott enters the years 1682-90 as poor years, but he notes that within this period the foreign trade is fairly prosperous, and (p. 315) he calls 1688 "the culmination of the good times." After the depression years 1704-8, marked as exceptionally severe, there came, according to the list, a few months of prosperity, but in the text (p. 468) 1709 is described as "the height of a relatively good period." Scott lists the plague as a factor in the marked depression of 1620-25—one of the instances of "random perturbations" which caused Mitchell to reject the whole series as outside the history of business cycles. But, in fact, the plague followed the depression by several years. Scott himself (on p. 186) says, "In spite of the plague in 1625, trade in that year began to improve," and the depression was "at an end." In the absence of quantitative evidence, contemporary statements of "poor trade" must be carefully examined. These run all the way from rhetorical complaints, made for the purpose of influencing the government toward favorable action for some particular locality or interest, to complaints true only of one locality or one industry, or to outcries from so many and so diverse sources that a general depression is clearly evidenced.

I have examined Scott's list with reference to the finding, for the nineteenth century, that on the long upward trends the shorter business cycles show more good than bad years, and vice versa. In 1558-1603, with a rapid upward movement of prices, there were, according to Scott, 16 good years and 29 poor, disagreeing with the general theory. In 1601-39, there were 25 good, 13 poor; for the whole period, 1558-1639, 41 good and 32 poor. In 1640-99 there were 20 good, 33 poor (plus 6 years undescribed), and in 1700-1720 there were 9 good, 12 poor. The totals, for 1640-1720, of 29 good and 45 poor conform to the expectation of a majority of poor years in a long downward trend. But the results for the period 1558-1639, when the secular trend of prices was markedly upward, do not conform. The

poor years outbalance the good, especially from 1558 to 1603. The contemporary complaints may in some instances have been misleading, but there can be no doubt that Elizabeth's reign was afflicted with a great many poor years. She started with a severe depression and a small treasury. Indeed, her foreign policy was largely dictated by her depleted resources. England was financially dependent on Antwerp, the banking center of Europe, until the great crisis of 1565— a crisis which had repercussions over the Continent. England managed to free herself from the dependence on foreign banking resources, and she apparently enjoyed a full decade of prosperity, from 1575 to 1585. But then followed a longer period of depression, studded with dark years, from 1586 to 1603. The reign of James I and the earlier years of Charles I (to the outbreak of the Civil War) were predominantly years of good trade and increasing wealth, but they were broken by the serious depression of 1620-24 and the poor years from 1637 to 1640. In 1640 the King's seizure of the bullion deposited in the mint, and the consequent bankruptcies, led to an increase in the practice of depositing gold with the goldsmiths—the beginning of banking. But the Civil War was a major "random perturbation," which needs study with more detail and more care. There were sufficient causes of general distress, such as the depredations of the troops on both sides, the heavy taxation, the cutting off of domestic and foreign trade; but the depression seems not to have been uniform or continuous. Some areas were less troubled than others, and there were ups and downs—for instance, there

WESLEY C. MITCHELL: Long-time professor of economics at Columbia University and a founder of the National Bureau of Economic Research (d. 1948). He wrote extensively on business cycles and did much to encourage their investigation. Although some of his conclusions have been questioned, there is no doubt that he stands as one of the pioneers in the study of economic fluctuations.
W. R. SCOTT: Author of the multivolume *Constitution and Finance of English, Scottish, and Irish Joint-Stock Companies to 1720* (1910-1912). The work is extremely well documented, and it is an invaluable study for anyone interested in the role played by the trading and planting companies in colonial expansion.

was a revival in 1645-46. After about 1650 complaints dropped off. Despite the interruptions of the Dutch and Spanish wars, domestic trade may be said to have enjoyed a period of rising prosperity. Notwithstanding some agricultural distress, rents were rising and land speculation was rife, followed by the depression from 1658 to 1660. Prosperity returned with the Restoration, but then came a break, in agricultural rents by 1663 and in trade by 1664, which inaugurated a decade of nearly unbroken disaster.

The economic prosperity of James I and of Charles I to 1640 fostered the rise of the agricultural and trading middle class. How does it happen, then, that most American historians ascribe the emigration to America, beginning in this period, to the economic distress of England? The depression of 1619-24 may have played a minor part, but chiefly we must look, so far as economic factors are concerned, to other causes than business cycles. The long secular trend of prices had social effects on the relations of classes. While the yeoman class as a whole, as well as the trades, benefited, the smaller tenant farms were being consolidated and the smaller tenants pressed down. Concurrently, the lesser landlords were suffering from a large prevalence of fixed rents at a time of rising prices and higher standards of living. So men like Winthrop, leaving impoverished estates, joined with the poorer yeomen and artificers, under the influence of religious dissent, the lure of adventure, and colonial propaganda, to settle the lands beyond the sea.

Modern studies of the business cycle are largely concerned with its causes. Research in the history of business fluctuations before the nineteenth century, because of the lack of adequate quantitative evidence, will probably contribute little to the quest for causes. But a detailed study of the cause and character of the earlier fluctuations should show that the "random perturbations" do not, after all, play a much more decisive part then than now. We may, therefore, considerably brighten the history of the "business cycles," and thereby give new emphasis to the long-persisting factors of causation.

But, in any case, such a study of economic fluctuations is required for the understanding, not merely of economic history, but of political and social changes, and even of literary and artistic activities.

WHEN JAMES VI OF SCOTLAND FOLLOWED ELIZABETH on the throne of England, in 1603, he did so with the general satisfaction and approval of the English people, in accordance with the expressed wish of the late queen, and as her heir at law. His accession was a notable victory for the principle of legitimacy as determining the royal succession, a principle which he had elaborated in a treatise, *The Trew Law of Free Monarchies,* published in 1598. In spite of the auspicious circumstances surrounding the beginning of the new dynasty, however, there were conditions that might well have given ground for serious apprehension of political and religious friction between the English crown and the interests represented in the House of Commons. For one thing, the long acquiescence of the nation in autocratic government was declining. The middle classes, always the main support of the Tudor system, had grown under Tudor rule in prosperity and self-reliance and no longer felt the need of a "strong monarchy" to repress aristocratic lawlessness and lower-class disturbances. The bad old days of "livery and maintenance" were far in the past, and the memory of earlier turbulence had faded. The growth of trade and industry, for which Tudor policies and administration were in no small measure responsible, gave the middle classes a sense of strength and self-sufficiency in 1603 which they had lacked in 1485. Even before the death of Queen Elizabeth, criticism of her government on political, religious, and economic grounds was expressed in the House of Commons, although the members of the House, as they informed James at the beginning of his reign, felt a tender regard for her sex and age, which, they implied, they could not feel for him. The sense of emergency and crisis in England's foreign relations, which had been favorable to the exaltation of the crown in the Tudor period, was diminished in the new reign. The Elizabethan war with Spain was terminated by a treaty in 1604, and the union of the crowns of England and Scotland in the person of James himself put an end to the old menace of Scottish invasions of England. In the essay that follows, Dr. Godfrey Davies, of the Huntington Library, an outstanding student of early-Stuart history, discusses James' traits and their effect upon the attitudes of his new subjects toward him.

THE CHARACTER OF JAMES VI AND I

GODFREY DAVIES

In his inimitable manner Sir Walter Scott drew the character of James VI of Scotland and I of England in *The Fortunes of Nigel*. His wizardry overcame the difficulties caused by the poor quality of his sources—some secret histories and partisan narratives—and helped him to paint a lifelike portrait. He realized that the inconsistencies of the royal character rendered it "the subject of doubt among his contemporaries" and "a problem to future historians."

Towards the solution of the problem, this article contributes sketches of James as he appeared successively during the four well-defined periods of his life—the first seventeen years, when tutors or governors directed his actions; the twenty years of his rule in Scotland, ending in 1603, when he became the first King of Great Britain; the nine years' ascendancy of Robert Cecil, Earl of Salisbury; and the last dozen years, when favorites dominated the King. No complete biography has been attempted for each of these periods, but, instead, stress has been laid on those traits which figured largely in contemporary writings. Such a procedure should demonstrate how far the child was father to the man and how far the adult's character differed from the boy's.

I. 1566-83

The circumstances of James's birth must surely have been unique. His father, Darnley, was one of the band that murdered Riccio, his mother Mary's favorite, a few months before the baby's birth. Shortly after it he was himself murdered by Bothwell, with the connivance of the mother, who then married Bothwell, a Protestant. In the midst of these tragedies, James was baptized in the Roman Catholic church. A year later Mary was turned off her throne by the confederate lords, marching under a banner representing her murdered husband and her fatherless infant crying, "Judge and avenge

Reprinted by special permission from *The Huntington Library Quarterly*, V (1941), 33-63. The footnotes which originally appeared with this essay have been omitted.

my cause, O Lord." On July 24, 1567, Mary, a prisoner in Lochleven Castle, was obliged to sign documents giving the crown to her son and nominating her illegitimate brother, Moray, as regent. Five days later the infant king was crowned at Stirling, where an oath to maintain the Protestant religion was taken on his behalf. In the following May Mary escaped, raised an army superior in numbers to the regent's, suffered defeat at Langside, and fled to England to throw herself on the mercy of Elizabeth, whose throne she had defiantly claimed as her own some years before. During the young king's boyhood, successive regents held power—Moray, assassinated in 1570; Lennox, mortally wounded by a pistol shot in 1571; Mar, who died peacefully in 1572; and Morton, executed in 1581.

From his fourth to his twelfth year James's education was intrusted to George Buchanan, the Scottish humanist, poet, and reformer. Buchanan held a most distinguished place in the councils of the advanced Protestants, and in his *Rerum Scoticarum historia* and *De jure regni apud Scotos* and other writings he emphasized the duty of kings to obey the laws and the right of subjects to dethrone tyrannical rulers. He is credited with a natural sympathy for youth, and his ideal of a good prince is recorded. A prince, he told Sir Thomas Randolph, the English resident in Scotland, should cherish true piety and should love peace but be ever ready for war; should be neither a miser nor a spendthrift, for each is equally harmful to his people; and should believe that a king exists for his subjects and not for himself, being the common father of the state. A prince's life should be the pattern for every citizen, and his countenance the terror of evildoers and the delight of those that do well. He should cultivate his mind carefully, his body reasonably, holding that good sense and good taste should keep extravagance in check.

The exact curriculum drawn up to translate these ideals into practice is not known, but obviously was classical. We have an account of one day's work. Morning prayers were followed by a course in Greek, the New Testament, Isocrates, and Plutarch. After breakfast came Latin—Cicero and Livy—or modern history. In the afternoon were composition and, if time permitted, arithmetic or cosmography, logic or rhetoric. The object of this system was the cultivation in speech and writing of a pure, elegant Latin style, and, if we may judge from the many eulogies which his subjects bestowed upon the King's Latinity, James learned his lessons well. Once he said that he followed Buchanan's pronunciation, both in Latin and Greek, which "I am sorry that my people of England do not like, for certainly their pronunciation utterly spoils the grace of these two learned languages." Opinions differed, even then, about the correct pronunciation of the classical tongues, and Ben Jonson boasted that he had told King James that Buchanan "had corrupted his ear when young, and learnt him to sing verses when he should have read them."

The first regency of Morton ended in 1578, when, at the age of twelve, James formally began to reign, though in fact he was under the control of governors for another five years. During this period he was the prey of contending factions, anxious to enjoy the prestige conferred by possession of the royal person. Twice he was the victim of *coups d'état*. In 1578 the young Earl of Mar seized the dual position of guardian of the King and governor of Stirling Castle, and thus restored Morton to power. During the struggle at Stirling the English ambassador reported that the King was in great fear, tearing his hair and sleeping restlessly.

The next year Esmé Stewart, Lord of Aubigny, a relative of the King, arrived in Scotland. As the agent of the Guises, he came from France to engineer the restoration of Mary Stuart and the Roman Catholic religion. His handsome figure and elegance established him as the first important favorite of James, who hugged to his breast the man whom, of all Scots, he had most to fear. He was created, first Earl, and then Duke, of Lennox, richly endowed with lands, made governor of Dumbarton Castle, Lord Chamberlain, and First Gentleman of the Bedchamber, and given the nomination and command of the standing guard now formed to secure the King's person. The King so loved Lennox that he could not bear to let him go out of his sight. After Lennox had had Morton executed on a charge of participation in Darnley's murder, he apparently believed that all he needed to restore the old religion was a foreign army, which, as Mary's champion, he offered to raise for her. But his lack of nerve at the decisive moment ruined his schemes. In 1582, while hunting, James was captured and induced to accompany the Earls of Mar and Gowrie, and others, to Ruthven Castle. Finding himself a prisoner, James began to cry, evoking from the Master of Glamis the bitter taunt, "Better bairns greet than bearded men"— a sneer never forgotten or forgiven. The Ruthven raiders forced James to issue a proclamation banishing Lennox, who, though his chances of rescuing the King by war seem to have been good, pusillanimously withdrew to England and thence to France, where he died a few months later.

The almost continual turmoil in which James· passed his youth left an indelible mark on him. It accentuated the hereditary tendency to fearfulness, and helps to explain the excessive dread of unruly crowds and drawn weapons, which astonished his contemporaries. Its evil effect might have been less had he been willing to let "malice domestic" do its worst until his coming of age. But by nature he could be neither neutral nor patient when his position in the state was in question. Too young and too unwarlike to prevail on the battlefield and too obstinate and vain to let others decide matters of state for him, he tried to get his own way by intrigue, and early acquired what a biographer calls "a precocious mastery of deceit." A striking proof is afforded by the contrast between the account of the English ambassador, Bowes, of the King's attitude toward Lennox, and that of the nobleman himself. According to the former, when the King and the lords at Ruthven had agreed to order the Duke's departure, the King

> showed such manifest signs, witnessing a great change and alteration in his conceit and favour towards the Duke, as the Lords are highly comforted therewith; for with unaccustomed oath he hath protested to and assured the noblemen with his colour changed, his hands lifted up, that if the Duke shall disobey this charge, then he shall never from henceforth have to do with the Duke, nor show favour to him nor to any of his favorers, but to esteem him and them as his enemies.

On the other hand, about a month later

WILLIAM CAMDEN: Historian and antiquary (d. 1623). His *Britannia* (1586), a classic historical study, was often revised and enlarged in his own lifetime. His *Annales* (1615-1627) is a useful account of the Elizabethan period. The Camden Society, founded in 1838 in his honor, publishes documents dealing with the early history and literature of England.

JOHN SELDEN: Lawyer, Parliamentarian, and scholar (d. 1654). Author of *History of Tythes* (1618), which was suppressed because it offended Anglican clergymen, he continued his criticisms of governmental policies in Parliament until 1649. The Selden Society, founded in 1887 in his honor, publishes early legal records.

SIR HENRY SPELMAN: Historian, antiquary, and member of Parliament (d. 1641). He was an active member of the Society of Antiquaries in late-Elizabethan times, and because of his scholarly talents he was appointed by James I to determine unsettled titles to land in Ireland. He was a devout Anglican and "no parliament man." His consuming interest was the collection of historical materials relating to English legal and ecclesiastical history.

Lennox was explaining to Mendoza, the Spanish ambassador in London, that he had left Scotland for two reasons: first, to comply with James's promise to Elizabeth; and second, because a plot Lennox had arranged to rescue the King had been divulged. As soon as the King had regained his liberty, Lennox was to reappear and occupy his former position at the King's side. James escaped from the raiders in June, 1583, and issued a proclamation that he meant to take unto himself "his awin place and state." From this time he may be said to rule as well as reign.

In some respects the King seemed well qualified to take the government into his own hands. As regards his education, he was very learned in many languages, sciences, and political theories. His understanding was ready if shallow, and his memory exact and well-stored. Yet, in spite of his quickness in learning, his undoubted abilities, and his large fund of knowledge, he gave little promise of ever being a profound scholar or great humanist. Perhaps the ease with which he learned prevented full assimilation. Certainly, he had already acquired a pragmatical self-conceit that often blinded him to broad issues. The rigidity of his mind made him cling to extreme positions, and the more he studied, the more arguments and illustrations he found to maintain his a priori assumptions. His learning did not enrich or enlarge his mind, but made him pedantic and pedagogic. It never induced in him the humility a true student feels when he contrasts what he knows with what might be known.

James was already as set and confident in politics as he was in learning. Observers blamed him severely for his ignorance of the poverty and weakness of his kingdom when compared with the wealth and strength of other nations. To overrate his native land might be judged patriotic but in reality was a form of self-inflation, so closely did he identify the state with himself. Consequently, James overestimated himself and despised other princes, never realizing that he was too young fully to understand matters of state. His wilfulness and obstinacy in choosing young, ambitious men as his councilors incurred the bitter criticism of so experienced a statesman as Walsingham. On his mission to Edinburgh, the English secretary of state bluntly told the Scottish king that young princes deceived themselves when they imagined themselves absolute and forgot that in exceeding the law they became tyrants. The history of both England and Scotland plainly showed, as Walsingham pointed out, that princes were as much bound to rule justly as were subjects to obey dutifully, and there were, he warned, many precedents for the deposition of rulers who had refused to remove evil councilors. He left the King "smarting like a whipped schoolboy," but otherwise unmoved and unconverted, for James always started a discussion convinced that he was right and always resented any advice that ran contrary to his preconceived ideas.

As for his capacity for business and affairs of state, we know that at an early age he was regarded as lazy and negligent. When reminded that in medieval France royal indolence had bred mayors of the palace, who reduced kings to mere monks at St. Denis, James replied that he never signed anything of importance until he had mastered it. He boasted that, even if he did spend much time in hunting, he could transact more business in an hour than others could in a day, because he could do five different things at once. And he professed to know beforehand, from his spies at their doors morning and evening, what his councilors would propose. His third explanation for his dilatory methods was that, when he had sat continuously at his desk for a week, he had never failed to be ill. This excuse served throughout his life, and he always justified his hunting as necessary to his health.

Pictures of James in childhood or early manhood leave the impression that he was shy, sensitive, and scared. These deductions from his portraits are confirmed by one of his mother's agents, who visited him in the summer of 1584. According to his account, James, having been brought up in fear, has still the defect that "he does not dare very often to contradict great lords; nevertheless, he loves extremely to be thought bold and formidable. In later years James abandoned this ambition to be a martial hero, substituting for it the role of great peacemaker. His anxiety to be other than he was persisted through life. What is today called an inferiority complex no doubt urged him to aspire to heights he had not the ability, strength, or resolution to attain.

II.   1583-1603

The second period of James's life yielded most of his contributions to literature. The first was *The Essayes of a Prentise, in the Divine Art of Poesie* (1584 or 1585). The contents of this work are twofold: there are poems and there are rules for versification. James's sonnets are not worse than many written in the pre-Spenser era, but in no single poem is there a spark of fire or ranging imagination. The explanation is supplied by the treatise James published with his poems. Clearly, his chief concern was with rules about the technical details of versification, which achieve metrical correctness. The rules, good or bad, were not his own. "His indebtedness to Gascoigne's excellent *Notes of Instruction* (1575) is obvious in every page." The desire to instruct others, even by appropriating what was already in print, is noteworthy in a royal youth of eighteen.

The King's prompt recognition of the new school of divine poetry which Saluste du Bartas originated in France in the late sixteenth century was more creditable. After commending Homer and Virgil as inimitable in a barbarous and corrupt tongue like the English, the King praised "the loftie phrase, the grave inditement, the facound termes of the French Salust" and assigned *La Judith* to Thomas Hudson as an agreeable subject to be turned into English verse. Not content with this commission, James himself took a hand and inserted in his *Essayes of a Prentise* both the French original and his own rendering of *L'Uranie*. In an un-

usually modest preface he confessed his unfitness to translate so fine a poem but hoped that his example would move others, better equipped, to improve on his poor effort. The King's interest in the Christian muse was lasting, not a passing whim induced by the visit of Du Bartas to Scotland, for he was the only modern poet whose works James commended to his son as being "most worthie to bee read by any Prince."

Meanwhile his mother, Mary Queen of Scots, was approaching her tragical end. When he learned that her life was in danger, James, who had never shown any filial love toward her, wrote many letters to Elizabeth and others, to try to save it. Obviously, he was moved by two considerations: the danger to the cause of monarchy if a queen were executed, and the loss of his own reputation if he suffered his mother to die shamefully. It is clear that he had already become a firm believer in the divine right of kings. He reminded Elizabeth that no law of God permits justice to strike upon crowned heads, whom he "hath called gods, and therefore subjected to the censure of none in earth . . . Who, being supreme and immediate lieutenant of God in heaven, cannot therefore be judged by their equals on earth." What monstrous thing is it, he asked, that sovereign princes themselves should be the example-givers in the profaning of their own sacred diadem? He complained to his ambassador in England that Elizabeth had acted so contrary to her good fame as "by subjects' mouth to condemn a sovereign." And, arguing that he deserved well at the Queen's hands, he proceeded: "You can guess in what sort my honor will be if this unhappy execution comes to pass, since already I scarcely dare go abroad for the reviling of the whole people. But all of Scotland is incensed, and condemns the English Queen, whom I dare not defend lest I dethrone myself." Nevertheless, having set his whole heart upon succeeding Elizabeth, James dared not offend her and her people, and he had to be content with verbal protests. According to a hostile witness, the

Presbyterian historian, David Calderwood, he could not, though he tried, conceal his joy at the news of his mother's execution. After all, she had named the Infanta of Spain as her successor, instead of her own son. Perhaps James's indifference to his mother was not greater than hers to him.

Two years later James married. How he chose his bride is described by Sir James Melville:

> Now the King being suited in marriage by many great princes, and his ambassadors being come back both out of Denmark and Navarre, with the pictures of the young Princesses; his Majesty determined first to ask council of God by earnest prayer, to direct him where it would be meetest for the weal of himself, and his country. So that after fifteen days advisement and devout prayer, as said is, he called his Council together in his cabinet, and told them how he had been advising about that matter of so great concernment to himself and his country the space of fifteen days, and that he was now resolute to marry in Denmark.

The marriage with Anne (1574-1619), the second daughter of Frederick II of Denmark, took place by proxy in 1589, and the bride was expected to cross the seas in September. She started but was driven back by storms—raised by witches, James thought. Thereupon, he determined to go himself and fetch her. The reasons that prompted this, his one truly romantic act, are perhaps hinted at in an unfinished poem. In it he explains that Christians well knew that God alone

>   . . . did before beginnings all
> on worldly things dispone.

No man, he said, can choose his destiny.

> For I as being a king by birth, it seemed
>   my lot was made
> There to reside where God my charge and
>   burthen on me laid,
> Lacking parents, brethren, bairns, or any
>   near of kin

> In case of death, or absences to supply my
>   place therein.

Nevertheless, he was going to leave his native land and seek his wife in Denmark. The line referring to his lonely state may voice a hope of finding solace in his consort. It is hard to say whether he was gratified or disappointed. He always treated Anne good-naturedly, tolerated her extravagances, forbore to grumble at her frivolity, and did not upbraid her for her vacillations in religion. Although six children were born to him, of whom three died in infancy, James was not uxorious. He was never unfaithful to Anne, and he showed her great generosity and kindliness, but there is no sign that he was ever passionately fond of her. They had too little in common to be good companions, for she did not especially care for hunting or sports, and had no interest in his theological or other treatises and discourses. Their relations are well illustrated by an incident that happened in July, 1613. At Theobalds the Queen, aiming at a deer, shot instead Jewel, the King's best hound. At first James stormed exceedingly but, after he learned who was responsible, he was soon pacified and "with much kindness wished her not to be troubled with it, for he should love her never the worse, and the next day sent her a diamond worth 2000*l.* as a legacy from his dead dog." The comment of the relater of the anecdote concludes, "Love and kindness increases daily between them, and it is thought they were never in better terms." The incident is very typical—the sudden anger, the surely unnecessary assurance that the accidental shooting of a dog would not lessen his love, and the extravagant gift.

The domestic history of Scotland helps to reveal a side of James's character that might otherwise escape emphasis—namely, his persistence. His efforts, continued until 1625, to suppress the age-long disorders of the Western Isles and the Border were strikingly successful, and he deserves full credit for making Scotland more peaceful, perhaps, than she had ever been, although his methods were sometimes dubious, even detestable. Another object on which James had set his heart was the establishment of the royal authority over the kirk. He accepted the doctrine of Presbyterianism but rejected its discipline as incompatible with his theory of monarchy. He hated its theory of the two kingdoms, with the corollary that the king was only a private member of the church. Both before and after 1603 he used every weapon in his armory to break the resistance of the kirk to the establishment of bishops, to bring about the cessation of meetings of the General Assembly except when he willed it to meet, and to suppress all criticism of his policies. By bribing the nobles with temporalities of the church and by appealing to their dislike of Presbyterian austerities, James triumphed after many years of embittered struggle, but entailed a terrible day of reckoning on his son.

Meanwhile, he was busily engaged in trying to mold his kingdom by his writings. He explained that he took up his pen very deliberately as "the great provost, and great schoolmaster of the whole land." He wrote to instruct his subjects, and told them that the best way he knew was to give them a mirror, not that they could see their own reflections but that they could see the heart of their king. He wanted to set *cor regis in oculis populi*. Inasmuch as James was unnaturally attracted by the horrible, and attributed to witches the storms that delayed his marriage, it is not surprising that he should have written *Daemonologie, in Forme of a Dialogue*. He tells us in his preface that the fearful abundance, at the time, of "these detestable slaves of the Devil, the witches or enchanters," had moved him to write, "not in any wise (as I protest) to show my learning and ingine [mother wit]," but merely to prove that such arts of Satan are most certainly practiced and that the instruments merit most severe punishment. James's next treatise, *The Trew Law of Free Monarchies* (1598), as the Advertisement stated, was intended to teach subjects the meaning of their allegiance—the most necessary of all knowledge except knowledge of

God. He claimed that the Scriptures, the fundamental law of Scotland, and the law of nature, alike proved that subjects ought to obey the king's commands, as the commands of God's minister, acknowledging him as a judge set over them, and realizing that he is accountable to God alone.

The last of James's prose works of this period is the *Basilikon Doron, or His Majesties Instructions to his Dearest Sonne, Henry the Prince*. This is in many respects the most interesting of all James's writings, because it sets forth his ideals of a Christian, a king, and a king's behavior in things indifferent. Much of the advice is admirable, and James's failure to attain the high standard he prescribed for his son is not surprising. What is astonishing is the complete contradiction between precept and example in matters on which great stress is laid, such as diligence in performing the office of a king or the careful selection of courtiers from among the old nobility. Indeed, a comparison between James's "Instructions" and his own actions, both then and later, would make a most severe criticism of his life. The discrepancy is probably due to several causes—to the vanity that made him boastful, to the self-deception that blinded him to his faults, and to the desire to be other than he was.

As the sixteenth century drew to a close, the prospect of succeeding Elizabeth absorbed James more and more. Though he had no serious rivals to fear, he became obsessed with the notion that he must either obtain official recognition as Elizabeth's heir or conciliate all parties that might otherwise oppose his succession. Failing to overcome the Queen's rooted objection to naming her successor, he intrigued in every direction. He made cautious overtures to Essex, and after the Earl's fall he entered into communication with Cecil and other members of the English Privy Council. More surprising, and certainly more tortuous, were his secret dealings with the Pope and the King of Spain. So devious were his approaches to these leaders of militant Roman Catholicism that even today it is difficult to be positive which of the messengers and letters that arrived at Rome and Madrid were authorized. James seems to have exaggerated, not only the power of the Pope and the possible effect of a papal excommunication as an obstacle to the English throne, but the strength of the English papists as well. His intrigues naturally caused the suspicion that he was either waiting for a favorable opportunity to become a convert or that at least he was strongly attracted by the Roman Catholic creed. Actually, he was a Calvinist—as his poetry shows—and he disliked the papal claim to the right of excommunicating and deposing heretical sovereigns as much as he disliked the claim the General Assembly made to the right to censure erring kings. The conclusion of Dr. Helen G. Stafford, the author of a very sound monograph entitled *James VI of Scotland and the Throne of England* (1940), is that, although in the last analysis James's "peaceful accession to the English throne may be attributed to factors beyond his control, his achievement in Scotland between 1587 and 1603 and his cautious handling of his relations with England and with Catholic Europe contributed somewhat to the realization of his dream." The conclusion is doubtful. He himself said, of the English throne, that "God by my birthright and lineal descent had in the course of time provided" it for him. Moreover, his intrigues may have had two most unfortunate results. One was to increase his confidence in his statecraft, which was to lead him to repose excessive hopes in the long-drawn-out Spanish match. The other was to spread abroad belief in his duplicity, and create among Roman Catholics the atmosphere in which the Gunpowder Plot was conceived.

III. 1603-12

James waited long, and impatiently, for the death of Queen Elizabeth, who had seemed as eternal as the sun and moon to the king anxious to enter the promised land. Actually, he became king of England on March 24, 1603, and in a week or so began his journey to London. His reception was extraordinarily warm everywhere, and the people greeted him on their knees, shouting "Welcome" and "God save King James." He declared to his first Parliament that he would ever remember with thankfulness "how at my first entry into this kingdom, the people of all sorts rid and ran, nay rather flew to meet me, their eyes flaming nothing but sparkles of affection, their mouths and tongues uttering nothing but sounds of joy; their hands, feet, and all the rest of their members in their gestures, discovering a passionate longing, and earnestness to meet and embrace their new sovereign." He may have been surprised at his hearty reception, and may have attributed too much to his personal qualities, and not enough to the inborn loyalty of his subjects and their relief at a peaceful succession when they had feared a civil war.

The King had certainly done his best to ingratiate himself with Englishmen. At York, for example, when offered a coach to take him to the Minster, he answered, "I will have no coach; for the people are desirous to see a King, and so they shall, for they shall as well see his body as his face." Accordingly, he went on foot to the church. At Theobalds, hearing that a multitude was assembled to see him, he showed himself at his chamber window half an hour on end.

James evidently had the best of intentions, and he was as anxious as ever to teach his subjects how to behave. By a new edition of the *Trew Law of Free Monarchies,* and by his speeches to Parliament, he set forth his theories of government. But he chose to publish his diagnosis of the social evils he found, in the preface to his work, *A Counterblaste to Tobacco* (1604). Peace and wealth, he argued, have brought forth a general slothfulness which makes us wallow in all sorts of idle delights. The clergy have become negligent and lazy, the nobility and gentry extravagant, lawyers covetous, and the common people prodigal and curious.

For remedie whereof, it is the Kings part (as the proper Phisician of his Politicke-body to purge it of all those diseases, by Medicines meete for the same . . . by the example of his owne Person and Court, to make us all ashamed of our sluggish delicacie . . . As likewise by his, and his Courts moderatenesse in Apparell, to make us ashamed of our prodigalitie . . . By the sharpe triall, and severe punishment of the partiall, covetous and bribing Lawyers, to reforme their corruptions: And generally by the example of his owne Person, and by the due execution of good Lawes, to reforme and abolish, piece and piece, these old and evill grounded abuses. . . . And surely in my opinion, there cannot be a more base, and yet hurtfull, corruption in a Countrey, then is the vile use (or other abuse) of taking Tobacco in this Kingdome, which hath mooved me, shortly to discover the abuses thereof in this following little Pamphlet.

The conclusion of this paragraph is as fine an example of bathos as can easily be imagined. The futility of the *Counterblaste* is proved by the ever increasing use of tobacco: it did not even keep his body free from "corruption," inasmuch as when his tomb was opened, in the nineteenth century, a pipe was found that had evidently been dropped at his interment.

But as early as June, 1603, the voice of criticism was heard saying that occasionally the King attended Council meetings, but most of the time he spent in fields and parks, chasing away idleness by violent exercise and early rising. Soon the King's addiction to hunting and his selfish absorption in his pleasures became more noticeable to his subjects than they had been in the first months of the reign. A well-known anecdote of James records that when he was hunting near Royston, one of his hounds, Jowler, was found with a paper about his neck and on it were the words, "Good Mr. Jowler, we pray you speak to the King (for he hears you every day, and so doth he not

us) it will please His Majesty to go back to London, or else the country will be undone; all our provision is spent already, and we are not able to entertain him longer."

James's character as a man is revealed very clearly in his recreations. He was passionately devoted to sports but he was not a good sportsman in either sense of the word. He was a notably indifferent performer at all exercises and games. He preferred hunting before other diversions, but his many falls show that he was a poor horseman. He never made it his chief pleasure, as a good sportsman should, to see that other participants in the day's pastime were enjoying themselves. On the contrary, if he found he was excelled by anyone, he either sulkily abandoned the exercise altogether or revealed his chagrin. When he and his guest, the King of Denmark, tilted at the ring, James showed his jealousy when the spectators applauded his royal brother more than him and when confused voices were heard saying, "Ah! if we only had such a king." When himself a spectator he soon made his lack of interest apparent, sometimes by going to sleep, as at a play, or by angry comments.

Henry IV of France sent De Vitry, a great hunter, to England, and he accompanied James on a hunting trip. De Vitry seems to have constituted himself the chief huntsman, following the hounds close at their heels, contrary to the English fashion, and frequently putting them on the right track when they went astray—to the shame of the royal huntsmen but to the admiration of the King and his friends. The French ambassador, who was present, reports that James loved his sport so passionately that he forgot his affairs of state and his own dignity. Being bothered by the crowds that ran from all sides to see him, he flew into a furious temper, cursing everyone he met and protesting that if they did not leave him free to enjoy his hunting he would abandon England. The Frenchman expressed the fear that these immoderate passions would scandalize the old councilors of Elizabeth. Actually, a few months earlier, an

Englishman had noted that the honest people desired of their king "some more of that generous affability which their good old Queen did afford them." James was apparently unaware of his failure to gratify his people's loyalty by gracious acknowledgements of their devotion, but he was conscious of his failure to remember his duty as a Christian. An ecclesiastical writer praises him for his constant prayers at night for forgiveness, when his hasty temper had escaped control. Unfortunately for his reputation, his anger and cursing were evident to many but his repentance was known to very few.

Defects like these soon undermined the King's popularity. Men began to make comparisons between James and Good Queen Bess. A bishop notes that, after a few years' experience of the "Scottish government," in disparagement and detestation of the Scots, Elizabeth's memory was much magnified— "such ringing of bells, such public joy and sermons in commemoration of her, the picture of her tomb painted in many churches, and in effect more solemnity and joy in memory of her coronation than was for the coming in of King James."

However discreetly James had behaved to his countrymen, they would not suddenly have lost their unpopularity in England, which centuries of conflict had engendered. Instead, he at once showed so marked a preference for the company of Scots that he intensified the rivalry between the nations. Not content with appointing Scots to prominent places about the court, he lavished thousands of pounds yearly upon them. The situation became acute enough not only to alarm Treasury officials at the King's profuseness but also to cause members of Parliament to complain of it at the very time that he was appealing to them for an increased revenue. Far from heeding their warnings, he gave a most conspicuous example of wilful obstinacy, for immediately after he had dissolved his first Parliament, in 1611, he distributed among six favorites, four of them Scots, no less than

£34,000, a thirteenth of the annual income —and this in spite of his heavy indebtedness. In addition to money or estates, he gave Scots some peculiar privileges for them to possess—as the patent for the alnage of wool, which he bestowed upon Lennox (son of his first favorite).

By itself, reckless generosity to a chosen few might argue nothing worse than foolish improvidence. But it was merely a visible sign of a much greater defect in James. One of the most remarkable features of his character was his extraordinary susceptibility to his immediate entourage. The importance to an ambitious subject of a place that afforded him daily contact with the King was widely recognized. Robert Carey, who brought James the first news of Elizabeth's death, was promised that whatever reward he sought would be granted. He immediately asked to be admitted a Gentleman of the Bedchamber. The opportunities for a small clique of household officers to take advantage of the weakness of the King were much increased by his habit of going off on a hunting trip with a small train. During the first nine years of the reign the sway of favorites was largely kept in check, in the most serious questions of policy, by the reliance James placed on Salisbury, but it is noteworthy that the French ambassador, La Boderie, couples Dunbar with Salisbury as the two important ministers. Dunbar was one of the conspicuous illustrations of the King's habit of rewarding Scots with English lands and salaries. As Lord Treasurer of Scotland his influence was paramount beyond the Border, but his eminence there can hardly have reconciled Englishmen to his appointment as Chancellor of the Exchequer and Master of the Wardrobe in London, or to James's acceptance of his dying recommendation of George Abbot as Archbishop of Canterbury. However, Dunbar was easily the most accomplished and respectable of the favorites. Others had little to recommend them expect prowess at sports and good looks. All his life James liked to have around him, and dependent upon his bounty, younger men of handsome appearance. He was very homely himself and had never enjoyed the spontaneous high spirits and irresponsibility of youth. At the age of eighteen he was described by an acute observer as "an old young man." Perhaps he saw embodied in these men his own unfulfilled aspirations.

One reason for James's addiction to favorites was his dislike and dread of strangers. Walton illustrates this foible when he describes Wotton's secret mission to James, in 1601. Wotton was requested to lay aside his rapier before entering the presence chamber, and found inside three or four Scots stationed in the corners of the room. Also, because James lacked the regal bearing, courtesy, dignity, and *savoir faire* that endear a sovereign to his people, he naturally preferred his own intimate circle. There seems no doubt that among his familiars James was good company. He was kindly and thoughtful toward those in direct contact with him. Several anecdotes support Laud's statement that the King in private was the best master that ever was, and the most free to his servants. He was temperate in his diet, and never intoxicated, though he did drink deeply at times. He enjoyed a jest even if broad and coarse, and had a store of pawky humor. His sayings were held in great reput for at least half a century. As Professor F. P. Wilson states, "The man whose table talk was most persistently reported in collection after collection and edition after edition was the Solomon of Great Britain, James I." A few specimens of the sole royal British contribution to a once popular series—the ana—follow: "I wonder not so much that women paint themselves as that when they are painted men can love them"; "Much money makes a countrie poore, for it sets a dearer price upon every thing"; "Let no man thinke that hee may frame and make his wife as he pleaseth, that deceived Solomon, the wisest king that ever was."

Not all of James's leisure hours were spent on boon companions or sports. He was genuinely interested in some politico-theological questions. Characteristically, his viewpoint toward his relations with the papacy was personal and monarchical. Much to his credit, he favored partial toleration for Roman Catholics, provided their loyalty was assured. In the new oath of allegiance framed in 1606, the test was not repudiation of transubstantiation or other doctrines, but willingness to deny the papal power to depose heretical princes and to promise assistance to the king if deposed and attacked by a papal champion. If the Pope would relinquish the claim to the power of deposition and would not insist on his precedence over monarchs, James seems to have believed that reconciliation with Rome was possible. Instead, he found himself embroiled in a controversy over papal claims which spread throughout Europe. Though he rose superior to the extreme hatred of Rome felt by many of his subjects, vulgar prejudice was in closer touch with reality than his erudite opinions. His attitude toward the papacy is a striking and typical example of the truth that much learning does not induce wisdom.

James's curious delusion about the possibility of reunion with Rome did not arise from ignorance or indifference. On the contrary, he was, like so many of his contemporaries, most interested in theological questions. Laud, who should have known, styled James "the most learned prince that this kingdom hath ever known for matters of religion." Walton tells how the King welcomed Donne's presence, especially at his meals, where there were usually "many deep discourses of general learning, and very often friendly disputes, or debates of religion, betwixt his Majesty and those divines, whose places required their attendance on him at these times: particularly . . . Montague (who edited his works in 1616) . . . and Andrews." Another biographer—of John Williams—assures us that not all the time spent at Royston and other hunting lodges was devoted to sports, for the King used to send thence to Cambridge for books to check quotations of Bellarmine, the great Catholic controversialist. An examination of James's writings reveals a very considerable knowledge of theological works, as well as of the classics. And yet, in spite of his learning, he never appreciated the strength of religious convictions. He erred because he was too concerned with the monarchical principle as he saw it, and judged creeds different from his own too exclusively from a constitutional point of view. He was a bigot, not for a religious doctrine but for a political theory.

The years of James's reign are the most famous in the annals of English literature. The wind bloweth where it listeth, and no theory of causation will fully explain the extraordinary literary output of those years. Writers on literature seem to be in agreement, however, that the accession of a king interested in letters and scholarship was advantageous to both, but none has placed a precise or detailed value upon the services James rendered to literature or learning. Ben Jonson, in his elegy in the First Folio, asserts that Shakespeare's plays were equally pleasing to Elizabeth and James. Certainly, in 1603, a license to perform was granted to the Lord Chamberlain's company—now the King's company —in the list of which Shakespeare's name stands second. His plays were frequently acted in the royal presence, and, about a century later, a story appeared in print that James had written "an amicable letter" to the dramatist. Ben Jonson's relations to the King were closer than those of Shakespeare. From 1604-5 onward, except when absent from London, he regularly wrote the Christmas masques for the court. In 1616 he was granted a pension of one hundred marks; according to Aubrey, James once gave him a hundred pounds for "drollery" —he seems to have been allowed a frankness of speech unusual at court. When he returned from his visit to Scotland he was warmly welcomed by the King, who expressed "some joy to see me, and is pleased to hear of the purpose of my book"—a poem descriptive of Scotland, which did not survive if ever written.

Unfortunately, no evidence exists to show James's opinion of the masterpieces Shakespeare and Jonson produced in his reign, but, though the argument from silence may be deceptive, the inference that he was not fully aware of their greatness may not be unfair. The play he liked best seems to have been George Ruggles' *Ignoramus,* acted at Cambridge in 1615. Then, we are told, he "was much delighted with the play, and laughed incessantly; and oftentimes, with his hands, and by words, applauded it." Perhaps an opportunity to display his knowledge of Latin by clapping all the topical hits in the play, and his delight at seeing ridicule heaped upon the common lawyers, account for his great pleasure. To have cried up *Ignoramus* and not to be known to have acclaimed Shakespeare's tragedies suggests at least an insensitiveness to true dramatic art. An attractive explanation is that the King was not really appreciative of literature as such, but only as a medium for the popularizing of his own convictions or prejudices.

The keen interest in poetry which James had shown, both by example and precept, before his accession to the English throne was maintained afterward, though to a slighter degree. He himself wrote few poems after 1603. There are, of course, many fulsome dedications to James in verse and in prose, but only occasional signs of his intercourse with poets. John Donne several times acknowledges his indebtedness to the "learnedest of Kings," but always for advising, even persuading, him to enter the ministry. Izaak Walton describes how James enjoyed "deep discourses of general learning . . . or debates of religion" with Donne and other divines. All in all, the King's relations with Donne are as creditable as anything recorded of him, but they concern the theologian and the scholar, not the poet.

Sir John Beaumont, in *Bosworth Field* (1629), has a poem, "To his late majesty, concerning the true form of English poetry," in which occur the lines:

Forgive my boldness that I here present
The life of muses yielding true content
In pondered numbers, which with ease
    I tried,
When your judicious rules have been
    my guide.

The historian of English poetry detected, in the hundred years following the defeat of the Armada, "a certain instinctive movement of thought and language in the nation under the leadership of the court, showing itself partly in the simplification of ideas, and partly in the harmonious mode of expressing them." The likelihood is that James exerted as much influence as his brother sovereigns in this movement, but at present there is no means of judging how much that was.

Toward the end of his life the King was the center of a small group assembled to versify the Psalms. Sir William Alexander, a member, soon found that James intended to be the head and that he himself should be merely an assistant. When Drummond of Hawthornden sent Alexander a version of a Psalm, the latter wrote: "I received your last letter, with the psalm you sent; which I think very well done. I had done the same long before it came; but he [the King] prefers his own to all else, though perchance, when you see it, you will think it the worst of the three." Drummond makes the judicious reply: "A Prince becomes jealous of possessors of those excellencies which he prideth in himself." The royal attitude thus described is typical: conceit impelled the King to be first, or to abandon any pursuit in which he might have to take a secondary place.

James's reign was a great age in English scholarship. The King himself, unquestionably a learned man, might well have been a generous patron of scholars. Once he had intended to be. In 1601 he had urged Casaubon to come to Edinburgh and assured him that, "besides the care of the church, it was his fixed resolve to encourage letters and learned men, as he considered them the strength, as well as the ornament of kingdoms." When the opportunity came he did not live up to his professions, as is proved by a brief survey of his relations with the giants of erudition of his time. He never fully appreciated Bacon, as statesman, jurist, or scholar. His slow promotion to the woolsack was in painful contrast to Buckingham's lightning advance to power. Bacon asked Northampton to present a copy of the *Advancement of Learning* to "his sacred majesty, whom I dare avouch (if the records and time err not) to be the learnedst king that hath reigned." When sending James a copy of the *Instauratio magna,* he wrote: "This, tending to enlarge the bounds of reason and to endow man's estate with new value, was no improper oblation to your Majesty, who, of men, is the greatest master of reason, and author of beneficence." What acknowledgment was made of the first gift is unknown; of the second, a newsletter reported that "the King cannot forbear sometimes in reading his last book to say that it is like the peace of God, that passeth all understanding."

James's relations with the remarkable group of antiquaries then alive were less cordial, on the whole, than might have been expected. Sir Henry Spelman relates that, when the Society of Antiquaries was revived in 1614, its members soon learned that "his majesty took a little mislike of our society, not being inform'd that we had resolv'd to decline all matters of state. Yet hereupon we forbore to meet again." As an offset may be mentioned the King's favor to Cotton, whom he styled "cousin," probably jocosely on account of a claim to descent from Robert Bruce. The antiquary was consulted on such questions as the proposed union of England and Scotland, the abuses in the navy, the possible augmentation of the royal revenue, and the new order of baronets (himself being the thirty-sixth created). His rash dabblings in political intrigues with the Spanish ambassador and the assistance he gave to Somerset—even forging the dates of some letters to aid the Earl's defense against the charge of complicity in Overbury's murder—were the causes of an imprisonment during parts of 1615 and 1616, but did not wholly lose him his position at court. However, apart from the occasional recognitions of his eminence as a scholar, he owed little to royal favor.

William Camden was befriended to a certain extent by James, who refused to allow Ralph Brooke to publish a second "Discoverie" of the errors of *Britannia*. He persuaded or ordered Camden to write the *Animadverisones* on De Thou, because, as Camden's biographer asserts, the King was infuriated with the French historian because he had stated that in Scotland power emanates from the people and that kings could be coerced there if they broke the laws, and had written calumnies against Mary Queen of Scots. If James approved of the biography of his mother by Will Stranguage (or Udall)—and it is dedicated to him—he clearly demanded a vindication at the expense of historic truth. Mary is thus characterized:

A woman most constant in her religion, adorned with a wonderful pietie towards God, wisdome above her sex, and was also very faire and beautifull. . . . Tossed and turmoiled by Murrey, her bastard brother, and other her ungrate and ambitious subjects, deposed from her Kingdome, and driven to flie into England, and circumvented and entrapped (as men speaking indifferently thinke) by sundry Englishmen, carefull of the conservation of their religion, and of the safetie of Queen Elisabeth.

After the publication of his *History of Tythes,* John Selden was summoned to Theobalds. There the King was pleased on two occasions to argue with him, "learnedly, humourously, and sometimes angrily," about passages in that work, especially about celebrating the birth of Christ on December 25. James said he suspected that Selden leaned toward the views of the seditious Scots who refused to celebrate Christmas on a fixed day. Selden replied that so far was this from being true that he had already more or less finished a little work proving that the observance of Christmas on December 25 was correct. James, most serenely, demanded immediately that it be brought to him. Notwithstanding the favorable issue of these audiences, the King later told him, after the publication of Richard Montagu's answer to the *History of Tythes:* "If you or any of your friends answer that refutation, I shall throw you into prison." Selden's treatise, *Mare Clausum,* was presented to James and he was on the point of ordering it to be printed when he remarked: "I remember that something is said about the North Sea which would displease very much my royal brother of Denmark which I would willingly avoid just now because I owe him a large sum of money, and, in turn, he may be about to ask me shortly for a larger sum." Accordingly, publication was postponed some seventeen years.

In 1610 Casaubon came to England and James gave him a pension of £300 a year. He at once impressed the King with his scholarship, and paid a penalty that he soon began to find burdensome—on Sundays he was expected to be a member of the royal circle, even when James was at a hunting seat. Casaubon formed a high opinion of his royal patron: "He is a lover of learning to a degree beyond belief; his judgment of books, old and new, is such as would become a professed scholar, rather than a mighty prince." But his interest in books was limited, at least during the years in which the antipapal controversy absorbed him. Therefore, Casaubon sorrowfully decided: "As long as I shall stay in England, I see that I must make up my mind to forego classical letters. Our excellent and most religious king is so fond of theology, that he cares very little to attend to any literary subject."

This passage gives one explanation of James's comparative neglect of historiography—his greater interest in theology. A second explanation is in the *Basilikon Doron.* There the King had especially advised Prince Henry to be well versed in authentic histories and in the chronicles of all nations, but he was to avoid infamous libels like the works of Buchanan and Knox, and punish the possessors of such books. In other words, while James wanted histories in favor of monarchs to be read, those that exposed the vices or misfortunes of kings were to be destroyed. When Selden was attacked for his *History of Tythes* he urged that his only concern had been to discover the facts about the origin of tithes, but he was obliged to express his regret that he had published his findings, and the book was suppressed. James must have been in complete agreement with that kind of procedure. Facts which contradicted his beliefs must not be uncovered; indeed, they were not facts and would only deceive the unwary.

IV. 1612-25

In the last of the four periods into which this study of James's character has been divided, the dominance of favorites becomes more marked. His portraits prepare us for such a situation, because they show that he deteriorated rapidly as his reign drew to a close. In middle age he appears watchful and disillusioned, without candor, sympathy, or tolerance. He seems to have been habitually uneasy or at least ill at ease, but defensively arrogant and obstinate. He possessed a sort of bonhomie, even a rowdy geniality. Toward the end he looks rather a careworn, loose-lipped wreck, inclined to let things slip, and incapable of sustained effort. And, though opinions may differ about the reliability of portraits as guides to character or about the correct interpretation of the portraits of James, there can be little dispute about the deterioration of the last half of the reign and the King's almost complete surrender to the dictates of favorites.

The rise of Robert Carr to eminence in the court circles was comparatively slow. He had followed James from Scotland as a page, and early in the reign had attracted attention by breaking his arm at a tilting match in the King's presence; thenceforth, he received many marks of the royal favor.

He was given Raleigh's manor of Sherborne in 1609, and created Viscount Rochester in 1611 (being the first Scot to take his seat in the English House of Lords in this reign) and Earl of Somerset in 1613. The ascendancy he established over James may be judged from a letter the King wrote him early in 1615—one of the most revealing extant letters from a sovereign to a subject. The tone is that of a weak man in the grip of a strange infatuation, but there are in the letter some characteristic boastings. The force and intensity of the style are very different from the philosophic or jesting attitude James usually assumed, and betray real feeling. And yet he may already have admitted Villiers to his favor—the exact date of the letter is unknown, so we cannot tell whether the appointment of Villiers as a Gentleman of the Bedchamber (April 13, 1615) immediately preceded or followed the letter's composition. Apparently, it was written after Somerset in a fit of temper had deserted the King. James rebukes him for the "strange streams of unquietness, passion, fury, and insolent pride, and (which is worst of all) with a settled kind of induced obstinacy," although he confessed that the greatness of the trust and privacy between them allowed Somerset infinite liberty and freedom of speech. Equally bad was the Earl's attempt to persuade James "that you mean not so much to hold me by love as by awe, and that you have me so far in our reverence, as that I dare not offend you, or resist your appetites." The King said he had long borne this grief, but now he can suffer it no longer without committing unpardonable sin against God "in consuming myself wilfully, not only myself, but in perilling thereby not only the good estate of mine own people, but even the state of religion through all Christendom, which almost wholly, under God, rests now upon my shoulders." Do not, therefore, he urges Somerset, hasten through grief the death of him who is the only author of your greatness. "Never let it appear that you disdain my person and undervalue my qualities, but hold me to your heart and you may build upon my favour as upon a rock. Recommend yourself to me by love and humble obedience. It hath ever been my common answer to any, that would plead for favour, to a Puritan minister by reason of his rare gifts, that I had rather have a conformable man with but ordinary parts, than the rarest men in the world, that will not be obedient; for that leaven of pride sours the whole loaf. Do not you and your father-in-law hedge in all the court to a dependency upon me and is not one of your nearest kinsmen in my son's bedchamber? It lies in your hands to make of me what you please, either the best master and truest friend or, if I find you ungrateful, no earthly plague so great can light upon you." What would have been the end of this extraordinary relationship between king and subject, but for a hideous scandal, cannot be guessed. James had incurred much odium by supporting the notorious divorce of Frances Howard from the Earl of Essex, so that she could marry Somerset. When Somerset and his wife were plainly implicated in Overbury's murder, the King had to abandon his favorite.

James's last and greatest favorite was George Villiers, whom he created Duke of Buckingham and gave lands and offices worth £17,000 a year. Villiers, the second son of a Leicestershire knight, owed his rise solely to his attractive, graceful person, which was sufficient to captivate the aging King. He ruled James not by arrogance (though he had much) but by flattery. On the other hand, Gondomar, the Spanish ambassador, maintained great influence over the King, for ten years, by firmness instead of flattery. He early discovered that James could be browbeaten, and relied upon his Spanish gravity virtually to control the foreign policy of England. These two instances prove that the King could be both coerced and cajoled. The correspondence between Buckingham and his sovereign is as revealing as the letter from James to Somerset. The Duke told the King that "kinder letters never servant received from master." What

return can I make, he asks, when so great a king descends so low as to communicate to his humblest slave and servant in terms of good fellowship, with expressions of greater care than servants have of masters or physicians of patients, of more tenderness than fathers have of children, of more friendship than between equals, of more affection than between lovers in the best kind, man and wife. I thank you for all you do and all I have. The writer struck the right note here. What Somerset forgot and Buckingham always remembered was that James loved his own creations—men of mean estate raised to the highest places in the realm—provided they frequently expressed their indebtedness to their only begetter.

An even more repulsive specimen of Buckingham's epistolary technique is his letter telling the King that Prince Charles and he were leaving Madrid and hastening home. "Sir, my heart and very soul dances for joy; for the change will be no less than to leap from trouble to care, from sadness to mirth, nay, from hell to heaven. I cannot now think of giving thanks for friend, wife, or child; my thoughts are only bent of having my dear Dad and Master's legs soon in my arms." James's letters to Buckingham are few and not much less revolting. One, concerning an interview Buckingham had promised to have with a Spanish agent, begins, "My sweet dear child, scholar, and friend." Buckingham redeemed his promise at the cost of absence from the King's side. The gullible monarch rewarded this self-denial with disgusting sentimentality: "Alas, sweet heart, I find by this how precise thou art to keep thy word to me, when thou prefers it to thy own greatest comfort in coming to me."

James's public behavior harmonized with his private letters. The Venetian representative describes how, at the end of the masque on Twelfth Night in 1617, the tired dancers began to lag,

whereupon the king, who is naturally choleric, got impatient and shouted aloud

Why don't they dance? What did they make me come here for? Devil take you all, dance. Upon this, the Marquis of Buckingham, his Majesty's favourite, immediately sprang forward, cutting a score of lofty and very minute capers, with so much grace and agility that he not only appeased the ire of his angry lord, but rendered himself the admiration and delight of everybody.

The King rewarded the Marquis with "marks of extraordinary affection, patting his face." The effect of such a scene can well be imagined. James, in his infatuation, had publicly affronted the nobility of England, including the Prince of Wales, one of the dancers, and openly shown his partiality for an upstart quite unknown four years before. *O tempora! O mores!*

The King's extreme partiality for his favorites, and the unseemly embraces he bestowed on them in public, naturally have given rise to suspicions, or even charges, that his behavior in private was still worse. One of the few modern works to make such charges is *The Complete Peerage*. After mentioning the Gowrie conspiracy in 1600, when Gowrie's brother, the Master of Ruthven, was slain while struggling with his sovereign, the passage continues: "What is unknown is the cause of the *fracas* between King and Master, but those who are acquainted with the King's vices, *inter Christianos non nominanda,* and with the fact that the Master was a singularly handsome lad, can make a shrewd guess." Notes of this character explain why G. E. C.'s work is sometimes called "the scandalous peerage." Certainly, the insinuation is unjustified in the present case, because, amid the obscurity that encompasses the conspiracy, almost the only undisputed facts are: that the Master of Ruthven persuaded James to go to Gowrie House and induced him to proceed unattended to the little study where he (the Master) was later slain by an attendant of the King's, and that James shouted for help. To disprove the above accusation is

not necessarily to clear the King's reputation entirely. Surely, however, on a candid review of the evidence, the verdict likely to be given when James is charged with unnatural vices is "not guilty"—even "not proven" seems unfair.

Much of the difficulty of interpreting James's character arises from the inconsistency between the king and the man. Throughout his life he held fast to a few maxims of state and followed a few main lines of policy. One instance has already been mentioned—his determination to subordinate the kirk to the crown. A second is to be found in the "Instructions" he wrote for his son about the functions of Parliament. "Hold no parliaments, but for necessitie of new lawes, which would be but seldome," was his concise direction. Therefore, all attempts of the estates to criticize or control policy were repulsed as *ultra vires*. In accordance with his own precept he angrily repulsed the House of Commons when it claimed, in the Protestation of 1621, the right to discuss foreign relations. His foreign policy was largely swayed by his excessive regard for the sacred cause of monarchy and by his ambition to be the peacemaker of Europe. Ambassadors resident at his court record many denunciations of rebels against their lawful sovereigns. Thus, he bitterly condemned the Spaniards for concluding the Twelve Years' Truce of 1609 with the rebellious Dutch, and upbraided his son-in-law's agent, Dohna, for the usurpation of the Bohemian throne. His attitude was strictly in accordance with another "Instruction"—to keep "that Christian rule, to doe as yee would be done to: especially in counting rebellion against any other Prince, a crime against your owne selfe." The lettering on the monument to him in the schools' quadrangle at Oxford, in which he took great interest and pride, begins *"Beati Pacifici";* and Anthony Wood, describing a visit of Charles II to Oxford, interprets the inscription exactly as the King would have wished—"the blessed peacemaker and the mirrour of the Christian world for his profound learning."

But in character James was much too weak to translate his tenacious theories into resolute action. A few cases are enough to show how his personal, private sentiments overrode his statecraft. In 1623 he terminated the long-drawn-out negotiations for a Spanish match, because "I like not to marry my son with a portion of my daughter's tears." In other words, James the father abandoned the projected marriage when it became clear that the Spaniards would do nothing to recover the Palatinate, the hereditary lands of his son-in-law, Frederick V. More startling, however, was his complete surrender to Buckingham's warlike ambitions. To gratify his favorite the King cast away his pacifism and began hostilities with Spain. He sanctioned an alliance with the Dutch, who were again "rebels." Also, to secure grants for the war and so forward Buckingham's schemes, he invited the Parliament to express its views and promised not to conclude peace without consulting it. In short, the convictions of a lifetime could not restrain his overmastering anxiety to please the ruling favorite. Hence, we have the paradox that the mind of James was usually controlled by fixed concepts, but his will was often swayed by changing personalities.

If a single epithet has to be selected to characterize James, it might well be "unkingly." Nature had denied him the power to appeal to the imagination of his subjects by a kingly bearing and he never cultivated their respect by strict attention to his duties. Always undignified in public, he appeared an odd mixture of a formal pedagogue and a fussy paterfamilias, of a philosopher and a jester. In private he was good-natured if irascible and obstinate, excessively generous, improvident, rather garrulous, gossip-loving, and witty. Obviously, he was ill-fitted to control the destinies of a nation. There are, however, many roles he might have filled. How happy he might have been, in the realm of fiction, with Mr. Oldbuck amid the curiosities of the den at Monkbarns. How congenial he would have found *Jorrocks' Jaunts and Jollities*. What an oracle he would have been at the Pickwick Club, and, to come back to realities, what a success he might have been at the Mermaid Tavern—if he would have refrained from instructing Shakespeare and Jonson in the art of versification.

WHEN CHARLES I CAME TO THE THRONE, in 1625, conditions were less favorable for a prosperous reign than they had been at the time of his father's accession. The growth of Puritanism had further associated religious elements with political opposition to the crown and had strengthened and intensified that opposition by adding to it a spirit of religious fervor. The most active Parliamentary critics of the government under James I had been Puritans, as they continued to be under his son. The great conflict between King and Parliament that was approaching had, to be sure, elements in it other than the religious, but the religious factor was powerful, and we usually speak of the "Puritan" Revolution. Certainly the outstanding foe of Puritanism and all its works among Charles I's councilors and advisers was the Anglican clergyman William Laud, who was appointed Archbishop of Canterbury in 1633. During the period of the Personal Rule, when Charles governed without Parliament (1629-1640), Laud was his principal adviser in matters political and social as well as religious, and his influence, under the King, was paramount at the Council table and in the courts of Star Chamber and High Commission. Indeed, he proved to be the last of a long line of English ecclesiastical statesmen that began in far-off Anglo-Saxon times. In the eyes of the Puritan majority in the House of Commons of the Long Parliament, which met in 1640, Laud was one of the main architects and pillars of the Personal Government, and he was put to death under Parliamentary attainder in 1645. Laud has of course been a highly controversial figure in English history and has been the subject of several biographies, the most penetrating of which is H. R. Trevor-Roper's *Archbishop Laud* (1940), a work in which Laud's religious and social policies are examined carefully and the reasons for their failure suggested. In the following essay, Mr. Trevor-Roper, who is best known for *The Last Days of Hitler* (1947), summarizes the conclusions reached in his book on Laud.

ARCHBISHOP LAUD

H. R. TREVOR-ROPER

It is now three hundred years since Archbishop Laud was beheaded on Tower Hill. For the first two hundred of those years his critics and commentators were unanimous in their opinion of him. The obviousness of his failure, the long success of the political system which he had in vain resisted, the cumbrous medievalism of his theological outlook, the absurdity of his personal foibles, all conspired against him in the golden age of liberal aristocracy. The whigs attacked him; the tories disowned him; he was an embarrassment even to the clergy, who were more disposed to apologise for his faults than to discover his virtues. The most his memory could expect was civility, the civility allowed to those whose ideals have long been dead and buried.

It was not till the nineteenth century that any voice was raised in his defence; and then it was not the voice of the historian. Then the loud, firm, sensible, but somewhat brassy voice of Macaulay, easily dismissing Laud as a "ridiculous old bigot," "a superstitious old driveller," was unexpectedly interrupted by a thin, clerical voice, emotional and nostalgic, tremulously insisting that Laud was "a character cast in a mould of proportions that are much above our own, and of a stature akin to the elder days of the Church." The voice came from Oxford, Laud's Oxford, the one spot where his ghost might still be thought to linger, among the belated gothic cloisters, the isolated medieval survivals, the outworn habits of thought of that backward-looking university. Of course Newman knew nothing, or almost nothing, about Laud, or the politics and history of the seventeenth, or any other century. To him Laud was a symbol, the last, most conspicuous victim of the liberal, scientific, secular society which he hated. As for "the science of history," he expressed his dislike of that, unless it included in its evidence such revealed facts as "the preservation of our race in Noah's Ark." If Macaulay was dogmatic and insensitive, unsympathetic with personal foibles, uncharitable to the weakness of the defeated, at least (like most of the great whig historians) he was a man of practical political experience; and these qualities are perhaps more valuable to the historian, who must interpret politics, than are those of Newman.

And yet it is by their fruits that movements must be judged; and, in spite of many

Reprinted by special permission from *History,* XXX (1945), 181-190. The author has made a few minor changes in the present version of his article.

extravagances, the Oxford Movement did something for the proper appreciation of Laud's character and history. If Newman was ignorant of history, Macaulay in fact knew very little about Laud. He had read Laud's diary, and laughed at its superstitious entries; he had probably looked at his apologia, *The History of his Troubles and Trial,* and thought it fussy and self-piteous; and he may have seen his few printed sermons, those of his papers noticed by Rushworth, and such of his letters as were included by Knowler in the Strafford correspondence. He may also have skipped impatiently through Heylin's tedious panegyric; and he had doubtless relished a number of libels and broadsheets. But all these are seventeenth-century compilations, the products of contemporary journalism; no systematic scholar, no Dalrymple, no Fox, no Mackintosh had collected the materials for a complete study. What those great whig collectors had done for the Glorious Revolution, in which they so firmly believed, the Oxford Movement ultimately did for its hero, Laud. From 1847 to 1860, in the Library of Anglo-Catholic Theology, appeared the seven volumes of his collected works: his sermons, his devotions, his diary, his apologia, his controversy with Fisher, the documents of his chancellorship of Oxford University, his state papers and memoranda, and, finally, his vast and various correspondence; all in an edition so complete and so scholarly (mainly the work of James Bliss) that the piety of a century has found only fragments to supplement it.[1]

No man remains altogether inhuman after his correspondence has been published; and the brutal epithets of Macaulay seem particularly unjust to anyone who has worked

[1] A few of Laud's letters have since been turned up. W. H. Hutton printed one in *English Hist. Rev.* (Oct. 1892); Mr. Godfrey Davies has revealed the existence of 21 letters from Laud to Bramhall among the Hastings MSS. (see *Bulletin of the Huntington Library,* April 1934); his correspondence with Lord Scudamore is printed in my book *Archbishop Laud,* 1940, of which this article summarises the conclusions.

through that series of letters, and seen forming behind them the image of that "little, low, red-faced man," meticulous and superstitious indeed, but indefatigable, disinterested, and consumed by a not ignoble ideal. S. R. Gardiner made use of this collection for his great history; and though Gardiner, by his method of deliberately denying himself the advantages of afterknowledge, seems now to have over-simplified the nature of the Rebellion (and thereby overrated the merits of Laud's opportunist rival, Williams), he is the first historian to do justice to the character, the honesty, and the idealism of Laud.

Meanwhile another change in English life was indirectly turning attention to Laud. Oxford University, the last stronghold of his ideas, was being reformed. A series of commissions was removing the last traces of his now superannuated regime. The exclusive Anglicanism, the clerical monopoly, the Laudian statutes, were changed; and when the compromising rubbish had been swept away, it was easier to appraise the neglected treasures which it had obscured. So when, in 1895, a commemorative volume of *Lectures on Laud* was produced, under the editorship of W. E. Collins, bishop of Gibraltar, due recognition was given to the great work he had performed for the constitution, the learning, and the fabric of the University which, since then, has not ceased to recognise him as a benefactor. (Laud's charitable foundations in Berkshire had already been fully described by J. B. Bruce, for the Berkshire Record Society in 1841.)

Their debt of piety to scholarship discharged, the publicists of the Oxford Movement withdrew again to the more congenial occupation of hagiography. Their criteria were not historical, and though they might restore a character, they could not seriously challenge the whig interpretation of history which was at least based on political (even if narrowly political) conceptions. The biographies of Laud by W. H. Hutton (1895) and A. S. Duncan-Jones (1927) make no advance on the interpretation of Gardiner. They record his uncontested virtues, slide discreetly over his incontestable faults, and, in general, use him as a peg on which to hang high-church doctrines. The whig charges that Laud was constitutionally retrograde and intellectually obscurantist are not refuted by the facts that King Charles had a fine collection of pictures and Laud commissioned Inigo Jones; nor even by the fact that the puritans were very nasty characters.

The real challenge to the traditional whig interpretation did not therefore come from the clerical school which narrowed its interest to church history. It was others who laid the foundations of a new historical system, and so changed the whole basis of historical study that no subsequent student can altogether ignore them. From the time when the German Marxists proclaimed their new gospel of the fundamental importance of social, and the relative or "ideological" character of legal and religious history, the whole period from the Reformation to the Revolution in England assumed a new significance. It was no longer a merely constitutional struggle, which could have been avoided if the Stuarts had had a little more political sense; it was the crisis in the change from medieval to "capitalist" society; and as such it needed a complete overhauling. While Anglican writers continued to redraft the personal portrait of Laud, the whole background against which he must appear, and by which the portrait must be conditioned, was being changed by secular writers who had perhaps little interest in that troublesome theologian, but a deep concern with the structure of English society. Under their hands the character of the age was transformed. The sociologists equated (perhaps too crudely) capitalism and calvinism; the economic strains of the Reformation were exposed by Mr. Tawney in his *Agrarian Problem in the Sixteenth Century,* and the reaction to them of religious thought in his *Religion and the Rise of Capitalism;* constitutional writers redirected their attention to the "Prerogative Courts," and found them socially constructive as well as politically repressive; economic historians (of whom Mr. J. U. Nef has drawn the conclusion most plainly) have pushed back the industrial revolution into the sixteenth century, and students of ideas have found medieval systems of thought lingering on in the seventeenth. In political history Dr. Feiling has shown that the differences between English parties were neither so well defined, nor so impersonal, as had traditionally been assumed. On all sides the solid-seeming dogmas of the classical whig school have been assailed by what may (considering their intellectual predominance) be called the Fabian school of English historians. Roman Catholics, too, have been encouraged by this movement to reconsider their part in English history; and Fr. Gordon Albion's *Charles I and the Court of Rome* (1935) deserves notice, both for the light it sheds on Laud's relations with the Romanists at court, and as an exception

SAMUEL R. GARDINER: English scholar (d. 1902) who wrote the standard account of English political history from the accession of James I to the age of Cromwell. His historical writing has often been criticized for its dullness and colorlessness, but these criticisms are basically unfair. Gardiner, a descendant of Cromwell, made a noble effort to deal impartially with the most controversial period in English history.
INIGO JONES: English architect (d. 1652) who designed many London buildings as well as theatrical scenes, machines, and dress for masques by Ben Jonson and others. He was highly regarded by both James I and Charles I.
EDWARD PUSEY: Nineteenth-century clergyman and scholar whose fear of the growth of rationalism in Anglican circles helped to shape the Oxford movement. He joined Newman and Keble in preparing the *Tracts for the Times* in order to defend the High Anglican position. He opposed those who joined the Church of Rome, but one of his objectives was to unite the English and Roman churches.

to the general standard of Roman Catholic works on this period.

Every great movement has its parasites, and there is no end to the nonsense that has been produced by neo-catholics and neo-tories operating safely behind the front lines. If whigs were the patrons of capitalism, then (by a slightly elliptical extension of the equation) tories, anglo-catholics, and Roman Catholics, being the enemies of the whigs, were clearly the far-seeing champions of all who resisted capitalist abuses. On this weak logical basis many pretentious efforts have been made to rehabilitate the casualties of history, of whom Laud is one. Mr. Wingfield-Stratford for instance, in his prolix *King Charles and the Conspirators* (1937), which contains a sympathetic portrait of Laud, has invalidated his whole argument by such reasoning. It is of course true that the Great Rebellion, like all great revolutions, was controlled by a group of conspirators; but this does not prevent the conspirators from being patriots as well, or make heroes of the defeated. No one would now maintain that the English grandees of 1688, or the American rebels of 1776, were pure-souled and disinterested idealists, and Cavour admitted that his methods, if applied in personal relations, would be those of a cad. But it will take more than these admissions to make statesmen of James II, George III, and the Neapolitan Bourbons. At least the whigs were never as foolish as this; being politicians, they knew that political ends call for political means, and judged accordingly.

Where, then, has this reorientation of ideas left the historical position of Laud? Has it overthrown, or merely modified, the whig interpretation? And if it has modified it, how significant is the modification? In the following pages an attempt will be made to give a summarised view of the present position, to answer, in terms of recent historical scholarship, the crucial question— why was Laud executed? What policy, what actions, made him at once so formidable, and so hateful, to his contemporaries that they held him worthy of a long imprison-

ment, a state trial, and an illegal death? To answer this question, it is not enough to say that he preached and enforced a form of ecclesiastical order and discipline which his enemies believed to be wrong; or that he was intolerant and cruel—that he invariably imposed savage sentences as a judge, that he believed in, and practised, religious persecution, and officiated at the last religious burning in England; or that he imposed a rigorous censorship on the Press. All these statements are true; but they are equally true of his opponents, whose theology was just as controversial, whose cruelty was no less vindictive, and against whose censorship the most famous English vindication of intellectual freedom was directed. Nor is it a valid argument that Laud's acts were illegal. The English constitution was not yet crystallised, and there was as much legal authority for the acts of Charles I's government as for the claims of its enemies. One party appealed to the precedents of Tudor times, when the Crown was strong; the other to those of Lancastrian times, when it was weak. There were precedents favouring both, and the decision between them was made by the Revolution, not before it. Certainly no act of Laud's was as outrageous, legally speaking, as his execution by a revolutionary party on a novel and unsubstantiated charge. It was not the formal illegalities, or supposed illegalities, of Laud's policy which caused his downfall, although these were naturally made the pretexts of the attack on him; it was that policy itself, its very aim and substance, that was his offence; and the generality of the charge, that he had "subverted the fundamental laws of the kingdom," was merely the lawyers' attempt to give a legal colour to such an offence.

What then was Laud's policy? He set out to halt, and in many ways to reverse, a process which had been going on for a century; a process which the majority of the articulate classes in England believed, with some justice, to be progressive, and in which many of them had, by then, a strong material interest; but which he believed, also with some justice (since no movement is wholly good or bad), to be disruptive of society; and for twelve years he wielded such extensive power that he was able, during that time, to achieve an artificial reaction.

The process which Laud sought to check was the vast and complex change in English society collectively included under the title of the Reformation, the process by which the slower, more traditional society of the Middle Ages had been replaced, or was being replaced, by a modern, competitive, capitalist society. In the course of this change, new sources of wealth had called into being new forms of organisation; politics had become secular; the Church, as a separate estate of the realm, was in decline, and the independent wealth which had supported it as such had been diminished by confiscation and by the voluntary or semi-voluntary action of its leaders; the old framework, the old ideas, had been broken up; and new religious forms, the forms of protestantism, with its emphasis on the individual, had been evolved to supersede the old conception of a universal church and a united society.

This process was economically an advance; without it, England would not have become a great power. And it was an advance constitutionally and intellectually; the eighteenth-century conception of freedom, and the English parliamentary constitution, which has guaranteed and preserved that conception, spring from it. In seeking to undo the Reformation, Laud was therefore economically, constitutionally, and intellectually retrograde. This retrogression is what the whigs triumphantly emphasised; it is what the neo-tories and anglo-catholics too easily forget.

But this process was also, socially, disruptive. Like all great changes, it claimed its victims. These victims included the backward landlords, who had not kept up with the economic changes; they also included the poor, who lost the security provided by a more static, less competitive society. Not all of them, of course; for many were absorbed by the new manufactures, or the expanding navy and merchant marine, and, in the general rise in living standards, became better off than they would have remained as copyhold peasants. But this was a long-term advantage; at the time of the changes there were many who suffered, many who were turned adrift from their small, but safe, holdings to swell the ranks of the "sturdy vagabonds" so problematical to the governments of the time. The first hundred years after the Reformation, if they were a century of splendid intellectual and practical development, were also, in certain areas, a century of serious agrarian dislocation. This, which is the burden of the Fabian song, is what the whigs, complacent in the best of possible worlds, had quite forgotten.

Laud never forgot it. He saw it so clearly, so consistently, so passionately, that he probably never saw any other side of the movement. Where others saw economic, constitutional and intellectual progress, he only saw the price at which it was won—the unity of society broken up. And since he was a clergyman, in an age of religion, he saw it also as the breaking up of the visible Church on earth, the mystical body of Christ, by private and irresponsible interpretations of Scripture. The unity of Church and State, and the necessity of authority in both, was his constant theme. "The Church and State are so near united and knit together that though they may seem two bodies, yet indeed in some relations they may be accounted as but one." And his twin bugbears were, in religion, private judgments against the consensus of the Church, and in society, private interests at the expense of the commonwealth. The former, in his eyes, were represented by the puritans, the latter by parliament. To him the puritans were "those wasps," parliament "that noise." In his years of power the puritans were persecuted, and parliament was suspended. When it met, he fell.

In his twelve years of power, therefore, Laud, whose energy was insatiable, for whom no detail was too insignificant, set out to restore, as he thought, the equilibrium of society, and to restore it by exalting the Church once again into an independent estate of the realm; an estate surely grounded on its own wealth, deriving its independent authority from the divine appointment of its bishops, the undisputed interpreter of doctrine, the guardian of political morality, the protector of the poor. For a century, the Church had been steadily impoverished; he enriched it. Its fabric had decayed, its lands had been frittered away, its authority had been evaded, its credit had declined, its control over education, its influence in politics had gone or were going. Laud rebuilt churches, both cathedrals (including St. Paul's) and parish churches. He used the forms of law to recover lands which had been leased away, and to prevent a continuance of the process. He restored its authority through the special courts set up by the Tudors, and extended it over all exempt jurisdictions. He demanded a high standard among bishops and clergy, and ruthlessly bullied those (and they were the majority) who did not forward his ambitions. He reformed universities, especially Oxford and Trinity College, Dublin, of both of which he was chancellor, and patronised the old patristic learning (for he saw no good in the new humanist and scientific studies), endowing chairs of Arabic and Hebrew and collecting and presenting manuscripts and coins. He founded, and encouraged others to found, charitable institutions. As the most influential member of the King's Council, he intervened in politics and advanced clergymen or personal dependents to high political office. Windebank, the Secretary of State, and Juxon, the Lord Treasurer, were his personal nominees. "And now," he sighed after the latter appointment, "if the Church will not hold up themselves under God, I can do no more!"

The authority of the Church, thus restored, was used to undo the effects of the Reformation. Laud found two-thirds of the livings of the Church in the gift of lay patrons, sometimes puritans. Declaring that he hoped ere long not to leave so much as a lay-fee in England, he blustered at the patrons and hunted out the incumbents. In courts and at council-tables, which he claimed as his pulpits, he denounced the exploitation which he associated with the Reformation, "what the Prophet hath called, in a very energetical phrase, grinding of the faces of the poor." Landlords who converted tillage into pasture recognised in him their most inveterate enemy. All free intellectual speculation came under his suspicion. And his long arm reached and persecuted those who differed from him in theology, whether great landlords with political power, or poor artisans and apprentices, throughout the three kingdoms, even in Holland, even in America.

Nevertheless, if Laud was intellectually a medieval figure, in two respects, at least, he fully accepted the Tudor Reformation. Firstly, he believed in absolute, centralised monarchy. The medieval state and the medieval church were both mosaics of special franchises, exempt jurisdictions, liberties, and peculiars. There were numerous feudal tenures in which the King's writ did not run, numerous ecclesiastical anomalies in which the local bishop or archbishop might not interfere, numerous civic or other corporations with their own elective constitutions. These conflicting jurisdictions had provided some guarantees of such practical liberty as had existed in the Middle Ages. In Church and State Laud went further than the Tudors in destroying them. In his metropolitan visitation he forced his jurisdiction on many great institutions (including Cambridge University, the Dean and Chapter of St. Paul's and the diocese of Lincoln) which claimed to be exempt from it; and as a politician he supported the King in his similar invasions of feudal liberties. In this he was supported by the civil lawyers, who, under the early Tudors, had pushed forward the doctrines of administrative law; but in England, the old, untidy common law had not been defeated, as it had been on the continent; side by side with the new Tudor courts and statutes it survived, and had been revivified by a new content of which its crabbed and cantankerous pedants were perhaps unaware. The common lawyers were therefore included by Laud, together with the puritans and parliament men, among the instruments of darkness. They proved to be dangerous enemies.

Secondly, Laud never for a moment contemplated a return to the Roman allegiance. This exception baffled his contemporaries. Many influential Roman Catholics had hopes of him. He was twice, unofficially, offered a cardinal's hat, and, of course, refused. His enemies made desperate efforts to prove him a papist, at least at heart. It would have been very useful to them if they could have proved it, for only thus could they prove their charge of treason. But it was impossible. Laud was a typical insular Englishman; he had never been abroad, and felt uneasy in the society of more polished, cosmopolitan courtiers; he despised Rome of the Counter-Reformation, which had renounced social responsibility, and would have nothing whatever to do with it. He believed in a national church, catholic in doctrine, but absolutely independent of foreign influences; a church such as had been ideally delineated on the ramshackle basis of the Elizabethan compromise by his great intellectual predecessors, Jewel, Hooker, and Andrewes and by his great practical predecessor, Archbishop Bancroft. He believed church and state to be inseparable, complementary features of the same organic unity. He made them so inseparable that they fell together, with him.

Such then was his policy, a large, if hard policy, and though narrow, not ignoble in its aims. But it failed. Why did it fail?

Firstly, it was too purely reactionary. A reformer, whether he is destroying old or new abuses, must produce a policy which is a synthesis of old and new. If his policy has too few roots in the past, it will be revolutionary, and fail, as Joseph II's policy failed. Laud's policy failed because it had too little application to the present. He had the largeness of mind to conceive of an ideal society out of a romanticised past, but

lacked the understanding to translate it effectively into the terms of contemporary society. It may be said that in some ways he was more modern than the parliamentary lawyers, the Cokes and the Prynnes and the Maynards, with their black-letter learning and antiquarian precedents; but whereas they used these ancient forms, which had once been the guarantees of feudal liberties, to secure the totally different, and modern, liberties of "capitalist" society, Laud used the more modern conceptions of conciliar government and civil law to preserve the obsolescent relations of the *Ancien Régime*. In this he was doomed to failure. The forces which he challenged had already been victorious, and had been consolidating and extending their victory for a century. Laud challenged them directly, as if the issue were still in doubt, ignoring the new developments, the new traditions, the new interests which had grown up and taken root in the interim. He relied entirely on authority to impose his programme, and could scarcely complain if his adversaries relied entirely on force to destroy it.

Secondly, Laud made the fatal mistake of many idealists. He supposed that ends justify means. But ends are themselves conditioned by the means used towards them; and to attain his ends, Laud involved himself in courses that were fatal to those ends. To obtain power, he attached himself to an unscrupulous adventurer, the Duke of Buckingham, and needlessly compromised himself by supporting a disastrous foreign policy in which he had no interest. To keep power he relied (since he had no popular support) on one of the most ineffectual and irresponsible governments that England has ever had, and identified himself with all the political follies of that government, with its financial anachronisms, its wasteful monopolies, its weak and silly foreign policy. He even had to connive at the arrival of a Roman mission in England, and to see a hated emissary of the Vatican cutting him out at court. And when he declared, as a political axiom, that the government on which he depended might do anything for money, his great ideals begin to look distinctly shabby.

Thirdly, he made no effort to build up a party in support of his policy. This omission was recognised and deplored by his contemporary supporters, and Mr. W. C. Costin, in his commemorative lecture (January, 1945), mentions it as "one of the serious impediments to his effective action." He needlessly alienated possible supporters; he made no effort to win adherents; he offered no concessions; he had very few friends. In fair weather, he seemed supreme; but when the Long Parliament met, even royalists, even personal friends like Hyde and Selden, were agreed that the destruction of his whole system must precede any settlement. Strafford was the only man in England on whom he could rely, and his enemies saw to it that Strafford was in no position to help him. Even the clergy gave him no useful help. His clerical supporters were mostly irresponsible enthusiasts, who were more of a liability than an asset; when he died, he left neither continuators, nor defenders, of his work. And ranged against him were not only the new landlords and city merchants to whose interests he was fundamentally opposed, and the puritan clergy who perhaps did not matter much, but the old nobility, exasperated by his pretensions, the Scots, enraged by his invasion of their independence, some even of his own bishops, resentful of his exacting discipline. In fact, throughout his political career, he waged a ceaseless and public vendetta against the opportunist, but able, bishop of Lincoln, and indulged the enemies of the church with the pleasing spectacle of inter-episcopal war. And finally, he made himself ridiculous by the pedantry with which he used the vast machinery of repression to hunt out and persecute small fry who were not worth catching.

Enthusiastic high-churchmen, by an evident misuse of language, still refer to Laud as "the great archbishop." It is possible for a man to fail and yet be great, but only if some significant part of his work survives the failure of his more obvious ambitions, as the Code Napoléon and the emancipation of Europe from belated feudalisms survived the collapse of the Napoleonic empire. But Laud's programme has only to be examined for the finality, the universality, of its failure to be obvious.

The Restoration of 1660 is interesting largely for what it failed to restore. The King, the Lords and the Bishops returned to their thrones and titles; but the Church and society of which Laud had dreamed were no longer even a possibility. Never, since the Restoration, has the Church been in a position to pose as a separate estate of the realm. By a private agreement with Lord Chancellor Clarendon, Archbishop Sheldon renounced the claim of the Church to tax itself, and therewith the possibility of furthering a policy unsupported by Parliament. Laud's social policy was dropped, and the courts by which he had enforced it were destroyed. In 1689, when the divine right of bishops followed that of kings into limbo, even the theory of episcopal independence disappeared. In one respect only did Laud's policy seem to have succeeded, and that apparent success was in reality the confirmation of his failure. Laud had sought to increase the economic wealth and social status of the clergy. In this, during his own lifetime, he had failed; but with the Restoration an improvement in the economic position of the bishops (though not of the lower clergy) became evident. The long leases of episcopal lands extorted by Tudor courtiers were now falling in; the value of land was rising; and the bishops, having accepted the position of debenture-holders in the aristocracy, were allowed to enjoy their rewards. Social status followed closely upon wealth. When that magnificent toady, Lord Crewe, was ordained, Charles II expressed his pleasure that a gentleman was at last entering the Church. Crewe was soon bishop of Durham, and was the first aristocratic bishop since the Reformation. Bishop Compton was the second; and when Crewe died, full of years and compliance, a Talbot succeeded him on his throne at Durham. Thereafter the combination of mitre and ermine, of the Hon.

and the Rev., was too usual to excite notice. No inconvenient relics, no insistent voices, reminded the English church of its defeated prophet, William Laud. A few charities in Berkshire, some improvements in Oxford, a parish church or two restored—such were the lasting results of that tireless, devoted, impersonal, but narrow, bigoted and misguided career. Many a despised Elizabethan bishop, many a forgotten Victorian stockbroker, has left a more valuable legacy.

There are some who say that his conception of "the beauty of holiness," the decent, orderly ceremonial of the English Church, neither tawdry in its colour nor drab in its plainness, is his legacy. This may be so, or it may not. Such things derive more often from the long tradition of a people than from the policy of one man; and anyway there are other claimants. In Oxford, Laud certainly left his mark, in statutes, in organisation, and in stone. For two hundred years Oxford showed the impress of his mind; it was orthodox, clerical, and jacobite; and the only occasion when it strayed into intellectual originality, with its scientific studies in the days of Cromwell, was an exception which certainly cannot be charged to Laud.

It is sometimes said that the Oxford Movement was a Laudian revival, but this cannot be maintained except in trivial respects; for although it arose in Oxford, and although Laud was one of its heroes, there are fundamental differences between the two movements. Laud sought to control capitalist society, Newman to escape from it. Laud was practical, Newman contemplative. The one quality which redeems Laud's career, illuminating even his frailties, is his comprehensive conception of the unity of society, his sense of social justice, the very restlessness of his energy in seeking, however wrong-headedly, however unsuccessfully, to secure this practical end. The Oxford Movement had no social policy. The grinding of the faces of the poor never stretched the *pia mater* of Dr. Pusey.

It is this finality of failure, then, which really makes it impossible to do more than modify, and elaborate, the traditional view of Laud. However we turn him, from whatever angle we view the history of the seventeenth century, his failure is equally complete, and therefore his judgment of the forces he sought to control equally faulty. The anglo-catholics who dug him up from beneath the neglect of two centuries have indeed rescued his character from ignorant contempt; the Fabians have indeed re-interpreted the world which he sought so infelicitously to alter; but still his failure remains, clear, huge, and final—his gigantic misconception of the practical. It is impossible to refute altogether the charges of the puritan Lord Saye and the tory Lord Bolingbroke, that he never saw beyond the walls of St. John's College.

THE LONG PARLIAMENT IN ITS EARLY SESSIONS swept away those features of Charles I's Personal Rule that were most hateful to the Puritans. Such institutions of royal autocracy as the courts of Star Chamber and High Commission, such financial devices as ship money and impositions found few defenders, and it was not until the Puritan majority made clear its intention to reorganize the Established Church root and branch, abolishing the office of bishop, and to deprive the King of ancient and once undoubted prerogative powers that a royalist party came into existence. It was the formation of this party that made possible the Civil War, which broke out between the King's forces and those of Parliament in the summer of 1642. The noblemen who commanded the

Parliamentary armies early in the war did not desire to win a really decisive victory over the King's troops. An association was formed, however, comprising a number of the eastern counties of England, of which Oliver Cromwell was the guiding spirit, and a force which it raised, known as the "Ironsides," was put under his command. It became the most effective of the Parliamentary forces and won a great victory at Marston Moor in July, 1644. In the famous New Model Army, which was organized shortly thereafter and was to become eventually the dominant power in England, Cromwell held the office of lieutenant-general. It was this army that won the decisive battle of Naseby in June, 1645. Its extraordinary morale was inspired by religious fervor, and the great part played by Puritan preachers in building up this spirit is the subject of the following essay. The author, William Haller, now professor emeritus of English at Barnard College, has written and edited a number of indispensable volumes on the history of English Puritanism.

THE WORD OF GOD IN THE NEW MODEL ARMY
WILLIAM HALLER

At the close of 1644 the Long Parliament and the Westminster Assembly found themselves in a difficult position. The preachers had declared that, if they all did the will of the Lord in the church, He would surely bless the efforts of their army in the war against the King. But the church was still unreformed and the King undefeated. They could have peace at the risk of allowing Charles to regain control of the church. They could go on with the war at the cost of permitting religious differences among their own partisans to continue and spread. In other words, nothing could be settled so long as Charles kept the field and the fear of defeat hung over English and Scots, Parliament and Assembly, Presbyterians, Independents, and sectaries alike. The predicament was made to Cromwell's hand. The campaign of 1644, having ended in frustration, he returned to his place in the House of Commons and initiated the maneuvers which led to the reorganization of the army with Fairfax in command but in the event with Cromwell still as its driving force. The result was the victory the Assembly divines had looked for as the sign of

God's favor upon their efforts to reform the church but victory on terms which made reform of the church as they conceived it more difficult than ever. For Cromwell's accomplishment in war and politics was due to his gift for drawing upon those very energies of the spirit in himself and others which had been evoked in the people by Puritan preaching but which the ministerial caste was now striving to keep within bounds. He had succeeded in organizing victory not by curbing and containing the Puritan spirit but by giving it free play among the men under his command and by granting scope to its most characteristic modes of expression and organization. Hence the preaching of the Word in the parliamentary army as reconstituted in the New Model had not a little to do with the army's military success.

The Word had, of course, been preached in the army before Cromwell came to dominate it. Many noted divines went out with the regiments under Essex in 1642. They are described at Edgehill riding up and down and exhorting the soldiers "now if ever to stand to it, and fight for their Reli-

Reprinted by special permission from *Church History*, XIX (1950), 15-33. The footnotes which originally appeared with this essay have been omitted.

gion, Lawes, and Christian liberties." Edge-hill, however, settled nothing, and when the campaign was over, most of the preachers went back to their city pulpits and then presently to the great business of the Assembly. Baxter charges them with having quit the army out of desire for an easier, quieter life, but a deeper reason for their defection is indicated by an action of Baxter's own. We learn from him that at the beginning of the war the officers of Cromwell's newly raised troop of horse at Cambridge, "that famous Troop which he began his army with," about this time "purposed to make their Troop a gathered Church and they all subscribed an Invitation to me to be their Pastor." He refused the invitation with a reproof, in which he made plain "wherein my Judgement was against the Lawfulnesse and Convenience of their way."

Baxter heard no more of Cromwell's troop until after Naseby, and apparently thought no more of it, but Baillie took note that as the campaign of 1644 dragged on more and more of the soldiery were, as he said, seduced to Independency and worse. As to Cromwell, he admitted with his unfailing candor that the man was "a very wise and active head, universally well beloved, as religious and stout" and that "most of the sojours who loved new wayes putt themselves under his command." The new ways, however, were not so new as they appeared in Scottish eyes. They were the natural out-come of the Puritan movement, and they were supremely apposite to the situation at hand. Looking back on this time, after the Restoration, Baxter thought that all the mischief that had befallen in his time had started with the seduction of honest, ignorant men in the army by a few self-conceited fellows, "hatcht up among the old Separatists," and that all the trouble might have been prevented if moderate, sound, learned ministers had stayed with the troops from the beginning. But his notion that "then all the Fire was in one Spark" and might easily have been stamped out was a delusion. Actually not all the ministers did leave the army after 1642; not all who remained or joined later were extreme heretics or separatists; not all who deviated from orthodoxy were ignorant conceited firebrands. But aside from that, those who did desert would probably have been no more successful in quenching the Word as preached among the soldiery than they were elsewhere. Not every man recruited or impressed into the New Model was a Puritan saint, but the men favored by Cromwell for positions of trust and leadership had the root of the matter in them and the rest at least knew how saints were supposed to feel and behave and what rewards they might expect here and hereafter. All were familiar with the common procedures of the godly for banding together in order to help themselves to edification by the Word.

RICHARD BAXTER: Presbyterian writer and divine who served as a chaplain in the Parliamentary army during the Civil War. He believed in limited monarchy, and when Charles I was beheaded he favored the accession of Prince Charles. He lived until 1691 —long enough to rejoice in the accession of William III.

GANGRAENA: Work by the Puritan pamphleteer Thomas Edwards. Published in three parts in 1646, it is a valuable historical source. Writing at a time of intense sectarian activity, Edwards estimated that there were almost two hundred sects in England. His work aimed to catalogue and expose their "errors, heresies, blasphemies, and pernicious practices."

WESTMINSTER ASSEMBLY: Group of English and Scottish divines and laymen which convened in 1643 and sat intermittently until 1649. It came into being as a result of a bargain. Parliament accepted the Solemn League and Covenant, and the Scots promised aid in the war against the King. The Assembly recommended the organization in England of a church of distinctly Presbyterian type.

Not Presbyterianism as conceived by the Westminster divines, with its rigid parochialism and its tight network of classes and synods, but Independency in all its protean manifestations, the irrepressible spontaneous aggregation of likeminded folk in shifting voluntary groups, seeking comfort and enlightenment for themselves from the preaching of the gospel, this was or was rapidly becoming the accustomed English way. It was a way adaptable to unprecedented conditions whether of civil war or life in the American wilderness, and not the least of its merits was that it gave scope for variations upon the doctrine of grace, better suited, or so it seemed, to the needs of men under such conditions than strict Calvinistic orthodoxy. Cromwell's troopers knew how to form themselves into what they chose to call gathered churches, and though Baxter refused to serve them, they had no trouble finding others to take the place he refused, ministers and graduates as well as men from their own ranks, officers and common soldiers, graced with gifts for expounding Scripture, without benefit of clergy but not without benefit of clerical example.

Unauthorized preaching had, of course, steadily increased everywhere ever since the fall of prelacy, and the New Model army had hardly got under way in 1645 when Parliament at last adopted an ordinance, long pending, designed to impose stricter control. The ordinance provided that no one was to be allowed to preach unless he had been ordained or approved as a person intending to enter the ministry and seeking to make trial of his ability, and orders were given that the rule was to be strictly enforced in the army. Yet the ordinance soon appeared in print, accompanied by an anonymous but revealing statement, called a "vindication." This assured the people that Parliament did not intend to repress godly instruction in the army at a time when the need for and the shortage of preachers were both so great. To be sure, preaching according to the usual rule, opening, dividing, and applying texts, was work for ordained ministers only. But no one was

forbidden to read and expound God's Word to those under his charge, "as suppose a Master to his Family, a Captain to his Company, a Collonell to his Regiment, a Generall to his Army, a King to his People, if he hath the grace to do it." Nor were people forbidden to gather for prayer and mutual instruction or to use and improve their talents as occasion might arise, each in his proper sphere.

> You therefore Gentlemen of the Souldiery in the field . . . you may both pray and speak too in the head of your Companies, Regiments and Armies, you may deliver the piety of your souls, the welgrounded confidence of your hearts, the valour of your minds, in such Orations, in such Liberties of Speech, as may best inspirit the men that follow you, with such a religious and undaunted animation as may render them unconquerable before the proudest enemy.

Thus animated, the New Model army took the field in the early spring of 1645. On June 14 it overwhelmed the King at Naseby, and within a year had brought every remaining royal force and stronghold in England to surrender or destruction. Shortly after the victory at Naseby, Baxter, having spent the interval as lecturer to the garrison at Coventry, went to the army on business of his own and learned with consternation what he took to be the consequences of his own and his fellow ministers' neglect. In all chief places of command he found none but hot sectaries, Cromwell's chief favorites, and when he met Cromwell he was coldly received and rebuked for his former refusal to serve the now famous victorious regiment. Troubled in conscience, he accepted appointment as chaplain to Whalley's regiment, and followed the army during the remaining stages of the war, preaching and disputing, up to the fall of Worcester. He then dropped out and, exhausted, ill, alone, in fear of death, with no book at hand but the Bible, bent his thoughts, he says, on his everlasting rest and the drawing up of his own funeral sermon. When he had composed what finally amounted to the first sixty-eight printed pages of his *Saints Everlasting Rest,* he found himself still alive and still full of his recent experience and the thoughts it provoked. The result was the remaining 788 pages of that work. But this was not all. He continued to occupy himself up to the Restoration with preaching and writing against what he conceived to be the errors and confusion in the church which followed Cromwell's rise to power. In the first part of his autobiography, said to have been written "for the most part" in 1664, he set down the earliest circumstantial, though bitterly hostile, record of the activities and ideas of the leading preachers in the New Model army at the moment of victory.

As early as June 1646, in a letter which found its way into Edwards' *Gangraena,* Baxter was reporting upon these matters. He found preachers in the army, he says, telling the soldiers that Christ judges only by the heart, that magistrates have nothing to do with the conversion of sinners or the reformation of the church, that ministers require no authorization save anointment of the Spirit and the acceptation of the saints, that universities are useless, tithes should be abolished, and the punishment of blasphemy left to God.

He was distressed, he tells us, to find so many honest men of little knowledge and weak judgment making it "too much of their Religion to talk for this Opinion and for that," for free grace and free will, for democracy, but above everything else for liberty of conscience, "that is, that the Civil Magistrate had nothing to do to determine of anything in Matters of Religion, by constraint or restraint, but every Man might not only hold, but preach and do in Matters of Religion what he pleased." But perhaps the most distressing thing about this state of affairs was that every one of the notions by which men were being carried away seemed but a distortion of, or false deduction from, some truth which wiser teachers had been setting forth for the enlightenment of precisely such persons. *The Saints Everlasting Rest,* springing directly out of Baxter's own experience as an army preacher, illustrates the errors he abhorred hardly less than the truths he embraced and shows how nearly related the two were to one another. The vital element in Baxter's belief appears in the funeral sermon for himself which comprises the opening chapters of that work. This was the conviction that Christ, having entered into his soul, had given him the power to know what God required of him and to do as he was required. Blest by grace with faith and the ability to act by the light of faith, he was assured, as he thought on his deathbed, of the everlasting rest in paradise, where there would be no more need for him or anyone to pray or preach—". . . The Unregenerate past hope; the Saints past fear, for ever."

To Baxter, as to many another Puritan enthusiast who had come under the combined spell of Paul and Plato, saving truth was something that could be apprehended, paradise a state that could be regained, by little and little, but certainly in the end. And yet the too lively apprehension of bliss in the hereafter could lead to misunderstanding and much trouble in the here and now. He found too many men in the army so overpersuaded that they had Christ within that they concluded they had but to reach forth their hands and retake paradise, or whatever else they might erroneously conceive to be rightfully theirs, at once, just as they had taken Bristol or Basing or Worcester. That is to say, they were plunged into mortal error, from which he was to spend the years trying to rescue them, on the crucial point of justification. "A great difficulty," he says, "riseth in our way," the difficulty, namely, of determining "in what sense is our Improvement of our Talent, our well-doing, our overcoming . . . alleged as a Reason for our Coronation and Glory?" The Puritan preachers before Baxter had perhaps made too certain that common men should understand that the justification and glorification of the saints followed inevitably upon their vocation and sanctification, and that their calling was sealed in the gifts entrusted to them. At any rate, fired by such doctrine, the men of the New Model had shown that, whether gentlemen or not, they had a gift for winning battles, and whether ministers and graduates or not, a talent for expounding Scripture. And victory, without tarrying for magistrates or ministers, Parliament or Assembly, seemed to have justified their faith. Hence, or so it appeared to Baxter, they jumped to the conclusion that the effect of grace was immediate, total, and absolute, that the second coming of Christ was momentarily to be expected, and that the liberation and crowning of the saints was to be looked for not in the indefinite future or upon terms but at once and unconditionally.

The full effect of all this on the men in the New Model would become clearer as soon as Parliament supplied them with a practical grievance and pamphleteers and agitators showed them how to transpose their faith into political as well as military action. Our concern here is with the preachers who filled the soldiers' minds with the errors Baxter deplored and so prepared them for the Levellers. Who accepted the invitation to dispense the Word to Cromwell's troopers which Baxter rejected, we do not exactly know. Nor can we point to any sermon in print before 1645 which Cromwell or his men can be said to have heard. There is, however, no lack of evidence as to who the preachers were who carried all before them in the New Model at the moment of its triumph or as to the nature of their utterances. The two whom Baxter found holding sway at headquarters directly after Naseby were John Saltmarsh and William Dell. The former especially seemed to him the prime source of those errors concerning justification which led to the anarchy which presently ensued.

On the eve of the Long Parliament, Saltmarsh, a graduate of Magdalene College, Cambridge, was still the conforming incumbent of a Yorkshire parish, but after the spiritual awakening described in his *Holy Discoveries and Flames* (1640), he embraced the Puritan cause. Under the Parliament he was appointed to a rectory in Kent but refused to accept tithes and by 1645 had joined the army. The substance of his preaching from that point on is to be found in the dozen or more tracts which he published, some of them more than once, between January 1645 and May 1647, the year of his death, with titles such as *Dawnings of Light* (1644), *Free-Grace* (1645), *Smoke in the Temple* (1646), and *Sparkles of Glory* (1647). The antecedents of Saltmarsh's ideas, as Baxter and as Rutherford with pedantic thoroughness pointed out, were not to be mistaken. He supplied the current version of the type of heterodoxy which had dogged Calvinistic orthodoxy from Geneva to Naseby and had most recently been heard in England from such preachers as John Everard, Giles Randall, and John Eaton. These were the men whose ideas had attracted the interest and sympathy of Lord Brooke, the courtly idealist, and of William Walwyn, the middle-class humanist. The truth was that antinomians, Anabaptists, familists, or whatever they might be called, and however they might be assailed as upstart, unruly, ignorant eccentrics, represented as ancient and as vital a form of Christian piety and doctrine as did the most orthodox adherent of the Westminster Assembly. The Puritan brotherhood had long been telling the people that, unless grace came to them by the will of God through Jesus Christ, they could not hope to be saved from judgment upon the sin to which they were born. The preachers had described the inner experience by which alone a man might know that grace had indeed come to him. Saltmarsh was one of the long succession of eager souls who found liberation and strength in pressing on to the conclusion that the grace men were told to hope for was theirs for the taking and that they did not need to wait for certitude until learned divines had settled all the fine points among themselves. All a man needed for his salvation was to know and love Christ within his own breast, in his fellow-men, and in God's creation. Salvation came, Saltmarsh said, by "experiment of Jesus Christ," to each man for himself by himself, the experience of each being of equal validity with that of every other man and the sufficient key to the mysteries of God's printed word. "The spirits of such as possess Christ" were the "counterpane" of the Scriptures, wherein "truth answers to truth, as in water face answers to face." "And the more Christ is known, and that love of God to the Sons of men which was manifest in the flesh, the more that glorious liberty from the Law, Sin, and Satan, is manifested in the soul."

There is no truth but Christ and no Christ but the Christ within; yet Christ manifests himself to no man once and for all but to each only by degrees. Truth is single and entire; yet it "shines forth in many streams of glory, and opens like day."

All outward administrations, whether as to Religion, or to natural, civil, and moral things, are only the visible appearances of God. . . . And God does not fix himself upon any one form or outward dispensation, but at his own will and pleasure comes forth in such and such an administration, and goes out of it, and leaves it, and takes up another. . . . The pure, comprehensive Christian, is one who grows up with God from administration to administration, and so walks with God in all his removes and spiritual increasings and flowings; and such are weak and in the flesh who tarry behind, worshipping that form or administration out of which God is departed.

It follows that truth cannot be made to prevail by argument or by violence but only through its own successive manifestations in the spirits of men. Churches and ministers err when they suppose not that they possess truth but that they possess it once and for all in its entirety. Magistrates err when they forbid truth to shine as it will in the hearts of men. The duty of the state is simply to maintain peace so that every man may seek truth for himself and make it known in his own way. Hence every man must be free to preach, and the press should be free to those who lack pulpits to preach from. Hence, too, no man should be despised either for gifts and learning or for the lack of them; "the spirit is in Paul as well as Peter, in both as well as one." Baxter's comment on the dangers likely to arise from such extreme deductions from the doctrine of Christian liberty is significant.

Some think the truth will not thrive among us, till every man have leave to speak both in Presse and Pulpit that please: God forbid that we should ever see that day! If ten mens voyces be louder then one, then would the noyse of Errour drown the voyce of Truth: . . . For the godly, compared with the ungodly, are not neer so few as the men of cleer understanding, in comparison of the ignorant: And they are the most forward to speake, that know least.

Baxter perceived that, if the ideas Saltmarsh was preaching to the army were to prevail, the end would be to reduce the ecclesiastical state to the purest democracy, and democracy seemed to him nothing but anarchy.

Saltmarsh was half a poet and excelled in lyrical, hortatory, mystical expression of the ideas that inspired the saints of the New Model. But the saints of the New Model passed readily from the belief that Christ was imminent in their breasts to certainty that the Lord was present in their ranks; and since their opponents in the field proved in fact unable to stand against them, the matter seemed to be put beyond question. The sermons of William Dell gave positive expression to such practical deductions from the doctrine of free justification. After graduating from Emmanuel College, Dell underwent a change of heart and joined the New Model in 1645. In May of that year he was saying that, as Christ did not suffer the apostles to go forth until he had armed them with the Holy Ghost, so he still gives power to His servants, more to some than to others but enough to each for the task in hand, and a little "will inable a man to doe great things, far greater then the world suspects or imagines." The conclusion was inescapable. "We may judge of our calling to any business by the power we have received from Christ for it," which was to say, by our success.

The preacher was speaking at this point of ministers of the church. A year later he was saying the same sort of thing to the embattled saints of the New Model.

> I have seen more of the presence of God in that Army, then amongst any people that ever I conversed with in my life . . . we have seen his goings, and observed his very footsteps: for he hath dwelt among us, and marched in the head of us, and counsel'd us, and hath gone along with us step by step from Naseby.

From this Dell went on just as positively to apply to the problem of the church the ideas and practices which had produced such convincing results in the war. He arrived at a ringing statement of the conception of the church as based solely upon the purely voluntary association of the elect brought together by the Spirit alone. Thus he pointed clearly to that ecclesiastical anarchy which Baxter and many besides feared as the certain result of popular obsession with the doctrine of free justification. The true church consisted only of such as had the Spirit of God within them, and the Spirit, though manifested in a diversity of gifts and dispensations, is the same Spirit in all and brings all together in love and peace. But "God doth not now make any people, or kindred, or nation his Church." The church is gathered out of every people, "and none can be stones of this building, but those that are first elect, and after made precious, through a new birth, and the gift of the spirit."

This was, of course, to welcome the disintegration of the ecclesiastical state and extend indefinitely the principle which had worked so well in the army. It was to declare that there could be no true church which was not a "gathered" church, and Dell drove the point home in a fast-day sermon delivered to the members of Parliament at St. Margaret's in November 1646. He told them that reformation could begin only with the reformation of sinners. But since only Christ can deal with sin, reformation must wait upon his continuing progressive triumph over the evil that harbors in every human breast. Rulers are as helpless against Antichrist as other men, and any attempt by the state to govern or reform the church is doomed to failure. "Clergy-power" formerly endeavored to claim support of the temporal authority by crying "Destroy one, Destroy both." The prelates were wont to say, "No Bishop, no King." Their successors still cry, "No minister, no Magistrate." So he admonishes Parliament not to suffer the victorious saints of the army to be oppressed by those "who would use your power against us, not for you, but for themselves."

Thus in November 1646 Parliament heard from the pulpit of St. Margaret's the same doctrine it had heard so roundly condemned in the same place two years before when set forth by Roger Williams in *The Bloudy Tenent* and by William Walwyn in *The Compassionate Samaritane*. When Dell said that only Christ could deal with sin, he meant in effect that sin could be dealt with only through the preaching of the gospel. The effect of Cromwell's leadership in reorganizing the army for victory over the King was to remove the last restrictions upon preaching in both the army and the community. Practically everyone was free to use whatever gifts he possessed for attracting listeners eager to hear that Christ was at hand, that no matter what the learned or well-placed might say to the contrary, they might be his chosen ones, his true church. It was still true that many preachers were ordained ministers, but from now on the gathered church was not necessarily derived from, or associated with, a parish church or settled congregation. Nor had such groups become as yet firmly organized into the dissenting communions of a later period. They were still shifting, amorphous groups, made up of people uprooted and set adrift by revolution and civil war, congregating about individual preachers and flocking at will from one to another. The preacher was all-important and essentially uncontrolled by any authority. Given a man with the necessary qualities of leadership, and the group presently cohered, joined with other groups similarly circumstanced, and formed a sect. Sects flourished by offering their proselytes the sense of distinction and security that came from feeling themselves a peculiar people, called to mount the ark of salvation in a doomed and perishing world. From being lowly and despised, they expected to see their situation reversed when Christ came to rule the world, purified and renewed. Or, unconvinced by the claims of any single group to be the true church, though recognizing the claims of each to some measure of Christ's spirit, one might choose to wait, content to possess Christ within oneself while still seeking for the visible manifestation of Him according to His own will in His own time. Practically speaking, this was to resolve the church completely and finally into the individual, every man becoming, so to speak, a church to himself. For the seeker, the only solution to the problem of the church was the toleration of churches within the framework of the state. A logical corollary to that conception was one which called for representative civil government democratically elected.

Many other preachers, though not all in exact agreement with Saltmarsh and Dell, arose in the army or on its periphery after 1645, but the most famous and the closest to Cromwell was Hugh Peters. He sprang from the same origins, subject to the same influences, as other members of the Puritan brotherhood. After graduating from Trinity College, Cambridge, he was first struck, he tells us, with a sense of his sinful estate upon hearing a sermon at St. Paul's, after which he was "quieted" by Thomas Hooker, further enlightened by Sibbes, Gouge, and Davenport, and then presented by a disciple to a lectureship in London. In 1627 he fled to Holland, where he associated briefly with William Ames and ministered to an English congregation. In 1635 he emigrated to New England and succeeded Roger Williams at Salem. He was intimate with the Winthrops, father and son. He witnessed the excitement caused by the antinomians and took part in the examination and trial of Mrs. Hutchinson. He was an active preacher, approved by his congregation, but he also busied himself in public affairs and was sent back to England as colony agent in 1641, just in time to take active part in the revolutionary cause. After serving as an army chaplain in the campaign of 1644, he joined the New Model, was probably present at Naseby, and served from this point on not only as chaplain and preacher but also as confidential agent and emissary, though the messenger sent up to London with the news of that victory was another preacher, Edward Bowles. But the two men went together as chaplains under Fairfax on the expedition that immediately followed for the recovery of the west. Both held forth to the troops the day before the storming of Bridgewater (July 20-22), and Peters was up and exhorting the men on the morning of the assault.

What Baillie called his "malapert rashness," his gifts of utterance and of showmanship, along with his interest in affairs, made Peters invaluable to the army commanders. He became the chief exponent and defender of their acts and policies in both church and state. "This man," Edwards wrote, "is an Ubiquitary, here and there, in this Countrey, and that Countrey, in the Army, and at London." He was called "Soliciter Generall for the Sectaries," "Vicar Generall and Metropolitane both in New and Old England," "the new Arch-bishop of Canterbury." Lilburne said that he was one of the principal guides and spokesmen of the great men of the army, that he lay in their bosoms, knew their secrets, and trumpeted abroad their principles and tenets. Of all the preachers who had spoken and written against the King, he was the only one who was made to pay the supreme penalty at the Restoration. The effect of all his stirrings and appearances and of the legends to which they gave rise has been, however, to obscure somewhat Peters' part in the religious life of the army. Though he busied himself with preaching along with all his other activities, none of his army sermons has come down to us in authentic form in print. His chief publications were the reports he brought up to London from time to time of the army's successes and needs. On March 21, 1646, he came with the news of the final putting down of all resistance in the west, issued in print as *Master Peters Messuage from Sir Thomas Fairfax.* Parliament voted that as his reward he should have an estate of £200 a year out of the lands of the Earl of Worcester, and it invited him, along with Joseph Caryl, to preach before both houses, the Assembly, and the lord mayor, aldermen, and common council at a special thanksgiving service in Christ Church. The sermon was presently published with the title *Gods Doings, and Mans Duty.* In theme and temper it gave premonition of the two tracts issued by Peters on behalf of the army and its commanders as their differences with Parliament grew acute. These were called *Mr. Peters Last Report of the English Wars* ([August 27] 1646) and *A Word for the Armie. And two words to the Kingdome* ([October 11] 1647).

Peters does not, in any of these writings, give direct expression to the doctrine of the indwelling Christ, but we are not to conclude that he had little interest or belief in free justification. He is the supreme example among the preachers of the manner in which acceptance of that doctrine relieved men from the confusions and inhibitions bred by doctrinal disputes and released them for revolutionary action. To believe was necessary if they were to act, but to act was impossible if they had to wait for all points of difference to be resolved by disputation among learned divines. "We know no more then we Practice," Peters said, "yet we shall never practice without knowledge." In his sermon to Parliament he made plain that knowledge as he conceived it and as the army preachers had set it forth to the soldiers had been confirmed by practical results, the force of which there was no mistaking. Now, however, the problem was different, not merely how to draw upon faith for motives to effective military action but how to compose the differences which had been so enormously complicated and exacerbated by the army's success and by the authority which that success gave to the religious conceptions prevailing in its ranks. The problem, for which the army leaders, especially Cromwell, felt a peculiar responsibility, was to make peace among the victors in the struggle against the King, and Peters' task for the moment was to present the army leaders' views on that subject. To this end he began in his thanksgiving sermon on April 2 by drawing the obvious deductions from his text, Psalm 31:23, "Love the Lord all ye his Saints: for the Lord preserveth the faithful, and plenteously rewardeth the proud doer." All the endeavors of the enemy have come to nothing: "the Parliament is not destroyed, the City stands, the Gospel is preached . . . Oh, my Lords you are not at Oxford, led up and down as Sampson, to be looked at by children."

> You have the Army you wished for, and the Successes you desired. Oh the blessed change we see, that can travell now from Edinburgh, to the lands end in Cornwall, who not long since were blockt up at our doors! To see the highways occupied again; to hear the Carter whistling to his toiling team; to see the weekly Carrier attend his constant mart; to see the hils rejoycing, the valleys laughing!

But the obvious deduction from all this was that the principles which had worked so well in war would work equally to everyone's advantage if applied to the vexed problem of religion. Were the issues that divided the church so important that they should be permitted to set Parliament against the men who had procured the liberty and safety of the kingdom? "You are still buzz'd in the ear with a desperate encrease of Errour," but there would be fewer errors, differences, and sects, if men did not think them so many. The only enemy was Antichrist, the only error pride, the only remedy love. The practical steps necessary for the establishment of peace were to promote preaching, relieve the poor, reform the laws, and regulate the press. But preaching, not discipline or polemics, came first. "If I know anything, what you have gotten by the sword, must be maintained by the word, by which English Christians are made."

Busybody though he was, Peters, nevertheless, as the editors of his autobiography said of him, had in him "a Root of Grace." That root of grace, the bottom of sheer godliness in the man which was probably what won Cromwell's confidence, appears best in the little book he wrote while waiting to be executed, *A Dying Fathers Last Legacy to an Onely Child* (1661). As Baxter had done, but without Baxter's superabundant rhetoric, Peters, believing death to be at hand, described the regeneration enjoyed by the saints through their union with Christ. Nothing could have been more perfectly in the vein of traditional Puritan piety. The child is told above all things to be "perfect in Romans 8," the starting point for so many sermons, spiritual biographies, and improving treatises. To the uncomprehending modern mind, no conception of man's destiny seems to offer less hope to the generality of men. To resilient saints like Peters, even while waiting to be hanged, drawn, and quartered, nothing offered greater comfort. The child is to note especially the first verse—"there is therefore now no condemnation to them which are in Jesus Christ"—and the twenty-eighth—"wee know that all things work together for good, to them that love God." "The preaching of these Truths," he says, "have been my greatest Advantage, and of most benefit to Others." For Peters, though he had sided against Mrs. Hutchinson, made after his return to England the easy demarche from Calvinist orthodoxy to the notion so alarming to Baxter that Christ comes to his chosen ones without limiting conditions and that the chosen are not the few but the many, the simple, the poor, and the young. He sends to fetch the fatherless child from the ditch, leads him from humiliation to glory, and seats him at the heavenly table.

The child for whom the book was intended is also instructed with many homely similitudes and pithy sayings, in the traditional code of behavior supposed to follow upon effectual calling. She is to gather "a Little English Library" of approved authors —Dod, Sibbes, Preston, Gouge, Thomas Hooker, Thomas Goodwin, Baxter himself. She is to keep a book in which she is to set down each night before she sleeps, "the Lords Gracious Providence and Dealings with you; and your dealings with him." She is to bear in mind that affliction keeps us waking, "as the Thorn to the singing Bird," that conscience calls us up to labor, "as the Day the Lark, and the Lark the Husbandman." Being a woman, she is to keep at home and not be like the squirrel, "leaping from Tree to Tree, and Bough to Bough." She is to remember that marriage "hath many Concernments in it, where Goodness and Suitableness are the primary ingredients," and that the conjugal yoke "must still be lin'd with more Love to make the draught easie." As "the little Needle will draw a long tail of Thread after it," so "little sins may be followed with great sorrows," but "a very very little Grace (if true) is saving: a little Growth (if right) is comforting," and "a little little grain" of faith "like Mustard-seed will do Wonders." But perhaps the best expression of the temper which enabled such sanguine, forth-putting, executive spirits to turn the doctrine and the piety of St. Paul to their own uses is Peters' disquisition, while waiting for the executioner, on the vanity of earthly things.

Many dying men speak much about the Vanity of the World: But truly, as I would not die in a pet, so I would not quarrel with or leave the World, because I could be no greater in it, but because I could not do, nor be better in it, and that God is pleased I should leave it for a better: I wish I had never been vain in a vain World, but I appeal to, and plead with, Christ for my peace. *So use the World, as if you used it not:* for the World hath a principle of decay in all the glory of it: Dote not on it, my poor Child.

But the greatest witness to the doctrine of free grace as preached by such men as Peters, Dell, and Saltmarsh in the army was Cromwell himself, as authentic a Puritan saint as ever confounded the Puritan brotherhood with the consequences of their own teachings. As early as 1638 he could declare "my soul is with the congregation of the firstborn, my body rests in hope, and if here I may honour my God either by doing or suffering, I shall be most glad." He said this while at the same time confessing, "I hated godliness, yet God had mercy on me." Many a man, after such an experience, turned to preaching, but Cromwell was an East Anglian squire, one of an extensive clan whose members characteristically became not preachers themselves, but patrons and supporters of preachers. Holding himself always accountable for the gifts that befell him, he sought relief for the tensions within him in vehement public activity, in his neighborhood, in Parliament, and finally in the army. Not with deaf ears had he heard Marshall, Calamy, and other preachers tell Parliament that the Lord had laid his command upon its members and had covenanted to acknowledge obedience with victory. Cromwell had taken to heart the argument that the law written by God in the breast must be heeded even at the cost of making war on the King. Consequently, with no taste for speculation and debate, he went off in 1642 and raised a troop of horse, which formed itself into a "gathered" church. By the time Presbyterians and Independents were locking horns in the Assembly, he was determining, by the same pragmatical test the preachers had commended, which elements in their teachings were useful and valid in the situation immediately at hand. He found that the habit his countrymen had learned of banding together in their own way in order to help themselves to the preaching of the Word was as though designed for the predicament that resulted from the dragging out of the war. His own religious position seems to have come most closely to that of the seekers who felt unable to accept in full the claims of any communion to be the true church. But this position was not incompatible with acceptance of the principle of the "gathered" church, and accepting that principle Cromwell was able to enlist the kind of men he needed to forge an effective instrument of war. That he knew what he was about, his own words testify. "You must get men of a spirit," he told John Hampden after Edgehill, "or else I am sure you will be beaten still . . . I raised such men as had the fear of God before them, and made some conscience what they did."

In Cromwell, however, as in other converts to the doctrine of grace, the dynamics of Puritan faith outran the restraints of Puritan discipline. In September 1644, when things looked black, he wrote, "the Lord is our strength, and in Him is all our hope. Pray for us." In April 1645, while the outcome still hung in the balance, he wrote, "God is not enough owned. We look too much to men and visible helps." And after Naseby, he could still write, "Sir, this is none other but the hand of God; and to him alone belongs the glory." Cromwell, like Peters, had a root of godliness in him. But he showed what strange alarming fruit that stock could produce. His first thought, always, was to get the business of the Lord, as he saw it, done rather than defined or thought out. Yet the inner compulsion to act and to defend what he had done or proposed to do drove him to take more and more extreme positions. These he arrived at pragmatically but none the less consistently with the logic and historic development of the Puritan movement. Thus he became the exponent in action of the most far-reaching tenets of the Puritan pulpit itself—the equality of men under God, the immanence of the Holy Spirit in the individual, the spiritual sufficiency of the individual without other mediation than the light within and perhaps the Scriptures, the liberty of conscience, the moral imperative implied in gifts and opportunities, the instant, unfailing supervention of providence in human affairs. These principles pointed inevitably to the attenuation of the ministerial function in religious life and of the state's responsibility for the integrity of the church. One would not dare to say that Cromwell had thought these things out to their remotest consequences before undertaking to raise his first troop of horse, if indeed he ever did, or that he kept strictly to them when the responsibility for restoring order to the nation fell into his hands, but the logic of events drove him to acknowledge, assert, and act upon such principles until he had beaten down every opponent he could reach.

His acknowledgements are famous. "I had rather have a plain russet-coated captain," he wrote to the Suffolk committee in August 1643, "that knows what he fights for, and loves what he knows, than that which you call a gentleman and is nothing else. I honour a gentleman that is so indeed." "Take heed of being sharp," he wrote to Crawford in March 1644, "or too easily sharpened by others, against those to whom you can object little but that they square not with you in every opinion concerning matters of religion." "He that ventures his life for the liberty of his country," he wrote to the House of Commons after Naseby, "I wish he trust God for the liberty of his conscience, and you for the liberty he fights for," and again, "when I saw the enemy draw up and march in gallant order toward us, and we a company of poor ignorant men . . . I could not . . . but smile out to God in praises, in assurance of victory, because God would, by things that are not, bring to naught things that are." And in the dispatch to Parliament after the taking of Bristol, he put into a single paragraph every essential point in the argument for spiritual liberty under the protection of the state. "Presbyterians, Independents, all had here the same spirit of faith and prayer; . . . they agree here, know no names of difference: pity it is it should be otherwise anywhere. All that believe, have the real unity, which is most glorious, because inward and spiritual, in the Body, and to the Head." Thus the spirit which the Puritan preachers had first evoked found the next stage for its development, after the Westminster Assembly, in the New Model army, and thus Cromwell, speaking from the experience of the army, voiced what was to prove in the end the only escape from the problem which the preachers had created but could not themselves remedy.

THE QUESTIONS THAT PRESENTED THEMSELVES to the minds of Englishmen at the outbreak of the Great Civil War and during its course (1642-1646) could not be reduced to the simple issue of liberty versus tyranny. Traditional attachment to the Church of England and traditional loyalty to the King counted for much, and many of those who had taken part in the overthrow of royal autocracy in the early days of the Long Parliament now took Charles' side. Disinterested patriots were to be found among Cavaliers and Roundheads alike, as were self-seeking adventurers. The issues of the day were naturally

STUART TIMES

reflected in the writings that were produced while the war was in progress. Most of these writings were propagandist and controversial in character, and they have long since been forgotten, except by historians who specialize in the period. As to the enduring body of English literature, it was enriched above all by John Milton's *Areopagitica* (1644), a classic defense of freedom of the press. For the most part, however, the literary tradition during the age of the Puritan Revolution was carried on by the Cavaliers; few eminent writers, other than Milton, were associated with the Roundhead cause. In the following essay, which originated as a radio program of the British Broadcasting Corporation, Miss C. V. Wedgwood examines the impact of the Puritan Revolution on the history of English literature. One of the most creative and productive historical writers in contemporary Britain, Miss Wedgwood is the author of *Strafford* (1935), *The Thirty Years' War* (1939), *Richelieu and the French Monarchy* (1950), and *Seventeenth-Century English Literature* (1950).

LITERATURE DURING THE GREAT CIVIL WAR
C. V. WEDGWOOD

I. CAVALIER SATIRISTS AND POETS

The Great Civil War between King Charles I and his Parliament could hardly have occurred at a happier moment in the history of the English language. This eccentric cause for congratulation was appreciated by at least one contemporary. A writer who in the midst of the conflict issued a pamphlet called *Vindex Anglicus,* or a Vindication of the English language, exclaims:

> What matchless and incomparable pieces of eloquence hath this time of Civil War afforded! Came there ever from a prince's pen such exact pieces as are His Majesty's declarations? Were there ever speeches uttered in better language, and sweeter expressions than those of the noble and learned Lord Digby and some other worthy personages?

No doubt exists as to this author's political views; he was certainly a Royalist. The matchless pieces of eloquence belong to the King and his friends. Dispassionate search among contemporary papers does not fail to show quite a number of exact pieces and sweet expressions from Parlia-

mentarian pens or lips. Milton's *Areopagitica* has, for instance, a stronger claim on the attention of posterity than anything by Digby or the King.

The author of *Vindex Anglicus* was none the less right in thinking that the Civil War came at a good time for literature. The English language had reached a rare perfection as an instrument both in prose and poetry, and still showed few signs of wear. Its idioms were in mint condition; it was not clogged with tired phrases, loaded with abstractions or weighted down with passive constructions. Moreover, writers had never before, and have perhaps never since, been quite so thick on the ground as they were in the decade which immediately preceded the war, the peaceful sixteen-thirties. They were not all very good writers; the purist might, and indeed did, complain that there were too many amateurs, especially at the universities—young men

> Pumping themselves for one term's noise as dry
> As if they made their wills in poetry.

They moved in cliques, almost in droves, about the Court, about the two universities and, in London, about the Inns of Court.

Reprinted by special permission from The Listener, May 11 and May 18, 1950.

They also circled about the great country houses where a surprising number of the English gentry and nobility were translating the classics, composing sonnets, meditating epigrammatically on death, or celebrating their own wives or each other's sisters in commendatory verses. This hubbub of writers, this perpetual interchange of verses and choice pieces in manuscript, could hardly be expected to die down merely because there was a civil war. *Inter arma silent poetae:* certainly not.

Moreover, most of these writers were men of active, enquiring minds who were deeply concerned with the issues of the war: with the legal question of right and wrong between King and Parliament, or still more with the religious question of Puritanism and Independency against an organised national church. Emotionally and philosophically almost every thinking man, and therefore almost every writer, was profoundly involved in the clash of opinion. Thus, there was an immediate diversion of these fresh, varied—if often rather light—talents into political controversy. One of the poets, John Hall, expresses what most of them felt:

Pray let m' alone. What, do you think can I
Be still while pamphlets thus like hailstones fly
About mine ears?

Evidently he could not, and neither could his contemporaries. Lyrical metre and metaphysical conceit were enlisted in political service. In the words of George Wither the conflict had changed

The bays of helicon and myrtles mild
To pricking hawthorns and to hollies wild.

The change did not necessarily alter the character or preoccupations of the writers. Private jokes and old rivalries were carried on into the war. Some old score was evidently being paid off in the most good-natured way imaginable when the Royalist Sir John Denham appealed to the King to spare the life of the Parliamentarian poet George Wither on the grounds that while Wither lived no one could say that *he* was the worst poet in England. Denham himself soon discovered in the war an easy talent for ironical verse very unlike the moralising of his peace-time vein. He wrote the best and one of the earliest of the Cavalier attacks on the lying newsletters which were issued by the hundred in London. Their readers expected at least one Royalist general slain for their pennyworth and the pamphleteers obliged, regardless of truth. A particular skirmish in a thunderstorm between the Royalist Hopton and the Roundhead Chudleigh in the west was widely and incorrectly represented as a miraculous victory for Parliament. Denham took this up in some light-hearted cantering verses:

Do you not know, not a fortnight ago,
How they bragged of a Western Wonder,
How a hundred and ten slew five thousand men

AREOPAGITICA: Pamphlet (1644) by John Milton written in the form of a speech addressed to Parliament for "the liberty of unlicensed printing." In it he penned one vast indictment of censorship; and in it he demonstrated his effectiveness as a prose writer, although he insisted that to write prose was for him to write with his left hand. One of the most frequently quoted statements in the pamphlet is the sentence "Give me the liberty to know, to utter, and to argue freely, according to conscience, above all liberties."

HUDIBRAS: Satire by the seventeenth-century poet Samuel Butler. Published during the Restoration, it was enormously popular in court circles. The poem ridiculed Puritanism for its hypocrisies and its imposition of restrictions on the human spirit. The leading characters in the poem are the Presbyterian knight Sir Hudibras and his squire Ralph.

With the help of lightning and thunder?
There Hopton was slain, again and again,
Unless my author did lie,
With a new thanksgiving for those who
    are living,
To God and his servant Chudleigh.

This kind of mockery filled many a popular broadsheet during the war. Other broadsheet poems made ingenious use of the poetic mannerism of the time. The echo poem, in which the last syllables of a line are repeated in order to give an answer or a comment, was frequently now taken over for political purposes. Echo gives typically Royalist answers to carefully phrased questions—

What did'st thou do when King left Parliament?
                Lament.
Tell me whereon this strength of faction lies?
                On lies.

The political poems, authored or anonymous, are full of metaphysical conceits and metaphors, sometimes startlingly effective. John Cleveland, describing the King's escape from Oxford disguised as a serving man, comes out with one of the most ingenious figures to be found in all his ingenious verse:

Oh, the accurst stenography of fate!
The princely eagle shrunk into a bat.

His comment on Prince Rupert, a general who recklessly exposed himself to enemy fire and time and again came off unhurt, is also expressed in a very choice conceit:

He gags their guns, defeats their dire
    intent,
The cannons do but lisp and compliment.

Cleveland was by far the best of the Royalist political poets in the early part of the war. He could command emotion without bombast and use literary devices—as he uses antithesis in his fine epitaph on Strafford—to force home a political point.

Here lies wise and valiant dust

Huddled up twixt fit and just
Strafford who was hurried hence
Twixt treason and convenience.
The prop and ruin of the state,
The people's violent love and hate,
One in extremes loved and abhorred,
Riddles lie here or in a word
Here lies blood and let it lie
Silent still and never cry.

Elegies on the dead had been one of the most frequent poetic exercises of the sixteen-thirties. They are not so frequent in the war as might be expected. Death became too ordinary. But the Oxford poet William Cartwright—for whose own death soon after King Charles himself went into mourning—eloquently lamented the death of the heroic Bevil Glenville whom he characterises in the opening lines as the pattern of a Cavalier:

Not to be wrought by malice, gain or
    pride
To a compliance with the thriving side;
Not to take arms for love of change, or
    spite,
But only to maintain afflicted right;
Not to die vainly in pursuit of fame
Perversely seeking after voice and name,
Is to resolve, fight, die as martyrs do
And thus did he, soldier and martyr too.

Robert Herrick introduces sympathetic but improbable fauna to mourn over the King's young cousin and captain of his Life Guard, Lord Bernard Stuart, killed in the Royalist rout before Chester:

Had wolves and tigers seen but thee,
They would have showed civility,
And in compassion of thy years
Washed these thy purple wounds with
    tears.

Henry Vaughan is ingeniously touching on the death of the young Princess Elizabeth as a prisoner in the hands of Parliament:

Thy portion here was grief, thy years
Distill'd no other rain but tears;
Thou seem'st a rosebud born in snow
A flower of purpose born to bow

To heedless tempests and the rage
Of an incensed and stormy age. . . .

Poems like Vaughan's and Herrick's are themselves not unlike rosebuds in snow. Their decorative gentleness hardly suits the harshness of the prevailing mood.

Tom Jordan's brisk talent in prose or poetry lent itself—or perhaps I should say hired itself, for he was willing to write for money—to political propaganda. He defended the Royalist point of view in a pamphlet called *Rules to know a Royal King from a disloyal subject with an exact account given of the Jewels of the Crown of England*. The Crown Jewels are the kingly virtues described under the figure of precious stones, Innocence, Fortitude, Patience, Mercy 'a stone of a delicious colour,' and finally Royal Anger 'a stone that shows a clear flame, yet appears burning and dangerous. It is not to be touched, but discerned at a distance. As you stand and look on it, it looks flaming; when you kneel, the fire seems to vanish.'

In the earlier years of the war we look in vain for the emergence of an outstanding satirical poet. Cleveland is essentially too complicated. Cartwright is too sincerely serious. Suckling, who would admirably have filled the part of Cavalier satirist in chief, died in Paris on the eve of the conflict. Denham's squibs and the anonymous doggerels hardly reach the level of satire, and the wits were on the whole inclined to content themselves with rhymed epigrams, of which a great number were passed about in manuscript. I have a weakness for Drummond's neat quatrain on the death of Pym, the leader of the House of Commons who was execrated by all the Royalists as the arch-incendiary of rebellion:

When Pym last night descended into Hell
Ere he his cups of Lethe did carouse—
'What place is this?' said he, 'I pray me
    tell,'
To whom a devil 'This is the Lower
    House.'

But in the disreputable person of Marcha-

mont Nedham a satirist of real power seems to have co-existed with a facile hack. Nedham's true sympathies, if he had any, were probably Royalist, but he was prepared to write for either side, and if he needed the money, for both at once. He had an easy gift in verse and prose—and worked it unsparingly, tossing off, among other pieces, a whole history of the Civil War in—largely deplorable—verses. Yet every now and again, in a snatch of six or eight lines, there emerges from his copious shoddy pages a sequence of sharp images, which for a moment foreshadows the major satirists of a later generation. Thus he excoriates the Marquis of Hamilton, Charles' most trusted and most untrustworthy adviser, whose folly and ambition had been largely responsible for the rebellion in Scotland and the rise of the Presbyterian party against the King:

'Twas he that first alarmed the kirk
To this preposterous bloody work:
Taught zeal a hundred tumbling tricks
And Sculpture twined with politics;
The pulpit made a juggler's box,
Set law and gospel in the stocks;
'Twas he patcht up the new Divine,
Part Calvin and part Catiline,
Rather than he his ends would miss,
Betrayed his master with a kiss,
And buried in one common fate
The glory of our Church and State.

This is sharp enough to have been claimed for Samuel Butler, whose incomparable satiric talent matured during these years although he did not publish *Hudibras* until after the Restoration. This is to anticipate. For the Royalists comic and satirical verse ceases almost altogether from the King's death until after the Restoration. Their situation had grown too tragic. That dreadful event itself called forth a chorus of poetry, much of it strident and despairing, almost all pitched in too high a key of anguish. Cleveland tautens the strings till they come near to cracking. Thus he imagines the King's last moments:

And so he looked upon the axe as one

Weapon yet left to guard him to his
    throne.
In his great name then may his subjects
    cry:
'Death thou art swallowed up in
    victory . . .'
His crown was fallen unto too low a thing
For him who has become so great a
    King . . .
And thus his soul of this her triumph
    proud
Broke like a flash of lightning through
    the cloud
Of flesh and blood; and from the highest
    line
Of human virtue, passed to the divine. . . .

Henry King, Bishop of Chichester, leads
up to the subject of the King's death with
a strange apostrophe to the Puritans, whom
he accuses of having substituted the atrocious
sport of King-hunting for the more innocent
sports and May-games once practised by the
English.

    The royal game dislodged and under chase
    Your hot pursuit dogs him from place to
        place.
    Not Saul with greater fury or disdain
    Did flying David from Jeshimon's plain
    Unto the barren wilderness pursue
    Than cours'd and hunted is the King by
        you.
    The mountain partridge and the chased roe
    Might now for emblems of his fortune go,
    And since all other May-games of the
        town
    (Save those yourselves should make) are
        voted down,
    The clam'rous pulpit hollas in resort,
    Inviting men to your King-catching sport.

The Royalist resistance persisted underground in England throughout the Commonwealth. More popular among its members
than the long elegies was an eight-line stanza
widely circulated in manuscript and set to
music at least twice—once by Samuel
Pepys:

Great, good and just, could I but rate
My grief and thy too rigid fate,
I'd weep the world in such a strain
As it should once deluge again.
But since thy loud-tongued blood de-
    mands supplies
More from Briareus' hands than Argus'
    eyes
I'll tune thy elegies to trumpet sounds
And write thy epitaph with blood and
    wounds.

The lines were sometimes attributed to
Cleveland, but they lack his ingenious economy and have more passion. Their authorship was claimed for Montrose by his
chaplain and biographer George Wishart
and there seems no reason for doubting
his word. Montrose himself was hanged in
Edinburgh after a vain attempt to raise
Scotland. It would doubtless have given him
some cause for pride had he known the
extent to which his unfathered lines were
being copied in England.

Paradoxically enough, the noblest and
today the best known lines on the King's
death were written by the Puritan Marvell
and in the course of a poem in praise of
Cromwell:

    He nothing common did or mean
    Upon that memorable scene,
    But with his keener eye
    The axe's edge did try,
    Nor called the gods in vulgar spite
    To vindicate his helpless right
    But bowed his comely head
    Down as upon a bed.

A strange freak in literature that all the
Royalist elegies should be surpassed by the
verse of a rebel.

For my present purposes I have kept company almost exclusively with Cavaliers.
Marvell can be a rebel, though it should be
emphasised that those who sided with Parliament never thought of themselves as that.
They represented constitutional government;
the King's party were the rebels. They, too,

had their quota of writers, indeed the greatest. Of that more at another time

II. ROUNDHEADS' VERSE AND PROSE

The Royalist writers, in the early part of the Civil War at least, are distinguished by their inexhaustible good humour, their light-hearted capacity for turning bitterness into laughter. A greater solemnity reigned among the Roundheads. They did not make fun of the Cavaliers, because they did not think the war or the Cavaliers particularly funny. In this no doubt they were right; the war was not a laughing matter, although few of them were able to express its tragedy with the lyrical sweetness that Marvell devoted to it:

O thou, that dear and happy isle
The garden of the world erewhile,
. Thou paradise of four seas
Which Heaven planted us to please,
But to exclude the world did guard
With wat'ry if not flaming sword;
What luckless apple did we taste
To make us mortal, and thee waste . . .

They were not without writers and counted John Milton, the greatest luminary of the epoch, as one of theirs. The young Marvell was with them in heart; as well as George Wither and Tom May. Yet there was among the extremists of the party a certain suspicion of literature—

No oracle of Delphos but of Sion,
No books, but that of God, must we
    rely on . . .

Among them, far more than among the Cavaliers, the ingenuous, almost, one might say, the unlettered broadsheet flourished. With the break-down of the Established Church every tailor and cobbler claimed a vocation for preaching. A very large number also claimed a vocation for writing, and because of the freshness of the language and the innocent approach, they often produced singularly effective phrases. The

greatest master of this unsophisticated style belongs to a later period, but John Bunyan was the inheritor of the unlettered muse which found so much expression in the Civil War.

The huge literature of religious polemic and political theory, lettered and unlettered, ignorant and erudite, which poured out from every sect and schism, belongs to politics rather than to literature. In the frequent pamphlets of moral instruction put out to encourage the soldiers of Parliament there are many phrases of touching or ingenious effectiveness. 'Every fellow is not a soldier who struts and looks big, wears a broad blade and takes tobacco'—this was a very usual opening note; the soldiers of the cause, the soldiers of what ultimately became—and really was—a New Model Army, were to be of a different stamp. The pamphlets addressed to them unconsciously echo that famous letter of Cromwell's: 'I had rather have a plain russet-coated captain that knows what he fights for, and loves what he knows, than that which you call a gentleman and is nothing else.'

Drill Orders in Rhyme

For such an army, whose soldiers were issued with pocket editions of the metrical psalms, it was not remarkable that one pamphleteer argued that even the ordinary words of command could be turned into so many instructions for right thinking, thus: 'Ere you Make Ready, remember the cause; when you Present, be not bloodthirsty; when you Give Fire, consider against whom.' On a lower level a helpful patriot had the idea of making drill easier for a raw young officer by putting all the orders into rhyme. Such innocent efforts compare favourably—if not from the literary at least from the ethical point of view—with the works of the vituperative and polemical writers who

. . . added fuel to the direful flame
Of civil discord and domestick blows
By the incentives of malicious prose.

A good deal of the prose—or verse for that matter—which appeared in the news-sheets was indeed malicious. Contradicting, blackening and shouting down the other party was the principal purpose of the greater number of the pamphlets produced. The Cavalier paper *Mercurius Aulicus* and the Roundhead *Mercurius Britannicus* barked and snarled at each other from Oxford and London respectively, and very funny they can be—as good as a Punch and Judy show. The arrows of reviling words, as George Wither lamented, flew hither and thither on paper wings increasing the discord. Reviling words were not eschewed by John Milton; far from it. Some of his pamphlets consist of little else. Take his first and second *Defence of the English People* in which he worries the Leyden Scholar Claude de Saumaise like a dog with a bone. Saumaise—*Salmasius* in his Latin-ised form—had expended a mass of learning in support of the King. Milton, in reply, expresses withering amazement that 'such a witless, senseless bawler, one that was born but to spoil or transcribe good authors, should think himself able to write anything of his own that will reach posterity . . . unless this defence of the King perhaps may be beholden to the answer I give to it, for being looked into now and then . . . .' Milton's arrogant prediction has been confirmed by time.

Milton's Reply to 'Eikon Basilike'

The same is not true of the *Eikon Basilike*, to which Milton was commissioned to write the official reply. This collection of prayers and reflections on the causes and course of the war, purporting to come from the King's hand, does in fact very closely represent his personality. Published immediately after his death, it enjoyed an immediate and resounding, if rather melancholy, success, and it stands today four-square both on its literary merit and historical interest. Milton, in answering it, laboured under serious difficulties. The solemnity of the circumstances prevented a too outra-geous use of the merely abusive technique, since the King was dead and the majority of his subjects regarded him as having been murdered. Milton recognises the delicacy of the situation—'To descant on the misfortunes of a person fallen from so high a dignity, who hath also paid his final debt to nature, is neither of itself a thing commendable, nor the intention of this discourse.' Yet the sneering personal note soon creeps in. *Eikonoclastes* does not rank among the great contributions to the prose literature of the war. It lacks the surge of republican patriotism which occasionally breaks through the concentrated abuse of the *Defence of the English People* or the controlled power of *Areopagitica*.

Areopagitica was partly the outcome of the pamphlet war. In its initial attack on the royal prerogative, Parliament had swept away among other things the royal power of censorship. This seems to have been more or less of an accident, and the snowstorm of pamphlets, from all sides and all points of view, which followed soon set them wondering whether a new censorship of some kind had not better be imposed. This provoked Milton's most famous prose work. It contains some of the most often quoted passages in English literature and I make no excuse for quoting one of them again. The well-known words on the English convey, better than anything else written in the war, that inspiring sense of elation and re-birth which undoubtedly swept through a great part of the people at the time, which was largely responsible for the victory of the New Model Army and for the immense revival of English prestige in Europe under Cromwellian rule:

Methinks I see in my mind a noble and puissant Nation rousing herself like a strong man after sleep, and shaking her invincible locks. Methinks I see her as an eagle mewing her mighty youth, and kindling her undazzled eyes at the full midday beam; purging and unscaling her long abused sight at the fountain itself of heavenly radiance; while the whole noise of timorous and flocking birds, with those also that love the twilight, flutter about amazed at what she means, and in their envious gabble would prognosticate a year of sects and schisms.

Early efforts at censorship were not effective. Pamphlets and newssheets continued to come out with false imprints or none to evade discovery; there was a flourishing resistance press. *The Man in the Moon,* a Royalist paper printed in London, pops up after a brief suppression like a Jack-in-the-Box, gaily challenging its suppressors—'By your leave, rebels and traitors, you have not lost me yet; I was but eclipsed for a week; and now have at you, 'tis not your pot gun act to suppress pamphlets that daunts me.'

As a counterpoise to such impertinences the Parliamentary party employed various more or less gifted hacks to defend its point of view. Among them was Marchamont Nedham of the elastic principles, and Tom May, a middle-aged poet who in his gayer youth in the sixteen-twenties and 'thirties had sometimes been charmingly and punningly known as 'our April poet Tom May.' It was not a very apt pun at the best of times for there was never anything very springlike in his voluminous writing. Tom May's Parliamentary opinions were probably sincere, but he was a disappointed man. He had hung about the Court before the war and was known to have expected the laureateship when Ben Jonson died. It was given to Davenant, however; and May, who had worked hard for it with two interminable historical poems, was bitterly disappointed. The Royalists naturally made the most of this when he began to turn out pamphlets and even the official history of the war in Latin and English for Parliament.

May's poetry had never been very good. His prose, however, is not without vitality and he catches the authentic echo of tavern argument, with its inconsistencies and its clichés, in his *Character of a Right Malignant*—one of the few pamphlets where a Roundhead makes the Cavaliers look fool-ish. The Cavalier, he writes, 'loves his freedom and would be loth to be a slave but he verily believes that the King may lawfully take away whatsoever he hath. He does not think that the King of England is as absolute a monarch as any in the world, but he thinks that the King may do what he will and that neither Parliament nor any human power may resist him in it. . . . He calls those hypocrites who lead a godly life and though he thinks it a great uncharitableness in those godly men to censure him for living loosely, he thinks it no uncharity in himself to censure them for professing godliness.'

Tom May was not, however, approved of by his own side. A useful writer he may have been, but his private life fell below the austere standards of the Roundhead. He was too fond of the bottle. In fact he is thought to have died by suffocating himself in his nightcap after a debauch, and his own party may have been glad to be rid of him. Andrew Marvell scrapes his name out of the Parliamentarian record with a singularly cruel epitaph beginning

> As one put drunk into the packet boat
> Tom May was hurried thence and did not
>   know't.

May's bibulous ghost, still hankering after the laureateship that Davenant had snatched from him, hurries to greet Ben Johnson in the shades and is repulsed by the illustrious dead in no uncertain terms:

> Far from these blessed shades tread back
>   again
> Most servile wit and mercenary pen
> Polydore, Lucan, Alan, Vandal, Goth
> Malignant poet and historian both.
> But thee nor ignorance nor seeming good
> Misled, but malice fixed and understood
> Because someone than thee more worthy
>   wears
> The sacred laurel, hence are all these
>   tears.
> Must therefore all the world be set on
>   flame
> Because a gazette writer missed his aim?

Yet wast thou taken hence with equal
fate
Before thou couldst great Charles's death
relate
But what will deeper wound thy little
mind
Hast left surviving Davenant behind. . . .

In the Commonwealth Marvell slips
easily into the place of the chief state poet.
But the clamour has very much died down
by that time. With the suppression of the
Royalist party the necessary opposition was
silenced. The censorship was at length organised and began to work effectively.
Marvell was later to develop a satirical
fighting vein but not until the Restoration.
With Cromwell in power he writes a marble-
smooth verse as handsome as monumental
sculpture. The famous Horatian Ode on
Cromwell's Return from Ireland still seems
to contain a faint hint of criticism:

'Tis madness to resist or blame
The face of angry Heaven's flame
And if we would speak true
Much to the man is due

Who from his private gardens where
He lived reserved and austere
As if his highest plot
To plant the bergamot

Could by industrious valour climb
To ruin the great work of time
And cast the kingdoms old
Into another mould.

Perhaps not wholly admiring, a note of
cynicism or doubt is somewhere there. But
eight years later, when he wrote his elegy
on Cromwell's death, no shadow darkens
the grandiose picture. Cromwell died on
September 3, 1658, the anniversary of his
victories at Dunbar and Worcester. Thus
Marvell:

No part of time but bore his mark away
Of honour; all the year was Cromwell's
day
But this of all the most auspicious found
Twice had in open field him victor crown'd

When up the arméd mountains of Dunbar
He marched, and through deep Severn
ending war.
What day should him eternise but the
same
That had before immortalised his name?

But it is in his description of Cromwell's
religion that he expresses in the majestic
language that characterises this period of
his poetry what the Puritan felt about his
cause and the war that had been fought:

He first put arms into religion's hand
And timorous conscience unto courage
mann'd
The soldiers taught that inward mail to
wear
And fearing God how they should noth-
ing fear
Those strokes, he said, will pierce through
all below
Where those that strike from Heaven
fetch the blow,
Astonished armies did their flight prepare
And cities strong were storméd by his
prayer.
Of that for ever Preston's field shall tell
The story and impregnable Clonmel. . . .
What man was ever so in Heaven obey'd
Since the commanded sun o'er Gibeon
stayed. . . .

The Puritans as the children of Israel and
Cromwell as Joshua—this was the parallel,
as the most stalwart of Cromwell's followers
were apt to see it. But with his death the
time for such parallels was at an end. The
country reverted without too long a delay
and fortunately without a new civil war to
its old habit of monarchy. The Cromwellian
dynasty in the person of Richard Cromwell
made itself scarce, and Marvell, who had
written some rather embarrassing praise of
the short-lived Richard, disappeared momentarily from the scenes to reenter as the
first major satirist of the reign of Charles II.

For a long time the last word on the war
seemed to have been spoken by Samuel
Butler whose lines provide a mocking com-

mentary on Marvell's. No praise from him for those who put arms into religion's hand:

                    that stubborn crew
Of errant saints whom all men grant
To be the true Church militant,
Such as do build their faith upon
The holy text of pike and gun,
Decide all controversies by
Infallible artillery
And prove their doctrine orthodox

By apostolick blows and knocks
Call fire and sword and desolation
A godly thorough Reformation
Which always must be carried on
And still be doing, never done,
As if religion were intended
For nothing else but to be mended.

In Butler's *Hudibras* the Cavaliers had the last word.

PURITANISM IS NOT THE NAME OF A DEFINITE BODY of religious doctrine or of a particular ecclesiastical system. It refers, rather, to attitudes and points of view with regard to man's relation to God. It existed within the Established Church of England as well as outside. In the reign of Queen Elizabeth the majority of Puritans were what might be called Low Churchmen, who advocated various reforms in the service, ritual, vestments, and discipline of the Church of England. When we speak of Puritans in the period of the Puritan Revolution, however, we usually have in mind religious groups *outside* the Church—Presbyterians, Independents, Anabaptists, for example. Among these groups, and even within them, there existed wide divergencies, even contradictions, in opinions and ideals. Puritanism exhibited libertarian and authoritarian elements, and within its ample confines a belief in equality and a belief in inequality existed side by side. It has been said that the Puritan believed in democracy in the Fall and aristocracy in the Redemption. But he believed, at any rate, in equality among the elect—those predestined by God's will to salvation—and this equality cut sharply across the social and economic distinctions of secular society. For the poor and the weak were quite as likely to be among the elect as the rich and the powerful, and perhaps more so. In the following essay, Professor A. S. P. Woodhouse, of the University of Toronto, concerns himself with the problem of how it came about that some Puritans were able to transfer to secular politics the liberal elements in Puritanism while discarding the illiberal elements. The reader will do well to note the author's *religious* approach to the study of Puritan thought, and to reflect upon the basis for the democracy of the Levellers which Professor Woodhouse finds in Puritan religion.

PURITANISM AND DEMOCRACY

A. S. P. WOODHOUSE

I

The period of the Puritan revolution was one in which religion and even theology dominated the common modes of thought and expression. Lord Acton, who (unlike some historians) was sufficiently unenlightened to know theology when he saw it, described the period as "the middle ages of Protestantism." It follows that the concepts whether of liberty or of authority which the Puritans developed can be fully understood only if they are studied in their proper setting, and their native terminology. Dogma formed that terminology and the Puritan church organization constituted the setting. Without denying the validity of other approaches (the constitutional approach for example, in which the liberals long had their own way, or the economic, in which the Marxists are taking theirs)—without denying the usefulness of these approaches, I suggest the value to the student who would know what really happened, of a third, namely the religious approach. For the Puritan concept of democracy, if it did not spring from Puritan religion, at least sprang up in closest contact with it. Puritan religion constituted the climate of opinion in which the concept was born and nourished. The religious approach has one advantage (shared in measure with the constitutional): it can stay within the period under discussion, and it can afford to rest its case on the actual words used. It does not require a transposition of terms, whereby theology is shown to be a roundabout way of saying economics. Nor does it ask us to make any large assumptions—to believe that Calvin

built better than he knew: he intended a church and it turned out to be a bank! One will no doubt be told that some of the theological argument with which the pamphlets in the Thomason Collection are filled, and most of the reasons urged in the Councils of the Army at Putney and Whitehall, are what are now called "rationalizations," and that we gain nothing by refusing to recognize this fact. So be it. But if these are rationalizations they involve the terms in which the Puritan viewed his world and they rest upon the convictions with which he was prepared to face not only his fellows but his Maker. We shall gain nothing by brushing those terms and those convictions aside, though to comprehend them requires patient study and a modicum of historical sympathy. "Nothing," says Lord David Cecil, "is more baffling to the imagination than the religion of another age."

What, then, are the features of the Puritan mind that are relevant to our thesis? What, for example, are the features which strike a reader of the debates in the Councils of the Army or of the pamphlets before mentioned? The first is the intrusion of dogma into every argument, and the constancy and directness of the scriptural reference. We shall have occasion presently to modify this statement in respect of half of the thinking of some of the Puritans. But for most of them it remains altogether true. Israel was ever before their eyes. Forget that and the policy of the Presbyterians becomes in part at least unintelligible. Had not God given to the Jews kings, and, whenever they could do so with impunity, had not that model people knocked them about? And so

Reprinted by special permission from *The Canadian Journal of Economics and Political Science,* IV (1938), 1-21. This essay was originally read to the Political Economy Seminar in the University of Toronto. To avoid quoting from inaccessible tracts, it selects most of its material from the author's *Puritanism and Liberty* (London: Dent, 1938; second edition, London: Dent, Chicago: University of Chicago Press, 1950). The footnotes which originally appeared with this essay have been omitted, but page references to *Puritanism and Liberty* are inserted in parentheses.

all along the line. Puritan religion in the various phases of the struggle with Charles, and beyond it, was a mighty revolutionary agent. Nothing indeed could withstand the divinity that hedged a king save the divinity of religion itself when it was ranged against him. Calvin is not thought of as a revolutionary or even a liberal. But between the lines of his injunction to Christian obedience may be read a strictly limited incitement to disobedience, which in the final words of the *Institutes* becomes perfectly specific:

> But in that obedience . . . due to . . . rulers we must always make this exception . . . : that it be not incompatible with obedience to Him to whose will . . . kings should be subject, to whose decrees their commands must yield, to whose majesty their sceptres must bow. And indeed how preposterous were it, in pleasing men, to incur the offence of Him for whose sake you obey men! . . . If they command anything against Him let us not pay the least regard to it, nor be moved by all the dignity which they possess as magistrates—a dignity to which no injury is done when it is subordinated to the special and truly supreme power of God.

Calvin enjoins Christian obedience *and fixes its limits.* Nor does he leave active resistance without recognition or a means of becoming effective: private citizens may not actively oppose their prince; but the inferior magistrates may, and when godliness is menaced, must. Here Calvin is at one with the more liberal thought of the Renaissance. His prescription might have been written for the Presbyterian party of the First Civil War. Charles is cast for the role of prince, and Parliament for that of the inferior magistrates: they fight by the book.

Extreme Puritanism soon leaves Calvin far behind, but not dogma and scripture. The Puritan knows no other means of counteracting scripture save by scripture. The model of Israel might become oppressive to the more extreme Puritan himself when it was urged to enforce the power and duty of the civil magistrate in religion, or urged against the separation of church and state and against the plea for liberty of conscience. What then did the extreme Puritan do? Did he rebel against the dogmatic principle? No, he merely denied its particular application; he called in the New Testament to counteract the teaching of the Old, and sought by a long and ingenious argument to demonstrate the distinction between the Law and the Gospel and to prove that what was the duty of the magistrate under the Law was no longer his duty under the Gospel. The mode of argument was thoroughly characteristic of the Puritan mind, and its substance (we shall observe) bears directly on the concept of liberty. But besides precept and model the Bible contained prophecy. Every party among the Puritans, save the Presbyterian, was in some degree touched by the Millenarian hope. It appears in such a sermon as *A Glimpse of Sion's Glory,* published before the outbreak of hostilities, or in discourses like Thomas Collier's to the Army at Putney in 1647,

HENRY IRETON: Officer in the New Model Army, son-in-law of Cromwell, and one of the signers of the death warrant of Charles I. A good deal is known of his political and social ideas owing to the preservation of the army debates in which he participated. Hostile to the beliefs of the Levellers, he opposed universal manhood suffrage, insisting that it would quickly be followed by attacks on private property.

THOMASON COLLECTION: Materials gathered by George Thomason and deposited in the British Museum. Invaluable for the study of the age of the Puritan Revolution, it consists of pamphlets, tracts, books, newspapers, and manuscripts. A *Catalogue* (1908) of the collection was prepared by G. K. Fortescue, but it leaves much to be desired from the standpoint of accuracy.

A Description of the New Creation, or in the most curious of all the petitions to Parliament and Army when Charles' death had thrown the constitution into the melting pot, *Certain Queries from Christian People,* in which government by the Saints in church-parliaments is seriously urged as a practical expedient and championed against an *Agreement of the People.* Millenarianism, with its ideal of the dictatorship of the Saints, was based on the prophecies of *Daniel* and *Revelation,* and it supplied at once a key to history and a programme of revolution.

It was also an extreme manifestation of one of the most constant and dominant features of the Puritan mind, its concern for positive reform. This concern springs from a quality (one might perhaps call it a defect) of Puritan religious experience: it is overwhelmingly active in character and scarcely contemplative at all. This is the stuff of which religious liberators are made, but it is also, and even more obviously, the stuff of religious tyrants. And the Puritan impulse towards liberty, which is a real and powerful impulse, very soon falls foul of the Puritan zeal for positive reform, so that the struggle in which the Puritans are engaged is a *civil* war indeed. Somewhere near the heart of Puritanism there exists in potential and unresolved conflict the impulse to freedom and the irresistible desire to dragoon men into righteousness for God's glory and the safety of his Church. The Levellers represent the full outworking of one impulse; the Millenarians, of the other. Too little attention has been paid to this second impulse by idealizers of the Puritan temper, who fail to recognize its dogmatic basis in Puritan theology—just as too little effort is made to understand the Puritan impulse to liberty by the other type of modern critic who can see in Puritanism nothing but the desire to make righteousness prevail. The impulse to liberty and the impulse to reform are both authentic notes of Puritanism. The latter, however, is the more pervasive. In the wide diversity of ideas uncovered by a survey of Puritanism from the Presbyterians, the party of the Right, to the sectaries, the parties of the Left, and through the Independents, the composite party of the Centre, which occupies the whole interval between the two extremes— in this wide diversity of ideas, there is one constant, namely, the acceptance of what Troeltsch has named the ideal of the holy community. Whether or not this operates against the impulse to liberty in secular politics, will depend on whether the ideal of the holy community is confined to the church or extends to dominate also the life of the state. To this, a central problem of our thesis, we shall return.

Whether libertarian or reforming, the Puritan is marked by varying degrees of utopianism and iconoclasm. Of the latter the concerted effort to destroy the religious institutions of a thousand years is an undeniable example. And such effort fosters an iconoclastic spirit. But all along the line religion is the Puritan's training ground, whether in liberty or reform, and theology lies at the basis of his thinking. If the Puritan learned anywhere to level institutions and build from the foundation up, it was not in the state but in the church. In regard to the utopianism (which is not the academic utopianism of Sir Thomas More) it is enough to remind ourselves of Charles I's indignant protest against "the utopia of religion and government into which they would reduce this kingdom"; to remind ourselves furthermore of how (as the period goes on) utopias become more frequent and more diverse. Religion lies at the root of many of them, as of Vane's *Healing Question;* and even where it is less obvious it is still a potent influence, as in Milton's *Ready and Easy Way to Establish a Free Commonwealth,* which embodies an individualistic, but not very democratic kind of republicanism, and in Winstanley's *Law of Freedom in a Platform,* which adumbrates a communistic and collectivist state.

With other documents of a utopian cast, such as the Levellers' *Agreements of the People* and the Millenarians' *Certain Queries* (already mentioned), these utopias reveal all the main tendencies of Puritan political thought, and put us on the track of their sometimes hidden theological foundations. The tendencies appear in a series of antitheses. First, the impulse to liberty and the concern for positive reform (the former almost identical with the very strong Puritan inclination to individualism and ultimately to anarchism; the latter counteracting this inclination and issuing generally in a tendency to junto and dictatorship, but in one instance, Winstanley, in a form of collectivism). This, then, is the second antithesis: individualism and some form of rule in which the interests of the individual, or at all events the unregenerate individual, are sacrificed to a loftier aim. Thirdly, equalitarianism subsisting beside the sternest and most unyielding form of inequality —the distinction between the elect and the reprobate, which is insuperable. "Men as men," said Ireton, "are corrupt and will be so." Nor is the distinction merely theoretic. In *Certain Queries* (for example) it becomes the foundation of a scheme of political settlement. Four of the queries will suggest the tone of the pamphlet and the implications of the doctrine (p. 246):

1. Consider whether it be not a far greater honour for parliaments, magistrates, &c. to rule as Christ's officers and the churches' representatives than as officers of a worldly kingdom and representatives of a mere natural and worldly people?
2. What right or claim mere natural and worldly men have to rule and government, that want a sanctified claim to the least outward blessings?
3. How can the kingdom be the Saints' when the ungodly are electors, and elected to govern?
4. Whether it be not a straitening of the Church's power, to limit it only to spiritual matters?

Evidently this doctrine stands in sharpest contrast with the equalitarianism of other Puritans of the Left, whether the individualist variety (of the Levellers) or the collectivist variety (of Winstanley and the Diggers). The last query quoted is even more searching than it appears; for (as we shall see) it is aimed directly against the principle or device which the Levellers employed to extend Christian liberty and equality from the religious to the secular sphere. The contrast is not the simple one between Puritanism of the Right (where one might expect some reactionary ideas) and that of the Left (where one might expect whatever ideas of liberty and equality Puritanism could muster). The contrast is within the parties of the Left, and as such it becomes very significant of the really divergent tendencies of Puritanism. Each of the tendencies glanced at has its recognizable source in the dogmas of Puritan theology. That is not surprising. But the divergent tendencies sometimes turn out on investigation to spring from the same dogma. And that, I think, is more surprising.

We have seen the basis of the idea of *inequality* in the doctrine of predestination. But the specifically Puritan idea of *equality* springs in part from the same source, and in part from the Protestant doctrine of the priesthood of the believer. All that Puritanism itself can say in the first instance is that *the elect are equal,* or (with the second, and less theoretic doctrine in view) that *all believers are equal.* And this, so far as it goes, is an idea of great potency. It is turned first against the elaborate hierarchy of the Christian Church and brings it crashing down. Then it is turned against the distinction of cleric from lay, and that too goes by the board. Finally it establishes a community in which, in spiritual things at least, absolute equality prevails (pp. 312-13):

The fifth rule [says William Dell] is to keep equality among Christians. For though according to our first nativity whereby we are born of men, there is great inequality, some being born high, some low, some honourable, some mean, some kings, some subjects, &c., yet according to our new or second birth whereby we are born of God, there is exact equality, for here are none better or worse, higher or lower, but all have the same faith, hope, love, the same God, Christ, Spirit, the same divine nature, the same precious promises, the same incorruptible crown and inheritance of Saints in light.

But such *equality* pertains only to the church order and cannot be separated from the *inequality* between Saint and sinner. This does not mean that it has not some levelling influence outside the church. The basic inequality, or the idea of Christian privilege, is something very different from inequality and privilege as the world knows them, and cuts sharply across the distinctions of caste and wealth. God (as Roger Williams observes) has "chosen a little flock out of the world, and those generally poor and mean." Truth in religion (say other writers) comes not from the learned, but often from "the meanest of the brethren." Christ does not rely on the great ones to forward his work, but can overthrow the wise by the foolish, and things that are mighty by things that are weak (pp. 282, 263, introd. p. 42). Again Puritanism claims for the conscience of the individual Christian (however humble his station) a new dignity and a new responsibility. Those in authority may demand an unquestioning obedience (say the Agents of the regiments to Fairfax) but a Christian is finally responsible to his own conscience; that is (in Ireton's phrase) to "conscience obliging above or against human and outward constitutions" (pp. 436, 459). The consciences of common men were a new phenomenon in politics, and one that has never since disappeared. But these Christian ideas, emphasized by the Puritans, while they were immensely important, still carried with them the basic notion of inequality. Every claim was made for the believer alone; and while this remained true, the destination of such thinking was not democracy, but the rule of the Saints. It is easy to see how one arrives at the ideal of the Millenarians from these premises, but not at the ideal of the Lev-

ellers. One can catch more than a Glimpse of Sion's Glory, but not of an Agreement of the People.

That is the fundamental problem, then: how did some of the Puritans manage to transfer to secular politics the liberal elements in Puritanism while discarding the reactionary elements—how did they develop the liberal inferences from dogma without the reactionary inferences? I have preferred to state the problem in terms of equality rather than of liberty (though the two ideas are almost inseparable) in order that we might reach a solution and then apply it in our discussion of liberty.

(1) A first and partial solution is found in the tendency of dogma to break down, a tendency which to a limited degree is seen in those Puritans of the Left who espouse the cause of political liberty and equality. There were some elements in the Puritan creed which might conceivably minister to that end. For example, there was the idea, fairly frequently and emphatically expressed, of the progressive interpretation of truth. No doubt the Bible was a complete revelation, but its meaning had been obscured until the Reformation, and the process of reformation was not yet complete; might not new light still break forth from the Holy Word? And this attitude of mind in some of the Puritans met and coalesced with impulses to free enquiry coming down from the Renaissance. In 1642 John Goodwin writes (introd. pp. 46-7):

If so great and considerable a part of the world as America . . . was yet unknown to all the world beside for so many generations together, well may it be conceived . . . that . . . many truths, yea and those of main concernment and importance, may be yet unborn. . . .

That is neither new nor unjustifiable by the practice of wise men, to examine . . . and . . . impugn received opinions. He that will please to peruse the first book of Dr. Hakewill's learned *Apology of the Power and Providence of God* . . . shall meet with great variety of instances,

. . . in divinity, philosophy, . . . history [and] . . . natural history, of opinions which had a long time been received, and yet were at last suspected, yea and many of them evicted and rejected upon due examination. . . . [Again] there are many errors (erroneously so called) in the Christian world which are made of the greatest and choicest truths; yea, and which doubtless will be redeemed from their captivity and restored to their thrones and kingdoms by [the] diligence, gifts, and faithfulness of the approaching generation.

Transferred to politics, this experimental spirit is itself a matter of great importance. It is essential to the ideal, shared by Independents and Levellers, of the arrival at truth and agreement through free discussion. But I cite it here rather as an example of an attitude which is finally hostile to dogma and dogmatism. Of the actual impairing of dogma the most striking instance is seen in a reaction among a minority of the Puritans against the Calvinistic doctrine of predestination (which parallels a much wider reaction in the Anglican Church), and this if it had been more general would have been highly significant because it undermines a chief foundation of Puritan *inequality*. Again there is a limited, but very interesting tendency to undermine dogma by a process of allegorical interpretation, of which we shall have a word to say later. This and other evidence might be brought forward to suggest two further features of the period which bear on the breakdown of dogma. The first is the alliance effected between extreme Puritanism and a current of thought which is not in origin or essence religious at all, but belongs rather to a libertine tradition. The second is a natural tendency, illustrated in all the Levellers, for interest to shift from religion to politics—a general secularizing of their thought anticipating the wider movement whose English beginning is conventionally assigned to 1660.

(2) But when all these things are added up, they do not suggest a sufficiently pronounced breakdown of dogma. And in the view of much evidence that liberal opinions could and did subsist with unrelieved dogmatism, we must turn elsewhere for the main solution of our problem, how the liberal inferences from dogma could be developed in the secular field without the reactionary inferences. An example will make the situation clearer. In politics Roger Williams is completely democratic in opinion, adopting the doctrine of natural rights, the sovereignty of the people, government by consent. But in religion he remains the strictest of the Separatists. Viewed in itself, his church is no doubt a religious democracy. Viewed in relation to the world, it is no democracy but an aristocracy of the elect. The world shall perish, but the Church shall remain always. It is instructive to notice the fate reserved for the sovereign people, from which no natural rights can save them, and to which they certainly do not consent (p. 271):

> When the world is ripe in sin . . . those holy and mighty officers and executioners, the angels, with their sharp and cutting sickles of eternal vengeance shall down with them and bundle them up for the everlasting burning. . . . Then shall that man of sin (2 Thess. 2. 8) *be consumed by the breath of the mouth of the Lord Jesus . . . and . . . be tormented with fire and brimstone in the presence of the holy angels. . . . And the smoke of their torment shall ascend up for ever and ever* (Rev. 14. 10, 11).

How can opinions so liberal in politics, so reactionary in religion, subsist peacefully together in one mind? Only by some principle or device which succeeds in completely isolating the spiritual and the secular, and permits the application of different standards of judgment in the two spheres. Failing that, the reactionary religion must communicate its quality to the political thinking and Williams must say that while the world lasts, the Saints should rule it. He says nothing of the kind. He insists upon the natural rights of natural men just as vehemently as upon the spiritual rights of spiritual men. And here the true relation of his religious and his political thought appears. First the separation of the spiritual and the secular; and then the influence of one upon the other, not by way of direct inference but by way of analogy.

This separation of the secular and the spiritual curiously parallels Bacon's division of the territory of thought between natural philosophy and divine. But in the Puritan the division rests on an altogether different foundation, a foundation of dogma. It is the result of a confident and extreme appeal to what I will call *the dogma of the two orders.* Man as man belongs to the order of nature; man as believer belongs to the order of grace. God is the creator and ruler of both orders; but they have different economies and are ruled by different laws. As one of the ablest of all the Puritan pamphlets on toleration, *The Ancient Bounds* (1645), puts it (pp. 247-8):

Christ Jesus, whose is the kingdom, the power and the glory, both in nature and in grace, hath given several maps and schemes of his dominions . . . : both of his great kingdom, the world, . . . which he hath committed to men to be administered in truth and righteousness, in a various form as they please; . . . and also his special and peculiar kingdom, the kingdom of grace. Which kingdoms though they differ essentially or formally, yet they agree in one common subject-matter, man and societies of men, though under a diverse consideration. And not only man in society, but every man individually, is an epitome, either of one only or of both these dominions: of one only, so every natural man (who in a natural consideration is called *microcosmus,* an epitome of the world), in whose conscience God hath his throne, ruling him by the light of nature to a civil outward good and end; of both, so every believer who, besides this natural conscience and rule, hath an enlightened

conscience carrying a more bright and lively stamp of the kingly place and power of the Lord Jesus, swaying him by the light of faith or scripture, and such a man may be called *microchristus,* the epitome of Christ mystical.

The dogma of the two orders was common to all the Puritans, and the differences in their political thinking turn in the last analysis on the different relations which they suppose to obtain between the two orders. To most of the Puritans it seems evident that the superior order, the order of grace, must rule the inferior. That is the position which receives extreme illustration in the Millenarians, and in such a document as *Certain Queries.* But to some of the Puritans this dogma means the total separation of the two orders, each with its own appropriate kind of goodness. For of goodness there are two kinds: the spiritual, or what we call piety, to which is attached the gift of salvation; and natural goodness (of various types) to which the unconverted and even the heathen can rise, but to which no such gift is attached. Williams writes (pp. 282-3):

. . . [T]his I must remember you of: that when the most high God created all things of nothing, he saw and acknowledged divers sorts of goodness, which must still be acknowledged in their distinct kinds—a good air, a good ground, a good tree. . . . I say the same in artificials, a good garment, a good house, . . . a good ship. I also add a good city, a good company or corporation, a good husband, father, master . . . ; that is, morally, civilly, good in their several civil respects and employments. . . . These I observe to prove that a subject, a magistrate, may be a good subject, a good magistrate, in respect of civil or moral goodness (which thousands want; and where it is it is commendable and beautiful) though godliness, which is infinitely more beautiful be wanting, and which is only proper to the Christian state, the commonweal of Israel, the true church, the holy nation (Ephes. 2; 1 Pet. 2).

It is not for the sake of the natural order that the distinction of the two orders is in the first place emphasized, but for the sake of the spiritual. In Williams, at least, it is a sense of the uniqueness of the spiritual experience that demands its sharp separation from everything else—but with momentous results in the order of nature and in politics. The separation indeed gets itself recorded (as we shall see) in the *Agreement of the People*.

In general terms the result of the separation of the two orders is to enable the Puritan who emphasizes the distinction between them to adopt in the secular sphere radical and naturalistic ideas, and to avoid (or rather, as the subsequent history of Dissent seems to show, to postpone) the repercussion of these ideas upon his dogmatic creed. In secular education, for example, the Puritan can accept the ideas of Bacon, while stoutly maintaining that for preaching the Word nothing is required but a knowledge of the English Bible and the gift of the Spirit. This fact is fully illustrated in William Dell's volume, *The Stumbling Stone* (1653), which has been hailed as a pioneer work in university reform, and condemned as Puritan obscurantism of a peculiarly vulgar variety. Both views are correct. But our concern is with politics. In politics the most obvious result of what I will for brevity call *the principle of segregation,* is the separation of church and state. And this has a twofold bearing on liberty: first, as it becomes the basis for the full Puritan doctrine of toleration; secondly, as it effects the complete secularizing of the state. The primary object is to spiritualize the church; but not less certainly it secularizes the state, and invites a new account of its origin, nature, and functions. The new account will not necessarily be democratic in character; but it may be so. The secularizing of the state is democracy's opportunity.

But the separation of the two orders, and of their social organs, the church and the state, does not mean the cessation of all influence one on the other. Religion will continue to influence politics—but not by direct inferences drawn from dogma; by analogy instead. The two orders are roughly parallel, and what is true *within* one is true *within* the other, though the basis in one instance is *grace* and the basis in the other is *nature*. There is (we have seen) a spiritual equality in the order of grace. Is there not an analogous equality in the order of nature? This is only one of a dozen points at which analogically Puritanism could reinforce the cause of liberty and equality. In a word, wherever one discovers within the order of grace, as the Puritan conceives it, ideas of liberty, of equality, of democratic organization, of government by the consent of the governed, of truth and agreement reached through free and equal discussion, there is also the possibility of their transfer to secular politics. Where, however, *the principle of segregation* is not emphasized, the inferences from dogma point towards the dictatorship of the Saints. Where the principle *is* emphasized this inference is prevented, and analogy points towards an Agreement of the People. It remains to see how.

II

As there is a specifically Christian idea of equality, so there is a specifically Christian idea of liberty. The doctrine of Christian liberty has been consistently overlooked by historians, though references to it abound in the seventeenth century, and there is a complete exposition of it in Milton, of its theological aspects in the *De Doctrina,* and of its practical bearings in *Of Civil Power in Ecclesiastical Causes.* In simplest terms the doctrine is something like this. The note of the old dispensation is bondage, for it means subjection to the letter of an external law. The note of the new dispensation, of the Gospel, is freedom, for it means the abrogation of this outward law, in favour of an inward law written by the Spirit in the heart of the believer. It will make a great deal of difference whether this abrogation of outward law is taken to mean the abrogation of the ceremonial law only, or of the ceremonial and judicial, or of these two and the moral law as well. According to Milton the whole Mosaic Law, in its three branches, is for the believer abrogated by the Gospel of Christ. Here one recognizes the basis of Antinomianism. But the doctrine need not, and in Milton does not, amount to Antinomianism. Nor is it original with Milton, as M. Saurat assumes; precisely the same doctrine is found in Luther, where it is turned against the papal tyranny, as Milton turns it against the tyranny of bishop and presbyter. But Luther, who originates, at least in its Protestant form, what I have called *the principle of segregation,* applies that principle so as to cut off all bearing of Christian upon civil liberty (pp. 221-5). Not so Milton, who does not apply the principle of segregation at all consistently. Milton makes the doctrine of Christian liberty a foundation of his plea for liberty of worship (which is quite compatible with the principle of segregation); but he also tends to transfer it directly, and not merely analogically, to the secular sphere (which is not compatible with that principle). This by the way. The fact to recognize is the tremendous force of the doctrine of Christian liberty itself, and its fundamental position in the struggle for religious toleration. This can best be seen by a quotation from Milton made up largely of texts from St. Paul (pp. 226-8):

I have shown that the civil power hath neither right nor can do right by forcing religious things. I will now show the wrong it doth by violating the fundamental privilege of the Gospel, the new birthright of every true believer, Christian liberty: *Where the spirit of the Lord is, there is liberty; Jerusalem which is above is free, which is the mother of us all.* . . .
For he [Christ] hath not only given us this gift as a special privilege and excellence of his free Gospel above the servile Law, but strictly also hath commanded

us to keep it and enjoy it: *You are called to liberty.* . . . *Stand fast therefore in the liberty wherewith Christ hath made us free, and be not entangled again with the yoke of bondage.* . . . *Ye are bought with a price: be not made the servants of men.* Some trivial price belike and for some frivolous pretences paid in their opinion if—bought and by him redeemed who is God, from what was once the service of God—we shall be enthralled again and forced by men to what now is but the service of men. . . . *Ye are complete in him which is the head of all principality and power;* not completed therefore or made the more religious by those ordinances of civil power from which Christ, their head, hath discharged us, *blotting out the handwriting of ordinances that was against us, which was contrary to us, and took it out of the way, nailing it to his cross.* . . . Hence it plainly appears that if we be not free, we are not sons but still servants unadopted. . . .

Ill was our condition changed from legal to evangelical and small advantage gotten by the Gospel, if for the spirit of adoption to freedom promised us we receive again the spirit of bondage to fear. . . . It will therefore not misbecome the meanest Christian to put in mind Christian magistrates . . . that they meddle not rashly with Christian liberty, the birthright and outward testimony of our adoption, lest, while they . . . think they do God service, they themselves, like the sons of that bondwoman, be found persecuting them who are free-born of the Spirit, and by a sacrilege of not the least aggravation, bereaving them of that sacred liberty which our Saviour with his own blood purchased for them.

It is thus that the Puritan counteracts the appeal to the Old Testament by an appeal to the New. The argument does not imply a departure from dogma and scripture; it is carried on within their confines, as could be proved just as conclusively from Roger Williams (cf. pp. 266-92).

One debt of liberty to the Puritan parties is the fact that they are always bringing the question of liberty forward for discussion. The subject of the Army debates in 1647-9 is religious liberty and political liberty. For the Puritan the priority of religious liberty is plain to read. It is in that protracted argument, carried on first with his opponents and then with his fellow Puritans, that his principles of freedom take shape. The object is to secure for the Christian his inalienable right, Christian liberty —the birthright of the second birth. Presently, however, two facts become evident. (1) You cannot guarantee the liberty of the Saint without at the same time guaranteeing the liberty of all men. In this one department, at least, the step forward from liberty to equality is logically forced upon the Puritans of the Left though only some of them take the step. (2) But secondly, it is not really possible to draw a sharp line between religious liberty and civil liberty. As Harrington observed, "Where civil liberty is entire, it includes liberty of conscience; where liberty of conscience is entire, it includes civil liberty." Thus the struggle for religious liberty holds, as it were, in solution the whole gift of Puritanism to the cause of freedom. But in order that the gift may be made, it is necessary that *the principle of segregation* (already applied in the interests of the Christian) should be carried to its logical conclusion and be applied also in the interests of the natural man. Roger Williams and the Levellers have done this so successfully that the modern reader tends to forget one fact: that in the first instance it is the Christian, and not the natural man, for whom they are concerned. The concern for the natural man follows. For Roger Williams religious liberty, resting on the total separation of church and state, is equally essential for the spiritual well-being of the church and for the internal peace of the civil state. In the Levellers the secular interest finally becomes paramount.

But to return to the doctrine of Christian liberty itself. It emphasizes the freedom of the believer. And we must add, his freedom not only from the bondage of the Law but from the bondage of sin. Thus Milton can say that "only good men can truly love liberty; the rest love not liberty, but licence." "Know that to be free is the same thing as to be pious, to be wise, to be temperate and just, to be frugal and abstinent, and lastly to be magnanimous and brave; so to be the opposite of all these is the same as to be a slave" (p. 231). But if only good men can be truly free, then Christian liberty is perfectly compatible with the rule of the regenerate over the unregenerate, as Milton increasingly came to believe. It is compatible even with the cruder notion of the dictatorship of the Saints. But this is true only if *the principle of segregation* is not applied. If the principle is applied, and is followed up by the *principle of analogy,* the result is totally different: Christian liberty for the Christian; natural liberty for the natural man. So that for the Levellers even liberty of worship becomes not merely an evangelical, but also a natural right. But the *principle of analogy,* once it is free to operate, will carry us further than that. Overton knows what he is about when, in his *Arrow Against All Tyrants,* he addresses the secretaries, men familiar with the ideas of Christian liberty and Christian equality, in these terms (introd. p. 69):

> For by natural birth all men are equal . . . born to like propriety, liberty and freedom, and as we are delivered of God by the hand of nature into this world, every one with a natural innate freedom and propriety, . . . even so we are to live, every one equally . . . to enjoy his birthright and privilege, even all whereof God by nature hath made him free . . . ; every man by nature being a king, priest, prophet, in his own natural circuit and compass, whereof no second may partake but by deputation, commission, and free consent from him whose right and freedom it is.

All save the last few words (and they have their own special relation to Puritanism) are virtually a statement of the doctrines of Christian liberty and equality, with *man* written over the word "believer," and *nature* written over the word "grace."

Analogy will lead from liberty and equality in the spiritual order to liberty and equality in the natural order. But what of the special features of Christian liberty? Do they reproduce themselves in politics? In measure they do. The marks of Christian liberty are twofold (though the two marks are perhaps in the last analysis one): (1) It is essentially individualistic, depending upon an inward spiritual state reached by the individual believer, and not upon any level of outward condition achieved by the community. And (2) liberty is defined in terms of the abrogation of outward law. It is not merely individualist, but at bottom anarchist in character. The ideal in Milton's phrase is to be able to live without laws because "our reason is our law." And in Milton's view of the state and of civil liberty precisely the same characteristics are seen. His is a laissez-faire state. It should guarantee the absolute separation of the ecclesiastical and political functions, removing from the church all state support and all power of persecution. It should guarantee complete freedom of discussion. It should provide for a state-supported, but not of course a compulsory, system of education —this, apart from the maintenance of order, being the one positive duty assigned to it. Finally, it will be well, he says (pp. 230-1),

since laws are usually worse in proportion as they are more numerous, if you shall not enact so many new laws as you abolish old, which do not operate so much as warnings against evil as impediments in the way of good; and if you shall retain only those which are necessary . . . which, while they prevent the frauds of the wicked, do not prohibit the innocent freedoms of the good, which punish crimes without interdicting those things which are lawful, only on account of the abuses to which they may occasionally be exposed. For the intention of

laws is to check the commission of vice, *but liberty is the best school of virtue.*

In this Milton is thoroughly typical. Individualism is part of the heritage of Puritanism. And up to a point both the Independents and the Levellers agree in advancing a laissez-faire ideal of the state. Distrust not only of corrupt government, but of over-much government, appears in both the *Heads of the Proposals* and the *Agreements of the People,* which set forth the individual's inalienable rights, and are obviously designed above all else to safeguard them (pp. 443-5, 355-67). Under the absolutist system of Charles I government had been everywhere, and under a self-perpetuating Parliament the old menace had assumed a new guise. On the practical level Independents and Levellers are reacting against this situation. On the theoretic level they are embodying in their constitutions an individualism which is at bottom religious in origin. And this twofold reference is indeed presented by the official *Agreement of the People* taken as a whole. It springs from a particular historical situation, and it embodies a set of principles which, if they are not derived from theology and the Puritan church order, are at least strongly reinforced thereby.

It must suffice to indicate what the points of contact between the *Agreement* and Puritan religion are; and by this statement to allow our thesis to stand or fall.

(1) The first point of contact is less a principle embodied in the *Agreement* than an assumption which underlies the document as a whole: namely the possibility of arriving at truth, and at agreement in the truth, through free discussion; for the *Agreements* (as Mr. Pease has shown) are designed to furnish a basis for discussion. The idea is indeed widespread in the Puritan revolution. It is the confident assumption of Milton in the *Areopagitica,* and (originally at least) of all parties in the Army debates. It is an idea thoroughly democratic in character. And one of its sources in seventeenth-century England (I do not claim this as the

only source) is the democratic practice of the Puritan congregations, Independent and Anabaptist. Moreover, there underlies the ideal of truth and agreement through discussion a view of truth as progressive in comprehension if not in revelation, which is precisely the view that we saw at the beginning of this paper to be characteristic of the Independents and which we illustrated by a quotation from John Goodwin.

(2) In the second place, the *Agreement* incorporates (as already hinted) the idea of the separation of the two orders, or what I have called *the principle of segregation.* After specifying the matters reserved as inalienable rights, it provides: "That the Representative have the supreme trust in order to the preservation and government of the whole, and that their power extend . . . to the enacting . . . [and] repealing . . . of laws, and the highest and final judgment, *concerning all natural or civil things, but not concerning things spiritual or evangelical.*"

(3) The *Agreement* itself, eschewing all effort at reform in the church, concentrates on the shaping of a perfect civil constitution. And here just below the surface lurks a very striking example of influence by analogy. Behind the idea of a free state composed of equals stood the model of a free church. And the mode of procedure in the two cases is identical, as Milton, in the *Ready and Easy Way to Establish a Free Commonwealth,* makes abundantly clear. Those who would reform the state, he remarks (introd. p. 72),

are not bound by any statute of preceding parliaments but by the law of nature only, which is the only law of laws truly and properly to all mankind fundamental, the beginning and end of all government, to which no parliament or people that will thoroughly reform but may and must have recourse, *as they had (and must yet have) in church reformation . . . to evangelic rules,* not to ecclesiastical canons though never so ancient, so ratified and established in the land by stat-

utes—which for the most part are mere positive laws, neither natural nor moral.

The model of ecclesiastical excellence, says the author of *Regal Tyranny Discovered* (1647), is founded on the law of God set forth in the New Testament and received by faith; that of civil excellence is "founded on the law of God engraven in nature and demonstrated by reason." In each case there is a primitive model of excellence, and underlying it a fundamental law; and in each case the injunction is to depart from, and if need be destroy, whatever conflicts with the law or fails to conform to the model. In the order of grace it is the law of Christ revealed in the New Testament (and, we may add, written in the heart of the believer) and so to be known by faith; in the parallel order of nature it is a parallel, but this time a natural law, discoverable and demonstrable by reason. In the church Puritan scripturism is a mighty agent of destruction and reconstruction. And whether operating directly, as in the Millenarians, or by analogy, as in the authors cited and in the Levellers, it is capable of having a similar effect in the state. Here are Puritan iconoclasm and utopianism with the principles from which they derive their strength. I am not, of course, suggesting that the concept of a law of nature is *derived* by the Independents and Levellers by analogy from the law of grace; but merely that it is reinforced and rendered acceptable by the analogy. Indeed throughout I am concerned to know how the Puritans came to adopt these liberal and often radical opinions, and not the actual sources of the opinions themselves.

(4) But the analogy between the purely spiritual church of extreme Puritanism and the purely secular state of the Levellers can be carried further. First there is the note of individualism, already observed, and expressed in the concept of inalienable rights. Secondly, if the Leveller emphasizes the *contract* on which the authority of all just government depends (not the contract between governor and governed, a form of

contract with which he was, of course, familiar, and which he had urged effectively against Charles; a contract rather among the sovereign people themselves as well as with their delegates)—if (I say) the Leveller emphasized this contract, and the principle of government by the consent of the governed, was it not because he had had, in his church, experience of a community organized upon these very principles? Behind the model of a free state stands the model of a free church, with its church covenant which embodies (and is conditioned by) the fundamental law, but which is freely consented to by every member of the church, and constitutes, so far as that congregation is concerned, an agreement of the people in spiritual things. There is, of course, one very real difference. In the church, government by consent is safeguarded by the power of withdrawal. In the state this power of withdrawal virtually disappears; its place is taken in part by a series of "reserves" (the inalienable rights mentioned above), which are not thus specified in the church covenant, and in part by the democratic device of biennial elections, so that (as Mr. Lindsay happily remarks) voting against the successful candidate is somehow thought of as a way of recording your consent to be governed by him.

(5) But, finally, the democratic order of the government to be established by the *Agreement* has a much wider significance. We spoke of the belief in the possibility of arriving at truth and agreement through free and equal discussion as something that underlay the very idea of an Agreement. It permeates the form of government to be set up. The *Agreement* may tend to reduce the members of the biennial Parliaments to the status of delegates, but if so, it is the interests of the democracy as a whole. Representative institutions are necessary in a national state; but the democracy in which the Leveller really believes, and which he wishes to perpetuate even at the expense of the Parliament, is the direct democracy of the Puritan congregation.

III

On a long view of the subject the conflict between this ideal and the sovereignty of Parliament, if not removed, is at least mitigated. For (as Mr. G. P. Gooch has observed in another connection) with the coming of democracy the old antithesis of the state and the individual loses much of its acuteness. Despite their defeat in practical politics, the Levellers' ideal persists as a valuable secondary tradition in English political thought and modifies the primary tradition for its good. But there is yet a third tradition in politics—happily never consolidated in English politics—between which and the Leveller ideal quarter is neither asked nor given: this is the tradition of dictatorship. It too has its representatives in the Puritan period, and (as we have seen) its place in the the pattern of Puritan thought. The terms in which that pattern is built up strike strangely upon the modern ear. Their study is a matter of historical—if you will, of antiquarian—interest; but the issues have not lost all their relevance to-day. "The consent of the governed is the only secure and lasting basis of government; and liberty is the condition of consent. Only free men can consent to their form of government. No enduring system can be established on the negation of liberty, even if it comes with the temporary gift of good government." Thus writes General Smuts in the 1930's; and that is precisely the Levellers' case against arbitrary government three hundred years ago—not merely against arbitrary and inefficient government by Charles, but against arbitrary though efficient government by Cromwell: against all those elements in Puritan thought which fostered dictatorship at the expense of democracy, and reform at the expense of freedom. But to concentrate on the extremes, on the Levellers with their doctrine of the sovereignty of the People and on the Millenarians with their doctrine of the privileges and the duties of the Saints, is to miss one of the most fascinating of the problems, too complicated to develop here: the problem of the conflict of ideas within the party of the Independents, and in Cromwell himself with his real feeling at least for religious liberty but his readiness to defy the will of the majority in the interests of reform—"That's the question: what's for their good, not what pleases them" (p. 420).

All this is not, of course, to deny the presence, conscious or half conscious, of motives far other than those on which our attention has been fixed. "All that I speak for," says Ireton, in the debates on the franchise, and naïvely enough—"All the main thing that I speak for is because I would have an eye to property." And Rainborough utters his immortal phrase: "The poorest he that is in England has a life to live, as the greatest he." But the Levellers, as Petty and Rainborough declare with justice, intend no attack upon the institution of private property, which is grounded in the law of nature and guaranteed by the law of God (see pp. 53, 57, 63, 59). One power withheld from the Representative in the *Agreement of the People* is the power of levelling estates: private property is an inalienable right (pp. 363, 340).

Communism in the period—of necessity we use the term rather loosely—is represented by the Diggers alone, whose position must in a word be made clear. The historian who chooses to assume that communism is the corollary of political democracy may regard the Diggers as carrying over to the economic sphere the principles of reason, justice, and equality advanced by the Levellers in the political. By the title, *The True Levellers' Standard Advanced* (pp. 379-85), Winstanley and his associates put forward some such claim. But the bases of Leveller and of Digger thinking are in truth as different as are their results. In the Levellers, as in the Independents, there is a strong, perhaps an exaggerated element of individualism: nothing could be more remote from collectivism than the *Agreements of the People*, in which Independent and Leveller collaborated and over which they wrangled in heated debate. But in the Independents, as distinct from the Levellers, the strong current of individualism which takes its rise in their common religious life is crossed and in measure thwarted by a desire to establish the reign of righteousness on earth and by a failure to apply without reserves *the principle of segregation*. With the Diggers the desire to establish the reign of righteousness, as they conceive it, obliterates every other motive. In them, as in the Millenarians, the principle of segregation is not invoked; the direct inferences from their religious thought are allowed to dominate their view of secular life, their interpretation of the past and their vision of the future; the ideal of the holy community, in the peculiar form which it takes in their minds, is not restricted to the order of grace but intrudes upon the order of nature. The Diggers are working for an economic millennium. And by them the liberty of the individual, so prized by the Levellers, is perhaps as little regarded as by the stern visionaries who hope on the battlefields of the Civil War to usher in the rule of Christ and his Saints. But instead of taking scripture, dogma, and prophecy with the terrifying literalness of Harrison and his fellows, Winstanley and his group subject them to a process of allegorical interpretation no less startling: the fall and its curse mean the emergence of pride and covetousness and the introduction of private property; the whole history of Israel and the coming of Christ are re-read in the light of this assumption; and the millennium (which, wherever emphasized, always carries some promise of perfectibility) is interpreted as the defeat of covetousness, the abolition of private property, and the establishment of communism throughout the world. Thus does the dogmatic scheme furnish a theological foundation for their social and political thought, even though their treatment of dogma undermines it in the very process of interpretation.

The Diggers do not contradict our thesis of the close connections in the Puritan revolution between religious and political thinking; rather they offer one more illustration of the variety of those connections. But instead of restating the thesis, I am disposed to formulate another: before we can arrive at the pattern of any period's thought we must surrender ourselves, at least temporarily, to its dominant terminology; only after so doing are we permitted (and perhaps constrained) to translate it into the terms of our own age—into those terms which it is our comfortable habit to regard as finally and even exclusively significant.

THE LEVELLER MOVEMENT WAS A PRODUCT of the form of Puritanism known as Independency, and it spread within the army, especially among the rank and file, as the army became predominantly Independent in religious opinion. The Levellers were democrats, believing in the sovereignty of the people under a higher, or fundamental, law which imposed limitations on the government in the interest of individual liberty. Their political program, never put into effect, was set forth in a document presented to the House of Commons just before the execution of Charles I. This draft constitution was called *An Agreement of the People,* and one of its specific restrictions upon the power of the representative legislature for which it provided was that the legislature should not "level men's estates, destroy property, or make all things common." Thus the Levellers, although advocates of political equality, explicitly repudiated communism and economic equality. There was, however, a short-lived communistic movement, whose adherents, inferior in numbers and in organization to the political Levellers, were known as Diggers or True Levellers. Their leader was Gerrard Winstanley, most of whose writings have been reprinted by Professor George H. Sabine, of Cornell University, in *The Works of Gerrard Winstanley* (1941). The modern writers who have dealt at any length with the Diggers have been for the most part Marxists who have seen in the activities of Winstanley and his followers a seventeenth-century expression of the Marxian class struggle and conclusive evidence that communism is not foreign to England but, on the contrary, deeply rooted in English tradition. In the following essay, Professor Winthrop S. Hudson, now of the Colgate-Rochester Divinity School, a penetrating American student of English religious history, concerns himself with the Digger movement. He sees Winstanley as a product of the radical Puritan thought of his time rather than as a precursor of Karl Marx.

ECONOMIC AND SOCIAL THOUGHT OF GERRARD WINSTANLEY

WAS HE A SEVENTEENTH-CENTURY MARXIST?

WINTHROP S. HUDSON

The resurrection from obscurity of Gerrard Winstanley, the "Digger," began in 1895 with Eduard Bernstein's *Socialismus und Demokratie in der grossen Englischen Revolution*[1] and was brought to completion in 1941 with the publication of his collected works.[2] One of the most colorful and interesting of the economic and religious radicals of seventeenth-century England, Winstanley long deserved a better fate than the neglect he received from succeeding generations of historians.

In 1648 Winstanley published several religious tracts which were typical of the chiliastic mysticism of left-wing Puritanism. The following year he began the "digging," which has captured the interest and imagination of his recent interpreters. Late in 1648 Winstanley had come to the conclusion that the imminent day of the Lord he had been proclaiming, as the beginning of the millennium, was to result in a communistic utopia, in which there would be neither buying, selling, working for hire, nor giving hire. The earth would be made "a common Treasury, without respect of persons." While in a trance, he had received a revelation that the saints were to work together and eat bread together, and he was told to "declare this all abroad."[3] This he did by word of mouth and by his pen; and he said that, when the Lord showed him the place where he would have him "manure and work upon the common Lands," he would "then go forth and declare it in my action."[4] The actual "digging" by Winstanley and his small band of followers began on April 1, 1649 at St. George's Hill in Surrey and continued for about a year before they were forced, largely as a result of local opposition, to discontinue their activity and admit defeat.

Except for the peculiarity of "digging," there is little in Winstanley's basic philosophy to distinguish him from the other religious radicals produced by the Puritan revolution who, as the representatives of the dispossessed, gave voice to the social discontent of the time and looked forward to a day of retribution when God would intervene and mete out justice to the oppressors. The similarities of the Diggers, the Quakers, the more enthusiastic Baptists, and the Fifth Monarchy men, with regard to both their theological points of view and their social attitudes, are more significant than their differences.[5] They were cut off the same piece, according to much the same pattern, and in large measure preached a common message of social redemption. They all believed in visions and dreams, in direct illumination and guidance by the

---

[1] Translated by H. J. Stenning as *Cromwell and communism* (London, 1930).

[2] George H. Sabine (ed.), *The works of Gerrard Winstanley* (Ithaca, N.Y., 1941). Winstanley's three earliest tracts are not reprinted, but abstracts are included. Sabine gives in his introduction an informative and well-balanced account of Winstanley's thought. He avoids many of the pitfalls into which Winstanley's other interpreters have stumbled. The fiction of Winstanley's rationalism, for example, is deftly demolished (pp. 40-41), and nowhere does Sabine disregard the millenarian framework on which Winstanley's thought is predicated.

[3] *The new law of righteousnes*, p. 190. All citations of Winstanley's tracts are to Sabine's edition of his works.

[4] *Ibid.*, p. 194.

[5] The agreements and similarities of these groups are set forth at length in William Y. Tindall, *John Bunyan, mechanick preacher* (New York, 1934), p. 5 and *passim*. Tindall makes a qualified exception of the Diggers (pp. 93-95), which is to be accounted for by his dependence upon Bernstein and Lewis H. Berens.

Reprinted by special permission from *The Journal of Modern History,* XVIII (1946), 1-21. Most of the footnotes which originally appeared with this essay have been omitted.

Spirit. They disagreed over the exact authority of Scripture—a disagreement more theoretical than real—but they were agreed that it was the possession of the Spirit, rather than education, which made possible correct interpretation. Pride and covetousness were regarded as the two cardinal sins. Millenarians all, they looked to God to bring an end to the present age of the Beast, and they were convinced that in this great work God would make use of the humble and despised in preference to the rich and powerful. While there was general agreement in the interpretation of the eschatological passages of the Bible,[6] there was some difference of opinion as to the manner in which Christ would appear and secure his victory. Some believed that he would appear in person to rule; others believed his coming would be in spirit within the saints through whom he would subdue the wicked; still others believed that he would appear within each individual to "bruise the head of the Serpent," subdue him, and cast him out. In addition to controversies over matters of emphasis and detail in their message of redemption, the radical groups were divided as to the validity of what they called "forms, ordinances, and customs" in worship and ecclesiastical government. Nevertheless, in spite of the fact that these differences were magnified by controversy, they were of small moment when placed over against the large areas of agreement that existed in left-wing Puritanism.

I

Unfortunately, from the point of view of a balanced appreciation of Winstanley, his initial resurrection from the limbo of forgotten men was accomplished by one who was a better Marxist than historian. Eduard

Bernstein found Winstanley interesting as an early exponent of the class struggle and as a class-conscious agitator in behalf of "a complete social system based on communistic principles." This is the pattern of interpretation that has been followed by most of those who have given attention to the Digger movement since that time. Indeed, much of the current interest in Winstanley is due to a desire to demonstrate that "the ideals of Socialism and Communism are not . . . . something of foreign origin . . . . , alien to the genius of the English people."[7] On the contrary, in the Diggers it becomes evident that left-wing socialism is indigenous to the British Isles and has its roots in "the native British tradition."[8]

To arrive at such a conclusion, however, requires a certain degree of sophistication. According to Christopher Hill, the usual approach to historical personalities is far from adequate. "The orthodox attitude to the seventeenth century revolution is misleading . . . . because it takes the actors in the revolution at their face value, and assumes that the best way to find out what people were fighting about is to consider what the leaders *said* they were fighting about."[9] Hence, much of what was said by the participants in the drama of seventeenth-century England must be regarded as mere camouflage without any real meaning or significance. Thus, Bernstein asserts that the Diggers' "mystical phraseology" served "as a cloak to conceal the revolutionary designs of the authors."[10] David W. Petegorsky speaks of Winstanley's "theological camouflage" and states that, although the Digger documents are "couched in the religious phraseology of the period," they lean "little on theological support for . . . . [their] validity."[11]

---

[6] The four beasts of Daniel were universally regarded as the Bablylonian, Persian, Greek, and Roman empires; the ten horns on the brow of the fourth beast were the remaining kingdoms; and the little horn, symbolizing the premature decay of a tenth part of Babylon, was identified with the Norman bondage in England.

[7] Henry Holorenshaw, *The Levellers and the English revolution* (London, 1939), p. 93.

[8] Christopher Hill (ed.), *The English revolution, 1640* (London, 1940), p. 100.

[9] *Ibid.,* pp. 9-10.

[10] P. 107.

[11] *Left-wing democracy in the English Civil War* (London, 1940), pp. 74 and 139.

The anticipations, resemblances, and parallels that the modern Marxist finds in Winstanley are numerous. Henry Holorenshaw, for example, discovered that Winstanley was "one of the pioneers in the conception of history as the history of class struggles," that "anticipations of modern Socialism are remarkably common in Winstanley's writings," and that "some of his remarks are reminiscent of the Soviet constitution of today."[12] Margaret James sees a "striking resemblance" in many of Winstanley's statements "to those enunciated two centuries later by Marx,"[13] while Christopher Hill finds in them "a very interesting anticipation of historical materialism and scientific communism."[14] Petegorsky, in his study of Winstanley, calls him "the most advanced radical of the century," who was "convinced that there is a law of development in social institutions" and who set forth "the one genuine proletarian ideology that the Civil War produced."[15]

[12] Pp. 28, 29, and 30.

[13] Hill, pp. 83 and 95.

[14] *Ibid.*, p. 69.

[15] Pp. 124, 145, and 73. A similar interpretation of Winstanley is to be found in *Gerrard Winstanley: selections from his writings*, ed. Leonard Hamilton (London, 1944). Lewis H. Berens, who made the first extended study of Winstanley, constitutes an important exception to the pattern of Marxist interpretation. But Berens, as a Single-taxer, had the point of view of his own particular hero to be read back into the mind of the seventeenth-century Digger. Henry George becomes Winstanley's "great modern representative." "What Winstanley discovered and proclaimed in the Seventeenth Century," says Berens, "Henry George rediscovered and again proclaimed in the Nineteenth Cenutry" (*The Digger move-*

While it is difficult to recognize the pre-Marxian Digger in the comparisons made by those who view him through post-Marxian eyes, it is not to be supposed that Winstanley was without genius and insight. He was much more than merely an average spokesman for the socially and economically dispossessed of his day. In many ways, in spite of his limited education, he stood head and shoulders above the other writers who came to grips with the situation created by a civil war that had benefited the landed and commercial classes while making the earning of a livelihood more difficult than ever for the laborers and artisans. He is distinguished from them by the clarity of his ethical judgments, by his thundering indictment and analysis of the results of private ownership of land, and by his always vivid and frequently penetrating insights into the character of other social institutions. Most surprising, perhaps, is his discussion of the source of wealth which describes, with some degree of accuracy, what nineteenth-century economists labeled "the labor theory of value."[16]

The basic misinterpretation of Winstanley's thought does not center in his specific insights with reference to the contemporary social situation. It is not his negative criticisms that trouble his interpreters; rather it is in the consideration of his positive proposals that misconceptions occur. The injustice is done in disregarding the fundamental intellectual framework within which he formulated his ideas. By suggesting that the

ment in the days of the Commonwealth [London, 1906], pp. 231, 234, and 229).

[16] *The law of freedom in a platform*, p. 511.

BATTLE OF WORCESTER: Decisive engagement of 1651, as a result of which the Cromwellian regime was secured. The Scots were defeated in their attempt to encourage Lancashire and Wales to rise in behalf of Prince Charles, the future Charles II.

EDUARD BERNSTEIN: German social reformer (d. 1932). Spokesman for the cause of Marxian revisionism, he attempted in his *Evolutionary Socialism* (1899) to eliminate from Marxian doctrines those features that the passage of time had shown to be erroneous. Often appealing to history in order to marshal evidence in support of his views, Bernstein in a work published in German in 1895 called attention to the Digger movement.

Digger movement "was an attempt to proceed by direct action to a form of agrarian
communism by members of the dispossessed
rural proletariat,"[17] the basic world view
upon which Winstanley's economic philosophy rested is completely distorted.

The best statement, perhaps, as to the
supposed methods by which Winstanley
hoped to realize his utopia is to be found
in Petegorsky, for *Left-wing democracy in
the English Civil War* is, on the whole, a
moderate and scholarly discussion of the
Digger movement.

> What more than anything else, I be-
> lieve, distinguishes Winstanley among the
> forerunners of modern socialism is his
> profound concern with the methods by
> which the communist order is to be
> achieved. The vision of a collectivist soci-
> ety . . . . is shared by many thinkers. But
> until the nineteenth century, ... few
> . . . . appreciated the problems its estab-
> lishment involved. . . . . Where they
> were aware of those difficulties, they
> despaired of their solution; and their
> communist societies were utopias set in
> another and distant world. Only God, by
> effecting a change in the hearts of men,
> could bring down those utopias from the
> realms of fancy. . . . . In Winstanley
> there is at once a keen perception of the
> problems . . . . , a consideration of the
> methods . . . . and the optimistic con-
> clusion that the task is not beyond the
> limits of human personality.[18]

Winstanley had faith, Petegorsky continues,
in the power of love and the efficacy of
rational persuasion in effecting social
change; "but it is nevertheless true to say"
that "the essence of his doctrine was the
realization that social change had to be
initiated neither by the spirit of love nor
by the force of reason, but only through
the direct action of politically-conscious individuals." The communist order was to be
established not by a "sudden miracle" but
by "the development of the waste and com-

[17] Hill, p. 69.
[18] Pp. 197-98.

mon lands by the poor." "The poor," Winstanley was convinced, "by their own unaided efforts, could remake the world."
Thus, in Winstanley, "both the tendency of
the mystic to await the intervention of the
Lord and the natural detachment of the
philosopher were conquered by the realism
of the practical reformer."[19]

Such a characterization makes Winstanley
seem eminently sensible and reasonable to
twentieth-century minds. As we shall see,
however, he was not a seventeenth-century
Marxist, nor was he even what we would
call a "practical reformer." He was acting
upon the assumption that God would intervene by "sudden miracle" to establish the
new order in society.

II

Winstanley's venture in digging and
planting the waste and common lands began
at a time when the failure of attempted
political reform[20] had reinforced the tendency to look to supernatural sources for
relief. All the left-wing religious groups had
been characterized by a more or less intense
millenarianism. In February 1649, with the
presentation of the Norwich petition requesting a government by the saints until
Christ should come, the Fifth Monarchy
movement came into being, and much of
the current apocalyptic sentiment began to
be channeled into a definite political program.[21] The Diggers represented a nonpolitical variation of this general eschatological
expectation, developing simultaneously with
the more widespread Fifth Monarchy movement.

Winstanley had begun his propagandist
career as an exponent of a chiliastic mysticism, and this interest constituted his chief
significance in his own day. Since he retained
this emphasis to the end, it is through the

[19] *Ibid.,* pp. 178, 199, 200, and 212.
[20] The Leveller agitation was largely brought
to an end by the defeat of the mutinous regiments at Burford, May 14, 1649.
[21] Louise F. Brown, *The political activities
of the Baptist and Fifth Monarchy men* (Washington, D.C., 1912), pp. 17-18.

framework of a mystical millenarianism that his social concern must be viewed.

The inclusion of a communistic emphasis in Winstanley's eschatological scheme was a relatively simple matter. The restoration of the Creation, as Winstanley had conceived it, was to result in a "Community of Mankind" in which men should be "of one heart and mind," knit together by an inner "Union and Communion of Love." When he was persuaded (by the radical Levellers of Buckinghamshire, we suspect) that the greatest sin in the world was "to lock up the treasuries of the Earth in Chests and houses: and suffer it to rust or moulder, while others starve," he concluded that the restoration would include a "Community of the Earth" as well as of mankind. No longer would men fight for possession of the objects of earth; they would share them "without using force or restraining one another." Actually, these "two Communities" were but "one in two branches," for there could be no true community of mankind without a community of the earth and no true community of the earth without a community of mankind.

The fourth chapter of Acts gave Winstanley his clue as to the way in which the new emphasis could be fitted into his eschatological pattern. When Christ first began "to spread himself in sons and daughters . . . ., the rich sold their possessions, and gave equality to the poor, and no man said, that any thing that he possessed was his own, for they had all things common." This was "a vexation" to the Serpent, and he sought to suppress this community. Whereupon the Lord, in order that "covetous, wise and lordly flesh" might demonstrate misery to be the only result of self-seeking ends, gave "this Beast a toleration to rule 42 months, or a time, times, and dividing time." Viewed in this light, all subsequent history and especially the history of England became illuminated as a phase of the great universal struggle of the Serpent in mankind for "propriety."

In the utopia of the Diggers, the "King of Righteousness" was to rule in every man;

buying and selling were to cease; distinctions of *mine* and *thine* would disappear; people no longer would "work for hire" or "give hire"; everyone would "work in love: one with and for another; and eat bread together, as being members of one household." The necessities of all would be supplied from a common storehouse to which all would contribute the products of their labor. There would be no beggars, no tears, no complaining, no oppression. Laws, lawyers, prisons, engines of punishment—even government itself—would be unnecessary, for "every one shal know the Law, and every one shal obey the Law, for it shal be writ in every ones heart." The only governor will be Christ; and the only magistracy "the love of Christ in us," constraining "all men to do his will."

Winstanley's social optimism, it is obvious, rested ultimately upon an expectation that human nature would be completely transformed. In the ideal society, all was dependent upon mankind's being restored to the "innocencie" and "plaine-heartedness" which prevailed before the Fall. The evils of life—war, misery, poverty, crime, fear, sorrow—all were due to the power of Satan in men's lives—a power expressing itself in covetousness and pride and resulting in the tyranny of kings, the pretensions of the clergy, the enclosures of the landlords, the thieving art of the merchants, and the chicanery of the lawyers. Hence, for any change to occur in social institutions, the power of Satan must first be extirpated in men's hearts; and this could be accomplished only by the direct action of a personal God.

To seek the blessed community by political action was, therefore, irrelevant; practical economic experiments were beside the point; an appeal to an individual's sense of decency was futile and naïve. Only the "Lord God Almighty" could do this great work, and he could do it only by changing "all things unto his own nature." Ideas of revolt were far from Winstanley's mind. Man could do nothing but *wait*—wait with meekness, patience, and quietness, until the

Lord "make forth himself in you." Redemption could be hindered and delayed by a failure to wait receptively upon the Lord, but man had no positive role to play in speeding the restoration. It is "the arm of the Lord onely," Winstanley constantly affirmed, that "shall bring these mighty things to passe."

Not only was human nature to be completely transformed; an even more startling change was to take place. The earth itself would be restored to its pristine glory. The barren places would become fertile, thorns and briars would disappear, violent storms would cease. These distempers of nature had been caused by the corruption of the flesh of evil men that infected the earth as their bodies decayed in the grave. The poison, in turn, was transmitted to the plants and, through them, to the animals that fed upon the plants. With the millennium all this would be changed. The source of infection would be gone, and the existing corruption "shall be removed from the Creation, Fire, Water, Earth, and Air." At that time, writes Winstanley: "The warm sun wil thaw the frost, and make the sap to bud out of every tender plant . . . . the tender grasse wil cover the earth, the Spirit wil cover al places *with the abundance of fruit . . . . ; The voice of mourning shall be heard no more, the birds shall sing merrily on every bough."*

The new order, then, was to be brought about "by the universall spreading of divine power," transforming mankind and renewing the earth. It was not, however, to be a long, drawn-out process. Winstanley was emphatic on this point. It will occur "as speedily as the *Midianites* Army was destroyed, and *Sodom* and *Gomorrah* burned. . . . . *Babylon* shall fall in one hour, Israel shall rise in one hour," and the "covetous oppressing Tyrants of the Earth" will tumble from power "on a sudden like a great tree that is undermined at the root." This was the hope he held forth to the oppressed and the dispossessed of his day.

III

Winstanley's activity in cultivating the commons placed against the millenarian

background of his thought has constituted a mystifying paradox to historians. If the new order was dependent upon God's decision, why should Winstanley embark upon a program of practical action? Varied answers have been given to this question. According to some, the chiliastic language was a mere "cloak" or "subterfuge" to conceal revolutionary designs. According to others, when Winstanley began his digging, his eschatological hope had begun to fade, and during the succeeding months it rapidly receded into the background. Still others have felt that the digging enterprise was an effort to anticipate God's act of redemption and thus constituted an alternative method for the realization of the new society. Another solution would be to conclude that Winstanley regarded the digging project as an interim procedure designed to secure immediate benefits prior to the time when God should act, recognizing, of course, that his perfect society in which "everyone will do as they would be done by" could not be achieved without divine intervention.

These answers to the problem posed by the apparent paradox in Winstanley's thought are of varying worth, but none of them can be accepted as an adequate explanation. We have no reason to suspect that Winstanley was insincere in his use of millenarian imagery. We have scarcely more reason to suppose that his millenarian expectations were diminishing. Nor can we be satisfied with the explanation that the cultivation of the common land constituted either an alternative or an interim procedure. As we have seen, Winstanley contemplated no extended period to elapse before the consummation of the new community. The half-day of the Beast was already expiring; the day of the Lord was at hand; its coming would not long be delayed. Mankind was to wait patiently and quietly for its appearance.

The idea of digging had originated in a trance, which Winstanley describes as follows: "I heard these words, *Worke together. Eat bread together;* declare this all abroad. Likewise I heard these words. *Whosoever it is that labours in the earth, for any person or persons, that lifts up themselves as Lords and Rulers over others : . . . , The hand of the Lord shall be upon that labourer: I the Lord have spoke it and I will do it:* Declare this all abroad." A few pages later, Winstanley reports:

> I have now obeyed the command of the Spirit that bid me declare this all abroad, and I have *declared* it, and I will declare it by word of mouth, I have now *declared* it by my pen. And when the Lord doth shew unto me the place and manner, how he wil have us that are called common people, to manure and work upon the common Lands, I will then go forth and *declare* it in my action, to eat my bread with the sweat of my brows, without either giving or taking hire, looking upon the Land as freely mine as anothers.

Anyone at all familiar with biblical thought will immediately recognize this declaration by action as an "eschatological sign."[35] Even if Ezekiel's oft-repeated refrain, "I the Lord have spoken it and I will do it," were lacking, it still would be obvious that the purpose of declaring the revelation by action was not to *do* something but to *say* something.

The true Levellers standard advanced contains Winstanley's only extended discussion of his purpose in digging on St. George's Hill. It was done, he says, as an act of obedience to a divine command, as a declaration of the divine will, as a demonstration

[35] An eschatological sign is usually either an event or an act whose purpose is to proclaim the will of God. It is a prophecy of what God will do. It is a pledge or an earnest of that which is to come. Frequently it is a demonstration of divine power which guarantees the existence of that which is to be, as well as the certainty of its coming. When an individual performs a sign, in obedience to a command of God, he becomes either an instrument by which God announces his purposes to the world, a witness to the divine power, or both. For a discussion of the deeds and sayings of Jesus as "eschatological signs," see Martin Dibelius, *The Sermon on the Mount* (New York, 1940), pp. 63, 82, 101, and 131–35.

of divine power, as a witness to the work of restoration God was to effect, as a fulfilment of scriptural prophecy, as a warning to the wicked, and as a test of sincerity. Winstanley's "third" reason—the fulfilment of the prophecies of Scripture—offers a clue as to the source from which he derived his idea of digging, for it directs our attention to the Book of Ezekiel.

The Book of Ezekiel, more than any other book in the Bible, seems to have provided the ideational pattern and program of the Diggers; and the thirty-sixth chapter, containing the promise of Israel's restoration, might well have been their charter. Ezekiel, of course, had been sent by God "for a sign unto the house of Israel" (Ezek. 12:6), and he was constantly directed to proclaim his message to them in the form of signs. He was told to say unto the Israelites: "I am your sign: Like as I have done, so shall it be done unto them [you]" (Ezek. 12:11). In his exposition of the purpose of digging, Winstanley cites a passage from the twenty-fourth chapter of Ezekiel: "Thus shall Ezekiel be unto you a sign; according to all that he hath done shall ye do: when this cometh, then shall ye know that I am the Lord . . . . ; so shalt thou be a sign unto them; and they shall know that I am the Lord" (Ezek. 24:24 and 27). If one places this apparent command beside the promise in the thirty-sixth chapter that the wastelands would be tilled and would become like the Garden of Eden in the day of restoration, the eschatological character of the digging becomes obvious.

One of the most interesting reasons Winstanley gives for the digging venture is that it would provide a demonstration of divine power. Although the "Earth, in view of Flesh, be very barren," we will "trust the spirit for a blessing." And he writes also: "Let the earth see . . . . to whom the Lord gives the blessing. . . . . Whether they that hold a civil propriety, saying, *This is mine* . . . . , or those that hold a common right, saying, *The earth is ours*. Let both sides waite with patience on the Lord, to see who he blessed." Had not the Lord said:

"I will make them and the places round about my hill a blessing. . . . . And the tree of the field shall yield its fruit, and the earth shall yield its increase . . . . ; and they shall know that I am the Lord" (Ezek. 34:26-27)?

An equally interesting function of the digging was to provide a test of sincerity. God had told Ezekiel: "[The people] sit before thee as my people, and they hear thy words, but do them not; for with their mouth they show much love, but their heart goeth after gain. And, lo, thou art unto them as a very lovely song of one that hath a pleasant voice . . . . ; for they hear thy words, but do them not" (Ezek. 33:31-32). Mere talk without corresponding action was, then, a mark of the Beast. Truth must be acted. Talking of love is no love. A righteous heart shall be known, not by his words, but by his actions. To say and not to do is a badge of hypocrisy. So said Winstanley, and the purpose of the digging was to test the sincerity of the Christian's professions. "By our hands truth is declar'd," affirmed Winstanley, and then continued in rhyme:

This tryal may our God see good
    to try, not us, but you;
That your profession of the Truth,
    may prove either false or true.

There were varying possible stages of response to this test for those who wished to escape the wrath to come. The only truly righteous response, of course, was to disown the landlords, join in the communal tilling of the common land, and thereby honor the Spirit and advance the work of restoration by bearing witness to the Light. Those who continued to lift up the Curse by working for hire participated in the work of unrighteousness, and the hand of the Lord would fall upon them. A second possible response is that made by those who are unable to participate personally in the work of righteousness but who further it by offering their moneys and opening their treasuries. They shall receive mercy. Finally, a dispensation of a sort will be granted to those who are passive and offer no opposition to the digging. But those who actively hinder and oppress the Diggers as they work together in righteousness shall be dealt with by the strong hand and stretched-out arm of the Lord. But whatever the response, men "shall be left without excuse in the day of Judgement," because their professions have been put to the test.

The major purpose of the digging, to be sure, was more fundamental. It was to declare the divine desire, intention, and purpose, and thereby warn the wicked and bring assurance to the righteous. The fact that the Spirit had risen up in these firstborn sons and daughters of the restoration, the fact that they had obeyed the Lord of Hosts who had revealed himself in them and to them, the fact that they had "cast off that oppression and outward bondage which the Creation groans under, as much as in us lies"—was a warrant, an earnest, a pledge that redemption would come and that it would not be long delayed. "This spirit of freedome being rising up in some already . . . . gives those bodies as pledges, that he will rise up in the whole and restore all mankinde to himselfe."

Actually, the digging project and the hostility it engendered were interpreted by Winstanley as the beginning of the "pitched battaile between the Lamb and the Dragon." These two powers are striving "in the heart of every single man" and make "men strive in opposition one against the other." These strivings will not cease "till the Dragon be cast out, and his judgement and downfall hastens apace, therefore let the righteous hearts wait with patience upon the Lord, to see what end he makes of all the confused hurley burleys of the world."

The Diggers, we may conclude, did not conceive of their venture as a means of effecting social change or as a way of gaining desired ends. They did not think of the practice of Christian love as a method for the achievement of the good society; rather, their intention was to live now as all will live after the restoration. They were bearing witness to the new life to come. Having done that, they waited for God to act. "I . . . .

have declared . . . . the whole light of that truth revealed to me by the word of the Lord," wrote Winstanley. "I shall now wait to see his hand, to do his own work in what time, and by what instruments he pleases." Elsewhere he declares: "I have Writ, I have Acted, I have Peace: and now I must wait to see the Spirit do his own work in the hearts of others, and whether England shall be the first Land, or some other, wherein Truth shall sit down in triumph."

The peace they experienced in their hearts was the final justification of the digging. They had been obedient to the Light, and a sweet contentment pervaded their spirits. Although "we have but a dish of roots and bread for our food," nevertheless "we have peace in our hearts, and quiet rejoycing in our work, and [are] filled with sweet content"; and this fact "does incourage us to go on in this work." Neither prison nor death shall "startle" us, while we are about the Spirit's work. "We have bin made to sit down and count what it may cost us . . . . , and we know the full sum, and are resolved to give all that we have to buy this Pearl which we see in the Field."

IV

Much of the confusion with regard to what the Diggers hoped to accomplish by their digging is due to the fact that the larger part of their literature is devoted to a plea for toleration that they might continue to dig as witnesses of the Lord. This plea has been misinterpreted as a positive program for the reconstruction of society, but they actually wanted only a liberty and freedom to work together as a "sign" upon what they regarded as communal property. The point at issue was the use of the commons and wastelands, and they based their claim to the use of these lands on a fourfold argument—theological, constitutional, moral, and practical.

The theological argument was constructed on both philosophical and biblical grounds.

From what we would call the "philosophical" point of view, Winstanley was convinced that every person had a "creation-right" to the earth, for it had been made a "common treasury" for all mankind. But the validity of this insight was not dependent upon his own intuitive apprehension or reflection. It had been revealed to him by the Spirit, but it was corroborated by the "plain Text of Scripture," which teaches that the "creation-right" was bestowed upon man in the beginning and was confirmed by covenant to Noah and his seed and to Abraham and his seed. The Bible, therefore, "gives a full warrant to all poore men, to build them houses, and plant corne upon the Commons and unnurtured land . . . . , being the right of their creation."

The constitutional argument—an effort to prove that the common people had a "legal," as well as a "creation-," right to the land—was somewhat more involved. Since the Scriptures confirm the fact that all mankind had a "creation-right" to the earth, it is evident that individual property rights were introduced by murder and theft and are dependent upon the laws of conquest. In England private ownership of land was the innovation of William the Conqueror and has been maintained since that time by the Norman power. When the monarchy was cast out, however, all rights dependent upon Norman laws were wiped out, and the earth reverted to its rightful condition as a "common treasury" for all. Parliament, furthermore, had given recognition to the right of the people to the land by declaring England to be a "free commonwealth"; and a free commonwealth was a meaningless term unless it meant free access to the land in order to gain a livelihood.

The common land, as the name implies, had remained as a residuary possession of the common people during the period of the Conqueror's rule. Nevertheless, this right had been partially subverted, for certain restrictions surrounded its use. But if the abolition of the kingly power had freed all the land of England from private ownership, then certainly that same act removed the restrictions upon the use of the commons by the poor, so long as they did not exclude anyone who wished to join them in the communal tilling of the soil.

The events of the Civil War were also involved in Winstanley's moral argument. At the beginning of the war, parliament had said in effect to the common people: "Come and help us against the King that enslaves us . . . . and we will make you a free people"; "Give us your taxes, free quarter, excise, and adventure your lives with us to cast out the oppressour Charles, and wee will make yow a free people." The common people had responded "with purse and person" and had joined wholeheartedly with parliament in casting off the Norman yoke. The fruits of the victory, however, had been garnered exclusively by the gentry, while the poor were "worse able to live than before." Such a situation was manifestly unjust. "If I adventure my life, and the fruit of my labour, equal with you, and obtain what we strive for; it is both Equity and Reason, that I should equally divide the Spoil with you, and not you to have all, and I none." The commoners had been promised that they would be made a "free people," but they were not free "so long as" they "lie under poverty, and must not be suffered to plant the commons and waste land" for their livelihood. Actually, there was a contract between parliament and people, confirmed by performance, by which the common people had a valid claim to the use of the commons. "Wee have bought it," Winstanley wrote to Fairfax, "by our blood and money."

Parliament and the people, however, had "not only joyned persons and purses together, but . . . . they took the Nationall Covenant, with joynt consent together." In the Solemn League and Covenant, they had sworn "to endeavour a Reformation according to the Word of God, which Reformation is to restore us to that Primitive freedom in the earth, in which the earth was first made and given to the sons of men, and that is to be a common treasury to all." If parliament and the Council of War refuse to carry through this reformation, they "wil be proved double hypocrites; First, to Almighty God, in breaking Covenant with him, for in his Name you made the Covenant. Secondly, to men, in breaking Covenant with them, for the matter of the Covenant was the freedom, peace, and safety of the people of *England,* taking in all sorts of people." The Diggers, however, will be content to "let the Freeholders have their freedom to work quietly in their Inclosures," if the common people are allowed to have the Commons and waste lands quiet to themselves." The very least parliament can do is to let the poor "dig" in peace.

If the plea of the Diggers for toleration should be ignored, declares Winstanley, parliament will be taking "part with such as have been either flat enemies, or ambidexterous all along the wars, and will cast out such as have been your true friends." By so doing, he tells them:

You pull the guilt of King *Charles* his blood upon your own heads; for then it will appear to the view of all men, That you cut off the Kings head, that you might establish your selves in his Chair of Government. . . . . Let it not be said in the ears of posterity, That the Gentry of England assembled in Parliament, proved Covenant-breakers . . . . to God, and the Common people, after their own turn was served; and killed the King for his power and government, as a thief kils a true man for his money. I do not say you have done so, but for shame dally no longer, ... let the poor oppressed go free.

Winstanley's practical argument for toleration rested upon three major contentions: the Diggers were not revolutionaries to be feared, their digging would provide certain immediate and obvious benefits, and finally those who persisted in opposing them would receive "like for like" in the day of judgment.

The Diggers took care to assure the authorities that there was "no intent of Tumult or Fighting" in their activity. On the contrary, they were a meek, harmless, inoffensive company, who hated no one and wished well to all. They constituted, therefore, no threat to the public peace and offered no reason for alarm or cause for fear. Furthermore, as Winstanley hastened to make clear, they had no intention of infringing upon existing property rights. They would restrict their digging to the common and wasteland and would not interfere with the right of the freeholders to the land within their enclosures.

As the months went by and opposition became more intense, the Diggers began to point out the material benefits that would accrue to the nation if they were allowed to continue the cultivation of the commons. They portrayed their work as something of a universal panacea: prices would be reduced, famine prevented, poverty wiped out, crime eliminated, prisons emptied, discontent quieted, and the nation strengthened; and the constant complaints and endless appeals to parliament for relief would be brought to an end. On the other hand, if liberty were not granted, a very great danger to the state would result: the people would begin to "mutter" against the government, they would never "trust the fair words of a Parliament any more," and "the Gentry of England assembled in Parliament" will find themselves in a precarious position.

Finally, the point is made again and again that the Diggers should be given freedom to dig because "judgement from the most High sleepeth not." The time "is very near" when Christ will rise in judgment, and "his appearance will be with power." It would be well for all to remember that on that day the Diggers will be "lively witnesses . . . . against . . . . all that have and may so furiously oppose us; and rebelliously fight against the Prince of Peace." Winstanley warns: "O ye Rulers of the earth, ... be wise, scorn not the Councell of the poor, least you be whipt with your own rod."

V

Winstanley had embarked upon the digging venture with high hopes. The end of the Beast's reign was very near. The millennium was about to be inaugurated by swift and decisive divine intervention. Nothing could obstruct God's imminent display of power, and England was destined to be the tenth part of Babylon that would be first to fall from the Beast. As time passed and the digging encountered increasing difficulties, Winstanley's optimistic expectations began to diminish. God would ultimately triumph, but perverse and stubborn flesh could delay his victory. "It shall take root," he said, "before many years passe over *Englands* head," but "I can set no time." England, to be sure, had been given the initial opportunity to embrace the righteous rule of God; but it was possible that the signal honor of being the first-fruit of the restoration might go by default to some other nation.

In the beginning the Diggers had not worried greatly about the means by which they would maintain themselves while digging. By cutting and selling wood from the common land, they had thought that they could provide food for themselves until "the first Crop comes up," but when they were prevented from harvesting what little they had been able to plant, their situation became critical. Their circular appeal for help, seized at Wellingborough in April 1650, reported that "their work is like to flagge and droppe"; it is "ready to die again for want of help. . . . . If you hear hereafter that there was a people appeared to stand up to advance publique freedome . . . . , and yet these men and their publique work was crushed, because they wanted assistance . . . . to keep them alive; . . . . if . . . . you had monies in your hands, and would not part with any of it . . . . , therefore you deservedly Grone under Tyranny and no Saviour appeares." Actually, at about the time the letter was seized, the digging had come to an end.

An humble request to the ministers of both universities and to all lawyers in every Inns-a-court, published in April 1650, was Winstanley's valedictory appeal in behalf of the digging; and it was, in reality, a confession that "self-loving flesh" had "for the present trod our weak flesh down." Yet the venture was not without results: it had put the pretensions of professing Christians to the test, and they would be without excuse in the day of judgment. "This work of digging, being freedom, or the appearance of Christ in the earth hath tried the Priests and professors to the uttermost, and hath ripped up the bottom of their Religion, and proves it meere witchcraft, and cosonage; . . . . when the Lamb turnes into the Lion, they will remember what they have done, and mourne. . . . . We have declared our Testimony, and now let freedom and bondage strive who shall rule in Mankind."

Within a few months, Winstanley sent to the printer a tract in which his bitterness of spirit overflowed. It was addressed "To the Severall Societies of People, Called Churches, in the Presbyterian, Independent, or any Other Forme of Profession," and the introductory epistle closes with a scathing exhortation: "He that hath eares to heare, let him heare, he that is filthie, let him be filthy still, till he be cast out as dung and unsavory salt." While *Fire in the bush* does not mention the unhappy attempt at cultivating the commons, the parties responsible for the ignominious end of that venture are paraded before the reader and scornfully indicted.

John Platt, rector of West Horsley, had taken the lead in marshaling the local opposition to the digging; and it is the clergy and the "professors" of religion who are the primary objects of Winstanley's bitter indictment. When Winstanley's thinking had begun to be colored by an economic concern, he had arrived at the conviction that the clergy were the creation and tools of the "kingly power"; now he reversed himself and adopted once more his earlier position. "The chiefe Beast is the Clergy."

It is "the most dreadful and terrible Beast" who bred the other Beasts—kingly power, legal power, and the thieving art of buying and selling.

While Winstanley's wrath was chiefly directed against those from whom much might be expected because of their professions, he still retains his old animosity toward the merchants, landlords, and lawyers. In addition, a new antagonism toward the soldiers appears, as well as a new hostility toward the Commonwealth government. Formerly, Winstanley had pled with parliament and the great officers of the army to keep their engagements and to effect a thorough-going reformation. Now this hope had vanished, and he tells them that they too are to be overthrown.

His disillusionment, however, was not long-lived. Within less than a year, government policy under Cromwell had taken a more favorable turn, and Winstanley was encouraged to present to the general a proposal he had been considering ever since the digging project had begun to go wrong. This proposal was set forth in *The law of freedom in a platform,* and it represents the adoption by Winstanley of a new program for the realization of his communist utopia.

VI

While the digging project was being carried forward, a somewhat similar millenarian movement was developing among the Baptists and Independents. Like the Diggers, the Fifth Monarchists capitalized upon the frustrated hopes of the Levellers. Beginning in Norfolk, early in 1649, the Fifth Monarchy movement spread rapidly both within the army and without. In 1651, directly after the battle of Worcester, representations in behalf of the Fifth Monarchy program began to be made to Cromwell; and since he received the suggestions with some show of interest, Fifth Monarchist hopes ran high for a few short weeks. Cromwell, however, was not yet ready to give serious consideration to their proposal.

It soon was apparent that he contemplated no move in the direction they sought; and by the latter part of December, the Fifth Monarchy leaders decided that appeals to the government should cease. Instead, they placed their complete trust in the Lord, whom they besought to speed the coming of Christ's kingdom by removing unfit magistrates from office, by ending the divisions among the saints, and by stirring up parliament, army, and people to keep their engagements.

The apocalyptic message of the Fifth Monarchists followed the generally accepted pattern of biblical interpretation. But, unlike most of the millenarians, who were content to discuss the time and circumstances of the "second-coming" and then to wait patiently for it to occur, the Fifth Monarchy men had a positive program to be put into effect by the saints. The point at which they departed from the prevailing millenarianism of the time was their conviction that the saints had the responsibility of making straight a highway for the Lord's return by reshaping the existing government to conform as closely as possible to divine requirements. Such a remodeling involved, among other things, the abolition of tithes, the substitution of the law of God for the existing laws, and the holding of office by none but godly men. These things having been done, the Lord would then return to rule in righteousness as king.

The immediate duty of the saints was clear. They must draw out of Scripture the godly frame of government and admonish the authorities to adopt it. If their advice went unheeded, the Fifth Monarchists were confident that the Lord would overturn the government and would continue to overturn succeeding governments until one arose which would do his work. Their confidence, in this respect, was based upon a passage from Ezekiel—a passage which became their rallying-cry: "Thus saith the Lord God; Remove the diadem, and take off the crown: this shall not be the same: exalt him that is low, and abase him that is high. I will overturn, overturn, overturn it: and it shall be no more, until he come whose right it is; and I will give it him" (Ezek. 21:26-27).

Winstanley compiled his final work, *The law of freedom in a platform,* and addressed the dedicatory epistle to Cromwell during October and the early days of November 1651. This was the period, following the battle of Worcester, when the Fifth Monarchists believed Cromwell to be favorably inclined toward their proposals; and Cromwell, reading the opening pages of Winstanley's recommended frame of government, would have readily recognized it as an alternative scheme to establish an interim Holy Commonwealth by executive action.

The dedicatory epistle makes obvious the character of Winstanley's proposal, for his use of the imagery of Ezek. 21:26-27 is a clear indication that he had been converted to the Fifth Monarchy point of view in so far as the method for the realization of his utopia was concerned. The "Crown of Honor," he told Cromwell, cannot be yours until you complete the reformation so well begun by casting out the "Oppressor's" power as well as his person. "You have the eyes of the People all the Land over . . . . waiting to see what you will do: And the eyes of your oppressed friends, who lie yet under Kingly power, are waiting to have the possession given to them of that Freedom in the Land, which was promised by you, if in case you prevailed. Lose not your Crown; take it up, and wear it. But know, that it is no Crown of Honor, till Promises and Engagements made by you be performed to your friends. *He that continues to the end, shall receive the Crown.*" It would be well for Cromwell to remember, Winstanley wrote, that when Charles was "in the height of his oppressing Power" the people dared only whisper "in private Chambers against him"; yet "he had his overturn." God has not changed. What he has done once, he will do again if necessary. "If," therefore, "you, and those in power with you, should be found walking in the

Kings steps, can you secure your selves or posterities from an overturn?" God is about his work of reformation, and he will carry it forward. "If he would not spare Kings, who have sat so long at his right hand, governing the World, neither will he regard you, unless your ways be found more righteous then the Kings." There are two alternatives, Winstanley told Cromwell: "You have the power of the Land in your hand, you must do one of these two things; First, ... fulfill the Scriptures and your own Engagements, and so take possession of your deserved Honor. Or secondly, ... remove the Conquerors Power out of the Kings hand into other mens, maintaining the old Laws still; And then your Wisdom and Honor is blasted for ever."

Winstanley had arrived at the conclusion that the reformation, necessary as a prelude to the "in-breaking" of divine power, must begin with the government rather than with the people. The straight highway that must be made before Christ could "come in power" was to consist not primarily of the receptive hearts of individuals but rather of the outward institutions of magistracy. When these were shaped according to the divine pattern, then God would infuse them with the Spirit of Righteousness, which was Christ in his "second-coming." It was foolish to think that Christ could come before this was done, for "the inward bondages of the minde, as covetousness, pride, hypocrisie, envy, sorrow, fears, desperation, and madness," which hinder his appearance, "are all occasioned by the outward bondage that one sort of people lay upon another." Not until "Commonwealths Freedom is established, and . . . . Kingly Slavery cast out" will the millennium arrive and *"knowledg cover the Earth, as the waters cover the Seas"* (Isa. 11:9; Hab. 2:14).

The new trend in Winstanley's thinking had been developing for some time. The earliest indication of it appears in *A New-Yeers gift for the parliament and armie,* written late in 1649, in which he says: "You Rulers of England, ... let no other Land take your Crown. You have set Christ

upon his throne in *England* by your Promises, Engagements, Oathes, and Two Acts of Parliament . . . . : Put all these into sincere Action, and you shall see the work is done, and you with others shall sing *Halelujah* to him that sits upon the Throne, and to the Lamb for everymore. But if you do not, the Lamb shall shew himself a Lion, and tear you in pieces for your most abominable dissembling Hypocrisie." A more explicit statement of Winstanley's emerging point of view is to be found in *Fire in the bush,* written during the summer of 1650. Here, in the bitterness of his frustration, he is sure that the so-called "Commonwealth government" will be overthrown, as every government has been "when it was universally proved a Devill, a destroyer, and waster. . . . . You oppressing powers of the world, who think God hath blessed you, because you sit down in that Chaire of Government, out of which the former Tyrants are gone: Doe you remember this? Your overturning, overturning, overturning, is come on to you, as well as to your fellow-break-promises, that are gone before. You that pretend to be saviours of the people . . . . , surely you must have your overturnings too."

According to Winstanley, the major portion of *The law of freedom* was written "above two years ago," which would be about the time of the composition of *A New-Yeers gift.* "The disorder of the Times," he declares, "caused me to lay it aside." More probably it was laid aside because Winstanley was becoming progressively more discouraged and disillusioned as the digging venture encountered increasing and more resolute opposition. From Winstanley's point of view, there would be little purpose in presenting such a document to a government that had been proved "a Devill, a destroyer, and waster" and which, therefore, was bound to be overthrown. Nevertheless, the text, *"Thou shalt not bury thy talent in the earth,"* Winstanley says, "was like fire in my bones." Consequently, after the battle of Worcester, when the situation seemed ripe for such an appeal to be made, Winstanley was "stirred up" to give his proposal a "resurrection." He gathered his papers together, compiled them into a "method," and dispatched it to Cromwell and the printer.

The proposal set forth in *The law of freedom* was definitely for an interim Holy Commonwealth, the purpose of which was to make the nation ready for God's final act of restoration. Although Winstanley occasionally bursts into rhapsody concerning the final glory of the commonwealth in its millennial estate, which would be the inevitable consequence of the adoption of his proposed frame of government, the interim character of his platform is everywhere apparent.

The form of government Winstanley proposed was designed throughout for the period prior to the final redemption of all mankind. Since some persons will be "foolish, some idle, ... some rash, some envyous, covetous," laws will be necessary to restrain them. This, in turn, will necessitate police officers and even capital punishment. Force will be used "to beat down the turbulency of any foolish or self-ended spirit that endeavors to break their common Peace." An army will be needed to wage war "either against an Invasion of a Forreign Enemy, or against an Insurrection at home."

It is possible, of course, that Winstanley had reverted from his universalism to an earlier Calvinistic particularism. If that were true, then, perhaps, there would be nothing incongruous in a Fifth Monarchy, with Christ as King, in which the saints ruled by the sword. But even a Calvinist would not consider such a situation the final state of the New Jerusalem. In a Calvinist millennium the reprobate would soon be banished to the netherworld. Actually, however, Winstanley still believed in a universal redemption.

The provision for regular worship in *The law of freedom* is further evidence that this was not the millennial society of Winstanley's apocalyptic expectations. For in the millennium, according to all ortho-dox interpretations, there were to be no formal or stated periods of worship; and, while Winstanley was heterodox at many points, he was orthodox in this respect. The provisions for worship in *The law of freedom* are, to be sure, somewhat unconventional; but it must be remembered that Winstanley was a left-wing Puritan and that there was little that was conventional in any of the left-wing groups. The unconventional character of Winstanley's religious proposals, however, has led most of his interpreters to assume that he gave very little room for religion in his commonwealth and that his interest in religion had been largely dissipated. This, however, is a misinterpretation, for his recommendations, on the whole, are those that would have been put forward by any Baptist or Quaker.

Winstanley did not believe in a "hireling" or paid ministry, nor did he believe in an educated ministry. It was to prevent the ministry from degenerating into a vocation that he suggested that ministers be chosen for a year at a time and that those who defied this provision and attempted "to make a Trade" of preaching be put to death. To scotch any idea that the minister enjoyed a monopoly of divine gifts, the practice of the gathered churches in permitting all members of the congregation to speak when moved by the Spirit was to be continued. The Sabbath was to be observed in the Puritan fashion as a requirement of the Mosaic Code, and on that day services of worship were to be held. As the gathered churches contended, the two primary functions of such services were fellowship and instruction, and the principal method of instruction was the sermon. Winstanley, as an exponent of the popular mysticism of the time, ruled out expository or textual preaching; but, aside from that, the sermons were to deal with the traditional subjects of religious inquiry. They were to deal with what we would call, in our academic fashion, "historical theology," "natural theology," and "philosophy of religion."

The law of freedom, then, was a platform for an interim Holy Commonwealth to be established by executive action as a necessary prerequisite to the divine act which would inaugurate the millennium. At a critical moment, when Winstanley had become utterly discouraged by the hostility of the Commonwealth authorities to his "declaration by action," Fifth Monarchist thought suggested to him that the obstacle blocking the path of a final restoration was an unreformed magistracy. Before he had had opportunity to submit his plan of reform, he became convinced that the present personnel of the Commonwealth was utterly corrupt and that the only remaining alternative was to wait for God to "overturn" them. Two years later, concluding that he had misjudged the situation and thinking that Cromwell might be the instrument God had chosen to complete the reformation, Winstanley hurriedly "set the candle" at his door to light the way. The candle, he told Cromwell, was roughly formed. The platform had been put together with dispatch, and it was "like a peece of Timber rough hewd, yet the discreet workmen may take it, and frame a handsome building out of it."

VII

Winstanley, as we have seen, was very much a man of his time. At times he displayed penetrating flashes of insight. Always he betrayed an acute sensitivity to the hopes and fears of the dispossessed, which he occasionally expressed in imaginative and beautiful prose. Nevertheless, his thought moved in the customary patterns of an age that saw supernatural direction of divine or demonic character in every event and viewed an unbalanced soul like Anna Trapnel as a prophetess and less fortunate victims of a similar malady as witches. It was a time when even such a hardheaded statesman as Oliver Cromwell would not lightly disregard the more moderated pretensions of self-styled prophets and would not scoff at any of them.

In spite of the limitations imposed upon him by his environment, Winstanley discharged successfully and effectively one of the most important functions of any true preacher of the gospel of Christ. He proclaimed a disturbing message. He made people uncomfortable. He made them uneasy—uneasy about themselves, about the professions they had made, and about the social order in which they lived. But a preacher he was, not an economist. And if his writings have been correctly interpreted, modern historians interested in Marxist parallels in English thought have superimposed upon Winstanley their own preconceptions. He was not interested primarily in a practical program of social reform but in the approaching reign of God, and it was that impending cataclysm which he proclaimed. The digging, therefore, had less significance as a communistic program than as a "sign" demanding attention to a message from the Lord. Winstanley stood in the succession of prophets who have measured men and their society with the plumb-line of God and found them wanting. And, like the prophets, he had great faith in the power of God to redeem the world from bondage, injustice, and oppression.

POLITICAL THEORIZING, like all reflective thinking, has usually originated in conditions of difficulty and perplexity, in periods of unrest and tension, when problems have been forced upon men and solutions demanded. In times of relative repose and contentment there has been little disposition to speculate on the subjects of which political and social theories take account. "The bulk of mankind," as Burke remarked, "are not excessively curious concerning any theories whilst they are really happy; and one sure symptom of an ill-conducted state is the propensity of the people to resort to them." It required the storm and stress, the disagreements and conflicts, of the Puritan Revolution to produce the body of controversial literature on questions of government, so momentous in consequence for the modern world, of which the works of Milton, Harrington, Filmer, and Hobbes are outstanding examples. It is difficult, however, to view the opinions and systems of the great thinkers of history except as they appear through the medium, inevitably more or less distorting, of what commentators and critics have said about them. In the following essay, Professor Sterling P. Lamprecht, of Amherst College, a learned and profound student of the history of English political thought, distinguishes between the ideas set forth by Hobbes himself in his own writings and "Hobbism," namely, the theories that can be formulated from the literature on Hobbes produced during his lifetime and soon after. He shows that Hobbes was far from being a Hobbist.

HOBBES AND HOBBISM

STERLING P. LAMPRECHT

Fearful of a committee appointed by the House of Commons to investigate the current tendencies towards atheism and profaneness, Hobbes in 1666 burned some of his private papers. The Great Plague and the Great Fire of London had just occurred. While many Englishmen were prone to blame the fire on those whom they considered the "treacherous Catholics," they tended to regard the plague as obviously an act of God. The House of Commons shared this widespread attitude and, desirous of ridding the country of the causes of the divine displeasure, named several persons whose wickedness might be the occasion of the display of God's wrath against the English people. The House included Hobbes in the list and specifically mentioned his *Leviathan.* Moreover, some bishops of the Church of England, at about the same time, suggested that it might be well to burn Hobbes as a heretic. Nothing came of the parliamentary investigation; indeed, the investigation seems not to have been begun. And no fires were lighted except that in

which Hobbes saw fit, as has been said, to burn some of his private papers.

It is interesting to conjecture, however, what the name of Hobbes would mean in the history of ideas if his works had happened all to perish in 1666 and we, then, had to judge him through the literature which his works provoked. The word *provoked* may here be used advisedly. For an amazing number of hostile writings against Hobbes were printed during his life-time and immediately after his death. Richard Blackbourne, in his *Vitae Hobbianae Auctarium* (1681), lists thirty-five authors who attacked Hobbes prior to that date, and then added: "In Hobbii defensionem unicum solummodo reperio scriptum, idque anonymum"! Of the thirty-five hostile writers, twenty-nine were concerned with Hobbes's political ideas, especially with the *Leviathan;* and the single favorable tract was, if not written by a foreigner, at least published in Amsterdam in defense of the *De cive.* After Blackbourne's report in 1681, the number of hostile references to Hobbes

Reprinted by special permission from *The American Political Science Review,* XXXIV (1940), 31-53. The footnotes which originally appeared with this essay have been omitted.

increased. The editor of *The Moral and Political Works of Thomas Hobbes of Malmesbury, Never Before Collected Together* (1750) has two long foot-notes to a preliminary biographical sketch in which, depending largely upon Blackbourne's list, he goes on to add eight more hostile writers and only one further (again a foreign) favorable writer. These lists are not exhaustive. Eight other hostile treatments of Hobbes can be given from the period of Hobbes's own lifetime and the ensuing decade. Added together, the lists give us fifty-one hostile and two favorable treatments.

Were we to formulate Hobbes's political theories from this contemporary literature about him (as, for example, we have to formulate our ideas of the Christian gnostics of the second century largely from the writings of the church fathers who attacked them), we should get a system of political philosophy which may be properly referred to as Hobbism—something quite different in most fundamental points from the theories Hobbes set forth in his writings, yet issuing from those writings as those writings were read by and impressed themselves on the minds of Hobbes's contemporaries. This system of Hobbism would in summary be as follows. (1) God made man such a beast and rascal that he inclines universally to malice and fraud. Man's typical acts, when he is unrestrained, are violent and ruthless, savagely disregarding the persons and property of his fellows. His greatest longing is to preserve himself by gaining power over others. And he deems the exercise of power honorable, no matter for what ends it be exercised. (2) There is no real distinction between moral right and moral wrong. Moral distinctions are artificial suppositions foisted upon the generality of men by some superior power; they are arbitrary conventions which rulers impose upon their subjects and have no validity beyond the frontiers within which those rulers exercise control. The state is thus the original of what men have come to deem virtue; and apart from the state there would be no moral distinctions or principles at all. (3) A *de facto* ruler is always justified in all his ways. Since the distinction between good and bad arises from the dictate of princes, the commands of princes are *ipso facto* the criterion of right and wrong for those whom they are strong enough to command. A ruler, being himself the source of morality, cannot be immoral. (4) Appeal to law as a protection of popular rights is essentially invalid. For not simply are there no popular rights, but the passing whims of rulers are of more force than what is alleged to be law.

These four points might well be taken as constituting the system of political Hobbism. Along with them would go the further position that both religion and personal character are to be despised by the discerning. Religion is a sham and a trick, whereby shrewd rulers buttress their wills by playing cleverly upon the fears of superstitious men. Character, too, is an idle notion. Men's inner motives are indifferent. What a man really seeks, what he hopes or wishes, what he secretly thinks, these are of no consequence provided that his outward acts conform to his ruler's will. No man can sin as long as he obeys his prince. On all matters on which he is not expressly forbidden to commit a deed, he is both legally and morally free to act as he chooses. As men are born savage beasts, so they remain savage beasts to the end, however much their bestiality is concealed beneath that thin veneer of legal conformity which can only ironically be called civilization.

Hobbism, thus defined, can find substantiation in the works of Hobbes, when those works are read hastily or separate sentences out of them are quoted out of context. That Hobbes was in his own day generally deemed a Hobbist is quite intelligible in the light of the psychology of the turbulent days of the Commonwealth and Restoration. That Hobbes continued to be deemed a Hobbist by many historians in subsequent centuries has been due both to the force of tradition and to the wide acceptance of a rival political philosophy which was sponsored with great power by Locke and was congenial to the currents of political change since the Glorious Revolution of 1688. Hobbes challenged, not merely with deep penetration but with caustic wit, many cherished political beliefs and party professions of his time; and his ideas run diametrically counter to much that is basic in the "natural rights" movement that gave constitutionalism its characteristic form in several of the great nations in the eighteenth and nineteenth centuries. He influenced the utilitarians and other nineteenth-century writers on specific points; but he has generally remained suspect, even to our own day, and is still pictured with many lingering traces of the Hobbism with which he was from the outset confused.

Among the factors which have tended to make Hobbes seem a Hobbist, three are perhaps most prominent. In the first place, Hobbes had a remarkable gift for trenchant utterance and a glee in exploiting this gift to the irritation of his opponents. During the years of his voluntary exile from his own country, he deliberately indulged his wit in antagonizing the clerical and royalist forces that had gathered in Paris about the person of the prince who later became Charles II. But he was not partial to any group in administering telling blows. Simultaneously with his expressions of anti-clericalism, he uttered defiances of the parties who were struggling for power in the Commonwealth at home—Presbyterians, Independents, agitators like the Levellers, republicans like Harrington. Consider, for example, the famous jibe that the papacy is "the ghost of the deceased Roman Empire, sitting crowned upon the grave thereof." Or the ironic condemnation of the Presbyterians as, jointly with the Roman clergy, "authors of this darknesse in religion." Or the attack upon the universities because they did no more than impose upon their students "the frivolous distinctions, barbarous terms, and obscure language of the Schoolmen," in order to "make men mistake the *ignis fatuus* of vain philosophy, for the light of the Gospel." Or the assault upon, not merely the preachers, but also the gentry of England, whose opinions, Hobbes said, were derived "from the venime of heathen politicians, and from the incantation of deceiving spirits." Or the cutting sarcasm in the brilliant half-truth that "the naturall seed of religion" lies "in these four things, opinion of ghosts, ignorance of second causes, devotion towards what men fear, and taking of things casuall for prognostiques." Could any author more directly and unsparingly assail every one of the respectable groups of his time? Could any author who so assailed these groups hope to escape in his turn the vitriolic misrepresentations to which his own words, wrested from their context, were capable of being put? It is no wonder that contemporary opinion about Hobbes was controlled more by indignation than by analysis and that subsequent opinion should follow along the lines of the hostile tradition that treated Hobbes as a Hobbist. Hobbism may not have been Hobbes's position; but the fury that led to its formulation was excited by the relentless irony of his barbed shafts and would not soon die out.

In the second place, Hobbes was known to his contemporaries, and even more generally to all subsequent generations, primarily by the *Leviathan*. The *Leviathan* is his greatest contribution to *belles lettres:* in suitability of style to content and in vigor of trenchant and dramatic utterance, it ranks among the finest classics of any literature. But intellectually and philosophically it is not as fine as the *De cive*. Eloquent as it is when taken paragraph by paragraph, quotable as it is when taken sentence by sentence, it lacks reasoned integrity and scholarly poise. It was written in the heat of controversy. It does not stay to achieve that balance of statement that is requisite to calm and fair consideration. Begun in a spirit of moderation, it passes in its middle chapters to passionate rhetoric, and closes in a burst of fury against the entrenched foes of Hobbes's program for securing a modicum of human happiness. The *De cive* indicates by its divisions the essential lines of its author's system of thought;

the *Leviathan* indicates rather the intensity of his hates. Constructive teaching is in the *Leviathan* submerged beneath the insistent fire of destructive attacks. It is still, even in these days when Hobbes is little more than the historian's subject of discourse, an insolent and provocative book. It chooses to state its thesis in its most controversial context, namely, in emphasis upon its claim that all churches are entirely subordinate to the power of civil authorities. It even indicates by its famous frontispiece opposite the title-page that it would humble the churches by making them merely an arm of secular jurisdiction. It thus drives many readers into protest before it informs them of its due intent, and this is true today to only a somewhat less extreme degree than in Hobbes's lifetime. There is no change in essential doctrine from the *De cive* to the *Leviathan*. But the *De cive* ought to be more read: it ought especially to be read as introductory to the later work. The *De cive*, if less eloquent in its rhetoric, is very much more methodical and clear in its philosophical import.

In the third place, Hobbes, as is typical of many another among the systematic philosophers, conceived an inclusive schematism which would enable him to place his political principles within the framework of a total theory of the universe. According to this schematism, the only ultimate facts are matter and motion; all else is but some special case of the basic realities of matter and motion. The schematism would, Hobbes thought, have three main parts, theory of body, theory of living body, theory of social body. So he wrote books with the titles *De corpore, De homine,* and *De cive*. The three books appeared in reverse order to their place in the allegedly controlling schematism, *De cive* in 1642, *De homine* in 1650, and *De corpore* only in 1655. Of course this matter of chronology is not conclusive; for Hobbes announced his general schematism in the "Preface to the Reader" of the *De cive,* and is known to have conceived it even earlier. Internal evidence, however, makes it highly probable that Hobbes did not deduce his political principles from his materialistic schematism, but derived them from observance of the actual actions of men and states and from his reading of others' (e.g., Thucydides's) similar observations. The grandiose schematism served, Hobbes hoped, to give his political principles the added convincingness that would ensue if they fell easily into their place in a comprehensive body of scientific knowledge; for were they not the political analogue to the new science that Galileo and Robert Boyle and others were making popular among the enlightened minds of the century? If such were Hobbes's hopes, such were not his actual reception and fate. His fate has been that his views on mathematics and physics have been regarded as unimportant. And his reception has been that his political principles, taken as corollaries of his materialistic scheme, have drawn from their place in that schematism only increased opprobrium. Hobbes's political ideas gain, when taken as deductive consequences of his physics, only an added brutality which his passionate statement of his principles had already suggested. And thus the tendency to treat Hobbes as a Hobbist, which arose in his own day from the controversial fury of his utterances, has persisted to our own day from the alleged dependence of them upon a schematism that was an afterthought, or at most a reinforcing addendum.

The distinction which has been asserted between Hobbism and Hobbes's genuinely intended meaning can best be exemplified by considering Hobbes's views in connection with each of the four points of Hobbism already summed up above. But before taking up these four points in turn, some preliminary remarks are needed about Hobbes's primary concern and practical objective. The central theme of Hobbes is that the raw material of human nature is such that it can be transformed into a degree of civilized decency through only one practical means, namely, through the provision of a genuinely sovereign authority within society. This theme is dramatically and symbolically portrayed in the superb frontispiece of the first (privately printed) edition of the *De cive*. In the upper part of the frontispiece is given a more or less conventional representation of the Last Judgment, with Christ in the center, the redeemed on his right, and the damned on his left. Probably no one will suppose that Hobbes wished to have his readers understand that his use of the traditional Christian iconography was indicative of his literal acceptance of the Christian mythology about the Last Judgment. Rather it doubtless means that whatever final and authoritative judgment can be passed upon human affairs will be in the light of the contrast between the two figures who stand respectively underneath the redeemed and the damned. Beneath the redeemed is the figure of *Imperium:* she is a stately woman, strong and fair; in her right hand are the scales of justice and in her left a drawn sword to enforce her decisions; on her head is a royal crown; behind her opens out an idyllic countryside where men reap in security the crops they had sown, and a noble city rests securely on a distant hill. Beneath the damned is the figure of *Libertas:* she is an old hag, sour in face, dejected in posture, mean in apparel; her weapons are primitive; behind her is visible a sordid vista, where assault and rape occur, and only a crude stockade offers a precarious refuge to the victims of open crimes. Hobbes seems to have wished to indicate that the antithesis of *imperium* and *libertas* is what the separation of redeemed and damned symbolizes. His intent is quite clearly to point out that we must choose irrevocably between *imperium* and her blessings on the one hand and on the other *libertas* and her attendant dangers. And if we translate Hobbes's Latin terms into current English, we cannot properly say that he is contrasting Empire and Liberty; for these words carry implications today that depart from his intent. We should rather say that he is contrasting Sovereignty and Anarchy. He is contrasting the possibilities of human life when firm rule establishes security for human enterprises with the doom that threatens all men alike when confusion and war are unrestrained.

The question that Hobbes raised in this frontispiece is an old one; the theme that he offers in its solution is a radical and uncompromising one. The question was how to guide the raw material of human nature into the ways of civilized life. This question confronts all serious and thoughtful moralists who do not entertain the notion that the human race began in a Garden of Eden and is subsequently guided by revelation and inspiration. Neither single men nor social groups originally possess such endowments as nobility, excellence, beauty, virtue. Men and societies come from barbarous backgrounds: they come with animal lusts, violent prejudices, wild passions, impulses which, uncontrolled, make for strife and discord. Whatever men come to exhibit in the way of worthy characters and ordered institutions and fine arts— whatever, in other words, they achieve in the way of civilization—is precarious in status and fragile in existence. This question of how to promote civilized ways in a precarious social world is a fundamental concern of many thinkers in all ages. But the solutions offered have varied considerably. Some thinkers have put their trust in educational schemes; others, in reliance upon natural reason; many, in supplications for divine grace; some, in appeal to law, whether *lex naturae* or Common Law; a credulous few, in the automatic balance of a welter of independent forces into an eventual happy synthesis. Hobbes brushed such solutions aside. Education is prone to corruption; reason is weak; divine grace is a bone of contention and a cause of controversy; law is often flouted when it is good and enforced when it is bad; custom is subject to periodic breakdowns; and the idea that the anarchy of individual lusts will iron themselves out into universal harmony is a silly dream. The only technique of order is discipline, discipline imposed from above, discipline that comes from power that cannot be challenged by either passion or ignorance. Sovereignty is thus the *sine qua non,* not merely of peace, but also of all excellence, both for individual men and for social groups.

In comparing Hobbes's position with Hobbism, one ought always to remember that all details in Hobbes's writings are subservient to a pressing home of this his central theme. Hobbes knew quite well that he fell at times into overstatement, but he evidently valued overstatement as useful to shock his readers out of their complacency. For example, he prefaced his first published work on political philosophy with the following very revealing words:

> Wherefore if ye shall meet with some things which have more of sharpness, and less of certainty than they ought to have, since they are not so much spoken for the maintenance of parties as the establishment of peace, and by one whose just grief for the present calamities of his country may very charitably be allowed some liberty; it is his only request to ye, Readers, ye will deign to receive them with an equal mind.

Of course Hobbes's contemporaries did not observe this warning and were shocked into violent opposition instead of into patient attention. But Hobbes's intent is none the less clear.

On the first point of Hobbism as outlined above, Hobbes was far from being a Hobbist. The picture which he gave of "man in the state of nature" is, to be sure, far from flattering. Every man in the state of nature is enemy to every other man; he exists in a constant state of war, friendless, neither giving nor receiving sympathy, beset by dire fears, driven by a lust for power after power that ceaseth only in death. But what is seldom noticed by Hobbes's readers is that the picture of "man in the state of nature" is not meant by Hobbes as a complete picture of human nature. The idea of man in a state of nature is, like the idea of a state of nature, not historical but analytical. Hobbes did not regard the state of nature as an early historical period from which men later departed; he rather

regarded it as a permanent factor within society, with which therefore all sound social theory must be constantly occupied— that is, as an ever-present menace against which men must be on their guard in both theory and practice. So the idea of man in a state of nature is an emphasis on an aspect of all human nature, an aspect that may be at times competently controlled but can never possibly be eradicated. Man in the state of nature is what man would be in the absence of all the normal associations of social life. It is really a picture of man as he is perhaps never, certainly seldom, found, though as he is in part forever tending to become. The idea is analogous to the scientific description of a body as continuing in a state of rest or of uniform motion in a straight line unless influenced by outside forces. Actually there is no such body, because all bodies are continually influenced by outside forces. Yet the concept of a body as it would be if left to itself is useful in enabling us to make more exact calculations of the various outside forces that influence any particular body we may wish to study. So the concept of man in the state of nature is useful in enabling us to estimate the importance of the social ties that qualify the conduct of any and every man we may wish to study. Hobbes was not so poor a psychologist as to overlook man's genuinely social interest. But the concept of man in a state of nature is important because it makes evident the gravity of the problem of securing a stable, and even moderately decent, society. Men do have lusts that do not easily submit to discipline; they are in continual need of being remade and controlled. The irruption of bestiality into human affairs is not to be glibly explained away as an unfortunate effect of bad social conditions: it is too often the very source of those bad conditions. We actually find men who are neither pure samples of man in the state of nature nor clear embodiments of perfect virtue. We have men of varying degrees of crudity and refinement; and our problem is to understand the causes of the crudity in order that we may then increase the amount of the refinement. A clear idea of man in the state of nature is a prerequisite to any formulation of an effective technique of social control; for the difficulties of social life are not functions of man's better aspects but rather functions of his basest lusts. The world is turbulent because men lie and cheat and murder. Thus the idea of man in a state of nature, while not a psychologically adequate analysis of human nature (which it was not Hobbes's purpose to give), is just that analysis of man that is most relevant to the political problem with which Hobbes is grappling.

Hobbes explicitly states that men are not naturally evil. But they are naturally passionate; and in the absence of means of security they are naturally the prey of hunting fears. Men's passions and fears may make them evil if conditions force them to aim primarily at defense against treachery and secret plotting. Men's passions will be qualified, however, and their fears may in large part be dissipated, if conditions surround them with ordered custom and lawful procedures. One cannot persuade water to run up hill, but one may pump it some distance upwards. So one cannot persuade men to be passionless; but one may so organize a state that men will gratify their passions within the definable bounds of civilized ways. In brief, excellence comes, not from romantic trust in human nature, but from realistic knowledge of what the forces are which require control. Hobbes really did for political theory at this point what scientific investigation of moving bodies was doing in the seventeenth century for mechanics. He did not discover any such existing person as a man in the state of nature, just as no one discovered a body that moved without influence from without. But he revealed what the nature is of that which we have to control, as others revealed the nature of that which outside forces affect. Hobbes therefore differs entirely from Hobbism, since he is not giving a picture of human nature in its entirety, but is fashioning a concept that is explicitly

relative to the central theme of securing a society in which incentives to violence are few and encouragements to virtue may abound.

The second point of Hobbism as outlined concerns the basis of morality. According to Hobbism, morality is the creature of the arbitrary fiat of princes and lacks all validity apart from sovereign control. It is easy to find the phrases in Hobbes, repeated from book to book and recurrently within each book, which led men to classify Hobbes as a Hobbist. For example, there are such passages as the following:

Nature hath given all to all. From whence we understand likewise, that in the state of nature profit is the measure of right.

Irresistible might, in the state of nature, is right.

Before the institution of sovereign power, *meum* and *tuum,* implied no propriety, but a community, where every man had right to every thing.

Seeing then that a just action . . . is that which is not against the law; it is manifest that before there was a law, there could be no injustice; and therefore laws are in their nature antecedent to justice and injustice.

Where there is no common-wealth, there is nothing unjust. So that the nature of justice, consisteth in keeping of valid covenants: but the validity of covenants begins not but with the constitution of a civill power sufficient to compel men to keep them.

These and other such phrases in Hobbes's writings are challenging. But they do not properly mean Hobbism. Two things need to be said in order to establish a correct interpretation of Hobbes's meaning. First, Hobbes is speaking in legal, not in moral, terms. Justice and right are being defined in terms of enforcement of a conformity to law. It is then an analytical proposition and admits of no dispute that where there is no law there can be no question of justice and right at all. Justice then begins only where law exists. And in the absence of law, might makes right, not in the sense that might proves wisdom or virtue to be resident in him who exercises the might, but in the sense that might, when irresistible, is the beginning of a régime in which the distinction between ruler and subjects is emerging, in which, hence, the existence of law is beginning to manifest itself and conformity to law is incipiently involved.

Secondly, and almost by corollary from the preceding remark, it is also clear that Hobbes is insisting that any significant morality is social in character and presupposes the occurrence of regularized procedures. Morality is not significantly present when men are considered in their separateness as atomic individuals; it is significantly present when men are considered in their interrelations in an integral situation in which questions of social adjustment arise. If one wants to press the point and insist that some minor problems of morality might arise in connection with the conduct of a single man in isolation from his fellows, Hobbes would grant the point. Indeed, he did expressly grant the point in a revealing fashion. Some critic evidently pressed this very point against Hobbes when the first privately printed edition of the *De cive* appeared in Paris in 1642. For in the Elzevir [Press] editions of 1647 footnotes appeared in answer to this criticism. Hobbes did not consider the point important enough to make any alterations in the text proper, but he did quite explicitly answer the criticism. Even apart from social institutions, a man may well find some conduct wiser and other conduct more foolish, so that "the laws of nature," i.e., the principles of reason or morality, apply to him considered alone. In his own words:

There are certain natural laws, whose exercise ceaseth not even in time of war itself. For I can not understand what drunkenness or cruelty, that is, revenge which respects not the future good, can advance towards peace, or the preservation of any man. Briefly, in the state of nature, what is just and unjust, is not to be esteemed by the actions but by the counsel and conscience of the actor.

There is here no reluctance to admit a minor kind of morality apart from social institutions; but Hobbes evidently considered such morality as of slight moment because hardly pertinent to any existing situation in which men actually live. All significant moral problems arise in the complex adjustments of men in civil society. So dominantly social is morality that one can practically equate the social and the moral; and Hobbes felt no compunction at such inconsequential over-statements as he, deeply stirred by his important theme, had made in the main text of his book.

The two comments just made in exposition of Hobbes's position are intimately involved in each other. It is precisely because justice and right have an important meaning as legal terms that morality can be viewed as a genuinely social affair. If men lived without a known law and a civil power to enforce it, they would have no guide except their individual judgments; consequently, opinions would clash, strife would ensue, and chaos would result. To recognize this is not to endorse ruthless, anti-social, and passionate acts: it is rather to indicate the indispensable rôle of law in the pursuit of the good life. If we supposed that individual men in their individuality are so many separate seats of moral prerogatives and moral obligations, then the nature of morality would be fixed antecedently to the enactment of laws, and the duty of law-makers would be merely to frame laws consistent with this fixed and antecedent standard. Such a philosophy would be an utterly superficial view of the intimate involvement of morals and law in each other. Not simply is it true that "where there is no judge, there is no end of controversy; and therefore the right of hostility remaineth," so that without law chaos would ensue and the possibility of genuinely moral achievement be annulled by universal strife. But also and more fundamentally it is true that the establishment of law creates a new situation in which sound reason or sound moral principle (two terms for the same idea) requires decisions such as would be ridiculous if there were no law or if there were a different law. Law does not by fiat create moral distinctions, and Hobbes never said that it did. But law does create significant moral situations, and Hobbes saw this more clearly than any prior political philosopher of modern times.

That Hobbes never regarded law as by fiat creating moral distinctions is so often overlooked that the point requires amplification. Hobbes repeatedly said that "the laws of nature," i.e., the principles of reason, "are the sum of moral philosophy." But for good and sufficient reason the law of nature demands the establishment of civil society (which of course includes law) and the operation of men within the structure thus established. As Hobbes said:

Theft, murder, adultery, and all injuries, are forbid by the law of nature; but what is to be called *theft,* what *murder,* what *adultery,* what *injury* in a citizen, this is not to be determined by the natural, but by civil law.

For the principles of reason are all of them abstract, and the acts of men are all of them concrete; and the passage from abstract principle to concrete act is possible only when considered in the social situation in which the concrete acts occur. Hobbes was far from the position of the Hobbist, who assumed that moral distinctions are artificial suppositions foisted upon men by arbitrary power. He was dramatically stressing the point that morality (aside from a few trivial exceptions) arises in social life as manifest in the existence of social instrumentalities or institutions to regularize human relations, of laws to define and modify these relations, and of authorities to enforce their observance. So far from being a denier of genuine moral distinctions, he was alert to specify exactly what

the conditions of morality are, in what context moral problems occur, and by what means some kind of practical solution of moral difficulties may be reached.

This fact anticipates and involves the third point on which Hobbes again must be distinguished from what has been called Hobbism. According to Hobbism, the lawmaker, since he creates moral distinctions, is *ipso facto* always morally justified in all of his acts, and a bad lawmaker is thus a contradiction in terms. Again, as in the case of the former point, it is easy to find the phrases in Hobbes's works which led hasty readers or prejudiced critics to interpret him as asserting this kind of Hobbism. Consider, for example, the following:

Legitimate kings therefore make the things they command just, by commanding them, and those which they forbid unjust, by forbidding them.

It belongs to the same chief power to make some common rules for all men, and to declare them publicly, by which every man may know what may be called his, what another's, what just, what unjust, what honest, what dishonest, what good, what evil.

There are no authentical doctrines concerning right and wrong, good and evil, besides the constituted laws in each realm and government.

Whatsoever he [i.e., the sovereign] doth, it can be no injury to any of his subjects; nor ought he to be by any of them accused of injustice.

These, again, are strong words; for Hobbes wished to drive home his point with vigor and to leave no loopholes for those who deem their private opinions superior to law. In one phrase, namely, in making the sovereign competent to determine good and evil, Hobbes might properly be said to have gone beyond his intent. For good and evil are ethical terms, even in Hobbes's usage; and his inclusion of them in the second and third sentences just quoted indicates how easy it was for Hobbes to slip into overstatement. With this exception granted, however, the passages quoted are thoroughly sound in the sense in which Hobbes used the terms. Hobbes was clearly employing the words in their strictly legal sense. His meaning is that the source of law can hardly be contrary to law (except in certain technical details, explanation of which he did not take time or burden himself to give). Civil society carries with it the obligation that it be respected as such. Even bad law is law, and even good citizens cannot properly flout bad law as if it were not really law at all. Since law establishes, in part at least, the situations which define our moral problems, it cannot, in any competent and incisive moral conduct, be treated as either inconsequential or irrelevant. He who ignores the legal purport of his acts *ipso facto* destroys the moral legitimacy of those acts.

Hobbes proceeded in all his writings to repudiate the Hobbist contention that "the king can do no wrong." He had much to say "concerning the duties of them who bear rule," to quote one of his chapter titles. Though a sovereign cannot, by definition, act unjustly, he "may by diverse ways transgress against the other laws of nature, as by cruelty, iniquity, contumely, and other like vices." A sovereign, as much as any other man, is subject to the law of nature or the dictates of reason; indeed he has greater responsibilities to these laws than other men because he is by function the person who "hath taken into his hands any portion of mankind to improve." "The duty of a sovereign," said Hobbes, "consisteth in the good government of the people." Good government involves provisions to increase the number of the people, to preserve peace at home, to provide defense against attack from without, and generally to safeguard "the commodity of living." And by commodity of living Hobbes meant such regulations as will give encouragement to trade, abundant opportunity for labor, ample supplies of food and other necessities, and such liberty of movement and of private affairs as is compatible with maintenance of public

order. Not simply may a sovereign violate his responsibilities to his people through indulgence in vice or through neglect, but even a conscientious sovereign may commit such vital mistakes of judgment that his rule involves serious moral disasters. All this Hobbes reiterated so frequently that at no point is he more obviously to be distinguished from Hobbism. One may agree or disagree with Hobbes on such points as whether increase of population is a good; but one can hardly identify him with Hobbism without ignoring long chapters of his political writings.

On the fourth point of Hobbism as outlined above, Hobbes may be said to have come fairly close to being a Hobbist. Yet even here a distinction must be carefully made. Hobbes did deny popular rights to the generality of men when they live in civil society. He granted to citizens only such rights as are conferred by law or as are not in any way dealt with by law. No rights inhere in citizens by virtue of their civil status which it would then be unjust to change or annul. Sovereign power must be, not only great, but also absolute. No check can be imposed on sovereign power; for then that person or group that imposes the check would be the sovereign, and the official on whom the check was imposed would be but a subordinate and dependent instrument. "The sovereign power . . . implieth an universal impunity."

Now it is only fair to grant to Hobbes all the validity that his words may have; and there are two things, in connection with this point, which ought to be said in his behalf and support. The first of these is that social problems often admit of no settlement by conference, by compromise, by mutual reconciliation of conflicting claims. In such cases, we have to choose between open strife and imposed settlement. Wise rulers, even prudent citizens, will seek to prevent the occasions of such embittered opposition. But rulers are not always wise nor citizens prudent; and even where wisdom and prudence are found in some men, intransigent discord may be found among others of their fellows. Often, perhaps usually, imposed settlement is in these cases preferable to continuance of strife. Well might Hobbes say: "The condition of man in this life shall never be without inconvenience." One of the conditions of civil life is the habit of conforming to governmental decisions as binding, whether they are or seem to be wisely made or not. To deny that civil authority is entitled to determine policy, even when it cannot give adequate demonstration of the soundness of that policy, is to "make it impossible for any nation in the world to preserve themselves from civil war."

The second thing to be said in Hobbes's support on the present point is that sovereign will inevitably lies behind law. Appeal from sovereign will to some law is virtually appeal from a present sovereign to a past sovereign; it is therefore virtually appeal to a fixed sovereignty and implies that past decisions of a former sovereign are preferable to decisions of a present sovereign who may take cognizance of changed conditions. Law is important, and no one saw this more clearly than Hobbes. But also no force in society is more human in its origin than law, more experimental in its course, more tentative in its objectives, more dependent in its meaning upon the authorities who use it. Veneration for law, whether common law, written or unwritten constitutions, or statutes of any kind, is a virtue which, pressed to an extreme, easily becomes a vice. Hobbes is at this point in sharp contrast with Locke, and is, it may well be maintained, the wiser political philosopher. The most significant thing about Locke's *Treatise of Civil Government* is really not what it says but what it avoids saying. Locke's most notable trait is that he could compose an entire treatise on government without so much as mentioning the word or introducing the idea of sovereignty. He hoped that laws might govern instead of men; and "liberals" have generally followed his lead. Locke evidently thought that an original contract could so determine for all time the best conditions for all future society that further exercise of sovereign power could be eliminated from

government in both theory and practice. He dared to hope that government might thus become merely the continued application of principles firmly established for every possible contingency. Hobbes had too much realism, too penetrating an insight, to entertain any such position. Even if he erred in overstatement, even if he made too little distinction between a sovereign's passing caprice and his studied decision, he is at least sound in refusing to take law as a final court of appeal. The complexity of social needs demands some authority other than law and custom to impose settlement and enforce it with power. Legalism ties a society to precedent, to the level of past achievement. Hobbes's appeal to sovereignty, with all the faults of its tendency to harsh overstatement, is in theory a release from outworn precedent. It is in theory a turning to the ultimate source of law in the interest of securing better and more pertinent law.

There yet remains something ruthless in Hobbes's words that sovereign power implies universal impunity, something ruthless enough to make it natural for hasty readers to misinterpret his words as a mere expression of Hobbism. Hobbes put the sovereign above not merely law but also criticism. Counsellors a sovereign may choose; but no one may offer unsolicited advice. Hobbes wrote that the subjects of a sovereign are not called upon to renounce their "natural reason," or to give "a submission of the intellectual faculty to the opinion of any other man." But he insisted upon such full obedience of every subject to his sovereign in all respects that for practical purposes he refuses to admit the right of independence of thought. We may well enjoy Hobbes's ironic comment that "in matter of government, when nothing else is turned up, clubs are trumps." We may even grant the truth behind the irony. But we can hardly brook the pretense of Hobbes that a sovereign is responsible to God alone, and hence beyond the legitimate right of human criticism. Hobbes seems too ready to let the sovereign use clubs as trumps on any and every occasion. The appeal to force may need to be implicit in any civil organization; but surely the exercise of force ought to be only a last resort when reason fails.

And exactly here is to be found that major fault that mars Hobbes's entire political philosophy. Hobbes's appeal to force was insistent because his distrust of human reason was excessive. Hobbes analyzed "the law of nature" with great skill and effect; but he did not believe that men are intelligent enough to follow the paths of reasonableness. Human reason may be fallible, as Hobbes pointed out; but so is any constituted authority or any *de facto* sovereignty. Because reason does not control men sufficiently, Hobbes denied it any proper play in human affairs. Hobbes had no sense for the social value of what we may call "His Majesty's Opposition." He had no sense for either the privilege or the duty of a sovereign to provide for criticism, to permit the free exchange and discussion of ideas to assist in clarifying policy and defining purposes. Since such criticism must at times be suspended, Hobbes would deny it altogether. Hobbes, himself given to forceful reasoning, yet regarded reasoning as weak and ineffective. He treated reasoning as sedition against authority, criticism as treason, discussion of policy as a mark of the dissolution of commonwealth. Hence he supported the strange thesis that strong government is one in which reasoning and criticism and discussion are not visible. When he wrote that "toleration of a professed hatred of tyranny, is a toleration of hatred to commonwealth in general," he so defined tyranny as to safeguard his statement. But he none the less gives even a sympathetic reader the impression that he would prefer an arbitrary fiat from any sovereign at all to a reasoned debate on matters of public policy. Only on such a supposition can one explain how he came to say that "the commands of them that have the right to command, are not by their subjects to be censured, nor disputed," or that "the law is all the right reason we have, and . . . the infallible rule of moral good-

ness." Hobbes, it might justifiably be said, took the same pessimistic view of human reason that was prevalent among the early Protestant reformers. But whereas the Protestant reformers looked to God's grace to re-endow human reason with more power, Hobbes looked to sovereign power to make human reason unnecessary.

An estimate of Hobbes's significance for political theory is possible by comparing his position with that of Plato. Plato held that "the best thing is, not that the laws prevail, but that a man prevail who has wisdom and royal quality." Here is the mean between Locke's appeal to law in fear of tyranny and Hobbes's appeal to tyranny in fear of anarchy. The historian may excuse Hobbes's fear of anarchy when he recalls the confusion of affairs in the seventeenth century and Hobbes's consequent desire to get something settled with finality. But the critic must weigh the merits of what the historian explains. And the critic may well see in Hobbes's distrust of reason a threat that Hobbes's political theory may easily slip into that very Hobbism from which Hobbes is carefully distinguished. For if reason be effete and insignificant, then the "natural man" tends to become the entire man, moral distinctions tend to become arbitrary fiats, and any sovereign may be justified in all his ways. Had the opponents of Hobbes focused their attack upon Hobbes's distrust of reason, they would have been able to make out a trenchant case. But of course they, too, distrusted reason, preferring to appeal to some principle of legitimacy or some ecclesiastical authoritarianism or some hereditary institution. Hobbes was so eager to solve the problem of political life that he chose one possible means of settlement of issues, one possibly correct means for the settlement of some issues. But he erred in generalizing about this means which competent reason might ratify relatively to some specific situations, and so regarded it as superseding for all occasions that critical reason which alone could justify it to a degree and for certain selected situations. We may need at times to enforce old law, to insist on some *de facto* settlement of moot issues, to precipitate revolution at the risk of disorder. But we cannot make ourselves victims of established law or submissive subjects of absolute power of facile inciters to violence. The one thing that Hobbes needed to complete his theory and to make it a defensible interpretation of civil and social life was an understanding of the rôle that reason may play in human affairs. With that addition, his political philosophy would become a definitive theory; but without that it still remains a monumental contribution that deserves to be differentiated from Hobbism, even while it is recognized as that from which hasty readers would be repelled as from Hobbism.

THE ENGLISH COMMON LAW WAS AN EVOLUTIONARY PRODUCT of the Middle Ages, and it was questionable whether its preservation would be compatible with the solution of the social, economic, and political problems which confronted English rulers and statesmen in the sixteenth and seventeenth centuries. Courts outside its domain—the Star Chamber, the Chancery, the Court of Requests, the High Commission, the Councils of the North and of Wales—acquired extensive jurisdiction and built up bodies of law that rivaled the common law. In fact, the greatest of English legal historians, Frederic William Maitland, was of the opinion that in the middle years of the sixteenth century England came close to a "reception" of the Roman law such as was experienced in France and other European countries and proved to be an effective instrument of despotic government. But that was not to be, and what actually came about was a remarkable renaissance of the common law in which the most celebrated of English judges, Sir Edward Coke, was the dominant figure. The early reforms of the Long Parliament, including as they did the abolition of the Star Chamber and other prerogative courts, represented a victory for the common law over its rivals no less than a victory for Parliament over the King. During the Interregnum, however, demands were made for reforms in the common law and in the courts. Under the Commonwealth and Protectorate, Parliamentary committees made many suggestions for change, some of which were adopted after the Restoration. In the period of the Puritan Revolution itself, the movement for law reform was a failure, but it is nevertheless worthy of historical attention, as Professor Goldwin Smith, of Wayne University, author of a recent textbook survey of English history, makes clear in the informative essay that follows.

THE REFORM OF THE LAWS OF ENGLAND, 1640–1660
GOLDWIN SMITH

The judicious Hooker, in sonorous phrases, vouched for a Tudor system of statecraft that won wide allegiance to the Crown, the Church, and the Law. "Of Law there can be no less acknowledged than that her seat is in the bosom of God, her voice the har-

Reprinted by special permission from *University of Toronto Quarterly*, X (1941), 469–481. The footnotes which originally appeared with this essay have been omitted.

mony of the world. All things in heaven and earth do her homage; all with uniform consent admire her as the mother of their peace and joy." With Hooker marched Sir Thomas Smith, and the two doughty champions of the harmonious and decently reasonable middle way have been given an honoured place in history. Few would challenge their right to stand as typical Elizabethan apologists, dedicated to the principles of law and degree and duty. The fact is, however, that the close and continued admiration and study of the golden age of Elizabeth has made inevitable the discovery of numberless contrasts between the rule of the Tudors and the sad destruction born of the Stuarts. These contrasts have been so frequently made and multiplied that the shaping spirit of the historians' imagination threatens at once to create and to destroy: to create a Tudor utopia that never existed; to destroy, in part at least, our ability to sense the temper of the last decades of the sixteenth century.

Obvious and vexatious abuses had their place in the Tudor strong monarchy. A study of the literature of complaint in sixteenth-century England casts a shadow over Froude's familiar picture of a nation filled with harmony and peace and founded in power and stability. The voices of Skelton, Fish, Roy, Starkey, Brinklow and Thomas Wentworth have been too frequently hushed by the historians. The whirlwind that the Stuarts could not ride was not wholly of their own making. Under Cromwell, the new heirs to a new power found themselves plagued by problems that had shadowed the horizon in the preceding century. A single illustration may be seen in the fact that the first concerted movement for law reform, apparently born in the turmoil of the Civil Wars, had its origins in the years when England emerged from the Middle Ages and the Tudors began to create a modern state.

The mediaeval common law had arisen to answer the needs of a mediaeval political and economic organization. In sixteenth-century England an attempt was made to supplement the deficiencies of an outworn legal system in an effort to solve the new and unfamiliar problems of a nascent modern society. Thus there occurred the creation of new bodies of rules, new courts, and new councils. By these creations, by the gradual adaptation of the old machinery to new uses, by the development of convenient legal fictions, by judicial decisions and parliamentary legislation, the expansion of the law proceeded at a bewildering pace. The result of these years of rapid growth and hasty grafting was a legal system twisted by contradictions and deformed by anomalous survivals. Rival courts disputed rights of jurisdiction. Difficulties that even those learned in the law could not resolve threatened on occasion completely to clog the channels by which the law of England was administered. By the early seventeenth century many advocates of reform declared the courts and the legal system to be the true embodiment of everything that was cumbersome, dilatory, and expensive.

When Cromwell and his allies had entrenched their forces, almost all existing institutions were put on trial. In the years when old idols were melted down and cast anew, it was inevitable that a demand should arise for a searching and strict examination of the law and the law courts. A multitude clamoured to reform, to overthrow, to threaten with final extinction, not only the body of enacted law but also the system of courts by which it was administered. "The major part of the laws made in this nation," declared William Cole, "are founded on principles of tyranny, fallacy and oppression. . . . The law in the generality is unjust and irrational, the execution desperately dangerous and changeable; it is easier to find a thousand evils in it, than one true principle in matter or form."

Extremists in religion carried their fanaticism into the spheres of government and legal theory. In agreement with these restless and unstable minds were many cautious and sober men who shared the general feeling of discontent and supported the demand for change in the form and administration of the law. If divers groups were united by a common opposition to the legal system, the unity of opinion went no further. Differences in the advocacy of means and methods, in the conception of a final, perfect and neatly articulated structure, these presented difficulties that were not easily overcome.

Many of the writers who commenced and continued assaults upon the established system of law were intellectually baffled by the operation of the legal machinery. Their phrases mutilated the language of the law and their plans for reform were frequently those of men stupefied by a body of knowledge whose secrets they had not plumbed. They were determined, however, to end their grievances even if the proposed panacea proved a mischief instead of a benefit. The law must be altered to conform to justice. It must become the instrument rather than the arbiter of human purposes. It must cease to be a legal and administrative device for binding with chains the unenlightened. In the maze of its complicated machinery all sense of simplicity had vanished. The common law was locked in the judges' breasts. It was difficult to believe that Sir Edward Coke had not nodded when he declared that the unwritten laws of England had been "divinely cast into the hearts of men and built upon the irremovable rock of reason." Surely the secret and intricate common law could be made to yield to the pressure of the

layman and be translated into a few rules, simple and easily understood. Certainly it seemed possible that the administration of justice could be made speedy and equitable. "Some real compensation is desired by the people for all their sufferings, losses and blood. The end of all just laws is safety and freedom . . . and equal and speedy distribution of right ought to be the abstract and epitome of all laws."

The genesis of much of the agitation may be found in the severity of the criminal code. "There is no necessity for the law to keep people in dread and awe." The fond and needless submission to harsh and unjust laws was a dishonourable badge of infamy. "Why do some laws exceed the offence?" asks Warr, in the pamphlet cited above.* "Why are men's lives forfeited by the law on light or trivial grounds? Why is our law a meander of intricacies? Why are so many men destroyed for want of formality and punctilio? . . . Is not trial by combat reasonless? Why should the laws of England be in an unknown tongue? Why should a murderer be allowed to live if a thief be condemned to die? This severity is one of the abominations of the time, for which the saints ought to mourn."

A second cause of complaint lay in the evils associated with the Court of Chancery. It had a bad origin and worse record. Years had been known to elapse before the

* ["The Corruption and Deficiency of the Laws of England" (1649).]

SIR MATTHEW HALE: Lord chief justice and prolific writer (d. 1676). His important studies in legal history—*History of the Common Law of England* and *Historia placitorum coronae*—were not published until the early eighteenth century.

EDMUND LUDLOW: Puritan general and regicide (d. 1692). His *Memoirs* (1698-1699) are a valuable source of information about the age of the Puritan Revolution, for they throw much light on the outlook of a Puritan republican. They are available in an admirable edition prepared by Sir Charles Firth.

HUGH PETERS: Puritan preacher who played an important part in encouraging the members of the court of commissioners, who were trying Charles I, to sign the death warrant. He was hanged during the Restoration as a regicide.

WILLIAM WALWYN: Reformer who, except for John Lilburne, was the most important leader of the Levellers. His writings reveal that his ideas concerning political and social change were profoundly influenced by his religious convictions.

final settlement of a case lost in the labyrinth of its intricate and cumbersome methods. "Quick justice"—thus went Samuel Chidley's epigram—"makes quiet commonwealths." "Away with it," cries another writer; "no greasing of the wheels; no patching and mending of the machine; destroy it, bolt and crank and lever, and end this engine of oppression and corruption."

A third evil, and one that came very near to the average man, was the expense involved in an appeal to the law. If a suit were instituted to recover a debt, it frequently happened that the cost of recovery was greater than the amount of the original debt. The changes in matters of land law and conveyance were equalled in injustice only by the amount of the sheriff's fee. Nor did the litigants in cases involving property rights escape unfleeced. "I have heard of two men, who fell at variance about a hive of bees, and went to law, until he that had spent least, had spent £500." The doubtful accuracy of the assertion does not alter the fact of evident irritation behind the determined challenge to the common, costly and offensive evils of the law.

Annoying and irksome as were these many manifestations of the oppressions of the law itself, the full weight of abuse fell not upon the law, but upon the administration of it. The lawyers were regarded as the defenders of a fortress behind whose walls were protected all the iniquities and inequalities of a hated system. Potent, rich and dreadful were the lawyers, and under their skilled manipulation the law became anything or nothing to serve their corrupt self-interest. "The law as it is now constituted," says Ludlow, "serves only to maintain the lawyers and to encourage the rich to destroy the poor." The lawyer, with his "great and questionable parchments," was an "insatiate cannibal" who stole, oppressed and went "clothed in a genteel garb and all his family." It was the lawyers who had disinherited the people of their common right. It was the lawyers who took the money and then departed.

Like careful bees, to their own hives
　　they flew
As he from fortune, they from him
　　withdrew.

"Be you at last instrumental," wrote Henry Parker to the Army, "to free your country from the intolerable burden of the needless lawyers, who love none but themselves." On the eve of the Restoration, in the pamphlet cited above,* William Cole, the most unrelenting opponent of the lawyers and their works, ended his labours with a note of warning and a message of optimism: "It is thy duty and every honest Englishman's in the land, to take care hereafter never to choose any of that generation to make laws for us. . . . I do not altogether despair, that before I die I may see the inns of courts, those dens of thieves, converted into hospitals."

For the judges as well as the lawyers there were words of censure and invective. John Pym, at the opening of the Parliament of 1640, had enumerated, among other grievances, "the extrajudicial decisions of the judges, without hearing of counsel or argument." William Sheppard in his famous tract, *England's Balme,* recommended that "all judges be beneath justice and accountable to some above them, by whom their judgement may be examined and miscarriage punished." Winstanley considered the law to be a badge of slavery to all but the gentry and clergy; the rest of the people "are left servants and bondsmen . . . ; none have freedom by the laws but those two sorts of people; all the common people have been, and still are, burdened under them."

There was one small but noisy group who spread their doctrines with vividness and force. They expressed the desire to repudiate all human law, to summon the people of England from the wilderness of sin and establish the rule of the Law of God. All things that were repugnant to His law were to be abolished. If the law were made in

* ["A Rod for the Lawyers: Who are hereby declared to be the Grand Robbers and Deceivers of the Nation" (1659).]

accordance with the will of the Almighty then the principle of justice would triumph indeed. With the zeal that their aims suggest they preached the doctrine of the forcible overthrow of all existing laws. Hugh Peters proposed that even the old records in the Tower be burned as monuments of tyranny and sin. In this, as in many a similar movement, Winstanley had his share. "The Reformation," he wrote to Fairfax, "is according to the word of God and that is the pure law of righteousness before the fall, which made all things and to which all things are to be restored." But it was not Winstanley whose voice was heard most often in the struggle. Perhaps in a moment of despair Samuel Chidley took a text from Hosea: "I have written to him the great things of my law; but they were counted a strange thing." He wrote to the Lord Mayor of London: "All laws which are not according to God's law and pure reason, are void and null; it is the word of God which is binding and yet is not bound." He wrote to the Commissioners of Oyer and Terminer: "It is time for thee Lord to work, for they have made void thy law." He wrote to the General Council of the Army: "God is the only law-maker and His law is the ancientest and best that ever was." He wrote to the Parliamentary Committee on Law Reform: "For doubtless, the standing of the statutes and judgements of the holy and blessed God is a most blessed work; and the establishment thereof will work a more blessed reformation, than hath yet been, or shall be spoken of, at this time." But no one heeded Samuel Chidley. The "blessed reformation" did not occur and the Law of God was not established.

The strenuous and persistent efforts of a few obscure individuals, such as John Hare, had resulted in the growth of another movement known as anti-Normanism. The declared purpose of the leaders was to bring England back to those laws "which were before William the Conqueror came in." To the laws that William introduced, "by the iniquity of precedent times and the ignorant negligence of the present we still remain subject." The figure of Winstanley appeared once more, declaiming against "the burden of the Norman yoke." By his side were Walwyn and Lilburne. It was John Hare, however, who became the moving spirit in the anti-Norman party. "The innovations of the conquest are a just cause of the disrelishment and contempt of our laws (so Normanized in matter and form) by understanding men; and no doubt they are the ground of that general and inbred hatred which still dwells in our common people against our laws and lawyers." "The Normans," observed John Warr, "established our laws and they were of all nations the most quarrelsome in contriving controversies and suits." An anonymous writer commented upon "the stupid degenerateness of these members of a Teutonic nation." "Let us remove this mountain of dishonour," he wrote, "and let us propose that all laws and usages introduced from Normandy be abolished and a supply made from St Edward's laws . . . unless it may seem honourable for Englishmen to imprison their laws in the language of their enemies." It is doubtful, however, if the anti-Normans ever constituted a large body of opinion. Fortescue had earlier observed that the changes at the Conquest had been "not so much in substance as in the names of things" and outside of the militant anti-Norman group there appears to have been little inclination to dispute that conclusion.

The former unity of the Army and Parliament, of Independents, Puritans and Presbyterians soon changed with victory to disunity and discord. As it had been the Army that had defeated the Royalists, so now it was the Army majority in the Rump Parliament that cut the knot of the problem of supremacy, decided the form of a new constitution, and dictated the policies of the Commonwealth.

Even before the dissolution of the Rump Parliament the campaign against the lawyers and their laws had commenced. In October, 1650, the first Parliamentary Committee report on law reform was presented to the House. "Whether the Rump passed these laws I do not find, but if they did not, they might have done, had they been let alone."

A second Committee was appointed on January 20, 1651, "to take into consideration what inconveniences were in the law, how the mischief that grows from delays, the changeableness and inequalities in the law may be prevented and the speediest way to prevent the same." It was difficult, however, for this group to undertake or complete any practicable policy of reform. There were few men among them who understood the technical complexities of the problems, or could have hoped for successful or effective action. Sir Matthew Hale and Anthony Ashley Cooper found it difficult to co-operate with such men as Hugh Peters. "Peters," observed Whitelocke, "understood very little of the law, but was very opinionative and would frequently mention some proceeding of law in Holland wherein he was altogether mistaken." The majority of the Committee feared and distrusted the lawyers. When the latter discoursed upon the necessity of restoring the known law in its "full and authentical force" their opponents saw the foes of reform in the advocates of restoration. If a civilian who had practised in the Court of Admiralty described in glowing terms the simplicity and uniformity of the civil law and desired its adoption in place of an abolished common law, the lay members of a Committee who knew not the civil law, suspected in the eulogy a veiled conspiracy to foist upon them a system unknown and undesirable. From the day of its first meeting the Committee was divided. The lawyers were determined to resist these ignorant men who had been placed in power to clear the channels of the law. "The people's safety," it was remarked, "is never at a greater hazard than when it is put into its own hands." It was indeed a strange and motley assembly; the laymen, many of the meanest rank in fortune and understanding, resolved not to be outwitted by the unscrupulous lawyers; they resolved to strike terror into the learned bodies of the clergy and the law. At first they were confident of their position and proficiency and were quite willing to rush in where lawyers feared to tread. It was not long, however, before they became lost in a maze of ill-concocted and worse-considered proposals. Their ambition was to make one complete and methodical abridgement of the whole common and statute law; to remove the difficulties and make clear and certain what was obscure. In vexation and despair Ludlow recorded that the Committee discussed the word "incumbrance" for three months before its meaning could be ascertained. "The reformation of the law," he wrote, "went on but slowly, it being in the interests of the lawyers to preserve the lives, liberties and estates of the whole nation in their hands." It may be remarked that the actions of the lawyers were not always justified; indeed, the adoption of some excellent suggestions was often hindered or prevented by their indiscriminate opposition.

Here for the first time an opportunity presented itself for the translation into law of one policy widely approved. As early as 1646 Hugh Peters preached a sermon before both Houses of Parliament, in which he expressed his desire that "some short way might be found to further justice." By the establishment of courts in every county the expense and delay resulting from the necessity of taking suits to the quarterly courts at Westminster would be brought to an end. Chancery would be deposed from its exalted position and the great common law courts would cease to oppress and terrify. "Why should wills be probated at London . . . at such a charge and distance? . . . Why is it not better to have a civil suit tried in the neighbourhood, while it is fresh and green and new, when the witnesses are alive, . . . than seven, ten or twenty years after the suit is commenced?" Finally, despite the opposition of the lawyers, a bill was prepared providing for the creation of county registries, but not for local courts. From the many weeks of discord there emerged other proposals for reform. The larger number were neither wise nor practicable. There were, however, some few drafts of bills worthy of consideration and debate. These included measures for the more easy and speedy recovery of debts, against duels and challenges, against bribery and extortion by lawyers and judges, for better procedure in cases civil and criminal. To this last draft was appended a table of maximum fees to be charged by members of the legal profession. On January 24, 1652, Parliament discussed the drafts sent up by Hale's Committee.

Barebones' assembly had already aroused the conservative instincts of the Army officers. The Saints, instead of making peace, were bringing a still greater unrest to England. Cromwell repented of his enthusiasms and the Saints, in December, 1653, were sent to join the motley and growing opposition. For the second time the cause of law reform had been halted by a political crisis.

To Cromwell the officers of the Army went in November, 1654, "to desire him to take care for the bringing about of a due regulating of the law." A third time the champions of reform believed that reform would be at last achieved. It was not until early in 1656 that the Protector finally appointed his Committee. "There are wicked and abominable laws," he declared, "which it will be in your power to alter. To hang a man for six and eight pence . . . to acquit murder . . . this is a thing God will reckon for." In this Committee, as in that of 1651, a large number of well-meaning but helpless amateurs were included. Many of these were opposed to Whitelocke because he was a lawyer and would trouble their proceedings by "telling them what was the law upon every occasion, and their affairs would not permit to tie themselves up in those rules of law."

It has been noted in another context that the Committee of 1651 passed several weeks in the discussion of the necessity for a system of local courts. The men of 1656 determined to end the intolerable stranglehold of the common law courts and of chancery. They assured the people that they would not be distracted from their purpose by any apprehension of what the lawyers might do, or suffer themselves to be hypnotized by the fine and flowery words of men more cunningly wise than they. A "new model for provincial courts," suggested in 1655 by William Sheppard, had been favourably received by Cromwell and his Council. A newsletter to the army in Scotland reported that the event "much startled the lawyers and the City." A dispatch of October, 1656, relates that "my Lord Lambert yesterday brought into the House an act for setting up courts of justice and equity at York, which startles the lawyers to see the administration of the law like to be carried into the provinces." In the same month the bill for establishing county registries was read. "It received a very large debate, because of the opposition it received from the long robe." Neither Lord Lambert's brave bill nor the County Registries bill passed. Two Acts were passed, however, of interest and importance. The first abolished *peine forte et dure.** The second provided for the translation of all laws into English and the use of English in all pleadings. "It is amazing," writes Whitelocke, "that so good a law should not have been continued after the Restoration." Yet there appeared, on the whole, to be reason for satisfaction. Cromwell was speaking with sincerity, though not with foresight, when he said to his last Parliament: "You have made many very good laws, the effect whereof the people of this commonwealth will with comfort find hereafter."

The period following the death of the Protector gave no opportunity for experiment or reform. With the story of Richard Cromwell and the rise and fall of successive groups in the months leading to the Restoration we are not here concerned. Of the long list of law reforms only a few were accepted after 1660. Since many of the grievances still continued, many of the proposals of the Interregnum Committees were adopted in the last quarter of the century;

* [Torture inflicted upon an indicted criminal to force him to submit to jury trial.]

others became law in the eighteenth and nineteenth centuries.

It is true that the Restoration swept away whatever hopes the law reform movement may have had for success. Yet there were other reasons for its failure. Time and conditions were unsuitable. There was little stability in government. Three committees of Parliament found their work brought to an unexpected termination by sudden dissolution. The spectre of foreign wars and the shadow of conspiracies at home were seldom absent. It is evident also that a period of emotional disturbances does not provide the atmosphere necessary for calm and unhurried judgment. Nor is this all. We cannot overlook the fact that there was little agreement among those who were demanding reform. As the sects in religion, so the groups of law reformers were passionately convinced of the perfection of their particular creed and greatly disturbed at the doctrines of others.

On one final question a word should be said. Even if the various reforms had been accomplished, it would not have been to the advantage of the law or the people. Many of these reforms were ingenious. It is equally certain they were not safe. Few noted the complexity of the forces with which they had to deal. Not seldom the result of the desired achievement would have been disillusion. Many of the reformers saw only in the foreground lawyers and unjust laws that sought to reduce the people to impotence. They were successful in transforming the national inertia of the masses into active sympathy; they transformed their complaints into commands. Beyond that they did not go. We cannot do better than conclude with Sir William Holdsworth that it was perhaps wise to suffer many of the evils of the old system of law "that its stability and orderly development might be secured; when the modern constitution, resting ultimately upon the supremacy of law, had been evolved, when the modern rules of private law had been more fully developed, then it would be time, with greater knowledge and deliberation, to take in hand those reformations which, amid the passion and turmoil of the seventeenth century, it had been possible to foreshadow, but impossible to effect."

IN NO DEPARTMENT OF HISTORICAL KNOWLEDGE are differences in interpretation more striking than in the biographical, and it is not difficult to understand why such differences should be most marked in the case of individuals who were involved in bitter controversies in their own day. In English history, for example, it is small wonder that a consensus of opinion has not been reached regarding the outstanding leaders in the age of the Puritan Revolution—Charles I, Strafford, Laud, Pym, Hyde, Cromwell. Charles II is another historical figure who has invited a variety of interpretations. His policy of religious toleration, for example, can be regarded as enlightened statesmanship or as the opening move in an attempt to bring about a Roman Catholic restoration. The Whig interpretation of the "Merry Monarch," which can be read in the pages of Macaulay or John Richard Green, has been challenged at many points by a number of biographers who have written during the past generation. Most of their biographies, however, are laudatory or apologetic but not scholarly, as the late Professor Clyde L. Grose, of Northwestern University, points out in the essay that follows. Author of the useful *Select Bibli-*

ography of British History, 1660-1760 (1939) and a witty and shrewd student of Restoration times, Professor Grose presents his own estimate of Charles "as head of the state, as head of the church, as promoter of the navy, as friend of science, as leader of court and society, and finally, in the best Hollywood fashion, as the Great Lover."

CHARLES THE SECOND OF ENGLAND
CLYDE L. GROSE

The seventeenth century in England was a period of constitutional and religious strain with such far-reaching consequences for the entire western world that partisans naturally wrote its history for many years. Not until Samuel Rawson Gardiner's great work of the second half of the nineteenth century did any scholar look steadily and with clear vision past both Whig and Tory historians of two centuries. His eighteen volumes, however, stop at 1656, and the late Sir Charles Firth continued them only to the death of Cromwell. The twenty-eight years of the Restoration remain to this day a period in which the amateur historian, the popular biographer, and the romanticist may roam undeterred and unchecked by a recognized guide.

The situation, however, is changing. No Gardiner of the Restoration has arisen, and it is improbable that one will appear. But the last fifteen years have produced scores of scholarly monographs and several good histories, lengthy if not of heroic proportions. The longest is David Ogg's *England in the Reign of Charles II* (2 vols., Oxford, 1934). Others are Keith Feiling's *British Foreign Policy* (London, 1930) and G. N. Clark's *Later Stuarts, 1660-1714* (Oxford, 1934), the latter in the promising Oxford History of England series.

Meanwhile Charles II had suddenly become the subject of many biographies which raised him from a state of comfortable infamy to the society of England's greatest. Explanation is not difficult. The World War

and its aftermath, like most crises, emphasized leadership. Peoples and parliaments grew dull and colorless compared to the outstanding personality. There arose a new interest in monarchy, somewhat by way of supporting what appeared to be a lost cause. With it came a revived interest in conservative institutions, including Catholicism; and Charles II, however he lived, died a Catholic. The postwar period also caused a relaxing of morals and standards, a dislike of the local and the customary, and a hankering after the exotic and the unusual. On most of these counts Charles II qualified for twentieth century fame.

This recent flood of laudatory biography, unscholarly as it is for the most part, can curiously enough be traced in large measure to the prefaces of a monumental work of scholarly editing. I refer to Dr. William A. Shaw's series of calendars of Treasury Books. The volumes for the reign of Charles II appeared during the years 1904-16. The editing is superb. No cheap apologia will spring directly therefrom. But in lengthy prefaces Dr. Shaw unwisely deserted the role of editor of financial documents and set forth striking generalizations about parliament and Charles II, from which the latter emerged triumphant and almost a patriot king, while parliament, niggard and inefficient, became the villain of the piece. What Dr. Shaw stated in strong but slightly restrained tones and only by way of preface became the central theme of recent biographers. Most of them recognize their debt to

Reprinted by special permission from *The American Historical Review*, XLIII (1938), 533–541. The footnotes which originally appeared with this essay have been omitted.

him. It is doubtful whether he is proud of his profuse progeny.

Eighteenth century historians tended to disregard Charles II in their emphasis on what preceded and followed. The same, with a few exceptions, may be said of the nineteenth century. Victorians naturally felt uneasy at the lax Restoration court, preferring the deprived Nonconformists and the immortal occupant of the Bedford jail. As late as 1901 Osmund Airy could write for the elaborately illustrated Goupil series of royal biographies a whiggish summary which would have satisfied most periods of the preceding two centuries.

Then came Dr. Shaw's more influential prefaces in 1904-11, and the World War. In 1917 Sir Henry Imbert-Terry portrayed this previously misunderstood monarch as a paragon of constitutional virtue who conformed to the best and noblest in English tradition. Then following the war, with publishers' demands for racy biography, there appeared in rapid succession the following lives of Charles II: Beresford Chancellor's in 1924; John Drinkwater's in 1926; Arthur Dasent's in 1927; David Loth's in 1930; Dennis Wheatley's and John Hayward's, both in 1933. All are interesting, laudatory, or apologetic. Not one is scholarly. Omitted from this list is Arthur Bryant's *King Charles II,* in 1931, which arrives at the same conclusions but by the way of some scholarship. His reading shows breadth if not any too much depth. His references are impressive in bulk if exasperating as to arrangement and usefulness. His work is not without merit in spite of its Tory bias, which is happily much less manifest in his more scholarly and important recent volumes on Pepys.

It is of interest and profit to compare these biographers with the best recent historians of the period. Not one of the latter shares their enthusiasm. All are unimpressed with Charles's suddenly-discovered patriotism, tireless energy, and sincere devotion to constitutionalism. All, basing their judgments on contemporary documents rather than prefaces thereto, find him easygoing,

undependable, more selfish than patriotic, not very far-sighted, and on the whole not very wise. It appears that Clarendon's wisdom was responsible for Charles's return to England surrounded by happy Englishmen rather than by Spanish soldiers, had he been able to get them. All admit his good nature, his gracious tact, his keen knowledge of men, and his occasional spurts of first-rate statesmanship, but they agree that he was neither a great nor a good king. Some writers have denied his indolence and his aversion to sustained effort. Their statements are in direct contrast to the witness of eight men who knew him well and who, regarding him in different ways and from different angles, some as friends, some as critics, all agree on this point. The eight men are Clarendon, Pepys, Evelyn, Grammont, Burnet, Halifax, and the two French ambassadors, Cominges and Barrillon. It is unbelievable that all should be wrong, especially when known facts agree considerably with their statements.

I shall now consider Charles successively as head of the state, as head of the church, as promoter of the navy, as friend of science, as leader of court and society, and finally, in the best Hollywood fashion, as the Great Lover. Recent events in England have somewhat dimmed his pre-eminence in this last regard, for even he would never have considered giving up a throne for the woman he loved—nor, incidentally, for anything else—but he nevertheless occupies a unique place among English monarchs who won women's hearts.

As head of the state Charles displayed easygoing indolence, marked neither by high principle nor striking accomplishment. His ability in time of crisis, however, to commandeer immense reserves of energy and leadership, combined with unusual tact and intuition, rates him among the abler kings of England. The way he rode the storms of 1678-81, stripped of experienced advisers and handicapped by three relatives—James, Monmouth, and William of Orange—is nothing short of masterly. It was about the only time he ever stood courageously in defense of a principle, that of hereditary succession. He had more brains than he ordinarily used, though this is scarcely a compliment. There may be personal satisfaction in possessing unused talents, but so far as society is concerned the result is nil.

The surroundings and discouragements of his early life left a permanent influence. Never again would he be a hungry, cold exile. Henceforth he would be comfortable. He never even dreamed of dying a martyr's death like his father. He longed for absolutism on the French model, but he never longed for it enough to exert himself in that direction to the limit of his powers. It was too hard work and might imperil his comfort. Except at the few times when he was aroused to great spurts of energy, he lacked courage, industry, and the serious resolve that persists against opposition. He manipulated ministries with consummate skill but seldom tried to dominate them. Extant records of council meetings show him a bored courtier, forced to listen to heavy discourse and at times forced to make decisions. When these decisions called for common sense and intuition, they were usually well made. When they required sustained application to a problem, they were usually poorly done. To a considerable degree he allowed things to drift, which may be another way of praising him for getting in the way very little. With the main currents of the day, commercialism, imperialism, and toleration, he moved gracefully and at times enthusiastically. He allowed the Committee on Foreign Affairs to become a sort of embryonic cabinet. In 1679 he permitted Sir William Temple and others to undertake a real pioneering venture in cabinet government, but he gave it little support and broke through all constitutional defenses at the first opportunity. This came in early 1681, when England was thoroughly enervated by the Popish Plot, the Exclusion struggle, and Shaftesbury's party strategems, the last a new and racking experience for the nation. He seized the opportunity, and the last four years of the reign represent a rapid return to absolutism: no parliaments, widespread destruction of municipal charters, interference with local governments and personal liberties, a tendency to the spirit of the French *dragonnades,* and the importation of a royal Swiss guard in the best Versailles fashion. Had it not been that Charles died in middle life, before the full import of his closing years became clear, and had it not been that James was such an "all-time low" in political wisdom as to unite everybody against him within three years of his accession, Englishmen would take more seriously the peril to their liberties represented by the period 1681-88. Just because it happened to end rather quickly, and without leaving serious scars, is no reason for diminishing the potential peril.

As head of the church Charles was a liability of the first order. Until his dying hours, when he was received into the Catholic faith, he had no serious religion but was a sort of indifferent deist who for political reasons preferred Catholicism. He conformed sufficiently to the established church to keep on friendly terms, but his conduct and that of his friends ruffled the better bishops. He could afford to be tolerant of

GILBERT BURNET: Clergyman and writer (d. 1715). He was relieved of his duties as king's chaplain because he complained about the dissolute life that Charles II was leading. During the reign of William III he became Bishop of Salisbury. His most important writings are his multivolume *History of the Reformation in England* and his posthumously published *History of My Own Times.*

JOHN EVELYN: Writer (d. 1706) whose reputation has rested above all on his admirable *Diary,* in which he discussed his continental travels and set forth his estimate of many of his notable contemporaries in Restoration times. He also wrote on engraving, architecture, agriculture, gardening, and commerce.

others' beliefs since it cost him no sacrifice of his own. The peoples' fear of his becoming a Catholic was enervating throughout the reign, particularly after the fall of Clarendon. The fear was of course wholly justified. His mother, sister, and wife were Catholics; his brother and heir was a Catholic, secretly from 1668, publicly from 1676; and he himself favored Catholics in 1662, 1670, and 1672 and became one himself in 1685. The tragic events of 1678-81 would never have occurred but for this atmosphere of suspicion, for which Charles was chiefly to blame.

It is really difficult to explain—more difficult still to justify—the Catholic clause of the Treaty of Dover. His common sense and intuition usually saved him from such steps. It is probable that Charles at this time actually expected to become a Catholic. If this was not the case, the clause is still more difficult to explain, for it was certainly not forced on him by Louis XIV. This is sometimes stated, but the supporting references usually refer less to the sixties than to the eighties, when Louis had aged and, having grown more religious, had deserted La Vallière and Montespan for Madame de Maintenon. In 1669-70 neither Louis XIV nor Colbert de Croissy pressed Catholicism on Charles or required it as a part of the alliance. To some degree they did the opposite. They were so bent on the prime purpose of the treaty, the joint war on the Dutch, that they warned Charles of the possible serious consequences within his kingdom if he should declare himself a Catholic. England's major interest at the moment should have been the rounding out of her maritime position by a final defeat of the Dutch—which was soon to occur— but it is highly astonishing that Charles should at that moment have unnecessarily risked terrible dangers at home. Any question as to the terribleness of the danger should be sufficiently answered by the events of 1678-81 and 1688. There is, furthermore, little excuse for Charles's possible ignorance of the danger, for his Declaration of Indulgence of 1662 and later events should al-

ready have given him proof of England's intolerance and dread of Rome. Many writers have put forth occult and complicated explanations of the Catholic clause of the treaty. None is convincing. Whatever it was, it was not statesmanship; and yet it stands as one of the chief personal accomplishments of the reign. It was unnecessary, unexecuted, and in the form of suspicions and rumors it bore malformed progeny for years to come.

As the promoter of the navy Charles stands out as did his father, who actually used his hard-won ship money for ships. Charles and James both liked ships and knew ships, and James was no mean admiral. Maritime pageants need not fear to feature either of them with historical accuracy, which, however, calls for few brilliant colors. The navy was one of Charles's chief interests, but it was a costly one, and he never had much money. He therefore supported it badly. His mistresses were not extravagant as mistresses go, but they were at least costly, and they were paid. Many a sailor and contractor went unpaid because Castlemaine or Kéroualle had first chance at the treasury. As to enlistment and impressment, the reign marked no improvement. There is stark tragedy in the statement of a Dutch captain that after the Four Days' Battle of June, 1666, many bodies of dead Englishmen floating in the water were in black Sunday clothes. They had been taken by the press gang at the church door the preceding Sunday.

Charles's interest in science, though superficial, was genuine and wholesome. His tolerance and skepticism put him in the current of the best thought of the day. His interest in the Royal Society helped it to brave early discouragements. Of its real work and purposes he showed little grasp. He ridiculed its efforts to weigh air, thinking it impractical, but the experiment was on the way to the steam engine.

As leader of court and society Charles introduced some refinement to a place much in need of it. It was, however, a Bourbon sort of refinement, never quite at home in

England, not even now. Its lax morals temporarily suited a period of reaction from Puritan restraints, but its foreign character ultimately became a thing from which England recoiled. Charles's conversation was ready and good. He may be excused for talking much because he talked well. His vulgarities had the saving grace of wit. He was the only Stuart king of England who had a sense of humor. His companions frequently shocked his ministers, and he often jested when serious problems were at hand. Pepys is our only authority (June 21, 1667) for the statement that on the night of the Medway disaster Charles and the Duchess of Castlemaine were playing at hunting a poor moth in Monmouth's lodgings, but at least he did things like that. During the Plague and the Fire he was not an example of sustained courage, as is often said. During the former he caroused considerably in safe Wiltshire.

At the close of an economic section in which Charles figured little, David Ogg says that "the scarlet woman was more in evidence than the economic man." Women were indeed an important aspect of the reign. Charles married a homely Portuguese infanta for political reasons and was, according to Continental standards of the day, not unkind to her. Following his first sight of her, he made a gallant effort to describe her in not too unflattering terms. The paragraph is worthy of quotation, for it shows his innate chivalry and honesty:

> Her face is not so exact as to be called a beuty, though her eyes are excellent good, and not anything in her face that in the least degree can shoque one . . . and if I have any skill in visiognimy, which I think I have, she must be as good a woman as ever was born. Her conversation, as much as I can perceive, is very good, for she hath wit enough and a most agreeable voyse. You would wonder to see how well we are acquainted already.

We may infer that Charles had not been swept off his feet. Nevertheless, he and this unattractive, barren Catherine of Braganza lived together until his death. Charles considered proposals of divorce but never approved them. She should have expected her ladies-in-waiting to be his mistresses, but he was unnecessarily instantaneous in forcing them upon her immediately after the marriage. Upon Clarendon's objections Charles penned one of the sharpest and most decisive notes of his whole life. In this there is significance. Greater decision and resolve on other matters than his private life would have made him a greater king.

Charles's mistresses were many and mostly of some quality. Though he did not restrict himself to ladies, he never stooped to the sort that intrigued Pepys. He had better taste in face and figure than his brother James, whose mistresses were so terrible looking that Charles once said he thought they must have been selected by his confessor as a form of penance. None of Charles's mistresses appears to have had much political influence. Foreign ministers tried to use them, but not very successfully and certainly not with much consistency or continuity. The Duchess of Mazarin, French as she was, represented a real problem to the French ambassador, for she was close to the colony of French exiles in London and a potential liability rather than an asset. Louise de Kéroualle, Duchess of Portsmouth, who came to England shortly after the Treaty of Dover and stayed to the end of the reign, undoubtedly had more influence than any other. The master of the royal backstairs during most of the reign was William Chiffinch. He did not write his memoirs, for which forbearance living Stuarts should possibly erect to him a monument. Nevertheless, were all known, Charles would probably receive considerable credit for seldom confusing mistresses and ministers.

One woman had influence with him, particularly in connection with the Treaty of Dover. This was his sister, Henrietta d'Orléans, sister-in-law of Louis XIV. Her he loved greatly. Their extant correspondence of one hundred and five letters, preserved wholly by accident, for Charles ordered it sent to him and destroyed, is interesting and unique. It is about the only part of Charles's correspondence worth reading. It shows him at his best. Time was kind to him in preserving it. Many of us would be pleased to have posterity judge us by the letters we write our sisters rather than those we write to some other women.

Restorations usually bring ills in their train and merely defer necessary solutions to problems. That of 1660 was no exception. But among restored monarchs Charles II was an unusually good one. He got in the way less than most of them do. He lived less in the past, much in the present, little in the future. If a breathing spell of thirty years was necessary for England to rise to the stature of her mid-seventeenth century leaders, England could easily have done worse than have Charles for twenty-five of them. But it is a defeatist's defense which can only refer to the possibility of something worse. There is no avoiding the conclusion that Charles's reign was filled with unnecessary religious tension and tragedy and ended in a constitutional disaster from which England escaped chiefly by accident. The convincing biographer who would portray Charles as a great and good king must have consummate literary skill and generous blindness to facts.

THE GLORIOUS REVOLUTION OF 1688 caused many Englishmen serious misgivings. They could hardly be expected to repudiate their convictions overnight, shed an allegiance long viewed as sacred, and yield to the radical notion that monarchs could be deposed. Scores of publicists, aware of the feeling of guilt that many Englishmen harbored, brought out pamphlets and books tending to vindicate the Revolution. The most famous and influential of these tracts was John Locke's *Two Treatises of Government* (1690), the preface to which made clear the author's major objectives: "These . . . I hope are sufficient to establish the Throne of our great Restorer, our present King *William;* to make good his title, in the Consent of the People; which being the only one of all lawful governments, he has more fully and clearly, than any prince in *Christendom;* and to justify to the World the People of *England,* whose love of their just and natural Rights, with their Resolution to preserve them, saved the Nation when it was on the very birth of Slavery and Ruin." Many others brought out works defending the Revolution, and still others wrote to condemn it. What helped to keep the great debate between the Williamites and the Jacobites a matter of urgency was that oaths of allegiance to William and Mary were required of all ecclesiastical and civil officeholders; those who refused to take the oaths were first to be suspended from office and then to be deprived of their position. In the essay that follows, Professor Charles F. Mullett, of the University of Missouri, examines the arguments set forth by English publicists at a time when the question of taking or not taking the new oaths was basic. Author of several books and many articles on modern British history, Professor Mullett stands out for the fair-mindedness of his approach to the past, for his ability to deal sympathetically with the upholders of a lost cause.

RELIGION, POLITICS, AND OATHS IN THE GLORIOUS REVOLUTION

CHARLES F. MULLETT

Although at the end of the seventeenth century men were shifting their political terminology from the spiritual to the secular, from God to nature, they still invoked the absolutes of history, law, and scripture. They did not lightly overturn their monarch, but when the necessity for such action arose they sought absolution in concepts which the most rigorous and learned mediaeval theologian would have understood. They appealed to the law of nature but they meant the law of God; and the shift involved no betrayal of absolute standards, no withdrawal from the same ethical doctrines that had nourished their forebears. The time was soon to come when secular phrases expressed a secular outlook, but in 1689 they continued to cover the religious convictions of centuries. As soon as the bars were down and men grappled in hectic controversy, the secular side of their politics diminished and the ethical and spiritual aspects became pronounced.

Whatever the particular dispute, the religious question was prominent and the aim was moral. History recorded the triumph of men over tyranny, law the triumph of right over injustice, scripture the triumph of good over evil. Whenever the instances were secular, the spirit was often religious; when they were spiritual, politics was never far below the surface. Dependence upon absolutes never entirely ruled out expediency. These men were not so foolish as to pose theory against practice, but their success in fitting theory to practice should not bring their dismissal as canting hypocrites. They married virtue to expediency and were convinced that God would bless the union.

The English Revolution of 1688 inspired an extensive political literature, but the concern here is with fugitive pieces, many of them sharply controversial, which reflect the emphasis of religion and politics, not with the classic theory of the Revolution. John Locke spoke not only for his own but for all time, and men quickly discerned that fact. The pamphleteers by contrast were so engrossed in the immediate struggle that they had no time and perhaps no capacity to inject a universal note. Nevertheless, in the white heat of controversy they phrased the persistent aspirations of citizens and the timeless truths of philosophers as well as contemporary motives and issues.

Despite the opprobrium that attached itself to James II soon after his succession to the throne—an opprobrium that mounted as his religious policies and personal characteristics became more clearly realized—men were loath to take revolutionary steps. Slow to open negotiations with William of Orange, slower still to join his ranks, they hoped that James would mend his ways in time to stay their hand. The irresponsible agitator was there, to be sure, but he was the exception, and men who deplored the actions and disliked the person of James II still held the crown in high esteem. They delayed because they understood full well that the remedy might be worse than the disease.

When, however, the Declaration of Indulgence, the appointment of Catholics to high places in the state and universities, and the attacks on bishops, boroughs, and lords-lieutenant repeatedly showed the royal purpose, and the birth of the young prince presaged a future of the same sort, men were willing to move. Even in that juncture they must needs find the soundest reasons for their conduct. They could not expel one ruler, and him legitimate, and set up another without a bulwark impregnable in its integrity. Not everyone who thought James tyrannical in church and state was

Reprinted by special permission from *The Review of Politics*, X (1948), 462-474. The footnotes which originally appeared with this essay have been omitted.

prepared to thrust him out, certainly not without reasons unimpeachable in their verity and historic in their validity. Willing to suffer martyrdom for their convictions men must find truth for their goal—and truth was not less truth when tinged with expediency. The casuist may be casuist and honest still.

Most of the reactions were anonymous, and often, so far as may be determined, ecclesiastical. Some indeed may have come from hired hacks but the majority bear the clear stamp of intense conviction. They fall into a pattern, and neither intellectual distinction nor spiritual dignity marks the generality. Some are for James but most oppose him, largely perhaps because his downfall has jeopardized the prospects if not the safety of his supporters. To most Englishmen of whatsoever political adherence or religious faith James II was the legitimate king, and for many—not avowed Jacobites alone—he continued king *de jure* even after he ceased to be king *de facto*. In the last years of Charles II, though religious bigotry had reached unanticipated heights in the Popish Plot and caused many to support Shaftesbury's campaign for excluding James in favor of the illegitimate Duke of Monmouth, as men cooled off they stood stanchly behind the legitimate succession, though its instrument was a Roman Catholic. The Rye House or Presbyterian Plot (1683) had strengthened this conviction. When Charles II died two years later the power of legitimacy was clearly registered in the indifference to Monmouth who indeed would have found even less support for his uprising had the west country wool trade been more thriving at the time.

Monmouth's own humiliating end would have contributed nothing to the revolutionary whirlwind if James had not overdone his penalties to the poor wretches who joined the pretender. But when he followed Kirke's Lambs with Jeffreys' Bloody Assize, and both with the violation of the spirit and letter of the constitution, invasion of the Church, and overt disregard for his oaths, men felt that here was a tyrant, a ruler willing to breach the law of the land and the law of God. A prince *lege solutus* had diminishing space in the constitutional theory and religious concepts of the late seventeenth century. To be sure some men denied that James had violated the law, others that it lay within human power to bring him to account, but the bulk of opinion, expressed in action and writing, took opposite views. The major concern then became how to establish a case against him, in what terms to justify acceptance of William and Mary. If in their running writers tripped over the rocks in their arguments, they did not hesitate to clamber upon their hands and knees to their destination. If thus they supply a worm's-eye rather than a bird's-eye view of the struggle, if they at times see a pebble as a mountain and the mountains not at all, they do convey details and impressions that the historian two and a half centuries later is apt to overlook.

The particular issue around which much of the controversy centered was the imposition of oaths of allegiance to William and Mary, rulers *de facto,* and the motives which prompted either acceptance or refusal of these oaths. Failure to take the oaths by August 1, 1689, brought suspension from office, ecclesiastical as well as civil. Full deprivation, in case of continued refusal, would follow six months later, on February 1, 1690. Some four hundred beneficed clergy, including Archbishop Sancroft and eight bishops, refused to take the oaths and became the core of the nonjuring schism. A few recanted in the time allowed but the overwhelming majority remained true to their original decision. That they did not decide lightly is evident from their record before and after. Some had already felt the weight of James's disapproval. All surrendered an established position in deference to their conviction that the king *de jure,* no matter how tyrannical, may not be deposed by his subjects. That their conduct was on the whole more admirable than that of the opposing group is not here contended. One may point out the expediency of those who accepted William without approving the action or subscribing to the reasons of those who clung to James. Rather the behavior of the latter is noticed as evidence of the degree to which men followed their convictions at whatever cost to themselves. Moreover, because they "constantly dragged their old party back to causes lost," they had an influence out of all proportion to their numbers.

The case of allegiance and the case of resistance to ruling powers had aroused ample discussion years before the Revolution tested generalizations framed under more academic, less decisive, conditions. Thus men quite naturally saw in the new oaths a specific application of earlier assertions. William and Mary were scarcely at Whitehall before the argument, that had now and again bobbed up for at least a century and a half and had been very close to the surface during the preceding decade, found literary expression and stimulated acrimonious debate. To whom should subjects give allegiance—an unworthy deserter but nonetheless *de jure* prince or *de facto* rulers who, no matter how deserving, represented a break in the succession and a deviation from divine law? The consequent affirmations sustained the dethroning not merely of a king but of the doctrine that might have kept him king.

Whichever view of monarchy these combatants took they were in deadly earnest: "on both sides we act upon Conscience." Yet not all saw the necessity "by any law of God to enquire cautiously into the nature of Princes Titles, whether they be Right or Wrong." Many rulers had occupied thrones without legal right. Kingship presumed allegiance, and subjects could take the new oath to William and Mary with good conscience toward James and the succession. The new oath contained nothing repugnant to the old since it could denote either acknowledgment of title or submission to government. The very words of the oath, "I A.B. do sincerely promise and swear, that I will be faithful, and bear true allegiance to their majesties . . . ," favored the second application. The oath, promissory and not assertive, made unnecessary any debate over the title of William and Mary, for they were already *de facto* rulers. While no oath could cancel former obligations or require impossibilities, nature intended government for the security of mankind and obedience for the preservation of the community. Rulers pursuing a contrary course must be opposed.

The first obligation of governors and governed alike was to the community. Parliament never sought adherence to oaths without exception, for to do so denied the legis-

---

BOYNE: River in Ireland; scene of battle in 1690. A defeat for the supporters of James II, this battle gave William possession of Dublin and helped to make his political status more secure. It stands out as one of the most important military engagements in the War of the League of Augsburg.

DRAGONNADES: Troops quartered in the homes of French Protestants during the reign of Louis XIV in order to "encourage" them to convert to Roman Catholicism. Many English Protestants feared that James II would use dragonnades to restore England to the Catholic fold.

RYE HOUSE PLOT: Unsuccessful conspiracy of 1683. Desperate Whigs, frustrated by the failure of the attempt to exclude the Duke of York from the succession to the throne, sought to assassinate Charles II and the Duke (the future James II). As a result of the plot, dissenters were rounded up on a large scale and punished for breaches of the Clarendon Code.

WILLIAM SANCROFT: Archbishop of Canterbury who was one of the "seven bishops" tried on the charge of seditious libel and acquitted in 1688. A High-churchman, he emerged after the Glorious Revolution as the leader of the nonjurors. Refusing to take the oaths to William and Mary, he gave up his office.

lature's importance. If the oaths to James were viewed strictly, Englishmen should not fight the French whom he had commissioned to invade England. The new oath did not require a man never to support James or to affirm the legal rights of William and Mary, but only to swear that he would obey the *de facto* rulers. It might be sworn because it demanded nothing vain or impossible. Whether James or William lawfully ruled England was irrelevant to the terms of the oath.

Yet the oath should be taken. The adherents of William and Mary and the nonjurors held identical principles concerning the Church of England; both opposed the extremes of arbitrary and republican government; and both deplored popery and fanaticism. They differed only as to whether, having given allegiance to James, one could lawfully swear an oath to William and Mary. The nonjuror should in this instance remember that he was living under and receiving protection from *de facto* rulers; either he must leave or stay. If he stayed he should take the oaths because in any case they would be required, and for the greater security of the country they were necessary. The truth could always be embraced and no disgrace attached to change. Already insignificant in numbers, nonjurors would grow steadily fewer; since they could not prevail they should take the oaths and rely no more on jesuitical promises. The oath to James no longer bound Englishmen, and those who now hesitated to give him up should have acted more boldly in the days of his downfall. A promise to live peaceably under the present rulers was not enough; without oaths to William and Mary men would still give allegiance to James and be ready to serve him. Union and oaths could alone forestall the popery and fanaticism which these very nonjurors freely admitted were threatening the country.

The imposition of oaths inspired some men to consider the dualism of crown and person. Did subjects swear allegiance to the king or the man? Though the utterances revealed no significant insight, they illustrated recognition of the problem. Those who opposed William and Mary saw no reason for discussing the matter since for them there was no division, but the defenders of the Revolution differentiated between James II and James Stuart. An old oath did not bind when subjects took a new one, for the pledge of allegiance meant service to the sovereign for the time being. In particular, the oaths to James no longer held since his government had ended: they were taken to him as king. Moreover, the government also included Lords and Commons. Subjects bore allegiance to the *king,* not the *man;* otherwise they might support a man who would cut their throats. When a ruler betrayed his crown he absolved his subjects from obligation; to obey the person against the crown contravened scripture, nature, and the ancient lawyers.

James's betrayal of his crown repeatedly occupied these writers as they sought to justify the Revolution. While they declared their views more succinctly and less philosophically than John Locke they did not fall short of his essential and central theme. By this subversion of the fundamental law James had already lost title to any Englishman's allegiance when he was asked to take the new oath. A king's right to the throne was a civil right, a contrivance of human laws and institutions. For years, philosophers had defended such actions as those taken against James, for when a king attempted to deliver his kingdom to another he might be resisted. His 'popery' and standing army both warranted James's overthrow and allegiance to the cause as well as the persons of William and Mary. He had suspended the law of the constitution, commissioned 'popish' officers, and deprived the Church of England of protection. On ceasing to accept the doctrine that the king was under the law as well as under God, he ceased to be king, and laws against resistance no longer applied. The Elizabethan oath of supremacy forbade allegiance to any foreign authority. By accepting papal control James had clearly violated English law and forfeited his right to allegiance. The king must govern according to law; if he broke God's law—which these writers identified with English law—he should not even retain the name of king. The careers of John, Edward II, and Richard II disclosed the treatment earlier Englishmen had meted out to rulers who had broken the law.

Those needing guidance in this hour of bewilderment should recall not only the dangers from 'popery' and arbitrary government but also the assistance Elizabeth had given rebellion against arbitrary rulers in Holland and France. Men now at the helm sought to protect, not to ruin, the church and state; in fact both were far safer under William than under James. William would not set up a Presbytery in preference to the Church of England, and Mary was a zealous Anglican. How could men compare 1688 with the '41? That affair had ended in regicide and a commonwealth; this one had preserved the monarchy in its essential integrity. To argue in behalf of James that he meant well was foolish. Would it have comforted the Romans if Nero had burned their city out of good intentions rather than as a frolic? So men sifted history and the principles of the English constitution and of government in general. They stressed the broken contract, the Dutch conquest, and James's usurpation; under the circumstances all Englishmen, and especially the clergy, should logically support his successors.

Many stainless characters, unconvinced by James's actions, had not yet taken the oaths to William and Mary. They stood in grave danger. What should be done for them? Did not these nonjurors see that the de jure ruler received allegiance so long as he acted lawfully, that if he broke the laws the people no longer owed him obedience and allegiance? To say that a king ruled by divine right gave the English government a divine origin, but the English constitution permitted no absolute ruler. In attempting to destroy that constitution James had absolved his subjects from allegiance. History

in general and the development of the English limited monarchy in particular proved that subjects could change their allegiance, and James's desertion made such a change necessary. Men ought not to obstruct a settlement (presumably to be regarded as fixed) that secured the Protestant religion and civil liberty. Acceptance of the Revolution and support for William and Mary would alone repel 'popish' tryanny, Irish conquest, and French dragonnades, and maintain order. James had violated the contract as summed up in Magna Carta, and he had abdicated when he dropped the Great Seal into the Thames.

Time and again *rex sub lege* came to the fore. How could one, men constantly inquired, be bound to a king who broke the laws and deserted his kingdom? James sought to establish absolutism and to oust the rightful heirs who could undoubtedly join parliament in securing the lawful succession and resisting the late king. Perhaps the nonjurors thought the Revolution unjustified to save English liberties and religion. How could the bishops now stressing their oaths to James and refusing them to William have aided in James's overthrow? They were hypocrites to make conscience of their oaths. Why not support the ruler who had saved the Church from 'popery'? Dissension only encouraged papists. When James lost his power he lost the allegiance of the people. Whether he would have reformed had he remained did not now apply. He had violated his oaths and would undoubtedly do so again.

From the outset, attention to the legality and propriety of the oaths heightened the question of allegiance to a *de facto* ruler. Many adherents of William and Mary did not deny that James was king *de jure* but they supported his *de facto* successors because history, law, and even scripture defended such action and because James had undeniably deserted his country. In substantiating the validity of allegiance to a *de facto* king, men cited the Bible, the conduct of primitive Christians, and continental history. English history showed the strongest assertors of passive obedience and non-resistance complying with *de facto* possession. English law in general defended allegiance to such rulers, and, more precisely, the statute, 25 Edward III (1352), with which great Coke had agreed, had defined treason as against the king *de facto*. Allegiance could not be paid to one legally dead; it must be paid to the *de facto* rulers. The statute of Henry VII (1495) declared that no persons "that attend upon the king and sovereign lord of this land for the time being in his person, and do him true and faithful service of allegiance" shall be convicted of high treason. Subjects were obligated to live peaceably and maintain the ruler *de facto* for the sake of the kingdom, so long as he kept the law. If to oppose William and Mary was treason, to defend them was a duty. This accorded with the letter and reason of the law and contravened no oath to James.

Englishmen could be faithful to William and Mary as they had been to James before his unlawful acts; although the king's authority stemmed from God, subjects should obey the *de facto* ruler. A king *de facto* was a king *de jure* and the lawful object of allegiance. He was a "king in possession." Had not Bishop John Overall in his "Convocation Book" declared that a government when "thoroughly settled" should be "reverenced and obeyed" no matter its rebellious origin? The measuring stick for a thorough settlement was pragmatic. When a government regularly collected taxes, when success crowned a just war, when the ruler demonstrated his ability to protect his subjects, then he was "thoroughly settled." By such standards most men were ready to acclaim William the proper king and to declare that he had lawful title.

These contentions did not go uncontested, for some opponents of the Revolution denied the validity of such pragmatic norms. One pointed to the cases of King David and Charles II as showing protection not necessary to allegiance. James's conduct did not extinguish allegiance to him: Christ accepted Pilate, and Paul, Nero. James in his zeal for his religion did nothing illegal, and only God could suspend allegiance. Another observed that although Englishmen might be grateful to William, breaking their allegiance to James was the road to the devil. They owed him obedience as the supreme authority by the word of God. The behavior of rebels and traitors was no foundation on which to justify taking up arms against the true and lawful king. Allegiance went to the *de jure* not the *de facto* prince, and no man-made arguments could alter this.

Occasionally an author sought to avoid committing himself to either side and in the guise of complete neutrality left his readers with the choice of either allegiance. One such began by declaring that the king in possession, that is the king *de facto*, was one invested with regal authority and actually exercising the powers of government. Subjects, for the good of the community, might lawfully pay him allegiance, as the greatest lawyers and the statute of Henry VII had proved and stated. Although allegiance was due the king *de facto*, for the very practical consideration that otherwise he would cut off heads and confiscate property, treason did not lie merely against the king in possession as English practice had shown. In spite of this affirmation the author denied any reciprocal relation between subjects and rulers by which subjects must obey him from whom they received actual protection. Apparently this writer believed that the law did not actually require allegiance to the *de facto* ruler, but he personally was risking no penalties from that ruler. It may indeed be that this pamphlet was written at a time when it appeared that James might recover his throne, say, just before the battle of the Boyne (July, 1690).

Running prominently through the arguments and declarations of the Williamites was James's desertion, an act as politically inept as his earlier conduct had been unconstitutional. It gave opponents an excellent excuse for supporting William; it deprived supporters of leadership; it alienated neutrals. It made him an arrant coward (which he was not) and a sorry ruler (which he was). Had James remained in England he could have embarrassed William no end. In addition to the substantial support he would have inspired as England's legitimate king against invading Dutch William, he might also have counted upon the favor of many avowed neutrals especially if William had projected any forcible action. The "horrid" crime against Charles I was still fresh in the memory, and rash indeed would have been the man to argue openly against James, "like father, like son." As it was, James's desertion completed what he had begun by violating the fundamental laws. His political *felo de se* had made meaningless allegiance to the *de jure* ruler.

Scarcely less troublesome in its limited way and always a factor in the acceptance of William and Mary was the problem of the succession. The leaders of the Revolution, it is true, had settled the matter in the Declaration of Right, but this did not prevent pamphleteers from adverting frequently to it. Many of them believed that allegiance to the new rulers did not injure the succession which was to go first through Mary, then through Anne, because they were in the Stuart line, and acceptance of William violated nothing. In any case James by abdicating the throne had lost any power to declare his successor, and the legitimacy of his newly claimed son was questionable.

Kings could abdicate, and James by his voluntary withdrawal had done just that, even though his action was a 'popish' plot to upset the country. William and Mary were the legal heirs; the pretended prince was no heir; a regency was impracticable. When James departed England needed a ruler. Who was more fitting than the instrument of deliverance? The rightful heir, Mary, had out of modesty associated William with herself; thus allegiance to them both was not sinful. James had forsaken the country; William had taken over. Considering the former's character a regent was impossible.

William and Mary had lawful title. Practical demands justified allegiance to them, for the kingdom must not in this juncture remain ungoverned while men argued over the legal technicalities of the succession.

This conclusion indeed was the substance of most arguments, affirmations, and vindications, whether couched in straightforward declarations or in dialogue. Although some pieces adduced virtually all the points possible and others concentrated on two or three, the essential stress was constant: James had broken the law and it only remained how to exploit and amplify that action into a defense of the Revolution and allegiance to William and Mary. A debate between two purported friends, a Jacobite and a Williamite, summed up most of the controversial issues, general and specific. Expediency and compromise were posed against strict legality and the absolutes, limited monarchy and the right of revolution against divine right, passive obedience, and non-resistance. The new oath was defended on the basis that the old did not oblige men to contravene justice and righteousness or to defend tyranny. Yet of course the Williamites did not have it all their own way, for an occasional Jacobite denied their contentions, insisting both that their facts and inferences were dubious or irrelevant and that many of them were now contradicting their own earlier declarations.

The controversy came to no sudden end but drifted into another, identical in its central themes if different in focus. When William Sherlock, Master of the Temple, who had refused to swear allegiance until August, 1690, six months after the day of deprivation for non-jurors, was appointed Dean of St. Paul's instead of being penalized, his conduct and supposed motives excited comment virulent and bitter as well as broadly political in character. Whether or not the contestants felt greater safety and freedom in stating their sentiments in terms of his behavior than in terms of the Revolution settlement, the debate became more vitriolic and verbose. At times it does appear that Sherlock's critics were using him as a whipping boy for their own consciences or pouring upon him the hostility they feared to direct against the *de facto* rulers. The arguments, when separated from Sherlock's conduct, did not change, though greater emphasis was placed on a "thorough settlement," Sherlock's own explanation for his delay. The controversy, which continued until 1692, complements what has been presented here in revealing the kinship of religion and politics in those electric years.

THE AGE OF THE RESTORATION, remarkably productive of imaginative literature, stands out likewise for its contributions to science. Indeed, the official history of the Royal Society of London for the Improving of Natural Knowledge, better known simply as the Royal Society, began in 1662, when Charles II, "the universal lover and patron of every kind of truth," granted it a charter. Filled with supporters of the King, the Society was granted numerous rights and privileges, among them, for example, the right to dissect the bodies of criminals. According to its statutes, it was to "question and canvass all opinions, adopting nor adhering to none, till by mature debate and clear arguments, chiefly such as are deduced from legitimate experience, the truth of such experiments be demonstrated invincibly." Among the early members of the Society were to be found not only scientists but also such men of letters as Samuel Pepys, John Dryden, John Evelyn, the diarist, and John Aubrey, the biographer; and one of the several aims of the Society was to improve English prose. Certainly its outstanding seventeenth-century member proved to be Isaac Newton, the English farm boy whose understanding family had not compelled him to remain on the farm. It is with Newton's contributions to science that the distinguished contemporary British scientist Professor E. N. da C. Andrade, director of the Davy Faraday Research Laboratory and author of an admirable recent biography of Newton, deals here.

NEWTON AND THE SCIENCE OF HIS AGE

E. N. da C. ANDRADE

It is my task—my honourable and inspiring task—to say something of Isaac Newton as seen against the background of the science of his time. I shall try to display briefly the position as he found it and to resume in a small space his great achievements and the changes in outlook which they produced. In praising Newton I shall endeavour not to do injustice to his great forerunners and to the men of his time who pursued worthily the same great ends as he did, and who would have held the centre of the stage in any other age than that dominated by him. For Newton, like Shakespeare, did not stand as a lonely adventurer into new realms, though he travelled further and straighter

Reprinted by special permission from *Proceedings of the Royal Society of London,* Series A, CLXXXI (1943), 227–243.

than the rest. Shakespeare was the supreme poet and playwright at a time when poetry and plays were part of the life of every cultivated man and occupied the attention of the brightest intellects. Newton was the supreme scientist in an age when the quantitative method of questioning Nature was abroad in the air. Each was the child of his time.

Let us consider the position when Newton went to Cambridge in 1661. The hold of Aristotle, whose works had for centuries been the ultimate resort of all those seeking knowledge of the working of nature, had been shaken off by such men as Galileo and Gilbert, but most of the learned still thought that those who relied on experiment were pursuing a futile and impudent course. The first resolve of Marlowe's Faustus

Having commenc'd, be a divine in shew,
Yet level at the end of every art,
And live and die in Aristotle's works

still represented the aim of many students. The foundation of the Royal Society in 1662 had been the occasion of many attacks on the experimental method, attacks stoutly met by Glanvill and by Sprat, and as late as 1692 Sir William Temple's *Essay upon the Ancient and Modern Learning,* satired by Swift in *The Battle of the Books,* set out to prove the superiority of the philosophers of the ancient world over all the moderns. Thus when Newton was a young man the new experimental method of questioning Nature was steadily making its way and the omniscience of the ancients was being called in doubt by a new school, but experimental science was by no means firmly established as a respectable study.

The great figures among the worthies of the exact sciences who had already appeared at that time were Copernicus, Tycho Brahe, Kepler, Gilbert, Galileo and Descartes. Kepler, following his great forerunners, had found the true laws of planetary motion, which were to be explained by Newton. Kepler's views as to the mechanism of the planetary motions were in his earlier writings largely mystical, involving the perfect properties of the five regular solids and also certain motivating souls or spirits, *animae motrices.* Throughout he held to the medieval point of view that a body could not maintain its motion unless there were a force propelling it. In his later writing he invoked a magnetic force, but it was not directed to the sun, like the true gravitational force, but pushed the planets on their way—*non est attractoria sed promotoria.* It was essentially bound up with the rotation of the sun. Thus he was ignorant of the basic laws of mechanics and his magnetic force had none of the true properties of magnetic forces. Kepler made no approach to a mechanical explanation of his laws.

Gilbert had not only established the basic principles of terrestrial magnetism and carried out fundamental work on electricity, but had invoked a force from the moon— a magnetic force it is true—to produce the tides. Galileo's greatest achievement had been to lay the foundations of mechanics.

RICHARD BENTLEY: English classical scholar (d. 1742) who served as Master of Trinity College, Cambridge. He was a friend of Newton, whose aid he sought in preparing his *Confutation of Atheism.* He engaged in a number of lively scholarly controversies, and Alexander Pope singled him out for a superb caricature in his *Dunciad.*
JOSEPH GLANVILL: Seventeenth-century scholar and clergyman who denounced the philosophy of scholasticism in *The Vanity of Dogmatizing.* On the other hand, he believed in the pre-existence of souls and in witchcraft.
SIR WILLIAM TEMPLE: Scholar, diplomat, and government official (d. 1699). His writings on Ireland and the Netherlands are valuable historical sources. The outstanding controversy in which he became involved was a debate over the relative merits of the ancients and the moderns. Bentley came to the defense of the moderns.

None of these men, however, had made any impression on the bulk of the learned: Francis Bacon, for instance, neglects Galileo and Kepler, and refuses to take Gilbert seriously. The great figure in the eye of natural philosophers was Descartes, who had developed a cosmogony based upon mechanical principles, not precise mechanical principles it is true, but principles very different from the mystical ones then in vogue. Joseph Glanvill used to lament that his friends had not sent him to Cambridge, where he might have learned the new philosophy of Descartes, rather than to Oxford, where Aristotelianism ruled. Descartes' system had acquired such a hold on men's minds that his views were still supported long after Newton's death. Both Jean Bernoulli, who died in 1748, and Fontenelle, who died in 1757, were Cartesians to the end. The demolition of the Cartesian system was, in contemporary eyes, one of Newton's greatest achievements. James Thomson said in his *Ode to the Memory of Sir Isaac Newton,* published immediately after his death:

> The heavens are all his own; from the
>   wild rule
> Of whirling vortices, and circling spheres,
> To their first great simplicity restored.
> The schools astonished stood.

From the *Principia* it is clear that Newton himself derived particular satisfaction from having invalidated the Cartesian system. It is fitting, then, that we start our consideration of contemporary science by a glance at this system, not only because it was the only attempt before Newton to explain the motions of heavenly bodies on general principles, but because it furnishes a contrast which brings out the essential Newtonian point of view.

Descartes starts, in the spirit of medieval thinkers, from certain general philosophical principles. He decides that the fundamental property of matter is extension—impenetrability, colour, hardness and so on are only secondary characteristics. Extension, which has three directions, is the subject of mathematics: motion is the subject of mechanics. All the different qualities of different kinds of matter are provided by different motions of the minute parts of which it is composed. 'Give me extension and motion,' declares Descartes, 'and I will construct the world.' One consequence of his fundamental belief is that there cannot be a vacuum, for extension without matter is a contradiction. He further considers, on theological grounds, that the quantity of motion in the heavens must be constant. He blames Galileo for founding his mechanics on experiments and not on reflexions on first causes. 'Everything Galileo says about the philosophy of bodies falling in empty space is built without foundation: he ought first to have determined the nature of weight.' Newton's point of view, of course, was the exact opposite to that of Descartes: he says in the famous letters to Bentley, ' . . . for the cause of gravity is what I do not pretend to know, and therefore would take some time to consider of it,' and again, 'gravity must be caused by an agent acting constantly according to certain laws, but whether this agent be material or immaterial, I have left to the consideration of my readers.' For Newton, as for the best of his successors, science was concerned with the question of 'How?': Descartes, like the ancients, was concerned with the insoluble question of a fundamental 'Why?'

It followed from the philosophic hypothesis of Descartes that the only kind of motion possible in a plenum was a motion in closed paths, more particularly a circular motion, since a particle could only move if another particle took its place. It was on grounds of this kind that he elaborated his vortex hypothesis. Certain very fine particles, which filled interplanetary space, moved round ceaselessly in huge vortices and carried the planets with them. The moon was carried round the earth by a minor vortex, and so on.

Descartes' cosmogony, then, was founded on a philosophical system: it was pictorial and unquantitative. The paths of the comets, handed on from one vortex to another, were in particular irreconcilable with observation. There was no attempt to deduce Kepler's laws, or to show how anything but circular motion could result from the vortices. The whole scheme was spun from the brain of Descartes, with more or less casual references to actual phenomena. No doubt it was referring to Descartes that Roger Cotes said in his Preface to the second edition of the *Principia,* 'Those who fetch from hypothesis the foundation on which they build their speculations may form indeed an ingenious romance, but a romance it will still be.' In spite of, or perhaps because of, this, Descartes' influence was immense, and when Newton was at Cambridge as a young man it was Descartes who was the great authority for all such progressive spirits as speculated on the structure of the universe.

We now turn to the astonishing story of the birth of the *Principia.* The time was ripe for the appearance of this great work. As regards the laws of motion, Galileo, whose services Newton freely acknowledges, and Descartes himself had done much to prepare the way for the more precise and particular formulation which Newton gives. Hooke among others had clearly expressed the protest of the most forward spirits of the time against the speculative method. 'The truth is, the Science of Nature has been already too long made only a work of the Brain and the Fancy: it is now high time that it should return to the plainness and soundness of *Observations* on *material* and *obvious* things.' The Royal Society was active in stimulating the pursuit of the new method and on the Continent the *Accademia del Cimento* had done excellent work, while the *Académie des Sciences* was founded in 1666. These continental societies had little influence on Newton, but are symptomatic of the general movement towards the experimental method. The stage was set for great things.

The story opens at Woolsthorpe, Newton's birthplace, whither Newton had come from Cambridge in June 1665 to escape the plague. He was then 22 years old and not yet a Master of Arts or Fellow of Trinity. He had read what he calls 'Schooten's *Miscellanies'* (probably the *Exercitationum Mathematicarum Libri V*), Descartes' *Geometria* and Wallis' works, and further was, of course, familiar with the work of his teacher Barrow. He had written his first treatise on the calculus, or 'fluxions' as he called it, but he had published nothing. The words which he wrote some fifty years later about this great springtime of his intellectual life have often been quoted but cannot well be omitted on an occasion like this. 'And the same year (1666) I began to think of gravity extending to the orb of the Moon, and having found out how to estimate the force with which a globe revolving within a sphere presses the surface of the sphere, from Kepler's Rule of the periodical times of the Planets being in a sesquialterate proportion of their distances from the centers of their orbs I deduced that the forces which keep the Planets in their Orbs must [be] reciprocally as the squares of their distances from the centers about which they revolve: and thereby compared the force requisite to keep the Moon in her orb with the force of gravity at the surface of the earth, and found them answer pretty nearly. All this was in the two plague years of 1665 and 1666, for in those days I was in the prime of my age for invention, and minded Mathematicks and Philosophy more than at any time since. What Mr Hugens has published since about centrifugal forces I suppose he had before me.'

It seems likely that he had already had his laws of motion in his head—in any case it is clear that he was convinced that every body would continue to move uniformly in a straight line unless some force acted on it, and that, therefore, there must be some force acting on the moon which drew it away from the straight line, tangential at any moment to its path, in the direction of the earth. Treating the moon's path as circular, from Kepler's third law, and from the law connecting the centrifugal force with the radius and the velocity, or the equivalent proposition to which Newton refers, it is easy to deduce the inverse square law. To show that the force keeping the moon in her orbit is the earth's gravitational force, assumed to diminish as the inverse square, is, however, a further step demanding a computation of how strong the gravitational force at the moon's orbit will be, compared to the measured force at the surface of the earth. Newton made this step and found it 'answer pretty nearly.' Why, then, did he delay the announcement of the law of gravity for twenty years or so?

There is always a ready answer to questions of this kind where Newton is concerned—that he never published anything until invited, in general strongly urged, to do so. It is, however, clear from many signs that Newton was not himself satisfied about the matter until some time about 1686. The usual story is that he took a wrong radius for the earth, namely one corresponding to 60 miles for 1° of latitude instead of the correct value of about 70, but this story is very improbable on many grounds, one of which is that good values were readily available to him.

The real reason for Newton putting the work aside seems to have been that the calculation, as far as the force at the earth's surface is concerned, depends essentially upon it being legitimate to assume that the earth's mass may be considered as concentrated at the centre. That this assumption is valid is far from obvious. It is fairly clear from certain passages in *De Motu* and in the *Principia* that it gave Newton some trouble to prove this assumption and that he did it late. In a letter to Halley of 20 June 1686 he says, 'I never extended the duplicate proportion lower than to the superficies of the earth, and before a certain demonstration I found the last year, have suspected that it did not reach accurately enough down so low.' Although this refers to the gravitational force within a sphere, this and the point under discussion are involved in the same mathematical demonstration, which Newton gives in the *Principia* in Book I, proposition LXXI and other

propositions following it. In any case Newton appears not to have been satisfied with his first calculations and to have turned to other things, possibly his optical experiments.

It is a strange thing that the *Principia* owes its publication largely to a quarrel with Hooke, and its sequel. In 1679 Hooke, then acting as Secretary of the Royal Society, wrote to Newton about various scientific matters and asked him very civilly for a philosophic communication—a paper, as we should say nowadays. He also asked for Newton's opinion on his *Potentia Restitutiva* and 'particularly if you will let me know your thoughts of that [hypothesis] of compounding the celestial motions of the planets of a direct motion by the tangent and an attractive motion towards the central body.' In his reply Newton made an extraordinary remark. 'But yet my affection to philosophy being worn out, so that I am almost as little concerned about it as one tradesman uses to be about another man's trade or a countryman about learning, I must acknowledge myself averse from spending that time in writing about it which I think I can spend otherwise more to my own content and the good of others: and I hope neither you nor any body else will blame for this averseness.' This is but one of many occasions on which Newton expresses his disinclination, almost distaste, for any further scientific work, his first antipathy having been aroused by the disputes and misunderstandings consequent on the publication of his first great paper on the prism.

To return, Newton did comply with Hooke's request for something for the Society by pointing out that a body let fall from on high should strike the earth slightly east of the perpendicular, and gave precise and excellent directions for carrying out the experiment. The purpose was to prove the diurnal rotation of the earth. Hooke, in reply, pointed out that the ball should fall to the south as well as to the east, and further corrected Newton in a point which is too complicated to discuss here and one on which differences of statement can be due to different interpretations of the problem. This correction, tactlessly expressed, irritated Newton in the highest degree and he answered curtly. In further letters, written in apparent unconsciousness of the annoyance he had given, Hooke suggested that the law needed to explain the planetary motions was the inverse square law.

Now other men had come to the same conclusion. In particular, Wren and Halley had discussed with Hooke the possibility of explaining the mechanism of the heavens on the basis of an inverse square law. Hooke declared that he could demonstrate mathematically that the path of a particle in a central inverse square field would be an ellipse, but it is clear that he never did so, and equally clear that he had not the mathematical equipment necessary to begin an attack on the problem. He was in the unfortunate position of being entirely convinced of a truth that he could not prove. In August 1684 Halley visited Cambridge and asked Newton what the path would be. He replied that it would be an ellipse and that he had formerly calculated it. He could not find the calculation but soon sent a proof (or apparently two different proofs) to Halley.

This incident seems to have aroused Newton from the distaste for science into which he had fallen, and he put together the treatise *De Motu,* founded on a course of lectures, which Halley presented to the Royal Society on 10 December 1684. The story of how Halley then coaxed and cajoled Newton into writing the *Principia* is familiar, but we in this Society ought not ever to celebrate the great work without a tribute to Halley, who not only realized at once the fundamental importance and significance of Newton's work but used all his tact to get the book written and made himself financially responsible for the production, the Royal Society being in financial difficulties at that time. We are not now in financial straits and shall, I believe, be glad to bear the expense of producing a second *Principia* when the genius of our age brings it forth. The book appeared in 1687, and bears the imprimatur of the then President, who, although he achieved nothing in science, is still remembered. He was Samuel Pepys.

The *Principia* is not an easy book to read. The proofs are all given in form of classical geometry, although, since it is certain that at the time when it was written Newton was in possession of the fundamental processes of the calculus and of the methods of analytical geometry, it is unlikely that this was the form in which he first derived them. Figure 4 [omitted] shows a typical geometrical diagram, dealing with the moon's motion, and a comparison with the pictures from Kepler and Descartes gives a graphic representation of the changed spirit in handling the mechanism of the heavens. With reference to the mathematical methods of the *Principia* Whewell has said 'Nobody since Newton has been able to use geometrical methods to the same extent for the like purposes; and as we read the *Principia* we feel as when we are in an ancient armoury where the weapons are of gigantic size; and as we look at them we marvel what manner of man he was who could use as a weapon what we can scarcely lift as a burden.' Various conjectures have been made by Rosenberger, Cantor, Giesel, Gerhardt and others as to why he did not use the new methods: Rouse Ball thinks that he was probably unwilling to add to the difficulties by introducing a new mathematical method. Be that as it may, he had a horror of unfounded criticism, and, as he told Dr Derham 'to avoid being baited by little smatterers in mathematics, he designedly made his *Principia's* abstruse; but yet so as to be understood by able mathematicians.' That he did not underrate the difficulty of the work is clear from what he says in the beginning of Book III: 'I chose to reduce the substance of that book into the form of propositions (in the mathematical way) which should be read by those only, who had first made themselves masters of the principles establish'd in the preceding books. Nor would I advise any one to the previous study of every proposition of those books. For they abound with such as might cost too much time, even to readers of good mathematical learning. It is enough if one carefully reads the definitions, the laws of motion, and the first three sections of the first book.'*

The first book contains certain definitions of space, mass and time which have often afforded a theme ample enough for discussion. But we will here let them pass uncommented. The famous laws of motion owe much to the labours of previous workers, in particular to Galileo, whose services Newton clearly acknowledges. The simple laws of central orbits under an inverse square law are worked out in much detail and the laws of pendulum motion are developed, with due acknowledgments to Huygens, who had published his *Horologium Oscillatorum* in 1673.

In the first book the motions are all supposed to take place in a non-resistant medium. In the second Newton considers motions in a resisting medium, always with his eye on the Cartesian world system which he was intent to demolish. He deals with a resistance proportional to the velocity and with a resistance proportional to the square of the velocity, and further points out different kinds of fluid resistance, which he later defines most clearly in the 28th Query appended to the third edition of the *Opticks,* 'for the resisting Power of the fluid Medium arises partly from the Attrition of the Parts of the Medium and partly from the *Vis inertiae* of the Matter,' that is, partly from the viscosity and partly from the bulk motion of the medium. The latter resistance he assumes proportional to the square of the velocity. In this book he opens the way to the hydrodynamics of real fluids. In the part dealing with hydrostatics he proves the law of the diminution of atmospheric pressure with height. He then further discusses the motion of the pendulum and is the first to suggest its use for making a survey of the gravitational accel-

* Andrew Motte's translation of 1729, volume 2, page 201.

eration. In another connexion he derives an expression for the velocity of sound, this being the first case of the calculation of the velocity of a wave from the properties of the medium. The only other point in this book to which I will refer is the calculation which Newton carries out on the motion of an infinitely extended viscous fluid in which a body rotating upon its axis is immersed. What he has in mind is the Cartesian vortex—'I have endeavoured in this proposition to investigate the properties of vortices, that I may find whether a celestial phenomenon can be explained by them.' He effectively defines the force 'arising from the want of lubricity in the parts of the fluid' as proportional to the velocity gradient, whence the term 'Newtonian viscosity.' He is thus the first to touch the mathematics of viscous fluids. He finds that the periodic time of circulation of the fluid carried round by a rotating sphere is proportional to the square of the distance from the centre of the sphere,* which is grossly inconsistent with Kepler's third law. Newton considers that his deduction is a clear refutation of the Cartesian vortices and, for once, almost gloats over his victory. 'Let philosophers then see how the phenomenon of the sesquiplicate ratio can be accounted for by vortices.' He brings many other objections against the Cartesian vortices: he points out, for instance, that a continuous supply of energy will have to be given to the sphere to maintain the motion, because 'it is plain that the motion is proportionally transferred from the centre to the circumference of the vortex, till it is quite swallowed up and lost in the boundless extent of that circumference.'

The second book of the *Principia* is the foundation stone of mathematical physics. In it Newton shows an extraordinary instinct for grasping the essentials of a problem—it would almost seem that he knew the

* Actually this is an error, which appears never to have been pointed out, although Stokes has indicated the like error in the case of the rotating cylinder, which Newton works out. It should be the *cube* of the distance.

solution in advance and added the proof as a concession to those less clear-sighted. As William Whiston, who knew him well, and succeeded him in the Lucasian chair, says: 'Sir Isaac, in mathematics, could sometimes see almost by intuition, even without demonstration. . . . And when he did but propose conjectures in natural philosophy, he almost always knew them to be true at the same time.' The manner of his refutation of the Cartesian vortices introduces a new spirit into the discussion: no hypothesis about the heavens is tenable unless the quantitative deductions from it agree with observation.

The third book opens with an introduction where, after stating what has been done in the first two books, Newton sets down the superb sentence—'Superstat ut ex iisdem principiis doceamus constitutionem systematis mundani'—it remains that from the same principles we demonstrate the form of the system of the world. It is this third book which based celestial mechanics so firmly that what was done in the next two hundred years was rather extension of, and improvements on, the Newtonian method than anything radically new. Not only does Newton establish the movements of the satellites of Jupiter, Saturn and the Earth, and of the planets round the Sun (or rather, as he points out, round the centre of gravity of the solar system) in terms of his gravitational theory, but he shows how to find the masses of the sun and planets in terms of the earth's mass, which he estimates quite closely; he accounts for the flattened shape of the earth and other planets; calculates the general variations of g over the surface of the earth; explains the precession of the equinoxes by consideration of the non-sphericity of the earth; calculates the main irregularities of the motion of the moon and of other satellites from the perturbing effect of the sun; explains the general features of the tides; and finally treats the orbits of comets in a way that shows that they are members of the solar system and enables the return of Halley's comet in 1759 to be accurately calculated. This brief and im-

perfect catalogue is merely a reminder of the scope of this extraordinary book, which drew from Laplace, no enthusiast, ' . . . all this, presented with much elegance, assures to the *Principia* preeminence over all the other productions of the human mind.' The book closes with the famous General Scholium which returns to the confutation of Descartes' vortices and says, concerning the cause of gravity, 'Hypotheses non fingo.'

We have a portrait of Newton, by Kneller, at about the time of the publication of the *Principia* which is particularly impressive. In contrast to most of the later and more formal portraits we see him in his own hair and in the casual clothing which we may suppose him to have worn when at work. The look of wild, almost hostile remoteness and of dominating and piercing intelligence seem to show that the artist has well read the features of his sitter and given us a true picture of the man in his hours of creative thought.

Although the book was eagerly bought, the Newtonian method and discoveries made way but slowly. Biot says that of Newton's contemporaries three or four only were capable of understanding the *Principia*, that Huygens only half adopted the ideas, Leibniz and Jean Bernoulli fought against them, and that fifty years had to pass before the great truth demonstrated by Newton was understood by the generality of men of science, let alone developed. No doubt the difficulty of the book had much to do with the tardy appreciation, outside a narrow circle, of its contents. The Cartesian scheme was easy, pictorial, general: the Newtonian difficult, mathematical, precise. The very method of attacking the problem was altogether new. The second edition appeared in 1713, edited by Roger Cotes, of whom Newton said 'if Mr Cotes had lived we might have known something.' The preface clearly shows that among the learned the Newtonian scheme had not been widely accepted. On the Continent the progress was still slower and it is generally held that it was Voltaire's *Elémens de la Philosophie de Newton,* which appeared in

1738, that led to Newton's work being appreciated in France. Incidentally, the story of the apple, which Voltaire had from Newton's niece, Mrs Conduitt, appeared in the second edition of Voltaire's book, in 1741. Later, it was in France that Newton's work was raised to great glory, when Lagrange and Laplace erected edifices of splendour and elegance on Newtonian foundations.

The optical work of Newton was perhaps his favourite study: at any rate it was that to which he made what is probably the only enthusiastic reference which he ever permitted himself, when he said, of his fundamental discovery in the matter of prismatic colours, 'being in my judgment the oddest, if not the most considerable detection which hath hitherto been made in the operations of nature.' The beautiful experiments which formed the background of this work will be dealt with by Lord Rayleigh, so I shall say nothing of them, but a few words as to the Newtonian attitude and theory may be permitted.

The nature of colour had from the days of Aristotle been the subject of philosophical speculation. According to Aristotle, colours are a mixture of light and darkness, or of white and black, a view which, embellished and modified in various ways, survived Newton and appeared again in, for instance, Goethe's writings. Descartes was apparently the first to break really new ground in comparing colours to notes in music: his view of light was that it was a pressure transmitted through the particles that filled all space, and he conjectured that a rotation of the particles might be the effective cause of colour, a view which presented inherent difficulties effectively exposed by Hooke. We may agree with Huygens that 'Descartes has said nothing that is not full of difficulties or even inconceivable, in dealing with light and its properties.' The medieval question as to whether light was a substance or an accident was still occupying the attention of even acute experimentalists such as Grimaldi, the discoverer of diffraction, whose book appeared

in 1665. It was Hooke again, who, with his extraordinary flair for the truth, combined with an inability to overcome the last difficulties that stood between him and a convincing conclusion, initiated the modern views. In his *Micrographia,* 1665, he expressed the view that light was a very quick vibration propagated with a finite velocity. He gave what resembles Huygens' construction for finding the wave front on refraction, but, since he thought that light travelled faster in a solid medium, e.g. glass, than in air, he found that in the medium the wave front must make an acute angle with the ray. It was with this 'obliquity' that he connected colour. 'Blue is an impression on the Retina of an oblique and confus'd pulse of light, whose weakest part precedes, and whose strongest follows. . . . Red is an impression on the Retina of an oblique and confus'd pulse of light, whose strongest part precedes and whose weakest follows.' For him blue and red were the primary colours, all others being mixed. There is no time to follow his extraordinarily acute experiments on the colours of thin plates, but it must be noted that his ill-tempered attacks were the cause of Newton expressing a disgust with science which nearly caused him to abandon her pursuit, and were, it is almost certain, the reason why the *Opticks* was not published until 1704, the year following Hooke's death. The quarrel between the two men, both, as is evident from their correspondence, capable of generous appreciation of the other's achievements, was exacerbated by Oldenberg, then Secretary of the Society, whose dislike of Hooke may have sprung from causes little creditable to him. Newton had been undoubtedly stimulated by his reading of Hooke's *Micrographia,* and he was always very remiss in acknowledgements to him. Let us pay a tribute to poor Hooke, sickly and without position or powerful friends. He had not Newton's power of thought, but he was probably the most ingenious contriver who ever lived and was a shrewd and daring speculator.

The experiments on the composition of

white light, which reduced the whole study to a quantitative basis, by showing that the refraction is a measure and index of the colour, will, as I have said, be dealt with by Lord Rayleigh. To the reflecting telescope, the explanation of the rainbow, the work on thin films, exemplified by Newton's rings, and the experiments on diffraction, this passing reference must suffice.

Nowhere more than in his writings on light does Newton stress his dislike of speculation not firmly rooted in experiment. The first words of the *Opticks* are 'My design in this Book is not to explain the Properties of Light by Hypotheses, but to propose and prove them by Reason and Experiments,' and again, in the 31st Query appended to the third edition of that book he makes his standpoint very clear, saying 'These Principles I consider not as occult Qualities, supposed to result from the specifick Forms of Things, but as general Laws of Nature, by which the Things themselves are form'd: their Truth appearing to us by Phaenomena, though their Causes be not yet discover'd. For these are manifest Qualities, and their Causes only are occult. And the *Aristotelians* gave the Name of occult Qualities not to manifest Qualities, but to such Qualities only as they supposed to lie hid in Bodies, and to be the unknown Causes of manifest Effects. . . . To tell us that every Species of Things is endow'd with an occult specifick Quality by which it acts and produces manifest Effects, is to tell us nothing.' It is in the light of this that we must read the famous 'Hypotheses non fingo.' Newton, of course, did make hypotheses, and even called them such—for instance in *Principia*, Book II, Section IX, his assumption as to the behaviour of viscous fluids is headed 'Hypothesis' and there are other instances. All he meant was that he was reluctant to speculate beyond any possibility of quantitative deduction, to form conjectures whose defence would be merely a matter of dialectics.

Newton's corpuscular hypothesis to account for the experimental behaviour of light is clearly a hypothesis, but we shall see how closely he adapts it to the observations. First, he points out that light cannot be a wave motion, or it would spread out on passing through an opening. Figure 5 [omitted] is the diagram with which he illustrates this point. He knew, it is true, the phenomena of diffraction, but he did not realize how by making the wave-length small enough this could be reconciled with the general facts of rectilinear propagation, for which a stream of particles seems best suited. He clearly saw that the phenomena of the colours of thin plates demanded a periodicity, and he introduced this into his theory by the hypothesis of fits of easy reflexion and easy transmission. It is clear that light is partly reflected and partly transmitted at the surface of a transparent body: Newton supposed that a light particle alternated at regular intervals between a state in which it was transmitted through the surface and one in which it was sent back. He put forward diffidently ('Those that are averse to assenting to any new Discoveries but such as they can explain by an Hypothesis, may for the present suppose') the idea that the impact of the particle on the surface excited vibrations in the medium which, overtaking the particles, put them into these alternating states. We are forcibly reminded of modern theories. The length of the interval of the fit, corresponding to our wave-length, was greater for the red than for the blue, and Newton gives the interval for yellow light incident normally as just about the actual wave-length of yellow light. However, of his whole theory he says 'But whether this Hypothesis be true or false I do not here consider. I content myself with the bare Discovery that the Rays of Light are by some cause or other alternately disposed to be reflected or refracted for many vicissitudes.' When he comes to consider polarization, he has to endow his particles with 'sides' so that there is a lack of complete symmetry about the direction of propagation. In short, he gave his particles just those properties which interpreted the experiment and hence was led to endow them with a periodicity and a polarity. This brought him to assume subsidiary waves accompanying the particles when they interacted with matter.

There seems to be a general belief that Huygens, as against Newton, advocated something very close to the wave theory of light, as it was accepted in, let us say, 1900. Huygens' wavelets, however, lack the essential properties with which Fresnel afterwards endowed them: they were not only longitudinal but had what were practically particle properties, as exemplified by the fact that the pole—the point of contact with the envelope—alone was efficacious. He was just as incapable as Newton of giving a satisfactory explanation of diffraction.

If we are asked to state in a sentence what was the main effect of Newton's work on the thought of his time, I think that the answer must be that it was to establish the power and universality of the methods of quantitative science. To Galileo we owe the great service, one that cannot be too highly praised, of having made particle dynamics into a science, but he did not look beyond the earth for its efficacy nor suggest the application of his methods to the relative movement of the parts of a continuous medium, such as water. Huygens founded the study of rigid dynamics. Hooke suggested and speculated with extraordinary ingenuity and acuteness. Newton, however, showed that three clearly enunciated laws of motion applied to all observable movements of inanimate nature: they governed the motion of waves and projectiles, visible solids and invisible air, resisted as well as free movements. Together with the inverse square law they explained not only the gross movement of planets and the movement of the comets, which before had seemed capricious, but also details which nobody before had ever considered as being mechanically explicable, such as the precession of the equinoxes. The problems of the tides and of the irregularities of the moon's motion he did not fully solve, it is true, but he did enough to convince mathematicians that they were soluble by his methods. After

Newton's work had been assimilated, the body of natural philosophers accepted it as a commonplace that all terrestrial and celestial movements were explicable in precise and numerical terms by calculations based on a few general laws: before Newton most thinkers were ready to invoke *ad hoc* principles and occult causes, based on human and divine analogies, for any but the simplest terrestrial phenomena, and the few who were in advance of their times were feeling tentatively for solutions which eluded their grasp.

Even in chemistry Newton was looking for an explanation in terms of attractions, though, strangely enough, in this science he never seems to have applied his own rule and made quantitative experiments. His work on light lies somewhat outside the mechanical scheme, but here again his insistence on the quantitative created a completely new attitude towards colour. It became a subject for measurement and calculation, rather than one for discussion in terms of generalities.

If we are to try to represent Newton's achievements by some modern analogy, to construct some imaginary figure who should be to our times what Newton was to his, we must credit this synthetic representative with, I think, the whole of relativity up to, and somewhat further than, the stage at present reached—we must suppose our modern Newton to have satisfactorily completed a unitary field theory. In light we must credit him both with having established the existence of spectral regularities and with their explanation in terms of the quantum theory. Possibly, too, we must give him the Rutherford atom model and its theoretical development, a simple astronomy in little to correspond to the solar system. Let us, then, think of one man who, starting in 1900, say, had done the fundamental work of Einstein, Planck, Bohr and Schroedinger, and much of that of Rutherford, Alfred Fowler and Paschen, say, by 1930, and had then become, say, Governor of the Bank of England, besides writing two books of Hibbert lectures and spending much of his time on psychical research, to correspond with Newton's theological and mystical interests. Let such a man represent our modern Newton and think how we should regard him. Only so, I think, can we see Newton as he appeared to his contemporaries at the end of his life.

There are no discontinuities in nature and there are none in the history of science. No discovery or fundamental innovation is absolutely new, unconnected with past thought and the stirring spirit of its own time. Newton was not uninfluenced by certain of his immediate predecessors and of his contemporaries. The revolt from the introspective method of constructing explanations of heavenly and earthly phenomena by appeals to philosophic necessity had begun before his birth, and his time was rich in brilliant exponents of the experimental philosophy, whose names will always stand as stars adorning the story of science. To compare him with other men of his time and to recognize their contributions to the development of the physical sciences does not, however, lead us to think less of Newton's achievements but rather to wonder at them all the more. It is easier to estimate the size of a colossus if there are statues of more than life size in its neighbourhood than if it stands alone in a desert.

Newton owed much to the pioneer labours of Galileo, who had founded the science of mechanics, and, in a different way, much to Barrow, whose great mathematical acuteness and sympathetic support were always at the disposal of the young Cambridge scholar. To Hooke he owed more than he was ever prepared to acknowledge. From his great continental contemporaries, Huygens and Leibniz, he borrowed little, if anything. Possibly if mathematical advances were alone in question Leibniz would have to be considered as a possible rival, but for Newton mathematics were merely a means to a physical end: his mathematical innovations may even be left out of consideration without grave injury to Newton's fame. There is no record of physical experimentation that can compare for mastery and elegance with the *Opticks,* no work in exact science that produces the impression of supreme greatness and power of thought that the *Principia* does.

The spirit of this age is a denigrating one, which, in a reaction from the earlier custom of representing great men as free from all blemish and weakness, delights in attempting to show that nobody much exceeds the common level. If an earlier painter might have left out Cromwell's warts, a painter of to-day might represent his face as one huge wart. I have read record of Newton's weaknesses and I know of the adumbrations of his discoveries that can be found in forerunners and contemporaries: I acknowledge that his earlier biographer shut his eyes to any incident, writing or action that might seem to detract from his perfection. Nevertheless, all things considered, I think that the contemporary judgment of his greatness can still stand, and that, if the Marquis de l'Hôpital's query as to whether Newton ate, drank or slept like ordinary men ('for I picture him to myself as a celestial genius') seems to our present-day sobriety an affectation, nevertheless we may agree that the line of Lucretius placed on the Trinity statue was well chosen and fitting—

Qui genus humanum ingenio superavit

'who excelled the human race in power of thought.'

THE

Eighteenth Century

PART SIX

DURING THE AGE OF QUEEN ANNE an extraordinary number of contributions were made to English literature. This was the age when such men as Addison, Steele, Defoe, Swift, and Pope were writing their masterpieces. It is, however, not only the student of literary development who finds much to prize in eighteenth-century writings; political, social, and economic historians are also deeply indebted to them. Consider the insights that Daniel Defoe's works, for example, offer into the life of the age. Now remembered mainly for his *Robinson Crusoe* (1719), Defoe was viewed by his contemporaries as a major journalist and publicist. He was also a shrewd and observant traveler who wrote the lengthy *Tour thro' the Whole Island of Great Britain*. Based on his travels during the early eighteenth century, the *Tour* is invaluable to the social and economic historian. As Defoe put it, "here is the present state of the country describ'd, the improvement, as well in culture, as in commerce, the encrease of people, and employment for them: Also here you have an account of the encrease of buildings, as well in great cities and towns, as in the new seats and dwellings of the nobility and gentry; also the encrease of wealth, in many eminent particulars." Defoe delighted in the description of such topics. A vigorous supporter of the merchant and manufacturer, he viewed it as part of his function to assert the glories of business life in what he regarded as "the most flourishing and opulent country in the world." In the essay that follows, the Reverend W. P. Witcutt, a British expert in the field of eighteenth-century literature, analyzes Defoe's *Tour,* and conveys to the reader some of his own enthusiasm for a work which for a long time after its publication served as a widely used travel guide.

DEFOE'S ENGLAND

W. P. WITCUTT

It is to the interest of the anti-traditionalist to belittle the past; and he never loses the opportunity of making the most of doing so. Pre-industrial England is constantly held up as poor, thinly-populated, and barbarous. The supporters of the existing Capitalist order and of the ideal Communist order alike draw this picture. It is essential for their conception of history. It is a hypothesis necessary for the acceptance of the dogma of Progress.

The traditionalist, therefore, should know his pre-industrial England. He should know it, if possible, from contemporary sources— not from source-books conveying, by means of carefully-selected extracts, the impression that the rulers of modern society desire, but from contemporary accounts taken whole and entire.

Defoe's "Travels through England," written about 1722, in the reign of George I, provide such an account. They give a picture of prosperity and security very different from that reflected in Cobbett's "Rural Rides" a hundred years later, or, for that matter, from the position reflected in modern newspapers.

Of course we are looking at the period through Defoe's eyes, and they were sanguine eyes. He was quite in harmony with his period, quite satisfied. Trade was the thing dearest to his heart, and trade was

Reprinted by special permission from *The English Review,* LX (1935), 69–76.

flourishing. There seems to have been no abject poverty to indicate that things were not as they should be, and he was no lover of the old order of things—no sentimental lover of the past, that is to say—he had a certain relish for the past. He had an eye for Gothic architecture; and a love for quaint old charters; he would spend several pages describing the tactics of a battle of the Civil Wars. Nevertheless, somewhere in his many pages, he enunciates a very modern-sounding heresy about "the main affair of Life, that is to say, getting Money."

This made him, perhaps, a more typical modern Englishman than Cobbett. All the same, he reminds one of Cobbett. One cannot help liking a man who, in describing the cellars cut out of the rock in Nottingham, informs us that "the bountiful Inhabitants generally keep these Cellars well stock'd with excellent Ale; nor are they uncommunicative in bestowing it among their Friends, as some in our Company experienc'd to a Degree not fit to be made Matter of History."

His book gives one the impression of a successful revolution. Ruined monasteries and dismantled fortifications give one a vivid impression of a fallen Church and a vanished feudal monarchy. London and Bristol, Liverpool and Manchester grow apace; the princes of the English countryside build their palaces at Belvoir and Burleigh; while Ludlow Castle, the Court of the President and Council of the Marches, crumbles to decay. It is a symbolical decay.

The Catholic Church lingers on, apart from the new order of things, in old Cathedral cities like Durham, where the Anglican clergy still wear the old priestly vestments on occasions, and the Catholics go openly to Mass; or in the pilgrimage town of Holywell, full of pious Welsh folk and priests in disguise. One is surprised, all the same, at the fear of the Catholic Church that still seems to exist. The triumph of Protestantism is still taken to be a very precarious thing.

"So long as this Island shall retain the Protestant Religion," says Defoe in one place, "how long that may be, as things are going, and if the Detestable Conspiracy of the Papists now on Foot should succeed, I will not pretend to say." This, in 1722!

Both Anglicanism and Dissent flourish in the new world of Trade. The Vicar of Halifax claims a hundred thousand communicants. Dissent, however, seems to go best with manufacturing. Wherever the ramifications of the great Woollen Trade spread, there are sure to be found Nonconformists. In the West Riding they are equal in numbers to the Anglicans; in Suffolk Southwold scarely any following remains to the Established Church; Devonshire is a Nonconformist stronghold. Defoe contrasts agricultural Cornwall, where scarcely any Dissenters are to be found. The main quarrel is, in fact, between Anglican and Nonconformist—Defoe is surprised at the lack of animosity between the two parties at Dorchester. The religious quarrel provides a basis for the political quarrel of Whig and Tory.

Mark on a map the areas where the Woollen Trade preponderates and you have the areas that were hot for the Parliament against the King—the West Riding, East Anglia, Devonshire. What identified Puritanism with Wool?

No historian ever seems to give the Woollen Trade its due weight in English history. It was Wool that smashed the Guilds; it was Wool that provided the sinews of war for the numberless foreign expeditions of the English monarchy; it was the weavers and the woollen merchants who spread first the Reformation and then Puritanism throughout the country, and provided a background for the defiance of the Parliament.

Probably the reason is that the historian generally shares the commonly accepted delusion that pre-industrial England was a thinly populated and almost purely agricultural country, where the bulk of what population there was lay entirely in the

South and East. We are constantly hearing that with the Industrial Revolution the centre of gravity in England shifted from the agricultural South to the new Industrial North. It is false. The great centres of population in the early 18th century, at any rate, lay not in the South and East, but in the North and West.

London, of course, is an exception. London was *the* great centre of population. It is curious that Defoe disliked London and its influence—not so whole-heartedly as Cobbett did, to be sure; but, still, he disliked it. Like Cobbett, he regarded its swollen size as due to the presence of those who battened on the interest of the public debt and the funds, and hoped that when these were paid off the population of London would automatically disperse back into the country. London in Defoe's time was reckoned to have a million inhabitants—and the calculation was based on burials and Anglican baptisms alone. If this is true, then the London of early Hanoverian times was a city as large as modern Birmingham.

After London came the West Riding— "one of the most populous parts of Britain, London and the adjacent parts excepted." Defoe sounds curiously modern when he speaks of the great manufacturing cities of the North. The phrase brings up visions of factories and smoke, but Defoe never praised an ugly city. Comeliness to him was almost as important a factor as Trade, for, after all, men had to live in these places. He praises the cities of the manufacturing North, curiously enough, for their beauty; and contrasts the finely built town of Liverpool with dirty, slummy towns like Hereford and Worcester.

Futhermore, a town to please Defoe had to be a cultural as well as a trading centre. He praises the purely commercial towns, but he would not have lived in them. He never omits to tell us where "good conversation" is to be had, as in the local culture-centres of York, Lichfield, and Derby. His ideal is Shrewsbury, a city full of Trade, and yet "really a Town of Mirth and Gallantry"— a regional capital of such prestige that almost with its backing alone King Charles had been able to put an army into the field "to the Surprize of the Parliament, and indeed of all the World."

But to return to the North. The type of manufacture Defoe describes sounds almost Utopian to us; there are no slums and no factories, no smoke and no crowded streets. The small woollen manufacturers lived each on their little plot of grass-land—small-holdings of from two to seven acres, where grazed the draught-horses and the family cow. In the centre of the holding stood the manufacturer's dwelling—a house and factory in one. "If we knock'd at the Door of any of the Master Manufacturers, we presently saw a House full of lusty Fellows, some at the Dye-vat, some dressing the Cloths, some in the Looms, some on one thing, some on another, all hard at work, and full employed upon the Manufacture, and all seeming to have sufficient Business." Between the houses of the master manufacturers lay scattered the cottages of the workmen; and everywhere ran little rills of water, which served the double purpose of

---

WILLIAM COBBETT: Early-nineteenth-century journalist, publicist, moralist, and reformer. Holding strong views on most of the public issues of his time, he frequently used his writings to demolish the position of those who did not share his opinions. He advocated Parliamentary reform and the repudiation of the national debt, and he fought against the Poor Law reform of 1834. His *Rural Rides* (1830), in addition to being a fundamental source of knowledge concerning farming conditions in early-nineteenth-century Britain, is a long eulogy of the agricultural laborer, for whom he considered himself the spokesman. Cobbett is the subject of an outstanding biography by Professor G. D. H. Cole.

carrying away the fats used in the preparation of the wool, and fertilising the land with them.

Thus the country round Halifax. "After we had mounted the third Hill, we found the Country, in short, one continued Village, tho' mountainous every way, as before; hardly a House standing out of speaking distance from another. Look which Way we would, high to the Tops, and low to the Bottoms, it was all the same; innumerable Houses and Tenters, and a white Piece upon every Tenter."

"The whole country is infinitely populous." Halifax had 100,000 Anglican inhabitants alone; and probably more Nonconformists. And this populousness was a traditional thing—back in Elizabethan times, Defoe tells us, this town could put 12,000 armed men into the field, and did do so at the time of the Rebellion of the Northern Earls. Nevertheless the process of draining the population of the countryside into the manufacturing districts was beginning. "In a word, the Country look'd as if all the People were transplanted to Leeds and Halifax, and that here was only a few just left at home to cultivate the Land, manage the Plough, and raise Corn for the rest."

Defoe is at great pains to explain how the huge population of the West Riding is fed. His explanation forms an essay in Regional Self-Sufficiency which would delight the heart of a Nazi autarchist. "Their Corn comes up in great Quantities out of Lincoln, Nottingham, and the East Riding, their Black Cattle and Horses from the North Riding, their Sheep and Mutton from the adjacent Counties every way." He even explains where the cheese comes from.

After London and the West Riding comes the third most populous district—Devonshire, "so full of great Towns, and those Towns so full of People, and those People so universally Employ'd in Trade, and Manufactures, that not only cannot it be equall'd in England, but perhaps in Europe." The Western Woollen district, however, stretched beyond Devonshire into S.W. Wilts and E. Somerset, which, rather than Devon,

formed its real centre. The system was different from that of the West Riding. "The spinning Work of all this Manufacture is performed by the poor People; the Master Clothiers, who generally live in the greater Towns, sending out the Work Weekly to their Houses, by their Servants and Horses, and, at the same time, bringing back the Yarn that they have spun and finished, which then is fitted for the Loom." "The Spinning is generally the Work of the Women and Children," while the men were engaged in agriculture.

The West Country is now a superseded part of England—its agony began in the days of Cobbett, who noted bitterly the distress of its people. In Defoe's time it was, if possible, a more individual and "separatist" part of England than the North. Its capital, Bristol—a town of 100,000 inhabitants, and the proud possessor of 3,000 sail of ships, was the only port in England that traded independently of London. It spoke a tongue more different from standard English than the dialect of any other region. "It cannot pass my Observation here," says Defoe, solemnly, "that when we are come this Length from London, the Dialect of the English Tongue, or the Country way of Expressing Themselves, is so strangely altered: it is true, that it is so in many parts of England besides, but in none in so gross a Degree as in this Part. This Way of Boorish Country Speech, as in Ireland, it is call'd the Brogue upon the Tongue; so here 'tis called 'Jouring'. . . . They carry it such a Length, that we see their 'Jouring' Speech even upon their Monuments and Grave-Stones." It was in a West Country school that Defoe's surprised ears heard the reader transform the verse of Cant. 5.3.: "I have put off my coat, how shall I put it on; I have washed my feet, how shall I defile them" into "Chav a doffed my cooat, how shall I don't; chav a washed my veet, how shall I moil 'em."

Fourthly came Norfolk, the centre of the Eastern Woollen district, where "we see a Face of Diligence spread over the whole Country; the vast Manufactures carry'd on (in chief) by the Norwich Weavers, employs all the Country round in spinning yarn for them."

Defoe has little to say about the purely agricultural districts of England. He was not very interested in agriculture, unlike Cobbett, who can tell us of the shape of Hertfordshire fields. Subsistence agriculture has no interest whatsoever for him. What does interest him, however, is the fact that the Eastern Midlands formed one "vast magazine of Wool for the rest of the Nation," and exported corn to Holland through the port of Lynn, as Hereford and Monmouth did to Portugal through their port of Chepstow. He takes a pride, moreover, in the princes of the English agrarian world—the great landowners; such as the Manners, whose estate was "equal to the Demesnes of some sovereign Princes," and the Cecils, whose palace at Burleigh "looks more like a Town than a House." At the same time he praises the sturdy independence of the English peasantry, then unbroken, and mentions the recent thwarting of a common-enclosing landlord "as an Instance of the popular Claim in England, which we call Right of Commonage, which the Poor take to be as much their Property, as a Rich Man's Land is his own."

The England of early Hanoverian time was, in fact, a strangely democratic world, where mine Host of the posthouse at Doncaster, who was mayor of the town, kept a pack of hounds, and "was Company for the best Gentlemen in the Town or in the Neighbourhood."; and where miners were not proletarians, but independent workmen who banded together to hew minerals out of the earth and sell them in the open market, like the Derbyshire lead miners, who required a special court to adjudge between their quarrels, "for they are of a strange turbulent, quarrelsome Temper, and very hard to be reconciled to one another in their subterraneous affairs."

It is indeed a strange England, as unlike our preconceived notions as possible; displaying vast trade and great manufacturing centres instead of agriculture and small market-towns alone; independent miners instead of the bond-slaves of legend; and, in the place of the bowing, servile innkeepers of historical fiction, mayors and keepers of hounds, and company for the best gentlemen in the town.

IF THE GLORIOUS REVOLUTION ushered in happy times for Defoe's England, it ushered in unhappy times for Swift's Ireland. It prepared the way not only for further religious, political, and constitutional disabilities but for greatly increased economic hardships. William III had said: "I shall do all that in me lies to discourage the woolen manufacture in Ireland, and to encourage the linen manufacture there, and to promote the trade of England." And by a series of acts—most notably a measure of 1698—Parliament virtually destroyed the Irish woolen industry and to a considerable extent the Irish middle class as well. Because Ireland became almost entirely a land of rack-rented peasants and absentee landlords, the population problem became especially pressing and depressing to Irish patriots. The irony, however, was that those who spoke and wrote on economic questions in the early eighteenth century were usually mercantilists in their outlook. They believed that government should regulate commerce, industry, and agriculture in order to increase the wealth and power of their nation; and they considered it axiomatic that if population grew, so, too, would wealth. This mercantilist idea throws much light on *A Modest Proposal,* the powerful tract in which Jonathan Swift suggested his solution for the alleviation of the poverty of the Irish: the sale of Irish children as food for the rich! In the essay that follows, Professor Louis A. Landa, of Princeton University, a learned student of the literature of the age of Pope, places Swift's tract in the context of early-eighteenth-century mercantilist thought.

A MODEST PROPOSAL AND POPULOUSNESS
LOUIS A. LANDA

In 1724, five years before the publication of *A modest proposal,* Swift wrote a tract entitled *Maxims controlled in Ireland,* in which he examined "certain maxims of state, founded upon long observation and experience, drawn from the constant practice of the wisest nations, and from the very principles of government." His purpose was to demonstrate that however much these maxims applied to other countries they had no application to Ireland. Among the maxims examined and confuted is one that was cherished by the mercantilist economic writers of the last half of the seventeenth and the first half of the eighteenth centuries: that people are the riches of a nation. The passage in which this maxim is presented would seem to be the germ of *A modest proposal:*

It is another undisputed maxim in government, 'That people are the riches of a nation'; which is so universally granted, that it will be hardly pardonable to bring it in doubt. And I will grant it to be so far true, even in this island, that if we had the African custom, or privilege, of selling our useless bodies for slaves to foreigners, it would be the most useful branch of our trade, by ridding us of a most unsupportable burthen, and bringing us money in the stead. But, in our present situation, at least five children in six who are born, lie a dead weight upon us, for want of employment. And a very skilful computer assured me,

that above one half of the souls in this kingdom supported themselves by begging and thievery; whereof two thirds would be able to get their bread in any other country upon earth. Trade is the only incitement to labour; where that fails the poor native must either beg, steal, or starve, or be forced to quit his country. This hath made me often wish, for some years past, that instead of discouraging our people from seeking foreign soil, the public would rather pay for transporting all our unnecessary mortals. . . . .

The parallelism in ideas between this passage and *A modest proposal* is striking. In each there is the complaint that the people, for want of employment, must turn to begging and thievery, that a portion of the population is a useless burden, and that under certain conditions these useless people could become a source of wealth to the nation. The ironic solution for Ireland's economic difficulties in each instance is the selling-off of human bodies, as slaves in the one case and as food in the other. In effect, Swift is maintaining that the maxim—people are the riches of a nation—applies to Ireland only if Ireland is permitted slavery or cannibalism. In both the *Maxims controlled in Ireland* and *A modest proposal* populousness is overtly and impliedly made a vicious economic condition for Ireland. The methods are, of course, different in the two, with *A modest proposal* gaining its effects through

Reprinted by special permission from *Modern Philology,* XL (1942), 161-170. Copyright, University of Chicago Press. The footnotes which originally appeared with this essay have been omitted.

broad and sustained irony; but for fear that the reader may miss his telling point, that people are not the riches of Ireland whatever they may be in other countries, Swift inserts at the close of *A modest proposal* a more direct statement of his purpose:

> I can think of no one objection, that will possibly be raised against this proposal, unless it should be urged that the number of people will be thereby much lessened in the kingdom. This I freely own, and was indeed one principle design in offering it to the world. I desire the reader will observe, that I calculate my remedy *for this one individual Kingdom of Ireland, and for no other that ever was, is, or, I think, ever can be upon earth.*

The satirical point of *A modest proposal* would have been sharpened for Swift's contemporaries to the extent to which they believed the maxim it refuted. How much more damaging to England that her drastic policies had forced Ireland outside the pale in which universally valid economic laws could operate!

An examination of economic tracts in the second half of the seventeenth century reveals constant iteration of the principle that people are the riches of a nation. Sir William Petty, whose views on Ireland were widely quoted in Swift's day, wrote that "Fewness of people is real poverty; and a Nation wherein are Eight Millions of People, are more than twice as rich as the same scope of Land wherein are but Four." People, wrote William Petyt, the supposed author of *Britannia languens* (1680), are "in truth the chiefest, most fundamental, and precious commodity." Sir Josiah Child, great merchant and expounder of mercantilist ideas, maintained that "most Nations in the Civilized Parts of the World, are more or less Rich or Poor proportionably to the Paucity or Plenty of their People, and not to the Sterility or Fruitfulness of their Lands." These statements are frequently repeated in the early eighteenth century. In *New essays on trade* (1702), Sir Francis Brewster wrote: "Nothing makes Kingdoms and Commonwealths, Mighty, Opulent and Rich, but multitudes of People; 'tis Crowds bring in Industry." From Defoe came a similar expression: ". . . . the glory, the strength, the riches, the trade, and all that is valuable in a nation as to its figure in the world, depends upon the number of its people, be they never so mean and poor. . . . ." These are typical expressions and could be multiplied. In their context and with their supporting arguments, these expressions, it is true, are not tantamount to an unqualified assertion that people are the riches of a nation. People are conceived of as a source of riches; their labor is potential wealth but it must be utilized. As one writer expressed it, the people are *"capital material . . . . raw* and indigested."

SIR JOSIAH CHILD: British merchant, governor of the East India Company, and writer on economic problems. His *New Discourse of Trade* is valuable for the light it throws on the economic ideas of one of the wealthiest businessmen in late-seventeenth-century Europe.

BERNARD DE MANDEVILLE: Early-eighteenth-century British moralist whose *The Fable of the Bees: or Private Vices Public Benefits* stressed the importance of self-interest as a force in economic life and the desirability of a minimum of government interference in the affairs of businessmen. His work was widely read in eighteenth-century intellectual circles and helped to counteract the prevailing mercantilist views of the time.

SIR WILLIAM PETTY: Versatile seventeenth-century economist, statistician, and charter member of the Council of the Royal Society. His *Treatise of Taxes and Contributions* (1662) earned him his reputation as the leading English writer on problems of taxation. His *Political Arithmetic* (1690) was an attempt to compare various countries from the standpoint of their economic condition and wealth.

Yet often the maxim was stated without qualification or without any attempt to equate the number of people and the employment available to them, although there was likely to be an assumption that employment could be provided. The mercantilist wanted a large or dense population in order to keep wages low and manufactures cheap, a condition by which a country gained an advantage in export trade, the great desideratum of the mercantilist. As William Petyt wrote: "The *odds in Populacy* must also produce the like odds in Manufacture; plenty of people must also cause *cheapnesse of wages:* which will cause cheapnesse of the Manufacture; in a scarcity of people wages must be dearer, which must cause the dearnesse of the Manufacture. . . . . Mandeville was thinking in the same terms when he declared that "in a free Nation where Slaves are not allow'd of, the surest Wealth consists in a Multitude of laborious Poor." Though the insistence on populousness received support from serious economic writers by serious arguments, the maxim was as likely as not to be set down in nontechnical and popular writings without consideration of the implications and assumptions involved, as it was, for example, in the *Weekly journal, or Saturday's post,* April 11, 1724, and in the Irish weekly, the *Tribune,* No. 17 (1729).

Against the uncritical enunciation of the maxim there were sporadic protests. In an *Essay upon the probable methods of making a people gainer in the ballance of trade* (1699), Charles Davenant declared: "Their's is a wrong Opinion who think all Mouths profit a Country that consume its Product; And it may more truthfully be affirmed, That he who does not some way serve the Commonwealth, either by being employed, or by employing Others, is not only a useless, but a hurtful member to it." A similar protest came from Laurence Braddon in 1723:

But tho' *Populousness be designed as the greatest Blessing to a Nation, yet, in fact, it proves a Blessing only to that Kingdom and State,* where due care is taken . . . . *that* none, who are willing to work, shall be forced to be Idle for want of Employment. . . . . And where none who are able are permitted to live idle, by begging, or other more Vicious Practices. . . . .

Swift, too, made a protest of the same nature. In *The history of the four last years of the queen,* which he was writing in the trying days near the end of Anne's reign, he complained that "The maxim, 'That people are the riches of a nation,' hath been crudely understood by many writers and reasoners upon that subject." At the moment his animus was directed against the Palatines, whose numbers immigrating into England had increased the population by just so many dissenters; yet he was also establishing a general point: that populousness per se is not a blessing; that a person who does not function productively in economic or political society makes the nation poorer, not richer; and that such a person is comparable, to use Swift's own figure, to a wen, which, although it makes a man fatter, is "unsightly and troublesome, at best, and intercepts that nourishment, which would otherwise diffuse itself through the whole body."

Viewed against this background, *A modest proposal* is seen to be another protest, in Swift's unique manner, against the unqualified maxim that people are the riches of a nation. The tract was written for a public in whose consciousness the maxim was firmly implanted, in the expectation that the ironic impact would thus be greater. The terrible irony in the bare maxim, divested of its supporting arguments, was even more apparent at this time than usual because of the famine conditions which prevailed in Ireland after three successive failures in harvests; and Swift takes occasion in two other tracts, one written in 1728 and one in 1729, to insist that "the uncontrolled maxim, 'That people are the riches of a Nation,' is no maxim here under our circumstances." Here, at least, was one country where populousness was not a virtue. Swift seemed to be aware—the evidence was before his eyes—of the contradiction in the mercantilist attitude that the wealth of a country was based on the poverty of the majority of its subjects. However, we must guard against endowing Swift with unusual knowledge of or insight into economic matters, or even seeing him as moving against the trend of mercantilist thought. His purpose was not primarily to expose an economic fallacy; it was purely propagandistic: to put the onus on England of vitiating the working of natural economic law in Ireland by denying Irishmen "the same natural rights common to the rest of mankind."

It would seem, on merely logical grounds, that Swift should have favored a reduction of the population to achieve a higher level of subsistence, that he should have defended, for example, the emigration of the Irish people to the American colonies; and he did pretend to see in emigration a partial solution. In *Maxims controlled in Ireland* he wrote that he has often wished "for some years past, that instead of discouraging our people from seeking foreign soil, the public would rather pay for transporting all our unnecessary mortals, whether Papists or Protestants, to America." He repeats the view in the *Intelligencer,* No. 19: "It must needs be a very comfortable circumstance, in the present juncture, that some thousand families are gone, or going, or preparing to go, from hence, and settle themselves in America." But these statements, viewed in their context, are seen to be ironic, their function being to emphasize the dire position of a country which must resort to emigration. In the light of contemporary economic theory, with its insistence on an increasing population, emigration could not be viewed with complacency; it was not acceptable as a solution. There was much concern that England's population was declining or was not increasing at a sufficiently rapid rate; and many mercantilists advocated encouragements to marriage, to achieve a higher birth rate, and laws to facilitate immigration. There were

complaints that emigration to the colonies has been detrimental to the nation. "The peopling of the American Plantations subject to the Crown of England," wrote Roger Coke, "hath diminished the strength of England." It is not, Slingsby Bethel maintained, in "the interest of State, to suffer such multitudes of people to pass out of his Majesties Kingdoms into other Princes Dominions, or the Western Plantations, thereby to disfurnish our selves of people; the sad consequences and effects whereof, are too visible in the misfortunes of *Spain.*" The author of *Britannia languens* argued in the same vein: ". . . . our *Plantation-Trade* hath robbed and prevented us of some Millions of our People, amongst which very many being, or might have been Manufacturers, the Nation hath also lost more Millions of Pounds in the loss of their Manufactures." Those Irishmen, Swift among them, who had observed the losses to Ireland resulting from the emigration of workers in the Irish woolen industry to France, Spain, Germany, and the Low Countries—an exodus caused by the restrictive acts passed by the English Parliament at the close of the seventeenth-century— would have read such complaints understandingly.

Many mercantilists found, however, that they could reconcile emigration to colonies with the desire for an increasing population and the fear of loss of numbers. It could not be denied that by reducing the number of laborers in the nation emigration tended to raise the costs of labor and manufactures and thus to put the country in a less favorable position for advantageous foreign trade; yet it could be and was argued that colonies compensated for the disadvantages created by providing raw materials to be manufactured in the mother-country and a market for the finished products. Emigration to colonies whose trade was carefully controlled by navigation acts was justifiable, therefore, if such colonies created employment at home and swelled the exports to a value greater than that lost by the numbers who emigrated. Thus Sir

Josiah Child wrote: "That all Colonies and foreign Plantations do endamage their Mother-Kingdom, whereof the Trades (of such Plantations) are not confined to their said Mother-Kingdom, by good Laws and severe Execution of those Laws." He continued:

> *Plantations* being at first furnished, and afterwards successively supplied with People from their Mother-Kingdoms, and People being Riches, that loss of People to the Mother-Kingdoms, be it more or less, is certainly a damage, except the employment of those People abroad, do cause the employment of so many more at home in their Mother-Kingdoms. . . . .

The argument is more fully expressed by John Cary:

> . . . . it having been a great question among many thoughtful Men whether our Foreign Plantations have been an advantage to this Nation, the reasons they give against them are, that they have drained us of Multitudes of our People who might have been serviceable at home and advanced Improvements in Husbandry and Manufacture; That the Kingdom of *England* is worse Peopled by so much as they are increased; and that Inhabitants being the Wealth of a Nation, by how much they are lessened, by so much we are poorer than when we first began to settle our Foreign Colonies; Though I allow the last Proposition to be true, that People are or may be made the Wealth of a Nation . . . . Its my Opinion that our Plantations are an Advantage . . . . every one more or less, as they take off our Product and Manufactures, supply us with Commodities which may be either wrought up here, or Exported again, or prevent fetching things of the same Nature from other Princes for our home Consumption, imploy our Poor, and encourage our Navigation. . . . .

Such justifications, as Swift was aware, had no application to Ireland, which was itself treated as a colony, with its trade strictly controlled by the Navigation Acts in the interests of England. An emigrant from England, Holland, or France might be looked upon as a unit of economic value who would eventually return his value to the mother-country; but one could hardly apply the same economic logic to the Irish emigrant, whose country was peculiarly removed from the operations of economic law. "I have often taken notice," Swift wrote, "both in print and in discourse, that there is no topic so fallacious . . . . as to argue how we ought to act in Ireland, from the example of England, Holland, France, or any other country, whose inhabitants are allowed the common rights and liberties of humankind." Public-spirited Irishmen were concerned at the numbers who were departing. Even Lord Primate Boulter, whose first thought was for the welfare of England rather than for Ireland, was disturbed in 1728, when famine was widespread, at the size of the emigration. In a letter written to the Duke of Newcastle, then Secretary of State, Boulter brought the problem before the English Cabinet for possible parliamentary action:

> I am very sorry I am obliged to give your Grace so melancholy an account of the state of this kingdom. . . . . For we have had three bad harvests together there [in the north], which has made oatmeal, which is their great subsistence, much dearer than ordinary. . . . . We have had for several years some agents from the colonies in *America,* and several masters of ships that have gone about the country, and deluded the people with stories of great plenty and estates to be had for going for in those parts of the world: and they have been better able to seduce people, by reason of the necessities of the poor so late. . . . . But whatever occasions their going, it is certain that above 4,200 men, women, and children have been shipped off from hence for the *West Indies* within three years, and of these above 3,100 this last sum-

mer. . . . . The whole north is in a ferment at present, and people every day engaging one another to go next year to the *West Indies*. The humour has spread like a contagious distemper, and the people will hardly hear any body that tries to cure them of their madness.

Swift, too, was genuinely perturbed. In 1728 and 1729 he refers several times to the subject of emigrating Irishmen, particularly to those who are leaving for America, which for several reasons he thinks no better than Ireland. Like Boulter, he believed that they had been given false representations and that they were doomed to disappointment; yet he is not at a loss to understand their motives for going, since "men in the extremest degree of misery, and want, will naturally fly to the first appearance of relief, let it be ever so vain, or visionary." It was at this time that Swift wrote *A modest proposal* and its lesser known companion piece, *An answer to the craftsman*. This last tract was occasioned by the license given to France to recruit Irishmen for military service in the French army; and it too is a bitter and ironic commentary, among other matters, on the sub-

ject of Ireland's depopulation by England. As he had done in *A modest proposal*, Swift makes in this tract an ironical computation of the monetary profit to Ireland from the reduction and destruction of its people. And he adds this recommendation: ". . . . for fear of increasing the natives in this island, that an annual draught, according to the number born every year, be exported to whatever prince will bear the carriage, or transplanted to the English dominions on the American continent, as a screen between his Majesty's English subjects and the savage Indians."

What Swift wanted for Ireland was not fewer people but more opportunities—opportunities that would present themselves if England adopted a less restrictive policy, if the Irish absentees were regulated, and if the Irish people could be made to see wherein their welfare lay. He maintained, as did many contemporary Irishmen, that Ireland possessed the potentialities of a rich country and could, under proper conditions, easily support its population. Ireland, he wrote, "is the poorest of all civilized countries in Europe, with every natural advantage to make it one of the richest."

TWO DEVELOPMENTS IN THE CONSTITUTIONAL HISTORY of Hanoverian times that usually receive considerable attention in textbooks are the evolution of the office of prime minister and the growth of the inner cabinet, or conciliabulum. If these developments are to be understood, however, they must be viewed in their historical context. It is important, in other words, not to search in the eighteenth century for the cabinet and the office of prime minister as they had evolved by the late nineteenth or twentieth century. It must be remembered that in Hanoverian England the prime minister and the cabinet were generally not regarded as limitations on the authority of the crown. On the contrary, they were instrumentalities employed by the crown in order to make more efficient its conduct of government and more harmonious its relations with the House of Commons and the House of Lords. Indeed, the widespread suspicion with which the prime minister and cabinet were regarded provides the best indication that in Hanoverian England they were considered instruments of royal power, not restrictions on royal power. Sir Robert

Walpole, for example, who is so often misnamed "the first British prime minister," complained that his enemies had "conferred upon me a kind of mock dignity and styled me the prime minister." In the following essay, E. T. Williams, Fellow of Balliol College, University of Oxford, considers some of the more important problems connected with the history of the eighteenth-century cabinet, and he makes it clear that much more detailed research needs to be done before the topic with which he deals can be adequately understood. Mr. Williams is warden of Rhodes House, Oxford, and present editor of the *Dictionary of National Biography*.

THE CABINET IN THE EIGHTEENTH CENTURY

E. T. WILLIAMS

The problem of interpreting the development and significance of the Cabinet in the eighteenth century is, in brief, this:[1] we know that earlier and, in the main, Whig historians, with the popular assistance of Disraeli, so distorted the question that their view is no longer acceptable. Yet no gen-

[1] BIBLIOGRAPHICAL NOTE: 1889, the date of Morley's *Walpole,* with its valuable seventh chapter, was perhaps the beginning of useful treatment of the subject. But publications treating directly of the matter from the point of view of the machinery of government may be dated, for convenience, from the first edition (1892) of W. R. Anson, *The Law and Custom of the Constitution,* vol. II. The fourth edition (1935), by A. Berriedale Keith, patches it a little in its discussion of the Cabinet. Detailed examination began with Professor Wolfgang Michael's first volume (1896, second edition, 1921), *Englische Geschichte im achtzehnten Jahrhundert* (translated, 1936, under the title *The Beginnings of the Hanoverian Dynasty*). His third volume (1934) contains (pp. 546-92) his conclusions on the Cabinet. Its translation is proceeding under the supervision of Professor L. B. Namier. D. A. Winstanley entered the field with "George III and his First Cabinet" in *Eng. Hist. Rev.,* vol. XVII (1902), followed by his *Personal and Party Government* (1910) and *Lord Chatham and the Whig Opposition* (1912).

Between 1912 and 1917 there appeared a series of articles beginning with that of H. W. V. Temperley, *Eng. Hist. Rev.,* vol. XXVII (1912), pp. 682-99, "Inner and Outer Cabinet and Privy Council, 1689-1783"; and continued by W. Michael, *Zeitschrift für Politik,* vol. VI (1913),

pp. 549-93, "Die Entstehung der Kabinettsregierung in England"; Sir William Anson, *Eng. Hist. Rev.,* vol. XXIX (1914), pp. 56-78, "The Cabinet in the Seventeenth and Eighteenth Centuries," and pp. 325-7, "The Development of the Cabinet, 1688-1760," commenting on Professor E. R. Turner's two articles with the same title in *Amer. Hist. Rev.,* vol. XVIII (1912-3), pp. 751-68 and vol. XIX (1913-4), pp. 27-43.

Mr. Temperley drew together the threads of the controversy and presented another suggestion to support his now modified view in *Eng. Hist. Rev.,* vol. XXXI (1916), pp. 291-6, "A Note on Inner and Outer Cabinets . . ." Yet Professor Turner remained critical in *Eng. Hist. Rev.,* vol. XXXII (1917), pp. 192-203, "The Cabinet in the Eighteenth Century." His views are to be found, at length, in his *Privy Council, 1603-1784* (vol. II, 1928) and *The Cabinet Council, 1622-1784,* the second volume of which was published posthumously (1932) with an introduction (pp. ix-xviii), by Professor E. R. Adair, briefly reviewing the literature of the controversy. R. R. Sedgwick, in a striking article, *Eng. Hist. Rev.,* vol. XXXIV (1919), pp. 290-302, "The Inner Cabinet from 1739 to 1741," joined Mr. Temperley in discerning a confidential Cabinet earlier than Professor Turner's hesitant *c.* 1745.

The argument was given a new twist, as, indeed, were all studies of English government in the eighteenth century, by Professor L. B. Namier in his remarkable two volumes *The Structure of Politics at the Accession of George III* (1929) and by his *England in the Age of the American Revolution* (1930). From another angle, M. A. Thomson, *Secretaries of State, 1681-1782* (1932), is very useful. W. Ivor Jennings, *Cabinet Government* (1936) is concerned with the subject only since 1832, but cf. his two

Reprinted by special permission from *History,* XXII (1937), 240-252. The author has made substantial changes in the present version of his essay.

erally satisfactory substitute has been produced, and the Whig ghost has been laid only to make its absence noticeable. The lack of precise nomenclature and practice by contemporaries increases the difficulty. Apart from Professor Turner's uncompleted monograph, printed contributions lie, for the most part, either dispersed in articles

or concealed in miscellaneous works not directly concerned with the problem. The aim of this article is to rehearse some of the arguments put forward upon disputed points and to attempt to integrate the scattered conclusions. It is essentially derivative. . . .[2] The intention is merely to suggest a possible interpretation and to point out the ambiguities which still surround any discussion of the epigenesis of the modern Cabinet.

There are four main questions in dispute, though they may be separated for convenience only, for they are interrelated and each, in addition, has its own attendant problems. First, the nineteenth-century interpretation of the constitutional powers of the Crown in the preceding century was an example of retrospective wish-fulfilment, and more modern historians have abandoned the habit of hissing George III as the villain

---

articles "Cabinet Government at the Accession of Queen Victoria," *Economica* vol. XI (1931), pp. 404-25, and vol. XII (1932), pp. 63-78. In the year 1938 the following were published: D. L. Keir, *Constitutional History of Modern Britain, 1485-1937* (4th ed., 1950); M. A. Thomson, *Constitutional History of England, 1642-1801;* and the eighteenth-century volumes (X-XII) of Sir William Holdsworth, *History of English Law.* Three recent articles are well worth attention: *The Times Literary Supplement,* 24 March, 1945, "Sir Robert Walpole" (evidently by Mr. Sedgwick); Professor A. S. Foord, *Eng. Hist. Rev.,* vol. LXII (1947), pp. 484-507, "The Waning of 'The Influence of the Crown'"; and Professor Richard Pares, *Royal Historical Society Transactions,* fifth series, vol. I (1951), pp. 127-51, "George III and the Politicians." Three skilfully edited collections of relevant documents have also been printed recently: A. Aspinall, *The Letters of George IV* (three vols., 1938); Mr. Sedgwick, *Letters from George III to Lord Bute, 1756-1766* (1939) (on which *vide,* especially, R. Pares, *Eng. Hist. Rev.,* vol. LV (1940), pp. 475-9), and Miss Ninetta Jucker, *The Jenkinson Papers* (1949).

There is no account for the eighteenth century similar to E. R. Adair, *The Sources for the History of the Council in the Sixteenth and*

Seventeenth Centuries (1924). Some help may be found in the *Report of the American · Historical Association,* 1911, which includes Professor Turner's notes on *Sources for the History of the English Cabinet in the Eighteenth Century* (vol. I, pp. 89-98). The principal sources may be found most conveniently in the bibliography (pp. 413-49) of his *Cabinet Council,* vol. II, which does not, however, pretend to completeness. Since 1951 it is possible to consult the invaluable *Bibliography of British History: the Eighteenth Century, 1714-1789,* edited by Stanley Pargellis and D. J. Medley.

[2] [Footnote omitted.]

WALTER BAGEHOT: Nineteenth-century writer on literature, politics, and economics whose *English Constitution* (1867), *Physics and Politics* (1872), *Lombard Street* (1873), *Literary Studies* (1879), and *Biographical Studies* (1881) placed him in the front rank of Victorian intellectuals.

LORD HARVEY: Eighteenth-century Whig and supporter of Robert Walpole. His frank and vitriolic *Some Materials towards Memoirs of the Reign of King George II* is an important source for an understanding of the 1730's.

L. B. NAMIER: Versatile twentieth-century British historian who has made major contributions to the study of eighteenth-century British history, the revolutions of 1848, Austro-Hungarian history, and the origins of World War II. His *Structure of Politics at the Accession of George III* (1929) and his uncompleted *England in the Age of the American Revolution* (1930) are invaluable for the student of modern English history.

HORACE WALPOLE: Gifted writer whose *Correspondence* and *Memoirs* are basic sources for the student of eighteenth-century Britain. From the standpoint of the historian, Walpole is at his best when he discusses Parliamentary events and political intrigues in the England of George II and George III.

of a Whig melodrama. Secondly, this doubt about the Crown naturally envelops any examination of the associated question of the evolution and recognition of the idea of a Prime Minister. Thirdly, concerning the Cabinet which really framed policy, and from which the modern Cabinet is derived, there are several controversial issues: the date of its separation from the larger body, membership of which became an honour entailing no governmental duties; its function and its membership; and the recognition of its separate organisation. Lastly, the development of the conception of collective responsibility was obviously retarded so long as there were merely nominal members of the Cabinet, and the question of individual responsibility complicated by uncertainty whether it was owed to the Crown, to the Courts or to Parliament.

The modern Cabinet is normally formed by the leader of the dominant party in the House of Commons, after summons by the King, whose constitutional power of choice in the matter is still in dispute, but is necessarily restricted.[3] Cabinet ministers accept a collective responsibility for their actions in office, which they hold so long as they maintain a majority in a House of Commons representative of a popular electorate. They are the political heads of government departments staffed by a non-political hierarchy of civil servants.[4]

The eighteenth century provides an almost complete contrast. The part played by the Crown was by no means insignificant. The King was no Doge, and Whig disgust with George III was born of this fact. The idea of a Prime Minister was not readily established, and the title itself was often a term of abuse. Party lines were indefinite, for ministerial politics in the century were "a scramble for office among a set of family groups."[5] Although a majority in

the House of Commons was important, resignation did not follow conventionally upon defeat. A popular electorate was alien to the century. Public opinion could not be entirely ignored, and made itself felt in isolated instances. But representation meant, to a remarkable extent, that the Crown and the House of Lords were represented in the House of Commons.[6] The civil service had not yet left politics; Professor Namier has made it clear that some, at least, of the too-famous "King's Friends" were but the embryonic "administrative class" of the modern civil service.[7] Not until the Crown lost control of policy, administration left the Household, and appointments

3 [Footnote omitted.]

4 Cf. D. N. Chester, "Development of the Cabinet, 1914-1949," in *British Government since 1918,* by Sir Gilbert Campion *et al.* (1950).

5 Anson, *Eng. Hist. Rev.,* vol. XXIX, p. 57. Despite Professor K. G. Feiling, *The Second Tory Party, 1714-1832* (1938), there is not yet a satisfactory history of the rise of party. "To sum up," says Professor Namier, "about 1750, 'Whig' meant 'an active politician,' and 'Tory' an 'independent'; and the Tories of about 1800 were, no less than the Whigs, spiritual and largely even lineal descendants of the Whigs of 1750. As for the system, it was not invented, but was fully developed by Walpole and the Pelhams; and it survived till 'party' replaced 'patronage' as the cement of Parliamentary politics."—*The Spectator,* 18 August, 1939, in a review of Professor Basil Williams, *The Whig Supremacy, 1714-1760* (1939). "We may say," with Professor Herbert Butterfield, "that the real 'party' in the Hanoverian period, the real structure of politics, was based on the principle of 'connection.' "—*George III, Lord North and the People, 1779-1780* (1949) p. 11, (on which study, however, cf. especially, *Times Lit. Supp.,* 6 January, 1950).

6 "The biggest body in the House of Commons (about 150 to 200 strong) consisted of men partly or wholly dependent on the Government for their seats or holding places—'who would support his Majesty's Government under any Minister not peculiarly unpopular'; and the next biggest, over a hundred strong, consisted of men entirely independent, who neither held nor wished for office or Government favours, the 'country gentlemen.' The men 'entrusted with his Majesty's business' had to look to these two bodies for 'numbers.' Ability and leadership were supplied by groups of politicians, the ever-shifting and re-forming 'factions.' . . . There were at all times 'flying squads' and intermediary formations. There were frequently problems and divisions which cut across the main alignments."—Namier, *Conflicts* (1942) p. 202.

7 [Footnote omitted.]

ceased to be due to jobbery, might the civil service be expected to be neutral. The eighteenth century had, then, none of the conventions which we like to associate with Cabinet government to-day. So long as the Crown and the civil service remained in politics, such constitutional conventions could scarcely arise.

In 1714 there were three consultative bodies under the Crown, competing, it might seem, for importance: the Privy Council, the Committee of the Council and the Cabinet Council. Of these, the Privy Council, as an active agent in government, was on the decline, and its functions became increasingly formal. Sir William Anson provided a useful example of the change in its position in his comparison of the meetings over the sale of Dunkirk in 1662 with Cholmondeley's unsuccessful attempt in 1713 to initiate a discussion of the Peace Treaties at a meeting summoned merely to register.[8] From the point of view of effective policy, in presiding over Anne's death-bed at Kensington, the Privy Council was presiding at the same time over its own.

The Committee of the Council,[9] a body dating from at least as early as 1693 and replacing in importance the temporary standing committees of privy councillors (which still, but decreasingly, continued to be formed in the eighteenth century), was given a formal sanction in 1714 which was confirmed on George II's accession. Its members were concerned with the Plantations, the Channel Islands "& other Matters that shalbe referred to them,"[10] such as, noticeably, Irish bills, quarantine requirements and royal funerals. It became, in short, the work-a-day aspect of the Privy Council, which gave official ratification to its decisions. It dealt with conciliar business only, and had no concern with important matters of policy. Foreign affairs,

in particular, were outside its sphere of influence. The lack of precise nomenclature, however, makes it difficult conclusively to distinguish it from the Cabinet Council. "The confusion is increased by the fact that the 'committee of council' is sometimes confused with 'private meetings,' and sometimes with the outer cabinet; in the same way the privy council is sometimes spoken of as 'the Cabinet.' When contemporaries themselves bestowed misnomers, it is not surprising that difficulties of identification are encountered by historians."[11] Professor Michael[12] attempted to draw a legal distinction between the Committee of the Council and the Cabinet Council in the first few years of George I's reign, but his test of royal presence is not conclusive.[13] With some reservation, then, because of its precision, may we accept the dictum that "the Cabinet determines policy; the Committee of Council does [some of] the work which to-day is done by the departments of government; the Council gives formal expression to the royal will."[14] The Cabinet Council may certainly be clearly distinguished from the Privy Council. They differ in title, function and mode of summons. The Cabinet Council is not a committee of the Privy Council, although, because of the oath, every member is a Privy Councillor.

The accession of George I is an important date in the development of the Cabinet, but it is far less important than some have pretended.[15] The Whigs put George on his throne; accordingly, he chose his ministers from among them. Anne had clung tenaciously, and with some success, to her ideal of a ministry on a broad bottom. George's ministries were Whig: but that is not to suggest that the King lost his control. They

[8] *Law and Custom* (4th ed.) vol. II, part i, p. 107.
[9] For this body, *vide* E. R. Turner, *Eng. Hist. Rev.,* vol. XXXI, pp. 545-72, and *Privy Council,* vol. II, pp. 367-432.
[10] *Privy Council Register LXXXV,* 1 October, 1714.

[11] Temperley, *Eng. Hist. Rev.,* vol. XXXI, pp. 294-5, n. 14.
[12] *Zeitschrift für Politik,* vol. VI, pp. 549-93.
[13] *Vide* Turner, *American Hist. Rev.,* vol. XVIII, p. 763, n. 86, and cf. pp. 766-7 for his distinction between the Cabinet Council and the Committee of Council.
[14] Anson, *Law and Custom,* vol. II, part i, p. 105.
[15] [Footnote omitted.]

remained the King's selection. Professor Michael[16] has proved clearly that the first two Georges did not lose their freedom of choice and that Walpole admitted it by implication.[17] Newcastle and Hardwicke, Professor Namier insists, "had no conception of a party-government unconnected with the King, and hence of a constitutional Parliamentary Opposition. For the King was to them a real factor in government, and not a mere figurehead . . ."[18] The King was not only an essential part of the constitution, but an integral part of politics. . . .[19] There were, of course, groups which were ready to oppose, but, in the majority of instances, when they hardened into effective organisation, they used the classical excuse of a national emergency or were liable to take shelter behind a member of the royal family whose nominal leadership removed the taint of disloyalty and added political fuel to the personal animosities of the Hanoverians and their heirs.[20] In the eighteenth century the rôle of father-image was not enough. The King was an active politician and played an important part, not merely because of Hanover, in framing foreign policy. In 1750, for example, by which time we have been taught that the oligarchs had dug themselves in, the strength of royal control was clearly shown. Halifax tried to gain admittance to membership of the Cabinet, and Newcastle wrote to his brother to say that "the whole council, all of us put together, could not make the king do it."[21] George III did not "attack" the constitution. The "crisis" of 1760-1 is a discredited legend: there was, of course, the usual jockeying for positions on the front-stairs at the beginning of a reign. George III's *Correspondence*[22] makes it apparent that he had an almost Whiggish reverence for, and no desire to go behind, the Revolution settlement. But he would not relinquish, and his intention was perfectly constitutional, those royal rights with which the Revolution had not been concerned. "In reality, George III never left the safe ground of Parliamentary government, and merely acted the *primus inter pares,* the first among the borough-mongering, electioneering gentlemen of England."[23]

Again, much has been made of the fact that George I ceased to attend Cabinet meetings after 1717 because of his ignorance of English.[24] Rather was it that ministers

[22] *1760-1783,* edited, unsatisfactorily, by Sir John Fortescue, in six volumes (1927-8); cf. Namier, *Additions and Corrections* to vol. I (1937).

[23] Namier, *England . . . ,* p. 4; cf. Pares, however, *op. cit.,* pp. 128-9: "It has lately been suggested that George III merely 'carried on, to the best of his more than limited ability the system of government which he had inherited from his predecessors.' This is quite true, in one sense: George III did not innovate. In another sense, I think it less true: George III did try to restore something which possibly ought to have existed but did not exist, when he came to the throne. He did what George II ought to have done, rather than what George II had done. If George III only did what George II had done, why did the politicians suddenly make a fuss about it?" "The truth seems to me to be," he says (*Eng. Hist. Rev.,* vol. LV., p. 479), "that, whereas the power of the executive was not less in George II's reign than in that of George III, the King's personal exercise of it was less frequent, direct and positive; that it was mainly confined in practice to certain personal proscriptions which his ministers could not overcome, and to helping ministries not inherently popular to keep themselves afloat by the use of the royal patronage. This was a good deal; it was more than some historians have admitted. But it was much less than George III did."

[24] Professor Michael has suggested (*op. cit.,* vol. III, pp. 575-6) that the King's lack of English was not the reason for his withdrawal, for his French was adequate, and later he conversed with Walpole in Latin. The juxtaposition, in Hallam, of this fact and the King's withdrawal led later historians, thinks Professor Michael, to make the first the reason for the second. George II, moreover, talked to his ministers in English.

[16] *Englische Geschichte im achtzehnten Jahrhundert,* vol. III, pp. 536-92.

[17] *Ibid.,* pp. 596-8.

[18] *England in the Age of the American Revolution,* p. 58.

[19] [Footnote omitted.]

[20] Cf. Sedgwick's introduction to *Letters of George III . . .* pp. XI-XVIII, and Pares, *op. cit.,* p. 129.

[21] Coxe, *Pelham* (1829), vol. II, p. 386.

were interested in pushing matters through Parliament, and the King was concerned, not with their discussions, but with their proposals. That the King ceased to preside over his Cabinet did not mean that, of constitutional necessity, he accepted its advice. He was influenced, no doubt, by the difficulty of finding new ministers, and recognised the advisability of having a parliamentary majority. But the King accepted the advice of his ministers, not because of any constitutional convention (for there was none), but because he had chosen them to advise him: that was their job. His absence must have robbed him somewhat, however, of that control based on detailed information which would have been provided more certainly by regular attendance at Cabinet meetings than by the politics of the Closet. George II occasionally presided over his Cabinet Council,[25] as he had done as Regent in 1716, when his father was in Hanover. But, as Waldegrave said of an instance in 1756, "it was unusual for the king himself to be present at such consultations."[26] It was customary, however, for him to be present at the formal meeting to approve the Speech before the session.[27] George III summoned and presided over at least two special meetings of the Cabinet: in 1779, when the ministers found the occasion so unusual that they imagined that their dismissal was intended; and in 1781.[28]

The royal absence had two obvious results. It meant that someone else presided, and that the King wanted reports of meetings. It thus made possible both a Prime Minister and a Cabinet minute-book. Neither resulted immediately. What was Walpole's position? He "did not, as his insecure position on George II's accession shows, enjoy any tenure independent of royal favour."[29] But, given that and because he persisted in remaining in the House of Commons, he was able to supply the essential "link, hitherto missing, between the two great centres of power" in the eighteenth century: the Closet, where the leading ministers had access to and worked with the King (and which was therefore, in Walpole's day, "a higher political level than the Cabinet") and the Commons, where financial business might be introduced, as today, only by a minister of the Crown. He fulfilled, therefore, "the dual function of 'Minister for the King in the House of Commons' and 'Minister for the House of Commons in the Closet.' "[30] Because his principal colleagues were in the Lords, Walpole came to answer in the Commons not just, as at first, for Treasury matters, but also, eventually, for the whole foreign and domestic policy which, as "the labouring oar," he had to defend there.[31] Royal favour, a masterful temperament, leadership of the House (best whipped from Treasury Chambers) and sheer administra-

[25] Cf. Temperley, *Eng. Hist. Rev.*, vol. XXVII, p. 693; Michael, *op. cit.*, vol. III, pp. 578-9; Turner, *Cabinet Council*, vol. II, p. 98; *The Times*, 15, 17, and 19 December, 1928, letters from G. M. Trevelyan, Paget Toynbee, R. R. Sedgwick and H. W. V. Temperley.

[26] *Memoirs from 1754 to 1758* (1821), p. 66.

[27] In the course of time these Cabinet Councils for the Speech were attached to meetings of the Privy Council. The custom of royal attendance there to give formal approval to the speech ceased in 1921. *Vide* "The End of the Nominal Cabinet," by L. B. Namier, *In the Margin of History*, pp. 105-14.

[28] *Report on MSS. in Various Collections, VI: MSS. of Capt. H. V. Knox*, pp. 263 and 272; cf. C. Grant Robertson, *England under the Hanoverians* (10th ed., 1930), appendix xiv, pp. 509-12.

[29] Keir, *op. cit.*, p. 332.

[30] *Times Lit. Supp.*, 24 March, 1945, p. 133, "Sir Robert Walpole" (no doubt by Mr. Romney Sedgwick).

[31] *Ibid.*, p. 133; cf. too *Times Lit. Supp.*, 27 March, 1930. There was a correspondence 7,13,20 and 27 March, 1930 *re* the term "Premier" in which Sir Richard Lodge took the chief share. He suggested that the absurd geographical division of duty between the two Secretaries of State created the need for the First Lord of the Treasury to have the decisive voice in foreign policy under the first two Georges. This view underestimates royal power and ignores the facts that the Northern Department was admittedly the more important Secretaryship (cf. Thomson, *Secretaries of State*, pp. 3-4) and that Walpole's ascendancy, like that of the elder Pitt after him, was the result of his powerful personality rather than of his "constitutional" position.

tive ability combined to give him domination in the Cabinet; yet he did not choose his own colleagues (though he managed by pressure in the Closet to be rid of some); in 1740 he was overruled by them;[32] and, when he went out of office, he did not take them out *en bloc* with him. Walpole was not "the first *modern* Prime Minister,"[33] a title which, probably because of its French connotation, he sturdily repudiated; but he had set the precedent, by no means immediately established or invariably adhered to, that the First Lord of the Treasury should lead the ministry. The reason was not a constitutional convention born before its time but was based upon the control which that office held of the King, gave over patronage. One clue to the future is to observe the length of life of ministries headed by commoners compared with that of the short-lived administrations led from the other House. Although Newcastle was unwilling to let his brother be "the first person on all occasions,"[34] it is evident that Henry Pelham dominated the administration for much the same reasons as Walpole had done: indeed, he did it more economically. There were "two indispensable requisites for orderly government under eighteenth century conditions—namely that the Government should be agreeable to the majority of the House of Commons and also acceptable to the King."[35] George III took some time to find a man to fill both, until at length he pitched on North as a benign bailiff for the royal business. "War can't be carried on in departments," however, and soon revealed the need (fulfilled in the Seven Years' War by the elder Pitt) for "one directing minister," a demand resisted as much by North himself (though he recognised the exigency) as by the politicians who, "hunting in small packs, were naturally averse to such a 'sole or superintending Minis-

ter.' "[36] Eventually (war sharpening the development yet again), in the person of the younger Pitt, " 'the Sole Minister' becomes 'the Prime Minister,' a recognised and integral part of the constitution, and Walpole's system is made respectable":[37] still, of course, under the King, as the latter's stand against Catholic Emancipation was to emphasise.

There is ample evidence of formal minutes of the Cabinet Council,[38] but it was scarcely to be expected that the smaller body of ministers who really did the work would keep regular minutes of their private meetings, save for their own convenience, until such sessions had come to replace (and make unnecessary) meetings—and therefore minutes—of the Cabinet Council. "From the Cabinet Council over which the King had once presided he never completely withdrew," as we have seen; but "the one person who never joined the Ministers sitting, as it were, in their shirt sleeves was the Sovereign; he never dropped out completely from the original Cabinet, but he never entered the one from which the present Cabinet is lineally descended."[39] As the position of this "Efficient Cabinet" (as it came to be called) was regularised, both the royal need for information and the ordinary demands of business required the keeping of minutes. The resultant task of sending accounts of meetings to the King in the form of Cabinet minutes appears to have devolved upon a Secretary of State. Conway, Dartmouth, Stormont and Fox

---

[32] Hervey, *Memoirs* (ed. Sedgwick, 1931), vol. III, pp. 937-40.

[33] Yet cf. Michael, *Historische Zeitschrift,* vol. CIV (1910), "Walpole als Premierminister," especially pp. 515-19.

[34] Coxe, *Pelham,* vol. I, p. 205.

[35] *Times Lit. Supp.,* 24 March, 1945, p. 134.

[36] *Ibid.,* 6 January, 1950 (commenting on Butterfield, *George III, Lord North . . . , cit. supra,* n. 5), p. 1.

[37] *Ibid.,* 24 March, 1945, p. 134.

[38] *E.g.* Temperley, *Eng. Hist. Rev.,* vol. XXVII, p. 690, n. 31, and p. 696, n. 56. When the Cabinet Council sat as a collective regency, the Lords Justices (George I's remedy for his son's eagerness to try on the crown in 1716), not only did the King require reports in Hanover but the formality of the proceedings entailed the keeping of minutes. For the Lords Justices *vide* Turner, *Eng. Hist. Rev.,* vol. XXIX, pp. 453-76, and *Cabinet Council,* vol. II, pp. 184-267.

[39] Namier, *Margin,* pp. 107-8.

seem to have done it in turn.[40] Stormont, describing in 1788 his own practice eight years before, said that he "regularly delivered to the King a copy of each minute of Cabinet."[41] The practice continued under George IV; but it would appear to have broken down when Melbourne began to brief the young Queen Victoria in more colloquial terms; and with the development of the letter from the Prime Minister to the Sovereign, formal minutes of Cabinet meetings seem to have lapsed in 1839, not to be revived until Lloyd George introduced the methods of the City into Downing Street in 1916.[42]

The political history of one generation produces the constitutional practice of its successors. Of the combination of the changes in political power and the demand by its possessors for increased and unrestricted executive efficiency, the British constitution is the distorted mirror. In their turn, royal executive expedients have gained an official sanction which, in the course of time, has atrophied their utility. The formalism and lack of elasticity with which administrative habit and general acceptance endow governmental institutions have made them in turn less adaptable to fresh circumstance and new control. From the effective, they decline into the ornamental. Their status is retained, though their function disappears. The history of the Privy Council is an example of a body whose dignity remains as its power declines. Nor was the trend confined to the Privy Council. A similar development took place within the Cabinet and, later, affected the Crown too. It may be suggested that the Parliament Act of 1911 marked a similar change in the position of the House of Lords, and that administrative technique since the First World War is likewise affecting the House of Commons. But the dating of a tendency is always

difficult, for constitutional conventions have no patentee.

In the eighteenth century, the real work of the Cabinet tended to be concentrated in the hands of a small knot of effective office-holders, whereas, for the rest, membership was merely an additional honour. Throughout the century decisions in crucial matters were taken by a few; with more, speed and secrecy were alike impossible. The distinction between the effective and nominal ministers was irregular and based on convenience, not convention. When did the division become clear, and how clear was it? The question is not whether a small group of leading ministers did the work, for that is generally admitted, but rather whether and, if so, when, there developed within, or alongside, the Cabinet Council a smaller group recognised as an organisation distinct from the formal body. Numerical tests thus cease to apply. The point is not that attendance at Cabinet meetings was small, but whether the small number attending comprised an integrated group linked to the principal offices and recognised as distinct from those whom Lady Cowper had described as "the Mob of the Cabinet" in 1720.[43]

The first Cabinet of George I had fifteen members,[44] including Marlborough, who was rarely invited, Somers, who was an invalid, and the Archbishop, who failed to attend. It showed a tendency to enlarge. Increased business demanded more officials, and membership might be retained despite loss of office. "This was a Council of State rather than an Administration."[45] The controlling agency in government under the Crown lay, therefore, in a smaller and more secret body of at least the five chief ministers: the First Lord of the Treasury, the two Secretaries of State, the Lord Chancellor, the leader of the House of Lords, and the Lord President, the link with the Privy Council. Frequently, too, we find them

[40] Turner, *Cabinet Council*, vol. II, pp. 118-9.
[41] *Hist. MSS Comm. Laing MSS.*, vol. II, p. 527; Turner, *ibid.*, vol. II, p. 124.
[42] *Vide* Lord Hankey, *Diplomacy by Conference* (1946), pp. 51-2, where the last Cabinet Minute is dated 10 May, 1839, the first letter from the Prime Minister 27 December, 1837.

[43] *Diary* (1864), p. 154; Turner, *Cabinet Council*, vol. II, p. 25.
[44] Anson, *Law and Custom*, vol. II, part i, p. 111.
[45] Namier, *Margin,* p. 107.

being joined by the First Lord of the Admiralty and the Lord Privy Seal. It is difficult to date with any certainty the beginnings of such a group and doubtful whether it was always formally separate from the Cabinet Council. Professor Temperley[46] noted the existence of a small and secret clique of ministers in 1702-3. There is a lack of clear evidence for the unbroken continuance to 1739-40 of a small and secret group of effective ministers. Private meetings of ministers were, and are, frequent. But the moment when the private meetings of the efficient Cabinet ministers were accepted as official has been long in dispute. Sir William Anson[47] dated it from the Pelham ministry. All the controversialists appear to agree[48] that it had obtained recognition by then; indeed, in the course of time, contemporaries themselves helped to clarify the question by giving a particular name, such as *conciliabulum,* to the smaller group. But dispute remains concerning meetings earlier than *c.* 1745, the date to which Professor Turner[49] tentatively assented as the earliest acceptable for a distinctive recognition of a separate body from the honorific Cabinet. In 1916 (and the date of the article is perhaps significant) Professor Temperley suggested[50] that we do not notice a *conciliabulum* under the Hanoverians until war tightened the executive again in 1739. Mr. Romney Sedgwick[51] showed clearly that there was a generally recognised body of five ministers in 1740 and 1741, meeting regularly and keeping memoranda of their proceedings, *i.e.* not just a series of informal meetings, but a small Cabinet communicating its decisions to the King, who approved of this restriction.

Pulteney had said in 1738, "We have in this kingdom several councils; we have a privy council; a cabinet council; and, for all I know, a more secret and less numerous council still, by which the other two are directed,"[52] and Hardwicke observed that the restriction of important business to a few was "the usual practice."[53] Walpole preferred this, and disliked formal Cabinet Council meetings, "for no good ever came of them."[54] But the peculiar circumstances of 1739-41, with war in Europe and the King part of the time in Hanover, may explain the formalisation of the group, in Harrington's words, of "the Lords whom the King has usually consulted in all secret affairs."[55] The Lords Justices (the Cabinet Council sitting as a collective regency in the King's absence) only ratified the decisions of this smaller and more confidential body. In 1740, "the Cabinet, unknown to law under its own name, was legalised. The inner Cabinet, not only unknown to law but unrecognised by the constitution, was regularised."[56] Their membership differed in title, size, and regularity and place of meeting. The ensuing struggle for Walpole's seat between Carteret, Pulteney and the Pelhams naturally prevented a recognised *conciliabulum,* but by 1748 we find Hardwicke echoing Harrington's phrase in alluding to "those points which the King has directed should be particularly considered by such of his servants as are consulted on the most secret affairs . . . ,"[57] and in 1750, presumably through the jealousy of the Pelhams, the group was narrowed. George II told Newcastle that Pelham and Hardwicke were "the only ministers; the others are for shew."[58]

[46] *Eng. Hist. Rev.,* vol. XXXI, pp. 293-4, but Turner (*Eng. Hist. Rev.,* vol. XXXII, p. 195) doubted whether the meetings of the "Secret Council" of 1702-3 were those of an "inner" Cabinet. There are, of course, several earlier instances of unofficial meetings of ministerial groups.

[47] *Ibid.,* vol. XXIX, p. 71.

[48] [Footnote omitted.]

[49] *American Hist. Rev.,* vol. XIX, pp. 42-3.

[50] *Eng. Hist. Rev.,* vol. XXXI, p. 295.

[51] *Ibid.,* XXXIV, pp. 290-302.

[52] *Parl. Hist.,* vol. X, p. 591; Sedgwick, *Eng. Hist. Rev.,* vol. XXXIV, p. 290.

[53] Sedgwick, *ibid.,* p. 294.

[54] *Ibid.,* p. 300.

[55] *Ibid.,* p. 291.

[56] *Ibid.,* p. 301. Mr. J. B. Owen once described this group to me as "the Closet without the King."

[57] *Bedford Correspondence,* vol. I (ed. Russell, 1842), p. 376; Turner, *Cabinet Council,* vol. II, p. 400.

[58] Coxe, *Pelham,* vol. II, p. 371; Sedgwick, p. 302.

In 1757, when Henry Fox advised a reconstruction of the ministry, Newcastle informed Hardwicke that "the Conciliabulum, that silly term, is to be the D. of Devonshire, the Duke of Bedford, Ld. Halifax, & the two Secretaries of State."[59] The practice continued under George III. "The whole cabinet would only be summoned to give a formal ratification to what had been decided by the few,"[60] and it is doubtful if even that was necessary save when "the lords of confidence" wished to spread the possible blame. With the King's approval, Grenville started weekly dinners of the confidential Cabinet in 1764.[61] The conception of an efficient Cabinet had become so accepted, despite the temporary exception of Chatham's "government by departments," that Burke was able to include the "double cabinet"[62] among his *Discontents,* and Temple could refer, four years earlier, to the titular body as "the hanging Committee,"[63] as its duties had become so perfunctory that questions of pardon were almost the only important matters with which it dealt. Yet it may be suggested that Burke was either muddled or disingenuous in his treatment of the subject,[64] for he appears to imply that the larger body was the proper Cabinet, and that "the interior Cabinet" was a collection of royal hirelings who confused and reduced the power of the principal ministers. Now it is clear that "the interior Cabinet" did, in fact, consist of the principal ministers, and this had been good Whig practice, as we have seen, under George II. Much of Whig objection to George III was due to his adaptation of their technique to his own constitutional purposes.[65] Either Burke failed to catch the trend of Cabinet development, or he was wilfully blind in his eagerness to attack "the court cabal," perhaps partly because he could hope himself only for inclusion in "the exterior Cabinet" if the Rockinghams came into office.

When did the nominal Cabinet disappear to leave membership confined to "the lords of confidence"? At the beginning of George III's reign the honorific body was so large that Horace Walpole prophesied that it was "a rank that will soon become indistinct from Privy Counsellor by growing as numerous,"[66] a comment which suggests that he noted the tendency which eluded Burke nine years later. It is noticeable that, from 1760 to 1783, the Privy Council increased in size, while the size of the Cabinet decreased, and it is reasonable to suppose that the reward of the increased dignity of titular Cabinet membership began to change to that of election to the rank of Privy Councillor. But that the nominal Cabinet did not disappear rapidly may be explained by the suggestion,[67] (which is the reverse of Burke's view) that George III used it as a lever against a *conciliabulum* with which he was dissatisfied. The difficulty is that lists of attendance are not satisfactory evidence that the right, as distinct from the practice, of attending had disappeared. The Archbishop attended as late as 1763,[68] and the Lord Lieutenant of Ireland was present in 1767. But when a later holder of that office wished to attend in 1780, Hillsborough, a Secretary of State, was instructed to inform him that it was unusual.[69]

If the effective Cabinet was confined to the leading ministers, how far and how soon was its membership functionally determined? Hervey's list of the Cabinet in 1740 states that "the Duke of Montagu, made Master of the Ordnance in place of the Duke of Argyll, became of course one of

---

[59] Temperley, *Eng. Hist. Rev.,* vol. xxvii, p. 696.

[60] Winstanley, *ibid.,* vol. xvii, pp. 680-1.

[61] Turner, *op. cit.,* vol. ii, p. 288.

[62] *Works* (*World's Classics edition*), vol. ii, p. 29.

[63] Namier, *Margin,* p. 108.

[64] [Footnote omitted.]

[65] [Footnote omitted.]

[66] *Walpole Letters* (ed. Toynbee, 1903-5), vol. v, p. 36; Anson, *Law and Custom,* vol. ii, part i, p. 112.

[67] Anson, *Eng. Hist. Rev.,* vol. xxix, p. 77.

[68] Turner, *Cabinet Council,* vol. ii, pp. 359-60. But there is no mention of his membership after 1765 (p. 88).

[69] *Ibid.,* p. 360. [Footnote 70 omitted.]

the Cabinet Council."[71] There appears, then, to have been some idea that certain offices carried with them membership at least of the nominal Cabinet, and there is a suggestion in 1755 of tenure's being linked with membership of the effective group when it is seen that Henry Fox became a Cabinet member on becoming Secretary at War in December 1754, but that he did not join the confidential Cabinet until he became Secretary of State a year later.[72] The practice is made clearer still by an instance in 1765, when Newcastle wished to become Lord Privy Seal. "To which Lord Northumberland replied, that as His Majesty had a regard for my experience, the King wished to have the Duke of Newcastle of the *Conciliabulum* where all business of consequence was first settled; which the Privy Seal was not."[73] There were still anomalies, dependent on personalities: in the next year, for example, Hardwicke, on declining the Secretaryship, yet agreed to join the "Cabinet Council with the communication of papers."[74] "Cabinet procedure was extremely informal in the days of Lord North, but became ostentatiously definite and correct in 1782 and 1783, when the King and the ministers were at arm's length."[75] Jeremy Bentham was to remember the following description of the 1782 ministry from a conversation with Shelburne when the latter was opening a despatch box ". . . there were at that time three grades of power, distinguished by appropriate denominations: the Cabinet simply; the Cabinet with the circulation; and the Cabinet with the circulation and the Post Office. By the circulation was meant the privilege of a key to the box in which the foreign despatches, with or without other documents of the day, went their rounds: by the Post Office, the power of ordering the letters of individuals to be opened at the Post Office";[76] *i.e.* the Nominal Cabinet, the Efficient Cabinet and, within the latter, the special position of the Secretaries of State.[77]

Obviously, while ambiguities persisted, notions of secrecy and collective responsibility are difficult to perceive. Moreover, so long as a majority in the House was "made" by Crown patronage, which was usually wielded by Cabinet ministers, many members of the Commons thus depended for their existence as members, in fact, if not in constitutional theory, upon the Cabinet: a situation liable to make responsibility to Parliament merely a pious hope. To suggest, too—and it has been done very often—that the King was bound to accept the advice of the ministers whom he had chosen, whose tenure was during his good pleasure and whose majority in the House was conditioned by his patronage is equally preposterous. Ministerial responsibility in the eighteenth century came to be owed politically to the Crown and legally to the Courts, especially to the House of Lords, for impeachment had not yet rusted into disuse. Continuance in office entailed consideration of royal wishes and, before Indemnity Acts had become a routine, it was advisable to keep on the weather side of the law, which did not recognise the existence of the Cabinet as such. Responsible government, as we know it, was impossible before the Reform Act, and it was still a very far cry, as the American war showed, to the conceptions of the Durham Report. The doctrine of "the separation of powers," which was never political practice, still misled those seeking the underlying secret of the constitution. Cabinet government in England was not a self-conscious development: constitutional theory, as usual, lagged behind empiricist politics, and the motor of the constitution generally evaded the contemporary commentator. Responsible government, in Durham's sense,

[71] *Memoirs,* vol. III, p. 925.
[72] Anson, *Eng. Hist. Rev.,* vol. XXIX, p. 73.
[73] *A Narrative of the Changes in the Ministry, 1765-1767* (Camden Society, new series, vol. LIX, 1898, ed. Bateson), Newcastle to White, p. 7.
[74] *Rockingham Memoirs* (ed. Albemarle, 1852), vol. I, pp. 330-1; Anson, *Law and Custom,* vol. II, part i, p. 113.
[75] Pares, *op. cit.,* p. 138.

[76] *Works* (1843), vol. IX, p. 218, n. *a.*
[77] Cf. Thomson, *Secretaries,* pp. 153-5.

was alien to an age of senatorial government, and the notion of responsibility to
Parliament would receive little countenance
so long as the King regarded his ministers
as individually answerable to himself and
was touchy about "desertions." From the
point of view of the ministers, responsibility meant "something different from
what it means to us. To them it meant legal
responsibility, liability to impeachment: to
us, it means responsibility to public opinion,
liability to loss of office."[78] Merely honorary
members of the Cabinet were not to be held
liable for the actions of the effective ministers, and in 1741, for example, Henry Pelham advised his brother, who disapproved of
Hanoverian neutrality, to leave what he
had called "the active part of the administration," and to retreat from responsibility
into temporarily nominal membership.[79]
Again, in 1775, Mansfield disclaimed all
responsibility for the colonial mismanage-
ment, because he had ceased to be a member of the efficient Cabinet since the close
of the Grenville ministry.[80] We may date
the disappearance of this difficulty and the
definite limitation of the Cabinet, from
Addington's check to Loughborough in
1801, "though it probably did no more than
express the usage of the previous twenty
years."[81] In 1801 Eldon became Lord Chancellor in Loughborough's stead, but the
latter continued to attend Cabinet meetings,
perhaps as a royal spy. Addington informed
him that his appearance was no longer desirable, and that "the members of the Cabinet should not exceed that of the persons
whose responsible situations in office require
their being members of it."[82]

One must expect collective responsibility
—if recognised at all—to have been confined to the efficient Cabinet. Yet, in the
Grafton administration, for example, the
public dissension of the ministers made
collective responsibility a dubious doctrine
even there; although, because of Chatham's
illness, this was, of course, a peculiar ministry.[83] War deepened the solidarity of ministries and, by 1779, we find "every expedition" being described as "the result of the
collective wisdom of all his Majesty's confidential ministers" and the First Lord of
the Admiralty being regarded as "in no
situation . . . more or less responsible to
his country than his colleagues for any
misconduct which flows from a Cabinet
measure."[84] As late as 1806, however, as
Ellenborough's case showed, the notion of
corporate responsibility was still not accepted. Chief Justice of the King's Bench,
he accepted a seat in the Cabinet, and it was
suggested that he might thus be judge in the
Cabinet's cause. The Government view was
that responsibility was individual, not collective, and Anson noted the survival of this
conception of individual and legal, as distinct from collective and parliamentary, responsibility as late as 1827 in Hallam.[85]

Few ministries in the eighteenth century
were homogeneous in policy, however well
they may have combined for administrative purposes. Usually they were comprised
of coalitions of "connexions"; and the disciplines of party in the modern sense or of
parliamentary defeat played little part, although regimentation from above, by a
Walpole or a George III, might give a
veneer of integration. From Newcastle's fall,
George III's Cabinets represented a series
of royal attempts to find an administrative
group to the King's liking: with much stress
on 'the independency of the Crown' in the
choice of ministers. "By trying to foist Bute
into the inner political circle . . . , George
III began to create the belief that he was

---

[78] Anson, *Law and Custom,* vol. II, part i,
p. 118.
[79] Coxe, *Pelham,* vol. I, pp. 21-6; Sedgwick,
Eng. Hist. Rev., vol. XXXIV, pp. 301-2.
[80] Anson, *op. cit.,* vol. II, part i, p. 114.
[81] *Ibid.,* p. 116.
[82] Campbell, *Lives of the Chancellors*
(1847), vol. VI, p. 327; Anson, *ibid.,* p. 116.

[83] Anson, *ibid.,* p. 117. *Vide,* especially, Grafton's *Autobiography* (ed. Anson, 1898), pp.
126-7 (a passage to which Mr. Giles Alington
kindly drew my attention) and pp. 229-30.
[84] *Sandwich Papers* (Navy Records Society)
vol. II (ed. G. R. Barnes and J. H. Owen, 1933),
p. 255, cited by Mr. C. T. Atkinson; Keir,
op. cit., p. 382.
[85] *Op. cit.,* p. 118.

. . . returning to the practices of the Stuarts. George III and Bute were not ignorant of these feelings, but expressly denied their validity; and in doing so," says Professor Pares, "they were committing a slight anachronism. After all the water that had run under the bridges since 1688 it was hardly commonsense, when talking of . . . a First Lord of the Treasury, to say that it was a question whether his Majesty was to exercise 'the liberty that his poorest subject enjoys, of choosing his own menial servants.' "[86] The King's undoubtedly constitutional powers had to face political realities (as Charles I's had had to do). There is no evidence of royal attendance at meetings of the efficient Cabinet. Nor, from the origin and nature of that body, was that to be expected; but its results are important. We know that, time aiding utility, the *conciliabulum* grew to be the chief effective and constitutional executive organ: the efficient (and the only) Cabinet. This meant that George III was unable to gather to himself all the powers which, for example, William III had possessed, and tried instead to find royal henchmen to control or to spy on the efficient Cabinet for him. The period from Bute's entrance in 1760-1 to Loughborough's decisive expulsion in 1801 was thus the testing-time for the new executive body. And it is here that the younger Pitt's career becomes so important in constitutional development. True, he did not fulfil all the criteria of a modern Prime Minister. None before 1832 could. But his period of office tilted the scale away from royal power. Habitual royal interference in the efficient Cabinet began to disappear. So, as a distinct body, did the nominal Cabinet Council.[87] The waning of the "influence" of the Crown between 1780 and 1832, "by a long train of legislation, administrative reform and changed attitudes in public life,"[88] was one

factor in weakening royal control. The King's illness was another. "I must decline entering into a pressure of business," he came to tell Pitt in 1789, "and indeed for the rest of my life shall expect others to fulfill the Duties of their Employments and only keep that superintending Eye which can be effected without labour or fatigue."[89] He continued to interfere, but his former control was slipping.[90] On two issues, of course, he was beyond persuasion: his hatred of Charles James Fox and of Catholic Emancipation. From 1801 Emancipation was a disturbing under-current working against the homogeneity of ministries; and the Irish Question had begun its long career (which lasted till 1922) as the catalyst of the decomposition of English Cabinets.

Three changes in the working of the Cabinet in the last quarter of the century strengthened Pitt's position. The limitation of Cabinets to their efficient members concentrated power. Membership was increasingly connected with the active administration of the departments of government, the latter themselves, however, still resisting (for many years to come, with success) what was to become "Treasury control." The squeezing of the King from effective and regular control of *policy* opened the way for ministerial leadership instead. Significant of the change was Pitt's remark to Melville in 1803 that it was "an absolute necessity . . . that there should be an avowed and real Minister possessing the chief weight in the Council and the principal place in the confidence of the King."[91] A test case had arisen in 1792, when Thurlow, the Lord

---

[86] Pares, *op. cit.*, p. 141.
[87] *Vide* a joint note by the late Professor Temperley and myself, *History*, new series, vol. XXII (1938), p. 334.
[88] Foord, *Eng. Hist. Rev.*, vol. LXII, p. 506. "Influence" had a specialised meaning in the eighteenth century: it referred to those "instru-

ments of persuasion" by which the King (or his ministers) could oblige supporters and maintain a Parliamentary majority; and not to royal *power*. Dunning's famous motion of 1780 can be understood only in terms of this technical connotation.
[89] *Pitt Papers* (Public Record Office), 23 February, 1789, a passage to which Professor V. T. Harlow kindly drew my attention.
[90] But cf. D. G. Barnes, *George III and William Pitt, 1783-1806* (1939), *passim*.
[91] Stanhope, *Pitt*, vol. IV (1862) p. 24; Anson, *Eng. Hist. Rev.*, vol. XXIX, p. 67. Politicians who had learned their trade before 1832

Chancellor, opposed a Government measure in the Lords. When Pitt turned to the King, George instructed Dundas to inform Thurlow that, having to decide between him and Pitt, he preferred Pitt.[92] What probably clinched the issue was the usual Hanoverian fear of the heir-apparent with whom the King believed Thurlow to have been intriguing; and George III was grateful to Pitt for his stand in the Regency crisis of 1788. The immense increase in the volume of public business which war produced was decisive. It was one matter "to preside over the belfry quarrels of the connexions"[93]; it was quite another for a sick man to try to control British policy in a European war. "The younger Pitt, silently and decorously, but quite firmly and plainly, transferred the greater part of the royal authority to the Cabinet."[94] "In 1783 it was likely that the King's view would prevail in a question not covered by any previous engagement; in 1806, more likely the Cabinet's."[95]

In the attempt to clarify, it is important not to appear to codify the development of the Cabinet in neat and tidy stages. Were this fragmentary collation of other men's researches to seem to do that, it would be ungrateful to their learning. The executive

in the eighteenth century, as in any other century, was what weak, ordinary or masterful men made it (or got away with) in the circumstances, peace and war, in which they found themselves at the time. The English Cabinet did not fall into a fixed pattern at any particular date in the century; "its composition was extremely elastic and pragmatic and curious hybrid forms were developed at times."[96] It was a peculiarly domestic product: and so, throughout its protean existence, it has remained.

The essence of Cabinet government, as we have come to know it in England, had not been secured by the end of the eighteenth century; nor, indeed, by 1832. We may, however, trace its silhouette, from the turn of the century until the Reform Act, in four incomplete trends: (i) the gradual expulsion of the Crown from *control of policy*, although the King, as 1827 showed especially, remained an active politician;[97] (ii) the resultant development of the idea of a Prime Minister which Pitt's personal dominance had strengthened and which Liverpool's gentler but undoubted control assisted; (iii) the growth of a functional Cabinet which directed a civil service itself growing sturdily further away from both its Household origins and its Parliamentary places; and (iv) the increase of ministerial responsibility, not yet confessedly collective, to the Commons, a House still far from reflecting either a coherent party system or a popular electorate.

(Peel, for example) required some time thereafter before realising that "the confidence of the Crown" had ceased to be the political necessity it had been during their apprenticeship.

[92] Stanhope, *Pitt,* vol. II (1861) pp. 148-50; Anson, *Law and Custom,* vol. II, part i, pp. 137-8.

[93] A phrase used to me by the late Professor G. S. Veitch, who fathered the first version of this essay in 1936.

[94] G. M. Young, "Government," in *Last Essays* (1950), p. 172.

[95] Pares, *op. cit.,* p. 149.

[96] Namier (who knows more about it than anyone else), *Margin,* p. 107.

[97] *Vide* A. Aspinall, *The Formation of Canning's Ministry* (Camden Society, third series, vol. LIX, 1937) and *Letters of George IV, passim.*

THE AGE OF THE SEVEN YEARS' WAR WAS one of almost unbelievable glory in the history of the British Empire—a period when Horace Walpole could understandably proclaim: "I shall burn my Greek and Latin books. They are the histories of little people. We subdue the globe in three campaigns, and a globe as big again as it was in their days." But a dozen years after the conclusion of this great war for empire the *Annual Register* of 1775 could point out that "it is no longer our task to describe devastation in Poland or slaughter on the Danube. The evil is at home." The debate over the causes of the American Revolution has, of course, often been heated. It got under way before the colonies declared their independence, and it has continued through the present time. Two of the most popular of the interpretations were set forth in the course of the crisis by Edmund Burke and Adam Smith, respectively. Burke emphasized Parliamentary taxation of the colonies as the major cause of the Revolution; Smith concentrated above all on colonial opposition to British mercantilism. And many other forces and factors—political, constitutional, and military—have been emphasized through the decades. One of the most thoughtful attempts to explore the origins of American secession from the Old British Empire was made by the late Professor Charles M. Andrews, of Yale University, in his presidential address before the American Historical Association. A master of historical research, Professor Andrews did much to reorient the study and writing of American colonial history; and if the colonial era is no longer viewed by historians as a mere prelude to the War of Independence, the responsibility lies in no small measure with him.

THE AMERICAN REVOLUTION: AN INTERPRETATION

CHARLES M. ANDREWS

You will not, I trust, take it amiss if, on this the occasion of our annual meeting, I select as my topic the familiar subject of the American Revolution. Quite apart from the pleasure that comes from harping on an old string, there is the conviction, which I hold very strongly, that no matter how familiar a subject may be, it can always be re-examined with profit and viewed not infrequently from such points of vantage as to set the scene in quite a new light. The writing of history is always a progressive process, not merely or mainly because each age must write its own history from its own point of view, but rather because each generation of scholars is certain to contribute to historical knowledge and so to approach nearer than its predecessor to an understanding of the past. No one can accept as complete or final any rendering of history, no matter how plausible it may be, nor consider any period or phase of the past as closed against further

investigation. Our knowledge of history is and always will be in the making, and it has been well said that orthodox history and an orthodox historian involve a contradiction in terms.

The explanations of history have been characterized as a rule by overmuch simplicity. So wrote Maitland of the history of England and so with equal justice might he have written of the history of America. As with natural phenomena in the pre-Copernican days of celestial mechanics, when the world believed that the sun moved and the earth was flat, so it has been at all times, with historical phenomena, that what to the superficial observer has appeared to be true has been accepted far too often as containing the whole truth. Among these pre-Copernican convictions, for example, widely held in America to-day, is the belief that the American Revolution was brought about by British tyranny. Whatever explana-

Reprinted by special permission from *The American Historical Review*, XXXI (1926), 219–232.

tion of that great event comes to be accepted by competent historians and their intelligent readers as a near approach to the truth, it is quite certain that it will not be anything as easy and simple as all that. There was nothing simple about the Balance of Power or the Balance of Trade, even when construed in terms of such vulgar commodities as fish, furs, and molasses, and particularly when one must give due consideration to the doctrine, as seriously held in some quarters to-day as it was in the eighteenth century, that colonial possessions are the natural sources for home industries. Our history before 1783 was a much more complex and cosmopolitan affair than older writers would have us believe, for they have failed to account for many deep-lying and almost invisible factors and forces which influence and often determine human action and are always elusive and difficult to comprehend.

Recent writers have approached the subject with a full recognition of the complexity of the problems involved. They have found many and varied conflicting activities making for disagreement and misunderstanding between the mother country and her offspring, giving rise to impulses and convictions, ideas and practices, that were difficult, if not impossible, of reconciliation. Such scholars have expressed their conclusions in many different forms. Some have seen a struggle between two opposing historical tendencies—one imperialistic and expansive, the other domestic and intensive; others, a clash of ideas regarding the constitution of the British empire and the place that a colony should occupy in its relations with the mother country. Some have stressed the differences that were bound to arise between an old and settled country and one that was not only dominated by the ideas and habits of the frontier, but was opposed also to the continued supremacy of a governing authority three thousand miles away. Others have explained the situation in terms of an antagonism between the law and institutions of England and those, growing constantly more divergent, of the Puritan and non-Puritan colonies in America. All of these explanations are sound, because they are based on an understanding of the deeper issues involved; and taken together, they are illuminating in that they enable the reader to broaden his point of view, and to break away from the endless controversies over immediate causes and war guilt that have hitherto tended to dominate the American mind.

But elucidating as these explanations are, no one of them seems quite sufficient to resolve so complex a subject as the causes of the American Revolution. To-day we conjure with such words as evolution and psychology, and look for explanations of acts on the part of both individuals and groups in states of mind produced by inheritance and environment. Fielding, acknowledged expert in the study of human experience, can say that for a man "to act in direct contradiction to the dictates of his nature is, if not impossible, as improbable as anything which can well be conceived." The philosophers tell us that mind can be more resistant even than matter, and that it is easier to remove mountains than it is to change the ideas of a people. That the impact of convictions is one of the most frequent causes of revolution we must acknowledge; and I believe that we have not considered sufficiently the importance of this fact in determining the relations of England with colonial America. If I may, by way of illustrating my point, I should like to show that certain differences existing between England and her colonies in mental attitudes and convictions proved in the end more difficult to overcome than the diverging historical tendencies or the bridging the three thousand miles of the Atlantic itself.

The American Revolution marks the close of one great period of our history and the beginning of another of even greater significance. It is the red line across our years, because by it was brought about a fundamental change in the status of the communities on the American seaboard—a change from dependence to independence. We sometimes hear that revolutions are not made but happen. In their immediate causes this is not true—for revolutions do not happen, they are made, in that they are the creatures of propaganda and manipulation. But, in reality, revolutions are not made. They are the detonations of explosive materials, long accumulating and often long dormant. They are the resultants of a vast complex of economic, political, social, and legal forces, which taken collectively are the masters, not the servants, of statesmen and political agitators. They are never sudden in their origin, but look back to influences long in the making; and it is the business of the modern student of the subject to discover those remoter causes and to examine thoroughly and with an open mind the history, institutions, and mental past of the parties to the conflict. In pursuit of my purpose let me call to your attention certain aspects of that most important of all periods of our early history, the years from 1713 to 1775.

The middle period of the eighteenth century in England, resembling in some respects the mid-Victorian era of the next century, was intellectually, socially, and institutionally in a state of stable equilibrium. The impulses of the Revolution of 1689 had spent their force. English thought and life were tending to become formal, conventional, and artificial, and the English mind was acquiring the fatal habit of closing against novelty and change. The most enlightened men of the day regarded the existing order as the best that could be conceived, and in the main were content to let well enough alone. Those who held the reins of power were comfortable and irresponsible, steeped in their "old vulgar prejudices," and addicted to habits and modes of living that were approved by age and precedent. The miseries of the poor were accepted as due to inherent viciousness; class distinctions were sharply marked, and social relations were cast in a rigid mould; while, as far as the mass of the poor was concerned, the vagrancy laws and the narrow policy of the corporate towns made free movement in any direction practically impossible. Life at large was characterized by brutality and a widespread

sense of insecurity. Little thought was given to the education of the poor, the diseases of poverty and dirt, the baneful effects of overcrowding in the towns, or the corrupting influence of life in tenements and cellars. Excessive drinking and habitual resort to violence in human relations prevailed in urban sections; and while it is probably true that in rural districts, where life was simple and medieval, there was greater comfort and peace and less barbarity and coarseness, nevertheless, it is equally true that the scenes of English country life in the eighteenth century, that have come down to us in literature and painting, are more often conventional than real. Vested interests and the rights of property were deemed of greater importance than the rights of humanity, and society clung tenaciously to the old safeguards and defenses that checked the inrush of new ideas. There was a great absence of interest in technical invention and improvement. Because the landed classes were in the ascendant, agriculture was the only national interest receiving attention—drainage, rotation of crops, and the treatment of the soil being the only practical activities that attracted capital. The concerns and welfare of those without the right to vote were largely ignored; and it is no mere coincidence that the waste of human life, which was at its worst in London between 1720 and 1750, with the population of England declining during that period, should not have been checked until after 1780. The age was not one of progress in government, social organization, or humanitarianism; and it is important to note that the reconstruction of English manners and ways of living, and the movement leading to the diminution of crime, to sanitation, the greater abundance of food, and amelioration of living conditions—particularly in the towns and among the poorer classes—came after, and not before, the American Revolution.

The state of mind, to which were due the conditions thus described, permeated all phases of British life and government, and determined the attitude of the ruling classes toward the political, as well as the social, order. These classes were composed in a preponderant degree of landed proprietors, whose feeling of feudal superiority and tenacious adherence to the ideas and traditions of their class were determining factors in political life both in Parliament and the country. They believed that their institutions provided a sufficient panacea for all constitutional ills and could not imagine wherein these institutions needed serious revision. They were convinced that the existing system preserved men's liberties better than any that had gone before, and they wanted no experiments or dangerous leaps in the dark. They not only held as a tenet of faith that those who owned the land should wield political power, but they were certain that such an arrangement had the sanction of God. They revered the British system of government, its principles and philosophy, as the embodiment of human wisdom, grounded in righteousness and destined by nature to serve the purpose of man. They saw it admired abroad as the most enlightened government possessed by any nation in the world, and so credited it with their unprecedented prosperity and influence as a nation. They likened its critics to Milton's Lucifer, attacking "the sacred and immovable mount of the whole constitution," as a contemporary phrased it, and they guarded it as the Israelites guarded the ark of the covenant. Woe to him who would defile it!

Nor were they any less rigid in their attitude toward the colonies in America. Colonial policy had developed very slowly and did not take on systematic form until well on in the eighteenth century; but when once it became defined, the ruling classes regarded it in certain fundamental aspects—at least in official utterance—as fixed as was the constitution itself. At first England did not take her colonies seriously as assets of commercial importance, but when after 1704 naval stores were added to the tobacco and sugar of Virginia and the West Indies, and it was seen that these commodities enabled England to obtain a favorable balance of trade with European countries, the value of the plantations in British eyes increased enormously. However, it was not until after 1750, when a favorable balance of trade was reached with the colonies themselves, that the mercantilist deemed the situation entirely satisfactory; and from that time on for twenty years—epochal years in the history of England's relations with America—the mercantilist idea of the place that a colony should occupy in the British scheme of things became fixed and unalterable. Though the colonies were growing by leaps and bounds, the authorities in Great Britain retained unchanged the policy which had been adopted more than half a century before. They did not essentially alter the instructions to the Board of Trade in all the eighty-six years of its existence. They created no true colonial secretary, even in 1768, and no department of any kind at any time for the exclusive oversight of American affairs. They saw no necessity for adopting new methods of managing colonial trade, even though the colonial situation was constantly presenting new problems for solution. Manufacturing was undoubtedly more discouraged in 1770 than it had been in 1699, when the first restrictive act was passed; and the idea that the colonies by their very nature were ordained to occupy a position of commercial dependence to the advantage and profit of the mother country was never more firmly fixed in the British mind than just before our Revolution. In fact, that event altered in no essential particular the British conception of the status of a colony, for as late as 1823, Sir Charles Ellis, undoubtedly voicing the opinion of his day, could say in Parliament that the colonial system of England had not been established for the sake of the colonies, but for the encouragement of British trade and manufactures. Thus for more than a century England's idea of what a colony should be underwent no important alteration whatever.

Equally unchangeable was the British idea of how a colony should be governed. In the long list of commissions and instructions drawn up in England for the guidance of the royal governors in America, there is to be found, with one exception only, nothing that indicates any progressive advance in the spirit and method of administration from 1696 to 1782. Year after year, the same arrangements and phraseology appear, conforming to a common type, admitting, it is true, important modifications in matters of detail, but in principle undergoing at no time in eighty-six years serious revision or reconstruction. These documents were drawn up in Whitehall according to a fixed pattern; the governors and councils were allowed no discretion; the popular assemblies were confined within the narrow bounds of inelastic formulae, which repeated, time after time, the same injunctions and the same commands; while the crown reserved to itself the full right of interference in all matters that were construed as coming under its prerogative. These instructions represented the rigid eighteenth-century idea of how a colony should be retained in dependence on the mother country. And what was true of the instructions was true of other documents also that had to do with America. For instance, the lists of queries to the governors, the questionnaires to the commodore-governors of the Newfoundland fishery, and the whole routine business of the fishery itself had become a matter of form and precedent, as conventional and stereotyped as were the polite phrases of eighteenth-century social intercourse. Rarely was any attempt made to adapt these instructions to the needs of growing communities such as the colonies were showing themselves to be; and only with the Quebec instructions of 1775, issued after the passage of the Quebec Act and under the guidance of a colonial governor of unusual commonsense, was there any recognition of a new colonial situation. In this document, which appeared at the very end of our colonial period, do we find something of a break from the stiff and legalistic forms that were customary in the earlier royal instructions, some appreciation of the fact that the time was approaching when a colony should be treated with greater liberality and be allowed to have some part in saying how it should be administered.

Without going further with our analysis we can say that during the half-century preceding our Revolution English habits of thought and methods of administration and government, both at home and in the colonies, had reached a state of immobility. To all appearances the current of the national life had settled into a backwater, and as far as home affairs were concerned was seemingly becoming stagnant. At a time when Pitt was breaking France by land and sea, and men on waking were asking what new territories had been added during the night to the British dominions, occurrences at home were barren of adventure, either in society or politics. Ministers were not true statesmen; they had no policies, no future hopes, no spirit of advance, no gifts of foresight or prophecy. In all that concerned domestic interests, they were impervious to suggestions, even when phrased in the eloquence of Pitt and Burke. They wanted no change in existing conditions; their eyes were fixed on traditions and precedents rather than on the obligations and opportunities of the future. Their tenure of office was characterized by inactivity, a casual handling of situations they did not understand and could not control, and a willingness to let the ship of state drift for itself. As a modern critic has said, they were always turning in an unending circle, one out, one in, one in, one out, marking time and never going forward.

To a considerable extent the narrow point of view and rigidity of attitude exhibited by the men who held office at Whitehall or sat in Parliament at Westminster can be explained by the fact that at this time officials and members of Parliament were also territorial magnates, lords of manors, and country squires, who were influenced in their political life by ideas that governed their relations with their tenantry and the management of their landed estates. It is not necessary to think of them as bought by king or ministers and so bound and gagged against freedom of parliamentary action. In fact, they were bound and gagged already by devotion to their feudal privileges, their family prerogatives, and their pride of landed proprietorship. They viewed the colonies somewhat in the light of tenancies of the crown, and as they themselves lived on the rents from their estates, so they believed that the king and the kingdom should profit from the revenues and returns from America. The point of view was somewhat that of a later Duke of Newcastle, who when reproached for compelling his tenants to vote as he pleased said that he had a right to do as he liked with his own. This landed aristocracy reflected the eighteenth-century spirit. It was sonorous, conventional, and self-satisfied, and shameless of sparkle or humor. It clung to the laws of inheritance and property, fearful of anything that might in any way offend the shades of past generations. In its criticism of the manners of others it was insular and arrogant, and was mentally so impenetrable as never to understand why any one, even in the colonies, should wish things to be other than they were or refuse to accept the station of life to which by Providence he had been called.

A government, representative of a privileged social and political order that took existing conditions as a matter of course, setting nature at defiance and depending wholly on art, was bound sooner or later to come into conflict with a people, whose life in America was in closest touch with nature and characterized by growth and change and constant readjustments. In that country were groups of men, women, and children, the greater portion of whom were of English ancestry, numbering at first a few hundreds and eventually more than two millions, who were scattered over many miles of continent and island and were living under various forms of government. These people, more or less unconsciously, under the influence of new surroundings and imperative needs, were establishing a new order of society and laying the foundations of a new political system. The story of how this was done—how that which was

English slowly and imperceptibly merged into that which was American—has never been adequately told; but it is a fascinating phase of history, more interesting and enlightening when studied against the English background than when construed as an American problem only. It is the story of the gradual elimination of those elements, feudal and proprietary, that were foreign to the normal life of a frontier land, and of the gradual adjustment of the colonists to the restraints and restrictions that were imposed upon them by the commercial policy of the mother country. It is the story also of the growth of the colonial assemblies and of the education and experience that the colonists were receiving in the art of political self-government. It is above all—and no phase of colonial history is of greater significance—the story of the gradual transformation of these assemblies from the provincial councils that the home government intended them to be into miniature parliaments. At the end of a long struggle with the prerogative and other forms of outside interference, they emerged powerful legislative bodies, as self-conscious in their way as the House of Commons in England was becoming during the same eventful years.

Here was an *impasse,* for the British view that a colonial assembly partook of the character of a provincial or municipal council was never actually true of any assembly in British America at any time. in its history. From the beginning, each of these colonial bodies, in varying ways and under varying circumstances, assumed a position of leadership in its colony, and exercised, in a manner often as bewildering to the student of to-day as to an eighteenth-century royal governor, a great variety of executive, legislative, and judicial functions. Except in Connecticut and Rhode Island, requests for parliamentary privileges were made very early and were granted year after year by the governors—privileges that were essentially those of the English and Irish Houses of Commons and were consciously modelled after them. At times, the assemblies went beyond Parliament and made claims additional to the usual speaker's requests, claims first asked for as matters of favor but soon demanded as matters of right, as belonging to representative bodies and not acquired by royal gift or favor. One gets the impression that though the assemblies rarely failed to make the formal request, they did so with the intention of taking in any case what they asked for and anything more that they could secure. Gradually, with respect to privileges, they advanced to a position of amazing independence, freeing themselves step by step from the interfering power of the executive, that is, of the royal prerogative. They began to talk of these rights as ancient and inherent and necessary to the orderly existence of any representative body, and they became increasingly self-assertive and determined as the years passed.

Nor was this the only change affecting the assemblies to which the eighteenth-century Englishman was asked to adapt himself. The attitude of the assemblies in America found expression in the exercise of powers that had their origin in other sources than that of parliamentary privilege. They adopted rules of their own that were sometimes even more severe than those of Parliament itself. They regulated membership, conduct, and procedure; ruled against drinking, smoking, and profanity, against unseemly, unnecessary, and tedious debate, against absence, tardiness, and other forms of evasion. They punished with great severity all infringement of rules and acts of contempt, and defended their right to do so against the governor and council on one side and the courts of the colony on the other. Nor did they even pretend to be consistent in their opposition to the royal prerogative, as expressed in the instructions to the royal governors, and in their manœuvres they did not follow any uniform policy or plan. They conformed to these instructions willingly enough, whenever it was agreeable for them to do so; but if at any time they considered an instruction contrary to the best interest of a particular colony, they did not hesitate to oppose it directly or to nullify

it by avoidance. In general, it may be said that they evaded or warded off or deliberately disobeyed such instructions as they did not like. Thus both consciously and unconsciously they were carving out a *lex parliamenti* of their own, which, evolving naturally from the necessity of meeting the demands of self-governing communities, carried them beyond the bounds of their own membership and made them responsible for the welfare of the colony at large.

The important point to remember is that the plan of governmental control as laid down in England was never in accord with the actual situation in America; that the Privy Council, the Secretary of State, and the Board of Trade seem not to have realized that their system of colonial administration was breaking down at every point. Their minds ran in a fixed groove and they could construe the instances of colonial disobedience and aggression, which they often noted, in no other terms than those of persistent dereliction of duty. Either they did not see or else refused to see the wide divergence that was taking place between colonial administration as they planned it and colonial administration as the colonists were working it out. Englishmen saw in the American claims an attack upon an old, established, and approved system. They interpreted the attitude of the colonists as something radical and revolutionary, menacing British prosperity, British political integrity, and the British scheme of colonial government. Opposed by tradition and conviction to new experiments, even at home, they were unable to sympathize with, or even to understand, the great experiment, one of the greatest in the world's history, on trial across the sea. There in America was evolving a new idea of sovereignty, inherent not in crown and Parliament but in the people of a state, based on the principle—self-evident it may be to us to-day but not to the Englishman of the eighteenth century—that governments derive their just powers from the consent of the governed. There was emerging a new idea of the franchise, as a natural right, under certain conditions, of every adult citizen, an idea which theoretically is not even yet accepted in Great Britain. There was being established a new order of society, without caste or privilege, free from economic restrictions and social demarcations between class and class. There was taking shape a new idea of a colony, a self-governing dominion, the members of which were competent to develop along their own lines, while working together with the mother country as part of a common state.

For us to-day with out perspective it is easy to see the conflict approaching and some of us may think perhaps that the British ministers and members of Parliament ought to have realized that their own ideas and systems were fast outgrowing their usefulness even for Great Britain herself; and that their inflexible views of the colonial relationship were fast leading to disaster. Yet we must keep in mind that it is always extraordinarily difficult for a generation reared in the environment of modern democracy to deal sympathetically with the Englishman's point of view in the eighteenth century, or to understand why the ruling classes of that day so strenuously opposed the advance of liberalism both in England and America. The fact remains, however, that the privileged and governing classes in England saw none of these things. They were too close to events and too much a part of them to judge them dispassionately or to appreciate their real significance. These classes, within which we may well include the Loyalists in America, were possessed of inherited instincts, sentiments, and prejudices which they could no more change than they could have changed the color of their eyes or the texture of their skins. That which existed in government and society was to them a part of the fixed scheme of nature, and no more called for reconsideration than did the rising of the sun or the budding of the trees in spring. If Lord North had granted the claims of the colonists he probably would have been looked on by Parliament as having betrayed the constitution and impaired its stability, just as Peel was pilloried by a similar landowning Parliament in 1845, when he advocated the repeal of the corn laws. One has only to read the later debates on the subject of enclosures and the corn laws to understand the attitude of the British landowners toward the colonies from 1763 to 1776. To them in each instance it seemed as if the foundations of the universe were breaking up and the world in which they lived was sinking beneath their feet.

Primarily, the American Revolution was a political and constitutional movement and only secondarily one that was either financial, commercial, or social. At bottom the fundamental issue was the political independence of the colonies, and in the last analysis the conflict lay between the British Parliament and the colonial assemblies, each of which was probably more sensitive, self-conscious, and self-important than was the voting population that it represented. For many years these assemblies had fought the prerogative successfully and would have continued to do so, eventually reducing it to a minimum, as the later self-governing dominions have done; but in the end it was Parliament, whose powers they disputed, that became the great antagonist. Canning saw the situation clearly when, half a century later, he spoke of the Revolution as having been a test of the equality of strength "between the legislature of this mighty kingdom . . . and the colonial assemblies," adding further that he had no intention of repeating in the case of Jamaica, the colony then under debate, the mistakes that had been made in 1776. Of the mistakes to which he referred the greatest was the employment of the deadly expedient of coercion, and he showed his greater wisdom when he determined, as he said, to keep back "within the penetralia of the constitution the transcendental powers of Parliament over a dependency of the British crown" and not "to produce it upon trifling occasions or in cases of petty refractoriness and temporary misconduct." How he would have met the revolution in America, based as it was on "the fundamental principles of political liberty," we cannot say; but we know that he had no sympathy with any attempt to force opinion back into paths that were outworn. That he would have foreseen the solution of a later date and have granted the colonies absolute and responsible self-government, recognizing the equality of the assemblies in domestic matters and giving them the same control over their home affairs as the people of Great Britain had over theirs, can be conjectured only by inference from his liberal attitude toward the South American republics. He stood half-way between the ministers of the Revolutionary period—blind, sensitive, and mentally unprogressive—and the statesmen of the middle of the nineteenth century, who were willing to follow the lead of those courageous and far-sighted Englishmen who saved the empire from a second catastrophe after 1830 and were the founders of the British colonial policy of to-day.

The revolt of the colonies from Great Britain began long before the battles of Moore's Creek Bridge and Lexington; before the time of James Otis and the writs of assistance; before the dispute over the appointment of judges in North Carolina and New York; before the eloquence of Patrick Henry was first heard in the land; and even before the quarrel in Virginia over the Dinwiddie pistole fee. These were but the outward and visible signs of an inward and factual divergence. The separation from the mother country began just as soon as the mercantile system of commercial control, the governmental system of colonial administration, and the whole doctrine of the inferior status of a colonial assembly began to give way before the pressure exerted and the disruptive power exercised by these young and growing colonial communities. New soil had produced new wants, new desires, new points of view, and the colonists were demanding the right to live their own lives in their own way. As we see it to-day the situation was a dramatic one. On one side was the immutable, stereotyped system of the mother country, based on precedent and tradition and designed to keep things comfortably as they were; on the other, a vital, dynamic organism, containing the seed of a great nation, its forces untried, still to be proved. It is inconceivable that a connection should have continued long between two such yokefellows, one static, the other dynamic, separated by an ocean and bound only by the ties of a legal relationship.

If my diagnosis is correct of the British state of mind in the eighteenth century, and the evidence in its favor seems overwhelming, then the colonists were as justified in their movement of revolt as were the Englishmen themselves in their movement for reform in the next century. Yet in reality no great progressive movement needs justification at our hands, for great causes justify themselves and time renders the decision. The revolt in America and the later reforms in Great Britain herself were directed against the same dominant ruling class that in their colonial relations as well as in their social and political arrangements at home preferred that the world in which they lived should remain as it was. Reform or revolt is bound to follow attempts of a privileged class to conduct affairs according to unchanging rules and formulae. The colonies had developed a constitutional organization equally complete with Britain's own and one that in principle was far in advance of the British system, and they were qualified to co-operate with the mother country on terms similar to those of a brotherhood of free nations such as the British world is becoming to-day. But England was unable to see this fact or unwilling to recognize it, and consequently America became the scene of a political unrest, which might have been controlled by compromise, but was turned to revolt by coercion. The situation is a very interesting one, for England is famous for her ability to compromise at critical moments in her history. For once at least she failed. In 1832 and later years, when she faced other great constitutional crises at home and in her colonies, she saved herself from revolution by understanding the situation and adjusting herself to it.

Progress may be stemmed for a time, but it cannot be permanently stopped by force. A novelist has expressed the idea in saying: "You cannot fight and beat revolutions as you can fight and beat nations. You can kill a man, but you simply can't kill a rebel. For the proper rebel has an ideal of living, while your ideal is to kill him so that you may preserve yourself. And the reason why no revolution or religion has ever been beaten is that rebels die for something worth dying for, the future, but their enemies die only to preserve the past, and makers of history are always stronger than makers of empire." The American revolutionists had an ideal of living; it can hardly be said that in 1776 the Englishmen of the ruling classes were governed in their colonial relations by any ideals that were destined to be of service to the future of the human race.

THE WEAKENING OF THE INFLUENCE OF THE CROWN is one of the most impressive themes in modern British constitutional history. A complicated subject, it has often been ruthlessly oversimplified. Certainly the Reform Act of 1832 stands out as a milestone in the reduction of crown influence, for it deprived most of the old rotten and pocket boroughs of their seats in the House of Commons, and therefore it had the effect of reducing considerably the possibility of crown management of the House of Commons. Indeed, most nineteenth-century writers, following the examples of Lord Grey and Walter Bagehot, tended to emphasize the contribution of the Reform Act of 1832 to the diminution of crown influence. And this was not surprising. Nineteenth-century writers saw that the ministers of William IV and Victoria were in no position to manipulate majorities in the House of Commons as their predecessors during the reigns of the first three Georges had been able to do. They concluded, therefore, that the Reform Act was responsible for the changed situation. Recent research has made it clear, however, that to focus attention on the Reform Act of 1832 is to misunderstand the waning of the influence of the crown—the time when it occurred and the manner in which it took place. In the essay that follows, Professor Archibald S. Foord, of Yale University, tackles the problem of crown influence; he makes it clear that the orthodox discussions of the subject set forth in so many standard constitutional histories are antiquated and should be basically revised.

THE WANING OF 'THE INFLUENCE OF THE CROWN'
ARCHIBALD S. FOORD

'The crown has so many offices at its disposal,' wrote David Hume in 1741, 'that, when assisted by the honest and disinterested part of the house, it will always command the resolutions of the whole so far, at least, as to preserve the antient constitution from danger. We may, therefore, give to this influence what name we please; we

Reprinted by special permission from *The English Historical Review*, LXII (1947), 484-507. Publisher, Longmans, Green & Co. Ltd. The extensive documentation which originally appeared with this essay has been omitted.

may call it by the invidious appellations of *corruption* and *dependence;* but some degree and some kind of it are inseparable from the very nature of the constitution, and necessary to the preservation of our mixed government.'

The influence of the crown did, in the eighteenth century and long after, receive many 'invidious appellations.' Members in opposition cried out against the use of places, pensions, and peerages to make and maintain parliamentary majorities. Exponents of the theory of a free legislature deplored the 'subjection' of parliament to court influence, and even Blackstone displayed some concern over the power of this 'influence most amazingly extensive.' But Hume was not alone in his belief in the necessity of 'corruption.' Without exception the ministries of the eighteenth century employed court favours to maintain themselves in office, and practical politicians saw no way to 'get the King's business done' in parliament without the use of influence. Loud as were the protests of the Rockingham whigs against the methods of George III and Lord North, Dunning's resolution in 1780 stated only that the influence of the crown 'ought to be diminished,' not destroyed. Toward the end of the century there was doubtless much truth in the assertion of the pamphleteer, William Knox, that since there was 'an absolute necessity of vesting in the executive a *certain degree* of influence . . . the only question for reasonable men to discuss is what that degree ought to be.'

Yet in the reign of Queen Victoria the influence of the crown, known to be an undeniable fact and believed to be a constitutional necessity in the reigns of the first three Georges, no longer existed. Melbourne, Peel, Russell and Palmerston possessed no such electioneering machinery as had Walpole, Newcastle, North, and the younger Pitt. The crown's 'fund of influence with which nobody else could compete' did not provide the basis for Victorian parliamentary majorities, and while some like Bagehot looked back on the old system without

lament, others like the third Earl Grey cast a wistful eye on methods that appeared to have produced governments more stable than those of the 1850's.

The disappearance of the 'corrupt' influence of the crown, it is now recognised, effected a vital change in the British constitution. The court's inability to make and control majorities by means of the 'king's interest' reduced the sovereign's personal influence and lessened his control over the personnel of the ministry. At the same time, the way was cleared for the development of the cabinet and the two-party system in modern form. But, though the significance of the disappearance of crown influence is well understood, there is a considerable disagreement as to the time and manner in which it occurred. Perhaps the most common assumption is that the Reform Act of 1832 destroyed at a single stroke, or at least rendered largely impotent, the old system. The very nature of crown influence, so closely bound up with the ancient electoral order, makes its survival beyond even a limited extension of the franchise a strong improbability. The ministers of William IV and Victoria could not manage elections and majorities in the same manner as the servants of the first three Georges, and this fact suggests that the Reform Act was the agency of destruction. The other most widely accepted opinion is that, for a variety of reasons, the old system came to an end about 1782. George III's failure to establish 'personal government,' the salutary effect of exclusion acts, and the economical reforms of the Rockingham ministry have all been alleged as the reason for its destruction. According to these views, the younger Pitt ruled without employing 'corruption,' and thereafter the use of influence was largely confined to private boroughmongers.

Now, on the one hand, it is clearly established that the influence of the crown was not destroyed in 1782. The myth concerning George III's loss of power during Pitt's ministries has been dispelled, and no legislation prevented the most effective use of crown influence to secure a government majority in the election of 1784. Moreover, the economical reforms of the Rockinghamites, though they achieved a moderate diminution of the 'king's interest,' fell far short of the goal, and the reforms were so imperfectly conceived that much further legislation was required.

On the other hand, there is considerable evidence which indicates that the old system of making and controlling majorities had been broken before 1832. Though parliament remained unreformed during the regency and reign of George IV, Lord Liverpool did not command such a fund of influence nor did he exercise so great a measure of control over parliament as had the first ministers of an earlier day. During most of his regime the ministry retained a precarious control over the house of commons by the sufferance of independent members; patronage resources were comparatively meagre; and the government did not make the efforts characteristic of Newcastle or Henry Fox to extract the utmost political advantage from favours, pensions, and appointments. As early at 1809, Thomas Grenville pointed out that 'the influence of what they call corruption is, for practical purposes, too small rather than too great,' though he added that this could not be said in public. In the same year Pitt's old patronage secretary, George Rose, delivered a detailed speech, which he later expanded into a pamphlet, on the decline of crown influence. Henry Brougham subjected it to jocosely savage criticism in the *Edinburgh Review,* but Rose's arguments were not without weight: the government at this time was unquestionably denied the use of numerous types of influence employed by previous ministries.

The administration itself does not appear to have become seriously concerned about the decline of its influence until after the general election of 1818. From then on the printed manuscripts and memoirs of the time display numerous references to the decreased influence of the crown, and political transactions point continually to the weakening control of ministers over their followers. In May 1819 Lord Liverpool corresponded with the Regent concerning a means 'of recovering that weight and influence which ought to belong to every government' considering 'the evil temper and disposition which has been so apparent in some of the late proceedings of the house of commons'; and William Lamb openly taunted the government on the floor of the house at 'the failure of those means of patronage by which they were enabled to attach adherents.' That the resources of influence were by no means exhausted is witnessed by the purchase of the Grenville connection at the price of a dukedom and several offices in 1821-2. But when Henry Brougham tried to revive the clamour

BLACKWOOD'S: Tory periodical founded in 1817 by William Blackwood, of Edinburgh, in opposition to the Whig *Edinburgh Review*. Its stress on satire brought it not only libel suits but increased circulation.

HENRY BROUGHAM: British Whig leader and social reformer (d. 1868). He tended to exaggerate his own contribution to the passage of the Reform Act, but he helped greatly to bring about the prohibition of the slave trade, the abolition of slavery, the humanization of the penal code, and the extension of popular education.

EDINBURGH REVIEW: Influential periodical that was founded in Edinburgh in 1802 by Francis Jeffrey, Henry Brougham, and Sydney Smith. Disturbed by the strength of Toryism, they felt the need for a periodical that would back Whig reforms. Jeffrey, who served as editor until 1829, was able to obtain articles from many of the ablest writers of the time, although the articles were published anonymously. One contributor who broke with the *Edinburgh Review* was Sir Walter Scott. Finding it too Whiggish, he shifted his allegiance to the *Quarterly Review*.

against the influence of the crown, his efforts fell woefully flat. Moreover, the patronage secretaries of the period occasionally revealed their worries over their diminishing resources. Charles Arbuthnot circulated a 'treasury note' in 1822 in which he complained that if 'the just and necessary influence of the crown' were further reduced, 'it will be quite impossible for any set of men to conduct the government of this country.' In the ministerial crisis of March 1827 Stephen Lushington thought that 'considering how much the crown's powers of grace and favour have been diminished in latter years, it would be of great benefit that its first minister, who is to dispense the small residue of these favours, should be in the house of commons.' John Wilson Croker showed Canning in April how tenuous was the ministry's hold upon the great tory borough-owners, and his conclusions indicated that the Liverpool ministry had been considerably in their debt. When Wellington became prime minister he was forcibly struck by the lack of patronage at his disposal for 'the king's service in parliament.' He wrote to Sir Herbert Taylor in 1830, 'Yet I must say that no government can go on without some means of rewarding services. I have absolutely none!' The duke could be disingenuous, and his statement is an obvious exaggeration, even if considered only in its context. But the opposition stalwart, Henry Brougham, wrote in the same year of 'the diminished patronage of the crown.' Though radicals and the opposition still tried to make political capital out of the supposedly evil power of ministerial corruption, politicians in the days of George IV perceived that the old system of influence was breaking up.

It appears, then, that there existed before 1832 a considerable amount of opinion to the effect that the power of royal influence had greatly declined. How far was this opinion correct? Since knowing men often misjudge political factors in their own time, can we accept the conclusion suggested by their evidence? An examination of the actual resources of crown influence may provide the answer.

The chief resources employed about the middle of the eighteenth century may be grouped under four headings: money, patronage, honours, and 'imperceptible influence.' Government funds were used to subsidize the ministerial press, to provide pensions, to purchase close boroughs, and to carry on such electioneering devices as parades, free beer for electors, and the patronising of local tradesmen. Patronage provided jobs for electors, employment for parliamentary placemen, and positions for the friends, relatives, and dependents of those who could supply the government with votes in parliament and the constituencies. Honours attracted the 'many who cannot be caught by the bait of covetousness [but] are caught by the bait of vanity.' 'Imperceptible influence,' in the form of favours which government could distribute by means of contract awards, loan issues, and leases of crown lands, played an important part in securing the support of both mercantile and landed interests. An analysis of these resources will demonstrate the extent of the political influence to be derived from them during the regency and reign of George IV.

The government funds which had been employed for political purposes in the middle of the eighteenth century came from four main sources. First were the monies from the civil list which were charged against secret service, pensions, and the privy purse. From 1714 to 1780 annual disbursement for secret service averaged £57,106. Of this sum, £6000 was always divided equally between the two secretaries of state, who may or may not have devoted it to political purposes. Another portion of the secret service fund was issued 'without imprest, account, or other charge' to the secretaries of the treasury, who employed a large share of it to maintain ministerial majorities. In the reigns of the first two Georges another part of secret service money was handled by the disburser of 'the king's money,' a fund employed for charity, spies, and the government press. The pension list, which usually contained some members of parliament and their dependents, averaged £95,447 from 1721 to 1780. The privy purse did not provide funds for political purposes until November 1777, when George III decided to devote £12,000 a year from that source to financing elections.

A second source of money was the collection of the crown's hereditary revenues from the excise and the post office, the duchies of Lancaster and Cornwall, fines from the alienation and wine offices, the 4½ per cent. duties in the Leeward Islands and the Barbadoes, and numerous droits, escheats, quit-rents, and forfeitures at home and in the colonies. Some of the funds from these sources (apparently charged on the civil list as 'special service') were turned over to the secretaries of the treasury for election purposes. Owing to the nature of these revenues, the amount varied greatly. In the years 1761-8 the sum averaged £50,835.

Scotland and Ireland provided the two remaining sources of a ministry's political funds. The Irish pension list, which had grown to more than £122,000 by 1777, was international in composition and included Frenchmen, Dutchmen, Germans, Scots, and English members of parliament. The Scottish government provided the crown with an annual surplus, disposable at the absolute discretion of the crown as an hereditary revenue, which approached £10,000 toward the end of the century, and Scotland's small pension list included Scottish peers and the wives and widows of prominent politicians in the northern kingdom.

It was possible for ministries to employ monies from these four sources for political purposes because there was as yet no clearcut distinction between public property and the private property of the king, and because parliament possessed practically no control over expenditure. The ministry did not have to account for disbursements; and payments for secret service, pensions, and the like were kept secret. After 1780 the gradual modernization of the British financial system so greatly altered these conditions that it is doubtful if the income of the state could any longer be employed for 'corruption.'

In 1780 the house of commons resolved 'that it is competent to this house to examine into and to correct abuses in the expenditure of the civil list revenues, as well as in every other branch of the public revenue, whenever it shall seem expedient to the wisdom of this house to do so.' Parliament in the same session passed an act appointing a commission of public accounts, the first since the Hanoverian succession, with full power to inquire into the entire financial system and to recommend reorganization. The fifteen reports of this commission laid the basis for a series of reforms which followed. In 1785 were established five commissioners for auditing the public accounts. Thereafter their powers were continually broadened, and under their supervision audited expense accounts were laid annually before parliament. The first reform of the civil list took place in 1782. Burke's Act of that year divided all charges on the civil list into eight classes, to each of which was allotted a departmental budget. The responsibility for the maintenance of each was fixed on a designated royal official. The privy purse alone remained the sovereign's private fund; in all other departments accounts of expenditure were required. Although this measure did not prove immediately effectual, continued investigation and regulation gradually pared away the crown's independence in finance until, by 1830, the king had lost the last moiety of discretion over civil list expenditure.

The particular rivulets from which political funds had flowed were also dammed by reforms. Burke's Act limited disbursements from the civil list for home secret service and special service to £10,000 a year, and accounts of this expenditure were ordered to be kept and presented to parliament if called for. This reduction did not go into effect until after Pitt's election of 1784, but in 1785 home secret service expenditure dropped to £7364, and thereafter the fund was kept within the £10,000 limit. English civil list pensions were likewise restricted. The sum was not greatly curtailed, but Burke's Act required pensions to be paid publicly at the exchequer and the list to be presented annually to parliament. These practices prevented further circumvention of the old laws prohibiting pensioners from sitting in the commons. The first lord of the treasury was allowed to grant a secret pension only if he registered an oath that it was not given for a political reason, or to any member of parliament. In 1793 the Irish and in 1810 the Scottish pension funds were also reduced and the publication of lists required. The sums devoted to pensions declined further during the reign of George IV, and by the first civil list act of William IV the total amount which the king could devote to pensions from any source was limited to £75,000. The hereditary revenues, too, came gradually under control. During the latter years of George III's reign these revenues were subjected to an increasing number of encumbrances, and under George IV they were applied to regular government charges.

These reforms, which began in 1780, gradually dried up the sources from which the ministerial party could draw public funds for political purposes. Moreover, Curwen's Bribery Act of 1809 laid down regulations so stringent that Lord Liverpool declared it had 'put an end to all money transactions between government and the supposed proprietors of boroughs.' When Henry Brougham attacked the influence of the crown in 1822, he not once accused the government of diverting the income of the state to any 'corrupt' uses. There is, then, evidence to support the conclusion that the money influence of the crown, which had played a part in maintaining ministerial majorities in the middle of the eighteenth century, had been largely destroyed by the early years of the nine-

teenth. Conclusive proof that the Liverpool government never used public funds to acquire support is lacking. Peel seems to have used some in Ireland in the election of 1812, though his resources were admittedly meagre. But if the ministry could still tap the state treasury, reform had made it impossible for Arbuthnot or Planta to dispose of sums comparable to those available to Roberts or Robinson.

In contrast to the decline of money resources, the use of honours appears to have increased. While there seems to have been no increase in the bestowal of political baronetcies, the Thistle and order of St. Patrick remained political rewards. The peerage and the order of the Garter underwent considerable expansion, and George III adopted expedients to expand the order in 1786 and 1805 for obviously political reasons. Pitt's ninety-two peerage creations are notorious, and in 1797 Burke, observing the trend, is said to have accepted some of the blame 'for so disproportionate an increase of honours, by having deprived the crown and the minister of so many other sources of recompense or reward, which were extinguished by my bill of reform.' Burke may have overestimated the effect of his Act, but the high rate of peerage creations both during and after Pitt's time appears to confirm the general import of his assertion; namely, that honours were being used to compensate in part for the loss of other forms of patronage. Nevertheless, ministers continued to show considerable restraint in recommending creations. They expressed concern at the increase in peers, even as they made them, and yet applications far outnumbered their recommendations. In 1812 Peel and Liverpool agreed that it would be wrong to promise two peerages in return for seven votes in the commons. The dukedom which bought Lord Buckingham in 1821-2 appears to have been granted with reluctance. Toward the close of Liverpool's regime the crown was bestowing peerages upon royal favourites and as rewards to faithful followers in the fashion accepted in later periods which boasted their freedom from the 'corruption' attributed to the unreformed parliament.

Imperceptible influence, by its very nature, is extremely difficult to gauge. The position of the crown as a great landed and financial corporation and as the repository of a mass of minor discretionary powers provided the ministry with many means to oblige private citizens. There was seemingly no limit to the ways in which small favours could be employed to aid the ministerial 'interest.' Criminals were paroled to secure electoral votes, naval vessels were paid off in government constituencies, and scores of other favours which only government could bestow served as powerful inducements in securing political support. The use of many of these means continued long after the great Reform Act, and the research of a lifetime would be required to ferret out the whole extent of the use of such favours. But the record of what George Rose singled out as three important forms of 'imperceptible influence'— government contracts, loans, and leases of crown lands—will explain much of the story.

Government contracts, Rose observed, provided ministers with 'great as well as unobserved influence.' In the middle of the eighteenth century there existed no regulated form of competitive bidding. Many of the most profitable contracts were under the management of the treasury, the headquarters for the distribution of government patronage, and the treasury's practice was to award contracts largely on the basis of political 'recommendations.' Namier has estimated that of the fifty-one or fifty-two merchants in the parliament of 1761, thirty-seven 'can be proved to have had extensive business dealings with the government,' and patronage secretaries listed contractors as placemen whose votes would generally be given for the ministry of the day. In 1782 an Act introduced by the Rockingham ministry disqualified government contractors for seats in the commons and required in every contract a clause to the effect that no member of parliament was to receive any benefit thereby. Pitt later introduced open bidding and put an end to the system of letting out contracts for military stores with an eye to political interest. At the outbreak of the war with France he transferred the purchasing of army provisions to the victualling commissioners, who had formerly handled naval provisions alone, and the transport board was established to provide all other types of military stores. Then, as now, interested parties could find ways to frustrate the intent of such laws and regulations, and Pitt's reforms certainly did not put an end to peculation in government contracts. But after this time opposition protests against 'corrupt' contracting died away, and if the ministry continued to derive any appreciable 'interest' therefrom, it was far less than in the days when contracts were awarded 'by favour' to merchants who sat in the house.

Before Pitt's time government loans were handled in much the same manner as contracts. The general practice was 'for the minister to settle, with a few select friends in the city, the terms on which they should be made; and then to give these, lists of more private friends, intended to be favoured, with specific sums for each.' Financiers sought seats in parliament, and when government credit was sound, they eagerly applied for a 'slice' of government loans. In the course of his financial reforms Pitt did away with this system. Public notice of an intended loan was given through the Bank of England, and the treasury encouraged loans from all reputable firms. When competition did not exist, Pitt apparently tried to stir up rivalry among the great banking houses. In 1793 when money was scarce, he told the commons that in arranging for a loan 'he had done everything in his power to excite a competition among the monied men, but without effect; for it so happened that he had not received two offers on the occasion.' Pitt's impartial system received encomiums even from Fox. His new policy was so widely accepted by

1795 that mere suspicion of partiality in negotiating a loan in that year brought on a parliamentary inquiry and a pamphleteer's bitter protest. No Act ever excluded financiers from parliament, but Pitt's reforms destroyed the influence to be derived from the floating of government loans.

The leasing of the crown lands in Walpole's time was one of the treasury board's special prerogatives. Every lessee became directly dependent upon the treasury for his renewal, which must occur within thirty-one years, but at any intermediate date the treasury could renew a lease upon terms more favourable to the applicant. The influence involved in the control of crown leases becomes apparent when it is realized that in 1787 (the year of the first printed survey) more than eighty members of lords and commons rented royal property. Efforts made to curtail this influence had only a limited effect. The *Nullum Tempus* Act of 1768 was designed to prevent the treasury from revoking royal grants for political reasons, but it failed to weaken ministerial control of crown leases. Over the protests of several landed magnates, a royal commission was appointed to investigate the management of crown property in 1786. Upon the basis of its report Pitt introduced a bill to reorganize crown leases, but it proved ineffective. Further reorganization took place in 1810 and 1814, and several investigations were ordered in the 1820's. Their reports indicated that management remained inefficient and liable to political influence. Daniel Harvey's plaint in 1830 that the crown lands, as managed by the government, were 'quite sufficient to corrupt both houses of parliament' was no doubt an exaggeration. But when evidence even after 1832 indicates that the influence of crown leases was still effective in electoral contests, one must conclude that inquiries and legislation had not removed crown lands from the sphere of politics in the unreformed parliament.

Three of the four important forms of 'imperceptible influence' had thus been partially curtailed before the great Reform Act. Other forms continued in use. The Liverpool government, for example, dispensed taxation remittances through local supporters in the period after Waterloo, but the tendency of administrative and financial reforms was to reduce the old fund of special favours by which government could attach adherents.

The most important element in the influence of the crown in the eighteenth century was probably the system of patronage. Hume and Blackstone both stressed the influence derived from the large number of offices at the disposal of the government. So generally recognized was the power of patronage that from 1675 onward fairly persistent efforts had been made to prevent the government's use of 'placemen' to make majorities. Such endeavours were guided in two directions: to disfranchise placemen and to exclude placemen from seats in parliament. Before 1780 some success was achieved in both ways. Under Queen Anne postmasters were disfranchised, and a series of Place Acts from 1693 to 1742 excluded several categories of officers from the house of commons. Had certain provisions of the Act of Settlement gone into effect, all placemen, including cabinet ministers, would have been ineligible to sit in the commons, but 'West's expedient' in 1705 softened the exclusion clauses and established the system of re-election upon acceptance of 'an office or a place of profit under the king.' The other Place Acts of the period were strictly limited in character, and numerous exclusion bills brought in by the opposition were usually defeated. Lord Egmont explained the rejection of the bill of 1734 in this manner:

I found by discourse with the two Mr. Towers that they yesterday purposely avoided being at the House because they were in their judgments for the bill to limit the number of officers in Parliament, but yet were not willing to disoblige the ministry who warmly pressed the rejecting that Bill. Mr. Moore also told me he would not be there, because though he liked the Bill, he did not know if the passing it at this time might not embarrass the King's affairs as we are going into a war, when it will be necessary the next Parliament should consist of members that will concur in the Court measures as Placemen will be sure to do. Mr. Page told me he left the House as the question was going to be put, because he could not oppose so reasonable and popular a Bill.

My brother Parker did the same, and I was informed that of those present at the debate, there were counted twenty friends of the Court who left the House, for the eyes of men are very searching on such occasions. I own I avoided being there because I really think it is inconsistent with our Constitution and dangerous to our liberties; that so many Placemen should have seats among us . . . yet I apprehended some danger might arise from passing it, because parties are now so high and envenomed against each other, that were the new Parliament almost entirely independent of the Crown, I know not how violently they may behave against the public measures next year . . . especially considering the characters of Sir William Wyndham, Mr. Pulteney, Shippen and others who are the promoters of this Bill, some of whose principles are suspected to tend to a Commonwealth and others more than suspected to be Jacobites.

With such opinion prevalent at Westminster, it is easy to see why Place Acts were rarely passed. Furthermore, there is little evidence that those in the statute book had any real effect in curtailing the influence of the crown. A large majority of government officials could vote if otherwise qualified, and there remained a considerable number of places tenable with a seat in parliament. John Robinson made a list of them in 1774 which reveals that there were in England 425 offices and categories of offices, in Scotland 24, and in Ireland 14, which could be held with a seat in lords or commons. The total of 463, however, omits army officers and various petty officials in Ireland, who were also eligible and accounted placemen in the house. At no time during the eighteenth century did every eligible placeman occupy a seat in the commons, but the most cautious estimates indicate well over 100 placemen in each parliament from the days of Walpole through those of North.

After 1780, however, legislation and administrative reorganization inexorably broke up the old system of patronage. Here the same forces were at work which effected a reduction in both 'imperceptible influence' and the pecuniary influence of the crown, and a changing attitude toward the employment of patronage worked in the same direction. A comparison of the situation in the disposal of patronage in several of the most important fields before and after 1780 will indicate the nature of the great alterations which took place.

Sinecure offices, once termed by Castlereagh 'more likely than any others to secure parliamentary influence,' had played a considerable part before 1780 in attaching ministerial adherents. Though many sinecurists were not removable at pleasure, the desirability of a well paid job with little or no labour made sinecures valuable rewards for political service. There was a sizeable cluster of functionless offices in the royal household, the duchies of Lancaster and Cornwall, the country palatine of Lancaster, and the earldom of Chester. Another group existed in the exchequer and in the offices of the pipe, the pells, and the first fruits. There were roughly 200 sinecures in the customs. Although no move was made to weed out such functionless offices until the second Rockingham ministry, in 1782 there commenced a constant and unremitting attack upon sinecures. Burke's Act abolished 134 offices in household and ministry. Treasury regulations under Shelburne did away with 144 sinecures in the customs, and the Exchequer Act of 1783 condemned a large number of exchequer sinecures to extinction upon the death of their incumbents. George Rose estimated that Pitt's reforms abolished 765 needless revenue offices in 1789 and another 196 in 1798. Legislation in the early nineteenth century weeded out still more useless offices, many of which had been converted into sinecures by administrative reform. A select committee of the commons, appointed to investigate sinecures from 1810 to 1812, found that many of the 342 sinecures still existing were to be abolished upon the death of their holders. Another investigation in 1817 resulted in the abolition or 'regulation' of 313 other useless offices. In 1822 Castlereagh boasted that since 1815 more than 2000 civil offices rendered useless by the close of the war had been abolished. Finally, in 1834, another select committee found that of 108 offices alleged still to be useless, 8 were not sinecures, 2 had already been abolished, and 43 had been 'regulated.' The remaining 55 were condemned, and the committee wrote the epitaph of the sinecure by announcing the establishment of the principle 'that anything in the nature of a sinecure office, with emoluments attached to it at the public charge, is alike indefensible in principle, pernicious as a means of influence, and grievous as an undue addition to the general burthen of the nation.' The progress of reform since 1782 makes it clear that the epitaph of 1834 was inscribed over a body long moribund if not altogether defunct as a means of political influence.

The destruction of the sinecure accompanied that of the old method of granting offices in reversion. When demands for patronage were greater than the supply, the government had sometimes promised offices upon the death or removal of the incumbent. Thus in 1762 Lord Henley, desirous of holding posts then occupied, asked 'two reversions for signing the peace,' and patronage was thereby mortgaged to pay for present support in the future. But acts regulating sinecures commonly prohibited grants in reversion, and an Act of 1808 which temporarily suspended the power to grant any office in this way was later ex-

tended through 1814. Thereafter the use of reversions as a means of influence fell into desuetude.

Another great change in the system of patronage occurred in the revenue departments. Before 1780 the treasury had engrossed all appointments in customs and excise, and the numerous revenue officers had been turned into borough voters and electioneers for the ministry of the day. Reformers in Shelburne's administration complained that these officers were 'appointed from country fox-hunters, bankrupt merchants, and officers of the army and navy' with 'much more attention being paid to their interest as votes than to their abilities and education for the duty of their offices.' The revenue officer, more than any other factor, produced the 'treasury boroughs' of the eighteenth century. In 1782, however, Crewe's Act disfranchised the majority of revenue officers. John Robinson's calculations for the election of 1784 show how serious a blow this was to the old system of influence. Speaking of Hastings, he observed that 'the disfranchising bill has made great alterations in this and other boroughs'; and of Winchilsea he wrote, ' . . . the revenue officers having been struck off leaves scarce a good voter.' After the union with Ireland, disfranchisement was extended to Irish revenue officers, and henceforward the placeman-voter ceased to exist as a widespread institution. The development of preliminary qualifications for civil servants from 1787 onwards also worked to remove political influence from revenue appointments.

In other spheres the patronage system was weakened not by legislation but by custom. Earlier in the century, Walpole and the Pelhams had unhesitatingly dismissed army officers who voted against the ministry in parliament. Cobham, Bolton, Pitt, Erskine, and Conway had lost their commissions in notorious political cases, and Walpole once roundly declared that if any officer should 'even show aversion to a minister, that minister would be the most wretched of creatures if he did not cashier

him, and he left the practice as a legacy
to his successors.' George Grenville, accepting the legacy, insisted that 'the king cannot
trust his army in the hands of those who
are against his measures.' Lords lieutenant
were treated in the same fashion. Throughout the eighteenth century they were accounted placemen to be appointed and dismissed for political reasons, and even the
Rockingham whigs removed lords lieutenant in opposition to replace them with
friends. Early in the nineteenth century this
practice came to an end. The celebrated
dismissals during the regency and reign of
George IV—Sir Robert Wilson from the
army and Lord Fitzwilliam from the lieutenancy of Yorkshire—were based on allegations of sedition rather than political
opposition. In 1821 Lord Palmerston, then
secretary at war, asserted that during his
period in office 'no officer had ever been
dismissed the service for his conduct in
parliament.' Such a practice he declared 'a
pitiful principle' based on 'mean and miserable feelings of resentment.' Even in the
most severe political crises the Liverpool
government permitted army officers to vote
against them with impunity. Lords lieutenant were appointed when in opposition, as
was Buckingham in 1813 and Morpeth in
1824, and Liverpool retained Devonshire,
Darlington, and Portland in lieutenancies
despite their consistent voting against him.
The ministry still possessed the unquestioned right to cashier such opponents, but
declined to continue political patronage in
the army and county government.

There are evidences of similar if less
emphatic trends in appointments to the
church, the law, and the colonies. While
private jobbery and charity had played a
great part in such appointments before
1780, political influence had often been a
major factor. Bishop Gibson and the duke
of Newcastle erected complex systems of
clerical patronage, and George III once
seriously considered Lord Mansfield's proposal 'that I should pitch on some bishop
to recommend to me in ecclesiastical affairs,
that I might keep that great engine of power

in my own hands instead of in the ministry.'
The magnitude of 'that great engine of
power' in the middle of the eighteenth century was measured by the ministry's right
to control a large number of the appointments to 2 archbishops, 24 bishoprics, and
851 minor church appointments in England
and Wales. In Ireland there were 8 arch-
bishoprics, 35 bishoprics, and about 200
livings; and over 250 ministers in Scotland.
Scores of legal appointments were also
made with an eye to political interest, especially high-ranking law officers of the
crown, Welsh judges, and judges in the
admiralty court, all of whom were accounted placemen under ministerial influence. Colonial officials were part of government patronage, and during the century
the ministry constantly encroached upon
the patronage of the East India Company.
It cannot be said that the practice in these
appointments was reversed as it was in the
case of lords lieutenant or army officers,
but there are indications of moves in the
same direction. The crown had surrendered
all its patronage in the church of Scotland
by 1829. Wellington maintained that his
church appointments during the ministry
of 1828-30 were strictly non-political, and
a savage critic of the method of church
preferment, writing in *Blackwood's* in 1831,
admitted that 'of late years' the government
had filled many clerical offices 'with the
most disinterested views.' As early as 1811
Francis Horner thought that the appointment of judges without regard to political
interest had become 'established morality.'
The American revolution diminished the
number of colonial appointments, and reforms in 1782 and 1814 abolished practices
which had made many overseas posts desirable political rewards. Castlereagh assured
the commons in 1822 that the colonial service was no longer a source of influence
and pointed out that seven-eighths of colonial appointments were in the hands of
local officers. Pitt's endeavour 'to give the
crown the power of guiding the politics of
India with as little means of corrupt influence as possible' was hardly attended with

success, but the number of posts in India at the disposal of the government depended so much on the relationships between ministers and company directors that Indian patronage never became the source of influence that many feared. Wellington called on the board of control to provide him with some appointments for political purposes in 1828, though the president became concerned with a plan in which he 'considered it to be a settled point that the patronage of India should be separated from the government.'

The effect of reform and voluntary surrender of ministerial discipline over placemen was a distinct diminution, though not a total destruction, of the eighteenth-century system of patronage. In 1826 the treasury still possessed ten seats to which it could nominate supporters. An investigation in 1821 revealed that there were still 89 placemen in the commons; but of these, 19 were not removable by the ministry, 13 were not directly removable, and a half-dozen were then in opposition. Castlereagh pointed out that only 47 or 48 of them held offices 'in a sense to which influence could be fairly attached,' and the majority of these were members of the ministry.

This evidence of a decline in the resources of crown influence lends considerable weight to the plaints of politicians in the reign of George IV that the old system of government 'corruption' was then breaking up. Whereas Walpole had been confident in 1734 that the crown could always outspend the gentry in elections, the Liverpool administration employed little or none of the public funds for political purposes. Honours have continued to be political rewards down to the present day, but some of the sources of 'imperceptible influence' were extinguished in Pitt's time. The Irish union gave the ministry a strong hold on the 100 new members, but Irish Exclusion Acts weakened their grip, and Catholic emancipation pretty effectively destroyed government control in most Irish constituencies. The general trend of legislative reform and administrative reorganization

supports Feiling's contention that in the early years of the Liverpool government the 'old cement of patronage was more than half gone.'

Most convincing of all arguments is the plain fact that Wellington lost the election of 1830. Never since the Hanoverian succession had the ministry of the day, backed by the influence of the crown, been defeated at the polls. Walpole had emerged triumphant in 1734 despite the overwhelming unpopularity of his late excise bill. The younger Pitt, with the crown on his side, had been able to defy parliament and the whig grandees in 1784. Yet Wellington, professing himself satisfied with the backing of William IV, found that he could not elect a parliament to support his ministry. Lord Ellenborough thought the elections had 'not been attended to in time,' though the *Edinburgh Review* asserted that the treasury had estimated the government would gain ninety-three seats in the election. So poor were treasury calculations, however, that even after the election disasters Wellington thought he had sufficient support, and not until he met parliament did he realize the true weakness of his position. The duke had complained of the paucity of his patronage, and the election demonstrated how greatly the influence of the crown had diminished since Dunning's celebrated resolution.

A particular moment in time when the influence of the crown became insufficient to control parliament cannot be definitely determined. The process of diminution was gradual, not cataclysmic. Stemming from the Rockinghamite reform movement in 1780 was a steady flow of reforms which had a cumulative effect in reducing the 'king's interest.' Halévy's assertion that by 1815 the tories 'were pledged to the defence of all the abuses employed by the eighteenth-century whigs to secure their power' must be rejected, for the progress of reform continued unabated. Liverpool wrote to Bathurst in 1818 that ministers were going to cram reform down the regent's throat because 'economy and reduction are the passions of the day, and . . . if he wishes to preserve his government, he must allow them to manage the questions of establishments of all descriptions in such a way as to give no pretext to our friends to vote against us.' Hardly a pledge to maintain abuses! Liverpool's statement points to two other factors in the process of gradual diminution: the change in attitude toward the use of 'corruption' and the growing force of public opinion. Men in parliament no longer abstained from voting on place bills for fear of the ministry or the security of the state. Ministers no longer cashiered army officers and lords lieutenant in opposition, or carried out wholesale purges in the civil service for political reasons. At the same time, the development of the press and education had increased the weight of what contemporaries called 'the popular element of the constitution.' There was much greater concern for 'opinion out-of-doors,' and the effect of that opinion was certainly vital in the election of 1830. These factors lead to the conclusion that the gradual process of diminution probably began to have serious effects upon the ministry's control of parliament toward the end of the Napoleonic wars, the very time when Rose and Grenville voiced doubts about the strength of the powers of 'corruption.' How serious were these effects is impossible to estimate, for the ministry continued to hold its own with the support of independent members,

though there is room for considerable doubt whether Liverpool would have weathered the elections of 1818, 1820, and 1826, had the state of public opinion been different. But clearly by 1830 the process of diminution had weakened the effectiveness of the influence of the crown so far as to destroy its power to maintain a parliamentary majority.

The traditional versions expounded in the standard constitutional histories must therefore be revised. The destruction of the influence of the crown occurred, not in the 1780's nor in 1832, but in the period lying between. It was effected, not by any enactment or group of enactments, but by a long train of legislation, administrative reform, and changed attitudes in public life. The forces motivating these alterations were the constant pressure of opposition parties striving to reduce ministerial power, the need for economy and retrenchment after the American revolution and during and after the wars of the French revolution, and the social and economic changes in British life as reflected in the growth of the power of public opinion through a cheaper and more influential press. In its last years, ministers had managed the unreformed parliament without the whole system of influence thought so indispensable in the eighteenth century, and one vital obstacle to the development of cabinet government and the two-party system in modern form had already been removed.

MOST EIGHTEENTH-CENTURY ENGLISHMEN were inactive in the political life of their times. As a rule they regarded politics as the preserve of the leisured classes, and they cared little—if at all—about the office of prime minister, the growth of the cabinet, or the constitutional ideas of George III. The subject of greatest interest was still agriculture, and what concerned the great mass of Englishmen was the condition-of-farming question. In certain respects English rural life was changing in the course of the eighteenth century. Owing to the growth in the size of the population and to the rising prices of farm products in the last decades of the century, English farmers often tried to step up their production—a process to which some historians have applied the expression "agricultural revolution." The label leaves much to be desired, however, from the standpoint of historical accuracy; it is far too crisp, sensational, even melodramatic, and it makes too rapid a process that took decades to work out. The increase of production in the eighteenth century took several notable forms: more efficient methods of breeding, crop rotation, the use of improved farm implements, and an intensified enclosure movement. One sure reflection of the growth of interest in more efficient methods of agricultural production was the marked increase in the number of books on farming published in Hanoverian England. By far the best remembered of the writers on farming is Arthur Young, whose publications are numerous enough to keep the most diligent reader occupied for a long time. A major source for an understanding of eighteenth-century agricultural life, his writings are notable not only for content but for form. In the following essay, G. E. Fussell evaluates some of Young's contributions to the farming literature of his time. A member of the British Ministry of Agriculture and Fisheries, Fussell probably knows more about the history of modern English agriculture than any other man now living.

MY IMPRESSIONS OF ARTHUR YOUNG

G. E. FUSSELL

Arthur Young was an enthusiast, but his enthusiasm was tempered by a strong dash of realism. That was the reason why he was so anxious to collect facts and the figures which describe them. Political arithmetic was a century old when he was born, but, in spite of an intelligent use of the Bills of Mortality, such vital statistics as had been compiled were little more than intelligent guesses and often not even intelligent.

The fortunate accident that turned Young into a farmer rather than a citizen of literary parts led to the first attempt to obtain not only statistics of production but also costs of production in a particular industry. He did this by the lately recognized method, euphoniously entitled "field work," instead of by the Buddhistic method of concentration practiced by so many of his contemporaries.

Young was fortunate in his friends, particularly in his acquaintance with the Rev-

erend Walter Harte, whose sketch of the farming methods seen in the course of his Continental travels inspired one of Young's earliest essays, "Of the Usefulness of Acquiring a Knowledge of Foreign Practices in Husbandry." This essay strikes the keynote of the whole of Young's activities. He thought that the best way of learning about farming was to go out into the countryside and see how it was done by the men who were doing it. A record of the different methods used in various parts of the country and of their practical results in yields, in cash, and in profit, could not but be helpful to any working farmer who would take the trouble to read about them and compare them with his own.

There had been many tourists who wrote of England before Young set out on his travels and many geographies that contained scrappy economic data, but none of these works made more than occasional references to farming and these of a kind

Reprinted by special permission from *Agricultural History,* XVII (1943), 135–144. The footnotes which originally appeared with this essay have been omitted.

useless to a working man although not quite so useless for other purposes. When he had to go on private business from Bradfield to South Wales in 1767, Young, who was then only twenty-six years old, set out to remedy this defect for the country he passed through, and the result was his volume entitled *A Six Weeks' Tour, Through the Southern Counties of England and Wales* (London, 1768).

Young's own estimate of this book is that it is one "in which, for the first time, the facts and principles of Norfolk husbandry were laid before the public," but as important as these facts were, even two years before Coke of Holkham settled in the county, the book is much more valuable than Young would have us believe. It laid before the public "the facts and principles" of the husbandry of a line of country from Bradfield to London and from London to South Wales, and the details given were quite all inclusive. They comprised the crop rotations, the implements used including drawings of some novel to Young, the cost of labor and provisions which often varied surprisingly in a few miles, the size of farms, and the number of men and horses or oxen employed on the different-sized farms. As if this were not enough to occupy all his powers of observation and industry to record, passing reference is made to local industry, such as the manufacture of Witney

blankets, and useful facts and figures about it are mentioned. Even at that Young's passion for facts and figures could not allow him to rest, and what I regard as too much attention is paid to details of the size of rooms in great houses, e.g., Blenheim, visited in the course of the journey, and discussions of the details of pictures by well-known artists (old masters) which hung on their walls, but this may all have been a sop to the Cerberus of the intelligentsia of the day, whose attention Young desired to attract and divert to the problems of farming.

Young did not try to assemble the economic data he collected on his tour and draw any general conclusions from them, possibly because he realized that the area visited was narrow and the data correspondingly a poor sample. A much better sample was collected in the following year, 1768, when his Northern Tour was undertaken. On this tour Young traveled 2,500 miles from Bradfield to the northern boundary of England, across country westward, and so in a wide sweep back home, and he collected statistical data from some 250 farms of all sizes and descriptions. These data he attempted to assemble in what is perhaps the first farm survey ever undertaken by an individual in order to use them in the discussion of current farming problems. One of these was the size of farms, a problem

COKE OF HOLKHAM: Much publicized advocate of improved husbandry (1752-1842). He transformed his holdings into a model estate and encouraged his tenants to use the latest agricultural methods. He prided himself on having converted West Norfolk from a rye-producing to a wheat-growing area.

LORD ERNLE (R. E. PROTHERO): Author of *English Farming, Past and Present* (1912), a classic study that approaches agricultural history from the economic, social, political, and legal standpoints.

WILLIAM MARSHALL: Prolific English farming writer (d. 1818) who viewed it as his mission to spread knowledge of advanced agricultural methods. Less well known than Arthur Young among his contemporaries, he has come more and more into his own in the opinion of experts in the history of English agriculture.

J. E. THOROLD ROGERS: British economic historian and author of a pioneering multi-volume study called *History of Agriculture and Prices in England, 1259-1793* (1866-1902). His work has been much criticized, but it continues to stand as one of the great monuments in economic history.

which can hardly be said to have been solved until this day. He justly said:

> I must, in the next place, enter upon a review of perhaps the most important part of the intelligence I generally received, that of the particulars of farms. . . . There has not, of late years, been any subject in political oeconomy that has been more debated, than the size of farms that is most advantageous. . . . Upon this very important subject, the publick has hitherto received no other information or satisfaction, than what is to be had from reasoning; we have had volumes of reasons, arguments, and opinions, upon this point, but scarce any facts; it is, therefore, with peculiar satisfaction, that I shall endeavour to treat the subject in a new way, by presenting facts alone.

This he proceeded to do by tabulation of his figures and came to the not unreasonable conclusion, for his time as for today, that a farm of about 300 acres is probably the best economic unit. His exact figure is 287 acres, half arable and half grass.

The table which leads to this conclusion is provided with the heads: Soil and general rent; Acres; Grass; Arable; Rent; Draught; Cows; Fat; Young Sheep; Servants; Maids; Boys; Labourers; Wheat; Barley; Oats; Pease; Beans; Turnips; Clover; Average Product; Farms in general (size is given in rent per acre); and Medium (rental per acre in £). Totals are provided, but the average yield is only a figure unrelated to any crop and is, therefore, anomalous. I have elsewhere assumed it to relate to the average yield of wheat per acre. Perhaps I should also explain here that the term "servants" means farm laborers who lived in the house and got part of their wages in the form of board and lodging. It does not mean domestic or household servants.

In his comments on these tables Young disclosed in no ambiguous manner the utterly scientific cast of his mind.

Candour requires me to remark that the proportions of the crops are not drawn from equal authority with the other articles. In many instances I was not informed of the actual number of acres of each grain; in which case I supply the break by the mean proportions of the courses of crops in the neighborhood; a method that, probably, is not accurate, but which is undoubtedly more to be depended on, than any general calculations, or suppositions. . . .

Young's conclusion that about 300 acres was the most productive size of farm is supported by a further table giving the produce of the different sizes of farm in categories up to 50 acres, 50 to 100, 100 to 200, 200 to 300, 300 to 400, 400 to 500, 500 to 700, 700 to 1000, and above 1000 acres. There are other calculations which strike the modern reader as something of oddities, but there is also one in quite the modern vein showing cattle per 100 acres and cattle per £100 rental on different-sized farms, as well as one to determine the density of population in a similar relation. The financial side was not neglected, the capital required for various types of farming in the large number of counties visited being discussed as well as the cost of provisions in relation to the prevailing rates of laborer's wages. As he himself admitted, with admirable ingenuousness, "This method of gaining a knowledge of the rural oeconomy of the nation, although not perfect, is far more satisfactory than general calculations, founded on circumstances extremely foreign to the subject."

Similar material was collected for a wide range of country, and published in 1771 as the Eastern Tour, but Young did not tabulate it. Otherwise, he might have been able to emphasize the conclusions founded on the data in the Northern Tour. This is rather a pity because the optimum size of farms, for example, was a subject very close to his heart, and he had already discussed it in *The Farmer's Letters to the People of England,* issued in 1767. Here the argument was based on inquiries made on the farms in his neighborhood and is, in embryo, the same sort of thing as was done on the Northern Tour, but these early essays contained a good deal of reasoning. The *Farmer's Letters* includes "Sylvae," which consists of some very early essays that had appeared in the periodical, *Museum Rusticum et Commerciale,* and had been gathered together for publication on the advice of the Reverend Walter Harte. One of these is an attempt to compare the profit of arable and grassland, and here again, in his very nonage, is evidence of Young's passion for the precise fact disclosed by figures. However, I very much suspect that those presented here are obtained from common knowledge—yet farmers' knowledge withal—rather than actual costings of particular farms, although Young himself claimed that they were based on farms with which he was acquainted.

Even so, these early essays, some published in 1764, show that Young was already widely read and that he had not confined his reading narrowly to farming textbooks, although, of course, the main trend was in that direction. In spite of his authority, however, he did not disdain the then illiterate or semiliterate farmer, and went so far as to inscribe an essay, "The Common Farmer Vindicated," in his defense.

It was inevitable that a new method of controversy on the farming question, supported as it was by incontrovertible facts and figures, such as were not even in existence before, should arouse both admiration and intense disgust. The former showed itself in the widespread popularity of the books; the latter in acrimonious attacks both on the product and its author. Criticism and controversy were conducted in a rambunctious manner in those days, and it was, judging by contemporary writings, quite impossible to overstep the bounds of good taste. Young was, however, as well equipped as his opponents to deal in invective and slanderous assertion, so probably no harm was done to anybody and the publicity helped to sell the books.

Young's own estimate of them is worthy of record. It shows him as being possessed of no false modesty:

> In these works I particularly attended to the course of the farmer's crops, the point perhaps of all others the most important, and the more so at that period, because all preceding writers had neglected it in the most unaccountable manner. . . .
>
> It has been very justly said that I first excited the agricultural spirit which has since rendered Britain so famous; and I should observe that this is not so great a compliment as at first sight it may seem, since it was nothing more than publishing to the world the exertions of many capital cultivators and in various parts of the kingdom, and especially the local practice of common farmers who, with all their merit, were unknown beyond the limits of their immediate district, and whose operation wanted only to be known to be admired.

True it is that justice is here done to the common farmer, but earlier tourists had neglected to notice him, "confining their attention absolutely to towns and seats, without paying any more thought to agriculture than if that art had no existence between the towns they visited." Young certainly made up for their deficiencies and set a fashion which has been copied at intervals ever since.

It was a fashion which Young continued to follow himself. Nearly every volume of the *Annals of Agriculture and Other Useful Arts* contains notes on short journeys into some rural district or other, and taken together these brief tours alone cover a very respectable proportion of the whole country. Before this he had spent three years in Ireland, and produced *A Tour in Ireland* (1780) and during the time the *Annals*

(1783-1815) were appearing and he was making sporadic journeys to different parts of England and Wales, he found time to go to France and prepare an account of his travels there. It is a matter of recurrent astonishment to me that the French tour should have made so great an appeal to the literati as it has done. Augustine Birrell's essay on Arthur Young is devoted almost entirely to it, and even the centenary essay in the London *Times Literary Supplement* mentions little else of his widespread activities. Possibly in these writers' minds an atmosphere of romance surrounded a journey made at some personal risk when the French Revolution had already broken out, especially as the same horse was used for a very long tour. Having seen something of both the first World War and the blitz on London in 1940, I am doubtful whether there is ever any romance about slaughter, and the use of one horse for a long journey can be nothing new in America; indeed Tschiffely outstripped Young in this respect quite recently.

When the Board of Agriculture was formed and began its survey of farming by counties, Young, in spite of being appointed Secretary of the Board, undertook to write surveys of six counties and these were by no means the smallest in the country. They were: Suffolk, 1794; Lincoln, 1799; Herts, 1804; Norfolk, 1804; Essex, 1807; and Oxford, 1809.

Young was never tired of doing this sort of work, and in the introduction to his *General View . . . of Lincoln* he emphasized its importance. "I cannot conclude these observations," he wrote, "without remarking the extreme importance of examining the several provinces of the kingdom repeatedly, till all the singularities of their state, and practical husbandry, are well ascertained. I by no means pretend to have exhausted Lincolnshire. . . ." That was not a surprising admission coming from a man who confessed that he had been commissioned to stay in the county seven weeks, but had extended his visit to twelve. This report was most virulently attacked, not only by T. Stone, who had hoped to do the work himself and been superseded, but in the *Farmers' Magazine* of 1801 which commented:

Mr. Arthur Young, who amused and instructed us in our younger days, by his rural writings, is the author of this work: Indeed, whether the title-page had afforded us this information or not, the work itself contains intrinsic evidence of the source from whence it proceeded. We observe the same desultory way of writing, the like chaos of materials, and a similar quantity of political arithmetic, as characterize this gentleman's other performances. Considering the number of years he has been employed in such investigations, the public might have sanguinely expected a perfect view of the Lincolnshire husbandry, especially as the author had a full command of official information.

Much of this criticism was undoubtedly just, and Young defended himself against it in the introduction to his *General View . . . of Essex* (1807). He explained that he had made a journey of 1,000 miles to examine a county with a million acres—no bad achievement in itself for a man of sixty-six. His claim was that "In drawing up this General View of it, I have followed the same rule by which I acted upon former occasions—to let the reader have the authority, not only of Essex farmers in general, but of the individuals in particular. I take it for granted that he does not want my ideas, or proposals. He has accordingly only Essex authority; I offer myself rarely to his notice, and never without warning him." This method inevitably caused repetition in the matter presented, and Young thought that the reports should be useful tables rather than agreeable books. By the greater mass of detail they presented so would they simplify the task of the writers of the proposed condensed survey of the country as a whole. I don't know that this conclusion is incontrovertible, and the task of writing the *Code of Agriculture,* which appeared in 1817, can have been hardly less tedious than that self-imposed one of William Marshall's review of the Reports to the Board of Agriculture.

I have dealt with Young's work as an investigator of local farming methods in England and Wales at some length because it is his descriptive writing that is of most value to the historian, and because his desire to record the exact truth of what he had seen is so evident in his own remarks. Although, like everyone else, he had his prejudices, he was prepared to accept evidence against them, and to modify his ideas as the years went by and his knowledge and experience grew. There is a fashion today to compare his survey work with the *Rural Economy* series produced by William Marshall to its disadvantage. Some weight may be attached to a contemporary criticism that it is not possible to survey farming by looking at the fields while passing along the road in the comfort of a chaise traveling rapidly at less than 10 miles an hour, but Young did much more than this. He collected information from local people and while this method is not infallible because wide experience is necessary as a background and some local people are inclined, even today, to tell tall stories to test the gullibility of their interlocutors, yet it was then an innovation. Marshall's information may have been more deep-seated because, at any rate so far as his early work is concerned, he lived for some time in the places described, but he was not the originator of this type of work. Be that as it may, he was undoubtedly jealous of Young's appointment as Secretary to the Board of Agriculture, a post to which he thought that he himself had some claim.

A wise crack, or *bon mot* if you prefer, which holds that the only time when one is qualified to do a piece of research is when one has completed it, might have led a good many of us to erase early work had that proved possible. Young actually tried

it. *A Course of Experimental Agriculture* was published in two large quarto volumes in 1770. "Its author in after years regretted its publication and spent much time and money in buying up and destroying such copies as came upon the market." This book was partly the result of Young's unsuccessful farming at Samford Hall, Essex, which he took in 1767 in order to separate his wife from her mother-in-law. The two volumes of the *Course* have been estimated to contain nearly four million words. At the time Young said: "The principal part of the last seven years I have lived in such retirement, and given so unlimited an attention to matters of husbandry, that my constant employment, as well as amusement, when out on my fields, has been the registering experiments; . . . and my papers multiplied until they grew into volumes." Suspicious as one may be of the accuracy of some 3,000 experiments carried out in a few years, Young's mind was sufficiently critical to point out that certain types of experiment that had much to commend them omitted the factor which to the practical farmer was the most essential of all, the cash profit. This was the one yardstick by which to decide whether or not to adopt the experimental method on a farm worked "for to get a living." He recognized the value of knowing the exact details of how the work was done, but believed the cash profit to be unequivocal, while the yield alone meant nothing. Any increase might in fact have been secured at too great a cost. He pointed out that "It is impossible for single experiments, or from a great number, in different lands, separately considered, to deduce a satisfactory proof of the superiority of any method," and he disdained experiments for one or two years and calculations for many years based upon them. All this is very just, but I cannot help having a sneaking feeling that many of the costs given in Young's own record of experiments were like those in other types of farming treatise, to which he took such great exception. They were in fact estimates rather than actual costings. He probably knew very well how much it cost to plow an acre both at Bradfield and at Samford, and did not hesitate to use this cost as a guide to the expense of plowing for the purpose of an experiment. Probably his other costings were of the same type although, of course, there is no actual proof that it is so. He did, however, try to suppress the book, and that may have been partly because he was wholly satisfied neither with the way the experiments had been carried out in the field nor with the results he had recorded.

The mere bulk of the *Course of Experimental Agriculture* is a prelude of the indefatigable industry which produced the two hundred and fifty volumes about or bearing on farming problems in a longish life. Such an output could not but be unequal, and aroused admiration and contempt, both in his lifetime and later, although the later criticisms were more kindly than those published contemporarily. Ernle wrote enthusiastically:

> His careless ease of style, his racy forcible English, his gift of happy phrases, his quick observation, his wealth of miscellaneous detail, make him the first of English agricultural writers. Apart from the value of the facts which they contain, his tours, with their fresh word-pictures, their gossip, their personal incidents, and even their irrelevancies, have the charm of private diaries.

Ernle added that "Young was a man of strong prejudices. He was also wanting in a power of generalization. But he worked untiringly for what he believed to be the progress of good farming."

Thorold Rogers went even farther in his strictures. For him Young "is no economist at all in the most shadowy sense of the word, for he has no real conception of the harmony of interests, the exposition of which is the true function of the economist. His entire sympathy is with agricultural production. Everything must lend itself to this result."

Russell M. Garnier, whose *History of* *English Landed Interest* I admire, perhaps got closer to the crux of the question when he wrote, "He [Young] was not so much instrumental in conveying knowledge to the common farmer, as in becoming the vehicle by which the latter's want of knowledge was made known to the experts." It might be added that he told the experts what the common farmer already knew. Garnier added: "No history of English land would be complete without a careful analysis of his character, life and writings, and no chronicler of the agriculture practised a hundred years ago could ignore a man whose name stands out as a landmark between the communal husbandry of the middle ages [*sic*] and the scientific processes of the present day [1890]. He forms one of a trio with Cobbett and Caird," but he was the first and foremost of this trio. Young's "mind was not so expansive as to fit him for economical reasoning. . . . We hardly think, however, that Rogers has read Young's character aright. . . . Nor, again, does Mr. Prothero [Ernle] quite hit off his particular idiosyncracies." A little later he added a comment which greatly pleases me: "it is probably correct to say that the secret of Young's success in literature was an imperfect literary education. . . . But a college education would have just muzzled that audacity of thought and vigour of expression which lifted his powers of composition above those of more refined but insipid writers."

At almost the same time as these three writers were stating that Young was possessed of no powers of generalization, he was called "a severe political economist" by Pell.

> Beyond this his head was always nearer the ground than the skies. He was no 'mooner.' He understood first principles, and, having mastered them, they became with him fixed principles. . . . First in the ranks of writers on husbandry and rural economy, he was as complete a failure as a farmer. . . . In the business of farming, indeed, many are the ex-

amples of brilliant conceptions in the study and conspicuous blundering in the field. In the present day, more even than at the commencement of the century, quackery in the disguise of science prances and parades on the made-up advertising jade in heroic style; while poor time-worn practice, plodding along on the lines of honest study and experience, sometimes scarcely meets with the respect it deserves.

Pell was, of course, only a farmer, otherwise he would not have dared to call Young an economist. However, fashions change and the pure reasoning, so much detested of Young, must today be based on just such surveys as he was the first to make. Reasoning today, in applied economics at any rate, has to be based in facts. This was just what Young tried to do in his Northern Tour. If he was not so successful as he might have been, few pioneers are, but they line out the tracks which others may follow. If he had done no more than this Young would have some claim to the title which Rogers so scornfully denied him, but the field survey of farming soon leads to much wider interests. Farming touches humanity at all points. It provides food, leather, wool, clothing, and numerous other commodities. All these become industrial in processing, transport, and marketing, and the attempt to separate farm economics from industrial economics is quite arbitrary, only existing in the mind of man as an organization of his methods of thinking. Insofar as he was concerned with the cost of production of farm output, Young was an economist, and I am afraid I cannot see where he lacks the power of generalization unless it is because he failed to carry on with his statistical attempts, which may have been impossible for quite other reasons. He had to make a living out of his writings until he was appointed Secretary to the Board of Agriculture, and that alone drove him to a constant output. He had little time to stop and generalize. He was too busy with accumulating data and publishing it, a serious defect in character, no doubt, but the man had to eat. He was inclined to admit that he was prepared to leave collation of the data to others—as he did in the preface to his *General View . . . of Essex.*

It was natural for a temperament like Young's to be attracted by novelties. Helpless as he was in this respect, I think it was a more important defect than his inability, whether due to natural incapacity, or too little leisure for thinking, for generalization. Any novelty was bound to be extolled by Young, and I suspect that some of the novelties that he found so admirable may have deserved the oblivion into which they have since fallen. When he described them he probably raised a controversy about their merits and thus aided progress indirectly by stimulating ideas either antagonistic or favorable. If any harm was done it was to the credulous well-to-do, because the ordinary farmer would only adopt something well tried which he was convinced would bring him in a profit.

Young's early defense of the common farmer is another facet of his character. He was a "good mixer" and was at home in any society—dustmen or dukes. This universality enabled him to obtain information where another man would have failed, and he is likely to have secured some of it, as he said himself in a widely quoted passage, because he could, in an age of toping, hold his own at the bottle.

Young's life is an example of a chance which decides a man's interests. If he had never gone to Bradfield to farm, the improvements of the eighteenth century would still have happened because the steadily growing pressure of population demanded them. However, Young went to Bradfield because he had nowhere else to go, and from that chance he became the prophet of an improved agriculture of such industry that is is wonderful to relate. How he succeeded in finding the time to do all he did is puzzling, but he did it and so left an indelible mark on the history of his time, as well as a history of that time so far as its then major industry, farming, is concerned.

LIKE "THE AGRICULTURAL REVOLUTION," the expression "the industrial revolution" leaves much to be desired. As it has been applied to the economic development of eighteenth-century England, it has made more often for a misunderstanding than for an understanding of the past. For one thing, it minimizes or ignores the industrial growth of earlier centuries and overlooks the striking industrial changes that took place in the later Middle Ages and in the Tudor and Stuart periods. Furthermore, it distorts the changes that occurred in the last half of the eighteenth century—a time when industrial development was not nearly so rapid as the term "revolution" implies. In 1800, for example, more than two decades after Watt had patented his famous invention, there were only some three hundred steam engines in use in all Britain. Finally, the label is misleading because it differentiates much too sharply the industrial growth of England from that of the Continent and reads into the eighteenth century various conditions that were generally characteristic of the mid-nineteenth. For these reasons specialists in economic history have come increasingly to put the label in quotation marks or to avoid its use altogether. One authority has called it "an unhappily chosen epithet for a singularly constructive epoch." Another has stated that it was helpful when it originally came into use, but it has by now "served its turn." In the following article, Professor John U. Nef, of the University of Chicago, author of several books and many articles on early-modern economic history, examines the origin of the concept of the English industrial revolution and explains the reasons for his objections to it. The reader will note that, unlike most present-day historians, Professor Nef does not hesitate to moralize.

THE INDUSTRIAL REVOLUTION RECONSIDERED

JOHN U. NEF

I

Economic history, as a subject of separate study, is now nearly a hundred years old. No other idea which has emerged from it has gained a tithe of the attention that scholars, teachers, and the general public have focused on the "industrial revolution." Yet there is scarcely a conception in economic history more misleading than one which relates all the important problems of our modern civilization to economic changes that are represented as taking place in England between 1760 and 1832. There is scarcely a conception that rests on less

secure foundations than one which finds the key to an understanding of the modern industrialized world in these seventy-two years of English economic history.

Knowledge of the manner in which the conventional view of the industrial revolution originated should have made the careful scholar wary about treating it as an "open sesame" to modern history and to the constructive study of modern society. As a supposedly scientific generalization, it goes back to the early eighteen-eighties, when young Arnold Toynbee delivered some brilliant lectures at Oxford. He died prematurely at thirty, from overstrain in the social

Reprinted by special permission from *The Journal of Economic History*, III (1943), 1-25. The footnotes which originally appeared with this essay have been omitted.

and educational work into which he threw himself with extraordinary energy during the last five years of his life, in spite of his delicate health. He left nothing in a form intended for publication. He had spoken without notes. But it was decided to make use of notes taken by students who had attended his course. In 1884 a small volume was published posthumously, entitled *Lectures on the Industrial Revolution of the Eighteenth Century in England.*

Because of the chronological framework of Toynbee's lectures, the industrial revolution has been widely represented as beginning in 1760. If any of us as schoolboys, when our pliable young minds first met the conception, had taken the time to inquire into general political history, we should have seen that his reason for choosing that particular year was simply that it marked the accession of George III. But, in our youth, we were given to understand that great wars were things of the past, and that political history was a boring, almost an obsolete, subject. We were all too willing to accept this view because it relieved us of a part of our obligation to study. Our attitude toward past political events resembled that of the small boy who pleased his isolationist and Republican father, on the eve of our entering this war, by saying, "I hate wah." When asked why, he explained, "because wah makes history, and I hate history." So, if we thought about it at all, we assumed that there must be some economic reason for beginning the industrial revolution in 1760, and some economic reason for ending it, as Mr. and Mrs. Hammond did in their famous volumes, in 1832. But that particular date was also determined by political history. It marked the passage of the first Reform Act.

Yet the selection of the two dates was not as capricious from the point of view of economic history as their mere political significance suggests. The phrase "industrial revolution" had a long history before Toynbee's lectures fixed it in the form in which it has been fed through textbooks to the last two generations of students. As a phrase it goes back at least to the beginning of the nineteenth century. It was apparently first used by Frenchmen, and it was certainly much more common in France than in England during the 1820's and 1830's. When Frenchmen at that time spoke of an "industrial revolution," they usually had in mind changes that had been taking place in England during their lives. The phrase was convenient for describing industrial innovations which were startling and which spread with extraordinary rapidity from one industry to another.

The germ of the thesis that the course of economic progress in England from the middle of the eighteenth down to the thir-

---

SIR WILLIAM J. ASHLEY: British economist, historian, and public servant (d. 1927) who became the leading professorial advocate of Joseph Chamberlain's protective tariff policy. His *Introduction to English Economic History and Theory* (1888-1893), *The Economic Organisation of England* (1914), and *The Bread of Our Forefathers* (1928) are among his most important scholarly writings.

THOMAS MUN: English merchant and director of the East India Company (d. 1641). To defend the policies of the Company, he wrote two books that have become classics in the literature of mercantilism: *A Discourse of Trade* (1621) and the posthumously published *England's Treasure by Foreign Trade* (1664).

DEAN JOSIAH TUCKER: British clergyman and pamphleteer (d. 1799) who wrote extensively on the economic, colonial, and political questions of his time. He started out as a mercantilist in his economic views, but he moved increasingly in the direction of a belief in qualified *laissez faire*. The reason he is not better known is that he was overshadowed by his contemporary, Adam Smith. A selection from his economic and political writings, edited by R. L. Schuyler, was published in 1931.

ties of the nineteenth century revolutionized the life of the world is to be found in one of the most famous and widely read histories ever written. It is set forth in a conspicuous place, in the justly celebrated third chapter of Macaulay's *History of England,* first published in 1848. This is what Macaulay wrote:

It can easily be proved that, in our own land, the national wealth has, during at least six centuries, been almost uninterruptedly increasing; that it was greater under the Tudors than under the Plantagenets; that it was greater under the Stuarts than under the Tudors; that, in spite of battles, sieges, and confiscations, it was greater on the day of the Restoration than on the day that the Long Parliament met; that, in spite of maladministration, of extravagance, of public bankruptcy, of two costly and unsuccessful wars, of the pestilence and of the fire, it was greater on the day of the death of Charles the Second than on the day of his Restoration. This progress, having continued during many ages, became at length, about the middle of the eighteenth century, portentously rapid, and has proceeded, during the nineteenth, with accelerated velocity . . . . The consequence is that a change to which the history of the old world furnishes no parallel has taken place in our country. Could the England of 1685 be, by some magical process, set before our eyes, we should not know one landscape in a hundred or one building in ten thousand.

Toynbee may well have been influenced directly by this passage (he could hardly have failed to be influenced indirectly) for he lived when the reading public got most of its history from such works as Macaulay's. Now that the substantial histories of the nineteenth century have been superseded by popular biographies and up-to-date textbooks, flimsy and soon out-of-date, few would think to look for Macaulay as a father of the modern conception of the industrial revolution. By the time Toynbee

lectured, modern scientific history was coming into its own. It was beginning to narrow the treatment of historical subjects acceptable to the learned, to squeeze out much of the sparkle and dash, to diminish the scope. But, whatever research lies behind Toynbee's lectures, his framework of industrial history and the significance which he saw in the framework are in accord with this passage from Macaulay. And, whatever the merits of Macaulay's *History,* the picture of change which he painted was not derived from an extensive examination of economic documents and statistics, such as the careful modern scholar would demand before he took seriously any generalization like the one made by Macaulay and later by Toynbee in his *Lectures.*

I am one of those persons who think that ideas are important. I think that they influence the conduct of men and the course of history, although they are obviously only one of many determining factors. Among the important ideas, many are derived to a large extent from history. Ideas are never photographs of actual scenes and experiences. When we speak of a historical idea as true, we are thinking of the general impression conveyed by a writer which corresponds most perfectly to the facts as they are revealed by the materials accessible to us. But in order to present such an impression, it is not enough to be in possession of a vast quantity of materials on some special aspect of history in some special period; it is necessary to understand the relation of this special subject and period to history as a whole. Partly for want of such a general view of even the whole of industrial history from 1760 to 1832, a warped impression of the place of the period in economic and general history was retained by economic historians in the early twentieth century. Accurate specialization can produce inaccurate history no less than can the historical generalizations which preceded the age of accurate specialization. The warped impression of economic history, derived from the followers of Toynbee, became still more warped as it was dished up to high school and college students out of textbooks and popular biographies. It has become so warped that the present generation of economic historians, whose knowledge of the period from 1760 to 1832 is fuller than that of their predecessors, are faced with a formidable task when they attempt to correct the popular misconceptions. Their task is not made easier by the repetition of the misconceptions in most recent textbooks assigned to students.

What are these misconceptions? How do they stand in the way of a true knowledge of the relation of the western peoples today to their history, and an understanding of the role which the mind might play in the twentieth-century crisis of civilization? For one thing, we have been mistaken about the time when the industrial revolution began. Sir William Ashley, one of the two pupils whose notes were used to reconstruct Toynbee's *Lectures,* tells us that the lecturer used the word "revolution" in the sense of "a rapid and sweeping phase" of evolution. If such a change in the tempo of industrial development is the proper test, is the accession of George III the right date to select for the beginning of the industrial revolution?

"What a change [since] 1785!" wrote Stendhal. "In the two thousand years of recorded world history, so sharp a revolution in customs, ideas, and beliefs has perhaps never occurred before." During his life, Stendhal's most read book was neither the *Chartreuse de Parme* nor the *Rouge et le noir;* it was *Racine et Shakespeare,* an essay in which he examined the social changes that were leading in the arts from classicism to romanticism. The words I quoted occur in the second part of this book, which was published in 1825. Very likely Stendhal was not thinking of English industry when he wrote them. But, as we shall see, the striking speeding up in the industrial evolution of England began, not in 1750 or 1760, but in the 1780's. A flash of artistic insight enabled Stendhal to hit on the right date. His accuracy leads one to ask whether contemporary university teachers may not be excessively zealous in protecting their students against contaminating their "scientific" view of the world by reading enduring works of literature. For even in the matter of observable facts, the books of great artists are not always less true than those of modern specialists in the "social sciences" and the "humanities."

What does it matter, men may ask. What are twenty-five years one way or the other in the great ocean of time? The answer is that the conventional date for the beginning of the industrial revolution gives us a false view of the economic history of eighteenth-century Europe and of its relation to general eighteenth-century history. According to the popular misconception, English, or at any rate British industrial development, was in sharp contrast to Continental throughout the eighteenth century, and not simply at the very end of it. But, as we shall see, the rate of industrial change from about 1735 to 1785 was no more rapid in Great Britain than in France, a far larger country with nearly three times as many people. What is striking in eighteenth-century economic history is less the contrasts than the resemblances between Great Britain and the Continent, both in the rate of economic development and in the directions that development was taking. The resemblances more than the contrasts should arrest the historian concerned with eighteenth-century thought, art, and even politics. The conventional way of dating the beginning of the industrial revolution hinders us from recognizing how homogeneous European civilization became, in all its manifold aspects, during the two generations preceding the French Revolution.

In the sense of a phenomenal speeding up of economic evolution, the industrial revolution, which began in England in the 1780's, spread across the Channel only somewhat later. For nowhere on the Continent did the industrial revolution, in this sense, begin until after the fall of Napoleon in 1815. In Germany and the rest of central Europe it began only in the 1830's and 1840's, after the passage of the first English Reform Act. It was not until the second half of the nineteenth century that the industrial revolution became world-wide. "Il y a eu l'âge antique (et biblique). Il y a eu l'âge chrétien. Il y a l'âge moderne" ["There was the age of Antiquity (and the Bible). There was the Christian age. There is the modern age"], chanted Péguy on the eve of the World War of 1914. The modern age, he went on, not without some exaggeration, had come in with the Third Republic. At the time of the Franco-Prussian War, "une paroisse ordinaire . . . était infiniment plus près d'une paroisse du quinzième siècle, ou du quatrième siècle, mettons du cinquième ou du huitième, que d'une paroisse actuelle" ["an ordinary parish . . . was infinitely closer to a parish of the fifteenth or of the fourteenth century, even of the fifth or the eighth, than to a parish of the present day"].

Many great figures in the history of thought and the arts, who have been associated with the industrial revolution because it is supposed to have begun in 1760, were really part of a homogeneous and relatively stable eighteenth-century civilization, part of an age when economic changes were only moderately rapid. Adam Smith's "progressive state," of which I shall speak later, was not a state in the throes of the phenomenally rapid development that characterized the industrial revolution. Johnson, Sterne, and Fielding; Hogarth and Gainsborough; Voltaire, Rousseau, Montesquieu, and Buffon; Kant, Schiller, and Goethe; Haydn, Mozart, Schubert, and Beethoven—all lived in a pre-industrial-revolution world.

Economic determinism gives a false view of history. But one does not, for that reason, have to assume that the economic environment is without its relation to culture. The work of all the great men I mentioned can be better understood when it is recognized that none of them created their masterpieces in an atmosphere of phenomenally rapid material progress, phenomenally rapid mechanization of industry, or phenomenally rapid change in the speed of transport and communications. None of them created their masterpieces when

thought and even belief (as if belief can be at the mercy of world events) were expected to change as rapidly as the methods of performing labor changed during the industrial revolution.

The violence done to the cause of truth by the popular misconception of the industrial revolution is not limited to the matter of dating. The picture of the historical process produced by it has helped to bring about a general misunderstanding of the relation of western man in our time to the history of past ages. In the high schools and colleges most Americans of my generation were taught to think of this globe as a primitive and uncivilized place before the great changes brought about by the industrial revolution. We were given the impression that it had produced a world which was, in every important way, so great an improvement on that before inhabited by mankind, that men and women could afford to trust the future of philosophical truth, morality, and beauty to economic development which seemed everywhere to be following a most gratifying course. Many of our teachers, all our influential playmates, left us with the impression that the only important things in life were the material conveniences: Pullman cars, electricity, sanitation, remedies against disease, and machinery driven by steam and hydroelectric power. We associated them all with the changes produced by the industrial revolution. It was taken for granted that the Christian religious beliefs, which had flourished prior to the industrial revolution, were simply the superstitions of primitive men and women, without our advantages. If we needed a religion, Professor T. N. Carver, the well-known Harvard economist, told us that it ought properly to be a "religion worth having." He explained that he meant just what he said; that he used the term "worth" in the most narrow economic sense. He reduced art, along with religion, to economic terms. Thus the "worth" of a work of art was measured, in the last analysis, by the volume of production which it generated. It might stimulate the wealthy businessman, who contemplated it, to make more money than he would have done if he had never seen it. A person in Dresden gazing at the Sistine Madonna might get what the Viennese, in happier days, called a *Stimmung*. This—Professor Carver opined, without giving really scientific reasons for his opinion—might put the businessman in a mood to work an extra day at his office, and lead indirectly to the sinking of a new mining shaft near Villach.

While Ashley's recollection of Toynbee's thesis may be correct, the popular impression of the industrial revolution is of something far more cataclysmic than a simple speeding up of evolution. The popular impression is of a transformation of the conditions of life that has brought human beings into a new world which does not bear comparison with the world of their ancestors. It has been assumed even by professors of the social sciences that there were no earlier periods of remotely comparable economic change, although scholars are now coming to recognize that in England during the reigns of Elizabeth and James I an early industrial revolution occurred. For this was a period when the rate of growth in the output of coal and some other commodities was comparable to that at the end of the eighteenth and the beginning of the nineteenth century. Scholars are learning that the late twelfth and thirteenth centuries were also a time of remarkably rapid economic development. They are learning that earlier civilizations had several periods of economic change, comparable in many ways to those which western civilization has undergone, although there were of course important differences. Rapid change is not a new phenomenon. Dynamic societies existed before the nineteenth century.

It is true that the industrial changes of the last hundred and fifty years, and above all the changes at the juncture of the nineteenth and twentieth centuries, have been on a much faster scale than those of any other period of equal length. They have affected a larger part of the earth. But the inference widely drawn from these facts,

and from the widespread disposition to minimize the changes of earlier periods, has led to the assumption that nothing which was done or thought before the industrial revolution is of real importance for any of our present problems. Not only the scientific and the technological knowledge which existed before that time, but also the philosophy, the theology, the art, and the political thought of all earlier periods are regarded as irrelevant to us. It is conceded that the specialist may study these subjects as curiosities and that students may take college courses in them to pass examinations, but it is assumed that they cannot help to guide men and women in the world in which we live. They cannot help us to find again common principles, or even common concepts and problems, in the realms of theology, philosophy, politics, and art. As one genial and industrious sociologist has put it, in the modern world of change "morality, as it is generally conceived, will have no place." He might have said the same of beauty and of truth.

Thus the conventional idea of the industrial revolution has interposed itself like a dense fog between us and our traditions. The fog at our backs makes it difficult to take our bearings and plot our course. A more intelligent knowledge of the past and of the works of great thinkers of the past could help to reveal the unity and essential simplicity of all great intellectual problems. It could help us to see the true connections between the vast number of special disciplines, into which scholarship is now broken up. Such knowledge could help us to incorporate the valuable new material, together with the new theories, which recent specialized scholarship provides, into a fresh synthesis in the life of the mind, the need for which is dimly felt today in many intellectual circles. In the cultural life and thought of the eighteenth century there were still common concepts and propositions which artists and other men of culture throughout Europe understood. We have lost the art of living life as a whole and the art of looking with our minds at the whole of man's universe. The crisis of the twentieth century compels us to reconsider the meaning of the industrial revolution and the nature of the society which it helped to destroy.

II

When we look back upon the late seventeenth and early eighteenth centuries, without the prejudices of modern "progressive" men, we are confronted with a society in many ways more intelligent and sophisticated in its thought and its conduct than that of our own time. The men and women who move about France in the pages of Madame de Lafayette, Madame de Sévigné, Saint-Simon, and Marivaux possess a sense of fitness and form nowhere equaled today. Their taste and good manners were grounded partly in an intense belief in the value of high moral standards, whatever the actual state of morality may have been, and I am not suggesting that it was exceptionally good. It is no accident that the English eighteenth-century novelist who captured the attention of the French more than any other should have been the leading English moralist of the age—the author of *Clarissa*. Diderot thought Richardson worthy of comparison with Homer, and he was not given to excessive statements about most aesthetic matters.

In the seventeenth century, English society had differed from French in important respects. Two call for particular comment here. First, the social and political position of the mercantile class, which made its money in trade and finance and by the development of mining, manufacturing, and shipping, was higher in England than in France. Its influence on political policy, on thought, science, and art was much greater in England than in France. This had been true ever since the early Stuart period. By contrast, the weakness of the merchants in France had begun to concern some Frenchmen by the middle of the seventeenth century. Thus in 1646, four years after Richelieu's death, an obscure French subject,

Jean Eon, published a book called *Le Commerce honorable*.

The French have long since entertained [he wrote] a very disparaging opinion of commerce, which they consider suited only to debased souls . . . . This is the opinion which the majority of Frenchmen hold and especially those of the *tiers état,* who have means and desire to elevate their children to the most honorable stations . . . . They have ambitions to acquire the offices of justice which the state in its need has created in great numbers, so that the majority of those who are rich and have means to carry on commerce abandon it, in order to acquire such positions for their children . . . . It is for this reason that for the maintenance of trade there remain only those of low estate . . . . Whenever, from that small number of Frenchmen who are engaged in foreign commerce, some one amasses a fortune, which is the very moment when he is the most capable of pursuing foreign trade, he abandons it in order to place his children in some office of state.

Eon's book had a very small sale. It does not seem to have contributed much to the main currents of French political and economic thought, then concerned almost altogether with strengthening the power of the Crown. Conditions in England were very different. There economic writers, like Mun, held that it was a principal function of the government to support the interests of the merchants. By serving their own interest, Mun and other British writers assumed that the merchants naturally promoted the national interest.

The other difference between the two countries, which it is necessary to emphasize, relates to the condition and to the outlook of the landed classes. As Taine pointed out in the nineteenth century in his famous work, *Les Origines de la France contemporaine,* there was no real equivalent in early modern times in France (or for that matter in any other Continental country) for the

English squirearchy, a social class possessing intense vitality, and one that used its energy in developing the economic resources of the estates over which it presided. The squirearchy was essentially of mercantile origin. In his *Complete English Tradesman,* first published in 1726, Defoe gave the following title to Chapter XXIV: "Extracts from the genealogies of several illustrious families of our English nobility, some of which owe their rise to trade, and others their descent and fortunes to prudent alliances with the families of citizens." It was an age when authors nearly put the contents of a chapter into its title.

The English squirearchy was not created in the eighteenth century, any more than the political power of the English merchant class was first established at that time. In a fascinating article, Professor Tawney has recently shown that the rise of the squirearchy—or gentry—is associated with the period of the early industrial revolution, the period roughly from 1540 to 1640.

If that period was one in which the English nation was striking out in new directions, economically, socially, philosophically, and artistically, directions different from those taken by most of the Continental peoples the same thing can hardly be said of the period which separates the English Restoration from the French Revolution. In economic and social life, as in culture, the forces that were drawing the Continent and Great Britain together were stronger in this later period than those that continued to hold them apart. Although Protestants were sometimes persecuted on the Continent and Catholics in England, wars were no longer fought over religious issues as they had been in the sixteenth and early seventeenth centuries. According to Jordan, the principles of religious toleration had won the day in England by the Restoration in 1660. In the eighteenth century, it made great progress on the Continent. Dean Tucker, who, although a churchman, has left his mark chiefly as a forerunner of Adam Smith in political economy, thought ill of "the Romish religion" mainly because it interfered with the economic improvement he had so much at heart. But he remarked in 1750 that "the Bigotry of the Court of France is not near so great, as it was in former times."

As British ways of thinking and acting spread to the Continent, Continental, and particularly French ways, spread to Great Britain. Classicism in conduct, thought, and art was not only influencing the whole of Continental Europe in the early eighteenth century, but it was also making a great impression on the English. The differences between France and England remained important, of course. To a cultivated Frenchman, like Montesquieu, England was a country of coal smoke, of morose, beef-eating squires, of shopkeepers, and of clergymen who, like Tucker, made religion their trade and trade their religion. But the differences between Englishmen and Continentals were not being accentuated in the eighteenth century. With Hogarth and Gainsborough, an art of painting develops in England which would not be mistaken for French or Italian, but is nevertheless much closer in artistic quality to the work of Continental contemporaries—Watteau and Fragonard, Canaletto and Guardi—than any English seventeenth-century painting is to the work of the best French, Dutch, Flemish, Spanish, and Italian painters of that earlier period.

When we think of the rich world of the early eighteenth century, with its fine literature, painting, and architecture, its wonderful music as exemplified by Scarlatti, Rameau, Handel, and above all by Bach, its polite manners, its strong sense of moral standards, its love of splendor in living, its limited warfare, resulting (except in central Europe) in what seems to us today a small number of deaths and even of casualties, we are inclined to regard the view of that society prevalent in the United States as a caricature of historical truth. It is true that if we measure the "general goodness" of life "for good people" by the criterion recently employed by one of our leading psychologists in comparing the cities of the United States, we are not likely to regard the civilization of the eighteenth century as of a high order. The material standard of living was, generally speaking, far lower than it was at the beginning of the twentieth century. The differences, however, must not be exaggerated. If Mr. Colin Clark's calculations are roughly correct, the Englishman at the end of the seventeenth century had, on the average, a somewhat larger command of economic goods to console him than the Italian, the Japanese, or the Russian has had in the interval between the two world wars, after nearly a century of unparalleled economic progress all over the globe.

But the Englishman in the late seventeenth and early eighteenth centuries was only about a third as well off as the Englishman in the decade preceding the present war. He died sooner. For the people of Great Britain, France, Germany, and the Low Countries, life was then on the average more than twenty years shorter. Punishments for crimes and even for misdemeanors were harsh and sometimes gruesome. Yet the working hours of the industrial laborer, though longer, were generally less monotonous than they are today. Nor was there any real equivalent, except in the discipline of the Prussian army as organized by Frederick William I, for the concentration camp and the firing squad of the modern totalitarian state. The French *lettres de cachet,* while arbitrary and secret, were not administered wholesale. They weighed chiefly upon members of powerful families, and involved imprisonment or banishment, either from the country or, with greater moderation, only from the court. They seldom led to the deliberate infliction of physical pain. Sometimes these *lettres* disposed of daughters against the will of their parents, either by marrying them off or by sending them to a convent.

While men of great character and learning were sometimes hustled off to prison without cause, the treatment they received frequently had compensations. Monsieur de Saci, the last of the great directors of Port-Royal, considered himself fortunate in one way when he was shut up for two years in the Bastille, because the asylum gave him exceptional opportunities to carry on his learned work. The quiet and rest enabled him to make much more rapid progress with his translation of the Old Testament than he could have done if he had been free. Unlike modern totalitarianism, French absolutism did not set about systematically to destroy the freedom of creative minds.

Most European countries in the eighteenth century, at least after 1730 or 1740, were what Adam Smith called "progressive." He measured progress in terms of the growth of the national dividend of goods and services. "It deserves to be remarked perhaps," he wrote, "that it is in the progressive state, while the society is advancing to the further acquisition, rather than when it has acquired its full complement of riches, that the condition of the laboring poor, of the great body of the people, seems to be the happiest and most comfortable. It is hard in the stationary and miserable in the declining state. The progressive state is in reality the cheerful and hearty state to all the different orders of society. The stationary is dull; the declining, melancholy."

This passage indicates that Adam Smith thought that mankind is generally happiest in the progressive state. Few modern economists would disagree. From the material standpoint, which is not the only one that should be considered (some economists to the contrary notwithstanding), is it not, as the passage which I have quoted suggests, less the total amount of wealth that men have that makes them rejoice than the fact that their wealth is increasing? If some of us were carried into the eighteenth century by magic (like Ralph Pendrel in Henry James's novel, *The Sense of the Past*), we should doubtless feel lost without the material conveniences to which we have been accustomed. We should remember that the eighteenth-century man would not have made that kind of comparison. He did not know what he lacked. It is an open question (there is much dispute about it among historians) whether or not the wage earner was increasing his real earnings in the eighteenth century. Whatever the truth on this point may be, wage earners still formed a much smaller minority of the population than they do today. There can be little doubt that material wealth had been growing very notably, at least since 1735, growing in almost every part of Europe more rapidly than population, which was also growing. People were becoming richer even before the industrial revolution.

III

When we compare the rate of economic development during the eighteenth century in the two leading countries of Europe, France and England, we find that the resemblances are more striking than the differences. Hence, if we are concerned with economic progress, it is one-sided to focus our attention upon Great Britain and neglect Continental nations, France in particular. When the size of the countries is considered, the economic development of France during the middle decades of the eighteenth century was in some ways more striking than that of England. In fact, the disposition of economic historians to think that British history will suffice for the student of rapid industrial progress in the eighteenth century is an example of the warped view of history to which the conventional picture of the industrial revolution has contributed. For the American schoolboy, brought up to estimate happiness in terms of measurable wealth, that picture has suggested, not simply that the world was uncivilized before 1760; it has actually suggested that whatever civilization there was before the Napoleonic era was largely confined to England!

Admittedly, as a certain James Puckle wrote, in 1697, British "artisans were universally allow'd the best upon Earth for Improvements." His words describe a condition that probably goes back to the time of Charles I. But what was the state of the industrial arts in France during the eighteenth century? Frenchmen like Montesquieu and Voltaire, men born just before Puckle published his tract, would have agreed with him

up to the hilt, as late as the 1730's, which is to say when Voltaire was entering middle life. His correspondence shows that he regarded as scandalous French ignorance of natural science in general, and of the achievements of Newton in particular. "In truth," he wrote of his countrymen in 1735, "we are the whipped cream of Europe." For him, the grace, the precision, the sweetness, and the finesse of French culture could not make up entirely for what he called the more masculine virtues in which the English excelled.

Voltaire's words were a reflection of existing conditions. They were also a lash to drive his countrymen to change these conditions. The lash was not ineffective, for the will to change existed. Under English influence and inspiration, the achievements of Frenchmen in most branches of natural science during the second half of the eighteenth century were hardly inferior to those of Englishmen. The admiration of Frenchmen for English achievements was reflected in a great many phases of French life. Frenchmen were studying with almost passionate enthusiasm (both in books and as travelers) the techniques developed in England for mining, manufacturing, and farming. The results were being applied to French industry. France and the Continent were drawing closer to England in economic life, as in culture and thought, particularly after the thirties of the eighteenth century. The economic and cultural *rapprochements* continued down to the era of the French Revolution. They helped to bind the intelligence of Europe into a common understanding approaching that which had existed in the thirteenth century.

The change in attitude extended to the economic policies of the French Crown toward industry and commerce. Here, too, there was a definite attempt in the eighteenth century to copy English policies, which, it was assumed, had had something to do with the economic leadership attained for British heavy industry in the early seventeenth century. The new French policies were all in the direction of the kind of laissez faire which many Anglo-Saxon economists have regarded as the chief means for attaining human happiness. There was as yet no important break in the restrictions imposed on foreign trade by high tariffs and export duties, against which writers on economic subjects had written in France as well as in England long before Adam Smith's time. But there were important changes in the relation of political authority to economic enterprise within France. During the eighteenth century French economic thinkers began to express the opinion that industrial enterprise was too much fettered by the government for the material welfare of the country. The practical results obtained by this new movement in French thought ought not to be exaggerated. Before 1789 it was not strong enough to bring about any general suppression of the tolls imposed on the transport of raw materials and commodities within the country. Opposition to the control exercised by the gilds over industry was widespread. Indeed this opposition culminated in an edict of 1776, designed to throw all crafts and professions open to every one, whether or not he had served an apprenticeship or joined a gild. But that edict was short-lived; it was withdrawn after the fall of Turgot; the gilds were reëstablished, and the corporate regime was even extended to certain crafts which hitherto had been free. There survived only a disposition on the part of public officials in Paris and in the provinces to disregard the old regulations, both of the gilds and of the central government, whenever they interfered with industrial production and the introduction of cheaper methods of mining and manufacturing.

One can see the process at work in Languedoc. Restrictions on the output of the chief textile enterprises were abolished early in the eighteenth century, and each merchant or group of merchants was allowed to decide independently how much cloth to produce for the market in the Levant. The construction of large coal-burning factories for the manufacture of glass bottles was encouraged, even though this was clearly an infringement of the privileges of a closed craft, the gentlemen glass makers, whose rights had been established by letters patent of 1436, and confirmed by subsequent letters patent in 1475, 1655, and 1727. A decree of 1744 revoked the exclusive right to refine sugar in the province, granted earlier to two successive companies of Montpellier merchants. This decree threw the industry open to every one.

Similar changes in policy may be observed in all provinces. The manner of leasing coal mines throughout the realm was radically changed by a decree of 1744. Previously the Crown had granted widespread monopolies, often covering a number of provinces, to various noblemen and others. Now concessions for starting new collieries in particular places could be obtained by any person with sufficient capital. Traders, merchants, and landlords, whose only passport was their financial resources, found it increasingly easy to enter any industry.

At the same time, the burdens imposed by the financial policies of the Crown upon the resources of the private merchant were somewhat lightened. After 1725 industrial capital and the profits from industry were largely relieved from the obligation to pay the *vingtième*. This impost became almost exclusively a tax on land. After 1740, the precious metal contained in the *livre tournois,* which had been reduced in almost every generation at least since the late fifteenth century, was maintained until the Revolution. The risk to creditors of the Crown from debasement, if not from default, diminished.

There was only one aspect of industrial life with which government officials concerned themselves more than they had in the past. Experience seemed to show in this case that government interference was needed to promote prosperity. Ministers, *intendants, subdélégués,* and inspectors of manufactures all worked to introduce new machinery, new kinds of furnaces, and new chemical processes into mining and manufacturing. More freely than in the past, the government advanced capital to help in the establishment of new enterprises. Immigration of foreign technicians and capitalists was welcomed. Although a patent system, modeled on that of England, was not adopted until 1791, much was done by the state before the Revolution to encourage the scientist and the inventor. Persons were no longer locked up as insane, as Solomon de Caus, who speculated on the force in a jet of steam, had been locked up by Richelieu, when he sought support for his inventions; insane persons were kept at liberty if they could help to introduce labor-saving machinery.

IV

The remarkable changes in the French attitude toward the practical aspects of natural science, toward industrial technology, and toward the proper relations of government to economic enterprise were accompanied by an equally remarkable growth in the volume of industrial output and in the number of working people employed in mines and manufactures. The change in the tempo and in the nature of industrial development began in the thirties and forties of the eighteenth century, at just about the time when Frenchmen were complaining that the scissors and knives made by their artisans were "plus beau que solide" ["more attractive than solid"], and when Voltaire was telling his contemporaries about the astonishing exhibition of machines at the court of Lorraine, many of them made by a simple locksmith, who had been sent by the late duke to study in England. Voltaire said this locksmith had become, by study and training, "a philosopher." Voltaire used the word in the English sense. He meant by it a natural scientist. Putting a man in that category was the highest praise he could give.

Between 1735 and 1785 the rate of growth in industrial output and in large-scale industry in France was apparently at least as rapid as in England, and possibly more rapid. Since the thirteenth century, there had been no fifty years of comparably rapid growth in the volume of French production. No fifty years since the half century following the Hundred Years' War had even approached those from 1735 to 1785 in the rate of economic progress. We have excellent evidence, for example, that between 1735 and 1785 the output of coal and iron grew faster in France than in England, although it must be remembered in connection with coal, that England was already a coal-burning country at the beginning of the eighteenth century. Compared with the high mounds beside the collieries in Durham and Northumberland around 1710, the piles of coal beside the chief French pits resembled anthills. The ignorance of some educated Frenchmen concerning the nature of mineral fuel is not a little comical. In 1709, the *intendant* in Lyons was a certain M. Trudaine—not the famous *intendant* of the same name, who later ruled Auvergne. Along with other *intendants,* our M. Trudaine was asked by the *contrôleur général* to supply reports on the state of the coal mines. He reported on those about Saint-Etienne, which were at the time, with those in Lyonnais, the principal collieries in France. M. Trudaine sent the *contrôleur général* a very pessimistic account, but he combined his pessimism with delightfully ignorant optimism. Production had fallen off by half, he wrote. He attributed this to the exhaustion of the supplies of coal, but he told the *contrôleur général* not to let that bother him. Nature would mend matters. The mines would soon replenish themselves. Often, he wrote, colliers who return to pits they have abandoned a few months before find that coal has sprouted in their absence.

Such an ignorance of geological processes would have exposed any public man in England or the Low Countries to ridicule even a century earlier. Undoubtedly one reason for it was the small importance of coal mining in France in the first decade of the eighteenth century. From the reports of the *intendants* in 1709, it appears that the annual output of the entire country amounted to less than a hundred thousand tons. Great Britain, a country less than half as populous, was producing in the neighborhood of three million tons. But the progress of the coal-mining industry in France was very rapid after the discovery, about 1715, of mines in the rich coal fields of the north, along the Belgian frontier; progress was more rapid still after the decree of 1744, which made it easier for capitalists to get mining concessions on reasonable terms. During the decade preceding the French Revolution, 1780-1789, the annual output of coal in France probably exceeded 700,000 tons. It may possibly have amounted to a million tons, an increase of eight or tenfold, or even more, in eighty years. Meanwhile British production had grown too, but at a much slower pace. During the decade 1781-1790, the annual output in Great Britain was probably in the neighborhood of ten million tons, an increase of not much more than threefold in eighty years.

The progress of the iron manufacture in the two countries presents similar contrasts. In 1720, England and Wales were producing about twenty-five thousand tons of pig iron and eighteen thousand tons of bar iron, a considerable part of which had passed through the pig-iron stage. The iron output of France at this time is quite uncertain, but it is doubtful whether it much exceeded that of England and Wales, even if we include Lorraine, which was under the sovereignty, not of the king of France, but of the Duke Leopold. In 1789, the output of pig iron in France, according to a recent authoritative estimate, was about a hundred and thirty-six thousand tons, the output of bar iron about ninety-four thousand tons. Production had possibly tripled during the previous seventy years. On the eve of the French Revolution, the output of iron in England and Wales was less than half that of France. The figures for England, Wales, plus Scotland were only sixty-eight thousand tons of pig iron and thirty-three thousand tons of bar iron. As late as 1757, the output of iron in England and Wales had been no greater than in 1720; it was only a little

greater in 1775. Practically all the growth in the eighteenth century took place after that year. Between 1720 and 1775, while the output of iron in Great Britain hardly increased at all, that in France probably at least doubled.

It would be unsafe to generalize from these figures for coal and iron concerning the growth in the total volume of production in the two countries. France was especially backward in the use of coal fuel when the century opened, partly because of her abundant timber supplies. In certain regions the French turned to coal in the eighteenth century, as the English had turned in the Elizabethan Age, because of the exhaustion of the forests. The earlier exhaustion of timber in Great Britain is the chief explanation for the stationary condition of iron production during the first three quarters of the eighteenth century; indeed the general use of coal in making iron began only in the last quarter. The course of iron production is, furthermore, an imperfect guide to the prosperity of the English metal industries generally. English imports from Scandinavia and from America of iron, suitable for manufacturing into finished commodities, were increasing between 1720 and 1775. The production in England of tin, lead, and copper was also growing substantially, largely because the ores of all three metals were smelted extensively with coal fuel much earlier than was iron ore.

When we consider other important industrial products, there is apparently no case in which the rate of industrial growth in France from 1735 to 1785 was in such remarkable contrast to that in England, as it was in the cases of coal and iron. The output of cotton and woolen cloth probably grew more slowly in France than in England, but English capital, some English labor, and much English technical skill, were being introduced into the French textile industry, as they were also into mining, metallurgy, paper and glass making, and nearly all other heavy manufactures.

On the eve of the French Revolution several very large plants, each employing something like a thousand or more work-men and representing an investment of many millions of francs, were in operation in France. There was one for mining coal at Anzin in the north, another for metal-lurgy at Le Creusot in central France, and a third for making glass at Saint-Gobain in Picardy. Anzin was to be the inspiration for Zola's famous novel, *Germinal;* Le Creusot was to come into the hands of the Schneider family and to gain notoriety as the property of men who were called, between the two world wars, the "merchants of death." Establishments of this size were a novelty even in the second half of the eighteenth century, except perhaps in shipbuilding. It is doubtful whether there were any as large in England before the 1780's. Mines and factories employing more than a hundred workmen were no novelty in either country. In France the number of these increased very rapidly during the last fifty years of the *ancien régime,* so that by 1785 there were several score. While parts of the coun-try were not touched by this remarkable industrial development, and although Eng-land remained in 1785 the most important industrial nation in Europe, her lead over France in the volume of output per capita from mines and manufactures was possibly less striking than it had been fifty years before. The same may be said of her lead circa 1785 in the use of machinery and large furnaces, and in the prevalence of large privately owned enterprises. During the last half century of the *ancien régime,* France was not falling behind England in the development of heavy industry as she had been falling behind, except for very brief periods, ever since the Religious Wars.

Confirmation for this new view of eight-eenth-century economic progress can be found in the records of commerce and of population growth. Of course, one should be a little suspicious of official figures, if the ways of gathering them practised under the exigent demands of Napoleon are typi-cal. Napoleon's minister of the interior, Chaptal, no mean chemist in his own right, left a warning for posterity about the sta-tistics gathered in the Napoleonic era. "Il commandait quelquefois l'impossible et vou-lait être servi sur-le-champ. Il demandait des états qui, pour être exacts, auraient exigé un travail de plusieurs semaines, et il les demandait à l'heure parce qu'il ne savait pas ajourner ses besoins . . . . Il valait mieux mentir avec audace que de retarder pour pouvoir lui offrir la vérité. Je l'ai vu affecter une grande prédilection pour Reynaud de Saint-Jean d'Angely, parce que celui-ci ré-pondait hardiment à toutes ses questions et n'aurait pas été embarrassé s'il lui avait demandé combien de millions de mouches se trouvaient en Europe au mois d'août. C'est sur des bases aussi hasardées qu'on a établi plusieurs fois l'état des fabriques, celui de l'agriculture, etc., et c'est d'après cela qu'on donnait à la France pour quelques milliards de commerce et d'industrie dans les temps les plus calamiteux." ["He some-times ordered the impossible and wanted to be served at once. He demanded reports which, to be accurate, would have required several weeks' work, and he demanded them right away because he did not know how to defer his requirements. . . . It was better to lie audaciously than to delay in order to be able to offer him the truth. I have seen him display great partiality for Rey-naud de Saint-Jean d'Angely, because the latter answered all his questions boldly and would not have been at a loss if he had asked him how many million flies were to be found in Europe in the month of Au-gust. It is on this kind of risky foundation that, on several occasions, reports were drawn up on the condition of manufacture, of agriculture, etc., and it is on that account that billions in commerce and industry were ascribed to France during the most calami-tous times."]

The official statistics for the last seventy years of the *ancien régime* were not neces-sarily the result of this kind of guesswork; the times were not calamitous enough to require it. Older civil servants did not labor under the pressure of such an exigent task-master as Napoleon. His dynamic personal-ity was more in keeping with an age that was to come than with the spirit of the eighteenth century. For what they are worth, the eighteenth-century figures for the value of commerce show an increase of nearly three and a half fold in the period 1764-1776 over the period 1716-1720. The figure for the earlier period is 214.8 millions of livres per annum; that for the later period, 724.9. Comparable figures for England suggest that the rate of growth in trade was somewhat slower between 1720 and 1774 than it was in France. The figure for 1720 is approximately thirteen million pounds sterling per annum; that for 1774 is 29.2 million pounds sterling. This confirms my impression that the rate of economic change in France during most of the eighteenth century was no less remarkable than in England.

Adam Smith observed that "the most decisive mark of the prosperity of any country is the increase in the number of its inhabitants." According to the best available figures—which leave much to be desired, because they are not based on any census —the population of England and Wales in 1720 was a shade over six millions. In 1790 it was 8.2 millions. The figures for France leave even more to be desired. But taking all the provinces that were French between 1919 and 1940, the people in 1700 could hardly have numbered more than twenty-one millions. During the latter part of Louis XIV's reign, particularly between 1689 and 1713, the continual warfare waged against various European coalitions is generally supposed to have caused a reduction in the population, less the result of deaths in battle than of economic hardships involved in maintaining large armies in the field. It is possible, therefore, that a figure of twenty millions would be about right for the French population in 1720. In 1789 the probable figure for the same area is twenty-six millions. At least five million French had been added to the population of the world in seventy years, as compared to a little more than two million English and Welsh. The rate of growth in population was comparable in France and England during the middle decades of the eighteenth century. An increase among the European peoples, destined eventually to lift the western European population in Europe and America from about a hundred and thirty to more than seven hundred millions, began in the eighteenth century. It began simultaneously in France and England. The period from 1720 to 1789 is the only stretch of time during the past two hundred years when the inhabitants of France have multiplied as rapidly as those of the other major countries of Europe. After the real spurt began, in the nineteenth century, France soon dropped far behind. She failed to reduce her mortality rates as rapidly as the other principal western countries. This is a matter of much importance in explaining the reduction in the rate of growth of the French population. It was mainly by prolonging life that western peoples so greatly increased their numbers.

If, then, we measure progress in terms of the *rate* of growth, as Ashley and Toynbee would have us do, there is no more reason for speaking of the "industrial revolution" of the eighteenth century as English rather than as French. But ought that phrase to be retained in connection with the eighteenth century?

Three of the technical inventions which were most important in bringing about a phenomenal growth in British industrial output were: the "puddling" process which made possible the widespread use of coal in the manufacture of bar iron, the adoption of the steam engine for manufacturing, and the use of power-driven machinery for spinning. It was not until 1784 that fresh methods of puddling and rolling were combined and coördinated into a single new process by Henry Cort. James Watt took out a patent for his famous new type of steam engine in 1780. But Professor Gay tells me that this engine and the spinning machinery sponsored by Arkwright began greatly to stimulate industrial and commercial growth only after the quashing of Watt's and Arkwright's patents by the courts in 1785. After that date the powerful new machinery and the new method of making iron with the help of coal came into extensive use for the first time. The turning point in the production of cotton, coal, iron, and other industrial commodities in Great Britain was the middle 1780's. Foreign trade figures tell the story. British imports during the seventies hardly increased forty per cent in volume. In the eighties they increased more than three hundred per cent. In the nineties they were nearly tripled again. It was in the late 1780's that Great Britain began to forge ahead of France. In 1780 the Island was producing little more than a third as much iron as France. In 1840 it was producing over three times as much. The French Revolution and the Napoleonic Wars helped Great Britain to gain a tremendous lead over Continental countries in industrial development, just as the Religious Wars and the Thirty Years' War had helped England to become the foremost country of Europe in the development of heavy industry during the late sixteenth and early seventeenth centuries.

The progressive state of Adam Smith was replaced in the late nineteenth century by the industrial state, first in Great Britain and then in one country after another. By the beginning of the twentieth century industrialism had swept over the whole globe. During the past four decades, and especially since the outbreak of the world war in 1914, the rate of growth in the volume of industrial output (apart from war materials) has fallen almost, if not quite, as rapidly as it rose in the early nineteenth century. Production has continued to increase in volume, but the *pace* has slackened greatly. If our descendants take a world view and think of the industrial revolution as a phenomenal speeding up of industrial evolution, they will associate it primarily with the nineteenth century, and with the remarkable age of European peace which lasted, with few interruptions, from 1815 to 1914.

*   *   *   *   *

MANY ENGLISHMEN WERE DISSATISFIED with the legal status of their religion in the eighteenth century. Presbyterians, Congregationalists, Baptists, Roman Catholics, and Jews complained of the political, social, economic, and educational disabilities under which they labored. The Church of England was so strongly entrenched, however, that few political leaders were willing to attempt to improve the status of the non-Anglican elements in the English population. To do so would cause too great an uproar. Whereas the privileged position of the Established Church was not seriously endangered by the grievances of non-Anglicans in the eighteenth century, many Anglicans became convinced that they were being threatened within their own church by the ideas and techniques of John Wesley and his fellow Methodists. This is ironic, inasmuch as Wesley had no intention whatever of breaking away from the Established Church. It is ironic, too, that Wesley was often denounced not only as a heretic but as a barbarian by members of Anglican intellectual circles. Yet if he is to be understood in his own light, it is important to remember that he considered himself not only a religious and humanitarian reformer but also an educational reformer. He insisted on caring for the minds as well as the souls and the bodies of his followers. It is this point that Dr. Louis B. Wright stresses in the essay that follows.

JOHN WESLEY: SCHOLAR AND CRITIC

LOUIS B. WRIGHT

Students of the eighteenth century are familiar with John Wesley, the preacher, the evangelist who spread the fear of Hell and the hope of Heaven throughout the British Isles. To thousands of his followers he is known as the founder of the Methodist church, the formulator of rules of conduct, and the writer of a copious journal. Those who have read biographies of Wesley or know his life as portrayed in the *Journal* visualize him as a preacher of consuming zeal, riding from town to town despite storm and danger, preaching a gospel of repentance of sins. Wesley's services as a reformer in a critical period in England's history are recognized—a tablet in Westminster Abbey attests Britain's gratitude. But Wesley the student of books, the productive scholar, the critic of letters, and the adviser in matters of literature to countless numbers of the uninitiated has been sadly neglected.

Born in 1703 and dying in 1791, Wesley almost completely spans the eighteenth century. During that long and eventful life he took time to write down his opinions of men and letters. He edited a collected library of fifty volumes, an extended five-foot shelf for the faithful; he edited the *Arminian Magazine* and devoted much space to biography, poetry, criticism, and an occasional bit of fiction; standard works of literature he abridged and edited for school and general reading. Not only were these works widely circulated, but extracts from his journal, published in Wesley's lifetime and after, were eagerly read. His opinions of books and authors were vigorously stated, and without doubt exerted a powerful influence upon the reading of his followers.

While Pope and Johnson held in succession the dictatorship in the narrow circle of letters, Wesley preached salvation and intelligence to the teeming proletariat and lower middle-class. What Wesley said about books meant infinitely more to his followers than did Dr. Johnson's ponderous dicta. Although Wesley left no impress upon the literary development of the age, he did powerfully influence the developing literary taste of a large segment of the British and even of the American public. In view of the growth of the democratic spirit and the increase in the reading public, this influence cannot be ignored. As late at least as the past generation, certain Wesleyan ideas about books enforced themselves upon members of the church he founded. The writer remembers a white-haired old lady in the South who refused to read novels because, she averred, "Mr. Wesley thought such light reading wasteful and unprofitable."

But what did Wesley think and say about books and writers? What was his attitude toward the literature of his age? What did this ever-travelling preacher read? The stories of his reading as he rode horseback from town to town are familiar. One wonders what books beguiled the rough miles over British moors or Irish fens; this Wesley often reveals in the *Journal*.

Whatever detractors may have said, John Wesley was no ignorant fanatic. Grounded in classical learning, Wesley left Oxford with a taste for good literature which he was to carry through life. Linked with this was an eloquence and a logical acuteness which Macaulay declared might have rendered him eminent in literature.

Wesley's reading at Oxford seems to have been chiefly in the classics, the Bible, philosophy, and poetry. One day out of the week he devoted to the study and composition of poetry. Two full days he devoted to the classics. Two books read during his college days left a lasting impression: Thomas à

Reprinted by special permission from *The South Atlantic Quarterly*, **XXIX** (1930), 262-281. The footnotes which originally appeared with this essay have been omitted.

Kempis' *Imitation of Christ* and Jeremy Taylor's *Holy Living and Holy Dying.* From Taylor came his early conception of humility and devotion which was to shape his later life.

The activity and strain of Wesley's life from the time he left the University onward did not affect his propensity for reading. Few men have ever wasted so little time in purposeless pursuit. Every spare minute he utilized in study, reading, or writing. Although he had keen appreciation of the pleasures of reading, he required of literature something more than mere entertainment. The reforming spirit led Wesley to apply a moralistic measure to literature and caused a warping of his critical faculty in many instances, but usually his criticisms are just and frequently savored with more common sense than those of his more literary contemporaries. For Wesley had that quality of solid sense that saved him from frequent absurdities into which religious and reforming fervor would have led a less discriminating commentator on men and letters.

Possessed of an impelling desire to know the contents of the printed page, Wesley investigated the great books not only of the past but of his own age. He kept abreast of current literature, and his contemporary criticism is worthy of note.

As one might expect, much of Wesley's time was consumed with what we may call professional reading: Scriptural commentary, theology, controversial matter, and philosophy. He was, of course, well versed in classic philosophy, and he kept up with modern schools of thought. In a critique of Locke's *Essay on the Human Understanding,* published in 1781, Wesley remarks:

> For what a comparison is there between this deep, solid weighty treatise, and the lively, glittering trifle of Baron Montesquieu? As much as between tinsel and gold.

He then states his agreement with Locke's theory of sensationalism. Of Montesquieu's *Spirit of the Laws,* Wesley says that it is as "insipid as the travels of Thomas Coryat." He objects to Montesquieu principally on stylistic grounds but remarks that he scoffs at the inspired writers. Voltaire naturally he execrates for his infidelity; Rousseau he ranks two degrees below Voltaire. Yet it is worth noting that he hits the obvious weaknesses of Rousseau in an entry in the *Journal* for February 3, 1770:

> I read with much expectation a celebrated book—*Rousseau upon Education.* But how was I disappointed! Sure a more consummate coxcomb never saw the sun! How amazing full of himself! Whatever he speaks, he pronounces as an oracle. . . . But I object to his temper, more than his judgment: he is a mere misanthrope;

FENELON: French writer (d. 1715) on politics, education, and theology who—often quite incorrectly—was considered by the eighteenth-century *philosophes* as a harbinger of their own ideas. His novel *Telemachus,* designed to teach the Duke of Burgundy how to rule, was his most widely read work.

LORD HERBERT OF CHERBURY: English philosopher in the age of the early Stuarts and brother of the poet George Herbert. He viewed Christianity as the highest form of religion. At the same time, however, he repudiated revelation as a fabrication of clergymen, and he insisted that virtuous conduct sufficed to lead to eternal bliss. These religious ideas helped to explain the high esteem in which he was held by eighteenth-century deists.

THIRD EARL OF SHAFTESBURY: English philosopher (d. 1713) whose education had been guided by John Locke. The leading deist of his time, he repudiated miracles and divorced ethics from religion. He won numerous supporters in eighteenth-century intellectual circles, among them such luminaries as Alexander Pope, Diderot, Leibniz, and Lessing.

a cynic all over. So indeed is his brother-infidel, Voltaire; and well nigh as great a coxcomb. But he hides both his doggedness and vanity a little better; whereas here it stares us in the face continually.

He further condemns Rousseau's theories because they are grounded on neither "reason nor experience." Pascal's *Thoughts* Wesley read and enjoyed. He takes occasion in the *Journal* for October 3, 1752, to comment:

> What could possibly induce such a creature as Voltaire to give such an author as this a good word; unless it was, that he once wrote a satire? And so his being a satirist might atone even for his being a Christian.

Religious fervor in a writer was not sufficient to win Wesley's praise. Swedenborg he thought a lunatic. He comments on December 8, 1771:

> Yet I can't but think the fever he (Swedenborg) had twenty years ago when he supposes he was "introduced into the society of angels" really introduced him into the society of lunatics.

Yet Wesley quotes Milton to show that Swedenborg is "majestic though in ruin."

Wesley's comment on Hume and Shaftesbury on March 5, 1767, is characteristic of him. He states that he had read "Dr. Campbell's excellent answer to David Hume's insolent book against miracles: and Dr. Brown's keen animadversions on the Characteristics of Lord Shaftesbury, another lively, half-thinking writer." In his *Journal* for May 5, 1772, we find him praising Beattie's "ingenious *Enquiry after Truth*," far above Hume, "the most insolent despiser of truth and virtue that ever appeared in the world." Of Bolingbroke, he remarks on July 11, 1758:

> I read over the Analysis of Lord Bolingbroke's works. Surely never did any man so flatly contradict and so fully answer himself.

The foraging eye of the travelling preacher found much to interest him professionally. This reading was as diverse as Wesley's interests. He read the life of St. Katherine one day and the life of Mahomet the next. He revised Fox's *Acts and Monuments* and abridged Jonathan Edwards' *Treatise on Religious Affections*. Such material, however, is what one would expect a preacher to seek. It is Wesley's other reading which discloses the breadth of his intellectual curiosity.

The natural sciences were for Wesley a field of considerable interest. He read treatises on medicine, astronomy, geology, physics, biology, etc. His own well-meaning invasion into the realm of medicine as the author of a collection of home remedies added little to his credit but disclosed a worthy purpose. Among the scientific works which he read were: "Lord Bacon's *Ten Centuries of Experiment*," "Mr. Huygens' *Conjectures on the Planetary World*," "Dr. Priestley's ingenious book on Electricity," "Dr. Cheyne's *Natural Method of Curing Diseases*," "Dr. Hodge's account of the plague in London," "Dr. Cadogan's ingenious treatise on Chronical Distempers." Wesley objects in his *Journal* for September 9, 1771, that Dr. Cadogan unnecessarily condemns wine: "But why should he condemn wine *toto genere?* which is one of the noblest cordials in nature."

Wesley in the twentieth century would have been familiar with the Einstein theory. The *Journal* for October 9, 1765, states:

> I read Mr. Jones' ingenious Essay on the *Principles of Natural Philosophy*. He seems to have totally overthrown the Newtonian Principles. But whether he can establish the Hutchinson is another question.

Wesley was convinced by Dr. Roger's *Essay on the Learning of the Ancients* that "they had microscopes and telescopes." He was quite startled by a treatise on biology. The *Journal* for July 21, 1758, states:

> I met with a tract which utterly confounded all my philosophy: I had long

believed that all microscopic animals were generated like all other animals by parents of the same species. But Mr. Needham makes it highly probable that they constitute a peculiar class of animals, differing from all others in this, That they neither are generated or generate nor subsist by food in the ordinary way.

Later in the same year, December 11, 1758, he says:

Most of this week I spent in preparing materials for *A Survey of the Wisdom of God in the Creation;* or a full, plain, and correct system of Natural Philosophy.

To literal interpretationists among Wesley's followers, his speculations and beliefs concerning geology may seem heretical. The *Journal* for January 17, 1770, makes the following disclosure:

In a little journey, which I took into Bedfordshire, I finished Dr. Burnet's *Theory of the Earth.* He is doubtless one of the first rate writers, both as to sense and style; his language is remarkably clear, unaffected, nervous, and elegant. And as to his theory, none can deny that it is ingenious, and consistent with itself. And it is highly probable: (1) That the earth rose out of the chaos in some such manner as he describes; (2) That the antediluvian earth was without high or abrupt mountains, and without sea, being one uniform crust, enclosing the great abyss; (3) That the flood was caused by the breaking of this crust, and its sinking into the abyss of waters; and (4) That the present state of the earth both internal and external, shows it to be the ruins of the former earth. This is the substance of his two former books, and thus far I can go with him.

I have no objection to the substance of his third book upon the general conflagration, but think it one of the noblest tracts which is extant in our language. And I do not much object to the fourth, concerning the new heavens and the new earth. The substance of it is highly probable.

The literature of travel, history, and biography held an intense interest for Wesley. In the *Journal* of May 17, 1776, he comments upon Dr. Johnson's *Tour to the Western Isles:*

It is a very curious book, wrote with admirable sense, and, I think, great fidelity; although, in some respects, he is thought to bear hard on the nation, which I am satisfied he never intended.

A few years later he defends Johnson again, June 11, 1781:

I had time to consider Dr. Johnson's *Tour Through Scotland.* I had heard that he was severe upon the whole nation; but I could find nothing of it. He simply mentions (but without any bitterness) what he approved or disapproved: and many of his reflections are extremely judicious; some of them very affecting.

Perhaps Wesley agreed with Johnson in some of his reflections on the dour Scots. It is worth note that these two great leaders of the eighteenth century admired each other.

Wesley had something of an antiquarian interest. As he rides through Ireland in 1748 we find him reading Sir James Ware's *Antiquities of Ireland,* which proves, unfortunately, "an extremely dull book." Wesley's ire is frequently stirred because of the dullness and flat style of much of the history and the travel literature which he encountered. Verily, the style of travelogues has not changed since Wesley's day. He was disappointed by Captain Cook's travels because of their incredibility; Cook he ranked with Robinson Crusoe. Narden's *Travels into Egypt and Abyssinia* and Seller's *History of Palmyra,* he finds "two as dry and unsatisfying books as ever I read in my life." What an admission for a man who had read the church fathers! However dull the work might be, Wesley's curiosity led him to consume all the works of history, antiquarian research, and travels which came within his reach. Dr. Shaw's *Travels* he found dull but was surprised to learn that Mt. Atlas was no higher than the English mountains. After reading Pennant's *Tour Through Scotland,* Wesley exclaims in the *Journal* for June 14, 1781, "No man should be above writing correctly." He wonders how a man of sense and learning could have written bad English on every page.

Along with history, biography appealed to Wesley. He translated a biography of Martin Luther, and on the day of its completion, July 19, 1749, made this entry in the *Journal:*

> I finished the the translation of *Martin Luther's Life.* Doubtless he was a man highly favoured of God, and a blessed instrument in His hand. But O! what a pity that he had no faithful friend! None that would, at all hazards, rebuke him plainly and sharply for his rough, untractable spirit, and bitter zeal for opinions, so greatly obstructive of the work of God!

After reading Luther's comment on the *Epistle to the Galatians,* Wesley had commented that it was shallow and muddy, and that "he is deeply tinctured with mysticism throughout! and hence often dangerously wrong."

Wesley had, in spite of religious fervor, the eighteenth century distrust of enthusiasms. On April 22, 1779, he refutes in the *Journal* a statement from Smollett's *History of England* that the Wesleys, Whitefield, and other preachers who followed them, had infected the people with "enthusiasm." On December 15, 1788, referring to his brother's poems, he says, "But some still savour of that poisonous mysticism with which we were both not a little tainted before we went to America." Georgia they found sufficient to quench any mystical excesses.

Not only did Wesley read as he rode, but like stage Hamlets, he walked with a book in his hand. He records on April 3, 1754: ". . . In my hours of walking I read Dr.

Calamy's *Abridgement of Mr. Baxter's Life."* On December 10, 1756, he notes that during the following week he spent "fragments of time" in reading "Mr. Hanway's accurate history of Shah Nadir, commonly called Kouli Khan: . . . Alexander the Great, yea Nero or Domitian, was innocent in comparison of him." On March 30, 1756, Wesley is reading the life of Peter the Great: "Undoubtedly he was a soldier, a general, and a statesman scarce inferior to any. But why was he called a Christian?" In riding to Rosmeed, April 21, 1760, Wesley reads Sir John Davis's *Historical Relations Concerning Ireland.* In 1748 he had read a history of St. Patrick but had found that the whole thing smelled "strong of romance." On February 11, 1768, he records that he spent "scraps of time in reading Mr. Wodrow's *History of the Sufferings of the Church of Scotland."*

Wesley anticipated modern historians in a desire to vindicate the names of Mary Queen of Scots and Richard III. On April 29, 1768, he read "an extremely sensible book," *An Inquiry into the Proofs of the Charges Commonly Advanced against Mary Queen of Scots.* He praises the author for going back to original sources for proof. On June 17, 1769, he records:

> I finished *Historic Doubts on the Life and Reign of Richard the Third.* What an amazing monster both in body and mind have our Historians and Poets painted him! and yet I think Mr. Walpole makes it more clear than one would expect at this distance of time.

A vindication of Richard follows. By January 14, 1776, Wesley is at work completing a history of England which will repair the injured reputations of Richard and Mary:

> . . . at all my vacant hours in this and the following week, I endeavored to finish the *Concise History of England.* I am sensible it must give offence, as in many parts I am quite singular; particular with

regard to those injured characters, Richard III and Mary Queen of Scots.

The title of Wesley's history indicates his emphasis on brevity. On July 6, 1781, he condemns Robertson's *History of America* for its prolixity. On February 5, 1786, he mentions that Dr. Stuart in his *History of Scotland* proved a better writer than Robertson.

Wesley's historical reading ranged from the classics to contemporary treatises. He was thoroughly versed in the original of Livy, Tacitus, and other less known Latin historians. He also had an intelligent interest in international politics of the eighteenth century. In his old age, September 20, 1790, he writes in his *Journal:*

> I read over the King of Sweden's Tract upon the Ballance of Power in Europe. If it be really his, he is certainly one of the most sensible, as well as one of the bravest Princes in Europe. And if his account be true, what a woman is the Czarina! But still God is over all!

Wesley's interests were not narrowly insular. He kept in touch with Continental thought and literature. He believed in the value of language study, in the modern as well as the ancient tongues. Grammars he edited to further linguistic study. On his voyage to America, the *Journal* for October 21, 1735, records that he "usually *learned* German" from nine until twelve o'clock each day. On April 4, 1737, he began learning Spanish in order to converse with his Jewish parishioners in Georgia. French he already knew. On March 6, 1750, he began writing a short French grammar. On February 10, 1751, Wesley writes that he had spent the previous week writing a Hebrew grammar. For the school at Kingswood, he prepared English, French, Latin, Greek, and Hebrew grammars. In the latter language, Wesley was well equipped. On March 1, 1776, he reads Bishop Lowth's *Lectures de Poesi Hebraea* and is pleased to find that the "noblest poetry may subsist without

being beholden either to rhyme or fixed measures."

Linguist though Wesley was, Irish proved too much for him. After studying Major Vallancy's *Irish Grammar,* he writes in his *Journal* for May 18, 1785, that he finds the language "worse than any antient language I know anything about," or any modern tongue. He declares that the language has mute letters, "the like of which is not found under heaven."

At Oxford Wesley had been thoroughly grounded in Latin and Greek; he had read during school days the traditional classic authors. Later, in the midst of professional activity, he continued to read Greek and Latin literature. The *Journal* for August 12, 1748, records:

> In riding to Newcastle I finished the *Iliad* of Homer. What an amazing genius had this man! To write with such strength of thought and beauty of expression when he had none to go before him! And what a vein of piety runs through his whole work, in spite of his pagan prejudices. Yet one can't but observe such improprieties intermixt, as are shocking to the last degree.

Wesley then takes Homer to task for putting coarse language in the mouths of gods and goddesses. In this objection, Wesley is merely voicing the eighteenth century protest against a breach of decorum. The common sense of Wesley also rebelled at Homer's making a supposedly wise king boast of having given the baby Achilles wine.

Xenophon's Memorabilia shows want of judgment in the author, Wesley declares in a *Journal* entry for May 27, 1742:

> How many of these things (about Socrates) would Plato never have mentioned! But it may be well, that we see the shades too of the brightest picture in all heathen antiquity.

Frequent allusions prove his familiarity with Plato and other Greek philosophers.

Marcus Aurelius so impressed Wesley

that he ranked him in virtue with the patriarchs and enthroned him in Paradise. The *Journal* for October 11, 1745, states:

> I read today part of the Meditations of Marcus Antoninus. What a strange heathen! giving thanks to God for all his good inspirations. . . . I make no doubt, but this is one of those many who shall come from the East and the West, and sit down with Abraham, Isaac, and Jacob. . . .

In Lucian's *Dialogues* Wesley noted on June 19, 1776, that he found "a good deal of humour but wonderful little judgment. His great hero is Diogenes the Cynic, just such another brute as himself. Socrates . . . he reviles and ridicules."

On a journey into Wales in 1749, Wesley read over Statius' *Thebais* and wondered how one man could write "so well and so ill." "Sometimes he is scarce inferior to Virgil; sometimes as low as the dullest parts of Ovid."

Other Latin authors, chiefly historical, he frequently mentions. He compares the style of Dr. Bates' *Elenchus Motuum Nuperorum in Anglia* to Caesar's history "whom he seems studiously to imitate." Quintius Curtius he describes on September 5, 1747, as "a fine Writer both as to thought and language. But what a hero does he describe! . . . I doubt whether Judas claims so hot a place in hell, as Alexander the Great."

Not only did Wesley read widely in the classics, in history, in philosophy, in travels, and in biography, but he also devoted much of his spare time to belles lettres. His services to polite literature were many, and his tastes were varied. His criticisms of current literary productions were intelligent, if not always in accord with the views of Pope or Doctor Johnson. In an age of sentiment, Wesley reflected contemporary sentimentality, relieved, however, by a certain critical sanity which he maintained. Professor Winchester in his biography has pointed out that Wesley admired the graveyard school; that he was a friend of James Hervey,

author of the dolorous *Meditations Among the Tombs;* that of Pope's poems, he admired most the "Elegy on an Unfortunate Lady"; that Prior's "Henry and Emma" was such a poem as Wesley believed ought to move one to tears, etc. In his devotion to sentiment, Wesley again is merely a man of his age. As a preacher and a moralist, sentimental moralizing in literature appealed to him. In this, however, he was no different from the purely literary critics of the period of sentimentalism. Even with his own penchant for moralizing, Wesley's good sense ordinarily kept him from the sentimental excesses of his more literary contemporaries.

An example of Wesley's critical independence and his estimation of popular opinion occurs in a review of Montesquieu's *Spirit of the Laws:*

> But whence is it that such a multitude of people so hugely admire, and so highly applaud this treatise? Perhaps nine in ten of them do this because others do: they follow the cry without why or wherefore: they follow one another like a flock of sheep; they run on because many run before them. It is quite the fashion; and who would be out of fashion? As well be out of the world. Not one half of these have read the book over. Nor does one in ten of them understand it. But it is enough that "everyone commends it, and why should not I too?" especially as he seems greatly to admire himself, and upon occasion to commend himself too; though in a modest, decent way; not in that fulsome manner which is common among modern writers.

In a *Journal* passage for December 26, 1740, Wesley condemns pedantry, with which he had little patience. He believed in conciseness and clarity. Pungent is his criticism of John Edwards' *Deficiencies of Human Knowledge and Understanding:*

> Surely, never man wrote like this man! Stiff and trifling in the same breath: positive and opinionated to the last de-

gree, and of course treating others with no more good manners than justice. But above all, sour, ill-natured, morose without a parallel, which indeed is his distinguishing characteristic. Be his opinion right or wrong, if Dr. Edwards' temper were the Christian temper, I would abjure Christianity forever.

Again on November 9, 1773, he comments on "Dr. Lee's *Sophron*": "When he makes a pertinent remark, he knows not when to have done with it, but spins it out without any pity to the reader." His criticism of Fénelon's *Telemachus* is that it is "spun out too long" and "drawn into mere French wire." Twelve books would have contained the matter better, he asserts in the *Journal* for January 7, 1760. Twenty years later, August 24, 1780, Wesley is objecting to a writer because of his prim, affected style:

I now looked over a volume of Mr. K's Essays. He is a lively Writer of middling Understanding. But I can not admire his style at all. It is prim, affected, and highly frenchified. I object to the beginning of many sentences with participles. This does well in French, but not in English. . . . He depresses Cowley beyond all reason; who was far from being a mean poet.

In the late eighteenth century discussion of the Genius and the Imagination, Wesley took part. In a *Journal* entry for November 5, 1787, he comments:

I read Mr. Duff's Essay on Genius. It is beyond all comparison deeper and more judicious than Mr. G's (Gerard's) Essay on that subject. . . . For Genius is not Imagination any more than it is Invention. If we mean by it a quality of the soul, it is in its widest acceptation, an extraordinary capacity, either for some particular act or science, or for all, for whatever may be undertaken. So Euclid had a genius for mathematics, Tully for oratory; Aristotle and Lord Bacon had

an universal genius applicable to everything.

Wesley's reactions to literature were usually definite and his evaluations are concisely expressed. Among the poets of his day, we find him strangely championing Matthew Prior as his favorite. He defended Prior vigorously in an *Arminian Magazine* article in 1782 from an attack by Johnson:

What he frequently obtains, as far above Pope's *Messiah* as that is above Quarles's Emblems seems to be the effort of a genius not inferior in strength to any beside Milton . . . nay, I reply, most of his works are as natural and unconstrained, as even those of Waller: though they would certainly have done their duty better had he taken more pains with them.

Even against the criticism that Prior's "amorous effusions have neither gallantry nor tenderness," Wesley defends the poet: "For gallantry, I know not what it means. But never man wrote with more tenderness. . . . I know not what man of sensibility can read them ["Henry and Emma" and "Abraham"] without tears." He compares Prior's "Solomon" with Pope's "Verses to the Memory of an Unfortunate Lady" to the credit of the former:

Upon the whole, I cannot but think that the natural understanding of Mr. Prior was far stronger than that of Mr. Pope. . . . And I conceive his poetical abilities were at least equal to those either of Pope or Dryden.

In the *Journal* for December 15, 1775, Wesley writes: "Today I read Dr. Beattie's Poems, certainly one of the best Poets of the Age: He wants only the Ease and Simplicity of Mr. Pope.—I know one, and only one that has it." That one was Prior. On Christmas Eve of the same year Wesley records reading a Danish anthology of poems in Latin which contained two of Pope's *Epistles*.

Wesley modelled his own prose style

after Swift. In 1757 in a treatise on *The Doctrine of Original Sin,* he quotes copiously from *Gulliver's Travels.* In the *Journal* for April 14, 1756, Wesley compares Skelton with Swift: "When there is occasion, he shows all the wit of Dr. Swift, joined with ten times his judgment; and (what is far more) a deep fear of God."

If Wesley admired the wit of Swift, he abhorred that of Mandeville. Of *The Fable of the Bees,* he comments on April 14, 1756:

I looked over a celebrated book, *The Fable of the Bees.* Till now I imagined there had never appeared such a book as the works of Machiavel. But Dr. Mandeville goes far beyond it. The Italian recommends a few vices as useful to some particular men, and on some particular occasions. But the Englishman loves and cordially recommends vice of every kind not only as useful now and then, but as absolutely necessary at all times for all communities! Surely Voltaire would hardly have said so much! And even Mr. Sundiman could not have said more.

On his return voyage from Georgia, Wesley had read and condemned Machiavelli's *Prince.*

For Sterne, Wesley had little appreciation. He regarded *A Sentimental Journey* as sheer nonsense. To *Tristram Shandy* he makes only inconsequential references. The comment in the *Journal* for February 11, 1772, is characteristic:

I casually took a volume of what is called *A Sentimental Journey through France and Italy.* Sentimental! what is that? It is not English: he might as well say, Continental. It is not sense. It conveys no determinate idea; yet one fool makes many. And this nonsensical word (who would believe it?) is become a fashionable one! However, the book agrees full well with the title; for one is as queer as the other. For oddity, uncouthness, and unlikeness to all the world beside, I suppose, the writer is without a rival.

Gray's poems, Wesley found "not much inferior to either Prior or Pope." An entry in the *Journal* for December 5, 1776, shows that he regarded Gray as too morose and pessimistic. He also objected to Gray's contempt for Mason, "one full as ingenious as himself, yea full as good a Poet."

Richard Blackmore's *Prince Arthur,* Wesley notes in the *Journal* for October 18, 1773, is "not a contemptible poem but by no means equal to his poem on the Creation in which are many fine strokes." Lord Lyttleton he appraises in the *Journal* for February 28, 1776, as "really a fine writer both in verse and prose."

Wesley was taken in by the Ossianic forgeries of McPherson. But for that matter, so were most of his contemporaries. His belief in the authenticity of Fingal he records in the *Journal,* May 15, 1784: "But what a poet was Ossian. Little inferior to either Homer or Virgil: in some respects superior to both." A second reading only served to convince Wesley further of the worth of the poem.

Concern with current literature did not prevent Wesley's reading authors of the past. On October 21, 1771, as he drove to Chatham he read "Mr. Hoole's fine translation of Tasso's *Jerusalem Delivered,* allowed, I suppose, by most judges of poetry, to be not much inferior to the Aeneid." He objected, however, to Tasso's "Popish Fooleries." Wesley also read and admired Harrington's translation of *Orlando Furioso.*

In a *Journal* entry for December 6, 1773, he compares Lord Herbert of Cherbury to Don Quixote: "Was there ever so wild a Knight-Errant as this? Compared to him Don Quixote was a sober man." Wesley was familiar with Bacon and refers to *The New Atlantis* in a letter quoted in the *Journal,* May 27, 1749. With Shakespeare and Milton he was intimately acquainted and frequently quoted from them. He refers on June 22, 1759, to a hostile justice of the peace as "simple Master Shallow."

In his criticism of the drama and the stage, Wesley does not seem to have been the narrow bigot that he has been made out. His objections are directed rather against the contemporary degeneracy of the playhouse than against stage plays *per se.* Not even does theatrical lampooning and scurrility directed against his followers stir him to vituperation against plays or players. When a Scotch company at Newcastle in 1743 gave a farce called "Trick upon Trick, or Methodism Displayed" after a performance of *The Conscious Lovers,* Wesley merely writes in his *Journal* for November 2 of that year: "Which is the most surprising—that those players acted this farce the next week or that some hundreds of people came again to see it?" The players, led by Samuel Foote, did much to stir the wrath of Wesley's adherents; their reaction against the theatre was only natural after such performances as Foote's *The Minor,* acted in the Haymarket in 1760, in which Methodists were held up to ridicule. Foote followed this play with an unacted sequel called *The Methodist.*

On January 13, 1747, Wesley relates in the *Journal* an effort of players to break up a service in the town of Devise, where a pantomime of obscene nature "which a modest man cannot well repeat" was staged in the house where he was to preach. He makes no condemnation of the players. When he preached at Sadler's Wells on April 29, 1754, in an abandoned playhouse, he was glad, however, when "it pleases God to take possession of what Satan esteemed his own ground." The provincial stage in the mid-eighteenth century had little to recommend it and one can well understand Wesley's hope, expressed in the *Journal* for March 21, 1764, that all playhouses, like the one at Birmingham, could be turned into chapels. A letter written on December 20, 1764, to the mayor of Bristol betrays a certain shrewdness in Wesley's representing the possible demoralizing effects of the establishment of a playhouse, "hurtful to a trading city." Wesley makes no request of the mayor but merely calls his attention to the quality of "most of the *present* stage entertainments."

Wesley's fight on the theatre throughout seems to have been on grounds of present degeneracy of most of the entertainment. He himself had occasionally attended stage plays when the bill promised something worthwhile. In a *Journal* entry for March 25, 1750, he remarks of a certain heckler that his "countenance I could only compare to that (which I saw in Drury Lane thirty years ago) of one of the ruffians in *Macbeth.*" On November 17, 1755, he humorously remarks of a thunder storm which interrupted another performance of *Macbeth* at Drury Lane that "it might be suspected that the fear of God had crept into the very theatre!"

Apparently Wesley had a kindly regard for David Garrick. He refused to believe an anecdote told by Mrs. Bellamy of Garrick's throwing into the sea a volume of Charles Wesley's hymns. In the *Journal* for December 28, 1789, he remarks of Garrick: "I cannot believe it [Mrs. Bellamy's story]. I think Mr. G. had more sense. He knew my brother well; and he knew him to be not only far superior in learning, but in poetry, to Mr. Thomson, and all his theatrical writers put together."

A performance of Terence's *Adelphi* by the Westminster scholars excited Wesley's admiration. On December 14, 1768, he writes in the *Journal:*

> An entertainment not unworthy of a Christian! O how do these Heathen shame us! Their very comedies contain both excellent sense, the liveliest pictures of men and manners, and so fine strokes of genuine morality, as are seldom found in the writings of Christians.

Although he did not see it acted, in the *Journal* for June 9, 1757, Wesley pronounced John Home's *Douglas* "one of the finest tragedies I ever read. What pity that a few lines were not left out; and that it was ever acted at Edinburgh!" Of Thomson's poetry, Wesley had a low opinion until "looking into one of his tragedies, *Edward and Eleanora,*" he says on October 14, 1772, "I was agreeably surprised. The sentiments are just and noble; the diction strong, smooth, and elegant; and the plot conducted with the utmost art, and wrought off in a most surprising manner. It is quite his masterpiece, and I really think might vie with any modern performance of the kind."

Although Wesley preached against the corruption in the contemporary playhouse, he recognized the value of drama. He was not above commending a play, and he was so charitable that on one occasion he paid the board bill of a starveling player and his wife and sent them on their way.

Wesley did not permit the learning acquired in his voracious reading to go to waste. His services toward the promotion of popular reading were definite and far reaching. He insisted upon his preachers reading methodically. He founded in 1778 the *Arminian Magazine* which published in addition to religious matter, letters, anecdotes, biographical sketches, poetry, book reviews, etc. Wesley wrote treatises which popularized reading and stimulated intelligent curiosity in many other fields besides that of religion. Even fiction did not escape him; he highly recommended and edited Henry Brooke's sentimental novel, *The Fool of Quality.* Not least among Wesley's efforts was the fifty-volume *Christian Library,* the publication of which was begun in 1749 and completed in 1755. Its purpose was "to provide a complete library for those that fear God." In the *Journal* for November 29, 1753, Wesley refers wearily to the labor of preparing *The Christian Library,* "a work by which I have lost two hundred pounds. Perhaps the next generation may know the value of it."

A variety of other works Wesley edited for separate publication. His abridgment of *Pilgrim's Progress* in 52 pages had five editions by 1766. In 1763, Wesley published "An Extract from Milton's *Paradise Lost* with Notes." He placed a star by noteworthy passages "peculiarly excellent either with regard to sentiment or expression"; these passages he advised his readers to memorize. Perhaps the popular conception of Heaven and Hell among his followers received a more definite shaping from this

version of Milton than from any recommended Scriptural passages. In 1750, Wesley had selected passages from Milton for the pupils at Kingswood School to transcribe and repeat weekly.

In 1770, Wesley edited Young's *Night Thoughts* and left out what he "apprehended to be either childish, or flat, or turgid, or obscure." Curiously, some of the poem remained after this test. In 1779, Wesley wrote a life of Dr. John Donne for the *Arminian Magazine,* which published that year about 70 poetical pieces. Fourteen pages were devoted to Prior's "Henry and Emma." Wesley's own contributions to the magazine ranged from "Thoughts upon Taste" in which he refers to the "ingenious thoughts of Mr. Addison" upon the same subject, to religious exhortations.

Wesley was always sympathetic with literary efforts. In 1789, he aided an improvident Welsh lawyer to publish his poems, which were promptly damned by reviewers. Wesley had, however, small sympathy with intellectual coddling. He believed in supplying students with literature which they ought to read and insisting that they read it. Not novels but history, he advises in a letter of August 18, 1784, to a school mistress:

I would recommend very few novels to young persons, for fear they would be desirous of more. Mr. Brooke wrote one more beside the *Earl of Moreland (The Fool of Quality),* *The History of the Human Heart.* I think it is well worth reading, though it is not equal to his former production. The want of novels may be more than supplied by well chosen history: such as *The Concise History of England, The Concise History of the Church,* Rollins' *Ancient History,* Hooke's *Roman History* (the only impartial one extant), and a few more. For the older and more sensible children, Malebranche's *Search after Truth* is an excellent French book. Perhaps you might add Locke's *Essay on the Human Understanding,* with remarks upon it in the *Arminian Magazine.* I had forgotten that beautiful book, *The Travels of Cyrus,* whether in French or English.

Throughout Wesley's long life, he was scarcely more concerned over the souls than over the minds of his followers in Britain and America. He preached to his ministers the necessity of learning; if they failed to read, it was not for lack of their leader's example and exhortation. Wesley's published *Journal,* containing his vigorous criticism of books, had a wide-spread circulation; the *Arminian Magazine,* the *Christian Library,* and his various abridgments and editions of literary works were read by thousands. Through all these works, Wesley proves himself a popularizer of what he judges to be good literature. Certainly the reading public of the eighteenth century owed him a great debt. Through Wesley, literature began to reach proletarian thousands who had never read before.

SEVERAL YEARS BEFORE THE OUTBREAK of the French Revolution, Sir John Hawkins, the London magistrate and conservative friend of conservative Dr. Johnson, complained that Englishmen were living in a period when "humanity is in fashion." Although some of Hawkins' contemporaries would have questioned the validity of his complaint and although the word "humanitarian" did not find its way into Dr. Johnson's *Dictionary,* there is no doubt that humanity was relatively more "in fashion" in the late eighteenth century than it had been in the age of George I and George II. Individual reformers and such humanitarian organizations as the Society for the Propagation of the Gospel in Foreign Parts (S.P.G.) and the Society for the Promotion of Christian Knowledge (S.P.C.K.) attempted to make their countrymen aware of the desirability of remolding English society in the humanitarian image; and in advancing their proposals for change they frequently had recourse to patriotic appeals. Distressed by the ignorance, crime, immorality, and poverty they saw around them, they aimed to convert England into a more wholesome place in which to live—a green and pleasant land worthy of Jerusalem. Various reformers concentrated their efforts on such objectives as the reduction of gin drinking, the improvement of hospital facilities and prison management, the prevention of cruelty to foundlings and animals, the elimination of juvenile delinquency, the betterment of sanitary conditions in urban areas, and the abolition of the slave trade. Although their efforts often failed to attain the speedy results sought by the more impatient members in their ranks, the humanitarians did achieve a number of notable successes. Some of these are analyzed in the following essay by Frank J. Klingberg, professor emeritus of history at the University of California. Author of the important monograph *The Anti-Slavery Movement in England* (1926), Professor Klingberg has done much to further the study of the history of British humanitarianism; it was appropriate that when his former students decided to prepare a volume of essays in his honor (1950), they took this topic as their central theme.

THE EVOLUTION OF THE HUMANITARIAN SPIRIT IN EIGHTEENTH-CENTURY ENGLAND*

FRANK J. KLINGBERG

The many movements which resulted from or produced the eighteenth-century mood acted together. The separate studies of the specialist tend to become too separate. All the humanitarian currents and forces of the century may be thought of as the struggle for the organization of a civilized social life, with the economist, the churchman, the reformer, the poet, the satirist, and the legislator each working in many related "causes" for the change of social conditions.

The establishment of governmental supremacy over the international Church under the Tudors and of Parliamentary supremacy over the King under the Stuarts, had resulted, by the opening of the eighteenth century, in social conditions difficult to describe. An intense religious revival, rapid economic change, and appalling distress and suffering were fundamental factors during the century. The Anglican Church and the State had reached a stability amounting to rigidity while society was, so to speak, "on the boil." People, crossing the frontiers of fifteen thousand English parishes and crowding into industrial areas, overwhelmed the scanty administrative machinery of government.[1] The weakening of the Church and of the Royal Prerogative

brought about an economic regime dominated by certain powerful individuals and corporations, often called a Venetian oligarchy. The growth of these corporations as against the guilds, and the surrender of business to them, frequently left the individual shorn of his livelihood, without the protection of old customs and institutions, and without the benefit of new regulations, which often did not appear until the nineteenth century. Not only was there a centralization of capitalistic control in industry and commerce, but the enclosure movement was evidence of the steady growth of the monopoly of land and the loss of the cotter's rights. In Germany, where poverty was universal but destitution unknown, the feudal system still protected the unfortunate, whereas in England, the pioneer in the transition period between feudalism and the modern state, society had become barbaric and destitution widespread.[2]

Revolution in industry and in agriculture, the rapid increase of population in the second half of the century, in itself a revolution, a migration of people to new areas or outside of corporate towns, all combined to produce new social ideas and ex-

* An abridged version of this article was read at the annual meeting of the American Historical Association at Chicago on December 29, 1941.

[1] J. L. and Barbara Hammond, writing on "Poverty, Crime, and Philanthropy," in A. S. Turberville (ed.), *Johnson's England* (Oxford, 1933), I, 301-302, point out that "all the problems that had occupied the Elizabethan statesmen fell upon the parish . . . there were no fewer than 15,000, and we can form some estimate of the size of most of them when we learn that in 1831 four-fifths had a population under 800 and nearly 7,000 had a population of under 300."

[2] On London life and conditions see Wilmarth Sheldon Lewis, *Three Tours through London in the Years 1748-1776-1797* (New Haven, 1941), *passim*. Continental travelers have left an unforgettable record of the time. Of special interest are W. H. Quarrell and M. Mare (eds.), *London in 1710. From the Travels of Z. C. von Uffenbach* (London, 1934); J. A. Kelly, *England and the Englishman in German Literature of the 18th Century* (London, 1933); Clare Williams (trans.), *Sophie in London, 1786* (London, 1934); and Rudolph Reuss, *Londres et Angleterre en 1700* (Strasbourge, 1933). Characteristics which impressed these foreigners were the craze for brutal sports of all kinds and for betting and wagering.

Reprinted by special permission from *The Pennsylvania Magazine of History and Biography,* LXVI (1942), 260-278.

perimental proposals for humanitarian reforms. Society was in a state of flux.[3] But neither Church nor State was prepared to function as an ameliorative agency. Health facilities and sanitation may be described by the phrase "sewer rivers." The failure to protect women and children and the masses of the people, uprooted or in new or old distresses, was a national disgrace. Taxation was so slight as to baffle the modern investigator, in itself evidence of the limited activities of the State.

The success of powerful business corporations inevitably suggested to humanitarians that they incorporate their otherwise disjointed efforts to ease the impact of economic revolutions at home and to mitigate the evils of imperialism on black man and brown man. The friendly, the kindly man, found in all ranks of society and in all four kingdoms, thus met the mass cruelty around him by voluntary charity.[4] For the sick, the aged, the prisoner,

the foundling, and the sufferers from every major hazard, the humanitarian, in the course of the century, covered the English countryside with numerous institutions which still stand as active monuments to this age. Most of these hostelries are unknown to the general public, except as their anniversaries are celebrated or biographies of their founders are written.[5]

The publication of *The History of the Foundling Hospital*,[6] whose charter dates back to 1739, is a case in point. This volume gives a factual picture of the appalling social chaos of the eighteenth century and that in one field alone. The management of the abandoned child was a complex problem. Throughout its history, from the moment that the newly-born child was baptized at the Hospital, placed with a foster mother,

---

[3] Elizabeth W. Gilboy, in *Wages in Eighteenth Century England* (London, 1934), has shown, chiefly from county records of Quarter Sessions, that a comparative stability of wages existed throughout the century in all areas, as against the rapid and frequent fluctuations of prices up and down—the two entirely unrelated. An increase of wages in the northern area is associated with the rise of the factory industry, while contemporary stagnation of wages at a low level in the western area is associated with the transfer of the cloth industry from the West to the North.

[4] "Case studies" of this voluntary charity may be found in W. S. Lewis and Ralph M. Williams, *Private Charity in England, 1747-1757* (New Haven, 1938), *passim*. The editors

have defined "private charity" as "the giving of money, food, clothing, etc., to individuals who have no immediate claims upon the beneficence of their donors. This is something other than the care of a landlord for his tenantry or the rewarding of faithful servants."

[5] A recent study is F. G. Parsons, *The History of St. Thomas's Hospital* (London, 1934). In Volume II, covering the period from 1600 to 1800, Mr. Parsons has quoted from private diaries and casebooks, as well as from the minutes of the Court of Governors. During the eighteenth century, largely through the influence of Sir Robert Clayton, a prosperity was achieved which made possible growth and improvement in medical practice. Sir Christopher Wren, who was a governor, was probably consulted as to the design of the fine buildings in Southwark.

[6] R. H. Nichols and F. A. Wray, *The History of the Foundling Hospital* (London, 1935).

BEGGAR'S OPERA: Enormously successful burlesque (1728) by the genial humorist John Gay. By means of the adventures of a highwayman, Captain Macheath, Gay satirized Italian opera, the modes of the court, the marriage customs of the aristocracy, and the political life of the age of Sir Robert Walpole.

GEORGE CRABBE: English poet, admirer of Alexander Pope, and critic of the Romantics. His poetry stands out for its scornful treatment of the amenities of the life of his time and for its realistic account of the condition of poor and humble people.

WILLIAM HOGARTH: English artist (d. 1764) who stressed in his work the crude, coarse, and grotesque features of eighteenth-century English life. A social critic, satirist, and reformer, he reacted strongly against what he considered to be the loose morals of his age, attacking intemperance, licentiousness, hypocrisy, and political deception.

taken from her at the age of four or five and later apprenticed in industry or agriculture, the records show the horrors of the contractual system of the eighteenth century, the lack of trained inspectors, and the inability of Parliament to intervene intelligently. When, in 1756-1760, Parliament ordered the admission of all foundlings, the mortality rate rose from forty-one per cent to sixty-eight per cent.[7] The history of this Hospital documents the cruelty and the chaotic conditions of the century. Hogarth, one of its benefactors, in his painting of the barbarities of the age, it may be mentioned in passing, drew his themes of cruelty to man and beast, of bribery, corruption, and vice of all sorts from real life.[8] He showed the contemporary evils and expressed, as did the poets, both lay and clerical, the indignation which led to change and reform.

The long period of transition in England between the partial decay or the destruction of old remedial institutions for the handling of distress and the creation of new ones by governmental action, gave the British humanitarian spirit a bent of private generosity which has continued to the present day. The slowness with which society arrived at state intervention, committed the people to the founding of numerous private social agencies, which they have continued to support. These agencies have often furnished the foundations for the great public services or have continued to supplement the activities of the state. The Benthamite reformer of the nineteenth century did not build on vacant ground, in education for example, but found the land dotted with schools, hospitals, prisons, and other institutions.[9] This fact demanded an

adaptation to existing structure and personnel. A tax-supported school system might dominate an American state. In England, Church and private initiative had often preëmpted the ground.

In this age of great men and meager institutions, the economic revolutions produced a new rich and a new poor, in addition to the old poor. The man engaged in agricultural improvements and active in purchasing and enclosing land, normally paid scant attention to the evicted cottager. Unaware, too, of broad changes, the founder of new factories felt a glow of achievement in the creation of new goods, rather than dismay at the destruction of an artisan class and its way of life.

The Anglican Church, a part of the state, was adapted to a static society and not prepared to meet the needs of the mobile people moving by covered wagon into new industrial towns. In England and Wales the rector of the parish served as moderator of disputes, as Parson Woodforde's diary and other records show, and thus checked crime at its source.[10] But only an Act of Parliament could add a new parish or shift support from a rich to a poor one.

Recent research has tended to break down the sharp divisions of the eighteenth

---

[7] Ibid., 60, 62.

[8] Rosamond Bayne-Powell, in The English Child in the Eighteenth Century (London, 1939), gives a further picture of this period when an infant of six could be hanged, when teeth were pulled from the gums of poor boys to supply the vacant spaces in the jaws of the rich.

[9] Mary G. Jones, in The Charity School Movement, A Study of Eighteenth Century Puritanism in Action (London, 1938), 3-4, points out, "The common tendency to date the pro-

vision of elementary education from 1870, or from the foundation of the National and the British and Foreign School Societies in the early years of the nineteenth century, or from the establishment of Sunday schools at the end of the eighteenth century, has obscured the efforts of educational enthusiasts throughout the eighteenth century to provide a means of free education for the lower orders in the four countries of the British Isles." This careful study gives striking evidence of the work of the Society for the Promotion of Christian Knowledge which, with like organizations, applied "the new method of associated philanthropy and the new device of joint-stock finance." Ibid., 3.

[10] John Beresford (ed.), The Diary of a Country Parson (5 volumes) is a vivid day-by-day account of the role of the parson in the parish in the latter half of the century. Interspersed with comments on foods and health are the tales of local disputes and vandalism which came to Parson Woodforde's attention and in which he acts as an adviser.

century into two contrasting parts—the first half characterized by inhumanity, or a contemplation of misery, and the second half by an unaccounted for humanitarian spirit and action. To examine the split between the halves and to come to grips with events and assess the evolution of the humanitarian mood, this brief study will more particularly relate the activities on behalf of native peoples made by the Society for the Propagation of the Gospel, and for the abolition of the slave trade by the Anti-Slavery Society. Such societies, with a definite origin and a definite aim, furnish a clear-running narrative, free from the complexities of the poor law, for example. For the purpose of comparison a brief reference will be made to prison reform.

The slave trade yielded an estimated twenty-four per cent per annum. It was a gigantic business enterprise. It is, therefore, the best example in the century of the conflict between the humanitarian spirit and huge vested interests. A minor wrong in Great Britain, or a witch-hunt in the colonies, might be managed as an episode to be corrected by local authority, but the mitigation and abolition of the slave system involved every economic interest of the people of Great Britain and of the British Empire. It was entrenched in the international stakes for world-wide empire, and was regarded as a first line of defense by the great naval powers. It was universally believed to be a nursery for seamen, the bulwark of tropical production, and the means of supporting manufactures, shipping, and the home population. A torchlight procession in London, in 1713, celebrated the slave trade monopoly for British enterprise gained at the Peace of Utrecht. A national celebration of outlawry of the trade, a hundred years later at the end of the Napoleonic wars, revealed the turn of opinion within the century.

Before going further a few questions may be raised. Did the humanitarian mood manifest itself in reform on the home front or concern itself first with the wrongs of "native peoples" as trade or empire developed? Without too great hazard it may

be said that public conscience became aware of the rights of others, of the submerged lower orders at home, or of natives abroad and, once this concern was aroused, the unfortunate man at home and "the noble savage" in a distant land received attention from assorted groups. Reserving the question of priority of interest, whether home or foreign, it is only necessary now to discover the origin of the humanitarian spirit, and the reasons for its growth. Overwhelming evidence exists to demonstrate the widespreading growth of the people's mood in the care of the aged, debtor, orphan, prisoner, the sailor, the shipwrecked, and the native in Asia, Africa, and America.

Again it may be asked, does the reformer really succeed with his reform or do economic interests shift, give him a hearing, and follow his remedy as good business? Did the shift of the British Empire to India, in the course of the eighteenth century, play a decisive role in bringing about the abolition of the slave trade? Was the eventual complete abolition of the trade brought about by the opening up of Africa to European capitalism so that the Negro could be used as a laborer in his homeland? Was the humanitarian merely deceived into taking an actual part in the exploitation of native peoples by his missionary and other enterprises, which gave him a constructive role, a role supporting, and not interfering with the economic venture? Would the Bible, rather than the whip, produce more sugar?

Returning to the main narrative, the ship owner, the factor or agent in Africa, the manufacturer of slave goods, the planter in the West Indies, the capitalist in London, all the beneficiaries of enormous profits, defended the *status quo* with great determination. In the gigantic efforts of the S.P.G. the missionary went in person to all fronts in the colonial world. The slave world was never wholly hostile to the humanitarian interventionist, a fact which gave the missionary footing as a propagandist, among plantations or farm colonies from Newfoundland to the Mosquito Shore and Barbados.

The ideology of the Society was early given practical formula. Christianization was not emancipation, education was an economic benefit, and the wealth made in the trade was to be tithed into a fund to be spent on the Negro. When Colonel Codrington presented, in 1710, his plantations and the four hundred slaves thereon, the corporation could accept the gift, operate it as a slave plantation, educate and Christianize its slaves, and use them as teachers of the race.[11]

Made a slaveowner by the Codrington gift, the Society was compelled until 1833-34 to carry out its own program and was removed from the hazards of pure speculation at the expense of other slaveowners. Absentee idealism was checked by factual reports from Barbados. The Codrington estates can be used as a yardstick in the evolution of the humanitarian spirit and during the later decades before universal emancipation, as documentation for the fact that more aggressive groups had outrun the Society's program. This advance of opinion caused Sir George Stephen sarcastically to address the Bishops as the Honorable Bench of Bishops and Board of Slave Holders, Inc.

The importance of Codrington, and of the Society's educational activities in New York, Pennsylvania, South Carolina, and elsewhere, cannot be exaggerated when it is realized that one major result of all this energy was the education of the home front. Throughout the century, in every diocese and in every parish, the people were not merely informed, but were actual participants in the humanitarian program. They were contributors of money, and they read the mass of literature, tracts, famous sermons, the Abstracts of Proceedings, which showed actual accomplishment, and committed them to new steps. The sermon was one of the chief, if not the most important, means of communication, and a weapon which political and religious antagonists

used with great effect both in England and in the American Colonies.

The Abstract of Proceedings, usually bound with the Sermon, was widely distributed over the parishes of England. The Abstract did not devote itself to argument and philosophical discussion, but was a documentary of factual progress, similar to business reports made by directors of an eighteenth-century company. The Secretary ably summarized the reports of each region, citing each missionary and parish by name, in a colorful and indelible narrative style. The effect was to make a readable story, with the impression of success. The excellence of eighteenth-century writing, whether in prose or poetry, with its exactness and precision, was not confined to Defoe, Swift, Fielding, Goldsmith, but includes even company abstracts and reports of boards of directors. In the S.P.G. manuscripts this eighteenth-century flavor is distinct, not only in reports of voyages, shipwrecks, disasters, and adventurers, but in the narration of day by day activities.

The Bray Associates, organized in 1723, intensified interest in the Negro, and added their evidence that the Negro could be educated in arts, crafts, and letters and made a member of civilized society.[12] This Society, with its own organization, literature, and schools, can only be mentioned here. But the fact that the mood of England was changing, decade by decade, is seen in the voice of these important societies.

These religious and educational corporations of the Church, created not only a mood but a literature which was certain to fire revolutionary leaders. The first of these

---

[11] See Frank J. Klingberg, "British Humanitarianism at Codrington," in The Journal of Negro History, XXIII (1938), 451-486.

[12] Edgar Legare Pennington, in Thomas Bray's Associates and their Work among the Negroes (Worcester, 1939), traces the work done for the Negro in the American colonies from 1704 to the outbreak of the American Revolution. See also Richard I. Shelling, "Benjamin Franklin and the Dr. Bray Associates," in The Pennsylvania Magazine of History and Biography, LXIII (1939), 282-293; and "The Reverend William Sturgeon, Catechist to the Negroes of Philadelphia . . . ," in Historical Magazine of the Protestant Episcopal Church, VIII (1939), 388-401.

men of action was Granville Sharp. His interests included activity against dueling, the press gang, prison abuse, Parliamentary corruption, war, drink, flogging, and unemployment. He discovered, by a study of heraldry, lost pedigrees and put men into the House of Lords, as a pastime. He defended the Indians of Saint Vincent's of the Caribbean against extermination. He opposed *The Beggar's Opera* as too gay. He worked out a new defense system for London.[13]

For present purposes it is impossible to follow his varied career, but it is important to note the vigor which led to his most successful achievement in reform, which he accomplished singlehanded, viz., the abolition of slavery in England, by the Somersett decision in 1772. This stroke was the result of seven years of indefatigable effort. The lawyers and his friends were alike against him in this supposedly hopeless aim. Blackstone, wishing him Godspeed in the court of king's bench, plainly intimated that failure was inevitable. The court was hostile, for it did not wish to emancipate fourteen or fifteen thousand slaves by judicial fiat. Chief Justice Mansfield, therefore, evaded the direct question in a series of decisions. Even in the Somersett case, Mansfield adjourned the case several times and counseled the owner of Somersett to set him free, so that no decision would be necessary. However, both parties to the suit, confident of victory, forced a decision. Sharp's part lay chiefly in his skilled argument. His brief was sent to all the lawyers and the judges and convinced Mansfield that slavery could not exist in England. Based on extensive research from Magna Carta on, his main thesis was that the only method by which a man in England could be held in bondage was under serfdom. Serfdom had practically disappeared by this time, and, in any event, Somersett was not a serf, because the contractual obligations of serfdom were wholly missing. The exact

technicality need not concern us here, for no eighteenth-century judge would make a decision as clear-cut as it is here summarized. The decision, of immense length, in fact incorporated Sharp's antislavery tracts and arguments.[14]

This decision is, moreover, of interest in the formula of reform, for Sharp and others resorted to historical tradition and precedent to attain ends, an approach which Sharp perhaps derived from the method of Biblical criticism, as well as from his legal research. He did not leave the Church, but denounced certain tenets as not in its best tradition and practice. And thus he found fault with the law.

The ideology of the century is also revealed in Sharp's happy confidence in human nature, which assumed that others, when informed, would be as determined as he to see the right prevail.[15] Men were good, and only institutions might be bad. He won an opposing lawyer, Dunning, to his cause, but when Dunning deserted him Sharp blamed legal ethics, not the man.

It must be noted that the Somersett case applied to England, Wales, and Ireland, but did not apply to Scotland. The Joseph Knight decision of 1778 was therefore important in its own right because it freed the slaves of Scotland on the broader ground that the whole system of slavery was untenable, "the dominion assumed over this

---

[13] E. C. P. Lascelles, *Granville Sharp and the Freedom of Slaves in England* (London, 1928), *passim*.

[14] A further discussion of Granville Sharp, and of the legal aspects of this decision, can be found in Frank J. Klingberg, *The Anti-Slavery Movement in England* (New Haven, 1926), especially Chapter II, "The Formation of Public Opinion in Great Britain against Slavery and the Slave Trade. The New Determinant: Humanitarianism. Emancipation of the Slaves in Great Britain," and Chapter III, "The Attack on the Slave Trade 1783-1793. Aggressive Humanitarianism."

[15] A couplet quoted in a Bombay government resolution expresses the attitude happily and with finality:

Truth has such a look and such a mien,
As to be loved needs only to be seen.

Educational Records, II, 145, Bureau of Education, India.

Negro under the law of Jamaica, being unjust."[16]

Sharp, in 1768, had drawn heavily upon the publications of the S.P.G. as one of the chief "civilizing" agencies of the eighteenth century. He had read Bishop Gibson's tracts and addresses, had studied the Negro school in New York, and in general fortified himself with information made available by the Society. He was in touch with colonial reformers. A letter from Benezet, in Philadelphia in 1772, shows that Wesley, Benjamin Franklin, Sharp, Warburton, were all in close collaboration. The time was ripe for cooperation and action. Benezet proposed petitions to King and Parliament, which set forth all the arguments used in the eighteenth and nineteenth centuries for the abolition of the slave trade and slavery. Benezet's letter, moreover, characteristically presented an English argument stating that the chief victims of the slave system were not the Negroes, but the white operators. This view was amplified later by Thomas Clarkson, a resourceful field agent, who showed by the case studies of twenty thousand seamen that the slave trade was not the nursery of seamen, but their grave. Wilberforce and others maintained that slavery had impoverished and dehumanized the white masters.

Sharp was now famous and, urging that slavery was illegal in the West Indies, and that the decision covered the colonies as well as England, he visited Lord North to propound his view that the Somersett case had freed all the slaves in the Empire. North convinced him that slavery in the colonies had the protection of Parliament and colonial assemblies. The American Revolution

[16] Howell, *State Trials*, XX, 6, 7. A summary of the act of 1701 (p. 21) is: "That no person shall be transported forth of this kingdom, except with his own consent, given before a judge or by legal sentence, under the certification, that any judge or magistrate, who shall give order for such transportation, or any one, who shall transport another, shall . . . be liable in the pecuniary pains of wrongous imprisonment, . . . [and] shall lose their offices, and be declared incapable of all public trust."

intervened, and nothing more could be done until the war was over.

Then Sharp returned to the attack, as suggested by Benezet in 1772. The postwar atmosphere is shown in the fact that it was now possible to launch an assault, respectable as practical politics, in the view of friend and opponent. In 1787 the Society for the Abolition of the Slave Trade was organized with Sharp as President.

The question at once arose as to the method of attack: should it be on the whole slave system or should it proceed a step at a time? The vote in the executive council of twelve was eleven to one in favor of attacking the slave trade, but not slavery within the British Empire where it was legally established. Sharp alone held out for emancipation of slaves as well as for abolition of the slave trade. A ready argument was available for Parliament, in 1778, had passed a self-denying ordinance as part of its attempt to conciliate the revolting colonies; that under no circumstances would the imperial legislature interfere with the internal affairs of any of its colonies. Jamaica, Barbados, and other colonies, with colonial legislatures, were clearly under the provisions of this Act.

At this stage, with the two judicial decisions freeing slaves throughout Great Britain, two men joined in the attack who had abilities particularly suited for propaganda: Thomas Clarkson, who became the indefatigable field agent, and William Wilberforce, the parliamentary leader. The evolution of the humanitarian spirit and the triumph of evangelicalism are to be seen in the lives of these two men of action, each of whom created a body of literature which space prevents reviewing.

William Wilberforce, it may quickly be said, in his first famous speech of 1789, marshalled all the arguments, religious, philanthropical, and economic, in skilful combination for an effective appeal. For seventeen years he introduced his resolutions in Parliament. He was careful to document his thesis that humanitarianism was a peculiarly British idea, that his countrymen were historically a kindly people. This latter point was not only the winning one at the moment but proved indispensable during the whole of the next generation. His friend Pitt was willing to identify himself with the attack on the slave trade. No statesman, twenty-five or fifty years earlier, would have dreamed of daring this. Besides, his Whig opponents, Charles James Fox and Edmund Burke, instantly pledged their support, gauging the issue as practical and the mood as coming to flood tide. Thus Pitt, Fox, Clarkson, Wilberforce, James Stephen, Zachary Macaulay and others, ingeniously showing that the slave, the owner, the shipper, the merchant, the Negro in Africa, the sailor, the Empire itself, would profit, had put the British genius of salesmanship to the supreme test in making this sale of an economic revolution.

But the abolition of the slave trade was not accomplished without great bitterness. Clarkson was repeatedly threatened with death. Wilberforce had to count on his wealth, social position, and his friendships to protect him from the suppression which Clarkson suffered from 1794 to 1804. When James Ramsay died a West Indian leader boasted that he had killed him. As in the case of Robert Norris, men often changed sides, and an Anti-Slavery man might appear on the opposition side, as Burke did when alarmed by the French Revolution. Humanitarian leaders were often drawn from the middle class, and the French Revolution, by its violence and its financial bankruptcy, and by releasing the energies of the lower classes, frightened most reformers into their cellars.

Returning to the year 1789, Clarkson, in marshalling evidence against slavery in the West Indies, which the abolition of the slave trade was to humanize, encountered maximum difficulty. Inhuman practices were brought to his attention by the large West Indian interests in England for, as Frank Wesley Pitman has pointed out, the English planter and overseer, Army and Navy official, missionary and traveler, returned to England as a home,[17] and was therefore in a position to describe the slave system. This he was willing to do, provided his evidence was considered confidential and would not be presented to Parliament. This restriction harassed Clarkson but his collection of facts grew, and in two directions. Africa could produce unlimited quantities of economic goods by leaving the Negro there to work in his homeland. And West Indian economy, without new importations of slaves, could grow tropical products by means of better methods of farming, and by greater care of women and children.

In 1807, on both sides of the Atlantic, the slave trade was abolished. The writer has never found a reference in English debate to the fact of the American prohibition coming into effect on August first of that year. All of the American states had prohibited the slave trade before 1803, reflecting the mood that slavery and the slave trade were evils which would fall of their own weight. It is a striking fact that the abolition of the slave trade, accomplished in Great Britain only after a battle of twenty years, was accomplished quietly in the same year in America, according to the provisions written in the federal constitution in 1787. Two generations later an exact reversal of opinion had occurred in the two countries. In contrast to the peaceful emancipation of the British slaves in the West Indies in 1833, is Lincoln's proclamation of January 1, 1863, at the height of a bloody civil war with a million dead. Curiously, the number of men in Great Britain dependent on cotton for a livelihood was exactly the same as the number of slaves producing cotton in the South. Four million black slaves, who had sent cotton from the fields to four million factory workers for manufacture, were freed. These factors support the thesis that

[17] For a discussion of absentee-management, see Frank Wesley Pitman, *The Development of the British West Indies, 1700-1763* (New Haven, 1917) especially Chapter I, "British West India Society in the Eighteenth Century."

the growth of the population in Great Britain was strikingly dependent on the growth of America.

Just as the West Indian planter and merchant and banker were to be convinced of the benefits to themselves and the Empire of the abolition of the slave trade, so we find, in other fields, the same arguments for reform. The whole community would benefit by revolution in prison management. Voluntary enlistments, rather than impressment, with better food and treatment, would strengthen the Navy. A public health policy which took greater care of mothers and children would build up the stamina of the people, increase population, and therefore Britain's weight in the world. All reformers argued in these larger, and nationalistic terms, that the petty abuse must be transformed into the public good.

A glance at prison reforms confirms the pattern of fact-finding, agitation, legislation. Unlike the slave trade, this reform was internal, and involved eighteenth-century administration and management. John Howard was able to obtain a Parliamentary Committee report. The Act of 1774, based on the report, was excellent in its paper provisions. It required that prisoners should be kept clean, the cells whitewashed, and well ventilated, warm and cold baths were to be provided, separate rooms for the sick were to be maintained, dungeons were to be abolished. An experienced surgeon with a salary, and other medical attendants were required. The Justices of the Peace, those men of all work, who were to enforce the Act, ignored it for the most part and, as the poems of Crabbe indicate, neither doctor nor chaplain did his work. Coming at the moment of the American Revolution, it preceded an accumulation of prisoners who could no longer be sent to the thirteen colonies. In 1779 Parliament decided to build two model prisons in the vicinity of London, but a site was not agreed upon. However, so strong had the humanitarian mood become that when, in January, 1788, the first shipload of felons arrived at Botany Bay, indicating the revival of penal trans-

portation, the humanitarian challenge was immediate. Sir Samuel Romilly, of French Huguenot stock and a noted traveler, was the pioneer in Parliament, while the brain-truster was Jeremy Bentham. Their main success occurred between 1806 and 1818. The founding of Australia was a by-product of the penal system.[18]

An analysis points to the fact that in reform, where negative action was sufficient, as in the Somersett case of emancipation, success could be attained on a general scale. In the case of prison reform and the abolition of penal transportation, however, the whole institutional life of the country had to be changed. This involved legislation, taxation, prison building, reform of discipline, centralization of control, a new police system, and the organization of skilled prison administrators. Most important of all was the modification of the eighteenth-century contractual method of action. The Army and Navy were provided for by contract. The care and feeding of all the dispossessed and wards of society tended to fall into the national pattern of hiring out these services and provisions. The extreme localism of government function was an obstacle. The action of the Justices of Peace on police and economic matters varied from county to county and from time to time.[19] Briefly, prison reform involved the abandonment of the eighteenth-century form of

[18] The story of penal transportation, particularly as it affected Great Britain and Ireland, is told in Eris O'Brien, *The Foundation of Australia (1786-1800)* (London, 1937), *passim.* As O'Brien points out (p. 6), "The political conditions explain the code of laws; the social conditions explain, at least to an appreciable extent, the criminality of the lower classes." The abolition of penal transportation is almost an exact parallel of the abolition of the slave trade. This story has been told by Dr. Charles Stuart Blackton in *The Australian Colonial Movement Against Penal Transportation from Great Britain, 1837-1867* (Ph. D. thesis in the Library of the University of California, Los Angeles).

[19] Valuable for social detail and as a record of the Justices in action is E. G. Dowdell, *The Justices of the Peace: A Hundred Years of Quarter Sessions. The Government of Middlesex from 1660 to 1760* (London, 1932).

society and the development of the nine-teenth-century state paternalism. It is this basic fact which stood in the way of decisive change. Noted men in succession: James Oglethorpe (1696-1785), Jonas Hanway (1712-1786), John Howard (1726-1790), spent their lives in efforts which were rea-lized only in the nineteenth century. The eighteenth century was a pioneer laboratory for nineteenth-century reorganization and reform.

Matching the growth of humanitarianism in political theory and in social outlook, and the change from cold religious orthodoxy to evangelicalism, was the parallel develop-ment of English literature from classicism, during the first half of the eighteenth cen-tury, to what is called sentimentalism dur-ing the second half. Each quarter-century of literary record, in fact each decade, falls into the exact pattern of official or historical narrative of reform, and is here cited as con-firming the fact of the evolution of the humanitarian spirit.

Truth comes out in poetry. The eight-eenth century can be found in all its reality, in the poets from John Gay to William Blake. They seem to the scholar of today much more aware of the social revolutions of the century than were the statesmen. Few of the literary figures, great or small, ignored the scene around them. The familiar work of Gay, Gray, Burns, and William Blake is known to all, either for reformatory zeal or human tenderness. George Crabbe takes one to live in the English village of the eighteenth century. His description of the parish poorhouse, "Whose walls of mud scarce bear the broken door," indicts the social order.[20] Crabbe, Goldsmith, and Cowper were field observers.[21] Thomson,

too, left his ivory tower, and Swift and Defoe were among the most careful as-sessors and critics of the human scene. Swift, in his description of a city shower, furnished an unforgettable picture of Lon-don, more revealing of its lack of sanita-tion than any social engineer could give.[22]

During this period God, in the hands of the eighteenth-century poets, is brought more closely within the reach of all human beings, and is clearly made humane. In this transformation, no man more than William Blake removed so much of Milton's concep-tion of a hard, cost-accountant God. Men were committed to the tender care of a humane God, and therefore to a share in making a humanitarian world. Blake sang the democracy of religion, the equalitarian-ism of the human soul, the dignity of the common man. In addition to his genius as a poet was his skill as an artist and an en-graver. His series to illustrate Young's "Night Thoughts," Gray's poems, and "The Divine Comedy" retold in another art the equalitarian message of his fellow poets, and of his own writings. He rose, like Robert Burns, from the ranks, singing, as he as-cended, of the immortality of the human spirit, but never neglecting this world's joys and sufferings. The lyric gift of the eight-eenth-century poet, his wit and charm, iden-tified him with the normal man in such a way that, as a member of society, he could criticize it and challenge its abuses.

Then, to sum up, the formula of reform proceeded from the private charity of indi-viduals to a Parliamentary party, from in-vestigation to legislation and enforcement. The chimney sweep, children in the factory,

---

[20] Ronald S. Crane, *A Collection of English Poems, 1660-1800* (New York, 1932), 940. In "The Parish" Crabbe speaks with a modern brevity, clarity and satire. Like Hogarth, his detail is etched into the mind, and furnishes the challenge for his appeal to those more fortunate for alleviation of the conditions he describes.

[21] Goldsmith, in dedicating "The Deserted Village" to Sir Joshua Reynolds, wrote, "I have taken all possible pains, in my country ex-

cursions, . . . to be certain of what I alledge; . . . all my views and enquiries have led me to believe those miseries real, . . ." *Ibid.,* 851.

[22] Swift writes,
Filths of all Hues and Odours, . . .
Sweepings from Butchers Stalls, Dung, Guts, and Blood,
Drown'd Puppies, stinking Sprats, all drench'd in Mud,
Dead Cats, and Turnip-Tops come tumbling down the Flood.
Ibid., 254.

slaves in the hold, women in the coal mines, Irish immigrants crowded in the white man's middle passage, all became objects of the law's care, but ultimate enforcement was to be won only by the creation of skilled enforcement agencies. Often new inventions came to the aid of the reformer. A new machine could sweep the chimney better than a boy, steam took the white immigrant across the Atlantic in days rather than weeks. Myriad inventions shortened the working day as practical economies.

Humanitarian reform took full advantage of the bitter rivalry of competing business enterprises. The canal builder fought with the road builder, the water carrier with the railroad. These revolutions were in part mitigated by an expanding economy which could absorb some of the victims of rapid change. Reform never left the economic arena, could never function in an economic void. In other words, the economic versatility of the country and the emigration of men and of capital made it possible to pursue a certain reform technique.

The old rich reformed the new rich, the old industry the new. Wool was conservative, cotton a risky, questionable business for new men. Wool reformed cotton, both brought linen to better working conditions. The Wilberforce family, having become wealthy in the Baltic trade, viewed the slave trade as diabolical, plantation society as intolerable. The landed men viewed the capitalist with disfavor. Lord Shaftesbury pointed out the menace of slavery, but resented criticism of his farm labor and their housing, saying that ivy covered the leaks.[23]

The social reformers were usually landed men and therefore conducted reforms in factories. They were honestly unable to see that tenement conditions might prevail in the beautiful countryside as well as in the

[23] Later, in the same manner, President Tyler and the Southerners pointed out that no slave worked as a London seamstress did. And Calvin Stowe burst bounds and declared that the real support of cotton and the slave plantation was the English cotton industry with its four million dependents. See Forrest Wilson, *Crusader in Crinoline,* pp. 379-380 and *passim.*

city. The country worker fitted into the county tradition and therefore had a certain security. In a feudal society the well-to-do felt some responsibility, religious and otherwise, for the welfare of the community because it had been sufficiently stable for personal relationships to develop. The soup and flannels for the bedridden cottager helped him bear his arthritis in a house with damp walls which had dripped for generations. The slaves on a large plantation in the West Indies, and the masses of industrial labor in England, were more easily seen to be dehumanized and were viewed as a part of a unit of production which, strangely enough, made one economic society. Capitalism linked the two; in one case factories in the field, in the other factories packed within walls.

In a similar interplay the Anglican clergy vied with the dissenter in humanitarian activities,[24] and both were challenged by the deistic philosophy of the century which emphasized allegiance of man to man, as did orthodox Christianity, and demanded that social injustices be attacked head on, or as of this world, to be remedied here and now. These religious workingman's movements are indigenous and continue in ever-recurrent waves such as, in recent times, in the rise of the Salvation Army.

The taxpayer, too, became a reformer. Taxes, amounting to millions of pounds a year, were frittered away under the contractual system and the unfortunates of society did not receive what the people

[24] M. Dorothy George, in *London Life of the XVIIIth Century* (New York, 1926), 11, suggests that the growth of a spirit of humanity, which in France drew its strength from free thought, "is sometimes too exclusively identified with evangelicalism. In England a fundamental element in the new point of view was a greater knowledge of social conditions and a new scientific spirit in dealing with social questions." Mrs. George's study is, throughout, invaluable for the specific information gleaned from trials, depositions of witnesses, petitions to Quarter Sessions, reports of coroner's inquests, settlement cases, the publication of charities and the pamphlets of reformers. Of special interest is the appendix containing vital statistics on mortality and conditions of apprenticeship.

paid for their relief. Dissatisfaction, therefore, was not confined to a robbed recipient, but included the taxpayer. The "Thatched House Society," organized in 1772, had, by 1792, raised and spent £30,000 and released 12,590 prisoners held for small sums.[25] This is a striking illustration of the charity of the citizen who accepted the institution, but determined to mitigate its severity. The prison and the workhouse were not, in theory, institutions of permanent abode, but were designed to serve a temporary function. The prisoner was to be acquitted, hanged, or transported. The debtor was, in some mysterious way, to do in prison what he failed to do when free.

The institutions of eighteenth-century England were, in theory, extremely simple. Officials acted only when absolutely necessary. These facts make the problem of the student of humanitarianism not simple but difficult. He has few major sources, such as the S.P.G. with its two hundred thousand manuscripts, and the S.P.C.K. to scrutinize for his materials, but must gather his gleanings from a thousand individuals, from short-lived magazines, from obscure pamphleteers, from county records,[26] from tacit assumptions in poetry and fiction, from exact gifts of charity, and from relief rolls in varied places where they are discovered by modern scholars.

Although immeasurable, the most profound consideration must be given to the entrenched traditions of the eighteenth century. The new cruelties and the violence of the age ran counter to the deep-seated conviction that kindliness was British, not Jacobin; was native, not foreign. The wells of charity and the ideologies, whether Anglican or dissenting, deistic or evangelical, sprang from the silent accretions of centuries of kindliness. The long training of the people in earlier times, when the Church cared for the unfortunate, must not be forgotten in the intricate eighteenth-century mixtures of medievalism and modern state socialism. The power of self-criticism and entrenched traditions of independence were strong enough to change the climate of opinion within the resistant framework. A hardy character bred neither a spirit of fatalism nor of violent revolution. Active humanitarianism rebuilt society, changed Hogarth's London to Lamb's London, and laid foundations for the nineteenth-century state.

[25] J. L. and B. Hammond, "Poverty, Crime, and Philanthropy," in A. S. Turberville (ed.), *Johnson's England,* I, 331. This Society, originally known as the Society for the Discharge and Relief of Persons Imprisoned for Small Debts, had as its most active member James Neild (1774-1814), a jeweler who acted as treasurer of the Society and whose book, *The State of Prisons in England, Scotland, and Wales,* was used by Romilly, Bennet, and Peel in the later campaigns.

[26] Valuable are such studies as E. M. Hampson's *The Treatment of Poverty in Cambridgeshire, 1597-1834* (London, 1933), which furnish exact detail as to the relief of poverty and the administration of poor and settlement laws.

WHEN, IN 1731, EDWARD CAVE founded that landmark in the history of periodicals *The Gentleman's Magazine,* he stated that his purpose was "to give Monthly a View of all the Pieces of Wit, Humor, or Intelligence, daily offer'd to the Publick in the News-Papers, (which of late are so multiply'd, as to render it impossible, unless a Man makes it a Business, to consult them all)." Most of these eighteenth-century newspapers proved, of course, to be short-lived. Only the *Gazette* lasted through the entire half century from 1700 to 1750; but it was a hopeful sign that the *London Evening Post,* founded in 1727, and the *General Evening Post,* founded in 1733, lasted into the period of the Napoleonic Wars. To the student of literature, what is perhaps especially remarkable about eighteenth-century newspapers is that they were so often able to engage the services of the outstanding writers of the time—Defoe, Henry Fielding, the Earl of Chesterfield, Dr. Johnson, and Oliver Goldsmith, for example. Their leading articles were, indeed, often of a literary character, and poems, stories, and essays were frequently featured. Dr. Johnson's *Idler* essays and Goldsmith's *Chinese Letters* made their first appearance in the newspapers. Journalism itself, however, was not as a rule a safe profession, and the freedom of the press was often in danger, for newspapers were recognized as a powerful political force. In the following essay, Professor William T. Laprade, of Duke University, discusses the press in an age when the public was becoming more and more newspaper-minded. Professor Laprade is the author of *Public Opinion and Politics in Eighteenth Century England to the Fall of Walpole* (1936), an important monograph based on extensive research in newspaper files; and for many years he has been urging his fellow historians to exploit eighteenth-century newspapers more effectively as historical sources.

THE POWER OF THE ENGLISH PRESS IN THE EIGHTEENTH CENTURY
WILLIAM T. LAPRADE

In the past generation or two, students have begun habitually to use newspapers as sources for the history of the time in which they were published. The assumption seems to be that the papers were recorders of facts or reflectors of opinion and so yield information, though often of doubtful reliability, concerning the subjects reported in their columns. There is an element of truth in this assumption. But it is doubtful whether newspapers can be used to much advantage as sources of information until they receive more attention as being themselves part of the fabric of society. Newspapers are more in the nature of relics than chronicles of their times. They have not served identical functions at all stages in their history. In late years they have become media through which important individuals and groups communicate with each other and with the public at large, thus constituting a sort of cement for holding society together, without which it is difficult to see how it could exist in its present form. Thus newspapers have

grown with the society of which they are so vital a part. Their evolution from small beginnings to their present impressive importance is not only a fascinating subject for study; it is a necessary one, if we are to understand either the contents of the newspapers of a given time or the character of the society in which they flourished.

Of no time and place is this more true than eighteenth-century England, the country and the period in which newspapers as we know them were largely evolved. The transition from a society in which newspapers were unimportant and almost unknown to one in which they were accepted as a matter of course and as almost essential if existing conditions were not to be radically changed, occurred in England in that century. There were embryonic newspapers in 1700, to be sure. But the papers in which the subjects of George III read accounts of Napoleon's campaigns were more like those of today than like the insignificant sheets which brought to their

Reprinted by special permission from *The South Atlantic Quarterly*, XXVII (1928), 426-434.

grandfathers tidings of Marlborough's victories. In that interval occurred a world of experiment and struggle, sometimes against odds, which had much to do with forming the character of English newspapers—and also of English society as later generations know it.

From the beginning, English newspapers were primarily intended to mould opinion; that is, they carried facts (or assertions) and arguments designed to create in readers a state of mind favorable to the purposes of those sponsoring the several journals. Consequently, they need to be studied in close correlation with other information about the persons and causes they were meant to serve. Just as history written without reference to the newspapers (as is the case with much that has been written in the past) lacks an essential flavor and content necessary to give it verisimilitude, so quotations from papers apart from their setting in time and circumstance reveal very little of what was going on. The activities of the politicians and of the writers for the press must be considered together if we are to understand either.

This is not surprising when we reflect that most of the important statesmen of the eighteenth century inspired or even wrote for the press, and almost every writer of note contributed to it. From Harley and Bolingbroke to Canning and the younger Pitt, from Defoe, Swift, Addison, and Steele to Burke and Johnson,—unless we bear in mind the relations of notable eighteenth-century Englishmen with the newspapers, we are in danger of overlooking a vital aspect of their lives. From Defoe's *Review,* conducted to support, in Harley's interest, toleration and the union of England and Scotland, and the *Examiner* of Swift and Bolingbroke, in which they made war on their political rivals, to the *True Briton,* inspired by Pitt to arouse the country against France, and Canning's *Anti-Jacobin,* intended to stimulate conservative fears of foreign radicalism to support a lagging war, scarcely a year was without its cause, and never a cause without its support in the press. Many persons remembered for other things achieved a large part of their reputation as writers for newspapers. Among them were Horace Walpole (in his father's time), Fielding, Smollett, Arthur Murphy, Wilkes, and Burke. Others who deserve to be remembered have been largely forgotten because their best work appeared in these passing records of the day. Such men were John Trenchard, Thomas Gordon, Nicholas Amhurst, James Ralph, John Campbell, William Guthrie, John Almon. All of these and a host of others deserve to live in history because of their part in giving tone and quality to the society of their times and because they lent a hand in shaping the character of newspapers in their infancy and lusty youth.

GORDON RIOTS: Anti-Roman-Catholic outbursts of 1780. They were instigated by the demented Lord George Gordon, who was obsessed by the idea that a new Popish Plot was being aimed at him personally. Accompanied by a large and unruly crowd, he presented a petition in the House of Commons in opposition to a recent Catholic Relief Act. The next few days saw the pillaging and burning of many Catholic homes. Order was restored owing in large measure to the efforts of John Wilkes. Ironically, however, many of the disturbers of the peace were political supporters of Wilkes, and so his involvement in the crushing of the anti-Catholic disorders was intimately connected with his demise as a significant political figure.

BENJAMIN HOADLY: English theologian and Whig controversialist (d. 1761) who justified the right of the people to dethrone a popish ruler. He also defended the right of the sovereign to insist upon the allegiance of his clergy. Because of his individualistic conception of religion and his latitudinarianism, he aroused widespread hostility among his fellow clergymen.

Like most institutions of importance, the newspaper grew without much taking of thought or premeditated planning. Many of the more significant journals were started to support the cause of the day and were suspended when that work was done. John Tutchin's *Observator* and Charles Leslie's *Rehearsal* were on opposite sides of questions relating to claims of the monarchy and the national Church at a time when passions on these subjects ran so high as to threaten the peace of the country. Thomas Gordon, succeeding John Trenchard, labored with Walpole, Hoadly, and other statesmen and Churchmen of the time in a campaign in favor of religious toleration, the importance of which is not appreciated in later generations largely because they did their work so successfully that people forgot that the previous conditions ever existed. The questions at issue in their day cannot be understood without reference to the *Independent Whig*, "Cato's Letters" to the *London Journal*, and similar contemporary writings.

When Bolingbroke and Pulteney joined forces in 1725 in a campaign to drive Walpole from office, almost their first step was to establish the *Craftsman*. In doing this, they but followed the example of Swift and Bolingbroke in 1709, of their opponents in the late months of Anne's reign, and of Walpole and Steele in 1717, when the ministry of the day threatened to change the character of the House of Lords. The *Craftsman* was opposed by as able, though some of them less well known, writers on the side of the ministers. In 1735 these writers in Walpole's behalf discontinued several of their weeklies and joined in alternate contributions to the *Daily Gazetteer*, which was then established as the first paper on record to purvey essays of this type as a part of its daily offering. Before its work was done, the *Craftsman* was joined by *Common Sense*, inspired and in part written by Lyttleton of the Cobham cousinhood, and by the *Champion*, one of Fielding's several ventures in the field of political journalism. The agitation that attended the actual defeat of Walpole gave birth to the *Westminster Journal*. In their fight against Carteret, Chesterfield and his associates used *Old England*, or the *Constitutional Journal*, later the *Broadbottom Journal*, for which Guthrie and Chesterfield himself wrote.

In the time of Pelham, propaganda was confined largely to the daily vehicles of news. But the preliminaries to the Seven Years' War saw Henry Fox and the elder Pitt striving against each other in the *Test* and the *Con-Test*, conducted by Arthur Murphy and Owen Ruffhead respectively, with William Beckford's *Monitor*, conducted by John Entick, speaking for the City groups who were interested in the war. The aftermath of the war gave birth to Smollett's *Briton*, Wilkes's *North Briton*, and Murphy's *Auditor* among the papers that arose to keep the surviving *Monitor* company. Though the essays of propaganda were soon to take a different form, the story of the rise of papers to serve causes of the moment might be continued to the end of the century.

The method of these political writers was to hark back to general shibboleths or principles, while they provided facts and arguments suited to the needs of the hour. Pursuing what Dicey called the "astounding method of retrogressive progress," almost without exception they appealed to history both to support their assertions and to obtain analogies for making covertly and indirectly points it was not expedient to make directly. Needing better, or at any rate different history from that they had at hand, many writers for the press became historians also, themselves helping to supply the material of which they felt the lack. Gordon, Ralph, Campbell, Guthrie, Smollett, and Entick, to mention only a few, all wrote history or historical essays of a respectable character. Bolingbroke's pieces on the subject are well known, at least by reputation. Even Wilkes advertised and began a history, actually receiving subscriptions for the work, though he never found time to finish it. Needless to say, the works of all of these writers, like most histories in most times, need to be studied in relation to the questions of the day in which they were written in order to be understood or appreciated.

The appeal of these newspapers was not limited to the narrow circle of their readers. In fact, the earlier papers were not primarily intended for circulation to individual subscribers. They were "taken in" by the coffee-houses and other public places where men congregated. Often some one person read the essay of the week to groups seated about a table or gathered in front of the fire. The more fetching points became texts for discussions that frequently developed into heated arguments. Feeling aroused in these groups spread by oral communication to interested persons in every station in society. Both the printers of the papers and the promoters of causes were interested in the encouragement of such discussion, the printers in order to increase their profits from sales, the promoters of causes to accomplish their purposes. Therefore runners were frequently employed to visit the coffee-houses and take the initiative when discussion lagged, whispering now and then information, as likely to be fictitious as correct, about the identity of the author of a piece and communicating facts or allegations which it was impolitic to print.

These early journals were not intended primarily to influence voters in the exercise of the suffrage. They were rather designed to create an atmosphere which by a kind of intimidation would inhibit or promote action by statesmen and members of Parliament. If we bear in mind the inadequacy of the London police throughout the eighteenth century and the keen prejudice against a large army and against the use of the forces which existed for the suppression of domestic disorders, the threat of a mob as an inspirer or deterrent of action is apparent. Later generations have tended to lose sight of the surging crowds in the yard of St. Stephen's Chapel which awaited and in a measure determined the decision of parliament on critical questions. The defeat of the excise in 1733, the beginning of the war with Spain in 1739, the repeal of the Stamp Act in 1766, and the Gordon riots in 1780 are but better known examples of mob influence that was more nearly habitual than historians have led us to think. The mob was ever a powerful, though a somewhat hazardous weapon in political warfare, and the newspapers were effective, as they were intended to be, in creating an atmosphere productive of mobs.

There is no better evidence of the effectiveness of the press in playing this rôle than the steps meditated and actually taken by almost every statesman of the century who remained long in office for its suppression or at least the restriction of its activities. Bolingbroke and Harley sought by taxation to make opposition papers impossible. While Walpole was constantly urged to more positive action, he never did more than harry the publishers of papers opposed to him by prosecutions for seditious libel. In his time Hardwicke began to use the method of reserving to the courts the decision of whether matter was libellous, leaving to the jury only the question of publication. After the orgy of popular agitation from 1760 to the close of the war, Grenville and his associates seem to have seriously set about the task of restricting within very narrow limits political propaganda appearing in newspapers. For nearly a decade printers conducted their business in peril of ruinous fines and imprisonment.

That this campaign did not in the end accomplish its purpose was in part due to the fact that the press had by this time become a vested interest involving property in a considerable amount, and in part because people had come to depend upon the papers for certain services they could not obtain elsewhere. Moreover, on second thought, none of the opponents of the press ever went quite as far as he was tempted to go while in office, because he reflected that he might in time be again out of power himself. In that case, he did not wish to be deprived of the most effective weapon available for political warfare. This thought invariably disposed those in office to a greater tenderness in dealing with objectionable writers for newspapers than they would otherwise have shown.

The result was that by the close of the Seven Years' War the power of the press, or rather of those who knew how to use it and to supplement it with other appeals to the emotions of the day, became so great as to obstruct seriously the orderly conduct of the government. It was this fact in part which led the ministry to prosecute Entick, Wilkes, and others. Pitt, as the outstanding heroic figure of the time, and Bute, as its chief political villain, were largely creations of the press; neither owed his reputation to his real character and accomplishment. It was this reputation based on fiction rather than character and achievements that statesmen of the day had to consider in their efforts to govern the kingdom.

A part of the ease with which a fictitious reputation could thus be attached inseparably to political leaders was due to the mystery that concealed the proceedings in parliament. At no time in the eighteenth century was less known out of doors of what went on in the halls of the legislature. The debates were nowhere published. Even the monthly magazines ceased carrying, after the question was disposed of, their sketchy and fragmentary reports.

But this proved to be the darkest hour before dawn. Grenville himself, probably recognizing the unfortunate effects of some of the efforts to restrict the press, came to feel that it would be wiser to have the proceedings of parliament frankly reported in the papers as news. This was done increasingly after 1770. The way was opened for it in the following year by a contest between the House of Commons and the City over the publication of a fragment of a debate in a paper printed in London by one of its citizens. In the course of the dispute the Lord Mayor and one of his fellow magistrates were sent to the Tower. But they stood their ground. While nothing was decided formally, newspapers thereafter exercised more freedom in publishing the proceedings of parliament, and the houses felt it prudent not to do anything about it.

This implicit admission that the doings in parliament were legitimate news proved to be almost as revolutionary a step in the development of government as the rise of the newspapers themselves. The most noticeable effect was the decline in the direct power of the journals. The essays of the political writers were removed from the position of importance on the front page which they had been wont to occupy to make room for the sayings and doings of political leaders. In fact, the political writing that was carried by the papers came in time to consist largely of comments on the actions of these leaders or suggestions to them. Thus the newspaper tended to become more largely a mere medium of communication, a reporter of news. It had previously been a more dangerous political weapon, frequently in hands unknown except to the initiated. The lucubrations of Junius were among the last important examples of political writing of the older type. The struggle for publication of the parliamentary debates took place while Junius was still appearing.

Whether the contents of the newspapers were in the form of open comment on public questions and parliamentary discussion freely published, or appeals to feeling by indirect or covert allusion, no student of the history of England in the eighteenth century can afford to neglect them. But, to repeat, if he goes to the papers as mere records of the events of the time, he will usually find very little that is worth while, even of information. Eighteenth-century newspapers (whatever may be true of those in later times) were not simply reflectors of the atmosphere in which events occurred. They were among the most effective instruments used by leaders in imparting tone and quality to that atmosphere; frequently they were means of shaping the course of events. In short, they came to be themselves a vital part of the machinery of government.

That the cabinet as it is familiar in later generations largely took shape in the eighteenth century is well known. The cabinet, in an important sense, is a group of leaders united for the purpose of obtaining support for themselves from parliament and from the public at large in order that they may have power to carry on the government. It is scarcely conceivable that a cabinet in that sense could have come into existence or could have functioned without the aid of the press to make known the plans of the leaders and to create a favorable attitude towards them. Furthermore, had such a group obtained power, without the press it would have been almost impossible to un-horse it as long as it remained united in itself. That could only be done by circulat-ing criticism and arousing in the discon-tented a community of feeling sufficient to lead to common action. On that very account, while men in office might medi-tate the suppression of the press and might actually attempt to restrict its activities, there was never an opposition in the cen-tury but advocated its freedom. The subject was dwelt upon so constantly by all writers against ministers that it became in the high-est degree hackneyed, without becoming unimportant.

Thus English newspapers grew from small beginnings until they were accepted as a necessary part of the fabric of society. We take them so entirely for granted that we do not always appreciate the difficulty in-volved when we try to imagine life in a society where they did not exist. Perhaps it is almost as difficult for us to imagine what conditions were when newspapers were in the stage of their first rapid growth, chang-ing their character from time to time, fre-quently with almost startling suddenness. The student of the history of England in the eighteenth century must cultivate this difficult capacity for imagination in himself before he can describe or reflect upon events of that time with much insight.

THE

Nineteenth Century

PART SEVEN

HARDLY HAD THE FRENCH MIDDLE CLASS come to power in the summer of 1789 when a major controversy got under way in Britain—a controversy that centered on the meaning of the revolutionary events in France. British reformers were delighted to see their French counterparts leading a movement that might liberate the world by the "omnipotence of reason." British conservatives, on the other hand, feared the implications of such a document as the French Declaration of the Rights of Man and the Citizen, and they were alarmed by the destruction of privileges that was taking place across the Channel. Fear of French ideas was pronounced in Britain long before the Reign of Terror (1793-1794)—indeed, many months before the establishment in September, 1792, of the First French Republic. It is important, in fact, to remember that the most influential literary attack on the Revolution, Edmund Burke's *Reflections on the Revolution in France,* was published as early as November, 1790. A forceful and stirring statement of the conservative point of view, it deservedly attracted widespread attention and underwent numerous reprintings. Burke had many supporters who found in the *Reflections* ideas clothed in a brilliant prose that they could never hope to emulate. But Burke also had numerous critics who sought to demolish his case for conservatism. In the following essay, Professor Carl B. Cone, of the University of Kentucky, deftly analyzes the arguments advanced by some of the publicists who found Burke's position untenable.

PAMPHLET REPLIES TO BURKE'S *REFLECTIONS*
CARL CONE

The storm of pamphlet controversy that swept England after 1790 was centered around Edmund Burke, the intellectual leader of conservatism, the most profound, eloquent, and uncompromising enemy of the French Revolution. John Thelwall, popular lecturer on political subjects, singled out Burke as the only apologist for abuses who "in any literary point of view, can be regarded as formidable at all." True enough that Pitt was often vilified for apostasy to his earlier reforming sympathies, but Burke was held primarily responsible for the verbal furor, and some writers blamed him for England's entry into the war with France. Burke's opponents were all the more indignant because the *Reflections on the Revolution in France* appeared at a moment when prospects seemed to glow brightly for a moderate settlement of French affairs—November, 1790. Indeed, most liberal Englishmen assumed that the worst days of the Revolution were passed, that the old regime was abolished, and that France was entering on a peaceful and prosperous career under a government which, unlike the English, they said, was based on full recognition of the rights of men. Within a few years, however, when certain dire prophecies of "the preacher of St. Stephens" had become realities, some of the former friends of the Revolution were ashamed of their ardor. James Mackintosh, author of *Vindiciae Gallicae,* one of the best of the replies to the *Reflections,* later became an open admirer of Burke.

Reprinted by special permission from *The Southwestern Social Science Quarterly,* XXVI (1945), 22-34. The footnotes which originally appeared with this essay have been omitted.

Without going into a detailed analysis of the *Reflections,* one need only recall that Burke opposed the Revolution because it seemed to controvert all that in government, society, and religion, he held most dear. Rather from a clash of fundamental principles than as a matter of foreign policy and party politics, did Burke stand forth as the champion of the Anti-jacobins, to whom he preached a holy war in the name of religion and monarchy. Burke began the *Reflections* with an attack upon Dr. Richard Price and the Revolution Society, to whom Price, an eminent Unitarian divine, had preached the sermon that so disturbed Burke, and which Burke's tirade made famous. In the course of his refutation Burke had to expound his views on the Revolution of 1688. It was here that he came into conflict with the philosophy of the eighteenth century revolutionaries, For Burke denied the contract theory whose basic principle was the sovereignty of the people. The rest of the *Reflections,* much the larger portion, was devoted to an exposition of the errors of the French and the dangers inherent in the Revolution, as well as an exhortation to the English people to hold true to the established order of things. Without developing a systematic philosophy of conservatism, Burke's *Reflections,* along with his *Appeal from the New to the Old Whigs* (1791), remains as an eloquent statement of the creed of all conservatives, in every age.

In discussing the contents of the numerous pamphlet replies, two general subjects must be considered. The first, and more important in the history of ideas, is that relating to the Revolution of 1688, with its corollaries—the theory of revolution based on the social contract idea which either postulated or assumed the sovereignty of the people, and the implication of that theory, parliamentary reform. The second subject is the controversy relating specifically to France—whether the Revolution was justified, and what the Revolution had accomplished. To give the greater effect to their arguments, the pamphleteers brought in incidental matters. Many of them professed

an admiration for Burke conceived in the days when he had been a champion of liberty. Now there were regrets over Burke's apparent inconsistency with his former principles and deeds. Nor was it beyond some to hint that Burke's desertion of the cause of liberty was the result of secret Catholic affinities, and of a pension from the Court.

Whatever the views of Price and Burke upon the Revolution of 1688, that event had vindicated a doctrine which later revolutionaries seized upon as the historical justification of their abstract claims. In the sermon preached before the Revolution Society on November 4, 1789, Dr. Price, buoyant with enthusiasm for the French Revolution, which seemed to be progressing so gloriously, made this remark:

> Let us, in particular, take care not to forget the principles of the Revolution. This Society has, very properly, in its Reports, held out these principles, as an instruction to the public. I will only take notice of the three following:
> First; The right to liberty of conscience in religious matters.
> Secondly; The right to resist power when abused.
> Thirdly; The right to chuse our own governors; to cashier them for misconduct; and to frame a government for ourselves.

The right of the people to do these things was based upon the proposition that "all civil and political authority is derived from the people." Moreover, said Price, while the Test and Corporation Acts remain on the statute books, and while representation in Parliament is inadequate, the friends of the Revolution must continue the struggle for complete religious and civil freedom.

Burke attacked Price for uttering such statements, and attempted to refute him by reducing Price's arguments to an absurdity. Those who answered Burke saw through such tactics, for Price did not mean that the Crown was actually elective, as Burke seemed to think when he said George III wore his crown in contempt of the Revolution Society. Price merely recalled that "all power originates with the people, that it is delegated, but never alienated; that when power is abused, the people have a right to resume it." He said, in effect, that government and the Hanoverian succession were based on the consent of the people, tacit perhaps, but nonetheless real. Whether mankind had ever passed through the successive stages from a state of nature to a state of civil society, and whether men in civil society had ever resumed from a tyrannical government the rights they were supposed to have yielded in forming that government, is beside the point. It makes little difference whether or not the social contract was an historical fact, for the principle underlying the theory has an eternal validity. Burke objected to the implications which Price, quite logically and moderately, drew from the idea of the sovereignty of the people. If one assumed that principle, then Price's statements could not be refuted. One cannot escape the admission that if the will of the people is supreme, then anything the people will is legal. Burke's philosophy could not stand before that single idea. Speaking empirically and historically, Burke was correct in asserting that sudden and violent change could be disastrous, and that practical considerations made it difficult boldly to create a government that is not based to a considerable extent upon convention and tradition. But failure does not make reform unlawful, and the French, though committing blunders, had not violated the supreme

law that the people are the ultimate source of political authority. This principle is no guarantee that reform will be successful— Burke's precepts could well have been observed as valuable guides. Nevertheless, it did decree that changes could be undertaken, that the people had the power and the right to attempt reform, even of a radical kind, and that no authority but themselves, or one of their own creation, was to judge how far such attempts were to be carried.

In harking back to the Act of Settlement as settling for all time the line of descent to the throne, Burke only contradicted himself as well as the Revolution. He could not logically support the Revolution of 1688 and deny that the people were supreme. Though he justified that Revolution, as a good Whig would, on the grounds of extreme necessity and as a means of preserving the constitution, he could not avoid the possibility that an exigency just as urgent might once again occur. Nor could he deny, as his opponents delighted to remind him, that the direct hereditary line of succession had been deliberately set aside. To plead that this could never happen again would, as Paine showed, be giving a unique authority to one generation to bind all posterity to a particular form of government, while refusing the right of self preservation to all succeeding generations. For, said Paine, "it is the living and not the dead, that are to be accommodated."

Charles James Fox, though not a literary

SIR ROBERT FILMER: English publicist (d. 1653). Largely ignored during his lifetime, he gained widespread recognition in the age of the Restoration from Tories who found in his *Patriarcha* arguments that they could employ. Now he is remembered chiefly because John Locke singled him out for attack. Filmer viewed a limited monarchy as anarchical and argued in favor of absolute royal power.

RICHARD PRICE: Nonconformist clergyman and reformer (d. 1791) who wrote on economic and political questions. In his own time he was regarded as an authority on life insurance and the national debt. Now he is remembered for his activities as a political controversialist. He defended the American cause in the period of the War of Independence and the cause of the Revolutionists in the age of the French Revolution. A sermon which he preached in 1789 on the French Revolution elicited Burke's *Reflections*.

opponent, drew the same conclusion. In 1688 James II was cashiered by a convention "speaking the sense of the people," then a new king was chosen, a new dynasty marked out, and the conditions it was to observe laid down. Fox "could not admit the right to do all this but by acknowledging the sovereignty of the people as paramount to all other laws."

No opponent of Burke failed, either specifically or implicitly, to render homage to this simple but transcendent principle. One said the government should originate in the people. George Dyer, a Unitarian reformer, considered "every man's right to make laws, as his most sacred property, and the exercise of that right as essential to liberty." To Robert Hall, the Baptist pamphleteer, rational obedience meant that no man should have dominion over another without that person's consent. Capel Lofft was another ardent champion of Price and his principles. Despite their variety of expression, these writers all meant essentially the same thing—that the will of the people was the supreme law. The revolutionaries and the reformers of the period needed no other doctrine than this, for if it were accepted, political reforms must follow. But it was vital that such recognition be achieved. The reformers were not content, therefore, with asserting that the sovereignty of the people was an established fact, dating from the Revolution of 1688, or even, as some said, from the Anglo-Saxon period before Norman tyrants usurped power; they took pains to give philosophic demonstration.

At this point, the natural rights doctrine, combined with the contract idea, came to their aid. Men were created free and equal, possessed of inalienable rights. In order to safeguard these rights, men had chosen to associate in a civil society, surrendering that portion of their rights which, taken collectively, would guarantee the permanent possession of those retained. The general rule prevailed that one gave up those rights which, if exercised in civil society, would be harmful to other persons, and retained

those which could be enjoyed without interfering with the rights of anyone else. Another rule decreed that one retained the rights which he could execute as an individual, and contributed to the formation of civil authority those he could not enforce. Civil power was the aggregate of the rights surrendered. It could never invade those retained; on the contrary, its most solemn duty was to guarantee them. Government, then, originated in a compact among the people, and was their creature, existing at their sufferance, limited and defined by the constitution which sanctioned it, and responsible at all times to the will of the majority. How different from Burke! Tradition, experience, the gradual accretion of institutions, practices, conventions, and principles—all were swept away.

Politics are not a mystery, said Boothby, for after all there are some principles, readily understandable, upon which government rests. And, asked Paine,

What is government more than the management of the affairs of a Nation? It is not, and from its nature cannot be, the property of any particular man or family. . . . Sovereignty, as a matter of right, appertains to the Nation only, and to any individual; and a Nation has at all times an inherent indefeasible right to abolish any form of Government it finds inconvenient, and to establish such as accords with its interest, disposition, and happiness.

That political power was derived "either mediately, or immediately, from the People," and that it was a trust exercised in their behalf, could not be denied. The object of that trust was twofold, first, to protect the inalienable rights of the individual, and secondly, to work for the general good.

The differences among the pamphleteers lay in the relative lengths to which they would extend their principles. This absence of unity among the reformers was an important reason for the failure of reform in this period. Wyvil, for example, read Paine out of the reform movement although *The*

Rights of Man was the most widely read of all the replies to Burke. Paine was held to be, not a reformer, but one who would overturn the British constitution and substitute a republican government for it. But if the people are supreme, then all changes are valid, and any form of government, democratic, republican, or both, is legal, if that is what the majority of the people desire. Theoretically there is no limit to the extent to which reforms might go, and the conservatives had some reason to fear the implications of the idea of the sovereignty of the people. At the same time, if this principle is in operation, the right of resistance disappears. It is a logical contradiction, for how can the people resist themselves? In a truly representative system there is no need of resistance, for where the sovereignty of the people is recognized, the government cannot do otherwise than represent their will. This served to emphasize the necessity for reform. When a government is unrepresentative the right of resistance becomes a principle of action because the people are then resisting, not themselves, but usurpation, and are seeking to replace that government with one that does reflect their will. Two alternatives are open. One is revolution. The French, said the pamphleteers, had to choose that method because of the blind inertia of their rulers. The other is reform—the establishment of a truly representative government by means of a broadened franchise and more frequent parliamentary elections. This is what Burke's opponents advocated; the end, they said, fully justified what after all were very temperate means.

Burke did not believe in natural rights or social contract, and the whole tenor of his thought and career was opposed to the doctrine of the sovereignty of the people. It was not on those grounds that he defended the Revolution of 1688. Like the Whig party, he spoke of that Revolution as being the product of an extreme necessity, and was not concerned about setting up a philosophy to justify revolution in the abstract. But in admitting the necessity, Burke, under cover of eloquence and verbiage, really gave the decision to Price, for what is resorted to when necessity does arise, if not the right of the people to resist their rulers when power is abused? The dichotomy grew out of the definition of the word "necessary." Price, Burke believed, interpreted the word too loosely, and in consequence the necessity for revolution would appear too early and upon pretexts too flimsy to justify radical action. Actually, events and circumstances must determine the meaning of the word. Both Price and Burke agreed that in 1688 the necessity for revolution existed, but Burke refused to look upon that event as a precedent. He denied that the necessity existed in France in 1789 while Price and his champions, the pamphleteer enemies of Burke, insisted that the Revolution was necessary. Moreover, the need for parliamentary reform in England, which was not apparent to Burke, who was perfectly satisfied with the Constitution, appeared urgent to Burke's enemies. For that reason the pamphlet controversy was the literary side of the reform movement in the 1790's.

Burke refused to speak abstractly about the right of revolution, for he had a definition of "necessity." It was not an *a priori* rule of conduct, but an admonition that circumstances and expediency should determine actions. He denied that revolution was a matter of "positive rights," whereas Price held that the sovereignty of the people made revolution legal and moral. But self preservation also justified revolution, even when, as to Burke, it was "a question (like all other questions of state) of dispositions, and of means, and of probable consequences." The dividing line between obedience and resistance is "faint, obscure, and not easily definable. It is not a single act or a single event which determines it. Governments must be abused and deranged indeed, before it can be thought of; and the prospect of the future must be as bad as the experience of the past . . . with or without right, a revolution will be the very last resource of the thinking and the good." Here is no fundamental disagreement between Burke and his opponents who could have thanked him for stating the general conditions that called for remedial action. Again, the controversy hinged on a relative interpretation of the evils of government at any particular time. Price and his supporters would be a little readier than Burke to declare that the necessity for reforms had arisen; they would be less patient to tolerate abuses. Nevertheless the act of revolution bore just as heavy a responsibility for them as for Burke, and they would have said with him that resistance was justified only by "a necessity that is not chosen, but chooses, a necessity paramount to deliberation, that admits no discussion and demands no evidence." Such a necessity would "authorize a dispensation with any other moral duty, perhaps with all of them together." But awful as revolution was, it was justified when the necessity arose. With that admission, Burke met defeat.

Although Burke, when driven into a corner, admitted the basic principle of the reformer's creed, his philosophy of man and the state was a qualification, a restraining influence against the logical clarity and terrifying directness of the revolutionary doctrine. These limitations were the ones which historical experience and present expediency provided. Burke's conservatism surrounded reform with safeguards which made it the last resource and not the "daily remedy" of a people who, God forbid it in England, he would say, had fallen under the crushing tyranny of an arbitrary government. The reformers insisted that the necessity to invoke the sovereignty of the people had arisen in France, and would arise soon in England if reform were not forthcoming.

While the most important aspect of the controversy between Burke and his pamphleteer opponents lay in the application of their respective doctrines to the English situation, yet Burke's criticism of events in France did not go unanswered. A brief treatment will shed light on the positions of each side in the controversy. Burke had been alienated from the French Revolution almost from the beginning, because he thought the National Assembly had taken measures far more extreme than were justified in order to remove grievances, the existence of which he admitted. By invoking a constitution which, though hitherto unused, could easily have been adapted to the new circumstances, the French would have preserved the experience of history and France would thus have settled down to a new period of prosperity and harmony. The National Assembly chose instead to overturn everything already established, and to begin anew, on the basis of a high-sounding and meaningless Declaration of Rights.

Those who answered the *Reflections* commended France on the course she had taken. Some thought France had no ancient constitution or if she had, it was too antiquated to be of any practical use. Therefore, the debris had to be swept away so that France could found a new government based on liberty for the individual and equality of rights. What Mackintosh called the "Military, Sacerdotal, and Judicial Aristocracies," constituted the *ancien régime*. The privileged orders were the allies of despotism. It was necessary to attack them in their corporate natures. To wait for gradual reforms would have been to give counter-revolution an opportunity to strike before liberty had been won and abuses either removed or corrected. Paine said the revolution was directed against those despotic principles which permeated the French government to its very roots—an ecclesiastical, feudal, and monarchical system which could not be reformed but had to be exterminated. And all this was not "like a creation from a chaos, but no more than the consequence of a mental revolution priorily existing in France." In accomplishing these changes, the French had proceeded with striking moderation. Burke, argued his opponents, had been seduced by his own passion into exaggerating the so-called excesses of the French. None denied that Gallic zeal had resulted in certain indiscretions, but as one writer put it, these disturbances were a small price to pay for the elimination of the intolerable conditions under which the French had long suffered. The justified fear of counter-revolution, and the sudden emancipation of a "swinish multitude" long held in bondage were factors to be considered in judging of French excesses. In the light of historical perspective, the revolution would appear to be only a very mild episode so far as violence was concerned. Outbursts of public enthusiasm were only "transient anarchy" as the prelude to "established liberty."

Burke's criticism of the new constitution provoked the wrath of the English enthusiasts, for his shrill censures and dire predictions seemed to them the ravings of a modern Jeremiah. Burke's sympathy for the royal family, the nobility, and the clergy, incensed his pamphlet enemies, many of whom were Dissenters who saw no good in church establishments anyway. Paine summed up the argument by saying that Burke "pities the plumage, but forgets the dying bird." Burke was misinformed, both as to conditions under the old regime, and events within France. "The simple truth is that Burke did not know enough of the subject about which he was writing." The accuracy of some of his predictions is for that reason all the more striking. But Burke was out of harmony with the times, and in trying to stem the tide of growing democracy he was doomed to failure. Granted that the English were more fortunate in their political system than the French, the English government was hardly representative. So long as the right of the majority of men to participate in political affairs was denied, said the reformers, just so long would government be ineffective in safeguarding the rights of the individual. In reply Burke insisted that the system of representation was perfectly adequate for all the purposes it would be called to answer—an argument similar to that of Wellington forty years later. Perhaps Wyvill was too enthusiastic when he pronounced Burke's utter defeat in the controversy. Of Burke's opponents, "some . . . were completely victorious, and overthrew the positions of their Antagonist with a very superior force of reason and true masculine eloquence. Not one of them was wholly unsuccessful, and unable to prove him erroneous in any important instance; not one failed to produce some example of gross misinformation. . . . By these united efforts to support the Cause of Freedom, the authority of our modern Filmer has been reduced to its proper level." But as a statement of conservative principles, the *Reflections* will always be highly valued.

The opponents of Burke pointed out his misconceptions with regard to France. They argued from the achievement of the Revolution of 1688, and on the basis of the natural rights doctrine, that any government which did not represent the national will and was not established with the consent of the majority was not to be endured. They pointed out that the French Revolution was the result of accumulated abuses brought home to the people through the force of reason and philosophy. They warned that England might expect to witness a similar outburst if grievances continued to multiply without being redressed. And last of all, they pointed out the course England should take in order that abuses might be removed, equality restored, and the general happiness increased. That remedy was parliamentary reform.

THE FRENCH REVOLUTIONARY AND NAPOLEONIC WARS had far-reaching effects on the course of English economic history. Taxes rose markedly, and so did the public debt; the high price of agricultural goods encouraged the further growth of enclosures; and war needs stimulated the expansion of the cotton, coal, iron, and shipbuilding industries. The fact that the so-called agricultural and industrial revolutions coincided with the French Revolutionary and Napoleonic Wars was of the first importance, for many of the hardships and abuses suffered by dispossessed farmers and industrial workers were the products not so much of agricultural and industrial change itself as of agricultural and industrial change in an atmosphere of war. When Napoleon was finally defeated, in 1815, the English economy, which had been intermittently geared to war needs for more than two decades, had to readjust to a peacetime situation, and the adjustment was complicated by rapidly falling prices, housing shortages, a chaotic currency, loss of markets, and widespread unemployment. In the following essay, T. S. Ashton, professor of economic history at the University of London, discusses the standard of living of English industrial workers in the age of the French Revolutionary and Napoleonic Wars and in the postwar period. Few, if any, twentieth-century scholars have been so well equipped to investigate this difficult subject as Professor Ashton, author of such important volumes as *Iron and Steel in the Industrial Revolution* (1924) and *The Industrial Revolution, 1760-1830* (1948).

THE STANDARD OF LIFE OF THE WORKERS IN ENGLAND, 1790–1830

T. S. ASHTON

I

What happened to the standard of life of the British working classes in the late decades of the eighteenth and the early decades of the nineteenth centuries? Was the introduction of the factory system beneficial or harmful in its effect on the workers? These, though related, are distinct questions. For it is possible that employment in factories conduced to an increase of real wages but that the tendency was more than offset by other influences, such as the rapid increase of population, the immigration of Irishmen, the destruction of wealth by long years of warfare, ill-devised tariffs, and misconceived measures for the relief of distress. Both questions have a bearing on some political and economic disputes of our own day, and this makes it difficult to consider them with complete objectivity. An American scholar (so it is said) once produced a book entitled *An Impartial His-*

tory of the Civil War: From the Southern Point of View.[1] If I seek to emulate his impartiality I ought also to strive to equal his candor. Let me confess, therefore, at the start that I am of those who believe that, all in all, conditions of labor were becoming better, at least after 1820, and that the spread of the factory played a not inconsiderable part in the improvement.

There is, it must be admitted, weighty opinion to the contrary. Most of the economists who lived through the period of rapid economic changes took a somewhat gloomy view of the effect of these changes on the workers. "The increasing wealth of the nation," wrote Thomas Malthus in 1798, "has had little or no tendency to better the conditions of the labouring poor. They have not, I believe, a greater command of the necessaries and conveniences of life; and a much greater proportion of them, than at

[1] Referred to in Thomas Jones, *Rhymney Memories* (N.p.: Welsh Outlook, 1939), p. 142.

Reprinted by special permission from *The Journal of Economic History, Supplement*, IX (1949), 19-38.

the period of the Revolution, is employed in manufactories and crowded together in close and unwholesome rooms."[2] A couple of generations later J. R. McCulloch declared that "there seems, on the whole, little room for doubting that the factory system operates unfavourably on the bulk of those engaged in it."[3] And, in 1848, John Stuart Mill wrote words that, if they gave some glimmer of hope, were nevertheless highly critical of the society from which the technological changes had sprung. "Hitherto," he said, "it is questionable if all the mechanical inventions yet made have lightened the day's toil of any human being. They have enabled a greater proportion to live the same life of drudgery and imprisonment and an increased number of manufacturers and others to make fortunes. They have increased the comforts of the middle classes. But they have not yet begun to effect those great changes in human destiny, which it is in their nature and in their futurity to accomplish."[4] Alongside the economists was a miscellany of poets, philosophers, and demagogues; parsons,

deists, and infidels; conservatives, radicals, and revolutionaries—men differing widely one from another in fundamentals but united in their hatred of factories and in their belief that economic change had led to the degradation of labor.

In the opposing camp there were publicists whose opinions are no less worthy of respect and whose disinterestedness and zeal for reform can hardly be called in question—men like Sir Frederic Eden, John Wesley, George Chalmers, Patrick Colquohoun, John Rickman, and Edwin Chadwick. To offset the passage from Mill, let me quote two sentences from Chadwick, who surely knew as much as anyone else of the squalor and poverty of large numbers of town-dwellers in the forties: ". . . the fact is, that hitherto, in England, wages, or the means of obtaining the necessaries of life for the whole mass of the labouring community, have advanced, and the comforts within the reach of the labouring classes have increased with the late increase of population. . . . we have evidence of this advance even in many of the manufacturing districts now in a state of severe depression."[5] (He wrote in 1842.)

If a public-opinion poll could have been taken it is probable that the adherents of the first group would have been found to outnumber those of the second. But this

[2] Thomas Malthus, *First Essay on Population, 1798* (London: Macmillan & Co., 1926), pp. 312-13.
[3] J. R. McCulloch, *Treatises and Essays on Money, Exchange, Interest, the Letting of Land, Absenteeism, the History of Commerce, Manufactures, etc.* (Edinburgh, 1859), pp. 454-55.
[4] John Stuart Mill, *Principles of Political Economy*, ed. W. J. Ashley (London and New York, Longmans, Green & Co., 1909), p. 751.

[5] Edwin Chadwick, *Report on the Sanitary Condition of the Labouring Population of Great Britain* (London, 1843), p. 188.

EDWIN CHADWICK: English Benthamite, civil servant, and advocate of improved public health conditions. A vigorous crusader for state regulation of water supply, drainage, and sewage, he could claim credit for the establishment in 1848 of the first British Board of Health.

J. R. MCCULLOCH: British economist, controversialist, and government official. His *Principles of Political Economy* (1825), although it made few original contributions to economic theory, helped to disseminate many of the ideas of the classical economists. The labor writers of his time viewed McCulloch as an enemy of labor and as an apologist for the governing elements.

JOHN RICKMAN: English statistician and government servant who devised the methods used in early-nineteenth-century England in compiling the census returns. A close friend of Robert Southey, he shared the poet's conservative views and his dislike of Malthus and the other economists.

is not a matter to be settled by a show of hands. It has been said of the people of Herbert Heaton's native county that they like to speak the truth—especially when it is unpleasant; and there is some evidence that this engaging trait is not found exclusively in Yorkshiremen. Writing to Southey in 1816 Rickman observed, "If one listens to common assertion, everything in grumbling England grows worse and worse";[6] and in a later letter, to a Frenchman, in which he pointed to the way in which the poor had benefited from public relief and cheap food, Rickman was careful to add, "But these arguments would encounter contradiction in England."[7] The romantic revival in literature, which coincided in time with the industrial revolution, tended to strengthen the despondency. Popular writers, like William Cobbett, pictured an earlier England peopled with merry peasants or sturdy beef-eating, beer-drinking yeomen, just as their predecessors of the age of Dryden had conjured up the vision of a Patagonia peopled with noble savages. But neither native pessimism nor unhistorical romanticism is sufficient in itself to explain the prevalence of the view that the condition of the workers had deteriorated. It is part of my thesis that those who held this view had their eyes on one section of the working classes only.

II

It may be well to begin by making a rapid survey of the economic and demographic landscape. In these early decades of the nineteenth century population was increasing rapidly. Whether it is good or ill that more human beings should experience the happiness and misery, the hopes and anxieties, the ambitions and frustrations of life, may be left for the philosopher or the theologian to determine. But the increase in numbers was the result not of a rise of the

birth rate but of a fall of the death rate, and it might be thought that this was indicative of an improved quality of life. "Human comfort," said Rickman in his letter to Southey, "is to be estimated by human health, and that by the length of human life. . . . Since 1780 life has been prolonged by 5 to 4—and the poor form too large a portion of society to be excluded from this general effect; rather they are the main cause of it; for the upper classes had food and cleanliness abundant before."[8] Such an argument was not easy to refute; but Gaskell tried to meet it by declaring roundly that there was no direct connection between mortality and well-being. The noble savage was invoked. In his case, it was asserted, life was "physical enjoyment" and disease "hasty death." For the worker in the manufacturing town, on the other hand, life was "one long disease" and death "the result of physical exhaustion."

If only he had known it, Gaskell might have answered Rickman with a flat denial. For it is now held by statisticians that the fall in the crude death rate was the result of a change in the age distribution of the population and that there was, in fact, no prolongation of the average life. (The deaths per thousand fell simply because population changes in the later eighteenth century had produced a society in which the number of young adults was abnormally high.) But even if the expectation of life was not raised it may be urged that the fall of the death rate conduced in some measure to a higher standard of life. For the pomp and circumstance of death and burial swallowed up no small part of the annual income of the workers.[9] When the percentage of deaths to population fell the proportion of income devoted to the dead probably diminished, and resources were thus freed to add to the comforts of the living.

The growth of population, and, in particular, the increase in the number of people of working age, might well have

[6] Quoted by M. Dorothy George, *England in Transition* (London: George Routledge & Sons, Ltd., 1931), p. 104.
[7] *Ibid.*, p. 137.
[8] *Ibid.*, pp. 104-5.
[9] David Davies, *The Case of Labourers in Husbandry* (Bath, 1795), pp. 23-27.

resulted in a fall of wages. But there took place simultaneously an increase in the supply of other factors of production. Estimates of the national income for this period are few and unreliable. But the statistics of output, expenditure, and consumption all suggest that over the period as a whole it was growing somewhat more rapidly than population. Is there any reason to believe that the proportion of this increased income that went to the workers diminished and that other classes obtained a larger share? This is a question to which no sure answer can be given: all that is possible is to estimate probabilities. In attempting this it is important to distinguish between the period of the war, the period of deflation and readjustment, and the succeeding period of economic expansion.

During the war heavy government expenditure of an unproductive nature produced a high level of employment but a low standard of comfort. Difficulties of obtaining foodstuffs from abroad led to an extension of the margin of cultivation, and the profit of the farmer and the rent of the landowner increased.[10] Wartime shortages of timber, bricks, glass, and other materials limited the construction of houses; high rates of interest and a burdensome property tax reduced the incentives to build. With a growing population and an increased proportion of people of marriageable age the demand for homes increased; urban rents, like agricultural rents, rose. The growth of the national debt led to an expansion of the number of bondholders. The high rates at which loans were floated swelled the income of the passive investor, and, since the tax system was highly regressive, the gain to the rentier was largely at the expense of the poor. Prices in general rose, and though rates of wages also moved up they did so more slowly. This, as Earl Hamilton has

argued, put additional resources at the disposal of the entrepreneur, and the tendency was reinforced by other, institutional, factors.[11] The trader's or manufacturer's token, the "long pay," and the truck system had existed at earlier times. But it is probable that the shortage of coin, which became acute during the period of inflation, led to an extension of these and other devices, the effect of which was to shift purchasing power from the workers to their employers. During the war, then, there took place a whole series of transfers of income—to landlords, farmers, houseowners, bondholders, and entrepreneurs—and these almost certainly worsened the economic status of labor.

The five or six years that followed the peace brought little alleviation. The landlords obtained legislation that enabled them to perpetuate their windfall gains. House rents remained high. Rates of interest fell but slightly.[12] And though wage rates were less affected than profits the reduction of government expenditure, the contraction of the currency, banking failures, and a general reluctance to embark on long-term investment reduced the level of activity. Any gains that may have come from the lag of wage rates behind falling prices were probably offset by high unemployment. It is difficult to believe that these years of deflation and civil tumult saw any marked improvement in the condition of the wage earners.

After 1821, however, economic forces bore less harshly on labor. The gold standard had been restored. A larger quantity of silver and copper was available for the payment of wages. Reforms of the fiscal system were in train. A series of conversions reduced the burden of the national debt, and by 1824 the gilt-edge rate was down to

[10] Between 1809 and 1815 rents in the eastern counties and North Wales increased by 40 per cent. R. J. Thompson, "An Inquiry into the Rents of Agricultural Land in England and Wales during the Nineteenth Century," *Journal of the Royal Statistical Society*, LXX (1907), 587-616.

[11] Earl Hamilton, "Prices, Wages and the Industrial Revolution," in Wesley C. Mitchell and Others, *Studies in Economics and Industrial Relations* (Philadelphia: University of Pennsylvania Press, 1941).
[12] The yield on Consols was 4.9 per cent in 1814 and 4.5 in 1815. In 1820 it still stood as high as 4.4.

TABLE I
EXPORT AND IMPORT PRICES AND THE TERMS OF TRADE
(1829 = 100)

Year	Export Index of Values	Export Price Index	Import Price Index	Net Barter Terms of Trade	Income Terms of Trade
1798	90	264	176	150	51
1799	103	252	183	138	56
1800	105	253	183	138	57
1801	113	255	189	135	60
1802	128	280	150	187	85
1803	103	281	164	171	63
1804	107	262.5	172	153	62
1805	106	255	178	143	60
1806	114	247	164	151	70
1807	104	248	167	148	62
1808	104	237.5	159	149	65
1809	132	220	193	114	68
1810	135	221	188	118	72
1811	92	227	155	146	59
1812	116	220	173	127	67
1813	...	...	...	...	..
1814	127	208	194	107	64
1815	144	187.5	172	109	84
1816	116	183	148	124	78
1817	117	162.5	160	102	73
1818	130	170	178	96	73
1819	98	164	148	111	66
1820	102	148	136	109	75
1821	103	141	120	117.5	86
1822	103	131	119	110	87
1823	99	127	118	108	84
1824	107	123	112	110	96
1825	109	128	137	93	80
1826	88	120	108	111	81
1827	104	111	107	104	97
1828	103	109	103	106	100
1829	100	100	100	100	100
1830	107	98	98	100	109
1831	104	95	102	93	102
1832	102	87.5	96	91	106
1833	111	89	104	85	107
1834	116	87.5	107	82	108
1835	132	94	114	82	116
1836	149	98	120	82	124

its prewar level of 3.3. Wartime scarcities had disappeared. A more ample supply of bricks and timber combined with cheap money to stimulate the building of factories and dwellings. By the early thirties rents (in the north at least) had fallen about 10 per cent, and in spite of a number of disturbing reports on conditions in the towns it is fairly clear that the standard of housing was improving. The fall of prices—less marked than in the years immediately after the war—now represented not depression but a reduction of real costs. All in all the economic climate had become more genial: it was possible for the workers to look forward to better conditions of life and work.

III

So far attention has been directed only to forces internal to the economy. What of those that operated from outside? It has been suggested that over the greater part of this period the power of British exports to exchange for goods from abroad was diminishing and that the unfavorable movement of the net barter terms of trade must have resulted either in lower money incomes for those engaged in the export trades or in higher costs of imported goods. Hence, other things being equal, it must have led to a fall in the standard of life of the workers.

The defects of early British commercial statistics are well known. Since both imports and exports were officially measured by a scale of prices that had become stereotyped in the first half of the eighteenth century, the movements of the figures from year to year represent changes in the volume, and not in the value, of overseas trade. From 1798, it is true, there are annual figures of the values of exports, derived from the declarations of merchants; but until recently there have been no corresponding estimates of the values of imports for the years before 1854. Mr. Schlote and Mr. Imlah have now filled the gap.[13] I am

glad to have this opportunity of paying tribute to the industry and scholarship of Mr. Imlah; every student of the history of international trade must be grateful to him. I have ventured to use his figures to construct crude index numbers of, first, values of British exports, second, the prices of exports and retained imports, and third, the terms of trade from 1798 to 1836 (see Table I).[14]

From 1803 to 1834 the course of export prices was almost continuously downward. That of import prices was less consistent. From 1802 to 1812 there were wide fluctuations with no marked trend, but from 1814 there was a descent—steep to 1821, less steep thereafter. The terms of trade moved strongly against Britain during the second phase of the war and less strongly, though markedly, against her from 1816 to the middle thirties. Before jumping, however, to the conclusion that here was a factor pressing heavily on British labor it may be well to look at the composition of the price index for exports. Table II gives the price relatives for some important export commodi-

[13] Werner Schlote, "Entwicklung und Strukturwandlungen des englischen Aussenhandels von 1700 bis zur Gegenwart," *Probleme der Weltwirtschaft* (Jena: n.p., 1938). See in particular Appendix Table 17. Also Albert H. Imlah, "Real Values in British Foreign Trade," *The Journal of Economic History,* VIII (November 1948), 133-52.

[14] The index numbers of prices have been obtained by dividing the index of declared or computed values by that of official values in the case of both exports and imports. The method is open to criticism, for the weighting is curious. The degree of importance assigned to each commodity depends on the rate at which a unit of it was assessed by the inspector general at a time long before that to which the index relates. It depends also on the amount of the commodity imported or exported, and this means that the weighting changes from year to year. My nonmathematical mind is encouraged, however, to believe that this peculiarity does not completely destroy the value of the figures. For Mr. Schlote's index of the terms of trade from 1814 (obtained by dividing a price index of *manufactured* exports by a price index of imports as a whole) is constructed by similar, but more refined, methods, and when adjusted to the same base year it shows, at least until 1832, movements in striking conformity with those of the series offered here.

ties for the years 1814-1829.[15] It will be observed that the prices of cotton yarn and fabrics fell much more steeply than those of the products of the linen, woolen, and iron industries. During the war manufactured cotton had taken the place of manufactured wool as the British staple export, and during the whole of the first half of the nineteenth century its lead over other commodities lengthened. It was the fall in the price of cotton yarn and cotton cloth that was responsible for the adverse trend of the terms of trade: the prices of exports exclusive of cotton goods actually declined less steeply than those of imports.

The reason for this extraordinary fall is twofold. Instead of producing muslins, cambrics, and other goods of high quality for sale in Europe and the United States, the factories of Lancashire were increasingly concerned with cheap calicoes for Indian and Far Eastern markets: a large part of the fall in price is to be accounted for by a change in the nature of the product of the industry. The other reason was the cost-reducing effect of technical and economic progress. The new mills of the postwar years were driven by steam instead of by water; improvements were being made year after year in the mule and the spinning frame; the power loom was steadily taking the place of the less efficient hand loom; with falling rates of interest capital charges were reduced; and with innovations in transport and trade the expenses of moving and merchanting the goods were diminished. The fall of the prices of cotton yarn and fabrics was not, then, the result of any decline of foreign demand; it reflected a reduction of real costs. And, though the labor cost of a pound of yarn or a yard of calico fell in a spectacular manner, there was no corresponding drop in the earnings of labor. The downward trend of the terms of trade did not represent any worsening of the economic situation either for the nation as a whole or for that part of it that depended on wages.

Figures purporting to show changes in the terms of trade are of dubious value for long-period studies: it is only over short series of years, when the nature of the commodities entering into trade and the state of technique do not change very much, that any safe conclusion can be drawn from them. Even in the short run, indeed, it is far from clear that a downward movement of the index should be taken as a sign of adversity. According to Table I, the terms of trade moved sharply downward in 1809-1810, 1812-1815, 1817-1818, and 1825, all periods when the volume of trade rose to a peak. They moved sharply upward in 1811, 1816, 1819, and 1826, all years of diminished or stagnant trade. The explanation is, of course, that the prices of British exports rose in times of prosperity and fell in times of depression less violently than those of imports, for the raw materials and foodstuffs Britain imported were inelastic in demand and supply. It would be absurd, however, to suppose that the welfare of the workers diminished when trade was active and increased when trade declined.

An apparatus that is concerned only with prices is clearly inadequate as a measure of changes in the benefits derived from international trade. Not only the cost of living but also the opportunities of earning determine the degree of well-being. Incomes earned by exports provide employment and generate other incomes. How far these incomes will go in the purchase of goods from abroad depends on the prices of imports. In the light of such reasoning a colleague of mine, Mr. Dorrance, recently suggested that a better instrument for measuring the social effects of international trade may be obtained by dividing the indexes of the *values* of exports by those of the *prices* of imports.[16] I have applied his formula to the trade statistics of the period, again making

[15] The prices have been obtained by dividing the value of the export of each commodity by the quantity exported as recorded by Porter.

[16] G. S. Dorrance, "The Income Terms of Trade," *Review of Economic Studies,* XVI, No. 39 (1948-49), 50-56.

use of Mr. Imlah's figures. The results are shown in the final column of Table I under the not altogether satisfactory heading "Income Terms of Trade." Here we have a set of figures free from the paradoxes of those in the preceding column. Both the trend and the year-to-year changes are what our knowledge derived from other sources would lead us to expect. The index shows little change during the war. It rises sharply

believe that the workers had no share in the gain.

IV

It is time to pass from speculation and to say something about such figures as we have relating to wages and the cost of living. The outstanding contribution to our knowledge of the first of these was made

TABLE II

PRICE RELATIVES OF EXPORTS OF HOME-PRODUCED MANUFACTURES

(1814 = 100)

Year	Cotton Yarn	Cotton Manu-factured	Linen Manu-factured	Woolen Manu-factured	Iron	Total Exports	Total Excluding Cotton Goods
1814	100	100	100	100	100	100	100
1815	83	80	86	101	106	90.6	99
1816	77	77	85	107	98	87.8	95
1817	71	67	79	97	93	78.5	90
1818	74	63	82	99	94	81.9	91
1819	64	70	81	101	92	79.6	88
1820	56	64	77	99	89	71.4	83
1821	49	62	77	87	80	67.6	79
1822	47	57	76	81	71	62.9	76
1823	44	55	71	76	70	60.7	73
1824	42	54	67	73	72	59.3	71
1825	45	54	71	77	90	62.0	78
1826	38	47	65	73	79	57.9	72
1827	36	46	60	65	72	53.6	69

in 1815 but falls from 1816 to 1819. In these four years of low investment and unemployment forces operating from overseas trade added, it would seem, to the distress. But from 1820 there is a marked upward movement broken only by the slumps of 1825-1826 and 1831. In the twenties and thirties incomes derived from overseas trade were increasing, and these incomes purchased more of the goods that came in from abroad. Commerce was exerting an increasingly beneficial influence on the economic life of Britain; and in view of the fact that the imports consisted largely of such things as tea, coffee, sugar, and the raw materials of industry it is difficult to

forty years ago or more by A. L. Bowley and G. H. Wood. It is based mainly on printed sources, but it is unlikely that further research will invalidate it in any serious way. Nevertheless, it is greatly to be hoped that it may be supplemented by data derived from the wages books which, in spite of bombing and paper salvage, still exist in many scattered factories up and down England. In the hands of careful students these records may be made to yield much information not only about rates of payment but also about actual earnings and sometimes about hours of work and the rents of working-class houses. Until the task is performed it will continue to be impossible to speak with assurance on the topic on which, greatly daring, I have ventured in this paper.

For information about the cost of living we are dependent almost entirely on the work of American scholars. If some of the remarks that follow are critical I would add that I am filled with shame that English economic historians have done so little in this field and with admiration for the tenacity and skill which your statisticians have brought to the task.

No single contribution to the study of the industrial revolution in England exceeds in importance that made by Norman J. Silberling, whose untimely death has deprived both economic history and statistics of an outstanding exponent. His index number of wholesale prices must remain an indispensable tool for as long ahead as we need look. It is unfortunate that, in my opinion, the same cannot be said of that by-product of his labors, the annual cost-of-living index from 1799 to 1850. This, I need not remind you, is based on the prices of fifteen commodities selected because of their supposed significance to consumers. The prices, however, are chiefly those of the wholesale, not of the retail, market; the index is valid only on the assumption that retail prices moved in the same direction and at approximately the same time as wholesale prices and that the spread between the two remained fairly constant. Now it is true that the structure of retail prices seems to have been far less rigid than it is today. The shopkeeper had not yet fully assumed his function as a shock absorber between merchant and consumer, and the price of a loaf or a pound of beef might double or halve within the course of a few months or even weeks. Several of the commodities used in the index are, however, not consumer's goods at all but merely the raw materials of these. My ancestors of the period did not nourish themselves by munching wheat and oats; they did not cover their nakedness with raw wool and cotton and flax; they were not, literally, shod with leather. According

to Silberling this elementary fact is of small account. "It is well known," he wrote, "in the case of cotton goods that prices adjusted themselves with fair alacrity to the price of raw cotton." When, however, the price relatives of the two are set side by side we find, as most of us would expect, a considerably greater amplitude of fluctuation in the figures for raw cotton than in those for cotton fabrics. It is surely unrealistic to assume that the prices of food and clothing and footwear are faithfully reflected in those of the substances of which they were made. Also, the prices used by Silberling have been refined by the elimination of customs duties. In actual fact duties constituted a large proportion of the cost of nearly everything brought into the country, a proportion that, moreover (as Mr. Imlah has shown), increased steadily down to the 1840's.

Nor is this all. The man whose scheme of expenditure conformed to that drawn up by Silberling had many idiosyncrasies. He did not occupy a house, or at least he was not called upon to pay rent. He allowed himself only a moderate amount of bread and very little porridge, and he never touched potatoes or strong drink. On the other hand, he got through quite considerable quantities of beef and mutton and showed a fondness for butter. Perhaps he was a diabetic. The ordinary Englishman of the eighteenth century would have been puzzled by him. For this ordinary Englishman (like his descendant of 1949) was a granivorous and not a carnivorous animal. His staple of diet was bread or, in the north of England, oatmeal; meat was for him a luxury to be taken once, or at most twice, in the week. Silberling's creature who quenched his thirst only with tea and coffee (with sugar but without milk) would have seemed to him a poor sort of fish. For however abstemious the ordinary Englishman may have been in respect to meat and many other things, he took small beer with each main meal of the working day and ale, in no small measure, whenever he had occasion to celebrate.

The portrait that appears in the scholarly pages of Elizabeth Gilboy has somewhat different features.[17] In her index, cereals have a weight of 50 per cent of the total, as against 32 per cent assigned to them by Silberling, and animal products are rightly given a lower status. But her prices are those that were paid by hospitals, schools, and government departments and not by individual workmen: they are contract and not truly retail prices. Moreover they are mainly London prices. One of the outstanding features of English life was (and still is) its regional variety. The prices of foodstuffs varied greatly between one part of the country and another, and it was not uncommon for something approaching a local famine to coincide with conditions of relative abundance at places only a hundred miles or so away. As improvements were made in transport by river, road, and canal, prices in the provinces tended to come into line with those of the metropolis. "All the sensible people," wrote Arthur Young in 1769, "attributed the dearness of their country to the turnpike roads; and reason speaks the truth of their opinion . . . . make but a turnpike road through their country and all the cheapness vanishes at once." But even fifty or more years later there were many areas of England without turnpikes. In these areas the prices of foodstuffs might be either lower or higher than in London; they were certainly subject to wider fluctuations.

No one has done more than Mrs. Gilboy to make us aware of local variations in the price of labor. But she has not taken full account of the possibility of a similar variation of retail prices or of local peculiarities of diet. Oatmeal remained the staple food of the poor in the north, and rye bread the staple in the Midlands, long after wheaten bread had come into common use in London and the south. To apply contract prices derived from the metropolitan area, and a system of weights based on metropolitan

habits, to the earnings of workers in the provinces is indeed a hazardous procedure. What someone has unkindly called Mrs. Gilboy's bricklayers dressed up as bluecoat boys[18] would hardly have been recognized as brothers by the pitmen of Northumberland or the weavers of Lancashire or Somerset.

But if the scheme of expenditure varied from place to place it varied also from time to time. Rufus T. Tucker, whose gallant attempt to trace the course of real wages of London artisans over two centuries must excite admiration, shows himself alive to this difficulty. His solution is to abandon the use of a fixed yardstick. When some new commodity seems to become significant in the workers' budget a place is found for it and the weights attached to other things are adjusted. Mr. Tucker divided the figures in his index of wages (for our period the wages of four kinds of building labor at Greenwich and Chelsea) by his chain index of prices in order to determine "the ability of a typical, regularly employed London artisan to purchase commodities of the sort artisans customarily purchased."

This typical London artisan was no static figure. At first his consumption was limited to a few commodities, including some inferior grain stuffs. Later he spread his expenditure over a wider range of goods, some of which were relatively expensive ("the commodities of the sort artisans customarily purchased" had changed). One might have supposed that the wider choice now open to him was one element in a rising standard of living. But no. Mr. Colin Clark has used Tucker's figures to support his thesis that average real income fell "from a fairly high level in the seventeenth century to an Asiatic standard at the beginning of the nineteenth." That Asiatic standard, I may remark in passing, included tea and sugar and some other minor products of Asia hardly known to the London artisan of the seventeenth century. Would the man of the early nineteenth century really have

[17] Elizabeth W. Gilboy, "The Cost of Living and Real Wages in Eighteenth Century England," *Review of Economic Statistics,* XVIII (1936), 134-43.

[18] Boys attending a charity school, at which they wear long blue coats or gowns.

welcomed a return to the diet of his great-great-grandfather? The reception he gave to some well-intentioned efforts to induce him to use rye instead of wheat in his bread hardly leaves one in doubt regarding the answer. Like the laborers of Nottinghamshire, he replied that he had lost his rye teeth.[19]

Mr. Tucker's artisan was peculiar in another respect. Whatever his income he always spent one sixth of it on rent or one fifth on rent and services combined. This is a proportion far higher than any I have been able to discover in other areas, but, no doubt, dwellings were dear in London. It is the fixity of habit that is peculiar. Mr. Tucker says that his index "attempts to measure the workman's ability to purchase housing." But, if it is true that the workman always spent a fixed proportion of his income on housing, would not the figures of wages alone serve as a measure of that ability? In fact, rents are perhaps the most difficult of all prices to draw into an index number. Few consumer goods are completely standardized. A loaf of bread at a given time and place may be a very different commodity from a loaf at another time and place. "The veal that is sold so cheap in some distant counties at present," wrote Malthus, "bears little other resemblance than the name, to that which is bought in London."[20] But this variation of quality is especially marked in the case of houses. A cottage with a living room and a single bedroom is a different commodity from one with four rooms and an attached wash house or loom shed. A cottage near a factory would usually produce a higher rent than one far distant; for the tenant of the first not only avoided a long walk to and from work but was also able, if he wished, to increase his income by working overtime without trenching unduly on the hours of sleep.[21]

The truth is that it is not possible to compare the welfare of two groups of people separated widely in time and space. We cannot compare the satisfaction derived from a diet that includes bread, potatoes, tea, sugar, and meat with that derived from a diet consisting mainly of oatmeal, milk, cheese, and beer. In the early and middle decades of the eighteenth century only a narrow range of commodities competed for the surplus income of the workers. That is why (to the distress of the well-to-do observer) any easement of the position of the poor was taken out in the form of more drink and more leisure—or in "debauchery and idleness," as the sedate and leisured observer usually put it. Later in the century the range of commodities available widened, and after the French wars new opportunities of travel and education were opened up. No index number can possibly take full account of such matters.

I have made these criticisms and asked these questions in no carping spirit. My object is simply to point to the difficulties of measuring arithmetically changes in the standard of living. The pioneers, as so often happens, have attempted too much. We must restrict our ambitions, realize the limitations of our bag of tricks, and refrain from generalizations. We cannot measure changes in real wages by means of an index of wholesale or institutional prices. We cannot apply the price data of one area to the wage data of another. We cannot safely draw up a table to cover a long series of years during the course of which changes may have occurred not only in the nature and variety of the goods consumed but also in human needs and human wants. We require not a single index but many, each derived from retail prices, each confined to a short run of years, each relating to a single area, perhaps even to a single social or occupational group within an area.[22]

I cannot hope at this stage to meet these

<hr/>

[19] See C. R. Fay, *The Corn Laws and Social England* (Cambridge: The University Press, 1932), p. 4.

[20] Malthus, *Essay on Population*, p. 317.

[21] A point made in an unpublished thesis by Walter Lazenby, "The Social and Industrial History of Styal, 1750-1850," University of Manchester, 1949.

[22] This is a view taken by a distinguished

TABLE III
Index of Cost of Diet in Oldham
(1791 = 100)

Year	Oatmeal	Flour	Potatoes	Beef	Mutton	Bacon	Butter	Cheese	Total Cost of Diet
1791 Spring	100	100	100	100	100	100	100	100	100
1792 Spring	105	90	85	100	100	100	100	60	94
1793 Fall	126	102	154	80	100	100	106	90	113
1794	. . .	. . .	. . .	. . .	. . .	. . .	. . .	. . .	. . .
1795 January	121	110	154	110	110	94	112	100	117
1795 May-June	132	151	185	120	120	106	112	110	138
1796	. . .	. . .	. . .	. . .	. . .	. . .	. . .	. . .	. . .
1797	84	82	100	130	130	106	112	130	98
1798	. . .	. . .	. . .	. . .	. . .	. . .	. . .	. . .	. . .
1799 Spring	103	73	85	100	100	88	112	110	92
1800 May	316	245	309	180	180	131	175	200	249
1801 January	290	270	309	160	160	150	188	180	253
1801 October	112	122	92	160	170	150	125	140	124
1802 January	126	135	92	176	180	138	115	132	133
1803 January	100	116	123	160	160	138	138	132	123
1804 January	142	114	154	160	160	124	162	154	139
1805	. . .	. . .	. . .	. . .	. . .	. . .	. . .	. . .	. . .
1806 January	153	141	115	140	140	100	144	154	139
1807 January	. . .	. . .	. . .	. . .	. . .	. . .	. . .	. . .	. . .
1808 January	153	133	185	140	140	112	175	140	148
1809 January	163	176	123	154	154	112	175	170	158

requirements. All I have to offer are three short tables exhibiting the changes in the cost of staple articles of diet in the area that is often spoken of as the cradle of the factory system. Such virtue as they possess derives from the fact that they are based on retail prices recorded by contemporaries. The first relates to Oldham, a textile town five or six miles from Manchester. The figures are drawn from an unpublished manuscript entitled "The Chronology or Annals of Oldham" by William Rowbottom,[23] and I am greatly indebted to a former colleague, Miss Frances Collier of the University of Manchester, for the toil involved in extracting them. Like other annalists of the period, Rowbottom began by describing the more sensational events, such as murders and thefts, which occurred in the locality. For 1787 and the succeeding three years there is little of economic interest in his manuscript. But in 1791 he began to make jottings about the prices charged by shopkeepers in Oldham, and as time went on the range of his observations widened and the record became more systematic. There are many months and some years for which little or no information about prices is given; and there are several commodities,

statistician. "I do not believe that index numbers can serve over very long periods. If the same form is used throughout the difficulty of shifts in the 'preference map' cannot be overcome. If the index is obtained by drawing together different forms, then a bias is to be expected, a bias which tends to be amplified over time. In general, index numbers are to be limited to short-run comparisons."—R. G. D. Allen, "The Economic Theory of Index Numbers," *Economica*, XVI(N.S.), No. 63 (August, 1949), 197-203.

[23] Transcript by Giles Shaw now in the Manchester Public Reference Library.

such as sugar, treacle, malt, coal, and candles, the prices of which are given so infrequently as to make it impossible to include them in the index.

When Rowbottom began to keep his record most of his fellow townsmen were still domestic workers employed in weaving fustians, calicoes, and checks, or making hats. Their staple diet consisted of bread, oatmeal porridge, potatoes, and a little beef and mutton. In compiling the index I have accordingly given a weight of 4 each to

details of wages, the price of provisions, and expenditure on poor relief published in the *Manchester Mercury* of January 18, 1820. They relate to "Manchester and the other principal seats of the Cotton Manufacture," and, although the source is not disclosed, the prices are said to be "the average retail prices of each year, according to the best information that could be procured." Again it is clear that the prices of grain foods and potatoes were more volatile than those of meat, bacon, butter, and cheese. The table

TABLE IV

INDEX OF COST OF DIET IN MANCHESTER AND OTHER TEXTILE TOWNS
(1810 = 100)

Year	Oatmeal	Flour	Potatoes	Beef Best	Beef Coarse	Bacon	Butter	Cheese	Index of Cost of Diet
1810	100	100	100	100	100	100	100	100	100
1811	100	91	100	100	100	82	112	100	97
1812	150	127	165	100	100	91	108	100	129
1813	130	111	120	106	108	100	119	106	116
1814	93	76	110	112	117	100	119	100	96
1815	87	69	110	100	108	95	112	100	91
1816	83	80	110	94	92	73	85	79	86
1817	127	120	130	94	92	64	85	79	111
1818	107	91	135	100	100	91	108	94	97
1819	90	73	130	100	100	91	92	94	86

oatmeal and flour, 2 to potatoes and 1 each to beef, mutton, bacon, butter, and cheese. It will be noticed that the prices of the first three of these fluctuated more violently than those of the others. The very poor, who lived chiefly on meal and potatoes, suffered much in 1795 and were reduced to extremities in 1800-1801. In these two years of famine, Rowbottom records, new kinds of cereals, such as barley flour and "American flour" (presumably of corn) were on sale. The poor gathered docks, "green sauce," and water cresses to serve as a substitute for potatoes, and nettles were on sale in Oldham at twopence a pound.

The same picture of wide fluctuations in the cost of a standard diet is shown in the figures for the years 1810-1819 (See Table IV). These are drawn from a table giving

suggests that the cost of the standard diet fell little, if at all, in the four years of depression and distress that followed the end of the war.

The figures in Table V relate to Manchester. They are taken from an estimate of the retail cost of provisions made by the Manchester Chamber of Commerce and published in an appendix to *Manchester Merchants and Foreign Trade* by Arthur Redford.[24] They indicate that throughout the twenties the cost of the staple diet moved to a higher rather than to a lower level.

I have resisted the temptation to throw these three figures together so as to offer a single index of the cost of provisions from

[24] Published at Manchester by the Manchester University Press, 1934.

1791 to 1831, partly because of slight differences of area and of the range of commodities but mainly because the data are not derived from a common source. The outlines are, however, clear. Following a fall after the famine of 1800-1801, the upward movement of prices continued, to a peak in 1812. Thereafter food prices fell to about 1820 but rose again during the following decade. In 1831 the standard diet

the striking features of domestic production was the wide variations in the prices offered for labor. In December 1793, according to Rowbottom, the weavers of ginghams at Oldham received 10s. per end, in April 1794 they were paid 19s. and in August of the same year 24s. 4d. During the same period the price of weaving nankeens rose from 16s. to 26s. a piece. Generally, for reasons set forth by Adam Smith, the price of labor

TABLE V

INDEX OF COST OF DIET IN MANCHESTER

(1821 = 100)

Year	Oatmeal	Flour	Potatoes	Beef Best	Beef Coarse	Pork	Bacon	Cheese	Index of Cost of Diet
1821	100	100	100	100	100	100	100	100	100
1822	94	117	79	100	117	96	115	95	102
1823	100	92	88	100	108	135	112	121	101
1824	116	115	141	115	117	139	127	126	122
1825	116	119	106	125	158	135	138	137	120
1826	122	112	172	125	158	130	115	137	130
1827	128	112	84	120	133	139	115	147	119
1828	119	119	100	130	133	130	123	132	120
1829	106	127	115	120	125	130	100	132	118
1830	112	119	106	110	100	113	115	105	112
1831	112	115	110	120	117	122	123	116	115

of the poor can hardly have cost much less than in 1791.[25] If this was so, it would seem that any improvement in the standard of living must have come either from a rise in money wages or from a fall in the prices of things not included in this index. One of

[25] The first of each of the following figures is the price at Oldham in 1791, the second that at Manchester in 1831: meal (per peck) 19d., 18d.; flour (per peck) 24d., 30d.; potatoes (per load) 6s. 6d., 6s. 3d.; beef (per pound) 5d., 6d.; pork (per pound) 5d., 5½d.; bacon (per pound) 8d., 7d.; cheese (per pound) 5d., 8d. The cost of diet in 1810 was apparently about 5 per cent higher than in 1809 and 60 per cent higher than in 1791. For purposes of comparison with the figures in Table III the figures in Table IV should be increased by 60 per cent.

Between 1819 and 1821 there was a marked drop in the prices of most of the commodities in the index. Roughly the cost of diet in 1821

rose when the cost of provisions fell and years of dearth were usually years of low wages. In these circumstances the standard of life of the worker was subject to violent fluctuation. One of the merits of the factory system was that it offered, and required, regularity of employment and hence greater stability of consumption. During the period 1790-1830 factory production increased rapidly. A greater proportion of the people came to benefit from it both as producers and as consumers. The fall in the price of textiles reduced the price of clothing. Government contracts for uniforms and army

was the same as in 1791, and the figures in Table V are broadly on the same base as those in Table III. The sample basket of commodities cost about 15 per cent more in 1831 than in 1791.

boots called into being new industries, and after the war the products of these found a market among the better paid artisans. Boots began to take the place of clogs, hats replaced shawls, at least for wear on Sundays. Miscellaneous commodities, ranging from clocks to pocket handkerchiefs, began to enter into the scheme of expenditure, and after 1820 such things as tea and coffee and sugar fell in price substantially. The growth of trade-unions, friendly societies, savings banks, popular newspapers and pamphlets, schools and nonconformist chapels—all give evidence of the existence of a large class raised well above the level of mere subsistence.[26]

There were, however, masses of unskilled or poorly skilled workers—seasonally employed agricultural workers and hand-loom weavers in particular—whose incomes were almost wholly absorbed in paying for the bare necessaries of life, the prices of which, as we have seen, remained high. My guess would be that the number of those who were able to share in the benefits of economic progress was larger than the number of those who were shut out from these benefits and that it was steadily growing. But the existence of two groups within the working class needs to be recognized. Perhaps the explanation of the division of opinion, to which I called attention at the beginning of this paper, rests on this. John Stuart Mill and his fellow economists were thinking of the one group, Rickman and Chadwick had their eyes fixed on the other.

[26] In 1837 or 1838 Thomas Holmes, an old man of 87, born in 1760, gave to a member of the Liverpool Statistical Society his impressions of the changes that had taken place since his youth at Aldbrough (Holderness): "There has been a very great increase in the consumption of meat, wheaten bread, poultry, tea and sugar. But it has not reached the poorest, except tea, sugar, and wheaten bread. The poorest are not so well fed. But they are better clothed, lodged and provided with furniture, better taken care of in sickness and misfortune. So they are gainers. This, I think, is a plain statement of the whole case."

Referring to mechanics and artificers, he says, "The wages of almost all have increased in a proportion faster than the rise in the expenses of living." When asked, "Are the poorer classes more intelligent?," he replied, "Beyond all comparison."

PARLIAMENTARY REFORM WAS A SUBJECT of heated debate in the Britain of the 1770's. Some years before the outbreak of the French Revolution, however, it had become clear that the governing elements in British political life were interested neither in redistributing seats in the House of Commons nor in extending the suffrage. And once Britain became involved in the French Revolutionary Wars, the movement for Parliamentary reform was for all practical purposes ended, at least "for the duration"; to criticize the British constitution at a time when Britain was at war amounted to giving aid and comfort to the French enemy. The upshot was that any significant revival of the assault on the unreformed House of Commons had to await the end of the Napoleonic Wars. Only then could British reformers escape the suspicion of treason. Hence it was that in the years of economic depression after Waterloo the movement for Parliamentary reform gained momentum. Middle-class and working-class elements, joining forces in order to bring pressure to bear on the Tory government, sought to reduce the political power of the British agricultural interest. The fears aroused by the reformers were enormous, and the government imposed severe restrictions on freedom of speech, press, and assembly. Even in the 1820's the government remained firm in its refusal to alter the suffrage and to permit redistribution of Parliamentary seats. Although it granted important reforms in the economic, criminological, and religious spheres, it refused to change the old House of Commons. The reformers themselves lost heart in the 1820's: witness the startling decline that took place in the number of petitions requesting Parliamentary reform. How, then, are we to explain the Reform Act of 1832? In large measure by the contagion of foreign example. It was the French Revolution of 1830 which, in the words of the *Annual Register,* provided the key to "the outcry for reform in Britain." In the following essay, George Macaulay Trevelyan analyzes the significance of the Reform Act. Often considered the outstanding twentieth-century British historian, Trevelyan has been a champion of the readable historical prose and the Whig point of view that his ancestor, Lord Macaulay, had advocated with such vigor.

THE GREAT DAYS OF REFORM

G. M. TREVELYAN

I. WHIGS AND TORIES

One hundred years ago the great Reform Bill was passed, after 15 months of fierce convulsion in the body politic that made almost as great an impression on contemporaries as the Bill itself. Of the protagonists in that struggle *The Times* newspaper alone survives to-day, triumphing over chance and time.

By the consent alike of friends and foes, the Reform Bill began a new era in the political life of Britain. In our domestic history 1832 is the next great landmark after 1688. But, whereas the institutions in Church and State known as the Revolution Settlement lasted unchanged for nearly a century and a half, the Reform Bill ushered in an era of ceaseless change. We have long ago overthrown the nicely adjusted balance of forces set up by the actual terms of the Bill—a balance between the landlord class and the bourgeoisie, between privilege and modern enterprise. Since then country life has been offered up a sacrifice to the city populations; the squires have gone down before the town middle class; but the victors have to-day the less joy of their victory, because they in their turn are hard pressed upon by classes that were not enfranchised by the Bill of 1832. Contrary to the prophecies of extreme Tories and Radicals at the moment when the Bill became law, Crown, Established Church, and House of Lords still exist, but the last two have been deprived of many privileges that were then considered essential. The Crown, indeed, has greater security and prestige than it had when worn by the sons of George III. But it has less political power than in 1831, when Grey admitted that, if King William had not signified his approval, he could not, under the existing custom of the Constitution, have introduced the Reform Bill into Parliament at all, any more than Pitt could introduce Catholic Emancipation without the Royal consent.

Strictly interpreted, the new constitutional era begun in 1832 lasted only till the second Reform Bill of 1867. But in another sense it is still the era in which we live. For the epoch of political change dating from the first Reform Bill has never yet stopped; nor will it ever stop, so long as scientific inven-

Reprinted by special permission from the London *Times,* June 7 and 8, 1932.

tion, the blind titan that makes and moves the world, continues to recast the economic and social structure of the country as fast every decade as it used to change every century. It was to meet the pressure of new social conditions that the political floodgates were opened in 1832, and the water has never ceased to pour through them. If they had not been opened purposely and wisely by skilled and careful hands, the pent waters would soon have burst the barriers, carrying destruction far and wide. That the Reform Bill saved the land from revolution and civil strife, and made possible the quiet progress of the Victorian era, is its great claim to the gratitude of posterity.

Lord Grey's Meaning

When Lord Grey said that in passing the Bill he intended to "stand by his order"—meaning the nobility and the landlord class—the Tory Peers laughed bitterly at such a paradox. But he meant what he said; and in fact the Bill did save "his order" for at least as long as anything could have saved it, and it saved a great many other things besides. Owing to the passage of the Bill, the cultivated upper class was not driven out of politics by a violent revolution, as in America, France, and elsewhere. Like the Revolution of 1688, the Reform Bill was a great Conservative as well as a great Liberal measure.

The opponents of the Bill—Eldon, Wetherell, Walter Scott, and the Duke of Wellington—in their honest attachment to the country's noble past and not ignoble present, refused to consider the possibilities of the future and to take counsel how the best of the past could be preserved for service in a new age. Their mistake did not consist in preferring rural to city life, or aristocracy to bourgeoisie—matters of taste wherein many will agree with them to-day and most of the Whig leaders agreed with them then. Nor did their mistake lie in their prophecy that larger changes would follow in the wake of the Reform Bill if once it were passed. The Tory mistake consisted in

thinking that no changes would follow if it were thrown out. On the contrary such changes would then have followed as have been seen in less happy lands. Westminster would have been as the Tuileries, and the struggle of churches and classes in the nineteenth century would have been fought out by other weapons than the vote.

The fundamental mistake of the Tories lay in supposing that a world which the Industrial Revolution had already reconstructed socially could for ever retain the same political structure as in the days of Queen Anne. If the Tories wished to preserve the rotten boroughs and the aristocratic constitution in perpetuity, they should have stopped the Industrial Revolution; they should have passed Luddite laws to prohibit the new machines. To prosecute Tom Paine was a mere measure of delay, since they neglected the more important work of hanging James Watt and locking up George Stephenson. When once they had allowed the cotton mills of Lancashire to arise, Peterloo and the Six Acts were mere measures of postponement—strong sweeps of Mrs. Partington's broom against the incoming Atlantic, effective for a season but ultimately of no avail. For, when once the cotton lords had made their fortunes, when once the operatives had come together in great new communities around the factory doors, the old order of society was doomed. Thenceforth the problem of statesmen could only be the orderly and gradual conduct of the process of political change, to answer to social facts already accomplished.

The Whig Cabinet

It is the merit of the Whigs of 1830-32 that they saw this better than the able men who had been governing England for the previous 50 years. The rising generation of Whig opposition leaders in the twenties—Russell, Durham, Brougham, and Althorp—realized the need of the nation as regards Reform of Parliament better than the Tory Governmentalists, partly because the Whigs, being always in opposition, had been at more leisure to observe and were less bound to vested interests; partly because Charles Fox had a generation before inscribed Parliamentary Reform on the Whig banner in the days when "it was safer to be a felon than a Reformer," and Grey and Holland had preserved that tradition of the elders.

To the older and younger Whigs, who had all been brought up in at least a theoretic attachment to Reform of Parliament, were added in the winter of 1830 a powerful group of reforming Tories, some of them the followers of Canning and Huskisson, lately dead. These recruits of Reform— Melbourne, Palmerston, Graham, and Stanley, "the Rupert of debate"—were welded with the Whigs into the Cabinet that Grey so skilfully formed after the fall of the Duke of Wellington. It was more than a new Cabinet, it was a new party, a party of Whigs and former Tories brought together to reform Parliament. It was an aristocratic Cabinet, and the element of family alliance was stong in it. It was none the worse for that, for the Whig aristocrats, Durham, Russell, Althorp, and Grey himself, were not only able men but advanced reformers —more advanced, oddly enough, than the democratic leader Brougham, who boggled at the total abolition of the rotten boroughs.

It was a Cabinet formed to pass a Reform Bill, and it accomplished its task. It is much to be doubted whether in that moment of time any other set of men could have cajoled and forced King, Lords, and Commons into doing what the nation so imperatively demanded. If the aristocracy was to be persuaded to abdicate a portion of its powers, the unwelcome medicine had best be prepared and presented to it by aristocrats.

With the *ex post facto* criticisms of later Radicals that the Bill did not go far enough the historian need scarcely concern himself, for he knows that nothing more radical could have been passed by, or even introduced into, the then House of Commons. To contemporaries the only question was why the Bill went so far as it did. That was the surprise which rallied the nation and even the Radicals of the day to support the Whigs, whom otherwise they distrusted and disliked. There lay the wisdom of Lord Grey and the "Committee of Four" whom he appointed to draw up the Bill—Russell, Durham, Graham, and Duncannon. The Bill went far enough to arouse the enthusiasm of the nation because it was more than "bit-by-bit Reform"; it did not go so far as "Radical Reform," for if it had been

"ORATOR" HENRY HUNT: English radical (d. 1835) who figured prominently in the agitation for annual Parliaments, universal manhood suffrage, and voting by secret ballot. He helped to make the white hat the sign of the radical in the Britain of the 1820's. His opponents viewed him as an unprincipled demagogue.

PETERLOO: Massacre in 1819 of some Manchester reformers who had met in St. Peter's Fields in order to listen to a speech by the radical "Orator" Hunt and to draw up petitions in support of Parliamentary reform.

FRANCIS PLACE: English tailor, reformer, and trade-union leader (d. 1854) who was a friend of Bentham and James Mill. He was active in the struggle for the repeal of the Combination Laws, the repeal of the stamp duties on newspapers and periodicals, and the passage of the Reform Bill of 1832. His writings are a basic source for an understanding of radical movements in early-nineteenth-century Britain. His biography, written by Graham Wallas, is an important secondary work for any student of nineteenth-century Britain.

SIX ACTS: Repressive measures of 1819 designed to prevent a revolutionary outbreak in Britain. Enacted shortly after the Peterloo Massacre, they severely restricted the holding of public meetings, limited the freedom of the press, and extended the heavy tax on newspapers to periodical publications in general.

Radical it would have alienated those forces in Court and Parliament without whose initial aid it could not be passed. It was a bull's eye of legislative marksmanship, when an inch more to right or left would have been fatal.

After Waterloo

The reason why the country needed and demanded a measure so extensive, and why nothing short of the total abolition of the rotten boroughs would have united opinion behind the Bill, was that Reform had been so long postponed. Fifty years before milder measures would have sufficed. Between the American and the French Revolutions proposals to abolish some, but not all, the rotten boroughs had been urged by Pitt, Fox, and the Yorkshire Reformers. "Bit-by-bit Reform" would probably have been England's path of progress in the later years of George III., had it not been for the French Revolution and the long Napoleonic Wars. The anti-Jacobin reaction in England, an inevitable result of those foreign events, by stopping change, made rapid change necessary in 1830 if revolution was to be avoided.

The Reform movement, when it revived after Waterloo, revived first as a working-class movement only. In the years 1817-19 the Radical agitation for the abolition of the rotten boroughs and for universal suffrage, led by Cobbett and Hunt, had been a movement of the suffering working class. In their acute economic distress during the bad times after the war they took up Parliamentary Reform as a means of compelling politicians to pay attention to their miserable state. The Radical and social character of the movement prevented both the Whig Opposition and the middle-class manufacturers from joining at that time in the cry for Reform, although Lord Grey still declared that if ever the nation took up the question of Reform "seriously and affectionately" he would place himself at the head of the movement.

Since for the present both Whigs and middle classes held aloof, it was easy for the Tory Government in 1819 to suppress the workingclass movement by Peterloo and the Six Acts. After that the Tories carried on for another dozen years with renewed vitality under Peel and Canning, undergoing a change in a Liberal direction in every subject of home and foreign policy, except only on Parliamentary Reform and the allied question of Municipal Reform. On that the Tory Government, even at its most liberal moment, was adamant. That was the Ark of the Covenant. All else could be touched —Catholics, Test Act, trade union laws, police, foreign policy, tariff policy—but the rotten boroughs, Parliamentary and municipal, were to be sacred.

The Spirit of the Age

For this reason, owing to the Tory refusal to touch Parliamentary Reform, so unwisely emphasized by Wellington in the autumn of 1830, when he declared the British Constitution to be incapable of improvement, the liberal "spirit of the age" had to turn elsewhere and seek some other embodiment than the Liberal Toryism that had dominated the twenties. "The spirit of the age" breathed into the nostrils of the long-moribund Whig party and revived it for another great period of national leadership and government.

For in 1830, under the exasperating stimuli of bad times and of Wellington's Prime Ministership, and in the excitement caused by an orderly bourgeois revolution in France, the middle classes of England suddenly began to agitate "seriously and affectionately" for the destruction of the rotten boroughs—but not for universal suffrage. They cried out for Parliamentary Reform on different lines and in a different spirit from the Radical agitation of the Peterloo period. There was, however, one thing in common between working-class and middle-class Reformers—intense hatred of the rotten boroughs. "Down with the borough-mongers" was the cry in every street. On that platform, and on that alone, the much divided nation might yet be united by a bold and skilful appeal.

Lord Grey and his Whig colleagues put themselves at the head of this new agitation in the winter of 1830, and satisfied it by the Reform Bill of 1831-32. That Bill was a treaty of alliance between the Whig aristocrats and the middle classes, particularly the new middle classes created by the industrial revolution. Many bourgeois families passed over from neutrality or Toryism to Whig allegiance on this issue. They had supported the Tory Government against the Jacobins, against Napoleon, and more recently against the Radical Reformers, though with divided sympathies over the Peterloo massacre. Owing to the Reform Bill the Tories lost them again for a generation.

II. ENGLAND'S WAY

What, then, were the terms of the alliance struck between the middle classes and the Whig aristocracy? What, in other words, were the essential provisions of the great Reform Bill? First and foremost, the rotten boroughs were all abolished. The principle of appointment of members of Parliament by individual patrons disappeared from the practice of the Constitution. This was effected in two ways. In the first place 150 seats were abolished by the famous Schedules A and B of the Bill; towns or hamlets in Schedule A lost both their members, those in Schedule B lost one. Secondly, some rotten boroughs kept their representation, but ceased to be "rotten" because their franchise was extended, so that they ceased to be in the gift of patrons. This occurred automatically, because a uniform franchise of all householders paying £10 a year rent was established for all Parliamentary boroughs, whether they were old or newly created by the Bill. The redistribution of seats to make good the gaps left by Schedules A and B went partly to increase the county representation, and partly to enfranchise certain great centres of population, including Manchester, Birmingham, Rochdale, and other towns of the North and Midlands which had been raised to importance by the Industrial Revolution. In the counties, where ever since the fifteenth century the franchise had been confined to freeholders of forty shillings and upwards, the larger tenant farmers were also enfranchised by the Reform Bill.

Such were the main outlines of the Bill in the form in which it became law on June 7, 1832. The chief criticism that is sometimes directed against it to-day is the principle of uniformity. It is argued that Brougham was right when he wanted some of the rotten boroughs to be spared, as indispensable for party managers and Ministers to put in able young men and other persons useful to Government or to Opposition. It is also argued that if, instead of the uniform £10 franchise, the franchise had varied in the different boroughs, a considerable portion of the working class could at once have been admitted to the franchise in some places, while in others something nearer to the old patronage boroughs could have been continued with advantage.

Nothing but the Bill

These criticisms, though by no means devoid of weight, overlook the actual difficulty of making arbitrary discriminations, which would most certainly have been fiercely attacked by an envenomed Opposition, and would moreover have cooled the support of the Bill in the country. Ministers would have been accused, with truth, of "cooking" the new constituencies. Even as it was that charge was made, and was rebutted only because a principle of statistical uniformity had been adopted. Ministers would have had no right to abolish a number of vested interests in certain boroughs of immemorial antiquity if they had preserved others equally abusive and had created a number of new irregularities in the franchise. Such a system might have been ideally better, but it would not have appeared just to plain people, and it could never have been passed through Parliament.

For these reasons the principle of uniformity, which had existed in the county franchise ever since the Act of 1430, was now applied to boroughs also. It had the result of excluding the whole working class for the time being. On the other hand, it made it inevitable that when in the course of time the franchise was further extended, the whole working class would ultimately be enfranchised. The Radicals, Francis Place and Cobbett, foresaw this, and supported the Bill in the interest of their clients. They joined in the cry for "The Bill, the whole Bill, and nothing but the Bill," because the Bill would break down the immemorial barriers of antiquity—the first line of defence which was by far the most formidable; and also because the principle of uniformity, though now working in the interest of the bourgeoisie by the £10 franchise, must in the end work in the interest of the masses at present unenfranchised. Others among the working-class leaders, like Hunt, denounced the Bill because of the restricted franchise. But, though working-class opinion may be said to have been to that extent divided, it was solid against the rotten boroughs, and solid for a fight with the Lords when the Lords threw out the Bill.

The most vigorous and active support of the Bill—particularly in the Political Unions organized by Attwood—came from the middle classes. The term "middle class" was then a less vague description than it is to-day. It meant all who did not belong to the "gentlemen" of the landowning class and of the liberal professions on the one hand, and who were not, on the other hand, weekly wage-earners. The middle class, whom the Whig publicists idealized as "the solid part of the nation" and "the wealth and intelligence of the nation," included every one from the humblest clerk or village shopkeeper up to the wealthiest moneyed magnate. In 1832 the master manufacturers were seldom allied by matrimonial, social, or political ties with the aristocracy or landed interest. Many of them were Dissenters. The law did not allow them to shoot game, even if they hired a shooting; they

were not invited to the country houses; and very few of their class could obtain seats in Parliament, or had anything to do with the choice of members for the rotten boroughs. They regarded the "landed interest" with a modified English version of the jealousy that the French capitalists in 1789 felt for the privileged *noblesse:* and the distaste was mutual. These social divisions largely disappeared in the following generation, but they counted in 1832, and put a great mass of wealth and power behind "the Bill."

The World of Dickens

But, most of all, the multitudinous lower middle class, the world of Cruikshank and of Dickens, was stirred by the Bill like the ocean by the attraction of the moon. The £10 franchise seemed to offer them political power and therewith a cure for all their troubles. Yet in fact the £10 franchise did not include all the lower middle class. It left very many of them still unenfranchised; this was perhaps a fortunate circumstance, because the demand for a further extension of the franchise became in later years common ground, under Bright's leadership, between the excluded half of the middle class and the whole working class. That was one reason why Victorian England was not torn by a class conflict of the working class against the rest of society.

In those days politics turned almost as much on religious and denominational jealousies as on social and economic issues. The Dissenters were for the Bill, seeing in it the necessary prelude to the redressing of their grievances such as Church rates and University tests. And this time they had unwonted allies in all the roughs in the country. The mob outrages, which a generation before had been directed against Dissenters and Reformers, were now directed against Bishops and Tories.

The clergy of the Establishment, with a few exceptions like the Rev. Sydney Smith, were more solidly against the Bill than any other class of the community. But the influence of the Church was then at its lowest point and did not carry the congregations. The clergy thought that the Bill would lead to disestablishment and disendowment. Yet in fact the Church retained not only its endowments but even the much-challenged compulsory Church rates and the monopoly at Oxford and Cambridge till after the passing of the second Reform Bill. That is one of many proofs that the immediate change made by the first Reform Bill was less than many people expected it to be.

It is not, indeed, true that the middle classes attained in 1832 to full control of the State. Their power was increased, but so also was the power of the squirearchy proper as against the small oligarchy who until 1832 had owned the borough representation.

The Landed Interest

If opinion in the towns was united in favour of the Bill, the countryside was divided. Probably half the squires supported it. They feared revolution if it were lost. For that reason many of the propertied classes were "Bill men" in the sombre winter of 1831-32—the winter of the rejection of the Bill by the Lords, the Bristol riots, cholera, and hard times. Many squires, whether Whig or Tory, were pleased by the increase which the Bill made in the county representation at the expense of the rotten boroughs, in which 99 squires out of 100 had no personal interest. The "borough-mongers," 150 individuals all told, must not be confused with the landed class as a whole. Moreover, the squires were delighted at the "Chandos Clause" added in Committee, which enfranchised their large tenant farmers. Under the Bill thus amended the squires obtained even more control over the county representation than before; and at the same time the county representation, previously limited to 82 English seats, was increased to 139.

Yet, actually and relatively, the power of the landed interest was diminished by the Bill. For it would now have to meet, on the floor of the House, no longer the mere nominees of borough owners who were landlords themselves, but the representatives of the triumphant middle class, the members of the newly enfranchised or newly reformed boroughs, elected by £10 householders. The issue between the gentry and the middle class, between the landed interest and the commercial and industrial world, came to a head over the Corn Laws a dozen years after the passage of the Reform Bill. Only then was the full extent of the change apparent. And by then intermarriage and social intercourse were beginning to blur the line previously so visible between the two divisions of the owners of wealth.

Public Opinion

The total abolition of the rotten boroughs won for the Bill and its authors the fierce support of the great bulk of the nation, irrespective of class and party. Once the Whig Ministers had, in March, 1831, made public their quite unexpected resolve to abolish all patronage boroughs it was necessary to go on and give effect to the policy, or, in the then state of public opinion, chaos would come again. Some of the Ministers and their supporters, like Palmerston, Lansdowne, and Campbell, were frightened by the sweeping character of the Bill. But to retire in face of the popular storm they had aroused in their support would be far more dangerous to the State than to let themselves be driven forward. The dynamics of the situation were not overstated in the emphatic orations with which young Tom Macaulay sprang to House of Commons fame. From first to last public opinion was the decisive element in the situation, and that is a main reason why the first Reform Bill was so important a step in the passage from aristocratic to democratic government. It was not only the actual provisions of the measure and the change it made in representation, but the means by which it was carried in face of the Peers' opposition, which made the first Reform Bill a turning point in political development.

The resistance of the House of Lords to the Reform Bill called forth a tremendous display of popular feeling and determination—orderly and organized, with a few exceptions like the disgraceful Bristol riots. Had it not been for the display of organized popular determination which held the Ministers and the House of Commons to their task, the Lords could have maintained their right of veto and compelled a compromise. For the only constitutional way to overcome their veto was the threat of a wholesale creation of Peers by the King. And William IV., though favourable to the Bill in its early days, was turning hostile to it in the winter of 1831-32, and would never have consented to make the famous threat of Peer-making if it had been possible for him to carry on the Government peaceably in any other manner.

Days of May

The last stage was the famous crisis in "the days of May," 1832. The Duke of Wellington, ever loyal to his Sovereign, attempted to form a Ministry in order to save the King's face and pass something like the Reform Bill without the appearance of Royal coercion applied to the House of Lords. The country thought that the Duke intended to scrap the Bill, and under that impression, probably a mistaken one, prepared for civil resistance. Such resistance must have been formidable, since the Army was hardly large enough to hold down London, let alone the other cities of England. Fortunately the matter was not put to the test, for Peel and the Conservative minority in the House of Commons declined to face an impossible situation merely in order to save the face of King and Peers, since by that time it was clear that the Bill must in any case be passed.

During this crisis in May the Whig Ministers had never actually vacated their offices. So when the King gave the effective guarantee that he would make Peers if necessary, the machinery of State rolled smoothly forward again, and on June 7, 1832, the Reform Bill became law. A change that in other lands or in an earlier England would have caused bloodshed and the breaking up of laws had been carried like any other Act of Parliament, as the prelude to the great era of peaceful progress that we now know as the Victorian Age. As we look back on it after a hundred years, "all passion spent," it was an affair of which Englishmen of all classes and parties may be proud, and it was a characteristically English business from beginning to end.

THE INDUSTRIAL MIDDLE CLASSES saw in the Reform Act of 1832 a major victory for their cause, and they sought to follow it up with other legislative reforms that would serve to remake British government and society in the industrial-middle-class image. Upholders as a rule of the conception of Adam Smith that the wealth of a nation would increase if each individual was permitted to pursue his own self-interest, they advocated a minimum of government intervention in economic life. Their greatest victory came, of course, in 1846, with the repeal of the Corn Laws, an event that signalized the defeat of the British agricultural interest; and three years later came the repeal of the Navigation Laws. It is, nevertheless, misleading to view the decades that followed the Reform Act of 1832 as an age of thoroughgoing individualism and *laissez faire,* for the second third of the nineteenth century stands out not only for the lifting of old restrictions on economic life but for the imposition of new ones. After all, 1833 was the year of the first consequential Factory Act, 1842 the year of the Mines Act, and 1847 the year of the Ten Hours Act. In short, even in the heyday of the "Period of Individualism" the state was meddling in economic life on an extensive scale. This was partly because of the agitation of humanitarian reformers who viewed it as the function of government to lift the status of downtrodden factory workers; partly, too, it was because of agitation by the Benthamites, who believed they had principles of legislation and administration that would ensure the greatest happiness of the greatest number. This is the thesis advanced by Professor J. Bartlet Brebner, of Columbia University, in the following essay on the contribution of Benthamism to the growth of state intervention in nineteenth-century Britain. Author of *The Making of Modern Britain* (1943) and *North Atlantic Triangle* (1945), Professor Brebner stands out for his analytical and interpretative approach to historical study.

LAISSEZ FAIRE AND STATE INTERVENTION IN NINETEENTH-CENTURY BRITAIN
J. BARTLET BREBNER

I

Seven or eight years ago our Association and its common-law bride, the Committee for Research in Economic History, earnestly set about producing offspring. One cluster of them, it was expected, would look like examples of laissez faire in the United States. In 1943 we inspected these infants in the form of four papers read at our annual meeting; more recently they have been maturing into books. And now we are obliged to acknowledge that they have disappointed the anticipations of their parents by looking rather more like state intervention than like laissez faire. The announcement of Louis Hartz's study, *Economic Policy and Democratic Thought: Pennsylvania, 1774-1860,* is not untypical of the comments on all of them which have been consistently made by relatives, friends, and scholarly reviewers. That announcement says: "Through his critical appraisal of Pennsylvania, a leading state in the formative years of the Republic, Mr. Hartz advances the perhaps startling thesis that

the contemporary theory of 'laissez-faire' actually embraced a vigorous concept of state economic responsibility."

"The perhaps startling thesis" sounds as if grandfather's big ears or great-aunt Mary's snub nose had cropped up again after skipping a generation, yet the British ancestors of these American children have been reputed to be of pure and congruous Manchester stock, bred true from sire Adam Smith. Perhaps, however, that popular notion is wrong. If we were to find that the British strain also "embraced a vigorous concept of state economic responsibility," we might be less easily startled by these American physiognomies and more resigned to their looking about as variegated and contradictory as physiognomies generally.

Conceivably, British laissez faire was a political and economic myth in the sense formulated by Georges Sorel half a century ago, that is, a slogan or war cry employed by new forms of enterprise in their politico-economical war against the landed oligarchy. This seems the more likely when one discovers from their writings that

Reprinted by special permission from *The Journal of Economic History, Supplement,* VIII (1948), 59-73. The author has made a few minor changes in the present version of his essay.

Jeremy Bentham and John Stuart Mill, who have been commonly represented as typical, almost fundamental, formulators of laissez faire, were in fact the exact opposite, that is, the formulator of state intervention for collectivist ends and his devout apostle. The probability that we are dealing with a myth increases still more in the light of two indubitable courses of events during the heyday of laissez faire: the fact that as the state took its fingers off commerce during the first half of the nineteenth century it simultaneously put them on industry and its accompaniments; and the fact that industry, having by 1850 used its slogan with considerable success against the landed oligarchy, promptly directed it, with some Spencerian and Darwinian trimmings, against its former allies, the laborers, who were becoming convinced that the vote was a natural right of man.

This is not to argue that laissez faire was not a powerful myth. As Hume said: "Though men be much governed by interest, yet even interest itself, and all human affairs, are entirely governed by *opinion*." Although laissez faire never prevailed in Great Britain or in any other modern state, many men today have been led to believe that it did. One might go further and declare that today even some scholars believe that it did. Part of that misbelief in scholars may be attributed to taste or to temperamental preference, and part to their reliance upon the work of other scholars. In this matter A. V. Dicey of Oxford seems to have been the principal maintainer of the myth for others. His original and learned Harvard lectures of 1898, published in 1905 and revised in 1914, under the title of *Law and Public Opinion in England during the Nineteenth Century*, amounted to an argument against increasing collectivism. The lectures were so passionately motivated as to be a sincere, despairing, and warped reassertion of the myth in terms of legal and constitutional history.[1]

[1] The introduction and footnotes to the second edition, however, reveal a good deal of inner uncertainty, for example, p. xxx, n. 1.

Dicey professed to have read the one scholarly work that might have corroded his position, but his own book reveals that he had not digested it, preferring, as he did, to depend on his cousin, Leslie Stephen. The potential corrosive was an extraordinarily painstaking analysis of Bentham, published by Elie Halévy, 1901-1904, and entitled *La Formation du radicalisme philosophique*.[2] Yet, as Halévy half-proudly and half-ruefully confessed in 1936, he had been born five or six years too soon and was a nineteenth-century liberal, so that, although in this and in later works he faithfully presented the manifold theoretical and actual contradictions of British laissez faire from their Benthamite birth in 1776 down to 1915, he too gave greater emphasis to "hands off" than to "hands on" until two or three years before his death in 1937.[3] When Sir Cecil Carr gave his Carpentier Lectures at Columbia University in 1940 he could still refer to the question "whether Britain had gone off the Dicey standard."[4] Now, more than forty years after Dicey published his immensely influential, and in one respect equally misleading, book, it must be asserted that either he had not read enough Bentham to know what he was talking about, or that he was betrayed by his own susceptibility to the public opinion he so subtly analyzed. In using Bentham as the archetype of British individualism he was conveying the exact opposite of the truth. Jeremy Bentham was the archetype of British collectivism.

[2] Translated as *The Growth of Philosophic Radicalism* (New York: The Macmillan Company, 1928).

[3] For a summary view of his intellectual course, see J. B. Brebner, "Élie Halévy (1870-1937)," in Herman Ausubel, J. Bartlet Brebner, and Erling M. Hunt (eds.), *Some Modern Historians of Britain: Essays in Honor of R. L. Schuyler* (New York, The Dryden Press, 1951), pp. 235-254.

[4] Sir C. T. Carr, *Concerning English Administrative Law* (New York: Columbia University Press, 1941), p. 26. His first lecture is a witty, perceptive distillation from the revision in this matter upon which he had embarked twenty years earlier. See his *Delegated Legislation* (Cambridge: The University Press, 1921).

One can trace this confusion back to its taproots by recalling that in the *annus mirabilis*, 1776, three very different books were published: Jeremy Bentham's *Fragment on Government*, John Cartwright's *Take Your Choice*, and Adam Smith's *Wealth of Nations*. Noting for the moment merely that the second powerfully revived the seventeenth-century creed of democracy based upon universal suffrage, let us start from the fact that Bentham and Smith were fundamentally contradictory of each other in their ideas of how to secure the general good. Bentham argued that individual interest must be *artificially* identified or made one by the omnipotent lawmaker, employing the felicific calculus of "the greatest happiness of the greatest number." Smith, as his *Theory of Moral Sentiments* had to some degree foreshadowed, argued that the identification or unification would be a *natural* one, that is, that if each individual were left free to pursue what he regarded as his own interest he would be "led by an invisible hand" and by "more familiar causes" to collaborate in the achievement of the general good.[5]

How, then, could Dicey entitle one of his lectures, referring to the middle fifty years of the nineteenth century, "The Period of Benthamism or Individualism"? The explanation is that he, and Halévy to an only slightly lesser degree, attributed the extensive state intervention of that time mainly to humanitarianism, in spite of the fact that in practically all of its many *forms* it was basically Benthamite—Benthamite in the

[5] But consider the exceptions culled by Jacob Viner, *Adam Smith, 1776-1826* (Chicago: The University of Chicago Press, 1928), chap. v.

sense of conforming closely to that forbidding, detailed blueprint for a collectivist state, the *Constitutional Code*, which was written between 1820 and 1832. Moreover, the architect of most of the state intervention was that bureaucrat of purest essence, Edwin Chadwick, whom Bentham had set to work on the *Code*, along with Southwood Smith.

Dicey's "period" was also the period of the so-called Triumph of Laissez Faire, of the Repeal of the Corn Laws, and the Fall of the Old Colonial System. Furthermore, it was the period when the masses of the population were adroitly used again and again to terrorize the landed oligarchy, until in 1867 the governing classes had to concede to the urban group a substantial degree of political democracy. How can one disentangle this medley of contrary elements, the most antithetical of which Dicey so blandly reconciled?

II

The principal clue, aside from Dicey's failure to read Bentham, appears to lie in Bentham himself. About 1808 he came to a turning point in life and thought. For thirty years he had been a prophet not without honor save in his own country, for Continental Europe and the Americas had made him famous. For twenty years he had engaged his energies and his wealth toward the construction in England of a panopticon, or penal institution whose "architectural principle of universal inspection" epitomized its incorporation of the basic Utilitarian principles. When he learned that the British Government had decided to abandon

---

AUGUSTE COMTE: French social philosopher (d. 1857) who sought to reorganize human society. Because in his later years he came to view the process of social reorganization as basically a religious problem, he alienated some of his supporters—in particular his leading British disciple, John Stuart Mill.

SIR CHARLES TREVELYAN: English government official, governor of Madras, father of the historian Sir George Otto Trevelyan, and grandfather of the historian George Macaulay Trevelyan. He played a major role in the movements to abolish the system of purchase in the army and to bring about civil-service reform.

this scheme, he suddenly saw everything in a new light.[6] Hitherto it had not occurred to him to doubt that, if the governing class could be made to see what was for the good of the community, they would at once do it. Now it dawned on him that all governments had had for their object the greatest happiness, not of those *over* whom, but of those *by* whom they were exercised. "The interest not of the many but of the few, or even of the one, has been the prevalent interest; and to that interest all others have been at all times sacrificed." His new Scottish friend and protégé, James Mill, was at the same moment equally pessimistic about the prospect of hammering the new political economy of Smith and Malthus into the heads of the prosperous landed aristocracy, Whig or Tory. The thing for both of them to do, therefore, was to take up John Cartwright's democratic prescription and get "the greatest number" into government. In 1807, Sir Francis Burdett had topped the poll as an Independent in the very constituency where Bentham and Mill lived—Westminster, whose scot-and-lot franchise entitled all rate payers to the vote. With prompt unanimity Bentham and Mill began vigorously to promote democracy and Parliamentary reform. Their ends seemed to justify a means that was secondary rather than primary in their thinking. Mill also, with at least the assent of Bentham, performed the astounding feat of seeming to reconcile his friend's principle of the artificial identification of individual interests with Smith's principle of their natural identification and with Malthus' population principle. For a thorough analysis of this unconvincing performance we are indebted to Elie Halévy.[7]

It did not change Bentham. It did not change Chadwick or Southwood Smith. Yet James Mill spent the rest of his life preaching laissez faire and claiming that it was Benthamism.

Space does not permit a discussion of the expedient and often transitory alliances against the landed oligarchy involving Benthamism, Smithism, Cartwrightism, and Malthusianism. In fact, events showed again and again how fragile were these marriages of convenience. In particular, Bentham himself remained preferentially faithful to the "genius" he had tremblingly discovered in himself in 1769 at the age of 21—the genius of legislation, of legislation *for* human happiness, following the principle of utility. Until his death in 1832, he and his coteries at The Hermitage and Ford Abbey gave most of their energies to the *Codes,* those amazingly prophetic and precise anticipations of the collectivized polities under which so much of the world lives today.[8] And Chadwick, Bentham's most stubbornly orthodox disciple, lived on until 1890, with his insistent finger in every interventionist pie from poor law, factory acts, and police to the century-long battle over public responsibility for public health. His unrelenting bureaucratic Benthamism led to his enforced retirement in 1854—"We prefer

---

[6] His first glimpse of enlightenment seems to have come in 1788 (Halévy, *Philosophic Radicalism,* p. 147), but he was diverted until 1808, when, characteristically, he discovered the "principle of self-preference" (*ibid.,* p. 405). The anonymous author of the long review of Bentham's works in *Edinburgh Review,* CLVIII (1843), 460-516, seems mistaken in dating the discovery in 1814 or in 1822 (*ibid.,* 494-502).

[7] *Philosophic Radicalism,* Part I, chap. iii, and Part II. Compare J. S. Mill's assertion about the Philosophical Radicals: "Their mode

of thinking was not characterized by Benthamism in any sense which has relation to Bentham as a chief or guide, but rather by a combination of Bentham's point of view with that of modern political economy, and with the Hartleian metaphysics."—*Autobiography,* edited by J. J. Coss from the original manuscript in the Columbia University Library (New York: Columbia University Press, 1924), p. 73. James Mill's "mind and Bentham's were essentially of different construction."—*Ibid.,* pp. 142-43.

[8] The two hundredth anniversary of his birth. Bentham's own circle was small; James Mill's, particularly after the foundation of the *Westminster Review,* was larger. As J. S. Mill testified: "The influence which Bentham exercised was by his writings . . . . my father exercised a far greater personal ascendancy."—*Autobiography,* p. 71. The writings centered in the *Constitutional Code* and the *Procedure Code,* with parliamentary, judicial, and legal reform proposals emerging concurrently.

to take our chance of cholera and the rest, than to be bullied into health," commented *The Times*—but public-health intervention, like the other Benthamite interventions, could not be stopped. It grew like a rolling snowball and the unabashable Chadwick was knighted thirty-five years later.

It is difficult to summarize justly the interplay of laissez faire and state intervention in Great Britain during the nineteenth century. Much of the difficulty stems from the fact that it was interplay in terms of political power and therefore involved two other forces, the landed interest and the masses, evoking the most curious and impermanent alignments of the four figures in the political dance. Up to 1848 industry and the Philosophical Radicals repeatedly succeeded in using the masses against the land, but the land got its revenge by committing the state to positive intervention in nearly every economic activity, usually on humanitarian, anti-industrial grounds, but practically always keeping as close as possible to Bentham's model of the artificial identification of interests by central authority and local inspectability. The land had both motivation and votes; the pure Benthamites mustered few votes, but they dominated royal commissions and Parliamentary committees by their superb confidence that they knew exactly and scientifically what was to be done. Historically, of course, Toryism has been notably friendly to planning as well as to humanitarianism. The mid-nineteenth century dance, therefore, was like a minuet: Parliamentary reform in 1832, the first effective Factory Act in 1833; Peel's Budget in 1841, the Mines Act in 1842; repeal of the Corn Laws in 1846, the Ten Hours Act in 1847. McCulloch praised the Factory Act of 1833; Macaulay and Lord John Russell successfully defended the Ten Hours bill.

Eighteen hundred forty-eight was far more of an earthquake in Great Britain than the Whig historians would have us believe. It jarred J. S. Mill into forthright denial of his father's mixed creed; it instantly projected Charles Trevelyan and the Treasury into administrative reform. Chartism found new channels into which it carried the prevailing workers' conviction that a man was not a man without a vote. Now all kinds of property were on the defensive against encroaching democracy, and oligarchical paternalism cast about for new justifications. They came to hand with miraculous aptness in the writings of Lyell, Spencer, Wallace, and Darwin. The politically and economically entrenched thereupon boiled these up together into the ruthless form of laissez faire that it has now become fashionable to call Social Darwinism. The iron law of evolution supplanted the iron law of wages.

Already, however, it was too late, for even if the masses had read the authoritarian writings of Bagehot, Fitzjames Stephen, Maine, and Lecky, they would still have demanded and obtained the vote. Disraeli's gamble of 1867 failed to kill democracy by kindness, and Gladstone became a democrat by conviction during the Midlothian campaign of 1879-1880. The "great depression" of 1873-1896 generated the new trade-unionism, a unionism of numbers in place of oligarchy. The majority of the people set out to empower themselves to dictate the answer to Chamberlain's imprudent question: "What ransom will property pay for the security it enjoys?" The democratic revolution was to be a political revolution in the best British tradition. The potential political weight of Labour found expression in what Dicey called "dominant collectivism," "socialism," recognition of "the right to work," and unique legal immunities, thirty-five years before Labour could elect a majority to take over Parliament.

Looking back across the nineteenth century in Great Britain, it is possible to tabulate the parallel developments of laissez faire and state intervention almost year by year. What must be kept in mind in spite of our tendency to polarize opposites is that both were exercises of political power, that is, instrumentalities of several kinds of interest. These interests strove to be the state, to use the state for economic and social ends. Occasionally one or the other triumphed with considerable purity, but never for long, and usually the political enactments represented compromise among them. In the large, power passed from the land to other forms of wealth and from them to the people, but as it did so, and as these three politico-economical elements moved in and out of the possible combinations of two against one, there was an astonishingly consistent inclination to resort to the Benthamite formula for state intervention. Moreover, intervention was always cumulative, building up like a rolling snowball after 1832, whether in factories, railways, shipping, banking, company finance, education, or religion.[9] It might be halted, a chunk or two might even be knocked off the outside, but almost at once it was set going and growing again. What were the Fabians but latter-day Benthamites?

III

Perhaps the aptest commentary on the sturdiness of Benthamite interventionism is provided by John Stuart Mill, the man whose awareness and articulate expression stretched from his father's expedient alliance with Bentham to the Great Divide of 1848, and from 1848 to the Great Depression which spawned the Fabians. It is notorious that Mill has been used and abused by warring interests which have raided the arsenal of his writings with sometimes quite sinister selectivity and disregard of his transitions. This is no occasion for exhaustive exegesis, but an alternative is at hand in evidence drawn from what Mill himself said had happened to him and within him. His *Autobiography* is a very careful composition. Even the glowing references to Mrs. Taylor,

which have been used in order to discredit the whole, will be found to be generous or even extravagant only in generalization; the specific references to her share in his work are studiously measured and precise and made perhaps ten years after her death. Set against Mill's actions and other utterances, the *Autobiography* stands out as a surer guide than any commentator.[10]

As the second of three reasons for leaving his autobiography to posterity, Mill said: "It has also seemed to me that in an age of transition in opinions, there may be somewhat both of interest and of benefit in noting the successive phases of any mind which was always pressing forward, equally ready to learn and to unlearn either from its own thoughts or from those of others." From babyhood to the age of fourteen, he was subjected by a tyrannical, irascible, fanatical father to an inhuman regimen of study which isolated him from boys of his own age and culminated in "a complete course of political economy," that is, in James Mill's blending of Smith, Malthus, and Ricardo. John Mill at fifteen served as critic and proofreader of the first version of his father's *Elements of Political Economy*, which was published in 1821. Yet that same year, "an epoch in my life," he discovered what were to be woven into its central strand: Bentham's basic principles as they had taken form during the last quarter of the eighteenth century and had been communicated to the world in 1802 by Etienne Dumont in *Traités de législation*. "Here indeed was the commencement of a new era in thought. . . . . I had become a different being." He read everything else of Bentham that he could find. "This was my private reading: while, under my father's direction, my studies were carried into the higher branches of analytic psychology." From 1822 to 1826 he and a very few young men conducted the intimate discussions of their Utilitarian Society. In 1825, aged nineteen, he undertook to edit and publish in

[9] For instance, the factory inspectors of the thirties secured the co-operation of the "good" manufacturers, and thereby the growth of intervention, by agreeing to enforce the regulations upon their "rascally" competitors. Cf. the "Honest Manufacturer" and the "Reducer" (of wages) in L. S. Marshall, *The Development of Public Opinion in Manchester* (Syracuse: Syracuse University Press, 1947), pp. 215-17.

[10] It does not mention Marx, Engels, or Darwin, but neither, in effect, did Dicey, forty years later.

three volumes Bentham's writings on evidence.

In the autumn of 1826 this Benthamite son of a harsh laissez-faire father fell into deep disillusionment, "left stranded at the commencement of my voyage, with a well-equipped ship and a rudder, but no sail." During 1827 and 1828 he began to find his way out through arguments with Tories, Coleridgians, and Owenites of the Debating Society at the Freemasons' Tavern and through the poetry of Wordsworth. He became aware of feeling, discovered the narrowness of both James Mill and Macaulay, and began to sift from the writings of the Saint-Simonians and Comte what he found congenial. He acquired "a conviction that the true system [of political philosophy] was something much more complex and many-sided than I had previously had any idea of." Through Coleridge, Carlyle, and the French writers, his "eyes were opened to the very limited and temporary value of the old political economy, which assumes private property and inheritance as indefeasible facts." Before the French Revolution of 1830 broke out, before he met or could be influenced by Mrs. Taylor, before the grand campaign for the Reform Bill, John Stuart Mill had become what might be called a liberal socialist.

While, in his estimation, the Philosophical Radicals after 1832 were sinking "into a mere côté gauche of the Whig Party," Mill discovered Tocqueville and, during the Hungry Forties, moved with his only kindred spirit, Mrs. Taylor, into the "third period" of his mental progress. "I had now completely turned back from what there had been of excess in my reaction against Benthamism. . . . . We were now much less democrats than I had been, because so long as education continues to be so wretchedly imperfect, we dreaded the ignorance and especially the selfishness and brutality of the mass: but our ideal of ultimate improvement went far beyond Democracy, and would class us decidedly under the general designation of Socialists."

As he wrote his own *Principles of Politi-*

cal Economy between the autumn of 1845 and the end of 1847, he expressed these ideals very cautiously, but his subtitle read *With Some of Their Applications to Social Philosophy,* and the chapter on "The Probable Futurity of the Labouring Classes," he felt, gave the book its tone. "This tone consisted chiefly in making the proper distinction between the laws of the Production of Wealth, which are real laws of nature, dependent on the properties of objects, and the modes of its Distribution, which, subject to certain conditions, depend on human will." The Revolution of 1848 broke out in Paris while his book was in press; in the second edition he became more explicit; and in the third "quite unequivocal," for "the public mind became more open to the reception of novelties in opinion, and doctrines appeared moderate which would have been thought very startling a short time before." Thus, as Henry Sidgwick distastefully remarked: "In short, the study planted by Adam Smith and watered by Ricardo had, in the third quarter of the nineteenth century, imbibed a full measure of the spirit of Saint-Simon and Owen—and that in England, the home of what the Germans call *Manchestertum.*"

John Mill's subsequent writings fall naturally into place. *Liberty,* written 1854-1859, voiced his fears, both of complete democracy before general education and of "that tyranny of society over the individual which most Socialistic systems are supposed to involve." *Considerations on Representative Government* and *The Subjection of Women,* both written 1860-1861, stated some of the conditions necessary to make imminent complete democracy tolerable. *Utilitarianism,* revised from earlier articles during the same years, reaffirmed, with modifications chiefly concerning liberty, his essential Benthamism. *Sir William Hamilton's Philosophy,* written 1862-1863, was necessitated by "the prevailing tendency to regard all the marked distinctions of human character as innate, and in the main indelible." *Auguste Comte and Positivism,* 1865, represented "the task of sifting what is good from

what is bad in M. Comte's speculations."
The essay which we know as *On Social
Freedom*,[11] in which Mill abjured the
"fallacy" that law is the basic threat to
liberty, and which, like the essay *Socialism*
of 1869, reaffirmed "The Necessary Limits
of Individual Freedom Arising out of the
Conditions of our Social Life,"[12] may not
have been published because, up to his
death in 1873, Mill had not been able logically to reconcile the authoritarian and the
libertarian elements of the socialistic creed
to which he had become intellectually and
sincerely attached over forty years earlier.

Mill, then, throughout his independent
life and thought was at bottom the Benthamite interventionist, not the apostle of
laissez faire. Furthermore, he early acquired
a sense of humanity and a sense of history.
In 1830 he decided "that any general theory
or philosophy of politics presupposes a previous theory of human progress, and that
this is the same thing with a philosophy of
history." His was a world of transition,
transition which he did not specifically
attach to industrialism and its accompaniments, but which he refrained from per-
verting into the myths of Social Darwinism.
For, above all, he was honest, he was
humane, and he was humble. He sensed the
irresistible advent of democracy, and of
democracy's recourse to the state for equali-
zation of circumstance, long before either
became dominant,[13] but he chose, not to
scheme against them, but rather to welcome
them as just, and to rely upon education[14]
and upon his country's heritage of liberty

[11] First published in *Oxford and Cambridge
Review* in June 1907; and with an introduction
by Dorothy Fosdick (New York: Columbia
University Press, 1941).

[12] The subtitle of *On Social Freedom.*

[13] "That government is always in the hands,
or passing into the hands, of whatever is the
strongest power in society, and that what this
power is, does not depend on institutions, but
institutions on it . . . ."—*Autobiography,* p. 114.

[14] "Education, habit, and the cultivation of
the sentiments, will make a common man dig
or weave for his country, as readily as fight for
his country . . . . the hindrance is not in the
essential constitution of human nature . . . ."—
Ibid., p. 163.

to domesticate them in some new compromise between man and his environment.
Locke had made liberty inseparable from
property. Mill believed that the oncoming,
fully democratic state might be made to
operate in such a way that both might be
equitably shared among all of its citizens.

IV

In the historical view, neither laissez faire
nor state intervention was the engine of
change in nineteenth-century Britain. Instead, both were constant accompaniments
of the basic force—industrialization. Politics
was as usual the agency resorted to for the
adaptation of society to profound, pervasive
alterations, and the central state gradually
became vital in the lives of more and more
men. Industrialization had broken the cake
of custom, destroying the old, flexible, local
apparatus of community. The new enterprisers wanted new freedoms, but also new
services, and extracted both from the state.
The old enterprisers and the new workers
were stripped of old protections and used
their political weight to create new protections. Meanwhile, expanding industrialization was producing ever greater economic
and social interdependence, ever greater
needs for mutual action. Labor, that is to
say the majority of the people, moved
toward command of this situation, first as
agitators manipulated by others, then as
trade-unionists and co-operators acting for
themselves, and finally as voters bent upon
overlapping enough of the middle classes
to be able to direct the state into the comprehensive collective responsibilities of to-
day. The old local sense of community
and mutuality found new expression in centralized forms. Political mutualism, on a
national scale, was emerging as the British
ethic, and Jeremy Bentham, not Adam
Smith, was its prophet.

Appendix: State Intervention in
Nineteenth-Century Britain

Even a diagram of the parallels of laissez
faire and state intervention during the nineteenth century would be too large to be

feasible here, but the principal categories of the latter may be indicated and dated in order to be set against the more familiar examples of the former. Especially noteworthy are the scale and variety of state intervention during the years 1825-1870 which Dicey characterized "The Period of Individualism." It is manifestly impracticable to separate the humane, the political, the economic, and the religious objectives of these interventions, or to differentiate sharply one period from another. The one common characteristic is the consistent readiness of interested groups to use the state for collectivist ends.

In the regulation of labor and industry, the century began under the modified Elizabethan statutes and the panicky prohibition of workers' combinations. In 1802 the first Factory Act achieved little to protect "the health and morals of apprentices" in textile factories, and the repeal in 1813-1814 of important provisions of the Elizabethan statutes as to wages and apprenticeship was followed in 1824-1825 by the legalization of trade-unions and the first ineffectual arbitration act. The Factory Act of 1833 set up Bentham's prescription of central authority and subordinate local inspectors with powers to make and enforce regulations. It was followed next year by a Poor Law (also Benthamite in apparatus) which attempted vainly to prohibit outdoor relief and at the same time to make workhouse life "less eligible" than any other available employment. The Factory Act of 1833 was followed by a series of similar statutes (chimney sweeps, 1840; mines, 1842; ten hours acts, 1847-1850; etc.) which regulated the workers' hours, safety, education, and so on, thereby building the approaches to state-promoted arbitration of disputes (1867-1896), employers' liability (1880-1897), and minimum wages (1909-1912). The courts repeatedly used interpretations of conspiracy and of the master-servant relationship to wear away statutory legalization of trade-unions, thereby evoking new statutes (Tolpuddle Laborers, 1834; "New Model" unions, 1851 on; *Hornby* v. *Close,*

1867; Trade Union acts, 1867, 1871, 1875; Taff Vale, 1900; Trade Disputes Act, 1906; Osborne Judgment, 1910; Trade Union Act, 1911; and so on to 1946).

In the promotion and regulation of economic enterprise by the state, there might be listed the railway companies acts from 1823 on, involving compulsory sale of rights of way; abolition of the slave trade (1807) and of slavery (1833); the reformed post office (1840)[15] and nationalization of telegraphs, telephones, and broadcasting (1856-1869, 1878-1911, 1922); inspection and enforcement of standards of amenity, safety, legality, and so forth, in steam power, railways, mercantile marine, gas and water supply, weights and measures, food adulteration, patents, bankruptcy, and so on, by the metamorphosed Board of Trade and the Home Office (after 1825); and the facilitation and regulation of limited-liability joint-stock companies (1856-1862). A great variety of land acts notably restricted freedom of contract in a number of ways.

Closely connected with these activities were the reform and expansion of the civil service which began about 1800 and accelerated greatly with Peel's fiscal reforms (1841-1846) and the revolutions of 1848. There might also be added the so-called "municipal trading" in markets, docks, water, gas, bathhouses, tramways, electric power, housing, slum clearance, lodginghouses, hospitals, libraries, museums, and so forth, which grew rapidly from about 1850 on. Reform of the criminal law, of other law, of procedure, and of the courts (1816-1873) was regarded by Benthamites as positive state action, and was paralleled by permissive protective police (1829-1839) which became obligatory in 1856.

The "sanitary idea," or assumption by government (central or local) of preventive responsibility for public health, was originally (1820-1847) promoted by Southwood

[15] Always a great and irresistibly attractive engine of taxation. See Howard Robinson, *The British Post Office* (Princeton: Princeton University Press, 1948).

Smith and Chadwick in pure Benthamite terms and invigorated by the Asiatic cholera which struck England in 1831 and at intervals later, but this centralized program conflicted, not only with endlessly ramified private properties and privileges, but also with jealous local government. Thus their central Board of Health (1848-1854) gave way to local authority, which in turn came under the view of a central Local Government Board in 1871, of a new Sanitary Code in 1875, of a new Local Government Act in 1888, and went back under strong Benthamite central control in the twentieth century.

In some ways the most surprising intervention by the state was in the property and privileges of the Established Church. The exclusive civil and educational privileges of Anglicans were whittled away almost continuously from 1813 to 1891. Parliamentary grants to a Church Building Commission from 1818 on and grants toward education in Ireland furnished the precedents for grants in aid of British education, Anglican and non-Anglican, which expanded enormously from 1833 on to the provision of public education in 1870, which became compulsory in 1880, and free in 1891. The Whig, Sir James Graham, in his popular, but unsuccessful, scheme of 1843 for national education, followed the Benthamite model of the factory and poor law acts, if not the elaboration of Bentham's *Chresto-mathia* or the educational provisions of the *Constitutional Code*. Leading Tories and Whigs agreed, but other matters proved more pressing. Marriage was regulated in 1835, divorce in 1857, and burial in 1880. The greatest impact of the state, however, was on church property. The Ecclesiastical Commission of 1836 (further empowered in 1840 and 1850), a kind of perpetual corporation, set out to remedy the scandalous anomalies then existing. Acting on the assumption that the property of the bishops and chapters ought to be employed for the benefit of the church as a whole, they got rid of pluralism, sinecures, and other abuses and reapportioned ecclesiastical income equitably so as to improve the poorer benefices and to establish new ones. A persistent process, also begun in 1836, regulated tithes and church rates.

Other interventions by the state, as, for instance, in provision of small holdings or in extending the legal protection of married women's property from the rich and prudential to the poor and improvident, might be assembled, but the examples above, even if regarded narrowly in their economic aspects, constitute appreciable qualifications of "The Triumph of Laissez Faire." They furnish historical background for A. W. Macmahon's recent assertion that *"laissez-faire* is quite literally the only untried utopia."

J. B. B.

THE SOCIAL AND ECONOMIC CHANGES that Britain was undergoing in the nineteenth century were often mirrored in the imaginative literature of the time. Many nineteenth-century British writers were convinced that literature should serve as a weapon of reform, and in their works they voiced their indignation at existing conditions in the hope of making their readers aware of specific abuses. The use of English literature for purposes of social protest was, of course, nothing new. The fourteenth-century author of *Piers Plowman* had used literature in that way; so, too, had scores of writers in Tudor, Stuart, and eighteenth-century England. It was, however, in early Victorian times that the literature of social protest assumed unprecedented proportions.

Writer after writer made it part of his mission to expose the evils that marred English industrial society and to champion the oppressed. Of these writers probably the best known to American readers are, first, Charles Dickens and, second, Elizabeth Barrett Browning, whose stirring poem *The Cry of the Children* (1843) is rarely omitted from anthologies of English literature for American schools. But Dickens and Mrs. Browning were only two of many. In the essay that follows, Professor William O. Aydelotte, of the State University of Iowa, examines skillfully the social criticisms of some of the leading novelist-publicists of early-Victorian England. He centers his discussion on Dickens, but he has much of interest to say about the ideas of some of Dickens' contemporaries.

THE ENGLAND OF MARX AND MILL AS REFLECTED IN FICTION
WILLIAM O. AYDELOTTE

I

The economic distress and the new concern with social problems in England in the 1840's, which underlay the reformulations of political economy in that decade, had also an extensive and significant reflection in imaginative literature. While the novel with a thesis, even a social thesis, was nothing new, it was only in the forties that English literature began to deal on a major scale with the social problems raised by the industrial revolution. One can sense in the novels of this decade an increased urgency and pressure, a more daring and direct attack. This emphasis is so marked that one critic has attempted a correlation between literature and socialism, and has sought to find in the novels of Dickens the same type of social observation and emotional reaction that prompted the analyses of Karl Marx.[1] While such a thesis goes too far and is almost certainly invalid, one can nevertheless find in these novels a historical meaning of a different sort, more complex, but also more interesting and suggestive to the historian.

[1] T. A. Jackson, *Charles Dickens, the Progress of a Radical* (New York: International Publishers Co., 1938).

It is impossible to summarize in a few words what is really a considerable body of literature, but at least some notion can be given of its extent and scope. Four writers of the period are especially important: Charles Dickens in his novels of the 1840's developed a vein of social criticism that he was to intensify in his writings of the fifties and sixties. Mrs. Gaskell portrayed labor-management relations in *Mary Barton* (1848) and, a few years later, in *North and South* (1855). Charles Kingsley began to work out his attitude toward the rural poor in *Yeast* (1848) and dealt with the urban workers and the Chartists in *Alton Locke* (1850). Disraeli tried to survey the whole political, social, and spiritual malaise of the times in his trilogy of *Coningsby* (1844), *Sybil* (1845), and *Tancred* (1847). But these four were not the only ones. Mrs. Trollope opened the decade with a novel on factory conditions, *Michael Armstrong, the Factory Boy;* and even Charlotte Brontë in *Shirley* (1849) turned to the unfamiliar topic of troubles between millowners and operatives in the period 1810-1812. In a different but related field of social criticism, Thackeray was dissecting the values of fashionable society and the attitudes of *arrivistes* in his sketches for *Punch* and in *Vanity*

Reprinted by special permission from *The Journal of Economic History, Supplement,* VIII (1948), 42-58.

Fair (1847). The new social emphasis was by no means restricted to fiction; it might be illustrated in other forms of literature by the poems of Elizabeth Barrett Browning and Thomas Hood, or by the writings of Carlyle.

What can the historian learn from these novelists? Their range is wide and all together they deal with most of the important social questions of the period: the New Poor Law, slums, public health, factory conditions, unemployment, class hostilities, labor-management relations, and, above all, the economic distress of the petty *bourgeoisie* and the working classes. One would then expect them to be a mine of information for the social historian. Yet in effect they are not, for the factual information they provide about social conditions is highly suspect for the scholar's purposes; it is spotty, impressionistic, and inaccurate. These writers were primarily novelists and artists; their reporting of social conditions is always limited by the background and interests of the writer and, still more important, subordinate to his artistic purpose. It should be understood from the start that, for the facts about social conditions in this period, our other and more conventional sources are far more satisfactory; and the attempt to tell the social history of a period by quotations from its novels is a kind of dilettantism which the historian would do well to avoid.

The historical interest of these novels lies in something quite different: in what they reveal about the opinions and attitudes of the men who wrote them. A novel helps to show not the facts of the age, but the mind of the novelist, not social conditions, but attitudes toward social conditions. The historical value of fiction, often misconceived, unfortunately, is not for the history of facts but for the history of opinions. A novelist may not be typical of his age— more often he is not—but at least his attitudes constitute one datum in our total picture of a climate of opinion. In this delicate subject of the history of the formation of opinions, a novel is the more illuminating

because of its highly personal and subjective character; a novelist will sometimes reveal things about himself, basic attitudes, unconscious preconceptions, even motives, which other men would succeed in keeping hidden. A study of the novelists of the 1840's, this crucial decade in the formation of new ideas and attitudes, may throw a fresh light on the new concern of the educated classes for the sufferings of the poor in an industrial society.

Taking the four most important social novelists of the decade, Dickens, Kingsley, Disraeli, and Mrs. Gaskell, we will try first to say what were the social attitudes reflected in their writings, and second to trace as far as possible the factors that lay behind these attitudes.

II

Anyone who wants to discuss these novels of the 1840's starts with a great advantage because of the admirable study of them published by Louis François Cazamian forty-five years ago. There is no need to retraverse the ground that he has so well covered, and instead of dealing at length with his exposition, I should prefer to make a fresh start and try to put the whole matter in a different way, suggesting a few reformulations that seem important in the light of our present understanding of the period.

Even allowing for the individual differences that we find in any group of artists, it seems fair to say that in general terms all four of these novelists exhibit in their social opinions a common attitude. It is really a double attitude, the two halves of which might appear inconsistent to a modern reader. On the one hand, they display a great sympathy for and interest in the underprivileged, an indignant protest against the treatment of the poor in modern society. On the other hand, they show also a negative or conservative aspect which I shall describe more fully in a moment.

The positive aspect, the element of social protest, need not detain us, for it is the best-understood feature of this literature.

It manifests itself, of course, not in any restatement of economic theory, but in an emotional attitude. The student who, following A. V. Dicey's argument, seeks in this literature evidence of the impending change from individualism to socialism will find slim pickings. The practical proposals of these writers are amazingly tame in comparison with the vehemence of their social criticism, and they were more generally on the side of private philanthropy than of state action. Dickens' criticisms of philanthropy relate more to method than to principle, and philanthropy remained the solution he sought in his private life as well as in the denouements of his novels—the benevolent man with a long purse who rewards the virtuous. Dickens had a kind of horror of the state in all its aspects, Parliament and bureaucracy alike, and it is hard to imagine him wanting to entrust the welfare of the people of England to the Circumlocution Office. Kingsley at the end of *Alton Locke* proposes Christian philanthropy as a substitute for discredited Chartism, and Mrs. Gaskell seems to find her solution of the labor-management problem, not in acts of Parliament, but in charity and mutual sympathy. Some of these writers do support factory and public-health legislation, but these measures do not loom large in the total picture of what they wanted done. Their attitude is hardly surprising. The issue between state action and philanthropy, so important to us, was by no means so clear to the generality of men in the 1840's, who seem to have made no very sharp distinction between the two procedures. The collectivist aspects of the factory acts, which

now seem highly significant, were less apparent to men at the time, who thought of these acts more as limited measures to remedy particular grievances, not as a precedent for socialism. Factory legislation in the nineteenth century was even supported by the skilled trade-unions, "administrative nihilists" who were altogether opposed to any socialistic policy. In the forties private bills were still frequent in Parliament, and Parliamentary action on behalf of the poor could be regarded simply as a means of carrying further the policies of private philanthropy.

These four writers display, not so much a consistent demand for state action, but more what Cazamian happily describes as a sense of social solidarity. They repudiated rationalistic utilitarianism, often through the mouth of a principal character speaking obviously for the author: Disraeli through Sidonia; Dickens through Cissy Jupe; Mrs. Gaskell in Job's reply to Mr. Carson; Kingsley perhaps through Tregarva. Although they failed, like most of their contemporaries, to anticipate the potentialities of the state for social services, it is much more important that they gave expression to demands for social improvement which a later generation was to implement by state action. In this respect, this literature is of central importance, since it expresses the psychological or deeper aspects of the reaction against economic individualism.

We may now turn to the negative side, the framework or boundaries in which the social ideals of these authors were constrained, the factors which constituted a limitation on their demands for reform. Here again

THOMAS HOOD: English humanitarian poet (d. 1845) who in *The Lay of the Labourer, The Workhouse Clock, The Bridge of Sighs,* and *The Song of the Shirt* came to the defense of downtrodden elements in English society.

CHARLES KINGSLEY: English clergyman, journalist, novelist, and social reformer (d. 1875). Hostile to chartism because of its antireligious flavor, he helped to launch the Christian Socialist movement in Britain. His novels exposing the miseries of the working classes, *Yeast* (1848) and *Alton Locke* (1850), were widely read and discussed in early-Victorian England. In the latter part of his life he served as professor of modern history at Cambridge.

we must allow for wide individual differences. Even so, we can see fairly clearly three principal elements that all these novelists have in common: (1) they looked to the past instead of the future; (2) they favored a system of class distinctions; (3) they showed little sympathy for democracy. All this is the more surprising in that they occasionally displayed inclinations in a different direction. Disraeli co-operated with the Radicals against the New Poor Law. Mrs. Gaskell was rebuked by Greg and others for taking too strongly the line of the poor in *Mary Barton.* Kingsley described himself as a "Christian Socialist," and even on one occasion as a "Chartist." Dickens called himself a Radical and was undoubtedly so thought of by his contemporaries.

1. Yet when we analyze this literature, we find that so far from being revolutionary it has signs of what might almost be described as an archaic character: all these writers show a nostalgia for the past and a tendency to seek the solution of their problems in institutions or formulas borrowed from the past. This may be illustrated most simply by the vogue of the historical novel in the 1840's. The fashion had, of course, been set by Scott. But his example was followed in the mid-century period, not only by writers of straight historical romances like Harrison Ainsworth and G. P. R. James, but by most of the better-known novelists as well. Kingsley wrote three historical novels, Dickens two, and Mrs. Gaskell one. Charlotte Brontë went back a generation, to the Napoleonic age, for the scene of *Shirley.* Thackeray also reverted to that period in *Vanity Fair* and to the early eighteenth century in *Henry Esmond.* Disraeli's novels are soaked in historical background and constitute a kind of rhapsody upon the past. This reversion to a departed age is common enough also in other aspects of the intellectual history of the period; one thinks at once of the medieval interlude in *Past and Present,* or of the Oxford movement and the doctrine of apostolical succession.

A deeper current of nostalgia for the past shows in other ways, for example, in Disraeli's lengthy historical justifications for his ideas in *Sybil.* Or again, Mrs. Gaskell's theme in *North and South* is not simply a return to the labor-management problem of *Mary Barton;* it is also, and still more, as is pointed up in the title, a contrast between the old and new civilizations: the agricultural, patriarchal, traditional south as opposed to the bustling, industrial north. And Mrs. Gaskell clearly prefers the south, though she tries also to be fair to Mr. Thornton, the manufacturer. The romantic appeal to the Middle Ages is a common theme in Kingsley; he expresses it, to give one example, in a letter to a friend: "I would, if I could, restore the feudal system, the highest form of civilization—in ideal, not in practice—which Europe has ever seen."

2. All four of these writers lay a principal emphasis on the leadership of the upper classes in improving society; they are nonequalitarian and unwilling to see workingmen take part in determining their own destiny. Their frequent attacks on the higher orders do not conceal the general respect they all have for position and authority; they attack individuals rather than the upper class as a whole. There is never any suggestion that the well-to-do should abdicate the duties of government. On the contrary, all of these writers regard action by workingmen on their own initiative as suspect. Chartism seems to them a menace, and a trade-union, though they can sympathize with the needs and wants that lie behind it, is something mysterious and sinister. Dickens is at pains to show in *Hard Times* that unions do not help the workingman and that the union organizer is an unscrupulous agitator. And Kingsley, though he was willing to help in the founding of workingmen's co-operatives, posted a placard to the Chartists in April 1848 telling them in effect to cease their agitation and let their friends among the upper classes take care of things.

The working class cannot lead itself, as

Disraeli makes Egremont say to Sybil: "The People are not strong; the People never can be strong. Their attempts at self-vindication will end only in suffering and confusion. . . . . You deem you are in darkness, and I see a dawn. The new generation of the aristocracy of England are not tyrants, not oppressors, Sybil, as you persist in believing. Their intelligence, better than that, their hearts, are open to the responsibility of their position. . . . . Enough that their sympathies are awakened; time and thought will bring the rest. They are the natural leaders of the People, Sybil; believe me they are the only ones."

All these novelists see life from an upper-class angle, to such an extent that they even have difficulty in visualizing their proletarian characters. In contrast to the many successful portraits of middle-class figures, characters of the proletarian class are not vividly depicted, not completely realized; they tend to be one-dimensional. This is true for Kingsley; also to some extent for Dickens, whose Stephen Blackpool is no proletarian hero but a mere model of meekness. Mrs. Gaskell had perhaps the most extensive personal acquaintance of any of them with the industrial poor, yet one recent critic, Lord David Cecil, thinks she is least successful in exactly this aspect of her work, where she tries to report on the social situation she has observed. Even Disraeli's accounts of the working classes, though based on the latest information from the government blue books, do not ring true. They are well documented, but they are not alive. It was perhaps impossible for these writers to regard a working-class background as anything but a stigma; hence, a working-class character was someone they could not completely enter into or identify themselves with. Mrs. Gaskell chose a woman of this class as the heroine of one of her social novels, but she is much closer to Margaret Hale than she is to Mary Barton. Disraeli's proletarian heroine, Sybil, turns out to be the daughter of a nobleman. Her father, Stephen Gerard, whom Disraeli plays up as the possessor of the true proletarian virtues, proves in the end to be the rightful Earl of Marney.

3. Such an attitude implies a lack of sympathy with democracy, and the interest of these four writers in democracy is at best only lukewarm. Kingsley commiserated the Chartists on being excluded from "a Freeman's just right of voting," but he promised to get for them "something nobler than Charters and dozens of Acts of Parliament —more useful than this 'fifty thousandth share in a Talker in the National Palaver at Westminster' can give you." The borrowing of a phrase from Carlyle is significant. When Kingsley wrote in his first "Parson Lot" letter that "my only quarrel with the Charter is that it does not go far enough in reform," all he seems to have meant was that he thought reform should be spiritual rather than material. He was no enthusiast for unlimited democracy. Disraeli makes his sophistical plea against democracy when Coningsby protests to Oswald Millbank he has no wish to abjure the representative principle, but representation is not necessarily, nor even in a principal sense, parliamentary. The representation of the press is far more complete than the representation of Parliament. Parliamentary representation, says Coningsby, is the happy device of a ruder age to which it was well adapted; it now shows symptoms of desuetude.

The antipathy to democracy among Victorian intellectuals is, of course, by no means restricted to these four writers. One could add other novelists, the Trollopes and Charles Reade for example, and critical writers like Carlyle, Ruskin, Maine, and Lecky. The hostility of creative writers to democracy in the mid-nineteenth century has been brought out and interestingly treated by B. E. Lippincott in his *Victorian Critics of Democracy;* it was not just an exceptional affair, but a major phenomenon of the age.

We can get more closely into the problem by taking up in detail a single example. Dickens exemplifies all three of these tendencies, though in doing so he also shows a certain ambivalence, and seems at times to reverse them completely: he was impatient with the past, he violently attacked the governing classes, and he proclaimed himself a Radical in politics. Yet the pattern, though complex, is clear.

1. Toward the past, Dickens appears to share all the Radical prejudices. He was not historically minded, he had no gift for entering into the point of view of another epoch; like Thomas Paine he weighed the past by the standards of the present and found it all a great mistake. In his *Child's History of England,* as well as in his correspondence and in his historical novels, he attacked the past, the Middle Ages, and the Catholic church in true Benthamite fashion. Among the dummy books he had made for his library was a seven-volume set called The Wisdom of Our Ancestors, the different volumes being entitled Ignorance, Superstition, Dirt, Disease, and such names—an idea ultimately derived, whether Dickens knew it or not, from a passage in the writings of Bentham.

But behind this superficial modernism lurks an affection for the old preindustrial England. Though Dickens' intentions were not reactionary, his instinctive preferences led him to the past rather than to the future. The customs and habits he described have an archaic flavor; and he had a habit of putting the setting of his novels about twenty years back even when he was attacking contemporary abuses. Although he lived in the city and wrote about it and caught much of its atmosphere and poetry, he shows also a yearning and affection for the countryside. The country appears as a significant symbol in several of his books, generally associated with a lightening of mood. (See, for example, Little Nell's escape to the country with her grandfather, or David Copperfield's journey down the Dover Road.) His love for his country house at Gad's Hill, with its Falstaffian associations, forms a part of this. We sense consistently in Dickens a sentimental affection for an old rural England, an England perhaps that never was, represented by stagecoaches, cold milk punch, and Christmas at Dingley Dell.

2. Dickens is, of course, famous for his satire of the governing classes: in a series of sharp and bitter portraits he attacks both the aristocracy, which seems to him to be preying upon society, and the rich *bourgeoisie,* who play a larger and even more ominous role in his novels. In contrast to this, he glorifies the lower orders, apparently as the really decent people, the representatives of the basic values he tries to inculcate.

But Dickens' attitude to the upper classes may be very easily misunderstood. The great point—and one which may escape a modern reader at first glance—is that when Dickens describes a wicked rich man he is portraying a moral type and not a class type. The notion that a man's conduct could be determined by his economic position, that a rich man is compelled by his class affiliation to be a menace to society, is entirely alien to Dickens. The callousness and neglect shown by the upper classes toward the lower is for him, not the inevitable product of sociological relationships, but simply a moral lapse. He condemns not the bourgeois class as a whole, which is what some modern critics have tried to read into him, but rather the moral faults exhibited by individuals.

Dickens, like the others, has a disposition to view things from the upper-class angle. His lower-middle-class characters (he deals relatively little with the proletariat) receive in general sympathetic treatment, but they are seldom persons with whom the reader is tempted to identify himself. They may be virtuous in the highest degree, "nature's gentlemen," but they are also a little ridiculous—Miss La Creevy, Newman Noggs, Mrs. Todgers, Captain Cuttle, and the whole gallery. Dickens is friendly to them, but also condescending. His heroes and heroines, by contrast, who play for the most part "straight" and not comic roles, are almost invariably of gentle birth, above the general line of social demarcation that he seems to make. Little Nell is socially redeemed by having a rich relation, and Oliver Twist by being (like Gerard in *Sybil*) a missing heir. Barnaby Rudge, though he gives his name to the book, is not a hero in the usual sense, not a "young, walking gentleman." Even Pip, though he comes to despise some, not all, of the values his education has given him, has nevertheless acquired these values; they have become a part of him and help to make up the point of view from which the story is told.

Contrary to what is sometimes asserted, Dickens was no equalitarian. In *The Chimes* he satirizes those who expect the poor to know their station. But that is exactly what he does expect himself, and this unconscious demand of his may be illustrated by the fact that the "good" poor in his novels always do know their stations: Mark Tapley, Mr. Peggotty, Joe Gargery, and the others. Dickens, in other words, is not opposed to the upper class as a class; he hopes not to destroy it but to educate and reform it, to produce in it a change of heart. He preaches, not against the upper class, but to it. He has no wish to equalize ranks; in fact, he not only accepts the current distinctions but even seems to welcome them. He is sympathetic to the poor, but his object is, as Edmund Wilson well puts it, to make the poor real to the upper classes.

3. Dickens' attitude to democracy is of a piece with this. Although the reforms he occasionally demanded could be accomplished only by act of Parliament, his final position seems to have been to give Parliament up as hopeless, to reject it as a possible agency of reform. This rejection was not partial or conditional; it was absolute. "I solemnly declare to you," he wrote to Sir Joseph Paxton in 1857, "that direfully against my will, I have come to the conclusion that representative Government is a miserable failure among us." This could be paralleled by similar passages in other letters. Dickens expressed always for Parliament a horror and disgust, dating and partly deriving no doubt from his early thralldom as a Parliamentary reporter.

III

We come now to the explanation. All that has been said so far goes to show that the radical interpretation of these authors is wrong, that we can in no way describe them as being in the vanguard of revolution. Neither collectivism nor democracy has any particular appeal for them. Yet, since we are looking for attitudes rather than theories, we may claim to find in them an attitude that is logically not unconnected with the development of collectivism later. Although they foresee little of the functions the state was to assume toward the end of the century, they do show a new appreciation of social problems and a more vigorous concern about the condition of the people, the kind of concern that was part of the basis of an increased assumption of responsibility by the state in the generations that followed.

We do not on the other hand find in them attitudes that could be said to lead logically to any sympathy with democracy. The drift is nonequalitarian, and what little they have to say about democracy is either unfavorable or at best unenthusiastic. This is the puzzle. Why did these novelists, with their intense social concern, and living in an age when democratic liberalism was on the offensive, tend so strongly to the opposed point of view?

Part of the answer might be found in a closer analysis of the times. Democracy, even if it seemed the creed of the future, had still only a limited application in the 1840's. Universal suffrage was still far ahead, the working classes had almost no political power and were not to become any kind of a force in Parliament for another fifty years. What social reform there was, even when it came through Parliament, was from the top down, strictly benevolent and philanthropic. It is plausible to argue, then, that these writers simply took their cue from the time, and did not think of democracy as a serious possibility for practical politics. By this argument it would be anachronistic to regard them as making a choice between democracy and philanthropy, for democracy was not vividly enough presented to their imaginations for them to regard it as a possible alternative, or for them to have any sense of choosing. One might also argue that the liberal creed, which embraced democracy, also embraced economic individualism against which these writers were to varying degrees in rebellion. Yet this may be pushing things too hard; there is much doubt that men of the 1840's would be so keenly alive to this ideological alignment. More important, perhaps, is the effect of Tory propaganda for social reform in this decade, in which we could include not only the "Tory radicals" in politics, but also Carlyle, whose influence on all four of these novelists was substantial. One might argue, along this line, that Toryism was a synthesis to which a literary man concerned with problems of human suffering might naturally turn.

But this will not quite answer. To begin with, it goes much too far to say that no one in that age took democracy as a serious possibility. On the contrary, this was a period of aggressive liberalism, and universal suffrage was being advocated from many different sources. To mention three sources that come to mind at once: democratic proposals had issued from the Jacobins in France, from the Chartists in England, and, above all, formed a part of the philosophy of Bentham. The anti-Jacobin scare had lost a lot of its punch by the 1840's, and England was deeply stirred by events across the channel. Chartism was, far from being unfamiliar, an object of major concern to all four of these novelists —they were, of course, hostile to it. Benthamism was the dominating political philosophy of the age, and must have been present in some form in the minds of all of them, particularly Dickens, who had spent four years of his early manhood reporting debates in the newly reformed Parliament. Dickens indeed thought of himself as a Radical: he accepted the editorship of the *Daily News* in 1846, which had been founded to advocate the Cobden-Bright line, and he reflects Radical influence in other ways, as in the attack on the abuses of the past.

Nor does it take us very far to say that these writers were influenced by the propaganda of Tory reformism. The role of the Tories in economic reform, incidentally, may have been somewhat exaggerated by scholars in the last few years. In any case, it does not explain this literature to demonstrate that the attitudes it reflects bear a resemblance to attitudes displayed by other groups at the same time. We have to show further why these writers imitated one attitude and not another. To point out a resemblance is not to offer an explanation. And it would be hard to fit these writers, who were none of them (except Kingsley in a minor way) aristocrats, into the pattern of opportunistic Tory landowners, needling the Whig factory magnates for the sake of political advantage, or to see them as inheritors of the aristocratic tradition of feudal benevolence.

The difficulty in any interpretation of literature in the light of the times in which it was written is the simplistic assumption that literature takes its character from something we vaguely refer to as the "spirit of the age." This assumption is a fallacious short cut which closes the road to accurate analysis. Literature is, of course, affected by the age in which it is written, and it also affects the age. But the relationship is involved, and different in the case of each author. Nor, so far as we can speak of such a thing as the character of an age, does literature necessarily follow it. More often it is in rebellion: Gide defines the *raison d'être* of the writer as being at odds with his times. And these writers in particular seem to stand out against whatever we can name as the major trend of their era. They flew in the face of the generally accepted economic doctrine, and their deeper and more underlying ideas seem more allied to romanticism and opposed to the most noticeable intellectual current of the age, which was more rationalistic and scientific.

A different explanation of the archaism and class prejudice of these authors might be sought in the very fact that they were writers. An attractive hypothesis could be set up to the effect that there is inevitably a conflict between an artist and any mass movement. Although he may reject the values of the society he lives in, the artist yet hesitates to join a large general movement against this society. The highly personal nature of his work makes him an individualist, sensitive to his own laws of development; he is unwilling therefore to take part in a popular movement in which his own individuality is in danger of being lost. Or, when he does join it, it will be with ambivalent loyalties, perhaps just to cover his own failures and frustrations. Furthermore, and this may help to explain the matter of insistence on class distinctions, artists and intellectuals are in general very sensitive to questions of status, especially their own. Their material rewards are not large, they are highly conscious of their own individuality—and all this makes them preoccupied with the issue of status in their writings (it is a principal subject of Victorian literature), and in their own lives insistent on maintaining their position.[2]

But these explanations, though suggestive, may not be the whole story. These novelists reflect attitudes that cannot be entirely explained by saying that they were writers or that they were affected by the ideologies of their age. They display, not simply the crotchets of intellectuals nor the irresolution of men living in an era of transition, but something that was for them more fundamental and basic. The explanation in terms of status is promising, but may be capable of a wider application. We have not space to discuss in detail more than one of these authors, and even for Dickens, our principal example, I do not like to oversimplify what is a very complicated and interesting pattern. But perhaps one or two points can be suggested.

The apparent contradiction in Dickens, his genuine sympathy with the "lower

[2] For some of the suggestions in this paragraph I am indebted to my colleague, Walter Metzger.

orders" combined with his insistence on class boundaries separating them from those above, has led to fantastically divergent interpretations of him by different writers, some of whom, like Edwin Pugh and T. A. Jackson, find him a leftist, while others, such as Wilhelm Dibelius or even G. K. Chesterton, find him pretty much of a conservative. The trouble is that most critics have been unwilling to try to reconcile both aspects of Dickens' social ideas. Since the facts seemed inconsistent, many students have tended to ignore one body of evidence or the other. But I think that a solution to the puzzle can be found, that the two aspects of Dickens are consistent with each other, and are indeed closely related and help to explain each other. His ambiguity, rightly considered, makes sense.

The connection can be found in a closer study of Dickens himself. As I said earlier, literature reflects principally not the times but the author, and any attempt to use novels for history must undertake at some step in the process an intimate study of the novelist concerned. Edmund Wilson in his perceptive essay on Dickens in *The Wound and the Bow* has made an effort to show how Dickens' political and social ideas were related to his personal problems and experiences. While I cannot follow Mr. Wilson in some of his views, particularly when he tries to find in Dickens a left-wing alignment, I think his approach is fruitful and can do something to explain the special pattern of Dickens' social ideas. Without going all the way into a psychological interpretation, we can admit that Mr. Wilson's stress on the traumatic experiences of Dickens' childhood seems reasonable, for we know from many sources that Dickens was unhappily conscious of these experiences all his life and was searching for some means of counterbalancing them. This much is generally agreed, and indeed critics have harped so much on the troubles of Dickens' youth—the domestic-service background of his grandparents, his father's financial ruin and arrest for debt, his own brief experience as a member of the working class in

Warren's blacking establishment—that these matters have become hackneyed. There is no doubt of the enormous impact of these experiences on Dickens; the only question is their meaning for him. But this meaning is clear. The significance of these experiences for Dickens was unquestionably that they involved humiliation, loss of status. Dickens' experience of poverty, whatever else it did for him, gave him a horror of it, a determination to escape from being poor or losing status himself.

This basic insecurity is quite apparent in his frantic attempts to compensate for these earlier experiences during his years of artistic production. It comes out, for example, in his exceptional efforts to conceal his background. The truth about his grandparents was kept a strict secret and was first revealed only in 1939. He kept hidden even from members of his family that the Murdstone and Grimby episode in *David Copperfield* had been a personal experience of his own. In the same novel, which is semiautobiographical, he makes significant alterations and substitutions in the events of his own life: thus, as one illustration, his father, John Dickens, becomes Mr. Micawber, still somewhat disreputable, but now happily no blood relation of the hero. Along the same line, Dickens attempted to build himself up as a man of position: sending his son to Eton; adding field after field to the Gad's Hill estate; affecting an excessive dandyism of dress and a conspicuously lavish standard of living; undertaking a hazardous second trip to America to increase his already ample fortune. He shows a kind of self-dramatization (not unconnected probably with his passion for amateur theatricals), which sometimes emerges naïvely in his correspondence: at the time of his separation from his wife he wrote that he could not have been more generous if she had been a woman of high birth and he a gentleman of fortune.

The pattern emerges clearly. Whatever else we may find in Dickens, we also find a preoccupation with his own position, his status, which colors everything he does. A large part of the error of the radical interpretation of Dickens is the assumption that an experience of loss of status and a sense of social insecurity will drive a man toward the left. Such a state of mind may, as seems to be the case with Dickens, work very much in the opposite direction. Dickens' personal circumstances induced him, perhaps compelled him, to welome a class stratification, to think of the poor as something apart. In the same way, Dickens' aggressiveness and truculence toward the upper classes, of which radical critics have made so much, can, so far as this is an attitude directed against a whole class, be given a quite different and nonradical interpretation. It can be explained just as well (in fact this fits better the other things we know about him) as the result of insecurity, an inverted snobbishness, not a desire to reject society but a fear of being rejected by it. It may also be significant that he did not begin his bitterest attacks on the upper classes until well on in his career; his social criticism on the whole increases in intensity in the later novels. In his early years, when his poverty was close behind him, he wrote as one remote from the poor, friendly but condescending. Later, in his period of success and prosperity, he is more warm in their cause and more bitter against those above. In other words, he did not begin his strongest attacks on the upper class until he was financially secure and had established his position as a member of it; he became ultra-friendly to the poor only after it was no longer possible that he could be identified with them.

Thus, Dickens' background colored his whole social thinking and exerted, to a degree at least, a normative influence upon it. This is not to minimize the great undercurrent of rebellion and dissatisfaction which Dickens expresses, not so much through his formulated ideas as through his mood, atmosphere, and symbolism. To depict him as passively acquiescing in the existing order of things would be contrary to the whole spirit of the later novels. All I am trying to show is that when this mood of rebellion did get itself translated into more precise concepts, it was affected and limited by certain underlying elements that gave it a particular character. To say this is not to indulge in debunking or cynicism. In a problem of this kind no explanation can be exclusive. Furthermore, Dickens' awareness of the issue of status affected his social ideas in a more positive way too: it made him exceptionally sensitive to the effect of philanthropy on the personal dignity of the recipient—not always a common thing in his age. Hence, for example, the imaginative sympathy and the incredible humanity and decency he displayed in the plans that he drew up for that ill-starred experiment, Miss Burdett-Coutts' Home for Fallen Women.

We have not time to explore further the relations between these two strands in Dickens, his reformism and his drive for status, which seem so closely and so interestingly interwoven. The object of this paper is not so much to attempt any full interpretation of Dickens, which would be impossible in this brief scope, but rather to suggest by using him as an example the kind of information that the historian may extract from literature. What the historian can find, in a word, is a more intimate glimpse into the factors behind the formation of opinion; he can get a grasp of the influences bearing upon the attitude of one man, which may be suggestive for the entire period. Such an approach may take the historian more directly to the causes of events, the ideas in the minds of men, and may help to emancipate him from the psychological naïveté which since the days of Adam Smith has been the bane of economic history.

How far patterns of this kind could be set up for other novelists or other figures of the period is a difficult question to answer. We may not generalize from the individual to the group, especially when the individual concerned has so many special quirks as Dickens. Yet one might not unreasonably anticipate that patterns like this would occur fairly frequently in the Victorian age, when on the one hand status mattered, and on the other hand class boundaries were fluid enough so that status could be successfully pursued or so that there was danger of losing it. The case of Dickens is suggestive, and it is amusing to consider whether anything like it could be worked out for others. Disraeli seems a possibility; and Eric Russell Bentley has suggested how a similar line of criticism might be applied to Carlyle. Ranging more widely, a trend of thought of the kind here suggested might throw light on certain puzzling facts of modern English social history: why it is that conservative movements tend to draw their ideology, their formative ideas, from *homines novi;* or why "feudal benevolence" and *noblesse oblige* were in nineteenth-century England most enthusiastically expounded and practiced by those who were in origin conspicuously not noble or feudal. The role played by benevolence as a label of status offers interesting possibilities for criticism.

But these are speculations, attempts to suggest wider implications that this line of argument might have. All I have tried to show here is the kind of information the historian can get out of literature, the attitudes and preconceptions literature reveals—attitudes which, though they may be trivial in themselves, yet, to the extent that they are widely shared, underlie and motivate basic historical changes.

ONE EVENT THAT CAUSED A FUROR in Britain during the mid-Victorian age was the publication of *The Origin of Species.* No other scientific work of the nineteenth century, in fact, had nearly so many repercussions as Charles

Darwin's masterpiece. Published in 1859, it soon became the center of many disputes. And since Darwin himself was not a controversialist by temperament, it remained for Thomas Henry Huxley and Herbert Spencer to rush with missionary zeal to the defense of the *Origin*. Very early it became clear that the words Darwin had spoken as a naturalist were not to have a limited appeal. Darwin's impact on religion, social thought, psychology, anthropology, and historical writing was profound. His ideas were invoked "to explain social evolution in general and to support individualism and socialism, competition and cooperation, aristocracy and democracy, brute force and kindliness, militarism and pacifism, ethical pessimism and optimism, creative emergent evolutionism and evolutionary naturalism." In much of the discussion generated by the *Origin,* the essential nature of Darwin's achievement was overlooked: that by his patient gathering of data he had marshaled evidence to establish evolution as a fact, and that he had set forth the theory of natural selection to explain the method of evolution. Indeed, it is remarkable that now—almost a century since the publication of the *Origin*—Darwin's conception of natural selection as the key to evolution in general is not only unimpaired but substantiated and implemented in many ways. His fundamental idea, in short, is still living science. In the following essay, the eminent British biologist Julian Huxley examines the critical years in the evolution of Darwin's thought. It is perhaps especially appropriate that Professor Huxley should write on Darwin, for it was his grandfather who fought so vigorously in Victorian England for the acceptance of the *Origin*.

CHARLES DARWIN: THE DECISIVE YEARS

JULIAN S. HUXLEY

It was Darwin himself who, looking back on his life, wrote in his autobiography, "The voyage of the Beagle has been by far the most important event in my life, and has determined my whole career"; and there can be no doubt that he was right. Thus every additional gleam of light on this period of his life is bound to be of interest.

Lady Barlow, Darwin's granddaughter, who in 1933 published Darwin's "Diary of the Voyage of H.M.S. *Beagle,*" has now given us further valuable material, in the shape of annotated extracts from the actual notebooks which Darwin kept during the voyage, together with the thirty-nine letters he wrote home from the *Beagle,* of which thirty-one (save for a few extracts of some) have not been previously published.*

These notebooks were the raw material out of which he fashioned the "Diary," written aboard the *Beagle* and not intended for publication. Later the "Diary," together with the notebooks, formed the foundation for the famous "Journal of Researches," or, as it is more generally called, "The Voyage of the *Beagle,*" as well as for the technical volumes on the zoological and geological results of the cruise. They were written day by day on the spot, in the form of hasty compressed notes, often difficult to follow, but sometimes eliciting a vivid picture of a scene or a state of mind, in the

* Charles Darwin and the Voyage of the *Beagle*. Edited with an Introduction by Nora Barlow. Pp. vii+280+16 plates. (London: Pilot Press, Ltd., 1945.) 15s. net.

Reprinted by special permission from *Nature,* CLVII (1946), 536-538.

same way that a sketch may sometimes be more immediately effective than a finished painting.

In a scientific journal, a reviewer must concentrate on points of scientific interest. Accordingly, I can merely record the fact that the letters and notebooks also reveal many other facets of Darwin's character— his love of home, his strong family affections, his deep emotional reaction to fine scenery, his shrewd comments on the social life and the human inhabitants of the countries he visited. In these pages, we can see the young Darwin as he was before chronic ill-health and the burden of the enormous intellectual task he set himself had damped down his vitality and blunted some of his sensibilities.

One of the first impressions left by these pages is of the young Darwin's immense capacity for scientific enjoyment—a capacity which he shared with other great men of science, such as Rutherford. New observations, new problems, new theories were capable of inspiring him with the same kind of sublime excitement that he experienced from great scenery or great poetry. Let me quote one or two passages (I retain Darwin's often curious punctuation and spelling). To his sister he writes from the Rio Plata: "How many magnificent and characteristic views, how many and curious tribes of men we shall see, what fine opportunities for geology and for studying the infinite host of beings:—is not this a prospect to keep up the most flagging spirit? If I was to throw it away, I don't think I should ever rest quiet in my grave; I certainly should be a ghost and haunt the British Museum." To another sister, from Monte Video: "I wish any of you could enter into my feelings of excessive pleasure which Geology gives as soon as one *partly*

understands the nature of the country." Five months later: "There is nothing like Geology; the pleasure of the first day's partridge shooting or first day's hunting cannot be compared to finding a fine group of fossil bones, which tell their story of former times with almost a living tongue." Three months later: "I have found the Geology of these countries so different from what I read about Europe, and in consequence when compared with it so instructive to myself, that I cannot help hoping that even imperfect descriptions may be of some general utility. Of one thing I am sure; that such pursuits are sources of the very highest pleasures I am capable of enjoying."

After visiting Concepcion in Chile shortly after a great earthquake there, he wrote: "I am very glad we happened to call at Concepcion so shortly afterwards: it is one of the three most interesting spectacles I have beheld since leaving England.—A Fuegian Savage; Tropical Vegetation; and the ruins of Concepcion. It is indeed most wonderful to witness such desolation produced in minutes of time."

This is how he describes his trip to the Andes: "I cannot express the delight which I felt at such a famous winding up of all my Geology in South America. I literally could hardly sleep at nights for thinking over my day's work. . . . To a Geologist . . . there are such manifest proofs of excessive violence; the strata of the highest pinnacles are tossed about like the crust of a broken pie."

In the "Journal of Researches" Darwin records the impression made on him by his first sight of primitive savages. The following unpublished letter gives added emphasis to that account: "We here saw the native Fuegian: an untamed savage is, I really think, one of the most extraordinary spectacles in the world:—the difference between

ROBERT FITZROY: Vice-admiral, hydrographer, and meteorologist (d. 1865). In 1828 he was placed in command of the *Beagle,* a brig that was used to survey the coasts of Patagonia, Tierra del Fuego, and the Straits of Magellan. On what proved to be Fitzroy's most famous voyage, Charles Darwin served as naturalist. The voyage began in December, 1831, and ended nearly five years later.

a domesticated and wild animal is far more strikingly marked in Man: in the naked barbarian, with his body coated with paint, whose very gestures, whether they may be peaceable or hostile, are unintelligible, with difficulty we see a fellow creature. No drawing or description will at all explain the extreme interest which is created by the first sight of savages. It is an interest which almost repays one for a cruize in these latitudes: and this I assure you is saying a good deal."

The notebooks are for the most part confined to factual records. But sometimes fact is combined with feeling, as in this extraordinary sketch of the tropical forest in Brazil: "Ap. 17th, Sosego. Twiners entwining twiners—tresses like hair—beautiful lepidoptera—Silence—hosannah—Frog, habits like toad, iris copper-coloured, colour became faint . . . musky shell, stain fingers red." Or this on "ostriches" [rheas]: "Ostriches tame, made sail. . . . Many ostriches, flocks from 20-30, beautiful on the brow of a hill."

The factual records are often pungent and vivid, and give evidence of acute and intense observation. Take this note on his trip inland from Valparaiso: "Near Luxan noticed as I thought heavy smoke, turned out to be locusts—clouds quite impervious [to light], ragged reddish brown, all flying north: many scattered outlyers lying on ground; in their advanced guards, sky like mezzotint engraving—main body about 20 feet above ground—perhaps 10 miles an hour. . . . Noise that of strong breeze through rigging of a ship. Where a cloud had alighted, far more than leaves on the trees—field tinged with their colour—people, sticks and shouts." Or this, "Immense herd of Guanaco—1000! . . . Guanaco sleep tail in centre in same places on different nights; then dung and dust in saucer-shaped cavities." Or this on the land iguana of the Galapagos: "Iguana—shakes head vertically; sea one [that is, the marine iguana] no. . . . Eats much cactus— . . . eats very deliberately without chewing. Small finch pecking from same piece often

alights on back. . . . Very fond of cactus, run away like dog from one another with pieces. Excavate burrow (shallow), first on one side and then on other—two or three times. Throw dirt with one arm and kick it out with well-adapted hind leg—then other side." Or this, "Capincha [capybara, the giant rodent] dung smells very sweet."

But the main interest of the notebooks and letters lies in the light they throw on the succession of Darwin's interests, the development of his scientific views, and the steadily increasing maturity of his intellectual outlook. In the first place they re-emphasize the priority of geology in his mind at the outset of his career. Thus on his way home he writes to Caroline Darwin: "I am in high spirits about my Geology, and even aspire to the hope that my observations will be considered of some utility by real geologists. . . . It is a rare piece of good fortune for me that of the many errant (in ships) Naturalists there have been few, or rather no, Geologists."

As Lady Barlow rightly points out, the voyage posed him with a tremendous problem—nothing less than the geological history of an entire continent. But this was also his opportunity: to have such large questions posed was to be driven to think of answers on a correspondingly large scale, in terms of bold, simple, and above all general ideas.

The entries in the latest of the notebooks, when he is drafting a geological paper, are illuminating. "In a Preface it might be well to urge Geologists to compare whole history of Europe with America; . . . and when we see conclusions substantiated over S. America and Europe, we may believe them to be applicable to the world." Again, "Earthquake part of necessary process of terrestrial renovation—and so is Volcano a useful chemical instrument. . . . Earthquakes act as ploughs, Volcanoes as Marl-pits." And a little later the splendidly assured entry "Read Geology of N. America, India—and remembering S. Africa, Australia, and Oceanic Isles, Geology of whole world will turn out simple."

This preoccupation with broad geological problems, involving as they do not only large areas but also huge lapses of time, during which small and for the most part continuous causes can accumulate to produce enormous effects, paved the way for a general evolutionary approach to the problems of life. The voyage also stimulated such a broad biological approach, by taking him to all parts of a great continent and so bringing forcibly before his eyes the facts of the geographical distribution of animals.

It is, of course, well known that two particular incidents of the voyage were the starting-point for Darwin's belief in organic evolution as against the immutability of species—the resemblance of the extinct species from the late Tertiary of the east coast of the continent to existing members of the peculiar South American fauna, and, to quote the autobiography, "the South American character of most of the productions of the Galapagos archipelago, more especially by the manner in which they differ slightly on each island of the group" —and, we may add, the fact that the majority of them are endemic species or even genera. But it has generally been supposed that the evolutionary bearing of the facts did not strike him until he had begun going over his collections and notes after his return, a supposition which was strengthened by the fact that in the "Diary" of the voyage, which he wrote up from the notebooks, the Galapagos ground-finches are not even mentioned. However, Lady Barlow reprints the passage, written probably in September 1835, and quoted by her in *Nature* of September 7, 1935, from Darwin's otherwise unpublished ornithological notebooks, which refers to the Galapagos ground-finches. This ends, "If there is the slightest foundation for these remarks, the Zoology of Archipelagoes will be well worth examining: for such facts would undermine the stability of species"—a conclusion expressed with typical Darwinian caution, but clearly indicating that he was already leaning towards an evolutionary interpretation.

There was, however, a remarkable delay in publishing anything which might even suggest that species were not immutable (the first hint of this was the sentence in the 1845 (2nd) edition of the "Voyage of the *Beagle*": "seeing this gradation and diversity of structure in one small, intimately related group of birds, one might really fancy that from an original paucity of birds in this archipelago, one species had been taken and modified for different ends"). Lady Barlow suggests that this delay may have been due not merely to Darwin's intellectual temperament and "the need in his own mind to marshal all the facts in logical sequence," but also to deference to Fitz-Roy's "emphatically creationist opinions." It was indeed an irony of fate that FitzRoy's belief that through new scientific knowledge, in his own words, "sooner or later the truth of every statement in the Bible would be proved," was one of the reasons leading him to press for the appointment of a naturalist to the *Beagle!*

In any event, here is another example of the influence of chance in deciding events. As is well known, it was only by a series of chances that Darwin found himself aboard the *Beagle* at all, the final hazard being FitzRoy's objection to the shape of Darwin's nose, which he, as a disciple of Lavater, considered as an indicator of insufficient determination. It is interesting to speculate what would have happened if Darwin had not taken part in the voyage. We can be pretty certain that it would not have been he who first successfully advanced a theory of evolution. I personally think it probable that, though evolution was in the intellectual air, its acceptance would have been delayed by several decades, for Alfred Russel Wallace's essay on a theory of evolution by natural selection, however brilliant, would not, I believe, have commanded the attention of the leaders of biology such as T. H. Huxley, much less converted them overnight, as did the "Origin of Species." The formulation of the theory of natural selection might well have been different, with less emphasis on the struggle for existence, and if so, the reaction against selectionism in the early years of this century might have been less violent.

But we may remind ourselves that modern evolution theory envisages three distinct kinds of process as contributing to evolution. There are single essentially unpredictable or 'chance' events, such as mutations; there are processes and laws of statistical type, giving quantitative accuracy when sufficient numbers are involved, such as Mendel's laws of inheritance, or the results of selection on variants of measurably different survival value; and there are unpredictable fluctuations (in the mathematical sense) or deviations from a statistical law, which occur owing to the small numbers involved, such as the chance fixation or elimination of genes by Sewall Wright's 'drift' in populations below a certain size, or the merely approximate regularities of such 'laws' as that of adaptive radiation.

The same sort of thing doubtless applies to the history of science. There are unpredictable single events, such as those which finally put Darwin aboard the *Beagle;* there are general 'statistical' trends, such as that towards the formulation of an evolutionary theory of life, which would in any event undoubtedly have come to pass some time during the nineteenth century; and there are unpredictable particular deviations from such trends, such as those due to the small number and diverse gifts of the men available to put forward an adequate and convincing theory of evolution. These notebooks confirm me in the feeling, which I expect most biologists share, that it was a very fortunate chance that made of Charles Darwin the protagonist of this great and fundamental revolution in biological thought.

UPON SEEING HER GROOM-IN-WAITING do an imitation of her, Queen Victoria is supposed to have said in reproof, "We are not amused." This comment of the Queen has often been taken to symbolize her era and to sum up the outlook of her subjects. Indeed, especially in the years following the publication of that triumph of iconoclastic biography, Lytton Strachey's *Eminent Victorians* (1918), it became fashionable to ridicule the Victorians, to poke fun at their alleged fastidiousness, prudishness, self-satisfaction, smugness, stuffiness, solemnity, and narrowness of view. Although the detractors and debunkers gained much publicity and seemed to dominate the field, the Victorians did, of course, occasionally find their defenders. In 1922, for example, Sir James Barrie admonished in *Courage, Rectorial Address at St. Andrews,* "Don't forget to speak scornfully of the Victorian Age; there will be time for meekness when you try to better it." Eleven years later, in 1933, the gifted literary historian Professor Howard Mumford Jones, now of Harvard University, also came to the defense of the Victorians, in a widely discussed article that was published in *Scribner's Magazine.* The essay that follows, based in large measure on this article, exposes the absurdities that have often figured so prominently in discussions of the Victorians.

THE COMIC SPIRIT AND VICTORIAN SANITY*
HOWARD MUMFORD JONES

I

We are all too familiar with the attacks on the Victorians. They conjure up the hair-cloth sofa, the Sunday-school tract, the antimacassar, the what-not, the bustle, and the unhygienic skirt. Victorianism is the elder generation. Victorianism is the pretense that if you do not name a thing, it isn't there. Those who dislike to discuss sex merely in terms of biology are apt to be classified with the lady who noted sadly the difference between the home life of Cleopatra and that of our dear Queen. Those who admire Gladstone (if anybody does) are Victorians, albeit those who admire Disraeli (and the Victorians admired him enough to make him premier) are not. To talk of duty, honor, the obligations of being a gentleman, the responsibilities of matrimony, or the sacredness of religious belief is to be Victorian. The Victorians were so bent on being moral that they ignored the unpleasant aspects of life. They had no use for art which was not ethical; they displayed, it is alleged, an embarrassing familiarity with the purposes of the Almighty. Did not one of them proclaim that God's in his heaven and all's right with the world, though the world was palpably maladjusted? Did not another sing aloud that he was going to be Queen of the May? Victorian stuffiness, Victorian decorum, Victorian prudery, Victorian solemnity!

Well, in one sense they had a right to be solemn. The first half of the century, like our own, was a period of recurrent crises, but whereas we have confined our discussions principally to "serious weeklies" and long-

Note: The substance of this chapter was originally published in *Scribner's Magazine*, February, 1933, under the title: "Those Eminent Victorians."

faced conferences and ineffectual newspaper editorials, the Victorians were of the opinion that the national conscience was concerned, and sought in their writings to arouse thinking on the subject. Our own fiction has been monotonously compounded of sex, horror, and psychology. The Victorians thought otherwise. From the day when Bulwer Lytton in his first novel converted Pelham to utilitarian thought, to the day when George Gissing laid down his pen, a consciousness of the importance of man to society and of society to man is a constant theme in nineteenth-century fiction. Mrs. Gaskell and Charles Kingsley cry out against social injustice. Thackeray studies the adjustment of the parvenus and the upper classes. Disraeli outlines a political philosophy in the Young England novels, and Trollope, in the Parliamentary novels, uttered more than parliamentary wisdom. George Eliot bases her books on a social philosophy; to George Meredith a reading of life is a reading of earth. Similarly the poets—Tennyson, Mrs. Browning, Swinburne, Kipling—are aware of political issues and turn them into beautiful and enduring verse.

I am far from thinking that literature is any better for being sociological, but most of us will agree that literature tends to be better when it is written with a large discourse, and I confess that the relative thinness of American fiction after our own Victorian age had ended seems to me to arise from the fact that it was based on a very narrow reading of life—a reading which sees the be-all and the end-all of the novelist's business as sex and psychology. And I wonder, in view of the relative brittleness of that fiction, whether we are quite entitled to patronize the Victorian novelist? Have we mastered the art of the novel so completely that we can afford to dismiss as naïve a Dickens who, more than any other single figure, in the opinion of his contemporaries, made readers aware of social chaos in England? Our solitary exhibit in the way of broad canvases and social satire was for a long time Sinclair Lewis (perhaps some would add Dreiser), a humorist of great power, but is it not odd that whereas we produced only one of this kind, the Victorians produced a score?

I have said that the problems of that period and our own were similar. On the one hand, there was, for example, the inherited system of the universe. There was God, whose wondrous hand the nightly stars hymned as of old. There was an intricate and reasonably formed universe which He had invented, and everywhere traces of His handiwork could be found. There was the Anglican Church as by law established. There was man, who certainly had a body, and who was presumed, as even Shelley admitted, to have a spirit and probably a soul. There were the Queen, God bless her, and England's wooden walls, and the Duke of Wellington. In fact, there was a noble world inhabited by noble beings. And then there came crashing down on the Victorians a bewildering variety of changes, discoveries, and revolutions.

Startling theories of geology ruined the comfortable chronology of the King James Bible and reduced the life of man to an inconsiderable second in infinite time. Astronomical investigations extended the regions of heaven until earth was lost in infinite space. More and more it appeared that man was a great deal lower than the angels, and about the middle of the century he appeared to be a good deal closer to the animals. A succession of brilliant investigations in science smashed the good old comfortable mathematical universe of the eighteenth century into bits. In the heavens there was only anarchy, and on earth nature was red in tooth and claw. The Anglican faith was split by a schism which sent some of its most brilliant minds into the Roman Catholic fold, and Arnold later pleaded in vain with the Puritans to return

to the established church. Could it be that the old system was wrong? The system that seemed as certain as the Duke of Wellington and as invincible as the Life Guards at Waterloo? Amidst the wreck of matter and the crash of worlds the Victorians clung to one essential belief—they were not under any circumstances going to admit that human life was any less interesting or important or dignified or noble, even though the heavens fell and hell blew up—in fact, one of them, Frederick Denison Maurice, helped in the explosion. They did their best to reconcile the smashing impact of the new science, which threatened to reduce everything to anarchic materialism, with their inherited belief in the dignity of human life. If we are today anything more than certain worms writhing in mid-night, we owe our sanity to the Victorians. They conserved the human tradition, and without the human tradition, we should be stark, raving mad.

While the physical universe was crashing around them, the political and social world, too, seemed to be going to pieces, as Carlyle and others gloomily observed. The fixed and immutable laws of political economy, traced logically to their tragic conclusion by Ricardo, McCulloch, and the Manchester School, seemed to indicate that modern life would have to be one of increasing misery. They saw poverty in the streets and heard revolutions across the water. From 1820 to 1870 the Victorians struggled with depressions at home and counted a succession of crashes abroad; yet the streets of London, unlike the streets of Paris, Berlin, Vienna, or Richmond, never ran red with blood, nor echoed to the tread of a conquering army. The Victorians went into the nineteenth century with an England that was in many ways the little old England of Walpole's time, and they emerged with an empire that, with all its defects, was the most remarkable the world had seen since Rome. Theirs is one of the most extraordinary examples of national continuity and astonishing readjustments in the history of mankind.

How did they manage it? I suspect we have overstressed Victorian prejudice; for they managed it by a tolerance for unexpected developments which far surpasses ours. They were capable of absorbing strange food. They made a Jewish novelist prime minister of England, despite his curls and his waistcoats; and I need not comment on the chances of either a Jew or a novelist, much less both, being elected President of this enlightened republic. They elected an atheist to Parliament, and when Parliament threw him out, they continued to elect him until not atheism, but Parliament gave way; and I hardly need mention the possibility of electing a Charles Bradlaugh to the Senate of the United States. They suffered a group of aliens to tie up the business of the House of Commons night after night under the leadership of Parnell and his followers; and I cannot imagine delegates from the Hawaiian Islands and Puerto Rico enjoying the same liberty in the House of Representatives. Huxley told a bishop to his face in a public

meeting that he was a liar; yet Huxley served on more public commissions (so his biographer states) than any other British scientist. Would an American professor in a state university be similarly honored? I think we have talked too much about Victorian moral conformity.

II

You cannot, said Burke, indict a whole people; and it is difficult to indict a whole century. That the Victorians (to confine ourselves to them) had their characteristic weaknesses is evident; but one grows weary by and by of so monotonous and one-sided an argument and longs for a little more attention to a few obvious facts.

For example, one is confronted by the charge of moral prudery. It is evident one can retort that the Victorians were often refreshingly immoral, and if this form of argument is hilariously absurd, it will at least awake the jaded attention of modern critics. Against the charge that the Vic-

THOMAS HENRY HUXLEY: English biologist, brilliant prose writer, and controversialist. Author of a multitude of monographs on scientific subjects, he had stylistic gifts that enabled him to become a highly effective popularizer of scientific knowledge. An enthusiastic exponent of the Darwinian theory of evolution, he served, in his own words, as Darwin's "bull-dog," for Darwin was unaggressive and not constituted temperamentally for controversy.

MRS. HUMPHRY WARD: Prolific and popular English novelist (d. 1920) who dealt in her books with serious themes. Her work was highly rated by many of the critics of her own time but has been very much neglected in recent years. Delighting in the discussion of controversial subjects, Mrs. Ward rarely failed to introduce into her novels the messages she found timely. Her novels are therefore a valuable source for the historian.

SAMUEL WILBERFORCE: Bishop of Oxford who was a major force in the attack on *The Origin of Species*. At the Oxford meeting of the British Association for the Advancement of Science in 1860, he asked whether Huxley "was related by his grandfather's or grandmother's side to an ape." The exact wording of Huxley's rejoinder was not recorded. But he is said to have answered that a man had no reason to feel ashamed that he had an ape for a grandfather, but "if there were an ancestor whom I should feel shame in recalling, it would be a *man,* a man of restless and versatile intellect, who, not content with success in his own sphere of activity, plunges into scientific questions with which he has no real acquaintance, only to obscure them by an aimless rhetoric, and distract the attention of his hearers from the real point at issue by eloquent digressions and skilled appeals to religious prejudice."

torians insisted upon the standards of middle-class respectability for all forms of conduct, let us set some bits of biography. The period opens in 1837, with the arrest of Thomas Griffiths Wainewright, artist and designer (the friend of Charles Lamb), who poisoned various harmless persons, partly for cash and partly for pleasure, and closes with Oscar Wilde, who wrote charmingly of Wainewright, and whose particular form of vice even our advanced generation has not quite brought itself to condone. The philosophical thought of the age was largely shaped by John Stuart Mill, who ran off with another man's wife, and its most characteristic novelist is George Eliot, who lived for over twenty years quite openly with a man she was not married to, for the sufficient reason that he was another woman's husband. The most amusing essay of Thomas De Quincey, who did not die until 1859, is a whimsical defense of murder considered as one of the fine arts, and his best-known work is an aesthetic description of the dreams of an opium-eater. Rossetti took chloral; James Thompson drank himself to death; and from Ford Madox Hueffer's absorbing *Memories and Impressions* I cull the following pleasing anecdote concerning a visit paid by William Sharp to the house of Philip Marston, the blind poet: "He found the poor blind man in the clutches of the poet I have just omitted to name, crushed beneath him and, I think, severely bitten. The poet had had an attack of delirium tremens and imagined himself a Bengal tiger. Leaving Marston, he sprang on all fours toward Sharp, but he burst a blood-vessel and collapsed on the floor. Sharp lifted him onto the sofa, took Marston into another room, and then rushed hatless through the streets to the hospital that was around the corner. The surgeon in charge, himself drunk, seeing Sharp covered with blood, insisted on giving him in charge for murder; Sharp, always a delicate man, fainted. The poet was dead of hemorrhage before assistance reached him."

And in the same book I am reminded

that Madox Brown, "whose laudable desire it was at many stages of his career to redeem poets and others from dipsomania, was in the habit of providing several of them with labels upon which were inscribed his own name and address." The poets, when too drunk to get about, were then brought by cabmen or others to Fitzroy Square, where the maid and the cabman promptly put them into a bath and made them drink strong coffee, the bath being selected because the poet would "not be able to roll out and injure himself." But let us continue.

Charles Dickens, in the minds of many the chief purveyor of Victorian sentimentality, separated from his wife and quarreled incessantly with his publishers. George Meredith left his first wife, the daughter of Thomas Love Peacock, and celebrated in *Modern Love,* published in 1862, not a triangle situation, but a quadrilateral one. M. Lafourcade, the French student of Swinburne, points out that Richard Monckton Milnes owned a library of erotica, introduced the poet to the works of the Marquis de Sade, and encouraged him to write poems celebrating various sexual perversities, that are unpublished and unpublishable. Among Swinburne's friends was Sir Richard Burton, whose chief masterpiece cannot for obvious reasons go through the mails. Swinburne himself got drunk ("and how drunk he used to get!" writes Julian Field, an Oxford student who knew him); indulged in the most outrageous language; and was frequently referred to by the erudite Furnivall, the Shakespeare editor, as "Pigsbrook." As for the literary groups with which the Victorian period closes, their "morality," as any reader of Holbrook Jackson's *The Eighteen Nineties* knows, was a little to seek—Francis Thompson took opium, John Davidson killed himself, Aubrey Beardsley is remembered for decadent drawings, and Ernest Dowson's brief career was scarcely memorable for ethical balance.

Now of course these tergiversations do not prove anything except as they raise doubts about careless judgments on the Victorians. As it is sometimes argued, however, that facts like these are exceptional and that the true tone of Victorianism is to be sought in the work of Tennyson, Browning, Thackeray, and Dickens, let us look at some of it. There is no doubt that Dickens invented Little Nell and Paul Dombey; that George Eliot wrote a Sunday-school story in *Silas Marner;* that Tennyson was often sentimental; and that Browning was an irritating optimist. But is this all the story? Is there anywhere a more vigorous denunciation of cant and hypocrisy than in the novels of Dickens, the creator of Mr. Pecksniff and Mr. Chadband and Mr. Podsnap? Thackeray certainly complained that he could not write with the openness of Fielding, but if the author of Becky Sharp and Major Pendennis was really hampered in depicting them, the fact is not patent; if there is a more appalling picture in brief compass of human greed and depravity than in the story (too little read) of the Honorable Mr. Deuceace as set forth by Mr. Yellowplush, his footman—if there is anywhere a more succinct statement of the lack of connection between worldly success and the official principles of that success than *Pendennis,* I do not know where it is. George Eliot undoubtedly wrote *Silas Marner;* but exactly what moral lesson is to be drawn from the loss of Mr. Tulliver's fortune, and what is the precise application of the seventh commandment to the life of Dorothea Brooke? Has anybody surpassed the sharpness with which Trollope pictured worldly clergymen in the Barchester series, or worldly aristocrats and parvenus in the parliamentary novels? Does nobody read *The Way We Live Now?* Is any reader of Disraeli still of the opinion that cynicism was unknown in the nineteenth century? Did or did not the Victorians produce those great eccentrics, George Borrow and Edward Fitzgerald, the author of *Hajji Babba,* and the author of *The Way of All Flesh?* The Victorian novel begins, if you please, with Peacock the satirist and closes with Meredith volleying arrows of silvery laughter; it includes the great apology for the natural man

to be found in *Lavengro* and *The Romany Rye;* and it numbers among its principal exhibits (a fact frequently forgotten) the serried titles of one Thomas Hardy, who was emphatically of the opinion that God is not in His heaven and that all is not right with the world.

As for poetry, let us look at Tennyson, that arch example of all the Victorian qualities. Arthur, it must be admitted, is not much of a man, but what about Ulysses? *Enoch Arden* is rather bad, but what about the poem which reads:

> Raving politics, never at rest—as this poor
>   earth's pale history runs—
> What is it all but a trouble of ants in the
>   gleam of a million million suns?

I cheerfully surrender Galahad to anybody who wants him, but this same Tennyson wrote "The Revenge"; and if the true test of poetical worth is pessimism (for so our modern argument seems to run) I submit in evidence this product of Tennyson's last years:

> Act first, this Earth, a stage so gloom'd
>   with woe
>   You all but sicken at the shifting scenes.
> And yet be patient. Our Playwright may
>   show
>   In some fifth Act what this wild Drama
>   means.

And then there is Browning. On the literary exchange Browning stock has at present sunk to its lowest level since the organization of Browning clubs, and there are almost no takers. I do not count myself among the Browning enthusiasts, but even the author of *Pippa Passes* is entitled to fair play; and I would merely observe that the famous phrase about the exact whereabouts of God with respect to the rightness of earth is not spoken by Browning *in propria persona,* but sung by Pippa herself as part of the dramatic action of the story, which has for its end to show the unconscious effect that the words of one human being may have in the lives of others—a theme not unknown to our stream-of-consciousness novelists. And this same Browning, so cheery, so irritatingly glad, had a fine eye for a scoundrel, as witness "Mr. Sludge the Medium" and "Prince Hohenstiel-Schwangau" and "The Bishop Orders His Tomb at St. Praxed's Church"; argued on occasion that it was better to be vitally immoral than passively moral; stole an invalid woman from her father; and (unless I am much mistaken) set a fashion for writing dramatic monologues which the admirable E. A. Robinson and other modern poets are still following without surpassing.

III

The truth is that, instead of inventing "Victorianism," the Victorians engaged in incessant warfare against the cant and hypocrisy they inherited from the maudlin sentimentality of the eighteenth century. At the opening of that epoch Shaftesbury taught that there was inherent in the human heart a something which his disciple, Hutcheson, was to label the "moral Sense." In the innumerable volumes of Daniel Defoe England read that nothing succeeds like success; that when you have money you ought to invest it prudently; that a bad woman can be made good by putting her funds out at six per cent; and that a wicked pirate becomes respectable when he retires to trade and to overreaching his fellow man in a bargain. The fashionable pens of Steele and Addison were presently at work refining female manners in the direction of modesty, good sense, and prudery; admonishing noblemen not to duel, drink, or gamble, but to follow the example of Sir Roger de Coverley and look after their tenants benevolently and morally. On the stage you learned that female delicacy is always to be protected—read the Conscious Lovers for an example; and if you attended the London Merchant, which moved the acid Mr. Pope to tears, you learned a good sound moral lesson as to the fate of the idle boys—for the apprentice takes up with a prostitute, embezzles money,

shoots his good old uncle, is caught, repents, and is hanged, to the accompaniment of such a salvo of moral platitudes as no Victorian novelist ever dreamed of.

And the doctrine was continually preached throughout the eighteenth century. What are the novels of Richardson but involved Sunday-school lessons in a low and prudential order of morality? What is Fielding's *Amelia* but an object lesson in the domestic virtues? What are the *Night Thoughts* of Edward Young except lessons in religiosity? What is *The Vicar of Wakefield* (in this connection at least) but a lesson in impossible goodness, and what is Samuel Johnson, among other things, but a dispenser of ethical commonplaces? No, it is not in the Victorian age that heroines begin to faint on the slightest provocation; it is in the novels and plays that preceded the nineteenth century. Nineteenth-century writers, with all their faults, never preached so ostentatious a morality as did Richardson, nor taught, like Defoe, that money is the test of virtue. No religious poetry of the Victorian era is as lugubrious as Young's *Night Thoughts* or Hervey's prose *Meditations among the Tombs*. The moral story for the young was really founded by the heavily virtuous female writers of the eighteenth century, and the moral tale flowed from the pens of Samuel Johnson, Mrs. Barbauld, Hannah More, and John Gay long before Little Nell died and Colonel Newcome was called away and Tito ruined Romola's life.

Of course this is not the whole truth about the eighteenth century, but it is a truth critics of Victorianism ignore when they declare that the Victorians, forgetting the glorious freedom of Byron and Shelley, invented a pall of morality and snuffily turned from art to the sermon. Their leaders did nothing of the kind. They took what had been given them and made the best of it. They were a race of rebels. They had little use for ethical codes which had cramped average human conduct for a hundred years and which, reinforced by the eighteenth-century reasoning of the utilitarians and the laissez-faire economists, threatened to cramp human conduct still. Indeed, we read them ill if we continue to forget that they were struggling with the great burden of "morality" which they inherited from the century before them.

IV

There still remain, however, the undeniable Victorian Sunday, the black clothing, and the sober faces in the faded daguerreotypes; the solemn discourses of John Ruskin and Matthew Arnold; Herbert Spencer and Bishop Wilberforce, Mrs. Hemans and Mrs. Humphry Ward. But even granting them, there is yet another aspect of the Victorians which we all too often neglect. We fail to remember that this gloomy age is likewise the age of British humor and that the nineteenth century has actually given more first-rate humorists to English literature than any other century in the long roll of English letters.

The wit of the century which invented *Punch* is perhaps its most enviable possession. The Victorians did not take themselves half so seriously as we take them now. Anecdote after anecdote exists to prove that the period was a time of exuberance and gaiety. William Morris, for example, stepped to the head of the stairs in that amazing household which contained the pre-Raphaelites (when they were not joyously quarreling) and called down to the cook: "Mary, those six eggs you served me for breakfast were bad. I ate them, but don't let it happen again." There is Edmund Yates's biting comment on Thackeray's first lecture when, asked his opinion of the performance, he meditated solemnly and remarked with becoming laconicism: "Very good. Wants a piano." Swinburne on one celebrated occasion met Tennyson at the house of a friend and said, "We understand, of course, that Arthur is Prince Albert and Guinevere is Queen Victoria, but Tennyson, who is Launcelot?" There is

W. S. Gilbert's famous comment on Beerbohm Tree in *Hamlet:* "Funny, without being vulgar." There is, in short, an endless stream of anecdote and persiflage which makes Victorian letters and memoirs an infinite delight.

In fact, when drollery is almost a major theme in the Victorian period, it is wonderful to see how critics forget to account for it. The age begins with Sydney Smith, who once dryly remarked: "Benevolence is a natural instinct of the human mind; when A sees B in grievous distress, his conscience always urges him to entreat C to help him" —and from that witty punster goes its scintillating way to Oscar Wilde, the epigrammatist. Was there ever such a feast of humor as Victorian fiction alone presents— the brilliant pages of Disraeli; the inimitable Dickens; Thackeray, over whose "Victorian" novels there plays a constant stream of satire and fun; George Eliot with her great comic peasant creations; George Borrow with his joy in life and humor; Trollope and the vagaries of cathedral life; the wit and wisdom of George Meredith? And as if this were not enough, there are the great eccentric novelists from Peacock, the irresistable, to Mallock's *The New Republic,* Oliphant's *Piccadilly,* and John Davidson's half-mad concoctions. There is Browning, a master of grotesque satire; Tom Hood—and when next it is argued that the Victorians could not call a woman's "limb" by its right name, let the cynic read *Miss Kilmansegg and Her Precious Leg;* there is the long succession of verse humorists from Father Prout to Charles Stuart Calverley. How in the name of common sense can a period be writ down as unmitigatedly solemn which produced Edward Lear and the *Ingoldsby Legends,* Lewis Carroll, and W. S. Gilbert? Has anyone arisen in this earnest age to create another Pooh-Bah or a new *Pirates of Penzance?* Had anybody until *Of Thee I Sing* was written laughed at the Senate as Gilbert laughed at the House of Lords, and do we dare treat our bishops as airily as that great man depicted the Bishop of Rum-Ti-Foo? It would appear from all this that the Victorians were not all such grave deacons as the world imagines. In fact, I believe that the absurd seriousness with which we read novels based on the fairy-tales of Freud, and ponderous works of fiction based upon the insubstantial fabric of disordered syntax and stream-of-conscious-ness anarchy must awaken mirth among the departed Victorians. And I think we might profit from the Gargantuan gales of laughter which come to us across the what-nots and set the patent rocking-chairs a-rocking, and which, blowing more softly, sigh through the woods where Alice and the White Knight walk forever to the delectation of mankind.

THE PERIOD FROM 1873 TO ABOUT 1896 has frequently been called the Great Depression. Some specialists in the field of economic history, however, have been critical of this label, insisting that it is misleading and that it makes for confusion rather than understanding. They point out that production continued to mount impressively during the course of the depression and that real wages increased rapidly in the years from 1873 to 1896. At the same time, they recognize that the period was one of almost continuously falling prices, falling profit margins, and falling interest rates. It is of course these characteristics that have made it possible for the label to survive. It goes without saying that numerous suggestions have been advanced to ac-count for the origins and course of the depression, and economists continue to set forth explanations. What matters especially from the historian's point of view is that the depression had serious repercussions on many aspects of life in late-Victorian Britain. Some of these repercussions are considered by R. C. K. Ensor in the following paper, which he prepared for delivery before the Royal Historical Society. A penetrating student of Victorian and Edwardian history, Ensor is the author of an excellent volume in the "Oxford History of England" series: *England, 1870-1914* (1936).

SOME POLITICAL AND ECONOMIC INTERACTIONS IN LATER VICTORIAN ENGLAND

R. C. K. ENSOR

In 1870 the Government of the day had behind it the stronger party in the country; and among its followers in Parliament were the two members for the City of London. Pass a quarter of a century, and come to the Government brought into power by the general election of 1895. Exactly the same two things may be said of it; it too had behind it the stronger party in the country; it too numbered among its followers in Parliament the members for the City of London. Only, whereas the Government of 1870 was Liberal, the Government of 1895 was Conservative. That quarter of a century had witnessed the transfer of the City of London's political

Reprinted by special permission from *Transactions of the Royal Historical Society,* Fourth Series, XXXI (1949), 17-28.

allegiance from Liberalism to Conservatism; and therein the City's opinions corresponded to those of the business and moneyed classes generally. So it was, not only in the south of England, but also in the Midlands and Lancashire; though not yet at all to the same extent in Yorkshire, the north-east coast, or Scotland.

Now how and why did this change come about? It was, of course, a very important one. People born in this century have been accustomed all their lives to think of the City of London as a Conservative force, and it may not be easy for them to realize that down to so late as 1870 it was unmistakably a Liberal one. How unmistakably may be seen, if we recall that one of the City members of 1870 had a seat in the Cabinet, and his name was G. J. Goschen. Goschen, the son of a prosperous German who had settled in London, was at that time only 39, but already seven years earlier he had written and published a classical book, *The Theory of Foreign Exchanges*. His father had sent him to school at Rugby, and in that and other ways he became thoroughly anglicized. But at bottom he had the mind of his race, not only precocious and with a hereditary gift for finance, but logical, systematic and impatient of the intellectual untidiness so characteristic of England. These qualities made him in that first Gladstone Cabinet not a brake but a stimulus. It was he whose daring attempt to reform local government regardless of

the wishes of the country gentlemen raised the first storm of Conservative opposition to the Ministry. Such a Jacobin did he appear to the landowning class that Gladstone, who did not care enough about local government to stand up for his Bill, had to transfer him hastily to the non-controversial post of First Lord of the Admiralty. Two years later, however, the same Government passed the Ballot Act, and that probably gratified no one of its members more than Goschen, whose logical mind had always been impressed by the abstract case for the ballot, and who consequently had in his election addresses given it first preference on his list of reforms.

How, then, did it happen that not so many years later this keen Liberal became in effect, though not in name, a Conservative, and with him a great part of the well-to-do business class, who were then the political leaders of the English town populations? The fashionable answer of the Marxian school would run something like this. The class to which Goschen belonged, the so-called bourgeoisie, had been brought to the front by the Industrial Revolution and the development of capitalism. Its first struggle had been against the landed class, who till then ruled the country—a struggle represented in Victorian politics by that between the Liberal and Conservative parties. In it the bourgeoisie—i.e. the Liberals—were victorious; but their victory was soon challenged by a third class, the pro-

---

KILMAINHAM TREATY: Settlement of 1882 inspired largely by Joseph Chamberlain. By its terms Parnell was released from Kilmainham jail on the understanding that he would work to check crime in Ireland. For their part the British were to wipe out rent arrears and end the policy of coercion. But about a week after Parnell's release the Phoenix Park murders took place, and the policy of coercion was promptly resumed. LAND ACTS OF 1870 AND 1881: Measures sponsored by Gladstone in his attempt to solve the Irish problem. The Act of 1870 provided that tenants must be compensated for the improvements that they had made. If their tenure was disturbed for reasons other than nonpayment of rent, they were also to be compensated. Few evicted tenants, however, were in a position to bring their cases to the courts. The Act of 1881 embodied the principle of the "three F's" (fair rent, free sale, and fixity of tenure). By recognizing a dual right in the land, the measure represented a revolution in the British conception of property.

letariat, whom the development of capitalism had also brought forth. Faced by this new challenge, which threatened the landed and bourgeois classes alike, the parties representing them—the Conservatives and Liberals—were impelled to combine, the more intelligent Conservatives becoming liberalized and the more intelligent Liberals conservatized. And Goschen's action, when he joined Lord Salisbury's Conservative Government in 1887, would be explained as an early, one might say a pioneer, example of this tendency. Despite its temporary interruption by the Liberal revival between 1900 and 1914, the tendency went on; and the subsequent development between 1919 and 1939 of a remodelled two-party system with Labour as the second party might be regarded as rounding it off.

The drawback to these attractive generalizations is that they so imperfectly correspond to the facts. When you have annotated them sufficiently, there is not much left. Take, to begin with, the initial assumption that the Conservative party stood for the landed interest and the Liberal party for the urban bourgeoisie. That can only be admitted with large reserves. The Conservative party developed in the nineteenth century out of the pre-existing Tory party, and the Liberal party out of the pre-existing Whigs. Now the distinction between Tories and Whigs was certainly not one between landowners and bourgeoisie. Both were parties of country gentlemen, but with the difference that, whereas the smaller landowners (squires or baronets with a few thousand acres apiece) were most commonly Tories, the larger landowners (and, in particular, most of the great ducal families) were usually Whigs. The chief doctrinal difference between them was that the Tory squires were strongly pro-Anglican and firmly upheld the civil disabilities imposed on Dissenters, while the Whig dukes, although themselves Churchmen by religion, were not in favour of Churchmen's secular privileges. In addition, it was the Whigs who had engineered the substitution of Parliamentary for absolutist government; and they had a tradition of loving liberty in that sense. Towards the end of the eighteenth century Burke and Fox and Adam Smith and Bentham between them developed it into something like Liberalism of the nineteenth-century type; and to this creed the then new bourgeoisie were commonly sympathetic, partly because so many of them were Dissenters in religion, and partly because the Adam Smith economics suited their business requirements. Yet it was not they, but the aristocrats and university teachers, who launched the Liberal doctrine. The first bourgeois business men to rank as prophets of this alleged bourgeois creed were Cobden and Bright—latecomers, who popularized rather than created, and who never came to the very top in the official party hierarchy.

Similar corrections are due on the other side. The only British Prime Minister in the nineteenth century who was a manufacturer's son was Peel—the Conservative leader. Not merely did he lead, but it was he perhaps more than any other who moulded and fashioned Conservatism in its modern form out of the nebulous Toryism that preceded it. It is true that after he had split his party in 1846 by repealing the Corn Laws, the anti-repeal majority, led by Disraeli and Lord George Bentinck, very naturally did consist first and foremost of the country gentlemen; and in this way the Tory or Conservative party then became more distinctively the landowners' party than ever before. Lord George Bentinck, indeed, saw things so much in that light that he felt it essential to convert Disraeli himself into a landowner, and for that purpose, with the help of his two brothers and the Duke of Portland, his father, he financed Disraeli's purchase of the Hughenden estate. But though at Hughenden the new Conservative leader conformed almost ludicrously in all externals to the role of a country squire, his mental outlook continued to be a different and wider one; and when he took office, it was to the great towns much more than to the countryside that his principal attention was directed.

Conversely, when the real crisis confronted British agriculture from 1877 onwards, it was he and his party (this supposed landed-interest party) which in fact, as we shall see, let the landed interest down.

To that crisis—the transatlantic challenge to British, indeed to West European, agriculture from 1877—let us next turn our attention. Neither its complicated causes nor its far-reaching and many-sided effects have by most historians been adequately appreciated. Rarely has a development, almost purely economic in itself, had such wide and deep repercussions on the world's politics.

Cheap transatlantic grain production was essentially an economic, non-political affair. It originated in a series of inventions. The first of these was one of Great Britain's gifts to the world—the invention of railways. Between 85° and 100° west longitude the United States contained enormous expanses of uncultivated but easily cultivable land, which until railways were developed could only be reached and settled along the navigable inland waterways. Of these there were a great many, especially in the basin of the Mississippi, with its huge tributaries; but, helpful as they were, they could only give access to a relatively small square mileage in so vast an area. The new transport changed all that, and after the American Civil War there was a fever of railway construction. The number of railway miles in the United States, which had been about 30,800 in 1860, exceeded 94,000 by 1880, i.e., it was more than trebled in two decades. Most of the growth was across prairie; farmers could get land there for nothing, or nearly nothing; and the companies offered them transport below cost price for a period of years. The result was an ultra-rapid increase in the number of American farmers. Simultaneously a quite different set of inventions also multiplied their productivity per head. The prairie farmer had virtually unlimited land, and it was virgin, needing no manure. But he could get no hired labour, and the limit to his output was set by what machines would enable one pair of hands to do. Inventions were forthcoming to meet that need, and the most epoch-making, the self-binder, was brought out in 1873. Within five years it was very widely used indeed, and in principle doubled every user's crop. But the story does not end there. Yet another series of inventions synchronized its effect. They were in the sphere of marine engineering; and by them, between 1863 and 1872, the fuel consumption of merchant steamers was halved, and not only coal was saved, but cargo-space greatly increased. Thus in eleven years the cost of sending grain by water from Chicago to Liverpool fell by nearly 10s. a quarter—9s. 9d. to be exact. That alone would have been a sensational change, had neither of the other changes happened.

The present writer has recounted these facts at more length elsewhere; but it seemed advisable at least to summarize them here, in order to recall how purely economic and non-political were the forces at work. No statesman 'planned' the overwhelming invasion of Europe by American prairie-wheat in the late 'seventies of last century. Its political consequences, however, were most far-reaching; and among them may be found, it is suggested, the major part of the answer to the question posed at the beginning of this paper.

By 1879 it had become evident that no agriculture in Western Europe could stand up against the prairie on equal terms, and in every country affected the farming interest cried out for Protection. And in every one they obtained it, excepting Britain and Belgium. The Belgian case was not important; for, although Flanders and Brabant had relatively large arable acreages, they were already to a considerable extent specialized to other crops than corn. Omitting Belgium, we may say that the Continent protected its corn and saved its farmers, whereas the British Isles did not. These were political decisions, and they had a variety of political results.

Let us to-day examine the British ones. Since 1846 the country classes in this island had enjoyed great prosperity. It was the golden age of British farming; and all classes concerned had the feeling that they had never been so well off before. That was true even of the agricultural labourers, who had really made much progress since the 'hungry 'forties.' But it was still truer of the better-off classes dependent on the land—owners, agents, farmers, country clergy, blacksmiths, wheelwrights, and (then a very numerous, sturdy and distinct order) country millers. This flourishing and, on the whole, harmonious society was ruled by the country gentlemen, then, as we have seen, more definitely dominating the Conservative party than at any time before or since; and the only serious grumble they could have, was that for twenty-five years their party never had a proper innings at the Westminster wickets. In 1874 even this was made good; a strong Conservative team started batting with every prospect of a high score. And then came this totally unforeseen revolution from the prairies; and when the country people cried to their own Government for help, they got none; and so—not in a moment, but through a long, slow agony of never-ending losses, which with no real intermission lasted over eighteen years—the whole of that once-flourishing society went down into the pit.

Why did the Disraeli Government allow this to happen? Why did they act so differently from the Governments of Germany and France? For two reasons—one negative, the other positive. The negative one was that, unlike the Continental Powers, Great Britain was not interested in conscripts. At that time it was everywhere believed that country people made the best soldiers; and this supplied France and Germany with a motive, not shared by Britain, for saving their country-dwellers. The positive reason was that in Britain food taxes were uniquely unpopular. Their repeal in 1846 had been followed by a golden age in sharp contrast to the iron age immediately preceding it; and so they had become in the national imagination a symbol of bad old days, which nobody wished to see back.

Had not Disraeli himself said that 'Protection was not only dead but damned'? No Government resting on votes could flout a conviction so strongly and almost universally held. In this way Disraeli and his colleagues were really powerless to act otherwise than they did.

Some of the principal consequences may be listed:

(1) The conversion of arable to pasture (mostly poor pasture) over huge acreages of Great Britain, increasing correspondingly the island's dependence on imported food. The loss of grain was not compensated by any net increase of livestock.

(2) Greatly reduced numbers and lowered quality of the agricultural population.

(3) Impoverishment of the landowning class, resulting in the loss of its political position. This is often popularly ascribed to death duties, and was undoubtedly later accentuated by them; but it began from the earliest 'eighties, as soon as it was realized that the low corn prices had come to stay, and that the elaborate structure of life interests, mortgages, etc., built up on the assumption of a given income from rents could not be sustained when that income was halved.

(4) Heavy financial injury to the Church of England and eventual destruction of that country parsonage life which had meant so much to the nation in the nineteenth century.

Now those were all changes of such national scope that sooner or later politicians had to take account of them; while one of them—(3)—directly influenced the composition of parties, since it enabled, indeed compelled, the Conservatives to become a town party. But towering over them in its immediate political consequences came yet another effect—(5)—which we may summarize as the revolution in Ireland. It was this, far more than anything else, which took bourgeois politicians like Goschen out of the Liberal party and into co-operation with the Conservatives.

First let us see very broadly what was the effect of the prairie corn-prices upon Ireland. In England the agricultural industry was the most advanced and in many ways the strongest in Europe. Nevertheless, with all its reserves of capital and skill, it could not stand up to the storm. But in England agriculture was only one industry out of many; though it still had employed more workers than any other, the others taken together far outnumbered it. Now in Ireland both these situations were quite different. Where English agriculture was exceptionally strong, Irish was exceptionally weak; what wrecked English farmers must far more easily wreck Irish. Secondly, whereas in England there were a mass of alternative industries, in Ireland, save around Belfast, there were none. Ruin farming, and you ruined almost the whole Irish people. And in fact that was what happened.

Then let us see what the Irish situation was, upon which the catastrophe supervened. It was perhaps the most favourable to the English connection ever known till then. For centuries there had been two roots of disaffection in Ireland—agrarian and national. But the agrarian was much the more important. To-day we probably tend, in the light of what subsequently happened, to exaggerate the earlier extent of Irish nationalism. In the eighteenth century few, if any, thought of Ireland as a nation; how should they, seeing that since mythological times she had never been one? The Protestant squires wanted a Dublin Parliament that they might get their jobbing fingers deeper in the pie of Dublin Castle's affairs without going to distant London for the purpose. And the Catholic majority of the Irish population, groaning under penal laws, whose scope was defined by religion, not by race, wanted religious emancipation. But neither were truly national. All that time, and far into the nineteenth century, there was among the common Irish people a pervading British patriotism—a sense of the greatness of the Pan-Britannic community, in which the Burkes and Goldsmiths and Sheridans and Wellesleys came to play such conspicuous parts. It was perhaps particularly fostered by the army; and the famous nineteenth-century speech of Lalor Sheil extolling the Irish soldiers who fought at Waterloo still breathes the spirit of it. When the youthful Thomas Davis and his associates came out in the 'forties of last century with the slogan 'Ireland a Nation,' what helped to make it attractive was that it was new. Irishmen had seldom seen themselves in that light before.

But the abiding evil in Ireland throughout was the monstrous land system. It is often said that the Union of 1801 might have succeeded, if it had been accompanied, as was Pitt's intention, by Catholic Emancipation. May it not be equally true that, although Catholic Emancipation in 1829 was twenty-eight years late, it would have succeeded even then if it had been possible to combine with it a sufficient measure of land reform? The word 'possible' is used, because probably it was not possible. Just as it has been said above, that in 1878-9 no British Government could, having regard to all the circumstances, have intervened to save agriculture, so it is scarcely thinkable that anyone could in 1829, or at any time within that generation, have carried through the British Parliament the reforms needed in Irish land law. Nevertheless Irish history would have been very different had it been done. For the extreme of feckless poverty and degradation which then prevailed among so many millions of Irish peasants was essentially due to the rack-renting system. Had that been earlier removed, the Irish famine and pestilence of 1845-6 could never have run the course that they did, nor been followed, as they were, by the migration of millions of Irish to the United States. Thus the foundations of Irish separation would not have been laid.

In 1870, however, the Land Act of that year at last removed the root evil in Irish life. It is improbable that it could have been passed earlier; only the devoted courage and supreme parliamentary skill of Mr. Gladstone, then at the very top of his form, passed it then. Irish agrarian disorders had preceded it, in part conjunction with the new Irish nationalist force represented by the Fenians; but after the passing of the Act they did not long continue. A real tranquillization set in. In 1875 the Dublin correspondent of *The Times,* an observer of the highest authority, made a survey of the country, and in a considered report declared that the outlook was never better; that the Land Act of 1870, following the Disestablishment Act of 1869, had done its work; and that a contented Ireland was now for all to see. There seem no valid reasons for doubting the truth of that diagnosis. Writers after the event have impugned it on the ground that within three years the land trouble was greater than ever. But that criticism is as much beside the mark as it is to blame Gladstone for not covering in his 1870 Act what he covered in his Act of 1881. Both censures ignore the point, that from 1877 onwards an entirely new thing happened, which nobody could anticipate beforehand. When Gladstone passed his 1870 Act, agriculture in the British Isles was as yet on the upgrade. It was still proving worth while to bring new acres under the plough. The invasion by prairie corn, which put an end to that, was a sudden and complete surprise—a bolt from the blue. But once it came, it came to stay, and was —failing government intervention—irresistible.

In Ireland it meant that almost immediately every tenant was unable to pay his rent. And on the other side every landlord was unable to obtain the income which he needed to discharge his ordinary obligations. A certain number of Irish landlords were wealthy and eminent Englishmen—persons like the Marquess of Lansdowne or the Duke of Devonshire; but the bulk were wholly or mainly dependent on their Irish estates. Thus the case was not one in which either side could easily give way; and very quickly violence began. As early as April, 1878, the Earl of Leitrim was waylaid and murdered in Donegal. Then the Fenians became active on the tenants' side; and when the National Land League was formed in 1879, its two treasurers and its two secretaries were all four of them Fenians. Its

president was Parnell; and thus there was assured a close liaison between political nationalism and agrarian discontent. In this way the Irish land revolution was launched, and ran its stormy course for a number of years.

It is no part of the purpose of this paper to trace that course in detail. It will suffice, if we register certain facts about it. On both sides of the Irish Channel the horrors and barbarities produced profound though opposite effects. On the Irish side they raised the temperature of anti-English feeling to heats rarely known before, and at the same time caused a dulling of the moral sense. Crimes, from which at first the great majority of Irishmen recoiled, came to be less blamed as they grew more familiar; and so the standards, as one might call them, of cruelty and atrocity progressively rose. In England, on the other hand, an intense repugnance was aroused. English society began to be familiar with the hapless figures and piteous tales of Irish landlord refugees. Formerly members of cultivated society, they often now possessed little but the clothes they stood up in. Some had had their mansions burned over their heads; others had seen husbands or brothers murdered, or been forced at dead of night to dig their own graves; most could tell of barbarous cruelties to their cattle and horses and wanton desolation of their homes. Both English political creeds—and certainly not least the Liberal—regarded security of person and property and the reasonable enforcement of contracts as basic, whether for liberty or for civilization. And now under the British flag across only a few miles of the Irish Channel they saw all such principles abrogated by agrarian violence. The result throughout English society was a Conservative reaction, which was helped to become Conservative in the party sense by the fact that a Liberal Government was in power and had the responsibility for securing what in fact was not secured. The tendency was strengthened by divisions within the Cabinet. Its most typically bourgeois members—Forster, Bright and eventually Chamberlain—were the least sympathetic towards the Irish. On the other hand, the most sympathetic was the Prime Minister, Gladstone himself. He had appraised the Irish situation much more fully than his colleagues; his successive policies—the 1881 Land Act, the 1882 Kilmainham treaty, and finally the 1886 Home Rule Bill—we can recognize now as acts of supreme statesmanship. But at the time when he performed them he was acquiring in too many other spheres—notably in the Transvaal, in India and in Egypt—a reputation for weak knees. It was peculiarly unfortunate that his most blameable performance in that respect—the universally reprobated failure to save Gordon—should have happened early in 1885, only a year before he formed his Home Rule Cabinet. Thus the English bourgeoisie seemed to have its worst fears confirmed beforehand.

The conclusion, to which we are working, is that what turned the Liberal business class of 1870 into the Conservative—or Liberal Unionist—business class of 1895 really was the Irish agrarian revolution. We know, of course, that the actual split in the Liberal party occurred formally in 1886 over Home Rule. But there was more in that than a formal occasion; dissatisfaction about Ireland had long been preparing the change. If we take Goschen's own case, he had declined to join the Gladstone Cabinet in 1880 because of a purely personal dislike that he had to widening the franchise for the county constituencies. But after that issue was disposed of by the Act of 1884, Gladstone again invited him, and he again declined. His biographer's excerpts from his diary and letters suggest that Ireland was the dominant motive; and this is at least equally evident in the case of Lord Hartington, afterwards the great Duke of Devonshire. He, of course, was an aristocrat, not a bourgeois; but he kept very close to the bourgeoisie's point of view, and was restive about Ireland long before the split came.

So it will be seen that the *a priori* scheme of things, whereby the bourgeoisie after figuring as Liberals in their opposition to landed privilege came to figure as Conservatives in opposition to a rising proletariat, does not fit what actually happened. What impelled the British bourgeoisie towards Conservatism in the later Victorian period was not fear of the proletariat at all. In the political field the working-class stirrings of the 'eighties came to very little all told; and if in the trade union field they were less negligible, they wore there no revolutionary aspect. No, the source of alarm was agrarian, not proletarian; it was Irish, not British; it was due to sequences of cause and effect very different indeed from any which would fit into the dialectic of Karl Marx. If you ask why the English urban bourgeoisie were so much stirred by these Irish rural events, the answer must cover several points. Their motives were not those of the English aristocracy, of whom some had estates in Ireland, others were related to Irish landowners by marriage, and all had a sense of class-community. But one very strong bourgeois reaction was a moral horror at unprevented and largely unpunished crime. In those days English business men were still regular at church, and the churches still repeated the Ten Commandments, and Sunday after Sunday brought the solemn monition: 'Thou shalt do no murder.' Sensibilities on that side were then much sharper than twentieth-century developments, including two world wars, have since left them. Secondly, there was a widespread feeling that in Ireland justice had been overborne by force, and that England's reputation for fair dealing had been compromised. Thirdly (and this was a very strong factor), there was evoked a peculiar kind of patriotic impulse. In Ireland itself the effect of the land-war was to give a most powerful stimulus to separatist nationalism. Other things contributed, and notably the personality of Parnell; but Parnell could never have become the magnet that he was but for the Land League. Indeed, it does not seem too much to include among the results of the Disraelian refusal to protect agriculture in 1878 the whole stream of tendency which, starting thence, has ended by separating Eire from Great Britain. But—and this is our present point —just as the land-war stimulated nationalism in Ireland, so it did in England. The English business class was intensely patriotic; it resented the Irish events as an affront to England; and as the affront— with others, e.g. Majuba and the loss of Gordon—occurred under a Liberal Government, it withdrew its allegiance from the Liberal party.

That is the end of the story which we set out to tell; but perhaps it calls for a brief epilogue. In the early twentieth century an appreciable part of the business class, which had deserted the Liberal party, came at least temporarily back to it. The reasons again go back to the prairie-corn crisis of the late 'seventies. Then, as was shown above, the Continental governments (notably those of France and Germany) saved their farmers by putting tariff duties on corn. But things did not end there; for when their farmers had protection, their manufacturers claimed and secured it also;

and the two interests, alternately forcing the pace, landed most European countries by the end of the century in pretty high Protection. As a counter-stroke against this the Conservative party was induced by degrees to identify itself with a Protectionist policy; but in so doing, although it pleased many business interests, it displeased others—then a majority—which had a vested interest in Free Trade. The consequence was a return to a political order, in which both of the two main parties had a strong footing in the business class. The return was undoubtedly made easier by the partial assuagement of Ireland for the time being through the Land Purchase Acts.

This state of things lasted until the 1914 war. It would carry us too far afield to attempt to trace to-day the later sequences of events, which eventually dethroned the Liberal party from its position as one of the two parties in our two-party system, and raised the Labour party to that position in its stead.

IN THE ATMOSPHERE OF THE GREAT DEPRESSION, demands for tariff reform in the protectionist direction grew apace. Individual Britons became advocates of protection for a variety of reasons: they saw their economic security threatened; they were Conservatives who wanted to lash out at free-trade Liberals; they were imperialists. Understandably, the protectionists faced a vast amount of opposition. By the 1870's free trade had become an article of faith to most Britons, who were convinced that the prosperity that had followed the repeal of the Corn Laws had been caused above all by the repudiation of the protective system. If Britain had become the world's forge, carrier, shipbuilder, banker, workshop, clearing house, and entrepôt, the explanation was simple: Britain had repudiated the protective system. British free traders regarded protectionism as an economic heresy which was against the laws of nature and which must bring ruin. The fact remained, nevertheless, that anti-free-trade agitation mounted in Britain in the late 1870's and the 1880's, and the London *Echo* could comment: "It is strange, after thirty years of silence, to hear—issuing as it were from the tomb—the assertions and the fallacies . . . which most people supposed were buried beyond hope of resurrecting." Most active in the revival of interest in protectionism was the National Fair-Trade League, founded in 1881. It is with the origins, activities, and significance of the League that Professor Sydney H. Zebel, now of Rutgers University, deals in the essay that follows. An able young American scholar, Professor Zebel excels in his ability to organize material and to present it in clear prose.

FAIR TRADE: AN ENGLISH REACTION TO THE BREAKDOWN OF THE COBDEN TREATY SYSTEM

SYDNEY H. ZEBEL

The past few years have witnessed epoch-making developments in the history of Great Britain and her empire. The Statute of Westminster (1931) and the Ottawa trade agreements (1932) have transformed the historic Empire into a British Commonwealth of Nations held together by the centripetal forces of preferential trade agreements. Too often, however, modern British historians have tended to forget that this development was not activated solely by the political and commercial exigencies of the great world-wide crises of 1929. Many writers have traced these events to Joseph Chamberlain and his scheme for an imperial zollverein; but few have realized that the origin of Chamberlain's policy, as well as that of the new British Commonwealth, lies rooted in an obscure tariff-reform agitation of the eighteen eighties and early nineties, commonly known as the "fair-trade movement." In its commercial aspects, fair trade laid the groundwork for Chamberlain's plan of an imperial zoll-verein, for the system of preferential tariffs which began with the Canadian innovation of 1897, and, finally, for the Ottawa agreements of 1932. In fair trade's emphasis on maintenance of the union with the colonies, we may discern a sharp reaction from the colonial policies of the Manchester school. Together with the imperial federation movement, fair trade helped to lay the foundations of the revived interest in the Empire and eventually made possible a genuine acceptance of the Statute of Westminster.

The fair-trade movement was primarily an English protest against the breakdown of the so-called "Cobden treaty system" and the revival of protectionism abroad. The commercial policy of Europe in the sixties and seventies has been generally regarded as the most signal victory for the principles of free trade. The Anglo-French treaty of commerce of 1860, more often called the "Cobden treaty," had been followed by various other liberal commercial agreements negotiated by Great Britain, with Belgium, the Zollverein, Italy, Switzerland, and Austria. Through this group of treaties, and the similar ones which France, Belgium, the Zollverein, and Italy had made among themselves and with other countries, there came into existence a European network of treaties resting on the combination of independent tariff treaties and most-favored-nation clauses. These worked, in an ingenious way, to reduce the general level of tariff duties in the countries concerned, since every reduction of duties granted to one of these states came into force as regards the others also, owing to the independent operation of the most-favored-nation clause.

Stimulated by the favorable results of these commercial agreements, English hopes were high for the universal adoption of free trade. But these hopes were destined to meet with disappointment. The world-wide depression following 1873 saw the complete breakdown of the Cobden system. France, Germany, Russia, Austria, and Italy, during the succeeding decade, all raised their tariff duties. France, impelled by her financial needs after the disastrous war with Prussia and by what Professor Clapham has called "the mood of nationalism at war," denounced the Cobden treaty in 1872. Though the treaty was subsequently renewed for short periods, the way was paved for the high French tariff of 1882. In 1879, falling prices, increasing agrarian competition from overseas, and need for new sources of imperial revenue led Bismarck to raise the German tariff duties. Russia, whose trade had never been released from hampering restrictions, now began also in 1879 and 1880 a sharp upward tariff movement. Austria remodeled her tariff along protective lines in 1878, and Italy increased her duties in 1883 and 1887. The United States and Canada had even earlier evinced their faith in protection. Although duties still remained, on the whole, lower than before 1860, the English, who had cherished such high hopes for the eventual triumph of international free trade, now found their commercial policy rejected on all sides. Foreign markets were being closed to British exports, "a barrier erected behind which the new-born industries were maturing in safety, for the day when they should be sufficiently strong to invade the British market."

At the same time, too, a series of domestic crises in British industry inaugurated a widespread wave of uneasiness about future prospects for that country. British exports in 1873 began a period of uninterrupted decline, reaching the low figure of £192,000,000 in 1879. From that date on, there was a slow rise in export figures, broken, however, by sharp drops in 1884-86, in 1891-94, and in 1896-98. British conditions were made even more depressing by a new factor that now entered the situation. The opening of the great prairie wheatlands of the United States, the new transcontinental railroads which made profitable markets easily available, and new low freight charges rendered even more critical the distress of British agriculture, already suffering from an unprecedented series of bad harvests.

The apparent collapse of British agriculture, after 1874, laid fresh burdens on British industry—already being challenged by foreign producers. To pay for the increased importation of food from abroad without disturbing the economic structure of the country, it was necessary to export a great deal more manufactured goods or to earn more in shipping freights. And precisely when she needed to increase her exports, Great Britain found herself restricted by the rising tariffs abroad and by the growing competition of Germany, the United States, France, and Belgium.

It was no wonder, therefore, that doubts of the wisdom of continuing a policy of free imports were not confined to the continental countries alone. Protectionism had by no means entirely disappeared from England, just as across the Channel, the Cobden treaty had been received, in certain quarters, with much hostility. Protests against free trade had been heard in England again, in 1868, when, for the first time during the decade, a short period of industrial depression set in. Only with the rapid and extraordinary revival of trade and industry from 1870 to 1873 did the demands for "reciprocity" and "retaliatory duties" cease.

Now, however, with the trade collapse of the early seventies and the continued commercial and industrial difficulties which followed, it was only natural that there should appear among those who were suffering from the new developments a strong feeling of dissatisfaction with the traditional English commercial policy. It was only natural, as an eminent historian points out, that "plain men should begin to put the question—is it 'fair' to keep open market for nations who are closing theirs?" And though the situation in late-Victorian England has been called "remarkably stable," contemporaries were haunted by "apprehensions of foreign competition";

and numerous panaceas, in their unsuitability reminiscent of a later period, were offered for a revival of British agricultural and industrial prosperity. The most persistent demands were made for a departure from the free-trade policy which had earlier seemed likely to inaugurate an era of world peace and good will among nations. The period from 1877 to 1881 was characterized by several different movements of this kind, originating in the dissatisfaction with England's commercial isolation and in the internal disorders within her industrial and agricultural mechanism. Of these, the two most prominent were the movements for reciprocity and retaliation which coalesced in 1881 to form the fair-trade movement. There was little difference between the two philosophies; adherents of both were alarmed at the rising tariff barriers abroad and identified the causes of the trade depression with these manifestations of protectionism in countries which had earlier indicated their desire to follow a free-trade policy. Both movements were determined to force, by one method or another, a lowering of these tariff barriers in order to alleviate the distress at home. Although reciprocity and retaliation found some support in English industrial centers, the governments of both Beaconsfield and Gladstone remained quite unfavorable to their suggestions.

Dissatisfied by the prospects of the renewal of the commercial treaty with France, on distinctly unfavorable terms, David MacIver, a foremost parliamentary advocate of reciprocity, suggested early in 1881 the formation of an organization to direct an anti-free-trade agitation. He was able to obtain the support of a few industrialists who had already shown interest in the movement. Among them were Samuel Cunliffe Lister, owner of the great Manningham silk mills at Bradford and inventor of numerous labor-saving devices, and later a president of the National Fair-Trade League; Sampson S. Lloyd, M.P., a former chairman of the Chambers of Commerce of the United Kingdom, and later the chairman of the executive committee of the League; Edward Charles Healey, the first treasurer of the League; Sir Henry Mitchell, of Bradford, the active promoter of the Royal Colonial Institute and one of the earliest advocates of imperial federation; and R. A. Macfie, of Edinburgh, a former member of parliament for the Leith Boroughs and another early advocate of closer relations with the colonies. These six industrialists signed a circular which summoned the first meeting of the organization, in London on May 17, 1881. On May 31 a private conference, representing various industrial and financial interests, assembled and agreed that it was necessary to enlighten the public as to the effects of England's one-sided free-trade policy, and at the same time to determine how far the resources of the British Empire could be developed and England made independent of other countries with hostile tariffs. It was at this meeting that the name of the National Fair-Trade League was decided on; and a substantial fund was subscribed immediately for the purpose of organization and the carrying-on of activities.

The first achievement of the League was, in combination with the chambers of commerce, the defeat of the attempts of Sir Charles Dilke to negotiate the less favorable treaty of commerce with France. It was not, however, until early in August, 1881, that the League had prepared its

---

LORD RANDOLPH CHURCHILL: English statesman (d. 1895), for some twenty years a member of the House of Commons. A Conservative, he supported the monarchy, the Church of England, and the Irish Union. As a believer in Tory democracy, however, he insisted on the need to extend the suffrage and to promote social-welfare legislation. His views brought him into frequent conflict with his fellow Conservatives. He is the subject of a biography by his son Winston Churchill.

program of policy and opened its doors to the public. Its platform, laid before the country by means of communications to the *Times* and other newspapers, ran as follows:

I. That there be no Renewal of Commercial Treaties, unless terminable at a year's notice, so that no entanglements of this kind may stand in the way of our adopting such a fiscal policy as the interests of the Empire—and the action of foreign nations—may render needful.

II. Imports of Raw Materials for Home Industries Free, from every quarter, in order that we may compete successfully in the sale of our manufactures.

III. Adequate Import Duties to be Levied upon the Manufactures of Foreign States refusing to receive our manufactures in fair exchange, to be removed in the case of any nation agreeing to take British manufactures duty free.

IV. A very Moderate Duty to be Levied upon all Articles of Food from Foreign Countries, the same being admitted free from all parts of our Empire, prepared to take our manufactures in reasonably free interchange.

1. To develop the Resources of our own Empire, and to determine the flow of British capital skill, and industry henceforth into our own dominions, instead of into Foreign Protective States, where it becomes a force commercially hostile to us.

2. Thus to transfer the great food-growing industries which we employ, from Protective Foreign Nations, who refuse to give us their custom in return, to our own Colonies and Dependencies, where our goods will be taken, if not 'duty free,' yet subject only to revenue duties almost unavoidable in newly-settled countries, and probably not equal to one-third the protective duties levied by the United States, Spain, Russia, etc.

The National Fair-Trade League confidently advocates this Programme . . . .

as a great National Policy which, while stimulating trade at home, and promoting the prosperity of all classes, would bind together more closely, by the ties of a common interest, the mother country and her scattered populations, strengthening the foundations and consolidating the powers and greatness of the Empire.

The new organization came but little to the fore in the first years of its existence. It was no sooner founded than a period of revival and prosperity of trade set in, which lasted for several years and stifled once more in industrial circles the complaints as to the effects of free trade. Fair-traders wisely occupied themselves with preparation for a renewal of the agitation with the advent of conditions more favorable to them. Although numerous pamphlets and articles advocating fair trade were published during this period, little could be expected from Gladstone's government, which was unqualifiedly opposed to these heretical fiscal doctrines. Many Conservatives, however, under the leadership of Lord Salisbury and Lord Randolph Churchill, were more favorable to the new doctrines of tariff reform. Even Sir Stafford Northcote, the nominal leader of the party and a convinced free-trader, saw no objection to protection being accepted by the Conservatives as "a pious opinion," although the party was not putting this policy forward as an article of faith. Members of that party, eager to embarrass the Liberal government, and always notoriously sympathetic to the demands of the landed interest, united in parliament with the fair-traders, led by Sampson S. Lloyd, to demand a parliamentary inquiry into the causes of the depression of trade and industry. The Liberal government was opposed to any such request and refused to assent to any implied questioning of the value of the system of free imports despite the insistence of the Earl of Dunraven, the president of the Fair-Trade League, and of the other fair-traders.

In June, 1885, the Conservatives had a

chance to show how sincere they had really been in urging an inquiry into the causes of the prolonged depression. The sudden defeat of the Liberal cabinet on June 8 over the budget was followed by Gladstone's resignation. Almost immediately, the Conservative ministry, formed by Lord Salisbury, announced in parliament that the government had resolved upon an inquiry into the causes of the depression of trade and industry, and, despite the furious attacks of the Liberals, proceeded to name a royal commission, with Sir Stafford Northcote as chairman, to study the problem. The more prominent Liberals refused all invitations to participate, and it was only with difficulty that a satisfactory commission was finally assembled.

The term of this first Salisbury government was only a short one. In the autumn of 1885 a general election took place. Rendered confident by the favor shown them by the Conservatives, the fair-traders determined to appeal for support to the country. With the aid of their newly established organ, *Fair-trade,* a weekly which had commenced publication on October 16, 1885, they hoped to present their case for fiscal reform. Although the crucial issues in this general election of 1885 were, contrary to the Fair-Trade League manifesto, those dealing with the Irish problem, foreign affairs, and, above all, Joseph Chamberlain's "unauthorized programme" of rural allotments, yet the problem of fair trade was an important one. The Liberal leaders adopted an unequivocal attitude toward this movement. Together with the Cobden Club, an organization of extreme free-traders, the Liberals appealed to the country to defeat the advocates of a "dear loaf." The Conservatives were unable, however, to show any unanimity. Many found it wiser to declare themselves free-traders and opposed to any reversal of the fiscal legislation of 1846. Others attempted to gain fair-trade support in the constituencies by a frank espousal of that cause. Still others attempted to straddle the issue.

Despite the bad trade in 1885, the elec-

tions ended in a majority for the Liberals—provided they could retain the support of the Irish Nationalists. The defeat of the more prominent fair-traders—Sampson S. Lloyd, James Lowther, W. Farrer Ecroyd, Coleridge Kennard, and W. J. Harris—was a great discouragement to the cause of fiscal reform. The advent of the third Gladstone ministry meant an indefinite delay in obtaining favorable government action. In general, therefore, the position of the fair-trade movement after the defeat in 1885 was far from being a happy one. A long tenure of office by the Liberals was considered likely. And the return of many less prominent fair-traders did little to compensate for the defeat of the fair-trade leaders and for the defeat of their Conservative allies.

A combination of unusual circumstances was, however, to change the whole picture. From being a beaten faction in a minority party, the fair-traders were transformed into an influential group whose support was highly important to a coalition government. It was Gladstone's Irish Home-Rule Bill that brought a reorganization of the Liberal cabinet in 1886. The refusal of an important section of the Liberal party to support his plans for Ireland forced Gladstone to appeal once more to the electorate, in the summer of 1886, for their verdict. In this appeal, however, Gladstone met a crushing defeat. The Unionist group in the Liberal party threw their support to Salisbury in order to enable him to form a government which would maintain the union with Ireland. Although the Liberal Unionists refused to take office in this Conservative government, they could be counted upon for its support. In return, the Conservatives found themselves eager to consult the interests of their Liberal supporters.

The fair-traders now also found themselves in a favored position. In the bitterly fought campaign of 1886, the subject of fair trade had been practically ignored. In their efforts to block Irish home rule the fair-traders had shown, for the moment, an almost total neglect of their own doctrines of fiscal reform. All Conservative and Liberal Unionist candidates had been endorsed by the League, regardless of their earlier position on the fair-trade question. Despite this total affiliation with the Unionist cause, when the election returns were in, the *Fair-trade* weekly was able to list the names of sixty-four members of the new parliament whose votes, the fiscal reformers believed, might be counted upon to support fair trade. However that may be, even the Cobden Club admitted later that at the elections of 1886 a larger number of candidates professing protectionist principles had been returned by the constituencies than at any previous election since 1852. These gains had changed the status of the National Fair-Trade League. The fair-trade members could now exercise tremendous pressure in behalf of their views upon the government. But great difficulties still existed. The main problem, *Fair-trade* soon recognized, lay in the fact that the Conservatives were able to hold office only by the support of the Liberal Unionists. This last group, almost all free-traders, was likely to be alienated by any Conservative support of the fair-trade movement. These suspicions of future government indifference to their erstwhile allies were soon made more certain by the unfavorable attitude of the ministry toward any fair-trade resolution presented in parliament. Even Lord Randolph Churchill, in a speech at Dartford, declared that "the main principle and the guiding motive of the government in the future will be to maintain intact and unimpaired the union of the Unionist party."

This official disfavor now rendered a different mode of attack essential. Hitherto, the fair-traders had concentrated their attacks on free trade in parliament. It was now evident that little could be expected from the government. There was yet one method, however, whereby favorable action might be obtained. The fair-traders proceeded to carry on an impressive agitation in the country. With the aid of a new, more responsible branch organization, numerous meetings were held, and strong efforts were made to obtain resolutions endorsing fair trade from chambers of commerce and chambers of agriculture throughout the country; and, in many instances, success greeted their efforts.

These successes continued despite the final report of the Royal Commission on the Depression of Trade and Industry. Two reports were issued—a majority and a minority report, the former favoring free trade. Both reports agreed in stating that trade and industry were in a depressed state, and that they showed a diminution—in some cases an entire absence—of profits, and a corresponding decrease in the employment of labor, although neither the amount of trade nor the amount of capital invested in it had decreased, but only the value of the latter. The number of unemployed in some trades, such as shipbuilding, had risen to 50 per cent; and the conditions of the workers had, in general, become worse, owing to the scarcity of employment. The two reports were also fairly well agreed as to the causes of the depression. These were listed as overproduction, a fall in prices, protective duties and export bounties of foreign countries, the burden of English labor legislation, the cheaper cost of transport abroad, and the better preparatory, technical, and commercial training there. In the proposed means of remedy, however, there was a radical difference of opinion between the two reports, especially in regard to the future English trade policy and the method of meeting foreign tariffs. While the majority report did not desire any change in the traditional free-trade policy, the proposals of the minority rested throughout on the basis of the fair-trade policy.

The unfavorable report of the majority did little harm to the fair-trade movement. In the opinion of various students of the problem, the minority report took more account of the facts brought to light in the course of the investigation. In addition, the minority report served to give more definite form to the earlier fair-trade proposals. A duty of from 10 to 15 per cent on manufactured articles imported from foreign countries was now fixed upon; a similar duty was to be imposed upon those articles of food imported from foreign countries which might be furnished by the colonies. To conciliate the consumer for the higher food prices likely to follow the adoption of these restrictions, the minority members proposed the abolition of the unpopular duties on coffee, tea, and sugar.

In parliament the pressure of public business made impossible any opportunity for discussion of the findings of the commission or for renewed discussion of the problems of industrial and agricultural distress; but, in any case, there was little use in raising the issue there. The government was unable, even had it so wished, to endorse fair trade because of the hostility of the Liberal Unionists. Agitation in the country was the only safe method if the Conservative government were not prematurely to be upset.

The long-continued agitation did, finally, by 1887, arouse various interests in the country to demand fiscal reform. The agricultural interests, in particular, were vociferous in their claims for protection. The danger now existed, however, that their demands were forming for more than the fair-trade specifics. An undercurrent of conflict was continuously evident during this period between industrialists, many of whom wished to discard the unpopular plans for food duties, and the agriculturists, frankly eager for protective duties on food products alone. Despite the serious disagreements, the Fair-Trade League concealed fairly successfully the doctrinal disputes which were causing a serious rift in the organization.

A more hopeful aspect of the situation was the rising interest the English now took in their colonies. This, in itself, was a break with the anti-imperialism of the Manchester school. From the outset, the Fair-Trade League had recognized the importance of the colonies but had declared, unlike the leaders of the Imperial Federation League, that only by some form of commercial federation could the ties of empire be ef-

fectually strengthened. "From the outset of the Imperial Federation League," wrote *Fair-trade,* "Fair-Traders have indeed never hesitated to believe, and to say publicly, that their plan of knitting the empire together in the firmer bonds of business interests, is really the only one feasible to accomplish real federation."

The Colonial Conference of 1887 did much to strengthen this view, despite the fact that the two most important problems —imperial federation and commercial federation—were excluded, by the terms of the invitation, from the discussion. The opinions expressed by Jan Hendrick Hofmeyr, a delegate from the Cape of Good Hope, and by some of the other colonial delegates, in regard to fiscal federation of the Empire, fitted in extremely well with the views of the fair-traders. And at a banquet for the colonial representatives, given by the Fair-Trade League on April 28, several of the delegates lauded the work the League was doing to render the idea of commercial federation of the Empire more popular in England.

The year 1887 saw other successes achieved by the fair-trade movement. On June 27 the Grand Council of the Birmingham Conservative Association adopted a fair-trade resolution; and at the summer conference of the National Union of Conservative Associations of Scotland two fair-trade resolutions were passed. The fair-trade policy of "boring" from within the local organizations of the Conservative party appeared now to be bearing results. Even Mr. Goschen, the Liberal Unionist who had just replaced Lord Randolph Churchill at the exchequer, declared, in a speech in London on July 6, that "it may not unfairly be contended that a *prima facie* case is made out that the fiscal system ought to be reviewed," and promised that "no foregone conclusion, no received prejudices shall prevent me from bringing an independent judgment and open mind to all those great problems, social, industrial, and commercial, which are jostling and competing for public attention." Even the trade-unions, hitherto uncompromising in their opposition to any suggested departure from free trade, now pressed the government to remedy the evils resulting from foreign bounties.

The close of 1887 witnessed the climax of the fair-trade agitation. At the annual conference of the National Union of Conservative and Constitutional Associations at Oxford, on November 22, the fair-traders finally achieved what appeared, at the time, to be a notable success. Amid great applause, Howard Vincent, M.P. for Sheffield, a militant fair-trader, proposed a resolution, that

the continued depression in trade and agriculture, the increase in scarcity of employment, and the consequent distress among all classes, render speedy reform in the policy of the United Kingdom as regards foreign imports and the influx of indigent foreigners a matter of vital necessity to the people of Great Britain and Ireland.

And, despite the warnings of several Conservative members of parliament of the disastrous effects such a decision was likely to have on the government, Vincent's resolution was carried by an enormous majority —about 1,000 to 12. The *Times*, which from the first had endorsed the Liberal Unionist alliance with the Conservatives, now delivered a sharp warning to the ministry to repudiate the "Oxford vote." Salisbury was, indeed, in a difficult position. He could afford the alienation of none of his supporters; nor could he avoid expressing an opinion. According to custom, the prime minister had planned to address the conference the next day; and his reply to the fair-trade challenge was eagerly awaited. He skilfully avoided any direct reference to the resolution, but he did make apparent his displeasure with this embarrassing protectionist display. At the same time, however, he indicated that he would be perfectly willing to carry out the desired fiscal reforms, but only if he were certain that such

a course of action had received the general assent of the community.

Neither the fair-traders nor the Liberal Unionists were satisfied by Salisbury's statement at Oxford. The fair-traders recognized, to be sure, the difficulties of the government but were "firmly convinced that they [the government] need not fear a general election next spring, even without the support of the Liberal Unionists." The Liberal Unionists, for their part, were determined to force Salisbury to repudiate openly the fair-trade movement. John Bright was violent in his denunciation of the Oxford vote. "You have observed," he wrote to the *Times,* "what the Conservatives have been saying at Oxford. They return, shall I say, like a dog to his vomit. They very slowly accept new teachings and new opinions, and the old delusions still attach to them. . . . ." And the other leaders, although more measured in their remarks, gave Salisbury to understand that any official support given to fair trade was likely to lead to a breakup of the coalition. The Liberals had good reason to exult. Sir William Harcourt stated the situation neatly. "Now I want to know," he asked, "how these gentlemen [the Liberal Unionists] are going to deal with this protectionist resolution. The flag of protection has been raised by the Tory party as the first article of their creed at Oxford." And in gleeful anticipation he continued: "Now are we going to see Mr. John Bright declaring for protection?"

An unfavorable Conservative reaction, however, was totally unexpected by the fair-traders. Although Howard Vincent defiantly announced his intention to hold great public meetings to force the government to act on the resolution adopted at the Oxford conference, the vast majority of the Conservatives were definitely opposed to his actions. In the *Times* several letters were published stating that Vincent's resolution had taken the conference by surprise and that the vote represented individual expressions of opinion alone. Various Conservative leaders publicly called on the fair-traders to avoid harassing the government. The fair-traders were now placed in an unenviable position. Success had been close, indeed, when the annual conference of the Conservative party had passed, with such a large majority, a fair-trade resolution. The unexpected reaction, however, had weakened tremendously the fair-trade movement. The leaders were anxious to avoid the charge that their tactics were making possible the return to power of the Liberal party and their Irish allies. Their indecision as to the next action to be taken was easily apparent.

Lord Salisbury gave evidence of a desire to soften the blow to his fair-trade supporters by the adoption of a policy of retaliatory tariffs, but Goschen rendered such action difficult by his answer that retaliation would certainly be tainted with the evils of protection in the eyes of "absolute Free Traders." And by a speech at Derby on December 19 Lord Salisbury virtually repudiated the fair-trade movement. The occasion was also notable for a liquidation of the Oxford affair. On the same platform, Howard Vincent appeared and pledged his unqualified support to the party while there was still danger to the union. At the same time, therefore, that the Conservative prime minister repudiated the fair-trade movement, a prominent advocate of the spurned doctrines accepted the blow and pledged his loyal acquiescence in the decision.

The arrival of an era of prosperity from the close of 1887 prevented any effective agitation on the part of the more irreconcilable fair-traders. A sudden and marked prosperity in trade now took the place of the former long depression. This change was attributed by the fair-traders to the grant of £20,000,000 for new ships, which gave a lively impetus to all the industries connected with shipbuilding; to the construction of the great Manchester Canal, which gave work to many unemployed; and, lastly, to the rise of the electrical industries, which were only, at this comparatively late date, starting in England. Whatever the cause of it may have been, this change again militated in conjunction with the Pyrrhic-like victory at Oxford against the movement.

By January, 1888, therefore, the fair-trade leaders advised discontinuing militant mass meetings and suggested only education and propaganda in the constituencies.

The fair-trade movement was now definitely on the decline. Some successes had been gained, it is true, during the continuous agitation of the 1880's. The doctrine of "cheapness at any cost" was losing its old hold on English statesmen, and the new interest in the colonies was a decided break with free-trade dogmatists. Despite these great gains, the fiscal reformers were now unable to make further headway. The Sugar Convention of 1888, designed to meet complaints against foreign bounties, was never ratified, and at the annual conference of the Conservative party, at Wolverhampton on November 2 and 3, 1888, the delegates, obviously following the instructions of the party leaders, avoided the embarrassments of the previous year. Earlier in 1888, too, the government had done its best to discourage the advocates of fiscal reform. In response to Earl de la Warr's motion in the house of lords for tariff reform, Lord Salisbury had curtly replied that "I have simply to say with respect to the question of Protection that this country has adopted the opposite system after a controversy unexampled in its length, in its earnestness, and in the decision with which the ultimate issue was arrived at."

Tired of these humiliating rebuffs, many fair-traders decided to break with the Conservatives and to pursue an independent policy of action in the constituencies. In the Holborn election in December, 1888, the first open opposition took place. When the candidates of both parties expressed their opposition to the fair-trade policy, a circular was published calling upon workmen to abstain from voting for either candidate. Although the Conservative candidate was successful, *Fair-trade* confidently asserted that the unexpectedly narrow margin of victory over the Liberal candidate was due to the numerous abstentions of the fiscal reformers. But the future was not a happy one for the fair-traders. It was evident that conditions, since the advent of prosperity in 1887, were no longer propitious. Salisbury's opposition had also led many of the leaders to forsake their own organization. And after several more years of fruitless activity, the organ of the Fair-Trade League discontinued publication.

From the wreckage of the movement after 1888, however, one aspect of the fair-trade movement had been salvaged. That organization's stand on commercial federation made easy a general exodus from the Fair-Trade League into the ranks of the Imperial Federation League. Howard Vincent, David MacIver, Samuel Cunliffe Lister, James Lowther, and their followers found that this important part of their program, commercial federation of the Empire, might more easily attain success if supported by a group untainted with the stigma of protection. It was they who, in 1891, took the lead in founding the United Empire Trade League, which had for its object the formation of an imperial zollverein.

The renewed depression of trade in 1891 did a little to revive the fair-trade movement. There was a great decline in exports, complaints as to the depression began again, and fair trade came temporarily to the front once more. The principal cause alleged for the decline was the McKinley tariff of 1890, which pressed heavily on a section of British industry. There were rumors, besides, of a similar raising of protective duties in France and other countries. This state of affairs led the fair-traders to reiterate their arguments of 1881, that England's complete helplessness in regard to the trade-policy adopted by other countries rested primarily on the fact that, by free trade, she had completely lost her bargaining power, that the whole responsibility for the losses suffered by home industry rested on this policy, and that the only means of protection was to have recourse to retaliatory tariffs. And tempted by Lord Salisbury's speech at Hastings on May 18, 1892, in which he expressed once more his dissatisfaction with England's position under free trade, the fair-traders made a last desperate attempt to persuade the constituencies in the general election that only by a reversal of the traditional trade policy could England's position be improved. In alliance with the United Empire Trade League, they fought in the elections of 1892 to return candidates pledged to the cause of fiscal reform. The Liberal triumph at this general election marked the final deathblow of the fair-trade movement. A few meetings continued to be held; but, to all intents and purposes, the movement had died with the defeat in the election of 1892.

Although the fair-trade movement was now practically dead, it still contributed a great deal to the breakup of the Imperial Federation League. This League, founded in 1884, had agitated for closer ties with the colonies. But, under the control of free-traders, it had been averse to any form of imperial preference—possible only by England's adoption of some form of protection. The United Empire Trade League, formed in 1891 by prominent fair-traders to press for the adoption of commercial federation of the Empire, had contributed much to embarrass the free-trade leaders of the larger organization. This movement was so closely akin to the old Fair-Trade League that the *Times* continued to label their meetings "Fair Trade."

After Gladstone's rejection of its comprehensive scheme for imperial federation, on April 13, 1893, the Imperial Federation League had no longer sufficient strength to resist the importunities of Sir Charles Tupper and the other militant leaders of the United Empire Trade League. Recognizing, at last, that their differences were fundamental and irreconcilable, the free-traders took the only possible step to avoid losing control of League policy. On November 24, 1893, the Imperial Federation League was finally dissolved. After the dissolution of the League, the various branches continued, for a time, to operate. The United Empire Trade League also continued its agitation, but a period of stagnation had set in.

The reasons for this failure seem clear

enough. That the tariff-reform movements had failed to enlist the support of the English laboring classes was evident from the extensive revival of socialism in Great Britain during this period. To the great masses of unskilled labor, free trade or protection involved, according to John Burns, no question of principle, but only of expediency: "They are for Free Trade so long as this seems to further their interests; they will adopt Protection or Fair Trade, without dogmatic or theoretic scruples, should they at any time see any advantage in it." The unemployed demonstrations in February, 1886, and November, 1887, together with the great strikes of the late eighteen eighties and early nineties indicate the nature of the doctrines which the great masses, at this time, found more to their liking.

A general revival of interest in the problem of tariff reform was to occur only when Joseph Chamberlain, after the political and financial difficulties of the Boer War, promulgated his scheme for an imperial zollverein. But his plans are not to be considered new ones; they were essentially the same, in their emphasis on the commercial value of the colonies, as those of the National Fair-Trade League. "The League and the name he helped to snuff out," concludes Professor Clapham; "years afterwards the spirit entered into him. For its strength lay less in its economics, though they were not negligible, than in its sense of a changing world and in its nationalism."

WHEN VICTORIA BEGAN HER REIGN, in 1837, anti-imperialist sentiment was in the ascendant; when her reign ended, in 1901, anti-imperialist sentiment had not disappeared altogether, but it was unimportant as a force in British life. The intellectual father of the movement to dismember the Empire was, of course, Adam Smith, who in his *Wealth of Nations* (1776) had denounced mercantilism and criticized the imperialism that had developed historically with mercantilism. Smith had many disciples in nineteenth-century Britain— disciples with whose ideas and interests his position harmonized; and it was they who intensified the attack on imperialism. They argued that colonies were a financial and military blunder; that in time the colonies would insist on their independence in any case; and that it was best to anticipate this demand by freeing them. Anti-imperialist sentiment became especially glaring in the years after the repeal of the Corn Laws (1846). Now that Britain was moving toward free trade, what was the sense in keeping colonies that dated from the age of mercantilism? Even Disraeli, who in later years emerged as a leading hero of the imperialists, expressed the view in 1852 that colonies were nothing more than "a millstone round our necks." The climax of anti-imperialism occurred during the early part of Gladstone's first ministry (1868-1874). Shortly after Disraeli came to power, in 1874, however, a thoughtful observer could ask, "Who talks now of casting off the colonies? What more popular cry than the preservation of our colonial empire?" In the following essay, Professor D. G. Creighton, of the University of Toronto, one of the outstanding scholars in present-day Canadian historical circles, analyzes and explains the changes in Victorian conceptions of empire.

THE VICTORIANS AND THE EMPIRE

D. G. CREIGHTON

I

In their imperial aspect, the opening and the closing years of Queen Victoria's reign were deceptively similar. The first and the last decades were marked by crises in the colonies overseas and by concern for the colonies at home. And the apparent importance of colonial questions in both the 1830's and the 1890's is attested by the pre-occupation of ranking British statesmen in imperial affairs. The reign began with rebellions in the Canadas; it ended with the war in South Africa. Within a year of the accession, Lord Durham, the radical Whig, had been appointed high commissioner to British North America; and when the reign closed, Joseph Chamberlain, the hope of radical liberalism, was in command of the colonial office. These somewhat superficial analogies at least suggest an uninterrupted development of the empire and a continuous interest in imperial affairs. But in fact, of course, the empire which Queen Victoria bequeathed to her successor differed in kind from that which she had inherited; and the colonialism of the early Victorian period is essentially unlike the imperialism of the nineties. In between, lies a long period of decadence and growth; and this process, like so many others in Victoria's reign, has its culmination in the early seventies of the century. Before that lies the slow, sombre decline of the second empire; and after that comes the rapid, hectic growth of the third.

The difference between these two periods and these two attitudes can be suggested in a number of ways; and since historians, like economists, have an incurable tendency to moralizing, it has often been presented as a contrast between disinterested liberalism and ruthless acquisitiveness. There is revealed, on the one hand, the good imperialism of the 1840's which we are expected to venerate; and, on the other, the bad imperialism of the 1890's which we are required to deplore. The early Victorian period is made bright with the mild radiance of such liberal colonial reformers as Lord Durham, Charles Buller, Lord Elgin, and Lord Grey; and the late Victorian era is darkened by the sinister presence of such imperialists and capitalists as Disraeli, Chamberlain, and Cecil Rhodes. On the one hand, is a disinterested colonial statesmanship manifesting itself in the grant of responsible government and the concession of fiscal autonomy; and, on the other, is a greedy urge for exploitation revealing itself in the purchase of the Suez canal shares, the penetration of Egypt, the partition of Africa, and the assault on the Boers.

The Victorians themselves—at least the greater part of them—remained happily in ignorance of their descent from righteousness into moral turpitude. And we might possibly profit by copying their attitude, though with a difference. Anti-imperialists and imperialists followed each other in two great assaulting armies through Victorian England; but the one thing common to both the pros and the antis, and indeed to all Englishmen in their political capacity, is the undeviating consistency with which they invariably acted upon the strictest moral principles. When it was the fashion to cut colonial connections, British statesmen were concerned above all else to promote the manly independence of the colonists. When, on the contrary, it became the habit to acquire colonies, British statesmen became acutely sensible of their duty to assist the development of backward peoples. The Victorians claimed by implication a consistency which their liberal and radical historians are not prepared to concede them. But it is possible that the contemporaries have more justification than has posterity. It is the

Reprinted by special permission from *The Canadian Historical Review*, XIX (1938), 138-153.

motives of the Victorians, and not the consistency with which they upheld them, which can be called in question. Englishmen were accustomed to explain that they acted for the welfare of the colonists, when what they really and very sensibly did was to act in the interests of Englishmen. They destroyed the second empire and built up the third for mainly the same reason—because they wanted to.

＊

II

The first half of Queen Victoria's reign—the years from the coronation to the early seventies—was the period of lack of faith in the empire, lack of belief in its value, and lack of interest in its continuance. It saw the virtually complete destruction of the old colonial system: it left mainly those sentimental ties and connections, which in fact were felt chiefly by the colonies, and which could therefore be regarded with complacent indulgence by British statesmen trained in the Manchester school. The work of destruction was only finished in 1870; but in fact, of course, it had begun almost a century before, far back in the days of the American Revolution. For the second empire, the empire which survived the American War of Independence, was cursed from its birth. It was but a contemptible fragment of the first empire and like the first empire it was everywhere supposed to be destined for independence. But in the meantime it was the feeble basis of a great imperial system, both political and economic, which its unimportance and its impermanence alike made ridiculous. The colonies consumed endless time, occasioned ceaseless trouble, and created uninterrupted expense. And in return they gave nothing which could not be got more copiously, and far more cheaply, from free countries like the United States.

It was not however the colonies, but the mother country which made the discredit of the second empire. It was not the defects of the colonies which were responsible; it was rather the new virtues of the British which enabled them to view these defects with a more coldly critical eye. From the beginning, the second empire was certainly a feeble, ill-conditioned youngling in comparison with the brave fellow who had run away from home. But, what was even more important, he was compelled to grow up in the uncongenial home atmosphere of British industrial capitalism and his whole life was made miserable by the unfeeling discipline of the classical economists from Adam Smith down to John Stuart Mill. The century which followed the end of the American Revolution witnessed the rise and splendid maturity of British industrialism, based on the realities of coal and iron, and of British world commerce, based on the theory of free trade. This system, sprung upon an unsuspecting world, which was incapable of serious competition, reaped its gaudiest rewards in the decades after 1850; but it had other and more consoling justifications than that of mere material success. There are always plenty of economists, and there

JAMES ANTHONY FROUDE: Prolific English historian (d. 1894) whose multivolume account of Tudor history from the time of Henry VIII to the defeat of the Armada is a classic. He held strong views on the issues of his age, insisting that the Irish were not capable of self-rule and that the British had a civilizing mission in Ireland—and, indeed, all over the world.

SIR JOHN SEELEY: Publicist and historian (d. 1895) who believed in the British civilizing mission. His *Expansion of England* (1883) was a forceful attempt to arouse interest in imperial expansion and to justify British imperialism from the historical standpoint.

GOLDWIN SMITH: Anglo-Canadian historian, publicist, and controversialist (d. 1910). A vigorous defender of the ideas of the Manchester School, he was an ardent free trader and no less ardent an anti-imperialist.

are invariably hordes of economic vulgarizers, who are ready and willing to exalt the conditions peculiar to their age or the convictions personal to themselves, into economic and social dogmas, absolute, incontestible, and eternal. But it may be doubted whether even the Marxists afford a more brilliant example of this truth than do the classical economists of Great Britain. In the pages of Malthus, McCulloch, and Mill the principles of political economy became fixed and unchanging rules which one could only discuss in detail and which one could never refute in essence. In the mouths of Cobden, Bright, and other middle-class reformers, these rules became moral principles, which grew ever more sacrosanct and which took on by degrees the character of divine injunctions. It was intellectually criminal to refute these rules; it was profane and impious to flout them. And it is probable, that one would have to go back to James I and the scholars and doctors who developed the theory of the divine right of kings, to discover a more curious union of dogmatism and moral unction, or a more interesting mingling of the divine and the mundane.

For the second empire, the meaning of the new industrialism and the new political economy was all too clear. It was not that the English had unselfishly abandoned the urge for empire: it was simply that they had substituted the new, divinely-inspired imperialism for the old, simple-minded, sinful imperialism of the first empire. They looked beyond the limits of their stunted, contemptible little colonies to the trade and the economic domination of the world. Of what use were colonies, when the special economic privileges which they demanded conflicted with the mission of the English to sell cottons to the entire globe? Of what value were the discredited practices of the mercantile system when its errors had been exposed and refuted by the theorists of free trade? In this atmosphere, which was the air that everybody breathed and the air through which all problems of the age were visualized, the burdens laid upon Great Britain by the second empire began to assume enormous proportions, and the benefits which it conferred to contract within infinitesimal limits. It was these considerations which helped largely to persuade the British to assume their own major role in the dissolution of the second empire. It was these considerations which induced them to give only a half-hearted opposition to the efforts by which the colonies assisted in the breakdown. "One thing," wrote Carlyle in 1850, "strikes a remote spectator in these colonial questions: the singular placidity with which British statesmen at this time, backed by M'Croudy and the British moneyed classes, are prepared to surrender whatsoever interest Britain might pretend to have in the decision. 'If you want to go from us, go: we by no means want you to stay; you cost us money yearly, which is scarce; desperate quantities of trouble too; why not go, if you wish it?' Such is the humour of British statesmen at this time."

It is distinctly to the credit of the British that they half persuaded themselves and wholly convinced posterity that this was not an imperial dissolution, but a grand imperial reform. The whole series of changes, which completely altered the structure of the second empire, has often been presented as if it were the work of a few disinterested liberal imperialists, acting in a kind of a vacuum created by their own idealism and their devotion to the empire. Attention has been concentrated, not upon the breaches in the imperial system which the British made in despite of colonial protest, but upon the few concessions which they granted in response to colonial importunities. The work of statesmen who were prepared to anticipate the break-up of the empire with equanimity if not with enthusiasm, has been dignified as colonial reform; and almost any politician who was willing to give up imperial controls, upon which he placed no value, in order to be rid of imperial burdens which he desired to escape, can qualify for the title of colonial reformer. The truth is, that if the British had believed in their empire, they would have fought for it, as they fought in 1775. But since they were non-believers, they were prepared for capitulation; and since they were Victorians, they contrived to invest their surrender with an air of dignified and impressive liberalism.

There were, of course, a few genuine colonial reformers at the beginning of Victoria's reign—men, that is, who understood reform to be something a little superior to the gentlemanly huckstering by which one surrendered privileges in exchange for the cancellation of burdens. Lord Durham, Charles Buller, Gibbon Wakefield, and William Molesworth were members of this group; but by the middle of the nineteenth century their day was definitely over. A faint air of disrepute hung over them. They were young, or they were politically unmanageable, or they had become regrettably involved in marital difficulties; and concern for the colonies was thus vaguely associated with political instability and moral error. Finally, the colonial reformers committed the great mistake of dying early. Charles Buller, the man who wrote *Responsible government for colonies,* died when he was barely forty; but William Ewart Gladstone, the alleged colonial reformer who recalled the imperial troops at the moment when New Zealand was threatened with Maori war, lived stoutly on to become the very personification of enlightened Victorian statesmanship.

The ideas of the colonial reformers found echoes in a few curious places; but perhaps not altogether unexpectedly from Thomas Carlyle. Carlyle has even been called the father of modern imperialism; he will certainly be called the father of modern fascism by his next biographer; and the first description is just about as instructive as the second. Like the colonial reformers, Carlyle believed that emigration to the colonies might be the means of allaying the social evils in the mother country; but though he took a practical interest in the colonies as a possible solution for what he used to call the "Sallow or Yellow Emancipation" question, he frequently conceived of them in a more grandiosely romantic fashion. He expatiated proudly upon their vast spaces, their splendid future, and the blood and treasure and bravery which had been expended in their conquest. Finally, the colonies, like every other society in which Carlyle was interested, appeared an eminently suitable place for the beneficent operations of the Carlylean hero. Totally rejecting the reformer's idea of responsible government, Carlyle insisted that the queen should select "some gallant-minded, stout, well-gifted cadet" as the typical governor. To him she was to say: "See, I have scores and scores of 'Colonies,' all ungoverned, and nine tenths of them full of jungles, boa-constrictors, rattlesnakes, Parliamentary Eloquences, and Emancipated Niggers, ripening towards nothing but destruction; one of these you shall have, you as Vice-King; . . . go you and buckle with it, in the name of heaven; and let us see what you will build it to."

These odd, unimportant, discordant protests were the only thing that broke the silence of indifference or interrupted the steady, peevish whine of belittlement. Colonial historians are naturally though erroneously accustomed to evaluate British interest in the colonies on the basis of the reams of paper which were consumed in the writing of colonial dispatches. It may be observed that in general, colonial officials wrote dispatches because they were paid to do so; and being normal men, they took a normal interest in doing a good job. But their activities could, and sometimes did, have about as little significance for the mass of their fellow-countrymen as do the operations of the Indian department for the population of Canada. It was in parliament itself, as well as in the country in general, that the attitude of the English people to colonies was plainly revealed. The colonial portfolio was itself regarded as of secondary importance in the cabinet. It was looked upon either as a brief stopping-place for some gifted politician on the make, or as a somnolent sinecure for someone who had lost his ambition or his party usefulness.

And often it was very hard to fill. "Well, I'll take the office myself," Lord Palmerston is alleged to have said to a permanent official on one occasion. "Just come upstairs and show me on the map where these damned places are." Even as late as the nineties, it was a matter of some small wonderment that Joseph Chamberlain, of whom one naturally expected better things, should actually prefer to take the colonial portfolio.

The mere mention of things colonial was usually sufficient to clear the house of commons of all but the most obstinate parliamentarians; and the opening sentences of the colonial secretary were lost in the noise of members departing for the more intellectual atmosphere of the lobbies or neighbouring chop-houses. The few members who watched the British North America Act of 1867 in its speedy passage through parliament could scarcely conceal their excruciating boredom; and after the ordeal was over, they turned with lively zeal and manifest relief to the great national problem of the tax on dogs. Most of the permanent undersecretaries for the colonies during the early decades of Queen Victoria's reign subscribed to what may be called the pomological view of colonies—the view, that is, that all colonies, like ripe apples, were destined inevitably to drop off the parent tree. They and their contemporaries showed little disposition to arrest the fall. There was scarcely a front rank statesman in early Victorian England who was not prepared to view the departure of the colonies with cheerfulness decorously mingled with resignation. And Lord John Russell, Gladstone, and Disraeli were all at times jarred out of their habitual polite indifference into positive and indignant denunciations of the imperial tie.

The heart of the whole movement was Manchester—Manchester, the centre of the new imperialism masquerading in a sober anti-imperialist disguise. It was Manchester's machinery and capital which destroyed the second empire; it was Manchester's prophets and priests who justified the destruction to an impressed and attentive populace. The Manchester school produced Goldwin Smith, who throughout a long life, devoted himself to the task of assisting nature in breaking up the second empire; and although Messrs. Cobden and Bright could give only intermittent attention to the imperial problem, their whole philosophy was the sufficient basis for the anti-imperialist attack. As fanatically righteous free traders, they abhorred the whole tangle of tariffs, preferences, and shipping regulations which made up the old colonial system. As professional anti-militarists, they deplored the awful business of colonial defence. Their tone, the whole character of their argument was such a pleasantly acceptable mixture of practicality and unction, of pecuniary considerations and moral earnestness, that it commanded devout and grateful respect.

Under the inspired leadership of the Manchester school, the whole political and economic world of Great Britain made a determined assault upon the second empire. In the period between 1840 and 1870, it was systematically destroyed, in all aspects, economic, political, and military. Great Britain repealed the corn laws, the timber duties, and the navigation laws, and thereby destroyed at a blow the whole system of imperial preferences and shipping monopolies upon which the colonies had built up their economic existence. But when the colonies, emulating Great Britain's exclusive concern for her own material interests, sought to build up their puny national economies by means of tariffs, there was a great wail of shocked surprise from the mother country. None of the alleged colonial reformers would listen for a moment to the absurd argument that if it was permissible for Great Britain to destroy tariffs in what Englishmen considered to be the national interest, then it was equally permissible for the colonies to establish tariffs in what the colonists considered to be their national interest. The reason for this distinction was transparently clear. Free trade was not an advantage to England: it was a principle of political economy: and Mr. Cobden, who knew all about these matters, was aware that it had the sanction of the deity. Protection could never be an advantage to any state, for it was founded on economic error and was *prima facie* evidence of moral turpitude. Great Britain had embraced free trade, merely because she had seen the light; the colonies hankered after protection merely because they had an incurable tendency to sin. This point was beautifully put by Goldwin Smith, in a passage which combined intellectual and moral arrogance in nicely graduated quantities: "The colonies have a strong propensity to the commercial vice of Protectionism. . . . Protection is the natural resort of ignorant cupidity, and ignorant cupidity is the besetting sin of communities intensely commercial and wanting in education."

It was, however, upon the question of imperial defence that the Cobdenites trained their heaviest artillery. Dislike of the garrisons, which Great Britain maintained in the colonies for their protection, was strengthened by Cobden's desire for what he called retrenchment and by Bright's love of peace; and the opposition to imperial militarism evoked all the exquisite talent for moral argumentation which the reformers had developed in their other humanitarian crusades. Messrs. Cobden and Bright, as is well known, opposed the ten-hours' day for industry in England; but they did so, not merely out of pre-occupation with the pecuniary interests of the employer, but also out of deep concern for the moral fibre of the labourers. Cobden, as he was careful to point out, was one of labour's sincerest friends; but he deplored what he called "a spurious humanity" or "a morbid sympathy" with labour's woes; and he greatly preferred a "masculine species of charity" which would encourage among workmen an independence, a self-respect, and disdain of being patronized and petted. This argument, which had served so well in the relations between capitalist and employee, was used unaltered to elucidate the proper relations between the colonies and England; and in this case, of course, the thoughtful capitalist was the mother country and the workmen lacking moral fibre were the colonies. If Great Britain were to withdraw her troops from the empire, it would be admittedly a financial advantage to England; but it would also be—and was not this the real point?—a moral gain for the colonies. "If," said John Bright, "they are to be constantly applying to us for guarantees for railways, and for grants for fortresses, and for works of defence . . . then I think it would be far better for them and for us— cheaper for us, and less demoralizing for them—that they should become an independent State. . . ." It was, in fact, a matter of great consolation for the Victorian imperial reformers to realize how invariably the pecuniary advantage of England coincided with the moral betterment of the colonies.

British statesmen could take an unprejudiced and manly stand in the subject of imperial defence, for, of course, nobody expected that the colonies would ever move to the assistance of the mother country. Great Britain had no desire to aid the colonies; and she naturally assumed that the colonies, acting on correct Manchester principles, would never have any intention of aiding her. The few people who discussed the bare possibility of colonial assistance, did so merely with the obvious intention of being humorous. Sir Charles Dilke, who made a tour of the English-speaking world in 1866 and wrote a book called *Greater Britain,* could wax very indignant over the spectacle of "Dorsetshire agricultural labourers paying the cost of defending New Zealand colonists in Maori wars," for the simple reason that he had not the faintest expectation that New Zealanders would ever come in scores of thousands from the other side of the world to fight for Great Britain in Belgium. "It is not likely, nowadays," he wrote, "that our colonists would, for any long stretch of time, engage to aid us in our purely European wars. Australia would scarcely feel herself deeply interested in the guarantee of Luxemburg, nor Canada in the affairs of Servia." This peculiarly unfortunate prophecy was the calm assumption of all who were concerned at home in the empire's affairs. And in 1869-71, the Gladstone government recalled the troops, despite the bitter protests of New Zealand that they were left defenceless in the probable event of a Maori war. The Gladstone government, adopting a tone which they might have employed in addressing a tenth-rate foreign power, replied to these protests with long, hectoring lectures. The evacuation of the troops went on all over the empire; and when in November, 1871, the last imperial soldiers marched down the streets of Quebec singing "Auld Lang Syne," the second empire of Great Britain was ended forever.

III

At almost exactly the same moment the change began. The death of the old empire coincided with nearly complete exactitude with the birth of the new imperialism. The very country which had dropped a few of its possessions and had considered dropping a lot more, now became curiously interested in acquiring new colonies. The very people who had derided the sentimental affection by which the colonists had kept the empire together, now began to develop imperial emotions of their own. The Royal Colonial Institute was founded in 1868: the recall of the troops from New Zealand aroused a sudden curious burst of imperial sentiment. In 1872 the incredible Disraeli— the man who had talked angrily a few years before of the "colonial deadweights"—informed an impressed audience at the Crystal Palace that the preservation of the empire was one of the three great objectives of the Conservative party. In 1875 that unrepentant spendthrift, the Khedive Ismail of Egypt, brought his shares in the Suez canal to market: and Disraeli, prompted no doubt by that oriental imagination of which disapproving English historians make so much, overcame the opposition of the cabinet and used the Rothschild money to purchase the Khedive's interest. Moreover, he created

that strangely un-English title "The Empress of India" to the immense gratification of the queen and to the embarrassment, disapproval, or amusement of his colleagues. The Indian empire was new only in name; but the adventure into Egypt was a real, if apparently a modest, novelty. And it had been preceded, a few years before, by the even more inconspicuous beginning to an even wilder series of imperial adventures. In 1868 a Boer farmer in South Africa purchased a small stone from a native witch-doctor. He paid everything he had for it—500 sheep, 10 oxen, and a horse. But he sold it to a trader for £11,000; and the trader resold it for £25,000. The stone weighed 83 carats and it came to be called the Star of South Africa. Two years later, in 1870, diamonds were discovered in considerable quantities at Kimberley. And in the same year, by one of those beautiful coincidences of history, Cecil John Rhodes landed in South Africa.

The change from the commercial cosmopolitanism of the Cobdenites to the territorial imperialism of the later Victorians is one of the most fascinating and the most difficult problems of the nineteenth century. But in the main the change was due not to the altered stature of the colonies, but to the disturbed state of Europe in general and England in particular. It was not the novel importance of the colonies which created the new imperialism any more than it was their previous insignificance which had precipitated the collapse of the second empire; in the second case, as in the first, it was British interests and British necessities which dictated the change. It was obvious, of course, even to the Victorians, that the empire was changing in character. Few people, except freaks like Carlyle, had predicted that the settlement colonies would ever amount to anything. But the plain fact seemed to be that they were progressing; and there were even a few daring Englishmen who were willing to prophesy that in the remote future they might be of some slight consequence in world affairs. It came home to the Victorians with a great shock of surprise that other European powers—powers who were fortunately bereft of colonies—seemed actually to be making very strenuous efforts to acquire some. Could it be that the British had under-estimated their overseas possessions? The idea was, of course, nonsensical and anyway it could never be publicly acknowledged. But might there not be in it an infinitesimal grain of truth?

It was, in short, the changed economic and political balance of power in the world at large, rather than the growing consequence of the settlement colonies, which gave impetus to the new imperialism. The year 1870 lifted the curtain on a new and vaguely disturbing scene. The world was suddenly crowded—overcrowded—with great hulking and ambitious national states. Italy was no longer a congeries of petty principalities: it was a nation. The Civil War and Reconstruction had created a new United States. The German Empire had sprung into being. These great national states were destroying the early Victorian ideal of peaceful commercial cosmopolitanism. They were violating the principle of free trade which had been the basic theory of Manchester; they were breaking up the economic unity of the globe which had been Manchester's material objective. The new world was evincing a disappointing disinclination to remain an economic unit—open and passively ready for the exploitation of the British. France and Germany and the United States were intent on tariffs—and the magisterial rebukes of Earl Grey and William Ewart Gladstone were even more ineffectual here than they had been in the case of the colonies. Moreover—alarming thought—the great national states began to manufacture, and on a large scale. They developed technical skills and superior technical education. And in the last crucial test, the test of world trade, the results of this revolution were manifest. Great Britain lost that position of uncontested and commanding superiority which had been hers since the beginning of the industrial revolution and which she had

accepted complacently as the rightful reward of her pious adherence to the inspired doctrines of political economy. The new national states began to invade the markets of the world. They began to pre-empt these markets as colonies or as spheres of influence.

Urged on by the pressure of these material factors and goaded by her capitalists and publicists, Great Britain entered the race for empire once more. The new imperialism was not, of course, a really novel apparition, it was simply the older and even more arrogant imperialism of the Cobdenites, suitably altered to meet the changing conditions; but its spirit, its methods, and its territorial interests were profoundly different. The older settlement colonies—Canada, Australia, New Zealand, as well as the empire of India—were all swept into the movement and sometimes occupied a central position in it; but it was not those places which kept the interest of capitalists and aroused the imagination of the people: it was Afghanistan, Egypt, and above all Africa. The drama of the new empire was played out against a gaudy backdrop of tropical forests, and great sluggish rivers, and empty veldt and sand, and terrible mountain passes. It had its triumphs and its heroic tragedies. There was that lost hundred soldiers at Rorke's drift, nearly half of them ill and fevered, who fought all night against the massed thousands of Zulus. There was that mere handful of men—Alan Wilson's patrol—who were surrounded by the Matabele army and fired their last round of ammunition, and stood up, the few survivors, and sang "God Save the Queen" and fell where they stood. These deeds of simple and outrageous bravery were followed and preceded by other acts, some of unremitting devotion, others of greed, cunning, and unprovoked violence. Livingstone plunged into the depths of central Africa, but in other remote and barbaric places like old King Lobengula's court in Matabeleland, concession hunters, with tired, anxious, predatory faces, intrigued among themselves and imposed on native credulity, to win the contract which would give them the right to dig for imagined gold. The period had its heroes—simple, fearless soldiers like Kitchener and Gordon: it had its capitalists and picturesque adventurers like Beit, and Barney Barnato of Kimberley. And among these last was Dr. Leander Starr Jameson, the hero or the villain of the raid into the Transvaal, with his "I-suppose-I-must-do-this" expression and his "I-know-I-will-do-this" mind.

Of them, but above them all, was Rhodes. He summed up the entire new empire—he personified it—its diverse and contradictory characteristics are united and reconciled in the elemental fact of his personality. He was at once an absurd romantic, a cool and cynical realist. There is both a massiveness and a childish naïveté in his designs. He was a portent of those forces, both material and moral, which are even now effecting the transformation of modern politics. In a document which he wrote in 1877, when he was twenty-four, he declared that he would work "for the furtherance of the British Empire, for the bringing of the whole civilized world under British rule, for the recovery of the United States, for the making of the Anglo-Saxon race into one Empire." He was a visionary who dreamed dreams; but he was also a capitalist who kept his eye unerringly fixed on realities; and the grandiose clauses of the various wills, by which he bequeathed his fortune for the spread of Britain's empire, are paralleled by the cool, laconic phrases in which he described the brute facts of his time. "Cobden," said Rhodes tersely, "had his idea of Free trade for all the world, but that idea has not been realized. The question of the day is the tariff question, and no one tells the people anything about it. . . . These islands can only support six millions out of their thirty-six millions. . . . We cannot afford to part with an inch of the world's surface which affords a free and open market to the manufactures of our countrymen. . . . It must be brought home to you that your trade is the world, and your life is the

world, and not England. That is why you must deal with these questions of expansion and retention of the world." Rhodes, in short, aspired simply to win a universal empire for England; and to himself, as the first task, he allotted Africa. And he was in a hurry—in a desperate hurry. For beyond the Cape Colony were the Orange Free State, the Transvaal, Bechuanaland, Matabeleland, and the whole north—"My North," Rhodes used to call it.

In the meantime, while the soldiers and promoters and speculators were founding the new empire overseas, there was an increasing boom in imperialism at home. The imperialists began to get into the newspapers and periodicals: they started to hold conferences. J. A. Froude founded the school of philosophy which was to supersede Manchesterism, and in 1883 Seeley published *The expansion of England.* The change was observable, however, not merely in these new voices, but also in the strangely novel accents of the old. Charles Dilke, the man who had written *Greater Britain*—of which he evidently considered the United States to be the most important part—published a new treatise entitled *Problems of Greater Britain;* and to the altered Mr. Dilke the chief problem appeared to be, not the task of expediting imperial separation, but the labour of promoting imperial unity. Tennyson's *Hands all round,* when it was first published in 1852, was chiefly made up of a denunciation of France and an offer of friendship to America. But the laureate, in imperial matters as in so many others, moved resolutely with the times; and when *Hands all round* reappeared in 1882, it was found to contain a great hymn to empire, with Canada, Australia, and India all mentioned in terms of respectful admiration. With a rapidity which left the colonies dizzy and breathless, Great Britain passed from the novel conviction that she must keep her surviving colonies to the inspired reflection that she could federate the entire empire. The colonies, which had barely ceased to fear imperial dismemberment, were suddenly invited to declare their views on imperial federation. They were haled forth, blinking, into the sunshine of Britannic favour; they were invited to sit in colonial congresses and to participate in the colour and splendour of the jubilees.

The movement for closer imperial unity, which reached and passed its height in the last two decades of the century, travelled the old and difficult paths toward the old and almost forgotten objectives. The early Victorians, who had recalled the legions, broken the mercantile system, and conceded responsible government, were now succeeded by the late Victorians who hoped to establish a common system of imperial defence, who aspired to tighten the commercial relations and the political unity of the empire. The work of imperial unification was undertaken in the same disinterested and liberal spirit in which the process of imperial decentralization had been carried through; and it was assumed that, in some unexplained and not entirely explicable fashion, imperial federation would be a great concession to the older settlement colonies. It was a concession whose merits were more adequately appreciated in Great Britain than in the colonies; but even in Great Britain it encountered resistance from the established policies of the past. The new British imperialism was in large measure the response of the British national state to the new national state system of Europe; and it was not unfitting that the movement for imperial federation should be blocked by those very national forces which had helped to set it in motion. Great Britain was just as unwilling to surrender the remnants of imperial control as were the colonies to abandon their newly won political autonomy. Preferential tariffs were just as objectionable to free-trade England as were imperial *zollvereins* to protectionist colonies. The Imperial Federation League, which had tried vainly to reconcile these conflicting interests, wound up its affairs in 1893; and the imperial conference of 1897 dispelled some of the great dreams of formal reorganization upon which Victorian

imperialism had fed for the last two decades.

It was the war in South Africa and not the achievement of imperial federation which was to form the not inappropriate climax of the new Victorian imperialism. The issue of preferential trade remained and was to divide the British Unionist party in the near future; but the exponents of closer political unity had failed to find their formula and the new imperial association assumed the vaguer title of British Empire League. As its theories were tacitly abandoned, British imperialism took on a more cloudy grandeur; and, as the Boer War drew steadily closer, it acquired a kind of exalted truculence of tone. It was this spirit, disseminated unconsciously and deliberately through various channels to the receptive peoples of the empire, which decided one of the great questions which the imperial conference of 1897 had left unresolved. The words of Reid, of New South Wales, at the imperial conference were prophetic. "The great test of our relations . . . ," he said, "will be the next war in which England is engaged . . . that feeling of patriotism, we may call it—it would flame out just as practically in the Colonies, in the hour of danger, as in England; but it is only in those moments that you can make the people one in the sense of sacrifice." It was not through the grant of political and economic concessions, but through the sense of sacrifice in a great imperial effort, that the empire of the Victorians was united at the last; and the very consciousness of colonial nationalism which had checked the invasions of autonomy, now encouraged the colonies to take the important place to which they felt entitled in the great affairs of an empire of which they were morally a part. It was a tribute to the potency of the new imperialism that, thirty years after Great Britain had withdrawn the garrisons from the colonies, the colonial contingents should be fighting in their first imperialist war.

At the very time when anti-imperialist sentiment was reaching its climax, the British government was beginning at last to grapple in a significant way with the Irish question. When William Ewart Gladstone announced at the outset of his first ministry (1868-1874) that his mission was to pacify Ireland, one major reason was that American Fenians were causing a great deal of embarrassment to the British government. Gladstone's response to the Fenian attempt to publicize Irish grievances took the form of an act (1869) for the disestablishment and partial disendowment of the Church of Ireland (Protestant Episcopal) and of a Land Act (1870) designed to improve the position of the Irish tenant. Despite these reforms, the Irish question became more difficult than ever; and so Gladstone worked for additional economic reforms for Ireland during the course of his second ministry (1880-1885). The main concession this time was the Land Act of 1881, which embodied the principle of the "three F's" (fair rent, fixity of tenure, and free sale) and recognized the land rights of tenants as well as of landlords. But because economic reforms did not put an end to the Irish demand for the repeal of the Act of Union, Gladstone finally became converted to the cause of Home Rule; and during his last two ministries he fought, if unsuccessfully, for the Home Rule Bills of 1886 and 1893. By championing Home Rule, Gladstone in effect extended recognition to one of the fundamental developments in nineteenth-century Irish history: the growth of nationalism. In the essay that follows, the eminent Irish scholar and ardent Irish nationalist Michael Tierney, president of University College, Dublin, sets forth his conception of the historical evolution of Irish nationalism.

ORIGIN AND GROWTH OF MODERN IRISH NATIONALISM
MICHAEL TIERNEY

It is the purpose of this paper to deal as objectively as possible with the origins and character of the complex phenomenon known as Irish nationalism. Students of British history, and in particular of the British Commonwealth of Nations in its modern form, while necessarily recognising the existence of this phenomenon, can hardly be said as a general rule to understand it very fully or to judge its past importance and present potentialities in a very sure light. Yet it has been an influence in the modern development of British government whose force can scarcely be overestimated; and it is doubtful if any other single factor has contributed so much to the formation of the British Commonwealth of Nations as at present constituted. The setting up of the Irish Free State in 1922 and its recent transformation into the State of Ireland or Éire may seem to have, to some extent at least, eliminated this force from the field of British and Commonwealth politics; but its complete objectives are as yet unrealised, and its strength remains at least as great as before. It is therefore obvious that sooner or later, when the appropriate crisis occurs, it will again come into play and that its repercussions, as always, will be formidable.

Reprinted by special permission from *Studies: An Irish Quarterly Review*, XXX (1941), 321-332.

There are two common fallacies in relation to Irish nationalism upon which, apart from failure to judge its strength, most of the disastrous misunderstandings of its meaning may be said to have so far rested. It is thought that it can be understood without knowledge of the long history which has produced it; and it is taken for a purely political phenomenon, whereas in its essential nature it is much more a cultural and social one. A slighter misunderstanding than these is the common propagandist view that Irish unrest in the past has been produced by some kind of original sin peculiar to the Irish character. There is no doubt that this character has played an enormous part in the tragic history of the relations between Ireland and Great Britain. Nevertheless it is true to say, as has so often been vainly repeated, that the Irish problem is essentially a British creation, and this not merely in times long past. At this very moment conscious and deliberate British policy is maintaining in Ireland a strident challenge to one of the most powerful Irish instincts, the instinct for national unity. The obvious Parliamentary reply that the British Government has no responsibility for partition ignores the much more obvious presence of British troops, paid by the British exchequer, in Northern Ireland to maintain it. Sooner or later that challenge will be met. How it will be met is a question the answer to which circumstances will dictate, and upon which the pacific declarations of present-day statesmen have no bearing.

It is easy for students familiar with the history of recently-formed communities to make mistakes in their estimation of the problems that arise in those of far older origin. Nineteenth and twentieth century parliamentary politics, dealing as they have done to so great an extent with questions of immediate practical import, have all along shown a fatal tendency to ignore deep-seated historical instincts, often incapable of precise formulation and entirely immeasurable by practical or business standards. In this immeasurability lies a very large part of the trouble about Irish nationalism, whose roots go far back into history and whose instinctive motions are often reactions to forces once powerful but now entirely spent and almost forgotten. The proverbial long memory of the Irish for past wrongs is not at all the conscious perversity in unreasoning rancour that it is so often represented as being. It is the complex subconscious product of a centuries-old struggle. Only the *naiveté* of an uninstructed and unimaginative "businessman" could suppose that such historical forces are unreal. They are the most powerful thing in history, and nowhere more powerful than in the very English community which has so often denied their right to existence in Ireland. What is peculiar about them in Ireland is that they are the product of an arrested development, and that there have existed for many centuries no traditional or organic national institutions, such as do exist in England, to correspond to them. At the present day the sole traditional Irish public institution is the Church, upon which in

---

WILLIAM MOLYNEUX: Protestant member of the Irish Parliament, disciple of John Locke, leading opponent of English legislation for Ireland, and author of *The Case of Ireland being bound by Acts of Parliament in England, Stated* (1698). In this pamphlet, which he dedicated to King William, he used and abused history in an effort to "prove" that the English Parliament had no right to legislate for Ireland.

WOLFE TONE: Dublin barrister who led the Irish movement for independence in the age of the French Revolution. He appealed to peasants for backing, insisting that "if the men of property will not support us, they must fall: we will free ourselves by the aid of that large and respectable class of the community,—the men of no property." French aid was not forthcoming, however, and Tone was put in prison, where he committed suicide in order to avoid the gallows.

Ireland the native character has been indelibly stamped, so that if you want to meet the typical Irishman you must seek out the priest. Everything else in Ireland is nostalgia for the past or aspiration towards the future. It must above all be emphasised, with the greatest possible force, that English political and social institutions have no meaning for the Irishman and call forth no loyalty from him. This applies to all institutions from Crown to Commonwealth and from peer to county council. Some of these institutions are passively accepted; they are not respected and least of all can they be said to be loved.

The origins of Irish nationalism must be sought far back in history, in the existence of a distinctive Irish civilisation, which was itself produced by the impact of the Christian Church upon a much older native pagan culture. There is little or no analogy between this Irish civilisation and those of the normal European States, which go back in one form or another to the political and social institutions of the Roman Empire. Ireland, unlike England, Germany or the Latin States, was Romanised only to the extent that it was Christianised. What resulted was not political unity nor even any clear political idea, but a most powerful and permanent native literary, artistic and religious culture, taking its highest form in the deepest consciousness of national unity and national otherness. Unlike Scotland, which owed both its national monarchy and its native culture to Irish colonists, Ireland never achieved more than a transient and uneasy political union among its many local communities and provincial kingdoms. What it did achieve was more powerful, less liable to injury from external attack. Its native civilisation triumphed over Scandinavian and Norman invaders, assimilated both, put up a long struggle against the centralised Tudor State, held out in an attenuated form even against the triumphant English nationalism of the seventeenth and eighteenth centuries, and has survived to the present day to be perhaps the strongest element in the complex Irish national character. One of the strangest things about modern English historical scholarship is that it should have devoted so little attention to this highly original and remarkably vital civilisation, the remnants of which could transform British politics when the Empire was at its strongest. The explanation of this neglect can only lie in the tragic antipathy which goes back as far as the outlawing of the native Irish in their own country by the Norman invaders.

The nearest comparison which enables us to grasp the character of this historic Irish civilisation is that with the great non-political cultures of the Orient, such as those of India and especially of China. It need hardly be said that this comparison is one of essence rather than one in respect of either quality or quantity. No attempt is at all implied to place the products of Irish national culture on the same level as those of the East. What is intended is rather to point out the similarity, on a totally different scale, between the non-political but religious, literary and artistic culture of, say, China, which produced its own very original and peculiar national institutions and gave the Chinese character a permanent impress, and the phenomenon which produced an exactly similar result in the small island of Ireland. In both cases it was the strength imparted by originality and long-continued adaptation to the ideas of one people that enabled the native culture, with only a shaky political framework or with none, to withstand a long series of internal crises and attacks from without. Just as the great culture of China seems at the present moment to be transforming itself, under European, American and Japanese pressure, into a highly explosive and dangerous brand of nationalism, so, under English pressure since the fall of the Stuarts, has Irish culture been transferred into a product which, while it has lost a great deal of its cultural character, is as little capable of yielding to that pressure as was the culture itself.

Irish civilisation had already acquired its characteristic form before the Scandinavian invasions in the ninth century. The effect upon it of these invasions, for all the disastrous losses they entailed, was to set it off upon another very original and still highly creative phase. There was even an effort, caused by military exigencies, to establish a strong national political unity as a sort of expression for the cultural unity which had for centuries already prevailed. This effort came to nothing owing to the death of Murchad, Brian's son, at the Battle of Clontarf, 1014. The period which followed is known in Irish history as that of the Kings with Opposition; but although marked by great political disunion, it was a period of powerful reintegration in religion and culture, so that the modern dioceses and parishes, by far the most important and organic social units, as well as some of the finest products of the native art and literature, date from this time. The Normans came with a Papal commission to introduce order and civilisation to Ireland. What they really brought was a violent intensification of political anarchy, from which the country was not to emerge for centuries, and a very marked decline in all cultural activities. Nevertheless, the native way of life, language, and artistic as well as social traditions prevailed, and by the end of the fourteenth century the Normans were becoming "more Irish than the Irish themselves." This assimilative process, however, was never completed, and in the end led to the growth of a new and very important element in Irish history, the Anglo-Irish element, that "middle nation" which, reinforced by continual fresh arrivals from England and ultimately marked by the religious difference, was to become the Ascendancy of the eighteenth and nineteenth centuries and is still entrenched in a dominant position in the six counties of Ulster. This failure on the part of the native Irish to assimilate the Normans and the corresponding failure of the Normans and English to assimilate the Irish constitutes the great tragedy of Irish history. It left the country a perpetual battle-ground, and the battle was set long before the Reformation, which only intensified it. In the great wars of the sixteenth century what was at stake was the traditional Irish type of society, way of life, and distinctive cultural unity; and with the attempt to impose the reformed religion, this cultural unity acquired a more religious character than had marked it before.

The seventeenth century was in Ireland a strange transitional period. Down to the collapse of the national resistance to King William at the Battle of Aughrim in 1691, a great deal of the old order still survived in spite of the Cromwellian upheaval and the steady persecution of the Catholics. It could almost seem as if the Stuart monarchy, itself Gaelic in origin though very little in spirit, was a guarantee for the continuance in some form of Gaelic culture. This was certainly the view of the poets, whose order had for centuries been the mainstay and symbol of the traditional cultural unity of Gaelic Ireland. They gave all their allegiance to the Stuart dynasty; and when it fell, their greatest representatives saw that Gaeldom had fallen along with it. The full history of Ireland's relation to the Stuarts has yet to be written. It was even more decisive and more tragic than that of Scotland. English and Scottish historians of the Stuarts seem scarcely to realise that, even after the Williamite triumph and the almost complete banishment of the Irish aristocracy, there was continued, especially in the south of Ireland, a great volume of popular poetry which linked the hopes and aspirations of the downtrodden Gaelic peasantry, not merely with the traditions of a vanished past but with the expectation that sooner or later the "Merchant's Son," the heir of King James, would return in triumph across the sea. It was to Scotland that the heir at last did return, but it was in Ireland that he was awaited with more passionate, and more artistically expressed longing. The half-century from Aughrim and Limerick to the Forty-five was filled with the expression of this hope in an eventual restoration, which it was dreamt would bring with it not merely religious freedom and the restitution of the land to its immemorial owners, but the revival of the old proud aristocratic culture of the Gael with its poetry, its music, and its traditions going back beyond Christianity to Oisin, the Fianna, and the Red Branch Knights. Culloden was just as much an Irish as a Scottish disaster, but whereas Scotland thereafter lay helpless, Ireland's helplessness was to prove more apparent than real. There was to be another revival, more powerful than any before it, but this time it was to take an entirely new form and to be in many respects, like Sun Yat Sen's programme for new China, a negation of the old ideals.

This new form was what we now know as Irish nationalism, an amalgam of the political unrest, which began towards the end of the eighteenth century to develop amongst the Ascendancy class in Ireland, with the old instinctive aspirations of the populace. Already in the seventeenth century there had been a curious prefiguration of this new mixture, in the shape of a kind of aristocratic nationalism cemented by the religious bond between the Old Irish nobility and those of the Old English in Ireland (as they were called) who had remained Catholic. It was upon this brief but prophetic union that the Confederation of Kilkenny had rested. The religious bond, however, was too tenuous to last in face of intense racial antagonism, and the Old English rallied to the Stuarts or even to the Parliament cause. After Aughrim and Limerick there was no more native and very little Catholic aristocracy left. The ownership of land in Ireland was transferred almost entirely to Protestant hands, and this transference was completed during the next half-century by a long series of apostasies motivated by the desire to hold on to estates. By about 1750 Ireland was owned by an absentee aristocracy, mostly of foreign origin and almost exclusively Protestant in religion. The mass of the people were crushed down into a uniform condition of misery as tenants at will, their religion proscribed, their national traditions doomed to illiterate decay, their very language beginning to yield at last before the growing prestige of English. The triumph of this Ascendancy was bound up with the Stuart failure and the victory of the Hanoverian dynasty, as well as with the supremacy of the Protestant religion and the proscription of the Catholic. It was to combat this system that Irish nationalism came into being. What is little realised outside Ireland and less even inside it is that this system, in most of its essential features, lasted down to the Great War of 1914 in the South and is still entirely predominant in the North.

From the standpoint of nationalism, the gloomiest period in Irish history was the half-century which elapsed between 1745 and the Union in 1801. The old hope of a Stuart restoration, poor as it was, was dead with Culloden, and for the ordinary Irishman there was nothing to take its place. Indeed, so low had the great majority sunk by that time that it was questionable if the ordinary Irishman was any longer capable of caring very much. He had become that bizarre, illiterate, tattered product that we begin to meet in the novels of Maria Edgeworth, speaking a queer jargon and bearing himself towards his social superiors with that easy-going tolerance which was never exactly respect and never lacked its touch of humour. His political consciousness could only express itself in outlandish secret societies—Ribbonmen, Whiteboys, Caravats, Shanavests—some of the names of which continued to inspire terror as late as a generation or so ago. Yet he still kept his fierce resentment at the loss of his religious freedom, as well as a very full consciousness that the land of Ireland belonged to him; and even though his language decayed, there remained to him a wealth of traditional lore, of half-remembered poetry and of very ancient saga, which contributed far more than external observers could realise to give him his unique national character. He was unarmed and uninstructed, but if the chance came he could fight with remarkable determination, as the events of 1798 in Wexford, Mayo and Longford were to prove. When he did fight, the motives that drove him to it were still the old, half-conscious but very real aspirations towards the recovery of his old possessions: his religion, his land and his peculiar native way of life.

What gave a renewed opportunity to the mass of the Irish people in these aspirations was the development, in the ranks of the Ascendancy itself, of nationalism in the modern sense of the word. This development had begun early in the century with Molyneux and Swift, neither of them Irish in origin and both still less so in culture. It was powerfully reinforced by the successful revolt of the American colonies and was made painfully acute by the French Revolution. The new nationalism was essentially a product of the English mentality, and quite beyond the range whether of the ancient Irish aristocracy or of the depressed modern peasantry. It took two forms, which ever since have competed one with the other, the desire to establish an Irish state virtually independent of England but entirely on the English model and owing allegiance to the Crown, and the more revolutionary policy of establishing an Irish republic modelled on that of France. The second was partly produced by the failure of the first after 1783, and both were entirely evolved by the same type of mind, an English not an Irish one. Between them, as alternatives to be pursued according to opportunity, they gave a new, intensely political development to a force which from the earliest centuries had lacked any clear political aim. They came at a highly providential moment, when the Stuart failure had seemed to deprive Ireland of all hope. It is very remarkable that ever since the end of the eighteenth century the most successful Irish political leaders have been men of English race: Grattan and Flood, Wolfe Tone and Emmet, Davis and Mitchel, James Stephens, Parnell, Redmond, Pearse. Even when the men have been entirely of Irish origin, as is the case with O'Connell and Michael Collins, their political ideas have derived from Ascendancy sources.

The Union of 1801 was not at all the decisive moment in Irish history that popular propaganda has made it seem. In one sense Lord Clare was perfectly right when he offered it to the Irish House of Lords as their sole means of protection against "the old inhabitants of the island," whom he graphically depicted as awaiting their hour to recover what they had lost. Though accompanied by the promise of Catholic Emancipation—a promise which was not kept—its real effect was to strengthen and perpetuate the Ascendancy, which had been tottering for ten years before. A second, entirely unlooked-for result was the marshalling of the common people henceforward behind the alternative aims of the new nationalism: Repeal and the Republic. Indecision as between these two aims has been the great mark of Irish politics from that day to this. Repeal has in recent times taken the form, first of Home Rule and later of Dominion status, but the alternative has remained the same. The indecision, or rather the opportunism, which led the people to embrace with apparent unanimity now the one and now the other, has arisen from the fact that the real objectives of the nation have been all along more fundamental, while of course seldom more than instinctive: Catholic Emancipation, the recovery of the land, and the restoration of the old Irish way of life with all that this implies in tradition, literature, and art. These objectives might be summed up in one phrase: the abolition of the Ascendancy imposed upon Ireland after the Treaty of Limerick in October 1691. It goes without saying that, in the sense of anything like a complete restoration of the past, they are unattainable. Ireland, the home of Oisin, to whose name Macpherson gave a European renown, is also the home of political romanticism. Catholic Emancipation is now over a century old, and the land has for the past fifty years been rapidly passing back into the hands of the people. At the present moment a very powerful effort is being made to revive the Irish language, lost over the greater part of the country during the course of the struggle since the Union. Whether this effort succeeds or fails—and it is likely to do neither completely—it is bound to have the most far-reaching effects on the cultural future of Ireland and, ultimately, on its political future as well.

In another respect also the Union had unforeseen results. It transferred the Irish question to the centre of British politics, where it became inevitably a focus of intense and lasting disturbance. For nearly a generation there was apparently nothing but the profound quiet of exhaustion, but the peace was shattered by O'Connell's election as member of Parliament for Clare in 1828. Catholic Emancipation became at once the question of the hour, its solution a matter of life or death. The old inhabitants of the island had at last gained the first of their objectives; and although much of its value was taken away by electoral devices, it became the starting-point for the great political activities within the framework of the Union. The vast agitation for Repeal was premature and was defeated not less by the ultimate political incapacity of the people than by O'Connell's notorious unwillingness to shed blood. The famine was the terrible price the nation had to pay for its passivity; but once more disaster gave the impetus for a fresh advance. It was the sons of the Famine victims who organised the Fenian terror and provided the striking-force in the land agitation. By the seventies another leader of genius, very significantly of English origin, had arisen, who was to triumph over the native ineptitude for politics and to weld republicans and constitutionalists together into the most formidable political organisation Ireland had ever known. Parnell's work was to win the second native victory over Ascendancy, in the form of the Land Acts. It is significant enough that he himself was primarily only little interested in the land agitation and that, while possessed of a towering genius for practical politics, he was unable to give Irish political aspirations more than a vague and tentative form. The discrepancy between Anglo-Irish political and native social aspirations is nowhere more plainly marked. Parnell's achievement more than ever deflected the course of English politics; the Tory party came for a time to be known as the Unionist party, and if his career had not been cut short the Liberals might very likely have got a new name as the party of Home Rule. The Irish question was henceforth to be the dominant influence on the career of almost every English statesman of note, until by 1914 it had brought Great Britain to the verge of civil war.

After Parnell's death his policy was carried on with much energy and devotion in Parliament, and the Irish question still held the front of the stage. Meanwhile, as if by regular succession, the incipient settlement of the land problem had brought forward in Ireland the third great popular instinct, the desire for the restoration of the old language and way of life. The Gaelic League, founded in 1893, was far more than a piece of linguistic romanticism. It offered to its rapidly growing membership a whole outlook on life, a complete national philosophy which at once embraced and transcended politics, work, sport and leisure of every kind. Never since the downfall of the old Gaelic order had the native Irishman possessed so satisfying and inspiring an intellectual equipment. Naturally its tendency ran towards the rejection of everything English, but inevitably also it tended to ally itself with the most extreme political doctrines, whose essentially English origin passed unnoticed. It was a great misfortune that it came at least a whole generation too late, for the native language was already gone out of use over the great part of Ireland and everywhere seemed stricken with an incurable decay. None the less it rediscovered the typical Irishman in the Gaelic-speaking peasant of the west, who had still kept alive the language, poetry, music and dance, the characteristic outlook on life and mental idiom of the national past when they were only a remote memory elsewhere. Through him and the living tradition he embodied, which was made clearer and more significant by the intense study of Irish literature, the concept of the Gael became an abiding national ideal and was to have a powerful influence on the politics of the future. Thus the nationalism of the twentieth century was an amalgamation of the two most vigorous forces in Irish life, which had at last come together: the republican doctrine set in motion by Wolfe Tone and inherited by the Irish Republican Brotherhood and the ancient Gaelic consciousness revived and sharpened by the Gaelic League and similar movements subsidiary to it. Of these latter movements the most remarkable was the so-called Irish Literary Renaissance, with its chief product the Abbey Theatre. In this the Anglo-Irish element, most vital representative of the old Ascendancy, borrowed from Ireland's Gaelic past and the living idiom of its peasantry an artistic and literary equivalent for the powerful political impetus it had already lent to the popular cause.

These were the forces fermenting with great and growing vigour in the Ireland of the decade before the Great War.

* * * * *

DESPITE THE VIGOROUS EFFORTS of the supporters of protective tariffs in late-Victorian times, the laissez-faire approach continued to dominate Britain's trade relations with foreign countries. In other branches of economic life, however, state intervention grew appreciably in the age of the Great Depression. Increasingly, it was believed by both Conservatives and Liberals that the government should recognize that it had obligations toward the underprivileged elements in British society. Measures were enacted to improve the position of Irish tenants by recognizing that they, as well as the landlords, had rights in the land; and by a series of acts Parliament sought to convert Irish tenants into peasant proprietors. On the domestic front, bills were passed dealing with such a variety of subjects as artisans' dwellings, the welfare of merchant seamen, public health and sanitation, factory conditions, child labor, railroad regulation, and the status of trade unions. Compared with imperial Germany, Britain was, to be sure, relatively backward in the realm of social-security legislation. By the end of the nineteenth century she still lacked the sickness insurance and the old-age pensions which Bismarck had sponsored in order to give German working-class elements a stake in imperial society and to prevent the further growth of socialism. On the other hand, Britain did catch up with Germany by the end of the century in the sphere of accident insurance. In the essay that follows, Professor W. C. Mallalieu, of the University of Louisville, analyzes deftly the late-Victorian setting from which emerged the highly important Workmen's Compensation Acts.

JOSEPH CHAMBERLAIN AND WORKMEN'S COMPENSATION

W. C. MALLALIEU

I

The British Workmen's Compensation Acts of 1897 and 1899 were "astonishing" to contemporaries and have not been adequately explained by historians. Although passed under a Conservative-Liberal Unionist Cabinet, these acts put heavy burdens upon industry and agriculture, interests that were very influential in both of these parties. "It was no wonder that Tories asked themselves what they were coming to, nor that the usual answer to the question was that they were being swallowed by Mr. Chamberlain."

Before his break with the Liberals in 1886, Joseph Chamberlain had been a Radical (in the old, non-Marxian sense), and his presence in the Salisbury Cabinet as Colonial Secretary (1895-1903) was partly responsible for the advanced social legislation of the period. Even before his advent the Conservative party had been drifting toward a broader outlook, and in the general elections of 1895 Lord Salisbury had expressed approval of the principles of a program of social reform drawn up by Chamberlain. In particular, as Chamberlain said, it was "most desirable in the interests of the Unionist [Conservative] party that this question [of industrial accidents] should be finally settled."

The most puzzling aspect of the situation is that this "revolutionary" act had not been demanded by labor leaders or others interested in the welfare of the workers. British trade-unions were essentially conservative, much concerned with protecting their own hard-earned status. They wanted to improve the legal position of employees injured through the negligence of employers, but they opposed compulsory insurance as "against the interests of trade [unions] and

friendly societies." The Employers' Liability Act of 1880 went only a short way to meet labor's demands but, even if all had been met, little more than half of the injuries would have been covered. Chamberlain's novel proposal not only gave labor more than it had been asking but, together with similar developments in other fields, forced trade-union representatives to adopt a broader social outlook.

A review of the discussion leading to the act of 1897 will show that it was not really radical but merely put into law the wishes and, in some cases, the practices of the more enlightened employers and that it was acceptable to other employers because it eased an issue between them and the trade-unions.

II

The Employers' Liability Act of 1880 had not been satisfactory to employers any more than to employees. They had feared the expense and disturbance caused by litigation with their men. Some, including the Mining Association and the Chairman of the Coal Trade Association, had in 1880 supported an amendment for all-inclusive accident insurance presented by Lord Randolph Churchill. The three Liberal-Labor members, Alexander MacDonald, Henry Broadhurst, and Thomas Burt, had vigorously opposed this plan. MacDonald, leader of the Miners' National Union, declared:

> This newborn zeal for insurance was of a very questionable character . . . for a system of insurance would be simply a system to destroy life. . . . Real protection was only to be obtained when owners were compelled to pay in purse for negligence of those they employed.

Reprinted by special permission from *The Journal of Economic History*, X (1950), 45-57. The footnotes which originally appeared with this essay have been omitted.

When the Gladstone Cabinet was reported to be seriously considering supporting Churchill's amendment, Broadhurst, secretary of the Parliamentary Committee of the Trades Union Congress, warned against doing so. The government later announced its opposition to the amendment, which was dropped.

The Employers' Liability Act of 1880 provided compensation for injured workmen only when negligence on the part of the employer or his authorized agents could be proved. Most employers insured themselves against such claims, paying premiums of four to twelve shillings per man per annum. Others had their workers "contract out" of the act, that is, waive claims against the employer, in return for insurance against all work accidents. This practice of "contracting out" was opposed by the trade-unions and failed to gain a foothold where they were strong. The union leaders asserted that there was seldom, if ever, a real or fair contract. Moreover, "the main point was one of safety and they felt that to contract out of the act would be to weaken its effect in regard to life and limb." However, the statistics presented by labor representatives did not, when carefully analyzed, prove that "contracting out" caused increase of accidents.

The real motive, perhaps, of the labor leaders was one they seldom mentioned, though it was often charged by critics. *The Times* declared that trade-union leaders were:

. . . primarily concerned with the running of their machine, with the extension and consolidation of a highly centralized bureaucracy. They view with impatience and hostility every arrangement that fosters local and sectional independence, and they see in the great insurance scheme, by which large numbers of workers are now protected, nothing but so many obstacles to the assertion of their supreme control.

The substantial truth of this charge was tacitly admitted by Broadhurst when he asserted that to allow "contracting out" would be "to strike at the root of trade unionism." Another labor leader asserted that "by any outside agreement between themselves and the workmen, the employers, in a covert manner, control the independence of the workmen."

For seventeen years the Trades Union Congress (T.U.C.), the National Miners Conference, the Amalgamated Society of Railway Servants, and other labor organizations carried on agitation for the prohibition of "contracting out." Each year, Henry Broadhurst introduced the bill prepared by the Parliamentary Committee of the T.U.C. Against this bill a counter agitation was conducted by the Liberty and Property Defence League and various influential trade and vested interests. When the bill came up in the House of Commons in 1883 it was coolly received on both sides and readily defeated (149 to 38).

After the election of 1885, however, the Liberals tended more and more toward the trade-union point of view. In this election,

---

CHARLES BRADLAUGH: English reformer, champion of birth control, and organizer of the National Secular Society (d. 1891). Because of his atheistic beliefs, he became involved in a lengthy dispute which resulted finally in a change in the law which made it possible for atheists to sit in the House of Commons. Although he was critical of socialism, he was a strong supporter of trade unionism and land-law reform.

JAMES KEIR HARDIE: British labor leader (d. 1915) who favored the establishment of an independent labor party that would work to win trade-union support for socialism. He was in large measure responsible for the formation in 1900 of the Labor Representation Committee, which in 1906 became the Labor Party. He has sometimes been styled "the traditional hero of British labor."

the first in which most miners and many other laborers could vote, the Employers' Liability Act Amendment Bill was the first item of the program that trade unions presented to candidates and was especially pushed by the Miners National Union. The outcome increased the number of "labour representatives" from two to eleven. The chief Parliamentary representative of labor, Henry Broadhurst, was made secretary of the Board of Trade in the new Liberal government.

Under these circumstances it was not surprising that the members of the Liberal Cabinet were "sympathetic" toward the bill for forbidding "contracting out." But unwilling to commit themselves, they had the bill referred to a select committee, of which the leading members were the chairman, Sir Thomas Brassey, and Charles Bradlaugh, both long-time friends of labor. After questioning trade-unionists (mostly miners and railway employees), employers, and insurance experts, the committee reported in favor of wide concessions to labor. The majority, including Brassey and Bradlaugh, reported that "contracting out" did not make employers careless and that it should be allowed under certain conditions. This report was greeted by the Parliamentary Committee of the T.U.C. as "a great advance upon the present act." But further progress was delayed by the dissolution and general election of 1886 and when the new Conservative Cabinet sponsored a bill based on the committee's report it was opposed by the labor representatives.

The provisions of this Conservative bill were only a little narrower than those suggested by the Select Committee. Clerks, agents, and domestics were excluded, as also were seamen except under special conditions. The liability of employers was increased in case of negligence of those in charge of engines and tramways and for defects in arrangements, buildings, and premises. "Contracting out" was to be allowed only if the Home Secretary or the Board of Trade certified that the insurance for which the employer paid was equivalent

to compensation under the act. Though badly drafted and limited in scope, it was an attempt to relieve some of the grievances of the workers.

In the Standing Committee on Law, Broadhurst tried to insert amendments supported by the "labour party," but succeeded only in having the minimum compensation in case of death raised from £150 to £250. To the T.U.C. he reported that the bill was a considerable advance, "yet it has some disadvantages as compared with the present act." The reason for the last statement is not apparent; nevertheless, the T.U.C. approved his views and instructed the Parliamentary Committee to do all it could to defeat the bill unless amended. Deputations of trade-unionists tried to impress their views upon the government, but they were counteracted by a deputation from the insurance societies of the London and North-Western Railway.

When the labor proposals regarding the insurance clauses were rejected by the government, Broadhurst moved the rejection of the bill. The unions affected by the bill, he said, were ready to allow existing insurance agreements to stand but they were determined to have no further "contracting out." "It was [he declared] an attempt to impose on the working people of this country the German system of compulsory insurance [and] to strike at the root of trade unionism." His motion was voted down (202 to 141), but its presentation, by showing that the bill would antagonize the very element for whose benefit it had been framed, assured the defeat of the bill. A week later it was withdrawn.

Much the same bill was introduced by the Conservative government in 1890. Slight concessions, such as making employers liable for their subcontractors and foremen, failed to conciliate the labor representatives. The T.U.C. Parliamentary Committee instructed Broadhurst to move the rejection of the bill; they would await, they said, a new Parliament and a new government "when the ballot box will clear men's minds with regard to our just demands . . . the same law as . . . the general public." This attitude, fully supported by the next Congress, caused the early withdrawal of the bill. Likewise, in 1892, the Conservatives announced they would introduce a new employers' liability bill, over which Home Secretary Matthews had "spent much time and trouble," but Broadhurst again announced his opposition, and the bill never saw the light of day.

The opposition of the labor leaders to these Conservative bills laid them open to charges of partisanship. As *The Times* remarked, there was ground for strong suspicion that Broadhurst would have accepted the same bill if sponsored by a Liberal government. The Trades Union Congress professed to be nonpartisan, yet it really was, as Broadhurst admits, "the Radical wing of the Liberal party." Constantly, and generally unanimously, it endorsed the Liberal policies regarding such subjects as Ireland, taxation, land laws, and the House of Lords. All the labor members of Parliament were Liberals. Broadhurst was a faithful supporter of Gladstone, an active Liberal campaign speaker, and even a Liberal minister. At this very time he was being attacked for his close connection with the Liberals by Keir Hardie and others who soon after formed the Independent Labour party. Yet the policy of opposition to any bill allowing "contracting out" went unchallenged; the labor leaders, however divided on other questions, seemed agreed on this.

III

During the elections of 1892 the labor question was much discussed, and when the Liberals emerged victorious they were committed to amendment of the Employers' Liability Law and to other labor reforms. Liberal legislation of the period 1892-1895 exempted trade-union funds from income tax, limited hours of railway and shop employees, and increased factory regulation, but the Liberal bills relating to miners' hours and employers' liability were blocked by controversies over amendments.

The Employers' Liability Bill, as originally framed by Herbert Asquith, met the trade-union demands in essentials by abolishing the judicial doctrine of nonliability for injuries to fellow employees and by prohibiting any future contracting out. It extended its benefits to all workmen except seamen and did away with required notice of accidents, time limits on suits, and limits on amount of compensation. In the Standing Committee, Asquith also accepted amendments extending the bill to domestic servants and to injuries to health and even allowing compensation when the workman failed to notify his employer of a dangerous defect in equipment. The final form of the bill was such a surrender to labor demands that its opponents, such as *The Times,* declared that it was intended "to buy the support of the trade-union leaders." *The Times* admitted that the bill would not ruin industry but preferred a scheme of insurance for all occupational accidents such as Chamberlain had recently brought before the public. In a magazine article, Chamberlain had warned the Conservatives:

> To adopt a purely negative attitude, to meet with destructive criticism every well meant suggestion without proposing any alternative—is neither statesman-like nor just, and will deservedly involve the defeat and discredit of any party which adopts it.

On the question of employers' liability, as on the other questions of the day, Chamberlain had ready his "alternative," which was not "inconsistent with . . . the permanent interests of the whole nation," which, in other words, was likely to prove acceptable to the coal operators, shipowners, and railway directors in the Unionist party. His argument was:

> That employers shall be legally compelled to pay compensation for injuries to workmen in all those cases in which the doctrine of common employment now limits their liability . . . is generally considered to be a large demand . . . . But it does not appear to have struck the

working class that, even if it were granted, there would still remain an immense number of injuries and fatal accidents for which no provision would be made. According to German statistics of the more serious accidents, 43 per cent are not attributable either to workmen or to masters, but are inherent in the work itself. The recognition of the universality of the right to compensation is the only equitable and indeed the only logical principle.

This proposal would not injure employers, who would recoup themselves in every case from the consumers. It would not injure the community, because they already . . . as a matter of charity or . . . under the poor law—pay the cost; and it would completely meet the claims of the working classes.

In moving to substitute his plan for the Liberal bill of 1893, Chamberlain declared that the government's plan did not go far enough:

By this bill you give up the idea of moral responsibility . . . you say that when a man is injured it is right that he should have compensation, and you are making the employer the channel for the payment of that compensation. That is my principle; but that is not adopted in its entirety by the Right Honourable gentleman [Asquith].

Chamberlain's proposal found some support among Conservatives and Liberal Unionists, but the trade-union leaders and labor representatives in joint session had resolved that "as the T.U.C. had not made a demand that all accidents should be met by a common insurance fund, they could not approve of the amendment." They charged that Chamberlain's move was intended to "strangle the bill," and the Speaker had, indeed, ruled that its adoption would mean the defeat of the measure. The Cabinet, Asquith stated, was not opposed to general compensation in principle. He argued, however, that the original bill was

necessary in any case to force employers to take proper precautions. Chamberlain disclaimed any idea of opposing the bill, however inadequate he might consider it, and when the debate had lasted long enough to publicize his plan he withdrew the amendment.

Thus the bill passed the House of Commons, but the real fight was between the two houses of Parliament. After the bill came to the House of Lords many petitions were presented from the insurance societies of the London and North-Western Railway, miners' insurance societies, and other workers' organizations. Lord Salisbury, the Conservative leader, promised to have the bill amended so as to allow insurance agreements. Such an amendment was proposed by the Earl of Dudley, one of the largest coal operators of the country, who had continued his contributions to the workers' insurance societies at their request and on the basis of "contracting out." It provided that "contracting out" be allowed if the employer in return contributed toward the men's insurance fund for all accidents and if the scheme was approved by a majority of the workmen and by the Board of Trade. At the request of the London and North-Western Railway the majority was later made two thirds and the employer was to be required to contribute one fourth of the insurance premium. Against this amendment the government could muster only 28 lords, while 148 voted for it, including some Liberal lords. This and other amendments, though upheld in the House of Commons by Chamberlain and other Unionists, were easily rejected there.

Believing that the Liberals were seeking a "cry for the country" against the House of Lords, Lord Salisbury consulted Chamberlain, who advised caution:

I think that amendments made by the House of Lords in any bill now before it should, if possible, have considerable popular support behind them, or should be of such a character as not to endanger the passing of the Bill . . . .

In this case [Employers' Liability Bill] although I have no doubt that all the official strength and influence of the Trades Unions is against contracting-out, yet there is a considerable amount of popular feeling in favour of voluntary arrangements . . . . The course which I have suggested to Mr. Balfour is that the Lords should maintain the principle of the Dudley amendment, and should further amend it so as to make it still more favorable to the workpeople.

Following this suggestion, a meeting of Conservative peers expressed their willingness to agree to additional safeguards for workmen who "contracted out" of the Act. The Liberals were willing to compromise on allowing existing contracts to stand for three years only. Against this amendment all the Conservatives and some of the Liberals (including labor representatives) voted, almost wiping out the government's majority (215 to 213). The Lords would not accept this compromise nor offer any other. Both parties issued urgent whips to their followers to be on hand for the final struggle in the Commons. The situation was unexpectedly changed, however, when instead of trying to agree with the Lords on a compromise allowing existing contracts to stand Gladstone moved that the order for consideration of the Lords' amendments be dropped, an action which meant the end of the bill. He declared that the Parliamentary Committee of the National Conference of Friendly Societies had expressed their opposition to the Lords' amendment and this must be taken as representing the feeling of the working class. The scheme for "contracting out" was harmful, he said:

. . . because it will tend by a subtle, but most extended, operation of causes, too efficient in their nature, to impair that independence and self-action on the part of the working man in the face of his employer which it is essential for the benefit of both that he should always be able to hold.

In this stand, Gladstone was upheld by the labor representatives, who had, indeed, probably instigated it, following the precedent of their action of 1888. Balfour, the Conservative leader, charged that the Liberals were killing their own bill and throwing away nine tenths of it because of the one tenth that they could not pass, merely for the sake of having another ground of complaint on which to appeal to the country against the Lords. The Conservatives and Liberal Unionists then left the House, leaving the government, 225 strong, to be opposed by six members, who still wanted to attempt some compromise with the Lords. Thus ended the last Employers' Liability Bill ever considered in Parliament.

IV

The Conservatives and Liberal Unionists prepared to take every possible advantage of the feeling of disappointment among the workers because of the failure of the Employers' Liability and other labor bills. Chamberlain in a speech at West Birmingham in the fall of 1894 advocated old-age pensions, arbitration of labor disputes, and compensation for all occupational injuries. His Memorandum of a Programme of Social Reforms, sent to Lord Salisbury, urged the necessity of these and other reforms. Salisbury's reply was somewhat evasive, but most of the reforms, he felt, were "salutary in themselves, and any difficulties are purely difficulties of strategy." When the new Conservative-Liberal Unionist Cabinet was formed in June 1895 the legislative program was still very indefinite. During the campaign that followed, several leading Conservatives endorsed Chamberlain's plan of compensation, but Lord Salisbury and others would not commit themselves. The Liberals warned workmen against being led into "the mists of a nebulous social program" and argued that the cost of Chamberlain's scheme would really come out of wages. On this and many other points, the Liberal position was practically identical with that of the Trades Union Congress; the sweeping victory of the Unionists showed, however, that many working-class voters had not followed their supposed leaders.

The new government had soon to come to a decision on workmen's compensation. The question had now attained such prominence that inaction would be dangerous. Yet, no matter what concessions were made to labor on other points, insistence upon "contracting out" would cause collision with the trade-unions. The Liberals would undoubtedly promise to repeal any such measure. On the other hand, the Unionists could not well abandon "contracting out" in view of their previous support and of the insistence of several influential members of the party. These considerations left a general compensation bill as the only alternative. The trade-union leaders and the Liberals might not like it, but they could hardly oppose a measure so beneficial to the working class.

The employers had to face a similar choice of alternatives. They knew that it was now certain that their liabilities would soon be largely increased. This would mean not only a financial burden but also constant litigation with their workers, with evil consequences upon their discipline and friendly relations. "Contracting out" would be more than ever necessary, yet a return of the Liberals to power would certainly result in its prohibition. These considerations led some employers to desire a general compensation scheme, which would both satisfy the workers and prevent litigation. Hence, when, toward the end of 1896, the bill that Chamberlain and Matthews, the Home Secretary, had endorsed was sent to large employers and chambers of commerce for their opinions, no great opposition was discovered. The exclusion of shipping and agriculture had the intended effect of preventing any opposition from these powerful interests.

The most serious opposition came from the various associations of coal-mine operators. The Mining Association of Great Britain unanimously decided to petition against the bill. The North of England Coal Trade Association declared that the bill would extinguish voluntary accident funds and ruin small colliery owners in case of serious accidents or explosions. They demanded that the royalty owners, the workers, and the state share the expense. Other coal associations passed similar resolutions. To these protests the government had to harden its heart though it incorporated certain amendments suggested by employers.

The attitudes of the "labour party" and the Liberal "front bench" were awaited with some interest. The T.U.C. Parliamentary Committee was divided, but a majority favored the bill. In a meeting with the executive of the Miners' Federation and the "advanced radical" members of Parliament, it was decided not to oppose the second reading but to offer amendments for the extension and improvement of the bill. Asquith's speech on the first reading indicated that the Liberals would not oppose the bill either. They still argued, however, that civil liability of employers would be necessary to enforce safety precautions and that the costs would come out of wages. They also criticized the government for not extending the bill to all trades.

Chamberlain frankly confessed that there was no logic in the exclusion of agriculture, shipping, and other industries but promised to deal with excluded trades in the near future. There was doubtless much truth in his taunt that the Liberals were "willing to wound, yet afraid to strike."

The bill passed without division in the House of Commons and with only six opponents in the House of Lords. The Earl of Wemyss, leader of the Liberty and Property Defence League, had offered to attempt the defeat of the bill, but the Mining Association thought it useless. Lord Londonderry, a prominent Conservative and large mineowner, appealed to Lord Salisbury not to "allow Conservative principles to be subordinated to Radical principles of the deepest dye." Later, resigning from a party association, he deplored the influence of Chamberlain, "whose radical views on home politics we have always regarded with disapproval, however much we may admire him as an imperialist."

The labor members had tried to show that the bill would be of little benefit to the working class, and the T.U.C. Parliamentary Committee stated that the act "scarcely touches the question of employers' liability." It is very significant that, in spite of this statement, the congress never again passed a resolution on employers' liability but instead confined its demands to extension and improvement of workmen's compensation and government inspection. Even wider vistas were opened by the presidential address of James O'Grady at the congress of 1898. In defending the compensation act, he acknowledged that it would injure friendly societies. But, he said:

They are usurping the functions of the state . . . . If . . . the national prosperity depends on the well-being of the worker, the necessary corollary is that the state should care for him in sickness . . . . And if preference will be given to young men

with whom the risks of accidents are less . . . pensions for old age will be advanced a considerable step nearer realization . . . .

There can be no doubt that the Workmen's Compensation Act was one of the most important ever passed by Parliament. The adoption of similar laws in all English-speaking countries is a tribute to the originality and political genius of Joseph Chamberlain. Other social legislation that he induced the Unionists to pass included conciliation of labor disputes, land reform, prohibition of child labor in mines, and improved housing. The limits of Conservative social reform were shown by the failure to pass old-age pensions and the eight-hour day in mines. These measures and others that deeply affected the interests of property owners were left for the succeeding Liberal Parliament (1906-1910). Back of both parties, however, stood the trade-unions and their national congress, exerting constant pressure which was fundamentally responsible for most legislation affecting labor.

THE CONTINUED DECLINE OF *laissez faire* and the further growth of state intervention in late-Victorian Britain were due in no small measure to the provisions of the Reform Act of 1867. The enfranchisement of urban workers made it imperative for political leaders—whether Conservative or Liberal—to seek working-class votes; and if these votes were to be obtained, political leaders had to support legislation to improve the status of workers. But the decline of *laissez faire* and the growth of state intervention also owed much to the disclosures of a long line of intellectuals who viewed it as their function to expose abuses in society and to demand social justice. Two Americans, Henry George and Edward Bellamy—the authors, respectively, of *Progress and Poverty* (1879) and *Looking Backward* (1888)—attracted far more attention and interest in Britain than in the United States. And there were many British intellectuals who caused considerable stir by their writings in defense of the particular social changes that they considered necessary or desirable. Especially prominent among these intellectuals were the members of the Fabian Society, who came increasingly into their own in the years following the publication of their *Fabian Essays* (1889). Since they numbered in their ranks such luminaries as George Bernard Shaw, H. G. Wells, and

Sydney and Beatrice Webb, it is understandable that an extensive literature has grown up around them. Few writers, however, have been better qualified to discuss their contributions than Margaret Cole. Wife of G. D. H. Cole and a leading Fabian in her own right, she is the biographer of Beatrice Webb, co-editor of Mrs. Webb's posthumously published *Our Partnership* (1948), and editor of *The Webbs and Their Work* (1949). The essay that follows was written by Mrs. Cole to commemorate the sixtieth anniversary of the founding of the Fabian Society.

THE FABIAN SOCIETY

MARGARET COLE

I

The Fabian Society, whose diamond jubilee was celebrated this January, has some claim to be a unique specimen in the political world. It is, since the dissolution of the Social-Democratic Federation, the oldest Socialist society in this country; it is almost certainly the oldest Socialist society in the world; and it is certainly in membership the smallest Society which has ever exercised so much political influence over so long a period. The membership and the activity of the Society have fluctuated from time to time; but, fluctuations notwithstanding, it has remained the Fabian Society, and the odd name which it chose for itself in 1884 has retained its significance throughout the sixty years which have followed.

The Society was born with no flourish of trumpets; it sidled into existence in the most unobtrusive way. In October of 1883 Edward Pease and Frank Podmore—who had met by chance while looking for a ghost in a house at Hampstead—were present at the first meeting of Thomas Davidson's Fellowship of the New Life, "whose ultimate aims shall be the reconstruction of Society in accordance with the highest moral principles," its first object being "the cultivation of a perfect character in each and all." This organisation (whose secretary for a time was Ramsay MacDonald) maintained a quiet existence for fifteen years; but in the meantime, in January, 1884, by a vote of nine members to two, it budded off a new body which called itself the Fabian Society, in allusion to the methods of the Roman general: "For the right moment you must wait, as Fabius did most patiently . . . but when the right moment comes you must strike hard, as Fabius did, or your waiting will be vain and fruitless."

The new Society, the names of whose original members are preserved in manuscript at the present Fabian offices, started operations with an Executive Committee of three members, a secretary (Pease) whose flat was its official address, and a capital of thirteen shillings and ninepence, contributed by the members present at the first meeting. It did not mention Socialism until it was ten weeks old; and only in its third Tract, published in June, did it publicly announce that it "had in view the advancement of Socialism in England." It issued no annual reports until 1889, and had no journal until *Fabian News* appeared in 1891. In 1889— the year of *Fabian Essays*—it had only 130-140 members, although these had for some years included the great quartette, Shaw, Webb, Olivier, and Graham Wallas, as well as Hubert Bland, the treasurer, and Pease, its secretary and guardian watch-dog for over thirty years, and it had already issued

Reprinted by special permission from *The Political Quarterly*, XV (1944), 245-256. The footnotes have been renumbered.

the second most famous of all Fabian publications, *Facts for Socialists*.

II

From 1889, however, there came a two-fold change which put the Society into the middle of the political map. First was the publication of the *Essays*. These were delivered originally as a series of unadvertised lectures in the winter of 1888-9; they were subsequently co-operatively revised by the lecturers, edited by Bernard Shaw, and issued by the venturesome Society at its own expense in December, 1889. The instant success—a success prolonged for many years—of this attempt to provide a body of doctrine for an English Socialist movement needs no recapitulation here. Even to-day, with the exception of the contribution of Annie Besant (of whom more hereafter), the *Essays* date remarkably little. Their thought is the thought of Bentham, Mill, Ricardo, and all the tradition of English radicalism, pursued to its logical end in a Socialist community. What they do lack, as Webb pointed out in later years, is any sense of the means to the end, of the institutions of English life through which the change must come. The Essayists might have learnt this lesson from Marx, if they had not been temperamentally averse from reading him; as it was, they had to learn the second half of the Fabian contribution to social science from the other member of the great partnership—Beatrice Potter—who even at the moment of the publication of the *Essays* was feeling her way, in spite of Alfred Marshall's discouragement of her efforts, to a study of the Co-operative Movement and later of the Trade Unions.

Fabian Essays made an instant sensation. It was followed up by a lightning campaign of lectures on Socialism in the provinces, conducted largely by that brilliant propagandist Annie Besant, who in her reaction from Bradlaugh's secularist individualism made a rocket-like flight through the Fabian Society until before 1890 was over she had come to earth again and buried herself in the Theosophical Society. Whatever Annie Besant was, she was certainly not a typical Fabian; nor in the main were her converts; they were working-class people who were crying out for a simple Socialist creed.

While the influence lasted, it swelled the Fabian Society into a body of over three thousand members, five-sixths of them in the provinces; but with the disappearance of Mrs. Besant and the foundation of the I.L.P. (in which the Fabian Society played its part) the provincial membership joined Keir Hardie's new organisation, and the Fabian Society returned to its business of quietly building up its central membership, which by the time of the Boer War had reached nearly nine hundred. The most tangible results on the organisation were the starting of *Fabian News* and the daring decision to pay the secretary a pound a week.

The characteristics of this decade, which was possibly the most formative and the most influential in the Society's history, deserve rather closer study. What first emerges is the enormous amount of actual

MRS. ANNIE BESANT: Militant English reformer (1847-1933) who in the 1870's played an important role in the agitation for birth control and secularism. Converted to socialism in the early 1880's, she led a strike of match girls in 1888 and contributed to the *Fabian Essays*. By the late '80's she abandoned socialism and became a vigorous champion of theosophy and Indian nationalism.

NEWCASTLE PROGRAM: A variety of policies adopted in 1891 by the Liberal Party and accepted by Gladstone. The program included Home Rule for Ireland, church disestablishment in Wales and Scotland, the right of local veto on the sale of intoxicating liquors, the elimination of plural voting, triennial Parliaments, land-law reform, the extension of employers' liability for accidents, and shorter hours for labor.

work done by the members of the Society as well as by its leaders. "Two Fabian committee meetings a week" writes Bernard Shaw to Ellen Terry in 1897—what would the present Fabian Executive make of that? But beside this we have to set such facts as the 3,400 lectures given during 1892 by 117 members, the regularly-attended fortnightly meetings of members, and the searching way in which each Fabian Tract, even when written by those best known in the Society, was perused and criticised by the others.

Many have read Webb's observation that "the work of the Fabian Society is the sum of the work of individual Fabians"; but not so many realise how much this work was in itself a co-operation, extending even to the revision by the leaders of one another's books. To quote Shaw again: "the Webbs' great new treatise on Democracy,[1] which I have to help in revising"; and it was quite in keeping with the tradition that during the 1919 railway strike both Shaw and Webb should turn up with manifestoes to be issued under the signature of J. H. Thomas, though neither of their styles could have remained for a moment unrecognised.

It was this sense of continued and active partnership which partly accounted for the rather engaging parish-magazine quality of *Fabian News*—"Frank Podmore," says an early issue, "has married Miss E. O. Bramwell, and *vice versa*"—a characteristic which it maintained with little change until the present paper shortage reduced it to a cold compressed news-sheet about as sympathetic as a page of *Bradshaw;*[2] the same cause also certainly helped to account for the remarkable effectiveness of Fabian propaganda. During the period under review, to take only a few examples, the Fabian Society (a) won the new London County

Council for the Progressives by means of a barrage of facts and questions for candidates; (b) in the famous article "To Your Tents, O Israel," declared, seven years before the foundation of the Labour Representation Committee, the two capitalist parties were broken reeds and that the Trade Unions would have to provide their own members of Parliament; (c) succeeded, through the agency of a barely-known member of the Society, in forcing upon a startled Liberal Party the Newcastle Programme of 1891;[3] and (d) a year or two after the end of the period, was practically responsible for the better parts of the Balfour Education Act of 1902. It was on this occasion that the Education Office, taking a step without precedent (and, so far as I know, without recurrence) for a Government Office, asked for proofs of the Fabian Tract on Education to distribute in advance to its officials.

Furthermore, the Fabians were rapidly creating confidence in themselves as persons to whom it was safe to go for information and assistance and who, moreover, might safely be entrusted with the spending of large sums. They ran tuition by correspondence course—until the foundation of Ruskin College; they bought and circulated travelling book-boxes in the days before Carnegie and University Tutorial Classes had made books easy of access; in the midst of their production of Tracts, of which 103 were published between 1889 and 1901, they issued, in *What to Read on Social and Economic Subjects,* one of the first catalogues *raisonnés* of social studies. In 1885, a Mr. Millar of Edinburgh presented them with £1,000 to run a huge conference on Industrial Remuneration, and, more important, in 1894 the Hutchinson Trust, a legacy from an old Fabian, gave them nearly ten times as much, which the Executive Committee with great foresight decided not to put into current expenditure but to employ partly on financing provincial lectures on Socialism and partly on founding the body which is

[1] *Industrial Democracy,* their second big book.
[2] It is, perhaps, worth noticing that, in the days when to avow oneself a Socialist needed some considerable courage, the Fabian Society habitually issued a printed list of its membership, and only discontinued the practice because of the assistance it gave to advertising touts.

[3] The full story of the adoption of the Newcastle Programme, interesting as it is, is too long to tell here.

now the London School of Economics and Political Science.

In 1896, the Fabian Society was asked to take part, with the Trades Union Congress, in a Conference of International Socialist Workers. The *Report of Fabian Policy* which the Society submitted with its resolutions for that Conference[4] is so illuminating on the nature and the methods of the Society that it is worth quotation.

1.—*The Mission of the Fabians.*

The object of the Fabian Society is to persuade the English people to make their political constitution thoroughly democratic and so to socialise their industries as to make the livelihood of the people entirely independent of private Capitalism.

The Fabian Society endeavours to pursue its Socialist and Democratic objects with complete singleness of aim. For example:

It has no distinctive opinions on the Marriage Question, Religion, Art, abstract Economics (!), historic Evolution, Currency, or any other subject than its own special business of practical Democracy and Socialism.

It brings all the pressure and persuasion in its power to bear on existing forces, caring nothing by what name any party calls itself, or what principles, Socialist or other, it professes, but having regard solely to the tendency of its actions, supporting those which make for Socialism and Democracy, and opposing those which are reactionary.

It does not propose that the practical steps towards Social-Democracy should be carried out by itself, or by any other specially organised society or party.

It does not ask the English people to join the Fabian Society.[5]

[4] Written by Shaw and published as Tract No. 70. Well worth reading in full.

[5] This was very true. Up till 1912, at any rate, entry to the Fabian Society, while not as difficult as entry to the Russian Communist Party, was not easy. The present Leader of the Labour Party has told how, on penetrating in 1909 to a basement in Clement's Inn, he and a friend were greeted by the General Secretary

3.—*Fabian Toleration.*

The Fabian Society, far from holding aloof from other bodies, urges its members to lose no opportunity of joining them and permeating them with Fabian ideas as far as possible. Almost all organisations and movements contain elements making for Socialism, no matter how remote the sympathies and intentions of their founders may be from those of the Socialists. On the other hand, unintentionally reactionary proposals are constantly being brought forward in Socialist bodies. Fabians are therefore encouraged to join all other organisations, Socialist or non-Socialist, in which Fabian work can be done.

6.—*Fabian Compromise.*

The Fabian Society, having learnt from experience that Socialists cannot have their own way in everything any more than other people, recognises that in a Democratic Community Compromise is a necessary condition of political progress. (Other sections deal in the same style with Fabian views on democracy, individualism, freedom of thought, the Press, the middle class, etc.)

14.—*Finally.*

The Fabian Society does not put Socialism forward as a panacea for the ills of human society, but only for those produced by defective organisation of industry and by a radically bad distribution of wealth.

It did not, however, refuse collaboration for limited objectives with Societies whose views of their Socialist function were rather different from its own. Examples are: a not very happy association under the chairmanship of William Morris with the Hammersmith Socialist Society (all that was left of Morris's Socialist League) and the S.D.F.; the long-continued partnership with the I.L.P. and the Trade Unions, which turned eventually into the Labour Party; and a

as though they had been a couple of black-beetles and forced to give adequate reasons for their presence. Fabian practice, in this respect, has softened with the years.

joint committee on Socialist propaganda with the I.L.P., formed a few years before the last war and broken up when the I.L.P. adopted its anti-war line.

III

The Boer War brought about the first really sharp dispute in the Fabian Society. A number of influential members were strongly pro-Boer and desired the Society to align itself with the anti-war campaign. The leaders, including Webb and Shaw, were inclined to say "a plague on both your houses" and to point out that neither Dutch farmers nor gold-diggers of doubtful origin cared a button for the rights or the conditions of the natives.[6] After some hot debate, the members of the Society were asked whether they thought the Society ought to produce a statement on the war, and by a fairly narrow majority decided that it ought not. Between twenty and thirty members, including Henry Massingham and Ramsay MacDonald, resigned as a result; but the Society generally proceeded steadily on its way, busy with the Education Bill, but not taking much notice either of the progress of the Labour Representation Committee or of politics in general, and neither gaining nor losing much in membership until after the 1906 election.

The results of that election seem to have taken the Society by surprise, as they certainly did the Webbs. As a result of the great radical break-through and the seething social discontent of the years between 1906 and the outbreak of war, the membership began to rise again rapidly. Another rocket, this time bearing the name H. G. Wells, flew into the Society with a brilliant paper entitled *This Misery of Boots* and flew out again in a fury almost before there had been time for all the changes he wished to make even to be discussed. Old provincial societies revived and new ones were founded; young men and women from the Universities flocked to join; forty-eight Tracts were issued

[6] See Shaw, *Fabianism and the Empire,* for a statement of their point of view.

in seven years; Executive elections were hotly contested, one polling 78 per cent of the membership; by 1913 there were thirty-nine provincial and eleven university societies, six London groups and a membership of 2,800 with possibly another 800-1,000 who were members of provincial societies only.

But to the historian this revival has a febrile quality which is absent from the earlier movement. It was not peculiar to the Fabian Society; in all parts of the "progressive" world there was apparent the same half-articulate but bitter discontent described so well in George Dangerfield's *Strange Death of Liberal England,* which fulminated now against the Liberals, now against the embryo Labour Party, now against the opponents of women's suffrage, now against the Trade Unions, now against the family, the stage censorship, the marriage laws, or what you will, and now against the collectivist philosophy of the Fabian leaders. The world of Victoria was in fact breaking up, and no one knew quite what was coming.

What is noticeable in the Fabian Society records is the extent to which the new recruits, from Wells onwards, appeared to mislike and to distrust the Society's policy and its practice. They all wanted it to be or to do something different; the only difficulty was that they could not agree what. All sorts of proposals appear and disappear —that the Society should become an immensely large propagandist body, and that it should confine itself to doing research; that it should disaffiliate from the Labour Party, and that it should expel from membership all who belonged to either of the older parties. Under such circumstances, it was fairly easy for the Executive, aided by the natural conservatism of the older members, to defeat the successive waves of reform and revolt; but when the Old Gang, as Pease called it, triumphed over the last of these, the "Right Moment" group led by Clifford Allen and G. D. H. Cole, their victory was won at the price of losing for the Society the driving force of the new generation.

Beatrice Webb, who did not join the Executive Committee until 1912, and was not so deeply imbued with the collectivist tradition, saw to some extent what was happening. After the great campaign for the break-up of the Poor Law, in which, of course, many of the new recruits took part, had finally proved a failure and broken itself against Lloyd George's Insurance Bill, she made a great effort to come to terms with the rebels, particularly the Guild Socialist and Syndicalist rebels.[7] She tried to woo the university young men, and by initiating special inquiries, such as the inquiry into the Control of Industry, which was the beginning of the Fabian Research Department, she endeavoured to find the young men work on which they might spread themselves. But the rebels were unaccommodating; they would have nothing whatever to do with collectivism; they manned the Fabian Research Department—but they took it out of the control of the Executive and finally away from the Society altogether.[8] The split, accentuated by the blank hostility of the Webbs to the Russian Revolution in its early days, was not effectively healed until more than twenty years had passed.

IV

The War, then, found the Fabian Society with a great part of its new membership lost again, either to the Forces or to the growing and independent Research Department. Nor did it do much during the War to revive its prestige, other than initiating

[7] She had previously announced, at a public dinner, that she did not intend to be reckoned as one of the Old Gang, but would in future lead the Fabian Nursery—though she was fifty-one at the time.

[8] Eventually they in their turn lost control of the Labour Research Department (as it became) to a Communist group; but the Fabian tradition of accurate and trustworthy service proved so strong that even when anti-Communist feeling was at its height, the Labour Research Department's Trade Union affiliates largely stood by it in defiance of all menacing circulars from headquarters.

the very fruitful procedure of hiring skilled research workers to do a particular job. Leonard Woolf's two important books, *Empire and Commerce in Africa* and *International Government,* as well as studies of the rural problem in England, of State and private insurance, and of the British Commonwealth of Nations were produced in this way. But the two principal developments of British Labour in wartime—the War Emergency Workers' National Committee and the reconstitution of the Labour Party on its present basis and with a defined Socialist programme—were the work of Webb himself, not of the Fabian Society.

Consequently, the Labour revival after the war affected the Fabian Society hardly at all; those who might have joined it turned rather to the I.L.P., or the new Divisional Labour Parties, particularly the Westminster Labour Party. It continued to publish a lessening trickle of Tracts, and to circulate boxes of books which got steadily more and more out of date; its name meant something in the counsels of the Labour Party, and a good deal more to foreign Socialists; but it retired into a quiet backwater, supported financially by a regular Summer School—which the General Secretary seldom attended—the regular Autumn Lectures, filled to overflowing by the many who wanted to listen to Bernard Shaw, and a gradually diminishing number of faithful adherents; by 1939 the effective —i.e. paying—membership had fallen to less than a thousand; and it is an ironic comment that the last Tract issued before the new revival was entitled *Our Ageing Population.* Various new groups formed during the twenties and thirties failed to offset the growing inertia, the only exception being a Local Government Bureau, which under W. A. Robson maintained a lively existence until it was snuffed out in the 1932 slump. In the later years, the files of *Fabian News* and the Annual Reports show clear signs of somnolence, the phrasing, and even some of the figures, remaining unchanged from year to year, as though they had been kept in standing type.

Meantime, in 1931, the parlous state of the Labour Party after the election had set some of its leaders, notably Clement Attlee and Stafford Cripps, searching for more up-to-date lines of political thinking and research. They made contact with G. D. H. Cole, who had for some time been organising[9] a group of Socialists, including a number of young men recently down from Oxford. The result of these discussions was the foundation, with the approving support of the Webbs, Arthur Henderson, and Hugh Dalton, of the New Fabian Research Bureau which, devoting its main attention to research and leaving political propaganda to others, gradually built up a distinguished and hard-working membership, which by 1939 had reached over 800. By that time, it was clear that the existence of two bodies sharing the same name was unnecessary and confusing. Heroic efforts by Emil Davies, the treasurer, having succeeded in clearing off the clinging debt of the Fabian Society, the way was now clear for an amalgamation, which was completed by June, 1939. Beatrice Webb, now in her eighty-second year, emphasised the continuity by becoming President of the reformed Society. G. D. H. Cole became its Chairman, and John Parker, who is now on the Front Bench of the Parliamentary Labour Party, its general secretary.

V

The sequel, the raising of the membership to something between five and six thousand, the revival of fifty or sixty provincial societies, and the steady stream of tracts, pamphlets, and books which have poured out, is a matter of current politics rather than of history. The war, which has been a hindrance by restricting paper supplies and carrying off or overworking the best workers, has yet helped in that it has stimulated the public demand for Socialist thinking while the political truce has been hamstringing the local Labour Parties. One change, how-

ever, from the early days of the Society must be noted. Political research, and political education, is still the main business of the Society. But political research has become much more skilled and much more all-embracing since the days when the Fabian Society could observe that "it had no opinions on the currency"; at the same time, the type of worker upon whom the Society can draw has become much more fully occupied, at least in his active years.[10] It would be impossible, to-day, to hold Executive meetings twice a week, or, notwithstanding all the voluntary contributions of members, to answer inquiries, to provide material for Parliamentary speeches and questions and for books and pamphlets, by conscripting the E.C. or even leading members of the Society. Nor are there available now, as there were before 1914, young men and women who can afford to work voluntarily for a political organisation while they look round and take their pick of a career; competition is too keen. A paid research staff is therefore essential—and expensive even if underpaid. It is all part of the complication of modern society, and of our painfully slow (and still incomplete) realisation of the fact that social, no less than scientific, research needs proper apparatus. The Fabian Society of to-day is a body which costs a good deal to run; but it could no more carry out the job which the Fabian Society of 1896 set itself on the resources of that date than a modern politician could become Prime Minister at twenty-four.

VI

It only remains to add a brief summing-up. Since 1884, the Fabian Society has almost entirely changed its personnel, and to a very large extent its methods of working. It still endeavours, as it said in 1896, to employ incontrovertible facts and figures to show the British public that Socialism is

[9] Through the Society for Socialist Inquiry and Propaganda, whose separate existence came to an end in 1932.

[10] Some historian or some economist might one day evaluate the "social dividend" which has accrued to this country as a result of the unearned income of £1,000 a year which Richard Potter left to his eighth daughter.

the only thing that will cure the economic evils from which they suffer, and that if they want Socialism they can have it; to this end, it still endeavours to make sure that its facts and conclusions will stand up to any criticism which may be brought to bear; and this has been recognized, not always conveniently, by the number of requests which continually turn up that the Fabian Society should take up, investigate and pronounce on this or that question. Its impartiality, granted its Socialist principles, has been generally recognised.

But it has also recognised its limitations, and has realised the undesirability of meddling in matters which were not its proper concern and in which it had no special competence. Though it has issued Manifestoes and statements from time to time, it has never fallen into the delusion common to many organisations, particularly the smallest, that passing a resolution on war, peace, reconstruction or other large subjects is doing something. This attitude may upon occasion have caused the Society to take too narrow or too insular an attitude—Shaw, in an article in the current *Fabian Quarterly,* points out how difficult he found it to induce his colleagues in the first decade of this century to believe that events on the Continent of Europe concerned them in any way; but it certainly made for stability and effectiveness in its own chosen task. The extreme case, possibly, is the "self-denying ordinance" embodied in the present Rules, which prevents the Society, *as a Society,* from passing any resolution of a political character; though Committees of the Society may, and do, freely express their views upon the subjects with which they are concerned.

The refusal of the Society's membership to make a pronouncement on the Boer War may be an instance of this; it is also an instance of its extreme reluctance to force an issue which might result in a split. The Society has always set its face firmly against anything like heresy-hunting in its ranks, nor has it ever formulated a faith that was rigidly binding on its members. The Fabian Basis—first formulated in 1887 and finally abolished in 1939—was never a ful confession of faith, but more a statement of the main points upon which Fabians were agreed. Outside the Basis, every Fabian might hold what views he liked and do what he chose to advance them.

Furthermore—and this is very important—the Fabian Society was never solopsist; it never developed—and I trust it never will—the kind of institutional loyalty that behaves like a dog-in-the-manger to any other institution. It never felt that England could only be saved by the Fabian Society, or even that any particular job was the Fabian Society's private property. Where it felt others could do the work better, it retired from the scene, as when it gave up its early branches to the I.L.P., or its correspondence courses to Ruskin College, or economic education to the London School of Economics. It filled in gaps—sometimes very important gaps—but it never sought to acquire a vested interest in the work which it was doing.

Finally, it was as British as they make 'em. In the early days its membership was almost entirely British; a name like that of Sergius Stepniak stands out like a beacon in the regular monthly list of enrolments.[11] Since 1918, and still more since 1933, that is no longer true; nevertheless, the general character remains British, and this perhaps makes it more possible for foreign comrades of varying types and nationality to feel that the Fabian International Bureau is a place where they will be welcomed and their problems discussed without their having to undergo an examination of a Gestapo type. At any rate, as Louis de Brouckère, himself a life-long friend of the Society, said at the Jubilee Reunion in January: "You in England do not realise how much the Fabian name has meant to the Socialists of Europe." We who have taken over from the founders trust that it will never mean less.

[11] Though, of course, distinguished foreign Socialists, such as Anatole France, were always eagerly entertained.

THE ADVOCATES OF STATE INTERVENTION in behalf of the working-class population achieved a number of legislative victories in the years immediately preceding World War I. In 1906, as a result of the Trade Disputes Act, the position of trade unions was considerably improved and peaceful picketing was legalized. In the same year the Workingmen's Compensation Law extended further the principle of employers' liability. In 1908, after a long period of agitation, an old-age pension measure was finally enacted. And in 1911 came the important National Insurance Act, which aimed "to provide for insurance against loss of health and for the prevention and cure of sickness." It also introduced unemployment insurance for workers engaged in a number of specified industries that were particularly subject to business fluctuations. Finally, in 1912 a Minimum Wage Law was passed. If, despite these as well as other impressive attempts at social amelioration, labor unrest was pronounced in prewar Britain, the reason was that wages were often failing to keep pace with rising prices. In the following essay, which was specially written for this book, Professor Samuel J. Hurwitz, of Brooklyn College, examines the history of British social reform in the years that preceded the outbreak of World War I. Author of the valuable monograph *State Intervention in Great Britain: A Study of Economic Control and Social Response, 1914-1919* (1949), Professor Hurwitz is a stimulating and profound student of twentieth-century British history.

THE DEVELOPMENT OF THE SOCIAL WELFARE STATE IN PREWAR BRITAIN, 1906-1914

SAMUEL J. HURWITZ

The great era of social legislation in Great Britain, prior to 1945, was the period from 1906 to the outbreak of World War I, when, ironically, Britain was governed by the Liberal Party, the traditional foe of state intervention. Within a period of less than a decade a Liberal government, to the consternation and distress of many of its members, enacted social legislation of a scope and variety perhaps unparalleled in the history of any country up to that time. Bills were introduced and passed providing for the extension of government regulation of labor relations, the expansion of public services, and the introduction of compulsory social insurance.

The Liberal Party's overwhelming victory and the surprisingly large Labor vote in the General Election of 1906 had electrified the nation. The Liberals had hoped for and expected victory, but the very size of their majority as well as the impressive Labor vote was embarrassing. Though the Liberal Prime Minister, Sir Henry Campbell-Bannerman, had promised that his government would make Britain less "of a pleasure ground for the rich and more of a treasure house for the nation," many of his colleagues had regarded this merely as traditional campaign rhetoric. Now, clearly and firmly in power, the Liberals could not put off demands for social legislation with the claim that all attempts at reform would be obstructed by the Opposition. Paradoxically, the very fact that they had a large majority in the House of Commons forced the Lib-

Published by special permission of the author.

erals to bow to the pressure of that growing body of the electorate which demanded positive action by the state.

At the same time, imaginative and ambitious politicians, such as David Lloyd George and Winston Churchill, saw in the rising tide of demand for social reform an opportunity for self and party. In their enthusiasm, they ignored the warnings of Lord Rosebery, the Liberal leader and one-time Prime Minister, that the Liberal Party would be "squeezed out between Socialism and Conservatism. Socialism can promise much more to the predatory elements in politics; Conservatism can offer much more confidence to those who wish to keep things as they are." But the Liberalism of the nineteenth century, with its policy of "Peace, Retrenchment and Reform," had become outworn; in the words of Lord Morley, it had "done its work" and must now be replaced. If social legislation was inevitable, it was best directed along less treacherous channels. By playing the lyre of social reform the Liberals hoped to prevent the working masses from succumbing to the siren call of the newly organized Labor Party.

Arthur Balfour, head of the Conservative government which had given way to the Liberals, was also aware that "a new era" had been inaugurated with the election of 1906. The fastidious and aristocratic Balfour boasted of never reading a newspaper, but the implications of the election were clear without benefit of headlines. The "masses" were threatening to become the "masters"; it was the duty of prescient statesmen to delay and if possible to prevent this by making concessions to the aroused electorate, the bulk of which had been enfranchised within a period of less than forty years. In the words of Walter Bagehot, who was well aware of the dangers to Britain's ruling classes in the extension of the suffrage, the "higher classes" must, "while they have still the power, concede every claim which they can safely concede, in order that they may not have to concede unwillingly some claim which would impair" the position of the country and of themselves. As Bagehot pointed out, "in excited states of the public mind" statesmen "have scarcely a discretion at all; the tendency of the public perturbation determines what shall and what shall not be dealt with."

Faced with such a situation the Conservatives seemed to have the advantage: unlike the Liberals, they were not bound to a doctrinaire policy of non-intervention by the state; and the traditional duty of the landed gentleman to look after his "folk" could be extended, without much violence to tradition, to the state, whose duty it was to guarantee a minimum standard of living to each of its citizens. Ideologically, the party of Disraeli could much more readily support social legislation than the party of Gladstone.

For it was the Liberal Party, the first important political manifestation of industrialism, which was the party of *laisser-faire*. By one of those great paradoxes of history, industrialism, which resulted ultimately in the intervention of the state in the economic activities of modern society, gave, at first, enormous impetus to a revolutionary though transitory principle: the right of the individual to act, for weal or woe as he pleased, without help or hindrance from organized society as represented by the state. Thomas Jefferson, the

---

DENIS BROGAN: Present-day Scottish scholar who has written extensively on French, American, and British history and current events. Although his style is at times unduly allusive, his comments are often profound.

LORD ROSEBERY: Gladstone's foreign secretary in 1886 and 1892 and Liberal prime minister following the resignation of Gladstone, in 1894. Like other nineteenth-century prime ministers, he was a scholar as well as a statesman. He wrote books on Pitt, Peel, Napoleon, and Cromwell.

idol of free men, had proclaimed that state best which governs least, and the qualifications put forth by Adam Smith, one-time professor of moral philosophy, were overlooked in favor of his strictures against the evils of state control.

The new doctrine of "freedom" was incalculable in its effect on human personality and was of real significance in the development of the economic institutions of modern society. Later generations, shocked at the ills of industrial society, are apt to overlook the gains achieved under a system of "free capitalism." But even Karl Marx, that mordant critic of things capitalistic, was ever ready and eager to admit that unrestrained capitalistic enterprise not only made possible the oncoming of socialism, but was itself an enormous advance over previous systems of production.

Nevertheless, the principle of unlimited freedom in economic activities was always broader than its application: practice rarely approaches precept. The doctrine of *laisser-faire* waxed while the principle of intervention waned, but the practice of state control was never entirely abandoned. And as the hazards and misfortunes of industrial life became more pronounced, and it became apparent that the common welfare was often endangered by a policy of *laisser-faire,* objections became more numerous and demands for the reassertion of power by society increased in ever-swelling volume. The organized community had relaxed its hold reluctantly and only on the promise that the liberty of each would promote the welfare of all; only on the assurance that even private vices would somehow be transmuted into public virtue; that the energy released by the disintegration of the organic community, by the atomization of society, would somehow be harnessed by an "invisible hand" for the greater benefit of all. The slackening of common control over economic activities was not conceived of as an abdication of the power of society to ameliorate the lot of its members. Rather, it was believed that common aims could best be achieved by a policy of "hands off."

But the failure to realize the promised ends forced a re-examination of means. Though liberty in itself became for some the objective, for those whose sole privilege seemed to be the right to be overemployed, underemployed, or unemployed, it was but a mockery. The doctrine of the omnipotence of individual effort and self-help could offer little attraction for those who saw destitution as their fate. The voices that had been raised earlier in protest against a policy which permitted the exploitation of individuals powerless to "compete" in the market could not be stilled. At the same time, members of the aristocracy, whose position was being rudely challenged, looked back nostalgically to a golden age not long gone, when in a divinely ordered universe each man found that station to which God had called him. Feudal society had recognized that it was the duty of the privileged, as the vicars of God, to aid the poor and benighted. Some aristocrats, refusing to come to terms with the newer egalitarian philosophy of liberalism, never gave up the concept and practice of *noblesse oblige.* And as their personal political role became circumscribed by changes in society, they enlarged the concept of duty, asserting it to be the obligation of the state to assume the responsibility for the welfare of its inhabitants. Advancing the doctrine that was soon known as "Tory Socialism," they insisted that it was the right and the duty of the state to intervene in order to improve the condition of the working classes.

"Tory Socialism" did not everywhere take precisely the same form; its paternalistic, authoritarian character varied with the political setting. Its strength too was a function of the balance of political power: it was weakest wherever the middle classes, having seized political power, were able to enforce a policy of *laisser-faire.* In Germany, however, where the middle classes, having won economic might with the aid of the state, feared to rend the fabric of political power lest they endanger their position, the concept of the welfare or modern social service state was early effectively preached

and practiced. Germany having fallen heir
to all the problems carried in the train of
modern industry, Chancellor Bismarck
sought to inaugurate what was for his time
an essentially revolutionary program of
social reform. Striving for a unified national
state, he saw in a program of social legislation the mortar which might cement the
community to the newly organized Reich.
The liberal slogans of *"laisser-faire, laisser-
passer,"* and "every man for himself and
the Devil take the hindmost" could have no
place, he asserted, in "a monarchical, paternalistic state." (Especially, he might have
added, in an age of universal manhood
suffrage.). It was the task of the state to
prevent suffering even, as he put it, if it
had to interfere with the right to starve.

Other countries, some independently and
others utilizing the experiences of Germany,
subsequently established schemes of social
insurance. Social insurance is, however,
only one type of social legislation; perhaps
the *omega,* but not the *alpha.* And though
the doctrine of state intervention flourished
best in Germany, where rapid and large-
scale industrialization had occurred without
upsetting the basic hold of the aristocracy
on the political power, other countries also
witnessed the development of social legislation. There never was, even in that archetype of a liberal state, Great Britain, any
period in which there existed a policy of
complete non-interference. At the height of
the successful agitation for the lifting of
many governmental restrictions on economic
activity, legislation was enacted for the
benefit of groups unable to survive under
a regime of "free enterprise." Hence the
Factory Acts, the limitation on hours of
employment for women and children. Later
came the Education Acts, gradually making
education compulsory and free; and toward
the turn of the century the milestone was
the Workmen's Compensation Act (1897).
Acting on grounds of principle or expediency, the Conservatives and even the Liberals had been forced to permit the enlargement of the area of state control; both
parties were being pushed into the unknown

seas of state intervention by a seemingly
irresistible tide. But there is no doubt that
the Conservatives faced the unknown with
much better grace. And indeed, if throughout the prewar decade, the enthusiasm for
social legislation on the part of the Conservatives seemed at times less than marked,
they never seriously attempted to bar it. On
the other hand, the agitation of the Liberals,
who oscillated between the fear that their
own clamor would prove *too* effective and
the hope that each measure would be the
last, is very plain.

The lack of any real program of social
reform plus the pressure of the ever more
discontented workers were responsible for
the *ad hoc* character of British social legislation in the decade before 1914. Whatever
the proclaimed intentions, the promises, and
the plans, no cohesive pattern of social
policy emerged. What was provided was
rather a mosaic of services, simple and complex, detailed and general, effective and
futile, varying in character and importance.
Perhaps no other period in their history so
bears out the traditional contention of
Britons that their activity is practical, based,
in the words of an official commission, "on
trial and error," without reference to any
hard and fast scheme, or any "conscious
direction of the national activities to definite ends." The activities of the government
were reflexive rather than reflective—almost
like those of a sleepwalker who reacts to the
exigencies of a situation. Certainly in this
period there was general confusion and precipitate action. Campbell-Bannerman had
promised that "the Liberals, aided by the
special knowledge of the Labor members,
could devote special attention to the condition of the people," but just what was meant
by "attention" was never clear. His successor as Prime Minister, Herbert Asquith,
recognized the "urgent, long-delayed, and
over-due problems of social reform," but he
seemed to do little without strong pressure.
Eager reformers agreed with him that there
was "a lot of country still to traverse, steep
hills to climb, stiff fences to take, deep and
even turbulent streams to cross before we

come to the end of our journey," but they became increasingly skeptical of his assertion that "we know where we are going and we shall not lose our way." Even with the perspective of two generations, it is still not possible to discern the road which the Liberal government consciously traveled.

Pledged though it was to social reform, the Liberal government which took office in December, 1905, was less than ardent in fulfilling promises so blithely put forth in vague generalities. When John Burns, of Dockers' Strike fame, had been given a seat in the government as President of the Local Government Board, there was alarm on the part of conservative citizens. His appointment, said the *Annual Register,* "might possibly raise expectations that it would be difficult or impossible to gratify." In office, however, Burns exhibited the lassitude that was to be characteristic of the government when it was not spurred on by fears of losing office. Soon the *Annual Register* could record that "the workingman President of the Local Government Board had delivered an interesting speech" with "little in it to cause real anxiety to sober people as to the likelihood of rash social and economic experiments." It was, continued the *Annual Register,* "remarkable for its full recognition that social amelioration could only be brought about by slow degrees." No professional politician, Burns was little moved by the popular clamor for social reform. Not so, however, many of his colleagues who were determined to stay in office. Burns was to demonstrate his lack of imagination in the next eight years; but he was also to give proof of his integrity by resigning from the Cabinet, along with John Morley, on the declaration of war by the British government, while his other colleagues, who had also opposed Britain's involvement, remained.

The government was not anxious to pass social legislation, but a series of unexpected Labor victories over both Conservatives and Liberals in by-elections made action imperative. As a result of popular pressure, three reform measures were enacted during the first year of office: the Workmen's Compensation Act, which extended the protection offered by the Acts of 1897 and 1899; the Trade Disputes Act, and the Provision of Meals Act.

The new Workmen's Compensation Act was demanded and on the whole welcomed by industrial workers. By its terms, all workers not expressly excluded were to receive protection against accidents and industrial diseases. The Act of 1897 had limited coverage to employees in specified dangerous trades; the Act of 1899 had extended protection to agricultural laborers and gardeners. The Act of 1906 further widened the coverage to embrace an estimated six million additional workers. The waiting time for benefits was reduced from two weeks to one, and benefits of about 50 percent of earnings were provided.

The history of the Trade Disputes Bill of 1906 illustrates the dilemma of the Liberal Cabinet with respect to social legislation. The Taff Vale decision of 1901, by holding that a trade union could be held responsible for the illegal acts performed on its behalf by any of its members, whether these acts were authorized or not by the union, threatened the unions with bankruptcy and ruin. As introduced, the Trade Disputes Bill proposed to limit the liability of trade unions to cases where the illegal acts were committed by authorized agents. The Labor members, dissatisfied with the proposal, were instrumental in forcing through legislation which freed trade unions from all liability for any acts of their members. As Keir Hardie expressed it, the difference between the Labor and the government proposals was that the trade unions were not satisfied with only barbed wire entanglements for the protection of their funds but wanted the funds moved out of the range of the enemy guns. Although many Liberals were opposed to what was a revolutionary proposal of freeing the trade unions from all liability, the sentiment among organized workers, some of whom had already joined the Labor Party, ran strong. Hesitating to push more union members into the Labor Party fold, the Liberal government capitulated and the bill as finally enacted embodied the demands of the unions. The Conservatives were no happier than the Liberals with the final measure, but like the Liberals most of them were also naturally averse to being branded anti-labor at a time when the labor vote was becoming ever more important. Though Sir Edward Carson, one of the Conservative leaders, gibed that "the King can do no wrong; neither can trade unions," few Conservatives voted against the bill. A total of only twenty-nine votes was recorded as against the measure, though more than two hundred members of the House of Commons abstained from voting. Nor did the House of Lords dare to veto the measure.

Much less controversial was the Provision of Meals Act, which became law in December, 1906, despite the opposition of some Liberals. Typical of the argument against state intervention was the traditional contention that the bill (which allowed local education authorities to provide a daily meal for school children) would discourage initiative, and foster indolence and degradation. Improvement in the condition of the people, said opponents of the measure, would come about only when they raised themselves by their individual efforts. The main argument in favor of the bill advanced by the President of the Board of Education was that it was very difficult to teach a hungry child the elements of learning, "either human or divine." Scoffers might have dubbed the measure a "relief for teachers." The Provision of Meals Act as amended in 1907 authorized the establishment of play centers and the provision of free medical examinations for children. In the following year, the Children Act codified the laws dealing with juvenile delinquency.

The social reform measures of 1906 did not quell the prevailing discontent. Though the Liberals with their comfortable majority were little disturbed by the Conservatives, the stability of the government seemed to be threatened from quarters other than His Majesty's Loyal Opposition. In a "country rich beyond description there are people poverty-stricken beyond description," cried a Labor member. The growing Labor Party and the disappointed among its own members were of increasing concern to the Liberal Party. Bold action was imperative. Old age pensions, demanded by large sections of the population and the subject of one of the first resolutions introduced by the Labor members in the 1906 Parliament, seemed to offer an opportunity to rally the forces behind the government. As Asquith admitted in a speech promising old age pensions, "This is a House of Commons which was elected more clearly and definitely than any other House in our history in the hope and belief on the part of the electors that it would find the road and provide the means for social reform." Even to a self-confessed moderate such as Asquith, there was "nothing that called so loudly or so imperiously" for attention as social reform. The proposed "pension" plan might be, as an opponent of the measure charged, "an enormous gift of money to a very large section of the working classes," but he recognized that they "were possessed of very large electoral power." And they would hold the Liberals to account if the government did not deal, as it had promised, with this "most serious and most urgent of all demands."

The Old Age Pension Act of 1908, which provided a maximum allotment of 5s. per week to all needy persons of good character on their reaching the age of seventy, signalizes, despite its ungenerous provisions, a distinct advance in the field of social legislation. Noncontributory pensions, though not entirely an innovation, sharply departed from the German practice of requiring the recipients of state aid to bear the brunt of the burden. The principle laid down in the Act, that state aid for those who could not help themselves was a right rather than a "charity," marked a historic break with the tradition established by the Poor Law of 1834. To old-fashioned Liberals, it was the death-knell of self-reliance. "The State invites us every day to lean upon it," complained Lord Rosebery. He heard "the wheedling and alluring whisper, 'Sound as you may be, we [the State] bid you be a cripple. Do you see? Be blind. Do you hear? Be deaf. Do you walk? Be not so venturesome. Here is a crutch for one arm; when you get accustomed to it, you will soon want another—the sooner the better.' The strongest man if encouraged may soon accustom himself to the methods of an invalid; he may train himself to totter, or to be fed with a spoon." Yet even the noble Earl, who rated the measure as one of the most important ever presented to Parliament, with consequences "so great, so mystic, so incalculable," admitted that it was supported by both parties, and he advised the House of Lords to approve it.

Other acts passed in 1908 and 1909 seemed only to confirm the gloomy predictions of those who saw at hand the end of individualism. In 1908, the enactment of the Miners Eight Hours Day Bill, which limited the working day of a miner working underground to eight hours from portal to portal, was the first of many subsequent measures that limited the working hours of the adult male. The "freedom of contract" of women and children had long been abridged; now an adult male who worked in the mines lost his "freedom" to make any contract he wished with respect to hours of work. The Development and Road Improvement Funds Act, providing for scientific research in agriculture and afforestation, as well as for the reclamation of land and the building of roads, was hailed by Keir Hardie. The Act, he maintained, endorsed the principle of the Right to Work and was "the most revolutionary measure ever introduced into Parliament." Whatever its implications, the measure, in its workings, fell far short of such interpretation. Somewhat more important was the Housing and Town Planning Bill of 1909, which amended the existing law enabling local authorities to provide new houses for the destitute. Landlords were required to keep their holdings in repair, or, in the words of the statute, "reasonably fit for

human habitation." Every county council was to have a full-time medical officer. Here, too, however, the law in its operation failed to match the expectations of its proponents. More significant in the development of social legislation were the Labor Exchanges Act of 1909 and the Trade Boards Act of the same year.

In 1905, just before leaving office, the Conservative government had appointed a Commission to investigate the functioning of the Poor Law, still based on the principles of the Law of 1834. Under the chairmanship of Lord George Hamilton (described by Balfour as "not as stupid as he looks"), the Commission of eighteen, including among its members Beatrice Webb, interviewed a total of 1300 witnesses. Its Report, issued in 1909, is the longest ever drawn up by a royal commission. Strictly speaking, two reports were published: that of the majority, signed by fourteen members of the Commission, and a Minority Report, drawn up for the most part by Sidney Webb and signed by his wife and three other members of the Commission. Differing on many matters, the two reports agreed that the Poor Law required revision, though they disagreed as to the nature of the changes. They also concurred in the proposal to establish a national system of unemployment exchanges as the first step to cope with the problem of poverty and unemployment. The Labor Exchanges Act, introduced by Winston Churchill on behalf of the government, was based on this recommendation, though registration was made voluntary rather than compulsory as suggested by the Commission. With a frankness not always to be found among politicians in such instances, Churchill stated, "It would be to invest the policy with an air of humbug if we were to pretend that labor exchanges are going to make more work. They are not."

The Trade Boards Act of 1909 was somewhat more effective in alleviating distress and much more important in its implications. It broke new ground in British social legislation by establishing the principle of a living wage. Thirty years earlier, a committee of the House of Lords had made an elaborate study of industries noted—or notorious—for their low wages. Its report, released in 1890, set forth no exact definition of "sweating" but listed such evils as underlying low wage rates, excessive hours of labor, and unsanitary conditions as characteristic of "sweated" industries. Though in marginal cases there might have been difficulties in definition, it was generally accepted in 1909 that an industry in which the rate of wages was inadequate or disproportionately low for the work performed was "sweated." The Act of 1909 listed the tailoring, cardboard-box making, the lace industry, and the chain-making trade as "sweated trades" and empowered the government to designate other industries as such. Nothing precipitate was to be done, however. There was first to be a long interval of investigation, and even when the rate was fixed, no punishment for violation was to be imposed for at least six months. Rates were to be set by Boards composed of representatives of employers and workers in the respective industries, as well as members of the public. Not until 1912 were standards laid down. Yet the Act was a portent of things to come. Its principle of a living wage not only marked the change from legislation designed to *alleviate* distress to legislation intended to *prevent* distress, but also set the stage for what was to become a principle of public policy in Great Britain, namely, the encouragement to industry and to labor to establish employer associations and trade unions. Nine years later, the Act was amended; thereafter the establishment of a Trade Board depended more upon whether an industry was not organized than upon the rate of wages being paid. As a Conservative spokesman, the Marquess of Salisbury, had explained it in 1909, "These women have not made sufficient progress in the art of citizenship to be able to combine in a trade union and until they do I presume we must be content with this procedure." A far cry from the Combination Acts!

Perhaps appetite grows with the eating.

More likely, with respect to the social reform movement in Britain during this period, the legislation, revolutionary as it appeared to be to its opponents, did not meet the needs and aspirations of the working classes. The legislation could not allay "the disquiet that compelled it." The basic cause of the unrest was the rising level of prices. The opening of new gold fields at the turn of the last century had brought little but distress to many in Britain. Money wages had gone up almost steadily, but the relative position of the workers was now worse than during the so-called great depression of 1873-1896. As real wages failed to go up in what was on the whole an era of industrial prosperity, discontent mounted. At the same time, though recent studies have demonstrated that the rich were not getting richer, ostentatious expenditure by the well-to-do—Veblen's "conspicuous consumption"—was more glaring than ever. To the Nonconformist conscience, this was particularly evil. One of the members of the Liberal government was moved, in 1909, to exclaim: "More than an age of Adventure, more even than an age of reckless Wickedness, does time judge and condemn an age of ineffectual Pleasure."

What the government could do to redress the balance was, however, the stumbling block. To attempt to conciliate the rebellious workers seemed like the labor of Sisyphus. And the Liberals realized that to do more in the way of basic reform would split their own ranks, since reforms for the benefit of the industrial workers could be achieved only at the expense of the middle class. For the sake of party and power, many Liberals had reluctantly acquiesced in the social legislation of the preceding two years, but they felt that to go on with further measures would lead straight to socialism. Even Lloyd George was frank to admit that "with the present organization of society" no government could prevent unemployment. "Trade has its currents, and its tides, and its storms and its calms, like the sea, which seem to be almost just as little under human control." What he proposed to do, he said, was to recognize the perils and to attempt to prepare to meet them. In the words of a later critic, the Liberals sought "to medicine" but they could never cure the social ills. The Prime Minister might proclaim that "property must be associated in the mind of the masses of the people with the ideas of reason and justice," but if this goal was to be reached only at the constant expense of property, Asquith and his followers could never accept, much less act on, this conclusion. Taxes were necessary, but should not, in the words of Lloyd George, "reflect any injury on that trade and commerce which constitute the sources of our wealth." And both Lloyd George and Asquith refused to exempt even the poorest from the "duty" of paying taxes. On June 24, 1907, Balfour had summed up the situation to the discomfiture of the Liberals:

Many voted for the Government in the mistaken view that it was in the power of this Government to carry certain schemes, or at all events to attain to certain objects which they had much at heart. [The Liberals] gave them to understand that they had panaceas for all those evils if they came to office; but when they had to turn these panaceas from perorations into Bills they found it extremely difficult, if not in some cases impossible. . . . [It was] far easier for the Government to try to quarrel with the House of Lords, to say to people, Oh, if you only knew what wonderful schemes we have in our heads, what admirable means we have in our pigeon-holes! But there is the House of Lords which will certainly reject them if we send them up! Great is then the disappointment almost unaffected when the House of Lords passes a measure—not indeed the results of the brains of the Government, but the result of the Labor representatives—when the House of Lords, instead of doing what they were intended to do, does the opposite, then the right hon. Gentleman cannot control himself. Their flagitious, un-

scrupulous opportunism moves his wrath and arouses his indignation, and for the simple reason that the right hon. Gentleman's Bills, as I have said, were never brought in to pass, but to be rejected. And I think they were so drafted that there was great difficulty in some cases in not rejecting the Bills.

It is only against this background that the extravagances of the 1909 budget campaign can be understood. It is customary for political parties to be unrestrained in denouncing each other, to proclaim and by dint of repetition to become convinced themselves that the end of the world will come about if the opposition is successful in passing certain legislation, but here the breach between conviction and reality was unnatural. The agitation (including a Hyde Park demonstration numbering a quarter of a million people, which *The Times* said was "skilfully engineered") and the real terror aroused during the budget campaign are all the more astonishing in the light of the actual provisions of the much hailed "revolutionary" budget. It is difficult to bridge the gap between the sound and fury embalmed in contemporary accounts and the relative innocuousness of the budget. For the budget of 1909, if it "soaked the rich" more than did most previous budgets, burdened the poor to an even greater degree than did preceding and less "radical" budgets. The major innovations were a tax on undeveloped land and a tax on "unearned increment." But the test of a tax is in the incidence and in the collection; when the land taxes were finally repealed after eleven years, it was ascertained that they had brought in only £1,300,000, and had cost almost four times as much to collect. As one of the inner circle of the Liberals later admitted, the bill originally "was drafted by those who disliked it and each amendment made it more impossible."

The budget accomplished little else, but it did prolong the Liberal tenure of office. In the words of one important Conservative, Lord Birkenhead, "the death rattle" of the

Asquith Cabinet was already audible, until the Liberals were saved by the fight over the budget. Lloyd George, the "Welsh wizard," had promised to bring on the Millenium, but by threatening to create what seemed to many of the Conservatives like Pandemonium, he and his party remained in power. In the fight over the budget and the subsequent campaign over the powers of the House of Lords, the Conservatives abandoned all prudence and became determined men of principle rather than of expediency. As an acute observer, Denis Brogan, has pointed out, "The great secret of the [British] governing class has always been its knowledge, its prophetic knowledge of when it was necessary to retreat." But the Conservatives now proceeded to lose their heads, to develop an ideology and "to think of following principles to their logical conclusion. Few less English remarks can be thought of than the 'damn the consequences' of Lord Milner." Even the growing realization on the part of the more perceptive Conservatives that they were walking into a trap could not hold them back. Retreat appeared more and more impossible and they marched forth to defeat with fatal resolution. In June, 1908, Lloyd George had threatened: "I have no nest-eggs; I am looking for some one's hen-roost to rob next year." But in the light of events it is clear that his theft consisted only in robbing the Conservatives of their reason and pillaging the Scriptures for phrases with which to adorn his speeches.

Even the Liberals fell prey to Lloyd George's rhetoric. They were both fascinated and alarmed by the budget. John Burns has graphically described the Cabinet's deliberations: "like nineteen rag-pickers round a 'eap of muck." But it was an opportunity that perhaps no politician, no matter how scrupulous, could have foregone. The Lords must be convulsed in order to prevent the masses from being converted to Labor. As the Earl of Crewe admitted, when he denied that the Conservatives had been lured by "a sinister kind of conspiracy" into an impossible position, "Our political existence as a Party is involved." Though they disliked the budget and even feared it, few Liberals, faced with the alternative of political death, went so far as Lord Rosebery, who lamented that the budget was the "end of all things—religion, property, and family life."

In the debate over the budget and the subsequent debate over the Parliament Act of 1911, sight was temporarily lost of the "social question." But it could not long be put off. During the Revolution of 1848, Alexis de Tocqueville had warned the Chamber of Deputies that the "passions are no longer political but social." Bismarck, thirty years later, told the Reichstag that the political question was the social question. And Ramsay MacDonald in 1911 reminded the House of Commons that social affairs had become the main business of politics. That was the problem, but the solution was most difficult. To stay in power the Liberals had two alternatives: a coalition with the Conservatives or the continuation of a social reform policy. Turned down in their quest for a coalition by the Conservatives, who deemed time to be on their side, the Liberals in order to stay in power had to go along with an advanced social policy. Not prepared to go so far, they did nevertheless proceed to enact a limited program of social legislation. How long they could have struggled along in this fashion it is impossible to say, but, faced with immediate and pressing problems, they still had one measure in reserve: the Invalidity and Unemployment Insurance Bill. This measure of 1911 was in two parts, one providing for sickness and invalidity insurance, and the other setting up a limited program of unemployment insurance. The provisions for sickness and invalidity insurance covered about fifteen million wage earners, or practically the whole industrial population. Benefits were to be 10s. per week for men and 7s. 6d. for women; payments were to be for twenty-six weeks per year. The scheme was financed by contributions of 4d. per week by male workers and 2d. by women workers, with the employers paying 3*d*. per week and the state contributing 2*d*. for each worker. Unemployment insurance, in which field there was much less experience on which to draw, was limited to about two million workers in trades with high chronic unemployment. These were the construction, engineering, and shipbuilding industries, which together accounted for about half of all unemployment. The fund was financed by payments of 2½*d*. per week from each worker, payments of 2½*d*. by the employers for each of their workers (with provision for abatement for employers with good employment records), and contributions by the state of one fourth of the total sum. Benefits were to be about 7*s*. per week for fifteen weeks a year. In such a fashion did the British government intervene in a field left untouched by Bismarck. The recognition of unemployment as a problem of industry and the state was a decided advance in social legislation and perhaps excuses the rhetoric of the Prime Minister, who boasted that "we are conferring upon millions of our fellow countrymen by the joint operation of self-help and of State-help, the greatest alleviation of the risks and sufferings of life that Parliament has ever conferred upon any people." To the workers, however, the provision for contributory payments for both health and unemployment insurance seemed like many steps backward.

After 1911 the Liberals could only mark time. They were afraid of losing their future, yet they could not go beyond their past; they felt that they had done all they could and dared. The period of far-reaching reform under the aegis of the state seemed ended. Even under the pressure of a national coal strike of 800,000 miners, with another million and a quarter workers thrown out of work, the government refused to yield to the strikers' demand for a national minimum wage. The Coal Mines (Minimum Wage) Act of 1912, passed as a result of the emergency, merely provided for the setting of district minimum wages by joint boards of miners and mine oper-

ators, much after the fashion of the Trade Boards Bill of 1909.

Little wonder that the workers, increasingly restive because of their failure to raise their standard of living in a period of industrial prosperity, turned to direct action. In 1911 a speaker at the Trade Union Congress had implored, "Let those strike who have never struck before and those who have always struck strike all the more." Ramsay MacDonald describes the strike movement of the period: "The labor world responded to the call to strike in the same eager, spontaneous way as nature responds to the call of springtime. One felt as if some magical allurement seized upon them."

There were ample signs that the next year might be even more troubled. Searching for parallels, observers fell back on the revolutionary year of 1848. There was, among the workers, a lack of interest in such "political" issues as Home Rule and Welsh Disestablishment. Public attention was occupied "not with the familiar questions of the later Victorian era, but with issues far more immediately urgent and vital." So passed the years 1911 through 1913. The chronicler for the *Annual Register* noted that the year 1912 opened "in anxiety and gloom." Describing December, 1913, the author could only repeat: "the year closed with anxiety and gloom." Labor unrest was unabated, and there were signs that the trade boom of the seven preceding years was drawing to a close. Subscriptions to leading charities had decreased, but "there had never been such a year in London for costly Christmas presents, nor had the luxury of the wealthy ever been displayed so ostentatiously." What did all this presage?

The advent of the World War temporarily diverted men's passions from the social question. All ills were put aside, all evils swallowed up in the fraternity of common hatred. For old-fashioned Liberals the era of the "Wonderful Century" was over; the old virtues and values were gone. In the words of Sir Edward Grey, "the lamps of civilization were extinguished"; man would now have to wrestle in the darkness with fear and torment. New and great events would recast reality and underline changes in public opinion.

Yet, in fact, the Liberals had built better than they knew. Though they advanced "with noisy mouths and mouselike feet," the period from 1906 to 1911 was a revolutionary period in the history of British social reform. A system of social insurance had been enacted in five short years. Imperfect and limited though it was, especially by later standards, it furnished the basis for revision and extension. In 1895 the *Economist* had lamented the growth of state intervention. "Little by little, year by year, the fabric of State expenditure and State responsibility is built up like a coral island, cell on cell." What would it have said of the Liberal pre-war era?

EXCEPT FOR A SMALL GROUP OF CAMBRIDGE HISTORIANS, few scholars on the eve of World War I cared to study nineteenth-century British foreign policy. One reason was that so great a mass of source material existed that few historians were willing to devote to the study of diplomatic history the immense amount of labor and time which the subject involved. A second reason was that many historians shared Bismarck's view concerning the traditional sources for the study of foreign policy: that "nothing of any value" would be found in the usual diplomatic reports, that they were worthless as material for history. Really important matters, as Bismarck pointed out, "are always dealt with in private letters and confidential communications, also verbal ones, and these are not included in the archives." The upshot was that only in the period after the outbreak of World War I did the study of nineteenth-century British foreign policy begin to come into its own, attracting able scholars who in earlier years would have chosen to pursue subjects much more remote from the contemporary scene. Many of these scholars, impressed with the relative newness of their subject matter, wrote articles and books of a heavily factual nature. They insisted that the time had not yet come for the generalizations and interpretations that were possible in other fields of historical investigation. A few, however, despite all the difficulties involved, ventured to generalize in their writings. In the following essay, Dr. Godfrey Davies, who has done much to stimulate the American study of British foreign policy, analyzes the forces and factors that shaped British foreign policy from Waterloo to Serajevo. Indeed, Dr. Davies explains the unity with which Britain entered the war by reference to the collective operation of these forces and factors in the summer of 1914.

THE PATTERN OF BRITISH FOREIGN POLICY: 1815–1914[1]

GODFREY DAVIES

Lord Salisbury, a most experienced statesman, is reported to have advised students of British foreign policy to use large maps. With equal sagacity he might have counseled them to take a long view. During a short period so many deviations and inconsistencies appear that the main direction is obscured. A statesman's predilections or party exigencies, and changes in the European or world situation, may cause zigzags to be more apparent on a chart than the true course. But, when a century is surveyed, broad trends appear, and a clear pattern emerges.

The pattern has a number of threads, of different colors, which do not remain of equal brightness throughout. In other words, a factor in foreign policy may remain dormant for a generation or more and suddenly come to life again when questioned. Imagine sea power as a deep navy blue in 1815, and gradually fading until 1856, when the whole question of maritime rights is raised and partly settled by the Declaration of Paris. The Trent affair also deepens the color temporarily, but then it grows pale until in the twentieth century, with the German challenge to British supremacy at sea, navy blue is most prominent again. The pattern becomes more intricate when new threads are introduced which fail to harmonize on occasion with the old. Examples occur when the desire to give moral support to liberalism or nationality abroad may be in conflict with the principles of nonintervention or the balance of power. But in the end the pattern is once more clear, and its last state can be compared with its beginning.

[1] This address is printed substantially as delivered on Founder's Day, Mar. 1, 1943. No consideration was given to British relations with the United States and the Far East, because time did not permit discussion of them commensurate with their importance.

In 1815 there were about six threads, which for convenience of reference are numbered and labeled.

(1) Belgium. For strategic and commercial reasons England had been interested since the end of the thirteenth century in keeping the Netherlands from falling into the hands of a powerful continental state. Belgium has been called "the cockpit of Europe," and in most continental wars in which Britain has participated her troops have fought there. French conquest of the Low Countries and refusal to abandon them were the main causes both of the start of the struggle against revolutionary France and of its length, 1793-1815. After the war British insistence secured the union of Holland and Belgium in order to safeguard their independence.

(2) Balance of Power. This factor in British foreign policy may be defined as an attempt to prevent any one European nation or group of nations from treating the rest like conquered territory. The policy is usually said to have originated with Cardinal Wolsey in the 1510's and 1520's. The phrase started as "balance of Europe," but by the end of the seventeenth century changed to its present form. The failure of the Stuart kings to preserve the balance was one reason for the Revolution of 1688. This principle, and colonial rivalry, were largely responsible for the Second Hundred Years' War with France, 1689-1815.

(3) Naval Supremacy. Naval supremacy was gained by the defeat of the Armada in 1588, regained by Oliver Cromwell in the 1650's, and maintained ever since with a few exceptions, of which the most serious was loss of command of the seas during the American Revolution.

(4) Colonies and Commerce. This thread is dependent upon (3). Many of the large areas that modern British cartographers

Reprinted by special permission from *The Huntington Library Quarterly*, VI (1943), 367-377.

color red were already red, wholly or in part, in 1815—Canada, Australia, India, and the West Indies. Footholds had been established in Africa. The extent to which foreign policy has been influenced by considerations of trade is very debatable. Judging by such collections as *British Documents on the Origins of the War,* the influence was extremely slight. References are few, and almost without exception indicate aloofness on the part of the Foreign Office. A striking example is to be found in a reply Lansdowne sent to a remonstrance of the Manchester Chamber of Commerce complaining that British trade interests in Morocco had been sacrificed by the Anglo-French agreement of April 8, 1904. Lansdowne makes it clear that the Chamber of Commerce had not been consulted beforehand and that the agreement, having been signed, could not now be altered.[2]

(5) Turkey. The preservation of Turkey was a new principle, which dated from William Pitt's unsuccessful efforts to keep Russia from the shores of the Black Sea. English eyes had been opened to the importance of naval supremacy in the Mediterranean Sea by Napoleon Bonaparte's invasion of Egypt in 1798, and this impression was deepened by his treating Constantinople as the strategic center of the world, for which he quarreled with Tsar Alexander and embarked on his famous Moscow expedition in 1812. British diplomacy had been active at the Porte and had aided Russia to make peace with Turkey in 1812, so that she could marshall all her strength against France.

(6) Humanitarianism. Usually regarded

[2] [Footnote omitted.]

as a product of the eighteenth century, humanitarianism invaded the sphere of foreign policy from various sides. It remained a potent influence throughout the period and grew stronger as the British constitution slowly developed into a democratic form of government dependent upon public opinion. The antislavery movement was its most obvious activity and persisted throughout the nineteenth century. British foreign secretaries could not afford to ignore it even if they were so minded. At times it clashed with economic interests and won some resounding victories, notably the abolition of the slave trade in the British Empire in 1807, and of slavery in 1833—on each occasion triumphing over the West Indian merchants and planters. It supported all efforts to mitigate the horrors of war and to reduce armaments.

The first four of these threads settle the pattern's essential features. Britain's geographical situation as an island adjacent to western Europe compelled the adoption and maintenance of all, unless Britain resigned her position as a great power. They were necessities of existence and their occasional neglect was nearly disastrous. The outstanding diplomatic battle, from 1902 to 1914, to restore the equilibrium, and the narrow margin by which Germany was defeated during the First World War, prove the tremendous difficulty of recovering an equipoise if once upset. So long as the question of India and the protection of her North-West Frontier and of sea routes from Britain to her shores, loomed so large in British eyes, Turkey's integrity seemed of the first importance. When in the 1880's and 1890's

---

LORD LANSDOWNE: Governor-general of Canada, viceroy of India, and British foreign secretary (d. 1927). He helped to construct the Anglo-Japanese Alliance and arrange the Anglo-French Entente in the early twentieth century.

TRENT AFFAIR: Crisis in Anglo-American relations that grew out of the American Civil War. In 1861 Mason and Slidell, commissioners of the Confederate States to Britain and France, were removed from the British mail steamer *Trent.* The British government protested, and there was talk of war. Prince Albert and Secretary of State Seward played major roles in smoothing out Anglo-American relations.

the scramble for Africa had replaced anxiety for India's defense, Turkey no longer retained her old significance as the guardian of the Straits. This factor would seem to be optional, though events during 1914-18 and after the outbreak of war in 1939 render such a judgment doubtful.

Surprise may be felt that no suggestion has been made to include two other threads, Peace and The Sanctity of Treaties. Britain had every inducement to keep the peace and to preserve the sanctity of treaties, inasmuch as she has been numbered among the "have" nations and anxious on that account to preserve the status quo. But she can hardly arrogate to herself any exclusive concern for these two fundamentals of foreign policies, inasmuch as all, or nearly all, nations have professed to seek them.

Starting with six threads, my purpose is to illustrate what happens to them and what others are added, during five periods into which the years 1815-1914 can be somewhat arbitrarily divided.

(a) 1815-30. Britain was singularly fortunate in that, during these critical years, she enjoyed the guidance of two of her greatest foreign secretaries, Castlereagh and Canning. The former tried to introduce an entirely new system of arranging the foreign relations of European countries—periodical meetings of the great powers (Britain, France, Austria, Prussia, Russia, and Italy after her unification in 1859) to discuss matters of common interest. The system of congresses failed because the desires of the autocracies collided with Castlereagh's new principle, our thread Number 7—Nonintervention in the Domestic Affairs of Other Nations. Austria, Prussia, and Russia wanted to stifle any revolutionary movement at birth, lest it prove contagious and, like the French Revolution, embroil all neighboring states. Britain protested that the powers had no moral right to interfere unless the danger to other nations from the forcible propaganda of revolution was unmistakable. After Castlereagh's death, Canning failed to prevent the suppression of constitutionalism in Spain, but British sea power and the Monroe Doctrine safeguarded the newly won independence of South America.

(b) 1830-65. Our pattern now becomes more confused than at any other time. The first reason is that Palmerston, easily the most important figure in British foreign policy for a generation, so transformed nonintervention that Talleyrand's definition was often true—that nonintervention was a philosophical and political term that meant much the same as intervention. The second reason is the interest the middle classes in England, after the Reform Bill of 1832 which gave them political power, felt in two new threads, Number 8, Nationality, and Number 9, Liberalism. Both were dynamic forces that transformed Europe politically, just as the industrial revolution and technology transformed her economically and socially. Palmerston laid stress upon nationality, Russell, another Liberal leader, upon liberalism, but neither ever succeeded in weaving either thread harmoniously into the pattern, which consequently grows obscure. New and old threads become entangled. A few examples follow. In 1830 Belgium, under the influence of nationalism, demanded independence from Holland, secured it with British and French assistance, and in 1839 was declared by the powers, including Prussia, to be perpetually neutral. Here the threads, Belgium and Nationality, are in harmony with each other but not with nonintervention. In Spain in the 1830's and 1840's Tories upheld nonintervention, but the Liberals departed so far from that principle in their desire to support liberalism that they permitted a legion to be enrolled in England in order to fight on the Iberian Peninsula. An even more complicated stage was reached when Italian nationality tried in 1848, and largely succeeded in 1859, to achieve unification by driving out the Austrians. Britain rejoiced at Austria's defeat in Italy but wished to maintain a strong Austria in central Europe to preserve the balance of power and keep Russia out of the Balkans. In other words our old threads, Balance of Power and Turkey, become entangled with the more recent additions, Nationality and Liberalism. On the whole, the latter prevail, although the one European war in which Britain took part from 1815 to 1914, the Crimean War against Russia, was fought to preserve Turkey and the balance of power.

The period ends with a decisive defeat of Palmerstonian intervention over the Schleswig-Holstein question in 1864, when these two provinces were torn from Denmark by Austria and Prussia. The rash words Palmerston and Russell had uttered to encourage Denmark to resist were not based on military strength to make them good. Bismarck was not to be bluffed. He called the hand and won the game. The moral Britain drew from the incident was that she should isolate herself from the Continent. The lesson she failed to learn was that in Prussia nothing succeeds like military success.

(c) 1864-74. Belgium and Nonintervention are the only threads that retain their brightness through the shortest and simplest period. During the Franco-German war of 1870 Britain extorted from each belligerent a pledge to respect Belgian neutrality and promised that, if either invaded Belgium, she would join the other to help expel the intruder, though she did not intend to participate in the war elsewhere. Apart from this outstanding exception, and representation at a conference of the powers to condone Russia's repudiation of the clauses of the Treaty of Paris (1856) which had prohibited warships and fortifications in the Black Sea, Britain carried nonintervention to the point of isolation. With folded arms she watched Prussia establish her supremacy in central Europe by the Austro-Prussian war of 1866, and Germany gain by the Franco-German war a hegemony in Europe that lasted a generation. The balance of power was neglected and not restored until the twentieth century. Her leaders, wont to regard nationality and liberalism as natural allies, did not perceive that German nationality, achieved by military strength, had given liberalism the most decisive defeat it

suffered until the rise of Fascism and Nazism.

(d) 1874-1902. The dominant note was the new imperialism. Our pattern changes in a startling fashion. No new threads appear, though one disappears, but the color scheme is altered. During the three years from 1876 to 1878 the preservation of Turkey against Russia, undertaken with especial regard to Asia Minor, Persia, and even Afghanistan a year or so later—in other words, the approaches to India— seemed all-important. So far as purely British interests were concerned the Treaty of Berlin was satisfactory, but its failure to gratify the nationalistic ambitions of submerged races in the Balkans left the door open for racial antagonisms that still exist. But in the 1890's Turkey's integrity ceases to be an object of British foreign policy. Humanitarianism would no longer tolerate support for Abdul Hamid, "the great assassin" of the Armenians. It is noteworthy that the one thread that vanishes was destroyed by humanitarianism. It is equally noteworthy that German influence replaced British at Constantinople. The Kaiser's theatrical visit there in 1898 suggested that *Realpolitik* had no hesitation in shaking hands with murder.

Another, less disinterested explanation of the disappearance from our pattern of thread Number 5, Turkey, is that English eyes were riveted on Africa, and not India, from 1880 to 1902. Beginning with France's occupation of Tunisia in 1881, Africa absorbed the foreign offices of four of the great powers, Britain, France, Germany, and Italy, and even of smaller nations like Spain and Belgium. Suddenly the fourth thread of our pattern, Colonies and Commerce, assumes the brightest hue. Previously it had been badly faded. During nearly a half century, and especially since the triumph of free trade in 1846, colonies had been regarded as liabilities rather than assets. Calculations had been made purporting to prove that each square mile of the Empire involved a net loss to Britain of a pound a year. The common expectation was that every colony would become independent—some felt, the sooner the better. The only argument many used against cutting the painter was that Britain would be ungenerous if she turned her colonies adrift until they had been educated in self-government. This little-England attitude was abruptly replaced by an ardent expansionist policy. Time is too short to permit analysis of the new imperialism. But attention can be drawn to its global nature. It affected Japan and the United States as well as Europe. Indeed, President McKinley provided a classical exposition of the new imperialism in his explanation of why he decided that the Philippines should be annexed. He relates how he wrestled with the problem as he walked the floor of the White House night after night and prayed for guidance. Eventually he felt convinced that to give back the islands to Spain would be cowardly and dishonorable, to turn them over to a commercial rival would be bad business, and to leave them to their own devices when they were unfit for self-government would soon result in anarchy. Therefore, he decided, the United States must keep them and educate, uplift, civilize, and Christianize the Filipinos. After this conclusion, he says, he slept soundly. The consciences of expansionists throughout the world were equally at rest when they had assumed "the white man's burden." After all, President McKinley's justification means much the same as the phrase Cecil Rhodes is said to have applied to British motives for maintaining an empire, "Philanthropy plus five per cent" (on the capital sunk in colonial enterprises).

So far as European powers were concerned the main sphere of imperialism was Africa, which displaced India as the center of interest at the British Foreign Office. What is called the scramble for Africa began, in 1881, when the French occupied Tunisia, and by the close of the century most of the hitherto dark continent had been annexed or occupied. During the scramble British relations with France remained bad, and nearly ended in war, in

1898, over control of the sources of the Nile. It is noteworthy that, although there is no necessary connection between humanitarianism and colonization, yet the longing to suppress slavery and establish Christianity in Africa frequently united with the urge to expand. But after the Boer War, of 1899-1902, the new imperialism declined rapidly.

During this period preoccupation with colonial questions led Britain to continue her neglect of the balance of power. Indeed, she tilted the balance still further by siding with the Triple Alliance of Germany, Austria, and Italy against France in the 1880's. In the 1890's she maintained what a Canadian minister was the first to call a splendid isolation. If the balance of power was somewhat restored in the 1890's by the Dual Alliance of France and Russia, Britain did nothing to help.

(e) 1902-14. During these twelve years our pattern becomes clear again. None of its threads is dull but the brightest are the oldest. They are taken in order and their connection with the outbreak of war is briefly told. (1) Belgium. The immediate cause of the entry of Great Britain into the First World War was Germany's invasion of Belgium, on the plea that necessity knows no law, and that the treaty of 1839 was a scrap of paper. In 1793 and 1815, in 1914 and 1918, the first and last battles were fought on Belgian soil. The oldest tradition in British foreign policy was responsible for England's entry into her greatest wars. (2) Balance of Power. At the turn of the century, Britain abandoned her attitude of aloofness from the Continent, in order to restore the European equilibrium, and established ententes with France in 1904 and with Russia in 1907. The balance between the Triple Entente and the Triple Alliance was so delicate that even the adherence of Balkan states might sway it. Hence events in that troubled region were important enough to usher in Armageddon. Sir Edward Grey knew that to preserve the balance was imperative and he therefore felt that Britain should intervene to prevent the defeat of

France, which would leave Germany supreme on the Continent.

(3) Naval Supremacy. The German Naval Law of 1900 and supplementary laws were intended to create a fleet so formidable that the strongest navy would hesitate to engage it. Britain regarded the creation of a powerful German fleet as a challenge to her sea power which could not be declined. She felt that if her supremacy at sea were lost she would be at Germany's mercy. With her food supplies at home sufficient for only about six weeks, she could easily be starved into surrender. Her tiny army could scarcely hope to defend her shores, much less to confront on German soil the greatest army in the world. Convinced that her navy, her sure shield in many a life-and-death struggle, was essential not only for her own preservation but also for the maintenance of peace, she saw plainly that Germany's rejection of overtures for a naval holiday or slowing down of construction rendered inevitable a struggle for existence.

(4) Colonies and Commerce. There was no direct colonial issue with Germany in 1914, but at any time one might arise, for she was as ardent for a bigger place in the sun as the Kaiser for the spotlight. In July, when Germany made a bid for English neutrality, she was willing to promise to leave France intact after a successful war but would give no guarantee about her colonies. The loyalty of the dominions emphasized their value to Great Britain in her hour of need. Anglo-German trade rivalry was keen, but except for a short recession in 1908 British commerce was increasing rapidly. In 1914, whereas German industrialists are said to have favored war, their British rivals are reported to have favored neutrality. (5) Turkey. This thread had already disappeared. (6) Humanitarianism. Much of the old zeal against slavery was now against German militarism, though the severest criticisms of it were soon proved to have fallen short of the brutal reality. Germany's refusal to agree to plans for the limitation of armaments and compulsory arbitration of international disputes alienated many, while the teaching of German philosophers and historians that war was a biological necessity disgusted others.

(7) Nonintervention. Although not prominent in the pattern, this thread was involved in Austria's ultimatum to Serbia that her officials should participate in the inquiry on Serbian soil into the alleged connivance of officials in the assassination of Francis Ferdinand at Serajevo. (8) Nationality. The quarrel between Austria-Hungary and Serbs revolved round the desires of the Serbs to unite with men of the same race and language then living in Bosnia. France wished to regain Alsace-Lorraine, torn from her in 1871, and the Poles in East Prussia and Galicia longed to recover their freedom. As the war progressed it became largely a struggle for self-determination—the great principle of the Treaty of Versailles. (9) Liberalism. Inasmuch as Tsarist Russia was one of them, the Allies could hardly claim to be engaged in a crusade for liberty, though the German army was recognized as the great enemy of freedom. The United States' entry into the war was, according to a popular slogan, to make the world safe for democracy.

The brightest threads in our pattern in 1914 were unquestionably the first three, the oldest and defensive principles, the loss of which would have meant Britain's extinction as a great power. But as the war progressed the remaining threads became brighter. That all the threads were in harmony explains the unanimity with which Britain entered the war. Nevertheless, these threads should not be regarded as wires on which British foreign ministers were manipulated like marionettes. Within limits there was still room for personalities or public opinion to influence foreign relations. Yet, viewed as a whole, our pattern is well described by a French proverb—the more it changes, the more it remains the same.

THE

Twentieth Century

PART EIGHT

ESPECIALLY IN THE 1930's—a decade of depression, isolationism, and widespread disillusionment with war as an instrument of national policy—economic interpretations of the origins of World War I gained considerable currency. According to these interpretations capitalists were chiefly responsible for the coming of the war. Intent on capturing more and more markets, they found the world becoming too small to satisfy their needs, and war followed as the inevitable result of industrial overproduction and intense economic rivalry. In short, British and German capitalists were the leading villains of the piece; they stood condemned as the authors of a war of imperialist rivalry. Such an approach to the coming of the war of 1914 obviously leaves much to be desired from the standpoint of historical accuracy. Above all, it discounts the fundamental fact that, despite all their rivalries, the British and the Germans were each others' best European customers. It also overlooks the widespread conviction in business circles that war was synonymous with trade losses, high taxes, and personal hardships. As the British foreign secretary, Sir Edward Grey, put it, "We are going to suffer . . . terribly in this war, whether we are in it or whether we stand aside. Foreign trade is going to stop, not because the trade routes are closed, but because there is no trade at the other end. Continental nations engaged in war—all their populations, all their energies, all their wealth, engaged in a desperate struggle—they cannot carry on the trade with us that they are carrying on in times of peace, whether we are parties to the war or whether we are not." In the selection that follows, the late Sir John Clapham examines economic forces in relation to the coming of World War I. The most distinguished twentieth-century master of modern British economic history, Professor Clapham is the author of one of the monuments of recent historical scholarship—*An Economic History of Modern Britain* (1930-1938), in three volumes.

WAR AND ECONOMIC CAUSATION

SIR JOHN CLAPHAM

On the British industrial society with its subordinate agriculture there fell—to the intense surprise of by far the greater part of its members—war. Though surprised, the majority accepted or hotly approved the conduct of its political leaders; and a critical people recently disunited went into unexpected and unknown war with a singularly common consent. Kitchener, their new War Minister, told them to prepare for years of fighting; but few in any station of life took his warning to heart at the first. Soldiers in all European armies had apparently expected the next war to be a short if bitter struggle and had made their preparations accordingly—partly because all were planning swift decisions in the field; partly, it would seem, because Treasuries and their experts had been convinced that no country could stand for very long the

Reprinted by special permission from Sir John Clapham, *An Economic History of Modern Britain*, III, 511-518. Copyright, Cambridge University Press, 1938.

economic strain of modern warfare, and had advised their fighting departments in that sense. This was the dominant opinion among British economic practitioners, thinkers, and writers, great and small. Those who believed that the stronger combatants, and Britain in particular, could at need bear a prolonged strain fancied that economic pressures must bring a rift somewhere in the weaker parts of the opposed alliances within a year, or two at most, whatever happened in the field. They underrated the staying power of agrarian and the adaptability of industrial, or semi-industrial, civilisations when fighting for their lives. Those who looked out through war-hating, liberal, City eyes were convinced that more than a year's war was out of the question. Five days after the battle of the Marne, when Britain's daily expenditure was perhaps a quarter of what it ultimately became, the *Economist* wrote about "the economic and financial impossibility of carrying on hostilities many months on the present scale." To which at least one economic thinker, accustomed to looking through the film of money and finance to the underlying realities, replied: "Nonsense, the thing" (he may have said "the bloody thing") "can go on so long as there is something to eat and something to shoot off." And one of the great combatants fell out, after two and a half years, mainly because of a standing lack of things to shoot off. Two others, the two most industrial, tried in their different ways to deprive one another of things to eat; and few military considerations were more decisive in the last year than the relative measures of their success. A Belgian scholar, interned in the heart of Germany, noted how courage sank when that wheat from the Ukraine, which was to have been the contribution of a beaten Russia to German victory, never came. When hungry German troops overran British lines in Picardy in March 1918, they were surprised and delighted, but in the end discouraged, by the plenty of good food and soldiers' luxuries found in the canteens; for they had been told that it was Britain who was short of things to eat —as indeed she was, though her armies were not; but short only to discomfort, not to despondency or death.

The military and the diplomatic historians must settle whether the war of 1914-18 need have become a test of national economic endurance: the economist notes that it did. In a world noisy with glib economic explanations, an economic historian of modern Britain is naturally inclined to ask—at the risk of providing obvious comments on simple-minded questions—whether that industrial and capitalistic civilisation which he has been studying was more prone to war than other civilisations; whether the private control of the means of production *per se* made war more likely; and whether the entry of his own country into war in 1914 was determined, directly or indirectly, by economic factors or calculations.

His answers to the first two queries, or perhaps rather his speculations about their themes, will be affected by his estimate of the connection between modern industrial civilisation and the unprecedented growth of the world's population during the nineteenth century. If, with a living student of population, he holds that this growth was not mysterious but "merely the response to increase in skill"[1] he will debit to that civilisation, with its many inventions, those overcrowdings, overflowings, lamentations about *Völker ohne Raum,* demands for places in the sun and silent resolves to hold places already secured there, which although they did not directly bring about the war of 1914 at least prepared nations to stand up and take it. But even if he accepts without qualification the doctrine of response to increase in skill, he will bear in mind how the skill increased so fast that the growing populations of all the great combatant nations were beyond a doubt becoming more not less prosperous, though at varying speeds and with occasional setbacks. There was no economic compulsion to raid one another for food or comforts,

[1] Carr-Saunders, quoted in vol. 1. 57 n. 1.

such as there may well be among growing primitive tribes in barren lands.

Whether increasing skill is the single simply-working cause of the growth in population, or only one cause among a bundle, it has at best an indirect connection with the private ownership of the means of production. The critics of private property and private capital regularly argue that skill may progress without at least the second; and defenders of private capital will not deny that skill increased in the socialistic empire of the Incas, or is increasing in the Russia of to-day. If skill produced a superfluity of people, and the superfluity tended to produce frictions between their governments, the frictions need not be debited to capitalism; the less so seeing that, of all European countries to-day, population is growing fastest in that where capitalism is a term of contempt.

When growing nations have arrived at the point of dependence on export trade, either for their existence or for the maintenance of that standard of life to which they have become accustomed, competition for markets leads to clashes of interest and jealousies that may foster warlike emotions among those sections of the population— sections varying in size and influence from century to century and from country to country—which think instinctively in fighting terms. Hence the superstition once current in Germany that England meant to attack her, and in 1914 did attack her, out of commercial envy; or the corresponding belief in England, perhaps equally superstitious but not so easily proved so, that Germany would challenge her one day out of economico-political ambition and a belief in the rights of the strong man armed over the markets of the world. Some Ger-

mans had certainly talked and written in this strain. The stubborn dogma that there is a given amount of trade, so that if you have it I cannot have it too, the dogma of the older Mercantilism, has great vitality; and unhappily there are groups of circumstances, short-period situations, particular branches of trade, in which it is not superstitious. Lancashire and Japan cannot both have the major part of the trade in winding-sheets for the Chinese. Whether predominance in that trade is worth a great war is most doubtful, and probably at no time has Lancashire even fancied that it was; but the prospect of the loss of it stirs up unpleasant emotions which may take a warlike tincture.

These things have no essential connection with capitalism as a form of industrial and commercial organisation. No doubt those who before 1914 procured for Britain from overseas her luxuries, her raw materials, and much of her necessary food, and those who conducted the export trade which paid for them, were private controllers of capital working for gain. Historically, luxuries and gain came first, necessary food and raw materials later. But it was exactly in the nineteenth century that the provision of food and materials became the main function of the importer, and so indirectly of the exporter. Given the population and its level of wealth and desires, their work was essential; although in a collectivist or a managed economy exports connected with certain classes of foreign investments, or otherwise held to be undesirable, might have been regulated or curtailed—whether in the ultimate interests of the country or not would have depended on the wisdom of the responsible officials. The search for markets and the desire to retain them, with

LORD KITCHENER: British expert on the Arabs, Sudanese, and Egyptians, upholder of the British cause in the Fashoda episode, governor-general and pacifier of the Sudan, commander-in-chief who did much to bring the Boer War to a conclusion, commander-in-chief in India, and head of the War Office during the early years of World War I. He was one of the few European leaders who predicted that the war would not be short. His death at sea, in June, 1916, was viewed by his countrymen as a calamity.

all the frictions which they may set up in a world of expanding national economies, were not vicious products of capitalist greed. Russia to-day shows no less interest in her export trade of timber, oil, wheat and latterly gold than capitalist England did in hers of cotton, coal, or machinery. And if Russia should become sufficiently industrialised to desire widening markets for her manufactures it is not likely that she will deny herself the appropriate methods of securing, exploiting, and retaining them. The process has begun already in Sinkiang and other parts of inland Asia.

Export by private capitalists has often been reproached with producing friction between peoples, decay of primitive civilisations, and minor wars, by indiscreetly and perhaps immorally pushing its wares into unwilling markets, or among tribes which they demoralise, and then demanding support from its government. There are notorious cases—in the nineteenth and other centuries—in which the charge can easily be sustained. But governments are at least free to repudiate unprincipled merchants. They cannot well repudiate themselves. Except on the rather naive assumption that governments arc normally more discreet and more moral than individuals ("If we did for ourselves what we are doing for Italy," Cavour said, "we should be great knaves") it is unlikely that government control or management of foreign trade would have tended to reduce international friction. The great amount of such control in the world of to-day does not appear to increase international harmony. If Smith, Grant and Jones put up the prices of British coals the foreign buyer will grumble and go elsewhere if he can; but if the British Government puts up the prices, that is likely to be treated as an unfriendly act. It is sure at least to be frictional. Italy was estranged from England by the high prices demanded for British coals while the government still controlled the mines in 1919-20. France, so far as is known, bore no malice because of the equally high prices charged at that time by individual Yorkshiremen for their cloth.

Merchants and manufacturers of the nineteenth century thought of themselves as lovers of Peace, which they certainly were, and of their work as a fosterer of Peace, which has not yet been proved false in spite of secondary trade wars. The charge most often brought against them then was that they loved Peace too well, for their pockets' sake, Peace without Honour. High-spirited writers were glad when, against the wishes of the Manchester people, Britain fought Russia needlessly in the Crimea.

No more shall commerce be all in all, and Peace
Pipe on her pastoral hillock a languid note.

At least, during the generations when these economic men had most power, the world for ninety-nine years was free from that 'general war' with which the statesmen of the eighteenth century had been thoroughly familiar. After 1918 someone wrote a book called *The First World War,* and many people shuddered at his 'First'; but those older wars which reached from the Ohio to Manila, or from the Malay Archipelago by way of Egypt and the Cape of Good Hope to New Orleans and Buenos Ayres, were about as wide as the then known world would permit; and some European peoples were involved in them who in 1914-18 managed to stand aside.

Industrialists—and men of science and government arsenals—made terrible engines of war, while statesmen trained whole nations to fight. In most countries a limited group of industrialists, with attached shareholders and wage-earners, were interested directly, not so much in an outbreak of war on a great scale—as business men they had to weigh the risks of that—as in expensive preparations for it. But neither history nor the present state of the world suggests that the making of all the armaments in the arsenals would have done much to ensure peace. Philip of Spain and Louis XIV of France, the Venetian Republic in its fighting days and the First French Republic, all had fairly complete control, if not actual monopoly, of their national armaments industries. It was when England was most pugnacious that all the great ships were built in royal yards. Armaments industries in contemporary Italy, Germany and Japan, as in re-arming Britain, are semi-public in character. The reputedly efficient and very great armaments industry of Russia is inevitably a State monopoly. There may be good reasons of various sorts for a more complete nationalisation of armaments industries to-day; it can hardly be proved that the private, as opposed to the public, manufacture of arms and instruments of war in Britain had anything to do directly, or even remotely, with its outbreak in 1914.

That 'capitalists' in general worked for, or even favoured, war because it would bring high interest rates and handsome profits is a clumsy generalisation, hardly worth notice were it not to some extent current, from the observed fact that it did bring the rates to all and the profits to many. Very properly, no one has ever suggested that wage-earners accepted the war of 1914 because of the extraordinarily high pay eventually received by munition-workers and others, or because war and the social policies arising from it, or stimulated by it, would bring to them certain substantial and permanent gains, as in fact they did. The reasonable expectation of the 'capitalist' in 1914 was loss of trade, high taxes and, in his family, death; of the wage-earner, death, taxes and unemployment. Neither had second sight and neither must be judged as if he had.

Industrialists as a class were everywhere pacific, merchants and money-handlers even more so. The average German industrialist may have been a shade less peace-minded than others. Germans had a well-grounded confidence in their army. The two wars which made the second Reich had been short and were held to have been economically profitable. When, after 1914, he thought that his country was winning, or when in Russia and Roumania for a time she had won, the German industrialist's mouth was wide open for iron-fields, oil-fields, colonies and economic concessions of every kind. But greed for other people's good things, when it seems that they may legally be had for the taking, is not peculiarly German. That German industrialist who slightly disgusted a Prussian general by coveting a hundred years of peace in which to knock England out was fairly representative of his class all the world over. It was for the sake of the interests of men like him that Wilhelm II desired, with perhaps two-thirds of his will, to be remembered as The Peaceful. British industrialists had for years been worried over German competition. A great group of them now wanted to abate it by tariffs; but the notion that it would be expedient to abate it by war was remote from their ways of thinking.

As for the pure capitalists of the City and the Stock Exchange, the men who handled the abstract values, not the things, who knew, or in imagination multiplied, the havoc which war must make among foreign investments and credits given to foreigners —they were in an agony of anxiety in early August 1914. The policy of "strict neutrality" and the ultimate chance of mediating effectively "between exhausted combatants" was what a journal which represented them tolerably well was writing about on August 1. "Old women" the sturdy Asquith called them. Few of them, it may be surmised, had any great fear of losing a possible war; but they were shaken by the prospect of war losses.

It is hard to associate any thought of an economic calculation with the memory of the man who led Britain into a war that he hated. True, Edward Grey had been Chairman of the North Eastern Railway, and he went back to its chair from Whitehall. Behind those considerations of obligation and honour which would probably have led him to take sides for war in any event lay his conviction that a German hegemony in Europe, won by force, would be too dangerous for Britain to be allowed—and among the things endangered were Britain's economic interests; what she held, not anything she coveted; but she held much. Nothing suggests that this, rather than her freedom to develop as she desired, was in the forefront of his mind; yet, if to have it somewhere in the mind is to make an economic calculation, he made one. But in 1912 he had wondered whether, if he were God, he would not say "this boasted civilisation . . . is so abnominable that I will sweep it away." "If God does think that," he added, "then the great industrial countries will perish in catastrophe." And again in January, 1918: "I feel deep in me that the civilisation of the Victorian epoch ought to disappear."[1] Perhaps one day an ingenious man of letters, armed with these revelations of his mind, will set out to prove that he contrived a war to hasten its end.

[1] Trevelyan, G. M., *Grey of Fallodon,* pp. 177, 341.

Here it is suggested that this civilisation which Grey of Fallodon thought abominable was less warlike in spirit than most which had preceded it, although the crowding that it caused, or permitted, suggested violent solutions to violent minds—as it still does; that the individual selfishness to which it gave scope, in the ownership of property and other ways, was not more threatening to the peace of the world than that centralised, impersonal, property-controlling or property-owning state selfishness which shows signs of succeeding it for a time; and that the chief director of British foreign policy at the close, though bound by his position to defend the abominable civilisation with other British interests in his care, had no more thought of material gain for his country than for himself.

THE FIRST IMPORTANT PUBLIC STATEMENT of British war aims came on August 3, 1914, the day before Britain declared war on Germany. In a speech before the House of Commons, Sir Edward Grey, secretary for foreign affairs, urged that Britain join France in the struggle against Germany in order to prevent all of western Europe from "falling under the domination of a single Power." Grey's statement was followed by many more elaborate British public declarations of war aims—declarations the purpose of which was "to win friends and influence people." Just as German statements of war aims were designed to put the German case in the best possible light, so British statements were designed to put the British case in the best possible light. They were intended to make it clear that the enemy was responsible for the coming of the war and that Britain and her allies were struggling for the triumph of justice, humanity, and reason. The difficulty, however, was that the public statements of war aims often conflicted with the secret treaties that were arranged in the period of the war. It was these treaties that Woodrow Wilson denounced when he stressed in the first of his Fourteen Points that "diplomacy shall proceed always frankly and in the public view." In the essay that follows, the veteran historian G. P. Gooch, the leading British expert on the diplomatic origins of World War I, analyzes British aims in the period of the war and discusses their bearing on the peace treaties that concluded the struggle.

BRITISH WAR AIMS, 1914-19

G. P. GOOCH

Now that the Allies have passed to the offensive and our ultimate victory seems to be assured, the demand for a fuller exposition of our war aims may be expected to grow. The Atlantic Charter is an excellent outline, but it will need to be filled in. Whether and at what point a detailed declaration should be made is a matter for the Allied Governments. Though it is often argued that the military situation must become clearer before a step of such far-reaching importance is taken, it is certainly not too soon for unofficial bodies and private citizens to begin to work out an acceptable settlement. In approaching this difficult task it is of interest to recall the evolution of our programme during the First World War and to inquire how far it was carried out in the treaties of peace.

Our reasons for joining in the conflict were explained by Grey in his historic speech of Aug. 3, 1914, and the objectives were authoritatively stated by the Prime Minister in two notable speeches. During the Franco-German War of 1870 Gladstone had said that the greatest triumph of our time would be the enthronement of the idea of public right as a governing idea of European policy. That, declared Asquith at Dublin on Sept. 25, 1914, was the best definition of Britain's ultimate policy. The idea of public right meant the substitution for force, for the nourishing of competing ambition, for the groupings of alliances, for a precarious equipoise, of a real European partnership based upon the recognition of equal rights, established and enforced by common will. On Nov. 9, 1914, at the Guildhall banquet, the Prime Minister was more precise. 'We shall never sheathe the sword, which we have not lightly drawn, until Belgium recovers in full measure all and more than all she has sacrificed, until France is adequately secured against the menace of aggression, until the rights of the smaller nationalities of Europe are placed on an unassailable foundation, and until the military dominion of Prussia is wholly and finally destroyed.' From what was called the Guildhall declaration Britain never departed, and no attempt was made to fill in the outlines for nearly two years.

During this long interval four events occurred which were to necessitate further and fuller declarations. The first was the entry of Turkey into the ranks of the Central Powers. The second was the use made by Germany of her colonies as bases for attack on the British Empire and its lines of communication, and the resulting need for considerable military operations by Dominion, Indian, and Colonial troops. The third was the belligerence of Italy in May 1915, which had to be purchased in the Treaty of London by the recognition of her claim to coveted territory on the east side of the Adriatic. The fourth was the ever-increasing extent of the devastations in France, which rendered reparation by the invader a primary war aim.

On Oct. 11, 1916, Asquith declared that the aims of the Allies were not selfish or vindictive, but they required adequate reparation for the past and adequate security for the future. Grey's address to the Foreign Press Association on Oct. 23, 1916, carried the definition of war aims a stage further. 'For years before the war we were living under the deepening shadow of Prussian militarism extending itself over the whole of Germany and then extending itself over the whole of the Continent. There must be no end to this war except a peace which is going to ensure that the nations of Europe live in the future free from the shadow of the great anarchist. A neutral has asked me

Reprinted by special permission from *The Quarterly Review*, CCLXXX (1943), 168-179.

what neutrals can do. The best thing is to work upon opinion for such an agreement between nations as will prevent a war like this happening again. If they had been united in such an agreement and prompt and resolute to insist in July 1914, that the dispute must be referred to a conference or to the Hague, and that the Belgian Treaty must be observed there would have been no war.' Though Grey left office a few weeks later when Asquith was followed as Premier by Lloyd George, the idea of creating international machinery for the prevention of war was kept continually in mind, and the first scheme of a League of Nations was worked out by the Phillimore Committee.

After more than two years of indecisive struggle Germany inaugurated an exchange of views between the belligerents which continued almost without interruption till the end. On Dec. 12, 1916, Bethmann-Hollweg transmitted a note suggesting negotiations. The latest events, he declared, proved that the resistance of the Central Powers was unbreakable, but they did not seek to crush or annihilate their enemies. They felt sure that the propositions which they would bring forward would serve as a basis for the restoration of a lasting peace. The first reply came from Britain's new Prime Minister. To enter into a conference without any knowledge of Germany's proposals would be dangerous. Before such an invitation could be considered it was necessary to know that Germany was prepared to accede to the only terms on which peace could be obtained and maintained—complete restitution, full reparation, effectual guarantees. After individual rejoinders, the Allies on Dec. 30, 1916, sent a collective refusal of the invitation which they described as empty and insincere. 'Once again the Allies declare that no peace is possible till they have secured reparation of violated rights, recognition of the principle of nationalities and of the free existence of small states, and a settlement calculated to end forces which have constituted a perpetual menace to the nations.'

In this first exchange neither side had put their cards on the table. But at almost the same moment, on Dec. 18, 1916, President Wilson invited the belligerents to announce the terms on which they believed the war might be ended. The Allies replied on Jan. 10, 1917, in the first detailed statement of their aims. They were the restoration and compensation of Belgium, Servia, and Montenegro; the evacuation and compensation of France, Russia, and Roumania; the reorganisation of Europe by a regime based on respect for nationalities, the right to full security, liberty of economic development, territorial conventions and international settlements guaranteeing frontiers against aggression; the restitution of provinces formerly torn from the Allies by force or against the wish of their inhabitants; the liberation of the Italians, Slavs, Roumanians, and Czecho-Slovaks from foreign domination; the liberation of the populations subject to the Ottoman Empire and the expulsion from Europe of that Empire as alien to Western civilisation. The Tsar's intentions for Poland had been indicated in his manifesto to his armies. The Allies desired to defend Europe against the covetous brutality of Prussian militarism, but the extermination and political disappearance of the German peoples had never formed part of their designs. The reference to the expulsion of the Turks from Europe was plain enough, but the attitude to the Austro-Hungarian Empire was vague. The liberation of Italians from foreign domination could only mean annexation to Italy; but the liberation of Slavs, Roumanians, and Czecho-Slovaks might mean nothing more than autonomy. The most radical interpretation of the word 'liberation' was adopted, not only by spokesmen of the nationalities concerned, but by the Central Powers; yet on Aug. 14, 1917, Lord Robert Cecil stated that the British Government was not pledged to any form of liberation. In other words no decision had been reached concerning the preservation of the Hapsburg Empire in the event of victory. No reference was made to the future of the German colonies.

The reply of the Allies to President Wilson was followed on Jan. 16, 1917, by a despatch from Balfour, Grey's successor as Foreign Secretary, explaining that in the opinion of the British people a durable peace was impossible without the victory of the Allies, since it depended on three conditions. 'The first is that the existing causes of international unrest should be as far as possible removed or weakened. The second is that the aggressive aims and the unscrupulous methods of the Central Powers should fall into disrepute among their own people. The third is that behind International Law, and behind all treaty arrangements for preventing or limiting hostilities, some form of international sanction should be devised which would give pause to the hardiest aggressor.'

No further official announcement of British war aims was made during 1917. No notice was taken of the Reichstag Resolution of July 19, declaring that it strove for a peace of compromise and the permanent reconciliation of the peoples, but an appeal from the Vatican to the belligerents on August 1 was not wholly ignored. The struggle, declared the Pope, was becoming a useless massacre, and ought to be ended by a peace without annexations or indemnities, and followed by the reduction of armaments and a system of arbitration. President Wilson replied that the rulers of Germany could not be trusted; but Britain, like France and Italy, made no public response. The view of the British Government was conveyed in a letter of August 21 to our Special Envoy at the Vatican. Till the Central Powers and their allies stated officially how far they were willing to go in regard to reparation and restoration, announced their war aims, and suggested measures for guaranteeing that the world would not again be plunged into similar horrors, any progress towards peace was unlikely. 'It appears to be useless to endeavour to bring about an agreement between the belligerents until the points of difference between them are clearly known, and neither Germany nor Austria has as yet made any statement corresponding to that issued by the Allies in answer to the note of President Wilson.' The Pope asked for and received a copy of this letter.

Despite the statement that nothing could be done from the British side till the Central Powers announced their aims, the Prime Minister, in a speech to the Trade Unions on Jan. 5, 1918, set forth the war aims of Great Britain more fully than ever before. The programme had been submitted to Asquith and Grey, to the leaders of the Labour Party, and to representatives of the Dominions, and he claimed that he was speaking for the nation and the Empire. The moderation of tone was in marked contrast to the strident self-confidence of the Allied reply to President Wilson a year earlier. The collapse of Russia and the Italian disaster at Caporetto had improved the military prospects of the Central Powers; American troops were slow in arriving; and Lord Lansdowne's letter of Nov. 28, 1917, published in the 'Daily Telegraph,' had argued that an indefinite prolongation of the war would ruin the civilised world.

The British, began Lloyd George, were not aiming at the destruction or disruption of Germany, and would not fight merely to destroy her constitution; but military autocracy was dangerous and out of date. The adoption of a really democratic constitution would be the most convincing evidence that the old spirit of military dom-

TREATY OF BREST-LITOVSK: Agreement (March, 1918) by the terms of which the Bolsheviks abandoned Poland, Lithuania, the Ukraine, the Baltic provinces, Finland, and Transcaucasia to the Central Powers. The harshness of the treaty had the effect of convincing the Allies that, unless they defeated Germany, they too would be forced to accept a Carthaginian peace. By the provisions of the Armistice, Germany was compelled to renounce the treaty.

ination had died, and would make it easier to conclude a democratic peace. 'The first requirement always put forward by the British Government and their Allies has been the independence of Belgium, and such reparation as can be made for the devastation of its towns and provinces. Next comes the restoration of Servia, Montenegro, and the occupied parts of France, Italy, and Roumania. We mean to stand by the French democracy to the death in the demand for a reconsideration of the great wrong of 1871. We shall be proud to fight to the end side by side with the new democracy of Russia. But if her present rulers take action independent of the Allies, we have no means of intervening to arrest the catastrophe which is assuredly befalling their country. Russia can only be saved by her own people. We believe, however, that an independent Poland, comprising all those genuinely Polish elements who desire to form part of it, is an urgent necessity for the stability of Western Europe.'

The curious word 'reconsideration' applied to the problem of Alsace-Lorraine suggested the possibility of something less than the integral return of these provinces to France, and the reference to the Hapsburg Empire revealed a similar diminution of demands. 'The break-up of Austria-Hungary is no part of our war aims; but genuine self-government must be granted to those Austro-Hungarian nationalities who have long desired it.' In one case, however, complete emancipation was essential. 'We regard as vital the satisfaction of the legitimate claims of the Italians for union with those of their own tongue and race.' The declaration concerning Roumania, on the other hand, was studiously vague. 'We also mean to press that justice be done to men of Roumanian blood and speech in their legitimate aspirations.'

If the reference to Austria-Hungary merely explained and limited the formula of Jan. 10, 1917, the passage about Turkey was a definite retreat. 'We are not fighting to deprive Turkey of its capital, nor of the rich and renowned lands of Asia Minor and Thrace, which are predominantly Turkish in race.' The Straits, however, were to be internationalised and neutralised. Arabia, Armenia, Mesopotamia, Syria, and Palestine were entitled to a recognition of their separate national conditions. 'What the exact form of that recognition in each particular case should be need not be here discussed; but it would be impossible to restore these territories to their former sovereignty. Much has been said about the arrangements we have entered into with our Allies on this and other subjects. I can only say that, as new circumstances like the Russian collapse and the separate Russian negotiations have changed the conditions under which those arrangements were made, we are and always have been perfectly ready to discuss them with our Allies.' The 'arrangements' to which Lloyd George referred were recorded in the secret treaties concluded by the Tsarist Government and published by the Bolshevists after their accession to power in November 1917. The first reference to the German colonies made during the war was vague. They would be held at the disposal of a conference whose decision must have primary regard to the wishes and interests of the native inhabitants. The governing consideration should be 'to prevent their exploitation for the benefit of European capitalists or governments. The general principle of national self-determination is, therefore, as applicable in their cases as in those of other occupied European territories.' No decision was announced on the question whether any of the colonies should be allowed to remain in German hands.

After dealing with territorial problems the Prime Minister turned to other considerations. There must be reparation for injuries inflicted in violation of International Law, such as those on British seamen. In the world shortage of raw materials, those countries which controlled them would naturally help themselves and their friends first, but, as circumstances changed, the settlement would change also. Finally, a great attempt must be made to establish by some international organisation an alternative to war as a means of settling international disputes. Three conditions were essential to permanent peace—the re-establishment of the sanctity of treaties, a territorial settlement based on the right of self-determination or the consent of the governed, and the creation of some international organisation to limit the burden of armaments and diminish the probability of war. 'On those conditions the British Empire would welcome peace; to secure those conditions its peoples are prepared to make even greater sacrifices than those they have yet endured.'

During the whole course of the conflict no other belligerent, not even President Wilson in the Fourteen Points announced two days later, issued a declaration of war aims so elaborate and precise. The change of tone in the speech was recognised by the Central Powers; but the comments from Hertling, the German Chancellor, and Czernin, the Austro-Hungarian Foreign Minister, were pronounced unsatisfactory by the Supreme War Council of the Allies at Versailles on Feb. 4, 1918, and the negotiations then in progress at Brest-Litovsk were said to disclose plans of conquest and spoliation. The Supreme Council, therefore, decided that the only immediate task was the prosecution of the war with the utmost vigour till a change of temper appeared in the enemy governments and peoples. This declaration was repeated at the opening of Parliament on February 12, when the Prime Minister declared that insistence on the integrity of the possessions of the enemy Powers made negotiations impossible. There was no use crying peace, he declared, when there was no peace.

In referring to the peoples of the Hapsburg Empire on Jan. 5, 1918, Lloyd George demanded separation for the Italians alone. Five months later, on June 3, 1918, though the great German offensive launched on March 21 was still in progress, the Prime Ministers of Great Britain, France, and Italy, meeting at Versailles on June 3, issued an important declaration. 1. The creation of a united and independent Polish state, with free access to the sea, constitutes one of the conditions of a solid and just peace and of the rule of right in Europe. 2. The Allied Governments have noted with pleasure the declaration made by the Secretary of State of the United States Government: 'The national aspirations of Czecho-Slovakia and Jugo-Slavia for liberty have the liveliest sympathy of this Government, and they desire to associate themselves in an expression of earnest sympathy for the nationalistic aspirations towards freedom of the Czecho-Slovaks and Jugo-Slav peoples.' The phraseology was somewhat involved, but the formula registered a notable advance towards the recognition of an independent Czecho-Slovak state for which Masaryk and Benes had been working.

The tide of battle in France turned on August 8, and on October 5, Prince Max of Baden, the new German Chancellor, requested President Wilson to initiate the discussion of peace on the basis of the Fourteen Points. An exchange of Notes followed between Washington and Berlin, and on November 5 the Allies announced the conditions on which they would be ready to negotiate. 'Subject to the qualifications which follow, they declare their willingness to make peace with the Government of Germany on the terms of peace laid down in the President's Address of January 8 (1918), and the principles of settlement enunciated in his subsequent Addresses. They must point out that Clause II, relating to what is usually described as the freedom of the seas, is open to various interpretations, some of which they could not accept. They must therefore reserve to themselves complete freedom on this subject when they enter the Peace Conference. Further, the President declared on January 8, that the invaded territories must be restored as well as evacuated and freed, and the Allied Governments feel that no doubt ought to be allowed to exist as to what this provision implies. By it they understand that compensation will be made by Germany for all damage done to the civilian population of the Allies and their property by the aggression of Germany by land, by sea, and from the air.' President Wilson admitted this interpretation, and on November 11 Germany accepted the terms of the Armistice announced by Foch on November 9. Her allies had already laid down their arms.

The British Delegation arrived in Paris on Jan. 11, 1919, without a detailed programme, but knowing perfectly well what they wished to be done. The British people had expressed its feelings in a General Election. Germany should be made incapable of renewed attack by land and sea, should surrender her colonies, pay for the war to the limit of her ability, and hand over certain war criminals for trial. The Fourteen Points had been accepted by the British Government, subject to two exceptions. Moreover, the official declarations made during the war were on record. In Lloyd George's words, the main outlines of the Treaty of Versailles were defined and fixed, not in the hour of victory, but during the years in which the struggle was going on and when the issue was still in doubt. Great Britain, however, could not dictate to her allies, and the political position of France, as the seat of the Conference and the victim of invasion, was very strong. Thus the result of the discussions was bound to be a compromise. From the outset a difference of attitude between London and Paris was revealed. The British Delegation desired to avoid decisions which the new German Government might feel unwilling to accept, for in that case the war would be resumed and Central Europe, it was feared, might become Communist. Moreover, as Lloyd George explains, our peace aims were so framed as to convince America, and especially the peace-loving and anti-Imperialist President, that our objectives were fundamentally just. France, on the other hand, was prepared to take more risks in obtaining a settlement which in her opinion would guarantee her security.

The Prime Minister was blamed in some quarters for the violence of his speeches during the General Election, and he was held mainly responsible for the intransigent character of the new Parliament; but further reflection convinced him that it would be unwise to press the defeated enemy too hard. When the difference of outlook had become fully apparent, he drew up a Memorandum on March 26, 1919, setting forth his view of the conditions, not of a temporary settlement, but of a lasting peace. A few sentences will show the character of this important document, which was addressed in the first place to Clemenceau, but was also intended as a warning to his more impatient followers at home. 'You may strip Germany of her colonies, reduce her armaments to a mere police force, and her navy to that of a fifth-rate Power; all the same, in the end, if she feels that she has been unjustly treated in the Peace of 1919, she will find means of exacting retribution from her conquerors. The deep impression made upon the human heart by four years of unexampled slaughter will disappear with the hearts upon which it has been marked by the terrible sword of the Great War. The maintenance of peace will then depend upon there being no causes of exasperation constantly stirring up the spirit of patriotism, of justice, or of fair play. To achieve redress our terms may be severe, they may be stern and even ruthless; but at the same time they can be so just that the country on which they are imposed will feel in its heart that it has no right to complain. But injustice, arrogance, displayed in the hour of triumph, will never be forgotten or forgiven. For these reasons I am, therefore, strongly averse to transferring more Germans from German rule to the rule of some other nation than can possibly be helped. I cannot conceive any greater cause of future war than that the German people, who have certainly proved themselves one of the most vigorous and powerful races in the world, should be surrounded by a number of small states, many of them consisting of people who have never previously set up a stable government for themselves, but each of them containing large masses of Germans clamouring for reunion with their native land.' The victors, he added, should try to act as if they were impartial arbiters, forget-ful of the passions of the war. A just settlement must be supplemented by a League of Nations, a limitation of the armaments of the victors no less than of the vanquished, and the admission of Germany to the League after accepting the terms of the Allies and establishing a stable democratic government.

The chief difference between the British and French delegations was in regard to the left bank of the Rhine, which the latter believed to be the only effective barrier against invasion. To the creation of a new and larger Alsace-Lorraine the British were unalterably opposed, and they were supported by President Wilson. A partial equivalent was offered in the form of an Anglo-American promise of military support in the event of unprovoked German aggression. The compromise was reluctantly accepted by the French as the best they could get, and it was embodied in the treaty of guarantee signed on June 28, the same day as the Treaty of Versailles. Its inadequacy in French eyes arose from the fact that it was a joint, not a separate guarantee, since the British guarantee was only to come into force when the corresponding treaty between France and the United States was ratified—a condition which was not fulfilled.

In his authoritative work 'The Truth about the Peace Treaties' Lloyd George argues that the settlement was just and in accordance with the principles officially proclaimed during the struggle. The surrender of the German fleet appeared to remove the danger which had been the main factor driving England into the Franco-Russian camp. But how far had the four war aims announced by Asquith in November 1914 been fulfilled? Had Belgium 'recovered all and more than all that she had sacrificed'? She was liberated, compensated, and enlarged. Was France 'adequately secured against the menace of aggression'? Her security was buttressed by the permanent demilitarisation of the Rhineland, the occupation of the Saar territory for fifteen years, and an Anglo-American promise of military support in the event of German aggression. Had the rights of the smaller nationalities been 'placed on an unassailable foundation'? On the whole the new frontiers were more in accordance with the wishes of the various races of Central Europe than those existing in 1914, and provision was made for the protection of minorities; but their rights could not be said to be effectively guaranteed. Had the military dominion of Prussia been finally destroyed? The German army was limited to 100,000 men, the German navy was forbidden to possess capital ships and submarines, and only civilian aeroplanes were allowed. The return to France of Alsace-Lorraine with its valuable iron resources was a further obstacle to the revival of formidable German armaments. Finally, the League of Nations, in the making of which British statesmen had taken an important part, was expected to prevent or defeat aggression from any quarter and to facilitate peaceful change. Whether these and other measures would finally destroy Prussian militarism only time could show.

Regarding the Treaty of Versailles as a whole, British statesmen could claim to have accomplished their war aims so far as the opinion of the other signatories allowed. What they did not and could not foresee was the gradual disintegration of the Grand Alliance which had made a dictated settlement possible, and the consequential escape of defeated Germany from the weakness and isolation in which she found herself at the end of the war.

THE EARLY YEARS OF THE REIGN OF GEORGE V were filled with crises. The new king came to the throne in 1910—at a time when the great domestic issues in Britain were Lloyd George's People's Budget, the veto power of the House of Lords, and Home Rule for Ireland. Other domestic crises were soon added to these: the alarming epidemic of strikes and the hardly less alarming activities of the militant advocates of women's suffrage. By the summer of 1914, war with Germany doubtless came as a relief to many an Englishman who had forgotten the glories of domestic peace—who, indeed, was tired of ceaseless war on the home front. Although the defeat of Germany ended the most serious crisis that was to occur during the course of George's reign, there was an abundance of critical problems to be faced in the years from 1919 to the end of the reign, in January, 1936. Of these some of the most conspicuous were the growth of the national debt, the development of intense foreign competition, the plight of the coal industry, unemployment, the General Strike of 1926, the Great Depression, the dole, the abandonment of free trade, the implications of the coming to power of the Nazis, and the Ethiopian affair. In the essay that follows, the renowned historian of political thought Sir Ernest Barker analyzes the course of British history during a momentous quarter of a century. The essay itself, it should be noted, was originally published shortly before the conclusion of George's reign.

THE MOVEMENT OF NATIONAL LIFE: 1910-1935

SIR ERNEST BARKER

A centre of calm in a blowing wind of change—a signal of comfort and assurance on a ship driving rapidly forward—that is how we think of the King, when we listen to his voice diffused through all the airs of the world, as we did last Christmas. He has seen great changes unrolled before his eyes in the last quarter of a century, as he has stood on the bridge and watched the voyage of his people into a new age and a new temper of life. What stock can we take of the course we have traversed during his reign and under his flag?

I

A gust of mechanical changes has produced a revolution in our material way of life. There has been a great age of applied physics. Perhaps it will be succeeded by a great age of applied biology, which will breed a new race of men, new stocks of animals, new crops of plants and all the kindly fruits of the earth. But we are still in the age of applied physics and all its marvels. The pace of life has been quickened by the motor-car, the aeroplane, the telephone, wireless. We live at a different tempo. We can move more quickly by land, sea and air; we can communicate thoughts and visual images far more rapidly, by new methods of diffusing sound and sight.

A world in which transport, and all other means of communication, have been quickened from *andante* to *presto,* is also a world which is far more interconnected. Not only do things move faster and further than they used to do, men are also brought more together than they used to be, and they share more together in hearing and seeing the

Reprinted by special permission from *The Fortnightly,* CXLIII (1935), 513-526.

same thing. The same film is shown in London and Florence. The same music is heard on the wireless in Cambridge and Stockholm. Our minds are driven to a new rapidity and a new catholicity. More psychological elasticity is demanded of us. We have to stretch our faculties to a quicker exercise and a wider reach. It is a question whether we can keep pace with the pace of our own inventions. But they will not stop. And we, too, cannot stop.

Perhaps some of the social and political movements of our time on the continent of Europe are connected with the physical revolution through which we are going. They tend towards an idolization of the group—the race, the nation, the class. They use the new physical means of mass-propaganda—the staged demonstration of masses of men brought together by new and quicker means of transport: the film, the wireless— to produce the temper and feeling of the group. But perhaps we may also say that the new means use them, or at any rate help to produce them. Physics affects politics: physical inventions which make men move quicker, and in closer connection, tend to produce political movements of a rapid *élan* and a gregarious or collectivist temper. It is not clear, however, that such consequences have yet ensued, or are likely to ensue, in Great Britain. We are not easily stampeded, and we still have a certain phlegm. But the new physical changes have changed us; and they have changed us in a number of ways.

There has been a movement into new industries. From the building of ships, for example, we have turned to the making of gramophones and wireless sets. The change

is simple in itself: it is more complicated, and more serious, when we look at its consequences. One consequence is that the responsible work of a craftsman, whose mistake might cost his employer hundreds of pounds, has become repetitive work which follows an undeviating rule. Another consequence, not less serious than the change in technique and the nature of workmanship, is geographical. Changing its character, industry has also changed its residence. Its chosen home is the Midlands and the South. A process of "industrial transference" is automatically at work; and statesmanship has even addressed itself to the problem of directing and guiding this transference by schemes of internal migration. Along with this change in the character and the residence of industry there has also gone a change of commerce. Publicity and salesmanship have become major commercial arts. The uses of advertisement, never unknown, have been explored and extended. We have perhaps become more suggestible; we have certainly been exposed to a greater pressure and blare of suggestion. The development is not peculiar to us. But it is at work among us—in our politics as well as in our economics; in our newspapers as well as on our hoardings. It is helping to make us a different people from what we were a quarter of a century ago.

There has been a movement of tastes as well as a movement of industry and commerce. Here the shock of the War has collaborated with the physical revolution and its gust of mechanical change to alter our ways of living. We have become more experimental in our clothes, our food and our habits. Old and set ways were cracked

EDUCATION ACT OF 1902: Milestone in British educational history. The most important legislative measure passed by the Balfour government, it recognized the provision of secondary education as a government responsibility. Within five years of its enactment, secondary schools had doubled in number.

GUILD SOCIALISM: Early-twentieth-century British scheme of social reform that resembled French syndicalism in many respects. Associated especially with the name of G. D. H. Cole, it stressed the abolition of the wage-nexus, organization and control of industry by workers, and the utilization of the trade union as the key to the new society.

by the War and the years of experimentation which followed the end of the War.
But there have also been many changes in
the mechanism of our enjoyments, which
have had nothing to do with the War. The
cinema has become a common possession
of all classes. It is a leveller within; it is
also a link with the world without. The
same is true of broadcasting; the same—at
any rate in the matter of levelling, and of
giving a new access for all into fresh fields
of experience and appreciation—is also true
of the growth of motor-transport. Joy has
been spread in a wider commonalty; a new
understanding of one another, and a new
feeling for the aspect and the beauty of
our country, have been gained.

In particular, we are perhaps less urban
in spirit than we used to be. We have discovered that there is an English countryside which is worthy of being kept in its
native beauty as our common heritage. We
have begun to feel that there is a biological
call in our blood which summons us back
to the soil in which our life is rooted. Not
only is the town-dweller moving back into
the country for residence. That, in itself,
would be little gain and a dubious benefit.
He is also beginning to realize that the
countrydweller has to be helped and encouraged in the old country callings which
alone make the countryside a real and living
thing—the rearing of stock, the growing of
crops, the marketing of produce. All this
helps to make our nation better balanced
than it was some twenty-five years ago. We
may see this better balance even in the love
of sport, which is one of our national
obsessions. There is more sport and more
games than there ever were; but it is less
of a tyranny. Sport has fallen into a better
proportion in our lives. There is so much
else of which we can think, and so many
other things for which we have now to find
time.

In many ways we have progressed in the
art of life since 1910. Not only have we
found new tastes; we have also tried to give
a new security, by schemes of insurance and
pensions and other means, to those who

walk on the verge between livelihood and
starvation. But there is still a black shadow
which attends on all our progress in the art
of life; and it is greater now than it was in
1910. This is the shadow of unemployment.
A revolution of technique has altered the
conditions of production: the political revolutions and perturbations which followed
the War have altered the markets for
products. We are paying the price of both
alterations—or rather the unemployed are
paying it for us, and we are paying them
back, in benefit and assistance, some of the
price which they are vicariously paying in
their own persons.

That is one shadow on the last twenty-
five years. Is it also a shadow, or is it a
cloud with a silver lining, that our country
has begun to live more to itself than it did
when the King ascended the throne? There
is less emigration than there was. In 1913
about 320,000 persons emigrated to the
British Dominions; in 1933 the emigrants
were fewer than 90,000. The causes are
external as well as internal; they depend on
the Dominions as well as upon ourselves.
But it is the internal causes which illustrate
the movement of our national life; and
among them we may count partly a greater
framework of security, which makes men
and women less anxious to leave its shelter,
and partly a large provision of amenities
and amusements, which acts as a home-
keeping magnet. Not only is there less emigration of persons; there is also less export
and import of goods to connect us with
the world outside. The old England of Free
Trade, which depended on the markets of
the world, began to be modified after the
War, when the policy of safeguarding industries was introduced in 1921; it has been
modified still more drastically during the
last few years. We can never be a self-
sufficing country, with a purely national
economy; but we have moved some stages
in that direction during the last fifteen years.

We have not, however, developed any
exclusive type of nationalism. Toleration
(sometimes based on a healthy spirit of
sympathy and compromise, but sometimes

resting on mere acquiescence and apathy) has long been one of our qualities; but we have learned to practise the quality in new forms and new directions. Old religious differences have lost their edge. The various branches of Scottish Presbyterianism were united in 1929; the different bodies of the Wesleyan confession became a single Methodist Church in 1932. The people of the Irish Free State, long divided from us in feeling, and dividing us acutely among ourselves by the profound cleavage of Unionists and Home Rulers, has acquired Dominion status with general consent; and if there are still disagreements between its Government and the Government of Great Britain, they do not involve the old cleavage of parties in Great Britain, nor are they conducted with the old rancour between the Irish and the British side. Scotland has bred a new nationalism in the last few years; but no Englishman would ever say "Nay" to its demands if they were pressed with a general ardour and conviction.

Our nationalism in Great Britain, such as it is, is a federal nationalism; it has no unitarian zeal; it will tolerate, and even respect, the claims of its different branches and the feelings of its different nationalities. The same spirit of toleration is abroad in the Commonwealth. Few of us to-day would press the claims of Westminster; all of us would subscribe to the spirit of the Statute of Westminster, which gives legal force to Lord Balfour's definition, in 1926, of the nature of Dominion autonomy; most of us welcome the progressive devolution upon India of the responsibility for carrying the vast orb of her fate. Signor Mussolini has said that "peoples that rise, or re-arise, are imperialistic; peoples that die are renouncers." If it be a sign of death to renounce power, and to be content with the voluntary bonds of free association, the British people is a dying people. But the renunciation of power may well be the most signal proof of strength and vitality.

Toleration is not only a virtue when it is practised between different confessions and different peoples; it is also a virtue between different classes, between different sexes, and between youth and age. Is there more tolerance and more understanding between social classes than there was in 1910, or is there a truceless war which has only been accentuated? I remember, when I was a Proctor at Oxford just before 1910, seeking in vain to secure a hearing for Mr. Keir Hardie—not because I believed in his views, but because I believed in free speech. I do not think that there would be any difficulty in securing a hearing for a Labour leader to-day, either in Oxford or anywhere else. The cry of the Class War is still ingeminated in England to-day, as Lord Falkland ingeminated "Peace"; and it is all too true that there is still too great a gulf of classes among us—and not least in the field of education. But those who lived through the so-called "General Strike" will not readily believe in a truceless war; and I, for one, should note a growth of social equality, and of mutual respect of class for class, in the years since 1910—though I should also note the long road that has still to be travelled before we attain any satisfactory level of equality.

Sex is far more equal to sex than class to class. The enfranchisement of women, in 1918, was not only a political act; it was also a social and moral landmark. Meredith would rejoice in the women of to-day, the peers and the companions of men. There are few things in the King's reign that are more notable than the ending of the subjection of women.

Youth, too, has come more into its own. Perhaps the cause is partly the sinking of the birth rate, which makes the young fewer and therefore more precious; perhaps it is partly the memory of the young gallantry which sacrificed itself twenty years ago (let us hope, "Not in vain"; let us pray, "Never again") in the turmoil of battle and death. To-day the nation gives far more pains to the right training and education of youth. To-day the old are beginning to learn and to practise the doctrine of a fixed age of retirement. Age-limits are coming down; youth feels its freedom and acclaims its responsibility; it is even ready to write autobiographies in the early twenties. There is some effervescence and some bubbles of an imaginary revolt of youth; there is some decay of manners (a precious thing, and a near neighbour of morals), and some wild experimentation in art and literature. But the man of sixty and upwards who reads the young poets of to-day, and then remembers what he was reading in the nineties of the last century, will note a new gravity and power and responsibility—even if, with his old-fashioned ideas of lucidity and style, he cannot always understand what he reads, or often feel the glow of an intimate appreciation.

II

The movement of national life is pre-eminently a movement of social thought, social temper, social habits and social adjustment. But there is another sphere, which also invites and demands attention. This is the sphere of organized institutions, in all its ranges—political and economic; ecclesiastical and educational; internal, imperial, and international.

In 1910 we spoke of the United Kingdom. In 1935 we speak of Great Britain and Northern Ireland. The change in our speech reflects a great change in our political structure. In 1910 there was a single parliament at Westminster. In 1935 there is also a dominion parliament in Dublin, and a separate parliament in Belfast for the North of Ireland, which, however, still continues to send members to the Westminster Parliament. Besides this change in our political structure, there have also been great changes in our political machinery. There are three of these which are crucial. One was the passing of the Parliament Act of 1911. Thenceforth the duration of Parliament was for five years instead of seven; thenceforth the House of Commons had the sole control of Money Bills, and could send forward other Public Bills for the King's assent, without the concurrence of the House of Lords, if it passed them in three successive sessions; thenceforth (since the preamble of the Parliament Act referred to some future reform of that House) the problem of the proper composition of the House of Lords was a permanent political issue. The King won his spurs by the prudence with which he faced the constitutional crisis that attended the passing of the Act; the House of Commons won an acknowledged superiority; and the adjustment of the balance of the Constitution which was made in 1911 has remained, and is likely to remain, secure.

The second great change has been the increase of the electorate, under the Representation of the People Act of 1918 and the subsequent Act of 1928. Under these Acts men and women count alike, and (save that a second vote can still be exercised by those who possess the necessary qualification) each citizen counts as equal to every other. The number of the electorate, which in 1910 was 7,700,000 for the whole of the United Kingdom, is now over 30,000,000 for Great Britain and Northern Ireland; it has been more than quadrupled. It is one of the problems of the future to shape this vast electorate into an organ of political discussion and decision which shall be at least as effective, and as stable, as the smaller electorate of a quarter of a century ago.

The third great change, in addition to the changes in Parliament and the electorate, has been a change in the party system. The Liberal party, which had been triumphant in the election of 1906, and was still the largest single party in the two elections of 1910, has dwindled and dwindled since 1918 until it has sunk to a tenth, or less, of the House of Commons. The Labour party, which in 1910 numbered only some 40 members, has grown till its normal strength may be said to vary between one-third and one-half of the House. The strength of the Conservative party has remained tolerably constant; but the changes in the two other parties have profoundly affected the general working of the whole party system. There has been a tendency, since 1918, towards coalition ministries and formal or informal working agreements between different parties. What the eventual issue will be; whether the Liberal party, after nearly 300 years of history, will disappear; whether we shall have a system of two parties, each widened in scope and altered in character by the absorption of the Right and the Left wings of the old Liberal party —these are questions we have still to solve.

There are other changes in the world of politics since 1910 which might be chronicled, and not least the reform of Local Government in 1929. But politics, for many years past, has seemed to many to be *vieux jeu*. There has been a shifting of the centre of gravity, and a change in the balance of human interest. Economics has advanced into the foreground: "economics," as it was being said in Germany in 1920, "is destiny." For some fifteen years now there has been the temporary problem (so long protracted that it may almost be called permanent) of the crisis of unemployment; but over and above that there is the enduring problem, which is destined long to engage our thought, of the proper economic basis of our general society—capitalist, socialist, syndicalist, or some form of mixture and compromise. Guild Socialism was the new gospel about 1910; the Liberal party suggested a new eirenicon or *via media* in "Britain's Industrial Future" in 1928: the great and cardinal issue still remains.

Meanwhile the immediate and urgent problem of maintaining a stable and decent standard of life for the people, in a period of bewilderingly swift transition, has controlled our actual policies. It has controlled the policy and legislation of the State; it has controlled the policy and the efforts of the Trade Unions. The State, in the last 25 years, has moved towards the fixing of standard wages in unorganized industries; it has developed schemes of insurance against invalidity and unemployment; it has introduced new methods of pensions and new provision for housing; it has, in a word, guaranteed, by a variety of social services, new rights to security of life and health and livelihood. Public expenditure upon these purposes has been multiplied, and again multiplied; taxation has risen to meet the expenditure; and there has been achieved, in the course of social legislation and in the process of financing such legislation, no inconsiderable redistribution of wealth. The convinced Socialist feels that all these measures are, at the most, palliatives offered by a desperate capitalism; but it may at least be said, in answer, that for our day, and in our circumstances, they are indispensable, and they serve the cause of general human welfare.

Meanwhile the policy and efforts of the Trade Unions, which in our country, for the last hundred years, have always run parallel with the policy and legislation of the State, have been concentrated on defending, by the force of voluntary combination, the vital and "key" position of the wage-standard. The great question arose which here agitated Great Britain at the end of the war. It was a question of the extent to which the force of voluntary combination could be pushed. Was each Trade Union to fight its own battle, or might a number of great Trade Unions combine in alliance to fight a joint battle? The threat to the level of wages, particularly in the mining industry, impelled the Trade Unions towards the policy of the great combination. First, there was the Triple Alliance of the miners, railwaymen and transport workers. That alliance, powerful as it seemed, led to no actual result. But the mantel of the Triple Alliance was taken over by the Trades Union Council, acting as the directorate of the general Trades Union Congress in which the Trade Unions are all combined.

The Trades Union Council acted in 1926, and used the policy of the great combination in a general strike intended to protect the wages of the miners. The policy was a natural extension of the scope of Trade Union efforts; but it was dubious whether it was legal, and it was certain that its execution disorganized the general life of the community and tended to coerce the Government into the adoption of measures which it would not otherwise, and apart from such coercion, choose to adopt. The policy failed; the rest of the community carried on, behaving—as did also the part of the community which had gone on strike —with good temper and restraint; the Government organized the necessary services; and nine days saw the beginning and end of the General Strike. In 1927 there followed the Trade Unions and Trade Disputes Act, which declared illegal the policy of the great combination, limiting strikes to the furtherance of a dispute in a particular trade or industry, and proscribing them if they tended "to coerce the Government either directly or by inflicting hardship upon the community."

So ended, at any rate for the time being, one of the many crises which have marked the reign of the King. How numerous they have been! It would be idle to enumerate them. It is sufficient to remember the years 1910, 1914, 1926, and 1931—and that does not end the list. The prayer for peace comes naturally to the lips. But we live in an age of change; and such an age must, ever and again, rise to some great crescendo.

There has been change in our Churches as well as in our politics and economics. Mention has already been made of the new unions which have been achieved in Scottish Presbyterianism and English Wesleyanism. There has also been change and movement in the Church of England. An Enabling Act of 1919 prepared the way for a new National Assembly of the Church, including a new House of Laity as well as the two clerical Houses drawn from the old Convocations, and empowered the Assembly to prepare and pass measures subject to a veto of either House of Parliament.

The Church was thus equipped with a fresh ecclesiastical parliament; and that parliament set to work to overhaul the Church. Its main measure, introducing a new Book of Common Prayer, was twice rejected, in 1927 and 1928, by the House of Commons. A new question has thus been written across the future of the Church of England. What are to be its relations to the State? Is it to

exercise its own independent spiritual authority, free from political control, in questions of doctrine, ritual and discipline; or is it to remain, as of old, in partnership with the State, and limited by its partner? That is a question which was raised when the two Archbishops appointed a Committee on Church and State in the year before the War, and it is a question which still waits for an answer.

In the general movement of national life the growth of national education has been an important factor. The great Education Act of 1902 has gradually matured its consequences. It has issued in powerful and progressive local education authorities; it has issued in a large extension of secondary education, which has opened new opportunities of development to tens of thousands of boys and girls; it has issued, ultimately, in a new entry of students into the Universities, which have grown apace both in numbers and in resources, and have come to play a far larger part in the life of the nation.

III

There are two great developments of our national life which look outward beyond the seas. One is the development of our relations with the British Commonwealth to which we belong, and of which we are part. The other is the development of our relations with the new system of international organization which issued from the War.

In 1910 there were many thinkers who looked forward to a new integration of the Commonwealth under a new Imperial Parliament representative of all its parts. The actual development has followed another and different line. The Commonwealth has evolved, by a process of devolution, into a body of autonomous States or Dominions, connected by the link of common allegiance to the King. It is not a parliament, or the legislative authority of a parliament, which holds the Commonwealth together; it is the King, and the common and voluntary recognition of a unity of spirit and purpose symbolized in the King's person. The Commonwealth is now a body of nations which have become nation-States as well as nations, but which can combine a general federal nationalism with their own particular nationalisms.

A federal nationalism on this scale, linking together nations so physically distant, and with such different traditions, is something hitherto unknown, and something unpredictable in its future growth and tendencies. It is showing itself capable, in this year 1935, of fostering the growth of a united India, with a system of responsible central government, as one of its integral parts. If the Commonwealth can achieve the inclusion of India, on equal terms, within its system, and if it can reconcile the national feeling of India with its own spirit of federal nationalism, it will have celebrated a triumph which may well be its permanent consolidation.

But we have also to recognize, as we have already had reason to note, that the volume of migration between the parts of the Commonwealth is slackening. Each part tends more and more to settle in its own tradition, and to follow its own goal of autonomy and autarchy. Yet the King remains. The common tradition of the common law of England remains. The sense of the fraternity of different nations in a common federal nationalism remains. It is a great thing that the movement of our national life should thus be interconnected and interfolded with the movement of the lives of other and cognate nations. It gives us more balance, and it gives us more width. They are both precious gifts.

Behind all that has hitherto been said about the last twenty-five years there stands the fact—the sombre and profound fact—of the Great War. It has not been the only cause of change; but it has conspired with and accentuated every other cause. War, said a Greek writer, is a violent teacher. One lesson which the War has taught us is that we belong to the Continent of Europe, as well as to the British Commonwealth; that we are vitally concerned and profoundly interested in the development of Europe; that we have to collaborate, day by day, in the settlement of its destinies. To look back to 1910 is to realize that we were still, at that time, in the main, an insular people. To-day we know that we are drawn into the life of the Continent; we follow, with a far deeper attention, the progress of its life; we know that we are able, and that we are bound, to aid in its progress.

The entry of Great Britain into Europe is one of the permanent results of the War, and our duty to Europe is one of the permanent lessons which we have learned from it. Another lesson, or another aspect of the same lesson, is our duty to the cause of the organization of peace—the peace of Europe; the peace of the world. Perhaps there is no point on which our system of life in 1935 differs more from the system of 1910 than it does in our new and grave preoccupation with the cause of peace. We sought peace twenty-five years ago: we ensue it with all our hearts to-day. Our nation is now part of a League of Nations—the greatest of all the new things which have come to birth in the King's reign. We are involved in a common effort of the nations to provide a general framework of collective security in the shelter of which each can develop its life, unfold its talent, and pursue its mission. The movement of our national life has interlocked us in this common effort. No cause stands closer to the heart of youth, in our British Universities, than this cause. And it is the young who carry in their hands the keys of the future.

It is a stirring age through which we have travelled; it is a stirring age that lies ahead. The aim of any organized society of men is justice—social justice within, which is fair to all classes and persons; international justice without, which is fair to all States and nations. Can we say of our country, in these last twenty-five years, that it has helped to advance the cause of social and international justice? That is our ultimate criterion. If we apply it, we may fairly say that there has been progress. There is more social justice than there was—more recognition of the just claims of different classes, different sexes, different ages. There is more international justice than there was—more of an organized system for appraising, in terms of justice and not in terms of power, the claims of the different nations.

But the establishment of justice is a never-ending movement, which will last as long as the life of humanity. The fundamental thing is that the thought of each nation should be exercised by its problems, and should direct itself in free and patient discussion to their solution. It is the comfort and hope of our age that thought is at work on the problems of justice in our country. Public opinion is more frank and outspoken; any threat to freedom of the expression of thought is quickly resented: the tolerance which is necessary to free discussion of the problems of justice is in the air.

There is no need to be alarmed about this new liberty: it is a necessity of our salvation. But there is also another thing which is necessary; and that, too, we are beginning to do. We have not only to think out the demands of justice by a process of social thought; we have also to realize those demands for ourselves, as far as we can, by

a process of voluntary social co-operation. The State is the great organ of justice; but voluntary societies and voluntary effort can also help to build Jerusalem. That is an old English method; but the Prince of Wales, in recent years, has drawn our attention again to its value. Voluntary social effort and social service—in helping the unemployed to help themselves; in promoting community associations, for the betterment of social life, on the great new housing estates which our municipalities have recently built; in every field in which we can freely serve social purposes—these are the needs, and their increasing fulfilment is the promise of our times.

Our country is being rebuilt. The rebuilding was already at work in 1910: it has gone further, much further, in 1935; it has still to go on, and to go still further. The scope of State action has widened, and is likely to widen still more. But if we are true to our old tradition and our present temper, we shall all seek to join in thinking freely together about the plan of the rebuilding, and we shall all work together, in the free company of voluntary society, to aid in its realization. The State is not all.

THE CONCESSIONS EMBODIED IN THE MUNICH AGREEMENTS did not satisfy German ambitions; and in March, 1939, the Nazis took the Czech people "under the protection" of the Reich and brought Memel back into the "homeland." Clearly, Poland was to be the next victim of German aggression. So it was that Britain and France were compelled to take a strong stand. They promised aid to the Poles, and it seemed that German expansion might at last be stopped. But late in August came the announcement of the German-Russian pact, and on September 1 the German attack on Poland got under way. It is no exaggeration to say that the Nazi-Soviet pact shocked the world. After all the Nazi denunciations of Bolshevism as the great menace to the modern world and after all the Communist denunciations of Nazism as the last stand of German capitalism, it was difficult for contemporaries to understand the pact. To be sure, Communists all over the world quickly set forth neat "explanations," but these convinced only those who wanted to believe them. The full story of the origins of the pact will not be known for many

years to come, but the recent publication of many fundamental documents
has made it possible to find out more about the revolution in Nazi-Soviet
diplomatic relations that ushered in World War II. In the essay that follows,
Professor L. B. Namier, of the University of Manchester, gives his analysis
of the reasons for the failure of Britain and France to reach an understanding
with Russia and of the reasons for the success of Germany and Russia
in coming to terms with each other. Professor Namier, one of the giants
among present-day British historians, has written with insight and profundity
not only on the origins of World War II but on eighteenth-century England,
the Revolutions of 1848, and the Austria-Hungary of Francis Joseph.

THE RUSSO-GERMAN TREATY OF 1939

L. B. NAMIER

If there ever was a chance of avoiding a
second world war, that chance lay in a defensive alliance between the Western Powers
and Soviet Russia. If there was a way of
making sure that there should be war, it
was by concluding the agreement with the
Germans precisely in the way knowingly
chosen by the Soviet Government. The
Ribbentrop-Molotov treaty negotiated and
signed during the night of August 23 to 24,
1939, settled the issue. Looking back one
wonders what it was that caused the Soviet
Government to take that fateful decision
which ultimately brought them to the brink
of disaster, inflicted untold suffering on their
own people, and devastated a large part of
Russia.

This much must be said from the very
outset in justice to all the three Governments concerned in the Anglo-French-Soviet
negotiations of 1939, that circumstances
were basically unfavourable to an agreement between them. At the end of the first
world war, Soviet Russia had given up the
alien fringe of the Tsarist Empire, and had
moreover been forced to cede a wide stretch
of White Russian and Ukrainian territory to
Poland and Rumania. Even the voluntary
renunciations were made with a hope that
communist revolutions would re-integrate
those countries in the Soviet system: but
after twenty years the frontiers still remained

as fixed in 1917-20. They had not been
drawn by the Western Powers—in fact,
Great Britain had opposed the expansion
of Poland to the east beyond the so-called
Curzon Line. None the less, if Russia meant
to recapture certain territories, or forcibly
to Sovietise neighbouring countries, it was
not for Powers which entertained friendly
relations with them and professed League
principles, to assist or abet Soviet action.
The Germans, on the contrary, felt nowhere
committed to the post-war settlement, and
Hitler, devoid of moral scruples and unem-
barrassed even by his own passionate declarations of undying hatred of Bolshevism,
was capable of any *volte-face*.

The immediate aim of the Western
Powers in entering into negotiations with
Russia in April 1939 was to secure a
promise of aid should they become involved
in war in discharge of the obligations they
had assumed when guaranteeing Poland and
Rumania against unprovoked German aggression. But there was latent hostility
between these two countries and Russia,
which found expression in the Polish-Rumanian alliance directed solely against her.
Neither desired the Russian help which the
Western Powers were trying to secure for
them: they feared that Russian troops,
having entered their countries, would not
leave again; and that Russia would try to

Reprinted by special permission from *The Listener*, September 1, 1949.

recover certain territories and to Sovietise the rest. Those fears have been justified by subsequent events: yet they were as serious an obstacle to an Anglo-French-Soviet agreement as they would have been to action under it had it been concluded.

In the case of the Baltic states, it was a question of a neutrality which these tried scrupulously to preserve, but could not have defended. The Western Powers accepted the consequences of a similar awkward position in Belgium and Holland, which offered perfect cover to the Rhineland and Ruhr while Hitler was engaged elsewhere, but, without advance preparation, no effective obstacle to his offensive against France. The Soviet Government had no such delicacies. The guarantees which it tried to establish for the Baltic states, in spite of their protests, were to contain extensive safeguards even against German "indirect aggression," and to admit an occupation of military and naval bases in case of war. Britain was prepared to meet reasonable Russian demands by making "indirect aggression" cover "action accepted by the state in question under threat of force by another power and involving abandonment of its independence and neutrality." But the Soviet Government demanded that it should extend even to a *coup d'état* or to a political change favourable to the aggressor: which would have made Russia judge of the internal affairs of her small neighbours, and sanctioned her intervention. And this had a twist of its own as much as that of the Nazis. No complete agreement was ever reached about "indirect aggression"—a characteristic difficulty in the relations of the negotiating powers.

That difficulty sprang primarily from mutual lack of sympathy and from distrust. These were of course equally marked in Bolshevik-Nazi relations: yet in structure, spirit, and methods their two systems were nearer to each other than either was to Western democracy. Nazism was not incompatible with social revolution, nor Bolshevism with expansionist aggression; and one may well wonder what, except the special brand of nonsense which each had talked and fervently professed for years past, so deeply divided them. Perhaps without knowing it they continued, in fantastically irrelevant terms, the old contest of Slavs and Germans for the territories between the Baltic, the Adriatic, and the Black Sea. Still, agreements and conflicts between Nazis and Bolsheviks were possible in terms comprehensible and congenial to either; co-operation with the West would have put a serious strain on their temper and imagination.

The only inducement to the Soviet Government to close with the West would have been a feeling of certainty that such a diplomatic line-up would stop Hitler and save them from having to fight, for war—the favourite instrument of German policy—is not that of Bolshevism. But they had their usual doubts and suspicions. What if Hitler, encircled and curbed, attempted a coalition of "Imperialist capitalist Powers" against Soviet Russia? (That coalition is the perennial nightmare of the Bolsheviks.) Or alternatively, might he not, after all, risk an attack against the East, counting on the defensive military doctrine and mentality which the French had developed, and on the military unpreparedness of Britain? If the French sat tight in their Maginot Line, while Britain's main contribution was a naval blockade, Russia would have to bear the brunt of the fighting and of the defence of the Poles and Rumanians, who, to say the least, were no concern of hers. Further, extreme distrust undoubtedly suggested to the Russians the idea that the Western Powers, having got them into war with Germany, might leave them in the lurch, or finally make peace at their expense. A determined and sustained effort on the part of the Western Powers would have been required to dispel Russian doubts and suspicions, and even then it is by no means certain that it would have succeeded. But in fact the negotiations were conducted in a manner often inept and on the whole half-hearted (notwithstanding the many concessions ultimately made to the Russians): wherein a serious under-estimate of the Soviet military power, and over-estimate of that of Poland, played a part. And suspicions were a more formidable hindrance to an agreement between Russia and the West than between her and Germany: for the one might have meant to go tiger-shooting together, while the other did mean keeping away from the shooting and playing the jackal to the tiger.

"What could England offer Russia?" said a German diplomat to a Russian at the end of July, 1939, speaking from a brief. "At best, participation in a European war and the hostility of Germany, but not a single desirable end for Russia. What can we offer? Neutrality and staying out of a possible European conflict and, if Moscow wishes, a German-Russian understanding on common interests." . . . This pointed to territorial acquisitions in the Baltic area, in Poland, and in Rumania, such as it was morally impossible for the Western Powers to offer.

What, on the other hand, were the obstacles to a Nazi-Soviet agreement? Hitler victorious would clearly have been a deadly menace to Soviet Russia. And though the Russians probably, in common with everybody else including most German generals, overrated the defensive strength of France, and therefore the immunity or even advantages which they would be able to derive from a war between Germany and the West, the incalculable risks of a European war must have made them pause. Next there were the difficulties of approach between two parties long hostile and intensely suspicious of each other: each fearing that the other was not serious in any tentative advances which it made, but was merely fishing for material with which to blackmail the Western Powers into a more favourable agreement against the other side. Indeed, even after a Nazi-Soviet agreement had been concluded, Hitler, if given sufficient time, might have used it with a view to pulling off a super-Munich, ultimately, the Russians feared, directed against them. Supreme caution seemed therefore imperative.

It would in fact be difficult to imagine a more involved or a slyer game than that played by the Soviet Government between April and August, 1939. Whenever a step was taken toward the Western Powers or progress achieved in the negotiations with them, some counterbalancing approach was made to the Nazis, so that Hitler, in fear of effective encirclement, should not change front and attempt that coalition whose spectre obsessed the Bolshevik mind. As Western re-armament was proceeding apace, his best chance in a show-down with Poland was in 1939, and the season for it lay between the harvest and the autumn rains, that is, between the beginning of September and the middle of October. Therefore as the summer drew on, both the Western Powers and Hitler were becoming more intent on reaching an agreement with Russia. When at the end of July the announcement was made that the Allied Military Missions were proceeding to Moscow, the Germans redoubled their endeavours. And when on August 12, the day on which

---

CURZON LINE: Eastern frontier laid down in 1919 between Russia and Poland. The Poles refused to accept it and demanded their old frontier of 1772. By the terms of the Peace of Riga of 1921 Poland obtained an eastern boundary which approximated the boundary she had had on the eve of the partition of 1795. The German and Russian partition of Poland that followed the battle of Poland in World War II corresponded roughly to the division effected by the Curzon Line of 1919. By the provisions of the Yalta Agreement of 1945 the Line once more defined in general Poland's eastern frontier.

POLISH-RUMANIAN ALLIANCE: Treaty signed in 1921. Although expressed in general terms, it afforded protection specifically against Soviet Russia. The military convention which was annexed to it anticipated attack only by Russia.

the military negotiations were opened, the Soviet Government informed the Germans that it was prepared to start political talks with them, the Germans threw all restraint to the winds: Ribbentrop, to clinch the matter, offered to come immediately to Moseow, and went on pressing, day by day his offer on the Russians with ever growing insistence. The Russians now employed delaying tactics. It is by no means certain that they had meant to give their move of August 12 as far-reaching a significance as the Germans tried to put on it. At what exact juncture Stalin formed the decision to close with the Germans rather than with the West is not known even now, nor what it was that finally tipped the balance. But even if that decision had already been reached, the terrible weapon of an understanding with Russia had to be withheld from Hitler till the advanced season would no longer allow time for blackmail but would force him to use it for one purpose only: an attack against Poland. As late as August 19, Molotov still refused to fix even an approximate date for Ribbentrop's journey, and only later in the day, apparently by order from Stalin, agreed to August 26 or 27. Finally, renewed German pressure, in the form of a personal telegram from Hitler to Stalin, made the Russians advance the date to August 23.

The rest presented hardly any difficulties. Hitler conceded whatever the Russians asked for; in fact, Ribbentrop was authorized to leave the Russians a free hand even with regard to Turkey and the Straits, but at this juncture the Russians did not raise the question. A secret protocol delimited spheres of interest: Finland, Estonia, and Latvia were to be in the Russian sphere, Lithuania in the German; a demarcation line across Poland assigned to Russia her White Russian and Ukrainian provinces, and also some ethnically Polish districts (which a month later Russia exchanged against Lithuania). Russia registered her interest in Bessarabia, and Germany her *désintéressement* in that area. The overt treaty took the innocent form of a non-aggression pact; yet its sense was patent to all and sundry. Hitler thought that his agreement with Russia would stop the Western Powers from giving the promised help to Poland. When he saw that it would not, he made a last confused bid for a second Munich. But time pressed: and eight days after the Nazi-Soviet agreement had been signed, Hitler opened his Polish campaign.

WHEN WORLD WAR II CAME, in September, 1939, it was reassuring to the British that they could count not only on their European allies but on the British nations overseas. Hardly had Britain declared war on Germany when Canada, South Africa, Australia, and New Zealand, though not Eire, did so too. The reasons for this action were many. Certainly the British nations overseas were alarmed by German aggression and by the prospect of a German-dominated Europe and a German-dominated world. Hardly less important, they were concerned over the fate of Britain. And their loyalty to Britain was not difficult to explain. As members of the British Commonwealth of Nations, they enjoyed numerous rights and privileges. They were, after all, as had been formally declared, "autonomous communities within the British Empire, equal in status, in no way subordinate one to another in any aspect of their domestic or external affairs, though united by a common allegiance to the Crown, and freely associated as members of the British Commonwealth of

Nations." In short, British willingness to accept and to treat the British nations overseas as equals had served to breed loyalty, and loyalty was certainly what the British needed in their desperate struggle with Nazi Germany. Here, then, is an opportunity to review some of the main currents in British imperial development from Tudor times to the age of World War II. And probably no present-day British scholar is better qualified to undertake such a review than the author of the following essay. An enthusiastic champion of imperial studies, Dr. J. A. Williamson has written extensively in the field which he has so often encouraged other scholars to explore.

PHASES OF EMPIRE HISTORY

J. A. WILLIAMSON

Political controversy in the past has sometimes given the impression that the Empire has been the affair of a section of the people and not of the people as a whole, and that those who have served it have been in some sense exploiters or their dupes. Now that the last-remaining exponents of this view are coming to repentance and assuring us from the highest levels that they hold the Empire blessed, we may reasonably regard the view itself as obsolete. But we do, nevertheless, continue to accept some of its consequences. One need only consider the history syllabus in the majority of our schools, the requirements of public examining bodies, and the content of "English History" as studied in the universities, to realise that in the opinion of the learned the modern history of the British people has taken place almost entirely in the British Isles and that their enterprise and industry upon the seas and across the seas are comparatively negligible and have little bearing upon their fortunes. Amid the realities of to-day such a statement sounds ludicrous, yet it does fairly represent the academic attitude. The major part of the British Empire is now the British Commonwealth, consisting of connected, independent, self-governing states. Great Britain is the leading member of the combination; and we in this country give far less attention to the common history than do the peoples of the other member-states.

The reason is undoubtedly inertia. In universities and schools there is a traditional content of history whose expansion is resisted; and the public examiner, if he asks for anything beyond that content, is quickly told that he is violating a "gentleman's agreement," and finds himself and his examination unpopular. So that we who believe that Empire history ought to be studied have the discouraging task of trying to strike fire from a putty of passive resistance.

The history of the Empire-Commonwealth is rooted in the distant past. It springs from the trade of mediaeval England; and the trade sprang from the soil, which produced the wool wherewith Englishmen first made their way in the world. Wool paid for the mediaeval imports. In those days we imported only luxuries, wines and spices, sugar and fine raiment. The whole people were concerned in the wool business, the men on the land and the men in the towns, and they were all interested in the incoming sugar and spice. Their interest spread to the lands which produced those things. In the fifteenth century, trade with Portugal and Spain extended to the Azores, Madeira and the Canaries. Trade with Italy for the spices suggested thoughts of Asia, whence the spices came. Before the century was out, a Bristol expedition had found the continent beyond the Atlantic and claimed it as the Cathay of the Grand Khan, while next year

Reprinted by special permission from *History*, XXXIII (1948), 49-71.

London helped to follow up the discovery. With the Cabot voyages the story enters its transatlantic stage.

The Tudor century did a great deal of thinking, projecting and experimentation, and anything permanent that it produced owed its permanence to being an attempt to meet a substantial national need. Perhaps this accounts for the ineffectiveness of the first half of the period. Up to about 1540 it was a time of prosperity in which the old European trades were active enough to keep employment good. The need for oceanic expansion was only a need of the merchants to get the spice trade out of the foreign hands which controlled supply. Hence arose the various projects for a new route to eastern Asia by way of the North West Passage. They were bound to fail for reasons obvious now; but they were not followed with much persistence because the national interest in them was small.

From about 1540 there was a generation of hard times. Religious intolerance hampered trade with Spain; it is then that we first hear of Englishmen in the Inquisition. Spaniards and Flemings complained of English violations of their neutrality in the war of 1545, and a general arrest of English trade in the Low Countries inflicted lasting damage. The Protector Somerset mishandled foreign affairs, and trade suffered with them. The reign of Mary saw little recovery, and the loss of Calais was a mercantile as well as a military disaster. Elizabeth and Burghley had to put in years of skilful work to recover the lost ground. Bad foreign trade meant unemployment and social distress. When distress expressed itself in rebellion even the government of Edward VI had to seek a remedy. The duke of Northumberland was the most notable seeker, and, bad as his domestic record may be, he is entitled to recognition as an empire builder. Northumberland sketched and initiated the policies that are characteristic of the Elizabethan age. He founded a company to seek the North East Passage with hopes of reaching the spices of southern Asia and new cloth markets in the cold countries coasted by the way. The first hope failed and the second succeeded, and the company became the Muscovy Company selling cloth in Russia. He cancelled the excessive privileges which gave the Hanseatic League the control of our exports to Germany. He encouraged London merchants to open new trades with Morocco and the Gold Coast. He even mediated a plan for an English expedition to reach Peru by ascending the Amazon. It was a full record for a minister who had only three years of precarious power, and Northumberland as a founder of overseas expansion deserves more credit than he has generally received.

The Elizabethans continued the search for trade with tropical Asia and the expansion of trade in the tropical Atlantic. In the 1580's they elaborated yet a third design, that of founding colonies in North America. At first sight it may seem that this is the real beginning of our subject and that the others have not much to do with it. But that is not so. British expansion has always comprised the two elements, colonial and mercantile, interlinked but distinct. A number of merchant firms traded with Africa. John Hawkins and others traded with the Spanish West Indies. Sir Humphrey Gilbert publicized the North West Passage and lost his life in an attempt to found an American colony. Raleigh founded a colony, impermanently as it turned out, although the ill success was due to the outbreak of the Spanish War.

The Elizabethans justified their efforts by a doctrine. Their period witnessed a recovery from the mid-century depression. The recovery was tempered by the fact that population was increasing, while the number of places in a mainly agricultural society was almost fixed. For the surplus there was industry, dependent on the expansion of foreign trade. But Hakluyt and Gilbert and Raleigh went further and preached emigration as the remedy for social ills. American colonies, they said, will draw off the unemployed, they will establish trade with the natives and so produce more employment at home, they will be stepping-stones to the

North West Passage, which will also open new trades, and they will occupy much English shipping, giving yet more employment to seamen, shipwrights and other craftsmen. It was on these grounds that they founded Virginia.

Raleigh's Virginia was ruined by the Spanish War, which absorbed all the shipping at the critical juncture and left the colonists to perish unsupported. The war was a twenty years' interruption to the plans of the Elizabethans. It was, however, a necessary interruption, for it established the sea power without which nothing else could prosper. Hawkins and Drake made and used an ocean-going navy, whereas before their time English fleets had never served out of home waters.

After the war the early Stuart period resumed the Elizabethan plans. In many respects the early Stuart period is continuous with the Tudor, and the break comes with the Civil War and the Interregnum. So the England of James I returned to the doctrines of Hakluyt and Raleigh, and refounded Virginia to relieve unemployment. Economists still believed that the country was over-populated. They regarded the people as consumers and not as producers, and welcomed any plans for reducing their numbers. It would seem that these ideas reached the minds of multitudes who could never have read them at first hand. For there was a rush to emigrate, a mass-movement, which set in about 1620 and continued for over twenty years. Such a movement had never taken place before, and was not to occur again for two hundred years, until the early nineteenth century. The Stuart emigration, concentrated and purposeful, founded the British Empire in so far as it was a system of colonies.

We exaggerate if we think of it chiefly as a Puritan movement which founded New England for reasons of religion. That is true of the New England leaders, but probably not of the majority of their followers. Land-hunger rather than Calvinism was the motive of most of them. At the same time greater numbers were emigrating to the West Indies with no suggestion of religious incentive. Barbados, St. Kitts, Antigua and Nevis had, by the mid-century, a much larger white population than they have ever had since, and observers agree that its tone was the reverse of puritanical. Bermuda was another completely secular colony, and Virginia was growing fast. Maryland, although founded by Roman Catholics, contained from an early date a Protestant majority, so that religion cannot have been the general incentive of the emigration that peopled it. No, the Stuart emigration—the great exodus, as it has been fitly called—was not mainly sectional but national, a product of the social condition of England and the ideas and ambitions that influenced the people.

With the Interregnum we enter a new phase in which the national motives are mercantile rather than social, and some of the less pleasing features of the old colonial Empire grow prominent. During the great exodus the emphasis had been upon human beings, the individuals who found the old country too crowded or could not endure its religious attitude. They thought of emigration and settlement in terms of souls to save

CONTINENTAL SYSTEM: Scheme of commercial warfare by which Napoleon sought to defeat Britain. Napoleon's idea was that, if British goods were excluded from the Continent, British commerce and industry would be strangled, labor unrest would follow, and Britain would be "vanquished by excess." The Continental System is the subject of an admirable monograph by the great Swedish scholar Eli F. Heckscher.

RICHARD HAKLUYT: Elizabethan and early-Stuart geographer, historian, and spokesman for English overseas expansion. He saw in the establishment of an empire opportunities to spread Anglicanism, to overcome depression at home, to increase the revenues of the crown, to strike out at Spain, and to build up the navy.

and livings to get, and it was from this standpoint that public opinion in England regarded the colonies.

But when the founding had succeeded, and the adventurers had all gone forth and the exodus had ceased, there was inevitably a different outlook. In the Commonwealth period the colonies were no longer being planted, they were planted, and their relationship to the mother country became the topic of concern. In the period of movement England had thought about colonists; now the concern was with colonies. The outgoing colonists had been human beings and nothing else. The established colony was an economic organisation in a very important geographical setting. Thenceforward, public thought in England devoted itself to the functions, duties and economic relations of the colonies to the mother country, while public thought in the colonies ran largely on the avoidance of the said functions, duties and relations and on the promotion of the colony's freedom to make any contacts with any country as it saw fit.

The Commonwealth inaugurated the laws of trade and navigation which were to govern Empire relationships for two hundred years. It directed its committee on colonial affairs in 1649 to consider how the colonies "may be best managed and made useful for this Commonwealth; how the commodities thereof may be so multiplied and improved, as those Plantations alone may supply the Commonwealth with what it necessarily wants."

The Navigation Act of 1650 prohibited all foreign ships from entering any English colonial port. That of 1651 dealt with the non-colonial aspect of sea power and said that goods from the outer continents must be brought to England only in English ships, while European goods might be brought only in English ships or in those of the producing country. The Restoration Navigation Act of 1660 combined the above and added the enumeration clause, that specified colonial goods might be sent only to England and not to foreign countries. Finally, the Staple Act of 1663 declared that foreign manufactures might be sent to the colonies only from an English port. These were the key acts of the system, which was frequently altered in detail although to the end it remained constant in its object. The object was to cause the colonial empire to yield the maximum wealth to the mother country by the exclusion of foreigners from any share in the colonial trade. But that was not all, although many history books imply that it was. The system required the colonies to trade solely with the mother country, but not solely in the mother country's ships. The Navigation Acts gave privilege to all ships under the flag of England (or, after 1707, of Great Britain). Ships owned by the colonists enjoyed the full privilege; and some of the colonies, notably the New England group, owned a great many ships. Again, the customs duties were so arranged that colonial produce had virtually a monopoly of the English market. Foreign-grown tobacco, sugar, cotton and the rest were charged duties so high that they were practically excluded. Third and most important was the defence of the colonies by the powerful navy of England, which could be maintained only by the national profit from the colonial trade and manned only by the numerous seamen employed in peace-time in that trade. During the long century from the passing of the Navigation Acts to the Declaration of American Independence, no colony was permanently lost to a foreign enemy except the little plantation of Surinam. No other colonial empire had so successful a record of defence. In the building of the great sea power which achieved it lies the justification of the old colonial system.

Nevertheless, when that has been said, it remains true that there is no surer way to rot a society than to set every man calculating how much he makes out of the others and how much they make out of him, not as a result of his own talents or failings but by virtue of the system under which they all live. And the Empire, considered as a society, duly rotted in spirit under this obsession with the question of material profits.

A change in the economists' views on emigration tended in the same direction. The great exodus had been largely promoted by the conviction that England was over-populated and that prosperity demanded the emigration of the surplus. In the middle years of the seventeenth century that conviction was entirely abandoned. Economic thinkers began to emphasise the people as producers rather than as consumers. Manufactures were on the rise. It was believed, therefore, that an increase of population would mean an increase of national wealth and power, provided that its members were economically good citizens, industrious and law-abiding. The emigration policy, therefore, changed. No longer was the emigration of normal good citizens advocated. They were best retained at home. But the man who was a bad citizen by the standards of the majority was not only encouraged to emigrate, he was made to. So in the Commonwealth period the Royalist prisoners from Drogheda and Worcester were sent to the plantations, and under the Restoration the Quakers, the Roman Catholics, the Covenanters, and the west-country Nonconformists who fought for Monmouth, poured forth in an unhappy stream to America and the West Indies. Hanoverian England grew more tolerant, and no longer thrust out political and religious dissidents. But it did expel the social misfits. The death penalty, easily incurred in those days, was almost as easily commuted for exile in virtual slavery to the colonies. Transportation indeed became a primary sentence, without the commutation of a hanging. In the eighteenth century Great Britain recruited her colonial population largely with convicted felons. The virtuous in England even came to think of them as typical colonists. Established Americans regarded them as typical Englishmen. Mutual respect across the Atlantic suffered.

So far we have been considering the colonial side of the old Empire. There was another side to it, east of the Cape of Good Hope. The East India Company worked with fair profit through the early Stuart period. The Civil War almost destroyed it, for its privileges were of royal grant and not sacred to the Parliamentary party which controlled the port of London. Interlopers traded as they pleased, and the Company almost ceased business. Cromwell intervened to save it, and under the Restoration it had security and success. Security perished with the Stuart monarchy in 1688, and after long uncertainty the old company and its rivals coalesced as the United East India Company, destined to a career of one hundred and fifty years.

In the first half of the eighteenth century the company doubled its trade. In the second, Clive's conquests put it on the way to founding an empire. The eastern trade was reasonably lucrative to the company as such, and enormously so to the fortunate individuals among its servants who survived the Indian climate and were able to reach home with their gains. They were a small minority of those who went out young and full of hope, and for the most part died before they had been five years in the East. The survivors came home very rich and became, as the nabobs, a power in society and politics. The national effect was an increase of trade and employment, a growth of luxury, and a consciousness of "the East India interest" as an object of policy in more senses than one. In the early eighteenth century the great mercantile fortunes had been made in the West Indian plantations. After 1760 they came rather from the East. The balance of empire was inclining eastwards, and events in the west were to accelerate its movement.

The Bourbon wars filled the mid-eighteenth century from Jenkins' Ear in 1739 to the recognition of American independence at Versailles in 1783. Great Britain fought to achieve a dominant position in the opening of the oceans and the trade of great regions which were to be brought for the first time within the scope of European development. The greater statesmen had in mind the future rather than the present. Home industries were quickening and could do so unchecked only by having the outer regions at their disposal. Men like Chatham and Choiseul fought for the future greatness of their peoples. They risked less than they hoped to gain. Victory meant worldwide power. Defeat would mean a temporary smart, but not annihilation. This alternative of much to gain and little to lose may account for the attractiveness of war to eighteenth century minds.

The quest for future options is attested not only by the struggles for control of North America and India, but also by the arduous exploration of the Pacific which went on between the wars. The object of Bougainville and Cook and the other Pacific navigators was the revelation of the great southern continent, *Terra Australis Incognita*, and the capture by their own countries of a leading share in its exploitation. Cook demonstrated the non-existence of *Terra Australis* as an empire-building proposition to yield a vast accession of trade and sea power. His positive discoveries, of a moderately attractive eastern Australia and a New Zealand comparable to the Britain of Julius Caesar, were received with comparative indifference by a generation that was not looking for areas to colonise but for possessions to yield mercantile wealth.

The Bourbon wars passed, leaving the temporary smart of American independence and some gains in the form of options on the future. American independence was a grave humiliation but not the break-up of the old colonial empire. In the mercantile view the loss was small, because the Americans did become independent and so gave no increase of wealth and sea power to the Bourbons. If the British had been evicted from India, the result would have been far more serious, for India would not have become an independent state but a French Empire. And India, as events were to show, was the base of mercantile enterprise all over southern Asia, and the place of arms for its defence. That rich tropical field was essential to Great Britain entering the hectic stage of the industrial revolution. She could trade with the sovereign United States as

she had traded with her thirteen colonies, but her career as the world's workshop would have been crippled by an Indian Ocean under French control.

So we do wrong to emphasise too strongly the end of the old colonial or mercantile Empire in 1783. Some important things did end then, including a chapter of our domestic politics, but in the Empire the main result was to accelerate the shift to the east which had been in progress before the War of Independence began. The West Indian plantations were already past their prime, their soil exhausted and new sugar-bearing regions beginning to eclipse them, while the eastern expansion had all its greatest days to come. During the next forty years, to the fall of Napoleon, the tropical east was the prime area of empire. Colonisation in its true sense of emigration and settlement was out of fashion, as it had been since Stuart times, but its turn was to come again.

Meanwhile, the last great war with France ran for its twenty years and proved itself to be the first great war of a new kind. On our part it was fought not for Empire but for survival of the British way of life. Failure, the failure of sea power to keep open the ocean routes, would have meant the slow starvation of the industrial population who had come to depend on the manufacture of cotton and many other things for distant markets. By 1800 this part of the population was large enough for its agony to have affected the whole body politic and resulted in revolution. A more complete defeat at sea would have entailed invasion and conquest by the Jacobins or Napoleon. It would have been no such conquest as triumphant Bourbons would have made, with cession of colonies and change of dynasty, and then a polite departure of the victors, leaving a humiliated England to its own devices. Conquest in the last French war would have been worse than that. It would have meant the destruction not only of the dynasty but of society, and permanent occupation by the victors. We are well acquainted with the prospect. Our ancestors of Napoleon's time were the first to face it, and they were delivered by sea power. The navy of Nelson, the navy of Rodney and Hawke and Anson, was the saviour of our people. That navy was the child of the Navigation Acts and the old colonial Empire. So far as we can see, it could have been born of no other parents. We may criticise the old imperialism, its selfishness, its slave trade, its jingoism, its blindness to the things of the spirit. But we owe its misfortunes our sympathy and its valour our gratitude, for without it we should not be here.

The history of the Empire in the forty years after American independence is the least known passage in the whole story. Much research has been done, about which we are to hear in the course of this meeting, but the subject as a whole still awaits a broad survey which will pass into the body of general knowledge. The need has been partially met by the second volume of the *Cambridge History of the British Empire*. Although numbered the second, it is the most recent of the volumes, having been published in 1940. Its plan and method provide rather a series of monographs than the rounded synthesis which we look for; but it is a stage in the progress to that end.

It is not easy, therefore, to speak with confidence of this period, although we can say that it was fruitful and important, and not the hiatus which the older histories assumed it to be. It seems that the east, the Indian ocean, the Indonesian borderland, and the China seas were the decisive scene, more important than the West Indies, which were declining from their once supreme position in the oceanic economy.

Napoleon understood this. He knew that if he could not kill England by the direct blow across the Channel his surest means was to ruin her eastern trade. It was surer even than the exclusion from Europe by the Continental System, which was, in fact, his last resort when the promise in the east was fading. He tried first for the conquest of India, the keystone of the eastern position. Nelson at the Nile stopped that, while Wellesley and his brilliant successors made

the Indian position stronger. Then he tried commerce destruction in the eastern seas from the Cape to the Dutch Indies. The navy mastered the threat, and one by one the cruiser bases fell, Capetown, Mauritius, Malacca, Batavia. The importance of these actions was not local. They were steps in the salvation of the livelihood of hundreds of thousands of people in the British Isles. The loss of that livelihood, added to the privations inflicted by the loss of European trade, might well have turned the scale and have riveted the Napoleonic fetters permanently upon the western world.

The navy, the sea power of the old colonial Empire, foiled the attack. The Indian trade, the China trade, and the multifarious activities of the Persian Gulf, Mauritius, Ceylon, Rangoon, Malacca and Indonesia, and even of Cook's discoveries in the western Pacific, all grew greater and fed with their products and their markets the demands of the newer industries at home. Lancashire and the Clyde, the West Riding and the Birmingham country, and London as the world's exchange and counting-house, all drew strength from the east, which the navy made a British monopoly in the Napoleonic War. It forms a more significant aspect of the war than even the European coalitions and the fortunes of the Grand Army. The focus of Empire action had moved east and was to stay there until Disraeli's time. But the action itself was part of the history of the British Isles and demands its place in a proportioned view.

After the peace the eastern interests continued to be dominant. There was no idea of maintaining the war-time monopoly by a parade of supreme sea power, but there was a vigorous pursuit of competition as between equals. The British government restored Java, the richest island of Indonesia, and the Dutch in their recovered Indies resumed some of the old restrictive methods of handling trade. The British thereupon demonstrated that freedom was better than restriction; and Raffles's Singapore, freely open to all the shipping of the east, attracted trade like a magnet and provided a growing outlet for the new British manufactures. British India, saved by Nelson and Wellesley, continued to be consolidated and improved until it became the post-Mutiny Empire of peace and good government, the glory of Victoria's reign and the symbol of ability and character. The China trade, almost new since the early eighteenth century, was outstripping the Indian at the beginning of the nineteenth. It led to closer and continuous contact with the Chinese, and to faults of misunderstanding which had regrettable consequences. China and Far Eastern policy claimed a large place in British thought, as India had done a century before; and ministries which had no zest for colonisation were ready to extend sea power by acquiring trading posts and ports of call. In 1840 the Melbourne government was reluctant to sanction the settlement of New Zealand and was only pushed into doing so by the initiative of private Englishmen, but next year the same government thought Hong Kong very desirable as an outpost for the eastern trade.

Meanwhile two great forces had been manifesting themselves, together destined to shape a modern Commonwealth and Empire undreamed of by the statesmen who fought Napoleon—the humanitarian movement, and the second great exodus of emigrants.

The humanitarian movement was rooted in the eighteenth century, and its growth strengthened in the nineteenth. The protest against exploitation in India was its earliest imperial manifestation, causing uneasiness about the nabobs coming home too rich from the East, and inspiring Burke's well-meant though misdirected indictment of Warren Hastings. The campaign of Sharp and Wilberforce against the slave trade quickly followed, and then the foundation of the great missionary societies, movements which collected a large following throughout the country. The Indian administration grew steadily stronger in coping with abuses and making constructive improvements. The slave trade was made illegal in 1807 and slavery itself abolished in 1833. The victors

then organised themselves as the Aborigines' Protection Society, which sought to preserve and protect native interests wherever they seemed to be in danger. Wilberforce and his friends were an influential society, informally known as the Clapham Sect, which numbered among its adherents high officials, colonial governors and cabinet ministers. The Clapham Sect was not a denomination —most of its members belonged to the Church of England—but it did infuse the principles of evangelical Protestantism into the administration of the Empire. It was not solely external in its activities. The humanitarian cause had an equally powerful effect in home society. It was, in fact, like all the phases of Empire development, a part of British history in the true sense of that term. Christian humanitarianism remained the prime moral force at home and overseas until the last years of David Livingstone in the early 'seventies.

Emigration had not been massive and spontaneous since the time of the early Stuarts. It once more became both in the half century after 1815. Again, as two hundred years before, there was the sense of over-population, based this time on real statistics. The accepted Malthusian doctrine asserted that population would always increase to the limits of subsistence, and that the majority were doomed to be always near starvation. New people, it seemed, must well up in poor old England like water in a leaky boat, and the only palliative was to bale out the surplus. Emigration schemes therefore secured vigorous support, and many were put into operation. As in the Stuart period, they took the people away in appreciable numbers. There is a broad similarity in motive and method between the two emigration movements. On Plymouth waterside one may read adjacent inscriptions commemorating the departure of the Pilgrim Fathers of 1620 in the *Mayflower* and that of the pioneers of New Zealand in the *Tory* in 1839.

So the new colonists went out, most of them to Canada, a few to South Africa, some to New Zealand, many to Australia.

After the famine of 1845 the majority were Irish, but it is probable that the Irish did not predominate before that date. Who these emigrants really were is a question which has not been fully investigated. One would expect them to consist largely of the unemployed of the cities, but the indications are that they were mostly countrymen. In Canada and New South Wales they expanded an existing British population. In Western and South Australia and in New Zealand and South Africa they planted British stocks where none had been before. They founded the colonies which were to become the dominions of the twentieth-century Commonwealth.

They took with them a healthy aversion to the very class-conscious society of contemporary England and to the monopoly of political privilege by the smaller classes in that society. Thus it fell out that democracy was achieved earlier in the colonies than in the mother country, and that responsible government had no great difficulty in prevailing over the close corporation of the colonial service which had hitherto ruled both possessions and colonies.

The humanitarians and the colonists were sometimes mutually hostile. This was seen in New Zealand, where the missionaries held that land-hungry settlers would hinder efforts to evangelise the Maoris. Sir James Stephen, a member of the Clapham Sect and for many years a dominant administrator in the colonial office, sided with the missionaries and opposed plans for colonisation until his hand was forced by the radical and secular Gibbon Wakefield, whose methods of settlement conceded little to native interests. The division between settlers and missionaries was yet more serious in South Africa, where it grew into the long feud between the Boers and British governments.

The nineteenth century exodus was a greater extension of the habitat of the British people and involved a much smaller breach of relationship than did that of the seventeenth century. The Stuart colonists had quickly become Americans with inter-

ests and sentiments that parted them from the older nation, although it must be admitted that those interests and sentiments were provoked by the mercantile system of control. The Victorian colonists had nothing to complain of in that respect. The partial repeal of the Navigation Acts by Huskisson permitted the colonies to trade where they would. The surviving parts of the Acts had little restrictive effect, and even they were abolished in 1849. Ten years after that Canada showed that the fiscal freedom of the colonies was complete by enacting protective duties against British goods.

Responsible government on the political side and abandonment of all controls on the economic allowed the new colonies from about 1850 to grow up in a freedom which the old Empire had not known. Edmund Burke, contemplating the discontent of the Americans, had said that freedom was the strongest chain to bind the colonies to the mother country. No one believed it then, and in the mid-nineteenth century there were still many who did not believe it. The colonial office of that time—from about 1850 to about 1870—was quite committed to the freedom, but did not expect any bond to result from it, expecting rather complete disruption and the secession of the settlement colonies in the guise of independent republics. It is significant of the change of ideas since the eighteenth century that no one thought of resisting the disruption by armed force. The general opinion of political Englishmen was that the break-up was natural and inevitable—"the ripe fruit falls from the parent tree" was the metaphor— and should be effected with friendship and good humour. The free-trade economists went further and hailed the separation as not only inevitable but desirable. We should still, they said, trade with the former colonies when they had become independent states, and we should spend no money on armed forces and incur no risk of war in their defence. Those economic men never considered what would happen if a British community should be in desperate need of defence. Would they really have washed their hands of it?

The colonists of 1850 were thus told by some, in all courtesy, that if they were bent on going we should wish them godspeed, and by others that they were an encumbrance of which we wished ourselves good riddance. The assumption of all was that they wanted to go. And they did not. Canada had responsible government from the mid-'forties, Australia and New Zealand from the mid-'fifties. They could have seceded, had they wished it. Yet every colony of its own free will maintained the connection. Sixty years ago, after some rioting in Trafalgar Square, the government of the day gave permission for public demonstrations to be held there. *Punch* had a cartoon depicting two citizens discussing the concession. "What!" says one, "*allowed* to meet in the Square! Then we won't!" It is one of England's discoveries in applied politics.

The years about 1870 mark the turning-point in this and other concerns of British life. The second Reform Act, in 1867, enfranchised a large number of people who were the relatives of the emigrants of the previous decades. Cheap postage averted the severance of personal ties between friends at home and overseas. Cheaper, safer and swifter ocean passages were rendering visits from colony to mother country more possible than ever before. There was a sense of kinship in the new Empire that had not existed in the old. The extension of the parliamentary franchise gave it political weight. An example was seen when Gladstone's colonial secretary behaved ungenerously towards New Zealand in 1869. There was an outburst of public interest and sympathy in England and some sharp criticism of the government.

A political leader might see that some new material, imperial sentiment, was ready to his hand. Disraeli did see it. In 1872 he made a declaration on the subject which is rightly quoted as significant of the new attitude, although it may be doubted that Disraeli himself felt very deeply on the matter. He said that the Liberals in power had been

trying to break up the Empire, and implied that the Conservatives would try to strengthen it. He favoured an imperial council or parliament of some kind, an imperial military organisation for common defence, and the reservation of unoccupied lands in the colonies for emigrants from the British Isles. In the then emergent state of an imperial public opinion it was a good theme for a party leader, but, in fact, Disraeli did not further any of these policies when he came into power. His own imperialism was of the older sort, concern for India and the general Asiatic position, and for the great line of communication through the Mediterranean, which had more than doubled its importance with the opening of the Canal in 1869. That was what the Empire meant to Disraeli, who had been born before Trafalgar and had grown up to hold the east predominant and the colonies of small account.

Whatever Disraeli's values may have been, the new interest in the Empire became a permanent factor in English life. It was not only a question of maintaining touch with friends overseas. There were other motives working in the same direction. The humanitarians had once been hostile to British expansion. They had hoped to instruct and fortify the savage potentate until he and his newly evangelised people could take their place, with the missionaries at their side, among the independent states of the civilised world. The dream had faded. No christianised chief had proved strong enough to fill such a position, and the surge of Western enterprise was growing so powerful that the isolation requisite for the missionary experiment was ceasing to exist. The future of the tropics lay in tutelage to some European power; and the humanitarians agreed that it had best be the British. Livingstone's death in 1873, followed by the publication of his *Last Journals,* showed what vast humanitarian tasks were still to be done, and how necessary it was for the British state to do its share of them.

Trade and industry also, which had been hostile or indifferent earlier in the century, were now revising their views. Undeveloped regions of Africa and Asia were acquiring a potential value as sources of raw materials and future markets for European manufactures. So long as these countries were open to all comers, the British industrialist had no desire to annex them. But if his rivals in France, Germany or Russia should annex them, he would soon find himself excluded. In self-defence, therefore, he had to promote an active British policy of keeping watch on all the moves of the great powers in Asia and of taking a fair share in the partition of Africa and the Pacific islands.

British industry was by this time another term for the livelihood of the British people. Humanitarianism was the practical expression of their religion. When these two combined to regard the dependent Empire as a field of necessary endeavour, the people themselves became keen and proud to be reckoned among the progressive colonial powers. From the middle 'seventies to the general election of 1906 was the generation of ardent imperialism not only in the British Isles but in the British Empire. It is necessary to say that the word imperialism is here used in its legitimate sense of devotion to the Empire, and not with the degraded implications that Communist claptrap has attached to it.

The older humanitarianism developed into the sense of trusteeship with which we are now familiar, less evangelical and more scientific, concerned rather with sanitation than the soul, but devoted none the less to the education, personal freedom, just government and enrichment of peoples who were only on the threshold of such possibilities. In Malaya, Burma and large parts of Africa the trusteeship bore good fruit, and while there were other regions less conspicuously improved, it could be fairly claimed that the British trusteeship and the British colonial service had by the opening of the twentieth century a fine achievement to their credit. Much of that achievement belonged to the years when Joseph Chamberlain at the colonial office infused new life

into what he called "the undeveloped estate," the stagnant Negro colonies in West Africa and the West Indies. This, which may be called the first chapter of the record of the trusteeship, is one aspect of late Victorian imperialism.

In India trusteeship in early guises began with the nineteenth century, at first as an obligation to enforce peace and deliver the oppressed. By the revised charters of 1813 and 1833 the Company ceased to be a trading body and became solely a governing agency. Its supersession by the Crown in 1858 was not in fact revolutionary, since the revolution had already taken place. From the Company's later years dates the policy of providing a western education for Indians and of associating them with the administration of the country. That policy took one hundred and twenty years to reach the fruition which some think premature even to-day. In the nineteenth-century stages progression was slow, in the twentieth it has been rapid. The change from the one to the other was apparent in the viceroyalty of Lord Curzon, a splendid ruler of India by Victorian standards, but too rigid for the pace of development that followed.

In the settlement colonies which became the Dominions the post-1870 period runs on to the year 1914. It witnessed the completion of internal freedom by the adoption of responsible government in the last three to lack it, the Cape Colony, Natal and Western Australia. Great Britain had long ceased to exercise any mercantile control, and the colonies were free to enact their own tariffs, as most of them did, for the protection of their own industries. The general trend was to preserve the imperial connection and keep alive the duties and privileges of British citizenship, and at the same time to develop a regional nationalism that arose inevitably from the geographical conditions. Three of these regions, Canada, Australia and South Africa, comprised collocations of colonies which it seemed natural to combine into greater units. The earliest Dominion, that of Canada, began with four constituent colonies in 1867, and was completed by subsequent accessions in the early 'seventies. The Australian colonies discussed the matter for many years before achieving the final stage in the Australian Commonwealth proclaimed on the first day of the twentieth century. These decisions were reached in peace and good will and by common consent. The story of South Africa was different. But before considering it, we should note what Dominion status and colonial self-government meant before the war of 1914.

It was the period of the mother-and-daughters conception, the colony being thought of as grown-up daughter, mistress in her own house but subordinate to Mother England in the Empire. Internal autonomy was complete in each unit, but the relations of each and all to foreign powers were in the hands of the British government, just as the defence of all depended primarily upon the British navy. Pre-1914 self-government therefore did not extend to foreign relations. The deficiency was permanently felt to be an unfulfilled aspiration, and at times occasioned keen resentment, as in Canada over the Alaska settlement of 1904 and in Australia during the New Guinea transactions with Germany in the 'eighties. If there had been any acceptable way of remedying the grievance it would have been remedied. It seemed at the time that if half-a-dozen Empire authorities of equal status each pursued its own independent foreign policy the result would be in practice the disruption which no one desired. The alternative was to create a super-government, an imperial federation in which all would be represented; but this would have entailed a loss of local liberty which no unit of the Empire was prepared to sustain. So the matter went on unsolved, with the British government provisionally doing the job, amid frequent consultations between Empire statesmen in the Imperial Conferences which were a feature of the period.

These problems and developments, together with the advance of India and the achievements of the tropical trusteeship, represented the main content of late Vic-

torian imperialism, in which there was little evil and much good. But in South Africa the story was different, imperialism assumed another aspect, and that difficult region was mishandled with ill results. In reading that story we should not lose our sense of proportion. South African imperialism was only a part of a much larger whole, although it made noise enough to monopolise all the attention which should justly have been accorded to other aspects of the Empire. It may be said, briefly and therefore perhaps challengeably, that great wealth rapidly attained went to the heads of a group of successful men and deprived them of a certain soberness of judgment that was needful; and thus a series of unfortunate events was allowed to result in war becoming unavoidable. The fault was not all on one side, and if the antecedent provocations were fairly evenly divided, the final thrust to war was clearly made by Paul Kruger, who believed that a fight was inevitable and that he would grow weaker by waiting.

In the development of British opinion South African imperialism resembled a hot fit and a cold. The 'nineties witnessed a good deal of vulgar bragging and superman talk which some of us recognised with distaste as echoed in the vapourings of Mussolini and the maniac shouts of Hitler. It was unpleasant to realise that the things which nauseated us in the 1930's were things which England had not altogether disapproved when we were young. It must be said, however, that British governments did not approve of them. Certainly Lord Salisbury and Joseph Chamberlain dreaded a war and did their best to avoid it. The hot fit spent itself in the South African War, not in a blaze of straw but in much endurance and self-sacrifice in a service wherein every man was a volunteer. After the war the cold fit supervened. The South African imperialism of the 'nineties was of no esteem with a public capable of forgetting its own words; the Empire went out of fashion, and Joseph Chamberlain's work for closer union failed. The election of 1906 went heavily against those who had conducted the South African War, and placed in power those who had opposed it. South African imperialism may have deserved its fate, but it carried down with it, for the time being, the public interest in much other imperialism that was good. It did not revive until the approach of great and dangerous war in 1914.

The Empire went through both the German wars with enormous sacrifice and devotion to the common cause, and emerged from each with its unity unbroken. The constitutional positions in 1914 and 1939 were different, because large and important developments took place after the first-named year.

In 1914 the declaration of war by the Crown in Great Britain involved every subject of the King, and the Dominions were at war whether they would have chosen it or not. South Africa, which had become a Dominion with the voluntary union of the four provinces in 1909-10, had a minority who believed that a German victory would increase their freedom. So at least they persuaded themselves against all common sense, their true incentive being the hatred left over from the South African War. The South African majority quickly put down these dissidents, and the country thenceforward played its part in the united Empire. The other Dominions had no doubts from the beginning. Their statesmen had been warned of the approaching peril, and when the time came their adhesion was prompt and enduring.

In practice the men of the Dominions were free men who served by their own choice; for had they chosen otherwise no mother country could have compelled their sacrifice. Yet formally they had been committed to war by the decision of Great Britain, which controlled their foreign relations. The declaration of war is the most serious act of foreign policy, and the whole question became practical and pressing. During the war it was determined that soon after the peace an Imperial Conference should discuss and amend the imperial constitution. Before it could do so the matter was decided by events. The signing of peace is the next most serious act to the declaration of war. The general peace conference of 1919 followed immediately on the close of hostilities, and in it the Dominions were represented as sovereign states. In that character each of them (except Newfoundland) signed the treaties and became a separate and independent member of the new League of Nations. These events rendered superfluous the projected constitutional conference, so far as it was intended to give the Dominions control of their foreign policy, and it was never held.

Something different from the previous Empire had emerged from the war. It became known as the British Commonwealth of Nations, the more obvious word "League" having been already adopted by an organisation destined to be less enduring. The Commonwealth consisted of the United Kingdom and the self-governing nation states, the smallest being Newfoundland and the largest Canada. These were the former colonies now known as Dominions. The Empire, more strictly so called, continued in being. It consisted of the colonies and protectorates, most but not all with non-European peoples, which had not yet attained complete self-government. With them must be classed the territories mandated to British control by the League of Nations, the whole forming the dependent Empire in various stages of development under the trusteeship. There was nothing rigid or permanent about the distinction between Empire and Commonwealth members, and it was expected that countries would pass in due course from the one category into the other.

In these developments India followed a stormy course of its own. The aims of the British government and enlightened opinion on the one hand, and of the Indian leaders on the other, were in a sense identical, the attainment of self-government independent of British tutelage. But the two parties had very different ideas on the rate of development. For British statesmanship the attainment was to be ultimate, for Indian it was immediate. Through years of strife, denunciation and misinformed criticism by on-lookers, the British governments steadily pursued their policy. There are few to-day who would argue that their conception of the proper rate of progress was too slow.

So the Commonwealth and Empire entered the inter-war period, the Commonwealth already achieved, the Empire rapidly developing. Although achieved, the Commonwealth was not yet defined. "Forms and formulas," said General Smuts in 1919, "may still have to be adjusted, but the real work is done." The forms and formulas were provided by the constitutional definition adopted in the Imperial Conference of 1926 and by the Statute of Westminster of 1931. The Statute of Westminster was a brief declaration of Great Britain's relinquishment of legislative powers which she had already ceased to exercise. It contained little that had not been long agreed, neither did it mention foreign policy or define Dominion status. These matters had already been settled by constitutional practice.

As Empire-Commonwealth the British world entered the second German-provoked war. It emerged changed and changing, but alive as ever, with an appeal as living as ever to the imaginations of its peoples. In one word, its principle is freedom. Freedom is now assailed from many sides, and the Empire-Commonwealth has its part to play in the service of mankind.

Earlier in this survey it was emphasised that the history of the Empire is part of the history of Great Britain. That was increasingly evident until the nineteenth century stage of the story, when peace and de-control obscured the essential unity. The events of the twentieth century have caused the unity to be strongly realised again, but it needs to be differently described. In these latter years and in the years to come we must say not that the Empire is part of England, but that England is part of the Empire and a member of its Commonwealth. With that inspiration, and with the knowledge that broad continents share with us their citizenship, we of the island may face the future with equal mind.

THE BRITISH HOME FRONT DURING World War II differed strikingly in several ways from the home front in the years of World War I. For one thing, a vastly greater amount of physical destruction took place in Britain between 1939 and 1945. Hardly less important, the popular emotions aroused during the struggle against Nazi Germany contrasted markedly with those aroused in the struggle against the Germany of the Kaiser. In September, 1939, there was in Britain little of the martial enthusiasm that had followed the German invasion of Belgium in August, 1914. Indeed, Winston Churchill summed up in unforgettable words the expectations of many of his countrymen when he spoke in May, 1940, of a future of "blood and toil and tears and sweat." Instead of the short war that so many Britishers had anticipated in 1914, Churchill held forth in 1940 the prospect of "many, many long months of struggle and of suffering." And instead of voicing the lofty war aims that had been so often expressed during World War I, he emphasized above all that victory was the aim of Britain in World War II, for "without victory there is no survival." In the following essay, Professor Richard H. Tawney, of the University of London, sets forth his conception of the fundamental issues that were at stake in World War II. Author of two volumes that have become historical classics, *The Agrarian Problem in the Sixteenth Century* (1912) and *Religion and the Rise of Capitalism: A Historical Study* (1926), Professor Tawney ranks, along with Winston Churchill, G. M. Trevelyan, Sir John Clapham, and L. B. Namier, among the great British historians of the century.

THE CRISIS OF WESTERN CIVILIZATION
RICHARD H. TAWNEY

It is still possible to encounter persons who dismiss the present struggle with a tranquil air of effortless superiority, as merely the latest in an interminable series of wars between irreconcilable nations in an incorrigibly bellicose continent. The peoples tortured by it, from Poles, Czechs and Jugo-Slavs, to Dutch and Danes, Belgians and Norwegians, may be pardoned if at times they wish that such illusions were well-founded. The truth, unfortunately, is different. Due allowance must be made, no doubt, for the abiding disposition of combatants to veil vulgar ambitions behind a façade of glittering phrases; but, when the inevitable exaggerations have been discounted, the reality which remains is too formidable to be brushed aside. It is that for the first time since the wars of revolutionary France, and to a far greater degree than even in them, what confronts the world today is a struggle, not merely of incompatible interests and national ambitions, but of creeds, doctrines, and principles. Its outcome will determine, not only the relations between states, but the whole manner and quality of existence among the peoples concerned, from forms of economic and social organization to the most intimate aspects of domestic life, such as the choice of residence, marriage, the education of the young, and the very books which we may be permitted to read.

That such, and not questions of frontiers and markets, are the issues at stake should by now be a truism. It is proved by the reiterated declarations of those who launched the conflict, by the methods employed by them and the fate of their victims, by the reaction to their menaces of the peoples still unsubdued, by the verdict of nations not yet themselves involved. No tyrant known to history has ever told the world so clearly the future which he is preparing for it as has the Chancellor of the German Reich. If anyone doubts what that future is to be, let him read *Mein Kampf,* not in the expurgated edition prepared for Anglo-Saxon imbeciles, but in the original and authentic version.

The leaders of the totalitarian states have repeatedly affirmed that the enemy to be destroyed is not merely a stubborn nation which bars the way to their victory, but a way of life, a body of institutions, and a philosophy behind both, which they denounce at different times, for the edification of different audiences, under the agreeably contradictory names of Liberalism, Bolshevism, Capitalism, the principles of 1789, and pluto-democracy, but which, however described, they conceive of less as a foe of flesh and blood than a spiritual antagonist, whose destruction is the necessary condition of the triumph of their New Order. The idol of their devotion is not the unhappy German people, of whom its rulers have frequently spoken with unconcealed contempt, but an idea and a mission. The object of that mission is not merely conquest, but the propagation through conquest of a novel type of society, with an ethic, a jurisprudence, a political system, and social structure of its own.

Reprinted by special permission from *Social Education,* VI (1942), 154-156.

The motives of the peoples who stand in arms against them, if more soberly expressed, are not less explicit. If in Russia the invader finds a fortress in every village, and armies behind him as well as in front; if, in my own country, strongly organized workers, who are not easily driven, toil willingly till they drop; if miners vote to hew coal seven days a week, and girls throw up good jobs to turn shells and build planes; if sailors, after being torpedoed, go to sea again on the first boat they can find, and old people pass the night without grumbling in cellars and subways, and everybody "goes short," the reason is simple. What they fight for is not territorial aggrandisement or economic advantages. It is the right to preserve what they hold to be of value, both to themselves and to mankind, in their own manner of life; to reform what is not; to do both, not at the orders of a master, but by the free decision of plain men and women; to hold open a door through which they—or, if not they, at least their children—may pass undismayed to make a better world.

The attitude of the neutrals—or rather of those states which sacrificed everything in order to be neutral, and mostly sacrificed it in vain—has been determined by similar consideration. Spain welcomes Hitler's Myrmidons; every Pole, Czech, Norwegian, and Belgian—to mention no others—who can escape from his tormented country seeks refuge in England. The explanation is obvious. It is not that the former are in love with Nazi Germany, or the latter with my countrymen. It is that both are conscious of spiritual affinities transcending national boundaries; that a small despot naturally seeks shelter beneath the wings of a large one, and that the hearts of free peoples instinctively turn to a nation which, whatever its vices—Heaven knows, they're grave enough—they know to be defending both its freedom and their own. The very course and procedure of military operations underlines the same lesson. France—torn by class antagonisms—had allies of her enemy in the very council-chamber of her cabinet. She

crumbled from within before being bludgeoned from without. Greece, the schoolmaster of liberty to all mankind, both knew what she was fighting for and loved what she knew.

To ignore these truisms, and to interpret this conflict primarily in terms of a struggle between Germany and Great Britain is to make nonsense of the story. It is to forget that the bitterest foes of the present German regime are to be found among Germans, and the most passionate prayers for a British victory rise from the lips of a dozen different peoples, of whom countless individuals are now serving by land and sea with the British forces, and who do not today fight en masse side by side with my countrymen only because, being under the heel of the conqueror, they can not, till better days come, fight as peoples at all. The truth is that the present war resembles less the collisions between states which took place in the last century than those credal conflicts of earlier ages, which are conventionally known as the wars of religion. It is a struggle, on the one side, to destroy the fabric of Western civilization, and on the other side, to preserve it—to preserve it, not with the object of maintaining it, like a museum specimen, in petrified immobility, but in order that men may use such freedom as they have already won to enlarge the boundaries of freedom in the future.

Nor is it difficult to indicate the values which give Western civilization its special character. Generations of political theorists, on both sides of the Atlantic, have labored to formulate them. The rule of law; the rights of man; the greatest happiness of the greatest number; governments as servants, not masters; liberty of speech and person; equality and the abolition of economic privilege—such are a few of the rubrics they have employed for the purpose. All may be reduced to one—the Christian doctrine that the ultimate value is the free activity of the human spirit, and that institutions exist for men, not men for institutions. The powers of this world have frequently regarded it as both foolish and wicked, and have furnished its practitioners with torture and death. Almost everything that is admirable, however, in the public life of Western nations, and, in particular, the capacity they have shown for periodical regeneration, has its source in the temper which that principle has fostered. The respect for the individual conscience; the attempt to make law, not mere force, the arbiter of society; the effort, feeble and fitful, but none-the-less real, to try political systems and economic organization by moral criteria, are all the results of it.

Owing to the triumphs of the national state during the last two centuries, students and teachers of history have tended, it is perhaps fair to say, to give more space to the forces dividing peoples than to the spiritual bonds uniting them. It is time, it seems to me, that the balance should be redressed, and that more should be said of the values common to the whole of Western civilization, not in order, of course, to depreciate the excellence of other cultures, such as that of the Chinese, but to make men aware that the richest treasures of life are not those for which they strive against their fellows, but those which they share with them. It is these spiritual treasures which are now threatened with destruction. The causes and significance of the present crisis will occupy the best minds of many different nations for generations to come, and only a charlatan will dogmatise upon them. There are three points, however, which I would venture to underline.

In the first place Europe is the heir of a historical legacy at once splendid and tragic. The most important of her characteristics can be simply stated. It consists in a combination of cultured unity with political diversity not found to the same extent in Russia, China, or North America. Geography has made it difficult for different parts of Europe to live in peace; but it has also made it impossible for them to live in isolation. History has given her a culture super-

national as well as national. But the values which make that culture do not radiate from a single center. They derive their quality from the characteristics of different peoples, varying in experience, needs, ideals, and ambitions; and the smallest, as well as the greatest, have contributed.

The permanent problem is to preserve both the common values and the national individualities from crushing the diversities, and the diversities from degenerating into an anarchy which, since it leaves the weak at the mercy of the strong, leads by a longer road to the same ruinous end. In our own day two movements have sharpened its edge. The sovereign states of Europe numbered sixteen in 1875, and twenty-two in 1914. By 1920, twenty-nine such states were packed into an area smaller than that of the American Union. When the present century opened, the Industrial Revolution had refashioned the framework of life in western and central Europe; but it was still young and feeble in the agrarian East; today it has woven the whole of it into one web. Thus political development has gone one way, and economic development another. Interdependence has increased, but so also have frontiers.

Other things being equal, consolidation means an advance in security and well-being, while disintegration means a diminution of both. The classical expedient for combining the advantages of unity in those matters where united action is essential with a regional autonomy which offers free play to beneficial diversities, corresponding to differences of culture, traditions and needs, is, of course, federalism. The difficulties of applying that solution to the problems of Europe are not small, and I must not pause to examine it. It is clear however—to judge by experience—that the political existence of the smaller European states will be precarious except as members of some larger association, while the economic benefits of larger areas over which a single policy is pursued are hardly to be contested. It is significant that whereas, in 1919, the whole emphasis of the representatives of such states was laid on national independence, the current now shows signs of turning, and that certain of them have already discussed with their neighbors proposals for common action in matters of defense and economic policy.

The second point which I would make relates, not to one continent, but in different degrees to all. It is that the world is now too small for the affairs of mankind to be conducted without disaster on the assumption that the ultimate political reality is the sovereign state which knows no superior. Distance, for most purposes, is to be measured in terms of time rather than of space; and, judged by that standard, New York is nearer London, and London nearer Nanking, than was the former to Indianapolis, and the latter to Edinburgh, in the days of our grandfathers. If mankind is not yet economically one, it has advanced sufficiently far on the road to unification, to make the paralysis of one region or continent a matter of more than merely local concern. Here again I must not pause to enter into detail, but here again one general conclusion can hardly be resisted. It is that, while the blameless bystander who asks "Am I my brother's keeper?" may be admirable as a moralist, as an economist and political scientist he is half a century out of date. The price which we pay for participation in the increased prosperity made possible by interdependence is, when the links are snapped, collective disaster. Collective disaster can be averted or cured only by collective action, and collective action is impossible without a measure of collective organization far more extensive than mankind has yet been willing to adopt.

The third point to which I would refer is equally obvious. It is a commonplace that the last century has seen both in America and in Europe an increase in income per head unparalleled in any previous period of history. Of America I do not venture to speak; but few who reflect on the social order which most nations in Europe carried into the present war, with its riches and its poverty; its aggregations of economic power divorced from responsibility; its idolatry of wealth, its suspicious truce between classes, broken at times by bitter struggles, will feel much exhilaration at the thought of perpetuating into a new age so speckled a legacy from one which has known better how to face death than how to live. It is idle for a nation to blazon "Liberty, Fraternity, and Equality" on the façades of its public buildings, if to display the same motto in its factories and mines would provoke only cynical laughter that greets a reminder, not of victories won, but of idealisms turned sour and hopes unfulfilled. Whatever other tasks await us, one at least is plain. It is to extend the application of the principles of democracy from the political sphere, where they are now accepted, to industrial organization and economic life. It is to clothe freedom with the positive significance which belongs to it when it means, not the mere absence of restrictions, but the presence of conditions enabling all to participate according to their powers, in the treasures of civilization.

IN THE PERIOD OF WORLD WAR II Conservatives and Laborites worked together with remarkable harmony. With the capitulation of Germany early in May, 1945, however, the coalition government dissolved rapidly. In July the long-awaited general election—the first since 1935—took place, and the greatest electoral surprise in British history occurred. Winston Churchill's words on the subject are now classic: "I acquired [in 1940] the chief power in the State which . . . I wielded in ever growing measure for five years and three months of world war, at the end of which time, all our enemies having surrendered unconditionally or being about to do so, I was immediately dismissed by the British electorate from all further conduct of their affairs." Whereas the Conservatives won some two hundred seats, the Laborites returned some four hundred members to the House of Commons. The reasons for the election results were, of course, widely discussed. The defeat of the Conservative Party was explained, for example, by its fear of fundamental social reforms, by its identification historically with the appeasement of Germany, by its association in the 1930's with widespread unemployment and economic insecurity, by its alienation of middle-class support. In the United States especially the tendency was to view the defeat of Churchill's party as an astounding act of ingratitude on the part of British voters. In the essay that follows, the late Professor William T. Morgan, of Indiana University, analyzes the election of 1945. Known mainly for his writings on the age of Queen Anne, Professor Morgan liked now and then to get away from the early eighteenth century and deal with contemporary British politics.

THE BRITISH GENERAL ELECTION OF 1945
WILLIAM THOMAS MORGAN

As the war seemed in 1944 to be slowly reaching a triumphal conclusion, the British gave themselves furiously to think about such domestic problems as housing, coal, social security, and education.* They felt

* This article is based largely upon material derived from ten contemporary British daily papers, the *Observer,* the *New Leader,* and the more important weekly and monthly magazines. The dailies include one from North Ireland, one from Scotland, one from Wales (all Conservative), the Liberal *Manchester Guardian,* and six from London. Of the six, the *Express* and the *Telegraph* were decidedly Conservative, the *Mail* less so, the *News Chronicle* Liberal, the *Herald* Laborite, and the *Times* almost neutral.

For discussions of the background and results of British elections since 1923, the reader is referred to the following articles in the *Quarterly* by the same author: "The Amenities of an English Election," XXIV (1925), 16-33; "Great Britain—Nine Years after the Armistice," XXVII (1928), 229-246; "Recent Political Crises in Great Britain," XXX (1931), 1-18; "Recent British Politics and the Newspaper Barons, 1929-1935," XXXIV (1935), 419-443; and "Mr. Neville Chamberlain and the Dictators," XXXVIII (1939), 1-22.

that they had won World War I only to lose the peace and were haunted by memories of subsequent unemployment. Periodicals began seriously to discuss programs of social reconstruction. Postwar education received much attention, and a comprehensive education act was passed only to encounter Socialist criticism because of its tenderness toward denominational and "public" schools, and the long delay in implementing some of its important provisions.

Soon after the invasion of Normandy political parties began to plan an election to replace what the *Economist* described as a "stale and superannuated" House of Commons. In October, 1944, Mr. Churchill had given assurances that the election would not be rushed, but political events were moving rapidly before V-E Day, May 8, 1945; and a fortnight later the Labor Party Conference refused to remain in the Coalition until the end of the war with Japan. The Premier resigned forthwith and announced that Parliament would be dissolved June 15, with the poll July 5. He also ac-

Reprinted by special permission from *The South Atlantic Quarterly,* XLV (1946), 297-312.

cepted the King's invitation to form a "Caretaker" (interim) Government which, although predominantly Conservative, assumed the name "National."

Numerous by-elections in the previous eighteen months had occasioned much fluttering in political dovecotes. Although Socialists and Liberals refrained from opposing Conservatives, certain so-called "Splinter" groups, especially the radical Common Wealth Party, challenged them. In December, 1943, the Government saved a presumably safe Conservative seat at Darwen by only 70 from a Liberal woman who defied party headquarters. At Skipton, Common Wealth overcame a handsome Conservative majority to win. At Brighton an Independent reduced a Conservative majority from 40,000 to 4,000. Another Independent, despite the Premier's intervention, won by 4,500 in a pocket borough of the Cavendishes over a member of that family. At Bury St. Edmunds, Mrs. Corbett-Ashby, a leading Liberal figure, also defied her party by standing, albeit unsuccessfully, against a Conservative. A Laborite won easily at Clays Cross, but he was opposed by two "Splinter" groups. At Rusholme, Common Wealth, stressing Socialism in an area where it was presumably unpopular, polled 6,670 votes to a Conservative's 8,430. A Scottish Nationalist wrested a seat at Motherwell from Labor. Although Mr. Churchill again intervened at Chelmsford, Common Wealth overcame a Conservative majority of 16,000 to win by 6,000. At Neath, Labor was challenged unsuccessfully by two other minor factions. Of the 219 by-elections since 1935, 134 had occurred after the war began; between 1935 and 1939 the Conservative group lost 17 seats; Liberals and Laborites, none. Since 1939 the Conservatives had lost 8; Liberals and Laborites, none. Several seats were retained by greatly reduced Conservative majorities, and 69 were uncontested. Since June, 1941, wrote Mr. Peter Richards in the *Political Quarterly,* the Opposition's popular vote had been 49 per cent of the total.

The campaign formally opened with Mr. Churchill's broadcast, the first of twenty-four for all parties; the Premier himself spoke four times over the air. In his opener Mr. Churchill was most bellicose and insisted that no Socialist system could "be established without a political police. . . . Socialist policy is abhorrent to British ideas of freedom . . . inseparably interwoven with totalitarianism." He thereby inaugurated a campaign which has rarely been exceeded in virulence. Mr. Clement Attlee, broadcasting in reply, was much less bitter, but accused his opponent of departing from the position of a national leader by yielding to the pressure of Conservative politicians, "anxious to exploit your own great service to the nation."

This was among the least predictable elections in British history. Public opinion had not been tested in a decade. The political bias of voters aged from twenty-one to thirty was thus unknown. Moreover, twenty-five new constituencies had been created. The trend of the service vote was uncertain. A great shifting of population had completely altered the character of the electorate in many constituencies. The voters' register was so defective that it might prove to be a determining factor in close contests. It was not easy to foresee the effect of six years of war upon a very tired people. Finally, the women outnumbered the men in most constituencies and in many instances held proxies for their menfolk in the services. Large numbers of them were in the armed services or in war factories, where many had joined trade unions for the first time. Conservative leaders naturally worried lest this might influence their political alignment.

Although the results were unpredictable, Mr. Churchill's first broadcast made certain that the election would not be dull. No political leader seems fully to have appreciated how important a factor the microphone was to be. When already too late, it became evident that Mr. Churchill broadcasted not only too frequently but far from well. Whatever the role of personal vituperation in lively public meetings, it had no place in the quiet atmosphere surrounding the parlor radio. No British politician showed any of Mr. Roosevelt's mastery of radio technique.

The first lively issue was the responsibility for the "rush" election. The Premier and his leading advisers, Lord Beaverbrook and Mr. Brendan Bracken, seem to have been mainly responsible for the decision. International affairs played a small part, for all parties agreed that Britain's first duty was to end the Japanese war. During the canvass, indeed, Labor ministers in the late Coalition supported Mr. Churchill's policy in the Levant crisis, and the United Nations Charter was signed in San Francisco. Mr. Churchill's attitude towards the Leftists in Italy and Greece, however, was criticized caustically. The Big Three meeting at Potsdam indirectly produced the campaign's liveliest moments. While the election was still in progress, arrangements were being perfected to hold this Conference, and Mr. Churchill invited Mr. Attlee as leader of the Opposition to accompany him. Mr. Attlee accepted, but Professor Harold J. Laski, Chairman of the Executive Committee of the Labor Party, insisted that Mr. Attlee could go only as an "observer," without authority to commit his party. The Conservatives thereupon immediately claimed that if their opponents secured a majority, their M.P.'s would be controlled by an irresponsible Socialist caucus. Mr. Churchill specifically inquired of Mr. Attlee whether he was going only as "observer."

Although Mr. Attlee replied in the negative, the Conservative press expressed great dissatisfaction that he had not unequivocally disavowed the authority of the Socialist Committee over the Laborite M.P.'s, asserting that representative government would be a thing of the past if a caucus could dictate policy to members of Parliament. Lord Beaverbrook shouted that Professor Laski "is the head of the Socialist caucus. . . . This caucus evidently has some secret protocols. . . . You will see that this [caucus] list is made up largely of men who are not in Parliament." The Secretary for Air asked, "Who is this Gauleiter Laski to tell British statesmen what they are to do?" Labor leaders pronounced this just another red scare. The *Economist* wrote, "The Laski stunt, especially in its timing, irresistibly recalls the Zinoviev letter . . . , but the Zinoviev letter was not put out by a Prime Minister." The *Guardian* carried a "Red Letter" editorial. The *Western Mail* (Cardiff) warned the voters that the fundamental issue was "the diktat of irresponsibles on the Labour Party Executive, who would lord it over Parliament and Ministers."

The Laborites reminded their opponents that the caucus was Joseph Chamberlain's invention. The *News Chronicle* showed that the Conservatives, too, were

ruled by an Executive of 33, half of whom are men of title. There are four Lords and one Lady, ten Knights and Baronets, one "Honourable Mrs.," and 17 not so common Commoners, including three colonels and a brace of majors. . . . Were they balloted for in the open like

SANKEY REPORT: Report issued in 1919 by a royal commission of inquiry headed by Justice Sankey. It dealt with the problem of the mines, and recommended nationalization as the solution. Although the Lloyd George government had pledged itself in advance to accept the recommendations of the commission, it proceeded to ignore the report, and accordingly aroused widespread hostility, especially in labor circles.

ZINOVIEV LETTER: Forged "Red Letter" that was published in the *Daily Mail* and elsewhere during the election campaign of 1924. Supposedly written by the chairman of the Communist International, it gave instructions to British Communists on methods to be used in order to win control of the labor movement. It helped to bring about the defeat of the Labor Party and the victory of the Conservatives in the general election of October, 1924.

Laski's legions? Finally, the people are wondering which of the 33 represents the millions of trade unionists Mr. Churchill claims as his supporters.

Conservative party managers decided that Laski was their most fruitful issue, and the Premier returned to him in his last broadcast:

It appears that this Socialist Executive . . . would require the submission of Ministers to its will; . . . secrets might have to be divulged to this Committee of 27 members, very few of whom are Privy Councillors.

Mr. Attlee replied, terming Mr. Churchill's "insinuations" that Labor Ministers would reveal Cabinet secrets to "outsiders" as "vile," adding that he never dreamed his former chief "would descend to such depths of misrepresentation . . . towards men who had shown him such loyalty" in the late Coalition. To Mr. Attlee's reply the *Herald* added a trenchant postscript:

For five years the Prime Minister has worked in the most intimate contact with the Labour leaders. . . . Mr. Attlee . . . has been in charge during the frequent and prolonged absences of Mr. Churchill . . . , [who] never for a moment feared that Cabinet secrets were likely to be divulged by Labour Ministers to their Party Chairman . . . , nor does he, to this day, believe there is the slightest change.

Nevertheless, the Premier wrote Mr. Attlee again that in view of the "grave constitutional issue . . . the situation is extremely disquieting and [I] think it ought to be fully explained by you to the nation." Mr. Attlee answered categorically that "the Chairman [Laski] has not the power to give me instructions." The *Telegraph* sadly commented that this exchange of letters would precipitate a crisis in the Socialist ranks, "but not, it seems, until after the election."

Meanwhile Labor attempted to cast upon the Conservatives the onus for prewar appeasement. Referring to Chamberlain's statement in 1935 that if the League did not have its way as to Ethiopia, the English people would be held up to shame by their children and children's children, a Labor member of Parliament noted that four years later Chamberlain as Prime Minister was in Rome toasting Victor Emmanuel III as Emperor of Ethiopia. The Chicago *Daily News* published during the election a part of the diary of Count Ciano, Mussolini's son-in-law; and an English paper reprinted an extract of January 27, 1939:

British Ambassador has submitted for our approval the outline of a speech Chamberlain will make before the House of Commons so that we might suggest changes if necessary. Il Duce approved, and said: "I believe it is the first time the head of a British Government had submitted to a foreign power the outline of one of his speeches. It is a bad sign for them."

Mr. Wickham Steed in the *Contemporary* caustically accused Conservative leaders, the British press, and even Scotland Yard of an abject attitude towards the dictators. The *Herald* reprinted a statement from Beaverbrook's *Express* of March 10, 1938, three days before the Nazis invaded Austria: "Welcome Herr von Ribbentrop, Hitler's Foreign Minister. We have the right to believe that he comes here an Ambassador of Peace, sincerely seeking it." The same paper quoted Mr. Duncan Sandys, Mr. Churchill's son-in-law:

If the strength of the German *Wehrmacht* would help in any way to prevent Soviet Russia from supporting her cunning propaganda abroad by force, then, indeed, Germany renders a service to civilisation, which may demand recognition.

This most illuminating statement first appeared in a German review in 1936.

While the Laborites stressed war guilt, the Conservatives elaborated the pacificism of the Socialists and their reluctance to back rearmament. The best Conservative election tract, Mr. Quintin Hogg's *The Left was never Right,* cited pacifist utterances by Socialist leaders who must, he argued, share the blame for Britain's deficient armaments and ineffective diplomacy. In rebuttal Mr. A. V. Alexander quoted Mr. Churchill's statement on October 5, 1938, that such responsibility rested "with those who have the undisputed control of our political affairs. . . . They left us in the hour of trial without adequate defense and effective international security."

The official campaign lasted three weeks. Because of "Wakes" week holidays, elections in twenty-two Northern constituencies were postponed a week, and in one other constituency for a fortnight. Only one previous election had so many candidates: there were 1,674 for 640 seats as compared with 1,728 for 615 seats in 1929. Only 3 seats were uncontested—a new low—compared with 7 in 1929 and 38 in 1935. Of the 1,674 candidates, 300 were Liberals, 600 Labor, and 630 "National." Common Wealth had 22, Communists 21, Scottish Nationalists 8, Welsh Nationalists 7, Independent Labor 5, Independents 42, with a score more representing a record number of "eccentric candidatures." Seven constituencies had 5 candidates each, 39 had 4; there were 291 triangular contests. Every Caretaker Minister had to fight for his seat, including the Speaker and Prime Minister.

Of 350 Labor candidates studied, 120 were university graduates, half honors' men; 100 had been journalists or business managers, or had held high public offices; 43 were barristers, solicitors, or doctors; 31 professors, headmasters, or lecturers; 161 were members of local governing bodies; 129 had seen service during the war, ranging "from private to lieutenant-general, from seaman to commander, from L.A.C. to air vice-marshal"; barely a quarter were trade union or Co-operative officials. Fifty had previous official experience in the Labor or Coalition Governments; 40 were women, compared with a previous Laborite record of 33 in 1935; and 130 sought re-election. Taking the candidates as a whole, nearly

one third came from the services, including 541 officers of all ranks, 13 noncommissioned officers, "one L.A.C., one leading seaman, and one private"; the Army had 414, including 6 generals, 130 majors, and 47 lieutenants; the Navy 35: one admiral, 13 commanders, and 21 lieutenant commanders. Of the Liberal and Conservative candidates nearly half were servicemen in the war. Five candidates were less than 26 years old. Among the 87 women candidates were Lady Violet Bonham Carter, daughter of the late Earl of Oxford and now President of the Liberal Party organization, and Lady Megan Lloyd George, daughter of the late Earl. Mrs. Van der Elst, indefatigable opponent of capital punishment, not only prevailed on Corporal C. Deller to retire in her favor, but to act as her election agent.

Cambridge University had interesting candidates: Mr. J. B. Priestley, author and broadcaster; Mr. H. Wilson Harris, editor of the *Spectator;* the sitting member, Professor K. Pickthorn; and a "radio doctor." For Oxford University stood irrepressible Sir Alan P. Herbert of *Punch* and Mr. G. D. H. Cole, equally adept as British Labor's historian and writer of mystery novels. The "Independent Sportsmen's Candidate" had the highly intelligible slogan of "More Homes, More Food, More Clothes, More Beer." The Foot family was represented by a father and three sons ("Four Feet").

Disregarding the 25 new constituencies and those where shifting population made predictions hazardous, political leaders concentrated upon 130 won in 1935 by margins of from 80 to 3,000, where intensive efforts might prove exceptionally fruitful. In the London area Labor held 11 such seats and the Conservatives 8.

Attempting in characteristic English fashion to forget the past, the Conservatives made Mr. Churchill their "starred item," featuring him as the great "National" leader. He appealed, therefore, to the electorate to forget party and vote for him and his Caretaker followers. Since he had opposed a Coupon (Coalition) election, his opponents accused him of inconsistency. They also made much of his earlier description of Tories as representing "sentiment by the bucketful; patriotism by the Imperial pint; the open hand at the Exchequer; the open door at the public-houses; dear food for millions; and cheap labor for the millionaires." Mr. Michael Foot, one of the "Feet," wrote: "The whole future of the Conservative Party rests in the hands of a man, who could not muster six Tory votes in the . . . Commons a dozen years ago." Mr. F. Seymour Cocks (another M.P.) insisted that the Conservative leopard had not changed its spots, for in the "National" Government "are many former supporters of the pro-fascist, anti-Russian policy which nearly brought us to ruin," including Lord Simon, Lord Croft, Lord Dunglass, and Lord Beaverbrook. Labor quoted Mr. Baldwin in 1930 on newspaper barons who sought power without responsibility, "the prerogative of the harlot . . . of being able to suppress everything that a man says that they do not like . . . without . . . any possibility of being hit back." The *News Chronicle* analyzed the Caretaker Ministry of 81 with its Cabinet of 16. Of the 64 who did not hold office by virtue of Labor or Liberal affiliations or their administrative abilities, 14 were in the Cabinet, and 14 were peers, 17 married to the daughters of peers, 5 to baronets' daughters. Fifty-eight of the 64 were Public School men, including 25 Etonians, 8 Harrovians, 4 Wykehamists. Of the 16 Cabinet Members, 7 were from Eton and 3 from Harrow.

The Socialists maintained that the Tories were primarily champions of Big Business. Mr. Dingle Foot stated that the Government stood almost alone in its refusal to legislate against monopolies. A paper read before the Royal Statistical Society showed that in each of 33 different trades 70 per cent of the output was controlled by not more than 3 firms. Mr. Bevin, outstanding Labor leader, described the steel industry as "being slowly choked to death by its own steel rings." The American steel industry,

he said, paid wages "four times higher than ours," but British steel for Portal prefabricated houses cost 27½ per cent more than American, and firms which had not turned a wheel in four years still paid dividends from profits made by other members of the cartel. A Labor spokesman claimed that steel was controlled by four firms, magnesium by two, transparent plastics by one, and 80 per cent of aluminum by one; credit was the monopoly of five banks, and transport largely of a half dozen men. Mr. Shinwell, volatile Labor leader, charged that Britain's principal monopolists "were directly or indirectly in the Caretaker Government," mentioning Mr. Lyttelton, Sir Andrew Duncan, and Lord Leathers. Mr. Harry Pollitt, Communist leader, maintained that British food was "in the grip of 9 big combines." The Laborites resented Lord Beaverbrook's vitriolic attack upon the popular Co-operatives, particularly because they felt that the Co-ops were the only successful competitors of great monopolies like Unilevers and the Imperial Tobacco Company. A Gallup poll on the question of whether combines tended to raise prices reported, 56 per cent Yes, 27 per cent No, and 17 per cent Undecided.

The campaign concentrated upon domestic affairs. Labor bitterly criticized the Government's health program and accused the Conservatives of selling out to reactionaries in the British Medical Association and the voluntary hospitals. The Conservatives tried to make nationalization the leading domestic issue. They insinuated that the change from private enterprise might not be carried out peacefully and that once the electorate committed itself to nationalization, it would be impossible to return to a system of free enterprise, for the trend of nationalization was towards totalitarianism. They cited likewise the costly failure of nationalization schemes in the Dominions, Belgium, and France.

The people were thoroughly disgusted with the Coalition's handling of the coal industry, in which every householder and most manufacturers were vitally interested. The Government was much criticized for its extreme solicitude for mine-owners and for allowing miners to be drafted, so that, in the face of a threatened coal famine, it was necessary to conscript untrained young men for the pits. Meanwhile the *New Statesman* described a new scheme for reorganizing the industry as "Coal Fascism," and the *Liberal Magazine* called it a "mirage." The miners, meanwhile, completed the organization of the National Union of Mineworkers, with a membership of 650,000 and a reserve fund of half a million sterling. In his Labor broadcast, Mr. James Griffiths claimed that private ownership had made a "tragic mess" of this industry, for since Justice Sankey's report in 1919 favoring its nationalization, 1,000 pits had been closed and 50,000 miners relegated to the scrap heap. Mr. Bevin likewise stated that the mines required very many millions of pounds for re-equipment, which would not "be forthcoming if the present ownership is retained." The coal output was declining and the number of skilled miners decreasing. Labor conceded that British output per manshift had risen only 14 per cent from 1925 to 1935 as compared with 118 per cent in the Dutch mines (mostly state-owned), but attributed the slightness of the increase to inefficient management. Between 1893 and 1913, Socialists asserted, coal profits had repaid the original capital investment in the mines three times over. When the Government announced a decrease in output and an increase in price of coal, Labor maintained that the only solution was control by a National Board staffed by experienced pit managers, technicians, scientists, workers, and consumers.

Public interest in housing was even more intense. The air war had left a considerable fraction of the English population homeless, perhaps half a million in the London area alone. Legal difficulties over land titles, conflicting jurisdictions of local and central authorities, and the question whether houses should be built by local authorities or private enterprise caused delays. Labor consequently accused the Government of employing every subterfuge to delay construction, contrasting Britain's dilatoriness with Russia's speed in rebuilding cities, and asked what had become of Mr. Churchill's promise to rehabilitate devastated areas as a war measure. Friendliness toward private enterprise, Socialists urged, explained the Government's failure to erect prefabricated houses. Even when they sought to do so, the *Observer* noted that contracts were so split up as to lose all the "low-cost benefits of mass production," and wages in American building trades were "two to four times higher than they are here, yet building costs, in relation to the general price level, are about the same." The Portal steel houses were given up, Labor insinuated, because they required six tons of steel, which would build several automobiles for export. Labor clamored in vain for legislation to control the rapidly rising prices of houses. The Government's program was so utterly confused that all the Caretakers dared promise, even during the election, was 220,000 houses completed in two years, which was cold comfort to poor people who had already passed through five winters and had a desperate, immediate need of more than a million homes.

Mr. Churchill never really sensed that housing was the one crucial issue, yet Miss Wilkinson asserted that "women voters especially would consider housing to be the acid test of party sincerity." In a Gallup poll on the most important political issue, 41% put housing first, 13% full employment, 7% social security, and 6% nationalization. The *Times* warned, ". . . in London housing is the foremost election issue." Two professors from Birmingham University Medical School published a report on infant mortality from 1928 to 1938, covering about one third of the English population. Among the classes that were well off, the mortality was 23 per 1,000; for over-crowded poor, 108; for unemployed, overcrowded poor, 158: a more timely or more potent campaign document could scarcely be desired.

With such personal issues at stake, many election meetings were stormy, but there was little violence. Conservative leaders soon

660 THE TWENTIETH CENTURY

realized that their campaign was lagging and sent the Premier on a grand tour through the Midlands, the North, and Scotland. Plans were made for a final gigantic rally of 50,000 in the London area. Only 20,000 showed up, many of them hostile; Mr. Churchill's temper was very short; so the Conservative canvass ended on a low note.

A moderate paper like the *Guardian* held Mr. Churchill and his counselors responsible for the bad tone of the election.

This election is the most hateful in recent memory because this great leader . . . turned himself into a party leader who catches at any device for winning votes . . . hinting that unless they give him a tremendous majority he cannot serve. . . . Wellington, . . . bitterly as he struggled against reform, always kept in mind his favourite formula, "the King's Government must be carried on."

The *Economist* agreed, and the *Observer* sadly commented that

it has seldom been the fate of a Tory Prime Minister to receive from the *Times,* on polling day, a rebuke for his irresponsible conduct of the election campaign.

Most political forecasters felt that the only doubt was as to the size of the Conservative majority. Optimistic Tories, the *Mail's* political correspondent reported, expected a majority of 150, the more sober-minded 50; the Communists anticipated a working majority for the combined Socialist-Liberal-"Splinter" group; Labor expected to win a great many Conservative seats, but not even a bare plurality; the Liberals hoped for 25 additional seats. The *Western Mail, Northern Whig,* and *Glasgow Herald* estimated the Conservative majority from 40 to 150. An *Express* survey reported a steady Conservative drift late in June, and its poll found that 37 per cent expected to vote Conservative, 37 per cent Labor, 17 per cent doubtful; of this group, however, 55 per cent thought the Conservatives would win, and 39 per cent Labor. The *Guardian* conceded that Labor's chances of a clear

majority "are pretty remote." The *News Chronicle* felt that probably "the Liberals may hold the balance." The *Herald* agreed with the *New Leader* that "the war-time glamour of Churchill" would gain for the Tories "a slight majority." One Gallup poll, sampling civilian voters in 195 constituencies, gave Labor 47 per cent, Conservatives 41 per cent, Liberals 11 per cent; a later Gallup poll showed Labor with 45 per cent, Conservatives 32 per cent, and Liberals 15 per cent. Mr. Beverley Baxter in the April *Maclean's,* a Canadian magazine, suggested not only that the Tories might lose 100 seats, but a possible Labor landslide.

The caution universally displayed was largely due to the many uncertainties as to the electorate, but two other factors were also involved. First, even if a party received a popular majority, it might not gain even half the seats. Second, these forecasts came before the polling in twenty-three Northern constituencies. Since these seats might well turn the tide, there was a parade of a galaxy of ministerial and other stars to the "Little" election.

For the first time the British people waited three weeks to hear the election results in order to get in the service vote, estimated at 2,000,000 out of a total electorate of over 32,000,000. There were weeks of great suspense everywhere. The Potsdam deliberations were practically suspended to allow Messrs. Churchill and Attlee to return home for the election returns, which were to be broadcasted over 150 American stations. The *Western Mail* declared that no election had ever aroused "such world-wide interest. . . . Every country wants to know what sort of Government the next will be."

The results were not only most surprising, but among the most decisive in British annals. Labor polled twelve and a quarter million votes and elected 400 members; the Conservatives had ten million, with 214 members; the Liberals two and a quarter million, and 12 members. Labor secured half of the votes and more than five eighths of the seats; the Tories two fifths of the votes and less than one third of the seats;

the Liberals about one tenth of the votes and less than one fiftieth of the seats. The "Splinter" groups gained only 3 seats. The Independents secured 400,000 votes and 10 seats.

Labor suddenly found itself in power, fortified by a majority of 160. The Liberals were almost extinguished as a party. The Conservatives were stunned and the Socialists jubilant. The Tories lost half their members and nearly all their first-rank ministers. Churchill was returned, but a politically unknown opponent, standing on an independent platform, polled 10,000 votes. Both his son and son-in-law lost. Twenty-seven Caretaker ministers went down, including 8 Cabinet members, and only 73 former M.P.'s are now included in the Opposition. Three outstanding Liberals failed, but practically every Labor leader came through triumphantly.

The press reaction was clear-cut. Even Beaverbrook's *Express* faced up to the shock with characteristic British stoicism:

A tidal wave . . . has submerged a great party in circumstances which cannot be matched in political annals. . . . A political debacle which will have the most profound and far-reaching effect upon the history of Britain and the world. . . . The watching world stands amazed, and the people of Britain themselves are bewildered at the wholesale change in personalities and policies.

The *Western Mail* termed it Socialism's "greatest victory," and the *Telegraph,* a "victory of almost unprecedented magnitude." The *Glasgow Herald* described the first reaction as one of "stupefied surprise." The *Northern Whig* asserted that "not since 1906 has there been anything comparable in British political life. . . . through the ballot box the British people have brought about a bloodless revolution." The *News Chronicle* referred to it as the "most exhilarating moment in the long history of the British Labour movement." The *Herald* quite naturally was in a highly expansive mood:

Democracy has won the day. That above all is the pure essence of the election result. . . . The performance of the British people . . . deserves to rank in history alongside the mightiest of their achievements. Ignoring every distraction, . . . they have proclaimed . . . their policy with an emphasis which will hearten the lovers of freedom and social justice throughout the Earth.

A London dockworker walked along an East End London street with a placard reading "This is our finest hour." The *Guardian* saw in the results the widest implications:

Britain has undergone a silent revolution. . . . It is the kind of progressive opportunity that comes only once in every few generations—in 1832, in 1868, in 1885, in 1906. Those were internal revolutions; this is part of the European revolution.

It was an emphatic protest against Conservatism, and it was nation-wide, including the black-coated proletariat, country folk, and even many squires. In Birmingham, the Chamberlain preserve, Conservatives elected only three of their dozen candidates. At Manchester, Labor wrested five seats from them; in Liverpool, eight of eleven members; and at Leeds, all but one. At Tyneside and Teeside, the Socialists won by large majorities and gained twenty London borough seats. In its old centers in the North East, London, Midlands, North West, and Wales, Labor secured some 75 per cent of the vote; in the Eastern counties south of the Humber, 55 per cent; in Scotland, 57 per cent; in the South and South East, 50 per cent; and even in the South West, 25 per cent. Labor is now, as never before, truly representative of all areas and of all classes.

Northern Ireland and the three English Universities resisted the swing to the Left. All five University seats were retained by National candidates. In Ulster, as usual, the main issue was the continuance of the Union. Excluding Belfast University, the

Conservatives elected nine of the twelve members.

The change in the composition of the House of Commons is deeply significant. The average for the three dominant groups in the seven elections between 1918 and 1935 was company directors, 139; lawyers, 137; trade union officials, 79. The services now elected 170 members; lawyers and trade union officials, 84 each. The greatest casualties were of company directors—only 54 survived. Journalism has its largest contingent—39, of whom 33 are Laborites. Thirty-nine miners gained seats, 20 doctors, 14 professors and lecturers, 9 engineers, 20 schoolmasters, 5 accountants, and 4 clergymen. Twenty-four women succeeded, 21 of them Socialists. Labor's representatives, hitherto largely trade union and Co-op leaders, are now widely diversified, only about a fourth having such affiliations. Over half of their M.P.'s come from the professional and middle classes. Although a younger group, it is one with broader bases of experience. Eton lost much of its control over the Commons, for the aristocratic element there suffered severely. The University of London and the provincial universities, however, have gained in political influence.

What occasioned this political earthquake? Of the many factors that entered in, five appear decisive. First, Mr. Churchill's arrogance, particularly his captiousness over the Laski episode. He failed, also, to support the Tory reform program. Except for one broadcast two years earlier, Churchill has been, to quote the *Economist,* "consistently contemptuous toward the need of reform." Second, the Conservatives had to fight on their diplomatic record, which included Munich. Third, the populace, especially the women, had waited patiently for the Coalition to remedy, among other things, the housing situation. Despairing of their sponsoring any strong social program, the voters turned to the Socialist solution—nationalization. Fourth, voters remembered how the Conservatives had tricked and terrified them in 1924, 1931, and 1935, and had rushed them headlong into elections in 1918 and 1924. Finally, Labor was never so well served by the press. In addition to the neutrality of the *Times, Observer,* and *Spectator,* the moral support of the *Guardian,* the aid of the Liberal *News Chronicle* and of the *Daily Mirror* tabloid, its cause was ably championed by the *Daily Worker* and *Daily Herald,* the popular Sunday papers, *Reynolds* and *News of the World,* and weeklies such as the *New Statesman, New Leader,* and *Tribune.* Cartoonist Low even poked fun at his own press lord employer.

The results should not have surprised the initiated. The by-elections before July, 1945, the rise of vigorous "Splinter" groups in the year and a half before the election, and the obvious popular distrust of the Government's dilatory tactics as to social reform were clearly revealed, as far as the popular vote was concerned, in Gallup polls. This victory was not, however, just a flash in the pan, as is shown by a continued Leftist trend in the local elections in November. The results were due to a decade of bitter reflection and intensive education by the Socialists. After sixty years the Fabian Society's policy of "intellectual osmosis" has produced, not only a victory, but a most decisive one.

THE LABOR PARTY HAD a relatively short history behind it. Although the industrial working class had grown rapidly during the course of the nineteenth century, working-class leaders had almost always been wary of founding a labor party. They preferred to work within the existing party framework, playing off

Liberals and Conservatives against each other. Even when, in 1900, the Labor Representation Committee was at long last formed in order to establish a distinct labor group in Parliament, it encountered widespread indifference and outright hostility. Relatively few trade unions were willing to affiliate themselves with it, the miners opposed it, the Marxist Social Democratic Federation quickly repudiated it, and many Fabians showed little enthusiasm for it. What saved the Committee was the Taff Vale decision concerning the suability of trade unions; and by 1906, when the Committee adopted the name "Labor Party," it numbered only twenty-nine members in the House of Commons. Yet if the Labor Party got off to an inauspicious beginning, it was able to form a minority ministry for the first time in 1924 and for the second time in 1929. Its greatest victory took place in 1945. Five years later the British electorate authorized it, if with considerably less enthusiasm, to remain in office. In October, 1951, however, after six years and three months of Labor governments, the Conservatives were returned to office—although with only a small margin in Parliament. In the following essay, which was written on the eve of the election of 1950, the late Professor Harold J. Laski, of the University of London, sketched the main currents in Labor Party history. A long-time member of the Executive Committee of the Party, Professor Laski knew much about its inner workings. He was one of the most controversial figures of his time. A man of strong prejudices, he aroused the wrath of numerous critics. But even his critics were compelled to recognize that along with his talent for invective went rare intellectual power.

THE FIRST FIFTY YEARS

HAROLD J. LASKI

The British Labor Party was born on February 27, 1900, in the Memorial Hall, Farmington Street, London, at a conference summoned by the Trades Union Congress of the previous year. Some of its members were notable men—Keir Hardie, Ramsay MacDonald, Bernard Shaw, Will Thorne, J. R. Clynes. Most of them were not Socialists, and the unions from which they came would not have joined the new party then formed if it had been given that complexion. Some of them were Tories, others were devoted followers of Gladstone, a few did not see that trade unions had political interests of any kind. But the Socialist group in the conference, led by Keir Hardie, knew what they wanted, were shrewd enough to realize the virtue of waiting, and, though from different groups, acted with a persuasive unity. An executive committee was set up, and Ramsay MacDonald, already widely known as a journalist of competence and a rhetorician with a voice like music, was chosen secretary without salary. Organizations could affiliate to the new party and nominate parliamentary candidates under its auspices; they must agree to abide by the decisions of the new party where working-class interests were involved but were free on other matters. The Labor Representation Committee had no doctrine; it was thoroughly respectable; and its income in its first year of life was just over two hundred pounds. Obviously, it had little to lose; perhaps it might have a world to win.

The Labor Party hardly began auspi-

Reprinted by special permission from *The Nation*, CLXX (February 25, 1950), 171-174.

ciously. In the "khaki" election of 1900 it sponsored fifteen candidates, of whom Keir Hardie alone was successful; the noise of the guns in South Africa drowned, even in trade-union ears, the harsh verdict of the Court of Appeal in the famous Taff Vale case, in which the judges hoped they had found a way to jeopardize the very existence of trade unions. But in the next four years the party won four by-elections, in one of which Arthur Henderson, who was to become its greatest organizer as well as the outstanding British Foreign Secretary of modern times, was sent to Parliament. At the general election of 1906 it profited from the great shift of British opinion to the left. Twenty-nine of its members were returned, including men like MacDonald, Clynes, Snowden, and Will Thorne, all of whom were to be great figures in its history for a generation or more; it could, moreover, usually count upon the support of twenty-five other trade-union members elected as Liberals. Arthur Balfour, the defeated Prime Minister, said at once that the Labor Party victories marked a new era in the history of Great Britain.

In the Parliament of 1906 the Labor Party did two things. It secured from the Liberal government the repeal by statute of the Taff Vale decision, which the House of Lords had upheld in 1901, and it gave national standing in the Commons not only to Keir Hardie but to MacDonald, Snowden, Clynes, and Henderson. Its policy was not very original—it accepted most of the doctrine and measures of the Liberal government. It did, indeed, take a firm stand for peace, and it was suspicious of the foreign policy of Sir Edward Grey. Socialist ideas were swiftly permeating the rank and file of its supporters, though a careful analysis of the attitude of MacDonald and Snowden would have shown that if they wore red ties, their shirts were the product of a Liberal factory. The Labor members, with occasional exceptions, did not really do much more than emphasize Liberal measures. Now and again, especially in the epoch of great strikes in 1911-12, when Winston Churchill first showed his natural attitude to trade unions by sending troops to shoot down striking miners in Tonypandy, South Wales, there was a vigorous outburst from a handful of members in which there was a recognizably Socialist note; and Keir Hardie, Snowden, and MacDonald, all protested vigorously against repression in India and Egypt. But it is on the whole true to say that up to 1914 most Labor M.P.'s could be described as Liberals emphasizing with 15 per cent more urgency the need to grapple with working-class questions.

The great turning point in the history of the Labor Party was the war of 1914. The larger part of the membership accepted it on the ground that German militarism was a threat to democracy, and of these Arthur Henderson was the chief; others opposed it, like Keir Hardie and Philip Snowden, either on pacifist grounds or because they thought it, in essence, an imperialist war. MacDonald took a somewhat ambiguous attitude: he criticized the policy of making war but wrote letters supporting the recruiting effort. The great achievement of Arthur Henderson, who had become the general secretary of the party, was that he maintained its unity, even though the two major groups were in fierce conflict. Partly through his influence the party, by a majority, decided to enter the first coalition government in 1915; and when in December, 1916, Lloyd George replaced Asquith as Premier, Henderson became the Labor member of the War Cabinet. But he did not remain there long. In February, 1917, the Russian Revolution began, and its complexities made the War Cabinet decide to send Henderson to Moscow to report upon the vast issues to which it gave rise. He returned convinced not only that the revolution must be safeguarded but also that all European Socialists should meet to see whether some common formula of peace could not be found. But Lloyd George and his other colleagues were insistent on unconditional surrender and emphatic that the Russian withdrawal from the war was a betrayal. After a decisive quarrel Henderson resigned—though with the party's approval other Labor men remained in office—and began to devote his gifts for organization to preparing the Labor Party for the outbreak of peace.

It was at this point that he found his great partner in the famous Fabian sociologist, Sidney Webb. In association with Webb, he persuaded the party to accept the new constitution of 1918, which with some minor changes remains the constitution today. They not only secured for the constitution the support of all the important trade unions and chief Socialist societies but gained the acceptance of the ideas, first, that every parliamentary constituency should have its local party, with both individual members and affiliated trade-union branches, and second, that the national party should boldly declare itself a Socialist party and make the acceptance of Socialist principles a necessary condition of membership. They then got the agreement of the reorganized party to a declaration of war aims which stands out still as one of the two or three most remarkable documents of the war, being built on the realization that the age of international organization had arrived and that national egotism, if written into the peace treaty, would sow the dragon's teeth of new wars. Thirdly, they secured acceptance of the famous document "Labor and the New Social Order," mainly written by Webb. There is still no better statement of the principles of democratic socialism; and it remains the foundation of all subsequent Labor Party efforts.

In the midst of these great achievements the election of 1918, skilfully maneuvered by Lloyd George as a tribute to himself before the war excitement had died down, was a disappointment; the Labor Party obtained only fifty-seven seats. But within a

year the tide began to flow the other way. In 1920, under the joint leadership of George Lansbury and Ernest Bevin—the latter had just emerged as a national figure —the Councils of Action were formed and succeeded in putting an end to the ugly policy of armed intervention in Russia, of which the Lloyd George Cabinet, including Winston Churchill, approved. Two years later the Tories separated from Lloyd George, and their leader, Bonar Law, became Prime Minister. In the general election which followed, all the well-known Labor leaders retained their seats, and with them came a famous group from the Clydeside, of whom James Maxton was the most beloved and John Wheatley the ablest figure. A number of these—Attlee, Greenwood, Shinwell, Sidney Webb—entered the House for the first time. With 142 seats, Labor became for the first time the official Opposition. Within a year Bonar Law was dead, and Stanley Baldwin had become Prime Minister. As a strong protectionist Baldwin dissolved Parliament in the hope that he could get a mandate for abandoning free trade. Labor members now numbered 191, and in conjunction with the Liberals they turned out the Baldwin government as soon as the new House met. On January 21, 1924, Ramsay MacDonald became the first Labor Prime Minister.

He had been elected leader of the party in 1922 by the solid vote of the Clydesiders, who believed that he held strongly left-wing Socialist opinions. That was a completely mistaken judgment. MacDonald was in fact an ambitious charlatan who clothed all his opinions in a mass of metaphysical rhetoric; he disliked the left, feared opposition, and was far too timid even to dream of embarking upon a determined program of Socialist legislation. He was vain beyond words and

STRESA FRONT: An attempt in 1935 on the part of Britain, France, and Fascist Italy to establish a common policy toward Germany. It grew out of the formal Nazi denunciation in March, 1935, of the disarmament clauses of the Versailles Treaty and the reintroduction of conscription. The three powers expressed their opposition to "any unilateral repudiation of treaties which may endanger the peace of Europe."

easily captured by the glamor of "society" in London. His government lasted just over ten months, during which Wheatley, as Health Minister, put through an admirable housing act and Ponsonby, the Under Secretary for Foreign Affairs, obtained, in spite of MacDonald, both the recognition of Soviet Russia and a promising trade treaty with its government. Then the Labor Ministry fell, over the issue of a withdrawal of proceedings for sedition undertaken against an ex-soldier who combined a fine war record with strong Communist leanings. MacDonald lied to the House about his part in the whole affair, made the question one of confidence, and when beaten secured a dissolution of Parliament. In the election, which the Tories won by the well-timed "discovery" of the Zinoviev letter, the Labor Party lost forty seats.

The new Tory government was to hold office for nearly five years. Baldwin made Winston Churchill his Chancellor of the Exchequer, and the latter, whose ignorance of economics was one of the most remarkable features of his political equipment, at once returned to the gold standard, with immense deflation as a result. This caused widespread unemployment and a general lowering of wages. The miners, betrayed in 1919 by Lloyd George over their claims for nationalization, were hit with particular severity. They refused to accept either an increase of hours or a decrease of pay. Mr. Baldwin bought them off for some months by a subsidy while his hand-picked Royal Commission reexamined the industry, reported against nationalization, and recommended a decrease in wages. The miners refused to accept this and appealed to the Trades Union Congress, which decided on May 1, 1926, to support them by a massive general strike. The economic life of the country was brought to a standstill for ten days. At the end of them, as the result of some curious half-official negotiations with Sir Herbert Samuel and the fear, whipped up by Sir John Simon, that the congress's action was both unconstitutional and illegal, the unions capitulated, though the miners

themselves, with typical courage, remained out for six months longer until they were beaten by sheer starvation. The Baldwin government took its revenge by passing the Trade Union Law Amendment Act of 1927, which, broadly speaking, was an English version of the Taft-Hartley Act.

Labor had its revenge in 1929, when the Tory government dissolved and went to the country with a slogan which consisted of Mr. Baldwin smoking a pipe and asking for the confidence of the people. It was not much to offer; and the electorate returned 289 Labor members—only twenty short of an absolute majority. Baldwin resigned, and MacDonald became Prime Minister, with Arthur Henderson, to the Prime Minister's chagrin, as his Foreign Secretary. Henderson's handling of the office was the one outstanding success the second Labor government, beset by its own lack of courage and the growing economic depression, could claim.

As unemployment grew, MacDonald set up an Economy Committee which reported in favor of large cuts, even in unemployment relief. When the Cabinet would not accept such proposals, he proposed resignation. He had long thought of coalition government as the way out of his difficulties, and he now, to most people's amazement, formed a new Cabinet for the purpose of "saving the pound." Baldwin and Sir Herbert Samuel entered this Cabinet; Snowden and Thomas, with fourteen other Labor members, followed MacDonald into the prison camp where he hoped to find peace. Twelve days later his "National Government" went off the gold standard it was intended to preserve, and knowing that there was no way back for him, he decided on a general election, the necessity of which he had denied a few weeks before. MacDonald gained an immense victory. Of the best-known Labor front benchers only George Lansbury, C. R. Attlee, and Stafford Cripps remained to lead the 56 who were left from 289. MacDonald remained the nominal Prime Minister until 1934, when

Baldwin took over the power that had, all along, been his. In the three years 1931-34, despite furious opposition from Labor and the loss of its Liberal members, the MacDonald government abandoned free trade, cut down all the social services, compelled a reduction in wages, and treated the unemployed as, in MacDonald's own word, "scrap." The Cabinet also turned away from Geneva and the chance of disarmament to the policy of the Stresa front, which led inexorably first to appeasement and then to the isolationism which came to full fruition later.

The Labor Party recovered only slowly from the crisis of 1931. At the general election of 1935 it returned 154 members, but the Tory power was overwhelming. When Neville Chamberlain succeeded Baldwin as Prime Minister in 1936, the Labor Party entered one of the unhappiest periods of its history. George Lansbury's absolute pacifism compelled his resignation of the leadership, C. R. Attlee taking his place. But the party had to watch helplessly while Chamberlain acquiesced, first, in the conquest of Abyssinia, then in Hitler's annexation of Austria, then in the hypocrisy of non-intervention in Spain. Chamberlain went forward, despite the resignation of Eden and the passionate hostility of Churchill, with pride and complacency to the disaster of Munich. Neither dissension nor denunciation could turn him from his goal, until in March, 1939, Hitler devoured the last remnants of Czechoslovakia and got ready for an attack on Poland. At long last, and too late, the Labor Party was able to lead public opinion in Great Britain to make continuation of appeasement impossible. Chamberlain made a last-minute and half-hearted effort to come to terms with Russia, but he was too late. His choice now lay between a super-Munich and a war to preserve what was left of freedom and democracy in Europe. The whole nation responded to the Labor Party's lead in the House of Commons. On September 3, 1939, Chamberlain was compelled to ask for a declaration of war against Germany in the worst possible conditions. By the following May his futility and incompetence were decisively shown in the failure of the Norwegian campaign. He sought earnestly Labor support; the party replied with emphasis that it would serve only under Winston Churchill as Prime Minister, and then upon the vital condition that it was a full partner. The Churchill government was formed, with Attlee as Deputy Prime Minister, Bevin as Minister of Labor, and Herbert Morrison, after a brief period at the Ministry of Supply, as Home Secretary and Minister of Home Security. If Churchill was the leader—and a great war leader—the debt he owed to his Labor colleagues was immeasurable. None but they could have won for him the confidence of the common people, and without that confidence he could not have become the architect of destiny.

After its famous victory in 1945 the history of the British Labor Party is too well known to require detailed analysis. It is more useful to sum up, on the eve of the election, the party's general characteristics.

1. It has become a genuinely national party. Though the trade unions remain an integral part of it, it has the support of the Cooperative Union and of members of all trades and professions. Its M. P.'s represent a good cross-section of the national life.

2. Though as in all political parties leadership counts for much, in no political party in Great Britain is the influence of the rank and file so clear or so obviously recognized.

3. The party is strongly democratic and has consistently refused to have any dealings with organized communism. It is Socialist, but its socialism has varied shades. Unity is achieved by the program of the party, which is laid down by the Annual Conference.

4. The members of the party in Parliament, though broadly bound by the policy of the conference, have a large freedom of maneuver in the House, whether in government or in opposition. They are, however, expected to consult the National Executive Committee; this last body, more-

over, controls the discipline of the party. Subject to the will of the conference, it indorses the nomination of candidates, may expel members of the party who refuse to accept its decisions, and decides whether or not the circumstances make it desirable to accept the task of government. The parliamentary party elects the leader of the party each session, but the program of the party for a general election is formulated by the National Executive Committee.

5. While the party has now a considerable staff of paid officials both in London and in the provinces, it relies for by far the larger part of its work on the voluntary efforts of individual members of local constituencies, among whom the women's sections make a particularly notable contribution.

Looking back on the last fifty years, one is struck by how the Labor Party, starting as a small group of trade unionists, Socialists, and cooperatives, has become the greatest Socialist party in Europe, strongly democratic, empirically rather than dogmatically internationalist. It is conscious of the reality of the class war but rejects the Marxian theory of a community which can only be made Socialist by a revolution to establish the dictatorship of the proletariat, which then, by repressing all opposition, passes into the classless society. Since 1917 it has sought with great energy to come to a full understanding with Russia, but the Kremlin, after a brief effort to achieve a united front, has shown little interest in the Labor Party, preferring to support the British Communist Party. At present this situation seems unlikely to change.

The inspiration of British socialism is a compound of various elements, some of which go back to the Great Revolt of 1381, others to the civil wars of the seventeenth century, others to the Chartist movement of the nineteenth century. It has by no means been uninfluenced by Marx and Engels, by Lenin, and even by Henry George. But the outcome is a peculiarly English one, and the tradition of progress by constitutional consent lies at its roots. That tradition would be difficult to destroy unless it were attacked by the power of wealth or threatened by a third world war. It suffers, probably, by its insufficient attention to Socialist philosophy, which makes it excessively empirical, and by its geographical position, which makes it excessively insular. But nowhere is there a party in which the spirit of fellowship is more profound and the reserve of practical wisdom more remarkable. It may still save Europe by its energy, as it is likely to triumph over the difficulties of its economic position. With all their faults its leaders are notable both for their integrity and their sagacity; its rank and file for their acute sense of fair play. It may lack any figure with the romantic dash and color of Winston Churchill, but it is at least aware that it has to operate in the twentieth and not in the eighteenth century.

THE ECONOMIC DIFFICULTIES THAT FACED the Labor government in the years after World War II were enormous. Although opponents of the Labor Party often attributed many of these difficulties to the fact that Labor was in power, it is almost certain that even if the Conservatives had won the election of 1945 things would have been much the same; economic problems would have been no less distressing. After all, the amount of physical destruction wrought during the war had been staggering. Hardly less significant, Britain's economic position in the world had altered considerably. It became all-important, therefore—no matter who controlled the government—to check inflationary tendencies at home and to send more goods abroad. Britons, as Sir Stafford Cripps expressed it, were not going to be able to "indulge in luxuries." What served further to complicate the economic situation in postwar Britain was the commitment of both major parties to programs of social-welfare legislation. However desirable in a social sense, these expensive programs would inevitably impose serious strains on an already heavily strained economy. It is remarkable, however, that despite the unpropitious economic conditions the Labor government was able to carry through one of the most momentous and far-reaching programs of peaceful reform in all of European history. In the following essay, Professor C. L. Mowat, now of the University of Chicago, discusses the British social scene as he saw it when he revisited his native land in 1947-1948 as a Guggenheim Fellow. Author of some excellent articles on recent British history, Professor Mowat has that rare combination of gifts: sympathetic insight and critical power.

A RETURN TO ENGLAND
C. L. MOWAT

North America puts on her best face for the traveler arriving by sea. England does not. The Statue of Liberty, the Golden Gate, the rock of Quebec, all announce to the traveler the grandeur and the promise of the continent he has come to. The approaches to England, being in character with the country, have little about them that is outwardly impressive; their setting is casual, matter-of-fact. As the ship rounds the Isle of Wight into the Solent and passes up Southampton Water, the views of park and woodland and open country begin to revive old memories: one had forgotten that grass could be so green. But Southampton, with its nondescript quays and customs sheds and tall cranes, is dispiriting at first sight. How small it seems, how drab and slow; how tiny the motor cars on the roads, the freight cars on the sidings, how feeble the high-pitched whistle of that diminutive switching engine. The focusing-down of one's vision has to be done and is done quickly, and one soon accepts things as they are and forgets the comparisons.

After this the country and people begin to take on a more attractive, hopeful appearance. Externally things seem little changed from their state before the war. The damage caused by bombing seems much less than one had expected, now that it has been partly tidied up. One even ceases to notice occasional gaps in terraces of houses, the occasional shell of a detached house or church; these seem to have suffered most from the incendiary bombs. Towns where several blocks in the center have been razed and the main shops exist in improvised or patched-up buildings or have moved to the suburbs—Bristol, Plymouth, Swansea, Southampton, Sheffield, Manchester, for example—have a sense of emptiness in the wounded parts, though one soon looks at crumbling walls, floors overgrown with wild flowers and bushes, half-exposed cellars and vaults, as one might look at ruins caused by Cromwell's cannon in the Civil Wars. The patchiness of the damage is striking; next door to the wilderness around St. Paul's and Moorgate in London are the busy streets of the city, eastward from the Bank and the Royal Exchange, unscathed.

The changes one notices are mostly for the better. People look well and well dressed,

Reprinted by special permission from *The South Atlantic Quarterly*, XLVIII (1949), 229-241.

particularly the children. Ill-clad children with dirty faces and runny noses are still to be seen on the poorer streets, but there are fewer of them. In spite of all protests at its extravagant demands of material, the "New Look" has conquered the women completely, much to the improvement of feminine appearance. Bare legs and bare heads are much more frequently seen than they used to be, even in churches; and the bare heads are usually more comely than the behatted ones.

The visitor is soon conscious of queues, and interprets them, according to his preconceived notions, as evidence either of the orderliness and patience of the British or of their docility and lack of spirit. At least they are thoroughly democratic. It is said that a government minister, seeing how much of the war damage at Buckingham Palace was still unrepaired, remarked to the King that he had been neglected. "Oh, I suppose my turn will come," was the King's reply. There are queues and queues. The bus queue is wholly admirable and equitable and can even be moderately comfortable under one of the many queue shelters built along the sidewalks. Queues outside shops are rare and usually short, unless it be outside a favorite cake shop or a Lyons tea shop in the lunch hour. Queues at railway stations exist in London and other large cities only at holiday seasons and are then necessary if regrettable. Those outside cinemas are often long and correspondingly depressing when one looks at the posters to see the fare which Hollywood is offering its patrons; in spite of recent difficulties, there has been little shortage of American pictures in Britain, though many being shown are quite old. Queues outside museums only exist when Princess Elizabeth's wedding dress, which is being shown all over the country, is on display; this is an interesting commentary on the sentimentality of the people and the warmth of their feeling for the Royal Family.

The queues in the Food Offices are sometimes long and tedious and more likely to rouse one's ire, particularly since the lesser components of the huge governmental machine are often maddeningly slow, rulebound, and uncivil; this is sometimes true also of the clerks in the post offices. But of the virtues of the rationing system, granted the unavoidable necessity of means to insure the fair distribution of limited supplies, there can be little doubt. It is, once its method is grasped, simple, quick, and almost automatic when one is dealing at the shops at which he is registered; the amount of food which the average family gets each week, particularly where there are young children, is adequate. Old couples living by themselves are the most seriously pinched for food unless they take some meals in restaurants. Children under five are best off, with a pint of milk a day at a low, subsidized price, cheap orange juice, and free cod liver oil—in fact they are, and rightly, given priority in many things; for older children the free school lunches serve a similar purpose. There is no doubt that the mass of the people is getting more and better food than before, a fact demonstrated by the figures for the consumption of milk: 1939, 108,300,000 gallons; 1947, 121,300,000 gallons. For most people the meat ration will only last one or two days each week, though it can be supplemented by fish. Milk (2½ pints per week for an adult) is apt to run short in many households. Oranges and bananas are obtainable from time to time, sometimes only for children; fresh fruit is often scarce during the winter. Rice is unobtainable; raisins, cornstarch, and olive oil are scarce; some families find the rations of sugar, bacon, cheese, fats, and tea insufficient. These are perhaps the most acceptable items in the food parcels from the United States, Canada, Australia, or elsewhere, which nearly every middleclass family seems to receive and for which it is unfeignedly grateful.

In restaurants, whether those serving lunch and dinner at the fixed price of two shillings and three pence or at the five shilling price limit, the food is often uninteresting—soup, some fish or some meat product liberally extended with "cereal filler," and stewed fruit or steamed pudding; tea remains a solid and often a good meal. The cheaper restaurants are as good as they were before the war if not better, the more expensive ones much poorer; neither are as bad as foreign critics like to imagine, though one objects to finding that a "steak" is whale steak, thin, tough, and not especially appetizing. In general there has been a considerable increase in eating out; partly, no doubt, because of the cheap and good meals provided by the "civic restaurants" run by the municipalities, the heritage of the wartime British Restaurants. "Morning coffee," taken in restaurants at eleven, seems to be a spreading habit.

Cigarettes and tobacco are rationed only "by the purse" and scarcity. The high tax, which puts the price of twenty cigarettes at three shillings and six pence and an ounce of tobacco at four shillings was intended to discourage smoking, which burns up scarce American dollars; it seems merely to have given the government an increased and lucrative revenue from an indirect tax which is politically innocuous. Most tobacconists have signs permanently up, "No cigarettes," but can often supply a regular customer from under the counter; pipe tobacco is seldom scarce. One's impression is that smoking has greatly increased, and the figures bear this out: the average monthly consumption was 15,840,000 pounds in 1938, 20,860,000 in 1946, and 18,720,000 in 1947. Beer is also heavily taxed, a pint costing anything from a shilling to one and six pence. It is not what it was—an age-old complaint. But "pubs" are as heavily frequented as before by women and men, young as well as old; the average monthly consumption of beer has risen from 2,080,-000 barrels in 1938 to 2,540,000 in 1947. Wines are controlled in price, usually around a pound a bottle; whiskey, when obtainable, is sold at a fixed price of thirty-three shillings and four pence a bottle.

The amount of inflation in the price of other things varies greatly. Most foodstuffs seem cheap by American standards, partly because of the subsidies paid by the gov-ernment, which are now costing some £470,000,000 a year. Thus butter costs one shilling and four pence a pound, and the week's ration of meat for one person (a shilling's worth) may comprise two small chops or a piece of quite tolerable steak. Many rents are still controlled and seem low; in any case rent has always taken a smaller part of the family's budget in Britain than in the United States. Clothes, shoes, furniture, seem to cost about three times as much as they did before the war, which brings them close to current American prices; but part of the increased price is due to the purchase tax, which is usually not stated separately on the price tag. This tax is 100 per cent of the value of luxury goods such as furs, new silver, cosmetics, and $33\frac{1}{3}$ per cent to $66\frac{2}{3}$ per cent on taxable household goods, furniture, clothing, stationery, and so forth; but utility furniture and clothes, of fixed and limited but satisfactory styles and materials prescribed by the government, are not subject to the tax and cost about one third as much.

To meet the increased cost of living there has been a great increase of weekly wage rates, the index of which now stands at 172 as compared with September, 1939. Average weekly earnings from most unskilled and semi-skilled jobs seem to be about 5 pounds. Salaries have risen similarly, if not by so much. It is generally agreed that the average working-class family is considerably better off than before the war, the middle-class family somewhat less well-off, and the wealthier classes very much less well-off. A recent study quoted by the *Economist* (August 21, 1948, p. 295) showed that the cost of living index had risen between 1938 and May, 1948 to 174 for a working-class family, 179 for the lower middle class, 180 for those in clerical positions, 182 for all persons on salary, and 198 for the upper middle class (1938 = 100). Working and middle classes alike can expect to gain from the comprehensive and universal National Insurance system and from the benefits of the National Health Service, inaugurated on July 5, 1948.

The former, however, involves for the average family a weekly contribution of four shillings and seven pence. Family allowances, paid by the government since August, 1946, provide five shillings a week for every dependent child after the first and may be claimed by every family, furthermore, many salaries, particularly academic ones, now include an addition for each child as a family allowance. What is important is that the cost of living has been fairly stable; one does not have the feeling that he is at the mercy of prices which are constantly increasing, with no check in sight. But there has been some increase in the last year: the official index for June, 1948, put it at 10 per cent for all retail prices and 13.5 per cent for food. Some consumer resistance to increased prices of shoes and clothes has been shown and resulted in August in the abolition of coupon values for shoes and the lowering of coupon values for clothes; many people felt, however, that it was not shortage of coupons, but shortage of cash which was slowing down sales. Ultimately this should mean a cutting of prices and so the advance of the policy of deflation which the government is cautiously pushing; but its success depends on how far additional wage increases can be averted in the interval.

The wealthier classes have certainly benefited least from the changes in standard of living since the war. The complaints some of them make of poverty sound rather hollow when set against the obvious comforts of their homes and the sort of clothes and holidays to which they can still treat themselves; nonetheless, their way of life is usually on a more modest scale than before, particularly in the matter of domestic service—or its absence. On the other hand, the "public" schools are crowded as never before, and the "prep schools" which prepare for them and which they often exceed in expense are enjoying a decided boom. Perhaps the unvarying explanation, "living on capital," is true, even if overworked. The midday crowd on Sunday in a fashionable "pub" in the outer suburbs of London still, as before the war, comprises an odd array of sporting types in loud checks, girls with fur coats, expensive dresses, and perhaps a pet dog; one cannot help wondering for what services to society they receive recompense on the high scale suggested by the amount they must spend on drinks during that social hour. Some of these people are leaving the country for South Africa or Rhodesia or Kenya, where cheap native labor still may permit a standard of domestic comfort long since forgotten in England. So, too, large amounts of capital are said to have been sent to South Africa for investment and safety.

Most people, of course, are content to travel less far; there seems to be much more traveling about in Great Britain than previously. Most of it is over short distances; indeed, there was some falling off of long-distance travel in the summer of 1948 as well as a decline in bookings of rooms in hotels and lodging houses at the seaside, an indication that people had less to spend than the year before and were more content with day trips for their holiday. Bus services in the towns are frequent, the fares low; the old penny minimum fare is now often a penny halfpenny, as in London, but the penny fare frequently survives; and in Aberdeen and Newcastle-on-Tyne, if not elsewhere, there are still halfpenny fares. Trams in many towns have been entirely or partially replaced by busses or trolley busses. These, mostly double-deckers, are modern, comfortable, and fast; it is characteristic of a national trait that passengers may bring dogs into them. The London "tubes" remain the marvels of smooth yet complex organization which they always were, even if more crowded and at times more stuffy. Country busses are frequent and crowded, so that one may often get left behind at an intermediate stop even when "reliefs" are run. Long-distance motor coach services and motor coach excursion trips of half a day, a day, or even a week or more are very popular. Trains are now nearly as frequent as before the war; the main line expresses are longer and more crowded and are gradually returning to their prewar speeds and punctuality; restaurant cars are still often lacking. Railway fares are 55 per cent higher than before the war; since bus fares have usually been raised very little, this puts the railways at a serious competitive disadvantage. Private cars are of course still much less widely used than in North America, and many were immobilized in 1947 when the basic petrol ration sufficient for 180 miles (later 270 miles) per month for nonbusiness purposes was abolished; it was reinstated for 90 miles per month in June, 1948, though with a measure of injustice for those with supplementary rations for business purposes, who were told that they could use part of their existing ration for driving for pleasure. Holidays on the Continent were popular in 1947 and were so again in the summer of 1948 after the ban on taking any money out of the country was lifted and travelers were permitted to take out thirty-five pounds. For the holiday-maker at home a new attraction is the Butlin holiday camps and their rivals. Butlin now operates several camps at seaside places in Great Britain and one in Ireland. Accommodation is in many small "chalets"; for an inclusive charge for the week, lodging, meals, and varied entertainment are provided; there are also nurseries so that parents can enjoy some freedom while on holiday.

One thing the frequent traveler will notice as a sign of the times is the number of young soldiers and R.A.F. men and women in the armed forces constantly traveling up and down the country by train—bored, sleepy, or whiling away the time, the girls, at least, by reading cheap novelettes and pulp magazines. One hears it frequently said that there is little or nothing for the men conscripted into the army or the R.A.F. to do; hence they are shifted from place to place and given long and frequent leaves; it may be so. One also occasionally sees an airfield with its large gleaming runways and scattered hangars laid out amid fields of grain or pasture; but these are fewer than might be expected.

Another thing the traveler cannot help seeing is the number of new houses under construction or finished on the outskirts of the towns, both large and small. Whole colonies of prefabs have sprung up, trim, compact, small, one-story structures of concrete or aluminum painted to look like stucco, and rather gay two-story versions, with a first floor of concrete supporting a wooden upper floor of a warm brown color. Internally, the one-floor prefabs provide a living room, two bedrooms, bathroom, and a kitchen which in design and equipment almost approaches American standards. While the shortage of houses is still serious, it is diminishing: it was estimated at the end of the war that 750,000 homes were needed; since then, to the end of June, 1948, 306,394 permanent houses had been provided by new construction and repair of those damaged in the war, and 152,627 temporary houses built.

Inside the average middle-class house the maidservant and "nannie" of former days are not likely to be found; on the other hand, very few such homes, even of young couples with relatively small incomes, are without some form of help, usually that of a woman coming in one or two mornings a week to do some of the cleaning. The housewife also has one or two more gadgets than previously to help her; if not a refrigerator or an electric mixer, perhaps a fairly modern gas stove and an "Ascot"— a miniature gas hot-water heater which is fixed above the sink and provides hot water for washing dishes. Older traditions of deferential service, of being lavishly entertained and waited on hand and foot, may survive in the houses of the wealthy, as they do in the London clubs, in the dining rooms which some firms maintain in their factories for the executive staff, and, in a somewhat attenuated form, in the colleges at Oxford and Cambridge.

One reason why domestic service is scarce is that women now find employment in many more jobs than before the war; the total number at work has increased from 5,094,-000 to 5,721,000; during the war the figure was a good deal higher. There are many in the factories, though very few are now left in the machine shops; others are working on the land in the Women's Land Army; others are in the armed services. On the railways they serve as clerks and ticket collectors and as station announcers, often with annoyingly exaggerated diction; also as porters, guards, and occasionally as signalmen. On the Underground in London several of them, in unbecoming grey cotton slacks and overalls and with strident voices not unlike the men's, act as lift operators and station announcers. As bus conductors women of all ages, often addressing passengers male and female as "dearie" or "love," are very frequently met with.

One notices other things. During 1947 many German prisoners of war were still to be seen in the villages and country towns and in London enjoying a respite from farm work; by the summer of 1948 all had gone home. Many Poles have settled in England and Scotland and entered business and the professions; in certain parts of London one hears foreign languages spoken more than English. Newspapers are still very small— four or eight pages; but the reduction in size is mainly at the expense of advertisements rather than of news columns and features. Weekly and monthly periodicals are numerous and sought after, and several new ones have appeared. Many textbooks are very scarce, but of other books, old and new, there is little scarcity, though small printings often make some particular book hard to get. Prices have increased less than is the case with other articles, and the cheaper books like the excellent Penguin series and its numerous progeny (once sixpence, now thrice that price) are bought in very large numbers.

BBC broadcasts serve for many in place of magazines. By American standards the programs would perhaps be thought too highbrow, with a large amount of time given to talks on literary subjects, to concerts of classical music, to plays and dramatizations. This is true of the Home and Light programs, even more of the new Third Program

(6:00 P.M. to midnight), of which a typical day is: 6:00 P.M., Chamber Music; 7:00, The Search for Nature (news of recent writings on field natural history); 7:20, Interlude; 7:30, concert by Concertgebouw Orchestra from Edinburgh Festival; 8:25, Trout Poaching (a talk); 8:40, Concert (continued); 9:30, The Rise of Christianity (discussion between the Bishop of Birmingham, Dr. Barnes, and a canon of Durham); 10:20, organ music by Bach; 10:50, Pompeii (talk on a recent visit to the excavations); 11:05, Interlude; 11:10, Piano solo, Schumann, "Carnaval," Op. 9; 11:40, The Muse in the Nursery (discussion on the interest of contemporary novelists in the child mind). Interludes during that week in the latter part of August, 1948, were taken up with prose readings from Jane Austen's works. A regular weekly feature is "The Critic on the Air," when a critic reviews recent dramatic productions of the Third Program itself.

The BBC announcers, in the main, use a less exaggerated Oxford accent than used to be the case. The BBC is no longer afraid of local variations of accent; in fact, it welcomes them. Witness the success of Mr. Ralph Wightman with his delightful, robust Dorset speech, announcing the program "Country Magazine," in which a group of people, from a different village each week, talk of their lives in an entirely natural and authentic way. Programs do not seem to be harried by time; if there are two or three minutes to spare, a pause of silence is announced and occurs unless it is filled in by a recording of the typically English music of change-ringing on a peal of bells.

At first, certain expressions sound strange. In 1947 every other person, it seemed, was a "spiv," a word of uncertain derivation denoting someone who lived on the black market or prospered in some other parasitical fashion. The war left a legacy of expressions: "You've had it," i.e., lost your chance; and the bored avowal of indifference, "I couldn't care less."

Many towns may look rather shabby, but few show need of paint as much as London, whose predominant stucco, at the mercy of the smoky atmosphere and frequently peeling, is particularly in need of attention. Nothing will much brighten the streets of small, working-class houses—continuous rows of boxlike, two-story houses of brick or stone, flush with the sidewalk and, in the North, frowning at each other across a road paved with stone setts. But one feels there is life and vigor pulsing through the towns, particularly in the North, where cheerfulness and civility, for example from bus conductors, are commoner than in the South. All the towns have the old, familiar smells from the grocer's, the baker's, the greengrocer's, the fishmonger's, and the butcher's shop, where the meat hangs in the open window or lies on the broad chopping block or counter. Other shops—drapers, shoe shops, hardware shops, furniture stores—now give the appearance from their windows of being well stocked, though often they do not have just what one wants, such as choice of shoes in one's particular size. Horse-drawn vans are still common in London and elsewhere and are used in considerable numbers by the railways and the brewers; a rubber-tired, horse-drawn postal van in the customary scarlet hue is a common sight in London. In the country tractors are now very much in evidence. The curiously shaped concrete cooling-towers, resembling gigantic milk bottles, of the electricity generating stations are a new feature of the horizon outside many of the larger towns.

In the summer, indeed all through the year, outdoor life is more popular than ever. There are long lines of eager bicyclists of both sexes, sparsely clad, crouching over their low handlebars; there are hikers crowding the Youth Hostels; there are throngs on the beaches in the summer. Public parks and open spaces in the towns are crowded on a Saturday afternoon or a Sunday, when innumerable cricket matches or football games are played, model airplanes flown, or model yachts sailed. Regattas, flower shows, cattle shows, sheepdog trials, church fetes, and bazaars still beguile the holidaymaker and the inhabitants of the countryside.

Scotland still preserves most of the marks of a country distinct from England. Speech is different, and in the western Highlands and islands, where Gaelic still has great vitality, language also. If shortbread and bannocks are less abundant, baps (soft rolls), pancakes (drop scones), and small cakes still make the tea table much more festive than in England. Sunday is more strictly observed and the churches well attended, some of the older men still going in their morning coats, while in the Highlands several of all ages may be wearing kilts. The correspondence columns of the *Scotsman* and other papers show the continuing interest in doughty sectarian controversies and in the exposition of points of religious belief. There is also the feeling that Scotland deserves to have more of its own government in its own hands through a real measure of devolution; but the Scottish nationalist movement, with more radical demands, makes little headway.

What of the future? The political temperature is low in England, and a year which produced great events and decisions did not produce great debates and searching of hearts. The Empire diminished in size, the Indian Empire came to an end; the mandate for Palestine was surrendered; Burma won its independence. In Europe the conflict between the Western Powers and Russia over the future of Germany grew sharper and, in Berlin, led almost to a state of siege. The tightening of Russia's control over the countries of eastern Europe was shown by the establishment of the Cominform, the denunciation of Tito and his regime in Yugoslavia, and above all by the coup in Czechoslovakia in March, 1948. An act continuing military conscription in Britain in peacetime was passed. Yet all these things caused little stir in the newspapers and less discussion in the average home or in talk between friends over the lunch table or by the fireside. No wonder that the beginning of the "Western Union" made by Great Britain, France, and the

Benelux countries was equally little noticed.

The same lack of strong interest and violent partisanship is apparent in domestic matters. The economic crisis is serious enough in all conscience, with the gap between imports and exports continuing to be very wide; but the crisis is not dramatic. It is hard to make people believe the message of the government's posters, to be seen on every billboard in the winter of 1947-1948, "We work or want," when everyone is at work, food is obtainable in the shops, and many people are better off than they were before the war. Marshall aid is gratefully received; what things would be like without it is hardly understood. So, too, with the measures of the Labor Government: nationalization of coal mining, the railways, and electricity; the extension of National Insurance and the inauguration of the National Health Service; even the intention to nationalize part of the iron and steel industry and the consequent introduction of the bill to reduce the power of the House of Lords to delay legislation—all these things naturally cause more bitter feeling among the government's opponents than enthusiasm among its supporters, but neither feeling is really very strong. Positive achievements which are less controversial are received with equal indifference: the number of houses built, the remarkable increase in exports, freedom from black markets and from serious inflation, the small number of strikes, and the smoothness of the whole great transition from war to peace.

Perhaps this is the product of apathy, of numbness, of a shocking indifference to the things that matter. Perhaps it is the highest sanity and good sense to accept in so matter-of-fact a fashion the events of a postwar era which is confused, disillusioned, and without glamour. If the future is dark, thinking makes it no less so; therefore, do not think about it too much; do not talk about an unthinkable war; do not double the anguish of war by worrying as much over its possibility as one may have to over its actual tribulations; instead, get on with the job at hand. The trouble is that even this immediate and limited task is tackled with less than full energy in such an atmosphere. It is universally said that people do not work as hard as they used to, and incentives to increase production are hard to find.

But for the visitor this state of low tension, the absence of war talk, the feeling of being relaxed, calm, and leisurely is very pleasant. There is still the quiet loveliness of the countryside, the charm of old streets and houses in the country towns and villages, the civilized life of the larger towns, where good plays can be seen and good concerts listened to almost throughout the year; there is still the simple hospitality and the cultivation of good talk in many a home. In these days these are things to be thankful for and to enjoy.

THROUGH MOST OF THEIR MODERN HISTORY the articulate elements in British society were far more concerned with political liberty than with democracy. In fact, as compared with other European countries, Britain was remarkably slow in achieving one of the essential elements of democracy—universal manhood suffrage. As early as 1792 the election of the Convention in France was authorized on the basis of universal manhood suffrage; and again in 1848 the French attained universal manhood suffrage as a result of revolution. Universal manhood suffrage also came relatively early in central Europe. In Britain, on the other hand, agricultural workers were not enfranchised until the passage of the Reform Bill of 1884, and even then several categories of male adults still lacked the right to vote. Bachelors who did not maintain separate dwellings, for example, won the franchise only with the enactment of the Reform Bill of 1918. It is striking, however, that in the very years when universal manhood suffrage was in the process of being attained in Britain complaints were raised that without economic and social democracy political democracy was inadequate. In the essay that follows, Professor Carl F. Brand, of Stanford University, author of the valuable monograph *British Labor's Rise to Power* (1941), discusses the expanded meaning that democracy has taken on not only for Laborites but for Conservatives and Liberals. The essay itself was Professor Brand's presidential address before the Pacific Coast Branch of the American Historical Association.

DEMOCRACY IN GREAT BRITAIN

CARL F. BRAND

For some time the British have used the word "democracy" freely and approvingly, but normally with political democracy in mind. They have been justly proud of their government so flexible and responsive to public opinion, a system under which the liberty of the individual has been cherished and the right of opposition not only tolerated but recognized as essential to the constitution. Evidently political democracy alone does not suffice, however, for they are today engaged in experiments so far-reaching and fast-moving as to warrant the term "revolutionary." They have a bearing upon the interpretation of democracy for, to a degree hitherto unknown, the British are reading equality and fraternity into it: they speak now of social democracy, of economic democracy, and of democracy in industry.

A recent letter from an English school inspector reveals the character and speed of changes there:

Yesterday in Sunderland a great car with a chauffeur crossed my path. Behind was sitting a uniformed nurse and a little child. I wondered what great industrialist owned the equipage. I was wrong. My companion said it was the school nurse, a municipal car, and some unknown child (so far as we were concerned). It gave me quite a shock to realise how out of date my first surmise had been!

Well might this observer wonder at the sight, because to an extent without precedent does the future of a British child fail to depend upon birth and wealth. Remnants of feudal classes have long survived in Britain, their numbers recruited from and their position strengthened by the successful oligarchs of commerce, finance, and industry. There the terms "lady" and "gentleman" have denoted class distinctions. The social distance has been great between master and servant, officer and private, church and chapel, public school and board school. A century ago Disraeli complained that England was inhabited not by one nation but by two. Political power, graceful living, and cultured society were the prerogative of one, deference and subserviency the lot of the other. The latter was composed mainly of the working classes, alternatively "the poor," who accepted their status with as little thought of changing caste as they did of copying the accent of the ruling class. Although a detailed analysis might modify these generalizations somewhat, as recently

Reprinted by special permission from *Pacific Historical Review*, XIX (1950), 113-126. The footnotes which originally appeared with this essay have been omitted.

as 1913 Ambassador Page could write:

> To an American democrat the sad thing is the servile class. Before the law the chimney sweep and the peer have exactly the same standing. They have worked that out with absolute justice. But there it stops. The serving class is what we should call abject. It does not occur to them that they might ever become—or that their descendants might ever become—ladies and gentlemen.

If Page could have lived a few years longer to see coal miners in the Cabinet, trade unionists on boards governing major industries, and ex-laborers in the House of Lords, he would have been as startled as was the inspector in Sunderland at the sight of the great car socially owned and democratically used.

It is common knowledge that in spite of some monarchical decoration Great Britain is structurally a democratic republic, but few realize the relative newness of popular control. Nineteenth-century enthusiasts for Anglo-Saxon freedom read far too much democracy into Tacitus' account of primitive Germanic oligarchy, and failed to understand the limitations upon the freemen of King Alfred, who were so bound to lords that they did not have liberty of movement. Others noted that the later Middle Ages created some valuable institutions such as local juries and a central representative assembly, but in spite of the fact that they provided invaluable political training for some classes and ultimately became instruments for the people to use, they were originally tools of those in power and not intended for the hands of political democrats.

Some true democrats did exist in the seventeenth century when the victorious Roundheads were confronted with the task of remaking England's government, and in the effort drew upon their century-old experience of self-government in their nonconformist churches. Cromwell's army of thinking men contained Levellers with a very modern outlook. British Labourites today take as a text the words Colonel Rainborough uttered just over three hundred years ago: "The poorest he that is in England hath a life to live as the greatest he." They act upon the principles of philosopher James Harrington who pointed out the dependence of political equality upon economic equality. Even communists can find some antecedents in the tiny group of Social Levellers, although the ideas of the latter were rooted in religion and humanitarianism, and not in economic theory.

Seventeenth-century radicalism was premature, however, so that well into the nineteenth century Britain continued to be an oligarchy. The dominant political philosophy was found in Burke who said that property must be protected against numbers, in Lecky who scorned democracy as the rule of ignorance and incapacity, and in Walter Bagehot who dreaded political combination in the lower classes as an evil of the first magnitude.

It was barely a century and a half ago that the current of democracy set in that swelled into the high tide of today. The new proletariat of the industrial revolution demanded the suffrage, and in its trade unions, friendly societies, coöperative societies, and nonconformist churches both received training in the democratic process and proved its capacity for it. Middle-class reformers desired an electorate that would produce a better parliament. Religious dissenters wanted political power in order to achieve religious equality. Finally, even the British women demanded the vote. The result was the well-known series of acts which made Britain into a political democracy. In 1948, just three hundred years after Colonel Rainborough, the Labour government's Representation of the People Act abolished the dual vote and made parliamentary constituencies practically equal. In elections the voice of "the poorest he" is now of equal weight with that of "the greatest he."

In this evolution of democracy the role of British Conservatism should be noted.

While Conservatives have clung to what they deem to have been proved good and insisted that the case for experiment be fully demonstrated, they have neither set up insurmountable obstacles to change nor fully mobilized their power to prevent it. Seldom has an appreciable minority assumed a "die-hard" position. On the contrary, much of the initiative has come from Conservatives. Certainly the bill of 1867, the first real step in democracy, owes a great deal to Disraeli. Conservatives as well as their rivals can claim credit for the bill of 1884, the popularizing of local government, and for the extension of democracy throughout the empire. Conservatives have not been Bourbons. From the time of Sir Robert Peel they have accepted accomplished changes and proceeded to make them work. It suggests that, if the Conservatives win the next general election, they will undertake no counterrevolution, even though a reverence for tradition may result in the restoration of the university seats. Political democracy, in spite of its relative novelty, is evidently secure in Great Britain.

Today, however, political democracy is not enough. Social equality is a goal. This aspiration has a history, too, for it was heard faintly from John Ball during the Great Revolt of 1381, more loudly from the Levellers, significantly from the early nineteenth-century Owenite socialists, and now insistently from the British Labour party. In this connection, although British socialism has long been egalitarian, the communist definition of democracy and its reported practical applications in Russia have not been without influence on the British labor movement. In 1918 Sidney Webb wrote his concepts into *Labour and the New Social Order,* which declared for the maintenance of a national minimum standard of living and for the sharing of the nation's income by all its members. By accepting this program the Labour party became avowedly a social democratic one.

Labour's ideal would be to achieve equality of opportunity and equality of status, that is, equal rights and duties for all citizens. It would find no place for anyone merely because of wealth or inherited position. Its practical aspiration is for a relative equality and not an absolute one, however, as is manifest in an official statement of April, 1949, called *Labour Believes in Britain:*

> We believe that inequality of opportunity and gross inequality of wealth are both morally unjust and economically crippling. We have set out, therefore, to establish equality of opportunity for all and to abolish extremes of wealth and poverty.

This statement obviously contemplates differences in incentives and rewards and not rigid uniformity, although some voices, such as that of G. B. Shaw, have been heard in favor of equal incomes. The British so-

---

BEVERIDGE REPORT OF 1942: Most famous of the plans for social security drawn up during World War II. Issued by a committee under the chairmanship of the Liberal Sir William Beveridge, it urged that further steps be taken to combat distress arising from unemployment, sickness, disability, and old age; it recommended the adoption of a system of children's allowances and of health service for the entire population; and it suggested that the government assume responsibility for the maintenance of full employment.

WHITLEY REPORTS: Reports dealing with the relations of employers and workers that were issued, starting in 1917, by a committee under the chairmanship of J. H. Whitley. As a result of the reports, the Ministry of Labor was authorized to establish boards to deal with labor problems wherever wages were sweated or trade unions feeble. Furthermore, a number of Joint Industrial Councils were set up on the principle of workers' representation, and workers' representation was extended to some government offices.

cialist expects to compensate exceptional intelligence and productivity, but intends to abolish great inequality of wealth or income and with it the attendant class distinctions. The practical goal is a broad and genuine social equality with a range of difference not so great as to bar the achievement of a spirit of fraternity in the nation and the possibility of fellowship among its members.

Among the tools of the modern social levelers are taxation of incomes and wealth and redistribution of the proceeds through the social services. Although Labour did not originate these methods, it has become their chief exponent. Due to high taxation there are now only 250 people in Britain with an annual income of over £5,000 as compared with 11,000 before the war. The estate duty on inheritances, rising to 75 per cent in the case of those over £2,000,000, is ending a major source of inequality. The nationalization program lessens the opportunity for new concentrations of wealth. Expenditure on public services, national insurance, education, family allowances, and food subsidies has provided a social wage averaging two pounds fifteen shillings a week for a family of five, a factor which has appreciably elevated the position of the less fortunate members of society. Housing measures, food control, and full employment have helped in leveling up, so that poverty in the old sense has been banished from Great Britain. The formerly wealthy minority is less well off, but so are the pawnbrokers, for a third of those who a decade ago flourished at the expense of the poor have recently gone out of business. In spite of wartime shortages and postwar austerity, the Webbs' ideal of a national minimum has been realized, and that with a rapidity which warrants the term revolutionary. Once Beatrice Webb said, perhaps too pessimistically, that it required thirty years for a reform to travel from royal commission to statute book. Could she have lived a few years longer, she would have been amazed at the speed with which the bulk of the Beveridge report of 1942 has been legislated and implemented.

Although the new Labour party today is the most ardent exponent of social democracy, the Conservative party has a long tradition of social reform which goes far to account for its present outlook. Many of the nineteenth-century social reformers were Tories and Conservatives, such as Thomas Carlyle, the Earl of Shaftesbury, William Wilberforce, and Benjamin Disraeli, who stirred Britain's conscience on conditions in factory towns and in mines at home or on slavery abroad. In many respects they were actually closer to the masses and more understanding and sympathetic than were the Liberals. It was Disraeli who as prime minister, 1874-1880, enacted social legislation that set precedents for our century, for he not only remedied grievances, as Conservative Sir Robert Peel had done before him, but also, as in the Artisans Dwelling Act, he used the state positively and constructively in a manner that was new. This tradition was continued as the Tory Democracy of Lord Randolph Churchill. Such men were neither political democrats nor social levelers, however. The equalizing tendencies of their policies were not designed to destroy the class structure and produce equality.

The tradition of social reform, nevertheless, early in the present century facilitated Conservative acquiescence in the social aspects of the Lloyd George legislation. During the Conservatives' two decades of power between the wars it enabled them to take such long steps forward that some now speak of Tory Socialism in the same tone that an earlier generation referred to Tory Democracy. Upon their return to power after the war of 1914-1918 they did not repeal the Lloyd George legislation, but on the contrary enormously expanded it. Few realize that Britain's great social program, as it stood on the eve of the last war, was mainly the result of Conservative legislation, but such was the fact. In a recent statement of party policy, *The Right Road for Britain* (July, 1949), it requires three pages to list the Conservative-sponsored acts for insurance for pensions, unemployment, and health; for workmen's compensation, family allowances, housing, education, school meals, and maternal and child welfare. British Toryism has adhered neither to a theory nor practice of laissez-faire.

Today most Conservatives support equality of opportunity. They point with pride to the Education Act of 1944 as mainly theirs. They advocate the use of the taxing power to eliminate the extremes of poverty and wealth. Like the Webbs, they urge the policy of a national minimum, for *The Right Road for Britain* states:

> The Social Services are no longer even in theory a form of poor relief. They are a co-operative system of mutual aid and self-help provided by the whole nation and designed to give to all the basic minimum of security, of housing, of opportunity, of employment and of living standards below which our duty to one another forbids us to permit anyone to fall.

In both content and tone this statement holds something of fraternity as well as equality. Were Disraeli alive today, he would say that R. A. Butler and Quentin Hogg, inheritors of his tradition, were striving to heal the division of England of which he complained and achieve the ideal of one nation there.

The dominant social outlook in Conservatism today has enough in common with Labour that a lifelong member of the latter party could recently change sides, because of differences on another issue, but assert that in *The Right Road for Britain* were the social objectives for which he had always fought. Conservative party managers, seeking a strong tactical position for the next general election, have complained that there are not enough differences to provide good talking points, and the Liberals have been quick to assert that "Tory Socialism" does not present the country with a real alternative to Labour.

By the road of social reform the British Liberal party, likewise, has taken long steps toward social democracy, but it was harder for its members to set foot upon it than it was for Conservatives of the Shaftesbury-Disraeli tradition. As nineteenth-century Liberalism was the political expression of laissez-faire, those who listened to Richard Cobden and John Bright, read Herbert Spencer, and supported W. E. Gladstone sought to remove the state from the sphere of economics. There was a hint of the future in the radicalism of Joseph Chamberlain, but the transformation of Liberalism came only after the turn of the century. Then, due partly to awakened conscience and partly to a desire to cut the ground from under the newly formed Labour party, the Liberals followed Lloyd George and Winston Churchill in important social legislation. Some of the acts had precedents in earlier Conservative ones, but others were new in principle. All used the state as the agency to improve the condition of its poorer citizens.

Although this party soon lost power and today holds the allegiance of only a tenth of the electorate, its leaders are not without influence and their ideas are worth noting. In recent years they have gone far beyond Lloyd George in their intolerance of extremes of wealth and poverty and in the ideal of equality. In the election of 1945, Liberal candidates stressed the obligation of the state in such matters as social security and housing in a way that would have been unthinkable in the nineteenth century. The economics of Lord Keynes, a twentieth-century Liberal, would have been incomprehensible to Cobden and Gladstone. Significantly, when Lord Beveridge, author of the "cradle to grave" social program, sought a political home, it was the Liberal party which triumphantly received him. A president of the National Liberal Federation, Eliott Dodds, recently rejected the former concept of individualism as atomistic, selfish, and isolationist, and redefined it as self-development in coöperation. In spite of continuity of the party label, accordingly, on social democracy the Liberalism of today is poles apart from that of the last century.

This brief examination of programs reveals that on greater social equality the three parties have much in common. While none expects an absolute uniformity, all would establish a minimum standard of living on as high a level as possible and all would utilize the state in this redistribution of national income and wealth. All would add to the "social wage" through the social services, and the present eagerness of all parties to claim credit for the national health scheme would indicate that the newer services are here to stay. The greater danger to them is not from within, but from without, because a world economic crisis might diminish many of them as the dollar problem has already affected a few.

In the current discussion of democracy in Britain the frontiers of that concept are also being extended to include economic democracy and democracy in industry. All parties have shown an interest, but Labour has taken the lead. It regards the concentration of economic power as incompatible with democracy. As in the seventeenth century Harrington saw a relation between land ownership and oligarchy, so today Labour fears a plutocracy resulting from concentrated control of industry.

Labour's remedy is, in part, the socialist one of public ownership. Its 1945 program demanded nationalization of coal, the Bank of England, gas and electricity, telecommunications, inland transport, and iron and steel—measures which would affect about 20 per cent of British industry. This program has been written into legislation. In 1949, the party's annual conference, looking forward to a general election in 1950, did call for the addition of a few minor industries to this list, but it emphasized the desirability of a period of development and consolidation, while working parties of employers, workers, and government nominees representing the general public would continue to investigate the problems of individual industries.

With Labour this solution is experimental and each step is taken with Fabian gradualism. If a remedy does not work, another will be tried. If successful in these tests, nationalization will doubtless be pushed further where industries are basic for British economy or defense, monopolized by trusts, inefficient, or suffering from very bad industrial relations. Nationalization is not an inevitability for the whole of British industry, however, or possibly even for a major portion of it. According to *Let Us Face the Future,* the 1945 program, many small businesses are not in question as they do not convey the threat implied in bigness. The co-operators, highly important in the labor movement, demand, and are promised, a place for their activities. Municipal enterprise is encouraged. Even where the state steps in, no uniformity is contemplated. As in watch manufacturing, the state may content itself with ownership of capital equipment without assuming responsibility for operation. It may take over certain plants, while the main part of an industry will be left in private hands, or as with inland transport, those proportions may be reversed. This experimental and pragmatic view of nationalization is emphasized in a pronouncement of 1948: "Nationalization is not a rigid concept, and we should, in accord with the British tradition, welcome variety of method." The Labour party, accordingly, envisages a mixed economy for Great Britain, with the extent of state control a matter for democratic decision.

The idea of democracy in industry is at least as old as Robert Owen, who urged the trade unions to replace capitalist and entrepreneur by taking over both ownership and management. Under his inspiration many small associations of producers were started but they usually failed when trade slackened. Early in the present century syndicalism appeared among the workers, while guild socialism, expounded in the *New Age,* a weekly, and in G. D. H. Cole's *Self-Government in Industry,* had some following among the intellectuals. The only practical outcome was the Whitley report, which led in 1918 to the establishment of some consultative councils.

Today the demand is real, though not

clearly defined, and the emphasis has shifted from workers' control to workers' participation. This may be due in part to the sobering effects of power, and in part to the failure of attempts at workers' control in Russia, Mexico, and Czechoslovakia. In 1944 the Trades Union Congress Interim Report on Postwar Reconstruction dissociated the unions from the idea of control, as they preferred to keep their independence and to leave responsibility with Parliament as representative of the community. Later pronouncements, including *Labour Believes in Britain* (1949), have stressed the desirability of fuller consultation. They have pointed to the existence of a National Production Advisory Council for Industry, the boards controlling nationalized industries, development councils, pit committees, and works councils, on all of which labor has been represented. They have called for the extension of this system until every worker has the opportunity to become fully informed about the establishment in which he is employed, to contribute suggestions for its improvement, and to share the responsibility for the way in which his work is conducted. At the Labour party conference of June, 1949, the railwaymen did revive the old syndicalist position on control, but the miners expressed the dominant view of preference for consultation. The Labour executive stressed their responsibility to the community:

> If we are a Socialist body, we ought to realise that we have to make nationalised industries work with efficiency, with justice to the workers but, in particular, in the interests of all the people in the country and not necessarily in the interests only of the workers employed in those industries.

Modern Conservatives, especially their younger spokesmen, manifest hardly less interest than Labourites in economic democracy, and there is considerable overlap in their positions. As this party never rooted its principles in laissez-faire, it does not balk at planning. Says Quentin Hogg in *The Case for Conservatism:* "Conservatism teaches that economic life can be just as much the subject of conscious and deliberate planning in the sense of conscious and intelligent shaping of events as foreign policy or military strategy."

Under Conservative planning the role of the government would ordinarily be confined to the prescription of general objectives and to supervision, but it could become more directly involved if necessary. It was Conservative governments significantly that nationalized broadcasting, created the electric grid, and nationalized coal royalties, and by setting up a public corporation for the B.B.C. the Tories furnished Labour with a model followed in the case of the London Transport Board and most of the recently nationalized industries. Conservatives have not been "die-hards" on the measures of the Attlee government. They have not used the House of Lords, for example, as a citadel of privilege for indiscriminate resistance. The Lords, instead, consciously acted as a council of state and did their best to see that the measures were improved so as to be instruments fit to achieve the purpose of their framers. If Conservatives win the general election of 1950, their position is that there will be no denationalization, although there will be some modifying and decentralizing. Conservatives, like Labour, contemplate a mixed economy. They have no formula like "free enterprise" to remedy all ills any more than Labour prescribes universal nationalization. They proclaim that their type of mixed economy will produce economic democracy because it will prevent undue concentration of power—and they are fond of quoting Lord Acton about the corrupting influence of power. They believe it will lead to the diffusion of wealth and make Britain a property-owning democracy.

Many Conservatives are as aware of the contrast between political and economic development in the nineteenth century as are the Labourites. As R. A. Butler, chief sponsor of the Education Act of 1944, wrote in his *Fundamental Issues:*

This political democracy marches hand-in-hand with an economic system in which the democratic principle is only just beginning to raise its head. I feel that we have a great contribution to make in developing the growth along sound and sensible lines of industrial democracy.

Conservatives find the solution of this problem not in nationalizing industry, but in humanizing it. They want industry to take greater interest in the worker and provide the worker with better reasons for an interest in his work. A report of the party's Committee on Policy and Political Education (1944) emphasizes the desirability of a real partnership between employer and employee, not merely for joint bargaining, but for joint endeavor, and states that workers individually and collectively should share responsibility. To help prepare the worker for what they call "co-partnership" these Conservatives advocate a teaching system throughout industry for training promising young men and women for better positions and for management. In all this the trade unions, here envisaged as "a valuable school of democracy," would have a necessary place.

These views were accepted by the party conference of 1946, where they were elaborated as an *Industrial Charter,* and they were restated in *The Right Road for Britain* (1949). In equality of opportunity in industry, a big extension of joint production committees, and joint consultation not only for labor-management problems but also in a more positive partnership, Conservatism and Labour have much ground in common.

The Liberals of today are about as critical of the results of laissez-faire as their grandfathers were hopeful. They, too, proclaim that industrial feudalism cannot continue to exist alongside political democracy. A statement from the *Liberal Magazine* is typical: "A democratic way of life cannot become universally established without economic democracy. The battle for economic democracy is now being fought." As long ago as 1928 the Liberal *Yellow Book* ad-

vocated the diffusion of ownership and advanced some concrete proposals. These ideas were developed in 1938 in the *Ownership for All* report. The Liberal national assemblies of 1947 and 1948 again debated them, and the latter actually advocated a compulsory scheme of "co-ownership" for every sizable firm.

Truly the Liberals have moved far from nineteenth-century individualism and laissez-faire. They accept a substantial amount of central planning. In the campaign of 1945 their candidates advocated public ownership where it was economic or where it was a question of a monopoly. They continue to oppose the nationalization of all industry, but disavow any intention of undoing what has been done. Liberals, too, evidently contemplate a mixed system for British industry.

Democracy in industry is as freely discussed by Liberals as is "ownership for all." Since democratic ownership implies democratic control, it is argued, all boards of directors should contain representatives of shareholders, managers, and workers, while works councils should provide a meeting place for labor and management to settle their problems. So do Liberals hope to put an end to "industrial serfdom" and produce a better climate in industry.

All three parties, it would appear, share the belief in the shortcomings of the present structure of industry and would do something to democratize it. Just what will come of it remains to be seen because, except for joint consultation, most of the practical suggestions are still in the realm of ideas and are not specific pledges.

British democrats find themselves in a certain dilemma in that they wish to utilize the state and so enhance its power, and at the same time extend the freedom of the individual. They are keenly alive to the dangers of unbalance in pursuing the interests of either extreme unchecked. They have noted how laissez-faire subordinated the liberty of the many to the greed of the ruthless and acquisitive few. They have seen with dismay the course of the totalitarian state in fascist and communist lands, where political democracy was an early casualty. Those carrying through the British revolution, and this is true particularly of the Labour party, believe that it is possible to achieve security with freedom. Indeed, they are convinced that it is only by enlarging the area of democracy that the maximum of liberty can be found. That is why G. B. Shaw used to debate the affirmative of the question: "That a democrat who is not also a socialist is no gentleman." It is the theme of Labour's 1949 statement, *Labour Believes in Britain,* that social democracy and freedom go together. Neither slave state nor police state is in prospect in Britain.

Democracy is not something for the distant future in Britain, but something to be practiced now. The British labor movement advocates it as a means as well as an end. Although it does not deny the right of revolution, it does not preach the resort to force. It has no use for bombs, barricades, and dictatorship. Its tools are the ballot and the budget. The operations of the latter may not be exactly painless, but, as the pages of *Punch* prove, they are not without humor.

This concern for liberty is a major reason why another party claiming to be democratic has made so little impression in Great Britain. For thirty years the Communist party has tried, but in vain, to win an appreciable following among the electorate. It has sought repeatedly to affiliate with the Labour party, only to be just as frequently rejected, because Labour realizes that it has very little in common and much of difference with communism. The net result of the communist irruption, indeed, has been to strengthen the socialist faith in democracy and emphasis upon freedom. An English professor of Eastern European history writes:

Some knowledge of the state of affairs in the "People's Democracies" has, I think, helped to clarify English thinking about democracy, and to lead to a great insistence on its political aspects. Twelve years ago I was expounding the thesis that political liberty without economic democracy was futile; today in this country the reaction against communism has led to a reversal of emphasis, and to the insistence that a planned society without liberty is fundamentally undemocratic.

The following statement of the Labour party executive, issued after the Communist seizure of power in Czechoslovakia stresses the difference between the two concepts of democracy:

For Democratic Socialists still free to choose their future the fall of Czechoslovakia is a warning and a lesson. . . . The issue before us no longer permits of any prevarication. Socialism is meaningless without democracy. Democracy cannot live without freedom of speech, press and organization, without the right to protection against arbitrary arrest, the right of appeal to a nonpolitical judiciary. Any attempt to achieve Socialism by means which deny democracy and human rights, particularly by the operation of an all-powerful secret police, must lead inevitably to a dictatorship, indistinguishable in its impact on the common man from Fascism, as it existed in Italy and in Germany, as it still exists in Spain.

Czechoslovakia is an acid test of sincerity. Those who seek to condone this crime show that they are false to the principles of Democratic Socialism for which the Labour Party stands.

This statement illustrates the point that, while British Labour does not believe that there is any real necessity of making a choice between socialism and democracy, if it were compelled to do so, it would choose democracy. In fact, not many days hence it will submit its socialist case and program to the electorate, and it is perfectly safe to assume that it will accept the verdict of democracy.

It is fully evident from what has been said that a redefinition of democracy is under way in Great Britain. It appears in the words of statesmen and in the programs of parties, but it is more than a thing on paper. A budget debate today is a revelation of the nature and scope of British democracy. No longer is it a matter of receipts, expenditures, and taxation, but something that ranges over the whole field of British policy and economy, with the chancellor of the exchequer reporting on everything and the people's representatives probing everywhere. The *Parliamentary Debates* and the *Economic Survey* bear testimony to the wide range of democratic interest and power. The growth of democracy is revealed also by the extent to which Britain no longer depends upon a tiny minority for its leaders. Even the foreign office is no longer a closed preserve, for it has been occupied by the son of an agricultural laborer, an ironworker, and a transport worker. It has touched the army, for at Wellbeck Abbey all ranks study side by side. It has even affected Oxford and Cambridge, externally aristocratic and medieval, yet they now select their students on talent and support a larger percentage of them on scholarships than any American university.

The British, accordingly, have gone far in recent years. Already the 1920's and 1930's seem another world. What will happen in the near future, one cannot say, but one may hazard a guess that on social and economic democracy there will be some compromise short of a dead level. Looking farther ahead, all that can be safely predicted is that history will not stop, that, barring a major catastrophe, the process of evolutionary adjustment will continue, that all parties will have a hand in it, and that Britain will continue to be both a land of liberty and a laboratory of democracy.